the Latest "Hot" Topics

Working with Diversity

Call-Out Quotes

Short "words of wisdom" from professionals from all walks of life are included in the text margins.

Concept Checks

Each major section concludes with two questions that tie to the chapter concepts. The first question tests recall of a basic fact, definition, or concept. The second question asks the student to think critically about the concept presented and provides them with the opportunity to assess their mastery of the subject material.

Chapter Closing Cases

Each chapter concludes with a detailed case study that asks students to apply what they have learned in the reading to a real-world scenario.

"You Make The Call"

These end-of-chapter exercises ask students to refer back to the "First Things First" opening vignettes to make judgments based on various scenarios.

Test Prepper Quizzes

Located at the end of every chapter, these short multiple-choice and true/false self-tests allow students to gauge their retention and comprehension of chapter material. The answers are found at the end of the text.

management

management

Ricky W. Griffin

Texas A & M University

Houghton Mifflin Company   Boston   New York

For Glenda—The anchor of my life and the center of my universe.

Vice-President and Executive Publisher: George Hoffman
Senior Sponsoring Editor: Lise Johnson
Senior Marketing Manager: Mike Schenk
Marketing Coordinator: Erin Lane
Development Editor: Julia Perez
Editorial Assistant: John Powers
Senior Project Editor: Kerry Falvey
Editorial Assistant: Joanna Carter
Art and Design Manager: Jill Haber
Cover Design Manager: Anne S. Katzeff
Photo Editor: Marcy Kagan
Composition Buyer: Chuck Dutton

Cover image: © Volker Möhrke/CORBIS

All end of chapter exercises were prepared by Margaret Hill and are reprinted here with her permission.

Photo credits may be found on page 687.

Printed in the U.S.A.

Library of Congress Control Number: 2006925140

ISBNs:
Instructor's exam copy:
ISBN-13: 978-0-618-83345-0
ISBN-10: 0-618-83345-5

For orders, use student text ISBNs:
ISBN-13: 978-0-618-76795-3
ISBN-10: 0-618-76795-9

2 3 4 5 6 7 8 9—CRK— 10 09 08 07

Brief Contents

Contents

PART

2

The Environmental Context of Management

PART 3
Planning and Decision Making

8   Managing Strategy and Strategic Planning   199

9   Managing Decision Making and Problem Solving   232

10 Managing New Venture Formation and Entrepreneurship 257

PART

4 The Organizing Process

13 Managing Organization Change and Innovation   343

14 Managing Human Resources in Organizations   371

PART

5

The Leading Process

15 Basic Elements of Individual Behavior in Organizations   403

18 Managing Interpersonal Relations and Communication 497

19 Managing Work Groups and Teams 525

PART

6

The Controlling Process

20 Basic Elements of Control

553

21 Managing Operations, Quality, and Productivity 582

22 Managing Information and Information Technology 612

APPENDIX

Tools for Planning and Decision Making   641

Preface

Since the publication of its first edition in 1984, nearly 1½ million students have used *Management* in preparation for their careers in business. *Management* continues to be used in hundreds of universities, graduate programs, community colleges, and management development programs throughout the world today. Indeed, the last edition of the book was used in over 40 countries and translated into several foreign languages.

In this edition, I have retained all the elements that have contributed to the book's success in the past while also taking a clear look toward the future—the future of business, of management, and of textbooks.

Writing a survey book poses a number of challenges. First, because it is a survey, it has to be comprehensive. Second, it has to be accurate and objective. Third, because management is a real activity, the book has to be relevant. Fourth, it has to be timely and up-to-date. And fifth, it must be as interesting and as engaging as possible. Feedback on previous editions of my text has always suggested that I have done an effective job of meeting these goals. In this edition, I think these goals have been met even more effectively.

I believe that current and previous users of *Management* will be pleased with how we have retained the essential ingredients of a comprehensive management textbook while adding a variety of new elements and perspectives. I also believe that those new to this edition will be drawn to the solid foundations of management theory and practice combined with new and exciting material.

Highlights and Improvements in the Ninth Edition

The ninth edition of *Management* is a substantive revision of the earlier work. Rather than simply adding the "hot topics" of the moment, I continue to thoroughly revise this book with the long-term view in mind. There are significant revisions of key chapters; an increased emphasis on the service sector, ethics, global management, and information technology; and an integrated organization of chapters. These changes reflect what I believe, and what reviewers and employers have confirmed, students will need to know as they enter a brand-new world of management. In addition, several integrated pedagogical features such as "Concept Check" and "Test Prepper" will also prove to be invaluable.

Integrated Coverage

Many textbooks set certain material off from the rest of the text in a separate section at the end of the book called "Emerging Trends," "Special Challenges," or something similar. New and emerging topics, and other material that doesn't easily fit anywhere else, are covered in that section. Unfortunately, by setting those topics apart in this way, the material often gets ignored or receives low-priority treatment.

But I decided several editions back that if this material was really worth having in the book to begin with, it needed to be fully merged with the core material. Thus, all material—both traditional and contemporary—is integrated throughout the text in order to provide more uniform and cohesive coverage of the entire field of management. This framework also helps to streamline the book's overall organization into six logical and symmetrical parts. Because reviewers and students have responded so favorably to this approach, it has been retained in the ninth edition. Furthermore, cross-referencing strengthens the integrated coverage throughout the text.

Logical Chapter Organization

This integrated approach to management also results in a logical and very effective chapter organization. Part 1 introduces the field of management, while Part 2 focuses on the environment of management. The remaining four parts cover the basic managerial functions of planning and decision making, organizing, leading, and controlling.

Topical Coverage for a Brand-New World of Management

Management provides comprehensive and balanced coverage of both traditional material and new and emerging issues and topics. A variety of topics are new to this edition, and coverage of other areas has been increased and/or heavily revised. In addition, new research and new examples have been integrated throughout the book. A few of the highlights are noted below.

Chapter 1: Managing and the Manager's Job   This chapter introduces you to the nature of management. It outlines the organization of the book and includes a comprehensive managerial-skills framework. It also introduces and discusses critical contemporary topics that relate to the new workplace.

Chapter 2: Traditional and Contemporary Issues and Challenges   This chapter starts with a brief history of management thought. A discussion of contemporary applied perspectives introduces the work of Senge, Covey, Porter, Kotter, Adams, and other modern popular-press business authors. The section on contemporary management challenges also introduces today's critical management issues.

Chapter 3: The Environment and Culture of Organizations   This chapter includes new and expanded coverage of such critical contemporary issues as corporate governance, corporate culture, and the growing impact of enterprise resource planning.

Chapter 4: The Ethical and Social Environment   In light of recent controversies, this chapter continues to receive special attention. It includes coverage of the reasons for unethical behavior and a model for assessing ethical decisions.

Chapter 5: The Global Environment   This chapter has updated data and statistics, and expanded coverage of cultural issues in international business. In addition, the chapter covers current issues in the European Union, the General Agreement on Tariffs and Trade (GATT), and the World Trade Organization (WTO).

Chapter 6: The Multicultural Environment   All data, statistics, and trends have been updated. The strategic importance of multiculturalism is also discussed.

Chapter 7: Basic Elements of Planning and Decision Making   This chapter introduces the essential concepts of planning and decision making. It also includes coverage of contingency planning and a section on crisis management. In today's turbulent world, these issues have taken on even greater importance.

Chapter 8: Managing Strategy and Strategic Planning   In addition to complete coverage of business and corporate strategies, this chapter includes a major section on global strategy. This section reflects the continued and growing importance of international business.

Chapter 10: Managing New Venture Formation and Entrepreneurship   Coverage of new ventures, start-ups, and entrepreneurship has been expanded. There is also added coverage of international management.

Chapter 11: Basic Elements of Organizing   This chapter introduces the basic building blocks of organizations. It also includes a section on how organizations are increasingly using electronic coordination techniques.

Chapter 12: Managing Organization Design   Chapter 12 discusses different frameworks for structuring organizations. It also covers the team organization, the virtual organization, and the learning organization.

Chapter 13: Managing Organization Change and Innovation   This chapter discusses change management. It includes coverage of business process change and enterprise resource planning.

Chapter 14: Managing Human Resources in Organizations   Coverage of change and human resource management has been revamped and coverage of ADA and the management of high-skill workers has been substantially revised. In addition, this chapter features material about the concept of human capital as well as electronic recruiting and the growing importance of corporate universities.

Chapter 15: Basic Elements of Individual Behavior in Organizations   This chapter includes the "big five" model of personality, as well as discussions of affect and mood in organizations and individual creativity in organizations. In addition, coverage of emotional intelligence, the Myers-Briggs framework, and dysfunctional work behaviors is also included.

Chapter 16: Managing Employee Motivation and Performance   Coverage of the major theories of motivation has been improved. Coverage of reward systems and executive compensation also has been revised and expanded.

Chapter 17: Managing Leadership and Influence Processes   This chapter has been reorganized and includes coverage of the latest version of Vroom's decision-making model. In addition, a major section introduces and discusses the concepts of strategic leadership, cross-cultural issues in leadership, and the growing awareness of the importance of ethical leadership.

Chapter 18: Managing Interpersonal Relations and Communication   Coverage of communication in teams has been revised and reframed. This chapter also includes coverage of electronic communication and the pros and cons of e-mail.

Chapter 19: Managing Work Groups and Teams   This chapter covers basic elements of groups in organizations as well as the widespread use of teams. It also includes coverage of virtual teams.

Chapter 20: Basic Elements of Control   Chapter 20 introduces the basic elements of control. It also includes material addressing recent accounting and auditing scandals as they relate to the control function in organizations.

Chapter 21: Managing Operations, Quality, and Productivity   The organization of this chapter has been improved by first discussing operations management, then using it as a framework for introducing quality and productivity. Other key topics in this chapter include supply chain management, value-added analysis, ISO 9000:2000 and ISO 14000, and six sigma.

Chapter 22: Managing Information and Information Technology   This chapter includes new and expanded coverage of the Internet, corporate intranets, and instant messaging as they relate to management.

In addition to these content revisions and additions, all in-text examples have been carefully reviewed and most have been replaced or updated.

Features of the Book

Basic Themes

Several key themes are prominent in this edition of *Management*. One critical theme is the ethical scrutiny under which managers work today. While the book has always included substantial coverage of ethics and social responsibility, even more attention has been devoted this time to topics such as corporate governance, ethical leadership, and the proper role of auditing. Another continuing theme is the global character of the field of management, which is reinforced throughout the book by examples and cases. A third key theme, information technology, is covered in detail in Chapter 22; in addition, it is also highlighted in boxed inserts in other chapters, and is integrated into the text itself throughout the book. Still another theme is the balance of theory and practice: managers need to have a sound basis for their decisions, but the theories that provide that basis must be grounded in reality. Throughout the book I explain the theoretical frameworks that guide managerial activities, and provide illustrations and examples of how and when those theories do and do not work. A fifth theme is that management is a generic activity not confined to large businesses. I use examples and discuss management in both small and large businesses as well as in not-for-profit organizations.

A Pedagogical System That Works

The pedagogical elements built into *Management*, Ninth Edition, continue to be effective learning and teaching aids for students and instructors.

- Learning objectives preview key themes at the start of every chapter. Key terms and concepts are highlighted in boldface type, and most terms are defined in the margin next to where they are discussed. Effective figures, tables, and photographs with their own detailed captions help bring the material to life.

- Another exciting feature is called "Concept Check." Each major section in every chapter concludes with two questions tied back to that section. The first question tests recall of a basic fact, definition, or concept. The second is more thought-provoking and analytical in nature. These questions allow students to continuously assess their mastery of the subject as they are reading and studying the material.

- Three kinds of questions at the end of every chapter are designed to test different levels of student understanding. Questions for Review ask students to recall specific information, Questions for Analysis ask students to integrate and synthesize material, and Questions for Application ask students to apply what they've learned to their own experiences.

- Each chapter also includes useful skill-development exercises. These exercises give students insight into how they approach various management situations and how they can work to improve their management skills in the future. The exercises are derived from the overall managerial skills framework developed in Chapter 1. For this edition, many of the exercises were replaced or substantially revised.

- New to this edition, each chapter also concludes with a "Test Prepper," a set of true/false and multiple choice questions that allow students to immediately assess their understanding of the chapter.

Applications That Keep Students Engaged

To fully appreciate the role and scope of management in contemporary society, it is important to see examples and illustrations of how concepts apply in the real world. I rely heavily on fully researched examples to illustrate real-world applications. They vary in length, and all were carefully reviewed for their timeliness. To give the broadest view possible, I include examples of both traditional management roles and nontraditional roles; profit-seeking businesses and nonprofits; large corporations and small businesses; manufacturers and services; and international examples and United States examples.

Furthermore, in this edition I have developed a better balance of large and established businesses (such as Home Depot, Coca-Cola, Boeing, Intel, and General Electric) and new, emerging businesses (such as Google, Starbucks, Video Game Corporation, Facebook, and Abercrombie & Fitch). Other applications include:

- Opening incidents at the beginning of every chapter. These brief vignettes, titled "First Things First," draw the student into the chapter with a real-world scenario that introduces a particular management theme. All opening incidents are new to this edition.

- New to this edition is an end-of-chapter feature called "You Make the Call." This feature is tied back to the chapter-opening incident; it requires students to play the role of a consultant, a manager, or other stakeholder in the organization featured earlier. Students are asked to comment, critique, or make suggestions about how well the business is doing and/or what it needs to do differently.

- Also new to this edition is a set of 2–3 call-out quotations spread throughout each chapter. These quotations provide real insights into how managers and other experts see the world of business as it relates to the topics at hand.

- Boxed features. Each chapter includes two or three boxed features. These boxes are intended to depart briefly from the flow of the chapter to highlight or extend especially interesting or emerging points and issues. There are three types of featured boxes found throughout the text:

 "The Business of Ethics" (the increasing importance of ethics in management)

"Technology Toolkit" (new technology and its role in management)

 "Working with Diversity" (the role of diversity in organizations)

- End-of-chapter cases. Each chapter concludes with a detailed case study. All the cases in the ninth edition are new and have been especially written for this book.

I would also like to invite your feedback on this book. If you have any questions, suggestions, or issues to discuss, please feel free to contact me. The most efficient way to reach me is through e-mail. My address is rgriffin@tamu.edu.

R.W.G.

Acknowledgements

I am frequently asked by my colleagues why I write textbooks, and my answer is always, "Because I enjoy it." I've never enjoyed writing a book more than this one. For me, writing a textbook is a challenging and stimulating activity that brings with it a variety of rewards. My greatest reward continues to be the feedback I get from students and instructors about how much they like this book.

I owe an enormous debt to many different people for helping me create *Management*. My colleagues at Texas A&M have helped create a wonderful academic climate. The rich and varied culture at Texas A&M makes it a pleasure to go to the office every day.

The fine team of professionals at Houghton Mifflin has also been essential in the success of this book. George Hoffman, Lise Johnson, Julia Perez, and Kerry Falvey were instrumental in the production of this edition.

Many reviewers have played a critical role in the evolution of this project. They examined my work in detail and with a critical eye. I would like to tip my hat to the following reviewers, whose imprint can be found throughout this text:

Ramon J. Aldag
University of Wisconsin

Dr. Raymond E. Alie
Western Michigan University

William P. Anthony
Florida State University

Jeanne Aurelio
Stonehill College

Jay B. Barney
Ohio State University

Richard Bartlett
Muskigum Area Technical College

John D. Bigelow
Boise State University

Allen Bluedorn
University of Missouri

Thomas M. Bock
The Devry Institute

Henry C. Bohleke
Tarrant County College

Marv Borglett
University of Maryland

Gunther S. Boroschek
University of Massachusetts—Boston Harbor Campus

Gerald E. Calvasina
University of North Carolina, Charlotte

Joseph Cantrell
DeAnza College

George R. Carnahan
Northern Michigan University

Ron Cheek
University of New Orleans

Thomas G. Christoph
Clemson University

Charles W. Cole
University of Oregon

Elizabeth Cooper
University of Rhode Island

Carol Cumber
South Dakota State University

Joan Dahl
California State University, Northridge

Carol Danehower
University of Memphis

Satish Deshpande
Western Michigan University

Gregory G. Dess
University of Kentucky

Gary N. Dicer
University of Tennessee

Nicholas Dietz
State University of New York—Farmingdale

Thomas J. Dougherty
University of Missouri

Shad Dowlatshahi
University of Wisconsin—Platteville

John Drexler, Jr.
Oregon State University

Stan Elsea
Kansas State University

Douglas A. Elvers
University of South Carolina

Jim Fairbank
West Virginia University

Dan Farrell
Western Michigan University

Gerald L. Finch
Universidad Internacional del Ecuador and Universidad San Francisco de Quito

Charles Flaherty
University of Minnesota

Ari Ginsberg
New York University Graduate School of Business

Norma N. Givens
Fort Valley State University

David Glew
University of North Carolina at Wilmington

Carl Gooding
Georgia Southern College

George J. Gore
University of Cincinnati

Jonathan Gueverra
Lesley College

Stanley D. Guzell, Jr.
Youngstown State University

John Hall
University of Florida

Mark A. Hammer
Washington State University

Barry Hand
Indiana State University

Paul Harmon
University of Utah

Stephanie Henagan
Loiusiana State University

John Hughes
Texas Tech University

J.G. Hunt
Texas Tech University

John H. Jackson
University of Wyoming

Neil W. Jacobs
University of Denver

Arthur G. Jago
University of Missouri

Madge Jenkins
Lima Technical College

Gopol Joshi
Central Missouri State University

Norman F. Kallaus
University of Iowa

Ben L. Kedia
University of Memphis

Joan Keeley
Washington State University

Thomas L. Keon
University of Central Florida

Charles C. Kitzmiller
Indian River Community College

Barbara Kovach
Rutgers University

William R. LaFollete
Ball State University

Kenneth Lawrence
New Jersey Institute of Technology

Clayton G. Lifto
Kirkwood Community College

John E. Mack
Salem State University

Myrna P. Mandell, Ph.D.
California State University, Northridge

Patricia M. Manninen
North Shore Community College

Thomas Martin
University of Nebraska—Omaha

Barbara J. Marting
University of Southern Indiana

Lisa McConnell
Oklahoma State University

Melvin McKnight
Northern Arizona University

Wayne A. Meinhart
Oklahoma State University

Aratchige Molligoda
Drexel University

Linda L. Neider
University of Miami

Mary Lippitt Nichols
University of Minnesota

Winston Oberg
Michigan State University

David Oliver
Edison College

Michael Olivette
Syracuse University

Eugene Owens
Western Washington University

Sheila Pechinski
University of Maine

Monique Pelletier
San Francisco State University

E. Leroy Plumlee
Western Washington University

Raymond F. Polchow
Muskigum Area Technical College

Boris Porkovich
San Francisco State University

Paul Preston
University of Texas—San Antonio

John M. Purcell
State University of New York—Farmingdale

James C. Quick
University of Texas—Arlington

Ralph Roberts
University of West Florida

Nick Sarantakas
Austin Community College

Gene Schneider
Austin Community College

H. Schollhammer
University of California—Los Angeles

Diane R. Scott
Wichita State University

Harvey Shore
University of Connecticut

Marc Siegall
California State University

Nicholas Siropolis
Cuyahoga Community College

Michael J. Stahl
University of Tennessee

Diane Stone
Ivy Technical State College

Marc Street
University of Tulsa

Charlotte D. Sutton
Auburn University

Robert L. Taylor
University of Louisville

Mary Thibodeaux
University of North Texas

Joe Thomas
Middle Tennessee State University

Sean Valentine
University of Wyoming

Robert D. Van Auken
University of Oklahoma

Billy Ward
The University of West Alabama

Richard Warner
Lehigh Carbon Community College

Fred Williams
University of North Texas

Mary Williams
Community College of Southern Nevada

James Wilson
University of Texas—Pan American

Carl P. Zeithaml
University of Virginia

I would also like to make a few personal acknowledgments. The fine work of Rob Thomas, Roy Orbison, Lyle Lovett, Johnny Rivers, and the Nylons helped me make it through many late evenings and early mornings of work on the manuscript that became the book you hold in your hands. And Stephen King, Tom Clancy, James Lee Burke, Peter Straub, and Carl Barks provided me with a respite from my writings with their own.

Finally, there is the most important acknowledgement of all—my feelings for and gratitude to my family. My wife, Glenda, and our children, Dustin, Ashley, and Matt are the foundation of my professional and personal life. They help me keep work and play in perspective and give meaning to everything I do. It is with all my love that I dedicate this book to them.

R.W.G.

Managing and the Manager's Job

chapter 1

FIRST THINGS FIRST

Where Is Google Going?

"I would rather have people think we're confused than let our competitors know what we're going to do."

—LARRY PAGE, CO-FOUNDER AND PRESIDENT, GOOGLE

Google is today's most well-known Internet success story. After an initial public stock offering (IPO) in 2004, Google's market capitalization value grew to over $100 billion by early 2006.

Sergey Brin and Larry Page met at Stanford University in 1995, when both were graduate students in computer science. Page had started a software development project that created an index of websites by crawling—examining the sites themselves, looking for key words and linkages between sites. Brin joined the team, and the pair tried to license their technology to other search companies, but couldn't find a buyer. What a stroke of good fortune for the two friends! Investment capital allowed the company to refine and test its product for several years. Then, in 2000, Brin and Page discovered a profitable business model based on selling advertising in the form of sponsored links and search-specific ads.

LEARNING OBJECTIVES

After studying this chapter, you should be able to:

1. Describe the nature of management, define management and managers, and characterize their importance to contemporary organizations.

2. Identify and briefly explain the four basic management functions in organizations.

3. Describe the kinds of managers found at different levels and in different areas of the organization.

4. Identify the basic managerial roles that managers play and the skills they need to be successful.

5. Discuss the science and the art of management, describe how people become managers, and summarize the scope of management in organizations.

6. Characterize the new workplace that is emerging in organizations today.

Google is one of the most popular websites on the Internet. The firm's co-founders, Larry Page (left) and Sergey Brin, use a number of unusual management techniques to keep their firm profitable and competitive.

From that beginning, Brin and Page built Google into the world's largest search engine, with an index of over 10 billion webpages, helping 380 millions users per month, in 112 different countries. Yet Google is much more than just a search engine. Its services include searches for news, shopping, local businesses, interactive maps, discussion groups, software, and even items on the user's personal computer, as well as blogs, web-based e-mail and voice mail, discussion groups, and digital photo management. All of these results are viewable from the Google website, a user's toolbar, or a search box on the Windows taskbar, and on wireless devices such as phones and PDAs.

How did these two thirty-something computer scientists build this amazing firm, and how will they lead it in the future? Both Brin and Page have no formal business education. They sometimes seem naïve, often rejecting the advice of experienced managers and relying on their own untried, unorthodox methods. For example, the firm ran into trouble with its IPO when Brin and Page neglected to reveal key information, refused to pay the usual underwriting commission to banks, and unethically disclosed details of the process in a presale interview with *Playboy* magazine.

However, the duo excels in any number of other managerial areas. First, they both have remained at the forefront of Google's technological innovations. Google's founders believe in the power of mathematics, so much so that they have developed unique algorithms for just about every activity in the firm. One of the most successful is the unusual algorithm used for auctioning advertising, which ensures that the company receives the highest price for its advertising placements.

Second, Brin and Page have been remarkably successful at attracting talented and creative employees, and then providing a work environment and culture that foster innovation and productivity. At least half of Google's employees are scientists and engineers. Many are recruited from the country's top engineering universities, while others "win" their job by performing well in an online programming contest. Googlers work in small, flexible, self-directed teams. The company's website reinforces the playful atmosphere, saying, "Work and play are not mutually exclusive. It is possible to code and pass the puck at the same time." Workers may pursue projects of their own choosing for 20 percent of their time, and many of Google's most innovative ideas have sprung from those ideas. Pay for performance is standard and compensation is relatively high, although Brin and Page each collect $1 in salary annually with no bonuses, stock, or options.

Third, although the founders avoid formal strategic planning, they have diversified Google extensively through acquisitions and key alliances. Typically, Google absorbs an acquired firm and then improves on its technology, adding variety to the firm's online offerings. Strategic alliances include those with foreign online service providers that offer Google searches on their sites.

For the future, Google is doing more of the same, including making an offer to buy Facebook, competing head-to-head with financial service providers for stock information and with iTunes for music and videos, and inventing new features and services. Innovations in the works include an automated universal language translator, from any language to any language, and a personalized home page that allows users to design automatic searches and display a personal "newspaper" of results.

What else is planned? Nobody knows. Outsiders often criticize Google, calling it a "black box" and asking for more details of the firm's long-range strategy. Yet Page explains, "We don't talk about our strategy . . . because it's strategic. I would rather have people think we're confused than let our competitors know what we're going to do." Over the long term, it's up to Brin and Page to continue the company's success—by finding the next Brin and Page.[1]

Sergey Brin and Larry Page are clearly managers. So, too, are Philip Knight (chairman of Nike), Anne Mulcahy (CEO of Xerox), Mikio Sasaki (president of Mitsubishi), Neil MacGregor (director of the British Museum), Richard Hayne (president of Urban Outfitters), Bob Ferguson (general manager of the Seattle Seahawks football team), George W. Bush (president of the United States), Benedict XVI (pope of the Roman Catholic Church), and Marilyn Ferguson (owner of the Garden District Gift Shop in Bryan, Texas). As diverse as they and their organizations are, all of these managers are confronted by many of the same challenges, strive to achieve many of the same goals, and apply many of the same concepts of effective management in their work.

For better or worse, our society is strongly influenced by managers and their organizations. Most people in the United States are born in a hospital (an organization), educated by public or private schools (all organizations), and buy virtually all of their consumable products and services from businesses (organizations). And much of our behavior is influenced by various government agencies (also organizations). We define an ***organization*** as a group of people working together in a structured and coordinated fashion to achieve a set of goals. The goals may include profit (Starbucks Corporation), the discovery of knowledge (Iowa State University), national defense (the U.S. Army), coordination of various local charities (United Way of America), or social satisfaction (a sorority). Because organizations play such major roles in our lives, understanding how they operate and how they are managed is important.

This book is about managers and the work they do. In Chapter 1, we examine the general nature of management, its dimensions, and its challenges. We explain the concepts of management and managers, discuss the management process, present an overview of the book, and identify various kinds of managers. We describe the different roles and skills of managers, discuss the nature of managerial work, and examine the scope of management in contemporary organizations. In Chapter 2, we describe how both the practice and the theory of management have evolved. As a unit, then, these first two chapters provide an introduction to the field by introducing both contemporary and historical perspectives on management.

> *organization*
> A group of people working together in a structured and coordinated fashion to achieve a set of goals

An Introduction to Management

Although defining the term *organization* is relatively simple, the concept of *management* is a bit more elusive. It is perhaps best understood from a resource-based perspective. As we discuss more completely in Chapter 2, all organizations use four basic kinds of resources from their environment: human, financial, physical, and information. Human resources include managerial talent and labor. Financial resources are the capital used by the organization to finance both ongoing and long-term operations. Physical resources include raw materials, office and production facilities, and equipment. Information resources are usable data needed to make effective decisions. Examples of resources used in four very different kinds of organizations are shown in Table 1.1.

Managers are responsible for combining and coordinating these various resources to achieve the organization's goals. A manager at Royal Dutch/Shell Group, for example, uses the talents of executives and drilling platform workers, profits earmarked for reinvestment, existing refineries and office facilities, and sales forecasts to make decisions regarding the amount of petroleum to be refined and distributed during the next quarter. Similarly, the mayor (manager) of New York City might use police officers, a government grant (perhaps supplemented with surplus tax revenues), existing police stations, and detailed crime statistics to launch a major crime prevention program in the city.

How do these and other managers combine and coordinate the various kinds of resources? They do so by carrying out four basic managerial functions or activities: planning and decision making, organizing, leading, and controlling. ***Management***, then, as illustrated in Figure 1.1, can be defined as a set of activities (including planning and decision making, organizing, leading, and controlling) directed at an organization's resources (human, financial, physical, and information), with the aim of achieving organizational goals in an efficient and effective manner.

management
A set of activities (including planning and decision making, organizing, leading, and controlling) directed at an organization's resources (human, financial, physical, and information), with the aim of achieving organizational goals in an efficient and effective manner

Table 1.1

EXAMPLES OF RESOURCES USED BY ORGANIZATIONS

All organizations, regardless of whether they are large or small, profit-seeking or not-for-profit, domestic or multinational, use some combination of human, financial, physical, and information resources to achieve their goals. These resources are generally obtained from the organization's environment.

Organization	Human Resources	Financial Resources	Physical Resources	Information Resources
Royal Dutch/ Shell Group	Drilling platform workers Corporate executives	Profits Stockholder investments	Refineries Office buildings	Sales forecasts OPEC proclamations
Iowa State University	Faculty Administrative staff	Alumni contributions Government grants	Computers Campus facilities	Research reports Government publications
New York City	Police officers Municipal employees	Tax revenue Government grants	Sanitation equipment Municipal buildings	Economic forecasts Crime statistics
Susan's Corner Grocery Store	Grocery clerks Bookkeeper	Profits Owner investment	Building Display shelving	Price lists from suppliers Newspaper ads for competitors

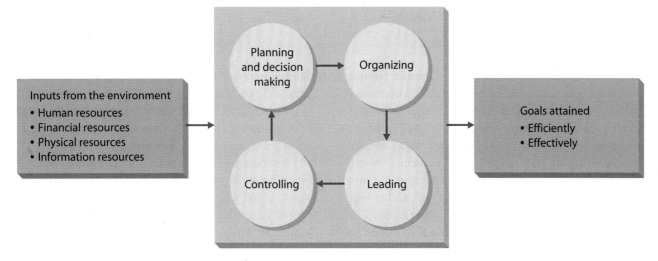

Figure 1.1
MANAGEMENT IN ORGANIZATIONS

Basic managerial activities include planning and decision making, organizing, leading, and controlling. Managers engage in these activities to combine human, financial, physical, and information resources efficiently and effectively and to work toward achieving the goals of the organization.

The last phrase in our definition is especially important because it highlights the basic purpose of management—to ensure that an organization's goals are achieved in an efficient and effective manner. By ***efficient***, we mean using resources wisely and in a cost-effective way. For example, a firm like Toyota Motor Corporation, which produces high-quality products at relatively low costs, is efficient. By ***effective***, we mean making the right decisions and successfully implementing them. Toyota also makes cars with the styling and quality to inspire consumer interest and confidence. A firm could very efficiently produce big-screen black-and-white televisions with few options and limited capabilities but still not succeed, because black-and-white televisions no longer have a market. A firm that produces products that no one wants is therefore not effective. In general, successful organizations are both efficient and effective.[2] *The Business of Ethics* highlights the impact businesses can have when they balance efficiency and effectiveness with social awareness about their role in protecting the natural environment.

With this basic understanding of management, defining the term *manager* becomes relatively simple—a ***manager*** is someone whose primary responsibility is to carry out the management process. In particular, a manager is someone who plans and makes decisions, organizes, leads, and controls human, financial, physical, and information resources. Today's managers face a variety of interesting and challenging situations. The average executive works 60 hours a week, has enormous demands placed on his or her time, and faces increased complexities posed by globalization, domestic competition, government regulation, shareholder pressure, and Internet-related uncertainties. The job is complicated even more by rapid changes, unexpected disruptions, and both minor and major crises. The manager's job is unpredictable and fraught with challenges, but it is also filled with opportunities to make a difference. Good managers can propel an organization into unprecedented realms of success, whereas poor managers can devastate even the strongest of organizations.[3]

---

efficient
Using resources wisely and in a cost-effective way

effective
Making the right decisions and successfully implementing them

manager
Someone whose primary responsibility is to carry out the management process

The Business of Ethics

"Green Is Green"

Or so says General Electric CEO Jeffrey Immelt. He means that companies can support the natural environment—by reducing waste, recycling, using less toxic materials, or cutting back on energy use—and at the same time, improve financial results. The U.S. federal government has been cutting back on pollution regulation. Yet many corporate leaders are voluntarily adopting environmentally friendly policies that they believe will lead to higher sales, cost savings, and, ultimately, greater profitability.

Among smaller, eco-friendly companies, efforts have been increased. Patagonia, a maker of outdoor clothing, already uses organic fibers. Now it's encouraging customers to return used clothes for recycling into new ones. Innovative firms recycle bamboo and wood window coverings, sell countertops made of recycled glass and concrete, and even offer reusable fabric diapers with biodegradable inserts!

Large traditional companies are also embracing the trend. In 2005, GE promised to improve energy efficiency by 4 percent annually and double revenues from "clean" products over the next decade. BP, the English oil and gas giant, created a new alternative energy division. Wal-Mart, which owns the largest fleet of trucks in the nation, plans to double its fuel efficiency. McDonald's is seeking its first green-building certification.

Starbucks and Whole Foods have both announced that they will purchase wind energy or wind energy credits to offset their electric usage. When mainstream companies get involved, they can have a significant impact on other firms, due to their size and power.

Technological innovations in batteries, wind turbines, solar devices and more are part of the reason for the change. For example, Corning has developed a "green glass" for use in liquid crystal displays, such as laptop screens, that doesn't contain toxic chemicals. As green technology becomes more affordable, more companies adopt it. Another important factor is buyer power. Educated customers who demand accountability from corporations have the ability to drive change.

However, the bottom line is the most critical element. Corporate CEOs and other top managers must answer to shareholders for profitability. When they have the option to increase profits with green methods, they will do the right thing for their shareholders, which also happens to be the right thing for the rest of the planet.

References: Chip Geller and David Roberts, "The Revolution Begins," *Fast Company*, March 2006, www.fastcompany.com on March 1, 2006; "Immelt Sees 'Green' Profit for GE," *Forbes*, May 13, 2005, www.forbes .com on March 1, 2006; Gene C. Marcial, "Corning Turns a Corner," *BusinessWeek*, April 17, 2006, www.businessweek.com on April 4, 2006.

Many of the characteristics that contribute to the complexity and uncertainty of management stem from the environment in which organizations function. For example, as shown in Figure 1.1, the resources used by organizations to create products and services all come from the environment. Thus it is critical that managers understand this environment. Part 2 of the text discusses the environmental context of management in detail. Chapter 3 provides a general overview and discussion of the organization's environment, and Chapters 4 through 6 address specific aspects of the environment more fully. In particular, Chapter 4 discusses the ethical and social context of management. Chapter 5 explores the global context of management. Chapter 6 describes the cultural and multicultural environment of management. After reading these chapters, you will be better prepared to study the essential activities that comprise the management process.

The Management Process

We note earlier that management involves the four basic functions of planning and decision making, organizing, leading, and controlling. Because these functions represent the framework around which this book is organized, we introduce them here

Figure 1.2
THE MANAGEMENT PROCESS

Management involves four basic activities—planning and decision making, organizing, leading, and controlling. Although there is a basic logic for describing these activities in this sequence (as indicated by the solid arrows), most managers engage in more than one activity at a time and often move back and forth between the activities in unpredictable ways (as shown by the dotted arrows).

and note where they are discussed more fully. Their basic definitions and interrelationships are shown in Figure 1.2. (Note that Figure 1.2 is an expanded version of the central part of Figure 1.1.)

Recall the details of the Google case discussed earlier. Sergey Brin and Larry Page must first create goals and plans that articulate what they want the company to become. Then they rely on effective organization to help make those goals and plans reality. Brin and Page also pay close attention to the people who work for the company. And they keep a close eye on how well the company is performing. Each of these activities represents one of the four basic managerial functions illustrated in the figure—setting goals is part of planning, setting up the organization is part of organizing, managing people is part of leading, and monitoring performance is part of controlling.

It is important to note, however, that the functions of management do not usually occur in a tidy, step-by-step fashion. Managers do not plan on Monday, make decisions on Tuesday, organize on Wednesday, lead on Thursday, and control on Friday. At any given time, for example, a manager is likely to be engaged in several different activities simultaneously. Indeed, from one setting to another, managerial work is as different as it is similar. The similarities that pervade most settings are the phases in the management process. Important differences include the emphasis, sequencing, and implications of each phase.[4] Thus the solid lines in Figure 1.2 indicate how, in theory, the functions of management are performed. The dotted lines, however, represent the true reality of management. In the sections that follow, we explore each of these activities.

Planning and Decision Making: Determining Courses of Action

In its simplest form, ***planning*** means setting an organization's goals and deciding how best to achieve them. ***Decision making***, a part of the planning process, involves selecting a course of action from a set of alternatives. Planning and decision making

planning
Setting an organization's goals and deciding how best to achieve them

decision making
Part of the planning process that involves selecting a course of action from a set of alternatives

help maintain managerial effectiveness by serving as guides for future activities. In other words, the organization's goals and plans clearly help managers know how to allocate their time and resources. Robert Nardelli is CEO of Home Depot. After joining the firm in 2000, he saw that Home Deport was losing market share to its chief rival Lowe's and to Wal-Mart. Since that time he has been working hard to revitalize the firm by remodeling many of its stores, adding new product lines, and refining its distribution network. Moreover, Nardelli has established a number of short- and long-term goals for Home Depot and outlined several strategic initiatives to achieve them. He has also set very high performance standards for everyone in the company.[5]

> **"I will never apologize for setting the bar high."**
> Robert Nardelli, CEO of Home Depot
> (*BusinessWeek*, March 6, 2006, p. 58)

Four chapters making up Part 3 of this text are devoted to planning and decision making. Chapter 7 examines the basic elements of planning and decision making, including the role and importance of organizational goals. Chapter 8 looks at strategy and strategic planning, which provide overall direction and focus for the organization. Chapter 9 explores managerial decision making and problem solving in detail. Finally, Chapter 10 addresses planning and decision making as they relate to the management of new ventures and entrepreneurial activities, increasingly important parts of managerial work.

Organizing: Coordinating Activities and Resources

organizing
Determining how activities and resources are to be grouped

Once a manager has set goals and developed a workable plan, the next management function is to organize people and the other resources necessary to carry out the plan. Specifically, **organizing** involves determining how activities and resources are to be grouped. Home Depot's Robert Nardelli believes that one reason the firm was underperforming before he arrived was that individual store managers had too much autonomy. Hence, he has systematically worked to centralize operations as much as possible at the corporate level. He has also clarified reporting relationships and implemented a 'command-and-control' mentality throughout Home Depot.

Organizing is the subject of Part 4. Chapter 11 introduces the basic elements of organizing, such as job design, departmentalization, authority relationships, span of control, and line and staff roles. Chapter 12 explains how managers fit these elements and concepts together to form an overall organization design. Organization change and innovation are the focus of Chapter 13. Finally, processes associated with managing the organization's workforce so as to most effectively carry out organizational roles and perform tasks are described in Chapter 14.

Leading: Motivating and Managing People

leading
The set of processes used to get members of the organization to work together to further the interests of the organization

The third basic managerial function is leading. Some people consider leading to be both the most important and the most challenging of all managerial activities. **Leading** is the set of processes used to get members of the organization to work together to further the interests of the organization. Robert Nardelli was in the military before he started his business career. His experiences there still shape his thinking about leadership. For instance, he wants everyone to know that he is in charge of all major decisions. He also never hesitates to reassign or fire managers whom he feels are not performing effectively.

Leading involves a number of different processes and activities, which are discussed in Part 5. The starting point is understanding basic individual and interpersonal processes, which we focus on in Chapter 15. Motivating employees is discussed in Chapter 16, and leadership itself and the leader's efforts to influence others are covered in Chapter 17. Managing interpersonal relations and communication is the subject of Chapter 18. Finally, managing work groups and teams, another important part of leading, is addressed in Chapter 19.

Controlling: Monitoring and Evaluating Activities

The final phase of the management process is **controlling**, or monitoring the organization's progress toward its goals. As the organization moves toward its goals, managers must monitor progress to ensure that it is performing in such a way as to arrive at its "destination" at the appointed time. A good analogy is that of a space mission to Mars. NASA does not simply shoot a rocket in the general direction of the planet and then look again in four months to see whether the rocket hit its mark. NASA monitors the spacecraft almost continuously and makes whatever course corrections are needed to keep it on track. Controlling similarly helps ensure the effectiveness and efficiency needed for successful management. At Home Depot, Robert Nardelli has implemented a far-reaching set of financial measures to maintain a current assessment of how the firm is doing as well as whether its performance is improving over time.

controlling
Monitoring organizational progress toward goal attainment

The control function is explored in Part 6. First, Chapter 20 explores the basic elements of the control process, including the increasing importance of strategic control. Managing operations, quality, and productivity is explored in Chapter 21. Finally, Chapter 22 addresses the management of information and information technology, which are also important areas of organizational control.

concept
CHECK

What is a manager, and what are the fundamental functions that comprise the management process?	*Describe examples of how the management functions might be performed in different sequences.*

Kinds of Managers

There are many different kinds of managers in organizations. As shown in Figure 1.3, some managers can be differentiated from others on the basis of their level in the organization. It is also possible to differentiate them across different areas.

Managing at Different Levels of the Organization

Managers can be differentiated according to their level in the organization. Although large organizations typically have a number of **levels of management**, the most common view considers three basic levels: top, middle, and first-line managers.

levels of management
The differentiation of managers into three basic categories—top, middle, and first-line

Top Managers   Top managers make up the relatively small group of executives who manage the overall organization. Titles found in this group include president, vice president, and chief executive officer (CEO). Top managers create the organization's goals, overall strategy, and operating policies. They also officially represent the organization to the external environment by meeting with government officials, executives

Figure 1.3

KINDS OF MANAGERS BY LEVEL AND AREA

Organizations generally have three levels of management, represented by top managers, middle managers, and first-line managers. Regardless of level, managers are also usually associated with a specific area within the organization, such as marketing, finance, operations, human resources, administration, or some other area.

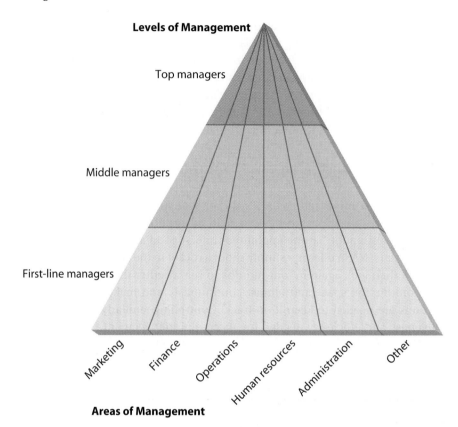

of other organizations, and so forth. *Working with Diversity* illustrates the impact that a top manager can have on both a company and the social context of that company.

Howard Schultz, CEO of Starbucks, is a top manager, as is Deidra Wager, the firm's executive vice president. The job of a top manager is likely to be complex and varied. Top managers make decisions about such activities as acquiring other companies, investing in research and development, entering or abandoning various markets, and building new plants and office facilities. They often work long hours and spend much of their time in meetings or on the telephone. In most cases, top managers are also very well paid. In fact, the elite top managers of very large firms sometimes make several million dollars a year in salary, bonuses, and stock.[6] Robert Nardelli, CEO of Home Depot, works 10 to 12 hours per day, 7 days a week; his 2005 compensation was $28.5 million.

Middle Managers   Middle management is probably the largest group of managers in most organizations. Common middle-management titles include plant manager, operations manager, and division head. Middle managers are responsible primarily for implementing the policies and plans developed by top managers and for supervising and coordinating the activities of lower-level managers.[7] Plant managers, for example, handle inventory management, quality control, equipment failures, and minor union problems. They also coordinate the work of supervisors within the plant. Jason Hernandez, a regional manager at Starbucks responsible for the firm's operations in three eastern states, is a middle manager.

In recent years, many organizations have thinned the ranks of middle managers to lower costs and eliminate excess bureaucracy. Still, middle managers are necessary to bridge the upper and lower levels of the organization and to implement the

Working with Diversity

Aetna's Diverse Leadership

Did you know that while 10 percent of white Americans have no health insurance, 18 percent of Asian Americans, 19 percent of African Americans, and 33 percent of Hispanics have none? When you add in that people of color are also less frequently diagnosed with major diseases and less likely to receive prescription medicines, you have a very unequal healthcare system.

Aetna is working to change that. The insurer, which provides coverage for health, life, disability, and long-term care, has created innovative programs to aid minorities. For example, one program focuses on the high rate of certain diseases in ethnic populations, for example, the prevalence of diabetes in African Americans. Aetna supplies special educational materials, case managers, health screenings, and online patient support. The Aetna Foundation takes the initiative further by funding research into better diagnostic tools and new treatments; in 2005, it spent $19 million toward this effort.

Aetna's interest in diversity also includes its employment practices. The company's workforce includes 27 percent people of color and 75 percent women. Aetna's top team includes one-third racial minorities and women. And Aetna president, Ronald A. Williams, is one of just 18 African Americans to attain the rank of CEO at a *Fortune* 500 corporation.

Williams's leadership revitalized Aetna. Williams is soft spoken, a master implementer who rejuvenates troubled firms. Williams meets quarterly with 20 percent of Aetna's workforce, approximately 5,000 managers. By choice, his office is on the first floor of the headquarters building, not on the top floor with the other executives. Williams is an innovator, focusing on improving the quality of products. Rewarding patients who choose top-ranked physicians is another innovation. "Quality costs less," Williams says, referring to the relatively lower costs when patients obtain better treatment outcomes.

Williams has led the way in addressing racial disparity too. With his encouragement, Aetna plans to increase its focus on better health care for minorities, which will seek to drive down costs and expand Aetna's customer base. Aetna is expected to earn $1.3 billion in 2006, up from a net loss of $280 million in 2001. It seems Williams and Aetna can continue to do well while doing good.

References: Jessi Hempel, "Aetna: Succession at Full Speed," *Business-Week*, January 16, 2006, www.businessweek.com on March 1, 2006; Kenneth Meeks, "The 75 Most Powerful African Americans in Corporate America," *Black Enterprise*, February 2005, www.blackenterprise.com on April 15, 2006; "Company Demographics," "Quality Care for All: Reducing Racial and Ethnic Disparities in Health Care," "Serving Diverse Populations," "The Aetna Foundation," Aetna website, www.aetna.com on March 1, 2006.

strategies developed at the top. Although many organizations have found that they can indeed survive with fewer middle managers, those who remain play an even more important role in determining how successful the organization will be.

First-Line Managers   First-line managers supervise and coordinate the activities of operating employees. Common titles for first-line managers are supervisor, coordinator, and office manager. Positions like these are often the first held by employees who enter management from the ranks of operating personnel. Wayne Maxwell and Jenny Wagner, managers of Starbucks coffee shops in Texas, are first-line managers. They oversee the day-to-day operations of their respective stores, hire operating employees to staff them, and handle other routine administrative duties required of them by the parent corporation. In contrast to top and middle managers, first-line managers typically spend a large proportion of their time supervising the work of subordinates.

Managing in Different Areas of the Organization

Regardless of their level, managers may work in various areas within an organization. In any given firm, for example, ***areas of management*** may include marketing, financial, operations, human resource, administrative, and other areas.

> *areas of management*
> Managers can be differentiated into marketing, financial, operating, human resource, administration, and other areas

Marketing Managers   Marketing managers work in areas related to the marketing function—getting consumers and clients to buy the organization's products or services (be they Motorola digital cell phones, Ford automobiles, *Newsweek* magazines, Associated Press news reports, flights on Southwest Airlines, or cups of latte at Starbucks). These areas include new-product development, promotion, and distribution. Given the importance of marketing for virtually all organizations, developing good managers in this area can be critical.

Financial Managers   Financial managers deal primarily with an organization's financial resources. They are responsible for such activities as accounting, cash management, and investments. In some businesses, such as banking and insurance, financial managers are found in especially large numbers.

Operations Managers   Operations managers are concerned with creating and managing the systems that create an organization's products and services. Typical responsibilities of operations managers include production control, inventory control, quality control, plant layout, and site selection.

Human Resource Managers   Human resource managers are responsible for hiring and developing employees. They are typically involved in human resource planning, recruiting and selecting employees, training and development, designing compensation and benefit systems, formulating performance appraisal systems, and discharging low-performing and problem employees.

Administrative Managers   Administrative, or general, managers are not associated with any particular management specialty. Probably the best example of an administrative management position is that of a hospital or clinic administrator. Administrative managers tend to be generalists; they have some basic familiarity with all functional areas of management rather than specialized training in any one area.[8]

Other Kinds of Managers   Many organizations have specialized management positions in addition to those already described. Public relations managers, for example, deal with the public and media for firms like Philip Morris Companies and the Dow Chemical Company to protect and enhance the image of the organization. Research and development (R&D) managers coordinate the activities of scientists and engineers working on scientific projects in organizations such as Monsanto Company, NASA, and Merck & Company. Internal consultants are used in organizations such as Prudential Insurance to provide specialized expert advice to operating managers. International operations are often coordinated by specialized managers in organizations like Eli Lilly and Rockwell International. The number, nature, and importance of these specialized managers vary tremendously from one organization to another. As contemporary organizations continue to grow in complexity and size, the number and importance of such managers are also likely to increase.

concept
CHECK

Identify different kinds of an organization's managers by level and area.

How might the importance of different areas of management vary as a function of the firm's business?

Basic Managerial Roles and Skills

Regardless of their levels or areas within an organization, all managers must play certain roles and exhibit certain skills if they are to be successful. The concept of a role, in this sense, is similar to the role an actor plays in a theatrical production. A person does certain things, meets certain needs, and has certain responsibilities in the organization. In the sections that follow, we first highlight the basic roles managers play and then discuss the skills they need to be effective.

Managerial Roles

Henry Mintzberg offers a number of interesting insights into the nature of managerial roles.[9] He closely observed the day-to-day activities of a group of CEOs by literally following them around and taking notes on what they did. From his observations, Mintzberg concluded that managers play ten different roles, as summarized in Table 1.2, and that these roles fall into three basic categories: interpersonal, informational, and decisional.

Interpersonal Roles   There are three **interpersonal roles** inherent in the manager's job. First, the manager is often expected to serve as a *figurehead*—taking visitors to dinner, attending ribbon-cutting ceremonies, and the like. These activities are typically more ceremonial and symbolic than substantive. The manager is also expected to serve as a *leader*—hiring, training, and motivating employees. A manager who formally or informally shows subordinates how to do things and how to perform under pressure is leading. Finally, managers can have a *liaison* role. This role often involves serving as a coordinator or link among people, groups, or organizations. For example, companies in the computer industry may use liaisons to keep other companies informed about their plans. This enables Microsoft, for example, to create software for interfacing with new Hewlett-Packard printers at the same time those printers are being developed. And, at the same time, managers at Hewlett-Packard can incorporate new Microsoft features into the printers they introduce.

Informational Roles   The three **informational roles** flow naturally from the interpersonal roles just discussed. The process of carrying out the interpersonal roles

> **interpersonal roles**
> The roles of figurehead, leader, and liaison, which involve dealing with other people

> **informational roles**
> The roles of monitor, disseminator, and spokesperson, which involve the processing of information

Category	Role	Sample Activities
Interpersonal	Figurehead	Attending ribbon-cutting ceremony for new plant
	Leader	Encouraging employees to improve productivity
	Liaison	Coordinating activities of two project groups
Informational	Monitor	Scanning industry reports to stay abreast of developments
	Disseminator	Sending memos outlining new organizational initiatives
	Spokesperson	Making a speech to discuss growth plans
Decisional	Entrepreneur	Developing new ideas for innovation
	Disturbance handler	Resolving conflict between two subordinates
	Resource allocator	Reviewing and revising budget requests
	Negotiator	Reaching agreement with a key supplier or labor union

Table 1.2

TEN BASIC MANAGERIAL ROLES

Research by Henry Mintzberg suggests that managers play ten basic managerial roles.

Managers play a number of different roles in organizations. One common role for top managers is that of figurehead. These individuals, for instance, are participating in the groundbreaking ceremony for the new U.S. embassy in Macedonia. They are (from left) Richard Graves of KBR Services (the general contractor), Macedonian President Branko Crvenkovski, U.S. Ambassador to Macedonia Gillian Milovanovic, Overseas Buildings Operations Director Charles Williams, and OBO Project Director Stephen Ziegenfuss.

---

decisional roles
The roles of entrepreneur, disturbance handler, resource allocator, and negotiator, which relate primarily to making decisions

---

places the manager at a strategic point to gather and disseminate information. The first informational role is that of *monitor*, one who actively seeks information that may be of value. The manager questions subordinates, is receptive to unsolicited information, and attempts to be as well informed as possible. The manager is also a *disseminator* of information, transmitting relevant information back to others in the workplace. When the roles of monitor and disseminator are viewed together, the manager emerges as a vital link in the organization's chain of communication. The third informational role focuses on external communication. The *spokesperson* formally relays information to people outside the unit or outside the organization. For example, a plant manager at Union Carbide may transmit information to top-level managers so that they will be better informed about the plant's activities. The manager may also represent the organization before a chamber of commerce or consumer group. Although the roles of spokesperson and figurehead are similar, there is one basic difference between them. When a manager acts as a figurehead, the manager's presence as a symbol of the organization is what is of interest. In the spokesperson role, however, the manager carries information and communicates it to others in a formal sense.

Decisional Roles The manager's informational roles typically lead to the **decisional roles**. The information acquired by the manager as a result of performing the informational roles has a major bearing on important decisions that he or she makes. Mintzberg identified four decisional roles. First, the manager has the role of *entrepreneur*, the voluntary initiator of change. A manager at 3M Company developed the idea for the Post-it note pad but had to "sell" it to other skeptical managers inside the company. A second decisional role is initiated not by the manager but by some other individual or group. The manager responds to her role as *disturbance handler* by handling such problems as strikes, copyright infringements, or problems in public relations or corporate image.

The third decisional role is that of *resource allocator*. As resource allocator, the manager decides how resources are distributed and with whom he or she will work most closely. For example, a manager typically allocates the funds in the unit's operating budget among the unit's members and projects. A fourth decisional role is that of *negotiator*. In this role the manager enters into negotiations with other groups or organizations as a representative of the company. For example, managers may negotiate a union contract, an agreement with a consultant, or a long-term relationship with a supplier. Negotiations may also be internal to the organization. The manager may, for instance, mediate a dispute between two subordinates or negotiate with another department for additional support.

Managerial Skills

In addition to fulfilling numerous roles, managers also need a number of specific skills if they are to succeed. The most fundamental management skills are technical, interpersonal, conceptual, diagnostic, communication, decision-making, and time-management skills.[10]

Technical Skills   *Technical skills* are the skills necessary to accomplish or understand the specific kind of work being done in an organization. Technical skills are especially important for first-line managers. These managers spend much of their time training subordinates and answering questions about work-related problems. They must know how to perform the tasks assigned to those they supervise if they are to be effective managers. Horst Schulze, former CEO of Ritz-Carlton, got his start washing dishes and waiting tables at hotels in Germany. Over the next several years, he also worked as a bellhop, a front desk clerk, and a concierge. These experiences gave him keen insight into the inner workings of a quality hotel operation, insights he used to take Ritz-Carlton to the top of its industry.[11]

Managers must exercise a variety of different skills. Technical skills are the skills necessary to accomplish specific kinds of work. The woman in the red jacket is a Wal-Mart manager. She is shown here training two new employees to function as checkout cashiers. While she may never perform this work herself, she has the technical skills necessary to train others.

Interpersonal Skills   Managers spend considerable time interacting with people both inside and outside the organization. For obvious reasons, then, the manager also needs *interpersonal skills*—the ability to communicate with, understand, and motivate both individuals and groups. As a manager climbs the organizational ladder, he or she must be able to get along with subordinates, peers, and those at higher levels of the organization. Because of the multitude of roles managers must fulfill, a manager must also be able to work with suppliers, customers, investors, and others outside of the organization. Although some managers have succeeded with poor interpersonal skills, a manager who has good interpersonal skills is likely to be more successful. When A. G. Lafley was recently appointed CEO of Procter & Gamble, observers were quick to praise him for his strong interpersonal skills. As one colleague put it, "A. G. has a reputation for both people skills and strategic thinking."[12]

Conceptual Skills   *Conceptual skills* depend on the manager's ability to think in the abstract. Managers need the mental capacity to understand the overall workings of the organization and its environment, to grasp how all the parts of the organization fit together, and to view the organization in a holistic manner. This allows them to think strategically, to see the "big picture," and to make broad-based decisions that serve the overall organization.

Diagnostic Skills   Successful managers also possess *diagnostic skills*, or skills that enable a manager to visualize the most appropriate response to a situation. A physician diagnoses a patient's illness by analyzing symptoms and determining their probable cause. Similarly, a manager can diagnose and analyze a problem in the organization by studying its symptoms and then developing a solution. When the original owners of Starbucks failed to make a success of the business, Howard Schultz took over and reoriented the business away from mail order and moved it into retail coffee outlets. His diagnostic skills enabled him to understand both why the current business model was not working and how to construct a better one.

technical skills
The skills necessary to accomplish or understand the specific kind of work being done in an organization

interpersonal skills
The ability to communicate with, understand, and motivate both individuals and groups

conceptual skills
The manager's ability to think in the abstract

diagnostic skills
The manager's ability to visualize the most appropriate response to a situation

communication skills
The manager's abilities both to effectively convey ideas and information to others and to effectively receive ideas and information from others

Communication Skills   *Communication skills* refer to the manager's abilities both to effectively convey ideas and information to others and to effectively receive ideas and information from others. These skills enable a manager to transmit ideas to subordinates so that they know what is expected, to coordinate work with peers and colleagues so that they work well together properly, and to keep higher-level managers informed about what is going on. In addition, communication skills help the manager listen to what others say and to understand the real meaning behind letters, reports, and other written communication.

decision-making skills
The manager's ability to correctly recognize and define problems and opportunities and to then select an appropriate course of action to solve problems and capitalize on opportunities

Decision-Making Skills   Effective managers also have good decision-making skills. *Decision-making skills* refer to the manager's ability to correctly recognize and define problems and opportunities and to then select an appropriate course of action to solve problems and capitalize on opportunities. No manager makes the right decision *all* the time. However, effective managers make good decisions *most* of the time. And, when they do make a bad decision, they usually recognize their mistake quickly and then make good decisions to recover with as little cost or damage to their organization as possible.

time-management skills
The manager's ability to prioritize work, to work efficiently, and to delegate appropriately

Time-Management Skills   Finally, effective managers usually have good time-management skills. *Time-management skills* refer to the manager's ability to prioritize work, to work efficiently, and to delegate appropriately. As already noted, managers face many different pressures and challenges. It is too easy for a manager to get bogged down doing work that can easily be postponed or delegated to others.[13] When this happens, unfortunately, more pressing and higher-priority work may get neglected.[14] Jeff Bezos, CEO of Amazon.com, schedules all his meetings on three days a week, but insists on keeping the other two days clear so that he can pursue his own ideas and maintain the flexibility to interact with his employees informally.[15]

concept
CHECK

| List and define the basic managerial skills that contribute to success. | How might the various managerial skills relate to different managerial roles? |

The Nature of Managerial Work

We have already noted that managerial work does not follow an orderly, systematic progression through the workweek. Indeed, the manager's job is fraught with uncertainty, change, interruption, and fragmented activities. Mintzberg's study, mentioned earlier, found that, in a typical day, CEOs were likely to spend 59 percent of their time in scheduled meetings, 22 percent doing "desk work," 10 percent in unscheduled meetings, 6 percent on the telephone, and the remaining 3 percent on tours of company facilities. (These proportions, of course, are different for managers at lower levels.) Moreover, the nature of managerial work continues to change in complex and often unpredictable ways.[16]

In addition, managers perform a wide variety of tasks. In the course of a single day, for example, a manager might have to make a decision about the design of a new product, settle a complaint between two subordinates, hire a new assistant, write a report for his boss, coordinate a joint venture with an overseas colleague, form a task force to investigate a problem, search for information on the Internet, and deal with a labor grievance. Moreover, the pace of the manager's job can be relentless. She may feel bombarded by mail, telephone calls, and people waiting to see her. Decisions may have to be made quickly and plans formulated with little time for reflection.[17] But, in many ways, these same characteristics of managerial work also contribute to its richness and meaningfulness. Making critical decisions under intense pressure, and making them well, can be a major source of intrinsic satisfaction. And managers are usually well paid for the pressures they bear.

> "Business is simple. Management's job is to take care of employees. The employees' job is to take care of the customers. Happy customers take care of the shareholders. It's a virtuous circle."
>
> John Mackey, Founder and CEO of Whole Foods
> (*Forbes*, February 14, 2005, p. 110)

The Science and the Art of Management

Given the complexity inherent in the manager's job, a reasonable question relates to whether management is a science or an art. In fact, effective management is a blend of both science and art. And successful executives recognize the importance of combining both the science and the art of management as they practice their craft.[18]

The Science of Management   Many management problems and issues can be approached in ways that are rational, logical, objective, and systematic. Managers can gather data, facts, and objective information. They can use quantitative models and decision-making techniques to arrive at "correct" decisions. And they need to take such a scientific approach to solving problems whenever possible, especially when they are dealing with relatively routine and straightforward issues. When Starbucks considers entering a new market, its managers look closely at a wide variety of objective details as they formulate their plans. Technical, diagnostic, and decision-making skills are especially important when practicing the science of management.

The Art of Management   Even though managers may try to be scientific as often as possible, they must frequently make decisions and solve problems on the basis of intuition, experience, instinct, and personal insights. Relying heavily on conceptual, communication, interpersonal, and time-management skills, for example, a manager may have to decide among multiple courses of action that look equally attractive. And even "objective facts" may prove to be wrong. When Starbucks was planning its first store in New York City, market research clearly showed that New Yorkers preferred drip coffee to more exotic espresso-style coffees. After first installing more drip coffee makers and fewer espresso makers than in their other stores, managers had to backtrack when the New Yorkers lined up clamoring for espresso. Starbucks now introduces a standard menu and layout in all its stores, regardless of presumed market differences, and then makes necessary adjustments later. Thus managers must blend an element of intuition and personal insight with hard data and objective facts.[19]

Becoming a Manager

How does one acquire the skills necessary to blend the science and art of management and to become a successful manager? Although there are as many variations as there are managers, the most common path involves a combination of education and experience.[20] Figure 1.4 illustrates how this generally happens.

Figure 1.4
**SOURCES OF MANAGEMENT
SKILLS**

*Most managers acquire their skills
as a result of education and experience. Though a few CEOs today do
not hold college degrees, most
students preparing for management
careers earn college degrees and
many go on to enroll in MBA
programs.*

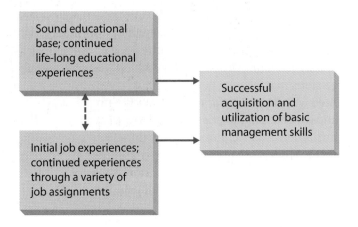

The Role of Education   Many of you reading this book right now are doing so
because you are enrolled in a management course at a college or university. Thus
you are acquiring management skills in an educational setting. When you complete
the course (and this book), you will have a foundation for developing your management skills in more advanced courses. A college degree has become almost a
requirement for career advancement in business, and virtually all CEOs in the
United States have a college degree. MBA degrees are also common among successful executives today. More and more foreign universities, especially in Europe,
are also beginning to offer academic programs in management.

Even after obtaining a degree, most prospective managers have not seen the
end of their management education. Many middle and top managers periodically
return to campus to participate in executive or management development programs ranging in duration from a few days to several weeks. First-line managers
also take advantage of extension and continuing education programs offered by
institutions of higher education. A recent innovation in extended management
education is the executive MBA program offered by many top business schools, in
which middle and top managers with several years of experience complete an
accelerated program of study on weekends.[21] Finally, many large companies have
in-house training programs for furthering managers' education. Indeed, some
firms have even created what are essentially corporate universities to provide the
specialized education they feel is required for their managers in order for them to
remain successful. McDonald's and Shell Oil are among the leaders in this area.
Regardless of the type of training, there is also a distinct trend toward online educational development for managers.[22]

The primary advantage of education as a source of management skills is that, as
a student, a person can follow a well-developed program of study, becoming familiar with current research and thinking on management. And many college students
can devote full-time energy and attention to learning. On the negative side, management education is often very general, to meet the needs of a wide variety of students, and specific know-how may be hard to obtain. Further, many aspects of the
manager's job can be discussed in a book but cannot really be appreciated and
understood until they are experienced.

The Role of Experience   This book will help provide you with a solid foundation
for enhancing your management skills. Even if you were to memorize every word
in every management book ever written, however, you could not then step into a

top-management position and be effective. The reason? Management skills must also be learned through experience. Most managers advanced to their present positions from other jobs. Only by experiencing the day-to-day pressures a manager faces and by meeting a variety of managerial challenges can an individual develop insights into the real nature and character of managerial work.

For this reason, most large companies, and many smaller ones as well, have developed management training programs for their prospective managers. People are hired from college campuses, from other organizations, or from the ranks of the organization's first-line managers and operating employees. These people are systematically assigned to a variety of jobs. Over time, the individual is exposed to most, if not all, of the major aspects of the organization. In this way the manager learns by experience. The training programs at some companies, such as Procter & Gamble, General Mills, and Shell Oil, are so good that other companies try to hire people who have graduated from them.[23] Even without formal training programs, managers can achieve success as they profit from varied experiences. For example, Herb Kelleher was a practicing attorney before he took over at Southwest Airlines. Of course, natural ability, drive, and self-motivation also play roles in acquiring experience and developing management skills.

Most effective managers learn their skills through a combination of education and experience. Some type of college degree, even if it is not in business administration, usually provides a foundation for a management career. The individual then gets his or her first job and subsequently progresses through a variety of management situations. During the manager's rise in the organization, occasional education "updates," such as management development programs, may supplement on-the-job experience. And, increasingly, managers need to acquire international expertise as part of their personal development. As with general managerial skills, international expertise can be acquired through a combination of education and experience.[24]

The Scope of Management

When most people think of managers and management, they think of profit-seeking organizations. Throughout this chapter, we use people like Sergey Brin and Larry Page of Google, Howard Schultz of Starbucks, and Robert Nardelli of Home Depot as examples. But we also mentioned examples from sports, religion, and other fields in which management is essential. Indeed, any group of two or more persons working together to achieve a goal and having human, material, financial, or informational resources at its disposal requires the practice of management.

Managing in Profit-Seeking Organizations Most of what we know about management comes from large profit-seeking organizations because their survival has long depended on efficiency and effectiveness. Examples of large businesses include industrial firms such as ExxonMobil, Toyota, BMW, Xerox, Unilever, and Levi Strauss;

Managers are needed in all manner of organizations, including voluntary ones. For instance, these volunteers from PacifiCare Health Systems came together from around Southern California to build one of three houses for families whose homes were destroyed during Hurricane Katrina. The houses were constructed, then disassembled and shipped to Texas, where they were rebuilt and completed on the site where the families are staying. A project manager was needed to oversee the work.

commercial banks such as Citicorp, Fuji Bank, and Wells Fargo; insurance companies such as Prudential, State Farm, and Metropolitan Life; retailers such as Sears, Safeway, and Target; transportation companies such as Continental Airlines and Consolidated Freightways; utilities such as Pacific Gas & Electric and Consolidated Edison of New York; communication companies such as CBS and the New York Times Company; and service organizations such as Kelly Services, KinderCare Learning Centers, and Century 21 Real Estate.

Although many people associate management primarily with large businesses, effective management is also essential for small businesses, which play an important role in the country's economy. In fact, most of this nation's businesses are small. In some respects, effective management is more important in a small business than in a large one. A large firm such as ExxonMobil or Monsanto can recover relatively easily from losing several thousand dollars on an incorrect decision; even losses of millions of dollars would not threaten their long-term survival. But a small business may ill afford even a much smaller loss. Of course, some small businesses become big ones. Dell Computer, for example, was started by one person—Michael Dell—in 1984. By 2005 it had become one of the largest businesses in the United States, with annual sales of almost $56 billion.

In recent years, the importance of international management has increased dramatically. The list of U.S. firms doing business in other countries is staggering. ExxonMobil, for example, derives almost 75 percent of its revenues from foreign markets, and Coca-Cola derives more than 80 percent of its sales from foreign markets. Other major U.S. exporters include General Motors, General Electric, Boeing, and Caterpillar. And even numbers like Ford's are deceptive. For example, the auto maker has large subsidiaries based in many European countries whose sales are not included as foreign revenue. Moreover, a number of major firms that do business in the United States have their headquarters in other countries. Firms in this category include the Royal Dutch/Shell Group (the Netherlands), Fiat S.p.A. (Italy), Nestlé S.A. (Switzerland), and Massey Ferguson (Canada). International management is not, however, confined to profit-seeking organizations. Several international sports federations (such as Little League Baseball), branches (embassies) of the federal government, and the Roman Catholic Church are established in most countries as well. In some respects, the military was one of the first multinational organizations. International management is covered in depth in Chapter 5.

Managing in Not-for-Profit Organizations   Intangible goals such as education, social services, public protection, and recreation are often the primary aim of not-for-profit organizations. Examples include United Way of America, the U.S. Postal Service, Girl Scouts of the U.S.A., the International Olympic Committee, art galleries, museums, and the Public Broadcasting System (PBS). Although these and similar organizations may not have to be profitable to attract investors, they must still employ sound management practices if they are to survive and work toward their goals.[25] And they must handle money in an efficient and effective way. If the United Way were to begin to spend large portions of its contributions on administration, contributors would lose confidence in the organization and make their charitable donations elsewhere.

The management of government organizations and agencies is often regarded as a separate specialty: public administration. Government organizations include the Federal Trade Commission (FTC), the Environmental Protection Agency (EPA), the National Science Foundation, all branches of the military, state highway departments, and federal and state prison systems. Tax dollars support government organizations, so politicians and citizens' groups are acutely sensitive to the need for efficiency and effectiveness.

Public and private schools, colleges, and universities all stand to benefit from the efficient use of resources. Taxpayer "revolts" in states such as California and Massachusetts have drastically cut back the tax money available for education, forcing administrators to make tough decisions about allocating remaining resources.

Managing healthcare facilities such as clinics, hospitals, and HMOs (health maintenance organizations) is now considered a separate field of management. Here, as in other organizations, scarce resources dictate an efficient and effective approach. In recent years many universities have established healthcare administration programs to train managers as specialists in this field.

Good management is also required in nontraditional settings to meet established goals. To one extent or another, management is practiced in religious organizations, terrorist groups, fraternities and sororities, organized crime, street gangs, neighborhood associations, and individual households. In short, as we note at the beginning of this chapter, management and managers have a profound influence on all of us.

Is management an art or a science? | *Identify four very different kinds of organizations and describe the role of management in their success.*   **concept** CHECK

The New Workplace

One of the most interesting characteristics of managerial work is the rapidly changing workplace. Indeed, this new workplace is accompanied by dramatic challenges and amazing opportunities. Among other things, workplace changes relate in part to both workforce reductions and expansion. But even more central to the idea of workplace change are such developments as workforce diversity and characteristics of new workers themselves.

The management of diversity is an important organizational challenge today. The term *diversity* refers to differences among people. Diversity may be reflected along numerous dimensions, but most managers tend to focus on age, gender, ethnicity, and physical abilities and disabilities.[26] For example, the average age of workers in the United States is gradually increasing. This is partly because of declining birthrates and partly because people are living and working longer. Many organizations are finding retirees to be excellent part-time and temporary employees. McDonald's has hired hundreds of elderly workers in recent years. Apple Computer has used many retired workers for temporary assignments and projects. By hiring retirees, the organization gets the expertise of skilled workers, and the individuals get extra income and an opportunity to continue to use their skills.

An increasing number of women have also entered the U.S. workforce. In 1950 only about one-third of U.S. women worked outside their homes; today, almost two-thirds work part time or full time outside the home. Many occupations traditionally dominated by women—nursing, teaching, secretarial work—continue to be popular with females. But women have also moved increasingly into occupations previously dominated by males, becoming lawyers, physicians, and executives. Further, many blue-collar jobs are increasingly being sought by women; and women are increasingly moving into positions of both business ownership as entrepreneurs and senior executives in major corporations. Similarly, more and more men are also entering occupations previously dominated by women. For example, there are more male office assistants and nurses today than ever before.

The ethnic composition of the workplace is also changing. One obvious change has been the increasing number of Hispanics and African Americans entering the workplace.[27] Further, many of these individuals now hold executive positions. In addition, there has been a dramatic influx of immigrant workers in the last few years. Immigrants and refugees from Central America and Asia have entered the U.S. workforce in record numbers.

The passage of the Americans with Disabilities Act also brought to the forefront the importance of providing equal employment opportunities for people with various disabilities. As a result, organizations are attracting qualified employees from groups that they may have once ignored. Clearly, then, along just about any dimension imaginable, the workforce is becoming more diverse. Workforce diversity enhances the effectiveness of most organizations, but it also provides special challenges for managers. We return to these issues in Chapter 6.

Aside from its demographic composition, the workforce today is changing in other ways. During the 1980s, many people entering the workforce were what came to be called yuppies, slang for "young urban professionals." These individuals were highly motivated by career prospects, sought employment with big corporations, and often were willing to make work their highest priority. Thus they put in long hours and could be expected to remain loyal to the company, regardless of what happened.

But younger people entering the workforce in the 1990s were frequently quite different from their predecessors. Sometimes called Generation X-ers, these workers were less devoted to long-term career prospects and less willing to adapt to a corporate mind-set that stresses conformity and uniformity. Instead, they often sought work in smaller, more entrepreneurial firms that allowed flexibility and individuality. They also placed a premium on lifestyle considerations, often putting location high on their list of priorities when selecting an employer. And, of course, new workers entering the workforce today are different from their counterparts in the 1980s and those in the 1990s.

Thus managers are increasingly faced with the challenge of first creating an environment that will be attractive to today's worker. Second, managers must address the challenge of providing new and different incentives to keep people motivated and interested in their work. Finally, they must build enough flexibility into the organization to accommodate an ever-changing set of lifestyles and preferences.

New technologies have greatly changed the way managers work. Jennifer Castagnier, for instance, is responsible for managing patient care in one unit of the Indiana Heart Hospital. She can use a bedside workstation to check a patient's medical history, monitor vital signs, order tests and medications, and issue discharge instructions. Work that once required hours of time and pages of paperwork can now be done in minutes and be handled electronically.

Managers must also be prepared to address organization change.[28] This has always been a concern, but the rapid, constant environmental change faced by businesses today has made change management even more critical. Simply put, an organization that fails to monitor its environment and to change to keep pace with that environment is doomed to failure. But more and more managers are seeing change as an opportunity, not a cause for alarm. Indeed, some managers think that if things get too calm in an organization and people start to become complacent, managers should shake things up to get everyone energized.

New technology, especially as it relates to information, also poses an increasingly important challenge for managers. Specific forms of technology, such as cellular telephones, personal digital assistants, and wireless communication networks, have made it easier than ever for managers to communicate with one another. At the same time, these innovations have increased the work pace for managers, cut into their time for thoughtful contemplation of decisions, and increased the amount of information they must process.

A final element of the new workplace we will note here is the complex array of new ways of organizing that managers can consider. Many organizations strive for greater flexibility and the ability to respond more quickly to their environments by adopting flatter structures. These flat structures are characterized by fewer levels of management, wider spans of management, and fewer rules and regulations. The increased use of work teams also goes hand in hand with this new approach to organizing. We will examine these new ways of organizing in Chapters 12 and 19.

concept
CHECK

What are the central components that characterize the new workplace? | *What are some even newer issues that managers today confront?*

Summary of Learning Objectives and Key Points

1. Describe the nature of management, define management and managers, and characterize their importance to contemporary organizations.
   - Management is a set of activities (including planning and decision making, organizing, leading, and controlling) directed at an organization's resources (human, financial, physical, and information) with the aim of achieving organizational goals in an efficient and effective manner.
   - A manager is someone whose primary responsibility is to carry out the management process within an organization.

2. Identify and briefly explain the four basic management functions in organizations.
   - Planning and decision making (determining courses of action)
   - Organizing (coordinating activities and resources)
   - Leading (motivating and managing people)
   - Controlling (monitoring and evaluating activities)
   - These activities are not performed on a systematic and predictable schedule.

3. Describe the kinds of managers found at different levels and in different areas of the organization.
   - By level, we can identify top, middle, and first-line managers.
   - Kinds of managers by area include marketing, financial, operations, human resource, administrative, and specialized managers.

4. Identify the basic managerial roles that managers play and the skills they need to be successful.
   - Interpersonal roles (figurehead, leader, and liaison)
   - Informational roles (monitor, disseminator, and spokesperson)

- Decisional roles (entrepreneur, disturbance handler, resource allocator, and negotiator).
- Key management skills are technical, interpersonal, conceptual, diagnostic, communication, decision-making, and time-management skills.

5. Discuss the science and the art of management, describe how people become managers, and summarize the scope of management in organizations.
   - The effective practice of management requires a synthesis of science and art, that is, a blend of rational objectivity and intuitive insight.
   - Most managers attain their skills and positions through a combination of education and experience.
   - Management processes are applicable in a wide variety of settings, including profit-seeking organizations (large, small, and start-up businesses and international businesses) and not-for-profit organizations (government organizations, educational organizations, healthcare facilities, and nontraditional organizations).

6. Characterize the new workplace that is emerging in organizations today.
   - The new workplace is characterized by workforce expansion and reduction.
   - Diversity is also a central component, as is the new worker.
   - Organization change is also more common, as are the effects of information technology and new ways of organizing.

Discussion Questions

Questions for Review

1. Contrast efficiency and effectiveness. Give an example of a time when an organization was effective but not efficient, efficient but not effective, both efficient and effective, and neither efficient nor effective.
2. What are the four basic activities that comprise the management process? How are they related to one another?

3. Briefly describe the ten managerial roles described by Henry Mintzberg. Give an example of each.
4. Describe a typical manager's day. What are some of the expected consequences of this type of daily experience?

Questions for Analysis

5. Recall a recent group project or task in which you have participated. Explain how members of the group displayed each of the managerial skills.
6. The text notes that management is both a science and an art. Recall an interaction you have had with a superior (manager, teacher, group leader). In that interaction, how did the superior use science? If he or she did not use science, what could have been done to use science? In that interaction, how did the superior use art? If he or she did not use art, what could have been done to use art?
7. Using the Internet, go to the websites of at least five large corporations and locate a biography of each CEO. What formal management education do these leaders have? In your opinion, what is the appropriate amount of formal education needed to be a corporate CEO? Why?

Questions for Application

8. Interview a manager from a local organization. Learn about how he or she performs each of the functions of management, the roles he or she plays, and the skills necessary to do the job.
9. Find an organization chart. You can find one in the library or by searching online. Locate top, middle, and first-line managers on the chart. What are some of the job titles held by persons at each level?
10. Watch a movie that involves an organization of some type. *Harry Potter, Training Day, Star Wars,* and *Minority Report* would all be good choices (or perhaps *Citizen Kane* for classic movie buffs). Identify as many management activities, skills, and roles as you can.

Building Effective Time-Management Skills

Exercise Overview

Time-management skills refer to the manager's ability to prioritize work, to work efficiently, and to delegate appropriately. This exercise allows you to assess your current time-management skills and to gain suggestions for how you can improve in this area.

Exercise Background

As described in this chapter, effective managers must be prepared to switch between the four basic activities in the management process. Managers must be able to fulfill a number of different roles in their organizations, and they must employ many different managerial skills as they do so. In addition, managers' schedules are busy and full of complex, unpredictable, and brief tasks, requiring managers to "switch gears" frequently throughout a workday.

Stephen Covey, management consultant and author of *The 7 Habits of Highly Effective People*, has developed a way of prioritizing tasks. He characterizes tasks using the terms *urgent* and *critical*. *Urgent* refers to tasks that must be done right away, such as tasks that have an approaching deadline. *Critical* tasks are those that have a high importance, that is, tasks that will have a big impact on critical areas of one's life. Thus, according to Covey, tasks fall into one of four quadrants: urgent, critical, urgent and critical, or not urgent and not critical.

Covey claims that most people spend too much time on tasks that are urgent, when they should instead be focused on tasks that are important. He asserts that workers who concentrate on urgent tasks meet their deadlines, but they may neglect critical areas such as long-term planning, and they may also neglect the critical areas of their personal lives. Effective managers can balance the demands of the urgent tasks with an understanding of the need to spend an appropriate amount of time on those that are critical.

Exercise Task

1. Visit the website of FranklinCovey (the firm co-founded by Stephen Covey) at www.franklincovey.com. Click on the tab marked "Effectiveness Zone," and then select "Assessment Sector." Take the Urgency Analysis Profile. This short online survey will require you to answer several questions and will take about 10 minutes.
2. Look at your profile. Explore the information available there, including the assessment of your current use of time and the suggestions for how you can improve your time management.
3. Do you agree with Covey's ideas about critical and urgent tasks? Explain your answer.
4. What is one thing that you can do today to make better use of your time? Try it and see if your time management improves.

Building Effective Conceptual Skills

Exercise Overview

Conceptual skills form the manager's ability to think in the abstract. This exercise will help you extend your conceptual skills by identifying potential generalizations of management functions, roles, and skills for different kinds of organizations.

Exercise Background

This introductory chapter discusses four basic management functions, ten common managerial roles, and seven vital management skills. The chapter also stresses that management is applicable across many different kinds of organizations.

Identify one large business, one small business, one educational organization, one healthcare organization, and one government organization. These might be organizations about which you have some personal knowledge or simply organizations that you recognize. Now imagine yourself in the position of a top manager in each organization.

Write the names of the five organizations across the top of a sheet of paper. List the four functions, ten roles, and seven skills down the left side of the paper. Now think of a situation, problem, or opportunity relevant to

the intersection of each row and column on the paper. For example, how might a manager in a government organization engage in planning and need diagnostic skills? Similarly, how might a manager in a small business carry out the organizing function and play the role of negotiator?

Exercise Task

1. What meaningful similarities can you identify across the five columns?

2. What meaningful differences can you identify across the five columns?

3. Based on your assessment of the similarities and differences as identified in Exercise Tasks 1 and 2, how easy or difficult do you think it might be for a manager to move from one type of organization to another?

CHAPTER CLOSING CASE

PLAYING HARDBALL AT HOME DEPOT

Home Depot CEO Robert Nardelli is taking his company in a radical direction: radical in its emphasis on a return to basics. At a time when many companies are exploring collaboration and decision making by consensus, Nardelli is pushing Home Depot to become more centralized. At a time when many companies are eliminating layers of management and reducing dependence on the formal organization hierarchy, Nardelli emphasizes a military-like discipline and obedience. At a time when many focus on progressive policies and experimentation, Nardelli rewards those who implement stringent plans to a high standard.

Nardelli's type of organization is one that used to be called command-and-control. Although widely popular throughout the economic expansion days of the 1950s and 1960s, its strict reliance on hierarchy and centralized decision making fell out of favor by the 1970s. Globalization, workplace diversity, rapid technological innovation, and even management consultants gradually shifted managerial attention toward

more "soft" topics, such as corporate culture and employee empowerment.

Nardelli adopted command-and-control to help the firm recover from problems with its former decentralized structure that gave store managers tremendous autonomy. Home Depot founders Bernie Marcus and Arthur Blank wanted to encourage innovation and initiative, but instead, the company "grew so fast the wheels were starting to come off," says Edward Lawler, a business professor at the University of Southern California. Today, the company has shifted again, back to where many firms started. "What worked 20 years ago may not work today," says Home Depot's head of North America, Carl Liebert.

"['Soft' issues] are extremely important issues, but the problem has been that they have generally been considered as stand-alone activities, almost as if they are strategies unto themselves," say authors George Stalk, Rob Lachenauer, and John Butman in their 2004 best-seller, *Hardball: Are You Playing to Play or Playing to*

Win? "But without a business strategy that will create or sustain competitive advantage, no amount of customer care or employee motivation will bring a company success or longevity. . . . Hardball companies have vitality because they go to the heart of the matter." Home Depot is one of the firms highlighted in the book as an example of a hardball company.

The principles that Nardelli uses are simple. First, centralize control over functions such as purchasing and information technology for better coordination and control, as well as lowered expenses due to high purchase volume. Second, slow growth to allow more time to recover from changes and to slow expansion expenses. Third, control by measuring every input and output carefully, instead of relying on instinct, as the founders often did. Fourth, ruthlessly eliminate underperforming managers. Nardelli has replaced 98 percent of top managers since he took control in 2001.

But Nardelli's ideas aren't solely focused on cost cutting. He's making a gutsy move into wholesale supply to contractors. The sales margins are lower and professional customers demand service and quality. Yet this industry is very fragmented, so Home Depot could gain an advantage by being the first large-scale competitor to enter. The CEO is also increasing Home Depot's service offerings, again, to move the company into an industry with weaker competitors. The firm has started to do its own product testing and new-product development. "Soft" issues aren't neglected entirely. Potential new hires, for example, who have passed an interview must then undergo a role-playing exercise. Only the best problem solvers and implementers make the cut.

Home Depot's sales have increased by 30 percent since 2002, yet the share price has dropped 20 percent, and customer satisfaction ratings are lower than Lowe's. One former manager claims that Nardelli

measures good customer service instead of inspiring it. "The mechanics are there. The soul isn't." The CEO must find a way to answer critics who say that he's turned a flexible, entrepreneurial employer into "a factory."

Nardelli knows that he is zigging when the rest of the industry is zagging, but he's betting on the strategic power of difference. There is rarely any advantage over competitors that comes from following the same strategy that everyone is using. Winning is almost always associated with unusual or contrary strategies. For years, observers have criticized many participants in the discount retail industry, asking, "Why try to out-Wal-Mart Wal-Mart? Why try to cut costs lower than the master at cost cutting?" If Nardelli has his way, people will soon be asking, "Why try to outdo Home Depot in home goods retailing? Why try to beat the master at his own game?"

CASE QUESTIONS

1. Give examples from the case of times when Bob Nardelli is planning, organizing, leading, and controlling.
2. What types of managerial roles does Nardelli fulfill? What managerial skills does he use?
3. In your opinion, does Nardelli tend to place more emphasis on the science of management or the art of management? What are some potential problems with his approach?

CASE REFERENCES

Brian Grow, "Renovating Home Depot," *BusinessWeek*, March 6, 2006, pp. 50–58; Jennifer Reingold, "Bob Nardelli Is Watching," *Fast Company*, December 2005, www.fastcompany on March 1, 2006; George Stalk, Rob Lachenauer, and John Butman, *Hardball: Are You Playing to Play or Playing to Win?* (Cambridge, Mass.: Harvard Business School Press, 2004).

YOU MAKE THE CALL

Where Is Google Going?

1. Assume that you are a Google employee. Sergey Brin has just stopped by your desk and asked you this question: "I'd be interested in knowing what you like most and least about working here." How do you think you might respond?
2. Assume that you are a major Google stockholder attending the firm's annual board meeting. You have bumped into Larry Page at a reception, and he asks you "How do you think we are doing running this company?" How would you respond?
3. Assume that you are the founder and owner of a small software company. Google has indicated an interest in buying your company. In addition to the price, what other factors (if any) might be important to you?
4. Assume that you have been contacted by a marketing research company. They want to know what you like and dislike most about using Google. What would you say?

Test Prepper

college.hmco.com/business/students

Choose the correct answer. Answers are found at the back of the book.

1. T F An organization that manufactures its product at the lowest possible cost is by definition effective.

2. T F Managers who spend too much time performing the controlling function are likely to lead the organization away from its goals.

3. T F Administrative managers are not associated with any particular management specialty.

4. T F In the spokesperson role, managers formally relay information to people outside the organization.

5. T F Modern management has become almost completely a science and almost not at all an art.

6. Organizations use all of the following kinds of resources, EXCEPT

   A. human resources.
   B. political resources.
   C. financial resources.
   D. information resources.
   E. physical resources.

7. Jim is a manager who recently merged the company's personnel and employee training departments into a single human resources department. Which management function has Jim performed?

   A. Empowerment
   B. Quality control
   C. Leading
   D. Organizing
   E. Planning and decision making

8. Managers are often expected to engage in ceremonial or symbolic activities, such as presenting awards and holding retirement ceremonies. Which role do managers fill in performing these activities?

   A. Spokesperson
   B. Liaison
   C. Figurehead
   D. Resource allocator
   E. Disseminator

9. A manager who knows how to perform the specific kind of work being performed in the organization has

   A. decision-making skills.
   B. conceptual skills.
   C. diagnostic skills.
   D. technical skills.
   E. informational skills.

10. Which of the following challenges and opportunities are managers in the new workforce unlikely to face?

   A. Organizations are attracting qualified disabled employees.
   B. An increasing number of ethnic minorities are entering the workforce.
   C. The average age of workers is gradually increasing.
   D. An increasing number of women have entered the workforce.
   E. New information-processing technology has slowed the pace of managers' work.

chapter 2

Traditional and Contemporary Issues and Challenges

FIRST THINGS FIRST

Coke Needs Shaking Up

"We feel pretty good about the way the company is moving. We just have bumps in the road that are so doggone visible."

—JIMMY WILLIAMS, DIRECTOR, COCA-COLA

At the peak of Coca-Cola's dominance of the soft-drink industry, about 1996, the company seemed invincible. Coke's then-CEO Roberto Goizueta and many industry observers dismissed PepsiCo as a loser in the cola wars. Goizueta convinced stockholders that cola purchases were steady through both strong and weak economic conditions, and that cola drinkers were willing to pay a premium price for the number one soft drink.

Yet over the last ten years, Coca-Cola's tale has been one of poor strategy, weak leadership, shoddy implementation, and innovation failures. Everyone failed to predict the coming health backlash against soft drinks, with water and sports drinks replacing cola as the trendiest beverages. Unfortunately for Coke,

LEARNING OBJECTIVES

After studying this chapter, you should be able to:

1. Justify the importance of history and theory to management and discuss precursors to modern management theory.

2. Summarize and evaluate the classical perspective on management, including scientific and administrative management, and note its relevance to contemporary managers.

3. Summarize and evaluate the behavioral perspective on management, including the Hawthorne studies, human relations movement, and organizational behavior, and note its relevance to contemporary managers.

4. Summarize and evaluate the quantitative perspective on management, including management science and operations management, and note its relevance to contemporary managers.

5. Discuss the systems and contingency approaches to management and explain their potential for integrating the other areas of management.

6. Identify and describe contemporary management issues and challenges.

Coca-Cola has struggled in recent years, in part because its top managers have focused too much attention on quantitative methods and not enough attention on the strategic and behavioral elements of their business.

Pepsi regrouped and emerged as a strong competitor. Pepsi's stock price has climbed by one-third since 2001, while Coke's dropped by one-third, showing the different investor perceptions of the two rivals. How did Coke, once considered to be the most powerful U.S. brand, fall so far so fast?

Lack of strong, consistent leadership is the heart of the problem. Coke has had four CEOs in the previous decade. Goizueta was an excellent manager, but following his death in 1997, Douglas Ivester led the firm for two years until he was ousted by the board of directors. Ivester inherited a well-run machine with excellent control systems that enabled Coke to manage far-flung global operations. Yet Ivester's analytical, hard-working approach relied heavily on numbers while neglecting to motivate and develop employees. Coke insiders claim he distanced himself, ignoring the people side of the business.

Next came Doug Daft, a former head of Coke Japan whose five-year tenure ended in 2004. Daft didn't improve matters much. He was a good salesman, but again, not much of a "people" person. He focused on operational details, yet lacked a long-term strategic vision and the skills to communicate it.

Both Daft and Ivester relied on quantitative management, while failing to consider alternative approaches that focus on behavior. Under their leadership, Coke developed superior technical and operational skills, but vision, motivation, group processes, and culture received little attention. As a result, many capable managers and workers have left Coke. Even worse, although the quantitative models effectively pinpointed trouble spots, poor attitudes and strategic confusion led to weak implementation. Implementation is critical in the soft-drink industry, where competitive gains are measured in fractions of a percent. Innovation has suffered too. There were two new low-calorie drinks, Diet Coke with Splenda and Coca-Cola Zero, yet there hasn't been a truly innovative beverage developed since the launch of Diet Coke in 1982.

Daft, along with Ivester, made a significant number of serious mistakes as CEO, including allowing a culture of racism to flourish, resulting in a $192 million settlement in 2000. Both CEOs replaced capable leaders with others who were less capable but perhaps more loyal to Daft and Ivester, which resulted in a loss of talent and experience at Coke. They both have been accused of ignoring the murders of union leaders at a Coke bottling plant in Colombia, South America, whom the union alleges may have been killed as a union-busting tactic with the implicit consent of Coke. Coke refused to compensate the workers' families for the deaths, and now faces union conflicts, a boycott, and several lawsuits in U.S. courts.

On the positive side, Coke's financial performance is currently quite good. Earnings are sharply up in 2006, costs are lower, bottlers are stronger. "We feel pretty good about the way the company is moving," says director Jimmy Williams. "We just have bumps in the road that are so doggone visible." Yet investors have little confidence in the firm's leadership and governance, as shown by the depressed stock price.

So far, even with the 2004 selection of insider Neville Isdell as CEO, Coke has not recovered. In fact, Isdell promises more of the same, spending his first few months replacing many regional managers with those loyal to him. No one doubts Isdell's devotion and skills, with 40 years' of experience at Coca-Cola.

The question is, Will he be able to maintain Coke's quantitative skills and strengths, while also introducing improvements in personal and interpersonal processes? So far, nobody knows the answer to that question, not even, apparently, Mr. Isdell himself.[1]

One lesson managers can learn from the mistakes made by Coca-Cola is that they need to understand keenly what makes their businesses work. As one part of this understanding, it is critically important that all managers focus on today's competitive environment and how that environment will change tomorrow. But it is also important that they use the past as context. Managers in a wide array of organizations can learn both effective and ineffective practices and strategies by understanding what managers have done in the past. Indeed, history plays an important role in many businesses today, and more and more managers are recognizing that many lessons of the past are important ingredients in future successes.

This chapter provides an overview of traditional management thought, so that you, too, can better appreciate the importance of history in today's business world. We set the stage by establishing the historical context of management. We then discuss the three traditional management perspectives—classical, behavioral, and quantitative. Next we describe the systems and contingency perspectives as approaches that help integrate the three traditional perspectives. Finally, we introduce and discuss a variety of contemporary management issues and challenges.

The Role of Theory and History in Management

Practicing managers are increasingly seeing the value of theory and history in their work. In this section, we first explain why theory and history are important and then identify important precursors to management theory.

The Importance of Theory and History

Some people question the value of history and theory. Their arguments are usually based on the assumptions that history is not relevant to contemporary society and that theory is abstract and of no practical use. In reality, however, both theory and history are important to all managers today.

Why Theory? A ***theory*** is simply a conceptual framework for organizing knowledge and providing a blueprint for action.[2] Although some theories seem abstract and irrelevant, others appear very simple and practical. Management theories, used to build organizations and guide them toward their goals, are grounded in reality.[3] Practically any organization that uses assembly lines (such as DaimlerChrysler, Black & Decker, and Fiat) is drawing on what we describe later in this chapter as "scientific management." Many organizations, including Monsanto, Texas

> **theory**
> A conceptual framework for organizing knowledge and providing a blueprint for action

The practice of management dates back many hundreds of years. For instance, consider the ruins of the Incan city of Machu Picchu in Peru. The city was built between 1460 and 1470 at an elevation of 8,000 feet. It housed 1,200 people in over 200 buildings. The design and construction of this city—without the aid of modern construction equipment—represented a gargantuan management challenge.

Instruments, and Seiko, use the behavioral perspective (also introduced later) to improve employee satisfaction and motivation. And naming a large company that does not use one or more techniques from the quantitative management perspective would be difficult. For example, retailers like Kroger and Target routinely use operations management to determine how many checkout stands they need to have.

In addition, most managers develop and refine their own theories of how they should run their organizations and manage the behavior of their employees. For example, both Douglas Ivester and Doug Daft believed that quantitative methods would lead to the most effective business solutions, with little regard for behavioral considerations. Their belief that business can be reduced to formulas and numeric indicators reflects their theory about business operations. Similarly, James Sinegal, founder and CEO of Costco Wholesale, believes that paying his employees well but otherwise keeping prices as low as possible are the key ingredients in success for his business. This belief is based essentially on his personal theory of competition in the warehouse retailing industry.

Why History? Awareness and understanding of important historical developments are also important to contemporary managers.[4] Understanding the historical context of management provides a sense of heritage and can help managers avoid the mistakes of others. Most courses in U.S. history devote time to business and economic developments in this country, including the Industrial Revolution, the early labor movement, and the Great Depression, and to such captains of U.S. industry as Cornelius Vanderbilt (railroads), John D. Rockefeller (oil), and Andrew Carnegie (steel). The contributions of those and other industrialists left a profound imprint on contemporary culture.[5]

Many managers are also realizing that they can benefit from a greater understanding of history in general. For example, Ian M. Ross of AT&T's Bell Laboratories cites *The Second World War* by Winston Churchill as a major influence on his approach to leadership. Other books often mentioned by managers for their relevance to today's business problems include such classics as Plato's *Republic,* Homer's *Iliad,* and Machiavelli's *The Prince*.[6] And, in recent years, new business history books are directed more at women managers and the lessons they can learn from the past.[7]

Managers at Wells Fargo clearly recognize the value of history. For example, the company maintains an extensive archival library of its old banking documents and records, and even employs a full-time corporate historian. As part of their orientation and training, new managers at Wells Fargo take courses to become acquainted with the bank's history.[8] Similarly, Shell Oil, Levi Strauss, Ford, Lloyd's of London, Disney, Honda, and Unilever all maintain significant archives about their pasts and frequently evoke images from those pasts in their orientation and training programs, advertising campaigns, and other public relations activities.

> **"**Business history lets us look at what we did right and, more important, it can help us be right the next time.**"**
>
> Alfred Chandler, noted business historian
> (*Audacity,* Fall 1992, p. 15)

Precursors to Management Theory

Even though large businesses have been around for only a few hundred years, management has been practiced for thousands of years. By examining management in antiquity and identifying some of the first management pioneers, we set the stage for a more detailed look at the emergence of management theory and practice over the last hundred years.

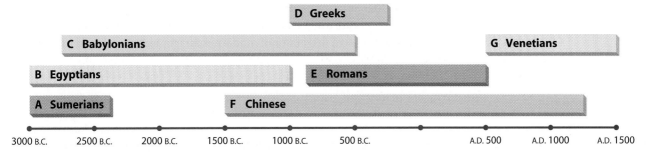

A Used written rules and regulations for governance

B Used management practices to construct pyramids

C Used extensive set of laws and policies for governance

D Used different governing systems for cities and state

E Used organized structure for communication and control

F Used extensive organization structure for government agencies and the arts

G Used organization design and planning concepts to control the seas

Figure 2.1

MANAGEMENT IN ANTIQUITY

Management has been practiced for thousands of years. For example, the ancient Babylonians used management in governing their empire, and the ancient Romans used management to facilitate communication and control throughout their far-flung territories. The Egyptians used planning and controlling techniques in the construction of their pyramids.

Management in Antiquity The practice of management can be traced back thousands of years. The Egyptians used the management functions of planning, organizing, and controlling when they constructed the pyramids. Alexander the Great employed a staff organization to coordinate activities during his military campaigns. The Roman Empire developed a well-defined organizational structure that greatly facilitated communication and control. Socrates discussed management practices and concepts in 400 B.C., Plato described job specialization in 350 B.C., and Alfarabi listed several leadership traits in A.D. 900.[9] Figure 2.1 is a simple time line showing a few of the most important management breakthroughs and practices over the last 4,000 years.

Early Management Pioneers In spite of this history, however, management per se was not given serious attention for several centuries. Indeed, the study of management did not begin until the nineteenth century. Robert Owen (1771–1858), a British industrialist and reformer, was one of the first managers to recognize the importance of an organization's human resources. Until his era, factory workers were generally viewed in much the same way that machinery and equipment were. A factory owner himself, Owen believed that workers deserved respect and dignity. He implemented better working conditions, a higher minimum working age for children, meals for employees, and reduced work hours. He assumed that giving more attention to workers would pay off in increased output.

Whereas Owen was interested primarily in employee welfare, Charles Babbage (1792–1871), an English mathematician, focused his attention on efficiencies of production. His primary contribution was his book *On the Economy of Machinery and Manufactures.*[10] Babbage placed great faith in the division of labor and advocated the application of mathematics to such problems as the efficient use of facilities and materials. In a sense, his work was a forerunner to both the classical and the quantitative management perspectives. Nor did he overlook the human element. He understood that a harmonious relationship between management and labor could serve to benefit both, and he favored such devices as profit-sharing plans. In many ways, Babbage was an originator of modern management theory and practice.

concept
CHECK

| Why are theory and history each important to managers? | Identify a key historical figure who interests you and then describe that person's contributions from a managerial or an organizational perspective. |

The Classical Management Perspective

At the dawn of the twentieth century, the preliminary ideas and writings of these and other managers and theorists converged with the emergence and evolution of large-scale businesses and management practices to create interest and focus attention on how businesses should be operated. The first important ideas to emerge are now called the ***classical management perspective***. This perspective actually includes two different viewpoints: scientific management and administrative management.

Scientific Management

Productivity emerged as a serious business problem during the first few years of this century. Business was expanding and capital was readily available, but labor was in short supply. Hence, managers began to search for ways to use existing labor more efficiently. In response to this need, experts began to focus on ways to improve the performance of individual workers. Their work led to the development of ***scientific management***. Some of the earliest advocates of scientific management included Frederick W. Taylor (1856–1915), Frank Gilbreth (1868–1924), Lillian Gilbreth (1878–1972), Henry Gantt (1861–1919), and Harrington Emerson (1853–1931).[11] Taylor played the dominant role.

One of Taylor's first jobs was as a foreman at the Midvale Steel Company in Philadelphia. It was there that he observed what he called ***soldiering***—employees deliberately working at a pace slower than their capabilities. Taylor studied and timed each element of the steelworkers' jobs. He determined what each worker should be producing, and then he designed the most efficient way of doing each part of the overall task. Next he implemented a piecework pay system. Rather than paying all employees the same wage, he began increasing the pay of each worker who met and exceeded the target level of output set for his or her job.

After Taylor left Midvale, he worked as a consultant for several companies, including Simonds Rolling Machine Company and Bethlehem Steel. At Simonds he studied and redesigned jobs, introduced rest periods to reduce fatigue, and implemented a piecework pay system. The results were higher quality and quantity of output, and improved morale. At Bethlehem Steel, Taylor studied efficient ways of loading and unloading railcars and applied his conclusions with equally impressive results. During these experiences, he formulated the basic ideas that he called "scientific management." Figure 2.2 illustrates the basic steps Taylor suggested. He believed that managers who followed his guidelines would improve the efficiency of their workers.[12]

Taylor's work had a major impact on U.S. industry. By applying his principles, many organizations achieved major gains in efficiency. Taylor was not without his

classical management perspective
Consists of two distinct branches—scientific management and administrative management

scientific management
Concerned with improving the performance of individual workers

soldiering
Employees deliberately working at a slow pace

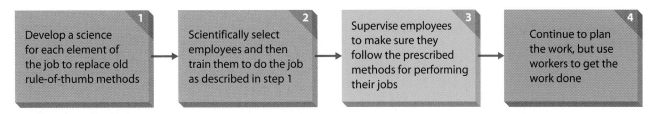

1	2	3	4
Develop a science for each element of the job to replace old rule-of-thumb methods	Scientifically select employees and then train them to do the job as described in step 1	Supervise employees to make sure they follow the prescribed methods for performing their jobs	Continue to plan the work, but use workers to get the work done

Figure 2.2

STEPS IN SCIENTIFIC MANAGEMENT

Frederick Taylor developed this system of scientific management, which he believed would lead to a more efficient and productive work-force. Bethlehem Steel was among the first organizations to profit from scientific management and still practices some parts of it today.

detractors, however. Labor argued that scientific management was just a device to get more work from each employee and to reduce the total number of workers needed by a firm. There was a congressional investigation into Taylor's ideas, and evidence suggests that he falsified some of his findings.[13] Nevertheless, Taylor's work left a lasting imprint on business.[14]

Frank and Lillian Gilbreth, contemporaries of Taylor, were a husband-and-wife team of industrial engineers. One of Frank Gilbreth's most interesting contributions was to the craft of bricklaying. After studying bricklayers at work, he developed several procedures for doing the job more efficiently. For example, he specified standard materials and techniques, including the positioning of the bricklayer, the bricks, and the mortar at different levels. The results of these changes were a reduction from 18 separate physical movements to 5 and an increase in output of about 200 percent. Lillian Gilbreth made equally important contributions to several different areas of work, helped shape the field of industrial psychology, and made substantive contributions to the field of personnel management. Working individually and together, the Gilbreths developed numerous techniques and strategies for eliminating inefficiency. They applied many of their ideas to their family and documented their experiences raising 12 children in the book and original movie *Cheaper by the Dozen.*

Henry Gantt, another contributor to scientific management, was an associate of Taylor at Midvale, Simonds, and Bethlehem Steel. Later, working alone, he developed other techniques for improving worker output. One, called the "Gantt chart," is still used today. A Gantt chart is essentially a means of scheduling work and can be generated for each worker or for a complex project as a whole. Gantt also refined Taylor's ideas about piecework pay systems.

Like Taylor, the Gilbreths, and Gantt, Harrington Emerson was a management consultant. He made quite a stir in 1910 when he appeared before the Interstate Commerce Commission to testify about a rate increase requested by the railroads. As an expert witness, Emerson asserted that the railroads could save $1 million a day by using scientific management. He was also a strong advocate of specialized management roles in organizations, believing that job specialization was as relevant to managerial work as it was to operating jobs.

Administrative Management

Whereas scientific management deals with the jobs of individual employees, ***administrative management*** focuses on managing the total organization. The primary contributors to administrative management were Henri Fayol (1841–1925), Lyndall Urwick (1891–1983), Max Weber (1864–1920), and Chester Barnard (1886–1961).

administrative management
Focuses on managing the total organization

Table 2.1

THE CLASSICAL MANAGEMENT
PERSPECTIVE

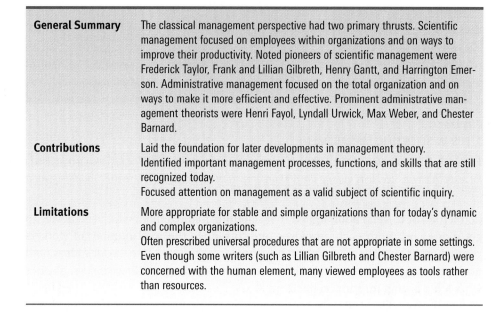

General Summary	The classical management perspective had two primary thrusts. Scientific management focused on employees within organizations and on ways to improve their productivity. Noted pioneers of scientific management were Frederick Taylor, Frank and Lillian Gilbreth, Henry Gantt, and Harrington Emerson. Administrative management focused on the total organization and on ways to make it more efficient and effective. Prominent administrative management theorists were Henri Fayol, Lyndall Urwick, Max Weber, and Chester Barnard.
Contributions	Laid the foundation for later developments in management theory. Identified important management processes, functions, and skills that are still recognized today. Focused attention on management as a valid subject of scientific inquiry.
Limitations	More appropriate for stable and simple organizations than for today's dynamic and complex organizations. Often prescribed universal procedures that are not appropriate in some settings. Even though some writers (such as Lillian Gilbreth and Chester Barnard) were concerned with the human element, many viewed employees as tools rather than resources.

Henri Fayol was administrative management's most articulate spokesperson. A French industrialist, Fayol was unknown to U.S. managers and scholars until his most important work, *General and Industrial Management,* was translated into English in 1930.[15] Drawing on his own managerial experience, he attempted to systematize the practice of management to provide guidance and direction to other managers. Fayol also was the first to identify the specific managerial functions of planning, organizing, leading, and controlling. He believed that these functions accurately reflect the core of the management process. Most contemporary management books (including this one) still use this framework, and practicing managers agree that these functions are a critical part of their jobs.

After a career as a British army officer, Lyndall Urwick became a noted management theorist and consultant. He integrated scientific management with the work of Fayol and other administrative management theorists. He also advanced modern thinking about the functions of planning, organizing, and controlling. Like Fayol, he developed a list of guidelines for improving managerial effectiveness. Urwick is noted not so much for his own contributions as for his synthesis and integration of the work of others.

Although Max Weber lived and worked at the same time as Fayol and Taylor, his contributions were not recognized until some years had passed. Weber was a German sociologist, and his most important work was not translated into English until 1947.[16] Weber's work on bureaucracy laid the foundation for contemporary organization theory, discussed in detail in Chapter 12. The concept of bureaucracy, as we discuss later, is based on a rational set of guidelines for structuring organizations in the most efficient manner.

Chester Barnard, former president of New Jersey Bell Telephone Company, made notable contributions to management in his book *The Functions of the Executive.*[17] The book proposes a major theory about the acceptance of authority. The theory suggests that subordinates weigh the legitimacy of a supervisor's directives and then decide whether to accept them. An order is accepted if the subordinate understands it, is able to comply with it, and views it as appropriate. The importance of Barnard's work is enhanced by his experience as a top manager.

The Classical Management Perspective Today

The contributions and limitations of the classical management perspective are summarized in Table 2.1. The classical perspective is the framework from which later theories evolved, and many of its insights still hold true today. For example, many of the job specialization techniques and scientific methods espoused by Taylor and his contemporaries are still reflected in the way that many industrial jobs are designed today.[18] Moreover, many contemporary organizations still use some of the bureaucratic procedures suggested by Weber. Also, these early theorists were the first to focus attention on management as a meaningful field of study. Several aspects of the classical perspective are also relevant to our later discussions of planning, organizing, and controlling. And recent advances in areas such as business-to-business (B2B) electronic commerce also have efficiency as their primary goal.

The limitations of the classical perspective, however, should not be overlooked. These early writers dealt with stable, simple organizations; many organizations today, in contrast, are changing and complex. They also proposed universal guidelines that we now recognize do not fit every organization. A third limitation of the classical management perspective is that it slighted the role of the individual in organizations. This role was much more fully developed by advocates of the

Technology Toolkit

A Tale of Two Compensation Plans

IBM and Google. Both are high-tech companies that attract and motivate the brightest engineers and computer scientists. Both run "campus-like" research facilities and compete against aggressive rivals. Yet the two firms couldn't be more different when it comes to their compensation plans, which are built on two different theories about how best to manage and motivate workers.

IBM, founded in 1888, adopts classical management theory, resulting in a traditional compensation plan. Money is assumed to be the primary motivator. The chief means of compensation are pay and financially valuable benefits, such as retirement plans and insurances. The company's website states, "Cash compensation opportunities include base pay, performance bonus, commissions, awards and other forms of earnings." Bonuses are related to workers' contribution as well as overall business unit performance, and usually equal 2 to 8 percent of annual pay. IBM offers generous paid vacation and holidays. Flexible schedules and telecommuting are options for some employees. IBM's website also lists "fun" benefits, which include, for example, reduced-price products, fitness centers, and cooking lessons.

Google, founded in 1998, takes a more behavioral approach to all of its operations, including its compensation plan. Money is just one motivator among many. Google offers generous base pay and stock options for many workers, common for high-tech startups. Other motivators include fun, friendship, intellectual challenge, and the chance to give back. There is a Google childcare center, on-site medical care and massages, reimbursement for using public transportation, and free meals and snacks all day. Employees can spend up to 20 percent of their time on projects of their choosing. There's beach volleyball, roller hockey, yoga, and pinball machines for relaxation. Google goes far beyond the traditional, offering live piano music, lava lamps, and a welcome to dogs, who share office space with their owners.

Of course, the difference between the two firms isn't absolute. Both offer some traditional and some nontraditional benefits. Both companies have been remarkably successful with their different policies. The comparison demonstrates that both a classical and a behavioral approach can be equally successful. The key is to choose the approach that best fits the company's management perspective and organization culture.

References: Julie Moran Alterio, "IBM Researchers Head to the Kitchen," *The Journal News* (Westchester, New York), December 31, 2003, www.thejournalnews.com on March 2, 2006; Alan Deutschman, "Can Google Stay Google?" *Fast Company*, August 2005, www.fastcompany.com on March 2, 2006; "Google Benefits," "The Google Culture," Google website, www.google.com on March 2, 2006; "Pay and Benefits," IBM website, www.ibm.com on March 2, 2006.

behavioral management perspective. Technology Toolkit highlights how one firm, IBM adheres to a classical framework in its approach to compensation, while Google uses an approach more consistent with the behavioral perspective.

concept
CHECK

| Summarize scientific management and describe the key ideas set forth by Taylor. | Compare and contrast scientific management and administrative management. |

The Behavioral Management Perspective

Early advocates of the classical management perspective viewed organizations and jobs from an essentially mechanistic point of view; that is, they essentially sought to conceptualize organizations as machines and workers as cogs within those machines. Even though many early writers recognized the role of individuals, their focus tended to be on how managers could control and standardize the behavior of their employees. In contrast, the ***behavioral management perspective*** placed much more emphasis on individual attitudes and behaviors and on group processes, and recognized the importance of behavioral processes in the workplace.

> **behavioral management perspective**
> Emphasizes individual attitudes and behaviors and group processes

The Hawthorne studies were a series of early experiments that focused on behavior in the workplace. In one experiment involving this group of workers, for example, researchers monitored how productivity changed as a result of changes in working conditions. The Hawthorne studies and subsequent experiments led scientists to the conclusion that the human element is very important in the workplace.

The behavioral management perspective was stimulated by a number of writers and theoretical movements. One of those movements was *industrial psychology,* the practice of applying psychological concepts to industrial settings. Hugo Munsterberg (1863–1916), a noted German psychologist, is recognized as the father of industrial psychology. He established a psychological laboratory at Harvard in 1892, and his pioneering book, *Psychology and Industrial Efficiency,* was translated into English in 1913.[19] Munsterberg suggested that psychologists could make valuable contributions to managers in the areas of employee selection and motivation. Industrial psychology is still a major course of study at many colleges and universities. Another early advocate of the behavioral approach to management was Mary Parker Follett (1868–1933).[20] Follett worked during the scientific management era, but quickly came to recognize the human element in the workplace. Indeed, her work clearly anticipated the behavioral management perspective, and she appreciated the need to understand the role of behavior in organizations.

Although Munsterberg and Follett made major contributions to the development of the behavioral approach to management, its primary catalyst was a series of studies conducted near Chicago at Western Electric's Hawthorne plant between 1927 and 1932. The research, originally sponsored by General Electric, was conducted by Elton Mayo and his associates.[21] Mayo was a faculty member and consultant at Harvard. The first study involved manipulating illumination for one group of workers and comparing their subsequent productivity with the productivity of another group whose illumination was not changed. Surprisingly, when

illumination was increased for the experimental group, productivity went up in both groups. Productivity continued to increase in both groups, even when the lighting for the experimental group was decreased. Not until the lighting was reduced to the level of moonlight did productivity begin to decline (and General Electric withdrew its sponsorship).

Another experiment established a piecework incentive pay plan for a group of nine men assembling terminal banks for telephone exchanges. Scientific management would have predicted that each man would try to maximize his pay by producing as many units as possible. Mayo and his associates, however, found that the group itself informally established an acceptable level of output for its members. Workers who overproduced were branded "rate busters," and underproducers were labeled "chiselers." To be accepted by the group, workers produced at the accepted level. As they approached this acceptable level of output, workers slacked off to avoid overproducing.

Other studies, including an interview program involving several thousand workers, led Mayo and his associates to conclude that human behavior was much more important in the workplace than had been previously believed. In the lighting experiment, for example, the results were attributed to the fact that both groups received special attention and sympathetic supervision for perhaps the first time. The incentive pay plans did not work because wage incentives were less important to the individual workers than was social acceptance in determining output. In short, individual and social processes played major roles in shaping worker attitudes and behavior.

The Human Relations Movement

The ***human relations movement***, which grew from the Hawthorne studies and was a popular approach to management for many years, proposed that workers respond primarily to the social context of the workplace, including social conditioning, group norms, and interpersonal dynamics. A basic assumption of the human relations movement was that the manager's concern for workers would lead to increased satisfaction, which would in turn result in improved performance. Two writers who helped advance the human relations movement were Abraham Maslow (1908–1970) and Douglas McGregor (1906–1964).

In 1943 Maslow advanced a theory suggesting that people are motivated by a hierarchy of needs, including monetary incentives and social acceptance.[22] Maslow's hierarchy, perhaps the best-known human relations theory, is described in detail in Chapter 16. Meanwhile, Douglas McGregor's Theory X and Theory Y model best represents the essence of the human relations movement (see Table 2.2).[23] According to McGregor, Theory X and Theory Y reflect two extreme belief sets that different managers have about their workers. ***Theory X*** is a relatively pessimistic and negative view of workers and is consistent with the views of scientific management. ***Theory Y*** is more positive and represents the assumptions that human relations advocates make. In McGregor's view, Theory Y was a more appropriate philosophy for managers to adhere to. Both Maslow and McGregor notably influenced the thinking of many practicing managers.

The Emergence of Organizational Behavior

Munsterberg, Mayo, Maslow, McGregor, and others have made valuable contributions to management. Contemporary theorists, however, have noted that many assertions of the human relationists were simplistic and provided inadequate

human relations movement
Argued that workers respond primarily to the social context of the workplace

Theory X
A pessimistic and negative view of workers consistent with the views of scientific management

Theory Y
A positive view of workers; it represents the assumptions that human relations advocates make

Table 2.2

THEORY X AND THEORY Y

Douglas McGregor developed Theory X and Theory Y. He argued that Theory X best represented the views of scientific management and Theory Y represented the human relations approach. McGregor believed that Theory Y was the best philosophy for all managers.

Theory X Assumptions	1. People do not like work and try to avoid it. 2. People do not like work, so managers have to control, direct, coerce, and threaten employees to get them to work toward organizational goals. 3. People prefer to be directed, to avoid responsibility, and to want security; they have little ambition.
Theory Y Assumptions	1. People do not naturally dislike work; work is a natural part of their lives. 2. People are internally motivated to reach objectives to which they are committed. 3. People are committed to goals to the degree that they receive personal rewards when they reach their objectives. 4. People will both seek and accept responsibility under favorable conditions. 5. People have the capacity to be innovative in solving organizational problems. 6. People are bright, but under most organizational conditions their potential is underutilized.

Source: D. McGregor and W. Bennis, *The Human Side of Enterprise: 25th Anniversary Printing,* 1985, Copyright © 1985 The McGraw-Hill Companies, Inc. Reprinted with permission.

descriptions of work behavior. For example, the assumption that worker satisfaction leads to improved performance has been shown to have little, if any, validity. If anything, satisfaction follows good performance rather than precedes it. (These issues are addressed in Chapters 15 and 16.)

Current behavioral perspectives on management, known as **organizational behavior**, acknowledge that human behavior in organizations is much more complex than the human relationists realized. The field of organizational behavior draws from a broad, interdisciplinary base of psychology, sociology, anthropology, economics, and medicine. Organizational behavior takes a holistic view of behavior and addresses individual, group, and organization processes. These processes are major elements in contemporary management theory.[24] Important topics in this field include job satisfaction, stress, motivation, leadership, group dynamics, organizational politics, interpersonal conflict, and the structure and design of organizations.[25] A contingency orientation also characterizes the field (discussed more fully later in this chapter). Our discussions of organizing (Chapters 11–14) and leading (Chapters 15–19) are heavily influenced by organizational behavior. And, finally, managers need a solid understanding of human behavior as they address such diversity-related issues as ethnicity and religion in the workplace. Indeed, all of these topics are useful to help managers better deal with fallout from the consequences of layoffs and job cuts and to motivate today's workers.

organizational behavior
Contemporary field focusing on behavioral perspectives on management

The Behavioral Management Perspective Today

Table 2.3 summarizes the behavioral management perspective and lists its contributions and limitations. The primary contributions relate to ways in which this approach has changed managerial thinking. Managers are now more likely to recognize the importance of behavioral processes and to view employees as valuable resources instead of mere tools. On the other hand, organizational behavior is still relatively imprecise in its ability to predict behavior, especially the behavior of a

Table 2.3
THE BEHAVIORAL MANAGEMENT
PERSPECTIVE

General Summary	The behavioral management perspective focuses on employee behavior in an organizational context. Stimulated by the birth of industrial psychology, the human relations movement supplanted scientific management as the dominant approach to management in the 1930s and 1940s. Prominent contributors to this movement were Elton Mayo, Abraham Maslow, and Douglas McGregor. Organizational behavior, the contemporary outgrowth of the behavioral management perspective, draws from an interdisciplinary base and recognizes the complexities of human behavior in organizational settings.
Contributions	Provided important insights into motivation, group dynamics, and other interpersonal processes in organizations. Focused managerial attention on these same processes. Challenged the view that employees are tools and furthered the belief that employees are valuable resources.
Limitations	The complexity of individual behavior makes prediction of that behavior difficult. Many behavioral concepts have not yet been put to use because some managers are reluctant to adopt them. Contemporary research findings by behavioral scientists are often not communicated to practicing managers in an understandable form.

specific individual. It is not always accepted or understood by practicing managers. Hence, the contributions of the behavioral school have yet to be fully realized.

concept
CHECK

What were the Hawthorne studies? What was learned from this research? | *What are the differences between the human relations movement and organizational behavior?*

The Quantitative Management Perspective

The third major school of management thought began to emerge during World War II. During the war, government officials and scientists in England and the United States worked to help the military deploy its resources more efficiently and effectively. These groups took some of the mathematical approaches to management developed decades earlier by Taylor and Gantt and applied them to logistical problems during the war.[26] They learned that problems regarding troop, equipment, and submarine deployment, for example, could all be solved through mathematical analysis. After the war, companies such as DuPont and General Electric began to use the same techniques for deploying employees, choosing plant locations, and planning warehouses. Basically, then, this perspective is concerned with applying quantitative techniques to management. More specifically, the **quantitative management perspective** focuses on decision making, economic effectiveness, mathematical models, and the use of computers. There are two branches of the quantitative approach: management science and operations management.

*quantitative management
perspective*
Applies quantitative techniques to
management

Management Science

Unfortunately, the term *management science* appears to be related to scientific management, the approach developed by Taylor and others early in the twentieth century.

But the two have little in common and should not be confused. ***Management science*** focuses specifically on the development of mathematical models. A mathematical model is a simplified representation of a system, process, or relationship.

At its most basic level, management science focuses on models, equations, and similar representations of reality. For example, managers at Detroit Edison use mathematical models to determine how best to route repair crews during blackouts. Citizens Bank of New England uses models to figure out how many tellers need to be on duty at each location at various times throughout the day. In recent years, paralleling the advent of the personal computer, management science techniques have become increasingly sophisticated. For example, automobile manufacturers DaimlerChrysler and General Motors use realistic computer simulations to study collision damage to cars. These simulations give them precise information and avoid the costs of crashing so many test cars.

Operations Management

Operations management is somewhat less mathematical and statistically sophisticated than management science and can be applied more directly to managerial situations. Indeed, we can think of ***operations management*** as a form of applied management science. Operations management techniques are generally concerned with helping the organization produce its products or services more efficiently and can be applied to a wide range of problems.

For example, Rubbermaid and Home Depot each use operations management techniques to manage their inventories. (Inventory management is concerned with specific inventory problems, such as balancing carrying costs and ordering costs, and determining the optimal order quantity.) Linear programming (which involves computing simultaneous solutions to a set of linear equations) helps United Airlines plan its flight schedules, Consolidated Freightways develop its shipping routes, and General Instrument Corporation plan what instruments to produce at various times. Other operations management techniques include queuing theory, break-even analysis, and simulation. All of these techniques and procedures apply directly to operations, but they are also helpful in such areas as finance, marketing, and human resource management.[27]

The Quantitative Management Perspective Today

Like the other management perspectives, the quantitative management perspective has made important contributions and has certain limitations. Both are summarized in Table 2.4. It has provided managers with an abundance of decision-making tools and techniques and has increased understanding of overall organizational processes. It has been particularly useful in the areas of planning and controlling. Relatively new management concepts such as supply chain management and new techniques such as enterprise resource planning, both discussed later in this book, also evolved from the quantitative management perspective. Even more recently, mathematicians are using tools and techniques from the quantitative perspective to develop models that might be helpful in the war against terrorism.[28] On the other hand, mathematical models cannot fully account for individual behaviors and attitudes. Some believe that the

General Summary	The quantitative management perspective focuses on applying mathematical models and processes to management situations. Management science deals specifically with the development of mathematical models to aid in decision making and problem solving. Operations management focuses more directly on the application of management science to organizations. Management information systems are developed to provide information to managers.
Contributions	Developed sophisticated quantitative techniques to assist in decision making. Application of models has increased our awareness and understanding of complex organizational processes and situations. Has been very useful in the planning and controlling processes.
Limitations	Cannot fully explain or predict the behavior of people in organizations. Mathematical sophistication may come at the expense of other important skills. Models may require unrealistic or unfounded assumptions.

Table 2.4

THE QUANTITATIVE MANAGEMENT PERSPECTIVE

time needed to develop competence in quantitative techniques retards the development of other managerial skills. Finally, mathematical models typically require a set of assumptions that may not be realistic.

concept
CHECK

What is management science? What is operations management?

What kinds of businesses are most and least likely to be affected by concepts from the quantitative perspective? Why?

Integrating Perspectives for Managers

It is important to recognize that the classical, behavioral, and quantitative approaches to management are not necessarily contradictory or mutually exclusive. Even though each of the three perspectives makes very different assumptions and predictions, each can also complement the others. Indeed, a complete understanding of management requires an appreciation of all three perspectives. The systems and contingency perspectives can help us integrate the earlier approaches and enlarge our understanding of all three.

The Systems Perspective

We briefly introduce the systems perspective in Chapter 1 in our definition of management. A **system** is an interrelated set of elements functioning as a whole.[29] As shown in Figure 2.3, by viewing an organization as a system, we can identify four basic elements: inputs, transformation processes, outputs, and feedback. First, inputs are the material, human, financial, and information resources the organization gets from its environment. Next, through technological and managerial processes, inputs are transformed into outputs. Outputs include products, services, or both (tangible and intangible); profits, losses, or both (even not-for-profit organizations must operate within their budgets); employee behaviors; and information. Finally, the environment reacts to these outputs and provides feedback to the system.

Thinking of organizations as systems provides us with a variety of important viewpoints on organizations, such as the concepts of open systems, subsystems, synergy, and entropy. **Open systems** are systems that interact with their environment,

system
An interrelated set of elements functioning as a whole

open system
A system that interacts with its environment

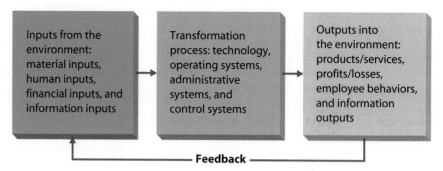

| Inputs from the environment: material inputs, human inputs, financial inputs, and information inputs | Transformation process: technology, operating systems, administrative systems, and control systems | Outputs into the environment: products/services, profits/losses, employee behaviors, and information outputs |

Feedback

Figure 2.3

THE SYSTEMS PERSPECTIVE OF ORGANIZATIONS

By viewing organizations as systems, managers can better understand the importance of their environment and the level of interdependence among subsystems within the organization. Managers must also understand how their decisions affect and are affected by other subsystems within the organization.

closed system
A system that does not interact with its environment

subsystem
A system within another system

synergy
Two or more subsystems working together to produce more than the total of what they might produce working alone

entropy
A normal process leading to system decline

whereas **closed systems** do not interact with their environment. Although organizations are open systems, some make the mistake of ignoring their environment and behaving as though their environment is not important.

The systems perspective also stresses the importance of **subsystems**—systems within a broader system. For example, the marketing, production, and finance functions within Mattel are systems in their own right but are also subsystems within the overall organization. Because they are interdependent, a change in one subsystem can affect other subsystems as well. If the production department at Mattel lowers the quality of the toys being made (by buying lower-quality materials, for example), the effects are felt in finance (improved cash flow in the short run owing to lower costs) and marketing (decreased sales in the long run because of customer dissatisfaction). Managers must therefore remember that although organizational subsystems can be managed with some degree of autonomy, their interdependence should not be overlooked.

Synergy suggests that organizational units (or subsystems) may often be more successful working together than working alone. The Walt Disney Company, for example, benefits greatly from synergy. The company's movies, theme parks, television programs, and merchandise-licensing programs all benefit one another. Children who enjoy a Disney movie like *Cars* want to go to Disney World, see the *Cars* attractions there, and buy stuffed toys and action figures of the film's characters. Music from the film generates additional revenues for the firm, as do computer games and other licensing arrangements for lunchboxes, clothing, and so forth. Synergy was also the major objective of Procter & Gamble's recent decision to buy Gillette—the firm decided it could use its own retailing presence and international distribution networks to substantially increase Gillette's sales. And Gillette's products are natural compliments to P&G's existing line of grooming products.[30] Synergy is an important concept for managers because it emphasizes the importance of working together in a cooperative and coordinated fashion.[31]

Finally, **entropy** is a normal process that leads to system decline. When an organization does not monitor feedback from its environment and make appropriate adjustments, it may fail. For example, witness the problems of Studebaker (an automobile manufacturer) and Kmart (a major retailer). Each of these organizations went bankrupt because it failed to revitalize itself and keep pace with changes in its environment. A primary objective of management, from a systems perspective, is to continually re-energize the organization to avoid entropy.

The Contingency Perspective

Another noteworthy recent addition to management thinking is the contingency perspective. The classical, behavioral, and quantitative approaches are considered **universal perspectives** because they try to identify the "one best way" to manage organizations. The **contingency perspective**, in contrast, suggests that universal theories cannot be applied to organizations because each organization is unique. Instead, the contingency perspective suggests that appropriate managerial behavior in a given situation depends on, or is contingent on, unique elements in that situation.[32]

Stated differently, effective managerial behavior in one situation cannot always be generalized to other situations. Recall, for example, that Frederick Taylor assumed that all workers would generate the highest possible level of output to maximize their own personal economic gain. We can imagine some people being motivated primarily by money—but we can just as easily imagine other people being motivated by the desire for leisure time, status, social acceptance, or any combination of these (as Mayo found at the Hawthorne plant). Leslie Wexner, founder and CEO of the Limited, used one managerial style when his firm was small and rapidly growing, but that style did not match as well when the Limited became a huge, mature enterprise. Thus Wexner had to alter his style at that point to better fit the changing needs of his business.

universal perspectives
An attempt to identify the one best way to do something

contingency perspective
Suggests that appropriate managerial behavior in a given situation depends on, or is contingent on, a wide variety of elements

An Integrating Framework

We noted earlier that the classical, behavioral, and quantitative management perspectives can be complementary and that the systems and contingency perspectives can help integrate them. Our framework for integrating the various approaches to management is shown in Figure 2.4. The initial premise of the framework is that

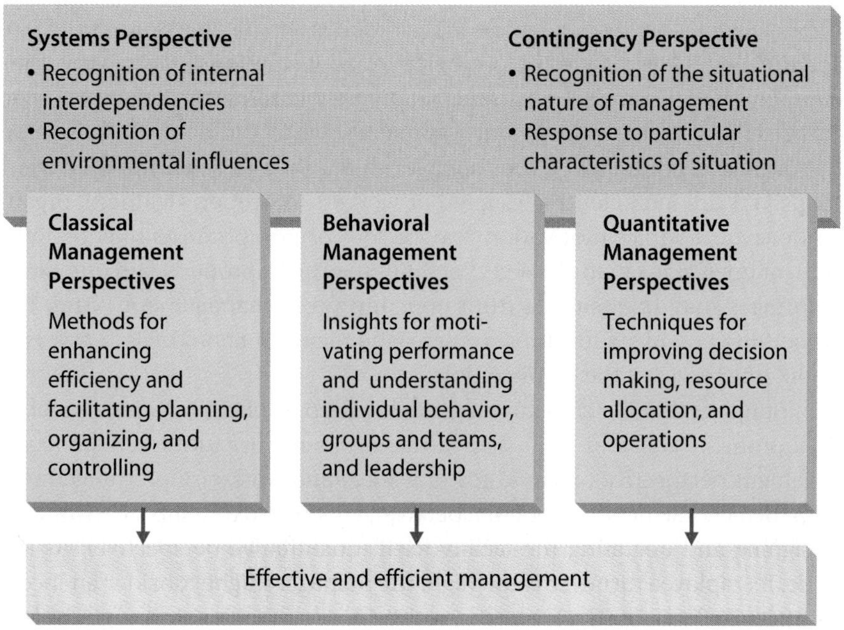

Figure 2.4
AN INTEGRATIVE FRAMEWORK OF MANAGEMENT PERSPECTIVES

Each of the major perspectives on management can be useful to modern managers. Before using any of them, however, managers should recognize the situational contexts within which they operate. The systems and contingency perspectives serve to integrate the classical, behavioral, and quantitative management perspectives.

Systems Perspective
- Recognition of internal interdependencies
- Recognition of environmental influences

Contingency Perspective
- Recognition of the situational nature of management
- Response to particular characteristics of situation

Classical Management Perspectives

Methods for enhancing efficiency and facilitating planning, organizing, and controlling

Behavioral Management Perspectives

Insights for motivating performance and understanding individual behavior, groups and teams, and leadership

Quantitative Management Perspectives

Techniques for improving decision making, resource allocation, and operations

Effective and efficient management

before attempting to apply any specific concepts or ideas from the three major perspectives, managers must recognize the interdependence of units within the organization, the effect of environmental influences, and the need to respond to the unique characteristics of each situation. The ideas of subsystem interdependencies and environmental influences are given to us by systems theory, and the situational view of management is derived from a contingency perspective.

With these ideas as basic assumptions, managers can use valid tools, techniques, concepts, and theories of the classical, behavioral, and quantitative management perspectives. For example, managers can still use many of the basic techniques from scientific management. In many contemporary settings, the scientific study of jobs and production techniques can enhance productivity. But managers should not rely solely on these techniques, nor should they ignore the human element. The behavioral perspective is also of use to managers today. By drawing on contemporary ideas of organizational behavior, managers can better appreciate the role of employee needs and behaviors in the workplace. Motivation, leadership, communication, and group processes are especially important. The quantitative perspective provides managers with a set of useful tools and techniques. The development and use of management science models and the application of operations management methods can help managers increase their efficiency and effectiveness.

Consider the new distribution manager of a large wholesale firm whose job is to manage 100 truck drivers and to coordinate standard truck routes in the most efficient fashion. This new manager, with little relevant experience, might attempt to increase productivity by employing strict work specialization and close supervision (as suggested by scientific management). But doing so may decrease employee satisfaction and morale, and increase turnover (as predicted by organizational behavior). The manager might also develop a statistical formula to use route driver time more efficiently (from management science). But this new system could disrupt existing work groups and social patterns (from organizational behavior). The manager might create even more problems by trying to impose programs and practices derived from her previous job. An incentive program welcomed by retail clerks, for example, might not work for truck drivers.

The manager should soon realize that a broader perspective is needed. Systems and contingency perspectives help provide broader solutions. Also, as the integrative framework in Figure 2.4 illustrates, applying techniques from several schools works better than trying to make one approach solve all problems. To solve a problem of declining productivity, the manager might look to scientific management (perhaps jobs are inefficiently designed or workers improperly trained), organizational behavior (worker motivation may be low, or group norms may be limiting output), or operations management (facilities may be improperly laid out, or material shortages may be resulting from poor inventory management). And, before implementing any plans for improvement, the manager should try to assess their effect on other areas of the organization.

Now suppose that the same manager is involved in planning a new warehouse. She will probably consider what type of management structure to create (classical management perspective), what kinds of leaders and work-group arrangements to develop (behavioral management perspective), and how to develop a network model for designing and operating the facility itself (quantitative perspective). As a final example, if employee turnover is too high, the manager might consider an incentive system (classical perspective), plan a motivational enhancement program (behavioral perspective), or use a mathematical model (quantitative perspective) to discover that turnover costs may actually be lower than the cost of making any changes at all.

What is the contingency perspective?

Select an organization and diagram its inputs, transformation processes, and outputs, consistent with the systems perspective.

Contemporary Management Issues and Challenges

Interest in management theory and practice has heightened in recent years as new issues and challenges have emerged. No new paradigm has been formulated that replaces the traditional views, but managers continue to strive toward a better understanding of how they can better compete and lead their organizations toward improved effectiveness. Figure 2.5 summarizes the historical development of the major models of management, described in the preceding sections, and puts into historical context the contemporary applied perspectives discussed in the next section.

Contemporary Applied Perspectives

In recent years, books written for the popular press have also had a major impact on both the field of organizational behavior and the practice of management. This trend first became noticeable in the early 1980s with the success of such classics as William Ouchi's *Theory Z* and Thomas Peters and Robert Waterman's *In Search of Excellence.* Each of these books spent time on the *New York Times* best-seller list and was required reading for any manager wanting to at least appear informed. Biographies of executives such as Lee Iacocca and Donald Trump also have received widespread attention. And bidding for the publishing rights to Jack Welch's memoirs, published when he retired as CEO from General Electric, exceeded $7 million.[33]

Other applied authors have greatly influenced management theory and practice. Among the most popular applied authors today are Peter Senge, Stephen Covey, Tom Peters, Jim Collins, Michael Porter, John Kotter, and Gary Hamel.[34] Their books highlight the management practices of successful firms such as Shell, Ford, IBM, and others, or outline conceptual or theoretical models or frameworks to guide managers as they formulate strategies or motivate their employees. Scott Adams, creator of the popular comic strip *Dilbert,* is also immensely popular today.

Outsourcing is a major issue facing managers today. By moving many jobs abroad, firms may lower their costs. But at the same time, they also reduce jobs available in their domestic environment. This worker is ironing clothing at the BonWorth factory in Mexico, which has 650 employees who produce about 10,000 garments a day to supply the company's 200-plus U.S. stores, which are scattered across 31 states.

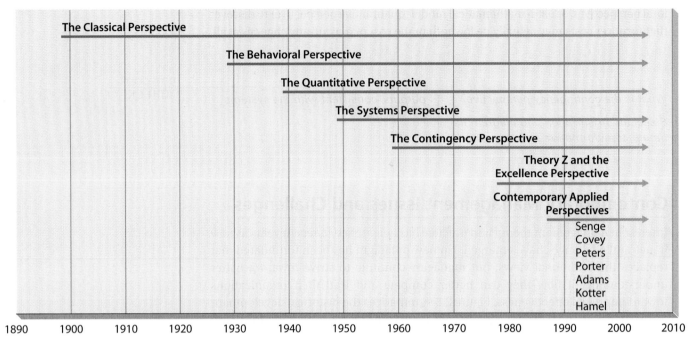

Figure 2.5

THE EMERGENCE OF MODERN MANAGEMENT PERSPECTIVES

Most contemporary management perspectives have emerged and evolved over the last hundred years or so. Beginning with the classical management perspective, first developed toward the end of the nineteenth century, and on through contemporary applied perspectives, managers have an array of useful techniques, methods, and approaches for solving problems and enhancing the effectiveness of their organizations. Of course, managers also need to recognize that not every idea set forth is valid, and that even those that are useful are not applicable in all settings. And new methods and approaches will continue to be developed in the future.

"You are what you read."
Martha Finney, business writer
(*HR Magazine*, June 1997, p. 141)

Adams is a former communications industry worker who developed his strip to illustrate some of the absurdities that occasionally afflict contemporary organizational life. The daily strip is routinely posted outside office doors, above copy machines, and beside water coolers in hundreds of offices.

Contemporary Management Challenges

Managers today also face an imposing set of challenges as they guide and direct the fortunes of their companies. Coverage of each of these is thoroughly integrated throughout this book. In addition, many of them are highlighted or given focused coverage in one or more special ways.

One of the most critical challenges facing managers today is an erratic economy that limits growth. A second important challenge is the management of diversity, as noted in Chapter 1. Another is employee privacy. A related issue has to do with the increased capabilities that technology provides for people to work at places other than their offices. The appropriate role of the Internet in business strategy is also a complex arena for managers.

Globalization is another significant contemporary challenge for managers. Managing in a global economy poses many different challenges and opportunities. For example, at a macro level, property ownership arrangements vary widely. So does the availability of natural resources and components of the infrastructure, as well as the role of government in business. Moreover, behavioral processes vary widely across cultural and national boundaries. For example, values, symbols, and beliefs differ sharply among cultures. Different work norms and the role that work plays in a person's life, for example, influence patterns of both work-related behavior and attitudes toward work. They also affect the nature of supervisory relationships, decision-making styles and processes, and organizational configurations. Group and intergroup processes, responses to stress, and the nature of political behaviors also differ from culture to culture. Chapter 5 is devoted to such global issues.

Another management challenge that has taken on renewed importance is ethics and social responsibility and their relationship to corporate governance. Unfortunately, business scandals involving unethical conduct have become almost commonplace today. From a social responsibility perspective, increasing attention has been focused on pollution and business's obligation to help clean up our environment, business contributions to social causes, and so forth. The proper framework for corporate governance is often at the center of these debates and discussions. Chapter 4 covers ethics and social responsibility in more detail.

Quality also continues to pose an important management challenge today. Quality is an important issue for several reasons. First, more and more organizations are using quality as a basis for competition. Continental Airlines, for example, stresses its high rankings in the J. D. Power survey of customer satisfaction in its print advertising. Second, improving quality tends to increase productivity because making higher-quality products generally results in less waste and rework. Third, enhancing quality lowers costs. Managers at Whistler Corporation once realized that the firm was using 100 of its 250 employees to repair defective radar detectors that had been built incorrectly in the first place. Quality is also important because of its relationship to productivity. Quality is highlighted in Chapter 21.

Finally, the shift toward a service economy also continues to be important. Traditionally, most businesses were manufacturers—they used tangible resources like raw materials and machinery to create tangible products like automobiles and steel. In the last few decades, however, the service sector of the economy has become much more important. Indeed, services now account for well over half of the gross domestic product in the United States and play a similarly important role in many other industrialized nations. Service technology involves the use of both tangible resources (such as machinery) and intangible resources (such as intellectual property) to create intangible services (such as a haircut, insurance protection, or transportation between two cities). Although there are obviously many similarities between managing in a manufacturing and a service organization, there are also many fundamental differences.

concept
CHECK

Besides Dilbert, *what other comic strips routinely reflect contemporary organizational life?*

Which contemporary management challenge interests you the most? Why?

Summary of Learning Objectives and Key Points

1. Justify the importance of history and theory to management and discuss precursors to modern management theory.
   - Theories are important as organizers of knowledge and as road maps for action.
   - Understanding the historical context and precursors of management and organizations provides a sense of heritage and can also help managers avoid repeating the mistakes of others.
   - Evidence suggests that interest in management dates back thousands of years, but a scientific approach to management has emerged only in the last hundred years.

2. Summarize and evaluate the classical perspective on management, including scientific and administrative management, and note its relevance to contemporary managers.
   - The classical management perspective had two major branches: scientific management and administrative management.
   - Scientific management was concerned with improving efficiency and work methods for individual workers.
   - Administrative management was more concerned with how organizations themselves should be structured and arranged for efficient operations.
   - Both branches paid little attention to the role of the worker.

3. Summarize and evaluate the behavioral perspective on management, including the Hawthorne studies, human relations movement, and organizational behavior, and note its relevance to contemporary managers.
   - The behavioral management perspective, characterized by a concern for individual and group behavior, emerged primarily as a result of the Hawthorne studies.

- The human relations movement recognized the importance and potential of behavioral processes in organizations but made many overly simplistic assumptions about those processes.
- Organizational behavior, a more realistic outgrowth of the behavioral perspective, is of interest to many contemporary managers.

4. Summarize and evaluate the quantitative perspective on management, including management science and operations management, and note its relevance to contemporary managers.
   - The quantitative management perspective and its two components, management science and operations management, attempt to apply quantitative techniques to decision making and problem solving.
   - Their contributions have been facilitated by the tremendous increase in the use of personal computers and integrated information networks.

5. Discuss the systems and contingency approaches to management and explain their potential for integrating the other areas of management.
   - The three major perspectives should be viewed in a complementary, not a contradictory, light. Each has something of value to offer.
   - Two relatively recent additions to management theory, the systems and contingency perspectives, appear to have great potential both as approaches to management and as frameworks for integrating the other perspectives.

6. Identify and describe contemporary management issues and challenges.
   - A variety of popular applied perspectives influence management practice today.
   - Important issues and challenges facing managers include employee retention, diversity, the new workforce, organization change, ethics and social responsibility, the importance of quality, and the continued shift toward a service economy.

Discussion Questions

Questions for Review

1. Briefly describe the principles of scientific management and administrative management. What assumptions are made about workers?

2. What are the differences between the contingency and the universal perspectives on management? How is the contingency perspective useful in the practice of management today?

3. Describe the systems perspective. Why is a business organization considered an open system?

Questions for Analysis

5. Young, innovative, or high-tech firms often adopt the strategy of ignoring history or attempting to do something radically new. In what ways might this strategy help them? In what ways might this strategy hinder them?
6. Can a manager use tools and techniques from several different perspectives at the same time? For example, can a manager use both classical and behavioral perspectives? Give an example of a time when a manager did this and explain how it enabled him or her to be effective.

Questions for Application

8. Go to the library or go online and locate material about Confucius. Outline his major ideas. Which seem to be applicable to management in the United States today?
9. Find a company that has laid off a significant number of workers in the last year. (*Hint:* Use the word *layoff* as a search term on the Internet.) Investigate that company. Why did the firm make the layoffs? In your opin-

4. For each of the contemporary management challenges, give at least one example, other than the examples found in the text.

7. Visit the website of Amazon.com. Select the tab that reads "See All 32 Product Categories" and then choose the link for "Books." Next select the link for "Bestsellers" and click on "Business & Investing" from the categories listed down the left side of the screen. Look at Amazon's list of best-selling business books. What ideas or themes do you see in the list? Which business leaders do you see?

ion, is the company likely to accomplish its intended goal by laying off so many workers? Why or why not?
10. Read about management pioneer Frederick Taylor at **www.cftech.com/BrainBank/TRIVIABITS/ FredWTaylor.html** or another source. Describe Taylor's background and experience. How does an understanding of Taylor's early career help you to better understand his ideas about scientific management?

Building Effective Decision-Making Skills

Exercise Overview

Decision-making skills refer to a manager's ability to recognize and define problems and opportunities correctly and then to select an appropriate course of action to solve those problems and capitalize on the opportunities. This exercise will help you develop your own decision-making skills while also helping you to better understand the importance of subsystem interdependencies in organizations.

Exercise Background

Assume you are the vice president for a large manufacturing company. Your firm makes home office furniture and cabinets for home theater systems. Because of the growth in each product line, the firm has also grown substantially in recent years. At the same time, this growth has not gone unnoticed, and several competitors have entered the market in the last two years. Your CEO has instructed you to determine how to cut costs by 10 percent so that prices can be cut by the same amount. She feels that this tactic is necessary to retain your market share in the face of new competition.

You have looked closely at the situation and have decided that there are three different ways you can accomplish this cost reduction. One option is to begin buying slightly lower-grade materials, such as wood, glue, and stain. Another option is to lay off a portion of your workforce and then pressure the remaining workers to work harder. As part of this same option, employees hired in the future will be selected from a lower-skill labor pool and thus be paid a lower wage. The third option is to replace your existing equipment with newer, more efficient equipment. Although this will require a substantial up-front investment, you are certain that lower production costs can be achieved.

Exercise Task

With this background in mind, respond to the following:

1. Carefully examine each of the three alternatives under consideration. In what ways might each alternative affect other parts of the organization?
2. Which is the most costly option (in terms of impact on other parts of the organization, not absolute dollars)? Which is the least costly?
3. What are the primary obstacles that you might face regarding each of the three alternatives?
4. Can you think of other alternatives that might accomplish the cost reduction goal?

Building Effective Conceptual Skills

Exercise Overview

Conceptual skills relate to a manager's ability to think in the abstract. This exercise allows you to practice your conceptual skills, while also giving you exposure to the management wisdom of another culture, conveyed in a way that is traditional in that culture.

Exercise Background

The scholarly study of management is a relatively new discipline. However, there have been managers as long as there have been organizations, and there is a great deal of management wisdom for you to discover from some very old sources.

One of these sources is Sun Tzu, a Chinese general who lived around 400 B.C. Sun Tzu rose from humble beginnings to become the most powerful general in the largest army on Earth during his time. This was a remarkable accomplishment for a peasant in a feudal society, and we can only speculate that Sun Tzu must have been an extraordinary person to have achieved this. Sometime after Sun Tzu's death, probably around 200 B.C., a book called *The Art of War* was written about him. This book describes principles that are ascribed to Sun Tzu and that are supposed to have formed the basis for his remarkable success.

Sun Tzu's book provided the organizing principles for the samurai warriors who emerged in medieval Japan, and it was used by Mao Zedong and Chiang Kai-shek in their fighting during the Chinese Communist revolution. The book was introduced to Western societies in 1772 after being translated by a Jesuit monk, and Napoleon is known to have read it. Today, the work is used extensively by U.S. military forces, as well as by many CEOs.

The book is written in an unusual style for today's tastes, and it deals exclusively with warfare, yet many contemporary treatments of the book relate Sun Tzu's principles in terms that can be useful in any competitive arena, such as war, business, or sports. Here is an example of Sun Tzu's ideas:

> With more careful calculations, one can win; with less, one cannot. How much less chance of victory has one who makes no calculations at all! Therefore, I say: Know the enemy and know yourself; in a hundred battles, you will never be defeated. When you are ignorant of the enemy but know yourself, your chances of winning or losing are equal. If ignorant both of your enemy and of yourself, you are sure to be defeated in every battle.

This is clearly a description of a principle of battle, yet it can be applied just as clearly to business.

If you are interested in reading more of Sun Tzu's ideas, an excellent translation of the full text of *The Art of War* is available online at **www.sonshi.com/learn.html**. Other translations can be found at many other sites or in books.

Exercise Task

1. Listen as your instructor tells you stories about Sun Tzu, in the Confucian style. Discuss your interpretation of these stories with your instructor and classmates.
2. Would a Confucian teaching style be appropriate for the courses taught at your school? Why or why not?

CHAPTER CLOSING CASE

GE'S CONTRIBUTIONS TO MANAGEMENT

In 1878, Thomas Edison founded General Electric (GE) as a private stock company. He used the company as a way to raise funds for his research into electric light. By 1879, he had created the first incandescent light. In that same year, GE developed the first machine capable of turning mechanical energy into enough electric energy to power a neighborhood of electric lights. Beginning with those innovations, GE became a company known for the quality of both its ideas and its implementation skills. Over the last 128 years, GE has produced innovative yet practical technologies, including the first electric-powered X-ray machine and television. The company was instrumental in developing a wide range of machines, from radios to locomotives, home appliances to radar systems. Medicine, manufacturing, and defense benefited from GE's inventions, as did households.

Yet these astonishing inventions are matched by GE's inventiveness in another arena—management. From its earliest days, GE has been a leader in developing new management techniques and practices. Many of these have been duplicated by other firms, but rarely does a firm surpass GE's skill in implementation or beat it to a new development.

GE's first management innovation was a corporate research and development lab, established in 1900. By the 1930s, the company was the first to offer pension and profit sharing plans. These were used to establish cooperative relations with labor, excluding unions from the relationship. The company

centralized decision making throughout its national operations in the 1950s, producing the unique "Blue Books" that governed managers' every move.

Strategic management was pioneered at GE in the 1960s and proved so popular that today the field is often the capstone course of an undergraduate degree in business. During this time, the company lent its name to the GE Business Screen, a technique developed jointly with consulting firm McKinsey. The Screen helped to identify the optimal portfolio of business units that can be held by a corporation. By the 1980s and 1990s, the company was building an effective global culture while being the first to offer programs such as Six Sigma quality initiatives and Work Out, a reengineering effort that simplified work and empowered employees.

There are other contributions from GE, in addition to its product and management innovations. They are able to change course frequently, abandoning whole programs. "Most people inside GE learn from the past but have a healthy disrespect for history," says CEO Jeff Immelt. "They have an ability to live in the moment and not be burdened by the past."

GE has also worked hard to develop leaders. One of its most controversial policies calls for the company to fire the lowest-performing 10 percent of workers each year. While some have called this policy inhumane, the remaining employees represent the best, and they are motivated to exceed their strategic

targets. Yet its training programs have produced many prominent alumni. CEOs who once were part of GE include Kevin Sharer of Amgen, Chris Kearney of SPX, Steven Bennett of Intuit, Larry Bossidy of Honeywell, and Larry Johnston of Albertson's.

GE doesn't have the fastest growth, most market value, highest profits, or largest size. Yet it's consistently ranked as one of the best firms. GE is the most admired firm in the world, according to 2006 surveys of business managers conducted by *Fortune*, *Barron's*, and the *Financial Times* of London. The firm has won that honor for 6 of the last 10 years. GE is the only one of the original Dow Jones Industrial Average 12, the dozen firms that made up the first DJIA in 1896, to remain on the list. The others have been acquired or gone out of business.

GE's important contributions to management are widely acknowledged. Many have been copied or used by other organizations. Dell Computer, for example, sends about 15 leaders through GE training programs each year. Larry Johnston, head of Albertson's, admires the firm's human resources skills the most. He says, "No one has better people. No one else's bench strength comes even close. It's that obsession with people that requires all GE leaders to spend a huge amount of time on human resources processes. . . . When you have the very best people, you don't have to worry as much about execution, because they make it happen." Others agree. "GE is the best school of management in the world bar none," is high praise from Dr. Clay Christensen, a management professor at Harvard Business School. The GE school has been teaching and leading businesses for over a century and will likely continue for the next 100 years.

CASE QUESTIONS

1. Do the various management developments at GE over the last century seem to follow the same pattern as the development of management theory, described in your text? Explain your answer.

2. Which of GE's management innovations seem to draw on a classical management perspective? Which seem to draw on a behavioral management perspective? Explain.

3. How does the contingency perspective explain the management changes that GE has made over the years?

CASE REFERENCES

"A History of the HR Race," *BusinessWeek*, October 10, 2005, www.businessweek.com on March 2, 2006; Geoffrey Colvin, "What Makes GE Great?" Fortune, March 6, 2006, pp. 89–96; Betsy Morris, "The GE Mystique," *Fortune*, March 6, 2006, pp. 98–104.

YOU MAKE THE CALL

Coke Needs Shaking Up

1. Assume you are a top manager at Coca-Cola. What might you do now to turn things around?

2. Assume you are a manager at Pepsi. What kinds of things might you do to capitalize on Coca-Cola's problems?

3. Assume that you are a personal confidant of Neville Isdell, who has asked your advice on what he might do to be a more effective leader. What would you tell him?

4. Assume you are the owner of a small local restaurant. You have had a long-standing contract to sell only Coca-Cola products. In what ways, if any, might Coke's problems affect you?

Test Prepper

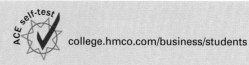

Choose the correct answer. Answers are found at the back of the book.

1. T/F   Scientific management deals with the jobs of individuals, and administrative management focuses on managing the total organization.

2. T/F   McGregor suggested the only way managers can operate efficiently is to acknowledge that people do not like work and try to avoid it.

3. T/F   A major limitation of the quantitative management perspective is that mathematical models cannot fully explain nor predict the behavior of people.

4. T/F   The contingency perspective helps managers find the "one best way" to manage.

5. T/F   Enhancing quality lowers costs for organizations.

6. Understanding the historical context of management

   A. will ensure managers make a profit in the future.

   B. may distract managers from solving their current organizational problems.

   C. is part of the management process.

   D. can help managers avoid the mistakes of others.

   E. should be a prerequisite for managers seeking promotions.

7. The basic assumption of the human relations movement was

   A. managers are most effective when they focus on their jobs rather than on employees.

   B. money is the greatest motivator of employee performance.

   C. all management theories are founded in an understanding of individuals.

   D. personal relations at work are the primary cause of inefficiency.

   E. increased satisfaction would result in improved performance.

8. Janice realizes her company is losing money because of poor inventory management procedures. Which of the following is most likely to help Janice?

   A. Classical management

   B. Operations management

   C. Behavioral management

   D. Scientific management

   E. Organizational behavior

9. Given the variety of management perspectives, how should managers determine their approach?

   A. Select the simplest perspective to implement and stay focused on efficiency.

   B. Allow employees to determine the appropriate perspective and delegate as many tasks as possible.

   C. Pursue effectiveness as the primary goal by picking one perspective and staying well within its guidelines.

   D. Rely most heavily on the most recent management perspectives and avoid relying on those that were developed long ago.

   E. Recognize the situational context and draw from any or all of the perspectives.

10. All of the following are contemporary challenges for managers EXCEPT

   A. an erratic economy.

   B. globalization.

   C. the shift towards a manufacturing economy.

   D. ethics and social responsibility.

   E. quality.

chapter 3

The Environment and Culture of Organizations

LEARNING OBJECTIVES

After studying this chapter, you should be able to:

1. Discuss the nature of the organizational environment and identify the environments of interest to most organizations.

2. Describe the components of the general and task environments and discuss their impact on organizations.

3. Identify the components of the internal environment and discuss their impact on organizations.

4. Discuss the importance and determinants of an organization's culture and how the culture can be managed.

5. Identify and describe how the environment affects organizations and how organizations adapt to their environment.

6. Describe the basic models of organizational effectiveness and provide contemporary examples of highly effective firms.

FIRST THINGS FIRST

The Powerful Mini

"[Small car design today is] about creating desire in a segment that has been sadly devoid of that in the U.S."

—FREEMAN THOMAS, DESIGNER, FORD

It began with the minivan. Then came monster pickup trucks and gas-guzzling SUVs. Finally, even the Army's big Humvee was adapted for household use. For more than a decade, the trend in automobiles has been toward big and bigger. Over the last few years, however, a new trend has emerged. Now, many auto buyers are looking for small cars, sometimes very small. Today's hottest rides include Toyota's Scion and new Yaris, the Rio from Kia, Chevy's Aveo, Nissan's new Versa, and more. One of the hottest is the Mini Cooper, with wait lists of three months or more for new buyers. Its website boldly claims, "Large. No Longer in Charge."

The Mini has been a major success because of its great fit with today's external environment. The newest Williams BMW Mini (left) is shown here passing an older model Mini on the streets of Manchester.

The move toward smaller autos has been fueled by a number of factors. One is the high price of gasoline, which encourages buyers to look for more fuel-efficient vehicles. While the behemoth Hummer H1 typically gets less than 10 miles per gallon of gasoline, the Toyota Echo achieves around 35. As gas prices continue to rise, the fuel-efficiency difference becomes ever more important.

Another economic consideration is the relatively lower sticker prices of many smaller cars. An SUV's price is usually 30 to 50 percent higher than the cost of a sedan, and small sedans are less expensive than large ones. Many buyers who cannot afford a new, large car welcome the option to purchase a small car. "People would still rather have a new car with a warranty over a used car, even if the used car is a bit bigger," says Kia Motors Chief Operating Officer Len Hunt.

Changing demographics also influences car buyers. Generation Y buyers are younger and more likely to delay marriage and children, so smaller cars meet their needs. Immigrants also tend to buy smaller cars, perhaps because they are more cost conscious or because they are more familiar with the smaller cars that prevail everywhere outside of the United States.

The Mini Cooper is one of the smallest of the small cars. It was originally designed and manufactured in England and now is made by BMW. To appeal to the needs of its unique market segment, the Mini can be customized online or at the dealer. About 80 percent of customers do so. After ordering, buyers use the "Where's My Baby?" tracking tool to follow the progress of their auto from the plant in Britain to delivery. After delivery, the owner becomes part of an online Mini club with e-mailed newsletters and special events. The car even receives a birthday card each year. Other clever marketing tools include racing games on the company's website and a just-for-fun "contract" that convertible owners must sign, promising to keep the top down at least 90 percent of the time.

The Mini offers features that small car buyers often desire. This includes convertible tops that can be operated from a button on the dash or from the key fob. The top goes up in just 15 seconds, allowing the driver to raise the roof at a traffic light. Design treats also include a "funky" 1950s-style dashboard and a sun roof that works even with the convertible. High-end MINI motion products offered on the company's website include a watch, driving shoe, and car tool kit.

The most important quality of the Mini may not be the design, special features, or fuel efficiency. It may simply be that the Mini is one of the first small cars that doesn't seem like a budget-driven compromise. Ford designer Freeman Thomas says that "[small car design today is] about creating desire in a segment that has been sadly devoid of that in the U.S." While only 10 percent of U.S. drivers bought small cars in 2005, that number seems sure to grow. And Mini seems destined to capture more than its fair share of this market segment.[1]

The world operates in what frequently appears to be mysterious ways. One day big vehicles are all the rage; in what seems like a day later, small and fuel-efficient alternatives are hot. Sometimes competition hurts, but sometimes it helps. When

Starbucks opens a new store, its closest competitors often benefit. Ford and General Motors compete with each other for consumer dollars, but work together to promote the interests of the U.S. auto industry. And CEOs face growing pressure to curb their salaries but grow their businesses. Clearly, the environmental context of business today is changing in unprecedented ways.

As we note in Chapter 1, managers must have a deep understanding and appreciation of the environments in which they and their organizations function. Without this understanding, they are like rudderless ships—moving along, but with no way of maneuvering or changing direction. This chapter is the first of four devoted to the environmental context of management. After introducing the nature of the organization's environment, we describe first the general and then the task environment in detail. We next discuss key parts of the internal environment of an organization. We then address organization-environment relationships and, finally, how these relationships determine the effectiveness of the organization.

The Organization's Environments

To illustrate the importance of the environment to an organization, consider the analogy of a swimmer crossing a wide stream. The swimmer must assess the current, obstacles, and distance before setting out. If these elements are properly evaluated, the swimmer will arrive at the expected point on the far bank of the stream. But if they are not properly understood, the swimmer might end up too far upstream or downstream. The organization is like a swimmer, and the environment is like the stream. Thus, just as the swimmer needs to understand conditions in the water, the organization must understand the basic elements of its environment to properly maneuver among them.[2] More specifically, a key element in the effective management of an organization is determining the ideal alignment between the environment and the organization and then working to achieve and maintain that alignment. To do so, however, the manager must first thoroughly understand the nature of the organization's environments.[3]

external environment
Everything outside an organization's boundaries that might affect it

internal environment
The conditions and forces within an organization

The **external environment** is everything outside an organization's boundaries that might affect it. As shown in Figure 3.1, there are actually two separate external environments: the general environment and the task environment. An organization's **internal environment** consists of conditions and forces within the organization. Of course, not all parts of these environments are equally important for all organizations. A small, two-person partnership does not have a board of directors, for example, whereas a large public corporation is required by law to have one. A private university with a large endowment (like Harvard) may be less concerned about general economic conditions than might a state university (like the University of Missouri), which is dependent on state funding from tax revenues. Still, organizations need to fully understand which environmental forces are important and how the importance of others might increase.

<u>**concept**</u>
CHECK

Define environment *as it relates to organizations.*

| *How easily differentiated are an organization's external and internal environments?*

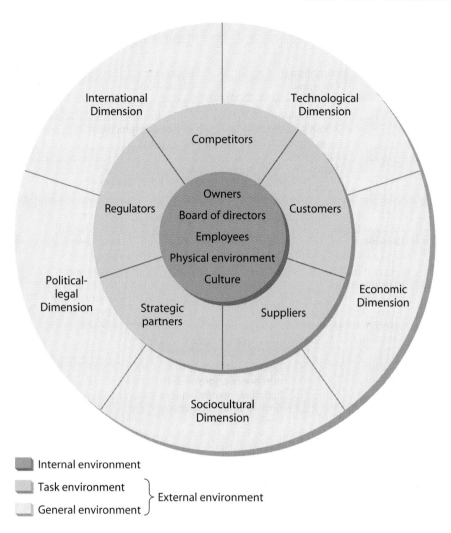

Figure 3.1

THE ORGANIZATION AND ITS ENVIRONMENTS

Organizations have both an external and an internal environment. The external environment consists of two layers: the general environment and the task environment.

The External Environment

As just noted, an organization's external environment consists of two parts. The ***general environment*** of an organization is the set of broad dimensions and forces in its surroundings that create its overall context. These dimensions and forces are not necessarily associated with other specific organizations. The general environment of most organizations has economic, technological, sociocultural, political-legal, and international dimensions. The other significant external environment for an organization is its task environment. The ***task environment*** consists of specific external organizations or groups that influence an organization.

The General Environment

Each of these dimensions embodies conditions and events that have the potential to influence the organization in important ways. Some examples to illustrate these dimensions as they relate to McDonald's Corporation are shown in Figure 3.2.

The Economic Dimension The ***economic dimension*** of an organization's general environment is the overall health and vitality of the economic system in which the organization operates.[4] Particularly important economic factors for business are

general environment
The set of broad dimensions and forces in an organization's surroundings that create its overall context

task environment
Specific organizations or groups that influence an organization

economic dimension
The overall health and vitality of the economic system in which the organization operates

Figure 3.2
MCDONALD'S GENERAL ENVIRONMENT

The general environment of an organization consists of economic, technological, sociocultural, political-legal, and international dimensions. This figure clearly illustrates how these dimensions are relevant to managers at McDonald's.

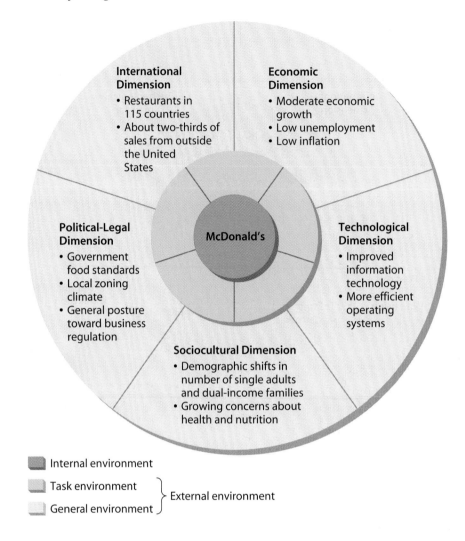

general economic growth, inflation, interest rates, and unemployment. As noted in Figure 3.2, McDonald's U.S. operation is functioning in an economy currently characterized by strong growth, low unemployment, and low inflation.[5] These conditions produce paradoxical problems. Low unemployment means that more people can eat out, but McDonald's also has to pay higher wages to attract new employees.[6] Similarly, low inflation means that the prices McDonald's must pay for its supplies remain relatively constant, but it also is somewhat constrained from increasing the prices it charges consumers for a hamburger or milkshake. The economic dimension is also important to nonbusiness organizations. For example, during weak economic conditions, funding for state universities may drop, and charitable organizations like the Salvation Army are asked to provide greater assistance at the same time that their incoming contributions dwindle. Similarly, hospitals are affected by the availability of government grants and the number of low-income patients they must treat free of charge.

The Technological Dimension   The ***technological dimension*** of the general environment refers to the methods available for converting resources into products or services. Although technology is applied within the organization, the forms and availability of that technology come from the general environment. Computer-assisted

---

technological dimension
The methods available for converting resources into products or services

manufacturing and design techniques, for example, allow Boeing to simulate the more than three miles of hydraulic tubing that run through a 777 aircraft. The results include decreased warehouse needs, higher-quality tube fittings, fewer employees, and major time savings. Although some people associate technology with manufacturing firms, it is also relevant in the service sector. For example, just as an automobile follows a predetermined path along an assembly line as it is built, a hamburger at McDonald's follows a predefined path as the meat is cooked, the burger assembled, and the finished product wrapped and bagged for a customer. The rapid infusion of the Internet into all areas of business is also a reflection of the technological dimension. Another recent advancement is the rapid growth of integrated business software systems.

The technological dimension of the general environment continues to evolve at breakneck speed. The pace of change and complexity involving computers and information technology is especially pronounced. Take this marketplace in Kampala, Uganda, for example. Buyers and sellers of fruits and vegetables have gathered here for centuries. But the presence of an Internet service provider is a new feature at the market, one that has the potential to revolutionize how the citizens of Africa live, work, and interact with the rest of the world.

The Sociocultural Dimension The ***sociocultural dimension*** of the general environment includes the customs, mores, values, and demographic characteristics of the society in which the organization functions. Sociocultural processes are important because they determine the products, services, and standards of conduct that the society is likely to value. In some countries, for example, consumers are willing to pay premium prices for designer clothes, whereas the same clothes have virtually no market in other countries. Consumer tastes also change over time. Preferences for color, style, taste, and so forth change from season to season, for example. Drinking hard liquor and smoking cigarettes are less common in the United States today than they were just a few years ago. And sociocultural factors influence how workers in a society feel about their jobs and organizations.

> **sociocultural dimension**
> The customs, mores, values, and demographic characteristics of the society in which the organization functions

Appropriate standards of business conduct also vary across cultures. In the United States, accepting bribes and bestowing political favors in return are considered unethical. In other countries, however, payments to local politicians may be expected in return for a favorable response to such common business transactions as applications for zoning and operating permits. The shape of the market, the ethics of political influence, and attitudes in the workforce are only a few of the many ways in which culture can affect an organization. Figure 3.2 shows that McDonald's is clearly affected by sociocultural factors. For example, in response to concerns about nutrition and health, McDonald's has added salads to its menus and experimented with other low-fat foods. And the firm was the first fast-food chain to provide customers with information about the ingredients used in its products. *The Business of Ethics* highlights how one firm—Hewlett-Packard—is aggressively working to have a positive impact on the sociocultural environment.

> "Everywhere, people are getting together and, using the Internet, disrupting whatever activities they're involved in."
>
> Pierre Omidyar, founder of eBay
> (*BusinessWeek*, June 20, 2005, p. 75)

The Business of Ethics

Hewlett-Packard Leads in Recycling

As many Americans switch to flat-screen models, 550 million analog TV sets and computer monitors will be discarded over the next three years. That will introduce millions of tons of toxic plastics and metals into landfills, including thousands of tons of deadly lead. Some state governments, such as those in California, Maine, and Washington, are taking action. Yet most manufacturers resist voluntarily taking responsibility for their old products. One company stepped forward as a leader in recycling—Hewlett-Packard (HP).

HP picks up discarded hardware and cartridges from the user's home or office for recycling. Cartridge recycling is free, while hardware costs between $13 and $34 per item. Another option is to trade in old but still working hardware for a credit toward new hardware or for cash. HP resells the equipment or recycles it if a buyer cannot be found. Yet another option is donation to charities, as HP will refurbish and ship donated hardware to schools and other needy groups.

HP was one of the first companies to recycle, beginning over ten years ago. Its interest in protecting the natural environment comes from the firm's organization culture, which emphasizes philanthropy. However, the company also wants to provide excellent customer service. The recycled products bring some modest income to HP, allow it to stay ahead of government mandates, and put pressure on the company's competitors to keep up.

In the end, though, it isn't about whether HP's motives are selfless or selfish. It's about the results. In 2005, HP recycled or refurbished almost 200 million pounds—about the weight of 350 jumbo airliners. The company has recycled 750 million pounds to date and expects to meet its goal of 1 billion pounds by 2007.

HP has a far-reaching influence. More companies are attempting recycling. HP's recycled materials end up as computer components, cell phones, and more, allowing those manufacturers to reduce plastics purchases. HP and others work with eBay in its Rethink Initiative, which offers incentives to sellers who recycle or reuse. HP actively lobbies for more inclusive take-back laws and wins against such powerful opponents as IBM and Apple Computer.

HP, long a leader in getting computer products into customers' hands, is now also the leader of taking those products back out of customers' hands at the end of their useful lives.

References: "HP Boosts Recycling Rate," "Product Return and Recycling," "Recycling HP Printers and Supplies," Hewlett Packard website, www.hp.com on March 3, 2006; "Rethink," eBay website, http://rethink.ebay.com on March 3, 2006; Lorraine Woellert, "HP Wants Your Old PCs Back," *BusinessWeek*, April 10, 2006, pp. 82–83.

> **political-legal dimension**
> The government regulation of business and the relationship between business and government

The Political-Legal Dimension   The ***political-legal dimension*** of the general environment refers to government regulation of business and the relationship between business and government. This dimension is important for three basic reasons. First, the legal system partially defines what an organization can and cannot do. Although the United States is basically a free market economy, there is still major regulation of business activity. McDonald's, for example, is subject to a variety of political and legal forces, including food preparation standards and local zoning requirements.

Second, pro- or antibusiness sentiment in government influences business activity. For example, during periods of probusiness sentiment, firms find it easier to compete and have fewer concerns about antitrust issues. On the other hand, during a period of antibusiness sentiment, firms may find their competitive strategies more restricted and have fewer opportunities for mergers and acquisitions because of antitrust concerns.

Finally, political stability has ramifications for planning. No business wants to set up shop in another country unless trade relationships with that country are relatively well defined and stable. Hence, U.S. firms are more likely to do business with England, Mexico, and Canada than with Haiti and Afghanistan. Similar issues are relevant to assessments of local and state governments. A new mayor or governor can affect many organizations, especially small firms that do business in only one location and are susceptible to deed and zoning restrictions, property and school taxes, and the like.

The International Dimension   Yet another component of the general environment for many organizations is the **international dimension**, or the extent to which an organization is involved in or affected by businesses in other countries.[7] As we discuss more fully in Chapter 5, multinational firms such as General Electric, Boeing, Nestlé, Sony, Siemens, and Hyundai clearly affect and are affected by international conditions and markets. For example, as noted in Figure 3.2, McDonald's operates restaurants in 115 countries and derives about two-thirds of its total sales from outside the United States. Even firms that do business in only one country may face foreign competition at home, and they may use materials or production equipment imported from abroad. The international dimension also has implications for not-for-profit organizations. For example, the Peace Corps sends representatives to underdeveloped countries. As a result of advances in transportation and information technology in the past century, almost no part of the world is cut off from the rest. As a result, virtually every organization is affected by the international dimension of its general environment.

> **international dimension**
> The extent to which an organization is involved in or affected by business in other countries

The Task Environment

Because the impact of the general environment is often vague, imprecise, and long term, most organizations tend to focus their attention on their task environments. These environments include competitors, customers, suppliers, strategic partners, and regulators. Although the task environment is also quite complex, it provides useful information more readily than does the general environment because the manager can identify environmental factors of specific interest to the organization, rather than having to deal with the more abstract dimensions of the general environment.[8] Figure 3.3 depicts the task environment of McDonald's.

Competitors   An organization's **competitors** are other organizations that compete with it for resources. The most obvious resources that competitors vie for are customer dollars. Reebok, Adidas, and Nike are competitors, as are Albertson's, Safeway, and Kroger. McDonald's competes with other fast-food operations, such as Burger King, Wendy's, Subway, and Dairy Queen. But competition also occurs between substitute products. Thus Ford competes with Yamaha (motorcycles) and Schwinn (bicycles) for your transportation dollars; and Walt Disney World, Club Med, and Carnival Cruise Lines compete for your vacation dollars. Nor is competition limited to business firms. Universities compete with trade schools, the military, other universities, and the external labor market to attract good students; and art galleries compete with each other to attract the best exhibits.

> **competitor**
> An organization that competes with other organizations for resources

Organizations may also compete for different kinds of resources besides consumer dollars. For example, two totally unrelated organizations might compete to acquire a loan from a bank that has only limited funds to lend. Two retailers might compete for the right to purchase a prime piece of real estate in a growing community. In a large city, the police and fire departments might compete for the same tax dollars. And businesses also compete for quality labor, technological breakthroughs and patents, and scarce raw materials.

> "As a business, you have to stay competitive. If we don't do it, our competitors will, and they're going to blow us away."
> Rosen Sharma, entrepreneur and founder of Solidcore, a small computer security firm
> (*Time*, March 1, 2005, p. 26)

Figure 3.3
MCDONALD'S TASK ENVIRONMENT

An organization's task environment includes its competitors, customers, suppliers, strategic partners, and regulators. This figure clearly highlights how managers at McDonald's can use this framework to identify and understand their key constituents.

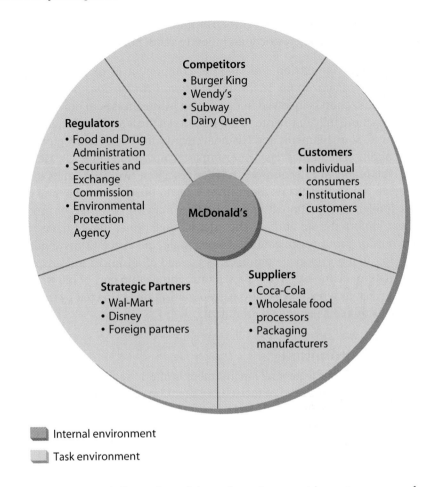

Internal environment

Task environment

---

customer
Whoever pays money to acquire an organization's products or services

Customers   A second dimension of the task environment is ***customers***, or whoever pays money to acquire an organization's products or services. Most of McDonald's customers are individuals who walk into a restaurant to buy food. But customers need not be individuals. Schools, hospitals, government agencies, wholesalers, retailers, and manufacturers are just a few of the many kinds of organizations that may be major customers of other organizations. Some institutional customers, such as schools, prisons, and hospitals, also buy food in bulk from restaurants like McDonald's.

Dealing with customers has become increasingly complex in recent years. New products and services, new methods of marketing, and more discriminating customers have all added uncertainty to how businesses relate to their customers, as has lower brand loyalty. A few years ago, McDonald's introduced a new sandwich called the Arch Deluxe, intended to appeal to adult customers. Unfortunately, the product failed because most adult customers preferred existing menu choices like the Quarter Pounder.

Companies face especially critical differences among customers as they expand internationally. McDonald's sells beer in its German restaurants, for example, and wine in its French restaurants. Customers in those countries see those particular beverages as normal parts of a meal, much as customers in the United States routinely drink water, tea, or soft drinks with their meals. The firm has even opened restaurants with no beef on the menu! Those restaurants are in India, where beef is not a popular menu option. Instead, the local McDonald's restaurants in that country use lamb in their sandwiches.

Suppliers *Suppliers* are organizations that provide resources for other organizations. McDonald's buys soft-drink products from Coca-Cola; individually packaged servings of ketchup from Heinz; ingredients from wholesale food processors; and napkins, sacks, and wrappers from packaging manufacturers. Common wisdom in the United States used to be that a business should try to avoid depending exclusively on particular suppliers. A firm that buys all of a certain resource from one supplier may be crippled if the supplier goes out of business or is faced with a strike. This practice can also help maintain a competitive relationship among suppliers, keeping costs down. But firms eager to emulate successful Japanese firms have recently tried to change their approach. Japanese firms have a history of building major ties with only one or two major suppliers. This enables them to work together better for their mutual benefit and makes the supplier more responsive to the customer's needs.

Honda picked Donnelly Corporation to make all the mirrors for its U.S.-manufactured cars. Honda chose Donnelly because it learned enough about the firm to know that it did high-quality work and that its corporate culture and values were consistent with those endorsed by Honda. Recognizing the value of Honda as a customer, Donnelly built an entirely new plant to make the mirrors. And all this was accomplished with only a handshake. Motorola goes even further, providing its principal suppliers with access to its own renowned quality training program and evaluating the performance of each supplier as a way of helping that firm boost its own quality.

> **supplier**
> An organization that provides resources for other organizations

> **strategic partners (strategic allies)**
> An organization working together with one or more other organizations in a joint venture or similar arrangement

> **regulator**
> A unit that has the potential to control, legislate, or otherwise influence the organization's policies and practices

Strategic Partners Another dimension of the task environment is *strategic partners* (also called *strategic allies*)—two or more companies that work together in joint ventures or other partnerships.[9] As shown in Figure 3.3, McDonald's has several strategic partners. For example, it has one arrangement with Wal-Mart whereby small McDonald's restaurants are built in many Wal-Mart stores. The firm also has a long-term deal with Disney: McDonald's will promote Disney movies in its stores, and Disney will build McDonald's restaurants or kiosks in its theme parks. And many of the firm's foreign stores are built in collaboration with local investors. Strategic partnerships help companies get from other companies the expertise they lack. They also help spread risk and open new market opportunities. Indeed, most strategic partnerships are actually among international firms. For example, Sony (a Japanese firm) and Samsung (a South Korean company) are fierce competitors in many sectors of the electronics industry but are also co-owners of a $2 billion factory that makes flat panel televisions and computer monitors.[10] *Technology Toolkit* highlights changing patterns of customers, suppliers, and strategic partners in television viewing patterns and options.

The regulatory environment affects businesses today in many different ways. This man is checking his son's height against a "standard" at Universal Studios theme park in Orlando, FL. Such standards are used to help Universal deal with liability issues that might arise if people are injured on a ride.

Regulators *Regulators* are elements of the task environment that have the potential to control, legislate, or otherwise influence an organization's policies and practices.

Technology Toolkit

Television for the People, by the People

Just a few years ago, the level of personalization that today's consumers enjoy would have been impossible to imagine. Personalized phone service? Design your own automobile? Made-to-measure blue jeans? Hundreds of coffee drink combinations? Unthinkable! Yet the ability to choose every aspect of virtually every product and service has become so important to buyers that every industry has been affected.

Television broadcasting is now under fire. John Hendricks, the CEO of Discovery Communications, likens the proliferation of programming to the variety of magazines available at a newsstand. "The next wave of media is to unleash the power of serving people's special interests," he states.

Although cable, satellite, and video recording technology increased options somewhat, 2005 brought the advent of online developments that will revolutionize TV. The first was the major media companies' adoption of Internet broadcasting. Apple's iTunes store, for example, offers mainstream shows such as *Law and Order* for prices as low $1 per episode. Other broadcasters, such as Trio, moved to online distribution. Trio then split its pop culture–focused audience into three segments for even higher levels of customization.

Another innovation is "slivercasting," broadcasting of narrowly focused channels over the Internet. Chan-

nels are devoted to sport sailing, vegetarian cooking, Alaska, and cancer treatments, among hundreds of others. Still other channels are re-broadcasts of programming from hundreds of foreign countries, very popular with immigrants and expatriates.

The biggest innovators are the websites that allow users to distribute videos of their own making. YouTube, founded in January 2005 by two friends who wanted to share party videos, is one example. After just one year of operation, YouTube now screens 30 million videos per day.

Internet broadcasting is less expensive than cable, and the potential worldwide audience is large, even for specialized channels. Advertising is limited, so most new channels make money from broadcast fees or product sales. YouTube co-founder Chad Hurley comments, "We're creating a new way to reach audiences in an era where the traditional TV time slot doesn't exist anymore." Consumers seeking high levels of personal service are unlikely to mourn the death of traditional television.

References: Heather Green, "Way Beyond Home Videos," *Business-Week*, April 10, 2006, pp. 64–65; Richard Siklos, "Death by Smiley Face: When Rivals Disdain Profits," *New York Times*, April 2, 2006, p. BU3; Saul Hansell, "Much for the Few," *New York Times*, March 12, 2006, pp. BU1, 4.

---

interest group
A group organized by its members to attempt to influence business

There are two important kinds of regulators. The first, **regulatory agencies**, are created by the government to protect the public from certain business practices or to protect organizations from one another. The second, **interest groups**, are organized by their members to attempt to influence organizations.

Powerful federal regulatory agencies include the Environmental Protection Agency (EPA), the Securities and Exchange Commission (SEC), the Food and Drug Administration (FDA), and the Equal Employment Opportunity Commission (EEOC). Many of these agencies play important roles in protecting the rights of individuals. The FDA, for example, helps ensure that the food we eat is free from contaminants and thus is an important regulator for McDonald's. At the same time, many managers complain that there is too much government regulation. Most large companies must dedicate thousands of labor hours and hundreds of thousands of dollars a year to complying with government regulations. To complicate the lives of managers even more, different regulatory agencies sometimes provide inconsistent—even contradictory—mandates.

For example, several years ago the *Exxon Valdez* tanker ran aground, spilling 11 million gallons of crude oil off the coast of Alaska. The EPA forced ExxonMobil to cover the costs of the ensuing cleanup. Because an investigation suggested that the ship's captain was drunk at the time, the EPA also mandated that ExxonMobil impose stricter hiring standards for employees in high-risk jobs. To comply with this mandate, ExxonMobil adopted a policy of not assigning anyone with a history of alcohol or substance abuse to certain jobs like tanker captain. However, another regulatory agency, the EEOC, then sued ExxonMobil on the grounds that restricting people who have been rehabilitated from alcohol abuse from any job violates their rights under the Americans with Disabilities Act. ExxonMobil was thus forced to change its policy, but was then again criticized by the EPA.

The regulatory environment in other countries, however, is even more stringent. When U.S. retailer Wal-Mart wants to open a new store, its regulatory requirements are actually quite low, and the procedures it must follow are clearly spelled out. In a sense, within reason and general basic ground rules, the firm can open a store just about anywhere it wants and operate it in just about any manner it wants. But conditions in Germany are quite different. That country's largest retailer, Allkauf, tried for over 15 years to open a store in one town—on land that it already owned. But the city government did not allow it because it feared that local competitors would suffer. And, by German law, Allkauf's existing stores can be open only 68.5 hours a week; they must close no later than 6:30 P.M. on weekdays and 2:00 P.M. on Saturday, and must remain closed on Sunday. They can hold large sales only twice a year and can never discount food items.

The other basic form of regulator is the interest group. Prominent interest groups include the National Organization for Women (NOW), Mothers Against Drunk Drivers (MADD), the National Rifle Association (NRA), the League of Women Voters, the Sierra Club, the Center for the Study of Responsive Law, Consumers Union, and industry self-regulation groups like the Council of Better Business Bureaus. Although interest groups lack the official power of government agencies, they can exert considerable influence by using the media to call attention to their positions. MADD, for example, puts considerable pressure on alcoholic-beverage producers (to put warning labels on their products), automobile companies (to make it more difficult for intoxicated people to start their cars), local governments (to stiffen drinking ordinances), and bars and restaurants (to refuse to sell alcohol to people who are drinking too much).

---

concept
CHECK

List the dimensions of the general and the task environments of a business.

Identify linkages between dimensions of the general environment and dimensions of the task environment.

The Internal Environment

As we show earlier in Figure 3.1, organizations also have internal environments that consists of their owners, boards of directors, employees, physical work environments, and cultures.

Owners

The ***owners*** of a business are, of course, the people who have legal property rights to that business. Owners can be a single individual who establishes and runs a

> **owner**
> Whoever can claim property rights to an organization

small business, partners who jointly own the business, individual investors who buy stock in a corporation, or other organizations. McDonald's has 700 million shares of stock, each of which represents one unit of ownership in the firm. The family of McDonald's founder Ray Kroc still owns a large block of this stock, as do several large institutional investors. In addition, there are thousands of individuals who own just a few shares each. McDonald's, in turn, owns other businesses. For example, it owns several large regional bakeries that supply its restaurants with buns. Each of these is incorporated as a separate legal entity and managed as a wholly owned subsidiary by the parent company. McDonald's also has partial ownership of Chipotle Mexican Grill and Donatos Pizza chain.

Board of Directors

board of directors
Governing body elected by a corporation's stockholders and charged with overseeing the general management of the firm to ensure that it is being run in a way that best serves the stockholders' interests

A corporate **board of directors** is a governing body elected by the stockholders and charged with overseeing the general management of the firm to ensure that it is being run in a way that best serves the stockholders' interests. Some boards are relatively passive. They perform a general oversight function but seldom get actively involved in how the company is really being run. But this trend is changing, as more and more boards are carefully scrutinizing the firms they oversee and exerting more influence over how they are being managed. This trend has in part been spurred by numerous recent business scandals. In some cases, board members have been accused of wrongdoing. In other cases, boards have been found negligent for failing to monitor the actions of firm executives.[11] At issue is the concept of corporate governance—who is responsible for governing the actions of a business.

Employees

An organization's employees are also a major element of its internal environment. Of particular interest to managers today is the changing nature of the workforce, as it becomes increasingly more diverse in terms of gender, ethnicity, age, and other dimensions. Workers are also calling for more job ownership—either partial ownership in the company or at least more say in how they perform their jobs.[12] Another trend in many firms is increased reliance on temporary workers—individuals hired for short periods of time with no expectation of permanent employment. Employers often prefer to use "temps" because they provide greater flexibility, earn lower wages, and often do not participate in benefits programs. But these managers also have to deal with what often amounts to a two-class workforce and with a growing number of employees who feel no loyalty to the organization where they work because they may be working for a different one tomorrow.[13]

The permanent employees of many organizations are organized into labor unions, representing yet another layer of complexity for managers. The National Labor Relations Act of 1935 requires organizations to recognize and bargain with a union if that union has been legally established by the organization's employees. Presently, around 12.5 percent of the U.S. labor force is represented by unions. Some large firms, such as Ford, Exxon, and General Motors, have several different unions. Even when an organization's labor force is not unionized, its managers do not ignore unions. For example, Honda of America, Wal-Mart, and Delta Air Lines all actively work to avoid unionization. And, even though people think primarily of blue-collar workers as union members, many white-collar workers, such as government employees and teachers, are also represented by unions.

Physical Work Environment

A final part of the internal environment is the actual physical environment of the organization and the work that people do. Some firms have their facilities in downtown skyscrapers, usually spread across several floors. Others locate in suburban or rural settings and may have facilities more closely resembling a college campus. Some facilities have long halls lined with traditional offices. Others have modular cubicles with partial walls and no doors. The top hundred managers at Mars, makers of Snickers and Milky Way, all work in a single vast room. Two co-presidents are located in the very center of the room, while others are arrayed in concentric circles around them. Increasingly, newer facilities have an even more open arrangement, where people work in large rooms, moving among different tables to interact with different people on different projects. Freestanding computer workstations are available for those who need them, and a few small rooms might be off to the side for private business.[14]

Employee safety and health regulations have caused many organizations to pay more attention to their internal environment. This concern, in turn, has also fostered new business opportunities. Rebecca Boenigk is shown here sitting on one of the products made by Neutral Posture in Bryan, Texas. Boenigk, founder and CEO of Neutral Posture, turned a small operation in her garage into an international company selling neutral body posture chairs designed by her father, Dr. Jerome Congleton.

Identify the main parts of an organization's internal environment.

What is corporate governance, and how is it related to the environment of business?

concept
CHECK

The Organization's Culture

An especially important part of the internal environment of an organization is its culture. ***Organization culture*** is the set of values, beliefs, behaviors, customs, and attitudes that helps the members of the organization understand what it stands for, how it does things, and what it considers important.[15] Culture is an amorphous concept that defies objective measurement or observation. Nevertheless, because it is the foundation of the organization's internal environment, it plays a major role in shaping managerial behavior.

> *organization culture*
> The set of values, beliefs, behaviors, customs, and attitudes that helps the members of the organization understand what it stands for, how it does things, and what it considers important

The Importance of Organization Culture

Executives at Ford Motor Company decided to move the firm's Lincoln Mercury division from Detroit to southern California. Interestingly, though, this move had little to do with costs or any of the other reasons most business relocations occur. Instead, they wanted to move Lincoln Mercury out from the corporate shadow of its dominating, larger corporate cousin, Ford itself. For years, Lincoln Mercury managers had complained that their business was always given short shrift and that most of Detroit's attention was focused on Ford. And, at least partially as a result, Mercury products all tended to look like clones of Ford products, and the division consistently failed to meet its goals or live up to its expectations. Finally, the company decided that the only way to turn the division around was to give it its own identity. And where better to start than by moving the whole operation—lock, stock, and barrel—to car-centric southern California, where its managers could be freer to hire new creative talent and start carving out a new and unique business niche for themselves.[16] In short, they wanted to create a new culture.

Culture determines the "feel" of the organization. The stereotypic image of Microsoft, for example, is a workplace where people dress very casually and work very long hours. In contrast, the image of Bank of America for some observers is a formal setting with rigid work rules and people dressed in conservative business attire. And Texas Instruments likes to talk about its "shirtsleeve" culture, in which ties are avoided and few managers ever wear jackets. Southwest Airlines maintains a culture that stresses fun and excitement.

Of course, the same culture is not necessarily found throughout an entire organization. For example, the sales and marketing department may have a culture quite different from that of the operations and manufacturing department. Regardless of its nature, however, culture is a powerful force in organizations, one that can shape the firm's overall effectiveness and long-term success. Companies that can develop and maintain a strong culture, such as Hewlett-Packard and Procter & Gamble, tend to be more effective than companies that have trouble developing and maintaining a strong culture, such as Kmart.[17]

Determinants of Organization Culture

Where does an organization's culture come from? Typically, it develops and blossoms over a long period of time. Its starting point is often the organization's founder. For example, James Cash Penney believed in treating employees and customers with respect and dignity. Employees at J. C. Penney are still called "associates" rather than "employees" (to reflect partnership), and customer satisfaction is of paramount importance. The impact of Sam Walton, Ross Perot, and Walt Disney is still felt in the organizations they founded.[18] As an organization grows, its culture is modified, shaped, and refined by symbols, stories, heroes, slogans, and ceremonies. For example, an important value at Hewlett-Packard is the avoidance of bank debt. A popular story still told at the company involves a new project that was being considered for several years. All objective criteria indicated that HP should borrow money from a bank to finance it, yet Bill Hewlett and David Packard rejected it out of hand simply because "HP avoids bank debt." This story, involving two corporate heroes and based on a slogan, dictates corporate culture today. And many decisions at Walt Disney Company today are still framed by asking, "What would Walt have done?"

Corporate success and shared experiences also shape culture. For example, Hallmark Cards has a strong culture derived from its years of success in the greeting card industry. Employees speak of "the Hallmark family" and care deeply about the company; many of them have worked at the company for years. At Kmart, in contrast, the culture is quite weak, the management team changes rapidly, and few people sense any direction or purpose in the company. The differences in culture at Hallmark and Kmart are in part attributable to past successes and shared experiences.

Managing Organization Culture

How can managers deal with culture, given its clear importance but intangible nature? Essentially, the manager must understand the current culture and then decide if it should be maintained or changed. By understanding the organization's current culture, managers can take appropriate actions. At Hewlett-Packard, the values represented by "the HP way" still exist, guiding and directing most important activities undertaken by the firm. Culture can also be maintained by rewarding and promoting people whose behaviors are consistent with the existing culture and by articulating the culture through slogans, ceremonies, and so forth.

But managers must walk a fine line between maintaining a culture that still works effectively and changing a culture that has become dysfunctional. For example, many of the firms already noted, as well as numerous others, take pride in perpetuating their culture. Shell Oil, for example, has an elaborate display in the lobby of its Houston headquarters that tells the story of the firm's past. But other companies may face situations in which their culture is no longer a strength. For example, some critics feel that General Motors' culture places too much emphasis on product development and internal competition among divisions, and not enough on marketing and competition with other firms.

Culture problems sometimes arise from mergers or the growth of rival factions within an organization. For example, Wells Fargo, which relies heavily on flashy technology and automated banking services, acquired another large bank, First Interstate, which had focused more attention on personal services and customer satisfaction. Blending the two disparate organization cultures was difficult for the firm, as managers argued over how best to serve customers and operate the new enterprise.[19]

To change culture, managers must have a clear idea of what they want to create. When Continental Airlines "reinvented" itself several years ago, employees were taken outside the corporate headquarters in Houston to watch the firm's old policies and procedures manuals set afire. The firm's new strategic direction is known throughout Continental as the "Go Forward" plan, intentionally named to avoid reminding people about the firm's troubled past and instead to focus on the future.

One major way to shape culture is by bringing outsiders into important managerial positions. The choice of a new CEO from outside the organization is often a clear signal that things will be changing. Indeed, a new CEO was the catalyst for the changes at Continental. Adopting new slogans, telling new stories, staging new ceremonies, and breaking with tradition can also alter culture. Culture can also be changed by methods discussed in Chapter 13.[20]

---

concept
CHECK

What is organization culture? | *Does your college or university have a culture? How would you describe it to someone?*

Organization-environment relationships can create complex issues. The Katrina Cottage is shown here being introduced by the Louisiana Recovery Authority. The Katrina Cottage is a small yet permanent house that can be built and installed on a site for about the same price as a FEMA trailer. Environmental conditions that arose in the aftermath of the hurricane led to the design and creation of this new approach to emergency housing.

Organization-Environment Relationships

Our discussion to this point identifies and describes the various dimensions of organizational environments. Because organizations are open systems, they interact with these various dimensions in many different ways. Hence, we will now examine those interactions. First we discuss how environments affect organizations, and then we note a number of ways in which organizations adapt to their environments.

How Environments Affect Organizations

Three basic perspectives can be used to describe how environments affect organizations: environmental change and complexity, competitive forces, and environmental turbulence.[21]

Environmental Change and Complexity   James D. Thompson was one of the first people to recognize the importance of the organization's environment.[22] Thompson suggested that the environment can be described along two dimensions: its degree of change and its degree of homogeneity. The degree of change is the extent to which the environment is relatively stable or relatively dynamic. The degree of homogeneity is the extent to which the environment is relatively simple (few elements, little segmentation) or relatively complex (many elements, much segmentation). These two dimensions interact to determine the level of uncertainty faced by the organization. **Uncertainty**, in turn, is a driving force that influences many organizational decisions. Figure 3.4 illustrates a simple view of the four levels of uncertainty defined by different degrees of homogeneity and change.

The least environmental uncertainty is faced by organizations with stable and simple environments. Although no environment is totally without uncertainty, some entrenched franchised food operations (such as Subway and Taco Bell) and many container manufacturers (like Ball Corporation and Federal Paper Board) have relatively low levels of uncertainty to contend with. Subway, for example, focuses on a certain segment of the consumer market, produces a limited product line, has a stable network of suppliers, and faces relatively consistent competition.

Organizations with dynamic but simple environments generally face a moderate degree of uncertainty. Examples of organizations functioning in such environments include clothing manufacturers (targeting a certain kind of clothing buyer but sensitive to fashion-induced changes) and CD producers (catering to certain kinds of music buyers but alert to changing tastes in music). Levi Strauss faces relatively few competitors (Diesel, Wrangler, and Lee), has few suppliers and few regulators, and uses limited distribution channels. This relatively simple task environment, however,

uncertainty
Unpredictability created by environmental change and complexity

"The world has changed and so you have to react dramatically and more aggressively, in a less forgiving, harsher way.**"**
Lee Scott, Wal-Mart CEO
(*Fortune*, April 18, 2005, p. 88)

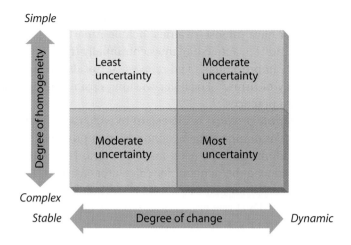

Simple

Complex

Degree of homogeneity

| Least uncertainty | Moderate uncertainty |
| Moderate uncertainty | Most uncertainty |

Stable — Degree of change — *Dynamic*

Figure 3.4
ENVIRONMENTAL CHANGE, COMPLEXITY, AND UNCERTAINTY

The degree of homogeneity and the degree of change combine to create uncertainty for organizations. For example, a simple and stable environment creates the least uncertainty, and a complex and dynamic environment creates the most uncertainty.

Source: From J. D. Thompson, *Organizations in Action,* 1967. Copyright © 1967 The McGraw-Hill Companies, Inc. Reprinted with permission.

also changes quite rapidly as competitors adjust prices and styles, consumer tastes change, and new fabrics become available.

Another combination of factors is one of stability and complexity. Again, a moderate amount of uncertainty results. Ford, DaimlerChrysler, and General Motors face these basic conditions. Overall, they must interact with myriad suppliers, regulators, consumer groups, and competitors. Change, however, occurs quite slowly in the automobile industry. Despite many stylistic changes, cars of today still have four wheels, a steering wheel, an internal combustion engine, a glass windshield, and many of the other basic features that have characterized cars for decades.

Finally, very dynamic and complex environmental conditions yield a high degree of uncertainty. The environment has a large number of elements, and the nature of those elements is constantly changing. Intel, Compaq, IBM, Sony, and other firms in the electronics field face these conditions because of the rapid rate of technological innovation and change in consumer markets that characterize their industry, their suppliers, and their competitors. Internet-based firms like eBay and Amazon.com face similarly high levels of uncertainty.

Competitive Forces   Although Thompson's general classifications are useful and provide some basic insights into organization-environment interactions, in many ways they lack the precision and specificity needed by managers who must deal with their environments on a day-to-day basis. Michael E. Porter, a Harvard professor and expert in strategic management, has proposed a more refined way to assess environments. In particular, he suggests that managers view the environments of their organization in terms of *five competitive forces*: the threat of new entrants, competitive rivalry, the threat of substitute products, the power of buyers, and the power of suppliers.[23]

The threat of new entrants is the extent to which new competitors can easily enter a market or market segment. It takes a relatively small amount of capital to open a dry-cleaning service or a pizza parlor, but it takes a tremendous investment in plant, equipment, and distribution systems to enter the automobile business. Thus the threat of new entrants is fairly high for a local hamburger restaurant but fairly low for Ford and Toyota. The advent of the Internet has reduced the costs and other barriers of entry in many market segments, however, so the threat of new entrants has increased for many firms in recent years.

Competitive rivalry is the nature of the competitive relationship between dominant firms in the industry. In the soft-drink industry, Coca-Cola and PepsiCo often

five competitive forces
The threat of new entrants, competitive rivalry, the threat of substitute products, the power of buyers, and the power of suppliers

engage in intense price wars, comparative advertising, and new-product introductions. Other firms that have intense rivalries include American Express and Visa, and Fuji and Kodak. And U.S. auto companies continually try to outmaneuver one another with warranty improvements and rebates. Xerox also faces extreme competition from a variety of firms.[24] Local car-washing establishments, in contrast, seldom engage in such practices.

The threat of substitute products is the extent to which alternative products or services may supplant or diminish the need for existing products or services. The electronic calculator eliminated the need for slide rules. The advent of personal computers, in turn, reduced the demand for calculators as well as for typewriters and large mainframe computers. NutraSweet is a viable substitute product threatening the sugar industry. DVD players are rendering VCRs obsolete, but high definition DVD technology is on the horizon and is likely to eventually replace today's DVD players.

The power of buyers is the extent to which buyers of the products or services in an industry have the ability to influence the suppliers. For example, a Boeing 777 has relatively few potential buyers. Only companies such as Delta, Northwest, and KLM Royal Dutch Airlines can purchase them. Hence, these buyers have considerable influence over the price they are willing to pay, the delivery date for the order, and so forth. On the other hand, during times of shortage, individual buyers have little power; if one buyer will not pay the asking price, others are waiting in line.

The power of suppliers is the extent to which suppliers have the ability to influence potential buyers. The local electric company is the only source of electricity in your community. Subject to local or state regulation (or both), it can therefore charge what it wants for its product, provide service at its convenience, and so forth. Likewise, even though Boeing has few potential customers, those same customers have only two suppliers that can sell them a 300-passenger jet (Boeing and Airbus, a European firm). So Boeing, too, has power. Indeed, the firm recently exercised its power by entering into long-term, sole-supplier agreements with three major U.S. airlines.[25] On the other hand, a small vegetable wholesaler has little power in selling to restaurants because if they do not like the produce, they can easily find an alternative supplier.

Environmental Turbulence   Although always subject to unexpected changes and upheavals, the five competitive forces can nevertheless be studied and assessed systematically, and plans can be developed for dealing with them. At the same time, though, organizations face the possibility of environmental change or turbulence, occasionally with no warning at all. The most common form of organizational turbulence is a crisis of some sort.

The terrorist attacks on September 11, 2001, are, of course, the most obvious illustration of environmental turbulence. Beyond the human and social costs, these events profoundly affected myriad businesses ranging from airlines, to New York's entertainment industry, to those firms with operations in the World Trade Center.[26] Another notable example of crisis was the crash of the space shuttle Columbia in 2003, which seemed likely to paralyze the U.S. space program for years. Another type of crisis that has captured the attention of managers in recent years is workplace violence—situations in which disgruntled workers or former workers assault other employees, often resulting in injury and sometimes in death. Finally, yet another kind of crisis that can affect business today is the rapid spread of computer viruses, such as the so-called love bug that shut down businesses around the world in early 2000.

Such crises affect organizations in different ways, and many organizations have developed crisis plans and teams.[27] When a Delta Air Lines plane crashed at the Dallas–Fort Worth airport, fire-fighting equipment was at the scene in minutes. Only a few flights were delayed, and none had to be canceled. Similarly, a grocery store in Boston once received a threat that someone had poisoned cans of its Campbell's tomato juice. Within six hours, a crisis team from Campbell Soup Company removed two truckloads of juice from all 84 stores in the grocery chain. Still, far too few companies in the United States have a plan for dealing with major crises.

How Organizations Adapt to Their Environments

Given the myriad issues, problems, and opportunities in an organization's environments, how should the organization adapt? Obviously, each organization must assess its own unique situation and then adapt according to the wisdom of its senior management. Figure 3.5 illustrates the six basic mechanisms through which organizations adapt to their environments. One of these, social responsibility, is given special consideration in Chapter 4.

Information Management   One way organizations adapt to their environments is through information management. Information management is especially important when forming an initial understanding of the environments and when monitoring the environments for signs of change. One technique for managing information is relying on boundary spanners. A *boundary spanner* is an employee, such as a sales representative or a purchasing agent, who spends much of his or her time in contact with others outside the organization. Such people are in a good position to learn what

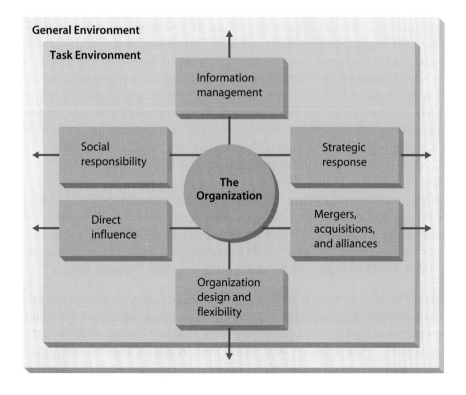

Figure 3.5

HOW ORGANIZATIONS ADAPT TO THEIR ENVIRONMENTS

Organizations attempt to adapt to their environments. The most common methods are information management; strategic response; mergers, acquisitions, and alliances; organization design and flexibility; direct influence; and social responsibility.

other organizations are doing. All effective managers engage in *environmental scanning,* the process of actively monitoring the environments through activities such as observation and reading. Within the organization, most firms have also established computer-based *information systems* to gather and organize relevant information for managers and to assist in summarizing that information in the form most pertinent to each manager's needs. (Information systems are covered more fully in Chapter 22.) Enterprise resource planning techniques are also useful methods for improving information management.

Strategic Response   Another way that an organization adapts to its environments is through a strategic response. Options include maintaining the status quo (for example, if its management believes that it is doing very well with its current approach), altering strategy a bit, or adopting an entirely new strategy. If the market that a company currently serves is growing rapidly, the firm might decide to invest even more heavily in products and services for that market. Likewise, if a market is shrinking or does not provide reasonable possibilities for growth, the company may decide to cut back. For example, a few years ago managers at Starbucks recognized that the firm's growth opportunities in the United States were slowing simply because there already were so many Starbucks shops. Accordingly, they devised a new plan to expand aggressively into international markets, thus providing an avenue for continued rapid growth.

Mergers, Acquisitions, and Alliances   A related strategic approach that some organizations use to adapt to their environments involves mergers, acquisitions, and alliances. A *merger* occurs when two or more firms combine to form a new firm. For example, DaimlerChrysler was created as a result of a merger between Daimler-Benz (a German firm) and Chrysler (a U.S. company). An *acquisition* occurs when one firm buys another, sometimes against its will (usually called a "hostile takeover"). The firm taken over may cease to exist and becomes part of the other company. For example, as part of its international expansion, Starbucks bought a British coffee shop chain called the Seattle Coffee Company. Starbucks has subsequently changed many Seattle Coffee outlets into Starbucks shops.

In other situations, the acquired firm may continue to operate as a subsidiary of the acquiring company. Royal Caribbean Cruise Lines bought a controlling interest in Celebrity Cruise Lines, but maintains it as a separate cruise line. And, as already discussed, in a *partnership* or *alliance* the firm undertakes a new venture with another firm. A company engages in these kinds of strategies for a variety of reasons, such as easing entry into new markets or expanding its presence in a current market.

In a somewhat unusual case, SBC Communications acquired AT&T in 2005. But even though SBC was the acquiring company, it adopted the AT&T name for the combined enterprise. Why? Because its managers felt that AT&T had more national brand recognition and the name would better enable the firm to gain market share. They felt it would be especially helpful in attracting new corporate clients.[28]

Organization Design and Flexibility   An organization may also adapt to environmental conditions by incorporating flexibility in its structural design. For example, a firm that operates in an environment with relatively low levels of uncertainty might choose to use a design with many basic rules, regulations, and standard operating procedures. Alternatively, a firm that faces a great deal of uncertainty might choose a design with relatively few standard operating procedures, instead allowing managers considerable discretion and flexibility with decisions. The former type, sometimes called a "mechanistic organization design," is characterized by formal and rigid rules and relationships. The latter, sometimes called an "organic design," is considerably more flexible and permits the organization to respond quickly to environmental change. We learn much more about these and related issues in Chapter 12.

Direct Influence Organizations are not necessarily helpless in the face of their environments. Indeed, many organizations are able to directly influence their environments in many different ways. For example, firms can influence their suppliers by signing long-term contracts with fixed prices as a hedge against inflation. Or a firm might become its own supplier. Sears, for example, owns some of the firms that produce the goods it sells, and Campbell Soup Company makes its own soup cans. Similarly, almost any major activity in which a firm engages affects its competitors. When Mitsubishi lowers the prices of its DVD players, Sony may be forced to follow suit. Organizations also influence their customers by creating new uses for a product, finding entirely new customers, taking customers away from competitors, and convincing customers that they need something new. Automobile manufacturers use this last strategy in their advertising to convince people that they need a new car every two or three years.

Organizations influence their regulators through lobbying and bargaining. Lobbying involves sending a company or industry representative to Washington in an effort to influence relevant agencies, groups, and committees. For example, the U.S. Chamber of Commerce lobby, the nation's largest business lobby, has an annual budget of more than $100 million. The automobile companies have been successful on several occasions in bargaining with the EPA to extend deadlines for compliance with pollution control and mileage standards. Continental Airlines routinely criticizes what it considers an antiquated air traffic control system in an effort to get the U.S. government to upgrade its technology and systems.

---

concept
CHECK

How do environments affect organizations? How do organizations affect their environments?	*What are some recent high-profile mergers? Why do you think they occurred?*

The Environment and Organizational Effectiveness

Earlier in this chapter we note the vital importance of maintaining proper alignment between the organization and its environments. The various mechanisms through which environments and organizations influence one another can cause this alignment to shift, however, and even the best-managed organizations sometimes slip from their preferred environmental position. But well-managed companies recognize when this happens and take corrective action to get back on track. Recall that we say in Chapter 1 that effectiveness involves doing the right things. Given the interactions between organizations and their environments, it follows that effectiveness is related ultimately to how well an organization understands, reacts to, and influences its environments.[29]

Models of Organizational Effectiveness

Unfortunately, there is no consensus on how to measure effectiveness. For example, an organization can make itself look extremely effective in the short term by ignoring research and development (R&D), buying cheap materials, ignoring quality control, and skimping on wages. Over time, though, the firm will no doubt falter. On the other hand, taking action consistent with a longer view, such as making appropriate investments in R&D, may displease investors who have a short-term outlook. Little wonder, then, that there are many different models of organizational effectiveness.

The *systems resource approach* to organizational effectiveness focuses on the extent to which the organization can acquire the resources it needs.[30] A firm that can get raw materials during a shortage is effective from this perspective. The *internal processes approach* deals with the internal mechanisms of the organization and focuses on minimizing strain, integrating individuals and the organization, and conducting smooth and efficient operations.[31] An organization that focuses primarily on maintaining employee satisfaction and morale and on being efficient subscribes to this view. *The goal approach* focuses on the degree to which an organization reaches its goals.[32] When a firm establishes a goal of increasing sales by 10 percent and then achieves that increase, the goal approach maintains that the organization is effective. Finally, the *strategic constituencies approach* focuses on the groups that have a stake in the organization.[33] In this view, effectiveness is the extent to which the organization satisfies the demands and expectations of all these groups.

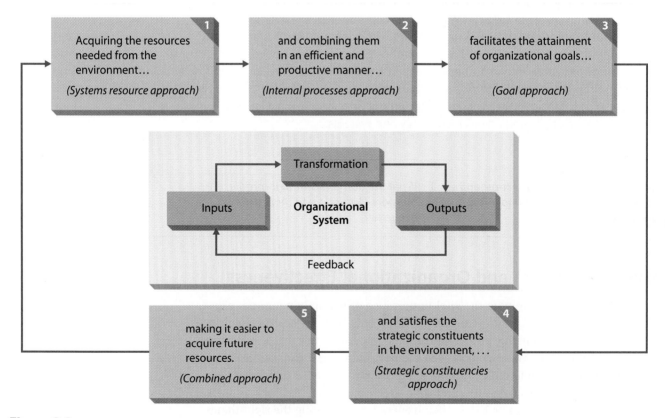

Figure 3.6

A MODEL OF ORGANIZATIONAL EFFECTIVENESS

The systems resource, internal processes, goal, and strategic constituencies each focuses on a different aspect of organizational effectiveness. Thus they can be combined to create an overall integrative perspective on effectiveness.

Although these four basic models of effectiveness are not necessarily contradictory, they do focus on different things. The systems resource approach focuses on inputs, the internal processes approach focuses on transformation processes, the goal approach focuses on outputs, and the strategic constituencies approach focuses on feedback. Thus, rather than adopting a single approach, one can best understand organizational effectiveness through an integrated perspective like that illustrated in Figure 3.6. At the core of this unifying model is the organizational system, with its inputs, transformations, outputs, and feedback. Surrounding this core are the four basic approaches to effectiveness as well as a combined approach, which incorporates each of the other four. The basic argument is essentially that an organization must satisfy the requirements imposed on it by each of the effectiveness perspectives.

Achieving organizational effectiveness is not an easy task. The key to doing so is understanding the environment in which the organization functions. With this understanding as a foundation, managers can then chart the "correct" path for the organization as it positions itself in that environment. If managers can identify where they want the organization to be relative to other parts of their environment, and how to best get there, they stand a good chance of achieving effectiveness. On the other hand, if they pick the wrong target to aim for, or if they go about achieving their goals in the wrong way, they are less likely to be effective.

Examples of Organizational Effectiveness

Given the various models of and perspectives on organizational effectiveness, it is not surprising that even the experts do not always agree on which companies are most effective. For example, for years *Fortune* has compiled an annual list of the "Most Admired" companies in the United States. Based on a large survey of leading executives, the rankings presumably reflect the organizations' innovativeness, quality of management, value as a long-term investment, community and environmental responsibility, quality of products and services, financial soundness, use of corporate assets, and ability to attract, develop, and keep talented people. The 2006 list of *Fortune*'s ten most admired firms is shown in Table 3.1.

Also illustrated in the table is part of a list published in *BusinessWeek,* also in 2006. This list represents the ten best-performing big companies in the United States as determined by revenue and profit growth, return on investment, net profit margins,

Fortune's Most Admired Companies (2006)	*BusinessWeek*'s Best Performing Companies (2006)
1. General Electric	1. Apple Computer
2. FedEx	2. WellPoint
3. Southwest Airlines	3. Caremark Rx
4. Procter & Gamble	4. United Health Group
5. Starbucks	5. Schlumberger
6. Johnson & Johnson	6. Occidental Petroleum
7. Berkshire Hathaway	7. Halliburton
8. Dell Computer	8. Qualcomm
9. Toyota Motors	9. Amgen
10. Microsoft	10. Aetna

Table 3.1

EXAMPLES OF ADMIRED AND HIGH-PERFORMING FIRMS

Source: "America's Most Admired Companies," *Fortune,* March 6, 2006, p. 65; "The Business Week 50," *BusinessWeek,* April 3, 2006, p. 65.

and return on equity over periods of one and three years. In some years there are some firms on both lists; in 2006, though, the two lists were unique. Given that both "admiration" and "performance" would seem to be highly related to effectiveness, a stronger correspondence between the two lists might be expected. It is important to note, of course, that different variables and methods are used to develop the two lists, and every firm included on either list is a very well-managed company. But the disparities in the lists also underscore the difficulties and judgment calls that are involved when trying to really evaluate the effectiveness of any given company or organization.

concept
CHECK

What are the four basic models of organizational effectiveness?

What local businesses do you especially admire? Why?

Summary of Learning Objectives and Key Points

1. Discuss the nature of the organizational environment and identify the environments of interest to most organizations.
   - Environmental factors play a major role in determining an organization's success or failure.
   - Managers should strive to maintain the proper alignment between their organization and its environments.
   - All organizations have both external and internal environments.

2. Describe the components of the general and task environments and discuss their impact on organizations. The external environment is composed of general and task environment layers.
   - The general environment consists of five dimensions: economic, technological, sociocultural, political-legal, and international.
   - The task environment consists of five elements: competitors, customers, suppliers, strategic partners, and regulators.

3. Identify the components of the internal environment and discuss their impact on organizations.
   - The internal environment consists of the organization's owners, board of directors, employees, physical environment, and culture.

4. Discuss the importance and determinants of an organization's culture and how the culture can be managed.
   - Organization culture is the set of values, beliefs, behaviors, customs, and attitudes that helps the

members of the organization understand what it stands for, how it does things, and what it considers important.
   - Managers must understand that culture is an important determinant of how well their organization will perform.
   - Culture can be determined and managed in a number of different ways.

5. Identify and describe how the environment affects organizations and how organizations adapt to their environment.
   - Environmental influences on the organization can occur through uncertainty, competitive forces, and turbulence.
   - Organizations use information management; strategic response; mergers, acquisitions, and alliances; organization design and flexibility; direct influence; and social responsibility to adapt to their environments.

6. Describe the basic models of organizational effectiveness and provide contemporary examples of highly effective firms.
   - Organizational effectiveness requires that the organization do a good job of acquiring resources, managing resources properly, achieving its goals, and satisfying its constituencies.
   - Because of the complexities associated with meeting these requirements, however, experts may disagree as to the effectiveness of any given organization at any given point in time.

Discussion Questions

Questions for Review

1. Consider the three environments of a firm. Which of the environments has the most direct and immediate impact on the firm? Which of the environments has a more diffuse and delayed impact? Explain.

2. Describe the organization's general environment. For each dimension, give at least one specific example, other than the examples mentioned in your text.

3. What are the major forces that affect organization-environment relationships? Describe those factors.

4. Describe the four approaches to organizational effectiveness. Give a specific example of something that a company should measure in order to evaluate its effectiveness under each approach.

Questions for Analysis

5. Elements from the general environment affect all organizations, but they may not affect all organizations in the same way. Choose an industry and discuss the impact of at least two different elements from the general environment on firms in that industry. Are all firms affected equally? Explain.

6. Which of the firm's environments is most readily changed by the firm? Which of the firm's environments is least amenable to change by the firm? How does this influence the actions that firms take?

Questions for Application

7. Go to Hoover's Online at **www.hoovers.com**. Enter a company name in the Search boxes. When that company's profile is shown, go to "Top Competitors." Here you can learn who the firm's top competitors are. Were you surprised by the list? How do you think Hoover's determines the list?

8. Go to the library or online and research a company. Characterize its level of effectiveness according to each of the four basic models. Share your results with the class.

9. Interview a manager from a local organization about his or her organization's internal environment, including owners, directors, employees, the physical work environment, and the organization culture. How do these various elements interact?

10. Consider an organization with which you are familiar. Outline its environments in detail. Then provide specific examples to illustrate how each dimension affects your organization.

Building Effective Time-Management Skills

Exercise Overview

Time-management skills refer to the manager's ability to prioritize work, to work efficiently, and to delegate appropriately. This exercise will provide you with an opportunity to relate time-management issues to environmental pressures and opportunities.

Exercise Background

As discussed in this chapter, managers and organizations must be sensitive to a variety of environment dimensions and forces reflected in the general, task, and internal environments. The general environment consists of the economic, technological, sociocultural, political-legal, and international dimensions. The task environment includes competitors, customers, suppliers, strategic partners, and regulators. The internal environment consists of owners, board of directors, employees, physical work environment, and organization culture.

One key problem faced by managers is that time is a finite resource. There are only so many hours in a day and only so many tasks that can be accomplished in a given period of time. Thus managers must constantly make choices about how they spend their time. Clearly, they should try to use their time wisely and direct it at the more important challenges and opportunities they face. Spending time on a trivial issue while neglecting an important one is a mistake.

Time-management experts often suggest that managers begin each day by listing what they need to accomplish that day. After the list is compiled, the manager is then advised to sort these daily tasks into three groups: those that must be addressed that day, those that should be addressed that day but could be postponed if necessary, and those that can easily be postponed. The manager is then advised to perform the tasks in order of priority.

Exercise Task

With the background information above as context, do the following:

1. Write across the top of a sheet of paper the three priority levels noted above.
2. Write down the left side of the same sheet of paper the various elements and dimensions of the task and internal environments of business.

3. At the intersection of each row and column, think of an appropriate example that a manager might face; that is, think of a higher-priority, moderate-priority, and lower-priority situation involving a customer.
4. Form a small group with two or three classmates and share the examples you have developed. Focus on whether there is agreement about the prioritization of each example.

Building Effective Communication Skills

Exercise Overview

Communication skills refer to a manager's ability to effectively receive information and ideas from others and to effectively convey information and ideas to others. This exercise will help you develop your communication skills while also helping you to understand the importance of knowing the customer segments in an organization's task environment.

Exercise Background

Assume that you are a newly hired middle manager in the marketing department of a large food manufacturer. You have just completed your formal study of management and are excited about the opportunity to apply some of those theories to the real-life problems of your firm. One problem in particular intrigues you. Your boss, the marketing vice president, developed a consumer survey to solicit feedback about products from customers. The feedback varies considerably, ranging from a 2 to a 5 on a scale of 1 to 5, which gives your firm no helpful data. In addition, sales of your company's products have been slowly but steadily declining over time, and the marketing department is under some pressure from upper management to determine why.

You have an idea that the survey is not an accurate reflection of consumer preferences, so you make a suggestion to your boss: "Why don't we gather some information about our customers, in order to understand their needs better? For example, our products are purchased by individual consumers, schools, restaurants, and other organizations. Maybe each type of consumer wants something different from our product." Your boss's response is to stare at you, perplexed, and say, "No. We're not changing anything about the survey." When you ask, "Why?" the boss responds that the product has been a best-seller for years, that "good quality is good quality," and thus that all customers must want the same thing. He then says, "I'll spare you the embarrassment of failure by refusing your request."

Exercise Task

1. With this background in mind, compose a written proposal for your boss, outlining your position. Be sure to emphasize your fundamental concern—that the marketing department needs to better understand the needs of each customer segment to provide products that meet those needs. Consider ways to persuade your boss to change his mind. (*Hint:* Telling him bluntly that he is wrong is unlikely to be effective.)
2. Based on what you wrote in response to Exercise Task 1, do you think your boss will change his mind? If yes, what persuaded him to change his mind? If no, what other actions could you take to attempt to have your ideas adopted by the firm?

CHAPTER CLOSING CASE

CULTURES WITHIN A CULTURE

Want Italian, seafood, or just a burger? Outback can satisfy any of these. Outback Steakhouse, Inc. is more than just a successful restaurant chain. It is a corporation that owns nine restaurant chains, each competing in a different segment of the casual (but not fast-food) dining market. The corporate parent has a unifying corporate identity and culture. Yet each of the chains also has a unique identity and culture. The challenge for corporate-level Outback managers is to provide support to each brand, while allowing each the flexibility to serve its particular segment.

Outback's corporate mission statement begins, "Our strength starts with our culture." Supporting that statement are three principles: "Our people are our most valuable resource. Focus on quality food and genuine hospitality. Success happens one meal, one person, one restaurant at a time." These values set the tone for the organization culture. Employees, products and services, and customers all receive attention in the mission statement.

Outback's website contains further clues to the organization culture. Regarding autonomy for each brand, the website states, "Although our brands are not homogeneous, common principles do exist across them all, as they were either seeded by the core principles of Outback Steakhouse or were chosen as viable partners because they share the same philosophies." The corporation's greatest strength is in its ability to recognize small, start-up eateries that have great potential. One

investment advisor compares Outback to a venture capital firm and notes that the talent to spot winners is much more rare than the talent of running a great restaurant.

Outback Inc. developed the restaurant concepts that became the Outback Steakhouse, as well as Lee Roy Selmon's and Cheeseburger in Paradise, created with signer/songwriter Jimmy Buffett. Others, such as Carraba's Italian Grill and Paul Lee's Chinese Kitchen, were developed by others but are now owned by Outback. Still other concepts, including Roy's Hawaiian Fusion, Fleming's, and Bonefish Grill, are in joint ventures with Outback.

The culture at Outback is embodied in the firm's slogan: "No Rules. Just Right." Founders Robert Basham, Tim Gannon, and Chris Sullivan had decades of combined experience in managing restaurants when they decided to sell Chili's and turn the profits to something more fun. The Australian theme of the restaurant was based on a U.S. fad for all things Aussie after the film *Crocodile Dundee*. The entrepreneurial venture was risky—the former corporate execs had to cover payroll with personal checks. The food was more adventurous too and the quality high. All three worked hard but had a great time doing it, and that attitude continues to this day.

Contrast that with Roy's, where chef Roy Yamaguchi, a Hawaiian of Japanese ancestry, creates "Hawaiian fusion" cuisine, melding seafood, European sauces, and Asian spices. Roy is an award-winning, classically trained chef, and he has been called "the father

of modern East-West cooking." His cuisine is always fresh, beautifully presented, and of very high quality. The atmosphere at Roy's is understated but elegant and the service attentive. Roy's organization culture is quite different from that at Outback. Food and wine are truly the focus of a Roy's dining experience, as Roy has personally trained every location's head chef.

Lee Roy Selmon's provides yet another dining experience, springing from a unique set of organizational values. Lee Roy, born the youngest of nine siblings in rural Oklahoma, was a three-time All-American as a Sooner and played 10 seasons as a Tampa Bay Buccaneer. After retirement, he was approached by Outback Inc. in 2000 with an idea for a southern-style soul food restaurant. Lee Roy's has a football theme, 27 big-screen televisions, and Mama Selmon's fried chicken, barbecued ribs, and Cajun shrimp. The menu highlights Mama Selmon's memorable advice: "Play hard. Eat well. And don't forget to share." The culture here? Well, it's family-style southern hospitality with good food and plenty of it.

Outback Inc. seems to be doing everything right. The stock value is rising, and some prominent analysts feel that it is still undervalued. When higher food and gas prices drove restaurant prices up, managers countered with some less expensive ingredients. Sales are increasing by 10 percent annually at some chains and revenues by 20 percent. The company is growing fairly rapidly, but is able to recruit a sufficient number of new managers.

At the previous year's end, Outback met its stated goals for the number of new locations, both domestic and international. It seems that a culture that combines fun, good food, hospitality, value, high quality, and customer service has made Outback a sure winner in the competitive casual dining industry.

CASE QUESTIONS

1. List some of the values held at Outback Inc., as well as some of its restaurant chains. How did these values come into being?

2. Why is it a challenge for Outback Inc. managers to maintain their own organization culture while not destroying the unique culture of each of the chains? What do you suggest Outback Inc. managers do to manage this assortment of cultures?

3. Using the four types of organizational effectiveness described in your text, evaluate Outback's effectiveness in each area and overall.

CASE REFERENCES

"2004 Annual Report," Outback website, www.outback.com on March 3, 2006; Gene G. Marcial, "Outback: Set to Sizzle," *BusinessWeek*, January 23, 2006, www.businessweek.com on March 3, 2006; Maggie Overfelt, "Steak Done Well," *Fortune Small Business*, June 1, 2005, www.fortune.com on March 3, 2006.

YOU MAKE THE CALL

The Powerful Mini

1. Assume you are a senior manager at Ford. Your boss has just asked you this question: "That Mini is doing so well—why didn't we think of it?" How might you respond?

2. An obvious tactic for carmakers today would be to try and imitate the Mini. What are the benefits and risks of this approach?

3. What factor or factors might cause a reversal in buying patterns back toward bigger cars and trucks?

4. Suppose you were in charge of the Mini product line. What might you do to keep the Mini "fresh" and at the forefront of its market niche?

Test Prepper

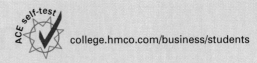

Choose the correct answer. Answers are found at the back of the book.

1. T F The economic dimension of the general environment affects both business and nonbusiness organizations.

2. T F Strategic partners are two or more companies that compete against each other for the same scarce resource.

3. T F Corporate boards of directors are increasingly taking more active roles in overseeing the management of publicly held organizations.

4. T F Organizations with simple and stable environments face the least uncertainty.

5. T F One strategic response an organization may adopt is maintaining the status quo.

6. The specific external organizations and groups that influence an organization are collectively known as the

    A. general environment.
    B. task environment.
    C. internal environment.
    D. external environment.
    E. sociocultural environment.

7. Francine works at a restaurant that is known for its extra-large portions of deep-fried foods. Sales in the past have been good but recently dropped dramatically as consumers indicated a preference for healthier meals. Which dimension of the general environment has changed?

    A. Economic dimension
    B. Technological dimension
    C. Sociocultural dimension
    D. Political-legal dimension
    E. Competitive dimension

8. Which of the following best explains the difference between regulatory agencies and interest groups?

    A. Regulatory agencies control competition; interest groups promote competition.
    B. Regulatory agencies operate in the task environment; interest groups operate in the general environment.
    C. Regulatory agencies are temporary; interest groups are permanent.
    D. Regulatory agencies are created by the government; interest groups are organized by their members.
    E. Regulatory agencies have little power to influence organizations; interest groups have a great amount of power to influence organizations.

9. Before managers attempt to change the organization's culture,

    A. they must understand the culture.
    B. they should place more emphasis on growth and competitiveness.
    C. they must protect the organization from "outsiders."
    D. they need to reduce the need for organizational culture.
    E. they must eliminate resistance to change in the task environment.

10. As chief executive officer, Diane ensures that her managers conduct smooth and efficient operations and maintain the satisfaction and morale of employees. Which model of organizational effectiveness does Diane follow?

    A. Systems resource approach
    B. Organizational culture approach
    C. Internal process approach
    D. Goal approach
    E. Strategic constituencies approach

The Ethical and Social Environment

LEARNING OBJECTIVES

After studying this chapter, you should be able to:

1. Discuss managerial ethics, three areas of special ethical concern for managers, and how organizations manage ethical behavior.

2. Identify and summarize several emerging ethical issues in organizations today.

3. Discuss the concept of social responsibility, specify to whom or what an organization might be considered responsible, and describe four types of organizational approaches to social responsibility.

4. Explain the relationship between the government and organizations regarding social responsibility.

5. Describe some of the activities organizations may engage in to manage social responsibility.

FIRST THINGS FIRST

Is Fair Trade Enough?

"There is no reason why fair trade [products] should cost astronomically more than traditional products."

—NICOLE CHETTERO, PUBLIC RELATIONS ASSOCIATE, TRANSFAIR USA

Our increasingly global economy raises many serious challenges for managers of multinational firms, including the issue of fair trade. "Fair trade" is the name given a variety of programs that attempt to ensure a fair price for their products to farmers who grow crops in developing countries for import to the developed nations.

Fair trade can alleviate the harsh conditions faced by foreign farm workers. For example, cocoa beans used in making chocolates are grown primarily in western Africa. A 2000 study found hundreds of thousands of children under the age of 14 involved in harvesting the cacao pods. The children work with machetes, are exposed to pesticides, and typically receive only food—not wages—for their efforts. Tens of thousands have been sold into forced labor by their destitute parents, who cannot feed them. The children are virtual slaves, with no legal rights, working 12 hours a day, 7 days per week. They lack health care, adequate nutrition, and, worst of all, the education that would allow them

Fair Trade is becoming an increasingly important consideration in less developed countries. These girls helped organize a fundraiser using Fair Trade products that give Latin American farmers more profit for their goods.

to improve their lives. Ironically, they have never eaten or even seen chocolate; they simply cannot afford it.

The farmers claim they are forced to use inexpensive child labor because there is an oversupply of cocoa worldwide and the price fluctuates wildly. Cargill and Archer Daniels Midland (ADM), two giant U.S. food companies, together purchase 25 percent of the world's cocoa supply, which they resell to manufacturers. U.S. chocolate makers Hershey's and Mars use a significant portion of the world cocoa supply. These corporations claim they are not responsible for conditions on the cocoa plantations, which they do not own. The result is a cycle of ignorance, hunger, and poverty in West Africa, with no end in sight.

Fair trade programs call for establishing a guaranteed minimum price for cocoa, guaranteeing an adequate return to plantation owners. While fair trade programs differ greatly, most also call for monitoring wages, enforcing anti-child-labor laws, requiring environmentally friendly policies, and providing education and healthcare services. The costs of the programs would be borne by the manufacturers who buy cocoa. In return, manufacturers could have the right to promote their chocolates as fair trade products, perhaps charging a premium price. The cost to consumers is pennies. "There is no reason why fair trade should cost astronomically more than traditional products," says Nicole Chettero, of TransFair USA, which certifies fair trade goods.

Although the chocolate industry has yet to implement industry-wide fair trade practices, coffee sellers have done more. Many large corporations, including Dunkin' Donuts and McDonald's, offer fair trade coffee at some locations. Others, such as Starbucks, have implemented their own fair trade policies with slightly different requirements. The cost difference per pound is a mere 16 cents, but that provides a living wage to the 800,000 small coffee farmers, mainly in Central and South America, that benefit from fair trade. Dozens of other foods, from bananas to sugar, also are impacted by fair trade policies.

Fair trade programs have been criticized for the price increase to consumers, the lack of effective monitoring, and the confusing differences between them. Yet the programs do begin to address the unequal power relationship between Third World farmers and large multinationals. That increases fairness, which meets the justice norm, one of the four ethical norms discussed in this chapter. Fair trade addresses the other three norms as well. It can dramatically improve the quality of life for small farmers while at the same time it maintains affordable prices for manufacturers and consumers. This meets the utility ethical norm. Fair trade meets the rights ethical norm by increasing the attention given to the rights of small farmers and workers, including their right to living wages, safe working conditions, healthcare, and education. Finally, fair trade is consistent with the caring ethical norm because it demonstrates the compassion that well-off individuals show toward those in need. A writer, Shel Horowitz, showed that compassion by purchasing fair trade chocolate after hearing about child slavery in Ivory Coast. "I don't want to be party to that," Horowitz says. "I try to minimize the impact of my consumerism on people who have very little."[1]

Businesses everywhere need to earn profits to remain in existence. But there are disparate views on how a firm can legitimately pursue and then use those profits. Some companies aggressively seek to maximize their profits, grow at any cost, and focus on nothing but what is best for the company. Others, like some of those mentioned above, take a much different approach to business and actively work for the betterment of society, even when it means less profit for the owners. Most businesses, however, adopt a position somewhere between these extremes. Decisions about which of these approaches to take are affected in turn by managerial ethics and social responsibility.

This chapter explores the basic issues of ethics and social responsibility in detail. We first look at individual ethics and their organizational context and then note several emerging ethical issues in organizations today. Next, we expand our discussion to the more general subject of social responsibility. After we explore the relationships between businesses and the government regarding socially responsible behavior, we examine the activities organizations sometimes undertake to be more socially responsible.

Individual Ethics in Organizations

ethics
An individual's personal beliefs about whether a behavior, action, or decision is right or wrong

ethical behavior
Behavior that conforms to generally accepted social norms

unethical behavior
Behavior that does not conform to generally accepted social norms

We define **ethics** as an individual's personal beliefs about whether a behavior, action, or decision is right or wrong.[2] Note that we define ethics in the context of the individual—people have ethics; organizations do not. Likewise, what constitutes ethical behavior varies from one person to another. For example, one person who finds a twenty-dollar bill on the floor of an empty room believes that it is okay to keep it, whereas another feels compelled to turn it in to the lost-and-found department. Further, although **ethical behavior** is in the eye of the beholder, it usually refers to behavior that conforms to generally accepted social norms. **Unethical behavior**, then, is behavior that does not conform to generally accepted social norms.

A society generally adopts formal laws that reflect the prevailing ethical standards—the social norms—of its citizens. For example, because most people consider theft to be unethical, laws have been passed to make such behaviors illegal and to prescribe ways of punishing those who do steal. But although laws attempt to be clear and unambiguous, their application and interpretation still lead to ethical ambiguities. For example, virtually everyone would agree that forcing employees to work excessive hours, especially for no extra compensation, is unethical. Accordingly, laws have been established to define work and pay standards. But applying the law to organizational settings can still result in ambiguous situations, which can be interpreted in different ways.

An individual's ethics are determined by a combination of factors. People start to form ethical standards as children, in response to their perceptions of their parents' and other adults' behaviors and in response to the behaviors they are allowed to choose. As children grow and enter school, they are also influenced by peers with whom they interact every day. Dozens of important individual events shape people's lives and contribute to their ethical beliefs and behavior as they grow into adulthood. Values and morals also contribute to ethical standards, as do religious beliefs. People who place financial gain and personal advancement at the top of their list of priorities, for example, will adopt personal codes of ethics that promote the pursuit of wealth. Thus they may be ruthless in efforts to gain these rewards, regardless of the costs to others. In contrast, people who clearly establish their family and friends as their top priorities will adopt different ethical standards.

Managerial Ethics

Managerial ethics are the standards of behavior that guide individual managers in their work.[3] Although ethics can affect managerial work in any number of ways, three areas of special concern for managers are shown in Figure 4.1.

managerial ethics
Standards of behavior that guide individual managers in their work

How an Organization Treats Its Employees One important area of managerial ethics is the treatment of employees by the organization. This area includes areas such as hiring and firing, wages and working conditions, and employee privacy and respect. For example, both ethical and legal guidelines suggest that hiring and firing decisions should be based solely on an individual's ability to perform the job. A manager who discriminates against African Americans in hiring is exhibiting both unethical and illegal behavior. But consider the case of a manager who does not discriminate in general, but who occasionally hires a close friend or relative when other applicants might be just as qualified. Although these hiring decisions may not be illegal, they may be objectionable on ethical grounds.

Figure 4.1
MANAGERIAL ETHICS

The three basic areas of concern for managerial ethics are the relationships of the firm to the employee, the employee to the firm, and the firm to other economic agents. Managers need to approach each set of relationships from an ethical and moral perspective.

Wages and working conditions, although tightly regulated, are also areas for potential controversy. For example, a manager paying an employee less than he deserves, simply because the manager knows the employee cannot afford to quit or risk losing his job by complaining, might be considered unethical. Finally, most observers would also agree that an organization is obligated to protect the privacy of its employees. A manager's divulging to employees that one of their coworkers has AIDS or is having an affair is generally seen as an unethical breach of privacy. Likewise, the manner in which an organization addresses issues associated with sexual harassment involves employee privacy and related rights.

How Employees Treat the Organization   Numerous ethical issues stem from how employees treat the organization, especially in regard to conflicts of interest, secrecy and confidentiality, and honesty. A conflict of interest occurs when a decision potentially benefits the individual to the possible detriment of the organization. To guard against such practices, most companies have policies that forbid their buyers from accepting gifts from suppliers. Divulging company secrets is also clearly unethical. Employees who work for businesses in highly competitive industries—electronics, software, and fashion apparel, for example—might be tempted to sell information about company plans to competitors. A third area of concern is honesty in general. Relatively common problems in this area include such activities as using a business telephone to make personal long-distance calls, stealing supplies, and padding expense accounts.

In recent years, new issues regarding such behaviors as personal Internet use at work have also become more pervasive. Another disturbing trend is that more workers are calling in sick simply to get extra time off. In one recent survey, for instance, between 2001 and 2002 the number of workers who reported taking more time off for personal needs increased by 21 percent. And, in that same study, 20 percent of those surveyed indicated that they try to take more vacation days than they are entitled to.[4] Although most employees are inherently honest, organizations must nevertheless be vigilant to avoid problems from such behaviors.

How Employees and the Organization Treat Other Economic Agents   Managerial ethics also come into play in the relationship between the firm and its employees with other economic agents. As listed previously in Figure 4.1, the primary agents of interest include customers, competitors, stockholders, suppliers, dealers, and unions. The behaviors between the organization and these agents that may be subject to ethical ambiguity include advertising and promotions, financial disclosures, ordering and purchasing, shipping and solicitations, bargaining and negotiation, and other business relationships.

For example, businesses in the pharmaceuticals industry have been under growing fire because of the rapid escalation of the prices they charge for many of their drugs. These firms counter that they need to invest more heavily in research and development programs to develop new drugs and that higher prices are needed to cover these costs. The key in situations like this, then, is to find the right balance between reasonable pricing and price gouging. And, as in so many other questions involving ethics, there are significant differences of opinion.[5] Another area of concern in recent years involves financial reporting by various e-commerce firms. Because of the complexities inherent in valuing the assets and revenues of these firms, some of them have been very aggressive in presenting their financial positions in highly positive lights. And, in at least a few cases, some firms have substantially overstated their earnings projections to entice more investment. Moreover, some of today's accounting scandals in traditional firms have stemmed from similarly questionable practices.[6]

Additional complexities faced by many firms today are the variations in ethical business practices in different countries. In some countries, bribes and side payments are a normal and customary part of doing business. However, U.S. laws forbid these practices, even if a firm's rivals from other countries are paying them. For example, a U.S. power-generating company once lost a $320 million contract in the Middle East because government officials demanded a $3 bribe. A Japanese firm paid the bribe and won the contract. Enron once had a big project in India cancelled because newly elected officials demanded bribes. Although these kinds of cases are illegal under U.S. law, other situations are more ambiguous. In China, for example, local journalists expect their cab fare to be paid if they are covering a business-sponsored news conference. In Indonesia, the normal time for a foreigner to get a driver's license is over a year, but it can be "expedited" for an extra $100. And in Romania, building inspectors routinely expect a "tip" for a favorable review.[7]

> "[Enron] took on the monopolies. I believe we were on the side of consumers. I was proud walking into the lobby . . . By making things happen, we were making the world better."
>
> Jeffrey Skilling, former Enron CEO
> (*USA Today,* April 11, 2006, p. 1B)

Ethics in an Organizational Context

Of course, although ethics are an individual phenomenon, ethical or unethical actions by particular managers do not occur in a vacuum. Indeed, they most often occur in an organizational context that is conducive to them. Actions of peer managers and top managers, as well as the organization's culture, all contribute to the ethical context of the organization.[8]

The starting point in understanding the ethical context of management is, of course, the individual's own ethical standards. Some people, for example, would risk personal embarrassment or lose their jobs before they would do something unethical. Other people are much more easily swayed by the unethical behavior they see around them and other situational factors, and they may even be willing to commit major crimes to further their own careers or for financial gains. Organizational practices may strongly influence the ethical standards of employees. Some organizations openly permit unethical business practices as long as they are in the firm's best interests.

If managers become aware of unethical practices and allow them to continue, they contribute to an organization culture that says such activity is permitted. For example, Hypercom Corporation, a Phoenix company that makes card-swiping machines for retailers, came under fire because of the actions and alleged wrongdoing of a senior marketing executive named Jairo Gonzalez. Gonzalez was accused of rape by his former secretary (she was paid a $100,000 settlement by the firm), and three other women accused him of sexual harassment. He also set up his own outside business—run by his father—to charge Hypercom for handling overseas shipping. Gonzalez got a job for his girlfriend at a video production firm used by Hypercom in Miami; when she moved to Phoenix, the firm switched its account to the video production firm she joined there. But the firm's CEO, George Wallner, defended his decision to retain Gonzalez because of the huge revenues Gonzalez generated. In Wallner's words, "He [is] bringing in $70 million a year. Do you fire your number one rock star because he's difficult?" And, regarding the payment to

Gonzalez's former secretary, Wallner asserted, "On a moral level this is confusing. But if you think of only the business decision, it was dead right." Perhaps it is not surprising, then, that another Hypercom manager married a temp and then got her a job at the firm, or that Wallner and his brother borrowed $4.5 million from the firm, some of it interest free.[9]

The organization's environment also contributes to the context for ethical behavior. In a highly competitive or regulated industry, for example, a manager may feel more pressure to achieve high performance. When managers feel pressure to meet goals or lower costs, they may explore a variety of alternatives to help achieve these ends. And, in some cases, the alternative they choose may be unethical or even illegal.

Managing Ethical Behavior

Spurred partially by increased awareness of ethical scandals in business and partially by a sense of enhanced corporate consciousness about the importance of ethical and unethical behaviors, many organizations have reemphasized ethical behavior on the part of employees. This emphasis takes many forms, but any effort to enhance ethical behavior must begin with top management. It is top managers, for example, who establish the organization's culture and define what will and will not be acceptable behavior. Some companies have also started offering employees training in how to cope with ethical dilemmas. At Boeing, for example, line managers lead training sessions for other employees, and the company also has an ethics committee that reports directly to the board of directors. The training sessions involve discussions of different ethical dilemmas that employees might face and how managers might handle those dilemmas. Chemical Bank and Xerox also have ethics training programs for their managers.

Organizations are also going to greater lengths to formalize their ethical standards. Some, such as General Mills and Johnson & Johnson, have prepared guidelines that detail how employees are to treat suppliers, customers, competitors, and other constituents. Others, such as Whirlpool, Texas Instruments, and Hewlett-Packard, have developed a formal ***code of ethics***—written statements of the values and ethical standards that guide the firms' actions. Of course, firms must adhere to such codes if they are to be of value. In one now-infamous case, Enron's board of directors voted to set aside the firm's code of ethics to implement a business plan that violated the code.[10]

> *code of ethics*
> A formal, written statement of the values and ethical standards that guide a firm's actions

And, of course, no code, guideline, or training program can truly make up for the quality of an individual's personal judgment about what is right behavior and what is wrong behavior in a particular situation. Such devices may prescribe what people should do, but they often fail to help people understand and live with the consequences of their choices. Making ethical choices may lead to very unpleasant outcomes—firing, rejection by colleagues, and the forfeiture of monetary gain, to name a few. Thus managers must be prepared to confront their own conscience and weigh the options available when making difficult ethical decisions.

Unfortunately, what distinguishes ethical from unethical behavior is often subjective and subject to differences of opinion. So how does one go about deciding whether a particular action or decision is ethical? Traditionally, experts have suggested a three-step model for applying ethical judgments to situations that may arise during the course of business activities. These steps are (1) gather the relevant factual information, (2) determine the most appropriate moral values, and (3) make an ethical judgment based on the rightness or wrongness of the proposed activity or policy.

But this analysis is seldom as simple as these steps might imply. For instance, what if the facts are not clear-cut? What if there are no agreed-upon moral values? Nevertheless, a judgment and a decision must be made. Experts point out that, otherwise, trust is impossible, and trust, they add, is indispensable to any business transaction. Thus, to more completely assess the ethics of a particular behavior, a more complex perspective is necessary. To illustrate this perspective, consider the following common dilemma faced by managers who are given expense accounts.[11]

Companies routinely provide their managers with accounts to cover their work-related expenses when they are traveling on company business or entertaining clients for business purposes. Common examples of such expenses include hotel bills, meals, rental cars or taxis, and so forth. But employees, of course, are expected to claim only expenses that are accurate and work related. For example, if a manager takes a client out to dinner while in another city on business and spends $100 for dinner, submitting a receipt for that $100 dinner is clearly accurate and appropriate. Suppose, however, that the manager has a $100 dinner the next night in that same city with a good friend for purely social purposes. Submitting that receipt for full reimbursement would be unethical. A few managers, however, might rationalize that it would be okay to submit a receipt for dinner with a friend. They might argue, for example, that they are underpaid, so this is just a way for them to increase their income.

Other principles that come into play in a case like this include various ethical norms. Four such norms involve utility, rights, justice, and caring. By utility, we mean whether a particular act optimizes what is best for its constituencies. By rights, we mean whether the act respects the rights of the individuals involved. By justice, we mean whether the act is consistent with what most people would see as fair. And by caring, we mean whether the act is consistent with people's responsibilities to one another. Figure 4.2 illustrates a model that incorporates these ethical norms.

Now, reconsider the case of the inflated expense account. Although the utility norm would acknowledge that the manager benefits from padding an expense account, others, such as coworkers and owners, would not. Similarly, most experts would agree that such an action does not respect the rights of others. Moreover, it is clearly unfair and compromises responsibilities to others. Thus this particular act would appear to be clearly unethical. However, the figure also provides mechanisms for considering unique circumstances that might fit only in certain limited situations. For example, suppose the manager loses the receipt for the legitimate dinner but has the receipt for the same amount for the social dinner. Some people would now argue that it is okay to submit the social dinner receipt because the manager is only doing so to get what he or she is entitled to. Others, however, would still argue that submitting the social receipt is wrong under any circumstances. The point, simply, is that changes in the situation can make things more or less clear-cut.

concept
CHECK

What are the three basic areas of managerial ethics?

Identify an ethical situation you have experienced or observed and analyze it in terms of the framework presented in Figure 4.2.

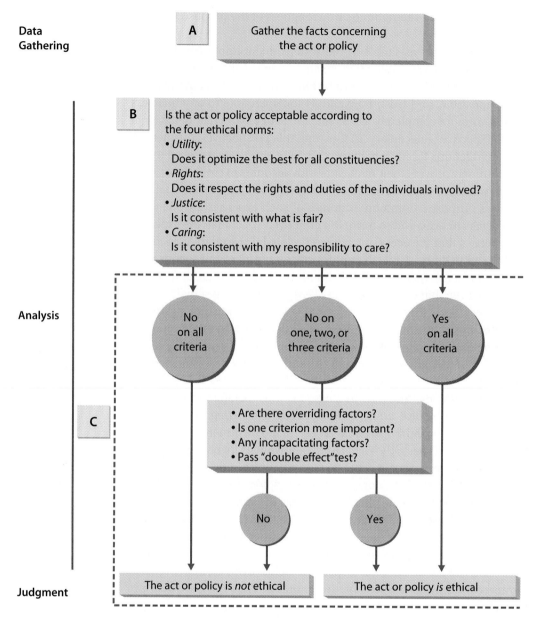

Data Gathering

A — Gather the facts concerning the act or policy

B — Is the act or policy acceptable according to the four ethical norms:
- *Utility*:
  Does it optimize the best for all constituencies?
- *Rights*:
  Does it respect the rights and duties of the individuals involved?
- *Justice*:
  Is it consistent with what is fair?
- *Caring*:
  Is it consistent with my responsibility to care?

Analysis

No on all criteria

No on one, two, or three criteria

Yes on all criteria

C —
- Are there overriding factors?
- Is one criterion more important?
- Any incapacitating factors?
- Pass "double effect" test?

No

Yes

Judgment

The act or policy is *not* ethical

The act or policy *is* ethical

Figure 4.2

A GUIDE FOR ETHICAL DECISION MAKING

Managers should attempt to apply ethical judgment to the decisions they make. For example, this useful framework for guiding ethical decision making suggests that managers apply a set of four criteria based on utility, rights, justice, and caring when assessing decision options. The resulting analysis allows a manager to make a clear assessment of whether a decision or policy is ethical.

Source: Adapted from Gerald F. Cavanagh, Dennis J. Moberg, and Manuel Velasquez, "Making Business Ethics Practical," *Business Ethics Quarterly*, 1995, vol. 5, no. 3, pp. 399–418; and Manuel Velasquez, Gerald F. Cavanagh, and Dennis Moberg, "Organizational Statesmanship and Dirty Politics," *Organizational Dynamics*, Autumn 1983, p. 84. Copyright 1983, with permission from Elsevier Science. Reprinted from Gerald F. Cavanagh, *American Business Values*, 4th ed. (Upper Saddle River, N.J.: Prentice-Hall, 1998). Reprinted by permission of Prentice-Hall, Inc.

Emerging Ethical Issues in Organizations

Ethical scandals have become almost commonplace in today's world. Ranging from business to sports to politics to the entertainment industry, these scandals have rocked stakeholder confidence and called into question the moral integrity of our society. But, at the same time, it is important to remember that most women and men today conduct themselves and their affairs with nothing but the highest ethical standards. Hence, as we summarize several emerging ethical issues in organizations, it is important to remember that one cannot judge everyone by the transgressions of a few.

Ethical Leadership

For every unethical senior manager, there are many highly ethical ones. But the actions of such high-profile deposed executives as Dennis Kozlowski (Tyco), Kenneth Lay (Enron), and Bernard Ebbers (WorldCom) have substantially increased the scrutiny directed at all executives. As a direct result, executives everywhere are being expected to exhibit nothing but the strongest ethical conduct. This leadership, in turn, is expected to help set the tone for the rest of the organization and to help establish both norms and a culture that reinforce the importance of ethical behavior.[12]

The basic premise behind ethical leadership is that because leaders serve as role models for others, their every action is subject to scrutiny. If a senior executive exercises questionable judgment, this sends a signal to others that such actions are acceptable. This signal may be remembered in turn by others when they face similar situations. As a result, CEOs like Aramark's Joseph Neubauer and Costco's James Sinegal are now being held up as the standard against which others are being measured. The basic premise is that a CEO must set the company's moral tone by being honest and straightforward and by taking responsibility for any identified shortcomings. And, to support this view, in 2002 Congress passed the **Sarbanes-Oxley Act**, requiring CEOs and CFOs to personally vouch for the truthfulness and fairness of their firms' financial disclosures. The law also imposes tough new measures to deter and punish corporate and accounting fraud and corruption.

Ethical Issues in Corporate Governance

A related area of emerging concern relates to ethical issues in corporate governance. As discussed in Chapter 3, the board of directors of a public corporation is expected to ensure that the business is being properly managed and that the decisions made by its senior management are in the best interests of shareholders and other stakeholders. But, in far too many cases, the recent ethical scandals alluded to above have actually started with a breakdown in the corporate governance structure. For instance, WorldCom's board approved a personal loan to the firm's CEO, Bernard Ebbers, for $366 million, when there was little evidence that he could repay it. Likewise, Tyco's board approved a $20 million bonus for one of its own members for helping with the acquisition of another firm.

But boards of directors are also increasingly being criticized even when they are not directly implicated in wrongdoing. The biggest complaint often relates to board independence. Disney,

Ken Lay, founder of Enron, became the iconic image of corporate disregard for shareholder welfare and unethical managerial conduct. Mr. Lay is shown here leaving the federal courthouse in the 11th week of his fraud and conspiracy trial in Houston. The jury found him guilty on all 6 counts of fraud and conspiracy. Mr. Lay died of a heart attack shortly after his conviction.

for instance, faced criticism on this front for years. Several key members of the firm's board of directors were from companies that do business with Disney, and others are longtime friends of former Disney CEO Michael Eisner. The concern was that Eisner may have been given more autonomy than might otherwise be warranted because of his various relationships with board members. Although board members need to have some familiarity with both the firm and its industry to function effectively, they also need to have sufficient independence to carry out their oversight function. And increasingly, corporate boards are creating strict rules dictating governance standards that provide a clear separation of authority between the board and the CEO.[13]

> "[New rules governing CEO conduct] . . . show dramatic change and it's all motivated by the desire for good corporate governance."
>
> Steve Odland, CEO of Office Depot
> (*USA Today,* March 20, 2006, p. 1B)

Ethical Issues in Information Technology

A final set of issues that has emerged in recent times involves information technology. Among the specific questions in this area are individual rights to privacy and the potential abuse of information technology by individuals. Indeed, online privacy has become a hot topic, as companies sort out the ethical and management issues. DoubleClick, an online advertising network, is one of the firms at the eye of the privacy storm. The company has collected data on the habits of millions of web surfers, recording which sites they visit and which ads they click on. DoubleClick insists the profiles are anonymous and are used to better match surfers with appropriate ads. However, after the company announced a plan to add names and addresses to its database, it was forced to back down because of public concerns over invasion of online privacy.

DoubleClick is not the only firm gathering personal data about people's Internet activities. People who register at Yahoo! are asked to list date of birth, among other details. Amazon.com, eBay, and other sites also ask for personal information. As Internet usage increases, however, surveys show that people are troubled by the amount of information being collected and who gets to see it.

One way management can address these concerns is to post a privacy policy on the website. The policy should explain exactly what data the company collects and who gets to see the data. It should also allow people a choice about having their information shared with others and indicate how people can opt out of data collection. Disney, IBM, and other companies support this position by refusing to advertise on websites that have no posted privacy policies.

In addition, companies can offer web surfers the opportunity to review and correct information that has been collected, especially medical and financial data. In the offline world, consumers are legally allowed to inspect credit and medical records. In the online world, this kind of access can be costly and cumbersome because data are often spread across several computer systems. Despite the technical difficulties, government agencies are already working on Internet privacy guidelines, which means that companies will need internal guidelines, training, and leadership to ensure compliance.

concept
CHECK

| *What are three emerging ethical issues in business today?* | *In what ways are information privacy and information technology relevant to you?* |

Social Responsibility and Organizations

As we have seen, ethics relate to individuals and their decisions and behaviors. Organizations themselves do not have ethics, but do relate to their environment in ways that often involve ethical dilemmas and decisions. These situations are generally referred to within the context of the organization's social responsibility. Specifically, **social responsibility** is the set of obligations an organization has to protect and enhance the societal context in which it functions.

social responsibility
The set of obligations an organization has to protect and enhance the societal context in which it functions

Areas of Social Responsibility

Organizations may exercise social responsibility toward their stakeholders, toward the natural environment, and toward general social welfare. Some organizations acknowledge their responsibilities in all three areas and strive diligently to meet each of them, whereas others emphasize only one or two areas of social responsibility. And a few acknowledge no social responsibility at all.

Organizational Stakeholders   In Chapter 3 we describe the task environment as comprising those elements in an organization's external environment that directly affect the organization in one or more ways. Another way to describe these same elements is from the perspective of **organizational stakeholders**, or those people and organizations who are directly affected by the practices of an organization and have a stake in its performance.[14] Major stakeholders are depicted in Figure 4.3.

organizational stakeholder
Person or organization who is directly affected by the practices of an organization and has a stake in its performance

Figure 4.3
ORGANIZATIONAL STAKEHOLDERS

All organizations have a variety of stakeholders who are directly affected by the organization and who have a stake in its performance. These are people and organizations to whom an organization should be responsible.

Most companies that strive to be responsible to their stakeholders concentrate first and foremost on three main groups: customers, employees, and investors. They then select other stakeholders that may be particularly relevant or significant to the organization and then attempt to address the needs and expectations of those stakeholders as well.

Organizations that are responsible to their customers strive to treat them fairly and honestly. They also seek to charge fair prices, to honor warranties, to meet delivery commitments, to advertise and promote their products in an honest and truthful manner, and to stand behind the quality of the products they sell. Companies that have established excellent reputations in this area include L.L. Bean, Lands' End, Dell Computer, and Johnson & Johnson.

Organizations that are socially responsible in their dealings with employees treat their workers fairly, make them a part of the team, and respect their dignity and basic human needs. Organizations such as 3M Company, Hoescht AG, SAS Institute, and Southwest Airlines have all established strong reputations in this area. In addition, they go to great lengths to find, hire, train, and promote qualified minorities.

To maintain a socially responsible stance toward investors, managers should follow proper accounting procedures, provide appropriate information to shareholders about the financial performance of the firm, and manage the organization to protect shareholder rights and investments. Moreover, they should be accurate and candid in their assessment of future growth and profitability, and avoid even the appearance of improprieties involving such sensitive areas as insider trading, stock price manipulation, and the withholding of financial data.

The Natural Environment   A second critical area of social responsibility relates to the natural environment.[15] Not long ago, many organizations indiscriminately dumped sewage, waste products from production, and trash into streams and rivers, into the air, and on vacant land. When Shell Oil first explored the Amazon River Basin for potential drilling sites in the late 1980s, its crews ripped down trees and left a trail of garbage in their wake. Now, however, many laws regulate the disposal of waste materials.

In many instances, companies themselves have become more socially responsible in their release of pollutants and general treatment of the environment. For example, when Shell launched its most recent exploratory expedition into another area of the Amazon Basin, the group included a biologist to oversee environmental protection and an anthropologist to help the team interact more effectively with native tribes.[16]

Still, much remains to be done. Companies need to develop economically feasible ways to avoid contributing to acid rain, global warming, and depletion of the ozone layer, and to develop alternative methods of handling sewage,

Respect for the natural environment is a key part of social responsibility. Vandana Shiva runs an organization called Navdanya (Nine Seeds). Her organization helps teach farmers in India how to produce hardy native varieties of crops that can be grown organically with natural fertilizer and no artificial chemicals.

hazardous wastes, and ordinary garbage.[17] Procter & Gamble, for example, is an industry leader in using recycled materials for containers. Hyatt Corporation established a new company to help recycle waste products from its hotels. Monsanto is launching an entire new product line aimed at improving the environment with genetically engineered crops.[18] Ford has also announced its intention to create a new brand to develop and market low-pollution and electrically powered vehicles.[19] The Internet is also seen as having the potential to play an important role in resource conservation, as many e-commerce businesses and transactions are reducing both energy costs and pollution.[20]

Companies also need to develop safety policies that cut down on accidents with potentially disastrous environmental results. When one of Ashland Oil's storage tanks ruptured several years ago, spilling more than 500,000 gallons of diesel fuel into Pennsylvania's Monongahela River, the company moved quickly to clean up the spill but was still indicted for violating U.S. environmental laws.[21] After the Exxon oil tanker *Valdez* spilled millions of gallons of oil off the coast of Alaska, the firm adopted new and more stringent procedures to keep another disaster from happening.

General Social Welfare   Some people believe that, in addition to treating constituents and the environment responsibly, business organizations also should promote the general welfare of society. Examples include contributing financially to charities, philanthropic organizations, and not-for-profit foundations and associations; providing other support (such as buying advertising space in programs) to museums, symphonies, and public radio and television; and taking a role in improving public health and education. Some people also believe that organizations should act even more broadly to correct the political inequities that exist in the world. For example, these observers would argue that businesses should not conduct operations in countries with a record of human rights violations. Thus they stand in opposition to companies' doing business in China and Vietnam. *The Business of Ethics* illustrates an organization that is dedicated specifically to promoting the general social welfare.

Arguments For and Against Social Responsibility

On the surface, there seems to be little disagreement about the need for organizations to be socially responsible. In truth, though, those who oppose broad interpretations of social responsibility use several convincing arguments.[22] Some of the more salient arguments on both sides of this contemporary debate are summarized in Figure 4.4 and further explained in the following sections.

Arguments For Social Responsibility   People who argue in favor of social responsibility claim that because organizations create many of the problems that need to be addressed, such as air and water pollution and resource depletion, they should play a major role in solving them. They also argue that because corporations are legally defined entities with most of the same privileges as private citizens, businesses should not try to avoid their obligations as citizens. Advocates of social responsibility point out that whereas governmental organizations have stretched their budgets to the limit, many large businesses often have surplus revenues that could be used to help solve social problems. For example, IBM

The Business of Ethics

The Innocence Project

Many organizations act ethically, but the Innocence Project is a set of organizations that exist solely to redress ethical and legal wrongs. The confederation of nonprofit legal clinics was established to "handle cases where post-conviction DNA testing of evidence can yield conclusive proof of innocence." Most of the clinics, which cover 29 states and the District of Columbia, are associated with a law school.

The clinic's clients were found guilty of committing felony crimes, usually assault, murder, or rape. Often, their convictions were aided by eyewitness testimony and physical evidence. Eyewitnesses, however, especially those under stress, are frequently mistaken. Criminal evidence laboratories make mistakes. New advances in DNA testing allow better accuracy than years ago.

Clients are accepted without regard to race, sex, or economic status. However, the typical client is an African American or Hispanic male who was young at the time of the alleged crime. Almost all clients are poor and were aided by public defenders at their trial. In contrast, many of those who work for Innocence Projects are law students or attorneys who are working pro bono, without charging a fee. Project staff are predominantly middle class or affluent and white. Many are female.

The close association between these two very diverse groups is aided by their empathy and mutual interest in justice. The convicts want to restore their reputations and regain their freedom. The volunteers gain practical experience while giving back. "What more can a person who hopes to enter the legal profession ask for but the opportunity to work for justice?" says Mike Cappell, a law student and Ohio Innocence Project volunteer.

It might be tempting to disapprove of the projects for aiding criminals. Others adopt the perspective that victims deserve more attention and sympathy than convicts do. Yet the clients of the Innocence Project, if they are proven to be innocent, are victims too. Even the original crime victims, whose testimony resulted in conviction, feel remorse when confronted with their mistake. "I had contributed to taking away 11 years of this man's life. . . . I felt so bad. I fell apart. I cried and cried and I wept and I was angry at me," says a rape victim about her alleged attacker, who was cleared by DNA evidence.

The numbers are huge, but thanks to the Innocence Project, 200 truly innocent people were freed from jail, saving several lives and thousand of years of wrongful imprisonment. Jacqueline McMurtrie, director of the University of Washington Innocence Project, says, "Few injustices compare to that of convicting an innocent person of a crime." What could be more ethical than righting that injustice?

References: "About the Innocence Project," "Causes and Remedies of Wrongful Convictions," The Innocence Project website, www .innocenceproject.org on March 4, 2006; Erik Laursen, "Ohio Innocence Project Gives Hands-On Legal Experience," University of Cincinnati Law School website, www.law.uc.edu on March 4, 2006; Amanda Schaffer, "Solving Puzzles with Body Parts as the Pieces," New York Times, February 28, 2006, www.nytimes.com on March 4, 2006.

routinely donates surplus computers to schools, and many restaurants give leftover food to homeless shelters.

Although each of the arguments just summarized is a distinct justification for socially responsible behaviors on the part of organizations, another more general reason for social responsibility is profit itself. For example, organizations that make clear and visible contributions to society can achieve an enhanced reputation and garner greater market share for their products. Although claims of socially responsible activities can haunt a company if they are exaggerated or untrue, they can also work to the benefit of both the organization and society if the advertised benefits are true and accurate.

Arguments Against Social Responsibility   Some people, however, including the famous economist Milton Friedman, argue that widening the interpretation of social responsibility will undermine the U.S. economy by detracting from the basic

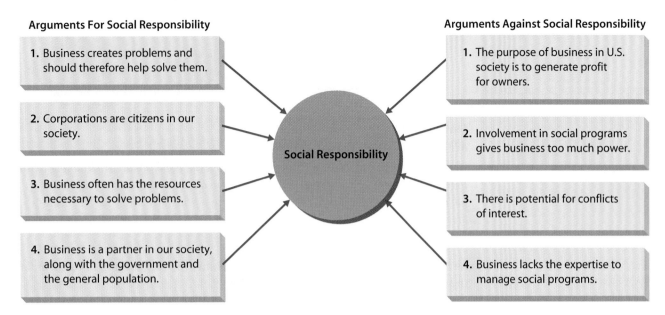

Arguments For Social Responsibility

1. Business creates problems and should therefore help solve them.

2. Corporations are citizens in our society.

3. Business often has the resources necessary to solve problems.

4. Business is a partner in our society, along with the government and the general population.

Social Responsibility

Arguments Against Social Responsibility

1. The purpose of business in U.S. society is to generate profit for owners.

2. Involvement in social programs gives business too much power.

3. There is potential for conflicts of interest.

4. Business lacks the expertise to manage social programs.

Figure 4.4

ARGUMENTS FOR AND AGAINST SOCIAL RESPONSIBILITY

While many people want everyone to see social responsibility as a desirable aim, there are several strong arguments that can be used both for and against social responsibility. Hence, organizations and their managers should carefully assess their own values, beliefs, and priorities when deciding which stance and approach to take regarding social responsibility.

mission of business: to earn profits for owners. For example, money that Chevron or General Electric contributes to social causes or charities is money that could otherwise be distributed to owners as a dividend. Shareholders of Ben & Jerry's Homemade Holdings once expressed outrage when the firm refused to accept a lucrative exporting deal to Japan simply because the Japanese distributor did not have a strong social agenda.[23]

Another objection to deepening the social responsibility of businesses points out that corporations already wield enormous power and that their activity in social programs gives them even more power. Still another argument against social responsibility focuses on the potential for conflicts of interest. Suppose, for example, that one manager is in charge of deciding which local social program or charity will receive a large grant from her business. The local civic opera company (a not-for-profit organization that relies on contributions for its existence) might offer her front-row tickets for the upcoming season in exchange for her support. If opera is her favorite form of music, she might be tempted to direct the money toward the local company, when it might actually be needed more in other areas.[24]

Finally, critics argue that organizations lack the expertise to understand how to assess and make decisions about worthy social programs. How can a company truly know, they ask, which cause or program is most deserving of its support or how money might best be spent? For example, ExxonMobil makes substantial contributions to help save the Bengal tiger, an endangered species that happens also to serve as the firm's corporate symbol. ExxonMobil gives most of the money to support breeding programs in zoos and to help educate people about the tiger. But conservationists criticize the firm and its activities, arguing that the money might

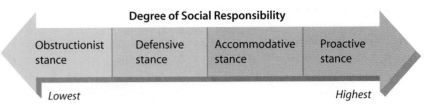

Degree of Social Responsibility

| Obstructionist stance | Defensive stance | Accommodative stance | Proactive stance |

Lowest   *Highest*

Figure 4.5
APPROACHES TO SOCIAL RESPONSIBILITY

Organizations can adopt a variety of approaches to social responsibility. For example, a firm that never considers the consequences of its decisions and tries to hide its transgressions is taking an obstructionist stance. At the other extreme, a firm that actively seeks to identify areas where it can help society is pursuing a proactive stance toward social responsibility.

be better spent instead on eliminating poaching, the illegal trade of tiger fur, and the destruction of the tiger's natural habitat.[25]

Organizational Approaches to Social Responsibility   As we have seen, some people advocate a larger social role for organizations, and others argue that the role is already too large. Not surprisingly, organizations themselves adopt a wide range of positions on social responsibility. As Figure 4.5 illustrates, the four stances that an organization can take concerning its obligations to society fall along a continuum ranging from the lowest to the highest degree of socially responsible practices.

Obstructionist Stance   The few organizations that take what might be called an ***obstructionist stance*** to social responsibility usually do as little as possible to solve social or environmental problems. When they cross the ethical or legal line that separates acceptable from unacceptable practices, their typical response is to deny or avoid accepting responsibility for their actions. For example, a senior executive of Astra USA, a subsidiary of a Swedish pharmaceutical firm, was once charged with sexual harassment and misusing corporate assets. When these problems were first reported, officials at both the U.S. company and its Swedish parent company denied any wrongdoing without even conducting an inquiry. They only acknowledged the problem when the executive was indicted and found guilty. More recently, both Enron and its auditor, Arthur Andersen, appear to have taken this approach, based on the numerous denials from officials at both firms regarding various charges of wrongdoing, as well as their intentional destruction of important legal and financial documents.

Defensive Stance   One step removed from the obstructionist stance is the ***defensive stance***, whereby the organization does everything that is required of it legally, but nothing more. This approach is most consistent with the arguments used against social responsibility. Managers in organizations that take a defensive stance insist that their job is to generate profits. For example, such a firm would install pollution control equipment dictated by law, but would not install higher-quality but slightly more expensive equipment even though it might limit pollution further. Tobacco companies like Philip Morris take this position in their marketing efforts. In the United States, they are legally required to include warnings to smokers on their products and to limit their advertising to prescribed media. Domestically they

obstructionist stance
An approach to social responsibility in which firms do as little as possible to solve social or environmental problems

defensive stance
A social responsibility stance in which an organization does everything that is required of it legally, but nothing more

follow these rules to the letter of the law but use stronger marketing methods in countries that have no such rules. In many African countries, for example, cigarettes are heavily promoted, contain higher levels of tar and nicotine than those sold in the United States, and carry few or no health warning labels.[26] Firms that take this position are also unlikely to cover up wrongdoing, and will generally admit their mistakes and take appropriate corrective actions.

Accommodative Stance   A firm that adopts an ***accommodative stance*** meets its legal and ethical obligations but will also go beyond these obligations in selected cases. Such firms voluntarily agree to participate in social programs, but solicitors have to convince the organization that the programs are worthy of its support. Both ExxonMobil and IBM, for example, will match contributions made by their employees to selected charitable causes. And many organizations will respond to requests for donations to Little League, Girl Scouts, youth soccer programs, and so forth. The point, though, is that someone has to knock on the door and ask—the organizations do not proactively seek such avenues for contributing.

> *accommodative stance*
> A social responsibility stance in which an organization meets its legal and ethical obligations but will also go beyond these obligations in selected cases

Proactive Stance   The highest degree of social responsibility that a firm can exhibit is the ***proactive stance***. Firms that adopt this approach take to heart the arguments in favor of social responsibility. They view themselves as citizens in a society and proactively seek opportunities to contribute. An excellent example of a proactive stance is the Ronald McDonald House program undertaken by McDonald's. These houses, located close to major medical centers, can be used by families for minimal cost while their sick children are receiving medical treatment nearby. Sears offers fellowships that support promising young performers while they develop their talents. Target stopped selling guns in its stores, and Toys "R" Us stopped selling realistic toy guns, both due to concerns about escalating violence. Increasingly, some firms, such as Mattel, Nike, and Home Depot are severing relationships with foreign suppliers found not to be treating their employees fairly.[27] These and related activities and programs exceed the accommodative stance—they indicate a sincere and potent commitment to improving the general social welfare in this country and thus represent a proactive stance to social responsibility.

> *proactive stance*
> A social responsibility stance in which an organization views itself as a citizen in a society and proactively seeks opportunities to contribute

"If we find evidence of systematic [worker abuse], we're not going to do business with you."
Jim Walter, Mattel Senior Vice President
(*USA Today,* March 27, 2006, p. 1B)

Remember that these categories are not discrete but merely define stages along a continuum of approaches. Organizations do not always fit neatly into one category. The Ronald McDonald House program has been widely applauded, for example, but McDonald's also came under fire a few years ago for allegedly misleading consumers about the nutritional value of its food products. And even though both Enron and Arthur Andersen took an obstructionist stance in the cases cited above, many individual employees and managers at both firms no doubt made substantial contributions to society in a number of different ways.

concept CHECK

What are the basic areas of social responsibility?

Which do you find most compelling: the arguments for or the arguments against social responsibility? Why?

The Government and Social Responsibility

An especially important element of social responsibility is the relationship between business and government. For example, in planned economies the government heavily regulates business activities, ostensibly to ensure that business supports some overarching set of social ideals. And even in market economies there is still considerable government control of business, much of it again directed at making sure that social interests are not damaged by business interests. On the other side of the coin, business also attempts to influence the government. Such influence attempts are usually undertaken in an effort to offset or reverse government restrictions. As Figure 4.6 shows, organizations and the government use several methods in their attempts to influence each other.

How Government Influences Organizations

The government attempts to shape social responsibility practices through both direct and indirect channels. Direct influence most frequently is manifested through regulation, whereas indirect influence can take a number of forms, most notably taxation policies.

regulation
Government's attempts to influence business by establishing laws and rules that dictate what businesses can and cannot do

Direct Regulation The government most often directly influences organizations through **regulation**, or the establishment of laws and rules that dictate what organizations can and cannot do. As noted earlier in the chapter, this regulation usually evolves from societal beliefs about what businesses should or should not be allowed to do. To implement legislation, the government generally creates special agencies to monitor and control certain aspects of business activity. For example, the Environmental Protection Agency handles environmental issues; the Federal Trade Commission and the Food and Drug Administration focus on consumer-related concerns; the Equal Employee Opportunity Commission, the National Labor Relations Board, and the Department of Labor help protect employees; and the Securities and Exchange Commission handles investor-related issues. These agencies have the power to levy fines or bring charges against organizations that violate regulations.

Indirect Regulation Other forms of regulation are indirect. For example, the government can indirectly influence the social responsibility of organizations through its tax codes. In effect, the government can influence how organizations spend their social responsibility dollars by providing greater or lesser tax incentives. For instance, suppose that the government wanted organizations to spend more on training the hard-core unemployed. Congress could then pass laws that provided tax

The government often plays a role in social responsibility. Lewis Perry from Seattle, WA is shown here sorting through boxes filled with used computer parts at Total Reclaim in Seattle. A network of state lawmakers wants to engineer a recycling program for these antiquated electronics, which have been dubbed "e-waste." The lawmakers hope to have the program up and running by 2009.

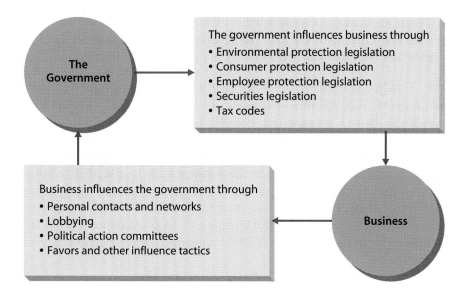

The Government

The government influences business through
• Environmental protection legislation
• Consumer protection legislation
• Employee protection legislation
• Securities legislation
• Tax codes

Business

Business influences the government through
• Personal contacts and networks
• Lobbying
• Political action committees
• Favors and other influence tactics

Figure 4.6

HOW BUSINESS AND THE GOVERNMENT INFLUENCE EACH OTHER

Business and the government influence each other in a variety of ways. Government influence can be direct or indirect. Business influence relies on personal contacts, lobbying, political action committees (PACs), and favors. Federal Express, for example, has a very active PAC.

incentives to companies that opened new training facilities. As a result, more businesses would probably do so. Of course, some critics argue that regulation is already excessive. They maintain that a free market system would eventually accomplish the same goals as regulation, with lower costs to both organizations and the government.

How Organizations Influence Government

As we mention in Chapter 3, organizations can influence their environment in many different ways. In particular, businesses have four main methods of addressing governmental pressures for more social responsibility.

Personal Contacts   Because many corporate executives and political leaders travel in the same social circles, personal contacts and networks offer one method of influence. A business executive, for example, may be able to contact a politician directly and present his or her case regarding a piece of legislation being considered.

Lobbying   *Lobbying*, or the use of persons or groups to formally represent an organization or group of organizations before political bodies, is also an effective way to influence the government. The National Rifle Association (NRA), for example, has a staff of lobbyists in Washington and a substantial annual budget. These lobbyists work to represent the NRA's position on gun control and to potentially influence members of Congress when they vote on legislation that affects the firearms industry and the rights of gun owners.

Political Action Committees   Companies themselves cannot legally make direct donations to political campaigns, so they influence the government through political action committees. *Political action committees (PACs)* are special organizations created to solicit money and then distribute it to political candidates. Employees of a firm may be encouraged to make donations to a particular PAC because managers know that it will support candidates with political views similar to their own. PACs, in turn, make the contributions themselves, usually to a broad

lobbying
The use of persons or groups to formally represent a company or group of companies before political bodies to influence the government

political action committee (PAC)
An organization created to solicit and distribute money to political candidates

slate of state and national candidates. For example, Federal Express's PAC is called Fed Expac. Fed Expac makes regular contributions to the campaign funds of political candidates who are most likely to work in the firm's best interests.

Favors Finally, organizations sometimes rely on favors and other influence tactics to gain support. Although these favors may be legal, they are still subject to criticism. A few years back, for example, two influential members of a House committee attending a fund-raising function in Miami were needed in Washington to finish work on a piece of legislation that Federal Express wanted passed. The law being drafted would allow the company and its competitors to give their employees standby seats on airlines as a tax-free benefit. As a favor, Federal Express provided one of its corporate jets to fly the committee members back to Washington. Federal Express was eventually reimbursed for its expenses, so its assistance was not illegal, but some people argue that such actions are dangerous because of how they might be perceived.

concept
CHECK

| *Identify the specific ways in which the government and organizations influence each other.* | *Do you think current levels of government regulation of business are excessive? Why or why not?* |

Managing Social Responsibility

The demands for social responsibility placed on contemporary organizations by an increasingly sophisticated and educated public are probably stronger than ever. As we have seen, there are pitfalls for managers who fail to adhere to high ethical standards and for companies that try to circumvent their legal obligations. Organizations therefore need to fashion an approach to social responsibility in the same way that they develop any other business strategy. In other words, they should view social responsibility as a major challenge that requires careful planning, decision making, consideration, and evaluation. They may accomplish this through both formal and informal dimensions of managing social responsibility.

Formal Organizational Dimensions

Some dimensions of managing social responsibility are a formal and planned activity on the part of the organization. Formal organizational dimensions that can help manage social responsibility are legal compliance, ethical compliance, and philanthropic giving.

legal compliance
The extent to which an organization complies with local, state, federal, and international laws

Legal Compliance *Legal compliance* is the extent to which the organization conforms to local, state, federal, and international laws. The task of managing legal compliance is generally assigned to the appropriate functional managers. For example, the organization's top human resource executive is responsible for ensuring compliance with regulations concerning hiring, pay, and workplace safety and health. Likewise, the top finance executive generally oversees compliance with securities and banking regulations. The organization's legal department is also likely to contribute to this effort by providing general oversight and answering queries from managers about the appropriate interpretation of laws and regulations. Unfortunately, though, legal compliance may not be enough—in some cases, for instance, perfectly legal accounting practices have still resulted in deception and other problems.[28]

Ethical Compliance   *Ethical compliance* is the extent to which the members of the organization follow basic ethical (and legal) standards of behavior. We note earlier that organizations have increased their efforts in this area—providing training in ethics and developing guidelines and codes of conduct, for example. These activities serve as vehicles for enhancing ethical compliance. Many organizations also establish formal ethics committees, which may be asked to review proposals for new projects, help evaluate new hiring strategies, or assess a new environmental protection plan. They might also serve as a peer review panel to evaluate alleged ethical misconduct by an employee.[29]

> *ethical compliance*
> The extent to which an organization and its members follow basic ethical standards of behavior

Philanthropic Giving   Finally, *philanthropic giving* is the awarding of funds or gifts to charities or other worthy causes. Target Corporation routinely gives 5 percent of its taxable income to charity and social programs. Giving across national boundaries is also becoming more common. For example, Alcoa gave $112,000 to a small town in Brazil to build a sewage treatment plant. And Japanese firms like Sony and Mitsubishi make contributions to a number of social programs in the United States. However, in the current climate of cutbacks, many corporations have also had to limit their charitable gifts over the past several years as they continue to trim their own budgets.[30] And many firms that continue to make contributions are increasingly targeting them to programs or areas where the firm will get something in return. For example, firms today are more likely to give money to job training programs than to the arts. The logic is that they get more direct payoff from the former type of contribution—in this instance, a better-trained workforce from which to hire new employees.[31]

> *philanthropic giving*
> Awarding funds or gifts to charities or other worthy causes

Informal Organizational Dimensions

In addition to these formal dimensions for managing social responsibility, there are also informal ones. Leadership, organization culture, and how the organization responds to whistleblowers all help shape and define people's perceptions of the organization's stance on social responsibility.

Organization Leadership and Culture   Leadership practices and organization culture can go a long way toward defining the social responsibility stance an organization and its members will adopt.[32] As described earlier, ethical leadership often sets the tone for the entire organization. For example, Johnson & Johnson executives for years provided a consistent message to employees that customers, employees, communities where the company did business, and shareholders were all important—and primarily in that order. Thus, when packages of poisoned Tylenol showed up on store shelves in the 1980s, Johnson & Johnson employees did not need to wait for orders from headquarters to know what to do: They immediately pulled all the packages from shelves before any other customers could buy them.[33] By contrast, the message sent to Hypercom employees by the actions of their top managers communicated much less regard for social responsibility.

Whistle-Blowing   *Whistle-blowing* is the disclosure by an employee of illegal or unethical conduct on the part of others within the organization.[34] How an organization responds to this practice often indicates its stance on social responsibility. Whistleblowers may have to proceed through a number of channels to be heard, and they may even get fired for their efforts.[35] Many organizations, however, welcome their contributions. A person who observes questionable behavior typically first reports the incident to his or her boss. If nothing is done, the whistleblower may then inform higher-level managers or an ethics committee, if one exists. Eventually, the person may have to go to a regulatory agency or even the media to be heard. For example, Charles W. Robinson, Jr., worked as a director of a SmithKline lab in San Antonio. One day he noticed a suspicious billing pattern that the firm was using to collect lab fees from Medicare: The bills were considerably higher than the firm's normal charges for those same tests. He pointed out the problem to higher-level managers, but his concerns were ignored. He subsequently took his findings to the U.S. government, which sued SmithKline and eventually reached a settlement of $325 million.[36]

Evaluating Social Responsibility

Any organization that is serious about social responsibility must ensure that its efforts are producing the desired benefits. Essentially this requires applying the concept of control to social responsibility. Many organizations now require current and new employees to read their guidelines or code of ethics and then sign a statement agreeing to abide by it. An organization should also evaluate how it responds to instances of questionable legal or ethical conduct. Does it follow up immediately? Does it punish those involved? Or does it use delay and cover-up tactics? Answers to these questions can help an organization form a picture of its approach to social responsibility.

More formally, an organization may sometimes actually evaluate the effectiveness of its social responsibility efforts. For example, when BP Amoco established a job-training program in Chicago, it allocated additional funds to evaluate how well the program was meeting its goals. Additionally, some organizations occasionally conduct corporate social audits. A *corporate social audit* is a formal and thorough analysis of the effectiveness of a firm's social performance. The audit is usually conducted by a task force of high-level managers from within the firm. It requires that the organization clearly define all of its social goals, analyze the resources it devotes to each goal, determine how well it is achieving the various goals, and make recommendations about which areas need additional attention. Recent estimates suggest that around 45 percent of the world's largest 250 firms and 36 of the largest 100 U.S. firms now issue annual reports summarizing their efforts in the areas of environmental and social responsibility; these percentages are expected to continue to increase in the years ahead.[37]

concept
CHECK

What formal and informal organizational dimensions can be used to manage social responsibility?	*What are the advantages and disadvantages of requiring organizations to perform annual social audits?*

Summary of Learning Objectives and Key Points

1. Discuss managerial ethics, three areas of special ethical concern for managers, and how organizations manage ethical behavior.
   * Ethics are an individual's personal beliefs about what constitutes right and wrong behavior.
   * Important areas of ethical concern for managers are how the organization treats its employees, how employees treat the organization, and how the organization and its employees treat other economic agents.
   * The ethical context of organizations consists of each manager's individual ethics and messages sent by organizational practices.
   * Organizations use leadership, culture, training, codes, and guidelines to help them manage ethical behavior.

2. Identify and summarize several emerging ethical issues in organizations today.
   * One emerging ethical issue is ethical leadership and its key role in shaping ethical norms and the culture of the organization.
   * Another involves corporate governance and focuses on the need for the board of directors to maintain appropriate oversight of senior management.
   * Third, ethical issues in information technology relate to issues such as individual privacy and the potential abuse of an organization's information technology resources by individuals.

3. Discuss the concept of social responsibility, specify to whom or what an organization might be considered responsible, and describe four types of organizational approaches to social responsibility.

   * Social responsibility is the set of obligations an organization has to protect and enhance the society in which it functions.
   * Organizations may be considered responsible to their stakeholders, to the natural environment, and to the general social welfare.
   * There are strong arguments both for and against social responsibility.
   * The approach an organization adopts toward social responsibility falls along a continuum of lesser to greater commitment: the obstructionist stance, the defensive stance, the accommodative stance, and the proactive stance.

4. Explain the relationship between the government and organizations regarding social responsibility.
   * Government influences organizations through regulation, which is the establishment of laws and rules that dictate what businesses can and cannot do in prescribed areas.
   * Organizations rely on personal contacts, lobbying, political action committees, and favors to influence the government.

5. Describe some of the activities organizations may engage in to manage social responsibility.
   * Organizations use three types of activities to formally manage social responsibility: legal compliance, ethical compliance, and philanthropic giving.
   * Leadership, culture, and allowing for whistle-blowing are informal means of managing social responsibility.
   * Organizations should evaluate the effectiveness of their socially responsible practices as they would any other strategy.

Discussion Questions

Questions for Review

1. Define ethical and unethical behavior. Give three specific examples of ethical behavior and three specific examples of unethical behavior.
2. Summarize the basic stances that an organization can take regarding social responsibility.
3. Who are the important stakeholders of your college or university? What does each stakeholder group get from the school? What does each give to the school?
4. Describe the formal and informal dimensions of social responsibility.

Questions for Analysis

5. What is the relationship between the law and ethical behavior? Can illegal behavior possibly be ethical?
6. Where do organizational ethics come from? Describe the contributions made by the organization's founder, managers, and workers, as well as laws and social norms. Which do you think is most influential? Why?
7. There are many worthy causes or programs that deserve support from socially responsible companies. In your opinion, which types of causes or programs are the most deserving? Explain your reasoning.

Questions for Application

8. Since 2000 a number of corporate scandals have been brought to light. Many organizations have responded by, for example, appointing a chief ethics officer, beginning an ethics training program for workers, writing a formal code of ethics, or setting up a hotline for whistleblowers. In your opinion, are these measures likely to increase organizational ethics in the long run? If so, why? If not, what would be effective in improving organizational ethics?
9. Review the arguments for and against social responsibility. On a scale of 1 to 10, rate the validity and importance of each point. Use these ratings to develop a position regarding how socially responsible an organization should be. Now compare your ratings and position with those of two of your classmates. Discuss your respective positions, focusing primarily on disagreements.
10. Give three specific examples of a way in which the government has influenced an organization. Then give three specific examples of a way in which an organization has influenced the government. Do you think the government's actions were ethical? Were the company's actions ethical? Why or why not?

Building Effective Diagnostic and Decision-Making Skills

Exercise Overview

Diagnostic skills are the skills that enable a manager to visualize the most appropriate response to a situation. Effective diagnosis of a situation then provides a foundation for effective decision making. Decision-making skills refer to the manager's ability to recognize and define problems and opportunities correctly and then to select an appropriate course of action to solve problems and capitalize on opportunities. This exercise will help you develop your diagnostic and decision-making skills by applying them to an ethical business dilemma.

Exercise Background

As businesses, industries, societies, and technologies become more complex, ethical dilemmas become more complicated. Consider the ethical dilemmas inherent in the online publication of music. The advent of fast Internet connections, the desire of many businesses to bypass intermediaries, and changing societal definitions of *theft* have all contributed to the difficult situation for the industry today. Use the Internet to investigate up-to-date information about online music publishing and then answer the following questions.

Exercise Task

1. Consider each of the stakeholders in the online music publishing industry—recording artists, recording companies, online file-sharing companies such as Napster, and consumers. From the point of view of each party, what are the ethical problems within the online music industry today?
2. What would be the "best" outcome for each of the parties?
3. Is there any way to satisfy the needs of all the stakeholders? If yes, tell how this can be accomplished. If no, tell why a mutually beneficial solution will not be possible.
4. What impact did your personal ethics have on your answer to question 3?

Building Effective Interpersonal Skills

Exercise Overview

Interpersonal skills refer to the ability to communicate with, understand, and motivate individuals and groups. Interpersonal skills may be especially important in a situation in which ethics and social responsibility issues are involved. This exercise will help you better relate interpersonal skills to ethical situations.

Exercise Background

Assume that you are a department manager in a large retail store. Your work group recently had a problem with sexual harassment. Specifically, one of your female employees reported to you that a male employee was telling off-color jokes and making mildly suggestive comments. When you asked him about the charges, he did not deny them but instead attributed them to a misunderstanding.

He was subsequently suspended with pay until the situation was investigated. The human resource manager who interviewed both parties, as well as other employees, concluded that the male employee should not be fired but should instead be placed on six months of probation. During this period, any further substantiated charges against him will result in immediate dismissal.

The basis for this decision included the following: (1) The male had worked in the store for over ten years, had a good performance record, and has had no earlier problems; (2) the female indicated that she did not believe that he was directly targeting her for harassment but instead was guilty of general insensitivity; and (3) the female did not think that his actions were sufficiently blatant as to warrant dismissal but simply wanted him to stop those behaviors.

Tomorrow will be his first day back at work. You are a bit worried about tensions in the group when he returns. You intend to meet with the female today and with the male tomorrow morning and attempt to minimize this tension.

Exercise Task

With the background information above as context, do the following:

1. Write general notes about what you will say to the male.
2. Write general notes about what you will say to the female.
3. What are the ethical issues in this situation?
4. If you have the option of having them work closely together or keeping them separated, which would you do? Why?

CHAPTER CLOSING CASE

BOEING GETS A SECOND CHANCE, AND A THIRD

Boeing is the world's largest aerospace firm, providing goods and services for military and industry buyers around the world. The company makes jets, helicopters, missiles, satellites, and more, and is the United States' largest exporter. With 153,000 employees and net earnings exceeding $1.5 billion in 2005, Boeing is one of the largest corporations in the world. Surely such a well-known and visible firm would not be able to get away with unethical actions. Yet an examination of the last five years reveals a company deeply troubled by immoral and illegal behavior, fostered by a culture that overlooks wrongdoing.

The problems stem from much earlier, but the extent of Boeing's troubles began to surface in 2002. At that time, Boeing was led by CEO Philip Condit, an engineer with a Ph.D. and 37 years of experience at Boeing. Following its 1997 acquisition of competitor McDonnell Douglas, Boeing experienced problems integrating the two firms' operations and cultures. A $2.6 billion loss related to the merger triggered a lawsuit from angry shareholders, who alleged that the firm covered up its true financial condition. In February 2002, Boeing settled the suit for $92 million but admitted no misconduct.

In 2003, Boeing managers were found to be in possession of documents that were stolen from rival Lockheed Martin. The documents may have given Boeing an advantage in bidding for defense contracts. The Pentagon revoked the resulting order, costing the firm $1 billion in sales, and barred them from bidding on federal contracts for 20 months. Boeing CFO Michael Sears was fired later that same year for illegally hiring an air force officer, Darleen Druyun, who had responsibility for Boeing's Pentagon contracts. Druyun purchased $20 billion of aircraft from Boeing just before she left the Pentagon. Sears and Druyun were later jailed for their roles and the contract was cancelled. Facing a growing crisis, the board of directors forced Condit to resign. His replacement was Harry Stonecipher, the former CEO of McDonnell Douglas, who had stepped aside following the Boeing merger. Stonecipher promised to clean up Boeing.

In 2005, the Pentagon cancelled more contracts that were issued by Druyun, worth billions of dollars. Female workers brought a class action sex-discrimination suit, claiming they were underpaid and denied promotion. The company settled for $73 million but admitted nothing. Stonecipher had an affair with a female subordinate at the company's annual executive retreat. The relationship was consensual, but Stonecipher was forced to resign for violating the company's code of conduct, a document he mandated for all employees. Stonecipher's behavior was "one of the dumbest moments in business," says *Fortune* magazine. He was replaced by outsider Jim McNerney, who vowed to clean up Boeing.

Sound familiar? McNerney may have a better chance of improving Boeing's ethics than either of his predecessors did. For one thing, he is an outsider who isn't afraid to bring sweeping change. There's no danger of "business as usual" with someone from outside the firm. Moreover, McNerney's experience at GE, where he was CEO of their aircraft engine division, and at 3M, where he turned around the struggling firm, demonstrates his leadership and ethical character. McNerney is known for his focus on employee development, in contrast to both Condit and Stonecipher, who were more interested in technical capabilities.

At the first executive retreat he led, McNerney sounded his warning. "I think the culture had morphed in dysfunctional ways," the CEO stated. "There are elements of our culture that I think we all would like to change." He claimed "management had gotten carried away with itself" and executives were "hiding in the bureaucracy." Previously, managers ignored others' mistakes, but McNerney insists on openness and accountability. He also plans to change compensation practices to eliminate illegal financial reporting. Teamwork is another emphasis and McNerney hopes to finally integrate McDonnell Douglas units with their Boeing counterparts. He says, "[Our problems aren't] something that happened in a separate part of the company."

McNerney wants to improve morals and the bottom line at the same time. He believes that improved legal and ethical conduct could increase stock price, boost sales, and improve motivation and morale. For McNerney, the ethical troubles are merely a reflection of more fundamental concerns. He hopes to spark a company-wide examination of Boeing's fundamental values and reason for being. "The definition of what we are is incomplete," says McNerney. "What do we do here? Do we all just live in the same building? Or are we going to figure out a way to help make this company greater than the sum of its parts?"

CASE QUESTIONS

1. Which organizational stakeholders were affected by ethical or unethical behavior at Boeing? Give specific examples.

2. What organizational approach to social responsibility did Boeing appear to use under the leadership of Condit and Stonecipher? How do you think the approach changed under McNerney's leadership?

3. Are the actions McNerney is proposing likely to improve ethics at Boeing? If yes, explain why. If no, tell what actions McNerney could take that would be effective.

CASE REFERENCES

"2005 Annual Report," Boeing website, www.boeing.com on March 4, 2006; "Boeing Fined in Sale of Restricted Parts," *New York Times*, April 10, 2006, www.nytimes.com on April 10, 2006; Stanley Holmes, "Cleaning Up Boeing," *BusinessWeek*, March 13, 2006, pp. 63–68; Stanley Holmes, "What Boeing Needs to Fly Right," *BusinessWeek*, March 8, 2005, www.businessweek.com on March 4, 2006; Adam Horowitz, "101 Dumbest Moments in Business," *Fortune*, February 1, 2006, www.fortune.com on March 4, 2006.

YOU MAKE THE CALL

Is Fair Trade Enough?

1. Do you pay attention to Fair Trade products in your own purchasing behaviors?
2. Do you think buying Fair Trade products really does any good?

3. Can you envision any circumstances in which unethical individuals could abuse the Fair Trade concept?
4. Can you envision any circumstances in which Fair Trade can actually cause harm?

Test Prepper

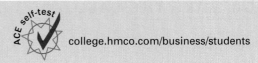

college.hmco.com/business/students

Choose the correct answer. Answers are found at the back of the book.

1. T F The first step to applying ethical judgments to business situations is to make an ethical judgment based on the rightness or wrongness of the proposed activity.

2. T F Business organizations may lack the expertise to understand how to assess and make decisions about worthy social programs.

3. T F The highest degree of social responsibility a firm can exhibit is the proactive stance.

4. T F Many firms that engage in philanthropic giving are increasingly channeling their contributions to programs that may ultimately benefit the firm in return.

5. T F Despite recent trends, legal liability has caused an increasing number of organizations to eliminate their annual reports on environmental and social responsibility.

6. At Jake's company, each new employee receives a formal statement of the company's values and ethical standards. This material is called the organization's
   A. code of ethics.
   B. declaration of managerial purpose.
   C. social responsibility statement.
   D. principled action guidelines.
   E. mission statement.

7. As a manager, Roxanne always tries to make decisions that optimize what is best for her constituencies—in this case, her employees. Roxanne follows which ethical norm?
   A. Responsibility
   B. Caring

   C. Justice
   D. Rights
   E. Utility

8. Which of the following is NOT an argument in support of organizations acting socially responsibly?
   A. Organizations create many of the problems that need to be addressed.
   B. Organizations are citizens of society.
   C. Large businesses have the money to help solve social problems.
   D. Solving social problems is part of the basic economic mission of business.
   E. Social responsibility can achieve an enhanced reputation and improve profits.

9. Ethical compliance is the extent to which the members of the organization follow basic ethical and _____ standards of behavior.
   A. philanthropic
   B. social
   C. legal
   D. cultural
   E. promised

10. A corporate social audit is a formal and thorough analysis of the effectiveness of a firm's social performance. Who usually conducts the social audit?
    A. A lobbying group
    B. A task force of high-level managers from within the firm
    C. A regulatory agency
    D. The board of directors
    E. A panel consisting of representatives from all major stakeholder groups

The Global Environment

chapter 5

FIRST THINGS FIRST

Coffee, Café, Kaffee, or Copi—Starbucks Spans the Globe

"We remain highly respectful of the culture and traditions of the countries in which we do business."

—HOWARD SCHULTZ, FOUNDER, STARBUCKS

Whether the customers are ordering in English, Spanish, German, or phonetic Chinese, Starbucks is known around the world for its coffeehouses. The first U.S. stores were begun in 1984 and internationalization started in 1995, with shops in Japan and Singapore. Starbucks expanded rapidly in Pacific Rim countries and by 2000 had outlets in Thailand, Australia, and the Philippines, among other countries. China's first locations were opened in 1999 in Beijing. The

Starbucks is becoming an increasingly global business. This thriving Starbucks coffeehouse, for instance, is in Shanghai, China.

LEARNING OBJECTIVES

After studying this chapter, you should be able to:

1. Describe the nature of international business, including its meaning, recent trends, management of globalization, and competition in a global market.

2. Discuss the structure of the global economy and describe the GATT and the WTO.

3. Identify and discuss the environmental challenges inherent in international management.

4. Describe the basic issues involved in competing in a global economy, including organization size and the management challenges in a global economy.

Middle East was the next region that Starbucks entered, and the first European outlets were opened in 2001. Latin America's first stores opened in 2002 in Puerto Rico and Mexico. Over the last five years, the company has expanded the number of international stores in both established and new markets.

Today, Starbucks has over 3,000 international stores in 36 countries. How does Starbucks choose international expansion targets? Size of the market is often important, but it's not used alone. For example, Starbucks has already entered most European countries and all of the developed economies in Asia. However, among the ten largest countries by population, Starbucks does business in just four, including China, Indonesia, Japan, and the United States. The other six—Bangladesh, Brazil, India, Nigeria, Pakistan, and Russia—have yet to see a Starbucks outlet. Other variables include the local standard of living and the similarity of the business environment. Countries with a very different business climate or with many very low-income individuals are not attractive targets. Starbucks also avoids expanding into countries with high levels of anti-U.S. sentiment.

In addition to choosing good candidate countries for global expansion, Starbucks has to decide whether to own the companies or whether to enter into joint venture or license arrangements with local partners. In the United States, about two-thirds of locations are company-owned. Starbucks does not franchise, but it does have joint venture agreements with vendors servicing bookstores, hotels, college campuses, and airports. Outside of the United States, however, Starbucks has adopted a slightly different policy. There, only about one-third of locations are company-owned; the rest are partnerships. This system allows the firm to gain local expertise while reducing its own investment and risk exposure.

Another set of decisions concern finding the optimal mix between standardization and adaptation for local tastes. For ease and efficiency in operations, as well as to ensure high quality, Starbucks would prefer standardization. However, the company has made changes when required by law or custom in overseas locations. "We remain highly respectful of the culture and traditions of the countries in which we do business," says founder Howard Schultz. "We recognize that our success is not an entitlement, and we must continue to earn the trust and respect of customers every day." Typically, the beverages remain the same, but the snacks are customized to suit local preferences. Green tea beverages, popular in many Asian countries, are offered by Starbucks to compete with local teahouses. In the Middle East, there are men-only and family areas in the shops. Sometimes the company refuses to change. It does not allow smoking even in smoking cultures, saying it interferes with the coffee aroma. Starbucks always insists on lots of space, even in crowded Tokyo.

Wherever it goes, Starbucks finds itself educating its customers about the very American experience it offers. When the company first entered China, for example, many consumers were unfamiliar with coffee. The drink had been unpopular there, perhaps because the proportions of coffee, milk, and sugar were often wrong. Starbucks employees provided information and taste samples to demonstrate the proper mixture. Starbucks should not find it hard to teach foreign customers to enjoy an "American" drink. After all, when the company was first founded, its goal was to introduce coffee drinkers in the United States to the Italian-style beverages Schulz enjoyed on his European vacations. With plans in the works to bring Starbucks to Brazil, Russia, and India, Starbucks may become the "first taste" of the United States for many individuals.[1]

Although every business is unique, the challenges and opportunities facing Starbucks are increasingly common among today's multinational corporations. Specifically, such businesses must make critical decisions regarding how they will allocate their resources in different markets and how they will strive to gain a competitive advantage in those markets. Indeed, to be successful today, managers have to understand the global context within which they function. And this holds true regardless of whether the manager runs a *Fortune* 500 firm or a small independent company.

This chapter explores the global context of management. We start by describing the nature of international business. We then discuss the structure of the global market in terms of different economies and economic systems. The basic environmental challenges of management are introduced and discussed next. We then focus on issues of competition in a global economy. Finally, we conclude by characterizing the managerial functions of planning and decision making, organizing, leading, and controlling as management challenges in a global economy.

It is also important to remember, though, that it is no longer feasible to segregate a discussion of "international" management from a discussion of "domestic" management as if they were unrelated activities. Hence, although we highlight the central issues of international management in this chapter, we also integrate international issues, examples, opportunities, and challenges throughout the rest of this book. This treatment provides the most realistic possible survey and discussion of the international environment of management.

The Nature of International Business

As you prepared breakfast this morning, you may have plugged in a coffee pot manufactured in Asia and perhaps ironed a shirt or blouse made in Taiwan with an iron made in Mexico. The coffee you drank was probably made from beans grown in South America. To get to school, you may have driven a Japanese car. Even if you drove a Ford or a Chevrolet, some of its parts were engineered or manufactured abroad. Perhaps you did not drive a car to school but rode a bus (manufactured by DaimlerChrysler, a German company) or a motorcycle (manufactured by Honda, Kawasaki, Suzuki, or Yamaha—all Japanese firms).

Our daily lives are strongly influenced by businesses from around the world. But no country is unique in this respect. For instance, people drive Fords in Germany, use Dell computers in China, eat McDonald's hamburgers in France, and snack on Mars candy bars in England. They drink Pepsi and wear Levi Strauss jeans in China and South Africa. The Japanese buy Kodak film and use American Express credit cards. People around the world fly on American Airlines in planes made by Boeing.

Their buildings are constructed with Caterpillar machinery, their factories are powered by General Electric engines, and they buy Chevron oil.

In truth, we have become part of a global village and have a global economy where no organization is insulated from the effects of foreign markets and competition.[2] Indeed, more and more firms are reshaping themselves for international competition and discovering new ways to exploit markets in every corner of the world. Failure to take a global perspective is one of the biggest mistakes managers can make.[3] Thus we start laying the foundation for our discussion by introducing and describing the basics of international business.

The Meaning of International Business

There are many different forms and levels of international business. Although the lines that distinguish one from another may be arbitrary, we can identify four general levels of international activity that differentiate organizations.[4] These are illustrated in Figure 5.1. A ***domestic business*** acquires essentially all of its resources and sells all of its products or services within a single country. Most small businesses are essentially domestic in nature; this category includes local retailers and restaurants, agricultural enterprises, and small service firms, such as dry cleaners and hair salons. However, there are very few large domestic businesses left in the world today.

Indeed, most large firms today are either international or multinational companies. An ***international business*** is one that is based primarily in a single country but acquires some meaningful share of its resources or revenues (or both) from other countries. Sears fits this description. Most of its stores are in the United States, for example, and the retailer earns around 90 percent of its revenues from its U.S. operations, with the remaining 10 percent coming from Sears stores in Canada. At the same time, however, many of the products it sells, such as tools and clothing, are made abroad.[5]

A ***multinational business*** has a worldwide marketplace from which it buys raw materials, borrows money, and manufactures its products and to which it subsequently sells its products. Ford Motor Company is an excellent example of a multinational company. It has design and production facilities around the world. The Ford Focus, for instance, was jointly designed by European and U.S. teams and is sold with only minor variations in dozens of foreign markets. Ford makes and sells other cars in Europe that are never seen in the United States. Ford cars are designed, produced, and sold for individual markets, wherever they are and without regard for national boundaries. Multinational businesses are often called *multinational corporations*, or *MNCs*.[6]

---

domestic business
A business that acquires all of its resources and sells all of its products or services within a single country

international business
A business that is based primarily in a single country but acquires some meaningful share of its resources or revenues (or both) from other countries

multinational business
A business that has a worldwide marketplace from which it buys raw materials, borrows money, and manufactures its products and to which it subsequently sells its products

---

Figure 5.1
LEVELS OF INTERNATIONAL BUSINESS ACTIVITY

There are four levels of international business activity. These range from domestic business (the lowest level of international activity) to global business (the highest level).

The final form of international business is the global business. A ***global business*** is one that transcends national boundaries and is not committed to a single home country. Although no business has truly achieved this level of internationalization, a few are edging closer and closer. For example, Hoechst AG, a large German chemical company, portrays itself as a "non-national company." Similarly, Unocal Corporation is legally headquartered in California, but in its company literature, Unocal says it "no longer considers itself as a U.S. company" but is, instead, a "global energy company."[7]

global business
A business that transcends national boundaries and is not committed to a single home country

"I was blessed to work for Sam Walton, and I am doubly blessed to work [for Wal-Mart] in China."

Joe Hatfield, Wal-Mart executive
(*Time*, June 27, 2005, p. 37)

Trends in International Business

To understand why and how these different levels of international business have emerged, we must look briefly to the past. Most of the industrialized countries in Europe were devastated during World War II. Many Asian countries, especially Japan, fared no better. There were few passable roads, few standing bridges, and even fewer factories dedicated to the manufacture of peacetime products. And those regions less affected by wartime destruction—Canada, Latin America, and Africa—had not yet developed the economic muscle to threaten the economic preeminence of the United States.

Businesses in war-torn countries like Germany and Japan had no choice but to rebuild from scratch. Because of this position, they essentially had to rethink every facet of their operations, including technology, production, finance, and marketing. Although it took many years for these countries to recover, they eventually did so, and their economic systems were subsequently poised for growth. During the same era, many U.S. companies grew somewhat complacent. Their customer base was growing rapidly. Increased population spurred by the baby boom and increased affluence resulting from the postwar economic boom greatly raised the average person's standard of living and expectations. The U.S. public continually wanted new and better products and services. Many U.S. companies profited greatly from this pattern, but most were also perhaps guilty of taking it for granted.

But U.S. firms are no longer isolated from global competition or the global market. A few simple numbers help tell the full story of international trade and industry. First of all, the volume of international trade increased more than 3,000 percent between 1960 and 2000. Further, although 176 of the world's largest corporations are headquartered in the United States, there are also 81 in Japan, 39 in France, 37 in Germany, and 35 in Britain.[8] Within certain industries, the preeminence of non-U.S. firms is even more striking. For example, only three each of the world's ten largest banks and ten largest electronics companies are based in the United States. Only two of the ten largest chemical companies are U.S. firms. On the other hand, U.S. firms comprise seven of the eleven largest aerospace companies, three of the seven largest airlines, four of the nine largest computer companies, four of the five largest diversified financial companies, and six of the ten largest retailers.[9]

U.S. firms are also finding that international operations are an increasingly important element of their sales and profits. For example, in 2004 Exxon Corporation realized 97 percent of its revenues and 72 percent of its profits abroad. For Avon, these percentages were 98 percent and 68 percent, respectively.[10] From any perspective, then, it is clear that we live in a truly global economy. Virtually all businesses today must be concerned with the competitive situations they face in lands far from home and with how companies from distant lands are competing in their homelands.

Licensing is an increasingly popular method for entering foreign markets. Franchising, a form of licensing, is especially popular these days. Pizza Hut, for example, is rapidly expanding into new markets around the world via franchising agreements with local investors and managers. The popular restaurants can now be found in over 100 different countries. St. Petersburg, Russia, is one of the more recent markets where Pizza Hut has set up shop.

---

exporting
Making a product in the firm's domestic marketplace and selling it in another country

---

importing
Bringing a good, service, or capital into the home country from abroad

---

licensing
An arrangement whereby one company allows another company to use its brand name, trademark, technology, patent, copyright, or other assets in exchange for a royalty based on sales

---

Managing the Process of Globalization

Managers should also recognize that their global context dictates two related but distinct sets of challenges. One set of challenges must be confronted when an organization chooses to change its level of international involvement. For example, a firm that wants to move from being an international to a multinational business has to manage that transition.[11] The other set of challenges occurs when the organization has achieved its desired level of international involvement and must then function effectively within that environment. This section highlights the first set of challenges, and the next section introduces the second set of challenges. When an organization makes the decision to increase its level of international activity, there are several alternative strategies that can be adopted. *Working with Diversity* illustrates some ways that Nokia has effectively managed its globalization activities.

Importing and Exporting   Importing or exporting (or both) is usually the first type of international business in which a firm gets involved. *Exporting*, or making the product in the firm's domestic marketplace and selling it in another country, can involve both merchandise and services. *Importing* is bringing a good, service, or capital into the home country from abroad. For example, automobiles (Mazda, Ford, Volkswagen, Mercedes-Benz, Ferrari) and stereo equipment (Sony, Bang & Olufsen, Sanyo) are routinely exported by their manufacturers to other countries. Likewise, many wine distributors buy products from vineyards in France, Italy, or California and import them into their own country for resale. U.S. sports brands have become one of the latest hot exports.[12]

An import/export operation has several advantages. For example, it is the easiest way of entering a market with a small outlay of capital. Because the products are sold "as is," there is no need to adapt the product to the local conditions, and little risk is involved. Nevertheless, there are also disadvantages. For example, imports and exports are subject to taxes, tariffs, and higher transportation expenses. Furthermore, because the products are not adapted to local conditions, they may miss the needs of a large segment of the market. Finally, some products may be restricted and thus can be neither imported nor exported.

Licensing   A company may prefer to arrange for a foreign company to manufacture or market its products under a licensing agreement. Factors that may lead to this decision include excessive transportation costs, government regulations, and home production costs. *Licensing* is an arrangement whereby a firm allows another company to use its brand name, trademark, technology, patent, copyright, or other assets. In return, the licensee pays a royalty, usually based on sales. For example, Kirin Brewery, Japan's largest producer of beer, wanted to expand its international operations but feared that the time involved in shipping it from Japan would cause the beer to lose its freshness. Thus it has entered into a number of licensing arrangements with breweries

Working with Diversity

Nokia Reclaims Asia

Nokia was one of the first entrants into the Indian cell phone market, yet growth soon fizzled. Nokia was an early mover into China, but lagged behind Motorola and several Chinese companies. But with other markets saturated and prices flat, the two largest Asian economies remain key elements in Nokia's growth strategy. Over the last few years, Nokia has made changes and regained its leadership position. With a market share of 30 percent and 60 percent, respectively, Nokia is today the largest seller of mobiles in both China and India.

The first big change was an increased seriousness given to the threat from domestic rivals. Local firms can market aggressively. Nokia had to watch and learn from local firms. In comparison, Motorola was slower to take locals seriously and lost market share quickly. Its share in India is just 5 percent today.

Nokia also changed its entry strategy. While many companies prefer to move slowly when entering an unfamiliar market, Nokia found this gave competitors too much breathing room. Their new, aggressive investment strategy saturates a local market. Instead of 8 national distributors in China, Nokia now has 50. Sales offices are up from just 3 to 70. The company is doubling its China plant, and a new factory is being built in southern India that will produce 20 million phones annually.

Another change was a switch to more local customization. Nokia designers were innovators, but they didn't often consider the unique needs of local customers. In India and in China, that adaptability was critical, resulting in a focus on less-expensive models. For the Chinese market, Nokia introduced a phone designed for messaging that included a stylus and touch pad, to facilitate entering Chinese characters. For the Indian market, Nokia upgraded with dust covers and a textured grip that was comfortable for sweaty hands. Even advertising materials and in-store displays were customized to reflect local preferences for language, colors, and themes.

The changes have paid off. In March 2006, Nokia had to make another big change. The company revised its sales estimates upwards. It now expects 15 percent growth in sales this year, up from its previous prediction of 10 percent.

References: Amanda Cantrell, "Wireless Stocks Take Off on Nokia Forecast," *Fortune,* March 30, 2006, www.fortune.com on April 1, 2006; "Cell Phone Market Set to Soar in 2005," *Fortune,* January 19, 2005, www.fortune.com on April 1, 2006; Bruce Einhorn and Nandina Lakshman, "Nokia Connects," *BusinessWeek,* March 27, 2006, pp. 44–45; "Nokia Profit Down in Quarter," *New York Times,* January 27, 2006, www.nytimes.com on April 1, 2006.

in other markets. These brewers make beer according to strict guidelines provided by the Japanese firm and then package and market it as Kirin Beer. They then pay a royalty back to Kirin for each case sold. Molson produces Kirin in Canada under such an agreement, while the Charles Wells Brewery does the same in England.[13]

Two advantages of licensing are increased profitability and extended profitability. This strategy is frequently used for entry into less-developed countries where older technology is still acceptable and, in fact, may be state of the art. A primary disadvantage of licensing is inflexibility. A firm can tie up control of its product or expertise for a long period of time. And, if the licensee does not develop the market effectively, the licensing firm can lose profits. A second disadvantage is that licensees can take the knowledge and skill to which they have been given access for a foreign market and exploit them in the licensing firm's home market. When this happens, what used to be a business partner becomes a business competitor.

Strategic Alliances In a ***strategic alliance***, two or more firms jointly cooperate for mutual gain.[14] For example, Kodak and Fuji, along with three other major Japanese camera manufacturers, collaborated on the development of a new film

strategic alliance
A cooperative arrangement between two or more firms for mutual gain

Almost overnight, or so it seems, Beijing is being transformed into a global business center. These workers queue for lunch at the Hyundai factory in Beijing. Hyundai is a South Korean company. This Beijing factory is a joint venture with the Beijing Automotive Industry Holding Company. It was the first automobile joint venture approved by China after the country joined the WTO in 2002. China produces more than 4 million cars a year. The surge in car sales in China reflects rapidly rising income levels fuelled by the country's economic boom.

---

joint venture
A special type of strategic alliance in which the partners share in the ownership of an operation on an equity basis

---

direct investment
When a firm headquartered in one country builds or purchases operating facilities or subsidiaries in a foreign country

---

maquiladoras
Light assembly plants built in northern Mexico close to the U.S. border that are given special tax breaks by the Mexican government

cartridge. This collaboration allowed Kodak and Fuji to share development costs, prevented an advertising war if they had developed different cartridges, and made it easier for new cameras to be introduced at the same time as the new film cartridges. A ***joint venture*** is a special type of strategic alliance in which the partners actually share ownership of a new enterprise. General Mills and Nestlé formed a new company called Cereal Partners Worldwide (CPW) to produce and market cereals. General Mills supplies the technology and proven formulas, while Nestlé provides its international distribution network. The two partners share equally in ownership and profits from CPW. Strategic alliances have enjoyed a tremendous upsurge in the past few years. In most cases, each party provides a portion of the equity or the equivalent in physical plant, raw materials, cash, or other assets. The proportion of the investment then determines the percentage of ownership in the venture.[15]

Strategic alliances have both advantages and disadvantages. For example, they can allow quick entry into a market by taking advantage of the existing strengths of participants. Japanese automobile manufacturers employed this strategy to their advantage to enter the U.S. market by using the already-established distribution systems of U.S. automobile manufacturers. Strategic alliances are also an effective way to gain access to technology or raw materials. And they allow the firms to share the risk and cost of the new venture. One major disadvantage of this approach lies with the shared ownership of joint ventures. Although it reduces the risk for each participant, it also limits the control and return that each firm can enjoy.[16]

Direct Investment Another level of commitment to internationalization is direct investment. ***Direct investment*** occurs when a firm headquartered in one country builds or purchases operating facilities or subsidiaries in a foreign country. The foreign operations then become wholly owned subsidiaries of the firm. Ford's acquisitions of Jaguar, Volvo, and Kia, as well as British Petroleum's acquisition of Amoco, were major forms of direct investment. Similarly, Dell Computer's new factory in China is a direct investment, as is the new Disney theme park in Hong Kong. And Coca-Cola spent $150 million to build a new bottling and distribution network in India.[17]

A major reason many firms make direct investments is to capitalize on lower labor costs. In other words, the goal is often to transfer production to locations where labor is cheap. Japanese businesses have moved much of their production to Thailand because labor costs are much lower there than in Japan. Many U.S. firms have been using maquiladoras for the same purpose. ***Maquiladoras*** are light assembly plants built in northern Mexico close to the U.S. border. The plants are given special tax breaks by the Mexican government, and the area is populated with workers willing to work for very low wages. More than 1,000 plants in the region employ 300,000 workers, and more are planned. The plants are owned by major corporations, primarily from the United States, Japan, South Korea, and major European industrial countries. This concentrated form of direct investment benefits the country of Mexico, the companies themselves, and workers who might otherwise be without jobs. Some critics argue, however, that the low wages paid by the maquiladoras amount to little more than slave labor.[18] In recent years, some of the production in this area has been moving to China, where there is also a large pool of talented workers, most of whom will work for even lower wages.

Like the other approaches for increasing a firm's level of internationalization, direct investment carries with it a number of benefits and liabilities. Managerial control is more complete, and profits do not have to be shared as they do in joint ventures. Purchasing an existing organization provides additional benefits in that the human resources and organizational infrastructure (administrative facilities, plants, warehouses, and so forth) are already in place. Acquisition is also a way to purchase the brand-name identification of a product. This could be particularly important if the cost of introducing a new brand is high. When Nestlé bought the U.S. firm Carnation Company, it retained the firm's brand names for all of its products sold in the United States. Likewise, when Daimler-Benz acquired Chrysler (and changed its corporate name to DaimlerChrysler), it kept all of Chrysler's product names. Notwithstanding these advantages, the company is now operating a part of itself entirely within the borders of a foreign country. The additional complexity in the decision making, the economic and political risks, and so forth may outweigh the advantages that can be obtained by international expansion.

Of course, we should also note that these approaches to internationalization are not mutually exclusive. Indeed, most large firms use all of them simultaneously. MNCs have a global orientation and worldwide approach to foreign markets and production. They search for opportunities all over the world and select the best strategy to serve each market. In some settings, they may use direct investment, in others licensing, in others strategic alliances; in still others, they might limit their involvement to exporting and importing. The advantages and disadvantages of each approach are summarized in Table 5.1.

Competing in a Global Market

Even when a firm is not actively seeking to increase its desired level of internationalization, its managers are still responsible for seeing that it functions effectively within whatever level of international involvement the organization has achieved. In one sense, the job of a manager in an international business may not be that much different from the job of a manager in a domestic business. Each may be responsible for acquiring resources and materials, making products, providing services, developing human resources, advertising, or monitoring cash flow.

Approach to Internationalization	Advantages	Disadvantages
Importing or Exporting	• Small cash outlay • Little risk • No adaptation necessary	• Tariffs and taxes • High transportation costs • Government restrictions
Licensing	• Increased profitability • Extended profitability	• Inflexibility • Competition
Strategic Alliances/Joint Ventures	• Quick market entry • Access to materials and technology	• Shared ownership (limits control and profits)
Direct Investment	• Enhanced control • Existing infrastructure	• Complexity • Greater economic and political risk • Greater uncertainty

Table 5.1

ADVANTAGES AND DISADVANTAGES OF DIFFERENT APPROACHES TO INTERNATIONALIZATION

When organizations decide to increase their level of internationalization, they can adopt several strategies. Each strategy is a matter of degree, as opposed to being a discrete and mutually exclusive category. And each has unique advantages and disadvantages that must be considered.

In another sense, however, the complexity associated with each of these activities may be much greater for managers in international firms. Rather than buying raw materials from sources in California, Texas, and Missouri, an international purchasing manager may buy materials from sources in Peru, India, and Spain. Rather than train managers for new plants in Michigan, Florida, and Oregon, the international human resources executive may be training new plant managers for facilities in China, Mexico, and Scotland. And, instead of developing a single marketing campaign for the United States, an advertising director may be working on promotional efforts in France, Brazil, and Japan.

The key question that must be addressed by any manager trying to be effective in an international market is whether to focus on globalization or on regionalism. A global thrust requires that activities be managed from an overall global perspective as part of an integrated system. Regionalism, on the other hand, involves managing within each region with less regard for the overall organization. In reality, most larger MNCs manage some activities globally (for example, finance and manufacturing are commonly addressed globally) and others locally (human resource management and advertising are frequently handled this way). *Technology Toolkit* highlights some of the ways in which Tesco, a British retailer, hopes to beat Wal-Mart at its own game in the U.S. market. We explore these approaches more fully later.

Technology Toolkit

Can Tesco Beat Wal-Mart at Its Own Game?

Wal-Mart is the largest corporation on the planet, with 2005 revenues nearing $316 billion and 1.5 million workers. Wal-Mart dominates its market with six times more sales than its nearest rival, Target. The firm's success comes from a combination of factors, including its use of technology. Wal-Mart was one of the first to use data mining, automated inventory control, and other cutting-edge technologies. The skillful deployment of technology helps Wal-Mart to cut costs, increase product availability and sales, and, ultimately, raise profits. The firm seems unbeatable. Yet a British retailing giant, Tesco, is challenging Wal-Mart on its home turf.

For Tesco, the fifth-largest retailer in the world, the decision to enter the U.S. retail market is surprising. U.S. sales are flat and show little potential for improvement. Tesco managers believe, however, that there is an opportunity for a unique type of store. They plan a series of Tesco Express outlets, starting in California. Express stores are mini-supermarkets that are slightly larger than convenience stores and offer more groceries, produce, and high-quality ready-to-eat foods. This segment of the retail industry is underserved in the United States, while the convenience store industry is fragmented and provides little threat.

To break into a market as an unknown brand, Tesco will use its strength in technology to drive costs down.

"Tesco is ruthless in supply chain management," notes industry consultant Scott Langdoc, referring to the firm's expertise in managing high-volume operations. A wireless network connects Tesco's British stores and allows real-time management of distribution and transportation. Workers use handheld PDAs for data entry and reporting. Radio Frequency Identification (RFID) tags allow tracking of each box and pallet. Supported by all of this technology, Tesco reportedly has the world's largest online grocery retailing operation, in which customers in the U.K. can order groceries online or even via their cell phone.

Tesco is likely to bring this technology to the United States. Some is already in place at other U.S. retailers, including Wal-Mart, but no one company currently has all of these capabilities. Due to its low costs, Tesco's operating margins are 5.7 percent, almost as good as Wal-Mart's 5.9 percent. If Tesco uses this entry as a foothold to enter the large store segment, then Wal-Mart, watch out!

References: Parija Bhatnagar, "Wal-Mart, Kroger, Safeway Better Watch Out. The British are Coming!" *Money*, February 27, 2006, www.cnnmoney.com on April 6, 2006; Kerry Capell, "Tesco: California Dreaming?" *BusinessWeek*, February 27, 2006, p. 38; Telis Demos, "The World's Most Admired Companies," *Fortune*, February 28, 2006, www.fortune.com on March 5, 2006; Barnaby J. Feder, "Out of Consumers' Sight, Radio Tags Gain Ground," *New York Times*, April 4, 2006, www.nytimes.com on April 6, 2006.

Identify and describe the four levels of international involvement.

Identify a product you recently purchased that was made in another country. What factors do you think caused it to be made there rather than at a domestic location?

concept
CHECK

The Structure of the Global Economy

One thing that can be helpful to managers seeking to operate in a global environment is to better understand the structure of the global economy. Although each country and indeed many regions within any given country are unique, we can still note some basic similarities and differences. We describe three different elements of the global economy: mature market economies and systems, high-potential/high-growth economies, and other economies.[19]

Mature Market Economies and Systems

A ***market economy*** is based on the private ownership of business and allows market factors such as supply and demand to determine business strategy. Mature market economies include the United States, Japan, the United Kingdom, France, Germany, and Sweden. These countries have several things in common. For example, they tend to employ market forces in the allocation of resources. They also tend to be characterized by private ownership of property, although there is some variance along this dimension. France, for example, has a relatively high level of government ownership among the market economies.

market economy
An economy based on the private ownership of business that allows market factors such as supply and demand to determine business strategy

U.S. managers have relatively few problems operating in market economies. Many of the business "rules of the game" that apply in the United States also apply, for example, in Germany or England. And consumers there often tend to buy the same kinds of products. For these reasons, it is not unusual for U.S. firms seeking to expand geographically to begin operations in other market economies. Although the task of managing an international business in an industrial market economy is somewhat less complicated than operating in some other type of economy, it still poses some challenges. Perhaps foremost among them is that the markets in these economies are typically quite mature. Many industries, for example, are already dominated by large and successful companies. Thus competing in these economies poses a major challenge.

The map in Figure 5.2 highlights three relatively mature market systems. ***Market systems*** are clusters of countries that engage in high levels of trade with one another. One mature

Cambodia provides a vivid example of how the structure of the global economy continues to evolve. This Cambodian farmer is walking his cattle on a rural road on the outskirts of Phnom Penh as two young women ride past on a motorcycle. High agricultural output, especially of rice, and expansion of international trade have led to consistent growth in the Cambodian economy. For instance, Cambodia received more than 1.4 million visitors and produced nearly 6 million tons of rice in 2005.

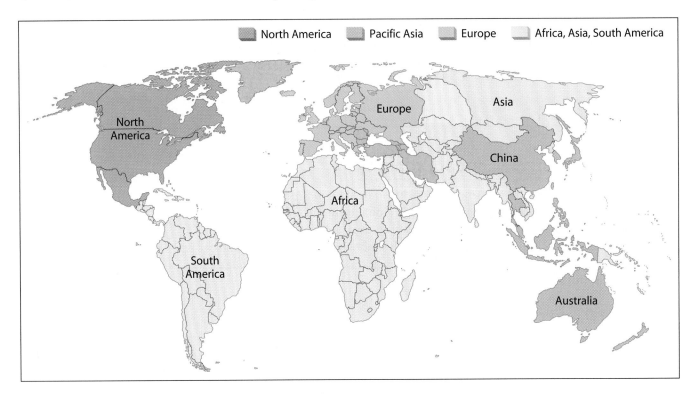

Figure 5.2
THE GLOBAL ECONOMY

The global economy is dominated by three relatively mature market systems. As illustrated here, these market systems consist of North America, Europe (especially those nations in the European Union), and Pacific Asia (parts of which are high-potential/high-growth economies). Other areas of Asia, as well as Africa and South America, have the potential for future growth but currently play only a relatively small role in the global economy.

---

market systems
Clusters of countries that engage in high levels of trade with one another

North American Free Trade Agreement (NAFTA)
An agreement made by the United States, Canada, and Mexico to promote trade with one another

European Union (EU)
The first and most important international market system

market system is North America. The United States, Canada, and Mexico are major trading partners with one another; more than 70 percent of Mexico's exports go to the United States, and more than 65 percent of what Mexico imports comes from the United States. During the last several years, these countries have negotiated a variety of agreements to make trade even easier. The most important of these, the ***North American Free Trade Agreement (NAFTA)***, eliminates many of the trade barriers—quotas and tariffs, for example—that existed previously.[20]

Another mature market system is Europe. Until recently, Europe was really two distinct economic areas. The eastern region consisted of communist countries such as Poland, Czechoslovakia, and Romania. These countries relied on government ownership of business and greatly restricted trade. In contrast, Western European countries with traditional market economies have been working together to promote international trade for decades. In particular, the ***European Union*** (or *EU*, as it is often called) has long been a formidable market system. The EU's origins can be traced to 1957 when Belgium, France, Luxembourg, Germany, Italy, and the Netherlands signed the Treaty of Rome to promote economic integration. Between 1973 and 1986, these countries were joined by Denmark, Ireland, the United Kingdom, Greece, Spain, and Portugal, and the group became known first as the European Committee and then the European Union. More recently, Austria, Finland, and Sweden joined the EU in 1995. For years these countries have followed a basic plan that led to the systematic elimination of most trade barriers. The new market system achieved significantly more potential when on January 1, 2002, 11 of the EU members eliminated their home currencies (such as French francs and Italian lira) and adopted a new common currency called the *euro*.

The European situation has recently grown more complex, however. Communism has collapsed in the Eastern countries, and they are trying to develop market economies. They also want greater participation in trade with the Western European countries. In some ways the emergence of the East has slowed and complicated business activities in the West. Twelve countries have applied for membership in the EU. This has led to controversy, as some current members want rapid expansion and others prefer a slower and more deliberate strategy. Sharp divisions among EU members regarding the U.S.-led war with Iraq in 2003 have also strained relations among such key nations as Spain and the United Kingdom (which supported the war) and France and Germany (which opposed the war). In the long term, however, the EU is almost certain to remain an important force in the global economy.

Yet another mature market system is ***Pacific Asia***. As shown in Figure 5.2, this market system includes Japan, China, Thailand, Malaysia, Singapore, Indonesia, South Korea, Taiwan, the Philippines, and Australia. Indeed, Japan, Taiwan, Singapore, Thailand, and South Korea were major economic powerhouses until a regional currency crisis slowed their growth in the late 1990s. That crisis appears to be coming to an end, however; trade among these nations is on the rise, and talk has started about an Asian economic community much like the EU.[21]

> *Pacific Asia*
> A market system located in Southeast Asia

High-Potential/High-Growth Economies

In contrast to the highly developed and mature market economies just described, other countries have what can be termed *high-potential/high-growth economies*. These economies have been relatively underdeveloped and immature and, until recently, were characterized by weak industry, weak currency, and relatively poor consumers.[22] The governments in these countries, however, have been actively working to strengthen their economies by opening their doors to foreign investment and by promoting international trade. Some of these countries have only recently adopted market economies, whereas others still use a command economy.

Even though it is technically part of Pacific Asia, the People's Republic of China is largely underdeveloped. But its market potential is enormous. For example, it is already the world's third largest automobile market. The transfer of control of Hong Kong from Great Britain to China focused even more attention on the market potential in the world's most populous country.[23] India is also emerging as a major force in the global economy. Vietnam has become a potentially important market, and Brazil is becoming more important as well.[24] Likewise, Russia and the other states and republics that previously made up the Commonwealth of Independent States are being closely watched by many companies for emerging market opportunities.[25] South Africa also holds considerable promise.

> " We will see China in a few years going from being a follower to a leader in defining consumer electronics trends. "
>
> Leon Husson, Philips Semiconductors Executive Vice-President
> (*BusinessWeek*, August 22, 2005, p. 57)

The primary challenges presented by the developing economies to those interested in conducting international business there are potential consumers' lack of wealth and an underdeveloped infrastructure. Developing economies have enormous economic potential, but much of it remains untapped. Thus international firms entering these markets often have to invest heavily in distribution systems, in training consumers how to use their products, and even in providing living facilities for their workers. They also run the risk of major policy changes that can greatly distort the value of their investments.[26]

Other Economies

There are some economic systems around the world that defy classification as either mature markets or high-potential/high-growth economies. One major area that falls outside of these categories is the oil-exporting region generally called the Middle East. The oil-exporting countries present mixed models of resource allocation, property ownership, and infrastructure development. These countries all have access to major amounts of crude oil, however, and thus are important players in the global economy.

These countries include Iran, Iraq, Kuwait, Saudi Arabia, Libya, Syria, and the United Arab Emirates. High oil prices in the last three decades have created enormous wealth in these countries. Many of them invested heavily in their infrastructures. Whole new cities were built, airports were constructed, and the population was educated. The per capita incomes of the United Arab Emirates and Qatar, for example, are among the highest in the world. Although there is great wealth in the oil-producing nations, they provide great challenges to managers. Political instability (as evidenced by the Persian Gulf War in 1991 and the U.S.-led war against Iraq in 2003) and tremendous cultural differences, for example, combine to make doing business in many parts of the Middle East both very risky and very difficult.

Other countries pose risks of a different sort to business. Politically and ethnically motivated violence, for example, still characterizes some countries. Foremost among these are Peru, El Salvador, Turkey, Colombia, and Northern Ireland. Cuba presents special challenges because it is so insulated from the outside world. With the demise of other communist regimes, some experts believe that Cuba will eventually join the ranks of the market economies. If so, its strategic location will quickly make it an important business center.

The Role of the GATT and the WTO

The global economy is also increasingly being influenced by the General Agreement on Tariffs and Trade (GATT) and the World Trade Organization (WTO).

General Agreement on Tariffs and Trade (GATT)   The General Agreement on Tariffs and Trade, or GATT, was first negotiated following World War II in an effort to avoid trade wars that would benefit rich nations and harm poorer ones. Essentially, the *GATT* is a trade agreement intended to promote international trade by reducing trade barriers and making it easier for all nations to compete in international markets. The GATT was a major stimulus to international trade after it was first ratified in 1948 by 23 countries.

One key component of the GATT was the identification of the so-called *most favored nation* (MFN) principle. This provision stipulates that if a country extends preferential treatment to any other nation that has signed the agreement, that preferential treatment must be extended to all signatories of the agreement. Members can extend such treatment to non-signatories as well, but are not required to do so.

GATT
A trade agreement intended to promote international trade by reducing trade barriers and making it easier for all nations to compete in international markets

World Trade Organization (WTO)   The *World Trade Organization,* or WTO, came into existence on January 1, 1995. The *WTO* replaced the GATT and absorbed its mission. The WTO is headquartered in Geneva, Switzerland, and currently includes 149 member nations and 32 observer countries. Members are required to open their markets to international trade and follow WTO rules. The WTO has three basic goals:

1. To promote trade flows by encouraging nations to adopt nondiscriminatory and predictable trade policies

2. To reduce remaining trade barriers through multilateral negotiations

3. To establish impartial procedures for resolving trade disputes among its members

The World Trade Organization is certain to continue to play a major role in the evolution of the global economy. At the same time, it has also become a lightning rod for protesters and other activists who argue that the WTO focuses too narrowly on globalization issues to the detriment of human rights and the environment.

> *World Trade Organization (WTO)*
> An organization, which currently includes 140 member nations and 32 observer countries, that requires members to open their markets to international trade and follow WTO rules

concept CHECK

What are the three major mature market systems? What are the GATT and WTO?

What impact has the U.S.-Iraq war had on international business?

Environmental Challenges of International Management

We note earlier that managing in a global context both poses and creates additional challenges for the manager. As illustrated in Figure 5.3, three environmental challenges in particular warrant additional exploration at this point—the economic environment, the political/legal environment, and the cultural environment of international management.[27]

The Economic Environment

Every country is unique and creates a unique set of challenges for managers trying to do business there. However, there are three aspects of the economic environment in particular that can help managers anticipate the kinds of economic challenges they are likely to face in working abroad.

Economic System   The first of these is the economic system used in the country. As we describe earlier, most countries today are moving toward a market economy. In a mature market economy, the key element for managers is freedom of choice. Consumers are free to make decisions about which products they prefer to purchase, and firms are free to decide what products and services to provide. As long as both the consumer and the firm are free to decide to be in the market, then supply and demand determine which firms and which products will be available.

A related characteristic of market economies that is relevant to managers concerns the nature of property ownership. There are two pure types—complete private ownership and complete public ownership. In systems with private ownership, individuals and organizations—not the government—own and operate the companies

Figure 5.3

ENVIRONMENTAL CHALLENGES OF INTERNATIONAL MANAGEMENT

Managers functioning in a global context must be aware of several environmental challenges. Three of the most important include economic, political/legal, and cultural challenges.

that conduct business. In systems with public ownership, the government directly owns the companies that manufacture and sell products. Few countries have pure systems of private ownership or pure systems of public ownership. Most countries tend toward one extreme or the other, but usually a mix of public and private ownership exists.

Natural Resources   Another important aspect of the economic environment in different countries is the availability of natural resources. A very broad range of resources is available in different countries. Some countries, like Japan, have few natural resources of their own. Japan is thus forced to import all of the oil, iron ore, and other natural resources it needs to manufacture products for its domestic and overseas markets. The United States, in contrast, has enormous natural resources and is a major producer of oil, natural gas, coal, iron ore, copper, uranium, and other metals and materials that are vital to the development of a modern economy.

One natural resource that is particularly important in the modern global economy is oil. As we noted earlier, a small set of countries in the Middle East, including Saudi Arabia, Iraq, Iran, and Kuwait, controls a very large percentage of the world's total known reserves of crude oil. Access to this single natural resource has given these oil-producing countries enormous clout in the international economy. One of the more controversial global issues today involving natural resources is the South American rain forest. Developers and farmers in Brazil, Peru, and other countries are clearing vast areas of rain forest, arguing that it is their land and that they can do what they want with it. Many environmentalists, however, fear the deforestation is wiping out entire species of animals and may so alter the environment as to affect weather patterns around the world.[28]

Infrastructure   Yet another important aspect of the economic environment of relevance to international management is infrastructure. A country's ***infrastructure*** comprises its schools, hospitals, power plants, railroads, highways, shipping ports, communication systems, air fields, commercial distribution systems, and so forth. The United States has a highly developed infrastructure. For example, its educational system is modern, roads and bridges are well developed, and most people have

infrastructure
The schools, hospitals, power plants, railroads, highways, ports, communication systems, air fields, and commercial distribution systems of a country

access to medical care. Overall, the United States has a relatively complete infrastructure sufficient to support most forms of economic development and activity.

Some countries, on the other hand, lack a well-developed infrastructure. Some countries do not have enough electrical generating capacity to meet demand. Such countries—Kenya, for example—often schedule periods of time during which power is turned off or reduced. These planned power failures reduce power demands but can be an enormous inconvenience to business. In the extreme, when a country's infrastructure is greatly underdeveloped, firms interested in beginning businesses may have to build an entire township, including housing, schools, hospitals, and perhaps even recreational facilities, to attract a sufficient overseas workforce.

The Political/Legal Environment

A second environmental challenge facing the international manager is the political/legal environment in which he or she will do business. Four especially important aspects of the political/legal environment of international management are government stability, incentives for multinational trade, controls on international trade, and the influence of economic communities on international trade.

> "Europe in many ways is the global regulatory superpower."
>
> Jeffrey Immelt, CEO of General Electric
> (*Fortune*, June 27, 2005, p. 160)

Government Stability Stability can be viewed in two ways—as the ability of a given government to stay in power against opposing factions in the country and as the permanence of government policies toward business. A country that is stable in both respects is preferable because managers have a higher probability of successfully predicting how government will affect their businesses. Civil war in countries such as Angola has made it virtually impossible for international managers to predict what government policies are likely to be and whether the government will be able to guarantee the safety of international workers. Consequently, international firms have been very reluctant to invest in Angola.

In many countries—the United States, Great Britain, and Japan, for example—changes in government occur with very little disruption. In other countries—India, Argentina, and Greece, for example—changes are likely to be somewhat chaotic. Even if a country's government remains stable, the risk remains that the policies adopted by that government might change. In some countries, foreign businesses may be **nationalized** (taken over by the government) with little or no warning. For example, the government of Peru nationalized Perulac, a domestic milk producer owned by Nestlé, because of a local milk shortage.

> **nationalized**
> Taken over by the government

Incentives for International Trade Another facet of the political environment is incentives to attract foreign business. For example, the state of Alabama offered Mercedes-Benz huge tax breaks and other incentives to entice the German firm to select a location for a new factory in that state. In like fashion, the French government sold land to the Walt Disney Company far below its market value and agreed to build a connecting freeway in exchange for the company's agreeing to build a European theme park outside of Paris.

Such incentives can take a variety of forms. Some of the most common include reduced interest rates on loans, construction subsidies, and tax incentives. Less-developed countries tend to offer different packages of incentives. In addition to lucrative tax breaks, for example, they can also attract investors with duty-fee entry of raw materials and equipment, market protection through limitations on other importers, and the right to take profits out of the country. They may also have to correct deficiencies in their infrastructures, as noted above, to satisfy the requirements of foreign firms.

Controls on International Trade   A third element of the political environment that managers need to consider is the extent to which there are controls on international trade. In some instances, a country's government might decide that foreign competition is hurting domestic trade. To protect domestic business, such governments may enact barriers to international trade. These barriers include tariffs, quotas, export restraint agreements, and "buy national" laws.

> *tariff*
> A tax collected on goods shipped across national boundaries

A ***tariff*** is a tax collected on goods shipped across national boundaries. Tariffs can be collected by the exporting country, countries through which goods pass, and the importing country. Import tariffs, which are the most common, can be levied to protect domestic companies by increasing the cost of foreign goods. Japan charges U.S. tobacco producers a tariff on cigarettes imported into Japan as a way to keep their prices higher than the prices charged by domestic firms. Tariffs can also be levied, usually by less-developed countries, to raise money for the government.

In the United States, the Byrd Amendment (named after West Virginia Senator Robert Byrd) stipulates that, if a domestic firm successfully demonstrates that a foreign company is dumping (selling for less than fair-market value) its products in the U.S. market, those products will be hit with a tariff and the proceeds given to the domestic company filing the complaint. U.S. ball-bearing maker Torrington recently received $63 million under provisions of this statute.[29]

> *quota*
> A limit on the number or value of goods that can be traded

Quotas are the most common form of trade restriction. A *quota* is a limit on the number or value of goods that can be traded. The quota amount is typically designed to ensure that domestic competitors will be able to maintain a certain market share. Honda is allowed to import 425,000 autos each year into the United States. This quota is one reason why Honda opened manufacturing facilities here. The quota applies to cars imported into the United States, but the company can produce as many cars within U.S. borders as it wants because those cars are not considered imports. ***Export restraint agreements*** are designed to convince other governments to voluntarily limit the volume or value of goods exported to or imported from a particular country. They are, in effect, export quotas. Japanese steel producers voluntarily limit the amount of steel they send to the United States each year.

> *export restraint agreements*
> Accords reached by governments in which countries voluntarily limit the volume or value of goods they export to or import from one another

"Buy national" legislation gives preference to domestic producers through content or price restrictions. Several countries have this type of legislation. Brazil requires that Brazilian companies purchase only Brazilian-made computers. The United States requires that the Department of Defense purchases only military uniforms manufactured in the United States, even though the price of foreign uniforms would be half as much. Mexico requires that 50 percent of the car parts sold in Mexico be manufactured inside its own borders.

Economic Communities   Just as government policies can either increase or decrease the political risk facing international managers, trade relations between countries can either help or hinder international business. Relations dictated by quotas, tariffs, and so forth can hurt international trade. There is currently a strong movement around the world to reduce many of these barriers. This movement takes its most obvious form in international economic communities.

An international ***economic community*** is a set of countries that agree to markedly reduce or eliminate trade barriers among member nations. The first and in many ways still the most important of these economic communities is the European Union (EU), discussed earlier. The passage of NAFTA, as also noted earlier, represents perhaps the first step toward the formation of a North American economic community. Other important economic communities include the Latin American Integration Association (Bolivia, Brazil, Colombia, Chile, Argentina, and other South American countries) and the Caribbean Common Market (the Bahamas, Belize, Jamaica, Antigua, Barbados, and twelve other countries).

> *economic community*
> A set of countries that agree to markedly reduce or eliminate trade barriers among member nations (a formalized market system)

The Cultural Environment

Another environmental challenge for the international manager is the cultural environment and how it affects business. A country's culture includes all the values, symbols, beliefs, and language that guide behavior.

Values, Symbols, Beliefs, and Language   Cultural values and beliefs are often unspoken; they may even be taken for granted by those who live in a particular country. Cultural factors do not necessarily cause problems for managers when the cultures of two countries are similar. Difficulties can arise, however, when there is little overlap between the home culture of a manager and the culture of the country in which business is to be conducted. For example, most U.S. managers find the culture and traditions of England relatively familiar. The people of both countries speak the same language and share strong historical roots, and there is a history of strong commerce between the two countries. When U.S. managers begin operations in Japan or the People's Republic of China, however, most of those commonalities disappear.

In Japanese, the word *hai* (pronounced "hi") means "yes." In conversation, however, this word is used much like people in the United States use "uh-huh"; it moves a conversation along or shows the person with whom you are talking that you are paying attention. So when does *hai* mean "yes" and when does it mean "uh-huh"? This turns out to be a relatively difficult question to answer. If a U.S. manager asks a Japanese manager if he agrees to some trade arrangement, the Japanese manager is likely to say, "Hai"—which may mean "Yes, I agree," "Yes, I understand," or "Yes, I am listening." Many U.S. managers become frustrated in negotiations with the Japanese because they believe that the Japanese continue to raise issues that have already been settled (because the Japanese managers said, "Yes"). What many of these managers fail to recognize is that "yes" does not always mean "yes" in Japan.

Cultural differences between countries can have a direct impact on business practice. For example, the religion of Islam teaches that people should not make a living by exploiting the misfortune of others; as a result, charging interest payments, for example, is seen as immoral. This means that in Saudi Arabia there are few businesses that provide auto-wrecking services to tow stalled cars to the garage (because that would be capitalizing on misfortune), and in the Sudan banks cannot pay or charge interest. Given these cultural and religious constraints, those two businesses—automobile towing and banking—do not seem to hold great promise for international managers in those particular countries!

Some cultural differences between countries can be even more subtle and yet have a major impact on business activities. For example, in the United States, most managers clearly agree about the value of time. Most U.S. managers schedule their activities very tightly and then adhere to their schedules. Other cultures do not put such a premium on time. In the Middle East, managers do not like to set appointments, and they rarely keep appointments set too far into the future. U.S. managers interacting with managers from the Middle East might misinterpret the late arrival of a potential business partner as a negotiation ploy or an insult, when it is rather a simple reflection of different views of time and its value.[30]

Language itself can be an important factor. Beyond the obvious and clear barriers posed by people who speak different languages, subtle differences in meaning can also play a major role. For example, Imperial Oil of Canada markets gasoline under the brand name Esso. When the firm tried to sell its gasoline in Japan, it learned that *esso* means "stalled car" in Japanese. Likewise, when Chevrolet first introduced a U.S. model called the Nova in Latin America, General Motors executives could not understand why the car sold poorly. They eventually learned, though, that, in Spanish, *no va* means "it doesn't go." The color green is used extensively in Muslim countries, but it signifies death in some other countries. The color associated with femininity in the United States is pink, but in many other countries, yellow is the most feminine color.

Individual Behaviors Across Cultures   There also appear to be clear differences in individual behaviors and attitudes across different cultures. For example, Geert Hofstede, a Dutch researcher, studied 116,000 people working in dozens of different countries and found several interesting differences.[31] Hofstede's initial work identified four important dimensions along which people seem to differ across cultures. More recently, he has added a fifth dimension. These dimensions are illustrated in Figure 5.4.

The first dimension identified by Hofstede is social orientation.[32] ***Social orientation*** is a person's beliefs about the relative importance of the individual versus groups to which that person belongs. The two extremes of social orientation are individualism and collectivism. *Individualism* is the cultural belief that the person comes first. Hofstede's research suggested that people in the United States, the United Kingdom, Australia, Canada, New Zealand, and the Netherlands tend to be relatively individualistic. *Collectivism*, the opposite of individualism, is the belief that the group comes first. Hofstede found that people from Mexico, Greece, Hong Kong, Taiwan, Peru, Singapore, Colombia, and Pakistan tend to be relatively collectivistic in their values. In countries with higher levels of individualism, many workers may prefer reward systems that link pay with the performance of individual employees. In a more collectivistic culture, such a reward system may in fact be counterproductive.

A second important dimension is ***power orientation***, the beliefs that people in a culture hold about the appropriateness of power and authority differences in hierarchies such as business organizations. Some cultures are characterized by *power respect*. This means that people tend to accept the power and authority of their superiors simply on the basis of their position in the hierarchy and to respect their right to control that power. Hofstede found that people in France, Spain, Mexico, Japan, Brazil, Indonesia, and Singapore are relatively power accepting. In contrast, people in cultures with a *power tolerance* orientation attach much less significance to a person's position in the hierarchy. These individuals are more willing to question a decision or

social orientation
A person's beliefs about the relative importance of the individual versus groups to which that person belongs

power orientation
The beliefs that people in a culture hold about the appropriateness of power and authority differences in hierarchies such as business organizations

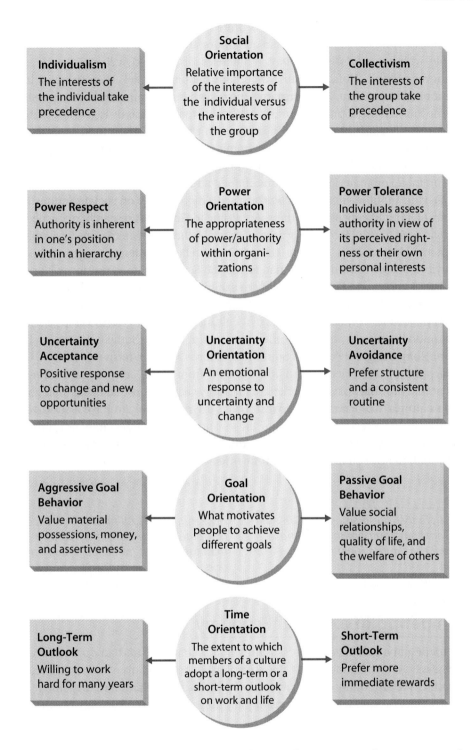

Figure 5.4
INDIVIDUAL DIFFERENCES ACROSS CULTURES

Hofstede identified five fundamental differences that can be used to characterize people in different cultures. These dimensions are social orientation, power orientation, uncertainty orientation, goal orientation, and time orientation. Different levels of each dimension affect the perceptions, attitudes, values, motivations, and behaviors of people in different cultures.

Source: R. W. Griffin and M. Pustay, *International Business,* 4th ed. © 2005. Reprinted by permission of Pearson Education, Inc. Upper Saddle River, NJ 07458.

mandate from someone at a higher level or perhaps even refuse to accept it. Hofstede's work suggested that people in the United States, Israel, Austria, Denmark, Ireland, Norway, Germany, and New Zealand tend to be more power tolerant.

The third basic dimension of individual differences studied by Hofstede was uncertainty orientation. **_Uncertainty orientation_** is the feeling individuals have regarding uncertain and ambiguous situations. People in cultures with *uncertainty acceptance* are stimulated by change and thrive on new opportunities. Hofstede

---

uncertainty orientation
The feeling individuals have regarding uncertain and ambiguous situations

suggested that many people from the United States, Denmark, Sweden, Canada, Singapore, Hong Kong, and Australia are among those in this category. In contrast, people with *uncertainty avoidance* tendencies dislike and will avoid ambiguity whenever possible. Hofstede found that many people in Israel, Austria, Japan, Italy, Columbia, France, Peru, and Germany tend to avoid uncertainty whenever possible.

The fourth dimension of cultural values measured by Hofstede is goal orientation. In this context, **goal orientation** is the manner in which people are motivated to work toward different kinds of goals. One extreme on the goal orientation continuum is *aggressive goal behavior*. People who exhibit aggressive goal behaviors tend to place a high premium on material possessions, money, and assertiveness. On the other hand, people who adopt *passive goal behavior* place a higher value on social relationships, quality of life, and concern for others. According to Hofstede's research, many people in Japan tend to exhibit relatively aggressive goal behaviors, whereas many people in Germany, Mexico, Italy, and the United States reflect moderately aggressive goal behaviors. People from the Netherlands and the Scandinavian countries of Norway, Sweden, Denmark, and Finland all tend to exhibit relatively passive goal behaviors.

A recently identified fifth dimension is called **time orientation**.[33] Time orientation is the extent to which members of a culture adopt a long-term versus a short-term outlook on work, life, and other elements of society. Some cultures, such as Japan, Hong Kong, Taiwan, and South Korea, have a longer-term orientation. One implication of this orientation is that people from these cultures are willing to accept that they may have to work hard for many years before achieving their goals. Other cultures, like Pakistan and West Africa, are more likely to have a short-term orientation. As a result, people from these cultures may prefer jobs that provide more immediate rewards. Hofstede's work suggests that the United States and Germany tend to have an intermediate time orientation.

goal orientation
The manner in which people are motivated to work toward different kinds of goals

time orientation
The extent to which members of a culture adopt a long-term versus a short-term outlook on work, life, and other elements of society

concept
CHECK

| What are the four elements of the political/legal environment that are most relevant to international managers? | How might cultural factors influence a computer manufacturer differently than they might influence a fashion-oriented apparel company? |

Competing in a Global Economy

Competing in a global economy is both a major challenge and an opportunity for businesses today. The nature of these challenges depends on a variety of factors, including the size of the organization. In addition, international management has implications for the basic functions of planning and decision making, organizing, leading, and controlling.

Globalization and Organization Size

Although organizations of any size may compete in international markets, there are some basic differences in the challenges and opportunities faced by MNCs, medium-size organizations, and small organizations.

Multinational Corporations   The large MNCs have long since made the choice to compete in a global marketplace. In general, these firms take a global perspective. They transfer capital, technology, human resources, inventory, and information from one market to another. They actively seek new expansion opportunities wherever feasible. MNCs tend to allow local managers a great deal of discretion in addressing local and regional issues. At the same time, each operation is ultimately accountable to a central authority. Managers at this central authority (headquarters, a central office) are responsible for setting the overall strategic direction for the firm, making major policy decisions, and so forth. MNCs need senior managers who understand the global economy and who are comfortable dealing with executives and government officials from a variety of cultures. Table 5.2 lists the world's largest multinational enterprises.

The dynamics of competing in the global economy grow both more exciting and more challenging every day. These cranes are loading containers onto an ocean cargo ship in the Persian Gulf in the container terminal at Jebel Ali Port in Dubai. Built in 1979, Jebel Ali is now the largest man-made harbor in the world and facilitates the movement of over 7 million containers a year. Shipping and distribution centers like Jebel Ali have opened new opportunities for large businesses everywhere.

Medium-Size Organizations Many medium-size businesses remain primarily domestic organizations. But they still may buy and sell products made abroad and compete with businesses from other countries in their own domestic markets. Increasingly, however, medium-size organizations are expanding into foreign markets as well. For example, Gold's Gym, a U.S. fitness chain, has opened a very successful facility in Moscow.[34] In contrast to MNCs, medium-size organizations doing business abroad are much more selective about the markets they enter. They also depend more on a few international specialists to help them manage their foreign operations.

Small Organizations More and more small organizations are also finding that they can benefit from the global economy. Some, for example, serve as local suppliers for MNCs. A dairy farmer who sells milk to Carnation Company, for example, is actually transacting business with Nestlé. Local parts suppliers also have been successfully selling products to the Toyota and Honda plants in the United States. Beyond serving as local suppliers, some small businesses buy and sell products and services abroad. For example, the Collin Street Bakery, based in Corsicana, Texas, ships fruitcakes around the world. In 2003 the firm shipped over 150,000 pounds of fruitcake to Japan. Most small businesses rely on simple importing or exporting operations (or both) for their international sales. Thus only a few specialized management positions are needed. Collin Street Bakery, for example, has one local manager who handles international activities. Mail-order activities within each country are subcontracted to local firms in each market.

Management Challenges in a Global Economy

The management functions that constitute the framework for this book—planning and decision making, organizing, leading, and controlling—are just as relevant to international managers as to domestic managers. International managers need to have a clear view of where they want their firm to be in the future; they have to organize to implement their plans; they have to motivate those who work for them; and they have to develop appropriate control mechanisms.[35]

Planning and Decision Making in a Global Economy To effectively plan and make decisions in a global economy, managers must have a broad-based understanding of both environmental issues and competitive issues. They need to understand local market conditions and technological factors that will affect their operations. At the

Table 5.2

THE WORLD'S LARGEST MNCs: INDUSTRIAL CORPORATIONS

Rank, 2005	2004	Company	Country	Revenues $ (millions)	% change
1	3	ExxonMobil	U.S.	339,938.0	25.5
2	1	Wal-Mart Stores	U.S.	315,654.0	9.6
3	4	Royal Dutch Shell	Netherlands	306,731.0	14.2
4	2	BP	Britain	267,600.0	(6.1)
5	5	General Motors	U.S.	192,604.0	(0.5)
6	11	Chevron	U.S.	189,481.0	28.1
7	6	DaimlerChrysler	Germany	186,106.3	5.3
8	7	Toyota Motor	Japan	185,805.0	7.6
9	8	Ford Motor	U.S.	177,210.0	2.9
10	12	ConocoPhillips	U.S.	166,683.0	37.0
11	9	General Electric	U.S.	157,153.0	2.8
12	10	Total	France	152,360.7	(0.2)
13	17	ING Group	Netherlands	138,235.3	30.6
14	16	Citigroup	U.S.	131,045.0	21.0
15	13	AXA	France	129,839.2	6.8
16	14	Allianz	Germany	121,406.0	2.1
17	15	Volkswagen	Germany	118,376.6	7.0
18	30	Fortis	Belgium/Netherlands	112,351.4	48.8
19	60	Crédit Agricole	France	110,764.6	87.6
20	19	American International Group	U.S.	108,905.0	11.1
21	24	Assicurazioni Generali	Italy	101,403.8	21.8
22	21	Siemens	Germany	100,098.7	9.4
23	31	Sinopec	China	98,784.9	31.6
24	18	Nippon Telegraph & Telephone	Japan	94,869.3	(5.6)
25	22	Carrefour	France	94,454.5	4.5
26	36	HSBC Holdings	Britain	93,494.0	28.9
27	33	Eni	Italy	92,603.3	24.8
28	35	Aviva	Britain	92,579.4	26.8
29	20	International Business Machines	U.S.	91,134.0	(5.4)
30	26	McKesson	U.S.	88,050.0	9.4
31	27	Honda Motor	Japan	87,510.7	8.7
32	40	State Grid	China	86,984.3	22.0
33	28	Hewlett-Packard	U.S.	86,696.0	8.5
34	45	BNP Paribas	France	85,687.2	24.8
35	N/A	PDVSA	Venezuela	85,618.0	32.2
36	66	UBS	Switzerland	84,707.6	48.8
37	52	Bank of America Corp.	U.S.	83,980.0	32.6
38	23	Hitachi	Japan	83,596.3	(0.5)
39	46	China National Petroleum	China	83,556.5	23.4
40	51	Pemex	Mexico	83,381.7	30.9
41	29	Nissan Motor	Japan	83,273.8	4.4
42	32	Berkshire Hathaway	U.S.	81,663.0	9.8
43	34	Home Depot	U.S.	81,511.0	11.5
44	73	Valero Energy	U.S.	81,362.0	50.9
45	65	J.P. Morgan Chase & Co.	U.S.	79,902.0	40.3
46	39	Samsung Electronics	South Korea	78,716.6	10.0
47	25	Matsushita Electric Industrial	Japan	78,557.7	(3.1)
48	68	Deutsche Bank	Germany	76,227.6	36.9
49	87	HBOS	Britain	75,798.8	58.7
50	38	Verizon Communications	U.S.	75,111.9	5.0
51	48	Cardinal Health	U.S.	74,915.1	15.0
52	89	Prudential	Britain	74,744.7	58.8
53	43	Nestlé	Switzerland	74,658.6	6.9
54	37	Deutsche Telekom	Germany	74,061.8	2.9
55	42	Metro	Germany	72,814.3	3.8
55	291	Dexia Group	Belgium	72,814.3	258.8
57	61	Credit Suisse	Switzerland	72,193.5	22.7
58	58	Royal Bank of Scotland	Britain	71,164.3	19.1
59	54	Tesco	Britain	71,127.6	13.9
60	41	Peugeot	France	69,915.4	(1.0)

Source: From *Fortune*, July 24, 2006, p. 113. Copyright © 2006 Time, Inc. All Rights Reserved.

corporate level, executives need a great deal of information to function effectively. Which markets are growing? Which markets are shrinking? What are our domestic and foreign competitors doing in each market? They must also make a variety of strategic decisions about their organizations. For example, if a firm wishes to enter the market in France, should it buy a local firm there, build a plant, or seek a strategic alliance? Critical issues include understanding environmental circumstances, the role of goals and planning in a global organization, and how decision making affects the global organization. We note special implications for global managers as we discuss planning and decision making in Chapters 7 through 10.

Organizing in a Global Economy   Managers in international businesses must also attend to a variety of organizing issues. For example, General Electric has operations scattered around the globe. The firm has made the decision to give local managers a great deal of responsibility for how they run their business. In contrast, many Japanese firms give managers of their foreign operations relatively little responsibility. As a result, those managers must frequently travel back to Japan to present problems or get decisions approved. Managers in an international business must address the basic issues of organization structure and design, managing change, and dealing with human resources. We address the special issues of organizing the international organization in Chapters 11 through 14.

Leading in a Global Economy   We noted earlier some of the cultural factors that affect international organizations. Individual managers must be prepared to deal with these and other factors as they interact with people from different cultural backgrounds. Supervising a group of five managers, each of whom is from a different state in the United States, is likely to be much simpler than supervising a group of five managers, each of whom is from a different culture. Managers must understand how cultural factors affect individuals, how motivational processes vary across cultures, how the role of leadership changes in different cultures, how communication varies across cultures, and how interpersonal and group processes depend on cultural background. In Chapters 15 through 19, we note special implications for international managers that relate to leading and interacting with others.

Controlling in a Global Economy   Finally, managers in international organizations must also be concerned with control. Distances, time zone differences, and cultural factors also play a role in control. For example, in some cultures, close supervision is seen as being appropriate, whereas in other cultures, it is not. Likewise, executives in the United States and Japan may find it difficult to communicate vital information to one another because of the time zone differences. Basic control issues for the international manager revolve around operations management, productivity, quality, technology, and information systems. These issues are integrated throughout our discussion of control in Chapters 20 through 22.

concept
CHECK

How do the four basic management functions relate to international business?

What kinds of small business might have the greatest success in international markets? What kinds might have the least success?

Summary of Learning Objectives and Key Points

1. Describe the nature of international business, including its meaning, recent trends, management of globalization, and competition in a global market.
   - Learning to operate in a global economy is an important challenge facing many managers today.
   - Businesses can be primarily domestic, international, multinational, or global in scope.
   - Managers need to understand both the process of internationalization and how to manage within a given level of international activity.

2. Discuss the structure of the global economy and describe the GATT and the WTO.
   - Mature market economies and systems dominate the global economy today.
   - North America, the European Union, and Pacific Asia are especially important.
   - High-potential/high-growth economies in Eastern Europe, Latin America, the People's Republic of China, India, and Vietnam are increasingly important to managers.
   - The oil-exporting economies in the Middle East are also important.

- The GATT and the WTO play critical roles in the evolution of the global economy.

3. Identify and discuss the environmental challenges inherent in international management.
   - Many of the challenges of management in a global context are unique issues associated with the international environmental context.
   - These challenges reflect the economic, political/legal, and cultural environments of international management.

4. Describe the basic issues involved in competing in a global economy, including organization size and the management challenges in a global economy.
   - Basic issues of competing in a global economy vary according to whether the organization is an MNC, a medium-size organization, or a small organization.
   - In addition, the basic managerial functions of planning and decision making, organizing, leading, and controlling must all be addressed in international organizations.

Discussion Questions

Questions for Review

1. Describe the four basic levels of international business activity. Do you think any organization will achieve the fourth level? Why or why not?
2. For each of the four globalization strategies, describe the risks associated with that strategy and the potential returns from that strategy.

3. Describe the various types of political controls on international trade. Be sure to highlight the differences between the types.
4. Explain the relationship between organizational size and globalization. Are large firms the only ones that are global?

Questions for Analysis

5. What are the advantages and disadvantages for a U.S.-based multinational firm entering a mature market economy? What are the advantages and disadvantages for such a firm entering a high-potential/high-growth economy?
6. Choose an industry. Describe the impact that international business has had on firms in that industry. Are there any industries that might not be affected by

the trend toward international business? If so, what are they? If not, why are there none?
7. You are the CEO of an up-and-coming toy company and have plans to go international soon. What steps would you take to carry out that strategy? What areas would you stress in your decision-making process? How would you organize your company?

Questions for Application

8. Use the Internet to locate information about a company that is using a global strategic alliance or global

joint venture. (*Hint:* Almost any large multinational firm will be involved in these ventures, and you can find information at corporate home pages.) What do you think are the major goals for the venture? Do you expect that the firm will accomplish its goals? If so, why? If not, what stands in its way?

9. Assume that you are the CEO of General Motors. What are the basic environmental challenges you face as your company continues its globalization efforts? Give some specific examples that relate to GM.

10. Review the following chart of Hofstede's cultural dimensions. Based on the chart, tell which country you would most like to work in and why. Tell which country you would like least to work in and why.

	Power Distance Range: 11–104	Individualism Range: 6–91	Uncertainty Avoidance Range: 8–112	Aggressiveness Range: 5–95
GERMANY	35	67	65	66
INDIA	77	48	40	56
ISRAEL	13	54	81	47
UNITED KINGDOM	35	89	35	66
UNITED STATES	40	91	46	62

Adapted from: Geert Hofstede, *Cultures and Organizations: Software of the Mind: Intercultural Cooperation and Its Importance for Survival* (London: HarperCollins, 1994), pp. 26, 55, 84, 113.

Building Effective Technical Skills

Exercise Overview

Technical skills are the skills necessary to accomplish or understand the specific kind of work being done in an organization. Companies must continually analyze population and trade data to form reasonable international strategies. This exercise will help you develop technical skills related to finding information and then see the impact that the information can have on a firm.

Exercise Background

In 2002, the five largest countries in the world, in population, were China, India, the United States, Indonesia, and Brazil, in that order. Assume you are the manager of a large multinational firm headquartered in the United States. Use the Internet to help you answer the questions below about trade and population in each of these countries. (Estimates of future population can be found at the U.S. Census Bureau, **www.census.gov/ipc/www/idbrank.html**.

Import/export data are also found at the U.S. Census Bureau, at **www.census.gov/foreign-trade/aip/index .html#profile**. From this main page, find the most recent figures. The remainder of the data can be found in the World Factbook, published by the Central Intelligence Agency, located at **www.cia.gov/cia/publications/factbook/index.html**.) Then consider the implications this information could have for your firm.

Exercise Task

1. List the five countries in the world that are estimated to have the largest populations in 2050. Describe how the list has changed since 2002.

2. What are the top five countries that receive exports from the United States?

3. What are the top five countries that import U.S. products?

4. What is the average life span (a measure of individual prosperity) in each of the largest countries and each of the top exporters and importers?

5. What is the gross domestic product per capita (a measure of economic health of an economy) in each of those countries, in U.S. dollars?

6. What are the implications for your firm? In other words, what do the data suggest about the desirability of various countries as trading partners today? What do the data suggest about the countries' desirability in the future?

Building Effective Communication Skills

Exercise Overview

Communication skills refer to the manager's ability both to convey ideas and information effectively to others and to receive ideas and information effectively from others. International managers have additional communication complexities due to differences in language, time zones, and so forth. This exercise will enable you to enhance your communication skills by better understanding the impact of different time zones.

Exercise Background

Assume that you are a manager in a large multinational firm. Your office is located in San Francisco. You need to arrange a conference call with several other managers to discuss an upcoming strategic change by your firm. The other managers are located in New York, London, Rome, Moscow, Tokyo, Singapore, and Sydney.

Exercise Task

Using the information above, do the following:

1. Determine the time zone differences in each of these cities.
2. Assuming that people in each city have a typical workday of 8:00 A.M. to 5:00 P.M., determine the optimal time for your conference call; that is, what time can you place the call and minimize the number of people who are inconvenienced?
3. Now assume that you need to visit each office in person. You need to spend one full day in each city. Using the Internet, review airline schedules, account for differences in time zones, and develop an efficient itinerary.

CHAPTER CLOSING CASE

GETTING P&G GROWING

Procter & Gamble (P&G) has long outgrown its original candle-making factory, built in Cincinnati in 1837. Today, the company makes consumer goods ranging from razors to diapers, shampoo to laundry detergent, coffee to antacids. This wide portfolio of business lines features more than 100 brands, 22 of which sell more than $1 billion annually. The firm's geographic reach is wide too. Over 100 million customers in 140 countries purchase P&G products each year. Manufacturing operations are dispersed across dozens of U.S. and overseas locations.

After decades of dramatic expansion, P&G hit a growth plateau in the 1990s. National and international expansion stalled, and product innovation slowed. P&G managers were not content with lowered expecta-

tions, however, and in 1998 they adopted a stringent set of global growth objectives. The company's globalization strategy became the primary driver of growth, although implementation raised a number of significant challenges.

The company's first international venture was a manufacturing plant built in Canada in 1915. By 1930, P&G was acquiring European firms. The following decades brought a string of overseas acquisitions as well as internally driven foreign growth. Today, P&G is a multinational corporation that is becoming a global one. About half of P&G's sales come from outside of the United States, and that percentage is increasing.

P&G has long dominated its U.S. and Western European markets. Its baby products, for example, have a

50 percent market share in Europe and a 60 percent share in the United States. Many of P&G's international markets are already huge—ten of them produce more than $1 billion in yearly revenues. To grow, P&G must seek out new "white space" opportunities. White space opportunities are "holes" in a company's offerings. They consist of geographic areas or new products with the potential for high growth that are related to the company's present offerings but aren't currently being exploited.

One area of white space for P&G is the development of new but related products. Since 2000, the company has introduced extensions of existing products, such as the SpinBrush addition to the Crest line of oral care merchandise. Some new pharmaceuticals have been developed through internal research and development, while others are over-the-counter drugs that were formerly available only by prescription. Some products are entirely new, such as the ThermaCare line of heat-producing wraps for pain treatment.

Another white space opportunity is the introduction of brands developed in one market into another market. For P&G, this has happened primarily through the introduction of the firm's U.S. brands to foreign countries. However, as the company increasingly becomes a truly global firm, it can combine ideas and resources from anywhere in the world to create new products. In 2005, for example, P&G introduced the U.S. brand Oil of Olay into Spain. The ideas don't even need to come from P&G employees. In 2005, P&G found an Italian professor who had perfected a way to print edible images on cakes using an ink jet printer. One year later, Pringles Prints were introduced—a potato chip with jokes printed on them.

A third white space opportunity is entry into new markets, either new regions, customer segments, or product lines. P&G is shifting its regional focus to developing economies. Basic products at a value price have been developed to appeal to buyers with lower incomes and simpler needs. Lower per unit prices translate into lower per unit revenues. However, the increased volume of sales enables P&G to achieve a growth rate in developing markets that is twice the rate in developed countries.

Another way that P&G tailors products for local needs is through acquisition. Throughout its history, the company has used acquisition of local manufacturers as a way to quickly and easily enter new regions. Customers continue to buy a familiar brand, while P&G instantly gains access to the market. In addition, a local brand is less likely to arouse anti-U.S. consumer backlash. Introduction of new product lines can also occur through acquisition. For example, in 2005, P&G bought Gillette, which owns the Braun and Gillette shaving brands, Oral-B dental care products, and Duracell batteries.

As P&G continues to implement its globalization growth strategy, it faces a number of economic, political, and cultural challenges. World energy prices are rising steeply, some nations limit foreign direct investment, and consumer preferences can be very different around the world. Yet P&G, with its long history of globalization and its effective growth strategies, is on its way to becoming a truly global enterprise.

CASE QUESTIONS

1. What are the potential advantages and disadvantages of P&G's global strategy of entering developing economies? How can P&G fully exploit the advantages? What can the company do to reduce or eliminate the disadvantages?

2. In your opinion, is P&G using the correct entry strategies to support its goal of rapid global expansion? If so, explain why. If not, explain why another strategy would be a better choice.

3. Consider some of the ways in which individual behavior differs across cultures. How might these differences influence P&G's product design or marketing approach in a culture that differs from U.S. culture?

CASE REFERENCES

"2005 Annual Report," Procter & Gamble website, www.pg.com on March 5, 2006; Steve Hamm, "Speed Demons," *BusinessWeek*, March 27, 2006, www.businessweek.com on April 1, 2006; Linda Sanford, "Businesses Must Learn to Let Go," *BusinessWeek*, January 9, 2006, www.businessweek.com on March 5, 2006; see also Larry Huston and Nabil Sakkab, "Connect and Develop: Inside Procter & Gamble's New Model for Innovation," *Harvard Business Review*, March 2006, pp. 58–67.

YOU MAKE THE CALL

Coffee, Café, Kaffee, or Copi—Starbucks Spans the Globe

1. Starbucks is an active participant in the Fair Trade concept (see First Things First in Chapter 4). Do you think their motivation is to be a good corporate citizen, or just to get favorable publicity? Why?

2. In what countries do you think Starbucks may encounter serious obstacles to success?

3. Even though Starbucks seems to be a socially responsible company, it is often the target of protests at WTO meetings. What are the possible explanations for this?

4. Starbucks does some peripheral business in areas such as music and movie promotions. Do you think these activities would travel well to foreign markets? Why or why not?

Test Prepper

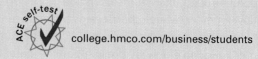

college.hmco.com/business/students

Choose the correct answer. Answers are found at the back of the book.

1. T   F   Exporting is selling a firm's product in a foreign country. Importing is selling the firm's product in its own country.

2. T   F   In market economies, governments determine the supply and demand of resources.

3. T   F   The primary challenges for developing countries interested in conducting international business are potential customers' lack of wealth and an underdeveloped infrastructure.

4. T   F   Most countries today are moving toward a market economy.

5. T   F   People in national cultures with a power tolerance orientation accept the authority of their superiors based simply on the superiors' position in the hierarchy and respect their right to control that power.

6. ImmunoLabs, Inc. has patented an efficient technique to manufacture flu vaccines. Rather than build its own facilities overseas, ImmunoLabs allows foreign companies to use this technology and pay a royalty based on sales. This situation represents

   A. a licensing arrangement.
   B. a strategic alliance.
   C. a joint venture.
   D. an exporting arrangement.
   E. an importing arrangement.

7. Which approach to internationalization involves a small cash outlay and little risk, but high transportation costs and potential government restrictions?

   A. Licensing
   B. Strategic alliances
   C. Joint ventures
   D. Direct investment
   E. Importing or exporting

8. Under the General Agreement on Tariffs and Trade (GATT), the most favored nation principle means

   A. trade barriers in this country are lower than in any other country.

   B. preferential treatment given to any nation that has signed the agreement must be extended to all nations that have signed the agreement.
   C. the countries that signed the agreement select one country that most benefits the others and give it preferential treatment during the following year.
   D. the countries that signed the agreement designate a new country that is not currently part of the agreement as the next to be admitted.
   E. tariffs and trade restrictions against this particular country will be lowered, if not eliminated.

9. The most common form of trade restriction is quotas. A quota is

   A. a tax collected on goods shipped across national boundaries.
   B. a limit on the number or value of goods that can be traded.
   C. a voluntary agreement not to sell more than a certain volume or value of goods.
   D. a minimum required volume or value of goods a country agrees to export.
   E. an estimate one country makes to another of the volume of value of goods it expects to sell.

10. Which of the following is most relevant to managers who are preparing to lead people in international organizations?

   A. Have a broad-based understanding of both environmental issues and competitive issues
   B. Address the basic issues of organizational structure and design
   C. Maintain effective inventory control systems
   D. Understand the differences across the cultures of employees
   E. Enter the global market cautiously and have a clear exit plan

The Multicultural Environment

FIRST THINGS FIRST

The Leadership of Debra Lee

"We're not PBS, and we'll never be PBS."

—DEBRA L. LEE, CEO, BLACK ENTERTAINMENT TELEVISION

Black Entertainment Television (BET) spent most of 2005 saying "Good-bye, Bob," to founder, CEO, and president Robert Johnson. Johnson launched the station in 1980, offering programming that appeals to African Americans. BET was enormously popular right from the start. Cable operators added the station to their line-ups and Johnson grew wealthy. He invested his profits in a number of other ventures, including an airline, a cell phone service provider, theme restaurants, and a cosmetics maker. All of these efforts failed and were abandoned. In 2000, Viacom purchased BET for $2.3 billion and left Johnson in command.

Debra L. Lee served as Johnson's chief operating officer (COO) at BET for more than a decade of this wild ride. In her tenure in that job, Lee developed a reputation as a master planner and implementer for her ability to carry out Johnson's sometimes overly ambitious dreams. While she was COO, Lee was responsible for expanding BET's coverage of music and news programming. She pioneered BET's presentation of original movies, concerts, and talk shows.

LEARNING OBJECTIVES

After studying this chapter, you should be able to:

1. Describe the nature of diversity and multiculturalism.

2. Identify and describe the major trends and dimensions of diversity and multiculturalism in organizations.

3. Discuss the primary effects of diversity and multiculturalism in organizations.

4. Describe individual strategies for and organizational approaches to managing diversity and multiculturalism in organizations.

5. Discuss the characteristics of the fully multicultural organization.

Debra L. Lee, CEO of Black Entertainment Television, has built on the foundation created by her predecessor, Bob Johnson, to turn BET into an entertainment powerhouse. Lee and Johnson are shown here at the 5th annual BET Awards at the Kodak Theatre in Hollywood.

She delivered record-setting ratings during a time of little growth in the cable market. In 2005, Johnson stepped down, and Lee moved into the top spot.

With this change, BET enters a new era. Lee seeks to broaden the station's programming appeal and expand beyond the 80 million homes that currently receive BET. Diverse programming has always been a strong selling point for media companies. Varied offerings attract a wider set of customers, increasing sales. African Americans account for about 13 percent of the U.S. population, a figure that continues to grow. Diversity also offers additional opportunities for cross-selling and cross-programming. For example, Viacom also owns MTV, so some of the same music videos can be played on both channels.

Another of Lee's initiatives is to continue to expand beyond television. The company already owns BET.com, which offers news, music, and more, all geared to the BET market. BET J (for Jazz) provides music for African American adults, with a focus on jazz, soul, blues, and R&B. BET books publishes African American–themed content in books and magazines. Lee envisions some new ventures too, such as a BET feature films division or an iTunes-like site to offer BET's music products.

Lee faced diversity issues of her own, but she didn't allow stereotyped thinking about women's roles to stop her rise. She graduated from Brown University and then earned a doctorate from Harvard's law school. She joined BET in 1986, after several years of practicing law in Washington, DC. Along the way to the CEO position, she married and had two children. While expecting her first child, she was in charge of construction of BET's corporate headquarters in Washington. At that time, she was also running the company's publishing division and serving as corporate general counsel. Lee's hard work and dedication paid off, for both her and her company. She is the recipient of numerous awards and honors, including a spot on *Black Enterprise's* list of the 50 most powerful women in business in 2006. In a world where only 1 percent of black female executives reach top management levels, Lee is a standout achiever.

BET's target audience is African American, ages 18 to 34, and male. Urban music makes up a large part of BET's programming, but some viewers are critical. "There has been such a pandering to young people," says writer Kevin Powell. "We [African Americans] have to stop participating in the one-dimensional portrayals of ourselves." Many agree and dislike an emphasis on hip-hop music videos that are often misogynistic and violent. Within BET, the criticism is dismissed as intellectual posturing and political correctness. Lee responds to critics, "We're not PBS, and we'll never be PBS."

However, in January 2004, Comcast launched TV One, another station geared toward African Americans. TV One is targeting older viewers, those who are 24- to 54-years-old. CEO Johnathan Rodgers says, "The mission of TV One is to be for African American adults what Lifetime is for women." For Lee and BET, TV One presents a challenge. How can BET effectively broaden its target market without alienating its loyal fans? For industry observers, the competition is a positive sign. Targeting specific demographic groups is an indicator that African American audiences are finally being taken seriously, as seriously as the mainstream audience.[1]

Like many other organizations in the world today, BET faces a variety of challenges, opportunities, and issues in its quest to remain competitive in its industry. One key ingredient in the firm's continued success is its ability to attract, motivate, and retain talented employees who reflect diversity from a variety of perspectives and to meld them into a focused and dedicated workforce. Their multicultural backgrounds pose challenges for the firm, but also provide enormous potential. This chapter is about diversity and multiculturalism in organizations. We begin by describing trends in diversity and multiculturalism, and identify and discuss several common dimensions of diversity. The effects of diversity and multiculturalism on organizations are then explored. We next address individual strategies for and organizational approaches to managing diversity and multiculturalism. Finally, we characterize and describe the fully multicultural organization.

The Nature of Diversity and Multiculturalism

We introduce the concept of organization culture in Chapter 3. We also note some of the basic managerial issues associated with doing business across national cultures in Chapter 5. At a much broader level, then, culture can be used to characterize the community of people who comprise an entire society. But a different set of issues involving social culture also arises within the boundaries of an organization. In other words, when the people comprising an organization represent different national cultures, their differences in values, beliefs, behaviors, customs, and attitudes pose unique opportunities and challenges for managers. These broad issues are generally referred to as *multiculturalism*.

A related area of interest is diversity. *Diversity* exists in a community of people when its members differ from one another along one or more important dimensions. These differences can obviously reflect the multicultural composition of a community. In the business world, however, the term *diversity* per se is more generally used to refer to demographic differences among people within a culture—differences in gender, age, ethnicity, and so forth. Diversity is not an absolute phenomenon, of course, wherein a group or organization is or is not diverse. Instead, diversity can be conceptualized as a continuum. If everyone in the community is exactly like everyone else, there is no diversity whatsoever. If everyone is different along every imaginable dimension, total diversity exists. In reality, of course, these extremes are more hypothetical than real. Most settings are characterized by a level of diversity somewhere between these extremes. Therefore, diversity should be thought of in terms of degree or level of diversity along relevant dimensions.

Organization culture, multiculturalism, and diversity are all closely interrelated. For example, the culture of an organization will affect the levels of diversity and multiculturalism that exist within its boundaries. Intel, for example, has an open and accepting culture that promotes diversity throughout its business. And similarities and differences arising from diversity and multicultural forces will also influence the culture of an organization. In addition, social culture and diversity are interrelated. For example, the norms reflected in a social culture will partially determine how that culture values demographic differences among people of that culture.

Each of these levels of culture represents important opportunities and challenges for managers. As we will see, if managers effectively understand, appreciate, and manage diversity and multiculturalism, their organization is more likely to be

multiculturalism
The broad issues associated with differences in values, beliefs, behaviors, customs, and attitudes held by people in different cultures.

diversity
Exists in a group or organization when its members differ from one another along one or more important dimensions, such as age, gender, or ethnicity

effective. But, if managers ignore cultural forces or, even worse, attempt to circumvent or control them, then their organization is almost certain to experience serious problems.

concept
CHECK

Define multiculturalism and diversity. | *How are multiculturalism and diversity related? How are they distinct?*

Diversity and Multiculturalism in Organizations

Beyond their strict definitions, diversity and multiculturalism essentially relate to differences among people. Therefore, because organizations today are becoming more diverse and multicultural, it is important that all managers understand the major trends and dimensions of diversity and multiculturalism.

Trends in Diversity and Multiculturalism

The most fundamental trend in diversity and multiculturalism is that virtually all organizations, simply put, are becoming more diverse and multicultural. The composition of their workforces is changing in many different ways. The basic reasons for this trend are illustrated in Figure 6.1.

One factor contributing specifically to increased diversity is changing demographics in the labor force. As more women and minorities have entered the labor force, for example, the available pool of talent from which organizations hire employees has changed in both size and composition. In 1955, for example, only 26.6 percent of the adult women in the United States worked outside the home. By 2005, however, that figure had grown to 59.1 percent.[2]

If talent within each segment of the labor pool is evenly distributed (for example, if the number of very talented men in the workforce as a percentage of all men in the workforce is the same as the number of very talented women in the labor force as a percentage of all women in the workforce), it follows logically that, over time, proportionately more women and proportionately fewer men will be hired by an organization. For example, suppose that a firm's top management team is 90 percent men and only 10 percent women. If the relevant labor pool is, say, 40 percent female, then women are clearly underrepresented in this firm. Over time, though, as men leave and are replaced by women at a percentage close to their representation in the labor pool, the composition of the top management team will gradually move closer to reflecting that labor pool.

A related factor contributing to diversity is organizations' increased awareness that they can improve the overall quality of their workforce by hiring and promoting the most talented people available. By casting a broader net in recruiting and looking beyond traditional sources for new

Workforce diversity is increasing in virtually all organizations today. For example, this group of sailors is working on the bridge of a new Navy transport ship, the USS San Antonio, as it leaves Port Aransas, Texas, on its maiden voyage. Not all that long ago, all three sailors would have been white males. But today's military reflects much greater gender and ethnic diversity.

employees, organizations are finding more broadly qualified and better-qualified employees from many different segments of society. Thus these organizations are finding that diversity can be a source of competitive advantage.[3]

Another reason for the increase in diversity is that both legislation and judicial decisions have forced organizations to hire more broadly. In earlier times, organizations in the United States were essentially free to discriminate against women, African Americans, and other minorities. Although not all organizations consciously or openly engaged in these practices, many firms nevertheless came to be dominated by white males. But starting with the passage of the Civil Rights Act in 1964, numerous laws have outlawed discrimination against these and most other groups. As we detail in Chapter 14, organizations must hire and promote people today solely on the basis of their qualifications.

A final factor contributing to increased multiculturalism in particular is the globalization movement. Organizations that have opened offices and related facilities in other countries have had to learn to deal with different customs, social norms, and mores. Strategic alliances and foreign ownership also contribute, as managers today are more likely to have job assignments in other countries or to work with foreign managers within their own countries. As employees and managers move from assignment to assignment across national boundaries, organizations and their subsidiaries within each country thus become more diverse and multicultural.

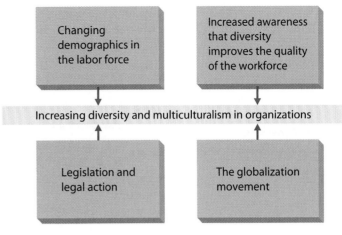

Figure 6.1

REASONS FOR INCREASING DIVERSITY AND MULTICULTURALISM

Diversity and multiculturalism are increasing in most organizations today for four basic reasons. These reasons promise to make diversity even greater in the future.

Dimensions of Diversity and Multiculturalism

As we indicate earlier, many different dimensions of diversity and multiculturalism can characterize an organization. In this section we discuss age, gender, ethnicity, and other dimensions of diversity.

Age Distributions   One important dimension of diversity in any organization is the age distribution of its workers. The average age of the U.S. workforce is gradually increasing and will continue to do so for the next several years. Figure 6.2 presents age distributions in the United States in 2000 and projected age distributions through the year 2025; over that span, the median age is expected to rise from 35.5 years to 38 years. Moreover, as shown in Figure 6.3, this trend is truly an international phenomenon, with Japan leading the way.

Several factors are contributing to this pattern. For one, the baby-boom generation (a term used to describe the unusually large number of people who were born in the 20-year period after World War II) continues to age. Declining birthrates among the post-baby-boom generations simultaneously account for smaller percentages of new entrants into the labor force. Another factor that contributes to the aging workforce is improved health and medical care. As a result of these improvements, people are able to remain productive and active for longer periods of time. Combined with higher legal limits for mandatory retirement,

Figure 6.2

AGE DISTRIBUTION TRENDS IN THE UNITED STATES

The U.S. population is gradually growing older. For example, in 1999 the median age in the United States was 35.5 years; by 2025, however, this figure will rise to 38 years. By that same year, more than one-third of the entire U.S. population will be over age 50.

Source: U.S. Census Bureau.

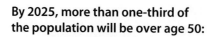

By 2025, more than one-third of the population will be over age 50:

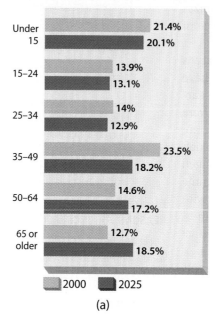

2000   2025

(a)

The median age will climb to 38:

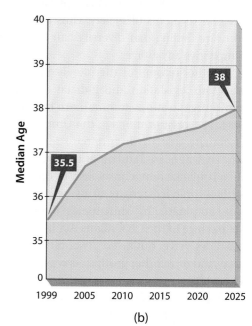

(b)

more and more people are working beyond the age at which they might have retired just a few years ago.

How does this trend affect organizations? Older workers tend to have more experience, to be more stable, and to make greater contributions to productivity than younger workers. On the other hand, despite the improvements in health and medical care, older workers are nevertheless likely to require higher levels of insurance coverage and medical benefits. And the declining labor pool of younger workers will continue to pose problems for organizations as they find fewer potential new entrants into the labor force.[4]

> "Practical intelligence stays with you. You don't lose it when you get older."
>
> Regina Colonia-Willner, psychologist and consultant
> (*BusinessWeek,* June 27, 2005, p. 82)

Gender As more and more women have entered the workforce, organizations have subsequently experienced changes in the relative proportions of male and female employees. In the United States, for example, the workforce in 1964 was 66 percent male and 34 percent female. By 2004 the proportions were around 54 percent male and 46 percent female.

These trends aside, a major gender-related problem that many organizations face today is the so-called glass ceiling. The *glass ceiling* describes a barrier that keeps women from advancing to top management positions in many organizations.[5] This ceiling is a real barrier that is difficult to break, but it is also so subtle as to be hard to see. Indeed, whereas women comprise over 38 percent of all managers, there are very few female CEOs among the thousand largest businesses in the United States. Similarly, the average pay of women in organizations is lower than that of men. Although the pay gap is gradually shrinking, inequalities are present nonetheless.

Why does the glass ceiling still seem to exist? One reason may be that real obstacles to advancement for women, such as subtle discrimination, may still exist in

glass ceiling

A perceived barrier that exists in some organizations that keeps women from advancing to top management positions

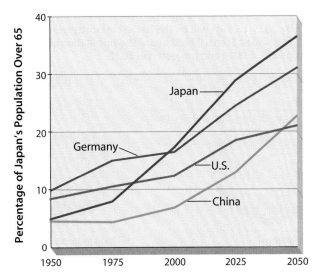

Figure 6.3

PERCENTAGE OF JAPAN'S POPULATION OVER 65

Aging populations represent new challenges for industrialized countries. As the proportion of working people drops, there are increased pressures on retirement funds, for example. An aging population also means higher healthcare costs. As this graph illustrates, the average age in Japan, Germany, China, and the United States continues to grow. Japan, with the world's longest average lifespan, has especially significant challenges ahead.

Source: From *Wall Street Journal*, February 11, 2003. Copyright © 2003 by Dow Jones & Co., Inc. Reproduced with permission of Dow Jones & Co., Inc. via Copyright Clearance Center.

some organizations.[6] Another is that many talented women choose to leave their job in a large organization and start their own business. Still another factor is that some women choose to suspend or slow their career progression to have children. But there are also many talented women continuing to work their way up the corporate ladder and getting closer and closer to a corporate "top spot."[7]

Ethnicity A third major dimension of cultural diversity in organizations is ethnicity. *Ethnicity* refers to the ethnic composition of a group or organization. Within the United States, most organizations reflect varying degrees of ethnicity, comprising whites, African Americans, Latinos, and Asians. Figure 6.4 shows the ethnic composition of the U.S. population in 1999 and as projected for the year 2025 in terms of these ethnic groups.[8]

The biggest projected changes involve whites and Latinos. In particular, the percentage of whites in the United States is expected to drop from 72 percent to 62.4 percent. At the same time, the percentage of Latinos is expected to climb from 11.5 percent to 17.6 percent.[9] The percentage of African Americans, Asians, and others is also expected to climb, but at lower rates. As with women, members of the African American, Latino, and Asian groups are generally underrepresented in the executive ranks of most organizations today. And their pay is similarly lower than might be expected. But, as is also the case for women, the differences are gradually disappearing as organizations fully embrace equal employment opportunity and recognize the higher overall level of talent available to them.[10]

ethnicity
The ethnic composition of a group or organization

Figure 6.4

ETHNICITY DISTRIBUTION TRENDS
IN THE UNITED STATES

*Ethnic diversity in the United States
is also increasing. For example,
although 72 percent of the U.S. population was white in 1999, this will
drop to 62.4 percent by 2025. Latinos will reflect the largest percentage increase, moving from 11.5
percent in 1999 to 17.6 percent of
the U.S. population by 2025.*

Source: U.S. Census Bureau.

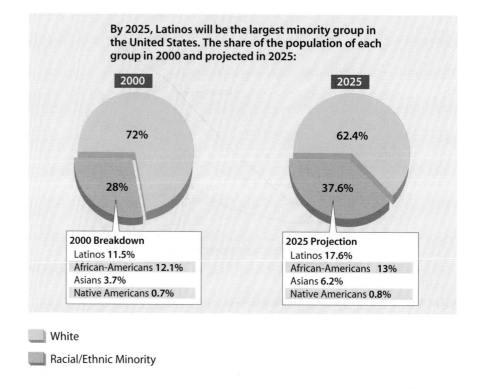

By 2025, Latinos will be the largest minority group in
the United States. The share of the population of each
group in 2000 and projected in 2025:

2000

72%

28%

2000 Breakdown
Latinos **11.5%**
African-Americans **12.1%**
Asians **3.7%**
Native Americans **0.7%**

2025

62.4%

37.6%

2025 Projection
Latinos **17.6%**
African-Americans **13%**
Asians **6.2%**
Native Americans **0.8%**

White

Racial/Ethnic Minority

Other Dimensions of Diversity   In addition to age, gender, and ethnicity, organizations are confronting other dimensions of diversity. Handicapped and physically
challenged employees are increasingly important in many organizations, especially
since the 1990 passage of the Americans with Disabilities Act. Different religious
beliefs also constitute an important dimension of diversity.[11] *Technology Toolkit*
provides more details about how disabled individuals can be productive members
of the workforce. And single parents, dual-career couples, gays and lesbians, people
with special dietary preferences (such as vegetarians), and people with different
political ideologies and viewpoints also represent major dimensions of diversity in
today's organizations.[12]

Multicultural Differences   In addition to these various diversity-related dimensions, organizations are increasingly being characterized by multicultural differences as well. Some organizations, especially international businesses, are actively
seeking to enhance the multiculturalism of their workforce. But even organizations
that are more passive in this regard may still become more multicultural because of
changes in the external labor market. Immigration into the United States is at its
highest rate since 1910, for example. Over 5 million people from Asia, Mexico,
Europe, and other parts of the world entered the United States between 1991 and
1995 alone.[13]

concept
CHECK

*Identify several dimensions of diversity
that are most relevant to organizations.*

*How might these dimensions be
related to one another?*

Technology Toolkit

Assistive Technology

Jamie developed multiple sclerosis and lost her strength. She uses a wheelchair and has movement in just one hand. Rick, a construction engineer, broke his back in an auto accident. He is now a paraplegic who also suffers from vocal cord damage that affects his ability to speak. Mumtaz has a degree in accounting but couldn't find a job because of severe visual impairment. These are tragic stories, but they have an upbeat ending. Jamie, Rick, and Mumtaz were all able to find rewarding, professional work, aided by assistive technology provided by their employers.

Jamie works from home, following up on customer service. Her standard PC is equipped with inexpensive off-the-shelf voice recognition software. She uses a voice-activated tape recorder and speakerphone, both purchased at Radio Shack. Rick manages complaints for building construction projects. At both home and office, he uses a mouse activated by one finger and an on-screen keyboard because his voice is too soft for most voice recognition software. Mumtaz found work in a bank. Her PC uses ZoomText, a screen magnification software bought off the shelf. ZoomText also includes voice recognition software, reducing the need for typing.

Adapting to the needs of employees with disabilities is an important human resources skill for corporations. Experts estimate that as many as 20 percent of individuals will suffer from disabilities at some time in their careers. While Jamie, Rick, and Mumtaz all suffer from permanent disabilities, some individuals will experience periods of disability. In addition, the aging of the labor force is another factor that corporations must consider, as older individuals are more likely to develop debilitating conditions like Parkinson's, which causes tremors, or arthritis, which makes movement painful.

Many companies, including Cisco, Nokia, Microsoft, and virtually every other high-tech firm, find that making and selling assistive hardware and software is rewarding and profitable. Many companies also find that employing individuals with disabilities is rewarding and provides critical sources of human resources during labor shortages. Disabled individuals, especially those whose employers purchase assistive technology, are often very loyal and motivated workers. Employers who are concerned about the cost of the technologies shouldn't worry—one-half total less than $50.

References: *Case Study Bulletin*, vol. 1, no. 5, Tech Connections website, Summer 2003, www.techconnections.org on March 6, 2006; "Cisco and Accessibility," Cisco website, www.cisco.com on March 6, 2006; "FAQ and Myths," Project Hired website, www.projecthired.org on March 6, 2006; "Nokia Helps Lead IT Industry to Customers with Disabilities," Nokia website, www.nokiaaccessibility.com on March 6, 2006; "ZoomText Provides Access for RBC Financial Group Employee with Visual Impairment," Microsoft website, www.microsoft.com on March 6, 2006.

Effects of Diversity and Multiculturalism in Organizations

There is no question that organizations are becoming ever more diverse and multicultural. But how does this affect organizations? As we see, diversity and management provide both opportunities and challenges for organizations. They also play a number of important roles in organizations today.

Diversity, Multiculturalism, and Competitive Advantage

Many organizations are finding that diversity and multiculturalism can be a source of competitive advantage in the marketplace. In general, six arguments have been proposed for how they contribute to competitiveness.[14] These are illustrated in Figure 6.5.

The *cost argument* suggests that organizations that learn to manage diversity and multiculturalism generally have higher levels of productivity and lower levels of turnover and absenteeism. Those organizations that do a poor job of managing

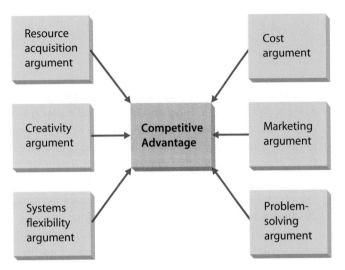

Figure 6.5

HOW DIVERSITY AND MULTICULTURALISM PROMOTE COMPETITIVE ADVANTAGE

Many organizations today are finding that diversity and multiculturalism can be sources of competitive advantage. Various arguments have been developed to support this viewpoint. For example, an African American sales representative for Revlon helped that firm improve its packaging and promotion for its line of darker skin-tone cosmetics.

diversity and multiculturalism, on the other hand, suffer from problems of lower productivity and higher levels of turnover and absenteeism. Because each of these factors has a direct impact on costs, the former types of organizations remain more competitive than will the latter. Ortho McNeil Pharmaceutical estimates that it has saved $500,000 by lowering turnover among women and ethnic minorities.[15]

The *resource acquisition argument* suggests that organizations that manage diversity and multiculturalism effectively become known among women and minorities as good places to work. These organizations are thus better able to attract qualified employees from among these groups. Given the increased importance of these groups in the overall labor force, organizations that can attract talented employees from all segments of society are likely to be more competitive.[16] Table 6.1 lists companies that have an especially good reputation as a good place for minorities to work.

The *marketing argument* suggests that organizations with a diverse and multicultural workforce are better able to understand different market segments than are less diverse organizations. For example, a cosmetics firm such as Avon, which wants to sell its products to women and African Americans, can better understand how to create such products and effectively market them if women and African American managers are available to provide inputs into product development, design, packaging, advertising, and so forth.[17] Similarly, both Sears and Target have profited by focusing part of their marketing efforts on building consumer awareness among Latinos.[18]

The *creativity argument* suggests that organizations with diverse and multicultural workforces are generally more creative and innovative than other organizations. If an organization is dominated by one population segment, it follows that its members will generally adhere to norms and ways of thinking that reflect that segment. Moreover, they have little insight or stimulus for new ideas that might be derived from different perspectives. The diverse and multicultural organization, in contrast, is characterized by multiple perspectives and ways of thinking and is therefore more likely to generate new ideas and ways of doing things.[19]

Related to the creativity argument is the *problem-solving argument*. Diversity and multiculturalism are accompanied by an increased pool of information. In virtually any organization there is some information that everyone has and other information that is unique to each individual. In an organization with little diversity, the larger pool of information is common, and the smaller pool is unique. But in a more diverse organization, the unique information is larger. Thus, because more information can be brought to bear on a problem, there is a higher probability that better solutions can be identified.[20]

Finally, the *systems flexibility argument* suggests that organizations must become more flexible as a way of managing a diverse and multicultural workforce. As a direct consequence, the overall organizational system also becomes more flexible. As we discuss in Chapters 3 and 13, organizational flexibility enables the

Table 6.1

AMERICA'S BEST COMPANIES FOR MINORITIES

Rank, 2003 (2002) Company 2002 Revenues (millions)	No. of Minorities		% Minorities	
	Board of Directors	**Top-paid 50**	**Officials and Managers**	**Workforce (Asian, Black, Hispanic, Native American)**
1 (5) **McDonald's** Oak Brook, Ill. **$15,406**	2 of 16	10	36.6%	52.6% (4.0%, 17.6%, 27.9%, 3.0%)
2 (1) **Fannie Mae** Washington, D.C. **$52,901**	5 of 17	11	32.6%	43.7% (13.6%, 25.5%, 4.2%, 0.4%)
3 (3) **Denny's** Spartanburg, S.C. **$1,128**	3 of 9	8	28.9%	46.7% (5.3%, 12.0%, 29.3%, 0.1%)
4 (11) **Union Bank of California** San Francisco **$2,592**	3 of 12	2	38.9%	55.8% (25.7%, 8.3%, 21.3%, 0.5%)
5 (2) **Sempra Energy** San Diego, Cal. **$6,020**	4 of 14	5	28.9%	47.6% (8.6%, 10.1%, 28.2%, 0.8%)
6 (7) **Southern California Edison** Rosemead, Cal. **$8,706**	2 of 11	9	28.5%	43.6% (8.5%, 8.7%, 25.5%, 0.9%)
7 (4) **SBC Communications** San Antonio **$43,138**	3 of 21	7	29.0%	37.8% (4.7%, 19.8%, 12.7%, 0.6%)
8 (9) **Freddie Mac** McLean, Va. **$39,663**	3 of 18	8	28.1%	32.5% (14.4%, 14.3%, 3.4%, 0.3%)
9 (15) **PepsiCo** Purchase, N.Y. **$25,112**	4 of 14	8	17.1%	26.9% (2.3%, 13.7%, 10.6%, 0.4%)
10 (6) **PNM Resources** Albuquerque **$1,169**	3 of 10	16	34.6%	47.9% (0.8%, 1.9%, 40.8%, 4.4%)

(continued)

Table 6.1

AMERICA'S BEST COMPANIES FOR MINORITIES (*continued*)

Rank, 2003 (2002) Company 2002 Revenues (millions)	No. of Minorities		% Minorities	
	Board of Directors	Top-paid 50	Officials and Managers	Workforce (Asian, Black, Hispanic, Native American)
11 (8) **U.S. Postal Service** Washington, D.C. **$66,463**	1 of 9	18	31.3%	36.3% (7.0%, 21.2%, 7.5%, 0.6%)
12 (17) **Wyndham International** Dallas **$1,871**	2 of 19	4	30.7%	61.6% (5.0%, 21.5%, 33.8%, 1.3%)
13 (14) **Xerox** Stamford, Conn. **$15,849**	2 of 8	12	22.2%	29.8% (5.3%, 15.6%, 8.1%, 0.7%)
14 (26) **Applied Materials** Santa Clara, Cal. **$5,062**	0 of 9	14	29.9%	38.9% (24.0%, 5.2%, 9.5%, 0.3%)

Source: Adapted from *Fortune*, July 7, 2003. Copyright © 2003 Time, Inc. All Rights Reserved.

organization to better respond to changes in its environment. Thus, by effectively managing diversity and multiculturalism within its workforce, an organization becomes better equipped to address its environment.[21]

Diversity, Multiculturalism, and Conflict

Unfortunately, diversity and multiculturalism in an organization can also create conflict. This conflict can arise for a variety of reasons.[22] One potential avenue for conflict occurs when an individual thinks that someone has been hired, promoted, or fired because of her or his diversity status. For example, suppose that a male executive loses a promotion to a female executive. If he believes that she was promoted because the organization simply wanted to have more female managers, rather than because she was the better candidate for the job, he will likely feel resentful toward both her and the organization.

Another source of conflict stemming from diversity or multiculturalism occurs through misunderstood, misinterpreted, or inappropriate interactions among people of different groups.[23] For example, suppose that a male executive tells a sexually explicit joke to a new female executive. He may be intentionally trying to embarrass her, he may be clumsily trying to show her that he treats everyone the same, or he may think he is making her feel part of the team. Regardless of his intent, however, if she finds the joke offensive, she will justifiably feel anger and

> "It strikes me as foreign to not have foreigners on a major U.S. corporation's board."
>
> Paul Anderson, Chairman of Duke Energy
> (*Wall Street Journal*, October 31, 2005, p. B1)

hostility. These feelings may be directed at only the offending individual or more generally toward the entire organization if she believes that its culture facilitates such behaviors. And, of course, sexual harassment is both unethical and illegal.

Conflict can also arise as a result of other elements of multiculturalism. For example, when a U.S. manager publicly praises a Japanese employee for his outstanding work, the action stems from the dominant cultural belief in the United States that such recognition is important and rewarding. But because the Japanese culture places a much higher premium on group loyalty and identity than on individual accomplishment, the employee likely will feel ashamed and embarrassed. Thus a well-intentioned action may backfire and result in unhappiness. A joint venture between IBM (a U.S. company), Siemens (a German company), and Toshiba (a Japanese company) had conflicts among team members attributed to cultural differences in work hours, working styles, and interpersonal relations.[24]

Conflict may also arise as a result of fear, distrust, or individual prejudice. Members of the dominant group in an organization may worry that newcomers from other groups pose a personal threat to their own positions in the organization. For example, when U.S. firms have been taken over by Japanese firms, U.S. managers have sometimes been resentful about or hostile toward Japanese managers assigned to work with them. People may also be unwilling to accept people who are different from themselves. And personal bias and prejudices are still very real among some people today and can lead to potentially harmful conflict.

Several high-profile problems involving diversity and multiculturalism have focused attention on the potential for conflict and how important it is that managers respond appropriately when problems occur. Shoney's, Inc., a southern restaurant chain, was charged with racism throughout its managerial ranks. At Texaco, senior executives used racial slurs on a tape subsequently released to the public. A class-action lawsuit against the financial brokerage giant Smith Barney alleged widespread hostilities and discrimination toward women throughout the firm. Wal-Mart is currently under scrutiny for similar practices.[25] In each of these cases, fortunately, the organization involved has undertaken major programs designed to eliminate such problems in the future. Denny's, for example, has taken such aggressive action that it has now become recognized as one of the best companies in the United States for minorities.[26]

---

concept
CHECK

How does diversity promote competitive advantage?

Which causes of diversity-related conflict are most likely to disappear in the future?

Managing Diversity and Multiculturalism in Organizations

Because of the tremendous potential that diversity and multiculturalism hold for competitive advantage, as well as the possible consequences of associated conflict, much attention has been focused in recent years on how individuals and organizations can better manage diversity and multiculturalism. In the sections that follow, we first discuss individual strategies for dealing with diversity and multiculturalism, and then summarize organizational approaches to managing diversity and multiculturalism.

Individual Strategies

One important element of managing diversity and multiculturalism in an organization consists of things that individuals themselves can do. The four basic attitudes that individuals can strive for are understanding, empathy, tolerance, and willingness to communicate.

Understanding   The first of these is understanding the nature and meaning of diversity and multiculturalism. Some managers, for example, have taken the basic concepts of equal employment opportunity to an unnecessary extreme. They know that, by law, they cannot discriminate against people on the basis of sex, race, and so forth. Thus, in following this mandate, they come to believe that they must treat everyone the same.

But this belief can cause problems when translated into workplace behaviors among people after they have been hired, because people are not the same. Although people need to be treated fairly and equitably, managers must understand that differences among people do, in fact, exist. Thus any effort to treat everyone the same, without regard for their fundamental human differences, will lead only to problems. Managers must understand that cultural factors cause people to behave in different ways and that these differences should be accepted.

Empathy   Related to understanding is empathy. People in an organization should try to understand the perspectives of others. For example, suppose a woman joins a group that has traditionally comprised white men. Each man may be a little self-conscious about how to act toward the new member and may be interested in making her feel comfortable and welcome. But they may be able to do this even more effectively by empathizing with how she may feel. For example, she may feel disappointed or elated about her new assignment, she may be confident or nervous about her position in the group, or she may be experienced or inexperienced in working with male colleagues. By learning more about her feelings, the group members can further facilitate their ability to work together effectively.

Tolerance   A third related individual strategy for dealing with diversity and multiculturalism is tolerance. Even though people learn to understand others, and even though they may try to empathize with others, the fact remains that they still may not accept or enjoy some aspect of their behavior. For example, one organization reported that it had experienced considerable conflict among its U.S. and Israeli employees. The Israeli employees always seemed to want to argue about every issue that arose. The U.S. managers preferred to conduct business more harmoniously and became uncomfortable with the conflict. Finally, after considerable discussion, it was learned that many of the Israeli employees simply enjoyed arguing and saw it as part of getting the work done. The firm's U.S. employees still do not enjoy the arguing, but they are more willing to tolerate it as a fundamental cultural difference between themselves and their colleagues from Israel.[27]

Willingness to Communicate   A final individual approach to dealing with diversity and multiculturalism is communication. Problems often get magnified over these issues because people are afraid or otherwise unwilling to openly discuss issues that relate to diversity or multiculturalism. For example, suppose that a young employee has a habit of making jokes about the age of an older colleague. Perhaps the young colleague means no harm and is just engaging in what she sees as good-natured kidding. But the older employee may find the jokes offensive. If the two do not communicate, the jokes will continue, and the resentment will grow. Eventually, what started as a minor problem may erupt into a much bigger one.

For communication to work, it must work two ways. If a person wonders whether a certain behavior on her or his part is offensive to someone else, the curious individual should just ask. Similarly, if someone is offended by the behavior of another person, he or she should explain to the offending individual how the behavior is perceived and request that it stop. As long as such exchanges are friendly, low key, and nonthreatening, they will generally have a positive outcome. Of course, if the same message is presented in an overly combative manner or if a person continues to engage in offensive behavior after having been asked to stop, problems will only escalate. At this point, third parties within the organization may have to intervene. Most organizations today, in fact, have one or more systems in place to address questions and problems that arise as a result of diversity. We now turn our attention to various ways that organizations can better manage diversity.

Organizational Approaches

Whereas individuals are important in managing diversity and multiculturalism, the organization itself must play a fundamental role.[28] Through the organization's various policies and practices, people in the organization come to understand what behaviors are and are not appropriate. Diversity and multicultural training is an even more direct method for managing diversity. And the organization's culture is the ultimate context in which diversity and multiculturalism must be addressed.

Organizational Policies   The starting point in managing diversity and multiculturalism is the policies that an organization adopts that directly or indirectly affect how people are treated. The extent to which an organization embraces the premise of equal employment opportunity, for instance, will help determine the potential diversity within it. But the organization that follows the law to the letter and practices only passive discrimination differs from the organization that actively seeks a diverse and varied workforce.

Like many families today, Madhavi Nerurkar and her husband face many challenges in their quest to make ends meet. Just as they bought their first home and had their first child, he lost his job. His new job paid less money and also required that he travel a lot. Hence, Madhavi needed to find a job to help with finances, but also needed flexibility to pick up their son from childcare. Fortunately, her new employer, RFB&D, recognizes the value of diversity and has been willing to accommodate her needs.

Another aspect of organizational policies that affects diversity and multiculturalism is how the organization addresses and responds to problems that arise from differences among people. For example, consider the example of a manager charged with sexual harassment. If the organization's policies put an excessive burden of proof on the individual being harassed and invoke only minor sanctions against the guilty party, it is sending a clear signal about the importance of such matters. But the organization that has a balanced set of policies for addressing questions like sexual harassment sends its employees a message that diversity and individual rights and privileges are important.

Indeed, perhaps the major policy through which an organization can reflect its stance on diversity and multiculturalism is its mission statement. If the organization's mission statement articulates a clear and direct commitment to differences among people, it follows that everyone who comes in contact with that mission statement will grow to understand and accept the importance of diversity and multiculturalism, at least to that particular organization.

Organizational Practices Organizations can also help manage diversity and multiculturalism through a variety of ongoing practices and procedures. Avon's creation of networks for various groups represents one example of an organizational practice that fosters diversity. In general, the idea is that, because diversity and multiculturalism are characterized by differences among people, organizations can more effectively manage that diversity by following practices and procedures that are based on flexibility rather than on rigidity.

Benefits packages, for example, can be structured to better accommodate individual situations. An employee who is part of a dual-career, childless couple may require relatively little health insurance (perhaps because his spouse's employer provides more complete coverage) and may request vacation time that coincides with those of his spouse. An employee who is a single parent may need a wide variety of health insurance coverage and prefer to schedule his vacation time to coincide with school holidays.

Flexible working hours are also a useful organizational practice for accommodating diversity. Differences in family arrangements, religious holidays, cultural events, and so forth may dictate that employees have some degree of flexibility in when they work. For example, a single parent may need to leave the office every day at 4:30 P.M. to pick up the children from their day-care center. An organization that truly values diversity will make every reasonable attempt to accommodate such a need.

Organizations can also facilitate diversity and multiculturalism by making sure that their important committees and executive teams are diverse. Even if diversity exists within the broader organizational context, an organization that does not reflect diversity in groups such as committees and teams implies that diversity is not a fully ingrained element of its culture. In contrast, if all major groups and related work assignments reflect diversity, the message is a quite different one.

diversity and multicultural training
Training that is designed to better enable members of an organization to function in a diverse and multicultural workforce

Diversity and Multicultural Training Many organizations are finding that diversity and multicultural training is an effective means for managing diversity and minimizing its associated conflict. More specifically, ***diversity and multicultural training*** is designed to better enable members of an organization to function in a diverse and multicultural workplace.[29] This training can take a variety of forms. For example, many organizations find it useful to help people learn more about their similarities to and differences from others. Men and women can be taught to work together more effectively and can gain insights into how their own behaviors affect and are interpreted by others. In one organization, a diversity training program helped male managers gain insights into how various remarks they made to one another could be interpreted by others as being sexist. In the same organization, female managers learned how to point out their discomfort with those remarks without appearing overly hostile.[30]

This group of Wells Fargo managers is going through a diversity training course in California. Diversity training is one strategy for helping to manage and promote diversity in organizations. While some experts question its effectiveness, many businesses nevertheless encourage or require their employees to participate in such training.

Similarly, white and African American managers may need training to better understand each other. Managers at Mobil Corporation (now a part of ExxonMobil) once noticed that four black colleagues never seemed to eat lunch together. After a diversity training program, they came to realize that the black managers felt that, if they ate together, their white colleagues would be overly curious about what they might be talking about. Thus they avoided close association with one another because they feared calling attention to themselves.[31]

Some organizations even go so far as to provide language training for their employees as a vehicle for managing diversity and multiculturalism. Motorola, for example, provides English-language training for its foreign employees on assignment in the United States. At Pace Foods in San Antonio, with a total payroll of over 450 employees, staff meetings and employee handbooks are translated into Spanish for the benefit of the company's 200 or so Latino employees.

Organization Culture   The ultimate test of an organization's commitment to managing diversity and multiculturalism, as discussed earlier in this chapter, is its culture.[32] Regardless of what managers say or put in writing, unless there is a basic and fundamental belief that diversity and multiculturalism are valued, it cannot ever become a truly integral part of an organization. An organization that really wants to promote diversity and multiculturalism must shape its culture so that it clearly underscores top management's commitment to and support of diversity and multiculturalism in all of its forms throughout every part of the organization. With top management's support, however, and reinforced with a clear and consistent set of organizational policies and practices, diversity and multiculturalism can become a fundamental part of an organization.[33]

concept
CHECK

Name the individual strategies for managing diversity and multiculturalism in organizations.

In your opinion, which organizational approaches to managing diversity and multiculturalism are most and least likely to be effective? Why?

Toward the Multicultural Organization

---

multicultural organization
An organization that has achieved high levels of diversity, is able to fully capitalize on the advantages of diversity, and has few diversity-related problems

---

Many organizations today are grappling with cultural diversity. We note in Chapter 5 that although many organizations are becoming increasingly global, no truly global organization exists. In similar fashion, although organizations are becoming ever more diverse, few are truly multicultural. The ***multicultural organization*** has achieved high levels of diversity, is able to fully capitalize on the advantages of diversity, and has few diversity-related problems. One article describes the six basic characteristics of such an organization.[34] These characteristics are illustrated in Figure 6.6.

First, the multicultural organization is characterized by *pluralism*. This means that every group represented in an organization works to better understand every other group. Thus African American employees try to understand white employees, and white employees try just as hard to understand their African American colleagues. In addition, every group represented within an organization has the potential to influence the organization's culture and fundamental norms.

Second, the multicultural organization achieves *full structural integration*. Full structural integration suggests that the diversity within an organization is a complete and accurate reflection of the organization's external labor market. If around half of the labor market is female, then about half of the organization's employees are female. Moreover, this same proportion is reflected at all levels of the organization. There are no glass ceilings or other subtle forms of discrimination.

Third, the multicultural organization achieves *full integration of the informal network*. This characteristic suggests that there are no barriers to entry or participation in any organizational activity. For example, people enter and exit lunch groups, social networks, communication grapevines, and other informal aspects of

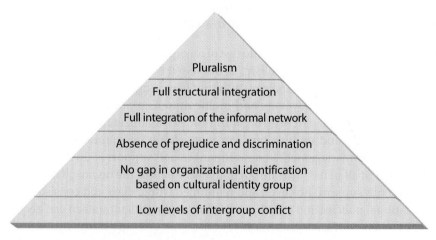

Figure 6.6
THE MULTICULTURAL ORGANIZATION

Few, if any, organizations have become truly multicultural. At the same time, more and more organizations are moving in this direction. When an organization becomes multicultural, it reflects the six basic characteristics shown here.

Source: Based on Taylor H. Cox, "The Multicultural Organization," *Academy of Management Executive,* May 1991, pp. 34–47. Reprinted with permission.

organizational activity without regard to age, gender, ethnicity, or other dimension of diversity.

Fourth, the multicultural organization is characterized by an *absence of prejudice and discrimination*. No traces of bias exist, and prejudice is eliminated. Discrimination is not practiced in any shape, form, or fashion. And discrimination is nonexistent, not because it is illegal, but because of the lack of prejudice and bias. People are valued, accepted, and rewarded purely on the basis of their skills and what they contribute to the organization.

Fifth, in the multicultural organization there is *no gap in organizational identification based on cultural identity group*. In many organizations today, people tend to make presumptions about organizational roles based on group identity. For example, many people walking into an office and seeing a man and woman conversing tend to assume that the woman is the secretary and the man is the manager. No such tendencies exist in the multicultural organization. People recognize that men and women are equally likely to be managers or secretaries.

Finally, there are *low levels of intergroup conflict* in the multicultural organization. We noted earlier that conflict is a likely outcome of increased diversity. The multicultural organization has evolved beyond this point to a state of virtually no conflict among people who differ. People within the organization fully understand, empathize with, have tolerance for, and openly communicate with everyone else. Values, premises, motives, attitudes, and perceptions are so well understood by everyone that any conflict that does arise is over meaningful and work-related issues as opposed to differences in age, gender, ethnicity, or other dimensions of diversity.

---

concept CHECK

What dimensions will reflect the multicultural organization?

Do you think a truly multicultural business organization will ever exist? Why or why not?

Summary of Learning Objectives and Key Points

1. Describe the nature of diversity and multiculturalism.
   - Diversity exists in a community of people when its members differ from one another along one or more important dimensions.
   - Multiculturalism is reflected when the people comprising an organization represent different cultures and have different values, beliefs, behaviors, customs, and attitudes.

2. Identify and describe the major trends and dimensions of diversity and multiculturalism in organizations.
   - Diversity and multiculturalism are increasing in organizations today because of changing demo-

   graphics, the desire by organizations to improve their workforces, legal pressures, and increased globalization.
   - There are several important dimensions of diversity, including age, gender, and ethnicity. The overall age of the workforce is increasing.

3. Discuss the primary effects of diversity and multiculturalism in organizations.
   - Diversity and multiculturalism can be a source of competitive advantage (cost, resource acquisition, marketing, creativity, problem-solving, and systems flexibility arguments).

- Diversity and multiculturalism can also be sources of conflict in an organization.
4. Describe individual strategies for and organizational approaches to managing diversity and multiculturalism in organizations.
   - Individual strategies include understanding, empathy, tolerance, and willingness to communicate.
   - Major organizational approaches are through policies, practices, diversity training, and culture.

5. Discuss the characteristics of the fully multicultural organization.
   - The major dimensions that characterize organizations as they eventually achieve this state are pluralism, full structural integration, full integration of the informal network, an absence of prejudice and discrimination, no gap in organizational identification based on cultural identity group, and low levels of intergroup conflict attributable to diversity.

Discussion Questions

Questions for Review

1. What are the primary dimensions of diversity?
2. Summarize the six arguments used to describe how the effective management of diversity can lead to a competitive advantage.
3. Discuss the four basic individual approaches and the four basic organizational approaches to diversity and multiculturalism.
4. What are the characteristics of a multicultural organization?

Questions for Analysis

5. In your opinion, are the "other" dimensions of diversity likely to have a greater or a lesser impact than the basic dimensions? Explain your answer.
6. The text outlines many different advantages of diversity and multiculturalism in organizations. Can you think of any disadvantages?
7. Think of a time when issues of diversity or multiculturalism created an advantage or led to positive outcomes at school or work. What actions did the participants take to lead to that positive outcome?

Questions for Application

8. Visit the registrar's office or admissions office at your college or university, or find information about admissions from your school's website. What actions, if any, is your school taking to increase diversity? If it is not taking any action, why do you think that is the case? If it is taking action, do you think the actions are likely to be effective, and why?
9. Consider the case of an employee who is part of a minority group on one dimension of diversity. What are some of the potential problems that this

employee might encounter? What are some ways that this employee's supervisor can help alleviate these problems?
10. Assume that you work for a large multinational organization. You have just learned that you are being transferred overseas, to an office in which you will be the first person of your ethnicity to work there. What steps might you take before you go to minimize problems that your presence might cause?

Building Effective Technical Skills

Exercise Overview

Technical skills are the skills necessary to accomplish or understand the specific kind of work being done in an organization. This exercise asks you to use the Internet to gather information about issues of diversity and multiculturalism, and then to consider those issues from a manager's point of view.

Exercise Background

An organization's definition and measurement of diversity are crucial to determining how diversity concerns are addressed. Assume that you are a top manager at your college or university. Your school is committed to maintaining an appropriate level of diversity within the student body. You are assigned the task of making a report to the school's policy-making board, describing the school's current level of diversity and any areas of concern.

Exercise Task

1. Use the Internet to gather information about the gender and ethnic diversity of your school's student body. Then gather information about your school's workforce—the faculty and staff. (*Hint:* Your school's webpages related to admissions and human resources might be helpful.)
2. Use the Internet to gather information about the diversity of your school's state and local communities, and about the United States as a nation.

(*Hint:* The U.S. Census Bureau's webpages devoted to Census 2000 have information for country, states, and counties. See **www.census.gov**.)
3. Based on the information you have gathered, is your school's student body at the appropriate level of diversity? Tell why or why not.
4. What are some areas, if any, that could reflect greater diversity among your school's student body?

Building Effective Time-Management Skills

Exercise Overview

Time-management skills refer to the manager's ability to prioritize work, to work efficiently, and to delegate appropriately. This exercise helps you explore your personal values and their relationship to the importance you place on various tasks.

Exercise Background

Each person is unique, based on unique characteristics, background, heritage, relationships, and experiences. Our uniqueness extends to our values, as each of us places more or less importance on different aspects of our life. For some, religion may be the primary motivator, whereas for others, a marriage or an occupation is extremely important.

Values play a key role in helping to assign priorities to tasks in daily life. In an ideal world, more time would be spent on tasks of greater importance and less time on relatively unimportant tasks. However, for many, mundane demands may take precedence. This in-class demonstration serves to clarify values and to encourage values-based time management.

Exercise Task

1. Listen as your instructor provides a demonstration to the class.
2. What are your "rocks"? What are your "pebbles"? What are your "grains of sand"?
3. Based on the above classification, what are your most important personal values?
4. Do you usually spend more time on tasks that support your most important values? Why or why not?
5. Describe some actions that you could take to ensure that more of your time is spent on tasks related to your most important values.

Building Effective Decision-Making Skills

Exercise Overview

Decision-making skills refer to the manager's ability to recognize and effectively define problems and opportunities and then to select an appropriate course of action for solving problems and capitalizing on opportunities. This exercise focuses on decision making about issues related to diversity and multiculturalism.

Exercise Background

For years your firm had relatively little diversity. The 1,000-member workforce was almost exclusively white and male. But in recent years you have succeeded in increasing diversity substantially. Almost one-third of your employees are now female, and over 40 percent are Latino or African American.

Unfortunately, your firm has recently met with some financial setbacks. You believe that you have no choice but to lay off about 300 employees for a period of at least six months. If everything goes well, you expect to be able to bring them back after six months.

Exercise Task

With the background information above as context, do the following:

1. Develop a layoff plan that will not substantially reduce your firm's diversity.

2. Decide how you will communicate your decision to the workforce.

3. What obstacles do you foresee in implementing your decision?

CHAPTER CLOSING CASE

UNIVERSITIES BECOME MORE DIVERSE, SLOWLY

Historically, universities have encouraged atmospheres of privilege and wealth, but over the last 30 years, the trend has intensified. At the 146 most selective universities in the United States, just 3 percent of the students come from families in the lowest economic quartile. Students from the top quartile make up 74 percent of the student bodies. This disparity has been particularly hard on ethnic minorities, who are overrepresented in lower economic brackets, resulting in colleges full of affluent, white students. The situation punishes gifted students from poorer backgrounds and contributes to a growing division between social classes.

Universities, in theory, prefer ethnically and economically balanced student bodies. Yet there are three problems that must be overcome. The first problem concerns admissions—how to encourage minorities to apply, how to appropriately consider race in a complex admissions process, and how to eliminate traditions that stand in the way of equality. For example, when "legacy" admissions processes are used, the racial distribution favors whites. Poor college preparation is also an issue for low-income students. Professors do not usually have the skills to bring a poorly prepared student up to speed.

Universities are improving admissions, but funding lags behind. Lower-class students, even with a "full ride," do not have the resources to purchase the extras, such as computers, trips home, or cell phones. Colleges, facing rising costs, cannot afford to have too many students on scholarship. One approach is to ask wealthy alumni and parents to contribute to an endowment fund marked for use by poorer students. They are likely to help because their contributions mean that there is sufficient funding to add extra enrollment slots, rather than taking a slot from one of the more elite students.

However, both the admissions and funding problems pale in comparison to the difficulty associated with integrating low-income students into the university culture, which is so strongly associated with affluence. A student from a disadvantaged background says, "When I heard my peers talking about Abercrombie, I thought they were talking about a person." Students with differing class backgrounds have different perceptions, attitudes, and customs. Everything, even table manners, becomes a means of sorting people by status. To make matters worse, some universities solve the funding problem by giving work-study jobs to lower-income students, who often find themselves serving meals to their peers in the dining hall.

Amherst is one of the first elite institutions to radically rethink the way it recruits and supports minority students. When professor Anthony Marx became the college's president in 2003, he brought a passion for equality in education. He worked building colleges in South Africa and saw some of his colleagues jailed, tortured, and murdered. Today, he says, "If you can [educate] kids who have suffered under apartheid, then you can't tell me we can't do better in the U.S., with all the resources we have." Marx vowed to save 25 percent of the admits for low-income students, a remarkable percentage. He's also sending admissions staff to low-income schools, raising $500 million in endowed funds, setting up tutoring centers, and holding fireside chats with diverse groups of students to discuss inequality.

West Point, the United States Military Academy, trains this nation's army officer corps. The majority of officers are white, but the army would like to change that. It too has a program for recruiting low-income students. The government covers all tuition and housing costs for every cadet, so funding is not a problem. Where West Point really excels is in its ability to prepare students for rigorous academic work, thanks to the U.S.M.A. Prep School. When a promising student does not have an adequate academic background, the Academy will send him or her to the Prep School for nine months' of remedial work. Prep School graduates find that the experience eases their transition into university life and gives them confidence.

Increasing diversity at colleges is certainly a benefit for those underprivileged students who would not otherwise have a chance for a university education. It's also a benefit to the other students, who learn to work with those from different backgrounds, an important skill in today's global, multicultural world. The biggest benefit, however, may be to U.S. society, which could see the class gap begin to close and individuals begin to be rewarded for what they can do, not for the colors of their skin or the thickness of their wallets.

CASE QUESTIONS

1. What advantages will come to universities that have high levels of diversity? What are some of the problems that highly diverse universities might face?

2. What types of approaches to diversity management are used at Amherst University and West Point?

3. Why does diversity in colleges and universities have such a large impact on diversity in government, business, and every other sector of society?

CASE REFERENCES

Francesca Di Meglio, "Building a Fire Under the Melting Pot," *BusinessWeek,* March 16, 2005, www.businessweek.com on March 6, 2006; Richard D. Kahlenberg, *America's Untapped Resource: Low-Income Students in Higher Education* (New York: Century Foundation Press, 2004); William Symond, "The Thinking at Harvard, West Point, and Smith," *BusinessWeek,* February 27, 2006, www.businessweek.com on March 6, 2006; William C. Symonds, "Amherst's A List: Affluence, Achievement, Athletics," *BusinessWeek,* February 27, 2006, www.businessweek.com on March 6, 2006; William C. Symonds, "Campus Revolutionary," *BusinessWeek,* February 27, 2006, pp. 65–70.

YOU MAKE THE CALL

The Leadership of Debra Lee

1. In general, do you think that an ethnically oriented business like BET is most effectively led by a member of that ethnic group? Why or why not?

2. Are there other ethnic groups that might profitably be served by a targeted television network?

3. What pitfalls must BET avoid if it is to maintain its success?

4. Compare and contrast the challenges faced by managers leading television channels targeted toward all ethnic groups versus managers leading BET.

Test Prepper

Choose the correct answer. Answers are found at the back of the book.

1. T   F   The average age of the U.S. workforce is gradually increasing.

2. T   F   The term *glass ceiling* describes an organization that allow outsiders to observe its inner workings.

3. T   F   The creativity argument for diversity suggests that organizations that manage diversity well will lower costs and increase productivity.

4. T   F   The best approach to diversity is to treat everyone exactly the same, without regard for their fundamental differences.

5. T   F   Perhaps the major policy by which an organization can reflect its stance on diversity is its code of ethics.

6. The marketing argument for diversity suggests organizations with a diverse and multicultural workforce
   - A. are better able to understand different market segments.
   - B. have access to an increased pool of information to solve problems.
   - C. become known among women and minorities as good places to work.
   - D. have higher levels of productivity and lower levels of turnover.
   - E. become more flexible and adaptable to changes in the market.

7. Conflict can arise in diverse and multicultural organization for all of the following reasons EXCEPT
   - A. misinterpreted actions among different groups of people.
   - B. organizational flexibility and adaptation to the environment.
   - C. different dominant cultural beliefs across ethnic groups.
   - D. fear or distrust across diverse groups.
   - E. personal bias and prejudice.

8. Individual employees can help better manage diversity by striving for each of the following attitudes EXCEPT
   - A. assimilation.
   - B. understanding.
   - C. empathy.
   - D. tolerance.
   - E. willingness to communicate.

9. The ultimate test of an organization's commitment to managing diversity and multiculturalism is
   - A. how many of its employees have completed diversity and multiculturalism training.
   - B. the reputation it has in the market.
   - C. its profitability.
   - D. the attitude of the CEO.
   - E. its culture.

10. A truly multicultural organization is characterized by a level of diversity that is a complete and accurate reflection of the organization's external labor market, at all levels of the organization. This is
    - A. pluralism.
    - B. full structural integration.
    - C. an absence of prejudice and discrimination.
    - D. full integration of the informal network.
    - E. complete organizational identification of cultural identity groups.

Basic Elements of Planning and Decision Making

chapter 7

FIRST THINGS FIRST

Steering Citigroup

"[It's] the catch-and-release decision making process: I thought we made that decision already, but here it is again, swimming around, like a fish."

—A FORMER TOP EXECUTIVE, CITIGROUP

Charles Prince took on the leadership of Citigroup, the world's largest financial services firm, knowing that the company needed change. The last several years had brought a wave of scandals to Citi and resulted in the resignation of the former CEO, Sandy Weill. To the surprise of many, Weill handpicked Prince, Citi's general counsel, as his successor. As he assumed the top spot in 2003, Prince described a number of new strategic goals and plans.

The change in leadership is the perfect time to make sweeping changes. Changes in the banking environment mandate updates too. Prince keeps a model ship in his office, one that was displayed by former Citibank CEO Walter Wriston. Wriston headed Citi in the 1970s, when shipping finance was the bank's most profitable service. Today Citigroup doesn't even have a shipping finance

LEARNING OBJECTIVES

After studying this chapter, you should be able to:

1. Summarize the function of decision making and the planning process.
2. Discuss the purpose of organizational goals, identify different kinds of goals, discuss who sets goals, and describe how to manage multiple goals.
3. Identify different kinds of organizational plans, note the time frames for planning, discuss who plans, and describe contingency planning.
4. Discuss how tactical plans are developed and executed.
5. Describe the basic types of operational plans used by organizations.
6. Identify the major barriers to goal setting and planning, how organizations overcome those barriers, and how to use goals to implement plans.

Charles Prince, Citigroup's Chief Executive Officer, has been developing plans and making decisions to enhance the firm's competitiveness.

department. Since the 1970s, Citigroup has been through dozens of acquisitions and divestitures. "The bank that Walter ran 30 years ago has disappeared," Prince states. "Citi is a battleship that needed to be turned around."

Citigroup needs an ethical culture shift. Prince defends Citi, saying, "Bad behavior is aberrational." At the same time, he is working to develop higher standards and stricter controls. The effort will certainly take time. Professor Rakesh Khurana says, "The culture can't change overnight. Citi is deeply rooted in past decisions and strongly held belief systems." Indeed, in 2005 two new scandals erupted, one in private banking in Japan and another over bond trading in the United Kingdom. Prince quickly apologized and fired the responsible managers immediately. Yet cynics note that both of these problems had been brewing for years, when Prince was the top lawyer for Citigroup.

Prince's two most important strategic goals for Citi are to stop the scandals and to grow the company. In a recent interview, Prince said his most urgent task was to "keep Citigroup out of the headlines." The culture change is Prince's approach to achieving that goal. His second task is to find a way to encourage growth at the already gigantic firm. Weill relied on acquisitions to grow Citi, making dozens in his five-year tenure as CEO. Prince believes that Citigroup has reached the limit of growth through acquisition, joking, "the only way we could do a transformational acquisition would be to buy Canada." Instead, he wants the company to grow internally, making change incrementally.

Citi's strategic plans must be updated to reflect its new goals. Prince hopes ethical improvements will result from tighter controls and better support from top management. To support internal growth, the company's culture will have to become more centralized and more efficient. Citi will also have to increase overseas revenues. The strategic changes are costly and have yet to show any results. Industry analyst John McDonald gives Prince credit for "making decisions that depress current results for the benefit of long-term growth potential."

Prince has always worked in staff positions, and has never had any operational banking experience. That makes it difficult for him to earn credibility and trust from the company's banking managers, who are responsible for the planning process at Citigroup. An effective planning process is critically important. To get a better perspective, Prince included more managers in the process. At the same time, he streamlined the process by creating some new higher-level committees. "Things get kicked around so much in these committees that many decisions are being made more slowly than ever," says one former top executive. "[It's] the catch-and-release decision making process: I thought we made that decision already, but here it is again, swimming around, like a fish."

Understandably, Prince faces many barriers in changing the values and strategic direction at Citigroup. The complex environment, resource constraints, and resistance to change all play a part. Hopefully, Prince's approach of communication, incremental change, inclusion, and consistency will win over Citi managers and investors. Then Prince may find that although the Citi ship is large and unwieldy, he can steer it into more favorable waters.[1]

Citigroup's Charles Prince took over a firm badly in need of an overhaul. To jump-start his efforts, he made several critical decisions as to how the firm's performance could be improved. For instance, he has worked to overhaul how the company develops plans and to focus on the broad strategic goals of enhancing ethical conduct and growing the business through expansion of current operations. Operationally, this has translated into more aggressive responses to unethical practices, a halt to acquisitions, and a focus on efficiency. As we note in Chapter 1, planning and decision making comprise the first managerial functions that organizations must address. This chapter is the first of four that explore the planning process in detail. We begin by briefly relating decision making and planning, and then explaining the planning process that most organizations follow. We then discuss the nature of organizational goals and introduce the basic concepts of planning. Next we discuss tactical and operational planning more fully. Finally, we conclude with a discussion of how to manage the goal-setting and planning processes.

Decision making and planning are vital processes in any organization. For instance, consider the myriad decisions and planning activities that go into preparations for hosting the Olympic Games. This is National Stadium, which will host several events in the 2008 Olympics in Beijing, China. Work on this single venue requires the efforts of dozens of managers and hundreds of workers. Moreover, the work must be coordinated so that the stadium is completed on time and within its budget. Complicating things even further for China's Olympic officials is the fact that this is only 1 of 31 competition venues that must be completed.

Decision Making and the Planning Process

Decision making is the cornerstone of planning. A few years ago, Procter & Gamble (P&G) set a goal of doubling its revenues over a ten-year period. The firm's top managers could have adopted an array of alternative options, including increasing revenues by only 25 percent or increasing revenues threefold. The time frame for the projected revenue growth could also have been somewhat shorter or longer than the ten-year period that was actually specified. Alternatively, the goal could have included diversifying into new markets, cutting costs, or buying competing businesses. Thus P&G's exact mix of goals and plans for growth rate and time frame reflected choices from among a variety of alternatives.

Clearly, then, decision making is the catalyst that drives the planning process. An organization's goals follow from decisions made by various managers. Likewise, deciding on the best plan for achieving particular goals also reflects a decision to adopt one course of action as opposed to others. We discuss decision making per se in Chapter 9. Our focus here is on the planning process itself. As we discuss goal setting and planning, however, keep in mind that decision making underlies every aspect of setting goals and formulating plans.[2]

The planning process itself can best be thought of as a generic activity. All organizations engage in planning activities, but no two organizations plan in exactly the same fashion. Figure 7.1 is a general representation of the planning

Figure 7.1

THE PLANNING PROCESS

The planning process takes place within an environmental context. Managers must develop a complete and thorough understanding of this context to determine the organization's mission and to develop its strategic, tactical, and operational goals and plans.

process that many organizations attempt to follow. But, although most firms follow this general framework, each also has its own nuances and variations.[3]

As Figure 7.1 shows, all planning occurs within an environmental context. If managers do not understand this context, they will be unable to develop effective plans. Thus understanding the environment is essentially the first step in planning. The four previous chapters cover many of the basic environmental issues that affect organizations and how they plan. With this understanding as a foundation, managers must then establish the organization's mission. The mission outlines the organization's purpose, premises, values, and directions. Flowing from the mission are parallel streams of goals and plans. Directly following the mission are strategic goals. These goals and the mission help determine strategic plans. Strategic goals and plans are primary inputs for developing tactical goals. Tactical goals and the original strategic plans help shape tactical plans. Tactical plans, in turn, combine with the tactical goals to shape operational goals. These goals and the appropriate tactical plans determine operational plans. Finally, goals and plans at each level can also be used as input for future activities at all levels. This chapter discusses goals and tactical and operational plans. Chapter 8 covers strategic plans.

CHECK

What is the relationship between decision making and planning?

Which do you think is easier for a top manager—making a decision or developing a plan?

Organizational Goals

Goals are critical to organizational effectiveness, and they serve a number of purposes. Organizations can also have several different kinds of goals, all of which must be appropriately managed. And a number of different kinds of managers must be involved in setting goals.

Purposes of Goals

Goals serve four important purposes.[4] First, they provide guidance and a unified direction for people in the organization. Goals can help everyone understand where the organization is going and why getting there is important.[5] Top managers at General Electric have set a goal that every business owned by the firm will be either number one or number two in its industry. This goal helps set the tone for decisions made by GE managers as it competes with other firms like Whirlpool and Electrolux.[6] Likewise, P&G's goal of doubling revenues, discussed in the section above, helps everyone in the firm recognize the strong emphasis on growth and expansion that is driving the firm.

Second, goal-setting practices strongly affect other aspects of planning. Effective goal setting promotes good planning, and good planning facilitates future goal setting. For example, the ambitious revenue goal set for P&G demonstrates how setting goals and developing plans to reach them should be seen as complementary activities. The strong growth goal should encourage managers to plan for expansion by looking for new market opportunities, for example. Similarly, they must also always be alert for competitive threats and new ideas that will help facilitate future expansion.

Third, goals can serve as a source of motivation for employees of the organization. Goals that are specific and moderately difficult can motivate people to work harder, especially if attaining the goal is likely to result in rewards.[7] The Italian furniture manufacturer Industrie Natuzzi SpA uses goals to motivate its workers. Each craftsperson has a goal for how long it should take to perform her or his job, such as sewing leather sheets together to make a sofa cushion or building wooden frames for chair arms. At the completion of assigned tasks, workers enter their ID numbers and job numbers into the firm's computer system. If they get a job done faster than their goal, a bonus is automatically added to their paycheck.[8]

Finally, goals provide an effective mechanism for evaluation and control. This means that performance can be assessed in the future in terms of how successfully today's goals are accomplished. For example, suppose that officials of the United Way of America set a goal of collecting $250,000 from a particular small community. If, midway through the campaign, they have raised only $50,000, they know that they need to change or intensify their efforts. If they raise only $100,000 by the end of their drive, they will need to carefully study why they did not reach their goal and what they need to do differently next year. On the other hand, if they succeed in raising $265,000, evaluations of their efforts will take on an entirely different character.

Kinds of Goals

Organizations establish many different kinds of goals. In general, these goals vary by level, area, and time frame.[9] Figure 7.2 provides examples of each type of goal for a fast-food chain.

Level

- Goals are set for and by different levels within an organization. As we noted earlier, the four basic levels of goals are the mission and strategic, tactical, and operational goals. An organization's **mission** is a statement of its "fundamental, unique purpose that sets a business apart from other firms of its

mission
A statement of an organization's fundamental purpose

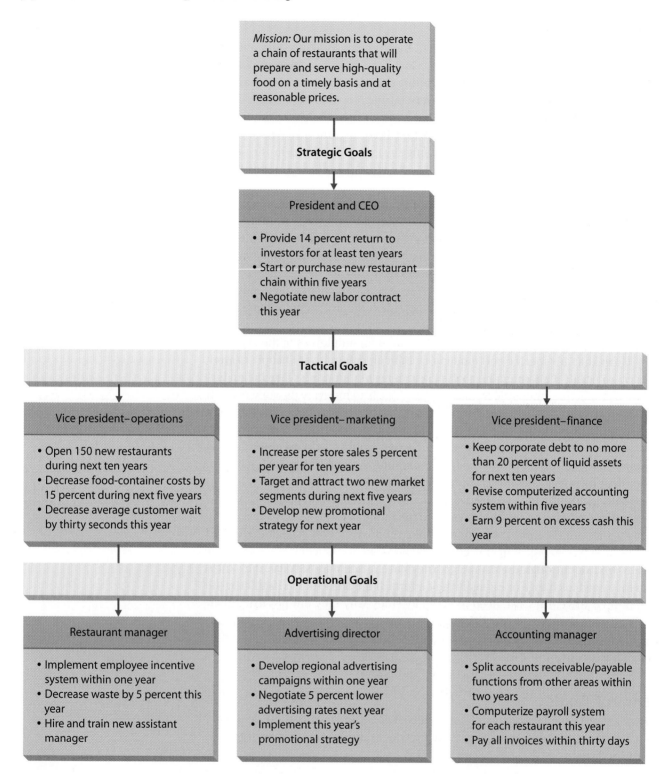

Figure 7.2
KINDS OF ORGANIZATIONAL GOALS FOR A REGIONAL FAST-FOOD CHAIN

Organizations develop many different types of goals. A regional fast-food chain, for example, might develop goals at several different levels and for several different areas.

type and identifies the scope of the business's operations in product and market terms."[10] For instance, Starbucks' mission statement is to be "the premier purveyor of the finest coffee in the world while maintaining our uncompromising principles while we grow." The principles referred to in the mission statement include: Provide a great work environment and treat each other with respect and dignity.

- Embrace diversity as an essential component in the way we do business.
- Apply the highest standards of excellence to the purchasing, roasting and fresh delivery of our coffee.
- Develop enthusiastically satisfied customers all of the time.
- Contribute positively to our communities and our environment.
- Recognize that profitability is essential to our future success.[11]

Hence, the mission statement and basic principles help managers at Starbucks make decisions and direct resources in clear and specific ways.

Strategic goals are goals set by and for top management of the organization. They focus on broad, general issues. For example, Starbucks has a strategic goal of increasing its number of worldwide retail outlets from around 10,000 today to 30,000.[12] ***Tactical goals*** are set by and for middle managers. Their focus is on how to operationalize actions necessary to achieve the strategic goals. To achieve Starbucks' goal of tripling its number of retail outlets, managers are working on tactical goals related to company-owned versus licensed stores and the global distribution of stores in different countries.

Operational goals are set by and for lower-level managers. Their concern is with shorter-term issues associated with the tactical goals. An operational goal for Starbucks might be a target number of new stores to open in each of the next five years. (Some managers use the words *objective* and *goal* interchangeably. When they are differentiated, however, the term *objective* is usually used instead of *operational goal*.)

Area   Organizations also set goals for different areas. The restaurant chain shown in Figure 7.2 has goals for operations, marketing, and finance. Hewlett-Packard (HP) routinely sets production goals for quality, productivity, and so forth. By keeping activities focused on these important areas, HP has managed to remain competitive against organizations from around the world. Human resource goals might be set for employee turnover and absenteeism. 3M and Rubbermaid set goals for product innovation. Similarly, Bath & Body Works has a goal that 30 percent of the products sold in its retail outlets each year will be new. In addition to its growth goals, Starbucks also has financial goals of maintaining a 20 percent annual growth rate in both revenues and profits.

Time Frame   Organizations also set goals across different time frames. In Figure 7.2, three goals are listed at the strategic, tactical, and operational levels. The first is a long-term goal, the second an intermediate-term goal, and the third a short-term goal. Some goals have an explicit time frame (open 150 new restaurants during the next ten years), and others have an open-ended time horizon (maintain 10 percent annual growth). Finally, we should also note that the meaning of different time frames varies by level. For example, at the strategic level, "long term" often means ten years or longer, "intermediate term" around five years or so, and "short term"

---

strategic goal
A goal set by and for top management of the organization

tactical goal
A goal set by and for middle managers of the organization

operational goal
A goal set by and for lower-level managers of the organization

around one year. But two or three years may be long term at the operational level, and short term may mean a matter of weeks or even days.

Responsibilities for Setting Goals

Who sets goals? The answer is actually quite simple: All managers should be involved in the goal-setting process. Each manager, however, generally has responsibilities for setting goals that correspond to his or her level in the organization. The mission and strategic goals are generally determined by the board of directors and top managers. Top and middle managers then work together to establish tactical goals. Finally, middle and lower-level managers are jointly responsible for operational goals. Many managers also set individual goals for themselves. These goals may involve career paths, informal work-related goals outside the normal array of official goals, or just about anything of interest or concern to the manager.

Managing Multiple Goals

Organizations set many different kinds of goals and sometimes experience conflicts or contradictions among goals. Nike had problems with inconsistent goals a few years ago. The firm was producing high-quality shoes (a manufacturing goal), but they were not particularly stylish (a marketing goal). As a result, the company lost substantial market share when Reebok and Adidas started making shoes that were both high quality and fashionable. When Nike management recognized and corrected the inconsistencies, Nike regained its industry standing.

> *optimizing*
> Balancing and reconciling possible conflicts among goals

To address such problems, managers must understand the concept of optimizing. **Optimizing** involves balancing and reconciling possible conflicts among goals. Because goals may conflict with one another, the manager must look for inconsistencies and decide whether to pursue one goal to the exclusion of another or to find a midrange target between the extremes. For example, Home Depot has achieved dramatic success in the retailing industry by offering do-it-yourselfers high-quality home improvement products at low prices and with good service. Now the firm is pursuing a goal of doubling its revenues from professional contractors. Among its plans have been to set up separate checkout areas and provide special products for contractors. The challenge, however, is to keep loyal individual customers while also satisfying professional contractors.[13] Home Depot's biggest competitor is also optimizing, but among different alternatives—trying to retain its core customer group while also appealing more to women.[14] Starbucks faces optimization challenges as it attempts to maintain its cache as an upscale purveyor of fine coffees while also opening roadside drive-through stores. And the airlines almost always seem to face a classic optimizing question—carrying more passengers for lower prices or fewer passengers for higher prices.[15]

> "If you explain to your subordinates the end state you want, and the timeline you'd like to get there, you can observe progress, provide resources, and know they're going to do things to get you to the goal."
>
> U.S. Marines General Peter Pace
> (*Fortune,* June 27, 2005, p. 56)

concept
CHECK

| What are the four fundamental purposes of goals in an organization? | Identify a recent situation in which you had to optimize among conflicting goals. |

Organizational Planning

Given the clear link between organizational goals and plans, we now turn our attention to various concepts and issues associated with planning itself. In particular, this section identifies kinds of plans, time frames for planning, who is responsible for planning, and contingency planning.

Kinds of Organizational Plans

Organizations establish many different kinds of plans. At a general level, these include strategic, tactical, and operational plans.

Strategic Plans   Strategic plans are the plans developed to achieve strategic goals. More precisely, a **strategic plan** is a general plan outlining decisions of resource allocation, priorities, and action steps necessary to reach strategic goals.[16] These plans are set by the board of directors and top management, generally have an extended time horizon, and address questions of scope, resource deployment, competitive advantage, and synergy. We discuss strategic planning further in Chapter 8.

Tactical Plans   A **tactical plan**, aimed at achieving tactical goals, is developed to implement specific parts of a strategic plan. Tactical plans typically involve upper and middle management and, compared with strategic plans, have a somewhat shorter time horizon and a more specific and concrete focus. Thus tactical plans are concerned more with actually getting things done than with deciding what to do. Tactical planning is covered in detail in a later section.

Operational Plans   An **operational plan** focuses on carrying out tactical plans to achieve operational goals. Developed by middle and lower-level managers, operational plans have a short-term focus and are relatively narrow in scope. Each one deals with a fairly small set of activities. We also cover operational planning in more detail later.

Time Frames for Planning

As we previously noted, strategic plans tend to have a long-term focus, tactical plans an intermediate-term focus, and operational plans a short-term focus. The sections that follow address these time frames in more detail. Of course, we should also remember that time frames vary widely from industry to industry.

Long-Range Plans   A **long-range plan** covers many years, perhaps even decades. The founder of Matsushita Electric (maker of Panasonic and JVC electronic products), Konosuke Matsushita, once wrote a 250-year plan for his company![17] Today, however, most managers recognize that environmental change makes it unfeasible to plan too far ahead, but large firms like General Motors and ExxonMobil still routinely develop plans for five- to ten-year intervals. GM executives, for example, have a pretty good idea today about new car models that they plan to introduce during the next decade. The time span for long-range planning varies from one organization to another. For our purposes, we regard any plan that extends beyond five years as long range. Managers of organizations in complex, volatile environments face a special dilemma. These organizations probably need a longer time horizon than do organizations in less dynamic environments, yet the complexity of their environment makes long-range planning difficult. Managers at these companies therefore develop long-range plans but also must constantly monitor their environment for possible changes.

strategic plan
A general plan outlining decisions of resource allocation, priorities, and action steps necessary to reach strategic goals

tactical plan
A plan aimed at achieving tactical goals and developed to implement parts of a strategic plan

operational plan
Focuses on carrying out tactical plans to achieve operational goals

long-range plan
A plan that covers many years, perhaps even decades; common long-range plans are for five years or more

intermediate plan
A plan that generally covers from one to five years

Intermediate Plans   An *intermediate plan* is somewhat less tentative and subject to change than is a long-range plan. Intermediate plans usually cover periods from one to five years and are especially important for middle and first-line managers. Thus they generally parallel tactical plans. For many organizations, intermediate planning has become the central focus of planning activities. Nissan, for example, fell behind its domestic rivals Toyota and Honda in profitability and productivity. To turn things around, the firm developed several plans ranging in duration from two to four years, each intended to improve some part of the company's operations. One plan (three years in duration) involved updating the manufacturing technology used in each Nissan assembly factory. Another (four years in duration) called for shifting more production to foreign plants to lower labor costs. And the successful implementation of these plans helped turn things around for Nissan.

short-range plan
A plan that generally covers a span of one year or less

action plan
A plan used to operationalize any other kind of plan

reaction plan
A plan developed to react to an unforeseen circumstance

Short-Range Plans   Managers also develop *short-range plans*, which have a time frame of one year or less. Short-range plans greatly affect the manager's day-to-day activities. There are two basic kinds of short-range plans. An *action plan* operationalizes any other kind of plan. When a specific Nissan plant was ready to have its technology overhauled, its managers focused their attention on replacing the existing equipment with new equipment as quickly and as efficiently as possible, to minimize lost production time. In most cases, this was done in a matter of a few months, with actual production halted for only a few weeks. An action plan thus coordinates the actual changes at a given factory. A *reaction plan*, in turn, is a plan designed to allow the company to react to an unforeseen circumstance. At one Nissan factory, the new equipment arrived earlier than expected, and plant managers had to shut down production more quickly than expected. These managers thus had to react to events beyond their control in ways that still allowed their goals to be achieved. In fact, reacting to any form of environmental turbulence, as described in Chapter 3, is a form of reaction planning.

Responsibilities for Planning

We earlier noted briefly who is responsible for setting goals. We can now expand that initial perspective and examine more fully how different parts of the organization participate in the overall planning process. All managers engage in planning to some degree. Marketing sales managers develop plans for target markets, market penetration, and sales increases. Operations managers plan cost-cutting programs and better inventory control methods. As a general rule, however, the larger an organization becomes, the more the primary planning activities become associated with groups of managers rather than with individual managers.

Planning Staff   Some large organizations maintain a professional planning staff. General Motors, Caterpillar, Raytheon, NCR, Ford, and Boeing all have planning staffs. And although the planning staff was pioneered in the United States, foreign firms like Nippon Telegraph and Telephone also started using them. Organizations might use a planning staff for a variety of reasons. In particular, a planning staff can reduce the workload of individual managers, help coordinate the planning activities of individual managers, bring to a particular problem many different tools and techniques, take a broader view than individual managers, and go beyond pet projects and particular departments. In recent years, though, some businesses have realized that they can plan more effectively by diffusing planning responsibility throughout their organization and/or by using planning task forces. For instance, Disney and Shell Oil have recently eliminated or downsized their centralized planning units.[18]

Planning Task Force   Organizations sometimes use a planning task force to help develop plans. Such a task force often comprises line managers with a special interest in the relevant area of planning. The task force may also have members from the planning staff if the organization has one. A planning task force is most often created when the organization wants to address a special circumstance. For example, when Electronic Data Systems (EDS) decided to expand its information management services to Europe, managers knew that the firm's normal planning approach would not suffice, and top management created a special planning task force. The task force included representatives from each of the major units within the company, the corporate planning staff, and the management team that would run the European operation. Once the plan for entering the European market was formulated and implemented, the task force was eliminated.

Board of Directors   Among its other responsibilities, the board of directors establishes the corporate mission and strategy. In some companies the board takes an active role in the planning process. At CBS, for example, the board of directors has traditionally played a major role in planning. In other companies the board selects a competent chief executive and delegates planning to that individual.

Chief Executive Officer   The chief executive officer (CEO) is usually the president or the chair of the board of directors. The CEO is probably the single most important individual in any organization's planning process. The CEO plays a major role in the complete planning process and is responsible for implementing the strategy. The board and CEO, then, assume direct roles in planning. The other organizational players involved in the planning process have more of an advisory or a consulting role.

Executive Committee   The executive committee is usually composed of the top executives in the organization working together as a group. Committee members usually meet regularly to provide input to the CEO on the proposals that affect their own units and to review the various strategic plans that develop from this input. Members of the executive committee are frequently assigned to various staff committees, subcommittees, and task forces to concentrate on specific projects or problems that might confront the entire organization at some time in the future.

Line Management   The final component of most organizations' planning activities is line management. Line managers are those persons with formal authority and responsibility for the management of the organization. They play an important role in an organization's planning process for two reasons. First, they are a valuable source of inside information for other managers as plans are formulated and implemented. Second, the line managers at the middle and lower levels of the organization usually must execute the plans developed by top management. Line management identifies, analyzes, and recommends program alternatives, develops budgets and submits them for approval, and finally sets the plans in motion.

Contingency Planning and Crisis Management

Another important type of planning is ***contingency planning***, or the determination of alternative courses of action to be taken if an intended plan of action is unexpectedly

contingency planning
The determination of alternative courses of action to be taken if an intended plan is unexpectedly disrupted or rendered inappropriate

Crisis planning has taken on new importance in recent years. In the large-scale emergency exercise shown here, Singapore Civil Defense personnel evacuate train passengers through a tunnel from a train carriage that was "bombed" in a staged attack. The government of Singapore staged this large-scale emergency exercise to test its readiness for terror attacks on its bus and subway systems, mindful that its role as a close U.S. ally makes it a potential target for Islamic extremists. The drill followed deadly bombings on the London transport system and the train network in Madrid, Spain.

crisis management
The set of procedures the organization uses in the event of a disaster or other unexpected calamity

disrupted or rendered inappropriate.[19] ***Crisis management***, a related concept, is the set of procedures the organization uses in the event of a disaster or other unexpected calamity. Some elements of crisis management may be orderly and systematic, whereas others may be more ad hoc and develop as events unfold. *The Business of Ethics* illustrates some of the problems facing paint manufacturers such as Sherwin Williams because of their poor contingency planning.

An excellent recent example of widespread contingency planning occurred during the late 1990s in anticipation of what was popularly known as the "Y2K bug." Concerns about the impact of technical glitches in computers stemming from their internal clocks' changing from 1999 to 2000 resulted in contingency planning for most organizations. Many banks and hospitals, for example, had extra staff available; some organizations created backup computer systems; and some even stockpiled inventory in case they could not purchase new products or materials.[20]

The devastating hurricanes that hit the Gulf Coast in 2005—Katrina and Rita—dramatically underscored the importance of effective crisis management. For example, inadequate and ineffective responses by the Federal Emergency Management Agency (FEMA) illustrated to many people that organization's weaknesses in coping with crisis situations. On the other hand, some organizations responded much more effectively. Wal-Mart began ramping up its emergency preparedness on the same day that Katrina was upgraded from a tropical depression to a tropical storm. In the days before the storm struck, Wal-Mart stores in the region were supplied with powerful generators and large supplies of dry ice so they could reopen as quickly as possible after the storm had passed. In neighboring states, The firm also had scores of trucks standing by crammed with both emergency-related inventory for its stores and emergency supplies it was prepared to donate—bottled water, medical supplies, and so forth. And Wal-Mart often beat FEMA by several days in getting those supplies delivered.[21]

Seeing the consequences of poor crisis management after the terrorist attacks of September 11, 2001, and the 2005 hurricanes, many firms today are actively working to create new and better crisis management plans and procedures. For example, both Reliant Energy and Duke Energy rely on computer trading centers where trading managers actively buy and sell energy-related commodities. If a terrorist attack or natural disaster such as a hurricane were to strike their trading centers, they would essentially be out of business. Prior to September 11, each firm had relatively vague and superficial crisis plans. But now they and most other companies have much more detailed and comprehensive plans in the event of another crisis. Both Reliant and Duke, for example, have created secondary trading centers at other locations. In the event of a shutdown at their main trading centers, these

The Business of Ethics

Lead Paint Liability

Contingency planning, by its very nature, is a challenge for organizations. How can a firm effectively anticipate and plan for an unexpected problem? Other contingencies are almost completely unpredictable. For example, how could any of the firms located in the World Trade Center buildings in New York City have anticipated the events of 9/11? Other contingencies may be more predictable. Companies that rely on oil, for example, should and do plan for prices to fluctuate.

In some cases, however, a lack of contingency planning can result from a failure of management. That is the situation for several firms that make paint or supply materials to paint manufacturers. Critics want paint companies to admit liability for lead contamination in older buildings. Once toxic lead paint is used, it remains forever. If paint flakes off, the chips can be breathed in or eaten by toddlers. Lead exposure causes severe health problems, including permanent nerve and brain damage and even death. Prosecutors have evidence that paint companies knew about lead's toxicity as early as 1900.

For their part, the paint companies claim that they voluntarily quit using lead in the 1960s, well before the federal ban of 1978. They also claim that no one can trace decades-old paint to its maker and that property owners should be required to keep lead paint safely covered up.

The state of Rhode Island is suing Sherwin-Williams, a paint maker, as well as NL Industries and Millennium Holdings, two firms that supplied lead. The problem there is huge. Rhode Island contains 250,000 homes with lead-based paint, and in 1993, 29 percent of children there had traces of lead in their blood.

Current law requires companies to set aside funds for contingencies, but the paint companies have not done so. That means that there are no funds for what could be the most expensive environmental cleanup effort ever attempted, expected to cost billions for Rhode Island alone.

The situation isn't unique. Similar difficulties have plagued the asbestos, tobacco, and pharmaceutical industries. Should paint company executives have foreseen the lawsuits? Should they have planned a response? Who will bear the cost of their failure to do so?

References: "2005 Annual Report," Sherwin-Williams Company website, www.sherwin-williams.com on March 6, 2006; Julie Creswell, "The Nuisance That May Cost Billions," *New York Times*, April 2, 2006, pp. NJ 1, 6; Peter B. Lord, "Second Lead Paint Trial Begins," *Providence* [Rhode Island] *Journal*, November 2, 2005, www.projo.com on March 7, 2006.

---

firms can quickly transfer virtually all their core trading activities to their secondary centers within 30 minutes or less.[22] Unfortunately, however, because it is impossible to forecast the future precisely, no organization can ever be perfectly prepared for all crises.

The mechanics of contingency planning are shown in Figure 7.3. In relation to an organization's other plans, contingency planning comes into play at four action points. At action point 1, management develops the basic plans of the organization. These may include strategic, tactical, and operational plans. As part of this development process, managers usually consider various contingency events. Some management groups even assign someone the role of devil's advocate to ask, "But what if . . ." about each course of action. A variety of contingencies is usually considered.

At action point 2, the plan that management chooses is put into effect. The most important contingency events are also defined. Only the events that are likely to occur and whose effects will have a substantial impact on the organization are used in the contingency-planning process. Next, at action point 3, the company specifies certain indicators or signs that suggest that a contingency event is about to take place. A bank might decide that a 2 percent drop in interest rates should be considered a contingency event. An indicator might be two consecutive months with a

> "In times of crisis, people crave strong and supportive leadership."
>
> David Kong, CEO of Best Western
> (*USA Today*, October 4, 2005, p. 2B)

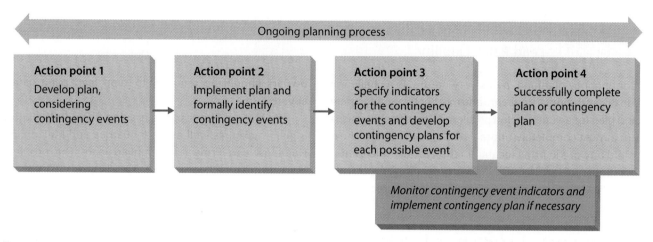

Figure 7.3
CONTINGENCY PLANNING

Most organizations develop contingency plans. These plans specify alternative courses of action to be taken if an intended plan is unexpectedly disrupted or rendered inappropriate.

drop of .5 percent in each. As indicators of contingency events are being defined, the contingency plans themselves should also be developed. Examples of contingency plans for various situations are delaying plant construction, developing a new manufacturing process, and cutting prices.

After this stage, the managers of the organization monitor the indicators identified at action point 3. If the situation dictates, a contingency plan is implemented. Otherwise, the primary plan of action continues in force. Finally, action point 4 marks the successful completion of either the original or a contingency plan.

Contingency planning is becoming increasingly important for most organizations, especially for those operating in particularly complex or dynamic environments. Few managers have such an accurate view of the future that they can anticipate and plan for everything. Contingency planning is a useful technique for helping managers cope with uncertainty and change. Crisis management, by its very nature, however, is more difficult to anticipate. But organizations that have a strong culture, strong leadership, and a capacity to deal with the unexpected stand a better chance of successfully weathering a crisis than do other organizations.[23]

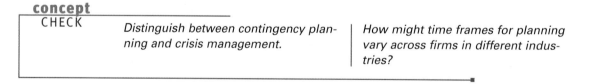

concept
CHECK

Distinguish between contingency planning and crisis management.

How might time frames for planning vary across firms in different industries?

Tactical Planning

tactical plan
A plan aimed at achieving tactical goals and developed to implement specific parts of a strategic plan

As we noted earlier, tactical plans are developed to implement specific parts of a strategic plan. You have probably heard the saying about winning the battle but losing the war. *Tactical plans* are to battles what strategy is to a war: an organized sequence of steps designed to execute strategic plans. Strategy focuses on

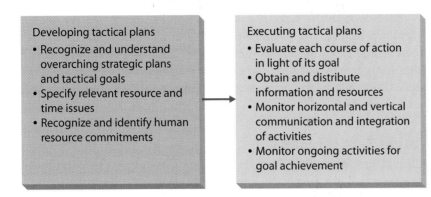

Developing tactical plans
- Recognize and understand overarching strategic plans and tactical goals
- Specify relevant resource and time issues
- Recognize and identify human resource commitments

Executing tactical plans
- Evaluate each course of action in light of its goal
- Obtain and distribute information and resources
- Monitor horizontal and vertical communication and integration of activities
- Monitor ongoing activities for goal achievement

Figure 7.4

DEVELOPING AND EXECUTING TACTICAL PLANS

Tactical plans are used to accomplish specific parts of a strategic plan. Each strategic plan is generally implemented through several tactical plans. Effective tactical planning involves both development and execution.

resources, environment, and mission, whereas tactics focus primarily on people and action.[24] Figure 7.4 identifies the major elements in developing and executing tactical plans.

Developing Tactical Plans

Although effective tactical planning depends on many factors, which vary from one situation to another, we can identify some basic guidelines. First, the manager needs to recognize that tactical planning must address a number of tactical goals derived from a broader strategic goal.[25] An occasional situation may call for a stand-alone tactical plan, but most of the time tactical plans flow from and must be consistent with a strategic plan.

For example, top managers at Coca-Cola developed a strategic plan for cementing the firm's dominance of the soft-drink industry. As part of developing the plan, they identified a critical environmental threat—considerable unrest and uncertainty among the independent bottlers that packaged and distributed Coca-Cola's products. To simultaneously counter this threat and strengthen the company's position, Coca-Cola bought several large independent bottlers and combined them into one new organization called "Coca-Cola Enterprises." Selling half of the new company's stock reaped millions in profits while effectively keeping control of the enterprise in Coca-Cola's hands. Thus the creation of the new business was a tactical plan developed to contribute to the achievement of an overarching strategic goal.[26]

Second, although strategies are often stated in general terms, tactics must specify resources and time frames. A strategy can call for being number one in a particular market or industry, but a tactical plan must specify precisely what activities will be undertaken to achieve that goal. Consider the Coca-Cola example again. Another element of its strategic plan involves increased worldwide market share. To facilitate additional sales in Europe, managers developed tactical plans for building a new plant in the south of France to make soft-drink concentrate and for building another canning plant in Dunkirk. The firm has also invested heavily in India.[27] Building these plants represents a concrete action involving measurable resources (funds to build the plants) and a clear time horizon (a target date for completion).

Finally, tactical planning requires the use of human resources. Managers involved in tactical planning spend a great deal of time working with other people. They must be in a position to receive information from others within and outside the organization, process that information in the most effective way, and then pass it on to others who might make use of it. Coca-Cola executives have been intensively involved in planning the new plants, setting up the new bottling venture noted earlier, and exploring a joint venture with Cadbury Schweppes in the United Kingdom. Each activity has required considerable time and effort from dozens of managers. One manager, for example, crossed the Atlantic 12 times while negotiating the Cadbury deal.

Executing Tactical Plans

Regardless of how well a tactical plan is formulated, its ultimate success depends on the way it is carried out. Successful implementation, in turn, depends on the astute use of resources, effective decision making, and insightful steps to ensure that the right things are done at the right times and in the right ways. A manager can see an absolutely brilliant idea fail because of improper execution.

Proper execution depends on a number of important factors. First, the manager needs to evaluate every possible course of action in light of the goal it is intended to reach. Next, he or she needs to make sure that each decision maker has the information and resources necessary to get the job done. Vertical and horizontal communication and integration of activities must be present to minimize conflict and inconsistent activities. And, finally, the manager must monitor ongoing activities derived from the plan to make sure they are achieving the desired results. This monitoring typically takes place within the context of the organization's ongoing control systems.

For example, managers at Walt Disney Company recently developed a new strategic plan aimed at spurring growth in and profits from foreign markets. One tactical plan developed to stimulate growth involves expanding the cable Disney Channel into more and more foreign markets; another involved building the new theme park near Hong Kong that opened in 2006. Although expanding cable television and building a new theme park are big undertakings in their own right, they are still tactical plans within the overall strategic plan focusing on international growth.[28]

concept
CHECK

How are tactical plans developed?

Which do you think is easier—developing tactical plans or implementing them? Why?

Operational Planning

Another critical element in effective organizational planning is the development and implementation of operational plans. Operational plans are derived from tactical plans and are aimed at achieving operational goals. Thus operational plans tend to be narrowly focused, have relatively short time horizons, and involve lower-level managers. The two most basic forms of operational plans and specific types of each are summarized in Table 7.1.

Single-Use Plans

single-use plan
Developed to carry out a course of action that is not likely to be repeated in the future

A **single-use plan** is developed to carry out a course of action that is not likely to be repeated in the future. As Disney planned its newest theme park in Hong Kong, it developed numerous single-use plans for individual rides, attractions, and hotels. The two most common forms of single-use plans are programs and projects.

Table 7.1

TYPES OF OPERATIONAL PLANS

Organizations develop various operational plans to help achieve operational goals. In general, there are two types of single-use plans and three types of standing plans.

PLAN	Description
Single-use plan	Developed to carry out a course of action not likely to be repeated in the future
Program	Single-use plan for a large set of activities
Project	Single-use plan of less scope and complexity than a program
Standing plan	Developed for activities that recur regularly over a period of time
Policy	Standing plan specifying the organization's general response to a designated problem or situation
Standard operating procedure	Standing plan outlining steps to be followed in particular circumstances
Rules and regulations	Standing plans describing exactly how specific activities are to be carried out

Programs   A ***program*** is a single-use plan for a large set of activities. It might consist of identifying procedures for introducing a new product line, opening a new facility, or changing the organization's mission. As part of its own strategic plans for growth, Black & Decker bought General Electric's small-appliance business. The deal involved the largest brand-name switch in history: 150 products were converted from the GE to the Black & Decker label. Each product was carefully studied, redesigned, and reintroduced with an extended warranty. A total of 140 steps were used for each product. It took three years to convert all 150 products over to Black & Decker. The total conversion of the product line was a program.

> *program*
> A single-use plan for a large set of activities

Projects   A ***project*** is similar to a program but is generally of less scope and complexity. A project may be a part of a broader program, or it may be a self-contained single-use plan. For Black & Decker, the conversion of each of the 150 products was

> *project*
> A single-use plan of less scope and complexity than a program

A program is a single-use plan for a large set of activities. Construction of the Three Gorges Dam in China certainly qualifies as a program! One of the largest construction programs ever undertaken, the Three Gorges Dam has taken years to complete, relied on the talents of hundreds of thousands of people, required millions of tons of concrete, and forced the displacement of thousands of people. Still, officials hope that the dam will help eliminate centuries-old flooding problems and provide a valuable and reliable source of electricity.

a separate project in its own right. Each product had its own manager, its own schedule, and so forth. Projects are also used to introduce a new product within an existing product line or to add a new benefit option to an existing salary package.

Standing Plans

standing plan

Developed for activities that recur regularly over a period of time

Whereas single-use plans are developed for nonrecurring situations, a ***standing plan*** is used for activities that recur regularly over a period of time. Standing plans can greatly enhance efficiency by making decision making routine. Policies, standard operating procedures, and rules and regulations are three kinds of standing plans.

Policies   As a general guide for action, a policy is the most general form of standing plan. A ***policy*** specifies the organization's general response to a designated problem or situation. For example, McDonald's has a policy that it will not grant a franchise to an

policy

A standing plan that specifies the organization's general response to a designated problem or situation

individual who already owns another fast-food restaurant. Similarly, Starbucks has a policy that it will not franchise at all, instead retaining ownership of all Starbucks coffee shops. Likewise, a university admissions office might establish a policy that admission will be granted only to applicants with a minimum SAT score of 1200 and a ranking in the top quarter of their high school class. Admissions officers may routinely deny admission to applicants who fail to reach these minimums. A policy is also likely to describe how exceptions are to be handled. The university's policy statement, for example, might create an admissions appeals committee to evaluate applicants who do not meet minimum requirements but may warrant special consideration.

standard operating procedure (SOP)

A standing plan that outlines the steps to be followed in particular circumstances

Standard Operating Procedures   Another type of standing plan is the ***standard operating procedure***, or ***SOP***. An SOP is more specific than a policy, in that it outlines the steps to be followed in particular circumstances. The admissions clerk at the university, for example, might be told that, when an application is received, he or she should (1) set up an electronic file for the applicant; (2) merge test-score records, transcripts, and letters of reference to the electronic file as they are received; and (3) forward the electronic file to the appropriate admissions director when it is complete. Gallo Vineyards in California has a 300-page manual of SOPs. This planning manual is credited with making Gallo one of the most efficient wine operations in the United States. McDonald's has SOPs explaining exactly how Big Macs are to be cooked, how long they can stay in the warming rack, and so forth.

rules and regulations

Describe exactly how specific activities are to be carried out

Rules and regulations are used to govern a variety of activities. California raisin farmers are subject to several rules and regulations created to help control raisin supply and demand. Raisin farmer Marvin Horne stands in a field of grapevines planted in 1918 next to his home in Kerman, California. Horne and other farmers are required to set aside a percentage of their crops to avoid a surplus. Unfortunately, Horne was recently accused of violating this rule by selling his entire crop.

Rules and Regulations   The narrowest of the standing plans, ***rules and regulations***, describe exactly how specific activities are to be carried out. Rather than guiding decision making, rules and regulations actually take the place of decision making in various situations. Each McDonald's restaurant has a rule prohibiting customers from using its telephones, for example.

The university admissions office might have a rule stipulating that if an applicant's file is not complete two months before the beginning of a semester, the student cannot be admitted until the next semester. Of course, in most organizations a manager at a higher level can suspend or bend the rules. If the high school transcript of the child of a prominent university alumnus and donor arrives a few days late, the director of admissions might waive the two-month rule. Indeed, rules and regulations can become problematic if they are excessive or enforced too rigidly.

Rules and regulations and SOPs are similar in many ways. They are both relatively narrow in scope, and each can serve as a substitute for decision making. An SOP typically describes a sequence of activities, however, whereas rules and regulations focus on one activity. Recall our examples: The admissions SOP consisted of three activities, whereas the two-month rule related to only one activity. In an industrial setting, the SOP for orienting a new employee could involve enrolling the person in various benefit options, introducing him or her to coworkers and supervisors, and providing a tour of the facilities. A pertinent rule for the new employee might involve when to come to work each day.

Distinguish between single-use and standing plans.

Identify a rule or regulation that relates to you but that you think is excessive or too restrictive.

concept
CHECK

Managing Goal-Setting and Planning Processes

Obviously, all of the elements of goal setting and planning discussed to this point involve managing these processes in some way or another. In addition, however, because major barriers sometimes impede effective goal setting and planning, knowing how to overcome some of the barriers is important.

Barriers to Goal Setting and Planning

Several circumstances can serve as barriers to effective goal setting and planning; the more common ones are listed in Table 7.2.

Table 7.2
BARRIERS TO GOAL SETTING AND PLANNING

As part of managing the goal-setting and planning processes, managers must understand the barriers that can disrupt them. Managers must also know how to overcome the barriers.

Major barriers	Inappropriate goals
	Improper reward system
	Dynamic and complex environment
	Reluctance to establish goals
	Resistance to change
	Constraints
Overcoming the barriers	Understanding the purposes of goals and planning
	Communication and participation
	Consistency, revision, and updating
	Effective reward system

Inappropriate Goals   Inappropriate goals come in many forms. Paying a large dividend to stockholders may be inappropriate if it comes at the expense of research and development. Goals may also be inappropriate if they are unattainable. If Kmart were to set a goal of having more revenues than Wal-Mart next year, people at the company would probably be embarrassed because achieving such a goal would be impossible. Goals may also be inappropriate if they place too much emphasis on either quantitative or qualitative measures of success. Some goals, especially those relating to financial areas, are quantifiable, objective, and verifiable. Other goals, such as employee satisfaction and development, are difficult, if not impossible, to quantify. Organizations are asking for trouble if they put too much emphasis on one type of goal to the exclusion of the other.

Improper Reward System   In some settings, an improper reward system acts as a barrier to goal setting and planning. For example, people may inadvertently be rewarded for poor goal-setting behavior or go unrewarded or even be punished for proper goal-setting behavior. Suppose that a manager sets a goal of decreasing turnover next year. If turnover is decreased by even a fraction, the manager can claim success and perhaps be rewarded for the accomplishment. In contrast, a manager who attempts to decrease turnover by 5 percent but actually achieves a decrease of only 4 percent may receive a smaller reward because of her or his failure to reach the established goal. And, if an organization places too much emphasis on short-term performance and results, managers may ignore longer-term issues as they set goals and formulate plans to achieve higher profits in the short term.

Dynamic and Complex Environment   The nature of an organization's environment is also a barrier to effective goal setting and planning. Rapid change, technological innovation, and intense competition can all increase the difficulty of an organization's accurately assessing future opportunities and threats. For example, when an electronics firm like IBM develops a long-range plan, it tries to take into account how much technological innovation is likely to occur during that interval. But forecasting such events is extremely difficult. During the early boom years of personal computers, data were stored primarily on floppy disks. Because these disks had a limited storage capacity, hard disks were developed. Whereas the typical floppy disk can hold hundreds of pages of information, a hard disk can store thousands of pages. Today, computers increasingly store information on optical disks that hold millions of pages. The manager attempting to set goals and plan in this rapidly changing environment faces a truly formidable task.

Reluctance to Establish Goals   Another barrier to effective planning is some managers' reluctance to establish goals for themselves and their units of responsibility. The reason for this reluctance may be lack of confidence or fear of failure. If a manager sets a goal that is specific, concise, and time related, then whether he or she attains it is obvious. Managers who consciously or unconsciously try to avoid this degree of accountability are likely to hinder the organization's planning efforts. Pfizer, a large pharmaceutical company, ran into problems because its managers did not set goals for research and development. Consequently, the organization fell further and further behind because managers had no way of knowing how effective their R&D efforts actually were.

Resistance to Change   Another barrier to goal setting and planning is resistance to change. Planning essentially involves changing something about the organization. As we will see in Chapter 13, people tend to resist change. Avon Products almost drove itself into bankruptcy several years ago because it insisted on continuing a policy of large dividend payments to its stockholders. When profits started to fall, managers resisted cutting the dividends and started borrowing to pay them. The company's debt grew from $3 million to $1.1 billion in eight years. Eventually, managers were forced to confront the problem and cut dividends.

Constraints   Constraints that limit what an organization can do are another major obstacle. Common constraints include a lack of resources, government restrictions, and strong competition. For example, Owens-Corning Fiberglass took on an enormous debt burden as part of its fight to avoid a takeover by Wickes Ltd. The company then had such a large debt that it was forced to cut back on capital expenditures and research and development. And those cutbacks greatly constrained what the firm could plan for the future. Time constraints are also a factor. It is easy to say, "I'm too busy to plan today; I'll do it tomorrow." Effective planning takes time, energy, and an unwavering belief in its importance.

> "My advice . . . is to be ready to revise any system, scrap any methods, abandon any theory if the success of the job demands it."
>
> Henry Ford
> (quoted in *Fortune*, June 27, 2005, p. 98)

Overcoming the Barriers

Fortunately, there are several guidelines for making goal setting and planning effective. Some of the guidelines are listed in Table 7.2.

Understand the Purposes of Goals and Planning   One of the best ways to facilitate goal-setting and planning processes is to recognize their basic purposes. Managers should also recognize that there are limits to the effectiveness of setting goals and making plans. Planning is not a panacea that will solve all of an organization's problems, nor is it an ironclad set of procedures to be followed at any cost. And effective goals and planning do not necessarily ensure success; adjustments and exceptions are to be expected as time passes. For example, Coca-Cola followed a logical and rational approach to setting goals and planning a few years ago when it introduced a new formula to combat Pepsi's increasing market share. But all the plans proved to be wrong as consumers rejected the new version of Coca-Cola. Managers quickly reversed the decision and reintroduced the old formula as Coca-Cola Classic. Thus, even though careful planning resulted in a big mistake, the company was able to recover from its blunder.

Communication and Participation   Although goals and plans may be initiated at high levels in the organization, they must also be communicated to others in the organization. Everyone involved in the planning process should know what the overriding organizational strategy is, what the various functional strategies are, and how they are all to be integrated and coordinated. People responsible for achieving goals and implementing plans must have a voice in developing them from the outset. These individuals almost always have valuable information to contribute, and because they will be implementing the plans, their involvement is critical: People are usually more committed to plans that they have helped shape. Even when an organization is somewhat centralized or uses a planning staff, managers from a variety of levels in the organization should be involved in the planning

Technology Toolkit

The Digital Dashboard

Top managers, especially CEOs, establish a firm's direction, set strategic goals, and formulate strategic plans. Today's technology allows any manager to access information contained in corporate databases. Yet there is an interesting debate: Should CEOs and other top executives use computers to get information they need to make effective decisions, or should they rely on written and verbal reports from subordinates?

Traditionally, top executives have not used computers. A desk that holds only a phone is a status symbol, indicating that the leader is occupied with deep thought and communications, not data grubbing. Jeff Immelt, CEO of General Electric, worries about missing the big picture if he's always on the computer. Instead, his deputies gather, interpret, and present data to him.

However, many modern CEOs are computer-savvy and tuned into technology. The digital dashboard, a cutting-edge tool for top executives, extracts and consolidates key pieces of information. The data is displayed on one computer screen that contains critical performance indicators and shows at a glance the overall functioning of the organization.

One system, designed by Verizon, allows communications managers to monitor their networks in real time. A green light signals OK status, while yellows or reds need attention. CEOs Larry Ellison of Oracle, Steve Ballmer at Microsoft, and Robert Nardelli of Home Depot all rely on dashboards.

Digital dashboards became a possibility only when corporations began to use software that integrates data about sales, profits, inventory, resource usage, production efficiency, and more. Unlike clunky decision support systems from the 1970s, the dashboard is user-friendly and requires no special training. Managers can quickly see the overview, then "drill down" into the details to pinpoint trouble spots. Many managers are enthusiastic and so is consultant Ken Rau. He says, "You can't manage something you can't measure." Another advantage of dashboards is data sharing, which aids in group decisions.

The dashboard concept has become so popular that several companies are offering versions for small businesses as "add-ons" to the popular Microsoft Office. The dashboard's technology provides data that aids in forming and evaluating strategic goals and plans. It's just one more step in the creation of the wired CEO.

References: Spencer E. Ante, "Giving the Boss the Big Picture," *Business-Week*, February 13, 2006, www.businessweek.com on March 7, 2006; Danny Bradbury, "Go Straight to the Info You Need," *Computer Weekly*, April 20, 2006, www.computerweekly.com on April 1, 2006; "Verizon Business Adds 'Dashboard' to Customer Center Portal," Verizon website, www.verizonbusiness.com on March 7, 2006.

process. *Technology Toolkit*, meanwhile, provides some interesting arguments both for and against intensive involvement by top managers in the planning process and discusses an emerging tool called the "digital dashboard."

Consistency, Revision, and Updating   Goals should be consistent both horizontally and vertically. Horizontal consistency means that goals should be consistent across the organization, from one department to the next. Vertical consistency means that goals should be consistent up and down the organization—strategic, tactical, and operational goals must agree with one another. Because goal setting and planning are dynamic processes, they must also be revised and updated regularly. Many organizations are seeing the need to revise and update on an increasingly frequent basis. Citigroup, for example, once used a three-year planning horizon for developing and providing new financial services. That cycle was subsequently cut to two years, and the bank now often uses a one-year horizon.

Effective Reward Systems   In general, people should be rewarded both for establishing effective goals and plans and for successfully achieving them. Because failure sometimes results from factors outside the manager's control, however, people should also be assured that failure to reach a goal will not necessarily bring punitive consequences. Frederick Smith, founder and CEO of Federal Express, has a stated goal of encouraging risk. Thus, when Federal Express lost $233 million on an unsuccessful service called ZapMail, no one was punished. Smith believed that the original idea was a good one but was unsuccessful for reasons beyond the company's control.

Using Goals to Implement Plans

Goals are often used to implement plans. Formal goal-setting programs represent one widely used method for managing the goal-setting and planning processes concurrently to ensure that both are done effectively. Some firms call this approach ***management by objectives***, or *MBO*. We should also note, however, that although many firms use this basic approach, they frequently tailor it to their own special circumstances and use a special term or name for it.[29] For example, Tenneco Automotive uses an MBO-type system but calls it the "Performance Agreement System," or PAS.

> *management by objectives (MBO)*
> A formal goal-setting process involving collaboration between managers and subordinates; the extent to which goals are accomplished is a major factor in evaluating and rewarding subordinates' performance

The Nature and Purpose of Formal Goal Setting The purpose of formal goal setting is generally to give subordinates a voice in the goal-setting and planning processes and to clarify for them exactly what they are expected to accomplish in a given time span. Thus formal goal setting is often concerned with goal setting and planning for individual managers and their units or work groups.

The Formal Goal-Setting Process The basic mechanics of the formal goal-setting process are shown in Figure 7.5. This process is described here from an ideal perspective. In any given organization, the steps of the process are likely to vary in importance and may even take a different sequence. As a starting point, however, most managers believe that, if a formal goal-setting program is to be successful, it

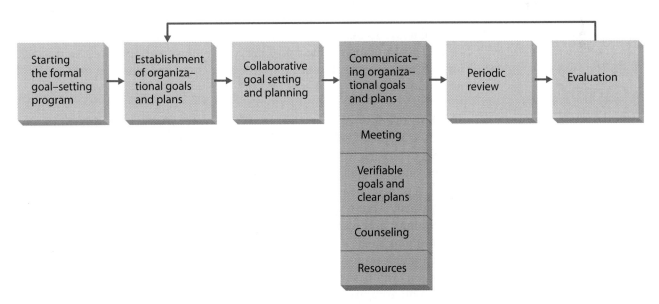

Figure 7.5

THE FORMAL GOAL-SETTING PROCESS

Formal goal setting is an effective technique for integrating goal setting and planning. This figure portrays the general steps that most organizations use when they adopt formal goal setting. Of course, most organizations adapt this general process to fit their own unique needs and circumstances.

must start at the top of the organization. Top managers must communicate why they have adopted the program, what they think it will do, and that they have accepted and are committed to formal goal setting. Employees must also be educated about what goal setting is and what their roles in it will be. Having committed to formal goal setting, managers must implement it in a way that is consistent with overall organizational goals and plans. The idea is that goals set at the top will systematically cascade down throughout the organization.

Although establishing the organization's basic goals and plans is extremely important, collaborative goal setting and planning are the essence of formal goal setting. The collaboration involves a series of distinct steps. First, managers tell their subordinates what organizational and unit goals and plans top management has established. Then managers meet with their subordinates on a one-to-one basis to arrive at a set of goals and plans for each subordinate that both the subordinate and the manager have helped develop and to which both are committed. Next, the goals are refined to be as verifiable (quantitative) as possible and to specify a time frame for their accomplishment. They should also be written. Further, the plans developed to achieve the goals need to be as clearly stated as possible and directly relate to each goal. Managers must play the role of counselors in the goal-setting and planning meeting. For example, they must ensure that the subordinates' goals and plans are attainable and workable and that they will facilitate both the unit's and the organization's goals and plans. Finally, the meeting should spell out the resources that the subordinate will need to implement his or her plans and work effectively toward goal attainment.

Conducting periodic reviews as subordinates are working toward their goals is advisable. If the goals and plans are for a one-year period, meeting quarterly to discuss progress may be a good idea. At the end of the period, the manager meets with each subordinate again to review the degree of goal attainment. They discuss which goals were met and which were not met in the context of the original plans. The reasons for both success and failure are explored, and the employee is rewarded on the basis of goal attainment. In an ongoing goal-setting program, the evaluation meeting may also serve as the collaborative goal-setting and planning meeting for the next time period.

The Effectiveness of Formal Goal Setting A large number of organizations, including Cypress Semiconductor, Alcoa, Tenneco, DuPont, General Motors, Boeing, Caterpillar, Westinghouse Electric, and Black & Decker, all use some form of goal setting. As might be expected, goal setting has both strengths and weaknesses. A primary benefit of goal setting is improved employee motivation. By clarifying exactly what is expected, by allowing the employee a voice in determining expectations, and by basing rewards on the achievement of those expectations, organizations create a powerful motivational system for their employees.

Communication is also enhanced through the process of discussion and collaboration. And performance appraisals may be done more objectively, with less reliance on arbitrary or subjective assessment. Goal setting focuses attention on appropriate goals and plans, helps identify superior managerial talent for future promotion, and provides a systematic management philosophy that can have a positive effect on the overall organization. Goal setting also facilitates control. The periodic development and subsequent evaluation of individual goals and plans helps keep the organization on course toward its own long-run goals and plans.

On the other hand, goal setting occasionally fails because of poor implementation. Perhaps the major problem that can derail a goal-setting program is lack of top-management support. Some organizations decide to use goal setting, but then its implementation is delegated to lower management. This limits the program's effectiveness because the goals and plans cascading throughout the organization may not actually be the goals and plans of top management and because others in the organization are not motivated to accept and become committed to them. Another problem with goal setting is that some firms overemphasize quantitative goals and plans and burden their systems with too much paperwork and record keeping. Some managers will not or cannot sit down to work out goals and plans with their subordinates. Rather, they "suggest" or even "assign" goals and plans to people. The result is resentment and a lack of commitment to the goal-setting program.[30]

concept
CHECK

What are the primary barriers to goal setting and planning?

Describe how a goal-setting system such as MBO might be used in a college classroom setting.

Summary of Learning Objectives and Key Points

1. Summarize the function of decision making and the planning process.
   - The planning process is the first basic managerial function that organizations must address.
   - With an understanding of the environmental context, managers develop a number of different types of goals and plans.
   - Decision making is the underlying framework of all planning because every step of the planning process involves a decision.

2. Discuss the purpose of organizational goals, identify different kinds of goals, discuss who sets goals, and describe how to manage multiple goals. Goals serve four basic purposes:
   - provide guidance and direction
   - facilitate planning
   - inspire motivation and commitment
   - promote evaluation and control
   - Goals can be differentiated by level, area, and time frame.
   - All managers within an organization need to be involved in the goal-setting process.
   - Managers need to pay special attention to the importance of managing multiple goals through optimizing and other approaches.

3. Identify different kinds of organizational plans, note the time frames for planning, discuss who plans, and describe contingency planning.
   - The major types of plans are strategic, tactical, and operational.
   - Plans are developed across a variety of time horizons, including long-range, intermediate, and short-range time frames.
   - Essential people in an organization responsible for effective planning are the planning staff, planning task forces, the board of directors, the CEO, the executive committee, and line management.
   - Contingency planning helps managers anticipate and plan for unexpected changes.

4. Discuss how tactical plans are developed and executed.
   - Tactical plans are at the middle of the organization, have an intermediate time horizon, and moderate scope.
   - Tactical plans are developed to implement specific parts of a strategic plan.
   - Tactical plans must flow from strategy, specify resource and time issues, and commit human resources.
   - Tactical plans must be effectively executed.

5. Describe the basic types of operational plans used by organizations.
   - Operational plans are at the lower levels of the organization, have a shorter time horizon, and are narrower in scope.
   - Operational plans are derived from a tactical plan and are aimed at achieving one or more operational goals.
   - Two major types of operational plans are single-use and standing plans.
     - Single-use plans are designed to carry out a course of action that is not likely to be repeated in the future. Programs and projects are examples of single-use plans.
     - Standing plans are designed to carry out a course of action that is likely to be repeated several times. Policies, standard operating procedures, and rules and regulations are all standing plans.

6. Identify the major barriers to goal setting and planning, how organizations overcome those barriers, and how to use goals to implement plans.
   - Several barriers exist to effective goal setting and planning:
     - improper reward system
     - dynamic and complex environment
     - reluctance to establish goals
     - resistance to change
     - various constraints
   - Methods for overcoming these barriers include:
     - understanding the purposes of goals and plans
     - communication and participation
     - consistency, revision, and updating
     - an effective reward system
   - One particularly useful technique for managing goal setting and planning is formal goal setting, a process of collaborative goal setting and planning.

Discussion Questions

Questions for Review

1. Describe the nature of organizational goals. Be certain to include both the purposes and the kinds of goals.
2. Describe the scope, responsible personnel, and time frames for each kind of organizational plan. How are plans of different kinds related?
3. Explain the various types of operational plans. Give a real or hypothetical business example for each type. Do not use examples from the text.
4. List the steps in the formal goal-setting process. What are some of the advantages for companies that use this approach? What are some of the problems that may arise from use of this approach?

Questions for Analysis

5. Managers are frequently criticized for focusing too much attention on the achievement of short-term goals. In your opinion, how much attention should be given to long-term versus short-term goals? In the event of a conflict, which should be given priority? Explain your answers.
6. What types of plans and decisions most likely require board of director involvement, and why? What types of decisions and plans are not appropriate for board involvement, and why?
7. Standing plans help make an organization more effective. However, they may inhibit experimentation and organizational learning. Under what conditions, if any, should organizations ignore their own standing plans? In the area of planning, how can an organization balance the need for effectiveness against the need for creativity?

Questions for Application

8. Interview the head of the department in which your major exists. What kinds of goals exist for the department and for the members of the department? Share your findings with the rest of the class.
9. Tell about a time when an organization was not able to fully achieve all of its goals simultaneously. Why did this occur? Is complete realization of all goals impossible for an organization? Why or why not?
10. From your library or the Internet, find information about a company's mission statement and goals. List its mission and some of its strategic, tactical, and operational goals. Explain the relationship you see among the goals at different levels.

Building Effective Communication and Interpersonal Skills

Exercise Overview

Interpersonal skills refer to the manager's ability to communicate with, understand, and motivate individuals and groups. Communication skills are used both to convey information to others effectively and to receive ideas and information effectively from others. Communicating and interacting effectively with many different types of individuals are essential skills for planning. This exercise allows you to think through issues of communication and interaction as they relate to an actual planning situation.

Exercise Background

Larger and more complex organizations require greater complexity of planning to achieve their goals. NASA is responsible for the very complex task of managing U.S. space exploration and therefore has very complex planning needs.

In April 1970, NASA launched the Apollo 13 manned space mission, charged with exploration of the lunar surface. On its way to the moon, the ship developed a malfunction that could have resulted in death for all the crew members. The crew members worked with scientists in Houston to develop a solution to the problem. The capsule was successful in returning to Earth, and no lives were lost.

Exercise Task

1. Watch and listen to the short clip from *Apollo 13*. (This movie was made by Universal Studios in 1995 and was directed by Ron Howard. The script was based on a memoir by astronaut and mission captain Jim Lovell.) Describe the various types of planning and decision-making activities taking place at NASA during the unfolding of the disaster.

2. The biggest obstacles to effective planning in the first few minutes of this crisis were the rapid and unexpected changes occurring in a dynamic and complex environment. List elements of the situation that contributed to dynamism (elements that were rapidly changing). List elements that contributed to complexity. What kinds of actions did NASA's planning staff take to overcome obstacles presented by the dynamic and complex environment? Suggest any other useful actions the staff could have taken.

3. NASA managers and astronauts did not use a formal planning process in their approach to this situation. Why not? Is there any part of the formal planning process that could have been helpful? What does this example suggest to you about the advantages and limitations of the formal planning process?

Building Effective Time-Management Skills

Exercise Overview

Time-management skills refer to the manager's ability to prioritize work, to work efficiently, and to delegate appropriately. This exercise will help you develop your time-management skills by relating them to the process of goal optimization.

Exercise Background

All managers face myriad goals, challenges, opportunities, and demands on their time. Juggling all these requires a clear understanding of priorities, time availability, and related factors. Assume that you are planning to open your own business, a retail store in a local shopping mall. You are starting from scratch, with no prior business connections. You do, however, have a strong and impressive business plan that you know will work.

In planning your business, you know that you need to meet with the following parties:

1. The mall manager, to negotiate a lease
2. A local banker, to arrange partial financing
3. An attorney, to incorporate your business
4. An accountant, to set up a bookkeeping system
5. Suppliers, to arrange credit terms and delivery schedules
6. An advertising agency, to start promoting your business
7. A staffing agency, to hire employees
8. A design firm, to plan the physical layout of the store

Exercise Task

With the background information above as a context, do the following:

1. Develop a schedule listing the sequence in which you need to meet with the eight parties above. Your

schedule should be developed to minimize back-tracking (seeing one party and then having to see him or her again after seeing someone else).

2. Compare your schedule with that of a classmate and discuss differences.

3. Are there different schedules that are equally valid?

CHAPTER CLOSING CASE

PLANNING THE SUBURBAN FUTURE

McMansions, condos, townhouses, golf resorts, retirement communities, and family-oriented suburban neighborhoods all spring from the vision of Bob Toll, founder and head of Toll Brothers, one of the largest home construction firms in the United States. Home construction projects require lots of planning, for materials, time, labor, and money. Toll's large developments require even more planning, to comply with building codes, provide roads and parks, and integrate with emergency services and schools. There is an additional layer of planning at Toll. Bob Toll has plans to expand his company beyond its current markets and products, to dominate the home building industry.

Bruce and Bob Toll began their partnership in 1967, building one-of-a-kind custom homes in the Philadelphia area. Each home was made to order for a specific client. The company developed several parcels of rural land into complete neighborhoods and by the early 1980s, expanded into neighboring states.

By the time Toll Brothers went public in 1986, the vision had evolved. A close examination of projects revealed that higher-end houses were more costly but less profitable. Too many choices led to errors and delays that drove expenses up. So Toll became a semi-custom builder, offering a few house styles and a limited number of customizable options. The proj-

ects were still luxurious, in a style Bob Toll calls "estate homes," but which most refer to as "McMansions."

This vision proved very profitable for Toll through 2000, and the company expanded into 18 states, primarily in the Northeast and mid-Atlantic regions. The vision evolved further into something broader. Toll properties are now found in Florida, the Midwest, and the West. The product line is broader too, spanning styles from single family homes to retirement villages to urban townhomes. Today, Bob Toll's vision is a company that "could build any luxury home, in any style, in any place where there was opportunity."

The vision translates into a set of strategic goals, which then inform Toll's tactical and operational goals. The most striking element of Toll's strategy is its national reach. Housing construction is one of the last industries in the United States not dominated by a few national or international companies. Only about 20 percent of the homes built in the United States each year are the product of a national homebuilder. So an important set of strategic goals at Toll relates to growth. The company would like to grow by 15 to 20 percent each year. Other strategic goals relate to developing new community housing concepts, entering new regions, and keeping expenses low.

Tactical goals support these strategic goals. Middle-level managers within Toll have the responsibility for identifying growth communities, for example. Design teams look at customer buying patterns and competitors' designs to determine regional design preferences. Designers also want to know which upgrades customers select. Toll has found that few buyers will pay for extra insulation, but whirlpool tubs and oversized wood moldings are popular. To reduce costs, Toll hires only through subcontractors, who often follow the company from site to site. Toll builds many of its own subcomponents, such as roof trusses, at regional factories, which improves quality, lowers cost, and ensures timely supply.

Toll has a team of buyers who scout for desirable properties. Newspaper ads, civic groups, and local property owners are all sources of tips. After purchase, other managers work with mayors and planning boards to design a development that will meet with community approval. These managers are implementing operational goals. Each development offers a few home models for buyers to choose from. If a new design is needed, it can be created in weeks, by designers who tweak a floor plan and adapt the exterior to meet local tastes.

Toll's tight integration of vision and goals does not guarantee success. One challenge is the nature of the industry itself. Housing markets are characterized by periods of rising prices and rapid growth, followed by a price collapse and growth slowdown, in a boom-and-bust cycle. Another challenge is the ability to guess correctly about the local economy and growth. High employment, mortgage interest rates, and even the price of gasoline influence home buyers' decisions.

Industry growth has been very strong for the last decade. The cost of building one of Toll's typical 2,700 square foot homes has remained fairly steady, at about $300,000. In the hot markets Toll favors, the average selling price was $425,000 in 2003; in 2006, this figure has ballooned to $695,000, before upgrades. One neighborhood development could net the firm as much as $100 million. Careful planning and efficient implementation keep Toll flourishing.

CASE QUESTIONS

1. What are the different time frames for planning at Toll? Give an example for each time frame that you identify.
2. How do managers at different levels in the organization contribute to planning at Toll?
3. Choose one element of Bob Toll's vision for his company. Show how it relates to goals at the strategic, tactical, and operational levels.

CASE REFERENCES

"2005 Annual Report," Toll Brothers website, www.tollbrothers.com on March 7, 2006; Maria Bartiromo, "Jitters on the Home Front," *BusinessWeek*, March 6, 2006, www .businessweek.com on March 7, 2006; Jon Birger, "Hang on to the Homebuilders," *Fortune*, August 22, 2005, www.fortune.com on March 7, 2006; Peter Coy, "Why Housing Looks Rickety," *BusinessWeek*, April 20, 2006, www. businessweek.com on April 10, 2006; Jon Gertner, "Chasing Ground," *New York Times Magazine*, October 16, 2005, pp. 46–82.

YOU MAKE THE CALL

Steering Citigroup

1. Assume you are Charles Prince; what kinds of goals and plans are most relevant to you and your job?
2. Assume that you are the manager of a small Citibank retail operation. What kinds of goals and plans are most relevant to you?
3. Explain how Citigroup might develop contingency plans related to its renewed focus on ethical conduct.
4. Citigroup recently bought a regional bank corporation in Texas as a way to establish retail operations in that state. The regional bank corporation operated 120 branches at the time it was bought by Citigroup. Discuss how Citigroup might have used various kinds of operational plans as it converted the regional corporation into a Citigroup operation.

Test Prepper

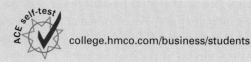

college.hmco.com/business/students

Choose the correct answer. Answers are found at the back of the book.

1. T   F   The cornerstone of planning is decision making.

2. T   F   When a manager optimizes, he or she attempts to solve a problem as quickly and as efficiently as possible.

3. T   F   The line managers at middle and lower levels of the organization usually execute the plans developed by top managers.

4. T   F   Rules, regulations, and standard operating procedures are all examples of standing plans.

5. T   F   Effective goal setting and comprehensive planning ensure organizational success.

6. Goals serve all of the following purposes EXCEPT
   A. to provide guidance and a unified direction for employees.
   B. to promote good planning.
   C. to serve as a source of motivation for employees.
   D. to provide an effective mechanism for evaluation and control.
   E. to test the commitment employees have to the organization.

7. Jennifer has developed the strategic plan for her organization and is now ready to implement a specific part of this plan. To do so, Jennifer should develop a
   A. mission statement.
   B. tactical plan.
   C. standing plan.
   D. strategic goal.
   E. long-range plan.

8. If you think of each college course you are required to complete to graduate as a project, the single-use plan that is the collection of these projects would be called a
   A. policy.
   B. program.
   C. standing plan.
   D. standard operating procedure.
   E. multiple-use plan.

9. All of the following are major barriers to effective goal setting and planning EXCEPT
   A. improper reward systems.
   B. dynamic and complex environments.
   C. revision and updating of goals.
   D. reluctance to establish goals.
   E. resistance to change.

10. Since failure sometimes results from factors outside the manager's control, people should be assured that failure to reach a goal
   A. will lead to less formal goal setting.
   B. will result in management by objectives.
   C. will not necessarily bring punitive consequences.
   D. will modify the mission of the organization.
   E. will reduce the need for contingency planning.

Managing Strategy and Strategic Planning

LEARNING OBJECTIVES

After studying this chapter, you should be able to:

1. Discuss the components of strategy, types of strategic alternatives, and the distinction between strategy formulation and strategy implementation.

2. Describe how to use SWOT analysis in formulating strategy.

3. Identify and describe various alternative approaches to business-level strategy formulation.

4. Describe how business-level strategies are implemented.

5. Identify and describe various alternative approaches to corporate-level strategy formulation.

6. Describe how corporate-level strategies are implemented.

7. Discuss international and global strategies.

FIRST THINGS FIRST

The Video Game Wars

"We think gamers will be spending most of their time . . . playing with others and with characters that they care about."

—HOWARD MARKS, CEO, VIDEO GAME MAKER ACCLAIM

Video games often portray war-fighting action, yet this is a different kind of war. It's a strategic war for dominance in the video game industry. As the industry matures, the number of competitors gets smaller because larger firms absorb smaller ones. Those remaining are more powerful, yet competition is more intense. Electronic Arts and Sony are the largest players in this industry, and each has adopted a different strategy for success.

Electronic Arts (EA) is the number 1 video game producer, making games for just about every game console, handheld game, PC, PDA, and mobile phone. Until this year, the company's strategy has been to develop games around popular movies or sports, such as *Lord of the Rings* and *Madden NFL*. EA's strategy minimizes the huge risk of creating a video game. It takes dozens of staff,

Electronic Arts uses a variety of strategies to compete in the market for electronic games. These are just a few of the firm's products.

millions of dollars, and 12 to 18 months to produce one new game. Sales revenues are unpredictable, and some expensive games have fizzled.

EA, under pressure from entrepreneurial rivals, must increase innovation, shifting to more internal development. However, developers are rotated freely among projects, helping out wherever they are needed. This increases productivity but hurts teamwork. In contrast, the teams at many small studios work on one game from start to finish. Small companies created many of gaming's biggest successes, including *Grand Theft Auto* and *Halo*. EA is switching to dedicated teams that can more readily improve just one segment of programming, for example, how weapons fire or how characters show emotions.

Sony is the number 2 video game producer and makes games solely for its PlayStation platforms. Video game hardware, not the games themselves, has always been its priority. Sony's approach is not focused on blockbusters. Instead, the company tries to manage the risky video game production process by investing less, which has led to lower expenses but also to fewer of the cutting-edge effects and graphics that video game fans love. Some of Sony's top-selling games include *The DaVinci Code*, *Field Commander*, and *Untold Legends*.

While both EA's new strategy and Sony's existing strategy could lead to success, EA's seems to be more in tune with industry changes. One important development is the growing popularity of massive multiplayer online games, known as MMOs. These games network thousands of players into an online community, where members interact through a role-playing scenario. Two of the most widely known MMOs are *EverQuest* and *Halo*. Both of these games allow individual play, group play, and individual or group play with online members. Writing MMO games is more difficult than writing games for individuals or small groups. EA's new emphasis on innovative concepts and increased use of teams should make it easier for them to develop MMOs, while Sony's emphasis on value will not help.

Which strategy is superior? It may not be either because other new strategies are also evolving. Small studio Acclaim is developing high-quality games that it gives away for free. Product endorsement fees for items highlighted within the game cover the cost. Acclaim hopes that users will understand that the ads pay for the game, much as TV advertising pays for broadcasts. Acclaim also sells virtual items, for real money. The users can resell the items when they are finished using them in the game. Acclaim's games are primarily MMOs. "We think gamers will be spending most of their time . . . playing with others and with characters that they care about," says Acclaim CEO Howard Marks. Instead of relying on medieval Dungeons-and-Dragons settings, the company offers games for all ages and with a wide variety of settings. Finally, Acclaim's games are available as online downloads. The games work on any platform that enables downloaded games. Thus far, only the Microsoft Xbox does so, but Acclaim hopes other game console makers will follow suit.

In a rapidly changing and complex environment, with competitors that have very different resources and weaknesses, using technology that is still evolving, there are a number of possible strategic responses. Only time will tell which company has adopted the correct approach.[1]

The video game market reflects one of the most critical concerns for an organization, managing strategy and strategic planning. One dominant company, Electronic Arts, has flourished by pursuing one strategy, while another dominant company, Sony, has found success with a very different strategy. Yet each firm must also continue to be vigilant to new strategic models being developed by other firms seeking a share of the lucrative video game market. If either EA or Sony stumbles it stands to lose millions of dollars in revenues. But those firms that most effectively manage their strategies are virtually certain to reap huge rewards. This chapter discusses how organizations manage strategy and strategic planning. We begin by examining the nature of strategic management, including its components and alternatives. We then describe the kinds of analysis needed for firms to formulate their strategies. Next we examine how organizations first formulate and then implement business-level strategies, followed by a parallel discussion at the corporate strategy level. We conclude with a discussion of international and global strategies.

The Nature of Strategic Management

A **strategy** is a comprehensive plan for accomplishing an organization's goals. **Strategic management**, in turn, is a way of approaching business opportunities and challenges—it is a comprehensive and ongoing management process aimed at formulating and implementing effective strategies. Finally, **effective strategies** are those that promote a superior alignment between the organization and its environment and the achievement of strategic goals.[2]

The Components of Strategy

In general, a well-conceived strategy addresses three areas: distinctive competence, scope, and resource deployment. A **distinctive competence** is something the organization does exceptionally well. (We discuss distinctive competencies more fully later.) A distinctive competence of the Limited is speed in moving inventory. It tracks consumer preferences daily with point-of-sale computers, electronically transmits orders to suppliers in Hong Kong, charters 747s to fly products to the United States, and has products in stores 48 hours later. Because other retailers take weeks or sometimes months to accomplish the same things, the Limited uses this distinctive competence to remain competitive.[3]

The **scope** of a strategy specifies the range of markets in which an organization will compete. Hershey Foods has essentially restricted its scope to the confectionery business, with a few related activities in other food-processing areas. In contrast, its biggest competitor, Mars, has adopted a broader scope by competing in the pet food business and the electronics industry, among others. Some organizations, called conglomerates, compete in dozens or even hundreds of markets.

A strategy should also include an outline of the organization's projected **resource deployment**—how it will distribute its resources across the areas in which it competes. General Electric, for example, has been using profits from its highly successful U.S. operations to invest heavily in new businesses in Europe and Asia. Alternatively, the firm might have chosen to invest in different industries in its domestic market or to invest more heavily in Latin America. The choices it makes as to where and how much to invest reflect issues of resource deployment.

---

strategy
A comprehensive plan for accomplishing an organization's goals

strategic management
A comprehensive and ongoing management process aimed at formulating and implementing effective strategies; a way of approaching business opportunities and challenges

effective strategy
A strategy that promotes a superior alignment between the organization and its environment and the achievement of strategic goals

distinctive competence
An organizational strength possessed by only a small number of competing firms

scope
When applied to strategy, it specifies the range of markets in which an organization will compete

resource deployment
How an organization distributes its resources across the areas in which it competes

Types of Strategic Alternatives

Most businesses today also develop strategies at two distinct levels. These levels provide a rich combination of strategic alternatives for organizations. The two general levels are business-level strategies and corporate-level strategies. **Business-level strategy** is the set of strategic alternatives from which an organization chooses as it conducts business in a particular industry or market. Such alternatives help the organization focus its competitive efforts for each industry or market in a targeted and focused manner.

Corporate-level strategy is the set of strategic alternatives from which an organization chooses as it manages its operations simultaneously across several industries and several markets.[4] As we discuss later, most large companies today compete in a variety of industries and markets. Thus, although they develop business-level strategies for each industry or market, they also develop an overall strategy that helps define the mix of industries and markets that are of interest to the firm.

Strategy Formulation and Implementation

Drawing a distinction between strategy formulation and strategy implementation is also instructive. **Strategy formulation** is the set of processes involved in creating or determining the strategies of the organization, whereas **strategy implementation** is the methods by which strategies are operationalized or executed within the organization. The primary distinction is along the lines of content versus process: The formulation stage determines what the strategy is, and the implementation stage focuses on how the strategy is achieved.

Sometimes the processes of formulating and implementing strategies are rational, systematic, and planned. This is often referred to as a **deliberate strategy**—a plan chosen and implemented to support specific goals.[5] Texas Instruments (TI) excels at formulating and implementing deliberate strategies. TI uses a planning process that assigns most senior managers two distinct responsibilities: an operational, short-term responsibility and a strategic, long-term responsibility. Thus one manager may be responsible for both increasing the efficiency of semiconductor operations over the next year (operational, short term) and investigating new materials for semiconductor manufacturing in the twenty-first century (strategic, long term). TI's objective is to help managers make short-term operational decisions while keeping in mind longer-term goals and objectives.

Other times, however, organizations use an **emergent strategy**—a pattern of action that develops over time in an organization in the absence of mission and goals or despite mission and goals.[6] Implementing emergent strategies involves allocating resources even though an organization has not explicitly chosen its strategies. 3M has at times benefited from emergent strategies. The invention of invisible tape, for instance, provides a good example. Entrepreneurial engineers working independently took the invention to their boss, who concluded that it did not have major market potential because it was not part of an approved research and development plan. Only when the product was evaluated at the highest levels in the organization was it accepted and made part of 3M's product mix. Of course, 3M's Scotch tape became a major success despite the fact that it arose outside of the firm's established practices. 3M now counts on emergent strategies to help expand its numerous businesses.

business-level strategy
The set of strategic alternatives from which an organization chooses as it conducts business in a particular industry or market

corporate-level strategy
The set of strategic alternatives from which an organization chooses as it manages its operations simultaneously across several industries and several markets

strategy formulation
The set of processes involved in creating or determining the strategies of the organization; it focuses on the content of strategies

strategy implementation
The methods by which strategies are operationalized or executed within the organization; it focuses on the processes through which strategies are achieved

deliberate strategy
A plan of action that an organization chooses and implements to support specific goals

emergent strategy
A pattern of action that develops over time in an organization in the absence of mission and goals or despite mission and goals

What are the basic components of strategy?	*Distinguish between business- and corporate-level strategies. Is one or the other more likely to be deliberate or emergent?*

Using SWOT Analysis to Formulate Strategy

The starting point in formulating strategy is usually SWOT analysis. **SWOT** is an acronym that stands for strengths, weaknesses, opportunities, and threats. As shown in Figure 8.1, SWOT analysis is a careful evaluation of an organization's internal strengths and weaknesses as well as its environmental opportunities and threats. In SWOT analysis, the best strategies accomplish an organization's mission by (1) exploiting an organization's opportunities and strengths while (2) neutralizing its threats and (3) avoiding (or correcting) its weaknesses.

> *SWOT*
> An acronym that stands for strengths, weaknesses, opportunities, and threats

Evaluating an Organization's Strengths

Organizational strengths are skills and capabilities that enable an organization to conceive of and implement its strategies. Sears, for example, has a nationwide network of trained service employees who repair Sears appliances. Jane Thompson, a Sears executive, conceived of a plan to consolidate repair and home improvement services nationwide under the well-known Sears brand name and to promote them as a general repair operation for all appliances, not just those purchased from Sears. Thus the firm capitalized on existing capabilities and the strength of its name to launch a new operation.[7] Different strategies call on different skills and capabilities.

> *organizational strength*
> A skill or capability that enables an organization to conceive of and implement its strategies

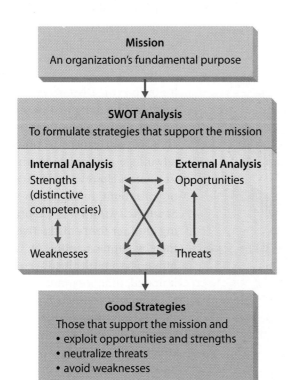

Figure 8.1
SWOT ANALYSIS

SWOT analysis is one of the most important steps in formulating strategy. Using the organization's mission as a context, managers assess internal strengths (distinctive competencies) and weaknesses as well as external opportunities and threats. The goal is then to develop good strategies that exploit opportunities and strengths, neutralize threats, and avoid weaknesses.

For example, Matsushita Electric has demonstrated strengths in manufacturing and selling consumer electronics under the brand name Panasonic. Matsushita's strength in electronics does not ensure success, however, if the firm expands into insurance, swimming pool manufacturing, or retail. Different strategies like these require different organizational strengths. SWOT analysis divides organizational strengths into two categories: common strengths and distinctive competencies.

Common Organizational Strengths A **common strength** is an organizational capability possessed by a large number of competing firms. For example, all the major Hollywood film studios possess common strengths in lighting, sound recording, set and costume design, and makeup. *Competitive parity* exists when large numbers of competing firms are able to implement the same strategy. In this situation, organizations generally attain only average levels of performance. Thus a film company that exploits only its common strengths in choosing and implementing strategies is not likely to go beyond average performance.

Distinctive Competencies A *distinctive competence* is a strength possessed by only a small number of competing firms. Distinctive competencies are rare among a set of competitors. George Lucas's Industrial Light & Magic (ILM), for example, brought the cinematic art of special effects to new heights. Some of ILM's special effects can be produced by no other organization; these rare special effects are thus ILM's distinctive competencies. Organizations that exploit their distinctive competencies often obtain a *competitive advantage* and attain above-normal economic performance.[8] Indeed, a main purpose of SWOT analysis is to discover an organization's distinctive competencies so that the organization can choose and implement strategies that exploit its unique organizational strengths.

Effective business strategies generally spell out such things as distinctive competencies, resource deployment, and scope. Consider, for instance, the success currently being enjoyed by Seth Goldman, owner and "Tea-EO" of Honest Tea. The distinctive competence of Honest Tea is its brewing technology: it uses real tea leaves and spring water, and adds only a minimum amount of sweetener. It invests heavily in building strong relations with key partners such as socially conscious suppliers and retailers. And it limits operations to packaged tea beverages. Honest Tea saw sales rise 67% in 2005 and seems headed toward long-term "prosperi-tea."

Imitation of Distinctive Competencies An organization that possesses distinctive competencies and exploits them in the strategies it chooses can expect to obtain a competitive advantage and above-normal economic performance. However, its success will lead other organizations to duplicate these advantages. **Strategic imitation** is the practice of duplicating another firm's distinctive competence and thereby implementing a valuable strategy. Although some distinctive competencies can be imitated, others cannot be. When a distinctive competence cannot be imitated, strategies that exploit these competencies generate sustained competitive advantage. A **sustained competitive advantage** is a competitive advantage that exists after all attempts at strategic imitation have ceased.[9]

A distinctive competence might not be imitated for three reasons. First, the acquisition or development of the distinctive competence may depend on unique historical circumstances that other organizations cannot replicate. Caterpillar, for example, obtained a sustained competitive advantage when the U.S. Army granted it a long-term contract during World War II. The army felt obligated to offer this contract because of the acute international construction requirements necessary to meet the army's needs. Caterpillar's current competitors, including Komatsu and John Deere & Company, cannot re-create these circumstances.

Second, a distinctive competence might be difficult to imitate because its nature and character might not be known or understood by competing firms. Procter & Gamble, for example, considers that its sustained competitive advantage is based on its manufacturing practices. Large sections of Procter & Gamble's plants are screened off to keep this information secure. Industrial Light & Magic also refuses to disclose how it creates some of its special effects.

Finally, a distinctive competence can be difficult to imitate if it is based on complex social phenomena, like organizational teamwork or culture. Competing organizations may know, for example, that a firm's success is directly traceable to the teamwork among its managers but, because teamwork is a difficult thing to create, may not be able to imitate this distinctive competence.

Evaluating an Organization's Weaknesses

Organizational weaknesses are skills and capabilities that do not enable an organization to choose and implement strategies that support its mission. An organization has essentially two ways of addressing weaknesses. First, it may need to make investments to obtain the strengths required to implement strategies that support its mission. Second, it may need to modify its mission so that it can be accomplished with the skills and capabilities that the organization already possesses.

In practice, organizations have a difficult time focusing on weaknesses, in part because organization members are often reluctant to admit that they do not possess all the skills and capabilities needed. Evaluating weaknesses also calls into question the judgment of managers who chose the organization's mission in the first place and who failed to invest in the skills and capabilities needed to accomplish it.

Organizations that fail either to recognize or to overcome their weaknesses are likely to suffer from competitive disadvantages. An organization has a **competitive disadvantage** when it is not implementing valuable strategies that are being implemented by competing organizations. Organizations with a competitive disadvantage can expect to attain below-average levels of performance.

Evaluating an Organization's Opportunities and Threats

Whereas evaluating strengths and weaknesses focuses attention on the internal workings of an organization, evaluating opportunities and threats requires analyzing an organization's environment. **Organizational opportunities** are areas that may generate higher performance. **Organizational threats** are areas that increase the difficulty of an organization's performing at a high level. *The Business of Ethics* shows how Toyota has used its organizational strengths to capitalize on environmental opportunities regarding consumer interest in fuel-efficient hybrid automobiles.

Porter's "five forces" model of the competitive environment, as discussed in Chapter 3, can be used to characterize the extent of opportunity and threat in an

organizational weaknesses
A skill or capability that does not enable an organization to choose and implement strategies that support its mission

competitive disadvantage
A situation in which an organization is not implementing valuable strategies that are being implemented by competing organizations

organizational opportunity
An area in the environment that, if exploited, may generate higher performance

organizational threat
An area in the environment that increases the difficulty of an organization's achieving high performance

The Business of Ethics

Toyota's Hybrid Autos

Japanese car makers are following a differentiation strategy. Led by Toyota, Japanese firms have created a number of small, innovative, and affordable autos. Toyota's hybrid Prius, with a fuel-efficient gas-electric engine, is the "Most Satisfying" car, according to *Consumer Reports*. Ninety-five percent of Prius owners would buy one again. A Prius spends just nine days on a dealer lot before being sold and goes for a 10 percent premium over sticker price. Apparently, everybody loves the Prius. But is Toyota as green as it claims?

Prius was introduced in 2000. The hybrid concept proved so popular that virtually every other auto maker now offers a hybrid, even GM and Ford. Hybrid vehicles have two engines, one gas and the other electric. Gas power starts the vehicle, and then the electric motor starts. Batteries are recharged by braking or coasting, and the gas motor kicks in while climbing hills or passing.

Hybrid engines use less gas. How much less depends on the ratio of gas to electric power. The 2005 Prius is rated by the EPA for 51 miles per gallon in the city and 60 miles per gallon on the highway. A non-hybrid Toyota of similar size, such as the Corolla, gets 30 and 38 mpg, respectively. Less gas translates into lower operating costs as well as less fuel exploration and refining, and therefore less environmental impact. Toyota estimates that by April 2006, 135 million fewer

gallons of gasoline were saved by the Prius. Hybrid engines also run more cleanly, producing fewer emissions. This helps hybrids meet stringent emissions testing, which is mandatory in California and becoming more common elsewhere.

Yet Toyota is fighting against some environmental causes. One problem is its strategy of offering a hybrid version of every vehicle it sells. While this may seem a noble cause, the results have been disappointing. Toyota's hybrid SUVs and trucks get only slightly better gas mileage than the non-hybrid versions. Therefore, consumers are misled about their vehicles' environmental effect. Also, Toyota's lobbyists are working to defeat federal and state legislation to mandate better fuel efficiency and cleaner emissions.

When Toyota, or any company, attempts to differentiate itself, it had better make sure that the facts support its claims. Conservationists, beware!

References: Bradley Berman, "Hybrid Talk: Big Auto Bandies the H Word," *BusinessWeek*, April 11, 2006, www.businessweek.com on March 8, 2006; Alex Taylor III, "The Birth of the Prius," *Fortune*, March 6, 2006, pp. 111–124; Peter Valdes-Dapena, "Consumer Reports: Prius, Corvette 'Most Satisfying' to Own," *Money*, March 2, 2006, www .cnnmoney.com on March 22, 2006; Peter Valdes-Dapena, "Toyota Tops Hottest Cars in America," *Money*, March 18, 2006, www.cnnmoney .com on March 22, 2006; Sarah A. Webster, "Ad Attacks Toyota's Record," *Detroit Free Press*, October 24, 2005, www.freep.com on March 22, 2006.

organization's environment. Recall that Porter's five forces are level of competitive rivalry, power of suppliers, power of buyers, threat of substitutes, and threat of new entrants. In general, when the level of competitive rivalry, the power of suppliers and buyers, and the threat of substitutes and new entrants are all high, an industry has relatively few opportunities and numerous threats. Firms in these types of industries typically have the potential to achieve only normal economic performance. On the other hand, when the level of rivalry, the power of suppliers and buyers, and the threat of substitutes and new entrants are all low, then an industry has numerous opportunities and relatively few threats. These industries hold the potential for above-normal performance for organizations in them.[10]

concept CHECK

What do the letters S, W, O, *and* T *represent when conducting a SWOT analysis?*

Under what circumstances might a firm find it advantageous to share with others the details of one of its distinctive competencies?

Formulating Business-Level Strategies

A number of frameworks have been developed for identifying the major strategic alternatives that organizations should consider when choosing their business-level strategies. Three important classification schemes are Porter's generic strategies, the Miles and Snow typology, and strategies based on the product life cycle.

Porter's Generic Strategies

According to Michael Porter, organizations may pursue a differentiation, overall cost leadership, or focus strategy at the business level.[11] Table 8.1 summarizes each of these strategies. An organization that pursues a ***differentiation strategy*** seeks to distinguish itself from competitors through the quality of its products or services. Firms that successfully implement a differentiation strategy are able to charge more than competitors because customers are willing to pay more to obtain the extra value they perceive.[12] Rolex pursues a differentiation strategy. Rolex watches are handmade of precious metals like gold or platinum and stainless steel, and are subjected to strenuous tests of quality and reliability. The firm's reputation enables it to charge thousands of dollars for its watches. Coca-Cola and Pepsi compete in the market for bottled water on the basis of differentiation. Coke touts its Dasani brand on the basis of its fresh taste, whereas Pepsi promotes its Aquafina brand on the basis of its purity.[13] Other firms that use differentiation strategies are Lexus, Nikon, Mont Blanc, and Ralph Lauren.

An organization implementing an ***overall cost leadership strategy*** attempts to gain a competitive advantage by reducing its costs below the costs of competing firms. By keeping costs low, the organization is able to sell its products at low prices and still make a profit. Timex uses an overall cost leadership strategy. For decades, this firm has specialized in manufacturing relatively simple, low-cost watches for the mass market. The price of Timex watches, starting around $39.95, is low

> **differentiation strategy**
> A strategy in which an organization seeks to distinguish itself from competitors through the quality of its products or services

> **overall cost leadership strategy**
> A strategy in which an organization attempts to gain a competitive advantage by reducing its costs below the costs of competing firms

Table 8.1
PORTER'S GENERIC STRATEGIES

Michael Porter has proposed three generic strategies. Each of these strategies—differentiation, overall cost leadership, and focus—is presumed to be widely applicable to many different competitive situations.

Strategy Type	Definition	Examples
Differentiation	Distinguish products or services	Rolex (watches) Mercedes-Benz (automobiles) Nikon (cameras) Cross (writing instruments) Hewlett-Packard (handheld calculators)
Overall cost leadership	Reduce manufacturing and other costs	Timex (watches) Hyundai (automobiles) Kodak (cameras) BIC (writing instruments) Texas Instruments (handheld calculators)
Focus	Concentrate on specific regional market, product market, or group of buyers	Tag Heuer (watches) Fiat, Alfa Romeo (automobiles) Polaroid (cameras) Waterman (writing instruments) Fisher-Price (handheld calculators)

because of the company's efficient high-volume manufacturing capacity. Poland Springs and Crystal Geyser bottled waters are promoted on the basis of their low cost. Other firms that implement overall cost leadership strategies are Hyundai, Eastman Kodak, BIC, and Old Navy.

A firm pursuing a ***focus strategy*** concentrates on a specific regional market, product line, or group of buyers. This strategy may have either a differentiation focus, whereby the firm differentiates its products in the focus market, or an overall cost leadership focus, whereby the firm manufactures and sells its products at low cost in the focus market. In the watch industry, Tag Heuer follows a focus differentiation strategy by selling only rugged waterproof watches to active consumers. Fiat follows a focus cost leadership strategy by selling its automobiles only in Italy and in selected regions of Europe; Alfa Romeo uses focus differentiation to sell its high-performance cars in these same markets. Fisher-Price uses focus differentiation to sell electronic calculators with large, brightly colored buttons to the parents of preschoolers; stockbroker Edward Jones focuses on small-town settings. General Mills focuses new-product development on consumers who eat meals while driving—their watchword is "Can we make it 'one-handed'?" so that drivers can safely eat or drink it.[14]

> **focus strategy**
> A strategy in which an organization concentrates on a specific regional market, product line, or group of buyers

The Miles and Snow Typology

A second classification of strategic options was developed by Raymond Miles and Charles Snow.[15] These authors suggested that business-level strategies generally fall into one of four categories: prospector, defender, analyzer, and reactor. Table 8.2 summarizes each of these strategies. Of course, different businesses within the same company might pursue different strategies.

A firm that follows a ***prospector strategy*** is a highly innovative firm that is constantly seeking out new markets and new opportunities and is oriented toward growth and risk taking. Over the years, 3M has prided itself on being one of the most innovative major corporations in the world. Employees at 3M are constantly encouraged to develop new products and ideas in a creative and

> **prospector strategy**
> A strategy in which the firm encourages creativity and flexibility and is often decentralized

Table 8.2
THE MILES AND SNOW TYPOLOGY

The Miles and Snow typology identifies four strategic types of organizations. Three of these—the prospector, the defender, and the analyzer—can all be effective in certain circumstances. The fourth type—the reactor—represents an ineffective approach to strategy.

Strategy Type	Definition	Examples
Prospector	Is innovative and growth oriented, searches for new markets and new growth opportunities, encourages risk taking	Amazon.com 3M Rubbermaid
Defender	Protects current markets, maintains stable growth, serves current customers	BIC eBay Mrs. Fields
Analyzer	Maintains current markets and current customer satisfaction with moderate emphasis on innovation	DuPont IBM Yahoo!
Reactor	No clear strategy, reacts to changes in the environment, drifts with events	International Harvester Joseph Schlitz Brewing Co. Kmart Montgomery Ward

entrepreneurial way. This focus on innovation has led 3M to develop a wide range of new products and markets, including invisible tape and anti-stain fabric treatments. Amazon.com is also following a prospector strategy as it constantly seeks new market opportunities for selling different kinds of products through its websites.[16]

Rather than seeking new growth opportunities and innovation, a company that follows a ***defender strategy*** concentrates on protecting its current markets, maintaining stable growth, and serving current customers, generally by lowering its costs and improving the performance of its existing products. With the maturity of the market for writing instruments, BIC has used this approach—it has adopted a less aggressive, less entrepreneurial style of management and has chosen to defend its substantial market share in the industry. It has done this by emphasizing efficient manufacturing and customer satisfaction. Although eBay is expanding aggressively into foreign markets, the online auctioneer is still pursuing what amounts to a defender strategy, in that it is keeping its focus primarily on the auction business. Thus, while it is prospecting for new markets, it is defending its core business focus.[17]

> **defender strategy**
> A strategy in which the firm focuses on lowering costs and improving the performance of current products

A business that uses an ***analyzer strategy***, in which it attempts to maintain its current businesses and to be somewhat innovative in new businesses, combines elements of prospectors and defenders. Most large companies use this approach because they want to both protect their base of operations and create new market opportunities. IBM uses analyzer strategies. DuPont is currently using an analyzer strategy; the firm is relying heavily on its existing chemical and fiber operations to fuel its earnings for the foreseeable future. At the same time, though, DuPont is moving systematically into new business areas such as biotech agriculture and pharmaceuticals. Yahoo! is also using this strategy by keeping its primary focus on its role as an Internet portal while simultaneously seeking to extend that portal into more and more applications.[18]

> **analyzer strategy**
> A strategy in which the firm attempts to maintain its current businesses and to be somewhat innovative in new businesses

Finally, a business that follows a ***reactor strategy*** has no consistent strategic approach; it drifts with environmental events, reacting to but failing to anticipate or influence those events. Not surprisingly, these firms usually do not perform as well as organizations that implement other strategies. Although most organizations would deny using reactor strategies, during the 1970s International Harvester Company (IH) was clearly a reactor. At a time when IH's market for trucks, construction equipment, and agricultural equipment was booming, IH failed to keep pace with its competitors. By the time a recession cut demand for its products, it was too late for IH to respond, and the company lost millions of dollars. The firm was forced to sell off virtually all of its businesses, except its truck-manufacturing business. IH, now renamed Navistar, moved from being a dominant firm in trucking, agriculture, and construction to a medium-size truck manufacturer because it failed to anticipate changes in its environment.

> **reactor strategy**
> A strategy in which a firm has no consistent approach to strategy

Strategies Based on the Product Life Cycle

The ***product life cycle*** is a model that shows how sales volume changes over the life of products. Understanding the four stages in the product life cycle helps managers recognize that strategies need to evolve over time. As Figure 8.2 shows, the cycle begins when a new product or technology is first introduced. In this *introduction stage,* demand may be very high and sometimes outpaces the firm's ability to supply

> **product life cycle**
> A model that portrays how sales volume for products changes over the life of products

Figure 8.2

THE PRODUCT LIFE CYCLE

Managers can use the framework of the product life cycle—introduction, growth, maturity, and decline—to plot strategy. For example, management may decide on a differentiation strategy for a product in the introduction stage and a prospector approach for a product in the growth stage. By understanding this cycle and where a particular product falls within it, managers can develop more effective strategies for extending product life.

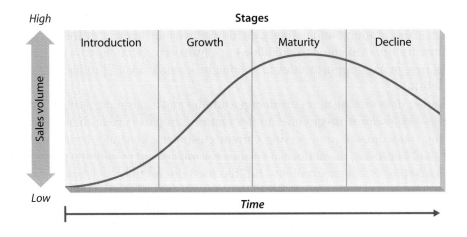

the product. At this stage, managers need to focus their efforts on "getting product out the door" without sacrificing quality. Managing growth by hiring new employees and managing inventories and cash flow are also concerns during this stage.

During the *growth stage,* more firms begin producing the product, and sales continue to grow. Important management issues include ensuring quality and delivery and beginning to differentiate an organization's product from competitors' products. Entry into the industry during the growth stage may threaten an organization's competitive advantage; thus strategies to slow the entry of competitors are important.

After a period of growth, products enter a third phase. During this *maturity stage,* overall demand growth for a product begins to slow down, and the number of new firms producing the product begins to decline. The number of established firms producing the product may also begin to decline. This period of maturity is essential if an organization is going to survive in the long run. Product differentiation concerns are still important during this stage, but keeping costs low and beginning the search for new products or services are also important strategic considerations.

In the *decline stage,* demand for the product or technology decreases, the number of organizations producing the product drops, and total sales drop. Demand often declines because all those who were interested in purchasing a particular product have already done so. Organizations that fail to anticipate the decline stage in earlier stages of the life cycle may go out of business. Those that differentiate their product, keep their costs low, or develop new products or services may do well during this stage.

concept

CHECK

Describe Porter's generic strategies and identify an example of each.

Identify examples beyond those noted above for each of the strategies in the Miles and Snow typology.

Implementing Business-Level Strategies

As we noted earlier, after business strategies are formulated, they must then be implemented. To do this effectively, managers must integrate the activities of several different functions. *Marketing* and *sales,* for example, are used to promote products or services and the overall public image of the organization (often through various types of advertising), price products or services, directly contact customers, and make sales. *Accounting* and *finance* control the flow of money both within the organization and from outside sources to the organization, and *manufacturing* creates the organization's products or services.[19] Organizational *culture,* as discussed in Chapter 3, also helps firms implement their strategies.[20]

Implementing Porter's Generic Strategies

Differentation and cost leadership can each be implemented through these basic organizational functions. (Focus is implemented through the same approaches, depending on which one it is based on.)

Differentiation Strategy In general, to support differentiation, marketing and sales must emphasize the high-quality, high-value image of the organization's products or services. Neiman Marcus, a department store for financially secure consumers, has excelled at using marketing to support its differentiation strategy. People do not go to Neiman Marcus just to buy clothes or to shop for home electronics. Instead, a trip to Neiman Marcus is advertised as a "total shopping experience." Customers who want to shop for $3,000 pet houses, $50,000 mink coats, and $7,000 exercise machines recognize that the store caters to their needs. Other organizations that have used their marketing function to implement a differentiation strategy include Chanel, Calvin Klein, and Bloomingdale's.

Companies use a variety of business-level strategies to enhance their competitiveness. For instance, Ben & Jerry's Homemade Ice Cream uses a differentiation strategy, promoting the image that their ice creams are of higher quality and thus worthy of higher prices. To help promote its products, the firm holds an annual free cone day on which its stores typically give away more than one million cones. Aleck Woodmaster is shown here serving up a free ice cream cone at the Ben & Jerry's shop in Montpelier, Vermont.

The function of accounting and finance in a business that is implementing a differentiation strategy is to control the flow of funds without discouraging the creativity needed to constantly develop new products and services to meet customer needs. If keeping track of and controlling the flow of money become more important than determining how money and resources are best spent to meet customer needs, then no organization, whether high-tech firm or fashion designer, will be able to implement a differentiation strategy effectively. In manufacturing, a firm implementing a differentiation strategy must emphasize quality and meeting specific customer needs, rather than simply reducing costs. Manufacturing may sometimes have to keep inventory on hand so that customers will have access to products when they want them. Manufacturing also may have to engage in costly customization to meet customer needs.

The culture of a firm implementing a differentiation strategy, like the firm's other functions, must also emphasize creativity, innovation, and response to customer needs. Lands' End's culture puts the needs of customers ahead of all other considerations. This firm, which sells men's and women's leisure clothing through a catalog service, offers a complete guarantee on merchandise. Dissatisfied customers may return clothes for a full refund or exchange, with no questions asked. Lands' End takes orders 24 hours a day and will ship most orders within 24 hours.

" . . . in the absence of sufficient product differentiation or innovation, it's harder to create consumer value and shareholder value."

A. G. Lafley, CEO of Procter & Gamble
(*Fortune,* February 21, 2005, p. 100)

Items with lost buttons and broken zippers are replaced immediately. The priority given to customer needs is typical of an organization that is successfully implementing a differentiation strategy.

Overall Cost Leadership Strategy   To support cost leadership, marketing and sales are likely to focus on simple product attributes and how these product attributes meet customer needs in a low-cost and effective manner. These organizations are very likely to engage in advertising. Throughout this effort, however, emphasis is on the value that an organization's products provide for the price, rather than on the special features of the product or service. Advertising for BIC pens ("Writes first time, every time"), Timex watches ("Takes a licking and keeps on ticking"), and Wal-Mart stores ("Always the low price brands you trust—always") helps these firms implement cost leadership strategies.

Proper emphasis in accounting and finance is also pivotal. Because the success of the organization depends on having costs lower than the competitors', management must take care to reduce costs wherever possible. Tight financial and accounting controls at Wal-Mart, Costco, and Wells Fargo have helped these organizations implement cost leadership strategies. Manufacturing typically helps, with large runs of highly standardized products. Products are designed both to meet customer needs and to be easily manufactured. Manufacturing emphasizes increased volume of production to reduce the per-unit costs of manufacturing. Organizations such as Toshiba (a Japanese semiconductor firm) and Texas Instruments have used this type of manufacturing to implement cost leadership strategies.

The culture of organizations implementing cost leadership strategies tends to focus on improving the efficiency of manufacturing, sales, and other business functions. Managers in these organizations are almost fanatical about keeping their costs low. Wal-Mart appeals to its customers to leave shopping carts in designated areas in its parking lots with signs that read, "Please—help us keep *your* costs low." Fujitsu Electronics, in its Tokyo manufacturing facilities, operates in plain, unpainted, cinderblock and cement facilities to keep its costs as low as possible.

Implementing Miles and Snow's Strategies

Similarly, a variety of issues must be considered when implementing any of Miles and Snow's strategic options. (Of course, no organization would purposefully choose to implement a reactor strategy.)

Prospector Strategy   An organization implementing a prospector strategy is innovative, seeks new market opportunities, and takes numerous risks. To implement this strategy, organizations need to encourage creativity and flexibility.[21] Creativity helps an organization perceive, or even create, new opportunities in its environment; flexibility enables it to change quickly to take advantage of these new opportunities. Organizations often increase creativity and flexibility by adopting a decentralized organization structure. (An organization is decentralized when major decision-making responsibility is delegated to middle- and lower-level managers.) Johnson & Johnson links decentralization with a prospector strategy. Each of the firm's different businesses is organized into a separate unit, and the managers of these units hold full decision-making responsibility and authority. Often these businesses develop new products for new markets. As the new products develop and sales grow, Johnson & Johnson reorganizes so that each new product is managed in a separate unit.

Defender Strategy   An organization implementing a defender strategy attempts to protect its market from new competitors. It tends to downplay creativity and innovation in bringing out new products or services and to focus its efforts instead on lowering costs or improving the performance of current products. Often a firm implementing a prospector strategy will switch to a defender strategy. This happens when the firm successfully creates a new market or business and then attempts to protect its market from competition. A good example is Mrs. Fields. One of the first firms to introduce high-quality, high-priced cookies, Mrs. Fields sold its product in special cookie stores and grew very rapidly. This success, however, encouraged numerous other companies to enter the market. Increased competition, plus reduced demand for high-priced cookies, threatened Mrs. Fields's market position. To maintain its profitability, the firm slowed its growth and focused on making its current operation more profitable. This behavior is consistent with the defender strategy.

Analyzer Strategy   An organization implementing an analyzer strategy attempts to maintain its current business and to be somewhat innovative in new businesses. Because the analyzer strategy falls somewhere between the prospector strategy (with focus on innovation) and the defender strategy (with focus on maintaining and improving current businesses), the attributes of organizations implementing the analyzer strategy tend to be similar to both of these other types of organizations. They have tight accounting and financial controls as well as high flexibility, efficient production as well as customized products, and creativity along with low costs. Organizations maintain these multiple and contradictory processes with difficulty.

   Starbucks is implementing an analyzer strategy. Although the firm is growing rapidly, its fundamental business is still coffee. At the same time, however, the firm is cautiously branching out into music and ice cream and other food products, and is experimenting with restaurants with more comprehensive menu selections. This approach is allowing Starbucks to remain focused on its core coffee business but to explore new business opportunities at the same time.[22] Similarly, Procter & Gamble has also revised some of its business strategies in an attempt to both protect its core businesses while also expanding into new ones.[23]

	concept CHECK
Identify common implementation issues for Porter's generic strategies and Miles and Snow's strategies.	*What role might organization culture play in implementing business-level strategies?*

Formulating Corporate-Level Strategies

Most large organizations are engaged in several businesses, industries, and markets. Each business or set of businesses within such an organization is frequently referred to as a *strategic business unit,* or *SBU.* An organization such as General Electric operates hundreds of different businesses, making and selling products as diverse as jet engines, nuclear power plants, and light bulbs. GE organizes these businesses into approximately 20 SBUs. Even organizations that sell only one product may operate in several distinct markets.

diversification
The number of different businesses that an organization is engaged in and the extent to which these businesses are related to one another

Decisions about which businesses, industries, and markets an organization will enter, and how to manage these different businesses, are based on an organization's corporate strategy. The most important strategic issue at the corporate level concerns the extent and nature of organizational diversification. ***Diversification*** describes the number of different businesses that an organization is engaged in and the extent to which these businesses are related to one another. There are three types of diversification strategies: single-product strategy, related diversification, and unrelated diversification.[24]

Single-Product Strategy

single-product strategy
A strategy in which an organization manufactures just one product or service and sells it in a single geographic market

An organization that pursues a ***single-product strategy*** manufactures just one product or service and sells it in a single geographic market. The WD-40 Company, for example, manufactures only a single product, WD-40 spray lubricant, and for years sold it in just one market, North America. WD-40 has started selling its lubricant in Europe and Asia, but it continues to center all manufacturing, sales, and marketing efforts on one product.

The single-product strategy has one major strength and one major weakness. By concentrating its efforts so completely on one product and market, a firm is likely to be very successful in manufacturing and marketing the product. Because it has staked its survival on a single product, the organization works very hard to make sure that the product is a success. Of course, if the product is not accepted by the market or is replaced by a new one, the firm will suffer. This happened to slide-rule manufacturers when electronic calculators became widely available and to companies that manufactured only black-and-white televisions when low-priced color televisions were first mass-marketed. Similarly, Wrigley has long practiced what amounts to a single-product strategy with its line of chewing gums. But, because younger consumers are buying less gum than earlier generations, Wrigley is facing declining revenues and lower profits.[25]

Related Diversification

related diversification
A strategy in which an organization operates in several businesses that are somehow linked with one another

Given the disadvantage of the single-product strategy, most large businesses today operate in several different businesses, industries, or markets.[26] If the businesses are somehow linked, that organization is implementing a strategy of ***related diversification***. Virtually all larger businesses in the United States use related diversification.

Bases of Relatedness   Organizations link their different businesses, industries, or markets in different ways. Table 8.3 gives some typical bases of relatedness. In com-

Table 8.3
BASES OF RELATEDNESS IN IMPLEMENTING RELATED DIVERSIFICATION

Firms that implement related diversification can do so using any number of bases of relatedness. Four frequently used bases of related uses for diversification are similar technology, common distribution and marketing skills, common brand name and reputation, and common customers.

Basis of Relatedness	Examples
Similar technology	Philips, Boeing, Westinghouse, Compaq
Common distribution and marketing skills	RJR Nabisco, Philip Morris, Procter & Gamble
Common brand name and reputation	Disney, Universal
Common customers	Merck, IBM, AMF-Head

panies such as Philips, a European consumer electronics company, a similar type of electronics technology underlies all the businesses. A common technology in aircraft design links Boeing's commercial and military aircraft divisions, and a common computer design technology links Dell's various computer products and peripherals.

Organizations such as Philip Morris, RJR Nabisco, and Procter & Gamble operate multiple businesses related by a common distribution network (grocery stores) and common marketing skills (advertising). Disney and Universal rely on strong brand names and reputations to link their diverse businesses, which include movie studios and theme parks. Pharmaceutical firms such as Merck sell numerous products to a single set of customers: hospitals, doctors, patients, and drugstores. Similarly, AMF-Head sells snow skis, tennis rackets, and sportswear to active, athletic customers.

Advantages of Related Diversification   Pursuing a strategy of related diversification has three primary advantages. First, it reduces an organization's dependence on any one of its business activities and thus reduces economic risk. Even if one or two of a firm's businesses lose money, the organization as a whole may still survive because the healthy businesses will generate enough cash to support the others.[27] At the Limited, sales declines at Lerners may be offset by sales increases at Express.

Second, by managing several businesses at the same time, an organization can reduce the overhead costs associated with managing any one business. In other words, if the normal administrative costs required to operate any business, such as legal services and accounting, can be spread over a large number of businesses, then the overhead costs *per business* will be lower than they would be if each business had to absorb all costs itself. Thus the overhead costs of businesses in a firm that pursues related diversification are usually lower than those of similar businesses that are not part of a larger corporation.[28]

Third, related diversification allows an organization to exploit its strengths and capabilities in more than one business. When organizations do this successfully, they capitalize on synergies, which are complementary effects that exist among their businesses. *Synergy* exists among a set of businesses when the businesses' economic value together is greater than their economic value separately. McDonald's is using synergy as it diversifies into other restaurant and food businesses. For example, its McCafe premium coffee stands in some McDonald's restaurants and investments in Donatos Pizza, Chipotle Mexican Grill, and Pret A Manger each allow the firm to create new revenue opportunities while using the firm's existing strengths in food-product purchasing and distribution.[29]

Unrelated Diversification

Firms that implement a strategy of **unrelated diversification** operate multiple businesses that are not logically associated with one another. At one time, for example, Quaker Oats owned clothing chains, toy companies, and a restaurant business. Unrelated diversification was a very popular strategy in the 1970s. During this time, several conglomerates like ITT and Transamerica grew by acquiring literally hundreds of other organizations and then running these numerous businesses as independent entities. Even if there are important potential synergies among their

> **unrelated diversification**
> A strategy in which an organization operates multiple businesses that are not logically associated with one another

different businesses, organizations implementing a strategy of unrelated diversification do not attempt to exploit them.

In theory, unrelated diversification has two advantages. First, a business that uses this strategy should have stable performance over time. During any given period, if some businesses owned by the organization are in a cycle of decline, others may be in a cycle of growth. Unrelated diversification is also thought to have resource allocation advantages. Every year, when a corporation allocates capital, people, and other resources among its various businesses, it must evaluate information about the future of those businesses so that it can place its resources where they have the highest potential for return. Given that it owns the businesses in question and thus has full access to information about the future of those businesses, a firm implementing unrelated diversification should be able to allocate capital to maximize corporate performance.

Despite these presumed advantages, research suggests that unrelated diversification usually does not lead to high performance. First, corporate-level managers in such a company usually do not know enough about the unrelated businesses to provide helpful strategic guidance or to allocate capital appropriately. To make strategic decisions, managers must have complete and subtle understanding of a business and its environment. Because corporate managers often have difficulty fully evaluating the economic importance of investments for all the businesses under their wing, they tend to concentrate only on a business's current performance. This narrow attention at the expense of broader planning eventually hobbles the entire organization. Many of International Harvester's problems noted earlier grew from an emphasis on current performance at the expense of investments for the future success of the firm.

Second, because organizations that implement unrelated diversification fail to exploit important synergies, they are at a competitive disadvantage compared to organizations that use related diversification. Universal Studios has been at a competitive disadvantage relative to Disney because its theme parks, movie studios, and licensing divisions are less integrated and therefore achieve less synergy.

For these reasons, almost all organizations have abandoned unrelated diversification as a corporate-level strategy. Transamerica has sold off numerous businesses and now concentrates on a core set of related businesses and markets. Large corporations that have not concentrated on a core set of businesses have eventually been acquired by other companies and then broken up. Research suggests that these organizations are actually worth more when broken up into smaller pieces than when joined.[30]

> "[Sara Lee] took a brand with pedigree and stretched it until it had no meaning at all."
>
> Pam Murtaugh, branding consultant
> (*USA Today,* February 11, 2005, p. 1B)

concept
CHECK

Distinguish between related and unrelated diversification.

The discussion above cites research that suggests that unrelated diversification is not likely to be a successful corporate strategy. If this is so, explain why General Electric remains so successful.

Implementing Corporate-Level Strategies

In implementing a diversification strategy, organizations face two important questions. First, how will the organization move from a single-product strategy to some form of diversification? Second, once the organization diversifies, how will it manage diversification effectively?

Becoming a Diversified Firm

Most organizations do not start out completely diversified. Rather, they begin operations in a single business, pursuing a particular business-level strategy. Success in this strategy then creates resources and strengths that the organization can use in related businesses.[31]

Development of New Products Some firms diversify by developing their own new products and services within the boundaries of their traditional business operations. Honda followed this path to diversification. Relying on its traditional strength in the motorcycle market, over the years Honda learned how to make fuel-efficient, highly reliable small engines. Honda began to apply its strengths in a new business: manufacturing small, fuel-efficient cars for the Japanese domestic market. These vehicles were first sold in the United States in the late 1960s. Honda's success in U.S. exports led the company to increase the size and improve the performance of its cars. Over the years, Honda has introduced automobiles of increasing quality, culminating in the Acura line of luxury cars. While diversifying into the market for automobiles, Honda also applied its engine-building strengths to produce a line of all-terrain vehicles, portable electric generators, and lawn mowers. In each case, Honda was able to parlay its strengths and resources into successful new businesses.

Replacement of Suppliers and Customers Firms can also become diversified by replacing their former suppliers and customers. A company that stops buying supplies (either manufactured goods or raw materials) from other companies and begins to provide its own supplies has diversified through ***backward vertical integration***. Campbell Soup once bought soup cans from several different manufacturers but later began manufacturing its own cans. In fact, Campbell is currently one of the largest can-manufacturing companies in the world, although almost all the cans it makes are used in its soup operations.

An organization that stops selling to one customer and sells instead to that customer's customers has diversified through ***forward vertical integration***. G. H. Bass used forward vertical integration to diversify its operations. Bass once sold its shoes and other products only to retail outlets. More recently, however, Bass opened numerous factory outlet stores, which now sell products directly to consumers. Nevertheless, Bass has not abandoned its former customers, retail outlets. Many firms are also employing forward vertical integration today, as they use the Internet to market their products and services directly to consumers.

Mergers and Acquisitions Another common way for businesses to diversify is through mergers and acquisitions—that is, through purchasing another organization. Such a purchase is called a ***merger*** when the two organizations being combined are approximately the same size. It is called an ***acquisition*** when one of the

backward vertical integration
An organization's beginning the business activities formerly conducted by its suppliers

forward vertical integration
An organization's beginning the business activities formerly conducted by its customers

merger
The purchase of one firm by another firm of approximately the same size

acquisition
The purchase of a firm by a firm that is considerably larger

organizations involved is considerably larger than the other. Organizations engage in mergers and acquisitions to diversify through vertical integration by acquiring former suppliers or former customers. Mergers and acquisitions are also becoming more common in other countries, such as Germany and China.[32]

Most organizations use mergers and acquisitions to acquire complementary products or complementary services, which are products or services linked by a common technology and common customers. The objective of most mergers and acquisitions is the creation or exploitation of synergies.[33] Synergy can reduce the combined organizations' costs of doing business; it can increase revenues; and it may open the way to entirely new businesses for the organization to enter. For example, MGM Grand paid $4.4 billion for its largest competitor in the gambling industry, Mirage Resorts. The deal allowed MGM Grand to compete with other firms more efficiently while eliminating a major rival.[34]

Managing Diversification

portfolio management technique
A method that diversified organizations use to determine which businesses to engage in and how to manage these businesses to maximize corporate performance

However an organization implements diversification—whether through internal development, vertical integration, or mergers and acquisitions—it must monitor and manage its strategy. The two major tools for managing diversification are (1) organization structure and (2) portfolio management techniques. How organization structure can be used to manage a diversification strategy is discussed in detail in Chapter 12.[35] *Portfolio management techniques* are methods that diversified organizations use to determine which businesses to engage in and how to manage these businesses to maximize corporate performance. Two important portfolio management techniques are the BCG matrix and the GE Business Screen.

BCG matrix
A method of evaluating businesses relative to the growth rate of their market and the organization's share of the market

BCG Matrix   The *BCG* (for Boston Consulting Group) *matrix* provides a framework for evaluating the relative performance of businesses in which a diversified organization operates. It also prescribes the preferred distribution of cash and other resources among these businesses.[36] The BCG matrix uses two factors to evaluate an organization's set of businesses: the growth rate of a particular market and the organization's share of that market. The matrix suggests that fast-growing markets in which an organization has the highest market share are more attractive business opportunities than slow-growing markets in which an organization has small market share. Dividing market growth and market share into two categories (low and high) creates the simple matrix shown in Figure 8.3.

The matrix classifies the types of businesses in which a diversified organization can engage as dogs, cash cows, question marks, and stars. *Dogs* are businesses that have a very small share of a market that is not expected to grow. Because these businesses do not hold much economic promise, the BCG matrix suggests that organizations either should not invest in them or should consider selling them as soon as possible. *Cash cows* are businesses that have a large share of a market that is not expected to grow substantially. These businesses characteristically generate high profits that the organization should use to support question marks and stars. (Cash cows are "milked" for cash to support businesses in markets that have greater growth potential.) *Question marks* are businesses that have only a small share of a quickly growing market. The future performance of these businesses is uncertain. A question mark that is able to capture increasing amounts of this growing market may be very profitable. On the other hand, a question mark unable to keep up with

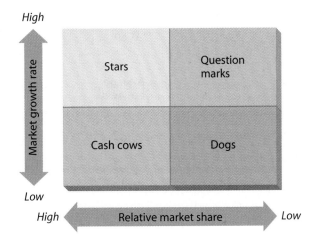

Figure 8.3
THE BCG MATRIX

The BCG matrix helps managers develop a better understanding of how different strategic business units contribute to the overall organization. By assessing each SBU on the basis of its market growth rate and relative market share, managers can make decisions about whether to commit further financial resources to the SBU or to sell or liquidate it.

Source: *Perspectives*, No. 66, "The Product Portfolio." Adapted by permission from The Boston Consulting Group, Inc., 1970.

market growth is likely to have low profits. The BCG matrix suggests that organizations should invest carefully in question marks. If their performance does not live up to expectations, question marks should be reclassified as dogs and divested. *Stars* are businesses that have the largest share of a rapidly growing market. Cash generated by cash cows should be invested in stars to ensure their preeminent position. For example, when BMW bought Rover a few years ago, experts thought its products would help the German auto maker reach new consumers. But the company was not able to capitalize on this opportunity, so it ended up selling Rover's car business to a British firm and Land Rover to Ford.[37]

GE Business Screen   Because the BCG matrix is relatively narrow and overly simplistic, General Electric (GE) developed the *GE Business Screen*, a more sophisticated approach to managing diversified business units. The Business Screen is a portfolio management technique that can also be represented in the form of a matrix. Rather than focusing solely on market growth and market share, however, the GE Business Screen considers industry attractiveness and competitive position. These two factors are divided into three categories, to make the nine-cell matrix shown in Figure 8.4.[38] These cells, in turn, classify business units as winners, losers, question marks, average businesses, or profit producers.

As Figure 8.4 shows, both market growth and market share appear in a broad list of factors that determine the overall attractiveness of an industry and the overall quality of a firm's competitive position. Other determinants of an industry's attractiveness (in addition to market growth) include market size, capital requirements, and competitive intensity. In general, the greater the market growth, the larger the market, the smaller the capital requirements, and the less the competitive intensity, the more attractive an industry will be. Other determinants of an organization's competitive position in an industry (besides market share) include technological know-how, product quality, service network, price competitiveness, and operating costs. In general, businesses with large market share, technological know-how, high product quality, a quality service network, competitive prices, and low operating costs are in a favorable competitive position.

Think of the GE Business Screen as a way of applying SWOT analysis to the implementation and management of a diversification strategy. The determinants of industry attractiveness are similar to the environmental opportunities and threats

> **GE Business Screen**
> A method of evaluating businesses along two dimensions: (1) industry attractiveness and (2) competitive position; in general, the more attractive the industry and the more competitive the position, the more an organization should invest in a business

Figure 8.4

THE GE BUSINESS SCREEN

The GE Business Screen is a more sophisticated approach to portfolio management than the BCG matrix. As shown here, several factors combine to determine a business's competitive position and the attractiveness of its industry. These two dimensions, in turn, can be used to classify businesses as winners, question marks, average businesses, losers, or profit producers. Such a classification enables managers to allocate the organization's resources more effectively across various business opportunities.

Source: From *Strategy Formulation: Analytical Concepts*, 1st edition, by Charles W. Hofer and Dan Schendel. Copyright (c) 1978. Reprinted with permission of South-Western, a division of Thomson Learning: www.thomsonrights.com. Fax 800-730-2215.

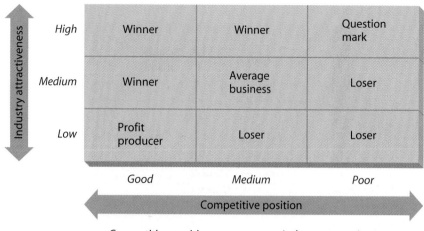

Competitive position
1. Market share
2. Technological know-how
3. Product quality
4. Service network
5. Price competitiveness
6. Operating costs

Industry attractiveness
1. Market growth
2. Market size
3. Capital requirements
4. Competitive intensity

in SWOT analysis, and the determinants of competitive position are similar to organizational strengths and weaknesses. By conducting this type of SWOT analysis across several businesses, a diversified organization can decide how to invest its resources to maximize corporate performance. In general, organizations should invest in winners and in question marks (where industry attractiveness and competitive position are both favorable); should maintain the market position of average businesses and profit producers (where industry attractiveness and competitive position are average); and should sell losers. For example, Unilever recently assessed its business portfolio using a similar framework and, as a result, decided to sell off several specialty chemical units that were not contributing to the firm's profitability as much as other businesses. The firm then used the revenues from these divestitures and bought more related businesses such as Ben & Jerry's Homemade and Slim-Fast.[39]

concept
CHECK

Compare and contrast the BCG matrix and the GE Business Screen.

When, if ever, would it make sense for a corporation to retain ownership of a money-losing business with limited opportunities for a turnaround?

International and Global Strategies

Strategic management is in many ways a continuing challenge for managers. But an increasingly important and special set of challenges confronting today's managers relates to international and global strategies.

Developing International and Global Strategies

Developing an international strategy is far more complex than developing a domestic one.[40] Managers developing a strategy for a domestic firm must deal with one national government, one currency, one accounting system, one political system, one legal system, and usually a single language and a comparatively homogeneous culture. Conversely, managers responsible for developing a strategy for an international firm must understand and deal with multiple governments, multiple currencies, multiple accounting systems, multiple political systems, multiple legal systems, and a variety of languages and cultures.

Moreover, managers in an international business must also coordinate the implementation of their firm's strategy among business units located in different parts of the world, with different time zones, different cultural contexts, and different economic conditions, as well as monitor and control their performance. Managers usually consider these complexities acceptable tradeoffs for the additional opportunities that come with global expansion. Indeed, international businesses have the ability to exploit three sources of competitive advantage unavailable to domestic firms.

International and global strategies are becoming increasingly important at many companies. Time Warner's Turner Network subsidiary, for example, has a thriving strategic alliance with a local partner in India. Executives from the two companies are shown here at a press conference where they announced plans to jointly build and operate theme parks in India based on popular Turner programming. The first two parks are called Cartoon Network Townsville and Planet Pogo.

Global Efficiencies International firms can improve their efficiency through several means not accessible to a domestic firm. They can capture *location efficiencies* by locating their facilities anywhere in the world that yields them the lowest production or distribution costs or that best improves the quality of service they offer their customers. Production of athletic shoes, for example, is very labor intensive, and Nike, like many of its competitors, centers its manufacturing in countries where labor costs are especially low.[41] Similarly, by building factories to serve more than one country, international firms may also lower their production costs by capturing *economies of scale*. Finally, by broadening their product lines in each of the countries they enter, international firms may enjoy *economies of scope*, lowering their production and marketing costs and enhancing their bottom line.

Multimarket Flexibility As we discuss in earlier chapters, there are wide variations in the political, economic, legal, and cultural environments of countries. Moreover, these environments are constantly changing: New laws are passed, new governments are elected, economic policies are changed, new competitors may enter (or leave) the national market, and so on. International businesses thus face the challenge of responding to these multiple diverse and changing environments. Often firms find it beneficial to empower local managers to respond quickly to such changes. However, unlike domestic firms, which operate in and respond to changes in the context of a single domestic environment, international businesses may also respond to a change in one country by implementing a change in another country. Chicken processor Tyson Foods, for example, has benefited from the increased demand by health-conscious U.S. consumers for chicken breasts. In producing more chicken breasts, Tyson also produced more chicken legs and thighs, which are considered less desirable by U.S. consumers. Tyson capitalized on its surplus by targeting the Russian market, where dark meat is preferred over light, and the Chinese market, where chicken feet are considered a tasty delicacy. Tyson exports over $250 million worth of chicken thighs and legs to Russia and China.[42]

Worldwide Learning   The diverse operating environments of multinational corporations (MNCs) may also contribute to organizational learning.[43] Differences in these operating environments may cause the firm to operate differently in one country than in another. An astute firm may learn from these differences and transfer this learning to its operations in other countries.[44] For example, McDonald's U.S. managers once believed that its restaurants should be freestanding entities located in suburbs and small towns. A Japanese franchisee convinced McDonald's to allow it to open a restaurant in an inner-city office building. That restaurant's success caused McDonald's executives to rethink their store location criteria. Nontraditional locations—office buildings, Wal-Mart superstores, even airplanes—are now an important source of new growth for the firm.

Unfortunately, it is difficult to exploit these three factors simultaneously. Global efficiencies can be more easily obtained when a single unit of a firm is given worldwide responsibility for the task at hand. BMW's engineering staff at headquarters in Munich, for example, is responsible for the research and design of the company's new automobiles. By focusing its research and development (R&D) efforts at one location, BMW engineers designing new transmissions are better able to coordinate their activities with their counterparts designing new engines. However, centralizing control of its R&D operations also hinders BMW's ability to customize its product to meet the differing needs of customers in different countries. Consider the simple question of whether to include cup holders in its cars. In designing cars to be driven safely at the prevailing high speeds of Germany's autobahn, the company's engineers decided that cup holders were both irrelevant and dangerous. Driving speeds in the United States, however, are much lower, and cup holders are an important comfort feature in autos sold to U.S. consumers. Lengthy battles were fought between BMW's German engineers and its U.S. marketing managers over this seemingly trivial issue. Only in the mid-1990s did cup holders finally become a standard feature in the firm's automobiles sold in North America.

As this example illustrates, if too much power is centralized in one unit of a firm, the unit may ignore the needs of consumers in other markets. Conversely, multimarket flexibility is enhanced when a firm delegates responsibility to the managers of local subsidiaries. Vesting power in local managers allows each subsidiary to tailor its products, personnel policies, marketing techniques, and other business practices to meet the specific needs and wants of potential customers in each market the firm serves. However, this increased flexibility will reduce the firm's ability to obtain global efficiencies in such areas as production, marketing, and R&D.

Furthermore, the unbridled pursuit of global efficiencies or multimarket flexibility may stifle the firm's attempts to promote worldwide learning. Centralizing power in a single unit of the firm to capture global efficiencies may cause the unit to ignore lessons and information acquired by other units of the firm. Moreover, the other units may have little incentive or ability to acquire such information if they know that the "experts" at headquarters will ignore them. Decentralizing power in the hands of local subsidiary managers may create similar problems. A decentralized structure may make it difficult to transfer learning from one subsidiary to another. Local subsidiaries may be disposed to automatically reject outside information as not being germane to the local situation. Firms wishing to promote worldwide learning must use an organizational structure that promotes knowledge transfer among its subsidiaries and corporate headquarters. The firms must also create incentive structures that motivate managers at headquarters and in subsidiaries to acquire, disseminate, and act on worldwide learning opportunities.

Consider the success of Nokia, headquartered in Helsinki, Finland, which is among the world's leaders in the cellular telephone and telecommunications industries. Nokia, like other telecommunications equipment manufacturers, was struggling to keep pace with rapid shifts in its worldwide markets. Managers in different regions had little idea what their counterparts in other markets were doing, and Nokia factories were grappling with excess inventories of some products and inventory shortages of others. In some instances, Nokia factories in one country would shut down for lack of a critical part that a Nokia factory in another country had in surplus. In response, the firm's CEO, Jorma Ollila, established what he called "commando teams" to attack these problems. The teams were charged with improving efficiency throughout the firm. Using a new worldwide information system, Nokia managers now monitor global, regional, and local sales and inventory on a real-time basis. This allows them to make internal transfers of parts and finished goods efficiently. More important, this approach has allowed Nokia to spot market trends and new product developments that arise in one region of the world and to transfer this knowledge to improve its competitiveness in other areas and product lines.[45]

> "From the very beginning, we decided we didn't want to export the same vision of beauty around the world. . . . We wanted to offer consumers the choice between very different options."
>
> Jean-Paul Agon, CEO of L'Oreal
> (*BizEd*, July/August 2005, p. 22)

Strategic Alternatives for International Business

International businesses typically adopt one of four strategic alternatives in their attempt to balance the three goals of global efficiencies, multimarket flexibility, and worldwide learning. The first of these strategic alternatives is the ***home replication strategy***. In this approach, a firm uses the core competency or firm-specific advantage it developed at home as its main competitive weapon in the foreign markets that it enters. In other words, the firm takes what it does exceptionally well in its home market and attempts to duplicate it in foreign markets. Mercedes-Benz's home replication strategy, for example, relies on its well-known brand name and its reputation for building well-engineered, luxurious cars capable of traveling safely at very high speeds. It is this market segment that Mercedes-Benz has chosen to exploit internationally, despite the fact that only a very few countries have both the high income levels and the high speed limits appropriate for its products. But consumers in Asia, the rest of Europe, and the Americas are nevertheless attracted by the car's mystique.

The ***multidomestic strategy*** is a second alternative available to international firms. A multidomestic corporation manages itself as a collection of relatively independent operating subsidiaries, each of which focuses on a specific domestic

home replication strategy
International strategy in which a company uses the core competency or firm-specific advantage it developed at home as its main competitive weapon in the foreign markets that it enters

multidomestic strategy
International strategy in which a company manages itself as a collection of relatively independent operating subsidiaries, each of which focuses on a specific domestic market

market. In addition, each of these subsidiaries is free to customize its products, its marketing campaigns, and its operating techniques to best meet the needs of its local customers. The multidomestic approach is particularly effective when there are clear differences among national markets; when economies of scale for production, distribution, and marketing are low; and when the cost of coordination between the parent corporation and its various foreign subsidiaries is high. Because each subsidiary must be responsive to the local market, the parent company usually delegates considerable power and authority to managers of its subsidiaries in various host countries. International businesses operating before World War II often adopted this approach because of the difficulties in controlling distant foreign subsidiaries, given the communication and transportation technologies of that time.

The **global strategy** is the third alternative philosophy available for international firms. A global corporation views the world as a single marketplace and has as its primary goal the creation of standardized goods and services that will address the needs of customers worldwide. The global strategy is almost the exact opposite of the multidomestic strategy. Whereas the multidomestic firm believes that its customers in every country are fundamentally different and must be approached from that perspective, a global corporation assumes that customers are fundamentally the same regardless of nationality. Thus the global corporation views the world market as a single entity as the corporation develops, produces, and sells its products. It tries to capture economies of scale in production and marketing by concentrating its production activities in a handful of highly efficient factories and then creating global advertising and marketing campaigns to sell the goods produced in those factories. Because the global corporation must coordinate its worldwide production and marketing strategies, it usually concentrates power and decision-making responsibility at a central headquarters.

The home replication strategy and the global strategy share an important similarity: Under either approach, a firm conducts business the same way anywhere in the world. There is also an important difference between the two approaches. A firm using the home replication strategy takes its domestic way of doing business and uses that approach in foreign markets as well. In essence, a firm using this strategy believes that, if its business practices work in its domestic market, then they should also work in foreign markets. Conversely, the starting point for a firm adopting a global strategy has no such home country bias. In fact, the concept of a home market is irrelevant because the global firm thinks of its market as a global one, not one divided into domestic and foreign segments. The global firm tries to figure out the best way to serve all of its customers in the global market and then does so.

A fourth approach available to international firms is the ***transnational strategy***. The transnational corporation attempts to combine the benefits of global scale efficiencies, such as those pursued by a global corporation, with the benefits and advantages of local responsiveness, which is the goal of a multidomestic corporation. To do so, the transnational corporation does not automatically centralize or decentralize authority. Rather, it carefully assigns responsibility for various organizational tasks to the unit of the organization best able to achieve the dual goals of efficiency and flexibility.

A transnational corporation may choose to centralize certain management functions and decision making, such as R&D and financial operations, at corporate

global strategy
International strategy in which a company views the world as a single marketplace and has as its primary goal the creation of standardized goods and services that will address the needs of customers worldwide

transnational strategy
International strategy in which a company attempts to combine the benefits of global scale efficiencies with the benefits and advantages of local responsiveness

headquarters. Other management functions, such as human resource management and marketing, may be decentralized, allowing managers of local subsidiaries to customize their business activities to better respond to the local culture and business environment. Microsoft, for example, locates most of its product development efforts in the United States, whereas responsibility for marketing is delegated to its foreign subsidiaries. Often, transnational corporations locate responsibility for one product line in one country and responsibility for a second product line in another country. To achieve an interdependent network of operations, transnational corporations focus considerable attention on integration and coordination among their various subsidiaries.

What are the basic strategic options available to multinational businesses?	*In what ways is international strategic planning most similar to and most different from domestic strategic planning?*	**concept** CHECK

Summary of Learning Objectives and Key Points

1. Discuss the components of strategy, types of strategic alternatives, and the distinction between strategy formulation and strategy implementation.
   - A strategy is a comprehensive plan for accomplishing the organization's goals.
   - Effective strategies address three organizational issues: distinctive competence, scope, and resource deployment.
   - Most large companies have both business-level and corporate-level strategies.
   - Strategy formulation is the set of processes involved in creating or determining the strategies of an organization.
   - Strategy implementation is the process of executing strategies.

2. Describe how to use SWOT analysis in formulating strategy.
   - SWOT analysis considers an organization's strengths, weaknesses, opportunities, and threats.
   - Using SWOT analysis, an organization chooses strategies that support its mission and
     - exploit its opportunities and strengths
     - neutralize its threats
     - avoid its weaknesses
   - Common strengths cannot be ignored, but distinctive competencies hold the greatest promise for superior performance.

3. Identify and describe various alternative approaches to business-level strategy formulation.
   - A business-level strategy is the plan an organization uses to conduct business in a particular industry or market.
   - Porter suggests that businesses may formulate:
     - a differentiation strategy
     - an overall cost leadership strategy
     - a focus strategy
   - According to Miles and Snow, organizations may choose one of four business-level strategies:
     - prospector
     - defender
     - analyzer
     - reactor
   - Business-level strategies may also take into account the stages in the product life cycle.

4. Describe how business-level strategies are implemented.
   - Strategy implementation at the business level takes place in the areas of marketing, sales, accounting and finance, and manufacturing.
   - Culture also influences strategy implementation.
   - Implementation of Porter's generic strategies requires different emphases in each of these organizational areas.

- Implementation of Miles and Snow's strategies affects organization structure and practices.

5. Identify and describe various alternative approaches to corporate-level strategy formulation.
   - A corporate-level strategy is the plan an organization uses to manage its operations across several businesses.
   - A firm that does not diversify is implementing a single-product strategy.
   - An organization pursues a strategy of related diversification when it operates a set of businesses that are somehow linked.
   - An organization pursues a strategy of unrelated diversification when it operates a set of businesses that are not logically associated with one another.

6. Describe how corporate-level strategies are implemented.
   - Strategy implementation at the corporate level addresses two issues:
     - how the organization will go about its diversification
     - the way an organization is managed once it has diversified
   - Businesses accomplish this in three ways:
     - developing new products internally
     - replacing suppliers (backward vertical integration) or customers (forward vertical integration)
     - engaging in mergers and acquisitions

- Organizations manage diversification through the organization structure that they adopt and through portfolio management techniques.
- The BCG matrix classifies an organization's diversified businesses as dogs, cash cows, question marks, or stars according to market share and market growth rate.
- The GE Business Screen classifies businesses as winners, losers, question marks, average businesses, or profit producers according to industry attractiveness and competitive position.

7. Discuss international and global strategies.
   - Although there are many similarities in developing domestic and international strategies, international firms have three additional sources of competitive advantage unavailable to domestic firms. These are
     - global efficiencies
     - multimarket flexibility
     - worldwide learning
   - Firms participating in international business usually adopt one of four strategic alternatives:
     - the home replication strategy
     - the multidomestic strategy
     - the global strategy
     - the transnational strategy
   - Each of these strategies has advantages and disadvantages in terms of its ability to help firms be responsive to local circumstances and to achieve the benefits of global efficiencies.

Discussion Questions

Questions for Review

1. Define the four parts of a SWOT analysis.
2. Describe the relationship between a distinctive competency, a competitive advantage, and a sustained competitive advantage.
3. List and describe Porter's generic strategies and the Miles and Snow typology of strategies.
4. What are the characteristics of businesses in each of the four cells of the BCG matrix?

Questions for Analysis

5. Describe the process that an organization follows when using a deliberate strategy. How does this process differ when an organization implements an emergent strategy?
6. Which strategy should a firm develop first—its business-level or its corporate-level strategy? Describe the relationship between a firm's business- and corporate-level strategies.
7. Volkswagen sold its original Beetle automobile in the United States until the 1970s. The original Beetle was made of inexpensive materials, was built using an efficient mass-production technology, and

offered few options. Then, in the 1990s Volkswagen introduced its new Beetle, which has a distinctive style, provides more optional features, and is priced for upscale buyers. What was Volkswagen's strategy with the original Beetle—product differentiation, low cost, or focus? Which strategy did Volkswagen implement with its new Beetle? Explain your answers.

Questions for Application

8. Assume that you are the owner and manager of a small business. Write a strategy for your business. Be sure to include each of the three primary strategic components.
9. Interview a manager and categorize the business- and corporate-level strategies of his or her organization according to Porter's generic strategies, the Miles and Snow typology, and extent of diversification.

10. Give an example of a corporation following a single-product strategy, a related diversification strategy, and an unrelated diversification strategy. What level of performance would you expect from each firm, based on its strategy? Examine the firm's profitability to see whether your expectations were accurate.

Building Effective Decision-Making Skills

Exercise Overview

Decision-making skills refer to the manager's ability to recognize and define problems and opportunities correctly and then to select an appropriate course of action to solve problems and capitalize on opportunities. As noted in the chapter, many organizations use SWOT analysis as part of the process of strategy formulation. This exercise will help you better understand how managers obtain the information they need to perform such an analysis and use it as a framework for making decisions.

Exercise Background

SWOT is an acronym for strengths, weaknesses, opportunities and threats. Good strategies are those that exploit an organization's opportunities and strengths while neutralizing threats and avoiding or correcting weaknesses.

Assume that you have just been hired to run a medium-size manufacturing company. The firm has been manufacturing electric motors, circuit breakers, and similar electronic components for industrial use. In recent years, the firm's financial performance has gradually eroded. You have been hired to turn things around.

Meetings with both current and former top managers of the firm have led you to believe that a new strategy is needed. In earlier times the firm was successful in part because its products were of top quality, which allowed the company to charge premium prices for them. Recently, however, various cost-cutting measures have resulted in a decrease in quality. Competition has also increased. As a result, your firm no longer has a reputation for top-quality products, but your manufacturing costs are still relatively high. The next thing you want to do is to conduct a SWOT analysis.

Exercise Task

With the situation described above as context, do the following:

1. List the sources you will use to obtain information about the firm's strengths, weaknesses, opportunities, and threats. If you are using the Internet, give specific websites or URLs.

2. For what types of information are data readily available on the Internet? What categories of data are difficult or impossible to find on the Internet?
3. Rate each source in terms of its probable reliability.
4. How confident should you be in making decisions based on the information obtained?

Building Effective Conceptual Skills

Exercise Overview

Conceptual skills refer to the manager's ability to think in the abstract. Strategic management is often thought of in terms of competition. For example, metaphors involving war or sports are often invoked by strategists. However, cooperation is another viable strategic alternative to competition. Cooperation has been a popular strategy in many countries for years, and the importance of cooperative strategic alliances and joint ventures is also rising in the United States. This game will provide you with an illustration of the advantages of a cooperative strategy in comparison with a competitive strategy.

Exercise Background

Competitive and cooperative strategies are quite complex when implemented in organizations. However, a simple and clear illustration of the principles underlying competition and cooperation can be given through the use of a game.

This game illustrates a "prisoner's dilemma" situation. The prisoner's dilemma is a classic situation used to demonstrate concepts related to game theory. In the original prisoner's dilemma, two criminals are suspected in a crime, but there is not enough evidence to convict either of them. The two criminals are separated and each is told that if he will "rat" on the other one, he will go free. Of course, if neither rats, both go free. If both rat, then both go to prison. The optimal outcome (for the prisoners!) occurs when neither rats on the other. However, in real situations, the most common outcome is just the opposite—that both "rat" and both go to jail.

The prisoner's dilemma case has been used by game theorists to describe how people make decisions about whether to act cooperatively or competitively. Although there are cases in which cooperation would be the most beneficial for both parties, individuals frequently choose competition instead, which often leads to the worst outcomes. In the game you are about to play, you will see how choices about competition versus cooperation affect outcomes.

Exercise Task

1. Break into small groups and play the board game according to the instructions you receive from your professor.

2. Present your group's results to the class.
3. After hearing the results from every group, be prepared to share your thoughts about the outcomes.

CHAPTER CLOSING CASE

THINKING OUTSIDE THE BIG BOX

Brad Anderson, CEO of Best Buy, creates winning strategies, and then he dismantles them. Anderson, head of Best Buy for ten years, oversaw the company's tremendous success as a big box retailer. In the same time period, revenues of rivals Radio Shack, CompUSA, and Circuit City remained flat or declined. However, Best Buy is now facing a new, tougher set of competitors, notably Dell and Wal-Mart. So Anderson embarked, on some ambitious strategic initiatives. A display at the firm's Minneapolis headquarters highlights prominent business failures. It is titled, "This is where companies go when their strategies get sick." To help Best Buy avoid that fate, Anderson has two promising ideas that will completely change the firm's strategic direction.

One strategic approach is to differentiate Best Buy from low-cost competitors by offering excellent customer service. Best Buy purchased the Geek Squad, which installed and repaired PCs, from a Minneapolis entrepreneur in October 2002. Today, the Geek Squad has rolled out to every store and consists of over 12,000 workers. The squad offers a flat-rate menu of services that includes repairs, networking, hardware and software installation, and training. Services are provided at the customer's location, in a Best Buy store, online, or over the phone. In addition, stand-alone Geek Squad Stores deliver an even wider range of products, focusing on small businesses.

Another new strategy is called "customer-centricity," or just "centricity." This customer-centered approach proposes that companies are so eager to increase sales that they don't bother to figure out which customers are profitable. However, some buyers are very lucrative and others cost more to sell to than their purchases are worth. By carefully scrutinizing customer traits and purchases, companies can identify "angel" customers and "demon" customers. Catering to the angels while ignoring the demons should increase profitability.

At Best Buy, centricity principles were used to identify five groups of angel customers, including an affluent technology fan, a busy mom, a young electronics enthusiast, a price-conscious dad, and a small business owner. A detailed description was developed for each group and their needs and preferences were extensively researched. Marketers created store designs and product/service mixes to meet each group's unique needs. Store's past sales led to the choice of one or more segments. For example, a store in a neighborhood of family homes might focus on just two segments: the technology fan and the busy mom. That location will carry a targeted line of products and have special displays and fixtures. Store personnel will receive specialized training. The technology fan can then receive information about

high-end home theater systems while the busy mom can use a personal shopping assistant to help her choose the right laptop for her teenager.

In addition to these hot concepts, Best Buy is pursuing a number of even more radical retailing ideas. One is the firm's line of eq-life shops that sell health-related electronic gear and also offer massages and fitness classes. Two other stand-alone concepts are in development. Another tactic is nurturing close relationships with venture capitalists who fund high-tech start-ups. The relationships allow Best Buy to stay informed about technology developments so it can better prepare for the future. The company is tapping into its human resources, too, by using employees' suggestions to help it create a line of house brands. Workers are responding favorably to the increased communication, training, and responsibility. Employee turnover dropped from 81 percent in 2005 to 69 percent in 2006.

Of course, the changes bring some sacrifices and challenges. In April 2006, Best Buy laid off 300 workers from its corporate staff. "We have to align our priorities and eliminate redundancies," says Kelly Groehler. "Despite the restructuring, we're still adding jobs this year, but in support of our strategic priorities." More layoffs are likely, especially in staff functions. In addition, industry observers are concerned about Best Buy's ability to implement many sweeping reforms in a short time. "I like that Best Buy has all these balls in the air, but they are not all going to work," notes analyst Greg Melich.

Right now the strategy appears to be paying off. Revenues rose by 7.3 percent over the last year, and shareholders are showing their confidence in the company by driving share price up from $44 in December 2005 to $58 by April 2006. The market and customers are both rewarding Best Buy's strategic experimentation. Best Buy is showing the innovative thinking that is required to stay competitive with powerhouses Dell and Wal-Mart.

CASE QUESTIONS

1. What are Best Buy's organizational strengths? Based on your response, which of Porter's generic strategies do you recommend Best Buy adopt? Why?

2. How do Anderson's two new strategies increase Best Buy's differentiation advantage? How do they increase Best Buy's low-cost advantage?

3. The home goods retailing industry is in the maturity stage of the product life cycle. Based on that information, what industry characteristics do you expect Best Buy to face? What strategy or strategies should Best Buy use to help it compete effectively in the maturity stage of the market?

CASE REFERENCES

"Best Buy Gains But Will Shed Jobs," *Money*, April 3, 2006, www.money.com on April 4, 2006; "Best Buy Cuts 300 Jobs," *Money*, April 3, 2006, www.money.com on April 4, 2006; Matthew Boyle, "Best Buy's Giant Gamble," *Fortune*, April 3, 2006, pp. 68–75; "How to Break Out of Commodity Hell," *BusinessWeek*, March 27, 2006, www.businessweek.com on March 8, 2006; "What We Do," Geek Squad website, www.geeksquad.com on March 8, 2006.

YOU MAKE THE CALL

The Video Game Wars

1. If you ran Electronic Arts, what changes, if any, would you make in the firm's strategy?

2. If you ran Sony's video game business, what changes, if any, would you make in its strategy?

3. If you ran a smaller video game start-up like Acclaim, how might you go about developing a strategy to more effectively compete with EA and Sony?

4. If you play video games now, what aspects of the strategies used by EA, Sony, and Acclaim tend to cause you to play more or fewer of each company's games?

5. If you do not currently play video games, what strategies, if any, might EA, Sony, and Acclaim adopt to increase your interest in playing?

Test Prepper

college.hmco.com/business/students

Choose the correct answer. Answers are found at the back of the book.

1. T F Multiple firms can simultaneously have the same sustained competitive advantage.

2. T F Organizations using a focus strategy attempt to sidetrack their competitors' efforts into less profitable businesses.

3. T F A business that follows a reactor strategy has no consistent strategic approach.

4. T F A tire manufacturer that opens its own retail stores to sell its tires has implemented forward vertical integration.

5. T F The BCG matrix is a more sophisticated approach to portfolio management than is the GE Business Screen.

6. Dovetech Company makes birdfeeders that include light-activated bird calls to lure birds to feed. Dovetech charges more for these unique birdfeeders than other manufacturers charge for theirs. Which of Porter's strategies is Dovetech following?

    A. Differentiation
    B. Focus
    C. Overall cost leadership
    D. Generic
    E. Competitive

7. All of the following are part of a defender strategy EXCEPT

    A. protecting current markets.
    B. maintaining stable growth.
    C. improving performance of existing products.
    D. lowering costs.
    E. seeking out new business opportunities.

8. The product life cycle model shows how sales volume changes over the life of products. In which stage is slowing the entry of competitors most important?

    A. Introduction
    B. Growth
    C. Adolescence
    D. Maturity
    E. Decline

9. An international firm may enjoy economies of scope by

    A. locating its facilities where production and distribution costs are the lowest.
    B. broadening its product lines in each of the countries it enters.
    C. building factories to serve more than one country at a time.
    D. empowering local managers to respond quickly to changes.
    E. transferring learning in one country to businesses in another country.

10. Managers who adopt a multidomestic strategy assume that

    A. responsibility for organizational tasks should be centralized.
    B. the core competency developed in the company's home country will be successful abroad.
    C. customers in every country are fundamentally different.
    D. business should be conducted the same way anywhere in the world.
    E. managers in every country are fundamentally the same.

chapter 9

Managing Decision Making and Problem Solving

LEARNING OBJECTIVES

After studying this chapter, you should be able to:

1. Define decision making and discuss types of decisions and decision-making conditions.

2. Discuss rational perspectives on decision making, including the steps in rational decision making.

3. Describe the behavioral aspects of decision making.

4. Discuss group and team decision making, including the advantages and disadvantages of group and team decision making and how it can be more effectively managed.

FIRST THINGS FIRST

Team Decision Making at Barclays

"[I] spend an awful lot of time with the business until I have tremendous confidence. . . . At that point, it is equally important to step away."

—BOB DIAMOND, PRESIDENT, BARCLAYS BANK

Barclays Bank, headquartered in the United Kingdom, eliminated almost all of its investment banking division in a sell-off ten years ago. Performance was so low that much of the operation was sold to rivals. The remains, a bond unit and some small leftovers, was nicknamed "the rump" of Barclays by British newspapers. U.S. manager Bob Diamond was picked to lead Barclays Capital, the group with the undignified alias. Diamond has built his unit into one of the stars of Barclays, with sales up 12 percent and leadership positions in many of its products. Appropriate use of teamwork is at the heart of his success.

When Diamond took over the discouraged and neglected division, he knew that growth was the only thing that would persuade Barclays' top managers that the unit was a valuable addition to the company's portfolio. He needed to

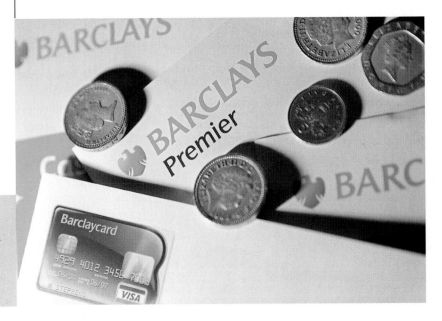

Once relegated to also-run status, Barclays is once again becoming a major player in the global banking market. Key strategic decisions have played a significant role in Barclays' turnaround.

quickly increase expertise so he turned to hiring from competitors. He hand-picked top performers from rivals, while at the same time letting go of under-performing workers. Diamond enjoys working in Barclays' meritocracy, saying that that system is "where we are all in competition with the same information and where the guy who works hardest or works smartest wins." Diamond is notorious for his competitive nature and his reliance on teamwork, developed during his days as a high school football star.

Once a good staff was in place, Diamond shifted focus to emphasize team-work. "My style has been to spend an awful lot of time with the business until I have tremendous confidence that I have the right people, who understand the plan," Diamond states. "At that point, it is equally important to step away and delegate." Diamond delegates many decisions to his team of executives, includ-ing the choice of who will make managing director. Thirty senior managers con-sider each candidate, anonymously voting on each via electronic buttons. Candidates must score at least 85 percent to be chosen, ensuring that every managing director has the support of the rest of the team.

Another innovation in group decision making is Diamond's approach to Bar-clays' customers, bond issuers such as large corporations or government enti-ties. While many banks allow employees from each product-related subunit to work directly with a client, Diamond feels that approach can be overwhelming. "We don't unleash everyone on a client—the loan salespeople, the debt capital market team, the commercial paper team, the institutional sales," says Diamond. Instead, the workers form into client-based teams that focus on understanding each organization's needs. Workers self-select for the teams where they can bring the most value.

Barclays' diversified teams, with members' varying backgrounds, help to boost creativity and improve the quality of decisions. Team decisions have led to the cre-ation of a number of innovative products, including unique derivatives, securitiza-tions, and convertible bonds. The new products are key to the success of the division. Barclays Capital is now the top bank in five of its most important products and is in the top five in an additional five categories. From being "the rump" in 1997, Barclays Capital today dominates capital raising for corporations. Diamond is a success too and was promoted to president of Barclays in June 2005. Yet it is the Barclays Capital employees who make the most significant contribution to Barclays' success, working together to make the decisions that guide the organization.[1]

Bob Diamond made several important decisions to get his division at Barclays turned around. And he continues to infuse effective decision-making methods in the business today. Making effective decisions, as well as recognizing when a bad decision has been made and quickly responding to mistakes, is a key ingredient in organizational effectiveness. Indeed, some experts believe that decision making is the most basic and fundamental of all managerial activities.[2] Thus we discuss it here, in the context of the first management function, planning. Keep in mind, however, that although decision making is perhaps most closely linked to the plan-ning function, it is also part of organizing, leading, and controlling.

State engineers in Florida have been struggling with decisions about how to best protect the endangered Everglades ecosystem. One option under consideration is storing polluted water on farmland until it can be cleaned and then pushed into the Everglades. Engineers believe that a consistent influx of clean water would help reduce phosphorous pollution that is choking wetlands life.

We begin our discussion by exploring the nature of decision making. We then describe rational perspectives on decision making. Behavioral aspects of decision making are then introduced and described. We conclude with a discussion of group and team decision making.

The Nature of Decision Making

Managers at Disney recently made the decision to buy Pixar Animation for $7.4 billion.[3] At about the same time, the general manager of the Ford dealership in Bryan, Texas, made a decision to sponsor a local youth soccer team for $200. Each of these examples reflects a decision, but the decisions differ in many ways. Thus, as a starting point in understanding decision making, we must first explore the meaning of decision making as well as types of decisions and conditions under which decisions are made.[4]

Decision Making Defined

Decision making can refer to either a specific act or a general process. ***Decision making*** per se is the act of choosing one alternative from among a set of alternatives. The decision-making process, however, is much more than this. One step of the process, for example, is that the person making the decision must both recognize that a decision is necessary and identify the set of feasible alternatives before selecting one. Hence, the ***decision-making process*** includes recognizing and defining the nature of a decision situation, identifying alternatives, choosing the "best" alternative, and putting it into practice.[5]

The word *best*, of course, implies effectiveness. Effective decision making requires that the decision maker understand the situation driving the decision. Most people would consider an effective decision to be one that optimizes some set of factors, such as profits, sales, employee welfare, and market share. In some situations, though, an effective decision may be one that minimizes loss, expenses, or employee turnover. It may even mean selecting the best method for going out of business, laying off employees, or terminating a strategic alliance.

We should also note that managers make decisions about both problems and opportunities. For example, making decisions about how to cut costs by 10 percent reflects a problem—an undesirable situation that requires a solution. But decisions are also necessary in situations of opportunity. Learning that the firm is earning higher-than-projected profits, for example, requires a subsequent decision. Should the extra funds be used to increase shareholder dividends, reinvest in current operations, or expand into new markets?

Of course, it may take a long time before a manager can know if the right decision was made. For example, the top management team at Eastman Kodak has

decision making
The act of choosing one alternative from among a set of alternatives

decision-making process
Recognizing and defining the nature of a decision situation, identifying alternatives, choosing the "best" alternative, and putting it into practice

❝The dumbest thing to do is sit on too much cash. It's not a good return on shareholder's capital.❞
Bryant Riley, market analyst
(*USA Today*, March 2, 2004, p. 1B)

made several major decisions that will affect the company for decades. Among other things, for example, it sold off several chemical- and health-related businesses, reduced the firm's debt by $7 billion in the process, launched a major new line of advanced cameras and film called Advantix, and made major new investments in new and emerging technology, such as digital photography. But analysts believe that the payoffs from these decisions will not be known for several years.[6]

Types of Decisions

Managers must make many different types of decisions. In general, however, most decisions fall into one of two categories: programmed and nonprogrammed.[7] A ***programmed decision*** is one that is relatively structured or recurs with some frequency (or both). Starbucks uses programmed decisions to purchase new supplies of coffee beans, cups, and napkins, and Starbucks employees are trained in exact procedures for brewing coffee. Likewise, the Bryan Ford dealer made a decision that he will sponsor a youth soccer team each year. Thus, when the soccer club president calls, the dealer already knows what he will do. Many decisions regarding basic operating systems and procedures and standard organizational transactions are of this variety and can therefore be programmed.[8]

programmed decision
A decision that is fairly structured or recurs with some frequency (or both)

   Nonprogrammed decisions, on the other hand, are relatively unstructured and occur much less often. Disney's decision to buy Pixar was a nonprogrammed decision. Managers faced with such decisions must treat each one as unique, investing enormous amounts of time, energy, and resources into exploring the situation from all perspectives. Intuition and experience are major factors in nonprogrammed decisions. Most of the decisions made by top managers involving strategy (including mergers, acquisitions, and takeovers) and organization design are nonprogrammed. So are decisions about new facilities, new products, labor contracts, and legal issues.

nonprogrammed decision
A decision that is relatively unstructured and occurs much less often than a programmed decision

Decision-Making Conditions

Just as there are different kinds of decisions, there are also different conditions in which decisions must be made. Managers sometimes have an almost perfect understanding of conditions surrounding a decision, but at other times they have few clues about those conditions. In general, as shown in Figure 9.1, the circumstances that exist for the decision maker are conditions of certainty, risk, or uncertainty.[9]

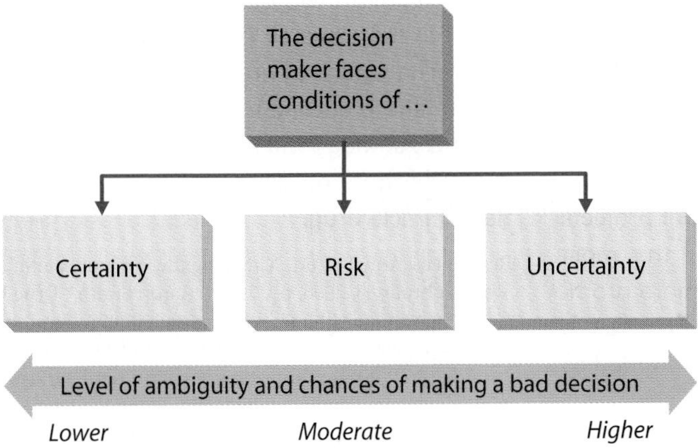

Figure 9.1
DECISION-MAKING CONDITIONS

Most major decisions in organizations today are made under a state of uncertainty. Managers making decisions in these circumstances must be sure to learn as much as possible about the situation and approach the decision from a logical and rational perspective.

Decision Making Under Certainty   When the decision maker knows with reasonable certainty what the alternatives are and what conditions are associated with each alternative, a ***state of certainty*** exists. Suppose, for example, that managers at Singapore Airlines make a decision to buy five new jumbo jets. Their next decision is from whom to buy them. Because there are only two companies in the world that make jumbo jets, Boeing and Airbus, Singapore Airlines knows its options exactly. Each has proven products and will guarantee prices and delivery dates. The airline thus knows the alternative conditions associated with each. There is little ambiguity and relatively little chance of making a bad decision.

Few organizational decisions, however, are made under conditions of true certainty. The complexity and turbulence of the contemporary business world make such situations rare. Even the airplane purchase decision we just considered has less certainty than it appears. The aircraft companies may not be able to really guarantee delivery dates, so they may write cost-increase or inflation clauses into contracts. Thus the airline may be only partially certain of the conditions surrounding each alternative.

> *state of certainty*
> A condition in which the decision maker knows with reasonable certainty what the alternatives are and what conditions are associated with each alternative

The Business of Ethics

Speeding Up Drug R&D

On the one hand, drug makers must ensure that products are thoroughly tested and safe. On the other hand, they also must take risks. If they do not, patients suffer from a lack of innovative new treatments. Robert Ruffolo, chief of research and development (R&D) at pharmaceutical maker Wyeth, is well aware of this dual nature of risk. He is changing the culture at Wyeth's laboratories to encourage more risk taking and creativity without undermining safety processes.

When Ruffolo assumed leadership of Wyeth's R&D in 2002, he established minimum quotas for new product creation. He began a first-ever review of every compound in development. Ruffolo wanted to increase innovation, but paradoxically, many of Wyeth's scientists feared that this approach would stifle creativity. "There was a lot of fear and loathing about going through that process," says researcher Steven Projan. "Everybody was convinced that this was a tool to kill off their favorite project."

As they examined project outcomes, Ruffolo and the 70 R&D scientists noted one fact. Development projects that appeared to be failing often received the most resources. Scientists were willing to starve more promising drugs to rescue those with the lowest chances of success. The best drugs were sometimes abandoned as resources were diverted elsewhere.

Ruffolo instituted annual reviews, examining costs, likelihood of success, and expected sales. In 2004 a group of scientists decided to stop development of a new drug that had disappointing results. Ruffolo gave the group an award, encouraging more review teams to do the same. Instead of advancing projects to the next stage based on one scientist's say-so, that decision is now made by a team that includes R&D and marketing specialists.

Scientists have learned that Ruffolo's tactics can work. They now deliver 12 new drugs annually, up from just 4 in 2002. Increased emphasis on speed and greater standardization of processes have cut trial periods from 18 months to just 6.

Will Ruffolo's approach increase new drug releases? It's too early to tell, but it has increased the number of drugs in the research pipeline, upping the odds of success. The entire pharmaceutical industry is suffering from a sharp decline in new product approvals. Maybe Ruffolo's strategy will help drug manufacturers get more products more quickly to those anxiously awaiting the next miracle drug.

References: Amy Barrett, "Cracking the Whip at Wyeth," *BusinessWeek*, February 6, 2006, pp. 70–71; Aaron Smith, "Drug Industry Could Use a Face Lift," *Money*, August 19, 2005, www.cnnmoney.com on April 10, 2006; "Wyeth's Profit Rises on Higher Drug Sales," *Fortune*, April 21, 2006, www.fortune.com on April 25, 2006.

Decision Making Under Risk   A more common decision-making condition is a state of risk. Under a ***state of risk***, the availability of each alternative and its potential payoffs and costs are all associated with probability estimates. Suppose, for example, that a labor contract negotiator for a company receives a "final" offer from the union right before a strike deadline. The negotiator has two alternatives: to accept or to reject the offer. The risk centers on whether the union representatives are bluffing. If the company negotiator accepts the offer, she avoids a strike but commits to a relatively costly labor contract. If she rejects the contract, she may get a more favorable contract if the union is bluffing, but she may provoke a strike if it is not.

On the basis of past experiences, relevant information, the advice of others, and her own judgment, she may conclude that there is about a 75 percent chance that union representatives are bluffing and about a 25 percent chance that they will back up their threats. Thus she can base a calculated decision on the two alternatives (accept or reject the contract demands) and the probable consequences of each. When making decisions under a state of risk, managers must reasonably estimate the probabilities associated with each alternative. For example, if the union negotiators are committed to a strike if their demands are not met, and the company negotiator rejects their demands because she guesses they will not strike, her miscalculation will prove costly. As indicated in Figure 9.1, decision making under conditions of risk is accompanied by moderate ambiguity and chances of a bad decision. Executives at Porsche have made several recent decisions under conditions of risk, starting with the question of whether the firm should join most of the world's other auto makers and build sport-utility vehicles (and potentially earn higher revenues) or maintain its focus on high-performance sports cars. Although the additional revenue is almost certain, the true risk in the firm's ultimate decision to build its Cayenne SUV is that the brand may lose some of its cachet among its existing customers. And now the firm is facing additional risky decisions regarding potential new products, including a four-door coupe, a smaller SUV, and even a minivan.[10] *The Business of Ethics* highlights how a manager at the pharmaceutical company Wyeth is attempting to increase the firm's willingness to make riskier decisions.

Decision Making Under Uncertainty   Most of the major decision making in contemporary organizations is done under a ***state of uncertainty***. The decision maker does not know all the alternatives, the risks associated with each, or the likely consequences of each alternative. This uncertainty stems from the complexity and dynamism of contemporary organizations and their environments. The emergence of the Internet as a significant force in today's competitive environment has served to increase both revenue potential and uncertainty for most managers.

> **state of risk**
> A condition in which the availability of each alternative and its potential payoffs and costs are all associated with probability estimates

> **state of uncertainty**
> A condition in which the decision maker does not know all the alternatives, the risks associated with each, or the consequences each alternative is likely to have

Managers today make many significant decisions under conditions of uncertainty. The skyrocketing costs of materials and labor have toppled several high-profile luxury condominium projects, dramatically increasing the uncertainty surrounding such ventures. These workers install exterior wall panels at Turnberry Place in Las Vegas, Nevada. At least six projects have publicly folded or stalled in a little more than a year, a fraction of the more than 100 projects once proposed, but enough to make some real estate watchers declare a bust to the boom.

To make effective decisions in these circumstances, managers must acquire as much relevant information as possible and approach the situation from a logical and rational perspective. Intuition, judgment, and experience always play major roles in the decision-making process under conditions of uncertainty. Even so, uncertainty is the most ambiguous condition for managers and the one most prone to error.[11] Indeed, many of the problems associated with the downfall of Arthur Andersen resulted from the firm's apparent difficulties in responding to ambiguous and uncertain decision parameters regarding the firm's moral, ethical, and legal responsibilities.[12]

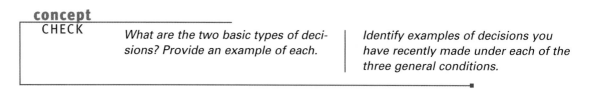

concept
CHECK

What are the two basic types of decisions? Provide an example of each.

Identify examples of decisions you have recently made under each of the three general conditions.

Rational Perspectives on Decision Making

Most managers like to think of themselves as rational decision makers. And, indeed, many experts argue that managers should try to be as rational as possible in making decisions.[13] This section highlights the fundamental and rational perspectives on decision making.

The Classical Model of Decision Making

classical decision model
A prescriptive approach to decision making that tells managers how they should make decisions; assumes that managers are logical and rational and that their decisions will be in the best interests of the organization

The **classical decision model** is a prescriptive approach that tells managers how they should make decisions. It rests on the assumptions that managers are logical and rational and that they make decisions that are in the best interests of the organization. Figure 9.2 shows how the classical model views the decision-making process.

1. Decision makers have complete information about the decision situation and possible alternatives.
2. They can effectively eliminate uncertainty to achieve a decision condition of certainty.
3. They evaluate all aspects of the decision situation logically and rationally.

As we see later, these conditions rarely, if ever, actually exist.

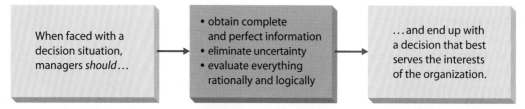

Figure 9.2
THE CLASSICAL MODEL OF DECISION MAKING

The classical model of decision making assumes that managers are rational and logical. It attempts to prescribe how managers should approach decision situations.

Steps in Rational Decision Making

A manager who really wants to approach a decision rationally and logically should try to follow the ***steps in rational decision making***, listed in Table 9.1. These steps in rational decision making help keep the decision maker focused on facts and logic and help guard against inappropriate assumptions and pitfalls.

Recognizing and Defining the Decision Situation   The first step in rational decision making is recognizing that a decision is necessary—that is, there must be some stimulus or spark to initiate the process. For many decisions and problem situations, the stimulus may occur without any prior warning. When equipment malfunctions, the manager must decide whether to repair or replace it. Or, when a major crisis erupts, as described in Chapter 3, the manager must quickly decide how to deal with it. As we already noted, the stimulus for a decision may be either positive or negative. A manager who must decide how to invest surplus funds, for example, faces a positive decision situation. A negative financial stimulus could involve having to trim budgets because of cost overruns.

Inherent in problem recognition is the need to define precisely what the problem is. The manager must develop a complete understanding of the problem, its

> *steps in rational decision making*
> Recognize and define the decision situation; identify appropriate alternatives; evaluate each alternative in terms of its feasibility, satisfactoriness, and consequences; select the best alternative; implement the chosen alternative; follow up and evaluate the results of the chosen alternative

Table 9.1

STEPS IN THE RATIONAL DECISION-MAKING PROCESS

Although the presumptions of the classical decision model rarely exist, managers can still approach decision making with rationality. By following the steps of rational decision making, managers ensure that they are learning as much as possible about the decision situation and its alternatives.

Step	Detail	Example
1. Recognizing and defining the decision situation	Some stimulus indicates that a decision must be made. The stimulus may be positive or negative.	A plant manager sees that employee turnover has increased by 5 percent.
2. Identifying alternatives	Both obvious and creative alternatives are desired. In general, the more important the decision, the more alternatives should be generated.	The plant manager can increase wages, increase benefits, or change hiring standards.
3. Evaluating alternatives	Each alternative is evaluated to determine its feasibility, its satisfactoriness, and its consequences.	Increasing benefits may not be feasible. Increasing wages and changing hiring standards may satisfy all conditions.
4. Selecting the best alternative	Consider all situational factors and choose the alternative that best fits the manager's situation.	Changing hiring standards will take an extended period of time to cut turnover, so increase wages.
5. Implementing the chosen alternative	The chosen alternative is implemented into the organizational system.	The plant manager may need permission from corporate headquarters. The human resource department establishes a new wage structure.
6. Following up and evaluating the results	At some time in the future, the manager should ascertain the extent to which the alternative chosen in step 4 and implemented in step 5 has worked.	The plant manager notes that, six months later, turnover dropped to its previous level.

causes, and its relationship to other factors. This understanding comes from careful analysis and thoughtful consideration of the situation. Consider the situation currently being faced in the international air travel industry. Because of the growth of international travel related to business, education, and tourism, global carriers like Singapore Airlines, KLM, JAL, British Airways, American Airlines, and others need to increase their capacity for international travel. Because most major international airports are already operating at or near capacity, adding a significant number of new flights to existing schedules is not feasible. As a result, the most logical alternative is to increase capacity on existing flights. Thus Boeing and Airbus, the world's only manufacturers of large commercial aircraft, have recognized an important opportunity and have defined their decision situation as how to best respond to the need for increased global travel capacity.[14]

Identifying Alternatives   Once the decision situation has been recognized and defined, the second step is to identify alternative courses of effective action. Developing both obvious, standard alternatives and creative, innovative alternatives is generally useful. In general, the more important the decision, the more attention is directed to developing alternatives.[15] If the decision involves a multimillion-dollar relocation, a great deal of time and expertise will be devoted to identifying the best locations. J. C. Penney spent two years searching before selecting the Dallas–Fort Worth area for its new corporate headquarters. If the problem is to choose a color for the company softball team uniforms, less time and expertise will be brought to bear.

Although managers should seek creative solutions, they must also recognize that various constraints often limit their alternatives. Common constraints include legal restrictions, moral and ethical norms, authority constraints, and constraints imposed by the power and authority of the manager, available technology, economic considerations, and unofficial social norms. Boeing and Airbus identified three different alternatives to address the decision situation of increasing international airline travel capacity: They could independently develop new large planes, they could collaborate in a joint venture to create a single new large plane, or they could modify their largest existing planes to increase their capacity.

Evaluating Alternatives   The third step in the decision-making process is evaluating each of the alternatives. Figure 9.3 presents a decision tree that can be used to

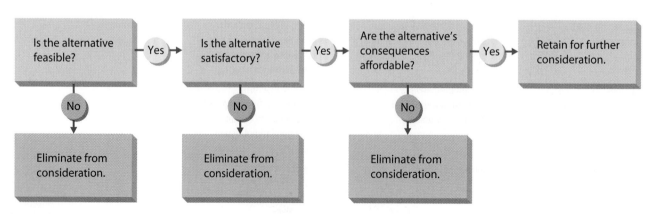

Figure 9.3

EVALUATING ALTERNATIVES IN THE DECISION-MAKING PROCESS

Managers must thoroughly evaluate all the alternatives, which increases the chances that the alternative finally chosen will be successful. Failure to evaluate an alternative's feasibility, satisfactoriness, and consequences can lead to a wrong decision.

judge different alternatives. The figure suggests that each alternative be evaluated in terms of its *feasibility,* its *satisfactoriness,* and its *consequences.* The first question to ask is whether an alternative is feasible. Is it within the realm of probability and practicality? For a small, struggling firm, an alternative requiring a huge financial outlay is probably out of the question. Other alternatives may not be feasible because of legal barriers. And limited human, material, and information resources may make other alternatives impractical.

When an alternative has passed the test of feasibility, it must next be examined to see how well it satisfies the conditions of the decision situation. For example, a manager searching for ways to double production capacity might initially consider purchasing an existing plant from another company. If more detailed analysis reveals that the new plant would increase production capacity by only 35 percent, this alternative may not be satisfactory. Finally, when an alternative has proven both feasible and satisfactory, its probable consequences must still be assessed. To what extent will a particular alternative influence other parts of the organization? What financial and nonfinancial costs will be associated with such influences? For example, a plan to boost sales by cutting prices may disrupt cash flows, require a new advertising program, and alter the behavior of sales representatives because it requires a different commission structure. The manager, then, must put "price tags" on the consequences of each alternative. Even an alternative that is both feasible and satisfactory must be eliminated if its consequences are too expensive for the total system. Airbus felt it would be at a disadvantage if it tried to simply enlarge its existing planes, because the Boeing 747 is already the largest aircraft being made and could readily be expanded to remain the largest. Boeing, meanwhile, was seriously concerned about the risk inherent in building a new and even larger plane, even if it shared the risk with Airbus as a joint venture.

> "We don't think [building the A380] is a very smart thing to do."
>
> Randy Baesler, Boeing executive
> (*Wall Street Journal,* May 27, 2005, p. A1)

Selecting an Alternative Even though many alternatives fail to pass the triple tests of feasibility, satisfactoriness, and affordable consequences, two or more alternatives may remain. Choosing the best of these is the real crux of decision making. One approach is to choose the alternative with the optimal combination of feasibility, satisfactoriness, and affordable consequences. Even though most situations do not lend themselves to objective, mathematical analysis, the manager can often develop subjective estimates and weights for choosing an alternative.

Optimization is also a frequent goal. Because a decision is likely to affect several individuals or units, any feasible alternative will probably not maximize all of the relevant goals. Suppose that the manager of the Kansas City Royals needs to select a new outfielder for the upcoming baseball season. Bill hits .350 but has difficulty catching fly balls; Joe hits only .175 but is outstanding in the field; and Sam hits .290 and is a solid but not outstanding fielder. The manager probably would select Sam because of the optimal balance of hitting and fielding. Decision makers should also remember that finding multiple acceptable alternatives may be possible; selecting just one alternative and rejecting all the others might not be necessary. For example, the Royals' manager might decide that Sam will start each game, Bill will be retained as a pinch hitter, and Joe will be retained as a defensive substitute. In many hiring decisions, the candidates remaining after evaluation are ranked. If the top candidate rejects the offer, it may be automatically extended to the number-two candidate and, if necessary, to the remaining candidates in order. For the reasons noted earlier, Airbus proposed a joint venture with Boeing. Boeing, meanwhile, decided that its best course of action was to modify its existing 747 to increase its capacity. As a result, Airbus then decided to proceed on its own to develop and manufacture a new jumbo jet. Boeing, however, also decided that in addition to modifying its 747 it would also develop a new plane to offer as an alternative, albeit one not as large as the 747 or the proposed Airbus plane. Implementing the Chosen Alternative.

After an alternative has been selected, the manager must put it into effect. In some decision situations, implementation is fairly easy; in others, it is more difficult. In the case of an acquisition, for example, managers must decide how to integrate all the activities of the new business, including purchasing, human resource practices, and distribution, into an ongoing organizational framework. For example, when Hewlett-Packard announced its acquisition of Compaq, managers also acknowledged that it would take at least a year to integrate the two firms into a single one. Operational plans, which we discuss in Chapter 7, are useful in implementing alternatives.

Managers must also consider people's resistance to change when implementing decisions. The reasons for such resistance include insecurity, inconvenience, and fear of the unknown. When J. C. Penney decided to move its headquarters from New York to Texas, many employees resigned rather than relocate. Managers should anticipate potential resistance at various stages of the implementation process. (Resistance to change is covered in Chapter 13.) Managers should also recognize that even when all alternatives have been evaluated as precisely as possible and the consequences of each alternative weighed, unanticipated consequences are still likely. Any number of factors—unexpected cost increases, a less-than-perfect fit with existing organizational subsystems, or unpredicted effects on cash flow or operating expenses, for example—could develop after implementation has begun. Boeing has set its engineers to work expanding the capacity of its 747 from today's 416 passengers to as many as 520 passengers by adding 30 feet to the plane's body. The company has also been developing its new plane intended for international travel, the 787. Airbus engineers, meanwhile, have been developing and constructing its new jumbo jet equipped with escalators and elevators, and capable of carrying 655 passengers. Airbus's development costs alone are estimated to be more than $12 billion.

Following Up and Evaluating the Results   The final step in the decision-making process requires that managers evaluate the effectiveness of their decision—that is, they should make sure that the chosen alternative has served its original purpose. If an implemented alternative appears not to be working, the manager can respond in several ways. Another previously identified alternative (the original second or third choice, for instance) could be adopted. Or the manager might recognize that the situation was not correctly defined to begin with and start the process all over again. Finally, the manager might decide that the original alternative is in fact appropriate but has not yet had time to work or should be implemented in a different way.[16]

Failure to evaluate decision effectiveness may have serious consequences. The Pentagon once spent $1.8 billion and eight years developing the Sergeant York anti-aircraft gun. From the beginning, tests revealed major problems with the weapon system, but not until it was in its final stages, when it was demonstrated to be completely ineffective, was the project scrapped.

At this point, both Boeing and Airbus are nearing the crucial period when they will learn whether they made good decisions. Airbus's A380 is scheduled to make its first commercial flight in 2007. Its final design allows seating for up to 850 people, and major airports around the world have been building new runways and terminal areas to accommodate the behemoth. Boeing's expanded 747 should be in service around the same time. Meanwhile, though, it appears that Boeing's secondary initiative for designing the new 787 may prove to be the best decision of all. A key element of the new plane is that it is much more fuel-efficient than other international airplanes. Given the dramatic surge in fuel costs in recent years, a fuel efficient option like the 787 is likely to be an enormous success. However, the 787 will not be available for passenger service until 2009, so its real impact will not be known for a few more years.[17]

concept
CHECK

What are the steps in rational decision making?

Recall a decision you recently made and believed to be rational. Trace the process through each of the steps noted above and reassess its real rationality.

Behavioral Aspects of Decision Making

If all decision situations were approached as logically as described in the previous section, more decisions might prove to be successful. Yet decisions are often made with little consideration for logic and rationality. Some experts have estimated that U.S. companies use rational decision-making techniques less than 20 percent of the time.[18] And, even when organizations try to be logical, they sometimes fail. For example, when Starbucks opened its first coffee shops in New York, it relied on scientific marketing research, taste tests, and rational deliberation in making a decision to emphasize drip over espresso coffee. However, that decision still proved wrong, as New Yorkers strongly preferred the same espresso-style coffees that were Starbucks mainstays in the West. Hence, the firm had to hastily reconfigure its stores to better meet customer preferences.

On the other hand, sometimes when a decision is made with little regard for logic, it can still turn out to be correct.[19] An important ingredient in how these forces work is the behavioral aspect of decision making. The administrative model better reflects these subjective considerations. Other behavioral aspects include political forces, intuition and escalation of commitment, risk propensity, and ethics.

The Administrative Model

Herbert A. Simon was one of the first experts to recognize that decisions are not always made with rationality and logic.[20] Simon was subsequently awarded the Nobel Prize in Economics. Rather than prescribing how decisions should be made, his view of decision making, now called the ***administrative model***, describes how decisions often actually are made. As illustrated in Figure 9.4, the model holds that managers (1) use incomplete and imperfect information, (2) are constrained by bounded rationality, and (3) tend to "satisfice" when making decisions.

administrative model
A decision-making model that argues that decision makers (1) use incomplete and imperfect information, (2) are constrained by bounded rationality, and (3) tend to "satisfice" when making decisions

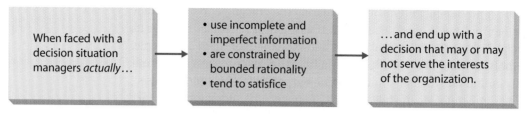

Figure 9.4
THE ADMINISTRATIVE MODEL OF DECISION MAKING

The administrative model is based on behavioral processes that affect how managers make decisions. Rather than prescribing how decisions should be made, it focuses more on describing how they are made.

> **bounded rationality**
> A concept suggesting that decision makers are limited by their values and unconscious reflexes, skills, and habits

> **satisficing**
> The tendency to search for alternatives only until one is found that meets some minimum standard of sufficiency

Bounded rationality suggests that decision makers are limited by their values and unconscious reflexes, skills, and habits. They are also limited by less-than-complete information and knowledge. Bounded rationality partially explains how U.S. auto executives allowed Japanese auto makers to get such a strong foothold in the U.S. domestic market. For years, executives at GM, Ford, and Chrysler compared their companies' performance only to one another's and ignored foreign imports. The foreign "threat" was not acknowledged until the domestic auto market had been changed forever. If managers had gathered complete information from the beginning, they might have been better able to thwart foreign competitors. Essentially, then, the concept of bounded rationality suggests that although people try to be rational decision makers, their rationality has limits.

Another important part of the administrative model is ***satisficing***. This concept suggests that rather than conducting an exhaustive search for the best possible alternative, decision makers tend to search only until they identify an alternative that meets some minimum standard of sufficiency. A manager looking for a site for a new plant, for example, may select the first site she finds that meets basic requirements for transportation, utilities, and price, even though further search might yield a better location. People satisfice for a variety of reasons. Managers may simply be unwilling to ignore their own motives (such as reluctance to spend time making a decision) and therefore not be able to continue searching after a minimally acceptable alternative is identified. The decision maker may be unable to weigh and evaluate large numbers of alternatives and criteria. Also, subjective and personal considerations often intervene in decision situations.

Because of the inherent imperfection of information, bounded rationality, and satisficing, the decisions made by a manager may or may not actually be in the best interests of the organization. A manager may choose a particular location for the new plant because it offers the lowest price and best availability of utilities and transportation. Or she may choose the location because it is located in a community where she wants to live.

In summary, then, the classical and administrative models paint quite different pictures of decision making. Which is more correct? Actually, each can be used to better understand how managers make decisions. The classical model is prescriptive: It explains how managers can at least attempt to be more rational and logical in their approaches to decisions. The administrative model can be used by managers to develop a better understanding of their inherent biases and limitations.[21] In the following sections, we describe more fully other behavioral forces that can influence decisions.

Political forces can play a major role in decision making. When the U.S. Congress was considering a decision regarding funding for smoking prevention and education programs, the American Cancer Society arranged to have yellow daffodils placed on every legislator's desk on the date the funding bill was coming to a vote. The purpose of the daffodils was, in part, to remind legislators that a number of public interest groups were planning to monitor the votes and publicize how each member of Congress voted.

Political Forces in Decision Making

Political forces are another major element that contributes to the behavioral nature of decision making. Organizational politics is covered in Chapter 17, but one major element of politics, coalitions, is especially relevant to decision making. A **coalition** is an informal alliance of individuals or groups formed to achieve a common goal. This common goal is often a preferred decision alternative. For example, coalitions of stockholders frequently band together to force a board of directors to make a certain decision.

> **coalition**
> An informal alliance of individuals or groups formed to achieve a common goal

The impact of coalitions can be either positive or negative. They can help astute managers get the organization on a path toward effectiveness and profitability, or they can strangle well-conceived strategies and decisions. Managers must recognize when to use coalitions, how to assess whether coalitions are acting in the best interests of the organization, and how to constrain their dysfunctional effects.[22]

Intuition and Escalation of Commitment

Two other important decision processes that go beyond logic and rationality are intuition and escalation of commitment to a chosen course of action.

Intuition **Intuition** is an innate belief about something, without conscious consideration. Managers sometimes decide to do something because it "feels right" or they have a "hunch." This feeling usually is not arbitrary, however. Rather, it is based on years of experience and practice in making decisions in similar situations.[23] An inner sense may help managers make an occasional decision without going through a full-blown rational sequence of steps. For example, the New York Yankees once contacted three major athletic shoes manufacturers—Nike, Reebok, and Adidas— and informed them that they were looking to make a sponsorship deal. While Nike and Reebok were carefully and rationally assessing the possibilities, managers at Adidas quickly realized that a partnership with the Yankees made a lot of sense for them. They responded very quickly to the idea and ended up hammering out a

> **intuition**
> An innate belief about something, without conscious consideration

> "Nothing is more difficult, and therefore more precious, than to be able to decide."
>
> Napoleon
> (quoted in *Fortune,* June 27, 2005, p. 55)

escalation of commitment
A decision maker's staying with a decision even when it appears to be wrong

contract while the competitors were still analyzing details.[24] Of course, all managers, but most especially inexperienced ones, should be careful not to rely too heavily on intuition. If rationality and logic are continually flouted for "what feels right," the odds are that disaster will strike one day.

Escalation of Commitment Another important behavioral process that influences decision making is **escalation of commitment** to a chosen course of action. In particular, decision makers sometimes make decisions and then become so committed to the courses of action suggested by those decisions that they stay with them, even when the decisions appear to have been wrong.[25] For example, when people buy stock in a company, they sometimes refuse to sell it even after repeated drops in price. They chose a course of action—buying the stock in anticipation of making a profit—and then stay with it even in the face of increasing losses. Moreover, after the value drops, they rationalize that they can't sell now because they will lose money.

For years Pan American World Airways ruled the skies and used its profits to diversify into real estate and other businesses. But, with the advent of deregulation, Pan Am began to struggle and lose market share to other carriers. Experts today point out that when Pan Am managers finally realized how ineffective their airline operations had become, the "rational" decision would have been to sell off the remaining airline operations and concentrate on the firm's more profitable businesses. But because they still saw the company as being first and foremost an airline, they instead began to slowly sell off the firm's profitable holdings to keep the airline flying. Eventually, the company was left with nothing but an ineffective and inefficient airline, and then had to sell off its more profitable routes before eventually being taken over by Delta. Had Pan Am managers made the more rational decision years earlier, chances are the firm could still be a profitable enterprise today, albeit one with no involvement in the airline industry.[26]

Thus decision makers must walk a fine line. On the one hand, they must guard against sticking too long with an incorrect decision. To do so can bring about financial decline. On the other hand, managers should not bail out of a seemingly incorrect decision too soon, as Adidas once did. Adidas had dominated the market for professional athletic shoes. It subsequently entered the market for amateur sports shoes and did well there also. But managers interpreted a sales slowdown as a sign that the boom in athletic shoes was over. They thought that they had made the wrong decision and ordered drastic cutbacks. The market took off again with Nike at the head of the pack, and Adidas never recovered. Fortunately, a new management team has changed the way Adidas makes decisions, and the firm is again on its way to becoming a force in the athletic shoe and apparel markets.

Risk Propensity and Decision Making

risk propensity
The extent to which a decision maker is willing to gamble when making a decision

The behavioral element of **risk propensity** is the extent to which a decision maker is willing to gamble when making a decision. Some managers are cautious about every decision they make. They try to adhere to the rational model and are extremely conservative in what they do. Such managers are more likely to avoid mistakes, and they infrequently make decisions that lead to big losses. Other managers are extremely aggressive in making decisions and are willing to take risks.[27] They rely heavily on intuition, reach decisions quickly, and often risk big investments on their decisions. As in gambling, these managers are more likely than their conservative counterparts to achieve big successes with their decisions; they are also more likely to incur greater losses.[28] The organization's culture is a prime ingredient in fostering different levels of risk propensity. *The Business of Ethics* feature that appears earlier in this chapter illustrates how an individual manager's risk propensity can be diffused in an organization.

Ethics and Decision Making

As we introduced in Chapter 4, individual ethics are personal beliefs about right and wrong behavior. Ethics are clearly related to decision making in a number of ways. For example, suppose that, after careful analysis, a manager realizes that his company could save money by closing his department and subcontracting with a supplier for the same services. But to recommend this course of action would result in the loss of several jobs, including his own. His own ethical standards will clearly shape how he proceeds.[29] Indeed, each component of managerial ethics (relationships of the firm to its employees, of employees to the firm, and of the firm to other economic agents) involves a wide variety of decisions, all of which are likely to have an ethical component. A manager must remember, then, that just as behavioral processes such as politics and risk propensity affect the decisions he makes, so, too, do his ethical beliefs.

concept
CHECK

Summarize the essential components of the administrative model of decision making.

Recall a recent decision that you observed or were involved in that had strong behavioral overtones. Describe how various behavioral elements affected the process or outcome.

Group and Team Decision Making in Organizations

In more and more organizations today, important decisions are made by groups and teams rather than by individuals. Examples include the executive committee of General Motors, product design teams at Texas Instruments, and marketing planning groups at Dell Computer. Managers can typically choose whether to have individuals or groups and teams make a particular decision. Thus knowing about forms of group and team decision making and their advantages and disadvantages is important.[30]

Group decision making and problem-solving are commonplace in organizations. These people are attending a recent international conference in Spain aimed at improving relations between different religious groups. They are participating in an offbeat brainstorming exercise that requires them to write down issues they see as critical for bringing about peace between their faiths.

Forms of Group and Team Decision Making

The most common methods of group and team decision making are interacting groups, Delphi groups, and nominal groups. Increasingly, these methods of group decision making are being conducted online.[31]

interacting group or team
A decision-making group or team in which members openly discuss, argue about, and agree on the best alternative

Interacting Groups and Teams *Interacting groups and teams* are the most common form of decision-making group. The format is simple—either an existing or a newly designated group or team is asked to make a decision. Existing groups or teams might be functional departments, regular work teams, or standing committees. Newly designated groups or teams can be ad hoc committees, task forces, or newly constituted work teams. The group or team members talk among themselves, argue, agree, argue some more, form internal coalitions, and so forth. Finally, after some period of deliberation, the group or team makes its decision. An advantage of this method is that the interaction among people often sparks new ideas and promotes understanding. A major disadvantage, though, is that political processes can play too big a role.

Delphi group
A form of group decision making in which a group is used to achieve a consensus of expert opinion

Delphi Groups A *Delphi group* is sometimes used to develop a consensus of expert opinion. Developed by the Rand Corporation, the Delphi procedure solicits input from a panel of experts who contribute individually. Their opinions are combined and, in effect, averaged. Assume, for example, that the problem is to establish an expected date for a major technological breakthrough in converting coal into usable energy. The first step in using the Delphi procedure is to obtain the cooperation of a panel of experts. For this situation, experts might include various research scientists, university researchers, and executives in a relevant energy industry. At first, the experts are asked to anonymously predict a time frame for the expected breakthrough. The persons coordinating the Delphi group collect the responses, average them, and ask the experts for another prediction. In this round, the experts who provided unusual or extreme predictions may be asked to justify them. These explanations may then be relayed to the other experts. When the predictions stabilize, the average prediction is taken to represent the decision of the group of experts. The time, expense, and logistics of the Delphi technique rule out its use for routine, everyday decisions, but it has been successfully used for forecasting technological breakthroughs at Boeing, market potential for new products at General Motors, research and development patterns at Eli Lilly, and future economic conditions by the U.S. government.[32]

nominal group
A structured technique used to generate creative and innovative alternatives or ideas

Nominal Groups Another useful group and team decision-making technique that is occasionally used is the *nominal group*. Unlike the Delphi method, in which group members do not see one another, nominal group members are brought together in a face-to-face setting. The members represent a group in name only, however; they do not talk to one another freely like the members of interacting groups. Nominal groups are used most often to generate creative and innovative alternatives or ideas. To begin, the manager assembles a group of knowledgeable experts and outlines the problem to them. The group members are then asked to individually write down as many alternatives as they can think of. The members then take turns stating their ideas, which are recorded on a flip chart or board at the front of the room. Discussion is limited to simple clarification. After all alternatives have been listed, more open discussion takes place. Group members then vote, usually by rank-ordering the various alternatives. The highest-ranking alternative represents the decision of the group. Of course, the manager in charge may retain the authority to accept or reject the group decision.

Advantages of Group and Team Decision Making

The advantages and disadvantages of group and team decision making relative to individual decision making are summarized in Table 9.2. *Working with Diversity* reinforces several of the advantages as they relate to diversity. One advantage is simply that more information is available in a group or team setting—as suggested by the old axiom, "Two heads are better than one." A group or team represents a variety of education, experience, and perspective. Partly as a result of this increased information, groups and teams typically can identify and evaluate more alternatives than can one person.[33] The people involved in a group or team decision understand the logic and rationale behind it, are more likely to accept it, and are equipped to communicate the decision to their work group or department.[34] Finally, research evidence suggests that groups may make better decisions than individuals.[35]

Working with Diversity

Diverse Groups Make Better Decisions

Behavioral factors have a profound effect on decision making. Those factors are heightened when diverse groups make decisions. Professor Samuel Sommers published a 2006 study showing diverse groups making better decisions. He staged mock trials with juries of all-white, all-black, and mixed members. The mixed juries "deliberated longer, raised more facts, and conducted broader and more wide-ranging deliberations," Sommers writes. In addition, the mixed juries made fewer factual errors, and any errors made were more quickly corrected.

Sommers adds, "Traditionally, [researchers] assumed that the influences of racial diversity result from the contributions of the minority members, who in effect bear the burden of bringing new perspectives . . . to the table." Yet his research points to a startling conclusion: Changes in white behavior made the difference. While black members behaved consistently, whites became more involved and focused in the mixed group, even before discussion began. When white members in mixed juries realized the group's mixed composition, they changed their behavior, for example, by taking better notes during the trial.

So how can organizations get the full benefits of inclusion in decision making? Here are some cases.

- A nonprofit's decision-making committees included persons with and without learning difficulties. Nondisabled members dominated group decisions. Therefore, members with disabilities served as "advisors," preparing remarks before the scheduled meeting. Everyone was heard, even those who needed extra help to participate. This technique could work for any group dominated by forceful members.

- Another technique for encouraging wider participation was used by a firm that designs public playgrounds. To allow children and adults an equal chance to contribute, meetings were held at the building site. Everyone explored the site and then expressed their views by drawings or notes attached to a detailed site map. Even children too young to write could participate in the group effectively.

- Even simple ideas are helpful. A city government was overwhelmed by too many volunteers when it asked for the public's help in evaluating community projects. Rather than limit involvement, the city formed a main committee and several subcommittees. This technique kept participation high, while maintaining a group size that facilitated discussion and consensus.

Diversity in decision-making groups can improve decision quality. Managers should find decision strategies that maximize the benefits of diversity for their organizations.

References: "Decision Making Case Studies," The Media Trust website, www.voluntarymatters3.com on April 10, 2006; Scott Dyer, "Leadership and Diversity in Louisiana," *Diverse Education*, April 21, 2005, www.diverseeducation.com on April 10, 2006; Samuel R. Sommers, "On Racial Diversity and Group Decision Making: Identifying Multiple Effects of Racial Composition on Jury Deliberations," *Journal of Personality and Social Psychology*, April 2006, vol. 90, no. 4, www.apa.org on April 10, 2006.

Table 9.2

ADVANTAGES AND DISADVANTAGES OF GROUP AND TEAM DECISION MAKING

To increase the chances that a group or team decision will be successful, managers must learn how to manage the process of group and team decision making. Federal Express and IBM are increasingly using groups and teams in the decision-making process.

Advantages	Disadvantages
1. More information and knowledge are available.	1. The process takes longer than individual decision making, so it is costlier.
2. More alternatives are likely to be generated.	2. Compromise decisions resulting from indecisiveness may emerge.
3. More acceptance of the final decision is likely.	3. One person may dominate the group.
4. Enhanced communication of the decision may result.	4. Groupthink may occur.
5. Better decisions generally emerge.	

Disadvantages of Group and Team Decision Making

Perhaps the biggest drawback of group and team decision making is the additional time and hence the greater expense entailed. The increased time stems from interaction and discussion among group or team members. If a given manager's time is worth $50 an hour, and if the manager spends two hours making a decision, the decision "costs" the organization $100. For the same decision, a group of five managers might require three hours of time. At the same $50-an-hour rate, the decision "costs" the organization $750. Assuming the group or team decision is better, the additional expense may be justified, but the fact remains that group and team decision making is more costly.

Group or team decisions may also represent undesirable compromises.[36] For example, hiring a compromise top manager may be a bad decision in the long run because he or she may not be able to respond adequately to various subunits in the organization nor have everyone's complete support. Sometimes one individual dominates the group process to the point where others cannot make a full contribution. This dominance may stem from a desire for power or from a naturally dominant personality. The problem is that what appears to emerge as a group decision may actually be the decision of one person.

Finally, a group or team may succumb to a phenomenon known as "groupthink." *Groupthink* occurs when the desire for consensus and cohesiveness overwhelms the goal of reaching the best possible decision.[37] Under the influence of groupthink, the group may arrive at decisions that are made not in the best interests of either the group or the organization, but rather to avoid conflict among group members. One of the most clearly documented examples of groupthink involved the space shuttle *Challenger* disaster. As NASA was preparing to launch the shuttle, numerous problems and questions arose. At each step of the way, however, decision makers argued that there was no reason to delay and that everything would be fine. Shortly after its launch, the shuttle exploded, killing all seven crew members.

groupthink
A situation that occurs when a group or team's desire for consensus and cohesiveness overwhelms its desire to reach the best possible decision

Managing Group and Team Decision-Making Processes

Managers can do several things to help promote the effectiveness of group and team decision making. One is simply being aware of the pros and cons of having a group or team make a decision to start with. Time and cost can be managed by setting a deadline by which the decision must be made final. Dominance can be at least partially avoided if a special group is formed just to make the decision. An astute manager, for example, should know who in the organization may try to dominate and can either avoid putting that person in the group or put several strong-willed people together.

To avoid groupthink, each member of the group or team should critically evaluate all alternatives. So that members present divergent viewpoints, the leader should not make his or her own position known too early. At least one member of the group or team might be assigned the role of devil's advocate. And, after reaching a preliminary decision, the group or team should hold a follow-up meeting wherein divergent viewpoints can be raised again if any group members wish to do so.[38] Gould Paper Corporation used these methods by assigning managers to two different teams. The teams then spent an entire day in a structured debate presenting the pros and cons of each side of an issue to ensure the best possible decision. Sun Microsystems makes most of its major decisions using this same approach.

---

concept CHECK

Summarize the advantages and disadvantages of group decision making.

Are some of the different types of decisions and decision-making conditions more amenable to group decision making than others? Explain how and why.

Summary of Learning Objectives and Key Points

1. Define decision making and discuss types of decisions and decision-making conditions.
   - Decision making is the act of choosing one alternative from among a set of alternatives.
   - The decision-making process includes recognizing and defining the nature of a decision situation, identifying alternatives, choosing the "best" alternative, and putting it into practice.
   - Two common types of decisions are programmed and nonprogrammed.
   - Decisions may be made under states of certainty, risk, or uncertainty.

2. Discuss rational perspectives on decision making, including the steps in rational decision making.
   - Rational perspectives on decision making rest on the classical model.
   - This model assumes that managers have complete information and that they will behave rationally. The primary steps in rational decision making are
     • recognizing and defining the situation
     • identifying alternatives
     • evaluating alternatives

   • selecting the best alternative
   • implementing the chosen alternative
   • following up and evaluating the effectiveness of the alternative after it is implemented

3. Describe the behavioral aspects of decision making.
   - Behavioral aspects of decision making rely on the administrative model.
   - This model recognizes that managers use incomplete information and that they do not always behave rationally.
   - The administrative model also recognizes the concepts of bounded rationality and satisficing.
   - Political activities by coalitions, managerial intuition, and the tendency to become increasingly committed to a chosen course of action are all important.
   - Risk propensity is also an important behavioral perspective on decision making.
   - Ethics also affect how managers make decisions.

4. Discuss group and team decision making, including the advantages and disadvantages of group and team

decision making and how it can be more effectively managed.

- To help enhance decision-making effectiveness, managers often use interacting, Delphi, or nominal groups or teams.

- Group and team decision making in general has several advantages as well as disadvantages relative to individual decision making.

- Managers can adopt a number of strategies to help groups and teams make better decisions.

Discussion Questions

Questions for Review

1. Describe the difference between programmed and nonprogrammed decisions. What are the implications of these differences for decision makers?
2. Describe the behavioral nature of decision making. Be certain to provide some detail about political forces, risk propensity, ethics, and commitment in your description.

3. What is meant by the term *escalation of commitment*? In your opinion, under what conditions is escalation of commitment likely to occur?
4. Explain the differences between three common methods of group decision making—interacting groups, Delphi groups, and nominal groups.

Questions for Analysis

5. Was your decision about what college or university to attend a rational decision? Did you go through each step in rational decision making? If not, why not?
6. Most business decisions are made under conditions of either risk or uncertainty. In your opinion, is it easier to make a decision under a condition of risk or a condition of uncertainty? Why?
7. Consider the following list of business decisions. Which decisions would be handled most effectively

by group or team decision making? Which would be handled most effectively by individual decision making? Explain your answers.
- A decision about switching pencil suppliers
- A decision about hiring a new CEO
- A decision about firing an employee for stealing
- A decision about calling 911 to report a fire in the warehouse
- A decision about introducing a brand new product

Questions for Application

8. Interview a local business manager about a major decision that he or she made recently. Try to determine whether the manager used a rational decision-making process or whether behavioral elements were also present. If the process was wholly rational, why do you think there was no behavioral component? If the process contained behavioral components, why were these components present?
9. Describe a recent decision you made that relied on intuition. In your opinion, what experiences formed

the source of your intuition? Did the decision lead to attainment of the desired outcomes? Did your intuition play a positive or negative role in goal attainment? Explain.
10. Interview a department head at your college or university to determine whether group or team decision making is used. If it is, how does the head attempt to overcome the disadvantages of a group decision making? Are the attempts successful? Why or why not?

Building Effective Conceptual Skills

Exercise Overview

Conceptual skills refer to the manager's ability to think in the abstract. This exercise will aid you in understanding the effect that nonrational biases and risk propensity can have on decision making.

Exercise Background

Two psychologists, Amos Tversky and Daniel Kahneman, conducted much of the research that led to our knowledge of decision-making biases. Tversky and Kahneman found that they could understand individuals' real-life choices by presenting experimental subjects with simulated decisions in a laboratory setting. They developed a theory they called prospect theory, which uses behavioral psychology to explain why individuals are nonrational when making economic decisions. Their work has contributed a great deal to the developing discipline of behavioral economics. In fact, Kahneman won the 2002 Nobel Prize in Economics for development of these concepts. (Tversky could not share in the award because the Nobel Prize cannot be given posthumously.)

Tversky and Kahneman's most important finding was that an individual's *perception* of gain or loss in a situation is more important than an objective measure of gain or loss. Thus individuals are nonrational; that is, they do not make decisions based purely on rational criteria. Related to this conclusion, Tversky and Kahneman found that humans think differently about gains and losses. This is called framing. Another finding is that people allow their perceptions to be skewed positively or negatively, depending on information they receive. Later, when new information becomes available, people have a hard time letting go of their initial perceptions, even if the new information contradicts their original impressions. This effect is referred to as anchoring and adjustment.

To answer the questions below, you must be able to calculate an expected value. To calculate an expected value, multiply each possible outcome value by the probability of its occurrence, and then sum all the results. Here is a simple example: You have a 50 percent chance of earning 80 points on an exam and a 50 percent chance of earning 70 points. The expected value can be calculated as $(.5 \times 80) + (.5 \times 70)$, or a .5 chance of 80 points (equal to 40 points) plus a .5 chance of 70 points (equal to 35 points). Therefore, the expected value of your exam is 75 points.

Exercise Task

1. Answer the list of brief questions that your professor provides to you. No answer is correct or incorrect; simply choose your most likely response. Then, when the professor asks, share your answers with the class.

2. Discuss the answers given by the class. Why do students' answers differ?

3. What have you learned about decision-making biases and risk propensity from these experiments?

Building Effective Decision-Making Skills

Exercise Overview

Decision-making skills refer to the manager's ability to recognize and define problems and opportunities correctly and then to select an appropriate course of action for solving problems and capitalizing on opportunities.

This exercise will allow you to compare individual decision making with decision making conducted through use of nominal groups.

Exercise Background

Individual decision making has some advantages—for example, speed, simplicity, and lack of conflict. However, there are times when these advantages are outweighed by other considerations. Innovation, in particular, is lower when one person makes a decision alone. A group decision is preferable when innovation is required because more input from more diverse individuals can generate more varied alternative courses of action.

Nominal groups are especially well suited for fostering creativity. Nominal groups allow individuals to have freedom in listing as many creative alternatives as they can, without worrying about criticism or political pressure. Nominal groups also pool input from many individuals and allow creative responses to the pooled input. Thus nominal groups foster creativity by combining techniques for improving both individual and group innovation.

Exercise Task

1. Listen as your professor describes the problem situation to the class.
2. Write down as many creative responses to the problem as you can. Do not worry about whether the alternatives you are generating are practical. In fact, try to list as many different, even "far-out," responses as you can.
3. When called on by your professor, share your list with the class.
4. Ask other students questions about their suggestions only for purposes of clarification. Do not, under any circumstances, reveal whether you think any idea is "good" or "bad."
5. After all the individual ideas are listed and clarified, add to the list any other ideas you have developed.
6. Vote on the list.
7. Did the nominal group technique generate alternatives that are more creative than those you generated on your own?
8. In your opinion, is the alternative chosen by the class vote a "better" solution than those you thought of on your own? Explain your answer.
9. Give some suggestions about what types of decisions in organizations could be effectively made using nominal group decision making. When should it *not* be used?

CHAPTER CLOSING CASE

THE ART AND SCIENCE OF DECISION MAKING

Some experts emphasize the importance of art in management. These scholars advocate more use of non-rational and behavioral factors, especially intuition, in decision making. Followers of this approach include author Malcolm Gladwell, whose book, *Blink: The Power of Thinking Without Thinking*, became a management best-seller. On the other hand, another group of scholars believes strongly in facts, measurable outcomes, and rational approaches. This group uses scientifically conducted studies to help managers improve their decision making using an approach called evidence-based management. Both approaches are leading managers to some unconventional insights about making decisions.

In corporations, intuition is often used, for example, to help loan officers determine whether an applicant is a good risk. Most loan managers consider rational data but, in the end, also give a lot of weight to their vague, undefined feelings about the applicant's creditworthiness. Gladwell calls these feelings "thin slices" because they are so small and subtle. Experts have found that officers who use both data and feelings make better choices than those who rely on the numbers alone. Other examples range from art appraisers to police officers, from CEOs to physicians. In each of these professions, the use of intuition is widely accepted and valued as a supplement to fact-based decision making.

How exactly does intuition aid in decision making? The "intuitionists" claim that individuals make better and faster decisions by focusing on the most relevant facts and ignoring the rest. What is often overlooked, though, is that intuition works best when it is based on experience. Experienced nurses can often sense, for example, when a patient needs urgent attention. What is really happening is that the experienced nurses seek out subtle clues and draw the correct conclusions from them. The intuitions of inexperienced workers are often faulty. Most of the battle casualties sustained in Iraq, for example, occur in the first 90 days of the soldier's deployment. Studies of airline crews show that 73 percent of serious mistakes happen when crews work together for the very first time.

There are other limitations of the intuition school of management. Critics points out that this approach focuses on quick action, but most decision making that takes place in organizations is not that time sensitive. While speed is an increasingly important part of many company's strategies, decision-making speed can be measured in days or weeks, not seconds or minutes. Except in emergencies, most organizational decision making allows time to gather information, generate alternative strategies, and discuss the merits of alternatives. Another negative of the intuition approach is its reliance on a single decision maker. Group members rarely experience the same intuitions, yet group decision making is becoming much more prevalent in today's organizations.

Many are concerned that the intuition approach gives managers an excuse for sloppy thinking and poor decision making. These critics, which include Stanford professors Jeffrey Pfeffer and Bob Sutton, are calling for an increased reliance on rationality. In their book, *Hard Facts, Dangerous Half-Truths, and Total Nonsense,* Pfeffer and Sutton highlight the importance of the science of management. Pfeffer and Sutton say, "Management decisions [should] be based on the best evidence, managers [should] systematically learn from experience, and organizational practices [should] reflect sound principles of thought and analysis."

Some of the insights that Pfeffer, Sutton, and other fans of evidence-based management have gained confirm traditional management practices, while others defy the current wisdom. Confirmed: Complainers hurt team performance more than incompetents. Busted: The common practice at many companies of giving large raises to a few top performers and small raises to everyone else is harmful. It does motivate the top performers, but they are the least loyal to the company and, in any case, are responsible for just a small portion of the total work. The harm comes because the rewards are perceived as unfair and therefore hurt the motivation of average workers, who do most of the tasks.

Cisco, the largest computer networking equipment maker, uses evidence-based management to identify good candidates for acquisitions. Cisco studied thousands of mergers and found that acquisitions work best when the acquired firm is the smaller, the two companies are located near each other, and the firms' cultures are similar. Cisco also found that effective post-acquisition integration was critical. Seventy percent of all mergers lead to a long-term loss of market value, yet Cisco completed 57 mergers over five years, all without any significant problems or loss of value.

New insights and approaches to decision making are constantly being conceived and publicized. Two of the most recent—intuition and evidence-based management—reflect the long-time debate among management scholars over the use of rational or behavior decision-making models. Savvy managers will find that each approach has something to offer.

CASE QUESTIONS

1. Is a rational decision process likely to produce the best outcomes when a situation is risky or when it is uncertain? Is an intuitive, behavioral process best used under risk or under certainty? Explain.

2. Consider the hypothetical case in which a company must choose one of two promising new products to develop and introduce to the market. There are not sufficient funds for both products. How might this company make use of intuition as it faces this decision?

3. Consider the hypothetical case in which a company must choose one of two promising new products to develop and introduce to the market. There are not sufficient funds for both products. How might this company make use of evidence-based management as it faces this decision?

CASE REFERENCES

Talis Demos, "Bestselling Wonks Square Off," *Fortune,* March 29, 2006, www.cnnmoney.com on March 30, 2006; "Forget Going with Your Gut," *BusinessWeek,* March 20, 2006, www.businessweek.com on March 30, 2006; Malcolm Gladwell, *Blink: The Power of Thinking Without Thinking* (Boston: Little, Brown, 2005); Jeffrey Pfeffer and Robert I. Sutton, *Hard Facts, Dangerous Half-Truths, and Total Nonsense* (Cambridge, Mass.: Harvard Business School Press, 2006).

YOU MAKE THE CALL

Team Decision Making at Barclays

1. Identify the specific decisions made at Barclays by Bob Diamond. In your opinion, which single decision made by Mr. Diamond contributed most to the turnaround at Barclays?

2. What event or events might cause Barclays to lose its momentum and competitiveness?

3. What part of Barclays' decision-making culture would be of most appeal to you as a prospective employee?

4. What part of Barclays' decision-making culture would be of least appeal to you as a prospective employee?

5. Does Bob Diamond seem like the kind of manager for whom you would like to work? Why or why not?

Test Prepper

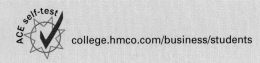

college.hmco.com/business/students

Choose the correct answer. Answers are found at the back of the book.

1. T F If a decision maker does not know what the odds of success are, he or she is operating under a condition of risk.

2. T F One part of evaluating an alternative solution is assessing whether it is feasible.

3. T F The classical decision-making model and the administrative model are based on the same fundamental assumptions.

4. T F One factor that influences the level of risk propensity in an organization is its culture.

5. T F To avoid groupthink, the group leader should make his or her own position known very early in the group decision-making process.

6. Rochelle is a human resource manager who regularly hires entry-level employees. This part of her job is so routine she knows immediately upon seeing someone's application whether he or she should be hired. Rochelle is making what kind of decision?

   A. Programmed
   B. Nonprogrammed
   C. Rational
   D. Behavioral
   E. Certain

7. In which order should the following criteria be used to evaluate an alternative?

   A. Feasibility, consequences, satisfactoriness
   B. Consequences, satisfactoriness, feasibility
   C. Satisfactoriness, feasibility, consequences
   D. Feasibility, satisfactoriness, consequences
   E. Consequences, feasibility, satisfactoriness

8. Managers must consider people's resistance to change during which step of rational decision making?

   A. Selecting the best alternative
   B. Evaluating alternatives
   C. Recognizing and defining the decision structure
   D. Implementing the chosen alternative
   E. Identifying alternatives

9. Keisha purchased 50 desktop computers for $500 each, and hoped to sell each for a $100 profit. However, a new model of computer soon came out and made Keisha's computers obsolete. Keisha is reluctant to sell her computers for any price below $500 because she'll lose money. This is an example of

   A. risk propensity.
   B. escalation of commitment.
   C. satisfactoriness.
   D. satisficing.
   E. bounded rationality.

10. In the nominal group technique,

   A. the group votes on alternatives that are generated by individual group members.
   B. a consensus of nonexpert opinion is achieved.
   C. programmed decisions are recast as nonprogrammed decisions.
   D. group members do not see each other.
   E. a critical evaluation of alternatives is avoided to facilitate the probability of groupthink.

Managing New Venture Formation and Entrepreneurship

chapter 10

FIRST THINGS FIRST

Founding Facebook

"We're not doing this to cash in. We're doing this to build something cool."

—MARK ZUCKERBERG, FOUNDER, FACEBOOK

Do you facebook? More likely than not, your answer is yes. Facebook was started by Mark Zuckerberg, a Harvard sophomore, in February 2004. Zuckerberg noted that each residence hall had a directory, but there was no college-wide listing, which hampered socializing. According to Zuckerberg, "I've always enjoyed building things and puttering around with computer code, so I sat down and in about a week I had produced the basic workings of the site." Zuckerberg was a computer prodigy who turned down a $1 million job offer at Microsoft after high school graduation, choosing Harvard instead.

As the Facebook website grew, more universities were added based on the recommendations of Harvard undergraduates. By November 2004, the site had 1 million users. Eighteen months later, membership included 7 million members at 2,100 colleges and 22,000 high schools. Facebook.com is the seventh-most

LEARNING OBJECTIVES

After studying this chapter, you should be able to:

1. Discuss the nature of entrepreneurship.
2. Describe the role of entrepreneurship in society.
3. Understand the major issues involved in choosing strategies for small firms and the role of international management in entrepreneurship.
4. Discuss the structural challenges unique to entrepreneurial firms.
5. Understand the determinants of the performance of small firms.

Facebook has become a campus phenomenon. This unidentified University of Missouri student is looking through Facebook while in class (instead of listening to the professor!).

visited Internet site and the second among college students, behind number one Google. Altogether, 53 percent of U.S. college students belong to Facebook.

Facebook began as a noncommercial enterprise, but as its popularity grew, so did its need for funds. Venture capitalists were generous in exchange for ownership shares. Another source of funding is advertising. Facebook allows its users to post online flyers for a flat fee of as little as $5 for 10,000 posts. Corporate online advertising is also available and constitutes a major source of income.

Anyone with an e-mail ending in the .edu suffix may register for free at Facebook. The Facebook system allows users to exchange photos and messages, as well as post personal information and view others' information. Facebook restricts access to students, granting a certain amount of security to users. In addition, users can contact only others through approved mechanisms, such as through the lists of mutual friends, through school affiliation, or by joining one of thousands of user-defined groups.

Facebook's college-oriented appeal is obvious to anyone who enters the site. On the one hand, that generates a high level of comfort and interest with the site's content. On the other hand, some disapprove of Facebook for glamorizing a "party" lifestyle. As *Rolling Stone* writer David Kushner says, "Surfing the site can feel like wandering through a giant dorm where every door is open and every kid is swilling Jack Daniel's." Facebook has a policy of not censoring users' posts, but that has led to criticism for including photos and descriptions of drug-taking, nudity, obscenity, and hate speech.

There are other drawbacks related to revealing too much information. Third-party advertisers can place "cookies" on users' computers, allowing the company to gather information about the user without permission. Some worry that Facebook facilitates identity theft or, even worse, stalking. Facebook warns users not to reveal too much personal information, and the site limits access to only known individuals, but some scary incidents have occurred.

Some colleges discipline students when their Facebook pages reveal evidence of underage drinking or sexual misconduct. At one evangelical university, students who admit in their Facebook profiles that they are gay are expelled. In addition, many employers and university admission committees routinely examine Facebook profiles. Workers who reveal company information or reveal bosses' incompetence have been caught in the act and fired. Facebook is even becoming an important tool for the police and has allowed the identification of several criminals on U.S. campuses. "[Facebook] is like putting stuff on the six o'clock news," says employment lawyer Garry Mathiason, who urges Facebook members to be discreet. "Once you've opened the drapes, people can see everything."

Facebook's increasing popularity with an important demographic segment shows no sign of slowing down. It comes as no surprise, then, that Facebook may be the target of a corporate acquisition. After MySpace.com was purchased by media giant News Corporation for $580 million, there was speculation that Facebook would be next. But Zuckerberg turned down an offer of $750 million in early 2006 and is holding out for $2 billion. Viacom, which owns MTV and Comedy Central, is one possible buyer, as is Google, which just raised $2.1 billion in an additional stock offering.

From a dorm-living Harvard sophomore to CEO of a firm valued at $2 billion, Zuckerberg has had an amazing two years. He insists, "We're not doing this to cash in. We're doing this to build something cool." Facebook is very cool, and it's also very hot. [1]

Just like Mark Zuckerberg, thousands of people all over the world start new businesses each year. And, like Facebook, some of these businesses succeed, while unfortunately, many others fail. Some of the people who fail in a new business try again, and sometimes it takes two or more failures before a successful business gets under way. Henry Ford, for example, went bankrupt twice before succeeding with Ford Motor Company.

This process of starting a new business, sometimes failing and sometimes succeeding, is part of what is called "entrepreneurship," the subject of this chapter. We begin by exploring the nature of entrepreneurship. We then examine the role of entrepreneurship in the business world and discuss strategies for entrepreneurial organizations. We then describe the structure and performance of entrepreneurial organizations.

The Nature of Entrepreneurship

Entrepreneurship is the process of planning, organizing, operating, and assuming the risk of a business venture. An *entrepreneur*, in turn, is someone who engages in entrepreneurship. Mark Zuckerberg, as highlighted in our opening incident, fits this description. He put his own resources on the line and took a personal stake in the success or failure of Facebook. Business owners who hire professional managers to run their businesses and then turn their attention to other interests are not true entrepreneurs. Although they are assuming the risk of the venture, they are not actively involved in organizing or operating it. Likewise, professional managers whose job is running someone else's business are not entrepreneurs, for they assume less-than-total personal risk for the success or failure of the business.

Entrepreneurs start new businesses. We define a *small business* as one that is privately owned by one individual or a small group of individuals and has sales and assets that are not large enough to influence its environment. A small, two-person software development company with annual sales of $100,000 would clearly be a small business, whereas Microsoft Corporation is just as clearly a large business. But the boundaries are not always this clear-cut. For example, a regional retailing chain with 20 stores and annual revenues of $30 million may sound large but is really very small when compared to such giants as Wal-Mart and Sears.

entrepreneurship
The process of planning, organizing, operating, and assuming the risk of a business venture

entrepreneur
Someone who engages in entrepreneurship

small business
A business that is privately owned by one individual or a small group of individuals and has sales and assets that are not large enough to influence its environment

What is a small business?

How easy or difficult is it to distinguish between a small and a large business?

concept
CHECK

The Role of Entrepreneurship in Society

> **"**The family name is on the door. It's more than just a job.**"**
>
> William Wrigley, CEO of Wrigley's Co.
> (*BusinessWeek*, November 10, 2003, p. 100)

The history of entrepreneurship and of the development of new businesses is in many ways the history of great wealth and of great failure. Some entrepreneurs have been very successful and have accumulated vast fortunes from their entrepreneurial efforts. For example, when Microsoft Corporation first sold its stock to the public in 1986, Bill Gates, then just 30 years old, received $350 million for his share of Microsoft.[2] Today his holdings—valued at over $60 billion—make him the richest person in the United States and one of the richest in the world.[3] Many more entrepreneurs, however, have lost a great deal of money. Research suggests that the majority of new businesses fail within the first few years of founding.[4] Many that last longer do so only because the entrepreneurs themselves work long hours for very little income.

As Figure 10.1 shows, most U.S. businesses employ fewer than 100 people, and most U.S. workers are employed by small firms. For example, Figure 10.1(a) shows that approximately 90 percent of all U.S. businesses employ 20 or fewer people; another 8 percent employ between 20 and 99 people. In contrast, only about 1 percent employs 1,000 or more workers. Figure 10.1(b) shows that 25.6 percent of all U.S. workers are employed by firms with fewer than 20 people; another 29.1 percent work in firms that employ between 20 and 99 people. The vast majority of these companies are owner operated.[5] Figure 10.1(b) also shows that 12.7 percent of U.S. workers are employed by firms with 1,000 or more total employees.

On the basis of numbers alone, then, small business is a strong presence in the economy, which is also true in virtually all of the world's mature economies. In

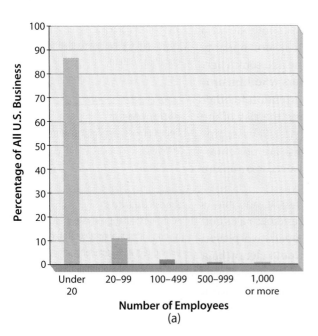

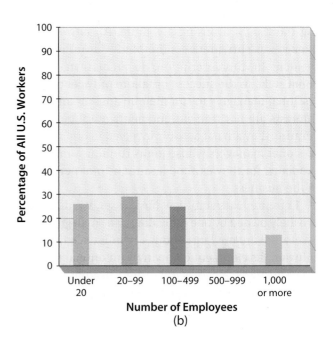

Figure 10.1

THE IMPORTANCE OF SMALL BUSINESS IN THE UNITED STATES

Over 86 percent of all U.S. businesses have no more than 20 employees. The total number of people employed by these small businesses is approximately one-fourth of the entire U.S. workforce. Another 29 percent work for companies with fewer than 100 employees.

Source: U.S. Census Bureau, *Statistical Abstract of the United States,* 2002 (Washington, DC: Government Printing Office, 2002).

Germany, for example, companies with fewer than 500 employees produce two-thirds of the nation's gross national product, train nine of ten apprentices, and employ four of every five workers. Small businesses also play major roles in the economies of Italy, France, and Brazil. In addition, experts agree that small businesses will be quite important in the emerging economies of countries such as Russia and Vietnam. The contribution of small business can be measured in terms of its effects on key aspects of an economic system. In the United States, these aspects include job creation, innovation, and importance to big business.

Job Creation

In the early 1980s, a widely cited study proposed that small businesses create eight of every ten new jobs in the United States. This contention touched off considerable interest in the fostering of small business as a matter of public policy. As we will see, though, relative job growth among businesses of different sizes is not easy to determine. But it is clear that small business—

New businesses are a prime source of new jobs. Marta Ballesteros, right, holds a stack of freshly made tortillas as she poses with her husband Alberto Piedrahita at their tortilla business run out of a warehouse in southwest Miami-Dade County in Florida. The couple immigrated from Colombia and opened the business out of their garage more than a decade ago. Today they sell about 31 million tortillas a year to supermarkets and restaurants throughout southern Florida. Their business employs several dozen workers.

especially in certain industries—is an important source of new (and often well-paid) jobs in the United States. According to the Small Business Administration (SBA), for example, seven of the ten industries that added the most new jobs in 1998 were in sectors dominated by small businesses. Moreover, small businesses currently account for 38 percent of all jobs in high-technology sectors of the economy.[6]

Note that new jobs are also being created by small firms specializing in international business. For example, Bob Knosp operates a small business in Bellevue, Washington, that makes computerized sign-making systems. Knosp gets over half his sales from abroad and has dedicated almost 75 percent of his workforce to handling international sales. Indeed, according to the SBA, small businesses account for 96 percent of all U.S. exporters.[7]

Although small businesses certainly create many new jobs each year, the importance of entrepreneurial big businesses in job creation should also not be overlooked. Although big businesses cut thousands of jobs in the late 1980s and early 1990s, the booming U.S. economy resulted in large-scale job creation in many larger businesses beginning in the mid-1990s. But this trend was reversed in recent years, as many larger companies began to downsize once again. Figure 10.2 details the changes in the number of jobs at 16 large U.S. companies during the ten-year period between 1996 and 2005. As you can see, General Motors eliminated 322,000 jobs while Kmart eliminated 132,000 jobs. Wal-Mart alone, however, created 671,910 new jobs during the same period, and Best Buy added an additional 75,500.

But even these data have to be interpreted with care. PepsiCo, for example, "officially" eliminated 273,000 jobs. But most of those losses came in 1997, when the firm sold its restaurant chains (KFC, Pizza Hut, and Taco Bell) to Tricon Global Restaurants (since renamed Yum! Brands). In reality, therefore, many of the

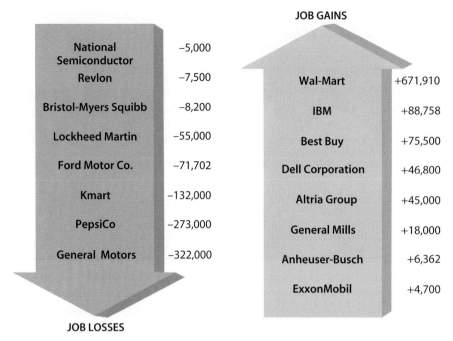

JOB GAINS

National Semiconductor	−5,000
Revlon	−7,500
Bristol-Myers Squibb	−8,200
Lockheed Martin	−55,000
Ford Motor Co.	−71,702
Kmart	−132,000
PepsiCo	−273,000
General Motors	−322,000

JOB LOSSES

Wal-Mart	+671,910
IBM	+88,758
Best Buy	+75,500
Dell Corporation	+46,800
Altria Group	+45,000
General Mills	+18,000
Anheuser-Busch	+6,362
ExxonMobil	+4,700

Figure 10.2

REPRESENTATIVE JOBS CREATED AND LOST BY BIG BUSINESS, 1996–2005

All businesses create and eliminate jobs. Because of their size, the magnitude of job creation and elimination is especially pronounced in bigger businesses. This figure provides several representative examples of job creation and elimination at many big U.S. businesses during the last decade. For example, while General Motors cut 322,000 jobs, Wal-Mart created 671,910 during this period.

jobs were not actually eliminated, but simply "transferred" to another employer. Likewise, although most of Wal-Mart's 671,910 new jobs were indeed "new," some came when the company acquired other businesses and thus were not net new jobs.

At least one message is clear: Entrepreneurial business success, more than business size, accounts for most new job creation. Whereas successful retailers like Wal-Mart and Best Buy have been growing and adding thousands of new jobs, struggling chains like Kmart have been eliminating thousands. At the same time, flourishing high-tech giants like Dell, Intel, and Microsoft continue to add jobs at a constant pace. It is also essential to take a long-term view when analyzing job growth. Figure 10.2, for example, shows that IBM has added over 88,000 new jobs. But this ten-year increase follows on the heels of major job cuts at the firm—163,381—between 1990 and 1994. Hence, most firms, especially those in complex and dynamic environments, go through periods of growth when they add new jobs but also have periods when they cut jobs.

The reality, then, is that jobs are created by entrepreneurial companies of all sizes, all of which hire workers and all of which lay them off. Although small firms often hire at a faster rate than large ones, they are also likely to eliminate jobs at a far higher rate. Small firms are also the first to hire in times of economic recovery, whereas large firms are the last. Conversely, however, big companies are also the last to lay off workers during economic downswings. Recent estimates suggest that over one-third of all small businesses in the United States have job openings, and almost 20 percent are planning to hire new employees. On the other hand, the SBA indicates that in 2000 large businesses employed more people than did small businesses for the first time since such statistics have been tracked.[8]

Innovation

History has shown that major innovations are as likely to come from small businesses (or individuals) as from big businesses. For example, small firms and individuals invented the personal computer and the stainless-steel razor blade, the transistor radio and the photocopying machine, the jet engine and the self-developing photograph. They also gave us the helicopter and power steering, automatic transmissions and air conditioning, cellophane, and the 19-cent ballpoint pen. Today, says the SBA, small businesses supply 55 percent of all "innovations" introduced into the U.S. marketplace.[9]

Not surprisingly, history is repeating itself infinitely more rapidly in the age of computers and high-tech communication. For example, much of today's most innovative software is being written at new start-up companies. Yahoo! and Netscape brought the Internet into the average U.S. living room, and online companies such as Amazon.com, eBay, and Google are using it to redefine our shopping habits. Each of these firms started out as a small business.

Of course, not all successful new start-ups are leading-edge dot-com enterprises. Drywall installer Jerry Free, for example, was frustrated by conventional methods of joining angled wallboard. In his spare time, he developed a simple handheld device that makes it easier and faster to perform this common task. He eventually licensed his invention to United States Gypsum, and it is now widely used throughout the construction industry. As for Free, the experience convinced him that "the cliché about invention being 1 percent inspiration and 99 percent perspiration is true."[10] Popular fashion designer Kate Spade has made it big by introducing a line of stylish purses and handbags sold through such exclusive retailers as Neiman Marcus. Rory Stear and Christopher Staines have succeeded with Freeplay Energy Group, a firm making environmentally friendly wind-up radios that need neither batteries nor electricity.[11] Eric Ludewig presides over fast-growing East of Chicago Pizza, a chain he founded when he was 22 years old and just out of college.[12] *Working with Diversity* highlights how some successful women entrepreneurs have also profited through innovative thinking.

Working with Diversity

Cosmetics Is a Woman's World

In the early 1900s, cosmetics were a man's world. Perfumes, soaps, lotions, and makeup were manufactured by large corporations such as Procter & Gamble. Following World War I, the cosmetics industry was changed forever by the advent of brands developed by women, including Elizabeth Arden, Helena Rubenstein, and Estée Lauder. Today a new generation of female entrepreneurs, sensing opportunity, are making their marks too.

One of these is Bobbi Brown. Brown came to New York in the 1980s to become a theatrical makeup artist, but was frustrated by the poor quality of the current products. She developed a best-selling line of more natural and flattering colors. As a girl interested in beauty, Brown compared herself to the thin, blonde models of the time and felt inadequate. "Then I saw Ali McGraw in 'Love Story' . . . and that epiphany impacted how I viewed myself, how I saw other women," she writes.

Another frustrated consumer was Iman, whose company produces cosmetics with an emphasis on darker skin tones. Iman, an African woman, was a top U.S. supermodel in the 1970s, but could not find makeup that looked good on women of color. Today, her makeup line is designed to suit African Americans, Latinas, Asians, and multicultural complexions, and is sold worldwide.

Entrepreneur Anita Roddick founded the Body Shop in 1976 in the United Kingdom. Roddick sold products made from natural ingredients that were not tested on animals. Today, the Body Shop is active in many causes, from recycling and packaging reduction to domestic violence and fair trade. The Body Shop has been phenomenally successful and, in March 2006, announced it will be acquired by giant French cosmetics firm L'Oreal.

Isabella Rossellini, an actress and model who bears an uncanny resemblance to her mother Ingrid Bergman, was the spokesperson for Lancôme cosmetics for 14 years. When she was let go because of her age, she defiantly started her own cosmetics line, called Manifesto.

Each of these entrepreneurial women has had a remarkable business career. Their experiences and training aided them, but the biggest boost came from other women—women who supported women-owned businesses by buying their cosmetics products.

References: "About Iman," Iman Cosmetics website, www.imancosmetics.com on April 10, 2006; "Bobbi Brown: Her Story," Estée Lauder website, www.bobbibrowncosmetics.com on March 25, 2006; "Isabella Rossellini's Fragrances," Isabella Rossellini's website, www "isabellarossellini.com" on April 10, 2006; "Where We Come From," The Body Shop website, www.thebodyshopinternational.com on April 10, 2006.

Importance to Big Business

Most of the products made by big manufacturers are sold to consumers by small businesses. For example, the majority of dealerships selling Fords, Chevrolets, Toyotas, and Volvos are independently owned and operated. Moreover, small businesses provide big businesses with many of the services, supplies, and raw materials they need. Likewise, Microsoft relies heavily on small businesses in the course of its routine business operations. For example, the software giant outsources much of its routine code-writing functions to hundreds of sole proprietorships and other small firms. It also outsources much of its packaging, delivery, and distribution to smaller companies. Dell Computer uses this same strategy, buying most of the parts and components used in its computers from small suppliers around the world.

concept
CHECK

Compare job creation success between small and large business in the United States.	*Why do so many innovations seem to come from entrepreneurs and small business?*

Strategy for Entrepreneurial Organizations

❝Entrepreneurship is certainly not the exclusive province of business. It can mushroom anywhere.❞
Barron Harvey, dean of Howard University's business school
(*USA Today*, April 7, 2004, p. 8B)

One of the most basic challenges facing an entrepreneurial organization is choosing a strategy. The three strategic challenges facing small firms, in turn, are choosing an industry in which to compete, emphasizing distinctive competencies, and writing a business plan.[13]

Choosing an Industry

Not surprisingly, small businesses are more common in some industries than in others. The major industry groups that include successful new ventures and small businesses are services, retailing, construction, financial and insurance, wholesaling, transportation, and manufacturing. Obviously, each group differs in its requirements for employees, money, materials, and machines. In general, the more resources an industry requires, the harder it is to start a business and the less likely that the industry is dominated by small firms. Remember, too, that *small* is a relative term: The criteria (number of employees and total annual sales) differ from industry to industry and are often meaningful only when compared with businesses that are truly large. Figure 10.3 shows the distribution of all U.S. businesses employing fewer than 20 people across industry groups.

Services Primarily because they require few resources, service businesses are the fastest-growing segment of small-business enterprise. In addition, no other industry group offers a higher return on time invested. Finally, services appeal to the talent for innovation typified by many small enterprises. As Figure 10.3 shows, 37.94 percent of all businesses with fewer than 20 employees are services.

Small-business services range from shoeshine parlors to car rental agencies, from marriage counseling to computer software, from accounting and management consulting to professional dog walking. In Dallas, for example, Jani-King has prospered by selling commercial cleaning services to local companies. In Virginia

Beach, Virginia, Jackson Hewitt Tax Services has found a profitable niche in providing computerized tax preparation and electronic tax-filing services. Great Clips, Inc. is a fast-growing family-run chain of hair salons headquartered in Minneapolis.

David Flanary, Richard Sorenson, and Michael Holloway recently established an Internet-based long distance telephone service in Austin, Texas, called PointOne Telecommunications. The basic idea was hatched during a tennis match. Recalls Sorenson, "We started getting excited, volleying at the net, and then finally we put the rackets down and went to the side to talk." The firm is off to a great start. Currently, it acts as a wholesale voice carrier, but as soon as its network is completed, PointOne will start signing up its own commercial customers. Investors agree that the company will soon be a major force in telecommunications.[14]

Retailing   A retail business sells directly to consumers products manufactured by other firms. There are hundreds of different kinds of retailers, ranging from wig shops and frozen yogurt stands to automobile dealerships and department stores. Usually, however, people who start small businesses favor specialty shops—for example, big-men's clothing or gourmet coffees—which let them focus limited resources on narrow market segments. Retailing accounts for 22.7 percent of all businesses with fewer than 20 employees.

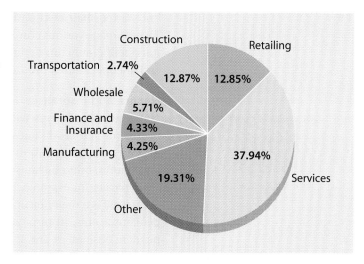

Figure 10.3

SMALL BUSINESSES (BUSINESSES WITH FEWER THAN 20 EMPLOYEES) BY INDUSTRY

Small businesses are especially strong in certain industries, such as retailing and services. On the other hand, there are relatively fewer small businesses in industries such as transportation and manufacturing. The differences are affected primarily by factors such as the investment costs necessary to enter markets in these industries. For example, starting a new airline would require the purchase of large passenger aircraft and airport gates, and hiring an expensive set of employees.

Source: U.S. Census Bureau, *Statistical Abstract of the United States:* 2005 (125th Edition), Washington, D.C., 2005.

John Mackey, for example, launched Whole Foods out of his own frustration at being unable to find a full range of natural foods at other stores. He soon found, however, that he had tapped a lucrative market and started an ambitious expansion program. Today, with 90 outlets in 20 states and Washington, D.C., Whole Foods is the largest natural-foods retailer in the United States, three times larger than its biggest competitor.[15] Likewise, when Olga Tereshko found it difficult to locate just the right cloth diapers and breast-feeding supplies for her newborn son, she decided to start selling them herself. Instead of taking the conventional retailing route, however, Tereshko set up shop on the Internet. Her business, called Little Koala, has continued to expand at a rate of about 10 percent a month, and she has established a customer base of 8,000 to 9,000 loyal customers.[16]

Construction   About 10 percent of businesses with fewer than 20 employees are involved in construction. Because many construction jobs are relatively small, local projects, local construction firms are often ideally suited as contractors. Many such firms are begun by skilled craftspeople who start out working for someone else and subsequently decide to work for themselves. Common examples of small construction firms include home builders, wood finishers, roofers, painters, and plumbing, electrical, and roofing contractors.

For example, Marek Brothers Construction in College Station, Texas, was started by two brothers, Pat and Joe Marek. They originally worked for other contractors but started their own partnership in 1980. Their only employee is a receptionist. They manage various construction projects, including new-home construction and remodeling, subcontracting out the actual work to other businesses or to individual craftspeople. Marek Brothers has annual gross income of about $5 million.

Finance and Insurance   Financial and insurance businesses also comprise about 10 percent of all firms with fewer than 20 employees. In most cases, these businesses are either affiliates of or sell products provided by larger national firms. Although the deregulation of the banking industry has reduced the number of small local banks, other businesses in this sector are still doing quite well.

Typically, for example, local State Farm Mutual offices are small businesses. State Farm itself is a major insurance company, but its local offices are run by 16,500 independent agents. In turn, agents hire their own staff, run their own offices as independent businesses, and so forth. They sell various State Farm insurance products and earn commissions from the premiums paid by their clients. Some local savings and loan operations, mortgage companies, and pawn shops also fall into this category.

Wholesaling   Small-business owners often do very well in wholesaling, too; about 8 percent of businesses with fewer than 20 employees are wholesalers. A wholesale business buys products from manufacturers or other producers and then sells them to retailers. Wholesalers usually buy goods in bulk and store them in quantity at locations that are convenient for retailers. For a given volume of business, therefore, they need fewer employees than manufacturers, retailers, or service providers.

They also serve fewer customers than other providers—usually those who repeatedly order large volumes of goods. Wholesalers in the grocery industry, for instance, buy packaged food in bulk from companies like Del Monte and Campbell and then sell it to both large grocery chains and smaller independent grocers. Luis Espinoza has found a promising niche for Inca Quality Foods, a midwestern wholesaler that imports and distributes Latino foods for consumers from Mexico, the Caribbean, and Central America. Partnered with the large grocery-store chain Kroger, Espinoza's firm continues to grow steadily.[17]

Transportation   Some small firms—about 5 percent of all companies with fewer than 20 employees—do well in transportation and transportation-related businesses. Such firms include local taxi and limousine companies, charter airplane services, and tour operators. In addition, in many smaller markets, bus companies and regional airlines subcontract local equipment maintenance to small businesses.

Consider, for example, some of the transportation-related small businesses at a ski resort like Steamboat Springs, Colorado. Most visitors fly to the town of Hayden, about 15 miles from Steamboat Springs. Although some visitors rent vehicles, many others use the services of Alpine Taxi, a small local operation, to transport them to their destinations in Steamboat Springs. While on vacation, they also rely on the local bus service, which is subcontracted by the town to another small business, to get to and from the ski slopes each day. Other small businesses offer van tours of the region, hot-air balloon rides, and helicopter lifts to remote areas for extreme skiers. Still others provide maintenance support at Hayden for Continental, American, and United aircraft that serve the area during ski season.

Manufacturing   More than any other industry, manufacturing lends itself to big business—and for good reason. Because of the investment normally required in equipment, energy, and raw materials, a good deal of money is usually needed to start a manufacturing business. Automobile manufacturing, for example, calls for billions of dollars of investment and thousands of workers before the first automobile rolls off the assembly line. Obviously, such requirements shut out most individuals. Although Henry Ford began with $28,000, it has been a long time since anyone started a new U.S. car company from scratch.

Research has shown that manufacturing costs often fall as the number of units produced by an organization increases. This relationship between cost and production is called an *economy of scale*.[18] Small organizations usually cannot compete effectively on the basis of economies of scale. As depicted in Figure 10.4(a), organizations with higher levels of production have a major cost advantage over those with lower levels of production. Given the cost positions of small and large firms when there are strong economies of scale in manufacturing, it is not surprising that small manufacturing organizations generally do not do as well as large ones.

Interestingly, when technology in an industry changes, it often shifts the economies-of-scale curve, thereby creating opportunities for smaller organizations. For example, steel manufacturing was historically dominated by a few large companies, which owned several huge facilities. With the development of mini-mill technology, however, extracting economies of scale at a much smaller level of production became possible. This type of shift is depicted in Figure 10.4(b). Point *A* in this panel is the low-cost point with the original economies of scale. Point *B* is the low-cost point with the economies of scale brought on by the new technology. Notice that the number of units needed for low costs is considerably lower for the new technology. This has allowed the entry of numerous smaller firms into the steel industry. Such entry would not have been possible with the older technology.

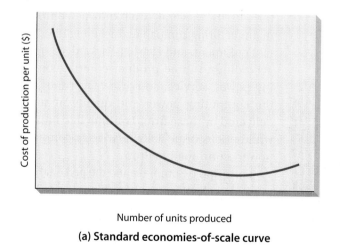

(a) **Standard economies-of-scale curve**

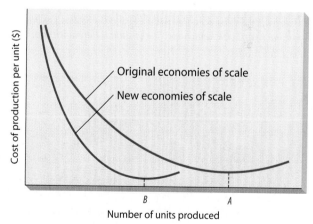

(b) **Change in technology that shifts economies of scale and may make small business production possible**

Figure 10.4

ECONOMIES OF SCALE IN SMALL-BUSINESS ORGANIZATIONS

Small businesses sometimes find it difficult to compete in manufacturing-related industries because of the economies of scale associated with plant, equipment, and technology. As shown in (a), firms that produce a large number of units (that is, larger businesses) can do so at a lower per-unit cost. At the same time, however, new forms of technology occasionally cause the economies-of-scale curve to shift, as illustrated in (b). In this case, smaller firms may be able to compete more effectively with larger ones because of the drop in per-unit manufacturing cost.

This is not to say that there are no small-business owners who do well in manufacturing—about 5 percent of businesses with fewer than 20 employees are involved in some aspect of manufacturing. Indeed, it is not uncommon for small manufacturers to outperform big business in such innovation-driven industries as chemistry, electronics, toys, and computer software. Some small manufacturers prosper by locating profitable niches. For example, brothers Dave and Dan Hanlon and Dave's wife Jennie recently started a new motorcycle-manufacturing business called Excelsior-Henderson. (Excelsior and Henderson are actually names of classic motorcycles from the early years of the twentieth century; the Hanlons acquired the rights to these brand names because of the images they evoke among motorcycle enthusiasts.) The Hanlons started by building 4,000 bikes in 1999 and will soon have annual production of 20,000 per year. So far, Excelsior-Henderson motorcycles have been well received (the top-end Excelsior-Henderson Super X sells for about $18,000), and many Harley-Davidson dealers have started to sell them as a means of diversifying their product line.[19]

Emphasizing Distinctive Competencies

As we defined in Chapter 8, an organization's distinctive competencies are the aspects of business that the firm performs better than its competitors. The distinctive competencies of small business usually fall into three areas: the ability to identify new niches in established markets, the ability to identify new markets, and the ability to move quickly to take advantage of new opportunities.

established market
A market in which several large firms compete according to relatively well-defined criteria

Recognizing market niches and creating new markets can be effective strategies for new businesses. Susan Medlin of Idaho learned that in some urban settings people were starting to keep a few chickens in their yard for producing eggs, so she decided there might be a market for small backyard chicken coops. She is shown here with a prototype of one of her models.

Identifying Niches in Established Markets An ***established market*** is one in which several large firms compete according to relatively well-defined criteria. For example, throughout the 1970s, several well-known computer-manufacturing companies, including IBM, Digital Equipment, and Hewlett-Packard, competed according to three product criteria: computing power, service, and price. Over the years, the computing power and quality of service delivered by these firms continued to improve, while prices (especially relative to computing power) continued to drop.

Enter Apple Computer and the personal computer. For Apple, user-friendliness, not computing power, service, or price, was to be the basis of competition. Apple targeted every manager, every student, and every home as the owner of a personal computer. Apple's major entrepreneurial act was not to invent a new technology (indeed, the first Apple computers used all standard parts taken from other computers), but to recognize a new kind of computer and a new way to compete in the computer industry.

Apple's approach to competition was to identify a new niche in an established market. A ***niche*** is simply a segment of a market that is not currently being exploited. In general, small entrepreneurial businesses are better at discovering these niches than are larger organizations. Large organizations usually have so many resources committed to older, established business practices that they may be unaware of new opportunities. Entrepreneurs can see these opportunities and move quickly to take advantage of them.[20]

niche
A segment of a market not currently being exploited

Identifying New Markets Successful entrepreneurs also excel at discovering whole new markets. Discovery can happen in at least two ways. First, an entrepreneur can transfer a product or service that is well established in one geographic market to a second market. This is what Marcel Bich did with ballpoint pens, which occupied a well-established market in Europe before Bich introduced them to this country. Bich's company, Société Bic, eventually came to dominate the U.S. market.

Second, entrepreneurs can sometimes create entire industries. Entrepreneurial inventions of the dry paper copying process and the semiconductor have created vast new industries. Not only have the first companies into these markets been very successful (Xerox and National Semiconductor, respectively), but their entrepreneurial activity has spawned the development of hundreds of other companies and hundreds of thousands of jobs. Again, because entrepreneurs are not encumbered with a history of doing business in a particular way, they are usually better at discovering new markets than are larger, more mature organizations.

First-Mover Advantages A ***first-mover advantage*** is any advantage that comes to a firm because it exploits an opportunity before any other firm does. Sometimes large firms discover niches within existing markets or new markets at just about the same time small entrepreneurial firms do, but are not able to move as quickly as small companies to take advantage of these opportunities.

first-mover advantage
Any advantage that comes to a firm because it exploits an opportunity before any other firm does

There are numerous reasons for this difference. For example, many large organizations make decisions slowly because each of their many layers of hierarchy has to approve an action before it can be implemented. Also, large organizations may sometimes put a great deal of their assets at risk when they take advantage of new opportunities. Every time Boeing decides to build a new model of a commercial jet, it is making a decision that could literally bankrupt the company if it does not turn out well. The size of the risk may make large organizations cautious. The dollar value of the assets at risk in a small organization, in contrast, is quite small. Managers may be willing to "bet the company" when the value of the company is only $100,000. They might be unwilling to "bet the company" when the value of the company is $1 billion.

Writing a Business Plan

Once an entrepreneur has chosen an industry to compete in and determined which distinctive competencies to emphasize, these choices are usually included in a document called a business plan. In a ***business plan*** the entrepreneur summarizes the business strategy and how that strategy is to be implemented. The very act of preparing a business plan forces prospective entrepreneurs to

business plan
A document that summarizes the business strategy and structure

crystallize their thinking about what they must do to launch their business successfully and obliges them to develop their business on paper before investing time and money in it. The idea of a business plan is not new. What is new is the growing use of specialized business plans by entrepreneurs, mostly because creditors and investors demand them for use in deciding whether to help finance a small business.

The plan should describe the match between the entrepreneur's abilities and the requirements for producing and marketing a particular product or service. It should define strategies for production and marketing, legal aspects and organization, and accounting and finance. In particular, it should answer three questions: (1) What are the entrepreneur's goals and objectives? (2) What strategies will the entrepreneur use to obtain these goals and objectives? (3) How will the entrepreneur implement these strategies?

Business plans should also account for the sequential nature of much strategic decision making in small businesses. For example, entrepreneurs cannot forecast sales revenues without first researching markets. The sales forecast itself is one of the most important elements in the business plan. Without such forecasts, it is all but impossible to estimate intelligently the size of a plant, store, or office, or to determine how much inventory to carry or how many employees to hire.

Another important component of the overall business plan is financial planning, which translates all other activities into dollars. Generally, the financial plan is made up of a cash budget, an income statement, balance sheets, and a breakeven chart. The most important of these statements is the cash budget because it tells entrepreneurs how much money they need before they open for business and how much money they need to keep the business operating.

Entrepreneurship and International Management

Finally, although many people associate international management with big business, many smaller companies are also finding expansion and growth opportunities in foreign countries. For example, Fuci Metals, a small but growing enterprise, buys metal from remote locations in areas such as Siberia and Africa, and then sells it to big auto makers like Ford and Toyota. Similarly, California-based Gold's Gym is expanding into foreign countries and has been especially successful in Russia.[21] And Markel Corporation, a small Philadelphia-based firm that manufactures tubing and insulated wiring, derives 40 percent of its annual revenues (currently around $26 million) from international sales.[22] Although such ventures are accompanied by considerable risks, they also give entrepreneurs new opportunities and can be a real catalyst for success.

concept
CHECK

Which industries seem most and least hospitable for entrepreneurship and small business?

Identifying a distinctive competence seems like a straightforward concept, yet many entrepreneurs fail to grasp its significance. Why do you think this is the case?

Structure of Entrepreneurial Organizations

With a strategy in place and a business plan in hand, the entrepreneur can then proceed to devise a structure that turns the vision of the business plan into a reality. Many of the same concerns in structuring any business, which are described in the next five chapters of this book, are also relevant to small businesses. For example, entrepreneurs need to consider organization design and develop job descriptions, organization charts, and management control systems.

The Internet, of course, is rewriting virtually all of the rules for starting and operating a small business. Getting into business is easier and faster than ever before, there are many more potential opportunities than at any other time in history, and the ability to gather and assimilate information is at an all-time high. Even so, would-be entrepreneurs must still make the right decisions when they start. They must decide, for example, precisely how to get into business. Should they buy an existing business or build from the ground up? In addition, would-be entrepreneurs must find appropriate sources of financing and decide when and how to seek the advice of experts.

Starting the New Business

The first step in starting a new business is the individual's commitment to becoming a business owner. Next comes choosing the goods or services to be offered—a process that means investigating one's chosen industry and market. Making this choice also requires would-be entrepreneurs to assess not only industry trends but also their own skills. Like the managers of existing businesses, new business owners must also be sure that they understand the true nature of the enterprise in which they are engaged.

Buying an Existing Business   After choosing a product and making sure that the choice fits their own skills and interests, entrepreneurs must decide whether to buy an existing business or to start from scratch. Consultants often recommend the first approach. Quite simply, the odds are better: If successful, an existing business has already proved its ability to draw customers at a profit. It has also established working relationships with lenders, suppliers, and the community. Moreover, the track record of an existing business gives potential buyers a much clearer picture of what to expect than any estimate of a new business's prospects. Around 30 percent of the new businesses started in the past decade were bought from someone else. The McDonald's empire, for example, was started when Ray Kroc bought an existing hamburger business and then turned it into a global phenomenon. Likewise, Starbucks was a struggling mail-order business when Howard Schultz bought it and turned his attention to retail expansion.

Starting from Scratch   Some people, however, prefer the satisfaction that comes from planting an idea, nurturing it, and making it grow into a strong and sturdy business. There are also practical reasons to start a business from scratch. A new business does not suffer the ill effects of a prior owner's errors. The start-up owner is also free to choose lenders, equipment, inventories, locations, suppliers, and workers, unbound by a predecessor's commitments and policies. Of the new businesses begun in the past decade, 64 percent were started from scratch.

Not surprisingly, though, the risks of starting a business from scratch are greater than those of buying an existing firm. Founders of new businesses can make only predictions and projections about their prospects. Success or failure thus depends heavily on identifying a genuine business opportunity—a product for which many customers will pay well but which is currently unavailable to them. To find openings, entrepreneurs must study markets and answer the following questions: (1) Who are my customers? (2) Where are they? (3) At what price will they buy my product? (4) In what quantities will they buy? (5) Who are my competitors? (6) How will my product differ from those of my competitors?

Finding answers to these questions is a difficult task even for large, well-established firms. But where can the new business owner get the necessary information? Other sources of assistance are discussed later in this chapter, but we briefly describe three of the most accessible here. For example, the best way to gain knowledge about a market is to work in it before going into business in it. For example, if you once worked in a bookstore and now plan to open one of your own, you probably already have some idea about the kinds of books people request and buy. Second, a quick scan of the local Yellow Pages or an Internet search will reveal many potential competitors, as will advertisements in trade journals. Personal visits to these establishments and websites can give you insights into their strengths and weaknesses. And, third, studying magazines, books, and websites aimed specifically at small businesses can also be of help, as can hiring professionals to survey the market for you.

Financing the New Business

Although the choice of how to start is obviously important, it is meaningless unless a new business owner can obtain the money to set up shop. Among the more common sources for funding are family and friends, personal savings, banks and similar lending institutions, investors, and government agencies. Lending institutions are more likely to help finance the purchase of an existing business than a new business because the risks are better understood. Individuals starting up new businesses, on the other hand, are more likely to have to rely on their personal resources.

Personal Resources   According to a study by the National Federation of Independent Business, an owner's personal resources, not loans, are the most important source of money. Including money borrowed from friends and relatives, personal resources account for over two-thirds of all money invested in new small businesses and one-half of that invested in the purchase of existing businesses. When Michael Dorf and his friends decided to launch a New York nightclub dubbed the Knitting Factory, he started with $30,000 of his own money. Within four months of opening, Dorf asked his father to co-sign the first of four consecutive Milwaukee bank loans (for $70,000, $200,000, $300,000, and to move to a new facility, $500,000, respectively). Dorf and his partners also engaged in creative bartering, such as putting a sound system company's logo on all its advertising in exchange for free equipment. Finally, because the Knitting Factory has become so successful, other investors are now stepping forward to provide funds—$650,000 from one investor and $4.2 million from another.[23]

Strategic Alliances   Strategic alliances are also becoming a popular method for financing business growth. When Steven and Andrew Grundy decided to launch an Internet CD-exchange business called Spun.com, they had very little capital and thus made extensive use of alliances with other firms. They partnered, for example, with wholesaler Alliance Entertainment Corporation as a CD supplier. Orders to Spun.com actually go to Alliance, which ships products to customers and bills Spun.com directly. This setup has allowed Spun.com to promote a vast inventory of labels without actually having to buy inventory. All told, the firm created an alliance network that has provided the equivalent of $40 million in capital.[24]

Lenders   Although banks, independent investors, and government loans all provide much smaller portions of start-up funds than the personal resources of owners, they are important in many cases. Getting money from these sources, however, requires some extra effort. Banks and private investors usually want to see formal business plans—detailed outlines of proposed businesses and markets, owners' backgrounds, and other sources of funding. Government loans have strict eligibility guidelines.

Venture Capital Companies   *Venture capital companies* are groups of small investors seeking to make profits on companies with rapid growth potential. Most of these firms do not lend money: They invest it, supplying capital in return for stock. The venture capital company may also demand a representative on the board of directors. In some cases, managers may even need approval from the venture capital company before making major decisions. Of all venture capital currently committed in the United States, 29 percent comes from true venture capital firms.[25] In 2005, venture capital firms invested $21 billion in new start-ups in the United States.

For example, Dr. Drew Pinsky, cohost of MTV's Loveline, got venture capital funding to extend his program to the Internet from a group of investors collectively known as Garage.com. Garage.com is comprised of several individuals and other investors who specialize in financing Internet start-ups.[26] Similarly, SOFTBANK is a venture capital firm that has provided funds to over 300 web companies, including Yahoo! and E*Trade. As founder Masayoshi Son puts it, "We're a strategic holding company, investing in companies that are very important in the digital information industry—in e-commerce, financial services, and media."

> **venture capital company**
> A group of small investors seeking to make profits on companies with rapid growth potential.

Small-Business Investment Companies   Taking a more balanced approach in their choices than venture capital companies, small-business investment companies (SBICs) seek profits by investing in companies with potential for rapid growth. Created by the Small Business Investment Act of 1958, SBICs are federally licensed to borrow money from the SBA and to invest it in or lend it to small businesses. They are themselves investments for their shareholders. Past beneficiaries of SBIC capital include Apple Computer, Intel, and Federal Express. In addition, the government has recently begun to sponsor minority enterprise small-business investment companies (MESBICs). As the name suggests, MESBICs specialize in financing businesses that are owned and operated by minorities.

SBA Financial Programs   Since its founding in 1953, the SBA has offered more than 20 financing programs to small businesses that meet standards of size and independence. Eligible firms must also be unable to get private financing at reasonable terms. Because of these and other restrictions, SBA loans have never been a major source of small-business financing. In addition, budget cutbacks at the SBA have reduced the number of firms benefiting from loans. Nevertheless, several SBA programs currently offer funds to qualified applicants.

For example, under the SBA's guaranteed loans program, small businesses can borrow from commercial lenders. The SBA guarantees to repay 75 to 85 percent of the loan amount, not to exceed $750,000. Under a related program, companies engaged in international trade can borrow up to $1.25 million. Such loans may be made for as long as 15 years. Most SBA lending activity flows through this program.

Sometimes, however, both desired bank and SBA-guaranteed loans are unavailable (perhaps because the business cannot meet stringent requirements). In such cases, the SBA may help finance the entrepreneur through its immediate participation loans program. Under this arrangement, the SBA and the bank each puts up a share of the money, with the SBA's share not to exceed $150,000. Under the local development companies (LDCs) program, the SBA works with a corporation (either for-profit or nonprofit) founded by local citizens who want to boost the local economy. The SBA can lend up to $500,000 for each small business to be helped by an LDC.

Spurred in large part by the boom in Internet businesses, both venture capital and loans are becoming easier to get. Most small businesses, for example, report that it has generally become increasingly easier to obtain loans over the last ten years. Indeed, some technology companies are being offered so much venture capital that they are turning down part of it to keep from unnecessarily diluting their ownership.

Entrepreneurs and small-business owners have an array of sources to which they can turn for information and advice. The Women's Business Enterprise National Council (WBENC), for instance, provides assistance to female business owners. Julie Rodriguez owns Epic Companies, a supplier of commercial divers and utility vessels to the oil and gas industry. WBENC has enabled her to expand her business into significant new markets by providing marketing research data and new industry contacts.

Sources of Management Advice

Financing is not the only area in which small businesses need help. Until World War II, for example, the business world involved few regulations, few taxes, few records, few big competitors, and no computers. Since then, simplicity has given way to complexity. Today, few entrepreneurs are equipped with all the business skills they need to survive. Small-business owners can no longer be their own troubleshooters, lawyers, bookkeepers, financiers, and tax experts. For these jobs, they rely on professional help. To survive and grow, however, small businesses also need advice regarding management. This advice is usually available from four sources: advisory boards, management consultants, the SBA, and a process called "networking."

Advisory Boards   All companies, even those that do not legally need boards of directors, can benefit from the problem-solving abilities of advisory boards. Thus some small businesses create boards to provide advice and assistance. For example, an advisory board might help an entrepreneur determine the best way to finance a plant expansion or to start exporting products to foreign markets.

Management Consultants   Opinions vary widely about the value of management consultants—experts who charge fees to help managers solve problems. They often specialize in one area, such as international business, small business, or manufacturing. Thus they can bring an objective and trained outlook to problems and provide logical recommendations. They can be quite expensive, however, as some consultants charge $1,000 or more for a day of assistance.

Like other professionals, consultants should be chosen with care. They can be found through major corporations that have used their services and that can provide references and reports on their work. Not surprisingly, they are most effective when the client helps (for instance, by providing schedules and written proposals for work to be done).

The Small Business Administration   Even more important than its financing role is the SBA's role in helping small-business owners improve their management skills. It is easy for entrepreneurs to spend money; SBA programs are designed to show them how to spend it wisely. The SBA offers small businesses four major management-counseling programs at virtually no cost.

A small-business owner who needs help in starting a new business can get it free through the Service Corps of Retired Executives (SCORE). All SCORE members are retired executives, and all are volunteers. Under this program, the SBA tries to match the expert to the need. For example, if a small-business owner needs help putting together a marketing plan, the SBA will send a SCORE counselor with marketing expertise.

Like SCORE, the Active Corps of Executives (ACE) program is designed to help small businesses that cannot afford consultants. The SBA recruits ACE volunteers from virtually every industry. All ACE volunteers are currently involved in successful activities, mostly as small-business owners themselves. Together, SCORE and ACE have more than 12,000 counselors working out of 350 chapters throughout the United States. They provide assistance to some 140,000 small businesses each year.

The talents and skills of students and instructors at colleges and universities are fundamental to the Small Business Institute (SBI). Under the guidance of seasoned professors of business administration, students seeking advanced degrees work closely with small-business owners to help solve specific problems, such as sagging sales or rising costs. Students earn credit toward their degree, with their grades depending on how well they handle a client's problems. Several hundred colleges and universities counsel thousands of small-business owners through this program every year.

Finally, the newest of the SBA's management counseling projects is its Small Business Development Center (SBDC) program. Begun in 1976, SBDCs are designed to consolidate information from various disciplines and institutions, including technical and professional schools. Then they make this knowledge available to new and existing small businesses. In 1995 universities in 45 states took part in the program.

Networking   More and more, small-business owners are discovering the value of networking—meeting regularly with one another to discuss common problems and opportunities and, perhaps most important, to pool resources. Businesspeople have long joined organizations such as the local chamber of commerce and the National Federation of Independent Businesses (NFIB) to make such contacts.

Today, organizations are springing up all over the United States to facilitate small-business networking. One such organization, the Council of Smaller Enterprises of Cleveland, boasts a total membership of more than 10,000 small-business owners, the largest number in the country. This organization offers its members not only networking possibilities but also educational programs and services tailored to their needs. In a typical year, its 85 educational programs draw more than 8,500 small-business owners.

In particular, women and minorities have found networking to be an effective problem-solving tool. The National Association of Women Business Owners (NAWBO), for example, provides a variety of networking forums. The NAWBO also has chapters in most major cities, where its members can meet regularly. Increasingly, women are relying more on other women to help locate venture capital, establish relationships with customers, and provide such essential services as accounting and legal advice. According to Patty Abramson of the Women's Growth Capital Fund, all of these tasks have traditionally been harder for women because, until now, they have never had friends in the right places. "I wouldn't say this is about discrimination," adds Abramson. "It's about not having the relationships, and business is about relationships."

Franchising

The next time you drive or walk around town, be on the alert for a McDonald's, Taco Bell, Subway, Denny's, or KFC restaurant; a 7-Eleven or Circle K convenience store; a RE/MAX or Coldwell Banker real estate office; a Super 8 or Ramada Inn motel; a Blockbuster Video store; a Sylvan Learning Center educational center; an Express Oil Change or Precision Auto Wash service center; or a Supercuts hair salon. What do these businesses have in common? In most cases, they are franchised operations, operating under licenses issued by parent companies to local entrepreneurs who own and manage them.

As many would-be businesspeople have discovered, ***franchising agreements*** are an accessible doorway to entrepreneurship. A franchise is an arrangement that permits the *franchisee* (buyer) to sell the product of the *franchiser* (seller, or parent company). Franchisees can thus benefit from the selling corporation's experience and expertise. They can also consult the franchiser for managerial and financial help.

For example, the franchiser may supply financing. It may pick the store location, negotiate the lease, design the store, and purchase necessary equipment. It may train the first set of employees and managers and provide standardized policies and procedures. Once the business is open, the franchiser may offer franchisees savings by allowing them to purchase from a central location. Marketing strategy (especially advertising) may also be handled by the franchiser. Finally, franchisees may benefit from continued management counseling. In short, franchisees receive—that is, invest in—not only their own ready-made business but also expert help in running it.

Franchises offer many advantages to both sellers and buyers. For example, franchisers benefit from the ability to grow rapidly by using the investment money provided by franchisees. This strategy has enabled giant franchisers such as McDonald's and Baskin-Robbins to mushroom into billion-dollar concerns in a brief time.

For the franchisee, the arrangement combines the incentive of owning a business with the advantage of access to big-business management skills. Unlike the person who starts from scratch, the franchisee does not have to build a business step by step. Instead, the business is established virtually overnight. Moreover, because each franchise outlet is probably a carbon copy of every other outlet, the chances of failure are reduced. McDonald's, for example, is a model of consistency—Big Macs taste the same everywhere.

---

franchising agreement
A contract between an entrepreneur (the franchisee) and a parent company (the franchiser); the entrepreneur pays the parent company for the use of its trademarks, products, formulas, and business plans

Of course, owning a franchise also involves certain disadvantages. Perhaps the most significant is the start-up cost. Franchise prices vary widely. Fantastic Sams hair salon franchise fees are $30,000, but a Gingiss Formalwear franchise can run as high as $125,000. Extremely profitable or hard-to-get franchises are even more expensive. A McDonald's franchise costs at least $650,000 to $750,000, and a professional sports team can cost several hundred million dollars. Franchisees may also have continued obligations to contribute percentages of sales to the parent corporation.

Buying a franchise also entails less tangible costs. For one thing, the small-business owner sacrifices some independence. A McDonald's franchisee cannot change the way its hamburgers or milkshakes are made. Nor can franchisees create an individual identity in their community; for all practical purposes, the McDonald's owner is anonymous. In addition, many franchise agreements are difficult to terminate.

Finally, although franchises minimize risks, they do not guarantee success. Many franchisees have seen their investments—and their dreams—disappear because of poor location, rising costs, or lack of continued franchiser commitment. Moreover, figures on failure rates are artificially low because they do not include failing franchisees bought out by their franchising parent companies. An additional risk is that the chain itself could collapse. In any given year, dozens—sometimes hundreds—of franchisers close shop or stop selling franchises.

concept
CHECK

What are the pros and cons of starting a new business from scratch versus buying an existing business?

Many people assume that Starbucks coffee shops are franchises, but in reality they are not. Why do you think Starbucks insists on owning all of its own retail outlets?

The Performance of Entrepreneurial Organizations

The formulation and implementation of an effective strategy plays a major role in determining the overall performance of an entrepreneurial organization. This section examines how entrepreneurial firms evolve over time and the attributes of these firms that enhance their chances of success. For every Henry Ford, Walt Disney, Mary Kay Ash, or Bill Gates—people who transformed small businesses into major corporations—there are many small-business owners and entrepreneurs who fail.

Figure 10.5 illustrates recent trends in new business start-ups and failures. As you can see, new business start-ups have generally run between around 150,000 and 190,000 per year. Business failures have generally run between 50,000 and 100,000, per year. In this section, we look first at a few key trends in small-business start-ups. Then we examine some of the main reasons for success and failure in small-business undertakings.

Trends in Small-Business Start-Ups
Thousands of new businesses are started in the United States every year. Several factors account for this trend, and in this section we focus on four of them.

Emergence of E-Commerce Clearly, one of the most significant recent trends in small-business start-ups is the rapid emergence of electronic commerce. Because

Figure 10.5

BUSINESS START-UP SUCCESSES AND FAILURES

Over the most recent ten-year period for which data are available, new business start-ups numbered between 150,000 and 190,000 per year. Business failures during this same period, meanwhile, ranged from about 50,000 to nearly 100,000 per year.

Source: U.S. Census Bureau, *Statistical Abstract of the United States,* 2002 (Washington, D.C.: Government Printing Office, 2002).

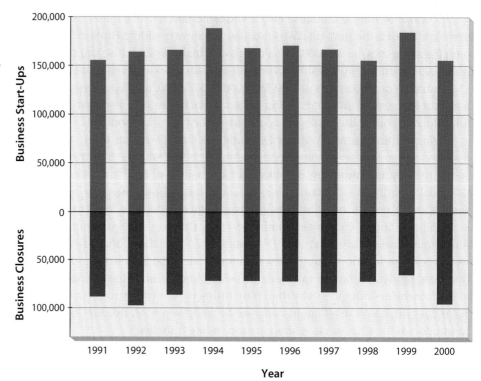

the Internet has provided fundamentally new ways of doing business, savvy entrepreneurs have been able to create and expand new businesses faster and more easily than ever before. Such leading-edge firms as America Online and eBay, for example, owe their very existence to the Internet. At the same time, however, many would-be Internet entrepreneurs have gone under in the last few years, as the so-called dot-com boom quickly faded. Figure 10.6 summarizes trends in online commerce from 2000 through 2003. In addition, one recent study reported that in 1999 the Internet economy grew overall by 62 percent over the previous year and provided jobs for 2.5 million people.[27]

Indeed, it seems as if new ideas emerge virtually every day. Andrew Beebe, for example, is scoring big with Bigstep, a web business that essentially creates, hosts, and maintains websites for other small businesses. So far, Bigstep has signed up 75,000 small-business clients. Beebe actually provides his basic services for free but earns money by charging for such so-called premium services as customer billing. Karl Jacob's Keen.com is a web business that matches people looking for advice with experts who have the answers. Keen got the idea when he and his father were struggling to fix a boat motor and did not know where to turn for help. Keen.com attracted 100,000 subscribers in just three months.[28]

Crossovers from Big Business   It is interesting to note that increasingly more businesses are being started by people who have opted to leave big corporations and put their experience and know-how to work for themselves. In some cases, these individuals see great new ideas they want to develop. Often, they get burned out working for a big corporation. Sometimes they have lost their job, only to discover that working for themselves was a better idea anyway.

Cisco Systems CEO John Chambers is acknowledged as one of the best entrepreneurs around. But he spent several years working first at IBM and then at Wang

Laboratories before he set out on his own. Under his leadership, Cisco has become one of the largest and most important technology companies in the world. Indeed, for a few days in March 2000, Cisco had the world's highest market capitalization, and it remains one of the world's most valuable companies.[29] In a more unusual case, Gilman Louie recently left an executive position at Hasbro toy company's online group to head up a CIA-backed venture capital firm called In-Q-It. The firm's mission is to help nurture high-tech companies making products of interest to the nation's intelligence community.[30] One of the women profiled in our *Working with Diversity* box earlier in this chapter was also a big-business crossover.

Opportunities for Minorities and Women In addition to big-business expatriates, minorities and women are starting more small businesses. For example, the number of African American-owned businesses has increased by 46 percent during the most recent five-year period for which data are available and now totals about 620,000. Chicago's Gardner family is just one of thousands of examples illustrating this trend. The Gardners are the founders of Soft Sheen Products, a firm specializing in ethnic hair products. Soft Sheen attained sales of $80 million in the year before the Gardners sold it to France's L'Oréal S.A. for more than $160 million. The emergence of such opportunities is hardly surprising, either to African American entrepreneurs or to the corporate marketers who have taken an interest in their companies. African American purchasing power recently topped $530 billion. Up from just over $300 billion in 1990, that increase of 73 percent far outstrips the 57 percent increase experienced by all Americans.[31]

Latino-owned businesses have grown at an even faster rate of 76 percent and now number about 862,000. Other ethnic groups are also making their presence felt among U.S. business owners. Business ownership among Asians and Pacific Islanders has increased 56 percent, to over 600,000. Although the number of businesses owned by American Indians and Alaska Natives is still somewhat small, at slightly over 100,000, the total nevertheless represents a five-year increase of 93 percent.[32]

The number of women entrepreneurs is also growing rapidly. Celeste Johnson, for example, left a management position at Pitney Bowes to launch Obex, Inc., which makes gardening and landscaping products from mixed recycled plastics. Katrina Garnett gave up a lucrative job at Oracle to start her own software company, Crossworlds Software. Laila Rubenstein closed her management-consulting practice to create Greeting Cards.com, Inc., an Internet-based business selling customizable electronic greetings. "Women-owned business," says Teresa Cavanaugh, director of the Women Entrepreneur's Connection at BankBoston, "is the largest emerging segment of the small-business market. Women-owned businesses are an economic force that no bank can afford to overlook."[33]

There are now 9.1 million businesses owned by women—about 40 percent of all

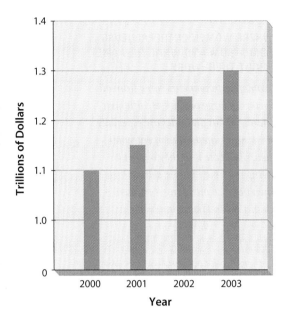

Figure 10.6

THE GROWTH OF ONLINE COMMERCE

Online commerce is becoming an increasingly important part of the U.S. economy. As shown here, for example, online commerce has grown from about $1.1 trillion in 2000 to an estimated $1.3 trillion by 2003. And most indicators suggest that this trend will continue.

Source: U.S. Census Bureau, *Statistical Abstract of the United States,* 2005 (Washington, D.C.: Government Printing Office, 2005).

 " Attitudes about women in the workplace, period, have changed, let alone women running their own businesses. "

Erin Fuller, executive director of the National Association of Women Business Owners
(AP wire story, January 29, 2006)

Figure 10.7

WHERE WOMEN ENTREPRENEURS COME FROM AND WHAT THEY LIKE ABOUT THEIR WORK

Women entrepreneurs come from all sectors of large businesses, although management and sales are especially well represented. Women entrepreneurs indicate that they really like being their own bosses, setting their own hours, controlling their own destinies, and being independent.

Source: From "Women Entrepreneurs," *Wall Street Journal*, May 24, 1999. Copyright ©1999 by Dow Jones & Co., Inc. Reproduced with permission of Dow Jones & Co., Inc. via Copyright Clearance Center.

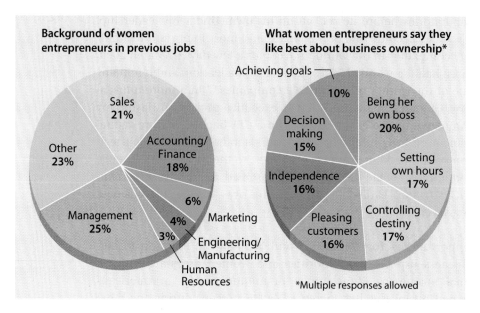

businesses in the United States. Combined, they generate nearly $4 trillion in revenue a year—an increase of 132 percent since 1992. The number of people employed nationwide at women-owned businesses since 1992 has grown to around 27.5 million—an increase of 108 percent.[34] Figure 10.7 summarizes the corporate backgrounds of women entrepreneurs and provides some insight into what they like about running their own businesses. Former corporate positions in general management (25 percent), sales (21 percent), and accounting and finance (18 percent) account for almost two-thirds of the women who start their own businesses. Once in charge of their own business, women also report that they like being their own bosses, setting their own hours, controlling their own destinies, pleasing customers, having independence, making decisions, and achieving goals.

Better Survival Rates   Finally, more people are encouraged to test their skills as entrepreneurs because the failure rate among small businesses has been declining in recent years. During the 1960s and 1970s, for example, less than half of all new start-ups survived more than 18 months; only one in five lasted 10 years. Now, however, new businesses have a better chance of surviving. Of new businesses started in the 1980s, for instance, over 77 percent remained in operation for at least 3 years. Today, the SBA estimates that at least 40 percent of all new businesses can expect to survive for 6 years. For the reasons discussed in the next section, small businesses suffer a higher mortality rate than larger concerns. Among those that manage to stay in business for 6 to 10 years, however, the survival rate levels off.

Reasons for Failure

Unfortunately, 63 percent of all new businesses will not celebrate a sixth anniversary. Why do some succeed and others fail? Although no set pattern has been established, four general factors contribute to new business failure. One factor is managerial incompetence or inexperience. Some would-be entrepreneurs assume that they can succeed through common sense, overestimate their own managerial acumen, or think that hard work alone will lead to success. But if managers do not know how to make basic business decisions or understand the basic concepts and principles of management, they are unlikely to be successful in the long run.

Neglect can also contribute to failure. Some entrepreneurs try either to launch their ventures in their spare time or to devote only a limited amount of time to a new business. But starting a new business requires an overwhelming time commitment. Entrepreneurs who are not willing to put in the time and effort that a business requires are unlikely to survive.

Third, weak control systems can lead to serious problems. Effective control systems are needed to keep a business on track and to help alert entrepreneurs to potential trouble. If control systems do not signal impending problems, managers may be in serious trouble before more visible difficulties alert them.

Finally, insufficient capital can contribute to new business failure. Some entrepreneurs are overly optimistic about how soon they will start earning profits. In most cases, however, it takes months or years before a business is likely to start turning a profit. Amazon.com, for example, has still not earned a profit. Most experts say that a new business should have enough capital to operate for at least six months without earning a profit; some recommend enough to last a year.[35]

Reasons for Success

Similarly, four basic factors are typically cited to explain new business success. One factor is hard work, drive, and dedication. New business owners must be committed to succeeding and be willing to put in the time and effort to make it happen. Gladys Edmunds, a single teen-age mother in Pittsburgh, washed laundry, made chicken dinners to sell to cab drivers, and sold fire extinguishers and Bibles door to door to earn money to launch her own business. Today, Edmunds Travel Consultants employs eight people and earns about $6 million in annual revenues.[36]

Careful analysis of market conditions can help new business owners assess the probable reception of their products in the marketplace. This will provide insights about market demand for proposed products and services. Whereas attempts to expand local restaurants specializing in baked potatoes, muffins, and gelato have been largely unsuccessful, hamburger and pizza chains continue to have an easier time expanding into new markets.

Managerial competence also contributes to success. Successful new business owners may acquire competence through training or experience or by using the expertise of others. Few successful entrepreneurs succeed alone or straight out of college. Most spend time working in successful companies or partner with others in order to bring more expertise to a new business.

Finally, luck also plays a role in the success of some firms. For example, after Alan McKim started Clean Harbors, an environmental cleanup firm based in New England, he struggled to keep his business afloat. Then the U.S. government committed $1.6 billion to toxic waste cleanup—McKim's specialty. He was able to get several large government contracts and put his business on solid financial footing. Had the government fund not been created at just the right time, McKim may well have failed.

concept
CHECK

What are the fundamental reasons for new business failure and success?

What current trends in business start-ups can you identify?

Summary of Learning Objectives and Key Points

1. Discuss the nature of entrepreneurship.
   - Entrepreneurship is the process of planning, organizing, operating, and assuming the risk of a business venture.
   - An entrepreneur is someone who engages in entrepreneurship. In general, entrepreneurs start small businesses.

2. Describe the role of entrepreneurship in society.
   - Small businesses are an important source of innovation
   - Small businesses create numerous jobs
   - Small businesses contribute to the success of large businesses.

3. Understand the major issues involved in choosing strategies for small firms and the role of international management in entrepreneurship.
   - In choosing strategies, entrepreneurs have to consider the characteristics of the industry in which they are going to conduct business.
   - Small businesses generally have several distinctive competencies that they should exploit in choosing their strategy. Small businesses are usually skilled at identifying niches in established markets, identifying new markets, and acting quickly to obtain first-mover advantages.
   - Small businesses are usually not skilled at exploiting economies of scale.
   - Once an entrepreneur has chosen a strategy, the strategy is normally written down in a business plan. Writing a business plan forces an entrepreneur to plan thoroughly and to anticipate problems that might occur.

4. Discuss the structural challenges unique to entrepreneurial firms.
   - With a strategy and business plan in place, entrepreneurs must choose a structure to implement them. All of the structural issues summarized in the next five chapters of this book are relevant to the entrepreneur.
   - In addition, the entrepreneur has some unique structural choices to make. For example, the entrepreneur can buy an existing business or start a new one.
   - In determining financial structure, an entrepreneur has to decide how much personal capital to invest in an organization, how much bank and government support to obtain, and whether to encourage venture capital firms to invest.
   - Entrepreneurs can also rely on various sources of advice.

5. Understand the determinants of the performance of small firms.
   - Several interesting trends characterize new business start-ups today.
   - There are several reasons why some new businesses fail and others succeed.

Discussion Questions

Questions for Review

1. Describe the similarities and differences between entrepreneurial firms and large firms in terms of their job creation and innovation.
2. What characteristics make an industry attractive to entrepreneurs? Based on these characteristics, which industries are most attractive to entrepreneurs?
3. Describe recent trends in new business start-ups.
4. What are the different sources of advice for entrepreneurs? What type of information would an entrepreneur be likely to get from each source? What are the drawbacks or limitations for each source?

Questions for Analysis

5. Entrepreneurs and small businesses play a variety of important roles in society. If these roles are so important, do you think that the government should do more to encourage the development of small business? Why or why not?

6. Consider the four major reasons for new business failure. What actions can entrepreneurs take to minimize or avoid each cause of failure?

7. The U.S. automotive industry is well established, with several large and many small competitors. Describe the unexploited niches in the U.S. auto industry and tell how entrepreneurs could offer products that fill those niches.

Questions for Application

8. Assume that you are opening a small business in your town. What are your financing options? Which option or options are you likely to choose, and why?

9. List five entrepreneur-owned businesses in your community. In which industry does each business compete? Based on the industry, how do you rate each business's long-term chances for success? Explain your answers.

10. Using the information about managing a small business presented in this chapter, analyze whether you would like to work in a small business—either as an employee or as a founder. Given your personality, background, and experience, does working in or starting a new business appeal to you? What are the reasons for your opinion?

Building Effective Diagnostic Skills

Exercise Overview

Diagnostic skills are the skills that enable a manager to visualize the most appropriate response to a situation. This exercise develops your diagnostic skills by asking you to consider the factors that increase your chances of choosing an entrepreneurial career.

Exercise Background

Scholars of entrepreneurship are concerned with understanding why some individuals choose to start a new business whereas others do not. Investigators have surveyed thousands of individuals, entrepreneurs and nonentrepreneurs, in an attempt to discover factors that can distinguish between the two groups. Hundreds of studies have been conducted, each with its own unique findings, but some consensus has emerged. Based on numerous studies, entrepreneurship is more likely among the following categories of individuals:

• Parents, children, spouses, or siblings of an entrepreneur.

• Immigrants to the United States or the children of an immigrant.
• Parents.
• Members of the Jewish or Protestant faith.
• Professional degree holders in fields such as medicine, law, or engineering.
• People who have recently experienced a life-changing event, such as getting married, having a child, moving to a new city, or losing a job.

Exercise Task

With the background information above as context, do the following:

1. Choose one of the categories above and explain why this factor might make an individual more likely to become a business owner.

2. From the categories listed above, choose one that is true of yourself. (Choose a different category than the one you discussed in your answer to question 1.) In your opinion, does that factor make it more likely that you will become an entrepreneur? Why or why not? If none of the categories above is true of yourself, tell whether that fact makes it *less* likely that you will become an entrepreneur, and why.

Building Effective Conceptual Skills

Exercise Overview

Conceptual skills refer to the manager's ability to think in the abstract. This exercise will help you relate conceptual skills to entrepreneurship.

Exercise Background

Assume that you have made the decision to open a small business in the local community when you graduate (the community where you are attending college, not your home). Assume that you have funds to start a business without having to worry about finding other investors.

Without regard for market potential, profitability, or similar considerations, list five businesses that you might want to open and operate based solely on your personal interests. For example, if you enjoy bicycling, you might enjoy opening a shop that caters to cyclists.

Next, without regard for personal attractiveness, list five businesses that you might want to open and operate based solely on market opportunity. Use the Internet to help you determine which businesses might be profitable in your community, based on factors such as population, local economic conditions, local competition, franchising opportunities, and so on.

Evaluate the prospects for success for each of the ten businesses.

Exercise Task

With this background information as context, do the following:

1. Form a small group with three or four classmates and discuss your respective lists. Look for instances where the same type of business appears on either the same or alternative lists. Also look for cases where the same business appears with similar or dissimilar prospects for success.

2. How important is personal interest in small-business success?

3. How important is market potential in small-business success?

CHAPTER CLOSING CASE

ENTREPRENEURIAL SPIRIT FLIES HIGH AT JETBLUE

JetBlue was founded by David Neeleman, an airline industry veteran, in 1999. The company began small, with just a few planes and one city pair. By the end of 2000, the company serviced cities around the country and more destinations were added each year. Today, JetBlue flies to 40 cities, including most regions of the United States and some Caribbean cities.

In the challenging environment of the modern airline industry,

JetBlue is one of the very few entrepreneurial success stories. While low-cost rivals Ted, owned by United Airlines, and Song, a now-failed venture of Delta Air Lines, struggle, JetBlue prospers. How does JetBlue succeed where other powerful firms fail?

JetBlue draws on a number of distinctive competencies. One strength springs from the talent and experience of Neeleman and his team of top managers. Neele-

man is a crossover from big business. The one-time travel agent started a Utah-based discount airline, Morris Air, in 1984, when he was just 24 years old. Morris Air was sold to Southwest Airlines in 1994 for $129 million in Southwest stock. Neeleman briefly worked at Southwest, but left after disputes with then-CEO Herb Kelleher. Neeleman helped to found Canadian-based WestJet Airlines and then developed the JetBlue concept. Neeleman recruited industry veterans such as COO Dave Barger and CFO John Owen, previously vice presidents at Continental and Southwest.

The airline's second-mover strategy, which imitates competitor Southwest, also provides advantages. The airline industry was traditionally composed of large international firms and some smaller, regional airlines. Both groups attempted to offer high levels of differentiated service and charged relatively high prices. Southwest was the first to offer discount air travel. Its strategy was an immediate success and spawned many imitators. Neeleman, thanks to his experiences, helped JetBlue to become the first copycat to duplicate every piece of Southwest's strategy, including low labor costs, a single type of aircraft and a single class of service, and lower-cost airports.

However, JetBlue adds its own unique take on Southwest's strategy. Neeleman improved on Southwest's formula by also offering differentiation. All of JetBlue's aircraft have luxurious leather seats and individual seat-back televisions, setting it apart from other low-fare carriers. Entertainment options include 36 channels of DirecTV, a selection of movies, and 100 channels of XM satellite radio. Flyers are pampered with a selection of fine wines, a Bliss Spa kit, and even Dunkin' Donuts coffee. Together, the low-cost strategy and differentiation allow JetBlue to reduce expenses while charging prices above other discount carriers, increasing profits. Neeleman identifies three important factors in developing a stable business model. "I always talk about the tripod—low costs, a great product, and capitalization," he says.

Neeleman was also able to avoid a common failing of many new businesses—insufficient capital. He had his personal fortune, which was considerable following the lucrative sale of Morris Air. Neeleman had many contacts from his previous ventures, and they were eager to give financial support to a new venture from a seasoned, capable entrepreneur. His investors sank $160 million into the start-up. In 2002, JetBlue held an initial public offering that raised $158 million and gave the company another source for future funding needs.

Today, Neeleman faces the biggest challenge of his career as he helps JetBlue make the transition from a small, entrepreneurial startup into the big leagues of major airlines. JetBlue's situation is reminiscent of People Express, a new airline that had $1 billion in sales within five years of start-up, and then went bankrupt just one year later. The company didn't have the funds or other resources to sustain rapid growth. Chris Collins, a former People Express manager, is now part of JetBlue's executive team. "[At People Express], we were the best thing going. A year later, we're gone because we couldn't sustain growth," Collins says. "You know what keeps me up at night [now]? Figuring out what we're going to need, not next year but five years from now."

Neeleman needs to figure out a way to grow while maintaining the cohesive culture and small-company feel of JetBlue. One way is through what he calls "visible leadership." Senior managers spend a day with crew members in different cities, working alongside them and talking about their concerns. Training managers in the JetBlue culture is important too.

Whether JetBlue can make the transition is still to be seen. Neeleman's focus on people, culture, strategy, and operations certainly has the company flying in the right direction.

CASE QUESTIONS

1. How does being a second mover contribute to JetBlue's success? How does its second-mover strategy present potential difficulties for the firm? Would a first-mover strategy have been better? Why or why not?

2. Consider the factors that lead to success for entrepreneurial firms. In your opinion, does JetBlue have what it takes to be a success? Explain.

3. Consider the factors that lead to failure for entrepreneurial firms. In your opinion, is JetBlue likely to experience failure? Explain.

CASE REFERENCES

"2005 Annual Report," "Fact Sheet," Jet-Blue website, www.jetblue.com on April 10, 2006; Stacy Perman, "How JetBlue Can Regain Its Golden Image," *BusinessWeek*, September 23, 2005, www.businessweek. com on April 10, 2006; Chuck Salter, "And Now the Hard Part," *Fast Company*, May 2004, www.fastcompany.com on April 10, 2006; Wendy Zellner, "Is JetBlue's Flight Plan Flawed?" *BusinessWeek*, February 16, 2004, www.businessweek.com on April 10, 2006.

YOU MAKE THE CALL

Founding Facebook

1. If you use Facebook, what are the properties of the site that cause you to use it?
2. If you do not use Facebook, what might cause you to become a user?
3. Identify the primary factors that led to Facebook's success.
4. What factors should Mark Zuckerberg keep in mind as possible threats to his firm?
5. Try to identify other potential networking concepts that might be extended from Facebook.
6. Would you be willing to invest in Facebook? Why or why not?

Test Prepper

college.hmco.com/business/students

Choose the correct answer. Answers are found at the back of the book.

1. T F Business owners who hire professional managers to run their businesses and then turn their own attention to other interests are still considered entrepreneurs.

2. T F Service businesses are the fastest-growing segment of small-business enterprise.

3. T F Consultants often recommend entrepreneurs buy a business rather than start one from scratch.

4. T F SBA loans are the most common source of small-business financing.

5. T F Every year about the same number of new businesses start as do fail.

6. Which of the following is true about small businesses and job creation in the United States?

   A. Small business creates jobs, but only in low-tech sectors of the economy.
   B. Small business increases the number of teenage workers, but not adult workers.
   C. Small business is rarely a source of jobs for international sales companies.
   D. Small business eliminates as many jobs as it creates.
   E. Small business is an important source of new jobs.

7. Patricia works in a furniture store and often meets customers who believe their sofas are still usable, but look bad because the fabric covering is worn. Patricia is not aware of anyone who currently performs in-home reupholstering of furniture, but thinks this might be a great idea for a new business. Patricia may have discovered a

   A. distinctive competence.
   B. niche.
   C. business plan.
   D. wholesaling opportunity.
   E. franchise.

8. The risks of starting a business from scratch are greater than those of buying an existing firm. To find an opening in the market, entrepreneurs must ask all of the following questions EXCEPT

   A. Who are my customers?
   B. At what price will my customers buy my product?
   C. Who are my competitors?
   D. How will my product differ from those of my competitors?
   E. Is my family completely behind me in this venture?

9. Which of the following is false about SBA financial programs?

   A. Eligible firms must also be unable to get private financing at reasonable terms.
   B. SBA loans have always been a major source of small-business financing.
   C. Sometimes the SBA and another bank will jointly make a loan.
   D. Budget cutbacks at the SBA have reduced the number of firms benefiting from loans.
   E. Under SBA's guaranteed loans programs, the SBA guarantees to repay 75 to 85 percent of the loan amount, not to exceed $750,000.

10. Tim is thinking about purchasing a franchised business. Which of the following should Tim NOT expect in his relationship with the franchiser?

    A. The franchiser may supply financing.
    B. The start-up costs of owning a franchise can be very significant.
    C. Most franchisers are reluctant to provide continued management counseling.
    D. A small-business owner sacrifices some independence as a franchisee.
    E. Franchises minimize risk, but do not guarantee success.

chapter 11

Basic Elements of Organizing

FIRST THINGS FIRST

LEARNING OBJECTIVES

After studying this chapter, you should be able to:

1. Identify the basic elements of organizations.
2. Describe alternative approaches to designing jobs.
3. Discuss the rationale and the most common bases for grouping jobs into departments.
4. Describe the basic elements involved in establishing reporting relationships.
5. Discuss how authority is distributed in organizations.
6. Discuss the basic coordinating activities undertaken by organizations.
7. Describe basic ways in which positions within an organization can be differentiated.

Did You Hear the One About . . . Delegation?

"You have to delegate when you're doing 22 episodes a season."

—ROB BURNETT, EXECUTIVE PRODUCER, WORLDWIDE PANTS, MAKER OF *EVERYBODY LOVES RAYMOND*

People say New Yorkers can't get along. Not true. I saw two New Yorkers, complete strangers, sharing a cab. One guy took the tires and the radio; the other guy took the engine.—David Letterman

Don't forget Mother's Day. Or as they call it in Beverly Hills, Dad's Third Wife Day.—Jay Leno

Critics have noted Schwarzenegger's only previous government experience was serving under President Bush senior as Chairman of the Council of Physical Fitness, a largely symbolic office, where Schwarzenegger's

David Letterman has been a late-night fixture for years. Part of his success is no doubt attributable to his effective delegation to his writers, producers, and staff.

only responsibility was doing hundreds of jumping jacks he was going to do anyway.—Jon Stewart

I cannot sing, dance or act; what else would I be but a talk show host?—David Letterman

Everybody who's anybody delegates. CEOs, the president, military commanders all delegate. Delegation can help leaders manage time better, bring more resources to bear, and develop subordinates' confidence and abilities. It is also risky. Some subordinates may not have the capability to make effective decisions. When that happens, managers are responsible for the results.

Imagine this: You are a television show host, known for your unique brand of humor. However, the reality is that you could never write enough material to fill an hour-long show every day. So you must delegate. From producers to directors to joke writers, your team makes most of the decisions that will have a high impact on your career. This is the situation facing late-night TV personalities such as David Letterman, Jon Stewart, and Jay Leno. They rely on a host of coworkers to make them appear funny, night after night.

Talk-show executive producers are the equivalent of corporate CEOs. They supervise lower-level employees, including producers, directors, and hosts. They delegate most of the decisions about the day-to-day running of the shows. Producers are the liaisons between directors and the studios, while directors are the heads of the production teams. Good producers and directors guarantee high-quality guests and a focused and effective staff.

Letterman's *Late Show* is produced by Worldwide Pants, a company he founded. The executive producer is Rob Burnett, who also produced *Everybody Loves Raymond* and *Ed,* also Worldwide Pants shows. Burnett claims that being responsible for enacting Letterman's vision and voice is "a gigantic responsibility fraught with an enormous amount of pressure."

Late Show employs teams of joke writers in addition to the host's material and ideas submitted by freelance writers. At the bottom of this hierarchy, freelance joke writers make $100 for each joke used on the air. Jokes are the comic's bottom line. Comedians use physical humor, voice control, and comic timing, but in the end, they are only as funny as their joke writers make them.

On *Late Show,* writers begin work in the late morning, with a brainstorming meeting that leaves everyone laughing and productive. Some are working on that night's show, some on later ones. Writers are given "setups," the serious straight line that begins the comic routine. The setups provide topics and shape the show. After a period of intense writing, there is a rehearsal and the host gives feedback. Letterman trusts his writers to plan a show that is varied, funny, and topical.

Burnett has learned what he can safely delegate and what he cannot. *Late Show* joke writers can write funny material that fits with Letterman's on-screen persona. On the other hand, *Everybody Loves Raymond* was Burnett's "baby," a concept he personally developed. *Raymond* contributors typically left after one season. "Writers are afraid to come to this show because they know how involved the creators are," one crew member relates. "You have to [delegate] when you're doing 22 episodes a season," Burnett adds. "But when we do, it's not the same. It's like a signature. We sign our names a certain way."

Interestingly, delegation at Worldwide Pants is sometimes a bit odd, as when Letterman delegates to Burnett who then delegates back to Letterman. When the *Raymond* character Phil Stubbs needed to utter a ridiculous catchphrase, Letterman supplied, "Shave my poodle."[1]

The relationships among talk show hosts and their writers in many ways mirrors the relationships between managers and their subordinates. All managers need the assistance of others to succeed and so must trust the members of their team to do their jobs and carry out their responsibilities. And the team members themselves need the support of their boss and a clear understanding of their role in the organization. The working relationship between managers and their subordinates is one of the most critical elements comprising an organization.[2] As you will see in this chapter, managing the basic frameworks that organizations use to get their work done—structure—is a fundamental part of the management process.

This chapter discusses many of the critical elements of organization structure that managers can control and is the first of five devoted to organizing, the second basic managerial function identified in Chapter 1. In Part Three, we describe managerial planning—deciding what to do. Organizing, the subject of Part Four, focuses on how to do it. We first elaborate on the meaning of organization structure. Subsequent sections explore the basic elements that managers use to create an organization.

The Elements of Organizing

Imagine asking a child to build a castle with a set of building blocks. She selects a few small blocks and other larger ones. She uses some square ones, some round ones, and some triangular ones. When she finishes, she has her own castle, unlike any other. Another child, presented with the same task, constructs a different castle. He selects different blocks, for example, and combines them in different ways. The children's activities—choosing certain combinations of blocks and then putting them together in unique ways—are in many ways analogous to the manager's job of organizing.[3]

organizing
Deciding how best to group organizational activities and resources

Organizing is deciding how best to group organizational elements.[4] Just as children select different kinds of building blocks, managers can choose a variety of structural possibilities. And, just as the children can assemble the blocks in any number of ways, so, too, can managers put the organization together in many different ways. Understanding the nature of these building blocks and the different ways in which they can be configured can have a powerful impact on a firm's competitiveness.[5] In this chapter, our focus is on the building blocks themselves—***organization structure***. In Chapter 12 we focus on how the blocks can be put together—organization design.

organization structure
The set of elements that can be used to configure an organization

There are six basic building blocks that managers can use in constructing an organization: designing jobs, grouping jobs, establishing reporting relationships between jobs, distributing authority among jobs, coordinating activities among jobs, and differentiating among positions. The logical starting point is the first building block—designing jobs for people within the organization.

concept
CHECK

What is the meaning of organizing as a management function? | Besides building blocks, what other analogies might seem to reflect organization structure?

Designing Jobs

The first building block of organization structure is job design. **Job design** is the determination of an individual's work-related responsibilities.[6] For a machinist at Caterpillar, job design might specify what machines are to be operated, how they are to be operated, and what performance standards are expected. For a manager at Caterpillar, job design might involve defining areas of decision-making responsibility, identifying goals and expectations, and establishing appropriate indicators of success. The natural starting point for designing jobs is determining the level of desired specialization.

> **job design**
> The determination of an individual's work-related responsibilities

Job Specialization

Job specialization is the degree to which the overall task of the organization is broken down and divided into smaller component parts. Job specialization evolved from the concept of *division of labor*. Adam Smith, an eighteenth-century economist, described how a pin factory used division of labor to improve productivity.[7] One man drew the wire, another straightened it, a third cut it, a fourth ground the point, and so on. Smith claimed that ten men working in this fashion were able to produce 48,000 pins in a day, whereas each man working alone could produce only 20 pins per day.

> **job specialization**
> The degree to which the overall task of the organization is broken down and divided into smaller component parts

More recently, the best example of the impact of specialization is the automobile assembly line pioneered by Henry Ford and his contemporaries. Mass-production capabilities stemming from job specialization techniques have had a profound impact throughout the world. High levels of low-cost production transformed U.S. society during the last century into one of the strongest economies in the history of the world.[8]

Job specialization is a normal extension of organizational growth. For example, when Walt Disney started his company, he did everything himself—wrote cartoons, drew them, and then marketed them to theaters. As the business grew, he eventually hired others to perform many of these same functions. As growth continued, so, too, did specialization. For example, as animation artists work on Disney movies today, they may specialize in generating computer images of a single character or doing only background scenery. And, today, the Walt Disney Company has thousands of different specialized jobs. Clearly, no one person could perform them all. *The Business of Ethics* describes a new specialized job being used in some organizations—the Chief Ethics Officer.

Job specialization can be found in a wide variety of settings. Consider, for instance, the various members of a racing crew. Each crew is comprised of specialists—someone is an expert on fuel mixtures, someone specializes in engine repairs, and someone specializes in tires. Lawrence Burch is a tire specialist for the Ryan Newman racing team. He is shown here checking the air pressure in a row of tires as he prepares for the Daytona 500 auto race at Daytona International Speedway in Daytona Beach, Florida.

The Business of Ethics

The New CEO (*Chief Ethics Officer*)

As the business environment, technology, and corporate strategies change, job designs must change to keep pace. One of the most interesting emerging new jobs is that of Chief Ethics Officer. Following a storm of corporate scandals in the early 2000s, many corporations voluntarily began ethics programs or enhanced already-existing ones. The need arose for someone to head the efforts, leading to the creation of a specialized position, the Chief Ethics Officer. Fannie Mae, the state of Connecticut, Mitsubishi, WorldCom, the New York Stock Exchange, and the U.S. Olympic Committee are just some of the organizations that now include an ethics officer in the top management team.

Ethics officers also come from a variety of backgrounds. About one-third have legal experience, while human resources, finance, accounting, and operations account for the rest. Most are long-time company employees who are internally promoted to the position. It's desirable to have an outsider in the role. Yet lack of trust from employees may keep outsiders from performing effectively.

Ethics officers may hold a wide range of responsibilities. According to the Ethics and Compliance Officer Association, a professional organization, the executives might be in charge of areas such as risk management, stakeholder relationships, whistle-blowing, ethics training, investigations, and preparation of financial statements, as well as overall responsibility for ethics and compliance programs. Some ethics officers also are involved in corporate social responsibility areas, such as the natural environment, diversity, human rights, and corporate philanthropy.

Ethics officers, therefore, perform functions that previously were the responsibility of directors, line personnel, or staff from the human resources, accounting, or legal areas. The trend toward the increased use of ethics officers has concentrated responsibility for corporate ethics in one individual or one small group of corporate-level staff.

Will use of an ethics officer result in more ethical behavior throughout a firm? The answer isn't clear. On the one hand, an expert at a high level may be very effective in making organization-wide changes. Yet on the other hand, employees may now feel that ethics is not their responsibility, creating a less ethical climate. Only time will tell if this ethics experiment works.

References: "Background of an Ethics Officer," "Responsibilities of an Ethics Officer," "What Is an Ethics & Compliance Officer?" Ethics and Compliance Officer Association, www.theecoa.org on April 12, 2006; Jonathan D. Glater, "Fannie Mae's Interim Chief Gets the Job Permanently," *The New York Times*, June 2, 2005, www.nytimes.com on April 12, 2006; David Henry, "Will Directors Morph into Corporate Constables?" *BusinessWeek*, June 14, 2004, www.businessweek.com on April 12, 2006; Joseph Weber, "Calling the Ethics Cops," *BusinessWeek*, February 13, 2006, www.businessweek.com on April 12, 2006.

Benefits and Limitations of Specialization

Job specialization provides four benefits to organizations.[9] First, workers performing small, simple tasks will become very proficient at each task. Second, transfer time between tasks decreases. If employees perform several different tasks, some time is lost as they stop doing the first task and start doing the next. Third, the more narrowly defined a job is, the easier it is to develop specialized equipment to assist with that job. Fourth, when an employee who performs a highly specialized job is absent or resigns, the manager is able to train someone new at relatively low cost. Although specialization is generally thought of in terms of operating jobs, many organizations have extended the basic elements of specialization to managerial and professional levels as well.[10] The job described in *The Business of Ethics* would be an example of just such a job.

On the other hand, job specialization can have negative consequences. The foremost criticism is that workers who perform highly specialized jobs may become bored and dissatisfied. The job may be so specialized that it offers no challenge or stimulation. Boredom and monotony set in, absenteeism rises, and the quality of the work may suffer. Furthermore, the anticipated benefits of specialization do not always occur. For example, a classic study conducted at Maytag found that the time spent moving work in process from one worker to another was greater than the time needed for the same individual to change from job to job.[11] Thus, although some degree of specialization is necessary, it should not be carried to extremes because of the possible negative consequences. Managers must be sensitive to situations in which extreme specialization should be avoided. And, indeed, several alternative approaches to designing jobs have been developed in recent years.

> "The best [Tour de France] teams have specialists to help position leaders for a win."
>
> Paul Hochman, business writer
> (*Fortune*, June 12, 2006, p. 150)

Alternatives to Specialization

To counter the problems associated with specialization, managers have sought other approaches to job design that achieve a better balance between organizational demands for efficiency and productivity and individual needs for creativity and autonomy. Five alternative approaches are job rotation, job enlargement, job enrichment, the job characteristics approach, and work teams.[12]

Job Rotation   *Job rotation* involves systematically moving employees from one job to another. A worker in a warehouse might unload trucks on Monday, carry incoming inventory to storage on Tuesday, verify invoices on Wednesday, pull outgoing inventory from storage on Thursday, and load trucks on Friday. Thus the jobs do not change, but instead, workers move from job to job. Unfortunately, for this very reason, job rotation has not been very successful in enhancing employee motivation or satisfaction. Jobs that are amenable to rotation tend to be relatively standard and routine. Workers who are rotated to a "new" job may be more satisfied at first, but satisfaction soon wanes. Although many companies (among them American Cyanamid, Bethlehem Steel, Ford, Prudential Insurance, TRW, and Western Electric) have tried job rotation, it is most often used today as a training device to improve worker skills and flexibility.

> *job rotation*
> An alternative to job specialization that involves systematically moving employees from one job to another

Job Enlargement   On the assumption that doing the same basic task over and over is the primary cause of worker dissatisfaction, *job enlargement* was developed to increase the total number of tasks workers perform. As a result, all workers perform a wide variety of tasks, which presumably reduces the level of job dissatisfaction. Many organizations have used job enlargement, including IBM, Detroit Edison, AT&T, the U.S. Civil Service, and Maytag. At Maytag, for example, the assembly line for producing washing-machine water pumps was systematically changed so that work that had originally been performed by six workers, who passed the work sequentially from one person to another, was performed by four workers, each of whom assembled a complete pump.[13] Unfortunately, although job enlargement does have some positive consequences, they are often offset by some disadvantages: (1) training costs usually increase, (2) unions have argued that pay should increase because the worker is doing more tasks, and (3) in many cases the work remains boring and routine even after job enlargement.

> *job enlargement*
> An alternative to job specialization that involves giving the employee more tasks to perform

Job Enrichment   A more comprehensive approach, *job enrichment*, assumes that increasing the range and variety of tasks is not sufficient by itself to improve employee motivation.[14] Thus job enrichment attempts to increase both the number of tasks a worker does and the control the worker has over the job. To

> *job enrichment*
> An alternative to job specialization that involves increasing both the number of tasks the worker does and the control the worker has over the job

implement job enrichment, managers remove some controls from the job, delegate more authority to employees, and structure the work in complete, natural units. These changes increase subordinates' sense of responsibility. Another part of job enrichment is to continually assign new and challenging tasks, thereby increasing employees' opportunity for growth and advancement.

AT&T was one of the earliest companies to try job enrichment. In one experiment, eight typists in a service unit prepared customer service orders. Faced with low output and high turnover, management determined that the typists felt little responsibility to clients and received little feedback. The unit was changed to create a typing team. Typists were matched with designated service representatives, the task was changed from ten specific steps to three more general steps, and job titles were upgraded. As a result, the frequency of order processing increased from 27 percent to 90 percent, the need for messenger service was eliminated, accuracy improved, and turnover became practically nil.[15] Other organizations that have tried job enrichment include Texas Instruments, IBM, and General Foods. This approach, however, also has disadvantages. For example, work systems need to be analyzed before enrichment, but this seldom happens, and managers rarely ask for employee preferences when enriching jobs.

Job Characteristics Approach   The *job characteristics approach* is an alternative to job specialization that does take into account the work system and employee preferences.[16] As illustrated in Figure 11.1, the job characteristics approach

job characteristics approach
An alternative to job specialization that suggests that jobs should be diagnosed and improved along five core dimensions, taking into account both the work system and employee preferences

Figure 11.1
THE JOB CHARACTERISTICS APPROACH

The job characteristics approach to job design provides a viable alternative to job specialization. Five core job dimensions may lead to critical psychological states that, in turn, may enhance motivation, performance, and satisfaction while also reducing absenteeism and turnover.

Source: J. R. Hackman and G. R. Oldham, "Motivation Through the Design of Work: Test of a Theory," *Organizational Behavior and Human Performance*, Vol. 16 (1976), pp. 250–279. Copyright © Academic Press, Inc. Reprinted by permission of Academic Press and the authors.

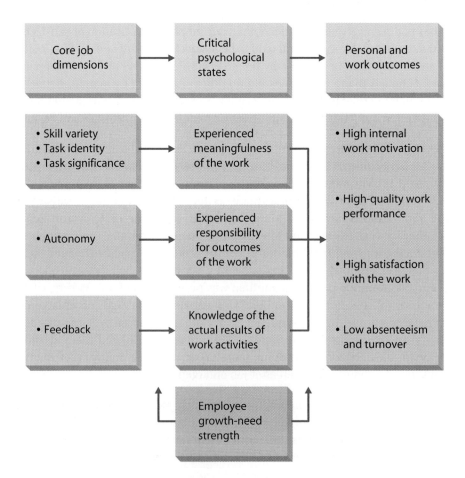

suggests that jobs should be diagnosed and improved along five core dimensions:

1. *Skill variety,* the number of things a person does in a job
2. *Task identity,* the extent to which the worker does a complete or identifiable portion of the total job
3. *Task significance,* the perceived importance of the task
4. *Autonomy,* the degree of control the worker has over how the work is performed
5. *Feedback,* the extent to which the worker knows how well the job is being performed

The higher a job rates on those dimensions, the more employees will experience various psychological states. Experiencing these states, in turn, presumably leads to high motivation, high-quality performance, high satisfaction, and low absenteeism and turnover. Finally, a concept called *growth-need strength* is presumed to affect how the model works for different people. People with a strong desire to grow, develop, and expand their capabilities (indicative of high growth-need strength) are expected to respond strongly to the presence or absence of the basic job characteristics; individuals with low growth-need strength are expected not to respond as strongly or consistently.

A large number of studies have been conducted to test the usefulness of the job characteristics approach. The Southwestern Division of Prudential Insurance, for example, used this approach in its claims division. Results included moderate declines in turnover and a small but measurable improvement in work quality. Other research findings have not supported this approach as strongly. Thus, although the job characteristics approach is one of the most promising alternatives to job specialization, it is probably not the final answer.

Work Teams   Another alternative to job specialization is ***work teams***. Under this arrangement, a group is given responsibility for designing the work system to be used in performing an interrelated set of tasks. In the typical assembly-line system, the work flows from one worker to the next, and each worker has a specified job to perform. In a work team, however, the group itself decides how jobs will be allocated. For example, the work team assigns specific tasks to members, monitors and controls its own performance, and has autonomy over work scheduling.[17] We discuss work teams more fully in Chapter 19.

> **work team**
> An alternative to job specialization that allows an entire group to design the work system it will use to perform an interrelated set of tasks

<table>
<tr><td>

What are the basic job design alternatives?

</td><td>

Which kind of job design best describes a job you have recently held? Do you agree or disagree with the text's assessment of that job design?

</td><td>

concept
CHECK

</td></tr>
</table>

Grouping Jobs: Departmentalization

The second building block of organization structure is the grouping of jobs according to some logical arrangement. The process of grouping jobs is called ***departmentalization***. After establishing the basic rationale for departmentalization, we identify some common bases along which departments are created.[18]

> **departmentalization**
> The process of grouping jobs according to some logical arrangement

Rationale for Departmentalization

When organizations are small, the owner-manager can personally oversee everyone who works there. As an organization grows, however, personally supervising all the employees becomes more and more difficult for the owner-manager. Consequently, new managerial positions are created to supervise the work of others. Employees are not assigned to particular managers randomly. Rather, jobs are grouped according to some plan. The logic embodied in such a plan is the basis for all departmentalization.[19]

Common Bases for Departmentalization

Figure 11.2 presents a partial organizational chart for Apex Computers, a hypothetical firm that manufactures and sells computers and software. The chart shows that Apex uses each of the four most common bases for departmentalization: function, product, customer, and location.

Functional Departmentalization   The most common base for departmentalization, especially among smaller organizations, is by function. ***Functional departmentalization*** groups together those jobs involving the same or similar activities. (The word *function* is used here to mean organizational functions such as finance and production, rather than the basic managerial functions, such as planning or controlling.) The computer department at Apex has manufacturing, finance, and marketing departments, each an organizational function.

> *functional departmentalization*
> Grouping jobs involving the same or similar activities

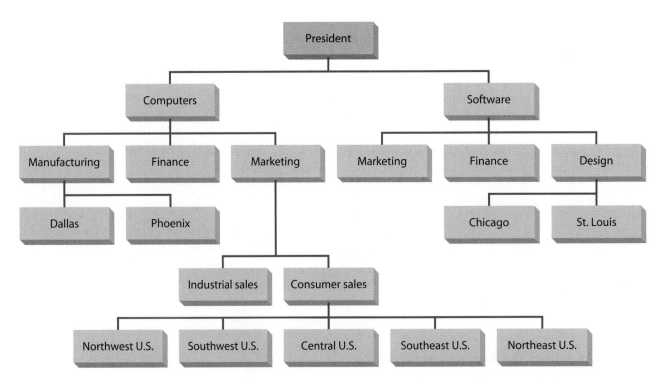

Figure 11.2
BASES FOR DEPARTMENTALIZATION

Organizations group jobs into departments. Apex, a hypothetical organization, uses all four of the primary bases of departmentalization—function, product, customer, and location. Like Apex, most large organizations use more than one type of departmentalization

This approach, which is most common in smaller organizations, has three primary advantages. First, each department can be staffed by experts in that functional area. Marketing experts can be hired to run the marketing function, for example. Second, supervision is also facilitated because an individual manager needs to be familiar with only a relatively narrow set of skills. And, third, coordinating activities inside each department is easier.

On the other hand, as an organization begins to grow in size, several disadvantages of this approach may emerge. For one, decision making tends to become slower and more bureaucratic. Employees may also begin to concentrate too narrowly on their own unit and lose sight of the total organizational system. Finally, accountability and performance become increasingly difficult to monitor. For example, determining whether a new product fails because of production deficiencies or a poor marketing campaign may not be possible.

Product Departmentalization   *Product departmentalization*, a second common approach, involves grouping and arranging activities around products or product groups. Apex Computers has two product-based departments at the highest level of the firm. One is responsible for all activities associated with Apex's personal computer business, and the other handles the software business. Most larger businesses adopt this form of departmentalization for grouping activities at the business or corporate level.

product departmentalization
Grouping activities around products or product groups

Product departmentalization has three major advantages. First, all activities associated with one product or product group can be easily integrated and coordinated. Second, the speed and effectiveness of decision making are enhanced. Third, the performance of individual products or product groups can be assessed more easily and objectively, thereby improving the accountability of departments for the results of their activities.

Product departmentalization also has two major disadvantages. For one, managers in each department may focus on their own product or product group to the exclusion of the rest of the organization. For example, a marketing manager may see her or his primary duty as helping the group rather than helping the overall organization. For another, administrative costs rise because each department must have its own functional specialists for areas such as market research and financial analysis.

Customer Departmentalization   Under *customer departmentalization*, the organization structures its activities to respond to and interact with specific customers or customer groups. The lending activities in most banks, for example, are usually tailored to meet the needs of different kinds of customers (business, consumer, mortgage, and agricultural loans). Figure 11.2 shows that the marketing branch of Apex's computer business has two distinct departments—industrial sales and consumer sales. The industrial sales department handles marketing activities aimed at business customers, whereas the consumer sales department is responsible for wholesaling computers to retail stores catering to individual purchasers.

customer departmentalization
Grouping activities to respond to and interact with specific customers or customer groups

The basic advantage of this approach is that the organization is able to use skilled specialists to deal with unique customers or customer groups. It takes one set of skills to evaluate a balance sheet and lend a business $500,000 for operating capital, and a different set of skills to evaluate an individual's creditworthiness and lend $20,000 for a new car. However, a fairly large administrative staff is required to integrate the activities of the various departments. In banks, for example, coordination is necessary to make sure that the organization does not overcommit itself in any one area and to handle collections on delinquent accounts from a diverse set of customers.

location departmentalization
Grouping jobs on the basis of defined geographic sites or areas

Location Departmentalization   *Location departmentalization* groups jobs on the basis of defined geographic sites or areas. The defined sites or areas may range in size from a hemisphere to only a few blocks of a large city. The manufacturing branch of Apex's computer business has two plants—one in Dallas and another in Phoenix. Similarly, the design division of its software design unit has two labs— one in Chicago and the other in St. Louis. Apex's consumer sales group has five sales territories corresponding to different regions of the United States. Transportation companies, police departments (precincts represent geographic areas of a city), and the Federal Reserve Bank all use location departmentalization.

The primary advantage of location departmentalization is that it enables the organization to respond easily to unique customer and environmental characteristics in the various regions. On the negative side, a larger administrative staff may be required if the organization must keep track of units in scattered locations.

Other Forms of Departmentalization   Although most organizations are departmentalized by function, product, customer, or location, other forms are occasionally used. Some organizations group certain activities by time. One of the machine shops of Baker Hughes in Houston, for example, operates on three shifts. Each shift has a superintendent who reports to the plant manager, and each shift has its own functional departments. Time is thus the framework for many organizational activities. Other organizations that use time as a basis for grouping jobs include some hospitals and many airlines. In other situations, departmentalization by sequence is appropriate. Many college students, for instance, must register in sequence: seniors on Monday, juniors on Tuesday, and so on. Other areas that may be organized in sequence include credit departments (specific employees run credit checks according to customer name) and insurance claims divisions (by policy number).

Other Considerations   Two final points about job grouping remain to be made. First, departments are often called something entirely different—*divisions, units, sections,* and *bureaus* are all common synonyms. The higher we look in an organization, the more likely we are to find departments referred to as divisions. H. J. Heinz, for example, is organized into five major divisions. Nevertheless, the underlying logic behind all the labels is the same: They represent groups of jobs that have been yoked together according to some unifying principle. Second, almost any organization is likely to employ multiple bases of departmentalization, depending on level. Although Apex Computer is a hypothetical firm that we created to explain departmentalization, it is quite similar to many real organizations in that it uses a variety of bases of departmentalization for different levels and different sets of activities.

concept
CHECK

What are the common bases of departmentalization?

Identify an organization with which you have some familiarity. Based on your knowledge of the firm, describe how it is departmentalized.

Establishing Reporting Relationships

The third basic element of organizing is the establishment of reporting relationships among positions. Suppose, for example, that the owner-manager of a small business has just hired two new employees, one to handle marketing and one to handle production. Will the marketing manager report to the production manager, will the production manager report to the marketing manager, or will each report directly to the owner-manager? These questions reflect the basic issues involved in establishing reporting relationships: clarifying the chain of command and the span of management. We should also note before proceeding, though, that in addition to formal departmental arrangements (as described earlier) and prescribed reporting relationships (as discussed below), there is also considerable informal interaction that takes place among people in any organization. *Technology Toolkit* explores this element of organizing more fully.

Technology Toolkit

Mapping Collaboration

Traditional organization charts display formal lines of reporting, but managers need to understand informal relationships too. Modern companies are complex, teams-based, and decentralized, with rapid turnover and remote workers, so the informal social network is difficult to directly observe. However, a new tool can help.

The technique is "social network analysis," SNA. SNA studies how people interact: who interacts, the type and frequency of interaction, the level of trust, and so on. Instead of a conventional organization chart, SNA charts resemble a spider web, with each node representing an individual and each line representing an interaction. Nion McEvoy, CEO of a small firm that underwent SNA, describes the resulting chart: "It looks like an advanced game of cat's cradle played by mice on speed."

SNA can identify, for example, valuable individuals regardless of their formal position, based on the lines that radiate from their nodes. Many top managers appear remote because their interactions are limited. SNA can diagnose when a key but overlooked employee needs recognition and when a top manager is too inaccessible. SAN can show "bottlenecks," or individuals that have too many links, indicating that too many people depend on them. They are overworked and slow down processes as others await their input. Units that become overly isolated show up in the charts as having too few links to other units.

NetForm, founded by corporate anthropologist Karen Stephenson, produces an SNA software targeted to businesses. Raw data is gathered from employees, who complete a survey asking questions such as "Whom do you go to for quick advice?" and "Whom do you hang out with socially?" Employees' answers are gathered online and analyzed. Results are then interpreted and shared.

SNA has been used at Mobil, J. P. Morgan, International Paper, and the Los Angeles Philharmonic. Benefits include more effective communications, better succession planning and talent spotting, increased innovation, and even more effective design of office space.

The results can be very surprising to managers and workers alike. "Some people you assumed are well connected . . . are totally out of touch," says International Paper manager P. J. Smoot. "You also discover people you never heard of who are key to holding the social network together."

References: Rob Cross, Andrew Parker, and Stephen P. Borgatti, "A Bird's-Eye View: Using Social Network Analysis to Improve Knowledge Creation and Sharing," IBM Institute for Business Value website, www.ibm.com on April 1, 2006; Jena McGregor, "The Office Chart That Really Counts," *BusinessWeek*, February 27, 2006, pp. 48–49; Ethan Watters, "The Organization Woman," *Business 2.0*, April 28, 2006, www.cnnmoney.com on April 1, 2006.

Most large businesses have a well-defined chain of command and rely on delegation of authority. Dan Gilbert is the principal owner of Quicken, a financial services firm, and the Cleveland Cavaliers professional basketball team. In order to take an active role in the management of both businesses, Gilbert has created a flexible but clear chain of command for each of his businesses. He also delegates authority to other key managers. For instance, Tony Nicholls, Quicken Loans' regional vice president, works at the firm's corporate campus in Livonia, Michigan. He oversees the work of dozens of employees but is also accountable to his own boss.

Chain of Command

Chain of command is an old concept, first popularized in the early years of the twentieth century. For example, early writers about the **chain of command** argued that clear and distinct lines of authority need to be established among all positions in an organization. The chain of command actually has two components. The first, called *unity of command,* suggests that each person within an organization must have a clear reporting relationship to one and only one boss (as we see in Chapter 11, newer models of organization design routinely—and successfully—violate this premise). The second, called the *scalar principle,* suggests that there must be a clear and unbroken line of authority that extends from the lowest to the highest position in the organization. The popular saying "The buck stops here" is derived from this idea—someone in the organization must ultimately be responsible for every decision.

Narrow Versus Wide Spans

Another part of establishing reporting relationships is determining how many people will report to each manager. This defines the **span of management** (sometimes called the *span of control*). For years, managers and researchers sought to determine the optimal span of management. For example, should it be relatively narrow (with few subordinates per manager) or relatively wide (with many subordinates)? One early writer, A. V. Graicunas, went so far as to quantify span of management issues.[20] Graicunas noted that a manager must deal with three kinds of interactions with and among subordinates: direct (the manager's one-to-one relationship with each subordinate), cross (among the subordinates themselves), and group (between groups of subordinates). The number of possible interactions of all types between a manager and subordinates can be determined by the following formula:

$$I = N(2^N/2 + N - 1)$$

where *I* is the total number of interactions with and among subordinates and *N* is the number of subordinates.

If a manager has only two subordinates, six potential interactions exist. If the number of subordinates increases to 3, the possible interactions total 18. With 5 subordinates there are 100 possible interactions. Although Graicunas offers no prescription for what *N* should be, his ideas demonstrate how complex the relationships become when more subordinates are added. The important point is that each additional subordinate adds more complexity than the previous one did. Going from 9 to 10 subordinates is very different from going from 3 to 4.

Another early writer, Ralph C. Davis, described two kinds of spans: an operative span for lower-level managers and an executive span for middle and top managers. He

---

chain of command
A clear and distinct line of authority among the positions in an organization

span of management
The number of people who report to a particular manager

argued that operative spans could approach 30 subordinates, whereas executive spans should be limited to between 3 and 9 (depending on the nature of the managers' jobs, the growth rate of the company, and similar factors). Lyndall F. Urwick suggested that an executive span should never exceed 6 subordinates, and General Ian Hamilton reached the same conclusion.[21] Today we recognize that the span of management is a crucial factor in structuring organizations but that there are no universal, cut-and-dried prescriptions for an ideal or optimal span.[22] Later we summarize some important variables that influence the appropriate span of management in a particular situation. First, however, we describe how the span of management affects the overall structure of an organization.

Tall Versus Flat Organizations

Imagine an organization with 31 managers and a narrow span of management. As shown in Figure 11.3, the result is a relatively tall organization with five layers of management. With a somewhat wider span of management, however, the flat organization shown in Figure 11.3 emerges. This configuration has only three layers of management.

What difference does it make whether the organization is tall or flat? One early study at Sears found that a flat structure led to higher levels of employee morale and productivity.[23] Researchers have also argued that a tall structure is more expensive (because of the larger number of managers involved) and that it fosters more communication problems (because of the increased number of people through

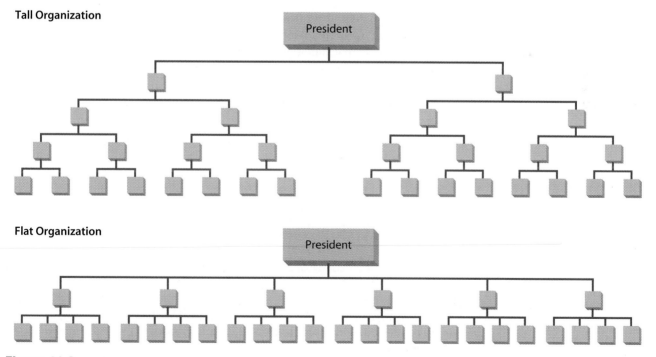

Figure 11.3

TALL VERSUS FLAT ORGANIZATIONS

Wide spans of management result in flat organizations, which may lead to improved employee morale and productivity as well as increased managerial responsibility. Many organizations today, including IBM and General Electric, are moving toward flat structures to improve communication and flexibility.

whom information must pass). On the other hand, a wide span of management in a flat organization may result in a manager's having more administrative responsibility (because there are fewer managers) and more supervisory responsibility (because there are more subordinates reporting to each manager). If these additional responsibilities become excessive, the flat organization may suffer.[24]

Many experts agree that businesses can function effectively with fewer layers of organization than they currently have. The Franklin Mint, for example, reduced its number of management layers from 6 to 4. At the same time, the CEO increased his span of management from 6 to 12. In similar fashion, IBM has eliminated several layers of management. One additional reason for this trend is that improved organizational communication networks allow managers to stay in touch with a larger number of subordinates than was possible even just a few years ago.[25]

Determining the Appropriate Span

Of course, the initial question remains: How do managers determine the appropriate span for their unique situation? Although no perfect formula exists, researchers have identified a set of factors that influence the span for a particular circumstance.[26] Some of these factors are listed in Table 11.1. For example, if the manager and subordinates are competent and well trained, a wide span may be effective. Physical dispersion is also important. The more widely subordinates are scattered, the narrower the span should be. On the other hand, if all the subordinates are in one location, the span can be somewhat wider. The amount of nonsupervisory work expected of the manager is also important. Some managers, especially at the lower levels of an organization, spend most or all of their time supervising subordinates. Other managers spend a lot of time doing paperwork, planning, and engaging in other managerial activities. Thus these managers may need a narrower span.

Some job situations also require a great deal of interaction between supervisor and subordinates. In general, the more interaction that is required, the narrower the span should be. Similarly, if there is a fairly comprehensive set of standard procedures, a relatively wide span is possible. If only a few standard procedures exist, however, the supervisor usually has to play a larger role in overseeing day-to-day activities and may find a narrower span more efficient. Task similarity is also important. If most of the jobs being supervised are similar, a supervisor can handle a wider span. When each employee is performing a different task, more of the supervisor's time is spent on individual supervision. Likewise, if new problems that require supervisory assistance arise frequently, a narrower span may be called for.

Table 11.1

FACTORS INFLUENCING THE SPAN OF MANAGEMENT

Although researchers have found advantages to the flat organization (less expensive and with fewer communication problems than a tall organization, for example), a number of factors may favor a tall organization.

1. Competence of supervisor and subordinates (the greater the competence, the wider the potential span)
2. Physical dispersion of subordinates (the greater the dispersion, the narrower the potential span)
3. Extent of nonsupervisory work in manager's job (the more nonsupervisory work, the narrower the potential span)
4. Degree of required interaction (the less required interaction, the wider the potential span)
5. Extent of standardized procedures (the more procedures, the wider the potential span)
6. Similarity of tasks being supervised (the more similar the tasks, the wider the potential span)
7. Frequency of new problems (the higher the frequency, the narrower the potential span)
8. Preferences of supervisors and subordinates

If new problems are relatively rare, though, a wider span can be established. Finally, the preferences of both supervisor and subordinates may affect the optimal span. Some managers prefer to spend less time actively supervising their employees, and many employees prefer to be more self-directed in their jobs. A wider span may be possible in these situations.

For example, the Case Corporation factory in Racine, Wisconsin, makes farm tractors exclusively to order in five to six weeks. Farmers can select from among a wide array of options, including engines, tires, power trains, and even a CD player. A wide assortment of machines and processes is used to construct each tractor. Although workers are highly skilled operators of their particular machines, each machine is different. In this kind of setup, the complexities of each machine and the advanced skills needed by each operator mean that one supervisor can oversee only a small number of employees.[27]

In some organizational settings, other factors may influence the optimal span of management. The relative importance of each factor also varies in different settings. It is unlikely that all eight factors will suggest the same span; some may suggest a wider span, and others may indicate a need for a narrow span. Hence, managers must assess the relative weight of each factor or set of factors when deciding the optimal span of management for their unique situation.

concept
CHECK

What factors determine the appropriate span of management for a particular setting?

In your opinion, how important is it to have a clear and unambiguous chain of command? Why?

Distributing Authority

Another important building block in structuring organizations is the determination of how authority is to be distributed among positions. **Authority** is power that has been legitimized by the organization.[28] Distributing authority is another normal outgrowth of increasing organizational size. For example, when an owner-manager hires a sales representative to market his products, he needs to give the new employee appropriate authority to make decisions about delivery dates, discounts, and so forth. If every decision requires the approval of the owner-manager, he is no better off than he was before he hired the sales representative. The power given to the sales representative to make certain kinds of decisions, then, represents the establishment of a pattern of authority—the sales representative can make some decisions alone and others in consultation with coworkers, and the sales representative must defer some decisions to the boss. Two specific issues that managers must address when distributing authority are delegation and decentralization.[29]

authority
Power that has been legitimized by the organization

The Delegation Process

Delegation is the establishment of a pattern of authority between a superior and one or more subordinates. Specifically, **delegation** is the process by which managers assign a portion of their total workload to others.[30]

delegation
The process by which a manager assigns a portion of his or her total workload to others

Reasons for Delegation   The primary reason for delegation is to enable the manager to get more work done. Subordinates help ease the manager's burden by doing major portions of the organization's work. In some instances, a subordinate may

Figure 11.4

STEPS IN THE DELEGATION PROCESS

Good communication skills can help a manager successfully delegate responsibility to subordinates. A manager must not be reluctant to delegate, nor should he or she fear that the subordinate will do the job so well that the manager's advancement is threatened.

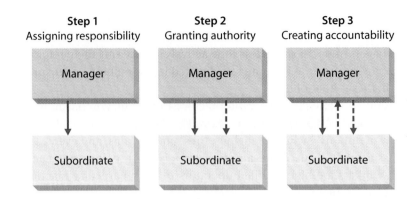

Step 1
Assigning responsibility

Step 2
Granting authority

Step 3
Creating accountability

Manager

Subordinate

have more expertise in addressing a particular problem than the manager does. For example, the subordinate may have had special training in developing information systems or may be more familiar with a particular product line or geographic area. Delegation also helps develop subordinates. By participating in decision making and problem solving, subordinates learn about overall operations and improve their managerial skills.

Parts of the Delegation Process   In theory, as shown in Figure 11.4, the delegation process involves three steps. First, the manager assigns responsibility or gives the subordinate a job to do. The assignment of responsibility might range from telling a subordinate to prepare a report to placing the person in charge of a task force. Along with the assignment, the individual is also given the authority to do the job. The manager may give the subordinate the power to requisition needed information from confidential files or to direct a group of other workers. Finally, the manager establishes the subordinate's accountability—that is, the subordinate accepts an obligation to carry out the task assigned by the manager. For instance, the CEO of AutoZone will sign off for the company on financial performance only when the individual manager responsible for each unit has certified his or her own results as being accurate. The firm believes that this high level of accountability will help it avoid the kind of accounting scandal that has hit many businesses in recent times.[31]

These three steps do not occur mechanically, however. Indeed, when a manager and a subordinate have developed a good working relationship, the major parts of the process may be implied rather than stated. The manager may simply mention that a particular job must be done. A perceptive subordinate may realize that the manager is actually assigning the job to her. From past experience with the boss, she may also know, without being told, that she has the necessary authority to do the job and that she is accountable to the boss for finishing the job as "agreed."

Problems in Delegation   Unfortunately, problems often arise in the delegation process. For example, a manager may be reluctant to delegate. Some managers are so disorganized that they are unable to plan work in advance and, as a result, cannot delegate appropriately. Similarly, some managers may worry that subordinates will do too well and pose a threat to their own advancement. And, finally, managers may not trust the

> "You can't do everything yourself. To be successful, you have to be willing to say, 'I don't know'."

Franny Martin, successful entrepreneur
(*USA Today,* January 18, 2005, p. 1B)

Distributing authority in an organization begins with delegation. At Yahoo!, the big Internet portal, extreme delegation is a fundamental management philosophy. When the firm hired Isabelle Bordry (left) and Clothilde de Mersan to launch and run Yahoo! France, U.S. managers were initially concerned about their ability to transfer its management style to the notoriously centralized, rigid French economy. But Bordry and de Mersan have enthusiastically embraced the notion of delegation and are aggressively working to encourage their employees to make their own decisions.

subordinate to do the job well. Similarly, some subordinates are reluctant to accept delegation. They may be afraid that failure will result in a reprimand. They may also perceive that there are no rewards for accepting additional responsibility. Or they may simply prefer to avoid risk and therefore want their boss to take all responsibility.

Norm Brodsky, a small-business owner who built six successful companies, learned firsthand what happens when the CEO cannot effectively delegate. It took Brodsky 7 years to build a messenger service into a $120 million operation—and just 14 months to go from $120 million into bankruptcy. "Where did I go wrong?" he asks rhetorically and then provides his own answer: "The company needed management, stability, and structure, and I kept it from getting them. I was so desperate to sustain the head rush of start-up chaos that I made all the final decisions and didn't let the managers do their jobs. In the end I paid a steep price."[32]

There are no quick fixes for these problems. The basic issue is communication. Subordinates must understand their own responsibility, authority, and accountability, and the manager must come to recognize the value of effective delegation. With the passage of time, subordinates should develop to the point at which they can make substantial contributions to the organization. At the same time, managers should recognize that a subordinate's satisfactory performance is not a threat to their own career, but an accomplishment by both the subordinate who did the job and the manager who trained the subordinate and was astute enough to entrust the subordinate with the project. Ultimate responsibility for the outcome, however, continues to reside with the manager.

Decentralization and Centralization

Just as authority can be delegated from one individual to another, organizations also develop patterns of authority across a wide variety of positions and departments. ***Decentralization*** is the process of systematically delegating power and authority throughout the organization to middle and lower-level managers. It is

decentralization
The process of systematically delegating power and authority throughout the organization to middle and lower-level managers

centralization
The process of systematically retaining power and authority in the hands of higher-level managers

important to remember that decentralization is actually one end of a continuum anchored at the other end by ***centralization***, the process of systematically retaining power and authority in the hands of higher-level managers. Hence, a decentralized organization is one in which decision-making power and authority are delegated as far down the chain of command as possible. Conversely, in a centralized organization, decision-making power and authority are retained at the higher levels of management. When H. Ross Perot ran EDS, he practiced centralization; his successors have used decentralization. No organization is ever completely decentralized or completely centralized; some firms position themselves toward one end of the continuum, and some lean the other way.[33]

What factors determine an organization's position on the decentralization-centralization continuum? One common determinant is the organization's external environment. Usually, the greater the complexity and uncertainty of the environment, the greater is the tendency to decentralize. Another crucial factor is the history of the organization. Firms have a tendency to do what they have done in the past, so there is likely to be some relationship between what an organization did in its early history and what it chooses to do today in terms of centralization or decentralization. The nature of the decisions being made is also considered. The costlier and riskier the decisions, the more pressure there is to centralize. Organizations also consider the abilities of lower-level managers. If lower-level managers do not have the ability to make high-quality decisions, there is likely to be a high level of centralization. If lower-level managers are well qualified, top management can take advantage of their talents by decentralizing; in fact, if top management does not, talented lower-level managers may leave the organization.[34]

A manager has no clear-cut guidelines for determining whether to centralize or decentralize. Many successful organizations, such as Sears and General Electric, are quite decentralized. Equally successful firms, such as McDonald's and Wal-Mart, have remained centralized. IBM has recently undergone a transformation from using a highly centralized approach to a much more decentralized approach to managing its operations. A great deal of decision-making authority was passed from the hands of a select group of top executives down to six product and marketing groups. The reason for the move was to speed the company's ability to make decisions, introduce new products, and respond to customers. For years, most Japanese firms have been highly centralized. Recently, though, many leading Japanese firms have moved toward decentralization.

concept
CHECK

What are the steps in the delegation process?

Under what circumstances would you prefer to work in a centralized organization? In a decentralized organization?

Coordinating Activities

A fifth major element of organizing is coordination. As we discuss earlier, job specialization and departmentalization involve breaking jobs down into small units and then combining those jobs into departments. Once this has been accomplished, the activities of the departments must be linked—systems must be put into place to keep the activities of each department focused on the attainment of organizational goals. This is accomplished by ***coordination*** —the process of linking the activities of the various departments of the organization.[35]

The Need for Coordination

The primary reason for coordination is that departments and work groups are interdependent—they depend on one another for information and resources to perform their respective activities. The greater the interdependence between departments, the more coordination the organization requires if departments are to be able to perform effectively. There are three major forms of interdependence: pooled, sequential, and reciprocal.[36]

Pooled interdependence represents the lowest level of interdependence. Units with pooled interdependence operate with little interaction—the output of the units is pooled at the organizational level. Gap clothing stores operate with pooled interdependence. Each store is considered a "department" by the parent corporation. Each has its own operating budget, staff, and so forth. The profits or losses from each store are "added together" at the organizational level. The stores are interdependent to the extent that the final success or failure of one store affects the others, but they do not generally interact on a day-to-day basis.

In ***sequential interdependence***, the output of one unit becomes the input for another in a sequential fashion. This creates a moderate level of interdependence. At Nissan, for example, one plant assembles engines and then ships them to a final assembly site at another plant, where the cars are completed. The plants are interdependent in that the final assembly plant must have the engines from engine assembly before it can perform its primary function of producing finished automobiles. But the level of interdependence is generally one way—the engine plant is not necessarily dependent on the final assembly plant.

Reciprocal interdependence exists when activities flow both ways between units. This form is clearly the most complex. Within a Marriott hotel, for example, the reservations department, front-desk check-in, and housekeeping are all reciprocally interdependent. Reservations has to provide front-desk employees with information about how many guests to expect each day, and housekeeping needs to know which rooms require priority cleaning. If any of the three units does not do its job properly, all the others will be affected.

Structural Coordination Techniques

Because of the obvious coordination requirements that characterize most organizations, many techniques for achieving coordination have been developed. Some of the most useful devices for maintaining coordination among interdependent units are the managerial hierarchy, rules and procedures, liaison roles, task forces, and integrating departments.[37]

The Managerial Hierarchy Organizations that use the hierarchy to achieve coordination place one manager in charge of interdependent departments or

---

coordination
The process of linking the activities of the various departments of the organization

pooled interdependence
When units operate with little interaction; their output is simply pooled

sequential interdependence
When the output of one unit becomes the input for another in sequential fashion

reciprocal interdependence
When activities flow both ways between units

Staple's, Inc. is the largest office products retailer in the United States. The firm's rapidly growing delivery business has become a major contributor to the firm's profitability. The delivery operation requires tight coordination among the firm's units responsible for taking customer orders and then filling, delivering, and billing for those orders. The firm relies on a variety of standard procedures for managing its delivery operation. It also uses electronic coordination to facilitate communication among the various units.

units. In Wal-Mart distribution centers, major activities include receiving and unloading bulk shipments from railroad cars and loading other shipments onto trucks for distribution to retail outlets. The two groups (receiving and shipping) are interdependent in that they share the loading docks and some equipment. To ensure coordination and minimize conflict, one manager is in charge of the whole operation.

Rules and Procedures   Routine coordination activities can be handled via rules and standard procedures. In the Wal-Mart distribution center, an outgoing truck shipment has priority over an incoming rail shipment. Thus, when trucks are to be loaded, the shipping unit is given access to all of the center's auxiliary forklifts. This priority is specifically stated in a rule. But, as useful as rules and procedures often are in routine situations, they are not particularly effective when coordination problems are complex or unusual.

Liaison Roles   We introduced the liaison role of management in Chapter 1. As a device for coordination, a manager in a liaison role coordinates interdependent units by acting as a common point of contact. This individual may not have any formal authority over the groups but instead simply facilitates the flow of information between units. Two engineering groups working on component systems for a large project might interact through a liaison. The liaison maintains familiarity with each group as well as with the overall project. She can answer questions and otherwise serve to integrate the activities of all the groups.

Task Forces   A task force may be created when the need for coordination is acute. When interdependence is complex and several units are involved, a single liaison person may not be sufficient. Instead, a task force might be assembled by drawing one representative from each group. The coordination function is thus spread across several individuals, each of whom has special information about one of the groups involved. When the project is completed, task force members return to their original position. For example, a college overhauling its degree requirements might establish a task force made up of representatives from each department affected by the change. Each person retains her or his regular departmental affiliation and duties but also serves on the special task force. After the new requirements are agreed on, the task force is dissolved.

Integrating Departments   Integrating departments are occasionally used for coordination. These are somewhat similar to task forces but are more permanent. An integrating department generally has some permanent members as well as members who are assigned temporarily from units that are particularly in need of coordination. One study found that successful firms in the plastics industry, which is characterized by complex and dynamic environments, used integrating departments to maintain internal integration and coordination.[38] An integrating department usually has more authority than a task force and may even be given some budgetary control by the organization.

In general, the greater the degree of interdependence, the more attention the organization must devote to coordination. When interdependence is pooled or simple sequential, the managerial hierarchy or rules and procedures are often sufficient. When more complex forms of sequential or simpler forms of reciprocal interdependence exist, liaisons or task forces may be more useful. When reciprocal interdependence is complex, task forces or integrating departments are needed. Of course, the manager must also rely on her or his own experience and insights when choosing coordination techniques for the organization. Moreover, informal interaction among people throughout the organization can also serve to effectively coordinate activities (recall the *Technology Toolkit* earlier in this chapter).

Electronic Coordination

Recent advances of electronic information technology are also providing useful mechanisms for coordination. E-mail, for example, makes it easier for people to communicate with one another. This communication, in turn, enhances coordination. Similarly, many people in organizations today use electronic scheduling, at least some of which is accessible to others. Hence, if someone needs to set up a meeting with two colleagues, he can often check their electronic schedules to determine their availability, making it easier to coordinate their activities.

Local networks, increasingly managed by hand-held electronic devices, are also making it easier to coordinate activities. Bechtel, for example, now requires its contractors, subcontractors, and suppliers to use a common web-based communication system to improve coordination among their myriad activities. The firm estimates that this improved coordination technology routinely saves it thousands of dollars on every big construction project it undertakes.

concept
CHECK

What are the three kinds of interdependence that necessitate coordination?

In the future, do you think electronic coordination will eliminate the need for structural coordination?

Differentiating Between Positions

The last building block of organization structure is differentiating between line and staff positions in the organization. A ***line position*** is a position in the direct chain of command that is responsible for the achievement of an organization's goals. A ***staff position*** is intended to provide expertise, advice, and support for line positions. In many modern organizations these differences are beginning to disappear, and in a few the difference has been eliminated altogether. However, there are still sufficient meaningful differences to warrant discussion.

> **line position**
> A position in the direct chain of command that is responsible for the achievement of an organization's goals

> **staff position**
> A position intended to provide expertise, advice, and support for line positions

Differences Between Line and Staff

The most obvious difference between line and staff is purpose—line managers work directly toward organizational goals, whereas staff managers advise and assist. But other distinctions exist as well. One important difference is authority. Line authority is generally thought of as the formal or legitimate authority created by the organizational hierarchy. Staff authority is less concrete and may take a variety of forms. One form is *advise authority*. In this instance, the line manager can choose whether to seek or to avoid input from staff; and even when advice is sought, the line manager might still choose to ignore it.

Another form of staff authority is called *compulsory advice*. In this case, the line manager must consider the advice but can choose to heed it or ignore it. For example, the pope is expected to listen to the advice of the Sacred College of Cardinals when dealing with church doctrine, but he may follow his own beliefs when making decisions. Perhaps the most important form of staff authority is called *functional authority*—formal or legitimate authority over activities related to the staff member's specialty. For example, a human resource staff manager may have functional authority when there is a question of discrimination in hiring. Conferring functional authority is probably the most effective way to use staff positions because the organization is able to take advantage of specialized expertise while also maintaining a chain of command.

Administrative Intensity

Organizations sometimes attempt to balance their emphasis on line versus staff positions in terms of administrative intensity. **Administrative intensity** is the degree to which managerial positions are concentrated in staff positions. An organization with high administrative intensity is one with many staff positions relative to the number of line positions; low administrative intensity reflects relatively more line positions. Although staff positions are important in many different areas, they tend to proliferate unnecessarily. All else being equal, organizations would like to devote most of their human resource investment to line managers because, by definition, they contribute to the organization's basic goals. A surplus of staff positions represents a drain on an organization's cash and an inefficient use of resources.

Many organizations have taken steps over the past few years to reduce their administrative intensity by eliminating staff positions. CBS cut hundreds of staff positions at its New York headquarters, and IBM cut its corporate staff workforce from 7,000 to 2,300. Burlington Northern generates almost $7 billion in annual sales and manages a workforce of 43,000 with a corporate staff of only 77 managers. Ford and General Motors have both downsized dramatically through job cuts and plant closings.

administrative intensity
The degree to which managerial positions are concentrated in staff positions

concept
CHECK

What is the basic difference between line and staff positions?

Do you think an organization can function effectively with no staff whatsoever?

Summary of Learning Objectives and Key Points

1. Identify the basic elements of organizations.
   - Organizations are made up of a series of elements:
     - designing jobs
     - grouping jobs
     - establishing reporting relationships
     - distributing authority
     - coordinating activities
     - differentiating between positions.

2. Describe alternative approaches to designing jobs.
   - Job design is the determination of an individual's work-related responsibilities.
   - The most common form is job specialization.
   - Other alternatives include job rotation, job enlargement, job enrichment, the job characteristics approach, and work teams.

3. Discuss the rationale and the most common bases for grouping jobs into departments.
   - The most common bases for departmentalization are:
     - function
     - product
     - customer
     - location
   - Large organizations employ multiple bases of departmentalization at different levels.

4. Describe the basic elements involved in establishing reporting relationships.
   - Establishing reporting relationships starts with clarifying the chain of command.
   - The span of management partially dictates whether the organization is relatively tall or flat.
   - In recent years there has been a trend toward flatter organizations.

   - Several situational factors influence the ideal span.

5. Discuss how authority is distributed in organizations.
   - Distributing authority starts with delegation.
   - Delegation is the process by which the manager assigns a portion of his or her total workload to others.
   - Systematic delegation throughout the organization is decentralization.
   - Centralization involves keeping power and authority at the top of the organization.
   - Several factors influence the appropriate degree of decentralization.

6. Discuss the basic coordinating activities undertaken by organizations.
   - Coordination is the process of linking the activities of the various departments of the organization.
   - Pooled, sequential, or reciprocal interdependence among departments is a primary reason for coordination.
   - Managers can draw on several techniques to help achieve coordination.
   - Electronic coordination is becoming increasingly important.

7. Describe basic ways in which positions within an organization can be differentiated.
   - A line position is a position in the direct chain of command that is responsible for the achievement of an organization's goals.
   - A staff position provides expertise, advice, and support for line positions.
   - Administrative intensity is the degree to which managerial positions are concentrated in staff positions.

Discussion Questions

Questions for Review

1. Describe the five alternatives to job specialization. What is the advantage of each, as compared to specialization?
2. What is meant by unity of command? By the scalar principle? Can an organization have one without the other? Explain.
3. Describe the organizational structure that results from each of the different bases of departmentaliza-

   tion. What implications does each of these structures have with regard to the distribution of authority within the organization?
4. Explain the differences between line and staff positions. What are the advantages and disadvantages of high versus low administrative intensity?

Questions for Analysis

5. Some people have claimed that the increasing technological sophistication required by many of today's corporations has led to a return to job specialization. In your opinion, what would be the consequences of a sharp increase in job specialization? Consider both positive and negative outcomes in your answer.

6. Try to develop a different way to departmentalize your college or university, a local fast-food restaurant, a manufacturing firm, or some other organization. What might be the advantages of your form of organization?

7. Consider the list of jobs below. In your opinion, what is the appropriate span of management for each?

Describe the factors you considered in reaching your conclusion.

- A physician practices medicine in a privately owned clinic, while also supervising a number of professional nurses and office staff.
- An owner-manager of an auto body shop deals with customers and directs several experienced mechanics, and also trains and oversees the work of some unskilled laborers.
- A manager in an international advertising agency directs a team of professionals who are located in offices around the world.

Questions for Application

8. Consider a job you have held. (Or, if you have not held a job, interview a worker.) Using the job characteristics approach, assess that job's core dimensions. Then describe how the core dimensions led to critical psychological states and, ultimately, to personal and work outcomes.

9. Use the Internet to locate organization charts for five different organizations. (Or use data from the Inter-

net to draw the organization charts yourself.) Look for similarities and differences among them and try to account for what you find.

10. Contact two very different local organizations (retailing firm, manufacturing firm, church, civic club, and so on) and interview top managers to develop organization charts for each organization. How do you account for the similarities and differences between them?

Building Effective Conceptual Skills

Exercise Overview

Conceptual skills refer to a person's abilities to think in the abstract. This exercise calls on your conceptual skills to address questions about appropriate span of management.

Exercise Background

Early management scholars believed that there was one optimal span of management or that an optimal span of management could be determined by looking at just one or a very few variables. Today, however, most experts agree that the optimal span of management depends on a number of complex questions. Discovery of the optimal span of management is important in ensuring an adequate, but not stifling, level of supervision, but it can be difficult to calculate.

Exercise Task

With the background information above as context, do the following:

1. Survey ten workers and managers about the span of management used in their workplaces. Notice the variation in the answers.

2. Choose one of these individuals for further investigation. Interview him or her to obtain information about the type of work he or she does, how much interaction with supervisors is required, how skilled the workers are, and other factors affecting the determination of optimal span of management. (See Table 11.1 for guidance.)

3. Does the span of management in use make sense, given the information you obtained in your answer to question 2? Why or why not?

4. If the span of management seems to be appropriate, what are some likely outcomes the organization might experience? If the span seems inappropriate, what are some likely outcomes?

Building Effective Diagnostic Skills

Exercise Overview

Diagnostic skills are the skills that enable a manager to visualize the most appropriate response to a situation. This exercise will enable you to develop your diagnostic skills as they relate to issues of centralization and decentralization in an organization.

Exercise Background

Managers often find it necessary to change the degree of centralization or decentralization in their organization. Begin this exercise by reflecting on two very different scenarios. In scenario A, assume that you are the top manager in a large organization. The organization has a long and well-known history of being very centralized. For valid reasons beyond the scope of this exercise, assume that you have decided to make the firm much more decentralized. For scenario B, assume the exact opposite situation; that is, assume that you are the top manager of a firm that has always used decentralization but has now decided to become much more centralized.

Exercise Task

With the background information above as context, do the following:

1. List the major barriers you see to implementing decentralization in scenario A.
2. List the major barriers you see to implementing centralization in scenario B.
3. Which scenario do you think would be easiest to implement in reality? In other words, is it likely to be easier to move from centralization to decentralization, or from decentralization to centralization? Why?
4. Given a choice of starting your own career in a firm that is either highly centralized or highly decentralized, which do you think you would prefer? Why?

CHAPTER CLOSING CASE

MANUFACTURING JOBS, JAPANESE-STYLE

Japanese auto manufacturers are winning the battle for U.S. buyers, dominating their U.S. competitors in sales, profits, and innovation. In 2005, Toyota's market share grew by 1.2 percent, or over 200,000 vehicles, while GM's dropped by 1.9 percent. Toyota's global profits for 2005 were $11 billion, as compared to a loss of $10.5 billion at GM. Toyota sells innovative, award-winning products including the popular Prius hybrid whereas GM's styles and technology are no longer cutting edge. Japanese firms use superior job designs and better reporting relationships while U.S. auto makers rely on narrowly defined, repetitive jobs and inflexible, hierarchical communications. These are only a few of the many complex reasons for the disparity.

Consider the Dundee, Michigan, engine-making plant of the Global Engine Manufacturing Alliance (GEMA), a partnership spearheaded by Japan-based Mitsubishi, along with DaimlerChrysler and Hyundai of South Korea. The Dundee plant is new and won't reach full capacity until early in 2007. It is clean and bright, contrasting sharply with traditional auto factories, which can be dark, greasy, and smelly. The plant makes extensive use of automation and robotics, reducing labor usage. The GEMA plant employs just 250 hourly workers to produce 840,000 engines. In the 1990s, it took 2,500 workers to staff a facility of similar size, and today, an older Detroit factory still used by Chrysler produces 350,000 engines with 750 workers.

Yet the most important innovation isn't the number of workers, but the way the work itself is designed. Instead of the phonebook-sized union contract used at traditional factories, the GEMA plant's contract with the United Auto Workers (UAW) is a slim booklet. Instead of the dozens of highly specialized jobs called for in most contracts, the GEMA contract uses just one category, "team member," for all hourly workers. Every worker learns every job on the assembly line, in keeping with the plant's philosophy of "anyone, anywhere, anything, anytime." Over the course of a typical 10-hour shift, one employee might be responsible for 15 to 20 different tasks.

Another Toyota joint venture, this time with GM, is organized around self-regulating teams. The plant was started in Fremont, California in 1984, by renovating a troubled GM plant and renaming it NUMMI, or New United Motor Manufacturing Inc. NUMMI's workforce makes decisions and assigns tasks without intervention from supervisors. Reporting relationships are not very hierarchical, and the most important communications take place with other team members, not superiors. Every worker's opinion is valued. For example, workers have the power to stop the assembly line when quality problems are occurring. Workers who stop the line are congratulated for taking responsibility for fixing the problems.

To coordinate the work, NUMMI relies on building strong personal relationships across workers. Supervisors have friendly interactions with employees and spend time socializing with them outside of work. These close relationships facilitate sharing information up, down, and across the management hierarchy. Toyota's approach builds strong bonds between managers and workers, so that the manager functions almost like a father to his employees.

In contrast, Honda uses teams extensively in its Marysville, Ohio, plant, but with an entirely different culture. Honda emphasizes innovation and encourages employees to challenge and question managers in order to make the company stronger. Honda's teams group quickly when a problem occurs and then are disbanded when the problem is solved. They are led by whichever team member has the most expertise relevant to the problem at hand. This approach works just as well as Toyota's in motivating workers.

The cooperation of U.S. labor unions is key to the success of the Japanese-style factories. The UAW is aware that auto makers are struggling in today's economy. It is showing support by being flexible about job design, allowing the same conditions that have been common in Japanese factories for years. U.S. workers are being flexible too and demonstrating that they prefer more autonomy and variety in their tasks.

Even Ford and GM, which are struggling to update their facilities and management practices, have taken notice of the Japanese auto makers' success. Both companies have announced plans to build a Japanese-style facility in the United States. Let's hope they don't miss the critical issue. The factory facility is important, the union contract is important, but most important is remaking the organization structure, starting with job design and coordination techniques.

CASE QUESTIONS

1. What benefits and potential disadvantages do U.S. firms gain from use of specialized job designs? What benefits and potential disadvantages do Japanese firms gain from use of broadly defined jobs?

2. Would you expect a traditional U.S. firm to have a relatively tall or flat organization structure? What about a traditional Japanese firm? Explain.

3. The Japanese firms described in the case use culture and relationships as coordination mechanisms. Do you think these are more or less effective than the more traditional coordination techniques mentioned in your text? Why or why not?

CASE REFERENCES

Gina Chon, "GM and Ford Lose More Market Share," *Wall Street Journal*, January 5, 2006, www.wsj.com on April 12, 2006; Roland Jones, "Road Ahead for Automotive Industry Still Bumpy," MSNBC website, www.msnbc.com on April 12, 2006; Micheline Maynard, "Carmakers' Big Idea: Think Small," *New York Times*, February 5, 2006, pp. BU 1, 7.

YOU MAKE THE CALL

Did You Hear the One About . . . Delegation?

1. What do you see as the potential major problems with the delegation relationship between talk show hosts and their writers?

2. Can you identify more traditional job settings that might have similar working relationships between managers and their subordinates?

3. In addition to delegation, how do other elements of organizing relate to the setting of talk show hosts?

4. How might new and emerging technologies change the working relationships between talk show hosts and their writers?

5. There are actually several different kinds of talk shows on television in addition to the late-night variety—afternoon shows, weekly shows, music talk shows, sports talk shows, and serious news shows, for example. Identify three such kinds of talk shows and comment on how delegation in those shows might be similar to and different from that used by the late-night shows.

Test Prepper

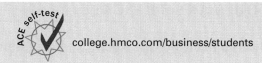

college.hmco.com/business/students

Choose the correct answer. Answers are found at the back of the book.

1. T   F   Using work teams is an alternative to using job specialization.

2. T   F   In an organization where employees have more than one boss, the scalar principle has been violated.

3. T   F   If all a manager's subordinates are in one location, the span of management will be more narrow than if the subordinates are spread out.

4. T   F   A shoe factory where workers start and complete each pair of shoes entirely by themselves and then place the shoes in the same large collection area is an example of pooled interdependence.

5. T   F   Rapid advances in information technology have made it more difficult for managers to coordinate in organizations.

6. Which of the following is NOT a basic element of organizational structure?
    A. Designing jobs
    B. Grouping jobs
    C. Establishing reporting relationships
    D. Increasing profitability
    E. Distributing authority

7. The job characteristics approach suggests that jobs should be diagnosed along each of the following core dimensions EXCEPT
    A. feedback.
    B. task identity.
    C. skill variety.
    D. autonomy.
    E. task specialization.

8. The unity of command principle suggests that
    A. each person within an organization should report to only one boss.

B. there must be an unbroken line of authority extending from the top to the bottom of an organization.
    C. managers are most effective when they maintain a wide span of control.
    D. the CEO of the organization must always have the final say in decision making.
    E. the chain of command should contain as few "links" or levels as possible.

9. Bhaskar needs to coordinate the efforts of a design team and a production team that are working on the same project. He doesn't have formal authority over either team. Which of the following structural coordination techniques would be the most appropriate for Bhaskar?
    A. Managerial hierarchy
    B. Rules and procedures
    C. Liaison role
    D. Task force
    E. Reciprocal interdependence

10. What is the most obvious difference between line and staff positions?
    A. Line managers work directly toward organizational goals; staff managers advise and assist.
    B. Line managers have higher administrative intensity than staff managers do.
    C. Line managers must heed the advice of staff managers, but staff managers can choose to ignore the advice of line managers.
    D. Line managers have less chance of being promoted up the organizational hierarchy than staff managers do.
    E. Line managers are an element of organizational structure; staff managers are an element of job design.

Managing Organization Design

FIRST THINGS FIRST

Organizing Abercrombie & Fitch

"Abercrombie's biggest weakness is that it is all about Mike."

—ROBERT BUCHANAN, ANALYST, A. G. EDWARDS & SONS

Abercrombie & Fitch is one of the "Three A's" of teen retailing, along with American Eagle and Aeropostale. These companies are the three largest specialty stores that cater to young adults ages 18 to 22. Look around any college classroom and you are likely to see more than one A&F cap, shirt, and pair of jeans. Abercrombie & Fitch is just one of the brands owned by the A&F Corporation, which follows a corporate strategy of related diversification. The corporation's other brands include Abercrombie, Hollister, and Ruehl 925. Based on its strategy, A&F Corporation probably should adopt a divisional, or M-form, organization design. Yet the company has chosen to retain a functional, or U-form, design instead.

Most companies pursuing a strategy of related diversification use an M-form structure. Limited Brands, a close competitor of Abercrombie & Fitch, uses a divisional structure, with units that include the Limited, Victoria's Secret, and Bath and Body Works. Each of these units can take advantage of staff support in

LEARNING OBJECTIVES

After studying this chapter, you should be able to:

1. Describe the basic nature of organization design.
2. Identify and explain the two basic universal perspectives on organization design.
3. Identify and explain several situational influences on organization design.
4. Discuss how an organization's strategy and its design are interrelated.
5. Describe the basic forms of organization design.
6. Describe emerging issues in organization design.

Abercrombie & Fitch is one of the nation's most successful retailers today. Its CEO, Michael Jeffries, uses a functional organization design in order to maintain tight control over the firm's operations.

areas such as logistics, information technology, real estate, and store design, but they can also make decisions autonomously. Abercrombie & Fitch, on the other hand, has a functional structure, with every employee assigned to a basic business function such as planning, purchasing, distribution, or stores. Executive or senior vice presidents head each of A&F's eight functions. The U-form helps employees to develop specialized, expert skills and makes it easy to coordinate within a function.

The company's history at least partially explains why A&F uses a functional structure. Abercrombie & Fitch was a high-end sporting goods retailer from 1892 until a bankruptcy in 1977. Oshman's, an up-and-coming sporting goods retailer, owned the brand for 11 years before selling it to Limited Brands. Limited Brands turned the brand into a preppy, upscale clothing retailer for young adults. In 1996, Limited Brands sold 16% of A&F through a public stock sale; its remaining shares were sold to the public in 1998, transforming A&F into a separate and independent company. Thus, the current incarnation of A&F started as a division of a larger firm. It makes sense, then, that its structure would look like the structure of one division of a multidivisional corporation.

Yet today, A&F has itself become a company that owns multiple brands. The Hollister brand sells similar types of merchandise as the A&F stores, but at a lower price point. The Abercrombie stores are targeted towards buyers from 10 to 14, while the Ruehl brand is for those 22 to 35 years old. As the firm has diversified, however, it hasn't switched to a different structure. The leadership of CEO Michael Jeffries is the reason. Stock analyst Robert Buchanan says, "Abercrombie's biggest weakness is that it is all about Mike."

Jeffries has headed A&F since it was part of Limited Brands and the firm is his life. He is always in control, personally approving every detail of store operations, even interviewing every advertising model himself. Jeffries is widely acknowledged to be a retailing genius. For example, when A&F faced a slump in sales in the late 1990s, Jeffries refused to lower prices. Instead, he raised them, confident that the higher costs would improve the brand's appeal. His strategy worked. He has also successfully predicted fashion trends for notoriously fickle teen buyers for more than 15 years. On the negative side, Jeffries' need for control coupled with the company's U-form structure has led to a leadership vacuum at A&F. The firm's functional managers do not usually have the broad experience and training to take over a general management position.

Abercrombie & Fitch started international expansion in 2006, increasing the complexity of the firm even more. So, is a U-form the right structure for Abercrombie & Fitch? That depends on how you feel about Michael Jeffries. If he can stay on top of trends and manage the growing company effectively, the U-form will be just fine. If the company loses him, or if he loses his grasp of the fashion preferences of today's teens, then the company may be wishing they had switched to an M-form structure years ago.[1]

One of the major ingredients in managing any business is the creation of an organization design to link the various elements that comprise the organization. There is a wide array of alternatives that managers in any given organization might select for its design. As we noted above, for instance, Abercrombie & Fitch uses a functional design but could also use a divisional design if Michael Jeffries chose to do so. In Chapter 11, we identified the basic elements that go into creating an organization. In this chapter, we explore how those elements can be combined to create an overall design for the organization. We first discuss the nature of organization design. We then describe early approaches aimed at identifying universal models of organization design. Situational factors, such as technology, environment, size, and life cycle, are then introduced. Next we discuss the relationship between an organization's strategy and its structure. Basic forms of organization design are described next. We conclude by presenting four emerging issues in organization design.

The Nature of Organization Design

What is organization design? In Chapter 11, we noted that job specialization and span of management are among the common elements of organization structure. We also described how the appropriate degree of specialization can vary, as can the appropriate span of management. Not really addressed, however, are questions of how specialization and span might be related to each other. For example, should a high level of specialization be matched with a certain span? And will different combinations of each work best with different bases of departmentalization? These and related issues are associated with questions of organization design.[2]

Organization design is the overall set of structural elements and the relationships among those elements used to manage the total organization. Thus organization design is a means to implement strategies and plans to achieve organizational goals.[3] As we discuss organization design, keep in mind two important points. First, organizations are not designed and then left intact. Most organizations change almost continuously as a result of factors such as situations and people. (The processes of organization change are discussed in Chapter 13.) Second, organization design for larger organizations is extremely complex and has so many nuances and variations that descriptions of it cannot be a full and complete explanation.

organization design
The overall set of structural elements and the relationships among those elements used to manage the total organization

concept
CHECK

What is organization design? | *How does organization design relate to organization structure?*

Universal Perspectives on Organization Design

In Chapter 2, we made the distinction between *contingency* and *universal* approaches to solving management problems. Recall, for example, that universal perspectives try to identify the "one best way" to manage organizations, and contingency perspectives suggest that appropriate managerial behavior in a given situation depends on, or is contingent on, unique elements in that situation. The foundation of contemporary thinking about organization design can be traced back to two early universal perspectives: the bureaucratic model and the behavioral model.

Bureaucratic Model

We also noted in Chapter 2 that Max Weber, an influential German sociologist, was a pioneer of classical organization theory. At the core of Weber's writings was

Dealing with bureaucratic organizations can be frustrating if that bureaucracy is too rigid, inflexible, and unresponsive. In the aftermath of Hurricane Katrina, many stories emerged about how bureaucracies slowed recovery efforts. For instance, dozens of federally insured medical providers were blocked from helping the Gulf Coast recover from the storm because their medical liability protection didn't apply outside their own states. Dr. Alvin Jackson, who spent about 10 days in the New Orleans area after Hurricane Katrina, is one of the many healthcare professionals calling for changes before another major medical emergency occurs.

---

bureaucracy
A model of organization design based on a legitimate and formal system of authority

---

the bureaucratic model of organizations.[4] The Weberian perspective suggests that a **bureaucracy** is a model of organization design based on a legitimate and formal system of authority. Many people associate bureaucracy with "red tape," rigidity, and passing the buck. For example, how many times have you heard people refer disparagingly to "the federal bureaucracy"? And many U.S. managers believe that bureaucracy in the Chinese government is a major impediment to U.S. firms' ability to do business there.

Weber viewed the bureaucratic form of organization as logical, rational, and efficient. He offered the model as a framework to which all organizations should aspire—the "one best way" of doing things. According to Weber, the ideal bureaucracy exhibits five basic characteristics:

1. The organization should adopt a distinct division of labor, and each position should be filled by an expert.

2. The organization should develop a consistent set of rules to ensure that task performance is uniform.

3. The organization should establish a hierarchy of positions or offices that creates a chain of command from the top of the organization to the bottom.

4. Managers should conduct business in an impersonal way and maintain an appropriate social distance between themselves and their subordinates.

5. Employment and advancement in the organization should be based on technical expertise, and employees should be protected from arbitrary dismissal.

Perhaps the best examples of bureaucracies today are government agencies and universities. Consider, for example, the steps you must go through and the forms you must fill out to apply for admission to college, request housing, register each semester, change majors, submit a degree plan, substitute a course, and file for graduation. Even when paper is replaced with electronic media, the steps are often the same. The reason these procedures are necessary is that universities deal with large numbers of people who must be treated equally and fairly. Hence, rules, regulations, and standard operating procedures are needed. Large labor unions are also usually organized as bureaucracies.[5]

Some bureaucracies, such as the U.S. Postal Service, are trying to portray themselves as less mechanistic and impersonal. The strategy of the Postal Service is to become more service oriented as a way to fight back against competitors like Federal Express and UPS.

A primary strength of the bureaucratic model is that several of its elements (such as reliance on rules and employment based on expertise) do, in fact, often improve efficiency. Bureaucracies also help prevent favoritism (because everyone must follow the rules) and make procedures and practices very clear to everyone. Unfortunately, however, this approach also has several disadvantages. One major disadvantage is that the bureaucratic model results in inflexibility and rigidity. Once rules are created and put in place, making exceptions or changing them is often difficult. In addition, the bureaucracy often results in the neglect of human and social processes within the organization.

Behavioral Model

Another important universal model of organization design was the ***behavioral model***, which paralleled the emergence of the human relations school of management thought. Rensis Likert, a management researcher, studied several large organizations to determine what made some more effective than others.[6] He found that the organizations in his sample that used the bureaucratic model of design tended to be less effective than those that used a more behaviorally oriented model consistent with the emerging human relations movement—in other words, organizations that paid more attention to developing work groups and were more concerned about interpersonal processes.

Likert developed a framework that characterized organizations in terms of eight important processes: leadership, motivation, communication, interactions, decision making, goal setting, control, and performance goals. Likert believed that all organizations could be measured and categorized along a continuum associated with each of these dimensions. He argued that the basic bureaucratic form of organization, which he called a ***System 1 design***, anchored one end of each dimension. The characteristics of the System 1 organization in Likert's framework are summarized in the left column of Table 12.1.

Also summarized in the right column of this table are characteristics of Likert's other extreme form of organization design, called ***System 4 design***, based on the behavioral model. For example, a System 4 organization uses a wide array of motivational processes, and its interaction processes are open and extensive. Other distinctions between System 1 and System 4 organizations are equally obvious. Between the System 1 and System 4 extremes lie the System 2 and System 3 organizations. Likert argued that System 4 should be adopted by all organizations. He suggested that managers should emphasize supportive relationships, establish high performance goals, and practice group decision making to achieve a System 4 organization. Many organizations attempted to adopt the System 4 design during its period of peak popularity. General Motors, for instance, converted a plant in the Atlanta area from a System 2 to a System 4 organization. Over a period of three years, direct and indirect labor efficiency improved, as did tool breakage rates, scrap costs, and quality.[7]

Like the bureaucratic model, the behavioral approach has both strengths and weaknesses. Its major strength is that it emphasizes human behavior by stressing the value of an organization's employees. Likert and his associates thus paved the way for a more humanistic approach to designing organizations. Unfortunately, the behavioral approach also argues that there is one best way to design an organization—as a System 4. As we see, however, evidence is strong that there is no one best approach to organization design.[8] What works for one organization may not work for another, and what works for one organization may change as that organization's situation changes. Hence, universal models like bureaucracy and System 4 have been largely supplanted by newer models that take contingency factors into account. In the next section, we identify a number of factors that help determine the best organization design for a particular situation.

> *behavioral model*
> A model of organization design consistent with the human relations movement and stressing attention to developing work groups and concern with interpersonal processes

> *System 1 design*
> Similar to the bureaucratic model

> *System 4 design*
> Similar to behavioral model

---

concept
CHECK

Distinguish between the bureaucratic model and the behavioral model of organization design.

Why do you think managers have often been concerned with identifying the "one best way" of doing something?

Table 12.1

SYSTEM 1 AND SYSTEM 4 ORGANIZATIONS

The behavioral model identifies two extreme types of organization design called System 1 and System 4. The two designs vary in eight fundamental processes. The System 1 design is considered to be somewhat rigid and inflexible.

System 1 Organization	System 4 Organization
1. Leadership process includes no perceived confidence and trust. Subordinates do not feel free to discuss job problems with their superiors, who in turn do not solicit their ideas and opinions.	1. Leadership process includes perceived confidence and trust between superiors and subordinates in all matters. Subordinates feel free to discuss job problems with their superiors, who in turn solicit their ideas and opinions.
2. Motivational process taps only physical, security, and economic motives through the use of fear and sanctions. Unfavorable attitudes toward the organization prevail among employees.	2. Motivational process taps a full range of motives through participatory methods. Attitudes are favorable toward the organization and its goals.
3. Communication process is such that information flows downward and tends to be distorted, inaccurate, and viewed with suspicion by subordinates.	3. Communication process is such that information flows freely throughout the organization—upward, downward, and laterally. The information is accurate and undistorted.
4. Interaction process is closed and restricted. Subordinates have little effect on departmental goals, methods, and activities.	4. Interaction process is open and extensive. Both superiors and subordinates are able to affect departmental goals, methods, and activities.
5. Decision process occurs only at the top of the organization; it is relatively centralized.	5. Decision process occurs at all levels through group processes; it is relatively decentralized.
6. Goal-setting process is located at the top of the organization; discourages group participation.	6. Goal-setting process encourages group participation in setting high, realistic objectives.
7. Control process is centralized and emphasizes fixing of blame for mistakes.	7. Control process is dispersed throughout the organization and emphasizes self-control and problem solving.
8. Performance goals are low and passively sought by managers who make no commitment to developing the human resources of the organization.	8. Performance goals are high and actively sought by superiors who recognize the necessity for making a full commitment to developing, through training, the human resources of the organization.

Source: Adapted from Rensis Likert, *The Human Organization*, 1967. Copyright © 1967 The McGraw-Hill Companies, Inc. Reprinted with permission.

Situational Influences on Organization Design

situational view of organization design
Based on the assumption that the optimal design for any given organization depends on a set of relevant situational factors

The **situational view of organization design** is based on the assumption that the optimal design for any given organization depends on a set of relevant situational factors. In other words, situational factors play a role in determining the best organization design for any particular circumstance. As discussed in *Working with Diversity*, practices such as offshoring are often affected by situational factors. Four basic situational factors—technology, environment, size, and organizational life cycle—are discussed here. Another strategy is described in the next section.

Core Technology

technology
Conversion processes used to transform inputs into outputs

Technology consists of the conversion processes used to transform inputs (such as materials or information) into outputs (such as products or services). Most

Working with Diversity

How to Offshore—and When Not to

Computer programmers in the Philippines, molecular biologists in Russia, customer service agents in India—outsourcing is bringing workers from around the world into U.S. corporations. When U.S. firms "offshore," that is, hire foreign firms to perform a business function, they alter their organization structures and increase diversity.

"In theory, it is becoming possible to buy, off the shelf, practically any function you need to run a company," says *BusinessWeek* writer Pete Engardio. Companies today choose which functions they will perform based on their value-creation capabilities. Some outsourcing processes are dizzying in their complexity. Drivers for Penske Truck Leasing send their paper logs to Mexico for data entry. Workers in Hyderabad, India, analyze and report the results to Penske's U.S. managers.

Sometimes, offshoring succeeds brilliantly, benefiting the contractor as well as the U.S. firm and local community. PCMC is a Wisconsin firm that designs and makes paper packaging. It often lost customers because its small engineering shop could not create new designs fast enough. The company could not afford to hire more engineers until it entered into an offshoring contract with an Indian company that built a 160-engineer center to support PCMC. The result? More orders and hiring in Wisconsin.

Offshoring seems to work best for manufacturing, technical, or financial functions. It can be a problem when there must be significant interaction between foreign contract personnel and U.S. customers or employees. Language and culture differences can make communication difficult, especially when using e-mail or the phone. For example, 1-800-Flowers tried outsourcing customer calls to India, with disastrous results. Florists not only have to process orders, they also console the grieving, offer interior design tips, and serve as relationship counselors. Indian workers simply did not understand the psychology of flower buying in the United States, and sales dropped.

Instead, 1-800-Flowers turned to "homeshoring," or hiring at-home contract workers. Homeshoring employees are more expensive than overseas contractors, but less expensive than company employees. Homeshoring workers connect with U.S. customers, and they alleviate concerns about private data going overseas. U.S. managers know it costs six times more to replace a customer as to keep him. If it keeps customers happy, saying no to offshoring may be the most cost-effective solution of all.

References: Michelle Conlin, "Call Centers in the Rec Room," *BusinessWeek*, January 23, 2006, www.businessweek.com on April 13, 2006; Pete Engardio, "The Future of Outsourcing," *BusinessWeek*, January 30, 2006, pp. 50–58; Manjeet Kripalani, "Spreading the Gospel," *BusinessWeek*, March 6, 2006, pp. 46–47.

---

organizations use multiple technologies, but an organization's most important one is called its *core technology*. Although most people visualize assembly lines and machinery when they think of technology, the term can also be applied to service organizations. For example, an investment firm like Vanguard uses technology to transform investment dollars into income in much the same way that Union Carbide uses natural resources to manufacture chemical products.

The link between technology and organization design was first recognized by Joan Woodward.[9] Woodward studied 100 manufacturing firms in southern England. She collected information about such aspects as the history of each organization, its manufacturing processes, its forms and procedures, and its financial performance. Woodward expected to find a relationship between the size of an organization and its design, but no such relationship emerged. As a result, she began to seek other explanations for differences. Close scrutiny of the firms in her sample led her to recognize a potential relationship between technology and organization design. This follow up analysis led Woodward to first classify the organizations according to their technology. Three basic forms of technology were identified by Woodward:

1. *Unit or small-batch technology.* The product is custom-made to customer specifications or produced in small quantities. Organizations using this form of technology include a tailor shop like Brooks Brothers (custom suits), a printing shop like Kinko's (business cards, company stationery), and a photography studio.

2. *Large-batch or mass-production technology.* The product is manufactured in assembly-line fashion by combining component parts into another part or finished product. Examples include automobile manufacturers like Subaru, appliance makers like Whirlpool Corporation, and electronics firms like Philips.

3. *Continuous-process technology.* Raw materials are transformed to a finished product by a series of machine or process transformations. The composition of the materials themselves is changed. Examples include petroleum refineries like ExxonMobil and Shell, and chemical refineries like Dow Chemical and Hoechst AG.

These forms of technology are listed in order of their assumed levels of complexity. In other words, unit or small-batch technology is presumed to be the least complex and continuous-process technology the most complex. Woodward found that different configurations of organization design were associated with each technology.

As technology became more complex in Woodward's sample, the number of levels of management increased (that is, the organization became taller). The executive span of management also increased, as did the relative size of its staff component. The supervisory span of management, however, first increased and then decreased as technology became more complex, primarily because much of the work in continuous-process technologies is automated. Fewer workers are needed, but the skills necessary to do the job increase. These findings are consistent with the discussion of the span of management in Chapter 11—the more complex the job, the narrower the span should be.

At a more general level of analysis, Woodward found that the two extremes (unit or small-batch and continuous-process) tended to be very similar to Likert's System 4 organization, whereas the middle-range organizations (large-batch or mass-production) were much more like bureaucracies or System 1. The large-batch and mass-production organizations also had a higher level of specialization.[10] Finally, she found that organizational success was related to the extent to which organizations followed the typical pattern. For example, successful continuous-process organizations tended to be more like System 4 organizations, whereas less-successful firms with the same technology were less like System 4 organizations.

Thus technology clearly appears to play an important role in determining organization design. As future technologies become more diverse and complex, managers will have to be even more aware of technologies' impact on the design of organizations. For example, the increased use of robotics may necessitate alterations in organization design to better accommodate different assembly methods. Likewise, increased usage of new forms of information technology will almost certainly cause organizations to redefine the nature of work and the reporting relationships among individuals.[11]

Environment

In addition to the various relationships described in Chapter 3, environmental elements and organization design are specifically linked in a number of ways.[12] The first widely recognized analysis of environment–organization design linkages was provided by Tom Burns and G. M. Stalker.[13] Like Woodward, Burns and Stalker worked in England. Their first step was identifying two extreme forms of organizational environment: stable (one that remains relatively constant over time) and unstable (subject to uncertainty and rapid change). Next they studied the designs of organizations in each type of environment. Not surprisingly, they found that organizations in stable environments tended to have a different kind of design than did organizations in unstable environments. The two kinds of design that emerged were called mechanistic and organic organization.

A *mechanistic organization*, quite similar to the bureaucratic or System 1 model, was most frequently found in stable environments. Free from uncertainty, organizations structured their activities in rather predictable ways by means of rules, specialized jobs, and centralized authority. Mechanistic organizations are also quite similar to bureaucracies. Although no environment is completely stable, Abercrombie & Fitch and Wendy's use mechanistic designs. Each A&F store, for example, has prescribed methods for store design and merchandise-ordering processes. No deviations are allowed from these methods. An *organic organization*, on the other hand, was most often found in unstable and unpredictable environments, in which constant change and uncertainty usually dictate a much higher level of fluidity and flexibility. Motorola (facing rapid technological change) and Limited Brands (facing constant change in consumer tastes) both use organic designs. A manager at Motorola, for example, has considerable discretion over how work is performed and how problems can be solved.

These ideas were extended in the United States by Paul R. Lawrence and Jay W. Lorsch.[14] They agreed that environmental factors influence organization design but believed that this influence varies between different units of the same organization. In fact, they predicted that each organizational unit has its own unique environment and responds by developing unique attributes. Lawrence and Lorsch suggested that organizations could be characterized along two primary dimensions.

One of these dimensions, *differentiation*, is the extent to which the organization is broken down into subunits. A firm with many subunits is highly differentiated; one with few subunits has a low level of differentiation. The second dimension, *integration*, is the degree to which the various subunits must work together in a coordinated

> " Networks are becoming the locus for innovation. Firms . . . are more porous and decentralized. "
>
> Walter Powell, Stanford professor
> (*BusinessWeek*, June 20, 2005, p. 81)

mechanistic organization
Similar to the bureaucratic or System 1 model, most frequently found in stable environments

organic organization
Very flexible and informal model of organization design, most often found in unstable and unpredictable environments

An organization's environment can affect how it should be designed. Starbucks works to balance mechanistic and organic design characteristics as it expands into international markets. It relies on mechanistic standardization to ensure product and quality service everywhere. But it also uses organic properties to accommodate local tastes and preferences. Heavily flavored coffees such as Caramel Macchiato are popular at this Puerto Rican store, but are not as popular in Japan. The firm's operating procedures as well as its supply chain are used to help Starbucks achieve this balance.

differentiation
Extent to which the organization is broken down into subunits

integration
Degree to which the various subunits must work together in a coordinated fashion

organizational size
Total number of full-time or full-time-equivalent employees

fashion. For example, if each unit competes in a different market and has its own production facilities, they may need little integration. Lawrence and Lorsch reasoned that the degree of differentiation and integration needed by an organization depends on the stability of the environments that its subunits face.

Organizational Size

The size of an organization is yet another factor that affects its design.[15] Although several definitions of size exist, we define **organizational size** as the total number of full-time or full-time-equivalent employees. A team of researchers at the University of Aston in Birmingham, England, believed that Woodward had failed to find a size-structure relationship (which was her original expectation) because almost all of the organizations she studied were relatively small (three-fourths had fewer than 500 employees).[16] Thus they decided to undertake a study of a wider array of organizations to determine how size and technology both individually and jointly affect an organization's design.

Their primary finding was that technology did in fact influence structural variables in small firms, probably because all of their activities tend to be centered on their core technologies. In large firms, however, the strong technology-design link broke down, most likely because technology is not as central to ongoing activities in large organizations. The Aston studies yielded a number of basic generalizations: When compared to small organizations, large organizations tend to be characterized by higher levels of job specialization, more standard operating procedures, more rules, more regulations, and a greater degree of decentralization. Wal-Mart is a good case in point. The firm expects to continue its dramatic growth for the foreseeable future, adding as many as 800,000 new jobs in the next few years. But, as it grows, the firm acknowledges that it will have to become more decentralized for its first-line managers to stay in tune with their customers.[17]

Organizational Life Cycle

Of course, size is not constant. As we noted in Chapter 10, for example, some small businesses are formed but soon disappear. Others remain as small, independently operated enterprises as long as their owner-manager lives. A few, like Dell Computer, JetBlue, and Starbucks, skyrocket to become organizational giants. And occasionally large organizations reduce their size through layoffs or divestitures. For example, Navistar is today far smaller than was its previous incarnation as International Harvester Company.

organizational life cycle
Progression through which organizations evolve as they grow and mature

Although no clear pattern explains changes in size, many organizations progress through a four-stage **organizational life cycle**.[18] The first stage is the *birth* of the organization. The second stage, *youth,* is characterized by growth and the expansion of organizational resources. *Midlife* is a period of gradual growth evolving eventually into stability. Finally, *maturity* is a period of stability, perhaps eventually evolving into decline.

Managers must confront a number of organization design issues as the organization progresses through these stages. In general, as an organization passes from one stage to the next, it becomes bigger, more mechanistic, and more decentralized. It also becomes more specialized, devotes more attention to planning, and takes on an increasingly large staff component. Finally, coordination demands increase, formalization increases, organizational units become geographically more dispersed, and control systems become more extensive. Thus an organization's size and design are clearly linked, and this link is dynamic because of the organizational life cycle.[19]

Strategy and Organization Design

Another important determinant of an organization's design is the strategy adopted by its top managers.[20] In general, corporate and business strategies both affect organization design. Basic organizational functions such as finance and marketing can also affect organization design in some cases.[21]

Corporate-Level Strategy

As we noted in Chapter 8, an organization can adopt a variety of corporate-level strategies. Its choice will partially determine what type of design will be most effective. For example, a firm that pursues a single-product strategy likely relies on functional departmentalization and can use a mechanistic design. If either unrelated or related diversification is used to spur growth, managers need to decide how to arrange the various units within the organizational umbrella. For example, if the firm is using related diversification, there must be a high level of coordination among the various units to capitalize on the presumed synergistic opportunities inherent in this strategy. On the other hand, firms using unrelated diversification more likely rely on a strong hierarchical reporting system, so that corporate managers can better monitor the performance of individual units with the firm.

An organization that adopts the portfolio approach to implement its corporate-level strategies must also ensure that its design fits its strategy. For example, each strategic business unit may remain a relatively autonomous unit within the organization. But managers at the corporate level need to decide how much decision-making latitude to give the head of each unit (a question of decentralization), how many corporate-level executives are needed to oversee the operations of various units (a question of span of management), and what information, if any, is shared among the units (a question of coordination).[22]

Business-Level Strategy

Business-level strategies affect the design of individual businesses within the organization as well as the overall organization itself. An organization pursuing a defender strategy, for example, is likely to be somewhat tall and centralized, have narrow spans of management, and perhaps take a functional approach to departmentalization. Thus it may generally follow the bureaucratic approach to organization design.

International organization design is becoming increasingly important for all large companies. Even a quintessential American firm like the Walt Disney Company must deal with theme parks in four countries and licensing agreements around the world. Rajat Jain, center, poses with Disney "stars" after their arrival in Mumbai, India. The characters will perform live in 24 shows in 6 different Indian cities as part of their six-nation promotional tour in the Asia-Pacific region. And as Disney's global empire continues to expand, continuous attention to organization design issues will be needed.

In contrast, a prospecting type of organization is more likely to be flatter and decentralized. With wider spans of management, it tries to be very flexible and adaptable in its approach to doing business. A business that uses an analyzer strategy is likely to have an organization design somewhere between these two extremes (perhaps being a System 2 or 3 organization). Given that a reactor is essentially a strategic failure, its presumed strategy is probably not logically connected to its design.

Generic competitive strategies can also affect organization design. A firm using a differentiation strategy, for example, may structure departments around whatever it is using as a basis for differentiating its products (such as marketing in the case of image or manufacturing in the case of quality). A cost leadership strategy necessitates a strong commitment to efficiency and control. Thus such a firm is more centralized as it attempts to control costs. And a firm using a focus strategy may design itself around the direction of its focus (location departmentalization if its focus is geographic region, customer departmentalization if its focus is customer groups).

Organizational Functions

The relationship between an organization's functional strategies and its design is less obvious and may be subsumed under corporate or business-level concerns. If the firm's marketing strategy calls for aggressive marketing and promotion, separate departments may be needed for advertising, direct sales, and promotion. If its financial strategy calls for low debt, it may need only a small finance department. If production strategy calls for manufacturing in diverse locations, organization design arrangements need to account for this geographic dispersion. Human resource strategy may call for greater or lesser degrees of decentralization as a way to develop skills of new managers at lower levels in the organization. And research and development strategy may dictate various designs for managing the R&D function itself. A heavy commitment to R&D, for example, may require a separate unit with a vice president in charge. A lesser commitment to R&D may be achieved with a director and a small staff.[23]

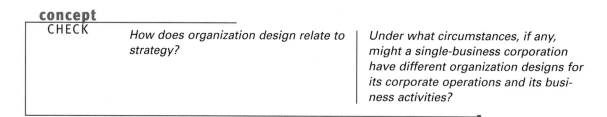

concept CHECK

How does organization design relate to strategy? | Under what circumstances, if any, might a single-business corporation have different organization designs for its corporate operations and its business activities?

Basic Forms of Organization Design

Because technology, environment, size, life cycle, and strategy can all influence organization design, it should come as no surprise that organizations adopt many different kinds of designs. Most designs, however, fall into one of four basic categories. Others are hybrids based on two or more of the basic forms.

Functional (U-Form) Design

functional (U-form) design
Based on the functional approach to departmentalization

The ***functional design*** is an arrangement based on the functional approach to departmentalization as detailed in Chapter 11. This design has been termed the

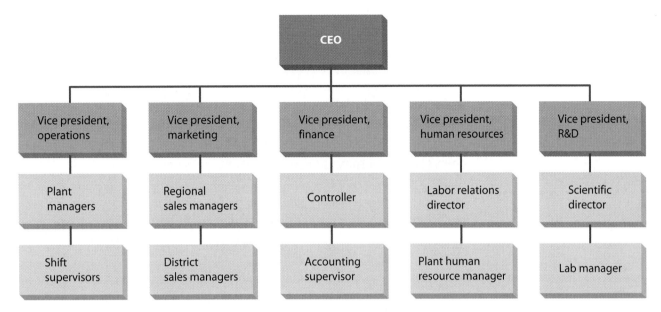

Figure 12.1

FUNCTIONAL OR U-FORM DESIGN FOR A SMALL MANUFACTURING COMPANY

The U-form design is based on functional departmentalization. This small manufacturing firm uses managers at the vice presidential level to coordinate activities within each functional area of the organization. Note that each functional area is dependent on the others.

U form (for unitary) by the noted economist Oliver E. Williamson.[24] Under the U-form arrangement, the members and units in the organization are grouped into functional departments such as marketing and production.

For the organization to operate efficiently in this design, there must be considerable coordination across departments. This integration and coordination are most commonly the responsibility of the CEO and members of senior management. Figure 12.1 shows the U-form design applied to the corporate level of a small manufacturing company. In a U-form organization, none of the functional areas can survive without the others. Marketing, for example, needs products from operations to sell and funds from finance to pay for advertising. The WD-40 Company, which makes a popular lubricating oil, and the McIlhenny Company, which makes Tabasco sauce, are both examples of firms that use the U-form design.

In general, this approach shares the basic advantages and disadvantages of functional departmentalization. Thus it allows the organization to staff all important positions with functional experts and facilitates coordination and integration. On the other hand, it also promotes a functional, rather than an organizational, focus and tends to promote centralization. And, as we noted in Chapter 11, functionally based designs are most commonly used in small organizations because an individual CEO can easily oversee and coordinate the entire organization. As an organization grows, the CEO finds staying on top of all functional areas increasingly difficult.

Conglomerate (H-Form) Design

Another common form of organization design is the **conglomerate,** or **H-form,** approach.[25] The **conglomerate design** is used by an organization made up of a

> **conglomerate (H-form) design**
> Used by an organization made up of a set of unrelated businesses

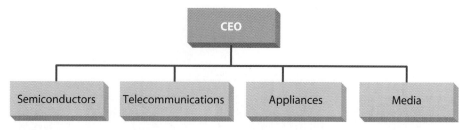

Figure 12.2

CONGLOMERATE (H-FORM) DESIGN AT SAMSUNG

Samsung Electronics Company, a South Korean firm, uses the conglomerate form of organization design. This design, which results from a strategy of unrelated diversification, is a complex one to manage. Managers find that comparing and integrating activities among the dissimilar operations are difficult. Companies may abandon this design for another approach, such as the M-form design.

set of unrelated businesses. Thus the H-form design is essentially a holding company that results from unrelated diversification. (The *H* in this term stands for holding.)

This approach is based loosely on the product form of departmentalization (see Chapter 11). Each business or set of businesses is operated by a general manager who is responsible for its profits or losses, and each general manager functions independently of the others. Samsung Electronics Company, a South Korean firm, uses the H-form design. As illustrated in Figure 12.2, Samsung consists of four basic business groups. Other firms that use the H-form design include General Electric (aircraft engines, appliances, broadcasting, financial services, lighting products, plastics, and other unrelated businesses) and Tenneco (pipelines, auto parts, financial services, and other unrelated businesses).

In an H-form organization, a corporate staff usually evaluates the performance of each business, allocates corporate resources across companies, and shapes decisions about buying and selling businesses. The basic shortcoming of the H-form design is the complexity associated with holding diverse and unrelated businesses. Managers usually find comparing and integrating activities across a large number of diverse operations difficult. Research by Michael Porter suggests that many organizations following this approach achieve only average-to-weak financial performance.[26] Thus, although some U.S. firms are still using the H-form design, many have also abandoned it for other approaches.

Divisional (M-Form) Design

In the divisional design, which is becoming increasingly popular, a product form of organization is also used; in contrast to the H-form, however, the divisions are related. Thus the **divisional design**, or **M-form** (for multidivisional), is based on multiple businesses in related areas operating within a larger organizational framework. This design results from a strategy of related diversification.

Some activities are extremely decentralized down to the divisional level; others are centralized at the corporate level.[27] For example, as shown in Figure 12.3, Limited Brands uses this approach. Each of its divisions is headed by a general manager and operates with reasonable autonomy, but the divisions also coordinate their

divisional (M-form) design
Based on multiple businesses in related areas operating within a larger organizational framework

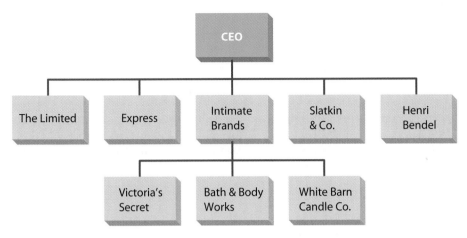

Figure 12.3

MULTIDIVISIONAL (M-FORM) DESIGN AT LIMITED BRANDS

Limited Brands uses the multidivisional approach to organization design. Although each unit operates with relative autonomy, all units function in the same general market. This design resulted from a strategy of related diversification. Other firms that use M-form designs include PepsiCo and the Walt Disney Company.

activities as is appropriate. Other firms that use this approach are the Walt Disney Company (theme parks, movies, and merchandising units, all interrelated) and Hewlett-Packard (computers, printers, scanners, electronic medical equipment, and other electronic instrumentation).

The opportunities for coordination and shared resources represent one of the biggest advantages of the M-form design. Limited Brand's market research and purchasing departments are centralized. Thus a buyer can inspect a manufacturer's entire product line, buy some designs for The Limited stores, others for Express, and still others for Henri Bendel. The M-form design's basic objective is to optimize internal competition and cooperation. Healthy competition for resources among divisions can enhance effectiveness, but cooperation should also be promoted. Research suggests that the M-form organization that can achieve and maintain this balance will outperform large U-form and all H-form organizations.[28]

Matrix Design

The **matrix design**, another common approach to organization design, is based on two overlapping bases of departmentalization.[29] The foundation of a matrix is a set of functional departments. A set of product groups, or temporary departments, is then superimposed across the functional departments. Employees in a matrix are simultaneously members of a functional department (such as engineering) and of a project team.

Figure 12.4 shows a basic matrix design. At the top of the organization are functional units headed by vice presidents of engineering, production, finance, and marketing. Each of these managers has several subordinates. Along the side of the organization are a number of positions called *project manager*. Each project manager heads a project group composed of representatives or workers from the functional departments. Note from the figure that a matrix reflects a *multiple-command*

matrix design
Based on two overlapping bases of departmentalization

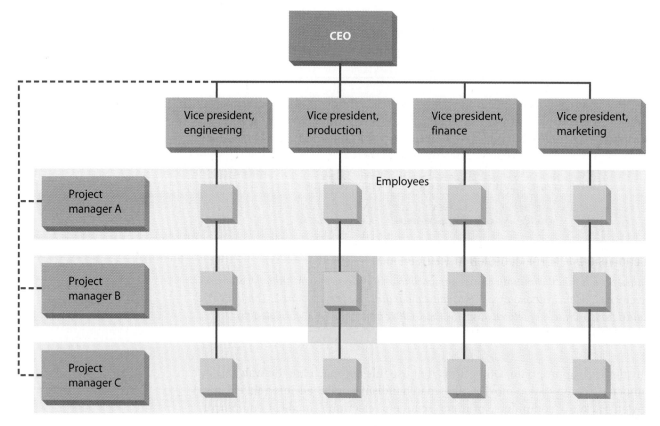

Figure 12.4

A MATRIX ORGANIZATION

A matrix organization design is created by superimposing a product form of departmentalization on an existing functional organization. Project managers coordinate teams of employees drawn from different functional departments. Thus a matrix relies on a multiple-command structure.

structure—any given individual reports to both a functional superior and one or more project managers.

The project groups, or teams, are assigned to designated projects or programs. For example, the company might be developing a new product. Representatives are chosen from each functional area to work as a team on the new product. They also retain membership in the original functional group. At any given time, a person may be a member of several teams as well as a member of a functional group. Ford used this approach in creating its popular Focus automobile. It formed a group called "Team Focus" made up of designers, engineers, production specialists, marketing specialists, and other experts from different areas of the company. This group facilitated getting a very successful product to the market at least a year earlier than would have been possible using Ford's previous approaches.

Martha Stewart also uses a matrix organization for her lifestyle business. The company was first organized broadly into media and merchandising groups, each of which has specific product and product groups. Layered on top of this structure are teams of lifestyle experts organized into groups such as cooking, crafts, weddings, and so forth. Each of these groups is targeted toward specific customer needs, but they work as necessary across all of the product groups. For example, a wedding expert might contribute to an article on wedding planning for a *Martha Stewart Living* magazine, contribute a story idea for a cable television program, and supply content for a Martha Stewart website. This same individual might also help select fabrics suitable for wedding gowns for retailing.[30]

Many other organizations have also used the matrix design. Notable among them are American Cyanamid, Monsanto, NCR, Chase Manhattan Bank, Prudential, General Motors, and several state and federal government agencies. Some organizations, however, such as Citibank and the Dutch firm Philips, adopted and then dropped the matrix design. Thus it is important to recognize that a matrix design is not always appropriate.

The matrix form of organization design is most often used in one of three situations.[31] First, a matrix may work when there is strong pressure from the environment. For example, intense external competition may dictate the sort of strong marketing thrust that is best spearheaded by a functional department, but the diversity of a company's products may argue for product departments. Second, a matrix may be appropriate when large amounts of information need to be processed. For example, creating lateral relationships by means of a matrix is one effective way to increase the organization's capacity for processing information. Third, the matrix design may work when there is pressure for shared resources. For example, a company with ten product departments may have resources for only three marketing specialists. A matrix design would allow all the departments to share the company's scarce marketing resources.

Both advantages and disadvantages are associated with the matrix design. Researchers have observed six primary advantages of matrix designs. First, they enhance flexibility because teams can be created, redefined, and dissolved as needed. Second, because they assume a major role in decision making, team members are likely to be highly motivated and committed to the organization. Third, employees in a matrix organization have considerable opportunity to learn new skills. A fourth advantage of a matrix design is that it provides an efficient way for the organization to take full advantage of its human resources. Fifth, team members retain membership in their functional unit so that they can serve as a bridge between the functional unit and the team, enhancing cooperation. Sixth, the matrix design gives top management a useful vehicle for decentralization. Once the day-to-day operations have been delegated, top management can devote more attention to areas such as long-range planning.

On the other hand, the matrix design also has some major disadvantages. Employees may be uncertain about reporting relationships, especially if they are simultaneously assigned to a functional manager and to several project managers. To complicate matters, some managers see the matrix as a form of anarchy in which they have unlimited freedom. Another set of problems is associated with the dynamics of group behavior. Groups take longer than individuals to make decisions, may be dominated by one individual, and may compromise too much. They may also get bogged down in discussion and not focus on their primary objectives. Finally, in a matrix, more time may also be required for coordinating task-related activities.[32]

Hybrid Designs

Some organizations use a design that represents a hybrid of two or more of the common forms of organization design.[33] For example, an organization may have five related divisions and one unrelated division, making its design a cross between an M-form and an H-form. Indeed, few companies use a design in its pure form; most firms have one basic organization design as a foundation for managing the business but maintain sufficient flexibility so that temporary or permanent modifications can be made for strategic purposes. Ford, for example, used the matrix approach to design the Focus and the newest Mustang, but the company is basically a U-form organization showing signs of moving to an M-form design. As we noted earlier, any combination of factors may dictate the appropriate form of design for any particular company.

concept
CHECK

| What are the basic forms of organization design? | Which basic organization designs are the most and the least clearly linked with strategy? |

Emerging Issues in Organization Design

In today's complex and ever-changing environment, it should come as no surprise that managers continue to explore and experiment with new forms of organization design. Many organizations today are creating designs for themselves that maximize their ability to adapt to changing circumstances and to a changing environment. They try to accomplish this by not becoming too compartmentalized or too rigid. As we noted earlier, bureaucratic organizations are hard to change, slow, and inflexible. To avoid these problems, then, organizations can try to be as different from bureaucracies as possible—relatively few rules, general job descriptions, and so forth. This final section highlights some of the more important emerging issues.[34]

The Team Organization

team organization
An approach to organization design that relies almost exclusively on project-type teams, with little or no underlying functional hierarchy

Some organizations today are using the ***team organization***, an approach to organization design that relies almost exclusively on project-type teams, with little or no underlying functional hierarchy. Within such an organization, people float from project to project as necessitated by their skills and the demands of those projects. At Cypress Semiconductor, T. J. Rodgers refuses to allow the organization to grow so large that it cannot function this way. Whenever a unit or group starts getting too large, he simply splits it into smaller units. Consequently, all units within the organization are small. This allows them to change direction, explore new ideas, and try new methods without dealing with a rigid bureaucratic organizational context. Although few organizations have actually reached this level of adaptability, Apple Computer and Xerox are among those moving toward it.[35]

The Virtual Organization

virtual organization
One that has little or no formal structure

Closely related to the team organization is the virtual organization. A ***virtual organization*** is one that has little or no formal structure. Such an organization typically has only a handful of permanent employees and a very small staff and administrative headquarters facility. As the needs of the organization change, its managers bring in temporary workers, lease facilities, and outsource basic support services to meet the demands of each unique situation. As the situation changes, the temporary workforce changes in parallel, with some people leaving the organization and others entering. Facilities and the services subcontracted to others change as well. Thus the organization exists only in response to its needs. And, increasingly, virtual organizations are conducting most—if not all—of their businesses online.[36]

> "When a company is as spread out as [MySQL] you have to think of virtual ways to imitate the dynamics of what goes on in a more familiar employment situation."
>
> Thomas Basil, MySQL executive
> (*Fortune*, June 12, 2006, p. 136)

For example, Global Research Consortium is a virtual organization. GRC offers research and consulting services to firms doing business in Asia. As clients request various services, GRC's staff of three permanent employees subcontracts the work to an appropriate set of several dozen independent consultants and researchers with whom it has relationships. At any given time, therefore, GRC may have several projects under way and 20 or 30 people working on projects. As the projects change, so, too, does the composition of the organization.

The Learning Organization

Another recent approach to organization design is the so-called learning organization. Organizations that adopt this approach work to integrate continuous improvement with continuous employee learning and development. Specifically, a **learning organization** is one that works to facilitate the lifelong learning and personal development of all of its employees while continually transforming itself to respond to changing demands and needs.[37]

> *learning organization*
> One that works to facilitate the lifelong learning and personal development of all of its employees while continually transforming itself to respond to changing demands and needs

Although managers might approach the concept of a learning organization from a variety of perspectives, improved quality, continuous improvement, and performance measurement are frequent goals. The idea is that the most consistent and logical strategy for achieving continuous improvement is by constantly upgrading employee talent, skill, and knowledge. For example, if each employee in an organization learns one new thing each day and can translate that knowledge into work-related practice, continuous improvement will logically follow. Indeed, organizations that wholeheartedly embrace this approach believe that only through constant learning by employees can continuous improvement really occur.

In recent years, many different organizations have implemented this approach. For example, Shell Oil recently purchased an executive conference center north of its headquarters in Houston. The center boasts state-of-the-art classrooms and instructional technology, lodging facilities, a restaurant, and recreational amenities such as a golf course, swimming pool, and tennis courts. Line managers at the firm rotate through the Shell Learning Center, as the facility has been renamed, and serve as teaching faculty. Such teaching assignments last anywhere from a few days to several months. At the same time, all Shell employees routinely attend training programs, seminars, and related activities, all the while learning the latest information that they need to contribute more effectively to the firm. Recent seminar topics have ranged from time management, to implications of the Americans with Disabilities Act, to balancing work and family demands, to international trade theory.

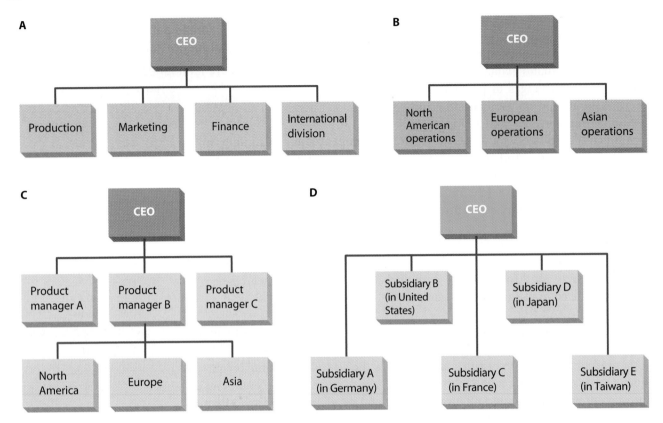

Figure 12.5

COMMON ORGANIZATION DESIGNS FOR INTERNATIONAL ORGANIZATIONS

Companies that compete in international markets must create an organization design that fits their own unique circumstances. These four general designs are representative of what many international organizations use. Each is derived from one of the basic forms of organization design.

Special Issues in International Organization Design

Another emerging issue in organization design is the trend toward the internationalization of business. As we discuss in Chapter 5, most businesses today interact with suppliers, customers, or competitors (or all three) from other countries. The relevant issue for organization design is how to design the firm to most effectively deal with international forces and compete in global markets. For example, consider a moderate-size company that has just decided to "go international." Should it set up an international division, retain its current structure and establish an international operating group, or make its international operations an autonomous subunit?[38]

Figure 12.5 illustrates four of the most common approaches to organization design used for international purposes. The design shown in A is the simplest, relying on a separate international division. Levi Strauss & Company uses this approach. The design shown in B, used by Ford Motor Company, is an extension of location departmentalization to international settings. An extension of product departmentalization, with each product manager being responsible for all product-related activities regardless of location, is shown in C. Finally, the design shown in D, most typical of larger multinational corporations, is an extension of the multidivisional structure with branches located in various foreign markets. Nestlé and Unilever use this type of design.

What is a team organization?

Do you think it is possible for a one-person operation, operating as a virtual organization, to grow large enough to compete with large businesses? Why or why not?

Summary of Learning Objectives and Key Points

1. Describe the basic nature of organization design.
   - Organization design is the overall set of structural elements and the relationships among those elements used to manage the total organization.

2. Identify and explain the two basic universal perspectives on organization design.
   - Two early universal models of organization design were the bureaucratic model and the behavioral model.
   - These models attempted to prescribe how all organizations should be designed.

3. Identify and explain several situational influences on organization design.
   - The situational view of organization design is based on the assumption that the optimal organization design is a function of situational factors.
   - Four important situational factors are:
     - technology
     - environment
     - size
     - organizational life cycle

4. Discuss how an organization's strategy and its design are interrelated.
   - An organization's strategy also helps shape its design.
   - In various ways, corporate- and business-level strategies both affect organization design.
   - Basic organizational functions like marketing and finance also play a role in shaping design.

5. Describe the basic forms of organization design.
   - Many organizations today adopt one of four basic organization designs:
     - functional (U-form)
     - conglomerate (H-form)
     - divisional (M-form)
     - matrix
   - Other organizations use a hybrid design derived from two or more of these basic designs.

6. Describe emerging issues in organization design.
   - Four emerging issues in organization design are
     - team organization
     - virtual organization
     - learning organization
     - international business organization

Discussion Questions

Questions for Review

1. Describe the three forms of core technology. Tell about the differences in organizational structure that occur in firms with each of the three types.
2. List the changes that occur as an organization grows in size. List the changes that occur as an organization ages over time. Are the two lists the same? Explain any differences you find.

3. Describe the basic forms of organization design. What are the advantages and disadvantages of each?
4. Compare and contrast the matrix organization and the team organization, telling about any similarities and differences.

Questions for Analysis

5. The business world today is increasingly complex and variable, in virtually every country and industry. Thus organizations must become more organic. What are some of the outcomes that companies will experience as they become more organic and less mechanistic? Be sure to include both positive and negative outcomes.

6. Each of the organization designs is appropriate for some firms but not for others. Describe the characteristics that a firm using the U form should have. Then do the same for the H-form, the M-form, and the matrix design. For each item, explain the relationship between that set of characteristics and the choice of organization design.

7. What are the benefits of using the learning organization approach to design? Now consider that, in order to learn, organizations must be willing to tolerate many mistakes because it is only through the effort of understanding mistakes that learning can occur. With this statement in mind, what are some of the potential problems with the use of the learning organization approach?

Questions for Application

8. Consider an organization (such as your workplace, a club or society, a sorority or fraternity, a church, and so on) of which you are a member. Describe some structural elements of that organization that reflect the bureaucratic model. Describe some elements that reflect the behavioral model. In your opinion, is that organization more bureaucratic or more behavioral in its structure? Why?

9. Use the Internet or library to investigate a corporation's strategy. Then use the Internet or library to obtain a description of the firm's organization design. Can you identify any links between the company's strategy and structure? Share your findings with the class.

10. What form of organization does your university or college use? What form does your city or town government use? What form do other organizations with which you are familiar use? What similarities and differences do you see? Explain your answers.

Building Effective Conceptual Skills

Exercise Overview

Conceptual skills refer to a person's abilities to think in the abstract. Conceptual skills are developed in this exercise, as you practice analyzing organizational structures.

Exercise Background

Looking at an organization chart allows one to understand the company's structure, such as its distribution of authority, its divisions, its levels of hierarchy, its reporting relationships, and more. The reverse is also true; that is, when one understands the elements of a company's structure, an organization chart can be drawn that reflects that structure. In this exercise, you will use the Internet to research a firm's structure and then draw the appropriate organization chart.

Exercise Task

1. Alone or with a partner, use the Internet to research a publicly traded U.S. firm in which you are interested. Gather information about the firm that will help you understand its structure. For example, if you researched Ford Motor Company, you would find information about different types of vehicles, different regions where Ford products are sold, different functions that are performed at Ford, and so on. (*Hint:* The firm's annual report is usually available online and usually contains a great deal of helpful information, particularly in the section that contains an editorial message from the chairman or CEO and in the section that summarizes financial information. "Segment" data also point to divisional structure in many cases.)

2. Draw an appropriate organization structure, based on your research.

3. Share your results with another group or with the class, justifying your decisions.

Building Effective Technical Skills

Exercise Overview

Technical skills are the skills necessary to accomplish or understand the specific work being done in an organization. This exercise asks you to develop technical skills related to understanding the impact of an organization's strategy on its structure.

Exercise Background

Assume that you are a manager of a firm that has developed a new, innovative system of personal transportation, such as the Segway HT. (If you are not familiar with the Segway, visit the website at **www.segway.com** and learn about the product.)

Exercise Task

Using the information about strategy given in each question below and your knowledge of the Segway product, choose the appropriate form of organization structure.

1. What would be the most appropriate organization structure if Segway's corporate-level strategy were to continue to produce a limited line of very similar products for sale in the United States?
2. What would be the most appropriate organization structure if Segway's corporate-level strategy were to continue to produce only its original product, but to sell it in Asia and Europe as well as North America?
3. What would be the most appropriate organization structure if Segway's corporate-level strategy were to move into related areas, using the innovations developed for the Segway to help design several other innovative products?
4. What would be the most appropriate organization structure if Segway's corporate-level strategy were to use its expertise in personal ground transportation to move into other areas, such as personal air or personal water transport?
5. What would be the most appropriate organization structure if Segway's corporate-level strategy were to use the funds generated by Segway sales to finance moves into several unrelated industries?
6. For each of the five strategies listed above, tell how that strategy influenced your choice of organization design.

CHAPTER CLOSING CASE

EBAY IS GROWING UP

In 1995, 28-year-old Pierre Omidyar conducted an intellectual experiment. "He launched eBay to experiment with how equal access to information and opportunities would affect the efficiency of a marketplace," according to the eBay website. Omidyar, a computer scientist, spent a weekend writing the software code that would permit online auctions. Enthusiastic response to his early efforts convinced Omidyar that somewhere, there was a buyer for every item.

He launched his site in 1995 and, two years later, changed the company's name to eBay.

The company's organization structure was the U-form, or functional, design that is typical of small businesses. Company presidents headed functional areas that included operations, finance, legal, and human resources. However, the most striking structural aspect of the startup was its reliance on a System 4 design, which emphasizes the importance of human resources and behavioral processes. Omidyar's personal values influenced the choice of a behavioral model for eBay. He wanted a company that let individuals be both buyer and seller, avoiding Big Business altogether. Omidyar envisioned his site as more than an auction space. eBay was intended to create an online community, similar to a small town. A behavioral model, with its lack of bureaucracy, democratic decision making, decentralization, open communication and interactions, and relationships of trust, was a perfect fit for Omidyar's vision.

eBay became wildly popular and grew rapidly. Omidyar stepped down as CEO in 1998, although he remained as chairman of the board of directors. He was replaced by Meg Whitman, a Harvard-trained MBA, management consultant, and manager in such Old Economy firms as Procter & Gamble, Disney, and Hasbro. Also in 1998, eBay held an initial public offering, becoming a publicly traded firm. As the company grew and matured, its organization design had to change too. New presidents were added to cover eBay's network of affiliated international sites, for example. New divisions were formed to manage PayPal, an online payment system, and Skype, an Internet phone service, when these businesses were acquired and integrated into eBay.

In addition, the reliance on a System 4 behavioral model was lessened, and the company became more bureaucratic. This change was due to a number of factors, including the growth of eBay, the change in leadership, and the involvement of outside investors. The company began to increase its reliance on rules and regulations, which were necessary to control the ever-larger number of buyers and sellers. Trust also became an issue. In eBay's early days, the rating system, based on buyer and seller user-generated performance ratings, communicated information that increased trust. However, users quickly found ways to exploit or manipulate the ratings system, and trust plummeted.

Additionally, eBay was sued for trademark infringement, as users posted text and photos that were owned by various companies. Other firms sued for fraud. Tiffany jewelers, for example, claimed that eBay was knowingly selling Tiffany knock-offs. eBay, with a culture of trust and a hands-off policy regarding the items sellers list, has not yet found an effective response to the property ownership issues.

For the first time, eBay was under pressure from investors to turn a profit. That led to cost-cutting measures and unpopular fee increases. One eBay seller criticized the company's lack of attention to sellers, saying, "The buyers seem far more important . . . than do the sellers. You cannot treat your base as a second class citizen and survive forever." Loss of motivation and low morale also began to spread among eBay employees. One former executive claims that working at eBay has become like working for Sears, referring to that firm's reputation for being an outdated and uninspiring organization.

eBay must find a way to grow, while still maintaining that "small-company" feel. Omidyar's company has changed a great deal already, and the firm must continue to evolve. Yet eBay must also be sensitive to the needs of buyers, sellers, investors, and outside companies.

Whitman and other top managers should carefully consider when and how they will update the organization design, which has a great impact on the culture and actions of the firm. Fortunately Whitman welcomes the opportunity. "I have one of the best jobs in cor-

porate America," she says. "It's this unique blend of commerce and community. The community of users is endlessly interesting and endlessly surprising. Every week, there is a different set of issues, a different challenge, something new to think about." This adolescent firm is gradually moving away from Omidyar's vision of community. eBay is in transition, growing up into one of the world's greatest online businesses.

CASE QUESTIONS

1. The online auction industry is fairly new and so it is rapidly changing in unpredictable ways. What impact would you expect this type of environment to have on an organization's design? Does eBay have the design you expect to see? Explain.

2. eBay today has a U-form, or functional, design. Will that change as the company grows? What kinds of changes do you think will occur?

3. eBay's current structure includes functional divisions as well as an international division. As eBay expands rapidly overseas, should the firm's organization structure change? If so, explain what changes will be needed. If not, explain why not.

CASE REFERENCES

Eryn Brown, "How Can a Dot-Com Be This Hot?" *Fortune*, January 21, 2002, www.cnnmoney.com on April 12, 2006; Adam Cohen, *The Perfect Store: Inside eBay* (Boston: Little, Brown, 2002); "Executive Team," eBay website, www.ebay.com on April 12, 2006; Robert D. Hof, "'The Constant Challenge' at eBay," *BusinessWeek*, June 30, 2004, www.businessweek.com on April 12, 2006.

YOU MAKE THE CALL

Organizing Abercrombie & Fitch

1. If you were hired to advise Michael Jeffries on A&F's organization design, what weaknesses and potential threats would you point out to him regarding the firm's current design?

2. What strengths would you identify for Jeffries?

3. Assuming you wanted a career in retailing, would you want to work for A&F? Why or why not?

4. If you worked at A&F part-time as a student, how might the firm's design affect your job?

5. It seems that mergers, acquisitions, and divestitures are commonplace in the retailing sector. Following such an event, does it make more sense to retain the current organization design for a while or to modify it right away? Why?

6. What differences might you expect to see between the organization designs used at traditional retailers like A&F and American Eagle versus online retailers such as Amazon and eBay?

Test Prepper

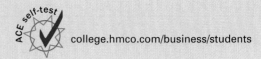
college.hmco.com/business/students

Choose the correct answer. Answers are found at the back of the book.

1. T   F   Another name for universal models of organization design is situational models of organization design.

2. T   F   A firm that pursues a single-product strategy will likely have a mechanistic design.

3. T   F   The divisional design, or M-form, results from a strategy of related diversification.

4. T   F   The matrix design is a hybrid of two other forms of organization design.

5. T   F   The simplest organization design for an international firm is to set up a separate international division.

6. Max Weber developed the bureaucratic model of organization design. Which of the following was not an element of Weber's model?

    A. Distinct division of labor
    B. "Red tape" and rigidity
    C. Consistent set of rules
    D. Clear chain of command
    E. Impersonal social relations

7. Which of the following is NOT a characteristic of a System 1 organization from Rensis Likert's behavioral model?

    A. Leadership is not based on confidence and trust.
    B. Motivation is based on economic motives.
    C. Decision making takes place at all levels.
    D. Communication flows downward.
    E. Subordinates have little effect on departmental goals.

8. All of the following occur as an organization becomes larger EXCEPT

    A. it becomes more decentralized.
    B. it becomes more specialized.
    C. it devotes more time to planning.
    D. it takes on an increasingly large staff component.
    E. it becomes less formalized.

9. In the functional (U-form) organization design, who holds the responsibility for integrating and coordinating across departments?

    A. The employees
    B. The lower-level managers
    C. The staff managers
    D. The middle-level managers
    E. The CEO

10. When Serena was made CEO of her company, she publicly vowed to facilitate the lifelong personal development of all the company's employees and committed to continually transform the organization to respond to changing demands and needs. Serena's intent is to create a(n)

    A. virtual organization.
    B. team organization.
    C. learning organization.
    D. international organization.
    E. System organization.

chapter 13

Managing Organization Change and Innovation

LEARNING OBJECTIVES

After studying this chapter, you should be able to:

1. Describe the nature of organization change, including forces for change and planned versus reactive change.

2. Discuss the steps in organization change and how to manage resistance to change.

3. Identify and describe major areas of organization change and discuss the assumptions, techniques, and effectiveness of organization development.

4. Describe the innovation process, forms of innovation, the failure to innovate, and how organizations can promote innovation.

FIRST THINGS FIRST

Innovative Ikea

"Designing beautiful-but-expensive products is easy. Designing products that are inexpensive and functional is a huge challenge."

—JOSEPHINE RYDBERG-DUMONT, PRESIDENT, IKEA SWEDEN

Ever craved a couch? Enough to camp outside a furniture store for a week? That's what customers did when modern design retailer Ikea opened a store in Atlanta. The brand is so popular that thousands lined up on grand opening day. In April 2006, Ikea's new Tokyo store, the first in Japan, attracted 35,000 customers on its first day. A store opening in Hong Kong created a day-long traffic jam.

In some ways Ikea is like a cult. Customers are fiercely loyal to the company's unique products that combine high style and low cost. Founder Ingvar Kamprad, who grew up on a small Swedish farm, started Ikea in 1943. He was just 17 when he began selling inexpensive small goods. Over time, his product line evolved to include furniture made by local carpenters. It took 16 years for Kamprad to open his first store, in 1957. After that slow start, Ikea's growth

Ikea has become a retailing powerhouse through innovation in products and store design and layout.

increased gradually at first but then more rapidly. The company now encompasses 231 stores in 33 countries with 15 new locations annually.

Ikea's vision statement is "Good design and function at low prices," so one important element of their business model is style. Scandinavian designers produce clean-lined, contemporary pieces. Ikea's style emphasizes light, natural wood tones and bright, clear colors. Curvy shapes, unusual materials, and whimsical designs predominate. Furniture is designed to fit in a variety of spaces and adapt to any decorating scheme. For example, one of Ikea's most popular products worldwide is the Klippan sofa, a simple two-seat couch covered in white cotton with silvery steel legs. Bright slipcovers customize the look.

The other important element of Ikea's business model is affordability. Kamprad is a frugal man who busses to work, although he is a multibillionaire and the richest man alive. His passion for reducing costs has led Ikea on a relentless quest for the best bargain. By looking for the lowest cost deal, whether made in-house or from a global supplier, Ikea drives prices down, sometimes by as much as 50 percent. The Klippan sofa, for example, cost $395 in 1985 but retails for $199 today.

Ikea's emphasis on design and low cost is innovative. "Designing beautiful-but-expensive products is easy," says Ikea Sweden president Josephine Rydberg-Dumont. "Designing products that are inexpensive and functional is a huge challenge."

Ikea is innovative in shaping buyer preferences. It encourages consumers to stop thinking of furniture as a durable good. Ikea manager Christian Mathieu claims that holding on to older furniture is a habit that makes no sense. "Americans change their spouse as often as their dining-room tables, about 1.5 times in a lifetime," he says. Of course, this risk-taking approach increases furniture sales for Ikea.

Product innovations go beyond the merely stylistic. Ikea supports the natural environment by using renewable soft woods like pine in most of its goods and publishing recycling instructions for every item. To save energy in transportation, most of the items are "knocked down," or shipped as parts that buyers assemble at home. Cheaper woods and knock-down design also save Ikea money, enabling lower prices and higher profit margins. Ikea's operating margin is 10 percent, above industry average and twice the level of rival Pier 1.

Even Ikea's store design is innovative. Displays are unique and fun. Customers walk through the store, writing down the items they want on a company-supplied notepad. Then they find items themselves in a warehouse section of the store. Stores include extras that both pamper shoppers and keep them in the store longer, including in-store restaurants with Swedish treats and a supervised play area for children. After purchase, buyers rent Ikea-owned vans to cart home large items.

Ikea's popularity has led to imitation by low-cost competitors Target and Kmart, which created their own lines of trendy but affordable furniture. The company's continued success will rely on its ability to stay innovative and keep one step ahead of the rest of the industry. With a staff personally trained by Kamprad and corporate assets valued at more than $50 billion, Ikea is poised to do just that.[1]

Managers at Ikea are keeping the firm at the forefront of its industry through the astute management of innovation. The firm uses innovative product designs, innovative cost structures, innovative marketing practices, and innovative store layouts to grow and prosper. At a broader level, Ikea also embraces change. As we will see, understanding when and how to implement change is a vital part of management. This chapter describes how organizations manage change. We first examine the nature of organization change and identify the basic issues of managing change. We then identify and describe major areas of change, including business process change, a major type of change undertaken by many firms recently. We then examine organization development and conclude by discussing organizational innovation as a vital form of change dramatically illustrated by Ikea.

The Nature of Organization Change

Organization change is any substantive modification to some part of the organization.[2] Thus change can involve virtually any aspect of an organization: work schedules, bases for departmentalization, span of management, machinery, organization design, people themselves, and so on. It is important to keep in mind that any change in an organization may have effects extending beyond the actual area where the change is implemented. For example, when Northrop Grumman recently installed a new automated production system at one of its plants, employees were trained to operate new equipment, the compensation system was adjusted to reflect new skill levels, the span of management for supervisors was altered, and several related jobs were redesigned. Selection criteria for new employees were also changed, and a new quality control system was installed.[3] In addition, it is quite common for multiple organization change activities to be going on simultaneously.[4]

> **organization change**
> Any substantive modification to some part of the organization

Forces for Change

Why do organizations find change necessary? The basic reason is that something relevant to the organization either has changed or is likely to change in the foreseeable future. The organization therefore may have little choice but to change as well. Indeed, a primary reason for the problems that organizations often face is failure to anticipate or respond properly to changing circumstances. The forces that compel change may be external or internal to the organization.[5]

> "If one wishes to start a major change, a sea change, a person who stayed away from the mainstream, who is from a remote area, may be called for."
>
> Dr. Ryoji Chubachi, Sony President
> (*Fortune,* June 12, 2006, p. 81)

External Forces External forces for change derive from the organization's general and task environments. For example, two energy crises, an aggressive Japanese automobile industry, floating currency exchange rates, and floating international interest rates—all manifestations of the international dimension of the general environment—profoundly influenced U.S. automobile companies. New rules of production and competition forced them to dramatically alter the way they do business. In the political area, new laws, court decisions, and regulations affect organizations. The technological dimension may yield new production techniques that the organization needs to explore. The economic dimension is affected by inflation, the cost of living, and money supplies. The sociocultural dimension, reflecting societal values, determines what kinds of products or services will be accepted in the market.

Because of its proximity to the organization, the task environment is an even more powerful force for change. Competitors influence an organization through

External forces are a common driver of change in organizations today. Pakistani pilot Ayesha Rabia Naveed, left, with her co-pilot Sadia Aziz, sit in the cockpit of a Pakistani International Airlines passenger plane in early 2006 in Islamabad, Pakistan. Airline officials reported that this was the first Pakistani passenger plane with a female pilot and all-woman crew to fly in this Islamic nation. An increased awareness of the value of and a new openness toward women in the workplace contributed to the airline changing its employment practices.

their price structures and product lines. When Dell lowers the prices it charges for computers, Gateway may have little choice but to follow suit. Because customers determine what products can be sold at what prices, organizations must be concerned with consumer tastes and preferences. Suppliers affect organizations by raising or lowering prices or changing product lines. Regulators can have dramatic effects on an organization. For example, if OSHA rules that a particular production process is dangerous to workers, it can force a firm to close a plant until it meets higher safety standards. Unions can force change when they negotiate for higher wages or go on strike.[6]

Internal Forces A variety of forces inside the organization may cause change. If top management revises the organization's strategy, organization change is likely to result. A decision by an electronics company to enter the home computer market or a decision to increase a ten-year product sales goal by 3 percent would occasion many organization changes. Other internal forces for change may be reflections of external forces. As sociocultural values shift, for example, workers' attitudes toward their job may also shift—and workers may demand a change in working hours or working conditions. In such a case, even though the force is rooted in the external environment, the organization must respond directly to the internal pressure it generates.[7]

Planned Versus Reactive Change

Some change is planned well in advance; other change comes about as a reaction to unexpected events. **Planned change** is change that is designed and implemented in an orderly and timely fashion in anticipation of future events. **Reactive change** is a piecemeal response to circumstances as they develop. Because reactive change may be hurried, the potential for poorly conceived and executed change is increased. Planned change is almost always preferable to reactive change.[8]

Georgia-Pacific, a large forest products business, is an excellent example of a firm that went through a planned and well-managed change process. When A. D. Correll became CEO, he quickly became alarmed at the firm's high accident rate—9 serious injuries per 100 employees each year, and 26 deaths during the most recent five-year period. Although the forest products business is inherently dangerous, Correll believed that the accident rate was far too high and set out on a major change effort to improve things. He and other top managers developed a multistage change program intended to educate workers about safety, improve safety equipment in the plant, and eliminate a long-standing part of the firm's culture that made injuries almost a badge of courage. As a result, Georgia-Pacific achieved the best safety record in the industry, with relatively few injuries.[9]

planned change
Change that is designed and implemented in an orderly and timely fashion in anticipation of future events

reactive change
A piecemeal response to circumstances as they develop

On the other hand, Caterpillar was caught flat-footed by a worldwide recession in the construction industry, suffered enormous losses, and took several years to recover. Had managers at Caterpillar anticipated the need for change earlier, they might have been able to respond more quickly. Similarly, Kodak had to cut 12,000 jobs in reaction to sluggish sales and profits.[10] Again, better anticipation might have forestalled those job cuts. The importance of approaching change from a planned perspective is reinforced by the frequency of organization change. Most companies or divisions of large companies implement some form of moderate change at least every year and one or more major changes every four to five years.[11] Managers who sit back and respond only when they have to are likely to spend a lot of time hastily changing and rechanging things. A more effective approach is to anticipate forces urging change and plan ahead to deal with them.[12]

concept
CHECK

What are the primary forces for change? Provide several examples of each.

Is it possible to eliminate the likelihood of reactive change altogether? Why or why not?

Managing Change in Organizations

Organization change is a complex phenomenon. A manager cannot simply wave a wand and implement a planned change like magic. Instead, any change must be systematic and logical to have a realistic opportunity to succeed.[13] To carry this off, the manager needs to understand the steps of effective change and how to counter employee resistance to change.[14]

Steps in the Change Process

Researchers have over the years developed a number of models or frameworks outlining steps for change.[15] The Lewin model was one of the first, although a more comprehensive approach is usually more useful in today's complex business environment.

The Lewin Model　Kurt Lewin, a noted organizational theorist, suggested that every change requires three steps.[16] The first step is *unfreezing*—individuals who will be affected by the impending change must be led to recognize why the change is necessary. Next, the *change itself* is implemented. Finally, *refreezing* involves reinforcing and supporting the change so that it becomes a part of the system.[17] For example, one of the changes Caterpillar faced in response to the recession noted earlier involved a massive workforce reduction. The first step (unfreezing) was convincing the United Auto Workers to support the reduction because of its importance to long-term effectiveness. After this unfreezing was accomplished, 30,000 jobs were eliminated (implementation). Then Caterpillar worked to improve its damaged relationship with its workers (refreezing) by guaranteeing future pay hikes and promising no more cutbacks. As interesting as Lewin's model is, it unfortunately lacks operational specificity. Thus a more comprehensive perspective is often needed.

A Comprehensive Approach to Change　The comprehensive approach to change takes a systems view and delineates a series of specific steps that often leads to

Figure 13.1

STEPS IN THE CHANGE PROCESS

Managers must understand how and why to implement change. A manager who, when implementing change, follows a logical and orderly sequence like the one shown here is more likely to succeed than a manager whose change process is haphazard and poorly conceived.

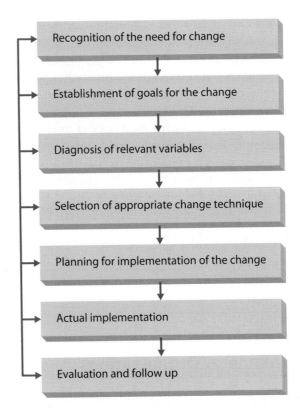

Recognition of the need for change

Establishment of goals for the change

Diagnosis of relevant variables

Selection of appropriate change technique

Planning for implementation of the change

Actual implementation

Evaluation and follow up

successful change. This expanded model is illustrated in Figure 13.1. The first step is recognizing the need for change. Reactive change might be triggered by employee complaints, declines in productivity or turnover, court injunctions, sales slumps, or labor strikes. Recognition may simply be managers' awareness that change in a certain area is inevitable. For example, managers may be aware of the general frequency of organizational change undertaken by most organizations and recognize that their organization should probably follow the same pattern. The immediate stimulus might be the result of a forecast indicating new market potential, the accumulation of a cash surplus for possible investment, or an opportunity to achieve and capitalize on a major technological breakthrough. Managers might also initiate change today because indicators suggest that it will be necessary in the near future.[18]

Managers must next set goals for the change. To increase market share, to enter new markets, to restore employee morale, to settle a strike, and to identify investment opportunities all might be goals for change. Third, managers must diagnose what brought on the need for change. Turnover, for example, might be caused by low pay, poor working conditions, poor supervisors, or employee dissatisfaction. Thus, although turnover may be the immediate stimulus for change, managers must understand its causes to make the right changes.

The next step is to select a change technique that will accomplish the intended goals. If turnover is caused by low pay, a new reward system may be needed. If the cause is poor supervision, interpersonal skills training may be called for. (Various change techniques are summarized later in this chapter.) After the appropriate technique has been chosen, its implementation must be planned. Issues to consider include the costs of the change, its effects on other areas of the organization, and the degree of employee participation appropriate for the situation. If the change is implemented as planned, the results should then be evaluated. If the change was intended to reduce turnover, managers must check turnover after the change has been in effect for a while. If turnover is still too high, other changes may be necessary.[19]

Understanding Resistance to Change

Another element in the effective management of change is understanding the resistance that often accompanies change.[20] Managers need to know why people resist change and what can be done about their resistance. When Westinghouse first provided all of its managers with personal computers, most people responded favorably. One manager, however, resisted the change to the point where he began leaving work every day at noon! It was some time before he began staying in the office all day again. Such resistance is common for a variety of reasons.[21]

Uncertainty   Perhaps the biggest cause of employee resistance to change is uncertainty. In the face of impending change, employees may become anxious and nervous. They may worry about their ability to meet new job demands, they may think that their job security is threatened, or they may simply dislike ambiguity. Nabisco was once the target of an extended and confusing takeover battle, and during the entire time, employees were nervous about the impending change. The *Wall Street Journal* described them this way: "Many are angry at their leaders and fearful for their jobs. They are swapping rumors and spinning scenarios for the ultimate outcome of the battle for the tobacco and food giant. Headquarters staffers in Atlanta know so little about what's happening in New York that some call their office 'the mushroom complex,' where they are kept in the dark."[22]

Threatened Self-Interests   Many impending changes threaten the self-interests of some managers within the organization. A change might diminish their power or influence within the company, so they fight it. Managers at Sears once developed a plan calling for a new type of store. The new stores would be somewhat smaller than a typical Sears store and would not be located in large shopping malls. Instead, they would be located in smaller strip centers. They would carry clothes and other "soft goods," but not hardware, appliances, furniture, or automotive products. When executives in charge of the excluded product lines heard about the plan, they raised such strong objections that the plan was cancelled.

Different Perceptions   A third reason that people resist change is due to different perceptions. A manager may make a decision and recommend a plan for change on the basis of her own assessment of a situation. Others in the organization may resist the change because they do not agree with the manager's assessment or perceive the situation differently.[23] Executives at 7-Eleven battled this problem as they attempted to enact a major organizational change. The corporation wanted to take its convenience stores a bit "upscale" and begin selling fancy fresh foods to go, the newest hardcover novels, some gourmet products, and higher-quality coffee. But many franchisees balked because they saw this move as taking the firm away from its core blue-collar customers.

Feelings of Loss   Many changes involve altering work arrangements in ways that disrupt existing social networks. Because social relationships are important, most people resist any change that might adversely affect those relationships. Other intangibles threatened by change include power, status, security, familiarity with existing procedures, and self-confidence.

Overcoming Resistance to Change

Of course, a manager should not give up in the face of resistance to change. Although there are no sure-fire cures, there are several techniques that at least have the potential to overcome resistance.[24]

Participation

Participation is often the most effective technique for overcoming resistance to change. Employees who participate in planning and implementing a change are better able to understand the reasons for the change. Uncertainty is reduced, and self-interests and social relationships are less threatened. Having had an opportunity to express their ideas and assume the perspectives of others, employees are more likely to accept the change gracefully. A classic study of participation monitored the introduction of a change in production methods among four groups in a Virginia pajama factory.[25] The two groups that were allowed to fully participate in planning and implementing the change improved significantly in their productivity and satisfaction, relative to the two groups that did not participate. 3M Company recently attributed $10 million in cost savings to employee participation in several organization change activities.[26]

Education and Communication   Educating employees about the need for and the expected results of an impending change should reduce their resistance. If open communication is established and maintained during the change process, uncertainty can be minimized. Caterpillar used these methods during many of its cutbacks to reduce resistance. First, it educated UAW representatives about the need for and potential value of the planned changes. Then management told all employees what was happening, when it would happen, and how it would affect them individually.

Facilitation   Several facilitation procedures are also advisable. For instance, making only necessary changes, announcing those changes well in advance, and allowing time for people to adjust to new ways of doing things can help reduce resistance to change.[27] One manager at a Prudential regional office spent several months systematically planning a change in work procedures and job design. He then became too hurried, coming in over the weekend with a work crew and rearranging the office layout. When employees walked in on Monday morning, they were hostile, anxious, and resentful. What was a promising change became a disaster, and the manager had to scrap the entire plan.

Force-Field Analysis   Although force-field analysis may sound like something out of a *Star Trek* movie, it can help overcome resistance to change. In almost any change situation, forces are acting for and against the change. To facilitate the change, managers start by listing each set of forces and then trying to tip the balance so that the forces facilitating the change outweigh those hindering the change. It is especially important to try to remove or at least minimize some of the forces acting against the change. Suppose, for example, that General Motors is considering a plant closing as part of a change. As shown in Figure 13.2, three factors are reinforcing the change: GM needs to cut costs, it has excess capacity, and the plant

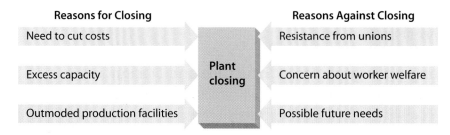

Figure 13.2

FORCE-FIELD ANALYSIS FOR PLANT CLOSING AT GENERAL MOTORS

A force-field analysis can help a manager facilitate change. A manager able to identify forces acting both for and against a change can see where to focus efforts to remove barriers to change (such as offering training and relocation to displaced workers). Removing the forces against the change can at least partially overcome resistance.

has outmoded production facilities. At the same time, there is resistance from the UAW, concern for workers being put out of their jobs, and a feeling that the plant might be needed again in the future. GM might start by convincing the UAW that the closing is necessary by presenting profit and loss figures. It could then offer relocation and retraining to displaced workers. And it might shut down the plant and put it in "mothballs" so that it can be renovated later. The three major factors hindering the change are thus eliminated or reduced in importance.[28]

Why do people resist change? How can managers help overcome this resistance?

How do you personally feel about change? Which, if any, of the techniques described above would help you be more receptive to change?

Areas of Organization Change

We noted earlier that change can involve virtually any part of an organization. In general, however, most change interventions involve organization structure and design, technology and operations, or people. The most common areas of change within each of these broad categories are listed in Table 13.1. In addition, many

Organization Structure and Design	Technology and Operations	People
Job design	Information technology	Abilities and skills
Departmentalization	Equipment	Performance
Reporting relationships	Work processes	Perceptions
Authority distribution	Work sequences	Expectations
Coordination mechanisms	Control systems	Attitudes
Line-staff structure	Enterprise resource planning (ERP)	Values
Overall design		
Culture		
Human resource management		

Table 13.1

AREAS OF ORGANIZATION CHANGE

Organization change can affect any part, area, or component of an organization. Most change, however, fits into one of three general areas: organization structure and design, technology and operations, and people.

organizations have gone through massive and comprehensive business process change programs.

Changing Organization Structure and Design

Organization change might be focused on any of the basic components of organization structure or on the organization's overall design. Thus the organization might change the way it designs its jobs or its bases of departmentalization. Likewise, it might change reporting relationships or the distribution of authority. For example, we noted in Chapter 11 the trend toward flatter organizations. Coordination mechanisms and line-and-staff configurations are also subject to change. On a larger scale, the organization might change its overall design. For example, a growing business could decide to drop its functional design and adopt a divisional design. Or it might transform itself into a matrix. Changes in culture usually involve the structure and design of the organization as well (recall that we discussed changing culture back in Chapter 3). Finally, the organization might change any part of its human resource management system, such as its selection criteria, its performance appraisal methods, or its compensation package.[29]

Changing Technology and Operations

Technology is the conversion process used by an organization to transform inputs into outputs. Because of the rapid rate of all technological innovation, technological changes are becoming increasingly important to many organizations. Table 13.1 lists several areas where technological change is likely to be experienced. One important area of change today revolves around information technology. The adoption and institutionalization of information technology innovations is almost constant in most firms today. Sun Microsystems, for example, adopted a very short-range planning cycle to be best prepared for environmental changes.[30] Another important form of technological change involves equipment. To keep pace with competitors, firms periodically find that replacing existing machinery and equipment with newer models is necessary.

A change in work processes or work activities may be necessary if new equipment is introduced or new products are manufactured. In manufacturing industries, the major reason for changing a work process is to accommodate a change in the materials used to produce a finished product. Consider a firm that manufactures battery-operated flashlights. For many years flashlights were made of metal, but now most are made of plastic. A firm might decide to move from metal to plastic flashlights because of consumer preferences, raw materials costs, or other reasons. Whatever the reason, the technology necessary to make flashlights from plastic differs importantly from that used to make flashlights from metal. Work process changes may occur in service organizations as well as in manufacturing firms. As traditional barbershops

Changing technology is a way of life in some parts of the world. For example, these commuters in Tokyo no longer need to purchase tickets to use the subway system. Instead, they simply flick a plastic card loaded with prepaid transfers through the turnstile ticket slot and move on. When they have used all of their transfers, they go to an automated vending machine and, using a credit card, reload their subway pass.

and beauty parlors are replaced by hair salons catering to both sexes, for example, the hybrid organizations have to develop new methods for handling appointments and setting prices.

A change in work sequence may or may not accompany a change in equipment or a change in work processes. Making a change in work sequence means altering the order or sequence of the workstations involved in a particular manufacturing process. For example, a manufacturer might have two parallel assembly lines producing two similar sets of machine parts. The lines might converge at one central quality control unit, where inspectors verify tolerances. The manager, however, might decide to change to periodic rather than final inspection. Under this arrangement, one or more inspections are established farther up the line. Work sequence changes can also be made in service organizations. The processing of insurance claims, for example, could be changed. The sequence of logging and verifying claims, requesting checks, getting countersignatures, and mailing checks could be altered in several ways, such as combining the first two steps or routing the claims through one person while another handles checks. Organizational control systems may also be targets of change.[31] For example, a firm attempting to improve the quality of its products might develop and implement a set of more rigorous and comprehensive quality-control procedures.

Finally, many businesses have been working to implement technological and operations change by installing and using complex and integrated software systems. Such systems—called *enterprise resource planning*—link virtually all facets of the business, making it easier for managers to keep abreast of related developments. **Enterprise resource planning,** or **ERP,** is a large-scale information system for integrating and synchronizing the many activities in the extended enterprise. In most cases these systems are purchased from external vendors who then tailor their products to the client's unique needs and requirements. Companywide processes—such as materials management, production planning, order management, and financial reporting—can all be managed via ERP. In effect, these are the processes that cut across product lines, departments, and geographic locations.

> *enterprise resource planning (ERP)*
> A large-scale information system for integrating and synchronizing the many activities in the extended enterprise

Developing the ERP system starts by identifying the key processes that need critical attention, such as supplier relationships, materials flows, or customer order fulfillment. The system could result, for instance, in sales processes' being integrated with production planning and then integrating both of these into the firm's financial accounting system. For example, a customer in Rome can place an order that is to be produced in Ireland, schedule it to be shipped via air cargo to Rome, and then have it picked up by a truck at the airport and delivered to the customer's warehouse by a specified date. All of these activities are synchronized by activities linkages in one massive database.

The ERP integrates all activities and information flows that relate to the firm's critical processes. It also keeps updated real-time information on their current status, reports recent past transactions and upcoming planned transactions, and provides electronic notices that action is required on some items if planned schedules are to be met. It coordinates internal operations with activities by outside suppliers and notifies business partners and customers of current status and upcoming deliveries and billings. It can integrate financial flows among the firm, its suppliers, its customers, and commercial bank deposits for up-to-the-minute status reports that can be used to create real-time financial reports at a moment's notice, rather than in the traditional one-month (or longer) time span for producing

Changing people's attitudes can be a slow but important process in any organization. For instance, the acceptance of women in the U.S. military has taken a long time, but now women such as U.S. Air Force Staff Sgt. Michelle Kelly, a technician with the 31st Maintenance Group, are becoming commonplace throughout the military. Kelly is part of the 555th Aerospace Ground Equipment Combat (AGE) Team at Aviano Air Base in Italy.

a financial statement. ERP's multilanguage capabilities also allow real-time correspondence in various languages to facilitate international transactions.

Changing People, Attitudes, and Behaviors

A third area of organization change has to do with human resources. For example, an organization might decide to change the skill level of its workforce. This change might be prompted by changes in technology or by a general desire to upgrade the quality of the workforce. Thus training programs and new selection criteria might be needed. The organization might also decide to improve its workers' performance level. In this instance, a new incentive system or performance-based training might be in order. *Reader's Digest* has attempted to implement significant changes in its workforce. For example, the firm eliminated 17 percent of its employees, reduced retirement benefits, and took away many of the "perks" (perquisites, or job benefits) that employees once enjoyed. Part of the reason for the changes was to instill in the remaining employees a sense of urgency and the need to adopt a new perspective on how they do their job.[32] Similarly, Saks Fifth Avenue recently changed its entire top management team as a way to breathe new life into the luxury retailer.[33]

Perceptions and expectations are also a common focus of organization change. Workers in an organization might believe that their wages and benefits are not as high as they should be. Management, however, might have evidence that shows the firm is paying a competitive wage and providing a superior benefit package. The change, then, would be centered on informing and educating the workforce about the comparative value of its compensation package. A common way to do this is to publish a statement that places an actual dollar value on each benefit provided and compares that amount to what other local organizations are providing their workers. Change might also be directed at employee attitudes and values. In many organizations today, managers are trying to eliminate adversarial relationships with workers and to adopt a more collaborative relationship. In many ways, changing attitudes and values is perhaps the hardest thing to do.

Changing Business Processes

Many organizations today have also gone through massive and comprehensive change programs involving all aspects of organization design, technology, and people. Although various descriptions are used, the terms currently in vogue for these changes are *business process change,* or *reengineering.* Specifically, **business process change**, or **reengineering**, is the radical redesign of all aspects of a business to achieve major gains in cost, service, or time.[34] ERP, as described above, is a common platform for changing business processes. However, business process change is a more comprehensive set of changes that goes beyond software and information systems.

business process change (reengineering)
The radical redesign of all aspects of a business to achieve major gains in cost, service, or time

Corning, for example, has undergone major reengineering over the last few years. Whereas the 150-year-old business once manufactured cookware and other durable consumer goods, it has transformed itself into a high-tech powerhouse making such products as the ultra-thin screens used in products like Palm Pilots and laptop computers.[35] Similarly, the dramatic overhauls of Kodak away from print film to other forms of optical imaging, of Yellow into a sophisticated freight delivery firm, and of UPS into a major international delivery giant all required business process changes throughout these organizations.

The Need for Business Process Change   Why are so many organizations finding it necessary to undergo business process change? We note in Chapter 2 that all systems, including organizations, are subject to entropy—a normal process leading to system decline. An organization is behaving most typically when it maintains the status quo, does not change in synch with its environment, and starts consuming its own resources to survive. In a sense, that is what happened to Kmart. In the early and mid-1970s, Kmart was in such a high-flying growth mode that it passed first J. C. Penney and then Sears to become the world's largest retailer. But then the firm's managers grew complacent and assumed that the discount retailer's prosperity would continue and that they need not worry about environmental shifts, the growth of Wal-Mart, and so forth—and entropy set in. The key is to recognize the beginning of the decline and immediately move toward changing relevant business processes. Major problems occur when managers either do not recognize the onset of entropy until it is well advanced or are complacent in taking steps to correct it.

Approaches to Business Process Change   Figure 13.3 shows general steps in changing business processes, or reengineering. The first step is setting goals and developing a strategy for the changes. The organization must know in advance what new business processes are supposed to accomplish and how those accomplishments will be achieved. Next, top managers must begin and direct the reengineering effort. If a CEO simply announces that business process change is to occur but does nothing else, the program is unlikely to be successful. But, if the CEO is

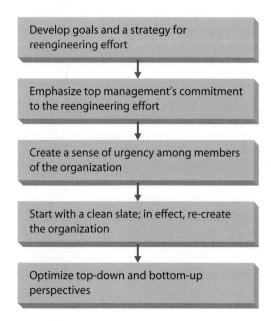

Figure 13.3
THE REENGINEERING PROCESS

Reengineering is a major redesign of all areas of an organization. To be successful, reengineering requires a systematic and comprehensive assessment of the entire organization. Goals, top management support, and a sense of urgency help the organization re-create itself and blend both top-level and bottom-up perspectives.

constantly involved in the process, underscoring its importance and taking the lead, business process change stands a much better chance of success.

Most experts also agree that successful business process change is usually accompanied by a sense of urgency. People in the organization must see the clear and present need for the changes being implemented and appreciate their importance. In addition, most successful reengineering efforts start with a new, clean slate. In other words, rather than assuming that the existing organization is a starting point and then trying to modify it, business process change usually starts by asking questions such as how customers are best served and competitors best neutralized. New approaches and systems are then created and imposed in place of existing ones.

Finally, business process change requires a careful blend of top-down and bottom-up involvement. On the one hand, strong leadership is necessary, but too much involvement by top management can make the changes seem autocratic. Similarly, employee participation is also important, but too little involvement by leaders can undermine the program's importance and create a sense that top managers do not care. Thus care must be taken to carefully balance these two countervailing forces. Our next section explores more fully one related but distinct approach called *organization development*.

Organization Development

We note in several places the importance of people and change. Beyond those change interests discussed above, a special area of interest that focuses almost exclusively on people is organization development (OD).

OD Assumptions   Organization development is concerned with changing attitudes, perceptions, behaviors, and expectations. More precisely, **organization development (OD)** is a planned effort that is organization-wide and managed from the top, intended to increase organizational effectiveness and health through planned interventions in the organization's process, using behavioral science knowledge.[36] The theory and practice of OD are based on several very important assumptions. The first is that employees have a desire to grow and develop. Another is that employees have a strong need to be accepted by others within the organization. Still another critical assumption of OD is that the total organization and the way it is designed will influence the way individuals and groups within the organization behave. Thus some form of collaboration between managers and their employees is necessary to (1) take advantage of the skills and abilities of the employees and (2) eliminate aspects of the organization that retard employee growth, development, and group acceptance. Because of the intense personal nature of many OD activities, many large organizations rely on one or more OD consultants (either full-time employees assigned to this function or outside experts hired specifically for OD purposes) to implement and manage their OD program.[37]

> *organization development (OD)*
> An effort that is planned, organization-wide, and managed from the top, intended to increase organizational effectiveness and health through planned interventions in the organization's process, using behavioral science knowledge

OD Techniques   Several kinds of interventions or activities are generally considered part of organization development.[38] Some OD programs may use only one or a few of these; other programs use several of them at once.

- *Diagnostic activities.* Just as a physician examines patients to diagnose their current condition, an OD diagnosis analyzes the current condition of an organization. To carry out this diagnosis, managers use questionnaires, opinion or attitude surveys, interviews, archival data, and meetings to assess various characteristics of the organization. The results of this diagnosis may generate profiles of the organization's activities, which can then be used to identify problem areas in need of correction.

- *Team building*. Team-building activities are intended to enhance the effectiveness and satisfaction of individuals who work in groups or teams and to promote overall group effectiveness. Given the widespread use of teams today, these activities have taken on increased importance. An OD consultant might interview team members to determine how they feel about the group; then an off-site meeting could be held to discuss the issues that surfaced and iron out any problem areas or member concerns. Caterpillar used team building as one method for changing the working relationships between workers and supervisors from confrontational to cooperative. An interesting new approach to team building involves having executive teams participate in group cooking classes to teach them the importance of interdependence and coordination.[39]

- *Survey feedback*. In survey feedback, each employee responds to a questionnaire intended to measure perceptions and attitudes (for example, satisfaction and supervisory style). Everyone involved, including the supervisor, receives the results of the survey. The aim of this approach is usually to change the behavior of supervisors by showing them how their subordinates view them. After the feedback has been provided, workshops may be conducted to evaluate results and suggest constructive changes.

- *Education*. Educational activities focus on classroom training. Although such activities can be used for technical or skill-related purposes, an OD educational activity typically focuses on "sensitivity skills"—that is, it teaches people to be more considerate and understanding of the people they work with. Participants often go through a series of experiential or role-playing exercises to learn better how others in the organization feel.

- *Intergroup activities*. The focus of intergroup activities is on improving the relationships between two or more groups. We noted in Chapter 11 that, as group interdependence increases, so do coordination difficulties. Intergroup OD activities are designed to promote cooperation or resolve conflicts that arise as a result of interdependence. Experiential or role-playing activities are often used to bring this about.

- *Third-party peacemaking*. Another approach to OD is through third-party peacemaking, which is most often used when substantial conflict exists within the organization. Third-party peacemaking can be appropriate on the individual, group, or organizational level. The third party, usually an OD consultant, uses a variety of mediation or negotiation techniques to resolve any problems or conflicts among individuals or groups.

- *Technostructural activities*. Technostructural activities are concerned with the design of the organization, the technology of the organization, and the interrelationship of design and technology with people on the job. A structural change such as an increase in decentralization, a job design change such as an increase in the use of automation, and a technological change involving a modification in work flow all qualify as technostructural OD activities if their objective is to improve group and interpersonal relationships within the organization.

- *Process consultation.* In process consultation, an OD consultant observes groups in the organization to develop an understanding of their communication patterns, decision-making and leadership processes, and methods of cooperation and conflict resolution. The consultant then provides feedback to the involved parties about the processes he or she has observed. The goal of this form of intervention is to improve the observed processes. A leader who is presented with feedback outlining deficiencies in his or her leadership style, for example, might be expected to change to overcome them.

- *Life and career planning.* Life and career planning helps employees formulate their personal goals and evaluate strategies for integrating their goals with the goals of the organization. Such activities might include specification of training needs and plotting a career map. General Electric has a reputation for doing an outstanding job in this area.

- *Coaching and counseling.* Coaching and counseling provide nonevaluative feedback to individuals. The purpose is to help people develop a better sense of how others see them and learn behaviors that will assist others in achieving their work-related goals. The focus is not on how the individual is performing today; instead, it is on how the person can perform better in the future.

- *Planning and goal setting.* More pragmatic than many other interventions are activities designed to help managers improve their planning and goal setting. Emphasis still falls on the individual, however, because the intent is to help individuals and groups integrate themselves into the overall planning process. The OD consultant might use the same approach as in process consultation, but the focus is more technically oriented, on the mechanics of planning and goal setting.

The Effectiveness of OD   Given the diversity of activities encompassed by OD, it is not surprising that managers report mixed results from various OD interventions. Organizations that actively practice some form of OD include American Airlines, Texas Instruments, Procter & Gamble, and BF Goodrich. Goodrich, for example, has trained 60 persons in OD processes and techniques. These trained experts have subsequently become internal OD consultants to assist other managers in applying the techniques.[40] Many other managers, in contrast, report that they have tried OD but discarded it.[41]

OD will probably remain an important part of management theory and practice. Of course, there are no sure things when dealing with social systems such as organizations, and the effectiveness of many OD techniques is difficult to evaluate. Because all organizations are open systems interacting with their environments, an improvement in an organization after an OD intervention may be attributable to the intervention, but it may also be attributable to changes in economic conditions, luck, or other factors.[42]

concept
CHECK

Identify each of the major areas of organization change and provide examples to illustrate each one.	*Based on your own knowledge and experiences, which, if any, of these areas of change is likely to become more prevalent in the future? Which, if any, is likely to become less prevalent? Why?*

Organizational Innovation

A final element of organization change that we address is innovation. ***Innovation*** is the managed effort of an organization to develop new products or services or new uses for existing products or services. Innovation is clearly important because, without new products or services, any organization will fall behind its competition.[43] First Things First highlighted the importance of innovation at Ikea. *Technology Toolkit* illustrates another example at a firm called Sportvision.

> **innovation**
> The managed effort of an organization to develop new products or services or new uses for existing products or services

The Innovation Process

The organizational innovation process consists of developing, applying, launching, growing, and managing the maturity and decline of creative ideas.[44] This process is depicted in Figure 13.4.

Innovation Development Innovation development involves the evaluation, modification, and improvement of creative ideas. Innovation development can transform a product or service with only modest potential into a product or service with significant potential. Parker Brothers, for example, decided during innovation development not to market an indoor volleyball game but instead to sell separately the appealing little foam ball designed for the game. The firm will never know how well the volleyball game would have sold, but the Nerf ball and numerous related products generated millions of dollars in revenues for Parker Brothers.

Innovation Application Innovation application is the stage in which an organization takes a developed idea and uses it in the design, manufacturing, or delivery of new products, services, or processes. At this point the innovation emerges from the laboratory and is transformed into tangible goods or services. One example of innovation application is the use of radar-based focusing systems in Polaroid's instant cameras. The idea of using radio waves to discover the location, speed, and direction of moving objects was first applied extensively by Allied forces during World War II. As radar technology developed during the following years, the electrical components needed became smaller and more streamlined. Researchers at Polaroid applied this well-developed technology in a new way.[45]

Application Launch Application launch is the stage at which an organization introduces new products or services to the marketplace. The important question is not "Does the innovation work?" but "Will customers want to purchase the innovative product and service?" History is full of creative ideas that did not generate enough interest among customers to be successful. Some notable innovation failures include Sony's seat warmer, the Edsel automobile, and Polaroid's SX-70 instant camera (which cost $3 billion to develop, but never sold more than 100,000 units in a year).[46] Thus, despite development and application, new products and services can still fail at the launch phase.

Innovation is a vital process in most businesses. Nike CEO Mark Parker, right, and Apple CEO Steve Jobs recently introduced the innovative Air Zoom Moire, the first footwear designed to talk to Apple's iPod nano. Its target market is tech-savvy people who exercise regularly. The Air Zoom Moire connects to an iPod through the wireless Nike + iPod Sport Kit. With Nike footwear connected to an iPod nano, information on time, distance, calories burned, and pace is stored on the iPod and displayed onscreen; real-time audible feedback is also provided through headphones. The kit, which includes an in-shoe sensor and a receiver that attaches to an iPod, sells in Apple stores for about $29.

Technology Toolkit

Sportvision: "Sports from the Fans' Perspective"

Remember September 27, 1998? On that day, a less-than-memorable NFL game unveiled a remarkable innovation: the virtual first-and-ten line. This bright yellow first-down line that appears on television screens is the first big innovation in football broadcasting since slow motion and instant replays, which debuted in the 1960s. The first-and-ten line is the product of Sportvision, which has come up with a pipeline of innovative products that are revolutionizing sports broadcasting, from golf to baseball to NASCAR.

Sportvision's marriage of sports and technology began during a 1995 meeting about ways to jazz up sports coverage on TV and raise ratings. Present were Stan Honey, an engineer who is chief technology officer of News Corporation, which owns Fox, and Fox Sports CEO David Hill. Hill conceived of a "glowing hockey puck" that would make the action easier to follow. The concept was a hit, and ratings improved.

By 1998, Honey started Sportvision, which soon figured out ways to transfer that innovation into other sports. The virtual first-and-ten line, as well as the kick and pass trackers, are made by Sportvision. For baseball, the KZone shows the virtual strike zone. Golf has virtual shot trails, course flyovers, and simulated putting zones. Sportvision appeals to motor sports fans with virtual dashboards and simulated pointers. There are also applications tailored to horse racing, soccer, bowling, Olympic sports, and extreme sports. StroMotion shows an athlete's movements over time and enhances many sports. Another application that works for various sports is the ability to display player or team statistics and virtual advertising.

Sportvision services don't come cheap. Exact prices are not disclosed, but Fox was paying about $25,000 per football game in 1998. Yet more and more shows purchase the products because fans demand them. "If people don't see it, their reaction is that the telecast is substandard," says Jed Drake, an ESPN senior vice president.

Sportvision is working on futuristic developments that meld technology and sports. One long-term project is a video racecar game that allows players at home to virtually compete against real NASCAR drivers running a real race. "We want to put you in the race," says Sportvision CEO Hank Adams. He's already shown that Sportvision can win the innovation race.

References: "Company Overview," "Management Team," Sportvision website, www.sportvision.com on April 16, 2006; Mark Hyman, "Stan Honey: Virtual Virtuoso," *BusinessWeek*, October 31, 2005, www.businessweek.com on April 16, 2006; Dan Williams, "Sportvision Enhances Fan Experiences and Provides New Revenue Streams," *Sport and Technology* newsletter, July 2003, www.sportandtechnology.com on April 16, 2006.

Application Growth   Once an innovation has been successfully launched, it then enters the stage of application growth. This is a period of high economic performance for an organization because demand for the product or service is often greater than supply. Organizations that fail to anticipate this stage may unintentionally limit their growth, as Apple did by not anticipating demand for its iMac computer.[47] At the same time, overestimating demand for a new product can be just as detrimental to performance. Unsold products can sit in warehouses for years.

Innovation Maturity   After a period of growing demand, an innovative product or service often enters a period of maturity. Innovation maturity is the stage at which most organizations in an industry have access to an innovation and are applying it in approximately the same way. The technological application of an innovation during this stage of the innovation process can be very sophisticated. Because most firms have access to the innovation, however, either as a result of their developing the innovation on their own or copying the innovation of others, it does not provide competitive advantage to any one of them. The time that elapses between innovation development and innovation maturity varies notably depending on the particular product or service.

Figure 13.4
THE INNOVATION PROCESS

Organizations actively seek to manage the innovation process. These steps illustrate the general life cycle that characterizes most innovations. Of course, as with creativity, the innovation process will suffer if it is approached too mechanically and rigidly.

Whenever an innovation involves the use of complex skills (such as a complicated manufacturing process or highly sophisticated teamwork), moving from the growth phase to the maturity phase will take longer. In addition, if the skills needed to implement these innovations are rare and difficult to imitate, then strategic imitation may be delayed, and the organization may enjoy a period of sustained competitive advantage.

Innovation Decline   Every successful innovation bears its own seeds of decline. Because an organization does not gain a competitive advantage from an innovation at maturity, it must encourage its creative scientists, engineers, and managers to begin looking for new innovations. This continued search for competitive advantage usually leads new products and services to move from the creative process through innovation maturity, and finally to innovation decline. Innovation decline is the stage during which demand for an innovation decreases and substitute innovations are developed and applied.

Forms of Innovation

Each creative idea that an organization develops poses a different challenge for the innovation process. Innovations can be radical or incremental, technical or managerial, and product or process.

Radical Versus Incremental Innovations   *Radical innovations* are new products, services, or technologies developed by an organization that completely replace the existing products, services, or technologies in an industry.[48] *Incremental innovations* are new products or processes that modify existing ones. Firms that implement radical innovations fundamentally shift the nature of competition and the interaction of firms within their environments. Firms that implement incremental innovations alter, but do not fundamentally change, competitive interaction in an industry.

Over the last several years, organizations have introduced many radical innovations. For example, compact disk technology has virtually replaced long-playing vinyl records in the recording industry, DVDs are replacing videocassettes, and

> *radical innovation*
> A new product, service, or technology that completely replaces an existing one

> *incremental innovation*
> A new product, service, or technology that modifies an existing one

> **"**Anytime you've got something radically different, there will be people who feel that we should be putting our resources on other stuff.**"**
>
> Roger Jellicoe, Motorola engineer
> (*Fortune*, June 12, 2006, p. 129)

high-definition television seems likely to replace regular television technology in the near future. Whereas radical innovations like these tend to be very visible and public, incremental innovations actually are more numerous. One example is Ford's sport-utility vehicle, Explorer. Although other companies had similar products, Ford more effectively combined the styling and engineering that resulted in increased demand for all sport-utility vehicles.

Technical Versus Managerial Innovations   ***Technical innovations*** are changes in the physical appearance or performance of a product or service, or of the physical processes through which a product or service is manufactured. Many of the most important innovations over the last 50 years have been technical. For example, the serial replacement of the vacuum tube with the transistor, the transistor with the integrated circuit, and the integrated circuit with the microchip has greatly enhanced the power, ease of use, and speed of operation of a wide variety of electronic products. Not all innovations developed by organizations are technical, however. ***Managerial innovations*** are changes in the management process by which products and services are conceived, built, and delivered to customers. Managerial innovations do not necessarily affect the physical appearance or performance of products or services directly. In effect, business process change or reengineering, as we discuss earlier, represents a managerial innovation.

Product Versus Process Innovations   Perhaps the two most important types of technical innovations are product innovations and process innovations. ***Product innovations*** are changes in the physical characteristics or performance of existing products or services or the creation of brand-new products or services. ***Process innovations*** are changes in the way products or services are manufactured, created, or distributed. Whereas managerial innovations generally affect the broader context of development, process innovations directly affect manufacturing.

The implementation of robotics, as we discuss earlier, is a process innovation. As Figure 13.5 shows, the effect of product and process innovations on economic return depends on the stage of the innovation process that a new product or service

---

technical innovation
A change in the appearance or performance of products or services, or of the physical processes through which a product or service passes

managerial innovation
A change in the management process in an organization

product innovation
A change in the physical characteristics or performance of an existing product or service or the creation of new ones

process innovation
A change in the way a product or service is manufactured, created, or distributed

---

Figure 13.5
EFFECTS OF PRODUCT AND PROCESS INNOVATION ON ECONOMIC RETURN

As the innovation process moves from development to decline, the economic return from product innovations gradually declines. In contrast, the economic return from process innovations increases during this same process.

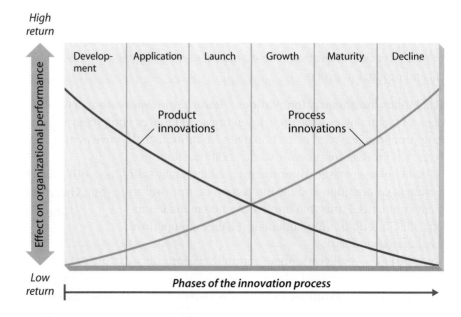

occupies. At first, during development, application, and launch, the physical attributes and capabilities of an innovation most affect organizational performance. Thus product innovations are particularly important during these beginning phases. Later, as an innovation enters the phases of growth, maturity, and decline, an organization's ability to develop process innovations, such as fine-tuning manufacturing, increasing product quality, and improving product distribution, becomes important to maintaining economic return.

Japanese organizations have often excelled at process innovation. The market for 35mm cameras was dominated by German and other European manufacturers when, in the early 1960s, Japanese organizations such as Canon and Nikon began making cameras. Some of these early Japanese products were not very successful, but these companies continued to invest in their process technology and eventually were able to increase quality and decrease manufacturing costs.[49] The Japanese organizations came to dominate the worldwide market for 35mm cameras, and the German companies, because they were not able to maintain the same pace of process innovation, struggled to maintain market share and profitability. And as film technology gives way to digital photography, the same Japanese firms are effectively transitioning to leadership in this market as well.

The Failure to Innovate

To remain competitive in today's economy, organizations must be innovative. And yet many organizations that should be innovative are not successful at bringing out new products or services or do so only after innovations created by others are very mature. Organizations may fail to innovate for at least three reasons.

Lack of Resources   Innovation is expensive in terms of dollars, time, and energy. If a firm does not have sufficient money to fund a program of innovation or does not currently employ the kinds of employees it needs to be innovative, it may lag behind in innovation. Even highly innovative organizations cannot become involved in every new product or service its employees think up. For example, numerous other commitments in the electronic instruments and computer industry forestalled Hewlett-Packard from investing in Steve Jobs and Steve Wozniak's original idea for a personal computer. With infinite resources of money, time, and technical and managerial expertise, HP might have entered this market early. Because the firm did not have this flexibility, however, it had to make some difficult choices about which innovations to invest in.

Failure to Recognize Opportunities   Because firms cannot pursue all innovations, they need to develop the capability to carefully evaluate innovations and to select the ones that hold the greatest potential. To obtain a competitive advantage, an organization usually must make investment decisions before the innovation process reaches the mature stage. The earlier the investment, however, the greater the risk. If organizations are not skilled at recognizing and evaluating opportunities, they may be overly cautious and fail to invest in innovations that later turn out to be successful for other firms.

Resistance to Change   As we discussed earlier, many organizations tend to resist change. Innovation means giving up old products and old ways of doing things in favor of new products and new ways of doing things. These kinds of changes can be personally difficult for managers and other members of an organization. Thus resistance to change can slow the innovation process.

Promoting Innovation in Organizations

A wide variety of ideas for promoting innovation in organizations has been developed over the years. Three specific ways for promoting innovation are through the reward system, through the organizational culture, and through a process called *intrapreneurship.*[50]

The Reward System   A firm's reward system is the means by which it encourages and discourages certain behaviors by employees. Major components of the reward system include salaries, bonuses, and perquisites. Using the reward system to promote innovation is a fairly mechanical but nevertheless effective management technique. The idea is to provide financial and nonfinancial rewards to people and groups who develop innovative ideas. Once the members of an organization understand that they will be rewarded for such activities, they are more likely to work creatively. With this end in mind, Monsanto gives a $50,000 award each year to the scientist or group of scientists who develop the biggest commercial breakthrough.

It is important for organizations to reward creative behavior, but it is vital to avoid punishing creativity when it does not result in highly successful innovations. It is the nature of the creative and innovative processes that many new product ideas will simply not work out in the marketplace. Each process is fraught with too many uncertainties to generate positive results every time. An individual may have prepared herself to be creative, but an insight may not be forthcoming. Or managers may attempt to apply a developed innovation, only to recognize that it does not work. Indeed, some organizations operate according to the assumption that, if all their innovative efforts succeed, then they are probably not taking enough risks in research and development. At 3M, nearly 60 percent of the creative ideas suggested each year do not succeed in the marketplace.

Managers need to be very careful in responding to innovative failure. If innovative failure is due to incompetence, systematic errors, or managerial sloppiness, then a firm should respond appropriately, for example, by withholding raises or reducing promotion opportunities. People who act in good faith to develop an innovation that simply does not work out, however, should not be punished for failure. If they are, they will probably not be creative in the future. A punitive reward system will discourage people from taking risks and therefore reduce the organization's ability to obtain competitive advantages.

Organization Culture   As we discussed in Chapter 3, an organization's culture is the set of values, beliefs, and symbols that help guide behavior. A strong, appropriately focused organizational culture can be used to support innovative activity. A well-managed culture can communicate a sense that innovation is valued and will be rewarded and that occasional failure in the pursuit of new ideas is not only acceptable but even expected. In addition to reward systems and intrapreneurial activities, firms such as 3M, Corning, Monsanto, Procter & Gamble, Texas Instruments, Johnson & Johnson, and Merck are all known to have strong, innovation-oriented cultures that value individual creativity, risk taking, and inventiveness.[51]

Intrapreneurship in Larger Organizations In recent years, many large businesses have realized that the entrepreneurial spirit that propelled their growth becomes stagnant after they transform themselves from a small but growing concern into a larger one.[52] To help revitalize this spirit, some firms today encourage what they call "intrapreneurship." **Intrapreneurs** are similar to entrepreneurs except that they develop a new business in the context of a large organization. There are three intrapreneurial roles in large organizations.[53] To successfully use intrapreneurship to encourage creativity and innovation, the organization must find one or more individuals to perform these roles.

> *intrapreneurs*
> Similar to entrepreneurs except that they develop new businesses in the context of a large organization

The *inventor* is the person who actually conceives of and develops the new idea, product, or service by means of the creative process. Because the inventor may lack the expertise or motivation to oversee the transformation of the product or service from an idea into a marketable entity, however, a second role comes into play. A *product champion* is usually a middle manager who learns about the project and becomes committed to it. He or she helps overcome organizational resistance and convinces others to take the innovation seriously. The product champion may have only limited understanding of the technological aspects of the innovation. Nevertheless, product champions are skilled at knowing how the organization works, whose support is needed to push the project forward, and where to go to secure the resources necessary for successful development. A *sponsor* is a top-level manager who approves of and supports a project. This person may fight for the budget needed to develop an idea, overcome arguments against a project, and use organizational politics to ensure the project's survival. With a sponsor in place, the inventor's idea has a much better chance of being successfully developed.

Several firms have embraced intrapreneurship as a way to encourage creativity and innovation. Colgate-Palmolive has created a separate unit, Colgate Venture Company, staffed with intrapreneurs who develop new products. General Foods developed Culinova as a unit to which employees can take their ideas for possible development. S. C. Johnson & Son established a $250,000 fund to support new product ideas, and Texas Instruments refuses to approve a new innovative project unless it has an acknowledged inventor, champion, and sponsor.

---

concept CHECK

Identify and describe the basic forms of innovation.

Identify several new products or variations of existing products that have been successful and several others that have been less successful.

Summary of Learning Objectives and Key Points

1. Describe the nature of organization change, including forces for change and planned versus reactive change.
   - Organization change is any substantive modification to some part of the organization.
   - Change may be prompted by forces internal or external to the organization.
   - In general, planned change is preferable to reactive change.

2. Discuss the steps in organization change and how to manage resistance to change.
   - The Lewin model provides a general perspective on the steps involved in change.
   - A comprehensive model is usually more effective.
   - People tend to resist change because of uncertainty, threatened self-interests, different perceptions, and feelings of loss.

- Participation, education and communication, facilitation, and force-field analysis are methods for overcoming this resistance.

3. Identify and describe major areas of organization change and discuss the assumptions, techniques, and effectiveness of organization development.
   - The most common areas of change involve changing organizational structure and design, technology, and people.
   - Business process change is a more massive and comprehensive change.
   - Organization development is concerned with changing attitudes, perceptions, behaviors, and expectations. Its effective use relies on an important set of assumptions.
   - There are conflicting opinions about the effectiveness of several OD techniques.

4. Describe the innovation process, forms of innovation, the failure to innovate, and how organizations can promote innovation.
   - The innovation process has six steps: development, application, launch, growth, maturity, and decline.
   - Basic categories of innovation include radical, incremental, technical, managerial, product, and process innovations.
   - Despite the importance of innovation, many organizations fail to innovate because they lack the required creative individuals or are committed to too many other creative activities, fail to recognize opportunities, or resist the change that innovation requires.
   - Organizations can use a variety of tools to overcome these problems, including the reward system, organizational culture, and intrapreneurship.

Discussion Questions

Questions for Review

1. What forces or kinds of events lead to organization change? Identify each force or event as a planned or a reactive change.
2. Compare planned and reactive change. What are the advantages of planned change, as compared to reactive change?
3. In a brief sentence or just a phrase, describe each of the organizational development (OD) techniques.
4. Consider the following list of products. Categorize each along all three dimensions of innovation, if possible (radical versus incremental, technical versus managerial, and product versus process). Explain your answers.
   - Teaching college courses by videotaping the instructor and sending the image over the Internet
   - The rise in popularity of virtual organizations (discussed in Chapter 12)
   - Checking the security of packages on airlines with the type of MRI scanning devices that are common in health care
   - A device combining features of a cell phone and a handheld computer with Internet capability
   - Robotic arms that can perform surgery that is too precise for a human surgeon's hands
   - Hybrid automobiles, which run on both batteries and gasoline
   - Using video games to teach soldiers how to plan and execute battles

Questions for Analysis

5. What are the symptoms that a manager should look for in determining whether an organization needs to change? What are the symptoms that indicate that an organization has been through too much change?
6. Assume that you are the manager of an organization that has a routine way of performing a task and now faces a major change in how it performs that task. Using Lewin's model, tell what steps you would take to implement the change. Using the comprehensive approach, tell what steps you would take. For each step, give specific examples of actions you would take at that step.
7. Think back to a time when a professor announced a change that you, the student, did not want to adopt. What were the reasons for your resistance to change? Was the professor able to overcome your resistance? If so, tell what he or she did. If not, tell what he or she could have done that might have been successful.

Questions for Application

8. Some people resist change, whereas others welcome it enthusiastically. To deal with the first group, one needs to overcome resistance to change; to deal with the second, one needs to overcome resistance to stability. What advice can you give a manager facing the latter situation?

9. Can a change made in one area of an organization—in technology, for instance—not lead to change in other areas? If you think that change in one area must lead to change in other areas, describe an example of an organization change to illustrate your point. If you think that change can occur in just one area without causing change in other areas, describe an example of an organization change that illustrates your point.

10. Research an innovation change that occurred in a real organization, by either interviewing an employee, reading the business press, or using the Internet. Describe the process by which the innovation was developed. Did the actual process follow the ideal process described in the chapter? Why or why not?

Building Effective Decision-Making Skills

Exercise Overview

Decision-making skills include the manager's ability to recognize and define problems and opportunities correctly and then to select an appropriate course of action to solve problems and capitalize on opportunities. This exercise gives you practice in making decisions related to organizational innovation.

Exercise Background

Assume that you are a manager at a venture capital firm. Your company actively seeks out promising new ideas for technological improvements and then provides financing, advice, and expertise to the start-up firms, in exchange for part ownership of the company. Your firm makes money when an idea is successfully brought to market because the value of your company's shares increases. Your compensation and your continued employment are therefore based on choosing the right ideas and giving the inventors appropriate help.

Exercise Task

1. Use the Internet to locate information about at least five promising new technologies. (*Hint:* Visit websites of publications that report technology news, such as *TechWeb*, or visit corporate websites of innovative companies like 3M. Or use "technology venture capital" as a search term to locate firms that are investing in new technologies and then read about their clients.) Choose the new technology that interests you the most.

2. Describe the innovation's current phase of the innovation process. Explain how you arrived at your answer.

3. Tell about the kinds of advice and expertise that this idea and its inventors need to grow into a successful start-up.

Building Effective Diagnostic Skills

Exercise Overview

Diagnostic skills help a manager visualize the most appropriate response to a situation. These skills are especially important during a period of organization change.

Exercise Background

Assume that you are the general manager of a hotel located on a tropical island. The hotel is situated along a beautiful stretch of beach and is one of six large resorts in the immediate area. The hotel is owned by a group of foreign investors and is one of the oldest on the island. For several years, the hotel has been operated as a franchise unit of a large international hotel chain, as are all of the others on the island.

For the last few years, the hotel's owners have been taking most of the profits for themselves and putting relatively little back into the hotel. They have also let you know that their business is not in good financial health; the money earned from your hotel is being used to offset losses they are incurring elsewhere. In contrast, most of the other hotels around have recently been refurbished, and plans have just been announced to build two new ones in the near future.

A team of executives from franchise headquarters has just visited your hotel. They expressed considerable disappointment in the property. They felt that it has not kept pace with the other resorts on the island. They also informed you that if the property is not brought up to their standards, the franchise agreement, up for review in a year, will be revoked. You see this move as potentially disastrous because you would lose their "brand name," access to their reservation system, and so forth.

Sitting alone in your office, you have identified several alternatives that seem viable:

1. Convince the owners to remodel the hotel. You estimate that it will take $5 million to meet the franchisor's minimum standards and another $5 million to bring the hotel up to the standards of the top resort on the island.
2. Convince the franchisor to give you more time and more options for upgrading the facility.
3. Allow the franchise agreement to terminate and try to succeed as an independent hotel.
4. Assume that the hotel will fail and start looking for another job. You have a good reputation, although you might have to start at a lower level (perhaps as an assistant manager) with another firm.

Exercise Task

With the background information presented above, do the following:

1. Rank-order the four alternatives in terms of their potential success. Make assumptions as appropriate.
2. Identify other alternatives not noted above.
3. Can any alternatives be pursued simultaneously?
4. Develop an overall strategy for trying to save the hotel while also protecting your own interests.

CHAPTER CLOSING CASE

CAN GM CHANGE?

General Motors (GM), the fifth largest corporation in the world, is in trouble. For decades, GM was the biggest auto maker in the world. That is, until 2006. GM's 2006 production is estimated to be 8.8 million, yet Toyota will likely produce 9 million vehicles. GM may lose the top spot for the first time in 74 years. Underlying the mess is an inability to change. Current troubles include

- Failure to develop innovative products. GM's strategy is to duplicate a successful design across several brands, known as "rebadging." This keeps costs low but also suppresses innovation. Buyers switch between GM brands, cannibalizing sales.

- Failure to create products with worldwide appeal. GM's design strategy is focused on U.S. consumers, yet global buyers have different needs. GM often relies on acquiring a national brand to gain entry into foreign markets. However, the new brands are quickly rebadged and become standardized.

- Failure to maintain distinct brands. Automobile buyers purchase the same auto brand repeatedly to reduce the risks inherent in a large purchase. Yet GM's rebadging strategy made all GM products resemble each other and brands lost their unique character. In 2004, GM was forced to cease production of Oldsmobile autos, the oldest U.S. car brand, due to low sales.

- Failure to predict buyer preferences. GM was slow to increase fuel efficiency in the 1970s. By the 1980s, GM's vehicles lagged behind Japanese products in quality. Today, GM lags in developing smaller, less expensive cars, has outdated designs, and is behind in development of fuel-efficient hybrids. "They need irresistibility and head-turners, and they haven't had them," says one industry observer.

- Failure to develop good labor relations. GM's workers, organized by the United Auto Workers union (UAW), resist plant closings, benefits reductions, and increased automation. Strikes occur regularly—16 of them between 1993 and 1998. Generous pay and benefits packages, which helped GM keep labor peace, are burdensome today. GM currently spends $5.7 billion annually on health care alone, adding $1,300 to the price of every vehicle.

These problems need solutions, but stakeholders' resistance to change is high. Customers buy imports because they perceive that GM products have outdated styling, poor performance, and low quality. GM has recently improved quality, yet buyers are now loyal to their imported brands. GM's average buyer incentive, designed to improve sales, was about $4,000 per vehicle in 2005, compared to Toyota's $1,000. The incentives were costly but mostly ineffective. GM's 2005 sales declined by 5 percent, while Toyota's grew by 10 percent.

GM workers are resisting change. GM will eliminate 30,000 workers and close a dozen plants by 2008. The remaining workers must accept lower pay and fewer benefits. In May 2006, GM workers may strike again. Even managers are feeling the pain. CEO Rick Wagoner's pay was cut in half, to $5.1 million, and no bonuses were paid to executives in 2005.

Dealers are resistant too. GM sells twice as many autos as Toyota, but has five times as many dealers. The auto maker wants to close dealers to cut costs but many of the family-owned dealers refuse to sell out. In addition, board members are deserting. Director A. G. Lafley, CEO of Procter & Gamble, resigned in 2005.

Shareholders are also resistant. GM recommends a 50 percent cut in dividends. This move will make the UAW happy because it shows that every stakeholder is making sacrifices. However, it will lead to annual savings of only $500 million, a pittance compared to GM's expenses.

The results of all this resistance are low morale, customer dissatisfaction, and sky-high costs. Change on these issues is so slow that outsiders wonder if GM is simply unaware of the challenges. Fritz Henderson, GM's chief financial officer and its head cost cutter, disputes that claim. He says, "I'm in crisis mode and have been for years."

That's a comforting idea, yet that way of thinking may be contributing to the problems. With an $8.6 billion loss in 2005, GM must change, and quickly. Small changes are not enough to keep GM from bank-

ruptcy. Yet thus far, GM has not met the demands of the union, dealers, customers, and shareholders. One dealer thinks that GM's current leaders will be unable to effect change. He expresses his desire for a change in leadership, saying "I can't really believe that the people who got GM into this mess are going to be the people who can get GM out."

CASE QUESTIONS

1. What are the external and internal forces that are calling for change at GM?
2. What are the reasons that each of the various GM stakeholders are resistant to change?
3. In your opinion, what should GM leaders do to overcome stakeholders' resistance to change?

CASE REFERENCES

"A Look at Auto Incentives," *New York Times*, May 5, 2006, www.nytimes.com on May 3, 2006; "G.M. Chief's Pay Cut Nearly in Half Last Year," *New York Times*, April 29, 2006, www.nytimes.com on May 1, 2006; Carol J. Loomis, "The Tragedy of General Motors," *Fortune*, February 20, 2006, pp. 59–75; David Welch, "The Other Club Battering GM," *BusinessWeek*, March 6, 2006, p. 38; David Welch, "You've Got the Floor, Kirk," *BusinessWeek*, February 20, 2006, p. 61.

YOU MAKE THE CALL

Innovative Ikea

1. Identify and key external and internal forces for change that affect Ikea.
2. Assume that you are the manager of an Ikea store and that corporate headquarters has instructed you to change the layout of your store in a dramatic new way but has left the details of the new design to your discretion. You want to manage this as a planned change. Describe the basic steps that you might employ.
3. Using the change process created in response to question 2, identify the major reasons that your

employees might resist the change and how you might best overcome that resistance.
4. What forces might cause Ikea to have to engage in reactive as opposed to planned change?
5. Using the various forms of innovation discussed in the chapter, identify a real or likely example of each as practiced at Ikea.
6. Would you want to manage an Ikea store? Why or why not?

Test Prepper

college.hmco.com/business/students

Choose the correct answer. Answers are found at the back of the book.

1. T   F   An organization's task environment is a more powerful force for change than is the general environment.

2. T   F   Organizational change is a fairly simple phenomenon.

3. T   F   Technological changes are becoming increasingly important to many organizations because of stringent governmental requirements.

4. T   F   In the OD technique of survey feedback, everyone who was involved in the survey receives the results of the survey.

5. T   F   Intrapreneurs are entrepreneurs who operate within the context of a larger organization.

6. Robert expects that in the near future his primary competitor will open a new retail store across the street. In anticipation of this, Robert begins designing and implementing a strategy to differentiate his product. This is an example of

   A. reactive change.
   B. planned change.
   C. piecemeal change.
   D. Lewin change.
   E. opportunistic change.

7. Managers must understand the resistance that often accompanies change if they are to manage change effectively. Which of the following is the biggest cause of resistance to change?

   A. Uncertainty
   B. Threatened self-interests
   C. Different perceptions
   D. Feelings of loss
   E. Poor education

8. Which of the following is an example of enterprise resource planning (ERP)?

   A. A business plan for a new product line
   B. A map of personnel needs over the length of a project, including succession plans if one or more employees were to leave
   C. A large-scale information system that integrates the many activities in the company
   D. A motivational technique to align the culture of the organization with the attitudes and preferences of the employees
   E. A change in work sequence that accompanies a change in technology

9. IBM's Selectric was one of the most popular typewriters ever. Once IBM began developing and marketing personal computers, its Selectric sales all but disappeared. The personal computer is an example of

   A. a radical innovation.
   B. an incremental innovation.
   C. a managerial innovation.
   D. an application innovation.
   E. an innovation decline.

10. Which of the following is NOT a common reason an organization may fail to innovate?

   A. Lack of resources
   B. Failure to recognize opportunities
   C. Incompetent intrapreneurs
   D. Resistance to change
   E. All of the above are common reasons an organization may fail to innovate.

Managing Human Resources in Organizations

chapter 14

FIRST THINGS FIRST

The "Try-Before-You-Buy" Workforce

"Without low-cost manual labor, how could you have the new economy?"

—RAJ JAYADEV, A FORMER TEMP WORKER, NOW AN ACTIVIST

You wouldn't get married after just one date, would you? So why would you accept a job, and why would an employer accept you, after just one interview? Temporary work provides time for both employer and employee to get familiar with each other.

The job market is heating up. Employers in many industries and regions cannot find enough good workers to fill available jobs. Those jobs aren't just clerical or blue-collar. More and more businesses say that they cannot fill positions for midlevel or even top executives. Hiring temporary help is one way to enlarge the pool of workers. Many companies then make offers of permanent employment to the best temps in a process called "temp-to-perm" or "temp-to-hire."

LEARNING OBJECTIVES

After studying this chapter, you should be able to:

1. Describe the environmental context of human resource management, including its strategic importance and its relationship with legal and social factors.

2. Discuss how organizations attract human resources, including human resource planning, recruiting, and selecting.

3. Describe how organizations develop human resources, including training and development, performance appraisal, and performance feedback.

4. Discuss how organizations maintain human resources, including the determination of compensation and benefits and career planning.

5. Discuss labor relations, including how employees form unions and the mechanics of collective bargaining.

6. Describe the issues associated with managing knowledge and contingent and temporary workers.

The use of temporary workers is becoming increasingly widespread. These job seekers, Eliseo Flores Canales (left) and Daisy Bonilla, have just applied for work at the Staffmark temp agency in Cypress, California.

Temp work is growing in importance. It accounts for about 2 percent of all employment in the United States today, up from 1.5 percent in 2001. In 2005, hiring of temporary workers grew by 200,000 positions over the previous year, resulting in a total of 2.6 million temporary workers in America.

The practice has advantages for employers. Companies that are fearful of making a commitment to untried employees get a chance to see those individuals in action. Firms that want to be selective "have learned to hire much more strategically," according to Richard Wahlquist, CEO of the American Staffing Association. Hiring workers into temporary positions can be less costly for companies that would otherwise pay a fee to a staffing agency. Employers usually do not offer benefits to temp workers, which can save an additional one-third of the total cost of the hire.

Temp-to-perm can also be beneficial to employees. Workers can "get to know if the boss is a pussycat or a tiger," says Marty Gargle, owner of a New York staffing service. Temp-to-perm hiring is also ideal for applicants with poor or outdated interviewing skills. Most temporary workers are hired through agencies, who conduct their own, less-stressful interviews. Temp workers have a chance to prove their abilities, an opportunity that might not come to those who do not interview well. Some temporary workers use their temporary jobs as a way to explore career options or to gain experience in a new industry.

Temporary work provides income during career transitions. It can also be a way to exercise control over work hours and conditions. Many temporary workers are pursuing outside interests that make it difficult for them to work long hours or commit to a permanent position. In addition, it is easier to leave a temp position. Workers can quit at any time without having that fact appear as a negative on their résumés.

Critics, however, note that temporary workers also face a number of challenges. Lack of benefits is certainly one. Wages can be lower too. Average hourly pay for temps rose just 1 percent in 2005, which does not keep pace with 3.2 percent inflation. Temp workers experienced declines totaling 6.7 percent from 2002 to 2003, resulting in earnings power that is lower than it was a decade ago. Temp workers report that their workplace injuries usually go unnoted and untreated. A recent documentary film titled *Secrets of Silicon Valley* revealed that over half of high-tech workers in temporary positions developed respiratory problems after exposure to harmful chemicals in a Hewlett-Packard assembly plant.

Clearly, some workers enjoy the freedom of temp work, but for most, full-time permanent employment is desirable. If temporary workers can use that position as an entry into full-time work, they will enjoy more workplace protection and be more highly compensated. But for those who cannot make the transition, the benefits can be elusive. "Without low-cost manual labor, how could you have the new economy?" questions Raj Jayadev, a temp worker turned activist. "The temp economy is extremely secretive. These exploits have to remain hidden, because the truth would completely burst this . . . belief that there is affluence for everybody."[1]

The decision to enter into an employment relationship is clearly complicated for both the individual seeking a job and the organization seeking an employee. While temporary workers have been around for a long time, the strategic use of temporary employment as a precursor to regular employment is a fairly new phenomenon. This emerging practice may become yet another of the many activities necessary to successfully manage an effective workforce.

This chapter is about how organizations manage the people that comprise them. This set of processes is called "human resource management," or HRM. We start by describing the environmental context of HRM. We then discuss how organizations attract human resources. Next we describe how organizations seek to further develop the capacities of their human resources. We also examine how high-quality human resources are maintained by organizations. We conclude by discussing labor relations.

The Environmental Context of Human Resource Management

Human resource management (HRM) is the set of organizational activities directed at attracting, developing, and maintaining an effective workforce.[2] Human resource management takes place within a complex and ever-changing environmental context. Three particularly vital components of this context are HRM's strategic importance and the legal and social environments of HRM.

> *human resource management (HRM)*
> The set of organizational activities directed at attracting, developing, and maintaining an effective workforce

The Strategic Importance of HRM

Human resources are critical for effective organizational functioning. HRM (or "personnel," as it is sometimes called) was once relegated to second-class status in many organizations, but its importance has grown dramatically in the last two decades. Its new importance stems from increased legal complexities, the recognition that human resources are a valuable means for improving productivity, and the awareness today of the costs associated with poor human resource management.[3]

Indeed, managers now realize that the effectiveness of their HR function has a substantial impact on the bottom-line performance of the firm. Poor human resource planning can result in spurts of hiring followed by layoffs—costly in terms of unemployment compensation payments, training expenses, and morale. Haphazard compensation systems do not attract, keep, and motivate good employees, and outmoded recruitment practices can expose the firm to expensive and embarrassing discrimination lawsuits. Consequently, the chief human resource executive of most large businesses is a vice president directly accountable to the CEO, and many firms are developing strategic HR plans and integrating those plans with other strategic planning activities.[4]

Even organizations with as few as 200 employees usually have a human resource manager and a human resource department charged with overseeing these activities. Responsibility for HR activities, however, is shared between the HR department and line managers. The HR department may recruit and initially screen candidates, but the final selection is usually made by managers in the department where the new employee will work. Similarly, although the HR department may establish performance appraisal policies and procedures, the actual evaluation and coaching of employees is done by their immediate superiors.

The growing awareness of the strategic significance of human resource management has even led to new terminology to reflect a firm's commitment to people. **Human capital** reflects the organization's investment in attracting, retaining, and motivating an effective workforce. Hence, just as the phrase *financial capital* is an indicator of a firm's financial resources and reserves, so, too, does *human capital* serve as a tangible indicator of the value of the people who comprise an organization.[5] *The Business of Ethics* discusses how some businesses used the Hurricane Katrina disaster to enhance their human capital and to demonstrate to their employees that they are caring and socially responsive companies.

> **human capital**
> Reflects the organization's investment in attracting, retaining, and motivating an effective workforce

The Legal Environment of HRM

A number of laws regulate various aspects of employee-employer relations, especially in the areas of equal employment opportunity, compensation and benefits, labor relations, and occupational safety and health. Several major ones are summarized in Table 14.1.

The Business of Ethics

After Katrina, a Helping Hand

When Hurricane Katrina struck the Gulf Coast in August 2005, millions of people lost everything they owned. The federal government's response was fraught with mistakes and shortcomings, but many businesses stepped forward to serve the Katrina victims.

Dozens of companies gave contributions of $1 million, including Apple, Citigroup, Enterprise Rent-a-Car, and the Gap. Some gave much more, with Wal-Mart's $17 million topping the list. Some employers promised funds to match employees' contributions.

Others donated goods or services. Abbott donated infant formula, while AT&T donated calling cards. Clorox gave 50,000 gallons of bleach to aid in removing mold. Albertson's donated $9 million in food, while pharmaceutical firms donated medicines. Other companies made more unusual offers. Banks promised home equity loans, even for homes that were not inhabitable. DirecTV began a Hurricane Katrina information channel. KB Homes, a national builder, committed to building thousands of new homes.

The outpouring of support helped residents rebuild shattered lives. In return, some companies got more than just a warm feeling. Entergy, a Gulf Coast electric utility, used Katrina to inspire employees. Company workers, even those who lost their homes, spent 16-hour days restoring power to a million customers. CEO Wayne Leonard sent motivating e-mails saying, for instance,

"Our response to this crisis will make the people we call Entergy remembered and revered for all time."

Domino's sugar factory was located in a flooded parish, and many workers were homeless. The plant produces almost 20 percent of the sugar consumed in the United States, so it was essential to get it running again. Within two weeks, Domino got trailers from the Federal Emergency Management Agency (FEMA) and built a park for 200 trailers in the factory's parking lot. They cleaned up 6.5 million pounds of wet sugar, built a water treatment plant, and powered up generators. Then Domino added a playground and community garden, and even gave a trailer to a nearby market owner to ensure food supplies.

These companies continue to provide hope, homes, and jobs to thousands and are helping communities to recover. In return, they gain a loyal and motivated staff. Mickey Seither, Domino's vice president, recognizes the company's dependence on its workers, saying, "We can fix anything; we can rebuild anything. But if we don't have employees, it's for naught."

References: Jon Birger, "Man on a Mission," *Fortune*, April 3, 2006, pp. 86–92; "Companies Pitch In," *Money*, September 15, 2005, www.cnnmoney.com on April 17, 2006; "Domino Sugar Plant Reopens," PBS NewsHour, March 8, 2006, www.pbs.org on April 17, 2006; Carmine Gallo, "Becoming a Chief Inspiration Officer," *BusinessWeek*, April 20, 2006, www.businessweek.com on April 20, 2006.

Table 14.1

THE LEGAL ENVIRONMENT OF HUMAN RESOURCE MANAGEMENT

As much as any area of management, HRM is subject to wide-ranging laws and court decisions. These laws and decisions affect the human resource function in many areas. For example, AT&T was once fined several million dollars for violating Title VII of the Civil Rights Act of 1964.

EQUAL EMPLOYMENT OPPORTUNITY

Title VII of the Civil Rights Act of 1964 (as amended by the Equal Employment Opportunity Act of 1972). Forbids discrimination in all areas of the employment relationship.

Age Discrimination in Employment Act. Outlaws discrimination against people older than 40 years.

Various executive orders, especially Executive Order 11246 in 1965. Requires employers with government contracts to engage in affirmative action.

Pregnancy Discrimination Act. Specifically outlaws discrimination on the basis of pregnancy.

Vietnam Era Veterans Readjustment Assistance Act. Extends affirmative action mandate to military veterans who served during the Vietnam War.

Americans with Disabilities Act. Specifically outlaws discrimination against disabled persons.

Civil Rights Act of 1991. Makes it easier for employees to sue an organization for discrimination but limits punitive damage awards if they win.

COMPENSATION AND BENEFITS

Fair Labor Standards Act. Establishes minimum wage and mandated overtime pay for work in excess of 40 hours per week.

Equal Pay Act of 1963. Requires that men and women be paid the same amount for doing the same job.

Employee Retirement Income Security Act of 1974 (ERISA). Regulates how organizations manage their pension funds.

Family and Medical Leave Act of 1993. Requires employers to provide up to 12 weeks of unpaid leave for family and medical emergencies.

LABOR RELATIONS

National Labor Relations Act. Spells out procedures by which employees can establish labor unions and requires organizations to bargain collectively with legally formed unions; also known as the *Wagner Act.*

Labor-Management Relations Act. Limits union power and specifies management rights during a union-organizing campaign; also known as the *Taft-Hartley Act.*

HEALTH AND SAFETY

Occupational Safety and Health Act of 1970 (OSHA). Mandates the provision of safe working conditions.

Equal Employment Opportunity *Title VII of the Civil Rights Act of 1964* forbids discrimination in all areas of the employment relationship. The intent of Title VII is to ensure that employment decisions are made on the basis of an individual's qualifications rather than on the basis of personal biases. The law has reduced direct forms of discrimination (refusing to promote African Americans into management, failing to hire men as flight attendants, refusing to hire women as construction workers) as well as indirect forms of discrimination (using employment tests that whites pass at a higher rate than African Americans).

Employment requirements such as test scores and other qualifications are legally defined as having an ***adverse impact*** on minorities and women when such individuals meet or pass the requirement at a rate less than 80 percent of the rate of majority group members. Criteria that have an adverse impact on protected groups can be used only when there is solid evidence that they effectively identify individuals who are better able than others to do the job. The ***Equal Employment Opportunity Commission*** is charged with enforcing Title VII as well as several other employment-related laws.

The ***Age Discrimination in Employment Act***, passed in 1967, amended in 1978, and amended again in 1986, is an attempt to prevent organizations from discriminating against older workers. In its current form, it outlaws discrimination against

> *Title VII of the Civil Rights Act of 1964*
> Forbids discrimination on the basis of sex, race, color, religion, or national origin in all areas of the employment relationship

> *adverse impact*
> When minority group members pass a selection standard at a rate less than 80 percent of the pass rate of majority group members

> *Equal Employment Opportunity Commission*
> Charged with enforcing Title VII of the Civil Rights Act of 1964

> *Age Discrimination in Employment Act*
> Outlaws discrimination against people older than forty years; passed in 1967, amended in 1978 and 1986

affirmative action
Intentionally seeking and hiring qualified or qualifiable employees from racial, sexual, and ethnic groups that are underrepresented in the organization

Americans with Disabilities Act
Prohibits discrimination against people with disabilities

Civil Rights Act of 1991
Amends the original Civil Rights Act, making it easier to bring discrimination lawsuits while also limiting punitive damages

Fair Labor Standards Act
Sets a minimum wage and requires overtime pay for work in excess of forty hours per week; passed in 1938 and amended frequently since then

people older than 40 years. Both the Age Discrimination in Employment Act and Title VII require passive nondiscrimination, or equal employment opportunity. Employers are not required to seek out and hire minorities, but they must treat all who apply fairly.

Several executive orders, however, require that employers holding government contracts engage in ***affirmative action***—intentionally seeking and hiring employees from groups that are underrepresented in the organization. These organizations must have a written affirmative action plan that spells out employment goals for underutilized groups and how those goals will be met. These employers are also required to act affirmatively in hiring Vietnam-era veterans (as a result of the Vietnam Era Veterans Readjustment Assistance Act) and qualified handicapped individuals. Finally, the Pregnancy Discrimination Act forbids discrimination against women who are pregnant.

In 1990 Congress passed the ***Americans with Disabilities Act***, which forbids discrimination on the basis of disabilities and requires employers to provide reasonable accommodations for disabled employees.

More recently, the ***Civil Rights Act of 1991*** amended the original Civil Rights Act as well as other related laws by both making it easier to bring discrimination lawsuits (which partially explains the aforementioned backlog of cases) while simultaneously limiting the amount of punitive damages that can be awarded in those lawsuits.

Compensation and Benefits   Laws also regulate compensation and benefits. ***The Fair Labor Standards Act***, passed in 1938 and amended frequently since then, sets a minimum wage and requires the payment of overtime rates for work in excess of 40 hours per week. Salaried professional, executive, and administrative employees are exempt from the minimum hourly wage and overtime provisions. The ***Equal Pay Act of 1963*** requires that men and women be paid the same amount for doing the same job. Attempts to circumvent the law by having different job titles and pay rates for men and women who perform the same work are also illegal. Basing an employee's pay on seniority or performance is legal, however, even if it means that a man and woman are paid different amounts for doing the same job.

The provision of benefits is also regulated in some ways by state and federal laws. Certain benefits are mandatory—for example, worker's compensation insurance for employees who are injured on the job. Employers who provide a pension plan for their employees are regulated by the ***Employee Retirement Income Security Act of 1974 (ERISA)***. The purpose of this act is to help ensure the financial security of pension funds by regulating how they can be invested. The ***Family and Medical Leave Act of 1993***

Images such as this one led to some of the earliest attempts to regulate human resource management practices in the United States. These young boys were working at a cotton mill in Macon, Georgia, in 1909. Their job was to replace bobbins as they got full and to repair broken threads. Child labor, substandard wages, hazardous working conditions, and blatant discrimination led lawmakers to pass numerous statutes intended to protect workers.

requires employers to provide up to 12 weeks of unpaid leave for family and medical emergencies.

In the last few years some large employers, most notably Wal-Mart, have come under fire because they do not provide health care for all of their employees. In response to this, the state of Maryland recently passed a law, informally called the "Wal-Mart bill," that requires employers with more than 10,000 workers to spend at least 8 percent of their payrolls on health care or else pay a comparable amount into a general fund for uninsured workers. Wal-Mart is considering appealing this ruling; meanwhile, several other states are considering the passage of similar laws.[6]

Labor Relations   Union activities and management's behavior toward unions constitute another heavily regulated area. The ***National Labor Relations Act*** (also known as the Wagner Act), passed in 1935, sets up a procedure for employees to vote on whether to have a union. If they vote for a union, management is required to bargain collectively with the union. The ***National Labor Relations Board (NLRB)*** was established by the Wagner Act to enforce its provisions. Following a series of severe strikes in 1946, the ***Labor-Management Relations Act*** (also known as the Taft-Hartley Act) was passed in 1947 to limit union power. The law increases management's rights during an organizing campaign. The Taft-Hartley Act also contains the National Emergency Strike provision, which allows the president of the United States to prevent or end a strike that endangers national security. Taken together, these laws balance union and management power. Employees can be represented by a legally created and managed union, but the business can make nonemployee-related business decisions without interference.

Health and Safety   ***The Occupational Safety and Health Act of 1970 (OSHA)*** directly mandates the provision of safe working conditions. It requires that employers (1) provide a place of employment that is free from hazards that may cause death or serious physical harm and (2) obey the safety and health standards established by the Department of Labor. Safety standards are intended to prevent accidents, whereas occupational health standards are concerned with preventing occupational disease. For example, standards limit the concentration of cotton dust in the air because this contaminant has been associated with lung disease in textile workers. The standards are enforced by OSHA inspections, which are conducted when an employee files a complaint of unsafe conditions or when a serious accident occurs. Spot inspections of plants in especially hazardous industries such as mining and chemicals are also made. Employers who fail to meet OSHA standards may be fined.

Investigators are currently looking into claims that chemical agents in the butter flavoring used in microwave popcorn are harmful to workers where such products are made. At least 30 workers at one plant in Jasper, Missouri, have contracted a rare lung disease, and some doctors believe that it resulted from conditions on their job site. Although federal health officials point out that there is no danger to those cooking or eating microwave popcorn, research is ongoing into potential hazards to those who work in the industry.[7]

Emerging Legal Issues   Several other areas of legal concern have emerged during the past few years. One is sexual harassment. Although sexual harassment is forbidden under Title VII, it has received additional attention in the courts recently, as

---

Equal Pay Act of 1963
Requires that men and women be paid the same amount for doing the same job

Employee Retirement Income Security Act of 1974 (ERISA)
Sets standards for pension plan management and provides federal insurance if pension funds go bankrupt

Family and Medical Leave Act of 1993
Requires employers to provide up to 12 weeks of unpaid leave for family and medical emergencies

National Labor Relations Act
Passed in 1935 to set up procedures for employees to vote on whether to have a union; also known as the Wagner Act

National Labor Relations Board (NLRB)
Established by the Wagner Act to enforce its provisions

Labor-Management Relations Act
Passed in 1947 to limit union power; also known as the Taft-Hartley Act

Occupational Safety and Health Act of 1970 (OSHA)
Directly mandates the provision of safe working conditions

more and more victims have decided to publicly confront the problem. Another emerging human resource management issue is alcohol and drug abuse. Both alcoholism and drug dependence are major problems today. Recent court rulings have tended to define alcoholics and drug addicts as disabled, protecting them under the same laws that protect other handicapped people. Finally, AIDS has emerged as an important legal issue as well. AIDS victims, too, are most often protected under various laws protecting the disabled.

Social Change and HRM

Beyond the objective legal context of HRM, various social changes are also affecting how organizations interact with their employees. First, many organizations are using more and more temporary workers today. This trend, discussed more fully later, allows them to add workers as necessary without the risk that they may have to eliminate their jobs in the future.

Second, dual-career families are much more common today than just a few years ago. Organizations are finding that they must make accommodations for employees who are dual-career partners. These accommodations may include delaying transfers, offering employment to the spouses of current employees to retain them, and providing more flexible work schedules and benefits packages. A related aspect of social change and HRM, workforce diversity, was covered more fully in Chapter 6.

Employment-at-will is also becoming an important issue. Although employment-at-will has legal implications, its emergence as an issue is socially driven. **Employment-at-will** is a traditional view of the workplace that says organizations can fire an employee for any reason. Increasingly, however, people are arguing that organizations should be able to fire only people who are poor performers or who violate rules and, conversely, should not be able to fire people who report safety violations to OSHA or refuse to perform unethical activities. Several court cases in recent years have upheld this emerging view and have limited many organizations' ability to terminate employees to those cases where there is clear and just cause or there is an organization-wide cutback.

employment-at-will
A traditional view of the workplace that says organizations can fire their employees for whatever reason they want; recent court judgments are limiting employment-at-will

concept
CHECK

Identify and briefly summarize the key laws that affect human resource management.	*How might the importance of human capital vary across different kinds of business?*

Attracting Human Resources

With an understanding of the environmental context of human resource management as a foundation, we are now ready to address its first substantive concern—attracting qualified people who are interested in employment with the organization.

Human Resource Planning

The starting point in attracting qualified human resources is planning. HR planning, in turn, involves job analysis and forecasting the demand and supply of labor.

Job Analysis *Job analysis* is a systematic analysis of jobs within an organization. A job analysis is made up of two parts. The job description lists the duties of a job, the job's working conditions, and the tools, materials, and equipment used to perform it. The job specification lists the skills, abilities, and other credentials needed to do the job. Job analysis information is used in many human resource activities. For instance, knowing about job content and job requirements is necessary to develop appropriate selection methods and job-relevant performance appraisal systems and to set equitable compensation rates.

> **job analysis**
> A systematized procedure for collecting and recording information about jobs within an organization

Forecasting Human Resource Demand and Supply After managers fully understand the jobs to be performed within the organization, they can start planning for the organization's future human resource needs. Figure 14.1 summarizes the steps most often followed. The manager starts by assessing trends in past human resources usage, future organizational plans, and general economic trends. A good sales forecast is often the foundation, especially for smaller organizations. Historical ratios can then be used to predict demand for such employees as operating employees and sales representatives. Of course, large organizations use much more complicated models to predict their future human resource needs. Wal-Mart completed an exhaustive planning process that projects that the firm will need to hire 1 million people by 2010. Of this total, 800,000 are for new positions created as the firm grows, and the other 200,000 will replace current workers who leave for various reasons.[8]

> "We are in the midst of a major structural shift in manufacturing. . . . The number of good-paying, middle-class jobs that have been the bulk of manufacturing is likely going to be less in the future."
>
> Harley Shaiken, Professor of Labor Relations,
> University of California, Berkeley
> (*USA Today*, March 28, 2006, p. 2B)

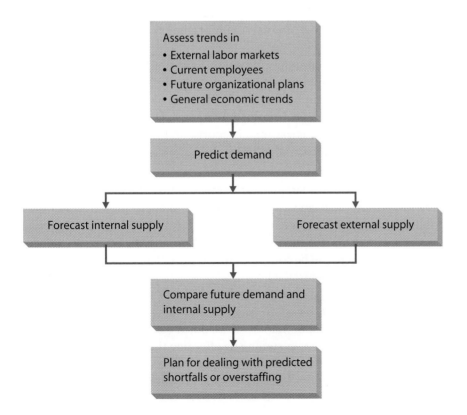

Figure 14.1
HUMAN RESOURCE PLANNING

Attracting human resources cannot be left to chance if an organization expects to function at peak efficiency. Human resource planning involves assessing trends, forecasting supply and demand of labor, and then developing appropriate strategies for addressing any differences.

Forecasting the supply of labor is really two tasks: forecasting the internal supply (the number and type of employees who will be in the firm at some future date) and forecasting the external supply (the number and type of people who will be available for hiring in the labor market at large). The simplest approach merely adjusts present staffing levels for anticipated turnover and promotions. Again, though, large organizations use extremely sophisticated models to make these forecasts. Union Oil Company of California, for example, has a complex forecasting system for keeping track of the present and future distributions of professionals and managers. The Union Oil system can spot areas where there will eventually be too many qualified professionals competing for too few promotions or, conversely, too few good people available to fill important positions.[9]

> **replacement chart**
> Lists each important managerial position in the organization, who occupies it, how long he or she will probably remain in the position, and who is or will be a qualified replacement

At higher levels of the organization, managers plan for specific people and positions. The technique most commonly used is the ***replacement chart***, which lists each important managerial position, who occupies it, how long he or she will probably stay in it before moving on, and who (by name) is now qualified or soon will be qualified to move into the position. This technique allows ample time to plan developmental experiences for persons identified as potential successors to critical managerial jobs.[10]

> **employee information system (skills inventory)**
> Contains information on each employee's education, skills, experience, and career aspirations; usually computerized

To facilitate both planning and identifying persons for current transfer or promotion, some organizations also have an ***employee information system***, or ***skills inventory***. Such systems are usually computerized and contain information on each employee's education, skills, work experience, and career aspirations. Such a system can quickly locate all the employees in the organization who are qualified to fill a position requiring, for instance, a degree in chemical engineering, three years of experience in an oil refinery, and fluency in Spanish. Enterprise resource planning (ERP) systems, as described in Chapter 13, generally include capabilities for measuring and managing the internal supply of labor in ways that best fit the needs of the organization.

Forecasting the external supply of labor is a different problem altogether. How does a manager, for example, predict how many electrical engineers will be seeking work in Georgia three years from now? To get an idea of the future availability of labor, planners must rely on information from such outside sources as state employment commissions, government reports, and figures supplied by colleges on the number of students in major fields.

Matching Human Resource Supply and Demand After comparing future demand and internal supply, managers can make plans to manage predicted shortfalls or overstaffing. If a shortfall is predicted, new employees can be hired, present employees can be retrained and transferred into the understaffed area, individuals approaching retirement can be convinced to stay on, or labor-saving or productivity-enhancing systems can be installed.

If the organization needs to hire, the external labor supply forecast helps managers plan how to recruit, based on whether the type of person needed is readily available or scarce in the labor market. As we noted earlier, the trend in temporary workers also helps managers in staffing by affording them extra flexibility. If overstaffing is expected to be a problem, the main options are transferring the extra employees, not replacing individuals who quit, encouraging early retirement, and laying people off.

Recruiting Human Resources

Once an organization has an idea of its future human resource needs, the next phase is usually recruiting new employees.[11] *Recruiting* is the process of attracting qualified persons to apply for jobs that are open. Where do recruits come from? Some recruits are found internally; others come from outside the organization.

Internal recruiting means considering present employees as candidates for openings. Promotion from within can help build morale and keep high-quality employees from leaving the firm. In unionized firms, the procedures for notifying employees of internal job change opportunities are usually spelled out in the union contract. For higher-level positions, a skills inventory system may be used to identify internal candidates, or managers may be asked to recommend individuals who should be considered. Most businesses today routinely post job openings on their internal communication network, or intranet. One disadvantage of internal recruiting is its ripple effect. When an employee moves to a different job, someone else must be found to take his or her old job. In one organization, 454 job movements were necessary as a result of filling 195 initial openings!

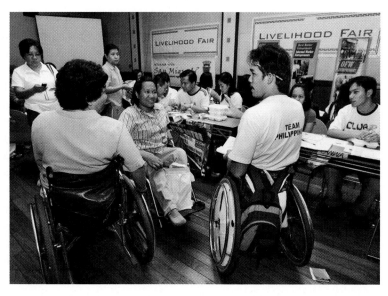

Job fairs are a common approach to recruiting, especially when employers are targeting certain groups of people. These applicants talk among themselves as they wait for their turn for an interview during a government-sponsored job fair for persons with disabilities in suburban Quezon City (north of Manila), Philippines. Thousands of job applicants with different forms of disabilities filed applications for a job during the job fair.

External recruiting involves attracting persons outside the organization to apply for jobs. External recruiting methods include advertising, campus interviews, employment agencies or executive search firms, union hiring halls, referrals by present employees, and hiring "walk-ins" or "gate-hires" (people who show up without being solicited). Increasingly, firms are using the Internet to post job openings and to solicit applicants. Of course, a manager must select the most appropriate methods, using the state employment service to find maintenance workers but not a nuclear physicist, for example. Private employment agencies can be a good source of clerical and technical employees, and executive search firms specialize in locating top-management talent. Newspaper ads are often used because they reach a wide audience and thus allow minorities equal opportunity to find out about and apply for job openings.

The organization must also keep in mind that recruiting decisions often go both ways—the organization is recruiting an employee, but the prospective employee is also selecting a job.[12] For instance, when unemployment is low (meaning there are fewer people seeking work), businesses may have to work harder to attract new employees. During the late 1990s, when unemployment dropped to a 25-year low, some recruiters at firms such as Sprint, PeopleSoft, and Cognex stressed how much "fun" it was to work for them, reinforcing this message with ice cream socials, karaoke contests, softball leagues, and free movie nights.[13] But when unemployment is higher (meaning there are more people looking for work), organizations may find it easier to recruit prospective employees without having to resort to expensive hiring incentives.

---

recruiting
The process of attracting individuals to apply for jobs that are open

---

internal recruiting
Considering current employees as applicants for higher-level jobs in the organization

---

external recruiting
Getting people from outside the organization to apply for jobs

---

Nevertheless, even if a firm can take its pick of the best potential employees, it still should put its best foot forward, treat all applicants with dignity, and strive for a good person-job fit. Recent estimates suggest that hiring the "wrong" operating employee—one who flops and either quits or must be fired—generally costs the organization at least $5,000 in lost productivity and training. Hiring the wrong manager can cost the organization far more.[14]

One generally successful method for facilitating a good person-job fit is the so-called **realistic job preview (RJP)**. As the term suggests, the RJP involves providing the applicant with a real picture of what performing the job that the organization is trying to fill would be like.[15] For example, it would not make sense for a firm to tell an applicant that the job is exciting and challenging when in fact it is routine and straightforward, yet some managers do this to hire the best people. The likely outcome will be a dissatisfied employee who will quickly be looking for a better job. If the company is more realistic about a job, though, the person hired will be more likely to remain in the job for a longer period of time.

> *realistic job preview (RJP)*
> Provides the applicant with a real picture of what performing the job that the organization is trying to fill would be like

Selecting Human Resources

Once the recruiting process has attracted a pool of applicants, the next step is to select whom to hire. The intent of the selection process is to gather from applicants information that will predict their job success and then to hire the candidates likely to be most successful. Of course, the organization can gather information only about factors that are predictive of future performance. The process of determining the predictive value of information is called **validation.**

Two basic approaches to validation are predictive validation and content validation. *Predictive validation* involves collecting the scores of employees or applicants on the device to be validated and correlating their scores with actual job performance. A significant correlation means that the selection device is a valid predictor of job performance. *Content validation* uses logic and job analysis data to establish that the selection device measures the exact skills needed for successful job performance. The most critical part of content validation is a careful job analysis showing exactly what duties are to be performed. The test is then developed to measure the applicant's ability to perform those duties.

> *validation*
> Determining the extent to which a selection device is really predictive of future job performance

Application Blanks   The first step in selection is usually asking the candidate to fill out an application blank. Application blanks are an efficient method of gathering information about the applicant's previous work history, educational background, and other job-related demographic data. They should not contain questions about areas not related to the job, such as gender, religion, or national origin. Application blank data are generally used informally to decide whether a candidate merits further evaluation, and interviewers use application blanks to familiarize themselves with candidates before interviewing them. Unfortunately, in recent years there has been a trend toward job applicants' either falsifying or inflating their credentials to stand a better chance of getting a job. Indeed, one recent survey of 2.6 million job applications found that an astounding 44 percent of them contained some false information.[16]

Tests   Tests of ability, skill, aptitude, or knowledge that is relevant to the particular job are usually the best predictors of job success, although tests of general intelligence or personality are occasionally useful as well. In addition to being validated, tests should be administered and scored consistently. All candidates should be given the same directions, should be allowed the same amount of time, and should experience the same testing environment (temperature, lighting, distractions).[17]

Interviews Although a popular selection device, interviews are sometimes poor predictors of job success. For example, biases inherent in the way people perceive and judge others at a first meeting affect subsequent evaluations by the interviewer. Interview validity can be improved by training interviewers to be aware of potential biases and by increasing the structure of the interview. In a structured interview, questions are written in advance, and all interviewers follow the same question list with each candidate they interview. This procedure introduces consistency into the interview procedure and allows the organization to validate the content of the questions to be asked.[18]

For interviewing managerial or professional candidates, a somewhat less structured approach can be used. Question areas and information-gathering objectives are still planned in advance, but the specific questions vary with the candidates' backgrounds. Trammell Crow Real Estate Investors uses a novel approach in hiring managers. Each applicant is interviewed not only by two or three other managers but also by a secretary or young leasing agent. This provides information about how the prospective manager relates to nonmanagers.

Assessment Centers Assessment centers are a popular method used to select managers and are particularly good for selecting current employees for promotion. The assessment center is a content-valid simulation of major parts of the managerial job. A typical center lasts two to three days, with groups of 6 to 12 persons participating in a variety of managerial exercises. Centers may also include interviews, public speaking, and standardized ability tests. Candidates are assessed by several trained observers, usually managers several levels above the job for which the candidates are being considered. Assessment centers are quite valid if properly designed and are fair to members of minority groups and women.[19] For some firms, the assessment center is a permanent facility created for these activities. For other firms, the assessment activities are performed in a multipurpose location such as a conference room. AT&T pioneered the assessment center concept. For years the firm has used assessment centers to make virtually all of its selection decisions for management positions.

Other Techniques Organizations also use other selection techniques depending on the circumstances. Polygraph tests, once popular, are declining in popularity. On the other hand, more and more organizations are requiring that applicants in whom they are interested take physical exams. Organizations are also increasingly using drug tests, especially in situations in which drug-related performance problems could create serious safety hazards. For example, applicants for jobs in a nuclear power plant would likely be tested for drug use. And some organizations today even run credit checks on prospective employees.

Describe the processes of human resource planning, recruiting, and selection.

As a potential employee, what things might a firm do in its recruiting efforts to impress you?

concept
CHECK

Developing Human Resources

Regardless of how effective a selection system is, however, most employees need additional training if they are to grow and develop in their jobs. Evaluating their performance and providing feedback are also necessary.

Training and Development

training
Teaching operational or technical employees how to do the job for which they were hired

development
Teaching managers and professionals the skills needed for both present and future jobs

In HRM, ***training*** usually refers to teaching operational or technical employees how to do the job for which they were hired. ***Development*** refers to teaching managers and professionals the skills needed for both present and future jobs. Most organizations provide regular training and development programs for managers and employees. For example, IBM spends more than $700 million annually on programs and has a vice president in charge of employee education. U.S. businesses spend more than $30 billion annually on training and development programs away from the workplace. And this figure does not include wages and benefits paid to employees while they are participating in such programs.

Assessing Training Needs   The first step in developing a training plan is to determine what needs exist. For example, if employees do not know how to operate the machinery necessary to do their job, a training program on how to operate the machinery is clearly needed. On the other hand, when a group of office workers is performing poorly, training may not be the answer. The problem could be motivation, aging equipment, poor supervision, inefficient work design, or a deficiency of skills and knowledge. Only the last could be remedied by training. As training programs are being developed, the manager should set specific and measurable goals specifying what participants are to learn. Managers should also plan to evaluate the training program after employees complete it. The training process from start to finish is diagrammed in Figure 14.2.

Common Training Methods   Many different training and development methods are available. Selection of methods depends on many considerations, but perhaps the most important is training content. When the training content is factual material (such as company rules or explanations for how to fill out forms), assigned reading, programmed learning, and lecture methods work well. When the content is interpersonal relations or group decision making, however, firms must use a method that allows interpersonal contact, such as role-playing or case discussion groups. When employees must learn a physical skill, methods allowing practice and the actual use of tools and materials are needed, as in on-the-job training or vestibule training. (Vestibule training enables participants to focus on safety, learning, and feedback rather than on productivity.)

Web-based and other electronic media-based training are becoming very popular. Such methods allow a mix of training content, are relatively easy to update and revise, let participants use a variable schedule, and lower travel costs.[20] On the other hand, they are limited in their capacity to simulate real activities and facilitate face-to-face interaction. Xerox, Massachusetts Mutual Life Insurance, and Ford have all reported tremendous success with these methods. In addition, most training programs actually rely on a mix of methods. Boeing, for example, sends managers to an intensive two-week training seminar involving tests, simulations, role-playing exercises, and CD-ROM flight simulation exercises.[21]

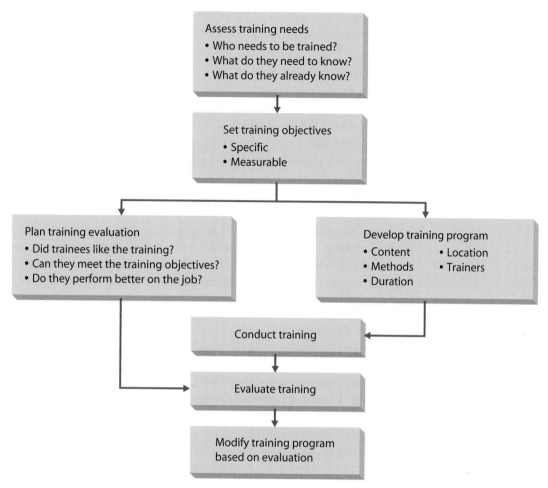

Figure 14.2
THE TRAINING PROCESS

Managing the training process can go a long way toward enhancing its effectiveness. If training programs are well conceived and well executed, both the organization and its employees benefit. Following a comprehensive process helps managers meet the objectives of the training program.

Finally, some larger businesses have started creating their own self-contained training facility, often called a *corporate university.* McDonald's was among the first to start this practice with its so-called Hamburger University in Illinois. All management trainees for the firm attend training programs there to learn exactly how long to grill a burger, how to maintain good customer service, and so on. Other firms that are using this approach include Shell Oil and General Electric.

> "You train people to thrive in adverse conditions by putting them into adverse conditions to prepare them."
> Astronaut John Grunsfeld
> (*Fortune*, June 12, 2006, p. 116)

Evaluation of Training Training and development programs should always be evaluated. Typical evaluation approaches include measuring one or more relevant criteria (such as attitudes or performance) before and after the training, and determining whether the criteria changed. Evaluation measures collected at the end of training are easy to get, but actual performance measures collected when the trainee is on the job are more important. Trainees may say that they enjoyed the training and learned a lot, but the true test is whether their job performance improves after their training.

Performance Appraisal

Once employees are trained and settled into their jobs, one of management's next concerns is performance appraisal. **Performance appraisal** is a formal assessment of how well employees are doing their jobs. Employees' performance should be evaluated regularly for many reasons. One reason is that performance appraisal may be necessary for validating selection devices or assessing the impact of training programs. A second reason is administrative—to aid in making decisions about pay raises, promotions, and training. Still another reason is to provide feedback to employees to help them improve their present performance and plan future careers.[22]

Because performance evaluations often help determine wages and promotions, they must be fair and nondiscriminatory. In the case of appraisals, content validation is used to show that the appraisal system accurately measures performance on important job elements and does not measure traits or behavior that are irrelevant to job performance.

Common Appraisal Methods   Two basic categories of appraisal methods commonly used in organizations are objective methods and judgmental methods. Objective measures of performance include actual output (that is, number of units produced), scrap rate, dollar volume of sales, and number of claims processed. Objective performance measures may be contaminated by "opportunity bias" if some persons have a better chance to perform than others. For example, a sales representative selling snow blowers in Michigan has a greater opportunity than does a colleague selling the same product in Arkansas. Fortunately, adjusting raw performance figures for the effect of opportunity bias and thereby arriving at figures that accurately represent each individual's performance is often possible.

Another type of objective measure, the special performance test, is a method in which each employee is assessed under standardized conditions. This kind of appraisal also eliminates opportunity bias. For example, Verizon Southwest has a series of prerecorded calls that operators in a test booth answer. The operators are graded on speed, accuracy, and courtesy in handling the calls. Performance tests measure ability but do not measure the extent to which one is motivated to use that ability on a daily basis. (A high-ability person may be a lazy performer except when being tested.) Special performance tests must therefore be supplemented by other appraisal methods to provide a complete picture of performance.

Judgmental methods, including ranking and rating techniques, are the most common way to measure performance. Ranking compares employees directly with one another and orders them from best to worst. Ranking has a number of drawbacks. Ranking is difficult for large groups, because the persons in the middle of the distribution may be hard to distinguish from one another accurately. Comparisons of people in different work groups are also difficult. For example, an employee ranked third in a strong group may be more valuable than an employee ranked first in a weak group. Another criticism of ranking is that the manager must rank people on the basis of overall performance, although each person likely has both strengths and weaknesses. Furthermore, rankings do not provide useful information for feedback. To be told that one is ranked third is not

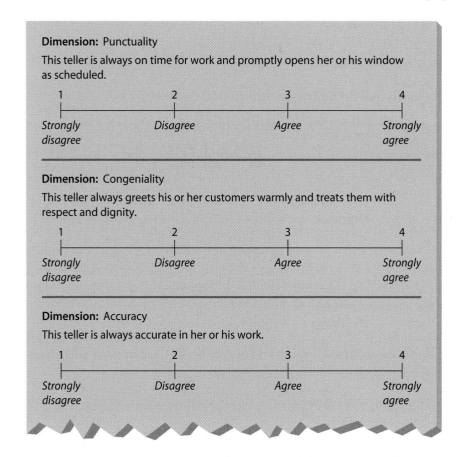

Figure 14.3

GRAPHIC RATING SCALES FOR A BANK TELLER

Graphic rating scales are very common methods for evaluating employee performance. The manager who is doing the rating circles the point on each scale that best reflects her or his assessment of the employee on that scale. Graphic rating scales are widely used for many different kinds of jobs.

nearly as helpful as to be told that the quality of one's work is outstanding, its quantity is satisfactory, one's punctuality could use improvement, or one's paperwork is seriously deficient.

Rating differs from ranking in that it compares each employee with a fixed standard rather than comparison with other employees. A rating scale provides the standard. Figure 14.3 gives examples of three graphic rating scales for a bank teller. Each consists of a performance dimension to be rated (punctuality, congeniality, and accuracy) followed by a scale on which to make the rating. In constructing graphic rating scales, performance dimensions that are relevant to job performance must be selected. In particular, they should focus on job behaviors and results rather than on personality traits or attitudes.

The ***Behaviorally Anchored Rating Scale (BARS)*** is a sophisticated and useful rating method. Supervisors construct rating scales with associated behavioral anchors. They first identify relevant performance dimensions and then generate anchors—specific, observable behaviors typical of each performance level. Figure 14.4 shows an example of a behaviorally anchored rating scale for the dimension "Inventory control."

The other scales in this set, developed for the job of department manager in a chain of specialty stores, include "Handling customer complaints," "Planning special promotions," "Following company procedures," "Supervising sales personnel," and "Diagnosing and solving special problems." BARS can be effective because they require that management take proper care in constructing the scales and they provide useful anchors for supervisors to use in evaluating people. They are costly,

> *Behaviorally Anchored Rating Scale (BARS)*
> A sophisticated rating method in which supervisors construct a rating scale associated with behavioral anchors

Figure 14.4

BEHAVIORALLY ANCHORED RATING SCALE

Behaviorally anchored rating scales help overcome some of the limitations of standard rating scales. Each point on the scale is accompanied by a behavioral anchor—a summary of an employee behavior that fits that spot on the scale.

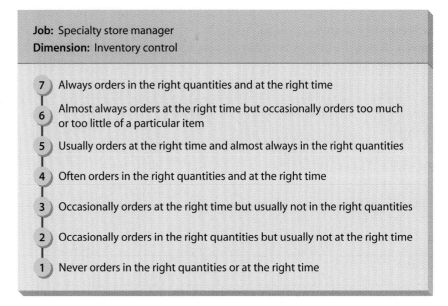

Job: Specialty store manager
Dimension: Inventory control

7 Always orders in the right quantities and at the right time

6 Almost always orders at the right time but occasionally orders too much or too little of a particular item

5 Usually orders at the right time and almost always in the right quantities

4 Often orders in the right quantities and at the right time

3 Occasionally orders at the right time but usually not in the right quantities

2 Occasionally orders in the right quantities but usually not at the right time

1 Never orders in the right quantities or at the right time

however, because outside expertise is usually needed and because scales must be developed for each job within the organization.

Errors in Performance Appraisal   Errors or biases can occur in any kind of rating or ranking system. One common problem is *recency error*—the tendency to base judgments on the subordinate's most recent performance because it is most easily recalled. Often a rating or ranking is intended to evaluate performance over an entire time period, such as six months or a year, so the recency error does introduce error into the judgment. Other errors include overuse of one part of the scale—being too lenient, being too severe, or giving everyone a rating of "average."

Halo error is allowing the assessment of an employee on one dimension to "spread" to ratings of that employee on other dimensions. For instance, if an employee is outstanding on quality of output, a rater might tend to give her or him higher marks than deserved on other dimensions. Errors can also occur because of race, sex, or age discrimination, intentionally or unintentionally. The best way to offset these errors is to ensure that a valid rating system is developed at the outset and then to train managers in how to use it.

A recent innovation in performance appraisal used in many organizations today is called **360-degree feedback**, in which managers are evaluated by everyone around them—their boss, their peers, and their subordinates. Such a complete and thorough approach provides people with a far richer array of information about their performance than does a conventional appraisal given just by the boss. Of course, such a system also takes considerable time and must be handled so as not to breed fear and mistrust in the workplace.[23]

360-degree feedback
A performance appraisal system in which managers are evaluated by everyone around them—their boss, their peers, and their subordinates

Performance Feedback

The last step in most performance appraisal systems is giving feedback to subordinates about their performance. This is usually done in a private meeting between the person being evaluated and his or her boss. The discussion should generally be focused on the facts—the assessed level of performance, how and why that assessment was made, and how it can be improved in the future. Feedback interviews are not easy to conduct. Many managers are uncomfortable with the task, especially if feedback is negative and subordinates are disappointed by what they hear. Properly training managers, however, can help them conduct more effective feedback interviews.[24]

Some firms use a very aggressive approach to terminating people who do not meet expectations. General Electric actually implemented a system whereby each year the bottom 10 percent of its workforce is terminated and replaced with new employees. Company executives claim that this approach, although stressful for all employees, helps it to continuously upgrade its workforce. Other firms have started using this same approach. However, both Ford and Goodyear recently agreed to abandon similar approaches in response to age discrimination lawsuits.[25]

concept CHECK

What are the most common methods for training employees and assessing their performance?

What kind of performance appraisal techniques or methods would you prefer to use as a manager? As someone being evaluated? Why?

Maintaining Human Resources

After organizations have attracted and developed an effective workforce, they must also make every effort to maintain that workforce. To do so requires effective compensation and benefits as well as career planning.

Determining Compensation

Compensation is the financial remuneration given by the organization to its employees in exchange for their work. There are three basic forms of compensation. *Wages* are the hourly compensation paid to operating employees. The minimum hourly wage paid in the United States today is $5.15. *Salary* refers to compensation paid for total contributions, as opposed to pay based on hours worked. For example, managers earn an annual salary, usually paid monthly. They receive the salary regardless of the number of hours they work. Some firms have started paying all their employees a salary instead of hourly wages. For example, all employees at Chaparral Steel earn a salary, starting at $30,000 a year for entry-level operating employees. Finally, *incentives* represent special compensation opportunities that are usually tied to performance. Sales commissions and bonuses are among the most common incentives.

Compensation is an important and complex part of the organization-employee relationship. Basic compensation is necessary to provide employees with the means to maintain a reasonable standard of living. Beyond this, however, compensation also provides a tangible measure of the value of the individual to the organization. If employees do not earn enough to meet their basic economic goals, they will seek employment elsewhere. Likewise, if they believe that their contributions are undervalued by the organization, they may leave or exhibit poor work habits, low morale, and little commitment to the organization. Thus designing an effective compensation system is clearly in the organization's best interests.[26]

A good compensation system can help attract qualified applicants, retain present employees, and stimulate high performance at a cost reasonable for one's

> **compensation**
> The financial remuneration given by the organization to its employees in exchange for their work

industry and geographic area. To set up a successful system, management must make decisions about wage levels, the wage structure, and the individual wage determination system.

Wage-Level Decision The wage-level decision is a management policy decision about whether the firm wants to pay above, at, or below the going rate for labor in the industry or the geographic area. Most firms choose to pay near the average, although those that cannot afford more pay below average. Large, successful firms may like to cultivate the image of being "wage leaders" by intentionally paying more than average and thus attracting and keeping high-quality employees. IBM, for example, pays top dollar to get the new employees it wants. McDonald's, on the other hand, often pays close to the minimum wage. The level of unemployment in the labor force also affects wage levels. Pay declines when labor is plentiful and increases when labor is scarce.

Once managers make the wage-level decision, they need information to help set actual wage rates. Managers need to know what the maximum, minimum, and average wages are for particular jobs in the appropriate labor market. This information is collected by means of a wage survey. Area wage surveys can be conducted by individual firms or by local HR or business associations. Professional and industry associations often conduct surveys and make the results available to employers.

> **job evaluation**
> An attempt to assess the worth of each job relative to other jobs

Wage Structure Decision Wage structures are usually set up through a procedure called ***job evaluation***—an attempt to assess the worth of each job relative to other jobs. At Ben & Jerry's Homemade, company policy once dictated that the highest-paid employee in the firm could not make more than seven times what the lowest-paid employee earned. But this policy had to be modified when the company found that it was simply unable to hire a new CEO without paying more than this amount. The simplest method for creating a wage structure is to rank jobs from those that should be paid the most (for example, the president) to those that should be paid the least (for example, a mail clerk or a janitor).

In a smaller firm with few jobs (like Ben & Jerry's, for example), this method is quick and practical, but larger firms with many job titles require more sophisticated methods. The next step is setting actual wage rates on the basis of a combination of survey data and the wage structure that results from job evaluation. Jobs of equal value are often grouped into wage grades for ease of administration.

Individual Wage Decisions After wage-level and wage structure decisions are made, the individual wage decision must be addressed. This decision concerns how much to pay each employee in a particular job. Although the easiest decision is to pay a single rate for each job, more typically a range of pay rates is associated with each job. For example, the pay range for an individual job might be $5.85 to $6.39 per hour, with different employees earning different rates within the range.

A system is then needed for setting individual rates. This may be done on the basis of seniority (enter the job at $6.85, for example, and increase 10 cents per hour every six months on the job), initial qualifications (inexperienced people start at $6.85; more experienced people start at a higher rate), or merit (raises above the entering rate are given for good performance). Combinations of these bases may also be used.

The Internet is also playing a key role in compensation patterns today because both job seekers and current employees can more easily get a sense of what their true market value is. If they can document the claim that their value is higher than what their current employer now pays or is offering, they are in a position to demand a higher salary. Consider the case of one compensation executive who met recently with a subordinate to discuss her raise. He was surprised when she produced data from five different websites backing up her claim for a bigger raise than he had intended to offer.[27]

Determining Benefits

Benefits are things of value other than compensation that the organization provides to its workers. (Benefits are sometimes called *indirect compensation*.) The average company spends an amount equal to more than one-third of its cash payroll on employee benefits. Thus an average employee who is paid $18,000 per year averages about $6,588 more per year in benefits.

Benefits come in several forms. Pay for time not worked includes sick leave, vacation, holidays, and unemployment compensation. Insurance benefits often include life and health insurance for employees and their dependents. Workers' compensation is a legally required insurance benefit that provides medical care and disability income for employees injured on the job. Social security is a government pension plan to which both employers and employees contribute. Many employers also provide a private pension plan to which they and their employees contribute. Employee service benefits include such extras as tuition reimbursement and recreational opportunities.

Some organizations have instituted "cafeteria benefit plans," whereby basic coverage is provided for all employees but employees are then allowed to choose which additional benefits they want (up to a cost limit based on salary). An employee with five children might choose medical and dental coverage for dependents, a single employee might prefer more vacation time, and an older employee might elect increased pension benefits. Flexible systems are expected to encourage people to stay in the organization and even help the company attract new employees.[28]

In recent years, companies have also started offering more innovative benefits as a way of accommodating different needs. On-site childcare, mortgage assistance, and paid leave programs are interesting new benefits that some firms offer.[29] A good benefits plan may encourage people to join and stay with an organization, but it seldom stimulates high performance, because benefits are tied more to membership in the organization than to performance. To manage their benefits programs effectively, companies should shop carefully, avoid redundant coverage, and provide only those benefits that employees want. Benefits programs should also be explained to employees in clear and straightforward language so that they can use the benefits appropriately and appreciate what the company is providing. Finally, as a result of economic pressures, some firms have started to reduce employee benefits in the last few years. In 2002, for example, 17 percent of employees in the United States with employer healthcare coverage saw their benefits cut. Some employers have also reduced their contributions to employee retirement plans, cut the amount of annual leave they offer to employees, or both.[30]

Career Planning

A final aspect of maintaining human resources is career planning. Few people work in the same jobs their entire careers. Some people change jobs within one organization, others change organizations, and many do both. When these movements are

> **benefits**
> Things of value other than compensation that an organization provides to its workers

haphazard and poorly conceived, both the individual and the organization suffer. Thus planning career progressions in advance is in everyone's best interests. Of course, planning a 30-year career for a newcomer just joining the organization is difficult. But planning can help map out what areas the individual is most interested in and help the person see what opportunities are available within the organization.[31]

Managing Labor Relations

labor relations
The process of dealing with employees who are represented by a union

Labor relations is the process of dealing with employees who are represented by a union.[32] Managing labor relations is an important part of HRM. However, most large firms have separate labor relations specialists to handle these activities apart from other human resource functions.

How Employees Form Unions

For employees to form a new local union, several things must occur. First, employees must become interested in having a union. Nonemployees who are professional organizers employed by a national union (such as the Teamsters or United Auto Workers) may generate interest by making speeches and distributing literature outside the workplace. Inside, employees who want a union try to convince other workers of the benefits of a union.

The second step is to collect employees' signatures on authorization cards. These cards state that the signer wishes to vote to determine whether the union will represent him or her. To show the National Labor Relations Board (NLRB) that interest is sufficient to justify holding an election, 30 percent of the employees in the potential bargaining unit must sign these cards. Before an election can be held, however, the bargaining unit must be defined. The bargaining unit consists of all employees who will be eligible to vote in the election and to join and be represented by the union if one is formed.

The election is supervised by an NLRB representative (or, if both parties agree, the American Arbitration Association—a professional association of arbitrators) and is conducted by secret ballot. If a simple majority of those voting (not of all those eligible to vote) votes for the union, then the union becomes certified as the official representative of the bargaining unit.[33] The new union then organizes itself by officially signing up members and electing officers; it will soon be ready to negotiate the first contract. The union-organizing process is diagrammed in Figure 14.5. If workers become disgruntled with their union or if management presents strong evidence that the union is not representing workers appropriately, the NLRB can arrange a decertification election. The results of such an election determine whether the union remains certified.

Organizations usually prefer that employees not be unionized because unions limit management's freedom in many areas. Management may thus wage its own

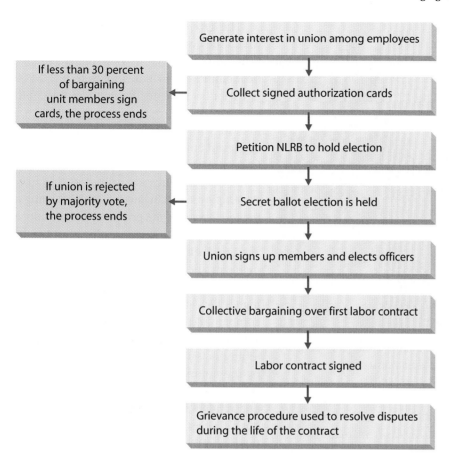

Figure 14.5
THE UNION-ORGANIZING PROCESS

If employees of an organization want to form a union, the law prescribes a specific set of procedures that both employees and the organization must follow. Assuming that these procedures are followed and the union is approved, the organization must engage in collective bargaining with the new union.

campaign to convince employees to vote against the union. "Unfair labor practices" are often committed at this point. For instance, it is an unfair labor practice for management to promise to give employees a raise (or any other benefit) if the union is defeated. Experts agree that the best way to avoid unionization is to practice good employee relations all the time—not just when threatened by a union election. Providing absolutely fair treatment with clear standards in the areas of pay, promotion, layoffs, and discipline; having a complaint or appeal system for persons who feel unfairly treated; and avoiding any kind of favoritism will help make employees feel that a union is unnecessary. Wal-Mart strives to avoid unionization through these practices.[34]

Collective Bargaining

The intent of **collective bargaining** is to agree on a labor contract between management and the union that is satisfactory to both parties. The contract contains agreements about such issues as wages, work hours, job security, promotion, layoffs, discipline, benefits, methods of allocating overtime, vacations, rest periods, and the grievance procedure. The process of bargaining may go on for weeks, months, or longer, with representatives of management and the union meeting to make proposals and counterproposals. The resulting agreement must be ratified by the union membership. If it is not approved, the union may strike to put pressure on management, or it may choose not to strike and simply continue negotiating until a more acceptable agreement is reached.

collective bargaining
The process of agreeing on a satisfactory labor contract between management and a union

A strike by a unionized workforce can be a debilitating event for any organization. Yvette Salazar, center, president of the local transit workers union, is cheered on by striking members as she asks Governor Bill Owens to order federal arbitration in hope of bringing an end to the strike during a rally at the Regional Transportation District's Market Street Station in Denver, Colorado, in April 2006. The strike shut down the city's light rail train system and reduced bus services.

The **grievance procedure** is the means by which the contract is enforced. Most of what is in a contract concerns how management will treat employees. When employees feel that they have not been treated fairly under the contract, they file a grievance to correct the problem. The first step in a grievance procedure is for the aggrieved employee to discuss the alleged contract violation with her immediate superior. Often the grievance is resolved at this stage. If the employee still believes that she is being mistreated, however, the grievance can be appealed to the next level. A union official can help an aggrieved employee present her case. If the manager's decision is also unsatisfactory to the employee, additional appeals to successively higher levels are made until, finally, all in-company steps are exhausted. The final step is to submit the grievance to binding arbitration. An arbitrator is a labor law expert who is paid jointly by the union and management. The arbitrator studies the contract, hears both sides of the case, and renders a decision that both parties must obey. The grievance system for resolving disputes about contract enforcement prevents any need to strike during the term of the contract.

concept CHECK

What are the basic steps employees follow to form a union?

In your opinion, do unions serve a useful purpose today? Why or why not?

New Challenges in the Changing Workplace

As we have seen throughout this chapter, human resource managers face several ongoing challenges in their efforts to keep their organizations staffed with effective workforces. To complicate matters, new challenges arise as the economic and social environments of business change. We conclude this chapter with a look at two of the most important human resource management issues facing business today.

Managing Knowledge Workers

Employees traditionally added value to organizations because of what they did or because of their experience. In the "information age," however, many employees add value because of what they know.[35]

The Nature of Knowledge Work   These employees are usually called **knowledge workers**, and the skill with which they are managed is a major factor in determin-

grievance procedure
The means by which a labor contract is enforced

knowledge workers
Workers whose contributions to an organization are based on what they know

ing which firms will be successful in the future. Knowledge workers, including computer scientists, engineers, and physical scientists, provide special challenges for the HR manager. They tend to work in high-technology firms and are usually experts in some abstract knowledge base. They often like to work independently and tend to identify more strongly with their profession than with any organization—even to the extent of defining performance in terms recognized by other members of their profession.

As the importance of information-driven jobs grows, the need for knowledge workers continues to grow as well. But these employees require extensive and highly specialized training, and not every organization is willing to make the human capital investments necessary to take advantage of these jobs. In fact, even after knowledge workers are on the job, retraining and training updates are critical to prevent their skills from becoming obsolete. It has been suggested, for example, that the "half-life" of a technical education in engineering is about three years. The failure to update such skills will not only result in the loss of competitive advantage but also increase the likelihood that the knowledge worker will go to another firm that is more committed to updating them.

> " The world is not the same as it used to be. Companies pay for skills in an era where brains are more important than brawn, and the forces of automation, globalization, deregulation, and competition have changed what this kind of work is worth in the world. "
>
> John Challenger, CEO of outplacement firm Challenger, Gray, & Christmas
> (*USA Today*, March 28, 2006, p. 2B)

Knowledge Worker Management and Labor Markets Even though overall demand for labor has slowed in recent years due to the economic downturn, the demand for knowledge workers remains strong. As a result, organizations that need these workers must introduce regular market adjustments (upward) in order to pay them enough to keep them. This is especially critical in areas in which demand is growing, as even entry-level salaries for these employees are high. Once an employee accepts a job with a firm, the employer faces yet another dilemma. Once hired, workers are more subject to the company's internal labor market, which is not likely to be growing as quickly as the external market for knowledge workers as a whole. Consequently, the longer an employee remains with a firm, the further behind the market his or her pay falls—unless, of course, it is regularly adjusted (upward).

Not surprisingly, the growing demand for these workers has inspired some fairly extreme measures for attracting them in the first place.[36] High starting salaries and sign-on bonuses are common. BP Exploration was recently paying starting petroleum engineers with undersea platform-drilling knowledge—not experience, just knowledge—salaries in the six figures, plus sign-on bonuses of over $50,000 and immediate profit sharing. Even with these incentives, HR managers complain that, in the Gulf Coast region, they cannot retain specialists because young engineers soon leave to accept sign-on bonuses with competitors. Laments one HR executive, "We wind up six months after we hire an engineer having to fight off offers for that same engineer for more money."[37]

Contingent and Temporary Workers

A final contemporary HR issue of note involves the use of contingent or temporary workers. Indeed, recent years have seen an explosion in the use of such workers by organizations. The FBI, for example, routinely employs a cadre of retired agents in various temporary jobs.[38]

Trends in Contingent and Temporary Employment   In recent years, the number of contingent workers in the workforce has increased dramatically. A contingent worker is a person who works for an organization on something other than a permanent or full-time basis. Categories of contingent workers include independent contractors, on-call workers, temporary employees (usually hired through outside agencies), and contract and leased employees. Another category is part-time workers. The financial services giant Citigroup, for example, makes extensive use of part-time sales agents to pursue new clients. About 10 percent of the U.S. workforce currently uses one of these alternative forms of employment relationships. Experts suggest, however, that this percentage is increasing at a consistent pace.

Managing Contingent and Temporary Workers   Given the widespread use of contingent and temporary workers, HR managers must understand how to use such employees most effectively. In other words, they need to understand how to manage contingent and temporary workers.

One key is careful planning. Even though one of the presumed benefits of using contingent workers is flexibility, it is still important to integrate such workers in a coordinated fashion. Rather than having to call in workers sporadically and with no prior notice, organizations try to bring in specified numbers of workers for well-defined periods of time. The ability to do so comes from careful planning.

A second key is understanding contingent workers and acknowledging both their advantages and their disadvantages. In other words, the organization must recognize what it can and cannot achieve from the use of contingent and temporary workers. Expecting too much from such workers, for example, is a mistake that managers should avoid.

Third, managers must carefully assess the real cost of using contingent workers. We noted above, for example, that many firms adopt this course of action to save labor costs. The organization should be able to document precisely its labor-cost savings. How much would it be paying people in wages and benefits if they were on permanent staff? How does this cost compare with the amount spent on contingent workers? This difference, however, could be misleading. We also noted, for instance, that contingent workers might be less effective performers than permanent and full-time employees. Comparing employee for employee on a direct-cost basis, therefore, is not necessarily valid. Organizations must learn to adjust the direct differences in labor costs to account for differences in productivity and performance.

Finally, managers must fully understand their own strategies and decide in advance how they intend to manage temporary workers, specifically focusing on how to integrate them into the organization. On a very simplistic level, for example, an organization with a large contingent workforce must make some decisions about the treatment of contingent workers relative to the treatment of permanent, full-time workers. Should contingent workers be invited to the company holiday party? Should they have the same access to such employee benefits as counseling services and childcare? There are no right or wrong answers to such questions. Managers must understand that they need to develop a strategy for integrating contingent workers according to some sound logic and then follow that strategy consistently over time.[39]

Indeed, this last point has become part of a legal battleground in recent years as some workers hired under the rubric of contingent workers have subsequently argued that this has been a title in name only, and that their employers use this title to discriminate against them in various ways. For instance, FedEx relies on over 13,000 "contract" drivers. These individuals wear FedEx uniforms, drive FedEx trucks, and must follow FedEx rules and procedures. However, because the firm has hired them under a different employment agreement than its "regular" employees, it does not provide them with benefits. Some of those individuals are currently suing FedEx on the grounds that, for all practical purposes, they are employees and should enjoy the same benefits as other drivers.[40]

		concept
		CHECK

What are the fundamental issues and considerations regarding the use of contingent and temporary employees? | *Have trends in employment for knowledge workers changed since the publication of this book?*

Summary of Learning Objectives and Key Points

1. Describe the environmental context of human resource management, including its strategic importance and its relationship with legal and social factors.
   - Human resource management is concerned with attracting, developing, and maintaining the human resources an organization needs.
   - Its environmental context consists of its strategic importance and the legal and social environments that affect human resource management.

2. Discuss how organizations attract human resources, including human resource planning, recruiting, and selecting.
   - Attracting human resources is an important part of the HRM function.
   - Human resource planning starts with job analysis and then focuses on forecasting the organization's future need for employees, forecasting the availability of employees both within and outside the organization, and planning programs to ensure that the proper number and type of employees will be available when needed.
   - Recruitment and selection are the processes by which job applicants are attracted, assessed, and hired.
   - Methods for selecting applicants include application blanks, tests, interviews, and assessment centers.
   - Any method used for selection should be properly validated.

3. Describe how organizations develop human resources, including training and development, performance appraisal, and performance feedback.
   - Organizations must also work to develop their human resources.
   - Training and development enable employees to perform their present job effectively and to prepare for future jobs.
   - Performance appraisals are important for validating selection devices, assessing the impact of training programs, deciding pay raises and promotions, and determining training needs.
   - Both objective and judgmental methods of appraisal can be applied, and a good system usually includes several methods.
   - The validity of appraisal information is always a concern, because it is difficult to accurately evaluate the many aspects of a person's job performance.

4. Discuss how organizations maintain human resources, including the determination of compensation and benefits and career planning.
   - Maintaining human resources is also important.
   - Compensation rates must be fair compared with rates for other jobs within the organization and with rates for the same or similar jobs in other organizations in the labor market.
   - Properly designed incentive or merit pay systems can encourage high performance, and a good benefits program can help attract and retain employees.

- Career planning is also a major aspect of human resource management.

5. Discuss labor relations, including how employees form unions and the mechanics of collective bargaining.
   - If a majority of a company's nonmanagement employees so desire, they have the right to be represented by a union.
   - Management must engage in collective bargaining with the union in an effort to agree on a contract.

- While a union contract is in effect, the grievance system is used to settle disputes with management.

6. Describe the issues associated with managing knowledge and contingent and temporary workers.
   - Two important new challenges in the workplace include
     - the management of knowledge workers
     - issues associated with the use of contingent and temporary workers

Discussion Questions

Questions for Review

1. Describe the steps in the process of human resource planning. Explain the relationships between the steps.
2. Describe the common selection methods. Which method or methods are the best predictors of future job performance? Which are the worst? Why?

3. Compare training and development, noting any similarities and differences. What are some commonly used training methods?
4. Define wages and benefits. List different benefits that organizations can offer. What are the three decisions that managers must make to determine compensation and benefits? Explain each decision.

Questions for Analysis

5. The Family and Medical Leave Act of 1993 is seen as providing much-needed flexibility and security for families and workers. Others think that it places an unnecessary burden on business. Yet another opinion is that the act hurts women, who are more likely to ask for leave, and shuffles them off to a low-paid "mommy track" career path. In your opinion, what are the likely consequences of the act? You can adopt one of the viewpoints expressed above or develop another. Explain your answer.
6. How do you know a selection device is valid? What are the possible consequences of using invalid selection methods? How can an organization ensure that its selection methods are valid?
7. In a right-to-work state, workers are permitted to decide for themselves whether to join a union. In

other states, workers may be required to join a union to obtain certain types of employment. If you live in a right-to-work state, do you agree that the choice to join a union should be made by each individual worker? If you do not live in a right-to-work state, do you agree that individuals should be required to join a union? Finally, if the choice were yours to make, would you join a union? Explain your answers. (*Hint:* Right-to-work states are generally in the South, Midwest, and parts of the West. If you do not know whether you live in a right-to-work state, visit the National Right to Work Legal Defense Foundation website, at **www.nrtw.org/rtws.htm**.)

Questions for Application

8. Choose three occupations that interest you. (The Labor Department's website has a full list, if you need help choosing.) Then access the Department of Labor, Bureau of Labor Statistics, online *Occupational Outlook Handbook*, at **www.bls.gov/oco**. What are the job prospects like in each of these fields? Based on what

you read at the website, do you think you would enjoy any of these occupations? Why or why not?
9. Consider a job that you have held or with which you are familiar. Describe how you think an organization could best provide a realistic job preview for that position. What types of information and experiences should be

conveyed to applicants? What techniques should be used to convey the information and experiences?

10. Contact a local organization to determine how that organization evaluates the performance of employees in complex jobs such as middle- or higher-level manager, scientist, lawyer, or market researcher. What problems with performance appraisal can you note?

Building Effective Decision-Making Skills

Exercise Overview

Decision-making skills include the manager's ability to recognize and define problems and opportunities correctly and then to select an appropriate course of action to solve problems and capitalize on opportunities. This exercise gives you practice in making career choices.

Exercise Background

Job seekers must understand a variety of information about their own abilities, preferences, and so on in order to make appropriate career choices. The problem is particularly acute for recent college graduates, who are often preparing to enter a career field that is largely unknown to them. Fortunately, a variety of sources of information can help. The Bureau of Labor Statistics maintains data about occupations, employment prospects, compensation, working conditions, and many other issues of interest to job seekers. The information is available by industry, occupation, employer type, and region.

Exercise Task

1. Access a summary of the Department of Labor's *National Compensation Survey*, at **http://stats.bls. gov/ncs/ocs/sp/ncbl0449.pdf**. (Or search for the survey's title, if the page has moved.) Find the detailed data related to the occupation that you think is your most likely career choice upon graduation. Then locate detailed data about two other occupations that you might consider—one with a higher salary than your most likely choice and one with a lower salary.

2. Record the hourly salary data for each of your three choices. Use the hourly salary to calculate an expected annual income. (*Hint:* Full-time jobs require about 2,000 hours annually.)

3. Based purely on salary information, which occupation would be the "best" for you?

4. Now access job descriptions for various occupations, at **www.bls.gov/oco**. Read the description for each of your three choices.

5. Based purely on job characteristics, which occupation would be the "best" for you?

6. Is there a conflict between your answers to questions 3 and 5? If so, how do you plan to resolve it?

7. Are there any job characteristics that you desire strongly enough to sacrifice pay to have them? What are they? What are the limits, if any, on your willingness to sacrifice pay?

Building Effective Technical Skills

Exercise Overview

Technical skills refer to the manager's abilities to accomplish or understand work done in an organization. Many managers must have technical skills to be able to hire appropriate people to work in the organization. This exercise will help you use technical skills as part of the selection process.

Exercise Background

Variation One. If you currently work or have worked in the past, select two jobs with which you have some familiarity. Select one job that is relatively low in skill level, responsibility, required education, and pay, and one job that is relatively high in the same categories. It will make the exercise more useful to you if you use real jobs that you can relate to on a personal level.

Variation Two. If you have never worked or are not personally familiar with an array of jobs, assume that you are a manager of a small manufacturing facility. You need to hire individuals to fill two jobs. One job is for the position of plant custodian. This individual will sweep floors, clean bathrooms, empty trash cans, and so forth. The other person will be an office manager. This individual will supervise a staff of three clerks and secretaries, administer the plant payroll, and coordinate the administrative operations of the plant.

Exercise Task

With the information above as background, do the following:

1. Identify the most basic skills that you think are necessary for someone to perform each job effectively.
2. Identify the general indicators or predictors of whether a given individual can perform each job.
3. Develop a brief set of interview questions that you might use to determine whether an applicant has the qualifications to perform each job.
4. How important is it that a manager hiring employees to perform a job has the technical skills to do that job him- or herself?

CHAPTER CLOSING CASE

USING HUMAN RESOURCES FOR COMPETITIVE ADVANTAGE

Nucor is a pioneer in the steelmaking industry, one of the first to make new steel from scrap metal. From a tiny upstart in the 1960s, the company today is the largest producer in the United States, shipping 21 million tons in 2005. The Nucor success story is all about the effective use of human resources.

In the 1960s, then-CEO Ken Iverson transformed the struggling firm with a unique management perspective. His philosophy required that employees earn according to their productivity, enjoy job security, and be treated fairly. These principles created an organization culture that is egalitarian, participative, and decentralized.

Iverson also designed a simple management structure, with few layers and few staff. General managers supervise department managers, line supervisors, and hourly personnel. There are just four layers and four job titles between a janitor and the current CEO, Daniel DiMicco. Nucor's headquarters staff consists of a mere 65 employees overseeing 12,000 workers, the smallest support staff of any multi-billion dollar firm.

Nucor has the best labor relations of any domestic steelmaker. None of the firm's plants are unionized, and employees do not feel they need a union for protection. On its part, Nucor has never engaged in union-busting tactics. Workers' contributions are recognized. In a gesture of appreciation, every single worker's name is printed on the cover of Nucor's annual reports.

Nucor also has an innovative compensation plan. Hourly workers at other mills earn $16 to $21 per hour, yet Nucor's make just $10. However, Nucor gives generous bonuses that are tied to the quality and productivity of the entire shift. Profit sharing adds an extra $18,000 annually. Bonuses and profit sharing in 2005 exceeded $220 million, in some cases, tripling take-home pay.

Compensation for managers is 75 to 90 percent of market average, but performance bonuses can double that amount. However, the hourly workers' bonuses and profit sharing are not offered to managers, creating greater pay equality. Even CEO DiMicco's pay is limited to 23 times the average hourly workers', compared to the typical CEO who makes 400 times the pay of a low-level worker. Executives have no perks—no company cars, extra holidays, enhanced insurance benefits, or reserved parking spaces.

Employment at Nucor can be lucrative, but high pay isn't guaranteed. If a bad batch of steel is identified before leaving the factory, the workers get no bonus. If the bad steel gets to the customer, they give up three times that amount. Bonuses are also dependent on the cyclical steel market. In 2005, when sales were strong, the average hourly worker made $91,000. In 2003, with steel sales down, the average was $59,000. "In average-to-bad years, we earn less than our peers in other companies," says James Coblin, Nucor's human resources vice president. "That's supposed to teach us that we don't want to be average or bad. We want to be good."

The nonunion workforce is flexible and participative. Workers take the initiative to improve operations in their areas. In fact, worker suggestions are the most important source of new ideas for the firm. Management has pushed decision making down to the lowest possible level. DiMicco refers to his executive vice presidents as "mini CEOs." Workers voluntarily assume responsibility because their pay is tied to overall performance. Trust is so high that divisions regularly compete for high performance, while still maintaining cooperation.

Nucor has grown through more than a dozen acquisitions over the last decade, yet the culture and practices have spread to each newly acquired plant. Leaders are promoted from within, which strengthens the culture. Nucor takes care to persuade new workers of the advantages of its system. At one newly acquired plant, Nucor based pay on the old system but posted what employees would have earned under the new system. After six months, employees realized the benefits and asked to switch to Nucor's formula.

Workers are passionate about Nucor. One vice president describes himself as "an apostle" for Iverson's methods and says, "Our culture is a living thing. It will not die because we will not let it die, ever." That passion has translated into profitability. Nucor has one of the highest returns to shareholders of almost all Standard & Poor's 500-stock index, at 387 percent over the past five years. Nucor managers routinely credit the workers for Nucor's high performance. General manager Ladd Hall says, "The people in the mills, that's what makes it Nucor."

CASE QUESTIONS

1. Instead of a separate performance appraisal system, Nucor judges performance based on the bottom line of quality, productivity, and profitability. What are the advantages and disadvantages of Nucor's choice?

2. What incentives does Nucor use to motivate and maintain its employees? Include both financial and nonfinancial incentives.

3. Many firms today use temporary, part-time, or virtual workers to reduce costs and gain flexibility. Nucor has not tried this. Should they? Why or why not?

CASE REFERENCES

"About Us," Nucor website, www.nucor.com on April 17, 2006; Nanette Byrnes, "The Art of Motivation," *BusinessWeek*, May 1, 2006, pp. 57–62; Gretchen Morgenson, "Companies Not Behaving Badly," *New York Times*, October 9, 2005, www.nytimes.com on April 17, 2006; Eduardo Porter, "Reinventing the Mill," *New York Times*, October 22, 2005, www.nytimes.com on April 17, 2006.

YOU MAKE THE CALL

The "Try-Before-You-Buy" Workforce

1. Assume you are a senior manager at a growing business in need of new employees. Your HR manager has recommended to you that you adopt a "temp-to-perm" practice. Our "First Things First" feature highlighted some of the advantages of this approach for employers. Are there disadvantages to your company? If so, what are they?

2. As a prospective job seeker, what are the advantages and disadvantages of accepting a "temp-to-perm" position as they relate to you personally?

3. Under what circumstances would you accept a "temp-to-perm" position?

4. Managing temporary employees who work with permanent employees poses a number of challenges for managers. In what ways are these challenges the same and in what ways are they different if the temporary workers are truly temporary versus being "auditioned" for permanent employment?

5. Would it be advisable to have a mix of three different types of employees—permanent, temporary, and "temp-to-perm"—working in the same setting? Why? What additional challenges might such an arrangement create?

Test Prepper

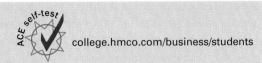

college.hmco.com/business/students

Choose the correct answer. Answers are found at the back of the book.

1. T   F   Under certain circumstances, employers are allowed to pay men and women doing the same job different amounts.

2. T   F   Several recent court cases have limited the ability of employers to terminate employees for virtually any reason.

3. T   F   Internal recruiting creates a ripple effect of open job positions.

4. T   F   Interviews are sometimes poor predictors of a job candidate's potential success.

5. T   F   An arbitrator is a financial planner who helps the firm determine the value of its human capital.

6. An employment requirement may create an adverse impact if

   A. members of the minority group meet or pass the requirement at a rate less than 80 percent of the rate of majority members.

   B. more than 20 members of a minority group have complained about the requirement.

   C. fewer than 20 percent of the majority group members fail the requirement.

   D. an executive order requires the employer to engage in affirmative action.

   E. the requirement makes it easier to bring a discrimination lawsuit, but also limits potential punitive damages.

7. The true test of whether a training and development program is effective is

   A. whether the training interfered with the production schedule.

   B. whether trainers met their learning goals.

   C. whether trainees' job performance improves after the training.

   D. whether trainees say they learned a lot from the training.

   E. whether trainees say they enjoyed the training.

8. Sandra has been asked to appraise the individual performance of a set of employees. She is having a difficult time because the group is large, the employees complete different kinds of work, and each employee has both strengths and weaknesses that will not be apparent in the appraisal method she is using. Sandra is likely using which technique?

   A. Rating
   B. Ranking
   C. Developmental
   D. Behavioral Anchored Rating Scale
   E. 360-degree feedback

9. Which of the following is necessary before a new local union can be formed?

   A. At least half of the employees must agree to collective bargaining.

   B. At least half of the managers in the affected unit must agree to collective bargaining.

   C. A majority of all those eligible to vote must vote for the union.

   D. Thirty percent of the employees in the potential bargaining unit must sign an authorization card.

   E. The existence of unfair labor practices must be established.

10. Which of the following steps is critical for an organization that relies on knowledge workers?

    A. Standardizing grievance procedures
    B. Retraining and updating training
    C. Preventing the formation of a union
    D. Encouraging the formation of a union
    E. Establishing informal assessment centers

chapter 15

Basic Elements of Individual Behavior in Organizations

FIRST THINGS FIRST

The Worst Bosses Ever

"There are certainly more [psychopaths] in the business world . . . than in the general population."

—DR. DAVID HARE, PSYCHOLOGY PROFESSOR,
UNIVERSITY OF BRITISH COLUMBIA

Bad bosses. Maybe you've had one or perhaps you've heard about some difficult, demanding, or just plain mean corporate leaders. Is meanness a temporary phase or an enduring personality trait? Managers are human, after all. Yet some bosses' behavior goes beyond the normal ups and downs. Psychologists studying corporate leadership describe the personalities of the worst bosses, the psychopaths and narcissists.

Dr. David Hare, professor of psychology, studies psychopaths. He consults with law enforcement and created questionnaires that reveal an individual's psychopathic tendencies. His research now includes corporate psychopaths. "If I wasn't studying psychopaths in prison, I'd do it at the stock exchange," says

LEARNING OBJECTIVES

After studying this chapter, you should be able to:

1. Explain the nature of the individual-organization relationship.

2. Define personality and describe personality attributes that affect behavior in organizations.

3. Discuss individual attitudes in organizations and how they affect behavior.

4. Describe basic perceptual processes and the role of attributions in organizations.

5. Discuss the causes and consequences of stress and describe how it can be managed.

6. Describe creativity and its role in organizations.

7. Explain how workplace behaviors can directly or indirectly influence organizational effectiveness.

Bad bosses can exhibit numerous dysfunctional characteristics. These staff members are clearly turned off by the behavior of their boss.

Hare. "There are certainly more people in the business world who would score high in the psychopathic dimension than in the general population."

According to Hare, psychopathic business leaders might include former Enron CFO Andrew Fastow and Al Dunlap, former CEO of Sunbeam, nicknamed "Chainsaw." Psychopaths' basic motive is the fulfillment of their own selfish desires, regardless of the consequences to others. They are superficially charming, insincere, lying, manipulative, guilt-free, lacking in empathy, ruthless, and unwilling to accept responsibility. Psychopaths are distinguished by two personality traits: "the callous, selfish, remorseless use of others" and "a chronically unstable and antisocial lifestyle." Psychopathic executives score high on the first factor but low on the second, turning them into high-functioning psychopaths. In contrast, criminal psychopaths are high on both factors, giving way to uncontrollable, violent impulses.

Unfortunately, business offers ample opportunities for successful psychopaths. American stockholders prefer top managers who are charismatic, visionary, and tough—traits of successful psychopaths. Psychologist Paul Babiak is the co-author, with Hare, of *Snakes in Suits: When Psychopaths Go to Work*. Rapid change does not dismay psychopaths. "Organization chaos provides both the necessary stimulation for psychopathic thrill seeking and sufficient cover for psychopathic manipulation and abuse," Babiak asserts.

Psychopaths are often likable and admired. Most individuals assume that others are like themselves, making them vulnerable to manipulation by a psychopath. "It goes against our intuition that a small percentage of people can be so different from the rest of us—and so evil. Good people don't want to believe it," claims Martha Stout, a psychologist. Yet behavior usually betrays the psychopath. Some have been known to punch or verbally abuse subordinates, while others delight in fraud or mass layoffs.

Narcissism is another problematic personality trait. Many leaders, in business and other fields, are narcissists. These individuals are egotistical and insensitive. They criticize others freely but have a tough time accepting criticism. Yet while psychopaths enjoy hurting others, narcissists think of themselves as visionaries who are trying to change the world for the better. They can't see through others' eyes but they do have good intentions. Babiak makes this distinction: "The psychopathy has no allegiance to the company at all, just to self. . . . [But narcissists'] identity is wrapped up with the company's existence. They're loyal."

Michael Maccoby, a psychotherapist and organizational consultant, names Bill Gates of Microsoft, Herb Kelleher of Southwest Airlines, and GE's Jack Welch as likely narcissists. He says, "[Narcissists] don't have much empathy. . . . They see other people as a means towards their ends. But they do have a sense of changing the world—in their eyes, improving the world." A moderate amount of narcissism may even be necessary to allow an entrepreneur to persist and excel in a difficult, risky environment.

How can organizations manage narcissists? Maccoby suggests that companies pair a narcissistic manager with a conscientious, steadying one. The behind-the-scenes good influence stops narcissists from becoming destructive or too out of touch. For example, Microsoft president Steve Ballmer is often seen as the reality check and implementer of Gates's visions.

However, organizations should not attempt to manage psychopaths. These individuals are so dangerous to organizations and coworkers that they should not have any place in a healthy organization. Robert Hare recommends screening and has developed an instrument for this purpose. "Why wouldn't we want to screen [executives]?" he asks. "We screen police officers, teachers. Why not people who are going to handle billions of dollars?" Employees suffering under the worst bosses surely agree. Why not eliminate managers whose personalities disqualify them for positions of trust?[1]

The people who populate today's business world are characterized by a wide variety of personalities and behaviors. While most people in business have relatively healthy and constructive personalities and behave in ethical and productive ways, there are some who reflect different profiles. Indeed, myriad different and unique characteristics reside in each and every employee. These affect how they feel about the organization, how they will alter their future attitudes about the firm, and how they perform their jobs. These characteristics reflect the basic elements of individual behavior in organizations.

This chapter describes several of these basic elements and is the first of several chapters designed to develop a more complete perspective on the leading function of management. In the next section we investigate the psychological nature of individuals in organizations. The following section introduces the concept of personality and discusses several important personality attributes that can influence behavior in organizations. We then examine individual attitudes and their role in organizations. The role of stress in the workplace is then discussed, followed by a discussion of individual creativity. Finally, we describe a number of basic individual behaviors that are important to organizations.

Understanding Individuals in Organizations

As a starting point in understanding human behavior in the workplace, we must consider the basic nature of the relationship between individuals and organizations. We must also gain an appreciation of the nature of individual differences.

The Psychological Contract

Most people have a basic understanding of a contract. Whenever we buy a car or sell a house, for example, both buyer and seller sign a contract that specifies the terms of the agreement. A psychological contract is similar in some ways to a standard legal contract but is less formal and well defined. In particular, a ***psychological contract*** is the overall set of expectations held by an individual with respect to what he or she will contribute to the organization and what the organization will provide in return.[2] Thus a psychological contract is not written on paper, nor are all of its terms explicitly negotiated.

The essential nature of a psychological contract is illustrated in Figure 15.1. The individual makes a variety of ***contributions*** to the organization—effort, skills, ability, time, loyalty, and so forth. These contributions presumably satisfy various needs and requirements of the organization. In other words, because the organization may have hired the person because of her skills, it is reasonable for

psychological contract
The overall set of expectations held by an individual with respect to what he or she will contribute to the organization and what the organization will provide in return

contributions
What the individual provides to the organization

Figure 15.1

THE PSYCHOLOGICAL CONTRACT

Psychological contracts are the basic assumptions that individuals have about their relationships with their organization. Such contracts are defined in terms of contributions by the individual relative to inducements from the organization.

Contributions from the Individual	Inducements from the Organization
• Effort	• Pay
• Ability	• Job security
• Loyalty	• Benefits
• Skills	• Career opportunities
• Time	• Status
• Competencies	• Promotion opportunities

inducements
What the organization provides to the individual

the organization to expect that she will subsequently display those skills in the performance of her job.

In return for these contributions, the organization provides **inducements** to the individual. Some inducements, like pay and career opportunities, are tangible rewards. Others, like job security and status, are more intangible. Just as the contributions available from the individual must satisfy the needs of the organization, the inducements offered by the organization must serve the needs of the individual. Thus, if a person accepts employment with an organization because he thinks he will earn an attractive salary and have an opportunity to advance, he will subsequently expect that those rewards will actually be forthcoming.

If both the individual and the organization perceive that the psychological contract is fair and equitable, they will be satisfied with the relationship and will likely continue it. On the other hand, if either party sees an imbalance or inequity in the contract, it may initiate a change. For example, the individual may request a pay raise or promotion, decrease her contributed effort, or look for a better job elsewhere. The organization can also initiate change by requesting that the individual improve his skills through training, transfer the person to another job, or terminate the person's employment altogether.

A basic challenge faced by the organization, then, is to manage psychological contracts. The organization must ensure that it is getting value from its employees. At the same time, it must be sure that it is providing employees with appropriate inducements. If the organization is underpaying its employees for their contributions, for example, they may perform poorly or leave for better jobs elsewhere. On the other hand, if they are being overpaid relative to their contributions, the organization is incurring unnecessary costs.[3]

> **❝**Take a reasonably intelligent worker who has been schooled in the idea that his employer is always out to take advantage of him, (and) he may not believe his company is really in jeopardy.**❞**
>
> Jay Waks, employment and labor attorney
> (*USA Today,* March 28, 2006, p. 2B)

The Person-Job Fit

Another reason for imprecise person-job fits is that both people and organizations change. An individual who finds a new job stimulating and exciting may find the same job boring and monotonous after a few years of performing it. And, when the organization adopts new technology, it has changed the skills it needs from its employees. Still another reason for imprecision in the person-job fit is that each individual is unique. Measuring skills and performance is difficult enough. Assessing needs, attitudes, and personality is far more complex. Each of these individual differences serves to make matching individuals with jobs a difficult and complex process.

The Nature of Individual Differences

Individual differences are personal attributes that vary from one person to another. Individual differences may be physical, psychological, or emotional. Taken together, all of the individual differences that characterize any specific person serve to make that individual unique from everyone else. Much of the remainder of this chapter is devoted to individual differences. Before proceeding, however, we must also note the importance of the situation in assessing the behavior of individuals.

Are specific differences that characterize a given individual good or bad? Do they contribute to or detract from performance? The answer, of course, is that it depends on the circumstances. One person may be very dissatisfied, withdrawn, and negative in one job setting, but very satisfied, outgoing, and positive in another. Working conditions, coworkers, and leadership are all important ingredients.

Thus, whenever an organization attempts to assess or account for individual differences among its employees, it must also be sure to consider the situation in which behavior occurs. Individuals who are satisfied or productive workers in one context may prove to be dissatisfied or unproductive workers in another context. Attempting to consider both individual differences and contributions in relation to inducements and contexts, then, is a major challenge for organizations as they attempt to establish effective psychological contracts with their employees and achieve optimal fits between people and jobs. *The Business of Ethics* discusses how one successful toy maker, BEKA, has excelled as a result of individual differences.

Person-job fit is an important element in individual behavior in organizations. Fine art restorer Thomas Cibelius works in a studio of the Historical Green Vault in Dresden, Germany, in preparation for the new opening of the famous treasure chamber in summer 2006. The masterworks of art once displayed there are being painstakingly restored to their original condition. Work such as this requires artistic ability, skill, and patience, qualities possessed by only a few people.

> **individual differences**
> Personal attributes that vary from one person to another

What is a psychological contract, and what are its fundamental components?

Describe different jobs that would result in both a very good and a very bad person-job fit for you personally.

concept
CHECK

Personality and Individual Behavior

Personality traits represent some of the most fundamental sets of individual differences in organizations. **Personality** is the relatively stable set of psychological attributes that distinguish one person from another.[4] Managers should strive to understand basic personality attributes and the ways they can affect people's behavior in organizational situations, not to mention their perceptions of and attitudes toward the organization.

> **personality**
> The relatively permanent set of psychological and behavioral attributes that distinguish one person from another

The Business of Ethics

Plays Well with Others

Play is serious business. Per child, Americans spend $242 on toys each year, and sales are growing at 6 percent. While most toys sold in the United States are designed there, large-scale production mainly occurs overseas, where labor costs are lower. The industry's U.S. workforce has shrunk by more than 50 percent over the last decade. Pressure from discount retail chains accelerates the trend toward foreign manufacturing. The three largest toy sellers make over one-half of total sales, with Wal-Mart cornering 30 percent of the toy market.

But in spite of cost pressure and offshoring, some toy makers play a different game. BEKA Inc. makes wooden blocks, art easels, puppet theatres, and play furniture. The firm, headed by brothers Jamie and Peter Kreisman, is successful with a creative yet traditional business model. For 30 years, BEKA has been a family-run, old-fashioned firm. Jamie Kreisman says, "Large companies . . . want to tell you how to cut corners to cut costs. . . . We could sell many more products, but it wouldn't be our product or what we want our name on. So we said, 'No, thank you.'" BEKA refuses to compromise, using durable hardwoods and expert woodworkers. Products are safe and durable. High-quality customer service offers personal attention and custom-made pieces.

BEKA's success is the result of the two founders' different temperaments and interests, as well as their creativity. The brothers share a spirit of independence, a love of craftsmanship, and service orientation. However, Jamie has an MBA while Peter has a PhD in physics. "I'll speak with customers about a product and mock up a sample, and then Peter will work out all the details and figure out how to build it safely, solidly, and as economically as possible," says Jamie. "He's the scientist, and I'm the people person and the number-cruncher." The brothers' complementary approaches are beneficial to BEKA.

Small toy stores are also endangered by the expansion of discount chains and low-cost products. They prefer toys such as BEKA's that are made by independent toy manufacturers. These toys allow the smaller stores to differentiate themselves from Wal-Mart and Toys "R" Us. The Kreismans, by using their unique personalities and pursuing their creative business model, are helping to keep the U.S. toy industry alive.

References: "2005 Dolls, Toys, Games, and Children's Vehicles Outlook," U.S. Department of Commerce website, trade.gov on April 24, 2006; "About BEKA," BEKA website, www.bekainc.com on April 24, 2006; Erin Chambers, "How a Toy Store Plays to Win," *BusinessWeek*, November 24, 2004, www.businessweek.com on April 24, 2006; Erin Chambers, "Playing by BEKA's Rules," *BusinessWeek*, December 8, 2004, www.businessweek.com on April 24, 2006.

The "Big Five" Personality Traits

"Big Five" personality traits
A popular personality framework based on five key traits

agreeableness
A person's ability to get along with others

Psychologists have identified literally thousands of personality traits and dimensions that differentiate one person from another. But, in recent years, researchers have identified five fundamental personality traits that are especially relevant to organizations. Because these five traits are so important and because they are currently the subject of so much attention, they are now commonly referred to as the ***"Big Five" personality traits***.[5] Figure 15.2 illustrates the Big Five traits.

Agreeableness refers to a person's ability to get along with others. Agreeableness causes some people to be gentle, cooperative, forgiving, understanding, and good-natured in their dealings with others. But it results in others' being irritable, short-tempered, uncooperative, and generally antagonistic toward other people. Although research has not yet fully investigated the effects of agreeableness, it would seem likely that highly agreeable people will be better able to develop good working relationships with coworkers, subordinates, and higher-level managers, whereas less agreeable people will not have particularly good working relationships. This same pattern might also extend to relationships with customers, suppliers, and other key organizational constituents.

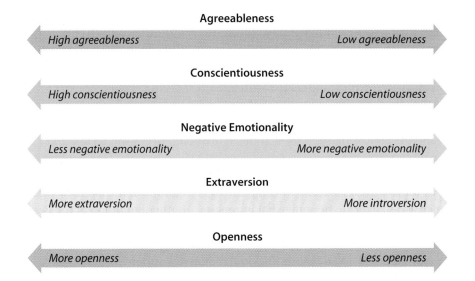

Figure 15.2

THE "BIG FIVE" MODEL OF PERSONALITY

The "Big Five" personality model represents an increasingly accepted framework for understanding personality traits in organizational settings. In general, experts tend to agree that personality traits toward the left end of each dimension, as illustrated in this figure, are more positive in organizational settings, whereas traits closer to the right are less positive.

Conscientiousness refers to the number of goals on which a person focuses. People who focus on relatively few goals at one time are likely to be organized, systematic, careful, thorough, responsible, and self-disciplined as they work to pursue those goals. Others, however, tend to take on a wider array of goals and, as a result, are more disorganized, careless, and irresponsible, as well as less thorough and self-disciplined. Research has found that more conscientious people tend to be higher performers than less conscientious people across a variety of different jobs. This pattern seems logical, of course, because more conscientious people will take their jobs seriously and will approach the performance of their jobs in highly responsible fashions.

The third of the Big Five personality dimensions is *negative emotionality*. People with less negative emotionality will be relatively poised, calm, resilient, and secure. But people with more negative emotionality will be more excitable, insecure, reactive, and subject to extreme mood swings. People with less negative emotionality might be expected to better handle job stress, pressure, and tension. Their stability might also lead them to be seen as more reliable than their less stable counterparts.

Extraversion refers to a person's comfort level with relationships. People who are called "extraverts" are sociable, talkative, assertive, and open to establishing new relationships. But introverts are much less sociable, talkative, and assertive, and less open to establishing new relationships. Research suggests that extraverts tend to be higher overall job performers than introverts and that they are also more likely to be attracted to jobs based on personal relationships, such as sales and marketing positions.

Finally, *openness* refers to a person's rigidity of beliefs and range of interests. People with high levels of openness are willing to listen to new ideas and to change their own ideas, beliefs, and attitudes as a result of new information. They also tend to have broad interests and to be curious, imaginative, and creative. On the other hand, people with low levels of openness tend to be less receptive to new ideas and less willing to change their minds. Further, they tend to have fewer and narrower interests and to be less curious and creative. People with more openness might be expected to be better performers, owing to their flexibility and the likelihood that they will be better accepted by others in the organization. Openness may also

conscientiousness
The number of goals on which a person focuses

negative emotionality
Extent to which a person is poised, calm, resilient, and secure

extraversion
A person's comfort level with relationships

openness
A person's rigidity of beliefs and range of interests

encompass an individual's willingness to accept change. For example, people with high levels of openness may be more receptive to change, whereas people with low levels of openness may be more likely to resist change.

The Big Five framework continues to attract the attention of both researchers and managers. The potential value of this framework is that it encompasses an integrated set of traits that appear to be valid predictors of certain behaviors in certain situations. Thus managers who can develop both an understanding of the framework and the ability to assess these traits in their employees will be in a good position to understand how and why employees behave as they do.[6] On the other hand, managers must also be careful not to overestimate their ability to assess the Big Five traits in others. Even assessment using the most rigorous and valid measures, for instance, is still likely to be somewhat imprecise. Another limitation of the Big Five framework is that it is based primarily on research conducted in the United States. Thus there are unanswered questions as to how accurately it applies to workers in other cultures. And, even within the United States, a variety of other factors and traits are also likely to affect behavior in organizations.

The Myers-Briggs Framework

Another interesting approach to understanding personalities in organizations is the Myers-Briggs framework. This framework, based on the classic work of Carl Jung, differentiates people in terms of four general dimensions. These are defined as follows.

- *Extraversion (E) Versus Introversion (I)*. Extraverts get their energy from being around other people, whereas introverts are worn out by others and need solitude to recharge their energy.
- *Sensing (S) Versus Intuition (N)*. The sensing type prefers concrete things, whereas intuitives prefer abstract concepts.
- *Thinking (T) Versus Feeling (F)*. Thinking individuals base their decisions more on logic and reason, whereas feeling individuals base their decisions more on feelings and emotions.
- *Judging (J) Versus Perceiving (P)*. People who are the judging type enjoy completion or being finished, whereas perceiving types enjoy the process and open-ended situations.

To use this framework, people complete a questionnaire designed to measure their personality on each dimension. Higher or lower scores in each of the dimensions are used to classify people into 1 of 16 different personality categories.

The Myers-Briggs Type Indicator (MBTI) is one popular questionnaire that some organizations use to assess personality types. Indeed, it is among the most popular selection instruments used today, with as many as 2 million people taking it each year. Research suggests that the MBTI is a useful method for determining communication styles and interaction preferences. In terms of personality attributes, however, questions exist about both the validity and the reliability of the MBTI.

Other Personality Traits at Work

Besides the Big Five and the Myers-Briggs framework, there are several other personality traits that influence behavior in organizations. Among the most important are locus of control, self-efficacy, authoritarianism, Machiavellianism, self-esteem, and risk propensity.

Locus of control is the extent to which people believe that their behavior has a real effect on what happens to them.[7]

Some people, for example, believe that, if they work hard, they will succeed. They also may believe that people who fail do so because they lack ability or motivation. People who believe that individuals are in control of their lives are said to have an *internal locus of control*. Other people think that fate, chance, luck, or other people's behavior determines what happens to them. For example, an employee who fails to get a promotion may attribute that failure to a politically motivated boss or just bad luck, rather than to her or his own lack of skills or poor performance record. People who think that forces beyond their control dictate what happens to them are said to have an *external locus of control*.

Locus of control is the degree to which an individual believes that behavior has a direct impact on the consequences of that behavior. Most professional athletes, for instance, are very self-confident and anticipate victory every time they enter an event. Venus Williams, for example, fully expects to win every time she steps on the tennis court. Thus, she clearly has an internal locus of control.

Self-efficacy is a related but subtly different personality characteristic. Self-efficacy is a person's beliefs about his or her capabilities to perform a task.[8] People with high self-efficacy believe that they can perform well on a specific task, whereas people with low self-efficacy tend to doubt their ability to perform a specific task. Although self-assessments of ability contribute to self-efficacy, so, too, does the individual's personality. Some people simply have more self-confidence than do others. This belief in their ability to perform a task effectively results in their being more self-assured and more able to focus their attention on performance.

Another important personality characteristic is ***authoritarianism***, the extent to which an individual believes that power and status differences are appropriate within hierarchical social systems like organizations.[9] For example, a person who is highly authoritarian may accept directives or orders from someone with more authority purely because the other person is "the boss." On the other hand, although a person who is not highly authoritarian may still carry out appropriate and reasonable directives from the boss, he or she is also more likely to question things, express disagreement with the boss, and even refuse to carry out orders if they are for some reason objectionable. A highly authoritarian manager may be autocratic and demanding, and highly authoritarian subordinates will be more likely to accept this behavior from their leader. On the other hand, a less authoritarian manager may allow subordinates a bigger role in making decisions, and less authoritarian subordinates will respond positively to this behavior.

Machiavellianism is another important personality trait. This concept is named after Niccolo Machiavelli, a sixteenth-century Italian political philosopher. In his book entitled *The Prince,* Machiavelli explained how the nobility could more easily gain and use power. *Machiavellianism* is now used to describe behavior directed at gaining power and controlling the behavior of others. Research suggests that Machiavellianism is a personality trait that varies from person to person. More Machiavellian individuals tend to be rational and nonemotional, may be willing to lie to attain

locus of control
The degree to which an individual believes that his or her behavior has a direct impact on the consequences of that behavior

self-efficacy
An individual's beliefs about her or his capabilities to perform a task

authoritarianism
The extent to which an individual believes that power and status differences are appropriate within hierarchical social systems like organizations

Machiavellianism
Behavior directed at gaining power and controlling the behavior of others

their personal goals, may put little weight on loyalty and friendship, and may enjoy manipulating others' behavior. Less Machiavellian individuals are more emotional, less willing to lie to succeed, value loyalty and friendship highly, and get little personal pleasure from manipulating others. By all accounts, Dennis Kozlowski, the indicted former CEO of Tyco International, had a high degree of Machiavellianism. He apparently came to believe that his position of power in the company gave him the right to do just about anything he wanted with company resources.[10]

Self-esteem
The extent to which a person believes that he or she is a worthwhile and deserving individual

Self-esteem is the extent to which a person believes that she is a worthwhile and deserving individual.[11] A person with high self-esteem is more likely to seek high-status jobs, be more confident in her ability to achieve higher levels of performance, and derive greater intrinsic satisfaction from her accomplishments. In contrast, a person with less self-esteem may be more content to remain in a lower-level job, be less confident of his ability, and focus more on extrinsic rewards. Among the major personality dimensions, self-esteem is the one that has been most widely studied in other countries. Although more research is clearly needed, the published evidence does suggest that self-esteem as a personality trait does indeed exist in a variety of countries and that its role in organizations is reasonably important across different cultures.[12]

risk propensity
The degree to which an individual is willing to take chances and make risky decisions

Risk propensity is the degree to which an individual is willing to take chances and make risky decisions. A manager with a high risk propensity, for example, might be expected to experiment with new ideas and gamble on new products. She might also lead the organization in new and different directions. This manager might also be a catalyst for innovation. On the other hand, the same individual might also jeopardize the continued well-being of the organization if the risky decisions prove to be bad ones. A manager with low risk propensity might lead to a stagnant and overly conservative organization or help the organization successfully weather turbulent and unpredictable times by maintaining stability and calm. Thus the potential consequences of risk propensity to an organization are heavily dependent on that organization's environment.

Emotional Intelligence

emotional intelligence (EQ)
The extent to which people are self-aware, manage their emotions, motivate themselves, express empathy for others, and possess social skills

The concept of emotional intelligence has been identified in recent years and provides some interesting insights into personality. **Emotional intelligence**, or **EQ**, refers to the extent to which people are self-aware, manage their emotions, motivate themselves, express empathy for others, and possess social skills.[13] These various dimensions can be described as follows:

- *Self-Awareness*. This is the basis for the other components. It refers to a person's capacity for being aware of how they are feeling. In general, more self-awareness allows people to more effectively guide their own lives and behaviors.

- *Managing Emotions*. This refers to a person's capacities to balance anxiety, fear, and anger so that they do not overly interfere with getting things accomplished.

- *Motivating Oneself*. This dimension refers to a person's ability to remain optimistic and to continue striving in the face of setbacks, barriers, and failure.

- *Empathy*. Empathy refers to a person's ability to understand how others are feeling, even without being explicitly told.

- *Social Skill*. This refers to a person's ability to get along with others and to establish positive relationships.

Preliminary research suggests that people with high EQs may perform better than others, especially in jobs that require a high degree of interpersonal interaction and that involve influencing or directing the work of others. Moreover, EQ appears to be something that is not biologically based but can be developed.[14]

concept
CHECK

What is personality? Identify several basic personality dimensions.

Describe your own personality in terms of the various personality dimensions discussed in this section. For instance, do you think you have an internal or an external locus of control?

Attitudes and Individual Behavior

Another important element of individual behavior in organizations is attitudes. ***Attitudes*** are complexes of beliefs and feelings that people have about specific ideas, situations, or other people. Attitudes are important because they are the mechanism through which most people express their feelings. An employee's statement that he feels underpaid by the organization reflects his feelings about his pay. Similarly, when a manager says that she likes the new advertising campaign, she is expressing her feelings about the organization's marketing efforts.

> *attitudes*
> Complexes of beliefs and feelings that people have about specific ideas, situations, or other people

Attitudes have three components. The *affective component* of an attitude reflects feelings and emotions an individual has toward a situation. The *cognitive component* of an attitude is derived from knowledge an individual has about a situation. It is important to note that cognition is subject to individual perceptions (something we discuss more fully later). Thus one person might "know" that a certain political candidate is better than another, whereas someone else might "know" just the opposite. Finally, the *intentional component* of an attitude reflects how an individual expects to behave toward or in the situation.

To illustrate these three components, consider the case of a manager who places an order for some supplies for his organization from a new office supply firm. Suppose many of the items he orders are out of stock, others are overpriced, and still others arrive damaged. When he calls someone at the supply firm for assistance, he is treated rudely and gets disconnected before his claim is resolved. When asked how he feels about the new office supply firm, he might respond, "I don't like that company [affective component]. They are the worst office supply firm I've ever dealt with [cognitive component]. I'll never do business with them again [intentional component]."

People try to maintain consistency among the three components of their attitudes as well as among all their attitudes. However, circumstances sometimes arise that lead to conflicts. The conflict individuals may experience among their own attitudes is called ***cognitive dissonance***.[15] Say, for example, that an individual who has vowed never to work for a big, impersonal corporation intends instead to open her own business and be her own boss. Unfortunately, a series of financial setbacks leads her to have no choice but to take a job with a large company and work for someone else. Thus cognitive dissonance occurs: The affective and cognitive components of the individual's attitude conflict with intended behavior. To reduce cognitive dissonance, which is usually an uncomfortable experience for most people, the individual might tell herself that the situation is only temporary and that she

> *cognitive dissonance*
> Caused when an individual has conflicting attitudes

can go back out on her own in the near future. Or she might revise her cognitions and decide that working for a large company is more pleasant than she had expected.

Work-Related Attitudes

People in organizations form attitudes about many different things. For example, employees are likely to have attitudes about their salary, promotion possibilities, their boss, employee benefits, the food in the company cafeteria, and the color of the company softball team uniforms. Of course, some of these attitudes are more important than others. Especially important attitudes are job satisfaction or dissatisfaction and organizational commitment.[16]

Job Satisfaction or Dissatisfaction *Job satisfaction* or *dissatisfaction* is an attitude that reflects the extent to which an individual is gratified by or fulfilled in his or her work. Extensive research conducted on job satisfaction has indicated that personal factors, such as an individual's needs and aspirations, determine this attitude, along with group and organizational factors, such as relationships with coworkers and supervisors, and working conditions, work policies, and compensation.[17]

> *job satisfaction* or *dissatisfaction*
> An attitude that reflects the extent to which an individual is gratified by or fulfilled in his or her work

A satisfied employee also tends to be absent less often, to make positive contributions, and to stay with the organization.[18] In contrast, a dissatisfied employee may be absent more often, may experience stress that disrupts coworkers, and may be continually looking for another job. Contrary to what many managers believe, however, high levels of job satisfaction do not necessarily lead to higher levels of performance. One survey has also indicated that, contrary to popular opinion, Japanese workers are less satisfied with their jobs than their counterparts in the United States.[19]

> "People don't feel good about flying an airline where the employees don't feel good about working for them."
> Richard Chaifetz, CEO of ComPsych
> (*USA Today,* November 30, 2004, p. 1B)

Organizational Commitment *Organizational commitment* is an attitude that reflects an individual's identification with and attachment to the organization itself. A person with a high level of commitment is likely to see herself as a true member of the organization (for example, referring to the organization in personal terms like "We make high-quality products"), to overlook minor sources of dissatisfaction with the organization, and to see herself remaining a member of the organization. In contrast, a person with less organizational commitment is more likely to see himself as an outsider (for example, referring to the organization in less personal terms like "They don't pay their employees very well"), to express more dissatisfaction about things, and to not see himself as a long-term member of the organization. Research suggests that Japanese workers may be more committed to their organizations than are American workers.[20]

> *organizational commitment*
> An attitude that reflects an individual's identification with and attachment to the organization itself

Research also suggests that commitment strengthens with an individual's age, years with the organization, sense of job security, and participation in decision making.[21] Employees who feel committed to an organization have highly reliable habits, plan a long tenure with the organization, and muster more effort in performance. Although there are few definitive things that organizations can do to create or promote commitment, there are a few specific guidelines available. For one thing, if the organization treats its employees fairly and provides reasonable rewards and job security, those employees will more likely be satisfied and committed. Allowing employees to have a say in how things are done can also promote all three attitudes.

Affect and Mood in Organizations

Researchers have recently started to focus renewed interest on the affective component of attitudes. Recall from our discussion above that the affective component of an attitude reflects our feelings and emotions. Although managers once believed that emotion and feelings varied among people from day to day, research now suggests that, although some short-term fluctuation does indeed occur, there are also underlying stable predispositions toward fairly constant and predictable moods and emotional states.[22]

Some people, for example, tend to have a higher degree of **positive affectivity**. This means that they are relatively upbeat and optimistic, have an overall sense of well-being, and usually see things in a positive light. Thus they always seem to be in a good mood. Other people, those with more **negative affectivity**, are just the opposite. They are generally downbeat and pessimistic, and they usually see things in a negative way. They seem to be in a bad mood most of the time.

Of course, as noted above, there can be short-term variations among even the most extreme types. People with a lot of positive affectivity, for example, may still be in a bad mood if they have just received some bad news—being passed over for a promotion, getting extremely negative performance feedback, or being laid off or fired, for instance. Similarly, those with negative affectivity may still be in a good mood—at least for a short time—if they have just been promoted, received very positive performance feedback, or had other good things befall them. After the initial impact of these events wears off, however, those with positive affectivity will generally return to their normal positive mood, whereas those with negative affectivity will gravitate back to their normal bad mood.

> **positive affectivity**
> A tendency to be relatively upbeat and optimistic, have an overall sense of well-being, see things in a positive light, and seem to be in a good mood

> **negative affectivity**
> A tendency to be generally downbeat and pessimistic, see things in a negative way, and seem to be in a bad mood

concept
CHECK

Identify and describe the three components of an attitude.

Using a job you have either held in the past or currently hold, describe the level of job satisfaction or dissatisfaction and organizational commitment you felt or feel. Describe what caused those attitudes and how they affected your behavior.

Perception and Individual Behavior

As noted earlier, an important element of an attitude is the individual's perception of the object about which the attitude is formed. Because perception plays a role in a variety of other workplace behaviors, managers need to have a general understanding of basic perceptual processes.[23] The role of attributions is also important.

Basic Perceptual Processes

Perception is the set of processes by which an individual becomes aware of and interprets information about the environment. As shown in Figure 15.3, basic perceptual processes that are particularly relevant to organizations are selective perception and stereotyping.

Selective Perception **Selective perception** is the process of screening out information that we are uncomfortable with or that contradicts our beliefs. For example, suppose a manager is exceptionally fond of a particular worker. The manager has a

> **perception**
> The set of processes by which an individual becomes aware of and interprets information about the environment

> **selective perception**
> The process of screening out information that we are uncomfortable with or that contradicts our beliefs

Figure 15.3
PERCEPTUAL PROCESSES

Two of the most basic perceptual processes are selective perception and stereotyping. As shown here, selective perception occurs when we screen out information (represented by the − symbols) that causes us discomfort or that contradicts our beliefs. Stereotyping occurs when we categorize or label people on the basis of a single attribute, illustrated here by color.

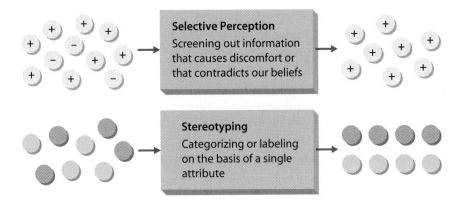

very positive attitude about the worker and thinks he is a top performer. One day the manager notices that the worker seems to be goofing off. Selective perception may cause the manager to quickly forget what he observed. Similarly, suppose a manager has formed a very negative image of a particular worker. She thinks this worker is a poor performer and never does a good job. When she happens to observe an example of high performance from the worker, she, too, may not remember it for very long. In one sense, selective perception is beneficial because it allows us to disregard minor bits of information. Of course, this holds true only if our basic perception is accurate. If selective perception causes us to ignore important information, however, it can become quite detrimental.

stereotyping
The process of categorizing or labeling people on the basis of a single attribute

Stereotyping   *Stereotyping* is the process of categorizing or labeling people on the basis of a single attribute. Common attributes from which people often stereotype are race and sex. Of course, stereotypes along these lines are inaccurate and can be harmful. For example, suppose a manager forms the stereotype that women can perform only certain tasks and that men are best suited for other tasks. To the extent that this affects the manager's hiring practices, the manager is (1) costing the organization valuable talent for both sets of jobs, (2) violating federal law, and (3) behaving unethically. On the other hand, certain forms of stereotyping can be useful and efficient. Suppose, for example, that a manager believes that communication skills are important for a particular job and that speech communication majors tend to have exceptionally good communication skills. As a result, whenever he interviews candidates for jobs, he pays especially close attention to speech communication majors. To the extent that communication skills truly predict job performance and that majoring in speech communication does indeed provide those skills, this form of stereotyping can be beneficial.

Perception and Attribution

attribution
The process of observing behavior and attributing causes to it

Perception is also closely linked with another process called attribution. ***Attribution*** is a mechanism through which we observe behavior and then attribute causes to it.[24] The behavior that is observed may be our own or that of others. For example, suppose someone realizes one day that she is working fewer hours than before, that she talks less about her work, and that she calls in sick more frequently. She might conclude from this that she must have become disenchanted with her job and subsequently decide to quit. Thus she observed her own behavior, attributed a cause to it, and developed what she thought was a consistent response.

More common is attributing cause to the behavior of others. For example, if the manager of the individual described above has observed the same behavior, he might form exactly the same attribution. On the other hand, he might instead decide that she has a serious illness, that he is driving her too hard, that she is experiencing too much stress, that she has a drug problem, or that she is having family problems.

The basic framework around which we form attributions is *consensus* (the extent to which other people in the same situation behave the same way), *consistency* (the extent to which the same person behaves in the same way at different times), and *distinctiveness* (the extent to which the same person behaves in the same way in other situations). For example, suppose a manager observes that an employee is late for a meeting. The manager might further realize that he is the only one who is late (low consensus), recall that he is often late for other meetings (high consistency), and subsequently realize that the same employee is sometimes late for work and returning from lunch (low distinctiveness). This pattern of attributions might cause the manager to decide that the individual's behavior is something that should be changed. As a result, the manager might meet with the subordinate and establish some punitive consequences for future tardiness.

concept
CHECK

Define perception and discuss two fundamental perceptual processes.

Recall a vivid example of behavior exhibited by someone and then describe that behavior from an attributional perspective.

Stress and Individual Behavior

Another important element of behavior in organizations is stress. **Stress** is an individual's response to a strong stimulus.[25] This stimulus is called a *stressor*. Stress generally follows a cycle referred to as the **General Adaptation Syndrome**, or GAS,[26] shown in Figure 15.4. According to this view, when an individual first encounters a stressor, the GAS is initiated, and the first stage, alarm, is activated. He may feel panic, wonder how to cope, and feel helpless. For example, suppose a manager is

> **stress**
> An individual's response to a strong stimulus, which is called a stressor

> **General Adaptation Syndrome (GAS)**
> General cycle of the stress process

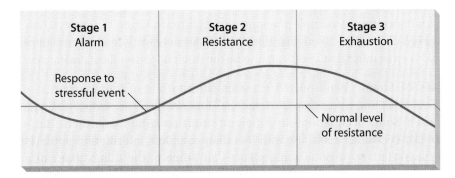

Figure 15.4
THE GENERAL ADAPTATION SYNDROME

The general adaptation syndrome represents the normal process by which we react to stressful events. At stage 1—alarm—we feel panic and alarm, and our level of resistance to stress drops. Stage 2—resistance—represents our efforts to confront and control the stressful circumstance. If we fail, we may eventually reach stage 3—exhaustion—and just give up or quit.

told to prepare a detailed evaluation of a plan by his firm to buy one of its competitors. His first reaction may be, "How will I ever get this done by tomorrow?"

If the stressor is too intense, the individual may feel unable to cope and never really try to respond to its demands. In most cases, however, after a short period of alarm, the individual gathers some strength and starts to resist the negative effects of the stressor. For example, the manager with the evaluation to write may calm down, call home to say he is working late, roll up his sleeves, order out for coffee, and get to work. Thus, at stage 2 of the GAS, the person is resisting the effects of the stressor.

In many cases, the resistance phase may end the GAS. If the manager is able to complete the evaluation earlier than expected, he may drop it in his briefcase, smile to himself, and head home tired but satisfied. On the other hand, prolonged exposure to a stressor without resolution may bring on stage 3 of the GAS—exhaustion. At this stage, the individual literally gives up and can no longer resist the stressor. The manager, for example, might fall asleep at his desk at 3:00 A.M. and never finish the evaluation.

We should note that stress is not all bad. In the absence of stress, we may experience lethargy and stagnation. An optimal level of stress, on the other hand, can result in motivation and excitement. Too much stress, however, can have negative consequences. It is also important to understand that stress can be caused by "good" as well as "bad" things. Excessive pressure, unreasonable demands on our time, and bad news can all cause stress. But even receiving a bonus and then having to decide what to do with the money can be stressful. So, too, can receiving a promotion, gaining recognition, and similar good things.

One important line of thinking about stress focuses on **Type A** and **Type B** personalities.[27] Type A individuals are extremely competitive, very devoted to work, and have a strong sense of time urgency. They are likely to be aggressive, impatient, and very work oriented. They have a lot of drive and want to accomplish as much as possible as quickly as possible. Type B individuals are less competitive, less devoted to work, and have a weaker sense of time urgency. Such individuals are less likely to experience conflict with other people and more likely to have a balanced, relaxed approach to life. They are able to work at a constant pace without time urgency. Type B people are not necessarily more or less successful than are Type A people. But they are less likely to experience stress.

> *Type A*
> Individuals who are extremely competitive, very devoted to work, and have a strong sense of time urgency

> *Type B*
> Individuals who are less competitive, less devoted to work, and have a weaker sense of time urgency

Causes and Consequences of Stress

Stress is obviously not a simple phenomenon. As listed in Figure 15.5, several different things can cause stress. Note that this list includes only work-related conditions. We should keep in mind that stress can also be the result of personal circumstances.[28]

Causes of Stress Work-related stressors fall into one of four categories—task, physical, role, and interpersonal demands. *Task demands* are associated with the task itself. Some occupations are inherently more stressful than others. Having to make fast decisions, decisions with less than complete information, or decisions that have relatively serious consequences are some of the things that can make some jobs stressful. The jobs of surgeon, airline pilot, and stockbroker are relatively more stressful than the jobs of general practitioner, baggage handler, and office receptionist. Although a general practitioner makes important decisions, he is also likely to have time to make a considered diagnosis and fully explore a number of different treatments. But, during surgery, the surgeon must make decisions quickly while realizing that the wrong one may endanger her patient's life.

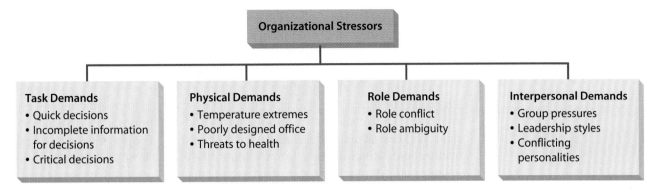

Figure 15.5

CAUSES OF WORK STRESS

There are several causes of work stress in organizations. Four general sets of organizational stressors are task demands, physical demands, role demands, and interpersonal demands.

Physical demands are stressors associated with the job setting. Working outdoors in extremely hot or cold temperatures, or even in an improperly heated or cooled office, can lead to stress. A poorly designed office, which makes it difficult for people to have privacy or promotes too little social interaction, can result in stress, as can poor lighting and inadequate work surfaces. Even more severe are actual threats to health. Examples include jobs like coal mining, poultry processing, and toxic waste handling.

Role demands can also cause stress. (Roles are discussed more fully in Chapter 18.) A role is a set of expected behaviors associated with a position in a group or organization. Stress can result from either role conflict or role ambiguity that people can experience in groups. For example, an employee who is feeling pressure from her boss to work longer hours or to travel more, while also being asked by her family for more time at home, will almost certainly experience stress as a result of role conflict.[29] Similarly, a new employee experiencing role ambiguity because of poor orientation and training practices by the organization will also suffer from stress. Excessive meetings are also a potential source of stress.[30]

Interpersonal demands are stressors associated with relationships that confront people in organizations. For example, group pressures regarding restriction of output and norm conformity can lead to stress. Leadership styles may also cause stress. An employee who feels a strong need to participate in decision making may feel stress if his boss refuses to allow participation. And individuals with conflicting personalities may experience stress if required to work too closely together. For example, a person with an internal locus of control might be frustrated when working with someone who prefers to wait and just let things happen.

Consequences of Stress As noted earlier, the results of stress may be positive or negative. The negative consequences may be behavioral, psychological, or medical. Behaviorally, for example, stress may lead to detrimental or harmful actions, such as smoking, alcohol or drug abuse, and overeating. Other stress-induced behaviors are accident proneness, violence toward self or others, and appetite disorders.

Psychological consequences of stress interfere with an individual's mental health and well-being. These outcomes include sleep disturbances, depression, family problems, and sexual dysfunction. Managers are especially prone to sleep disturbances when they experience stress at work.[31] Medical consequences of stress affect an individual's physiological well-being. Heart disease and stroke have been linked to stress, as have headaches, backaches, ulcers and related disorders, and skin conditions such as acne and hives.

Individual stress also has direct consequences for businesses. For an operating employee, stress may translate into poor-quality work and lower productivity. For a manager, it may mean faulty decision making and disruptions in working relationships. Withdrawal behaviors can also result from stress. People who are having difficulties with stress in their job are more likely to call in sick or to leave the organization. More subtle forms of withdrawal may also occur. A manager may start missing deadlines, for example, or taking longer lunch breaks. Employees may also withdraw by developing feelings of indifference. The irritation displayed by people under great stress can make them difficult to get along with. Job satisfaction, morale, and commitment can all suffer as a result of excessive levels of stress. So, too, can motivation to perform.

Another consequence of stress is **burnout**—a feeling of exhaustion that may develop when someone experiences too much stress for an extended period of time. Burnout results in constant fatigue, frustration, and helplessness. Increased rigidity follows, as do a loss of self-confidence and psychological withdrawal. The individual dreads going to work, often puts in longer hours but gets less accomplished than before, and exhibits mental and physical exhaustion. Because of the damaging effects of burnout, some firms are taking steps to help avoid it. For example, British Airways provides all of its employees with training designed to help them recognize the symptoms of burnout and develop strategies for avoiding it.

burnout
A feeling of exhaustion that may develop when someone experiences too much stress for an extended period of time

Managing Stress

Given the potential consequences of stress, it follows that both people and organizations should be concerned about how to limit its more damaging effects. Numerous ideas and approaches have been developed to help manage stress. Some are strategies for individuals; others are strategies for organizations.[32]

One way people manage stress is through exercise. People who exercise regularly feel less tension and stress, are more self-confident, and feel more optimistic. Their better physical condition also makes them less susceptible to many common illnesses. People who do not exercise regularly, on the other hand, tend to feel more stress and are more likely to be depressed. They are also more likely to have heart attacks. And, because of their physical condition, they are more likely to contract illnesses.

Another method people use to manage stress is relaxation. Relaxation allows individuals to adapt to, and therefore better deal with, their stress. Relaxation comes in many forms, such as taking regular vacations. A recent study found that people's attitudes toward a variety of workplace characteristics improved significantly following a vacation. People can also learn to relax while on the job. For example, some experts recommend that people take regular rest breaks during their normal workday.

People can also use time management to control stress. The idea behind time management is that many daily pressures can be reduced or eliminated if individuals do a better job of managing time. One approach to time management is to make a list every morning of the things to be done that day. The items on the list are then grouped into three categories: critical activities that must be performed, important activities that should be performed, and optional or trivial things that can be delegated or postponed. The individual performs the items on the list in their order of importance.

Finally, people can manage stress through support groups. A support group can be as simple as a group of family members or friends to enjoy leisure time with. Going out after work with a couple of coworkers to a basketball game or a movie, for example, can help relieve stress built up during the day. Family and friends can help people cope with stress on an ongoing basis and during times of crisis. For example, an employee who has just learned that she did not get the promotion she has been working toward for months may find it helpful to have a good friend to lean on, talk to, or yell at. People also may make use of more elaborate and formal support groups. Community centers or churches, for example, may sponsor support groups for people who have recently gone through a divorce, the death of a loved one, or some other tragedy.

Exercise and support groups can both be effective ways to manage stress. These U.S. Marines are playing basketball on a makeshift court at an abandoned train station on their base in Iraq. The sandstorms are brutal, the roadside bombs deadly, and the long separations from loved ones stressful. But the exertion of the basketball games and the camaraderie among the marines make it a little easier for them.

Organizations are also beginning to realize that they should be involved in helping employees cope with stress. One argument for this is that because the business is at least partially responsible for stress, it should also help relieve it. Another is that stress-related insurance claims by employees can cost the organization considerable sums of money. Still another is that workers experiencing lower levels of detrimental stress will be able to function more effectively. AT&T has initiated a series of seminars and workshops to help its employees cope with the stress they face in their jobs. The firm was prompted to develop these seminars for all three of the reasons noted above.

A wellness stress program is a special part of the organization specifically created to help deal with stress. Organizations have adopted stress-management programs, health promotion programs, and other kinds of programs for this purpose. The AT&T seminar program noted earlier is similar to this idea, but true wellness programs are ongoing activities that have a number of different components. They commonly include exercise-related activities as well as classroom instruction programs dealing with smoking cessation, weight reduction, and general stress management.

Some companies are developing their own programs or using existing programs of this type. Johns Manville, for example, has a gym at its corporate headquarters. Other firms negotiate discounted health club membership rates with local establishments. For the instructional part of the program, the organization can again either sponsor its own training or perhaps jointly sponsor seminars with a local YMCA, civic organization, or church. Organization-based fitness programs facilitate employee exercise, a very positive consideration, but such programs are also quite costly. Still, more and more companies are developing fitness programs for employees. Similarly, some companies are offering their employees periodic sabbaticals—extended breaks from work that presumably allow people to get revitalized and reenergized. Intel and McDonald's are among the firms offering the benefit.[33]

Define stress and list its primary causes and consequences.

Are you more of a Type A or a Type B person? How do you feel about this?

Creativity in Organizations

Creativity is yet another important component of individual behavior in organizations. **Creativity** is the ability of an individual to generate new ideas or to conceive of new perspectives on existing ideas. What makes a person creative? How do people become creative? How does the creative process work? Although psychologists have not yet discovered complete answers to these questions, examining a few general patterns can help us understand the sources of individual creativity within organizations.[34]

> **creativity**
> The ability of an individual to generate new ideas or to conceive of new perspectives on existing ideas

The Creative Individual

Numerous researchers have focused their efforts on attempting to describe the common attributes of creative individuals. These attributes generally fall into three categories: background experiences, personal traits, and cognitive abilities.

Some organizations actively seek ways to enhance creativity among their employees. For instance, at Electronic Arts, a videogame developer, creativity is a critical element in the firm's success. To help people both counteract the stress from their hectic work lives and provide a place for calm mental relaxation, Electronic Arts provides a most unusual amenity—a maze. Game developers can walk in the maze whenever they feel that their creative juices need a boost.

Background Experiences and Creativity   Researchers have observed that many creative individuals were raised in environments in which creativity was nurtured. Mozart was raised in a family of musicians and began composing and performing music at age six. Pierre and Marie Curie, great scientists in their own right, also raised a daughter, Irene, who won the Nobel Prize in chemistry. Thomas Edison's creativity was nurtured by his mother. However, people with background experiences very different from theirs have also been creative. Frederick Douglass was born into slavery in Tuckahoe, Maryland, and had very limited opportunities for education. Nonetheless, his powerful oratory and creative thinking helped lead to the Emancipation Proclamation, which outlawed slavery in the United States.

Personal Traits and Creativity   Certain personal traits have also been linked to creativity in individuals. The traits shared by most creative people are openness, an attraction to complexity, high levels of energy, independence and autonomy, strong self-confidence, and a strong belief that one is, in fact, creative. Individuals who possess these traits are more likely to be creative than are those who do not have them.

Cognitive Abilities and Creativity   Cognitive abilities are an individual's power to think intelligently and to analyze situations and data effectively. Intelligence may be a precondition for individual creativity—although most creative people are highly intelligent, not all intelligent people are necessarily creative. Creativity is also linked with the ability to think divergently and convergently. *Divergent thinking* is a skill that allows people to see differences among situations, phenomena, or events. *Convergent thinking* is a skill that allows people to see similarities among situations, phenomena, or events. Creative people are generally very skilled at both divergent and convergent thinking.

Interestingly, Japanese managers have come to question their own creative abilities. The concern is that their emphasis on group harmony may have stifled individual initiative and hampered the development of individual creativity. As a result, many Japanese firms, including Omron Corporation, Fuji Photo, and Shimizu Corporation, have launched employee training programs intended to boost the creativity of their employees.[35]

The Creative Process

Although creative people often report that ideas seem to come to them "in a flash," individual creative activity actually tends to progress through a series of stages. Not all creative activity has to follow these four stages, but much of it does.

Preparation The creative process normally begins with a period of *preparation*. To make a creative contribution to business management or business services, individuals must usually receive formal training and education in business. Formal education and training are usually the most efficient ways of becoming familiar with this vast amount of research and knowledge. This is one reason for the strong demand for undergraduate and master's level business education. Formal business education can be an effective way for an individual to get "up to speed" and begin making creative contributions quickly. Experiences that managers have on the job after their formal training has finished can also contribute to the creative process. In an important sense, the education and training of creative people never really ends. It continues as long as they remain interested in the world and curious about the way things work. Bruce Roth earned a Ph.D. in chemistry and then spent years working in the pharmaceutical industry learning more and more about chemical compounds and how they work in human beings.

Incubation The second phase of the creative process is *incubation*—a period of less intense conscious concentration during which the knowledge and ideas acquired during preparation mature and develop. A curious aspect of incubation is that it is often helped along by pauses in concentrated rational thought. Some creative people rely on physical activity such as jogging or swimming to provide a break from thinking. Others may read or listen to music. Sometimes sleep may even supply the needed pause. Bruce Roth eventually joined Warner-Lambert, an up-and-coming drug company, to help develop medication to lower cholesterol. In his spare time, Roth read mystery novels and hiked in the mountains. He later acknowledged that this was when he did his best thinking. Similarly, twice a year Bill Gates retreats to a secluded wooded cabin to reflect on trends in technology; it is during these weeks, he says, that he develops his sharpest insights into where Microsoft should be heading.[36]

> "You need time, just thinking time, to step out of the day to day to see what's going on in the world, and what's going on with your customers."
>
> Susan Schuman, CEO of Stone Yamashita Partners
> (*BusinessWeek*, April 24, 2006, p. 68)

Insight   Usually occurring after preparation and incubation, *insight* is a spontaneous breakthrough in which the creative person achieves a new understanding of some problem or situation. Insight represents a coming together of all the scattered thoughts and ideas that were maturing during incubation. It may occur suddenly or develop slowly over time. Insight can be triggered by some external event, such as a new experience or an encounter with new data, which forces the individual to think about old issues and problems in new ways, or it can be a completely internal event in which patterns of thought finally coalesce in ways that generate new understanding. One day Bruce Roth was reviewing some data from some earlier studies that had found the new drug under development to be no more effective than other drugs already available. But this time he saw some statistical relationships that had not been identified previously. He knew then that he had a major breakthrough on his hands.

Verification   Once an insight has occurred, *verification* determines the validity or truthfulness of the insight. For many creative ideas, verification includes scientific experiments to determine whether the insight actually leads to the results expected. Verification may also include the development of a product or service prototype. A prototype is one product or a very small number of products built just to see if the ideas behind this new product actually work. Product prototypes are rarely sold to the public but are very valuable in verifying the insights developed in the creative process. Once the new product or service is developed, verification in the marketplace is the ultimate test of the creative idea behind it. Bruce Roth and his colleagues set to work testing the new drug compound and eventually won FDA approval. The drug, named Lipitor, is already the largest-selling pharmaceutical in history. And Pfizer, the firm that bought Warner-Lambert in a hostile takeover, is expected to soon earn more than $10 billion a year on the drug.[37]

Enhancing Creativity in Organizations

Managers who wish to enhance and promote creativity in their organizations can do so in a variety of ways.[38] One important method for enhancing creativity is to make it a part of the organization's culture, often through explicit goals. Firms that truly want to stress creativity, like 3M and Rubbermaid, for example, state goals that some percentage of future revenues are to be gained from new products. This clearly communicates that creativity and innovation are valued.

Another important part of enhancing creativity is to reward creative successes, while being careful not to punish creative failures. Many ideas that seem worthwhile on paper fail to pan out in reality. If the first person to come up with an idea that fails is fired or otherwise punished, others in the organization will become more cautious in their own work. And, as a result, fewer creative ideas will emerge.

concept
CHECK

Define creativity and describe its likely causes.

Think of an important idea you recently had and try to explain how you derived it, based on the creative process discussed in this section.

Types of Workplace Behavior

Now that we have looked closely at how individual differences can influence behavior in organizations, let's turn our attention to what we mean by workplace behavior. *Workplace behavior* is a pattern of action by the members of an organization that directly or indirectly influences organizational effectiveness. Important workplace behaviors include performance and productivity, absenteeism and turnover, and organizational citizenship. Unfortunately, a variety of dysfunctional behaviors can also occur in organizational settings.

workplace behavior
A pattern of action by the members of an organization that directly or indirectly influences organizational effectiveness

Performance Behaviors

Performance behaviors are the total set of work-related behaviors that the organization expects the individual to display. Thus they derive from the psychological contract. For some jobs, performance behaviors can be narrowly defined and easily measured. For example, an assembly-line worker who sits by a moving conveyor and attaches parts to a product as it passes by has relatively few performance behaviors. He or she is expected to remain at the workstation and correctly attach the parts. Performance can often be assessed quantitatively by counting the percentage of parts correctly attached.

performance behaviors
The total set of work-related behaviors that the organization expects the individual to display

For many other jobs, however, performance behaviors are more diverse and much more difficult to assess. For example, consider the case of a research and development scientist at Merck. The scientist works in a lab trying to find new scientific breakthroughs that have commercial potential. The scientist must apply knowledge learned in graduate school with experience gained from previous research. Intuition and creativity are also important elements. And the desired breakthrough may take months or even years to accomplish. As we discussed in Chapter 14, organizations rely on a number of different methods for evaluating performance. The key, of course, is to match the evaluation mechanism with the job being performed.

Withdrawal Behaviors

Another important type of work-related behavior is that which results in withdrawal—absenteeism and turnover. *Absenteeism* occurs when an individual does not show up for work. The cause may be legitimate (illness, jury duty, death in the family, and so forth) or feigned (reported as legitimate but actually just an excuse to stay home). When an employee is absent, her or his work does not get done at all, or a substitute must be hired to do it. In either case, the quantity or quality of actual output is likely to suffer. Obviously, some absenteeism is expected. The key concern of organizations is to minimize feigned absenteeism and to reduce legitimate absences as much as possible. High absenteeism may be a symptom of other problems as well, such as job dissatisfaction and low morale.

absenteeism
When an individual does not show up for work

Turnover occurs when people quit their jobs. An organization usually incurs costs in replacing individuals who have quit, but if turnover involves especially productive people, it is even more costly. Turnover seems to result from a number of factors, including aspects of the job, the organization, the individual, the labor market, and family influences. In general, a poor person-job fit is also a likely cause

turnover
When people quit their jobs

of turnover. The current labor shortage is also resulting in higher turnover in many companies due to the abundance of more attractive alternative jobs that are available to highly qualified individuals.[39]

Efforts to directly manage turnover are frequently fraught with difficulty, even in organizations that concentrate on rewarding good performers. Of course, some turnover is inevitable, and in some cases it may even be desirable. For example, if the organization is trying to cut costs by reducing its staff, having people voluntarily choose to leave is preferable to having to terminate their jobs. And, if the people who choose to leave are low performers or express high levels of job dissatisfaction, the organization may also benefit from turnover.

Organizational Citizenship

organizational citizenship
The behavior of individuals that makes a positive overall contribution to the organization

Organizational citizenship is the behavior of individuals that makes a positive overall contribution to the organization.[40] Consider, for example, an employee who does work that is acceptable in terms of both quantity and quality. However, she refuses to work overtime, will not help newcomers learn the ropes, and is generally unwilling to make any contribution to the organization beyond the strict performance of her job. Although this person may be seen as a good performer, she is not likely to be seen as a good organizational citizen.

Another employee may exhibit a comparable level of performance. In addition, however, he will always work late when the boss asks him to, take time to help newcomers learn their way around, and is perceived as being helpful and committed to the organization's success. Although his level of performance may be seen as equal to that of the first worker, he is also likely to be seen as a better organizational citizen.

The determinant of organizational citizenship behaviors is likely to be a complex mosaic of individual, social, and organizational variables. For example, the personality, attitudes, and needs of the individual will have to be consistent with citizenship behaviors. Similarly, the social context in which the individual works, or work group, will need to facilitate and promote such behaviors (we discuss group dynamics in Chapter 18). And the organization itself, especially its culture, must be capable of promoting, recognizing, and rewarding these types of behaviors if they are to be maintained. Although the study of organizational citizenship is still in its infancy, preliminary research suggests that it may play a powerful role in organizational effectiveness.[41]

Dysfunctional Behaviors

dysfunctional behaviors
Those that detract from, rather than contribute to, organizational performance

Some work-related behaviors are dysfunctional in nature. ***Dysfunctional behaviors*** are those that detract from, rather than contribute to, organizational performance. Two of the more common ones, absenteeism and turnover, are discussed above. But other forms of dysfunctional behavior may be even more costly for an organization. Theft and sabotage, for example, result in direct financial costs for an organization. Sexual and racial harassment also cost an organization, both indirectly (by lowering morale, producing fear, and driving off valuable employees) and directly (through financial liability if the organization responds inappropriately). So, too, can politicized behavior, intentionally misleading others in the organization, spreading malicious rumors, and similar activities. Workplace violence is also a growing concern in many organizations. Violence by disgruntled workers or former workers results in dozens of deaths and injuries each year.[42]

concept
CHECK

Distinguish between performance behaviors, withdrawal behaviors, organizational citizenship, and dysfunctional behaviors.	Have you ever called in sick for work when you were well, or missed class using sickness as a false excuse? Can such actions be justified?

Summary of Learning Objectives and Key Points

1. Explain the nature of the individual-organization relationship.
   - A basic framework that can be used to facilitate this understanding is the psychological contract—the set of expectations held by people with respect to what they will contribute to the organization and what they expect to get in return.
   - Organizations strive to achieve an optimal person-job fit, but this process is complicated by the existence of individual differences.

2. Define personality and describe personality attributes that affect behavior in organizations.
   - Personality is the relatively stable set of psychological and behavioral attributes that distinguish one person from another.
   - The "Big Five" personality traits are:
     - agreeableness
     - conscientiousness
     - negative emotionality
     - extraversion
     - openness
   - The Myers-Briggs framework can also be a useful mechanism for understanding personality.
   - Other important traits are:
     - locus of control
     - self-efficacy
     - authoritarianism
     - Machiavellianism
     - self-esteem
     - risk propensity
   - Emotional intelligence, a fairly new concept, may provide additional insights into personality.

3. Discuss individual attitudes in organizations and how they affect behavior.
   - Attitudes are based on emotion, knowledge, and intended behavior.
   - Whereas personality is relatively stable, some attitudes can be formed and changed easily. Others are more constant.
   - Job satisfaction or dissatisfaction and organizational commitment are important work-related attitudes.

4. Describe basic perceptual processes and the role of attributions in organizations.
   - Perception is the set of processes by which an individual becomes aware of and interprets information about the environment.
   - Basic perceptual processes include selective perception and stereotyping.
   - Perception and attribution are also closely related.

5. Discuss the causes and consequences of stress and describe how it can be managed.
   - Stress is an individual's response to a strong stimulus.
   - The General Adaptation Syndrome outlines the basic stress process.
   - Stress can be caused by task, physical, role, and interpersonal demands.
   - Consequences of stress include organizational and individual outcomes, as well as burnout.
   - Several things can be done to manage stress.

6. Describe creativity and its role in organizations.
   - Creativity is the capacity to generate new ideas.
   - Creative people tend to have certain profiles of background experiences, personal traits, and cognitive abilities.

- The creative process itself includes preparation, incubation, insight, and verification.

7. Explain how workplace behaviors can directly or indirectly influence organizational effectiveness.
   - Workplace behavior is a pattern of action by the members of an organization that directly or indirectly influences organizational effectiveness.
   - Performance behaviors are the set of work-related behaviors that the organization expects the indi-

vidual to display to fulfill the psychological contract.
   - Basic withdrawal behaviors are absenteeism and turnover.
   - Organizational citizenship refers to behavior that makes a positive overall contribution to the organization.
   - Dysfunctional behaviors can be very harmful to an organization.

Discussion Questions

Questions for Review

1. What is a psychological contract? List the things that might be included in individual contributions. List the things that might be included in organizational inducements.
2. Describe the three components of attitudes and tell how the components are related. What is cognitive dissonance? How do individuals resolve cognitive dissonance?

3. Identify and discuss the steps in the creative process. What can an organization do to increase employees' creativity?
4. Identify and describe several important workplace behaviors.

Questions for Analysis

5. Organizations are increasing their use of personality tests to screen job applicants. What are the advantages and disadvantages of this approach? What can managers do to avoid some of the potential pitfalls?
6. As a manager, how can you tell that an employee is experiencing job satisfaction? How can you tell that employees are highly committed to the organization? If a worker is not satisfied, what can a

manager do to improve satisfaction? What can a manager do to improve organizational commitment?
7. Managers cannot pay equal attention to every piece of information, so selective perception is a fact of life. How does selective perception help managers? How does it create difficulties for them? How can managers increase their "good" selective perception and decrease the "bad"?

Questions for Application

8. Write the psychological contract you have in this class. In other words, what do you contribute, and what inducements are available? Ask your professor to tell the class about the psychological contract that he or she intended to establish with the students in your class. How does the professor's intended contract compare with the one you wrote? If there are differences, why do you think the differences exist? Share your ideas with the class.
9. Assume that you are going to hire three new employees for the department store you manage. One will sell shoes, one will manage the toy department, and

one will work in the stockroom. Identify the basic characteristics you want in each of the people, to achieve a good person-job fit.
10. Describe a time when someone displayed each one of the Big Five personality traits at either a very high or a very low level. For example, tell about someone who appeared to be highly agreeable or highly disagreeable. Then tell about the outcomes that person experienced as a result of displaying that particular personality trait. Do the outcomes seem logical; that is, do positive personality traits usually lead to good outcomes and negative traits to bad ones? Explain your answer.

Building Effective Interpersonal Skills

Exercise Overview

Interpersonal skills refer to the ability to communicate with, understand, and motivate individuals and groups. This exercise shows you a widely used tool for personality assessment. It shows how an understanding of personality can aid in developing effective interpersonal relationships within organizations.

Exercise Background

There are many different ways of viewing personality, but one that is widely used is called the Myers-Briggs Type Indicator. According to Isabel Myers, each individual's personality type varies in four dimensions:

1. *Extraversion (E) Versus Introversion (I).* Extraverts get their energy from being around other people, whereas introverts are worn out by others and need solitude to recharge their energy.
2. *Sensing (S) Versus Intuition (N).* The sensing type prefers concrete things, whereas the intuitivist prefers abstract concepts.
3. *Thinking (T) Versus Feeling (F).* Thinking individuals base their decisions more on logic and reason, whereas feeling individuals base their decisions more on feelings and emotions.
4. *Judging (J) Versus Perceiving (P).* People who are the judging types enjoy completion or being finished, whereas perceiving types enjoy the process and open-ended situations.

Based on answers to a survey, individuals are classified into 16 personality types—all the possible combinations of the four dimensions above. The resulting personality type is then expressed as a four-character code, such as ESTP or INFJ, for example. These four-character codes can then be used to describe an individual's preferred way of interacting with others.

Exercise Task

1. Use an online Meyers-Briggs assessment form to determine your own personality type. One place to find the form online is **www.keirsey.com/scripts/ newkts.cgi.** This website also contains additional information about personality type. (*Note:* You do *not* need to pay fees or agree to receive e-mails to take the Temperament Sorter.)
2. When you have determined the four-letter code for your personality type, obtain a handout from your professor. The handout will show how your personality type affects your preferred style of working and your leadership style.
3. Conclude by addressing the following questions:
   • How easy is it to measure personality?
   • Do you feel that the online test accurately assessed your personality?
   • Why or why not? Share your assessment results and your answers with the class.

Building Effective Time-Management Skills

Exercise Overview

Time-management skills help people prioritize work, work more efficiently, and delegate appropriately. Poor time-management skills, in turn, may result in stress. This exercise will help you relate time-management skills to stress reduction.

Exercise Background

List several of the major events or expectations that cause stress for you. Stressors might involve school (hard classes, too many exams), work (financial pressures, demanding work schedule), or personal circumstances (friends, romance, family). Try to be as specific as possible. Also try to identify at least ten different stressors.

Exercise Task

Using the list that you developed, do each of the following:

1. Evaluate the extent to which poor time-management skills on your part play a role in how each stressor affects you. For example, do exams cause stress because you delay studying?
2. Develop a strategy for using time more efficiently in relation to each stressor that relates to time.
3. Note interrelationships among different kinds of stressors and time. For example, financial pressures may cause you to work, but work may interfere with school. Can any of these interrelationships be managed more effectively vis-à-vis time?
4. How do you manage the stress in your life? Is it possible to manage stress in a more time-effective manner?

CHAPTER CLOSING CASE

STEVE JOBS: "THE LEADING-EDGE GUY IN THE WORLD"

Personality can describe a person of prominence or notoriety. Sometimes the word is used more correctly to refer to a set of enduring character traits. Steve Jobs, the charismatic, colorful, and controversial co-founder and head of Apple Computer, fits both definitions. He's a personality who has an interesting personality. Jobs is seen as an inspiring visionary on the one hand, and on the other hand, as difficult and abrasive. His complex personality encompasses many contradictions and yet is a source of his professional success, as well as the success of his several business ventures.

After one semester at Reed College, Jobs worked briefly at Hewlett-Packard, where he met fellow computer geek Steve Wozniak. Jobs had a short stint at Atari, an early video game maker, and backpacked around India. In 1976, when Jobs was 21, he convinced Wozniak to sell a personal computer Wozniak designed and built for himself. This was the first commercially available personal computer. Apple Computer's initial public offering in 1980 created many millionaires, including Jobs.

As CEO of Apple, Jobs oversaw the development of the enormously successful Macintosh. Apple Computer grew tremendously, but Jobs' tenure was marred by controversy and difficulties. His idealistic vision and impossibly high standards drove the firm to ever-greater achievements. Yet after several failed designs and cost overruns, Apple hired John Sculley, former CEO of Pepsi, to run Apple. Jobs and Sculley clashed continually, and in 1985, the Apple board of directors forced Jobs to resign. Larry Tesler, then Apple's chief scientist, describes the mood at Apple. "People in the company had very mixed feelings about it. Everyone had been terrorized by Steve Jobs at some point or another, and so there was a certain relief that the terrorist would be gone," says Tesler. "And on the other hand I think there was incredible respect for Steve Jobs by the very same people, and we were all very worried what would happen to this company without the visionary, without the founder, without the charisma."

Jobs protested by selling his Apple stock and starting NeXT, a high-end computer company. NeXT made the PC used by Tim Berners-Lee to write the software code called "WorldWideWeb 1.0," the basis for today's Internet. In 1986, Jobs purchased George Lucas's computer animation studio, Pixar. Jobs's management at Pixar was very hands-off, but he pushed NeXT constantly, resulting in many innovative products.

In 1996, Apple purchased NeXT for $400 million and Jobs returned to his now-ailing and almost bankrupt company. Within a year, he was named CEO of Apple. His leadership produced the iPod and launched the iTunes online music store. Meanwhile, Pixar released hit after hit, including *Toy Story, A Bug's Life, Finding Nemo,* and *The Incredibles,* in partnership with Disney. Disney's then-CEO Michael Eisner and Jobs fought bitterly and publicly, but in 2005, Bob Iger became CEO at Disney. Iger quickly established better relations with Jobs. In 2006, Disney purchased Pixar for $7.4 billion, making Jobs Disney's largest stockholder controlling 7 percent of stock and a board member.

Today, Jobs is a successful businessman—the 140th richest person in the world, with a net worth estimated at $4.4 billion. His personality has been instrumental in his achievements. "If Steve has a good relationship with you, there's nobody better in the world to work with. He trusts you, and he listens, and he bounces his ideas off you," says Edgar Woolard, Jr., a former Apple board member. Woolard says Jobs is "an absolute perfectionist" who is "incredibly creative with great vision." Colleagues portray Jobs as persuasive, charismatic, energetic, confident, and powerful.

These traits point to success, yet the darker side of these same traits can be problematic. Jobs is seen as both an evangelist and an *enfant terrible*. He can be erratic, tempestuous, mercurial, obsessive, aggressive, demanding, and grandiose. According to some, he's a control freak and a micromanager. He is often outspokenly critical and sar-

castic, with unrealistically high standards and a bad temper.

Apple is transformed into a powerhouse. New products are blockbusters. The firm's stock has doubled in the last year and Apple ranks 11th in *Fortune*'s list of "Most Admired Companies." Pixar, and now Disney, will undoubtedly continue to create award-winning films. These accomplishments spring from Jobs's drive to improve and innovate. *Fortune* writer Fred Vogelstein admires Jobs, saying, "[He] throws the status quo into disorder and rides that chaos to the front of the pack." "He wants to be the leading-edge guy—which he is," states Woolard, who is also a fan. "He's the leading-edge guy in the world."

CASE QUESTIONS

1. Describe Steve Jobs's personality using the Big Five traits and

other personality traits discussed in your text.
2. How does Jobs's personality help him to be a better leader? How does his personality detract from his ability to lead?
3. How do personality traits support creativity? What personality traits allow Jobs to be creative?

CASE REFERENCES

Peter Burrows, "An Insider's Take on Steve Jobs," *BusinessWeek*, January 30, 2006, www.businessweek.com on April 30, 2006; Peter Burrows, "iPods, Sure. But Don't Go Dissing Macs," *BusinessWeek*, April 3, 2006, pp. 68–69; Peter Burrows and Ronald Grover, "Steve Jobs' Magic Kingdom," *BusinessWeek*, February 6, 2006, pp. 63–69; *Triumph of the Nerds: The Rise of Accidental Empires*, dir. Robert X. Cringely, PBS, 1996; William C. Taylor and Polly LaBarre, "How Pixar Adds a New School of Thought to Disney," *New York Times*, January 29, 2006, p. BU 3; Fred Vogelstein, "Mastering the Art of Disruption," *Fortune*, February 6, 2006, pp. 23–24.

YOU MAKE THE CALL

The Worst Bosses Ever

1. Have you ever worked with or for someone who exhibited some of the dysfunctional characteristics of psychopaths or narcissists? If so, what were those characteristics?
2. If you came to realize after taking a new job that your boss exhibited psychopathic behaviors, what would you do?
3. What would you expect to happen if a middle manager with psychopathic or narcissistic characteristics was assigned to work for a more senior manager with the same or similar characteristics?

4. Assume that you are a top manager at a large company. You have come to realize that a "fast track" manager currently in line for your job when you are promoted is a psychopath. What would you do?
5. In the same situation as detailed in question 4, what if the other manager is a narcissist? Specifically, would you handle one differently from the other? Why or why not?
6. Some people might argue that narcissistic managers could actually be beneficial to an organization. What would be the basis for such an argument? Do you agree or disagree?

Test Prepper

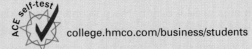

Choose the correct answer. Answers are found at the back of the book.

1. T F The psychological contract is typically written on paper.

2. T F Attitudes and personality characteristics are essentially the same thing.

3. T F People who have more negative affectivity also have high negative emotionality.

4. T F Type B people are less likely to experience stress than are Type A people.

5. T F Creative people are convergent thinkers; non-creative people are divergent thinkers.

6. Which of the following does NOT describe one of the "Big Five" personality traits?

    A. A person's belief in his or her ability to complete a task

    B. A person's rigidity of beliefs and range of interests

    C. A person's comfort level with relationships

    D. A person's ability to get along with others

    E. The number of goals on which a person focuses

7. Juliana is interested in increasing her emotional intelligence. Juliana should focus on improving all of the following dimensions EXCEPT

    A self-awareness.

    B. managing emotions.

    C. empathy.

    D. creativity.

    E. social skills.

8. Which of the following is NOT an example of a work-related stressor?

    A. The temperature in the office is too high.

    B. Decisions have to be made quickly and with incomplete information.

    C. Employees with conflicting personalities are required to work together.

    D. New employees receive insufficient orientation and training.

    E. Employees experience constant fatigue, frustration and helplessness.

9. While trying to find a solution to a product distribution problem, it occurs to Shoji that the source of the problem is similar to a kink in a garden hose—simply increasing pressure from the "faucet" (or manufacturing facility) won't solve the problem. This is an example of

    A. divergent thinking.

    B. vertical thinking.

    C. lateral thinking.

    D. convergent thinking.

    E. conscientiousness.

10. An employee who is seen as a good organizational citizen is one who

    A. behaves strictly within the formal performance requirements of the job.

    B. is committed to remaining with the organization.

    C. makes a positive overall contribution to the organization.

    D. is generally in a good mood.

    E. has positive attitudes about the organization, its culture, and other employees.

Managing Emplo[...] Motivation and Performance

FIRST THINGS FIRST

Better Work/Life Balance as a Motivator

*"We've created jobs that are literally impossible.
The human cost is profound."*

—LOWELL BRYAN, PARTNER, MCKINSEY & COMPANY

Many working women complain that a good balance between a corporate career and a fulfilling life is hard to achieve. Women, who make up an increasingly large proportion of executives, are justified in this complaint. The average workweek of a top manager has expanded, leaving little time for outside activities. However, it's clear that no real change will take place in executives' hours until men also clamor for change.

Fortunately, young men graduating from business schools today make time off one of their top requests. With a shortage of management talent in many industries, employers are beginning to change their demanding ways. A better work/life balance may be coming soon to a corporation near you. But until then, long hours remain the rule rather than the exception.

[...]scribe the major con[...] [...]ent perspectives on motivation.

3. Identify and describe the major process perspectives on motivation.

4. Describe reinforcement perspectives on motivation.

5. Identify and describe popular motivational strategies.

6. Describe the role of organizational reward systems in motivation.

A desirable work/life balance may be difficult to achieve in today's high-pressure business world. This woman, however, appears to have been successful.

Sixty-hour workweeks used to be the norm in the United States; now 80 hours is more typical, and even that may be inadequate in some career fields. Jack Welch, former CEO of GE, routinely worked Saturdays. "I thought these weekend hours were a blast," Welch says. "The idea just didn't dawn on me that anyone would want to be anywhere but at work." For the past 25 years, current GE CEO Jeffrey Immelt's regular hours have been 7 A.M. to 9 P.M. seven days a week, for a whopping 100 hours!

One culprit is managers' desire to get recognized for hard work. Another is the increased size and complexity of businesses. The world's largest firms generate three times as much revenue (adjusted for inflation) and sell 16 times more products than in 1970, yet the typical organizational workforce is not growing at the same pace.

Moreover, working longer hours doesn't increase production proportionally. A 2002 study showed that U.S. workers were less productive per hour worked than those from countries with shorter workweeks, including France and Germany. Experts hypothesize that overworked employees become tired, stressed, and less motivated. Lowell Bryan, a McKinsey & Company partner, claims, "We've created jobs that are literally impossible. The human cost is profound, and the opportunity cost is also great in terms of organizational effectiveness." Problems made worse by overwork are costly and can include injuries, mistakes, rework, workplace violence, stress-related diseases, absenteeism, and high turnover.

Hiring a new manager or law associate can cost hundreds of thousands of dollars, putting pressure on companies to develop more humane policies. Fox News, for example, split the job of president between two individuals, who both work full-time and share responsibilities equally. The editorship of the *Los Angeles Times* was held by one person—now three workers do that job. Part-time work is another option. JetBlue allows key managers to work part-time schedules in exchange for reduced compensation. It's not hard to implement these new working arrangements. Law associates can handle fewer cases; auditors can work with fewer clients.

Sabbaticals, regularly scheduled extended vacations with pay, are another approach. Normal vacations do not provide enough time off to truly relax and reflect, and about one-third of U.S. workers don't even use all of their time off. So Intel grants an eight-week paid holiday to every full-time worker every seven years, in addition to their regular three to four weeks' annual vacation.

Five percent of large corporations in the United States offer paid sabbaticals, while another 18 percent award unpaid leaves. Sabbaticals can be costly because vacant positions must be staffed. But managers whose employees use sabbaticals find that workers return refreshed and enthusiastic. Few workers quit, and managers can better evaluate the potential of employees who fill in for the absent worker.

It's accepted wisdom that willing workers are plentiful, no matter how demanding the schedule, but most companies note that there is a shortage of qualified managers. Increasingly, men, especially younger men, want time off and are willing to give up money and career advancement to get it. Both men and women now talk freely in many companies about wanting to "have it all," referring to a career and a rewarding life outside of work. As these conversations become more widespread and more intense, perhaps U.S. companies will respond. Alternate, flexible work arrangements are more acceptable to workers, and they can also create a more motivated, productive, and loyal workforce.[1]

Several different factors may cause managers to put in long hours—employer expectations, demanding workloads, or the sheer enjoyment of the work are all things that motivate some people to work nights and weekends. Likewise, a number of factors are also suggesting that change may be in the wind, factors such as a growing desire among younger people to lead more balanced lives and the recognition that long hours may not equate to higher performance. The trick is figuring out how to create a system in which employees can receive rewards that they genuinely want yet lead a balanced life while performing in ways that fit the organization's goals and objectives.

> **motivation**
> The set of forces that cause people to behave in certain ways

In most settings, people can actually choose how hard they work and how much effort they expend. Thus managers need to understand how and why employees make different choices regarding their own performance. The key ingredient behind this choice is motivation, the subject of this chapter. We first examine the nature of employee motivation and then explore the major perspectives on motivation. Newly emerging approaches are then discussed. We conclude with a description of rewards and their role in motivation.

The Nature of Motivation

Motivation is the set of forces that cause people to behave in certain ways.[2] On any given day, an employee may choose to work as hard as possible at a job, work just hard enough to avoid a reprimand, or do as little as possible. The goal for the manager is to maximize the likelihood of the first behavior and minimize the likelihood of the last. This goal becomes all the more important when we understand how important motivation is in the workplace.

The Importance of Employee Motivation in the Workplace

Individual performance is generally determined by three things: motivation (the desire to do the job), ability (the capability to do the job), and the work environment (the resources needed to do the job). If an employee lacks ability, the manager can provide training or replace the worker. If there is a resource problem, the manager can correct it. But, if motivation is the problem, the task for the manager is more challenging.[3] Individual behavior is a complex phenomenon, and the manager may be hard pressed to figure out the precise nature of the

Motivation is the set of forces that causes people to behave in certain ways. Japanese mountaineer Takao Arayama, in blue, is shown here scaling Mt. Everest, the world's highest peak. Arayama, of Kamakura, Japan, reached the 8,850-meter (29,035-foot) peak in May 2006, at age 70 years, 7 months, and 13 days, just 3 days older than the last record holder, another Japanese climber. Arayama was motivated both by the challenge of the climb and the desire for a new world's record.

Figure 16.1

THE MOTIVATION FRAMEWORK

The motivation process progresses through a series of discrete steps. Content, process, and reinforcement perspectives on motivation address different parts of this process.

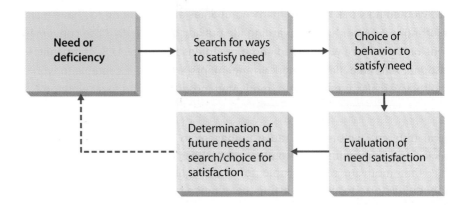

problem and how to solve it. Thus motivation is important because of its significance as a determinant of performance and because of its intangible character.[4]

The motivation framework in Figure 16.1 is a good starting point for understanding how motivated behavior occurs. The motivation process begins with a need deficiency. For example, when a worker feels that she is underpaid, she experiences a need for more income. In response, the worker searches for ways to satisfy the need, such as working harder to try to earn a raise or seeking a new job. Next she chooses an option to pursue. After carrying out the chosen option—working harder and putting in more hours for a reasonable period of time, for example—she then evaluates her success. If her hard work resulted in a pay raise, she probably feels good about things and will continue to work hard. But, if no raise has been provided, she is likely to try another option.

Historical Perspectives on Motivation

To appreciate what we know about employee motivation, it is helpful to review earlier approaches. The traditional, human relations, and human resource approaches have each shed partial light on motivation.[5]

The Traditional Approach The traditional approach is best represented by the work of Frederick W. Taylor.[6] As noted in Chapter 2, Taylor advocated an incentive pay system. He believed that managers knew more about the jobs being performed than did workers, and he assumed that economic gain was the primary thing that motivated everyone. Other assumptions of the traditional approach were that work is inherently unpleasant for most people and that the money they earn is more important to employees than the nature of the job they are performing. Hence, people could be expected to perform any kind of job if they were paid enough. Although the role of money as a motivating factor cannot be dismissed, proponents of the traditional approach took too narrow a view of the role of monetary compensation and failed to consider other motivational factors.

The Human Relations Approach The human relations approach was also summarized in Chapter 2.[7] The human relationists emphasized the role of social processes in the workplace. Their basic assumptions were that employees want to feel useful and important, that employees have strong social needs, and that these needs are more important than money in motivating them. Advocates of the human relations approach advised managers to make workers feel important and allow them a modicum of self-direction and self-control in carrying out routine activities. The illusion of involvement and importance was expected to satisfy workers' basic social needs and result in higher motivation to perform. For example, a manager might allow a work group to participate in making a decision, even though he or she had already determined what the decision would be. The symbolic gesture of seeming to allow participation was expected to enhance motivation, even though no real participation took place.

The Human Resource Approach   The human resource approach to motivation carries the concepts of needs and motivation one step farther. Whereas the human relationists believed that the illusion of contribution and participation would enhance motivation, the human resource view assumes that the contributions themselves are valuable to both individuals and organizations. It assumes that people want to contribute and are able to make genuine contributions. Management's task, then, is to encourage participation and to create a work environment that makes full use of the human resources available. This philosophy guides most contemporary thinking about employee motivation. At Ford, Westinghouse, Texas Instruments, and Hewlett-Packard, for example, work teams are being called on to solve a variety of problems and to make substantive contributions to the organization.

concept
CHECK

Summarize historical perspectives on employee motivation.

Use Figure 16.1 to trace through a motivational cycle you have recently experienced.

Content Perspectives on Motivation

Content perspectives on motivation deal with the first part of the motivation process—needs and need deficiencies. More specially, **content perspectives** address the question: What factors in the workplace motivate people? Labor leaders often argue that workers can be motivated by more pay, shorter working hours, and improved working conditions. Meanwhile, some experts suggest that motivation can be more effectively enhanced by providing employees with more autonomy and greater responsibility.[8] Both of these views represent content views of motivation. The former asserts that motivation is a function of pay, working hours, and working conditions; the latter suggests that autonomy and responsibility are the causes of motivation. *Diversity in Action* explores some of the factors that motivate many women coming out of law school today. Two widely known content perspectives on motivation are the needs hierarchy and the two-factor theory.

> *content perspectives*
> Approach to motivation that tries to answer the question: What factor or factors motivate people?

The Needs Hierarchy Approach
The needs hierarchy approach has been advanced by many theorists. Needs hierarchies assume that people have different needs that can be arranged in a hierarchy of importance. The two best known are Maslow's hierarchy of needs and the ERG theory.

Maslow's Hierarchy of Needs   Abraham Maslow, a human relationist, argued that people are motivated to satisfy five need levels.[9] ***Maslow's hierarchy of needs*** is shown in Figure 16.2. At the bottom of the hierarchy are the *physiological needs*—things like food, sex, and air, which represent basic issues of survival and biological

> *Maslow's hierarchy of needs*
> Suggests that people must satisfy five groups of needs in order—physiological, security, belongingness, esteem, and self-actualization

Working with Diversity

Breaking the Glass Ceiling at Law Firms

As the enrollment of women in law school skyrocketed after 1970, it was expected that the flood of young female associates would result in greatly increased numbers of female partners. Law school enrollment has been higher for years, yet there are still fairly few women partners.

"You have a given population of people who were significantly motivated to go through law school with a certain career goal in mind," says attorney Bettina Plevan. "What de-motivates them to want to continue working in the law?" Karen Lockwood, a law partner, also believes the problem is one of motivation, not access to opportunities. She adds, "Law firms are way beyond discrimination. Problems with advancement and retention are grounded in biases, not discrimination."

Some women prefer to reduce work as they raise families. However, most female attorneys would prefer to work and raise children, but are unable to do both effectively. Flexible or part-time work could help. The assumption that a working mother will be less available or dedicated is also a barrier. Most women do the majority of the housework and childrearing. For them, a more equitable distribution of household tasks or better access to quality childcare would make the difference.

"People explain it simply as the fact that women have children, but so many other factors play into it," claims Jane Pigott, a diversity consultant. She adds, "[Women] have a different style of self-promotion. But women need to learn how to be comfortable saying 'I want.'" In addition, women reentering the workforce should keep in touch with colleagues to ease their return.

Women are more likely to be motivated by informal mentoring, which is scarce for female attorneys. Female partners are lonely too, missing casual friendships at work. Lauren S. Rikleen, a partner, states, "I never felt like I belonged," even after more than two decades. Finally, women and men would be more motivated by reduced emphasis on billable hours and more on meaningful work.

Flexible and meaningful work, better mentoring, more training in communication, even more help at home. A combination of these factors will be more motivating to attorneys of both genders.

References: Stephen J. Adler, "Avon, the Net, and Glass Ceilings," *BusinessWeek*, February 6, 2006, www.businessweek.com on May 1, 2006; Timothy L. O'Brien, "Up the Down Staircase," *New York Times*, March 19, 2006, pp. BU 1, 4; Andrew Zolli, "Demographics: The Population Hourglass," *Fast Company*, March 2006, www.fastcompany.com on May 1, 2006.

Figure 16.2
MASLOW'S HIERARCHY OF NEEDS

Maslow's hierarchy suggests that human needs can be classified into five categories and that these categories can be arranged in a hierarchy of importance. A manager should understand that an employee may not be satisfied with only a salary and benefits; he or she may also need challenging job opportunities to experience self-growth and satisfaction.

Source: Adapted from Abraham H. Maslow, "A Theory of Human Motivation," *Psychology Review*, 1943, vol. 50, pp. 370–396.

function. In organizations, these needs are generally satisfied by adequate wages and the work environment itself, which provides restrooms, adequate lighting, comfortable temperatures, and ventilation.

Next are the *security needs* for a secure physical and emotional environment. Examples include the desire for housing and clothing and the need to be free from worry about money and job security. These needs can be satisfied in the workplace by job continuity (no layoffs), a grievance system (to protect against arbitrary supervisory actions), and an adequate insurance and retirement benefit package (for security against illness and provision of income in later life). Even today, however, depressed industries and economic decline can put people out of work and restore the primacy of security needs.

Belongingness needs relate to social processes. They include the need for love and affection and the need to be accepted by one's peers. These needs are satisfied for most people by family and community relationships outside of work and by friendships on the job. A manager can help satisfy these needs by allowing social interaction and by making employees feel like part of a team or work group.

Esteem needs actually comprise two different sets of needs: the need for a positive self-image and self-respect, and the need for recognition and respect from others. A manager can help address these needs by providing a variety of extrinsic symbols of accomplishment, such as job titles, nice offices, and similar rewards as appropriate. At a more intrinsic level, the manager can provide challenging job assignments and opportunities for the employee to feel a sense of accomplishment.

At the top of the hierarchy are the *self-actualization needs*. These involve realizing one's potential for continued growth and individual development. The self-actualization needs are perhaps the most difficult for a manager to address. In fact, it can be argued that these needs must be met entirely from within the individual. But a manager can help by promoting a culture wherein self-actualization is possible. For instance, a manager could give employees a chance to participate in making decisions about their work and the opportunity to learn new things.

> "I wanted to do something with my life where I felt I was contributing. Somehow, selling more tacos and margaritas than the week before wasn't."
>
> Cathey Gardner, former restaurant manager, on her decision to become a nurse
> (*USA Today*, August 16, 2004, p. 2B)

Maslow suggests that the five need categories constitute a hierarchy. An individual is motivated first and foremost to satisfy physiological needs. As long as they remain unsatisfied, the individual is motivated to fulfill only them. When satisfaction of physiological needs is achieved, they cease to act as primary motivational factors, and the individual moves "up" the hierarchy and becomes concerned with security needs. This process continues until the individual reaches the self-actualization level. Maslow's concept of the need hierarchy has a certain intuitive logic and has been accepted by many managers. But research has revealed certain shortcomings and defects in the theory. Some research has found that five levels of need are not always present and that the order of the levels is not always the same, as postulated by Maslow.[10] In addition, people from different cultures are likely to have different need categories and hierarchies.

The ERG Theory   In response to these and similar criticisms, an alternative hierarchy of needs, called the **ERG theory of motivation** was developed.[11] This theory collapses the need hierarchy developed by Maslow into three levels. *Existence needs* correspond to the physiological and security needs. *Relatedness needs* focus on how

> *ERG theory of motivation*
> Suggests that people's needs are grouped into three possibly overlapping categories—existence, relatedness, and growth

people relate to their social environment. In Maslow's hierarchy, these would encompass both the need to belong and the need to earn the esteem of others. *Growth needs,* the highest level in this schema, include the needs for self-esteem and self-actualization.

Although the ERG theory assumes that motivated behavior follows a hierarchy in somewhat the same fashion as suggested by Maslow, there are two important differences. First, the ERG theory suggests that more than one level of need can cause motivation at the same time. For example, it suggests that people can be motivated by a desire for money (existence), friendship (relatedness), and the opportunity to learn new skills (growth) all at once. Second, the ERG theory has what has been called a *frustration-regression* element. Thus, if needs remain unsatisfied, the individual will become frustrated, regress to a lower level, and begin to pursue those things again. For example, a worker previously motivated by money (existence needs) may have just been awarded a pay raise sufficient to satisfy those needs. Suppose that he then attempts to establish more friendships to satisfy relatedness needs. If for some reason he finds that it is impossible to become better friends with others in the workplace, he eventually gets frustrated and regresses to being motivated to earn even more money.

The Two-Factor Theory

two-factor theory of motivation
Suggests that people's satisfaction and dissatisfaction are influenced by two independent sets of factors—motivation factors and hygiene factors

Another popular content perspective is the **two-factor theory of motivation.**[12] Frederick Herzberg developed his theory by interviewing 200 accountants and engineers. He asked them to recall occasions when they had been satisfied and motivated and occasions when they had been dissatisfied and unmotivated. Surprisingly, he found that different sets of factors were associated with satisfaction and with dissatisfaction—that is, a person might identify "low pay" as causing dissatisfaction but would not necessarily mention "high pay" as a cause of satisfaction. Instead, different factors—such as recognition or accomplishment—were cited as causing satisfaction and motivation.

This finding led Herzberg to conclude that the traditional view of job satisfaction was incomplete. That view assumed that satisfaction and dissatisfaction are at opposite ends of a single continuum. People might be satisfied, dissatisfied, or somewhere in between. But Herzberg's interviews had identified two different dimensions altogether: one ranging from satisfaction to no satisfaction and the other ranging from dissatisfaction to no dissatisfaction. This perspective, along with several examples of factors that affect each continuum, is shown in Figure 16.3. Note that the factors influencing the satisfaction continuum—called *motivation factors*—are related specifically to the work content. The factors presumed to cause dissatisfaction—called *hygiene factors*—are related to the work environment.

Based on these findings, Herzberg argued that there are two stages in the process of motivating employees. First, managers must ensure that the hygiene factors are not deficient. Pay and security must be appropriate, working conditions must be safe, technical supervision must be acceptable, and so on. By providing hygiene factors at an appropriate level, managers do not stimulate motivation but merely ensure that employees are "not dissatisfied." Employees whom managers attempt to "satisfy" through hygiene factors alone will usually do just enough to get by. Thus managers should proceed to stage two—giving employees the opportunity to experience motivation factors such as achievement and recognition. The result

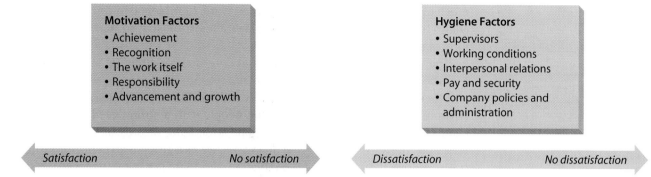

Figure 16.3

THE TWO-FACTOR THEORY OF MOTIVATION

The two-factor theory suggests that job satisfaction has two dimensions. A manager who tries to motivate an employee using only hygiene factors, such as pay and good working conditions, will likely not succeed. To motivate employees and produce a high level of satisfaction, managers must also offer factors such as responsibility and the opportunity for advancement (motivation factors).

is predicted to be a high level of satisfaction and motivation. Herzberg also went a step further than most other theorists and described exactly how to use the two-factor theory in the workplace. Specifically, he recommended job enrichment, as discussed in Chapter 11. He argued that jobs should be redesigned to provide higher levels of the motivation factors.

Although widely accepted by many managers, Herzberg's two-factor theory is not without its critics. One criticism is that the findings in Herzberg's initial interviews are subject to different explanations. Another charge is that his sample was not representative of the general population and that subsequent research often failed to uphold the theory.[13] At the present time, Herzberg's theory is not held in high esteem by researchers in the field. The theory has had a major impact on managers, however, and has played a key role in increasing their awareness of motivation and its importance in the workplace.

Individual Human Needs

In addition to these theories, research has focused on specific individual human needs that are important in organizations. The three most important individual needs are achievement, affiliation, and power.[14]

The ***need for achievement***, the best known of the three, is the desire to accomplish a goal or task more effectively than in the past. People with a high need for achievement have a desire to assume personal responsibility, a tendency to set moderately difficult goals, a desire for specific and immediate feedback, and a preoccupation with their task. David C. McClelland, the psychologist who first identified this need, argues that only about 10 percent of the U.S. population has a high need for achievement. In contrast, almost one-quarter of the workers in Japan have a high need for achievement.

The ***need for affiliation*** is less well understood. Like Maslow's belongingness need, the need for affiliation is a desire for human companionship and acceptance. People with a strong need for affiliation are likely to prefer (and perform better in) a job that entails a lot of social interaction and offers opportunities to make friends. One recent survey found that workers with one or more good friends at work are

need for achievement
The desire to accomplish a goal or task more effectively than in the past

need for affiliation
The desire for human companionship and acceptance

much more likely to be committed to their work. Continental Airlines, for instance, allows flight attendants to form their own teams; those who participate tend to form teams with their friends.[15]

The need for power has also received considerable attention as an important ingredient in managerial success.

The ***need for power*** is the desire to be influential in a group and to control one's environment. Research has shown that people with a strong need for power are likely to be superior performers, have good attendance records, and occupy supervisory positions. One study found that managers as a group tend to have a stronger power motive than the general population and that successful managers tend to have stronger power motives than less successful managers.[16] Dennis Kozlowski, disgraced former CEO of Tyco International, clearly had a strong need for power. This was reflected in the way he routinely took control over resources and used them for his own personal gain. Indeed, the things he bought with company money were probably intended to convey to the world the extent of his power.[17]

need for power
The desire to be influential in a group and to control one's environment

Implications of the Content Perspectives

Managers should remember that Maslow's needs hierarchy, the ERG theory, the two-factor theory, and the needs for achievement, affiliation, and power all provide useful insights into factors that cause motivation. What they do not do is shed much light on the process of motivation. They do not explain why people might be motivated by one factor rather than by another at a given level or how people might go about trying to satisfy the different needs. These questions involve behaviors or actions, goals, and feelings of satisfaction—concepts that are addressed by various process perspectives on motivation.

concept
CHECK

| Summarize the needs hierarchy approaches to employee motivation. | How would you assess yourself regarding the needs for achievement, affiliation, and power? |

Process Perspectives on Motivation

process perspectives
Approaches to motivation that focus on why people choose certain behavioral options to fulfill their needs and how they evaluate their satisfaction after they have attained these goals

Process perspectives are concerned with how motivation occurs. Rather than attempting to identify motivational stimuli, ***process perspectives*** focus on why people choose certain behavioral options to satisfy their needs and how they evaluate their satisfaction after they have attained these goals. Three useful process perspectives on motivation are the expectancy, equity, and goal-setting theories.

Expectancy Theory

expectancy theory
Suggests that motivation depends on two things—how much we want something and how likely we think we are to get it

Expectancy theory suggests that motivation depends on two things—how much we want something and how likely we think we are to get it.[18] Assume that you are approaching graduation and looking for a job. You see in the want ads that General Motors is seeking a new vice president with a starting salary of $500,000 per year. Even though you might want the job, you will not apply because you realize that you have little chance of getting it. The next ad you see is for someone to scrape bubble gum from underneath theater seats for a starting salary of $6 an hour. Even though you could probably get this job, you do not apply because you do not want it. Then you see an ad for a management trainee at a big company, with a starting salary of $40,000. You will probably apply for this job because you want it and because you think you have a reasonable chance of getting it.

Expectancy theory rests on four basic assumptions. First, it assumes that behavior is determined by a combination of forces in the individual and in the environment. Second, it assumes that people make decisions about their own behavior in organizations. Third, it assumes that different people have different types of needs, desires, and goals. Fourth, it assumes that people make choices from among alternative plans of behavior, based on their perceptions of the extent to which a given behavior will lead to desired outcomes.

Figure 16.4 summarizes the basic expectancy model. The model suggests that motivation leads to effort and that effort, combined with employee ability and environmental factors, results in performance. Performance, in turn, leads to various

Process perspectives on motivation suggest that people are motivated to pursue rewards they want and that they think they can achieve. New York Knicks guard Nate Robinson flies toward the basket during the 2006 NBA All-Star slam dunk contest. Athletes like Robinson believe that if they exert effort they will perform at a high level. Of course, they then expect to be rewarded for that performance.

outcomes, each of which has an associated value, called its *valence*. The most important parts of the expectancy model cannot be shown in the figure, however. These are the individual's expectation that effort will lead to high performance, that performance will lead to outcomes, and that each outcome will have some kind of value.

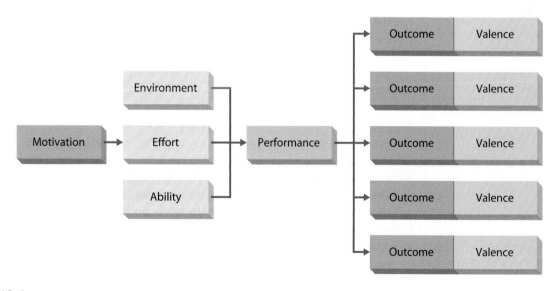

Figure 16.4
THE EXPECTANCY MODEL OF MOTIVATION

The expectancy model of motivation is a complex but relatively accurate portrayal of how motivation occurs. According to this model, a manager must understand what employees want (such as pay, promotions, or status) to begin to motivate them.

effort-to-performance expectancy
The individual's perception of the probability that effort will lead to high performance

performance-to-outcome expectancy
The individual's perception that performance will lead to a specific outcome

outcomes
Consequences of behaviors in an organizational setting, usually rewards

valence
An index of how much an individual desires a particular outcome; the attractiveness of the outcome to the individual

Effort-to-Performance Expectancy   The ***effort-to-performance expectancy*** is the individual's perception of the probability that effort will lead to high performance. When the individual believes that effort will lead directly to high performance, expectancy will be quite strong (close to 1.00). When the individual believes that effort and performance are unrelated, the effort-to-performance expectancy is very weak (close to 0). The belief that effort is somewhat but not strongly related to performance carries with it a moderate expectancy (somewhere between 0 and 1.00).

Performance-to-Outcome Expectancy   The ***performance-to-outcome expectancy*** is the individual's perception that performance will lead to a specific outcome. For example, if the individual believes that high performance *will* result in a pay raise, the performance-to-outcome expectancy is high (approaching 1.00). The individual who believes that high performance *may* lead to a pay raise has a moderate expectancy (between 1.00 and 0). The individual who believes that performance has no relationship to rewards has a low performance-to-outcome expectancy (close to 0).

Outcomes and Valences   Expectancy theory recognizes that an individual's behavior results in a variety of ***outcomes***, or consequences, in an organizational setting. A high performer, for example, may get bigger pay raises, faster promotions, and more praise from the boss. On the other hand, she may also be subject to more stress and incur resentment from coworkers. Each of these outcomes also has an associated value, or ***valence***—an index of how much an individual values a particular outcome. If the individual wants the outcome, its valence is positive; if the individual does not want the outcome, its valence is negative; and if the individual is indifferent to the outcome, its valence is zero.

It is this part of expectancy theory that goes beyond the content perspectives on motivation. Different people have different needs, and they will try to satisfy these needs in different ways. For an employee who has a high need for achievement and a low need for affiliation, the pay raise and promotions cited above as outcomes of high performance might have positive valences, the praise and resentment zero valences, and the stress a negative valence. For a different employee, with a low need for achievement and a high need for affiliation, the pay raise, promotions, and praise might all have positive valences, whereas both resentment and stress could have negative valences.

For motivated behavior to occur, three conditions must be met. First, the effort-to-performance must be greater than 0 (the individual must believe that if effort is expended, high performance will result). The performance-to-outcome expectancy must also be greater than 0 (the individual must believe that if high performance is achieved, certain outcomes will follow). And the sum of the valences for the outcomes must be greater than 0. (One or more outcomes may have negative valences if they are more than offset by the positive valences of other outcomes. For example, the attractiveness of a pay raise, a promotion, and praise from the boss may outweigh the unattractiveness of more stress and resentment from coworkers.) Expectancy theory suggests that when these conditions are met, the individual is motivated to expend effort.

Starbucks credits its unique stock ownership program with maintaining a dedicated and motivated workforce. Based on the fundamental concepts of expectancy theory, Starbucks employees earn stock as a function of their seniority and performance. Thus their hard work helps them earn shares of ownership in the company.[19]

The Porter-Lawler Extension   An interesting extension of expectancy theory has been proposed by Porter and Lawler.[20] Recall from Chapter 2 that the human

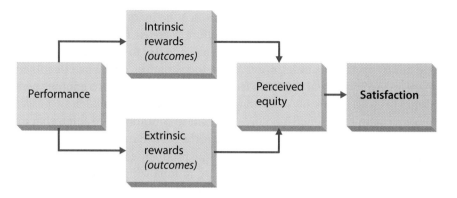

Source: Edward E. Lawler III and Lyman W. Porter, "The Effect of Performance on Job Satisfaction," *Industrial Relations*, October 1967, p. 23. Used with permission of the University of California.

Figure 16.5

THE PORTER-LAWLER EXTENSION OF EXPECTANCY THEORY

The Porter-Lawler extension of expectancy theory suggests that if performance results in equitable rewards, people will be more satisfied. Thus performance can lead to satisfaction. Managers must therefore be sure that any system of motivation includes rewards that are fair, or equitable, for all.

relationists assumed that employee satisfaction causes good performance. We also noted that research has not supported such a relationship. Porter and Lawler suggested that there may indeed be a relationship between satisfaction and performance but that it goes in the opposite direction—that is, high performance may lead to high satisfaction. Figure 16.5 summarizes Porter and Lawler's logic. Performance results in rewards for an individual. Some of these are extrinsic (such as pay and promotions); others are intrinsic (such as self-esteem and accomplishment). The individual evaluates the equity, or fairness, of the rewards relative to the effort expended and the level of performance attained. If the rewards are perceived to be equitable, the individual is satisfied.

Equity Theory

After needs have stimulated the motivation process and the individual has chosen an action that is expected to satisfy those needs, the individual assesses the fairness, or equity, of the resultant outcome. ***Equity theory*** contends that people are motivated to seek social equity in the rewards they receive for performance.[21] Equity is an individual's belief that the treatment he or she is receiving is fair relative to the treatment received by others. According to equity theory, outcomes from a job include pay, recognition, promotions, social relationships, and intrinsic rewards. To get these rewards, the individual makes inputs to the job, such as time, experience, effort, education, and loyalty. The theory suggests that people view their outcomes and inputs as a ratio and then compare it to someone else's ratio. This other "person" may be someone in the work group or some sort of group average or composite. The process of comparison looks like this:

> *equity theory*
> Suggests that people are motivated to seek social equity in the rewards they receive for performance

$$\frac{\text{Outcomes (self)}}{\text{Inputs (self)}} = \frac{\text{Outcomes (other)}}{\text{Inputs (other)}}$$

Both the formulation of the ratios and comparisons between them are very subjective and based on individual perceptions. As a result of comparisons, three conditions may result: The individual may feel equitably rewarded, underrewarded, or overrewarded. A feeling of equity will result when the two ratios are equal. This may occur even though the other person's outcomes are greater than the individual's own outcomes—provided that the other's inputs are also proportionately greater. Suppose that Mark has a high school education and earns $30,000. He may still feel equitably treated relative to Susan, who earns $35,000, because she has a college degree.

People who feel underrewarded try to reduce the inequity. Such an individual might decrease her inputs by exerting less effort, increase her outcomes by asking for a raise, distort the original ratios by rationalizing, try to get the other person to change her or his outcomes or inputs, leave the situation, or change the object of comparison. An individual may also feel overrewarded relative to another person. This is not likely to be terribly disturbing to most people, but research suggests that some people who experience inequity under these conditions are somewhat motivated to reduce it. Under such a circumstance, the person might increase his inputs by exerting more effort, reduce his outcomes by producing fewer units (if paid on a per-unit basis), distort the original ratios by rationalizing, or try to reduce the inputs or increase the outcomes of the other person.

Managers today may need to pay even greater attention to equity theory and its implications. Many firms, for example, are moving toward performance-based reward systems (discussed later in this chapter) as opposed to standard or across-the-board salary increases. Hence, they must ensure that the bases for rewarding some people more than others are clear and objective. Beyond legal issues such as discrimination, managers need to be sure that they are providing fair rewards and incentives to those who do the best work.[22]

Goal-Setting Theory

The goal-setting theory of motivation assumes that behavior is a result of conscious goals and intentions.[23] Therefore, by setting goals for people in the organization, a manager should be able to influence their behavior. Given this premise, the challenge is to develop a thorough understanding of the processes by which people set goals and then work to reach them. In the original version of goal-setting theory, two specific goal characteristics—goal difficulty and goal specificity—were expected to shape performance.

Goal Difficulty *Goal difficulty* is the extent to which a goal is challenging and requires effort. If people work to achieve goals, it is reasonable to assume that they will work harder to achieve more difficult goals. But a goal must not be so difficult that it is unattainable. If a new manager asks her sales force to increase sales by 300 percent, the group may become disillusioned. A more realistic but still difficult goal—perhaps a 30 percent increase—would be a better incentive. A substantial body of research supports the importance of goal difficulty. In one study, for example, managers at Weyerhauser set difficult goals for truck drivers hauling loads of timber from cutting sites to wood yards. Over a nine-month period, the drivers increased the quantity of wood they delivered by an amount that would have required $250,000 worth of new trucks at the previous per-truck average load.[24]

Goal Specificity *Goal specificity* is the clarity and precision of the goal. A goal of "increasing productivity" is not very specific; a goal of "increasing productivity by 3 percent in the next six months" is quite specific. Some goals, such as those involving costs, output, profitability, and growth, are readily amenable to specificity. Other goals, however, such as improving employee job satisfaction, morale, company image and reputation, ethics, and socially responsible behavior, may be much harder to state in specific terms. Like difficulty, specificity has been shown to be consistently related to performance. The study of timber truck drivers men-

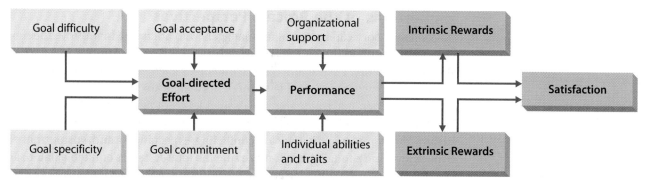

Figure 16.6

THE EXPANDED GOAL-SETTING THEORY OF MOTIVATION

One of the most important emerging theories of motivation is goal-setting theory. This theory suggests that goal difficulty, specificity, acceptance, and commitment combine to determine an individual's goal-directed effort. This effort, when complemented by appropriate organizational support and individual abilities and traits, results in performance. Finally, performance is seen as leading to intrinsic and extrinsic rewards that, in turn, result in employee satisfaction.

Source: Reprinted from *Organizational Dynamics*, Autumn 1979, Gary P. Latham and Edwin A. Locke, "A Motivational Technique That Works," p. 79, copyright © 1979 with permission from Elsevier Science.

tioned above, for example, also examined goal specificity. The initial loads the truck drivers were carrying were found to be 60 percent of the maximum weight each truck could haul. The managers set a new goal for drivers of 94 percent, which the drivers were soon able to reach. Thus the goal was both specific and difficult.

Because the theory attracted so much widespread interest and research support from researchers and managers alike, an expanded model of the goal-setting process was eventually proposed. The expanded model, shown in Figure 16.6, attempts to capture more fully the complexities of goal setting in organizations.

The expanded theory argues that goal-directed effort is a function of four goal attributes: difficulty and specificity, as already discussed, and acceptance and commitment. *Goal acceptance* is the extent to which a person accepts a goal as his or her own. *Goal commitment* is the extent to which she or he is personally interested in reaching the goal. The manager who vows to take whatever steps are necessary to cut costs by 10 percent has made a commitment to achieve the goal. Factors that can foster goal acceptance and commitment include participating in the goal-setting process, making goals challenging but realistic, and believing that goal achievement will lead to valued rewards.

The interaction of goal-directed effort, organizational support, and individual abilities and traits determines actual performance. Organizational support is whatever the organization does to help or hinder performance. Positive support might mean making available adequate personnel and a sufficient supply of raw materials; negative support might mean failing to fix damaged equipment. Individual abilities and traits are the skills and other personal characteristics necessary for doing a job. As a result of performance, a person receives various intrinsic and extrinsic rewards, which in turn influence satisfaction. Note that the latter stages of this model are quite similar to the Porter and Lawler expectancy model discussed earlier.[25]

Implications of the Process Perspectives

Expectancy theory can be useful for managers who are trying to improve the motivation of their subordinates. A series of steps can be followed to implement the basic ideas of the theory. First, figure out the outcomes each employee is likely to want. Second, decide what kinds and levels of performance are needed to meet organizational goals. Then make sure that the desired levels of performance are attainable. Also make sure that desired outcomes and desired performance are linked. Next, analyze the complete situation for conflicting expectancies and ensure that the rewards are large enough. Finally, make sure the total system is equitable (fair to all). The single most important idea for managers to remember from equity theory is that if rewards are to motivate employees, they must be perceived as being equitable and fair. A second implication is that managers need to consider the nature of the "other" to whom the employee is comparing her- or himself. Goal-setting theory can be used to implement both expectancy and equity theory concepts.

concept
CHECK

| *Describe the basic motivational process that employees go through as reflected in expectancy theory.* | *Recall a situation in which you experienced inequity. Analyze the situation in terms of equity theory. Was your feeling of inequity justified?* |

Reinforcement Perspectives on Motivation

A third element of the motivational process addresses why some behaviors are maintained over time and why other behaviors change. As we have seen, content perspectives deal with needs, whereas process perspectives explain why people choose various behaviors to satisfy needs and how they evaluate the equity of the rewards they get for those behaviors. Reinforcement perspectives explain the role of those rewards as they cause behavior to change or remain the same over time. Specifically, **reinforcement theory** argues that behavior that results in rewarding consequences is likely to be repeated, whereas behavior that results in punishing consequences is less likely to be repeated.[26]

Kinds of Reinforcement in Organizations

There are four basic kinds of reinforcement that can result from behavior—positive reinforcement, avoidance, punishment, and extinction.[27] These are summarized in Table 16.1. Two kinds of reinforcement strengthen or maintain behavior, whereas the other two weaken or decrease behavior.

Positive reinforcement, a method of strengthening behavior, is a reward or a positive outcome after a desired behavior is performed. When a manager observes an employee doing an especially good job and offers praise, the praise serves to positively reinforce the behavior of good work. Other positive reinforcers in organizations include pay raises, promotions, and awards. Employees who work at General Electric's customer service center receive clothing, sporting goods, and even trips to Disney World as rewards for outstanding performance. The other method of strengthening desired behavior is through **avoidance**. An employee may come to work on time to avoid a reprimand. In this instance, the employee is motivated to

---

reinforcement theory
Approach to motivation that argues that behavior that results in rewarding consequences is likely to be repeated, whereas behavior that results in punishing consequences is less likely to be repeated

positive reinforcement
A method of strengthening behavior with rewards or positive outcomes after a desired behavior is performed

avoidance
Used to strengthen behavior by avoiding unpleasant consequences that would result if the behavior were not performed

Arrangement of the Reinforcement Contingencies

1. *Positive Reinforcement.* Strengthens behavior by providing a desirable consequence.
2. *Avoidance.* Strengthens behavior by allowing escape from an undesirable consequence.
3. *Punishment.* Weakens behavior by providing an undesirable consequence.
4. *Extinction.* Weakens behavior by ignoring it.

Schedules for Applying Reinforcement

1. *Fixed-Interval.* Reinforcement is applied at fixed time intervals, regardless of behavior.
2. *Variable-Interval.* Reinforcement is applied at variable time intervals.
1. *Fixed-Ratio.* Reinforcement is applied after a fixed number of behaviors, regardless of time.
2. *Variable-Ratio.* Reinforcement is applied after a variable number of behaviors.

Table 16.1

ELEMENTS OF REINFORCEMENT THEORY

A manager who wants the best chance of reinforcing a behavior would likely offer the employee a positive reinforcement after a variable number of behaviors (variable-ratio reinforcement). For example, the manager could praise the employee after the third credit card application was received. Additional praise might be offered after the next five applications, then again after the next three, the next seven, the next four, and so on.

punishment
Used to weaken undesired behaviors by using negative outcomes or unpleasant consequences when the behavior is performed

extinction
Used to weaken undesired behaviors by simply ignoring or not reinforcing them

fixed-interval schedule
Provides reinforcement at fixed intervals of time, such as regular weekly paychecks

variable-interval schedule
Provides reinforcement at varying intervals of time, such as occasional visits by the supervisor

fixed-ratio schedule
Provides reinforcement after a fixed number of behaviors regardless of the time interval involved, such as a bonus for every fifth sale

variable-ratio schedule
Provide reinforcement after varying numbers of behaviors are performed, such as the use of complements by a supervisor on an irregular basis

perform the behavior of punctuality to avoid an unpleasant consequence that is likely to follow tardiness.

Punishment is used by some managers to weaken undesired behaviors. When an employee is loafing, coming to work late, doing poor work, or interfering with the work of others, the manager might resort to reprimands, discipline, or fines. The logic is that the unpleasant consequence will reduce the likelihood that the employee will choose that particular behavior again. Given the counterproductive side effects of punishment (such as resentment and hostility), it is often advisable to use the other kinds of reinforcement if at all possible. *Extinction* can also be used to weaken behavior, especially behavior that has previously been rewarded. When an employee tells an off-color joke and the boss laughs, the laughter reinforces the behavior and the employee may continue to tell off-color jokes. By simply ignoring this behavior and not reinforcing it, the boss can cause the behavior to subside and eventually become "extinct."

Providing Reinforcement in Organizations

Not only is the kind of reinforcement important, but so is when or how often it occurs. Various strategies are possible for providing reinforcement. These are also listed in Table 16.1. The *fixed-interval schedule* provides reinforcement at fixed intervals of time, regardless of behavior. A good example of this schedule is the weekly or monthly paycheck. This method provides the least incentive for good work because employees know they will be paid regularly regardless of their efforts. A *variable-interval schedule* also uses time as the basis for reinforcement, but the time interval varies from one reinforcement to the next. This schedule is appropriate for praise or other rewards based on visits or inspections. When employees do not know when the boss is going to drop by, they tend to maintain a reasonably high level of effort all the time.

A *fixed-ratio schedule* gives reinforcement after a fixed number of behaviors, regardless of the time that elapses between behaviors. This results in an even higher level of effort. For example, when Sears is recruiting new credit card customers, salespersons get a small bonus for every fifth application returned from their department. Under this arrangement, motivation will be high because each application gets the person closer to the next bonus. The *variable-ratio schedule*, the most powerful schedule in terms of maintaining desired behaviors, varies the number of behaviors needed for each reinforcement. A supervisor who praises an employee for her second order, the seventh order after that, the ninth after that, then the fifth, and then the third is using a variable-ratio schedule. The employee is motivated to increase the frequency of the desired behavior because each performance increases the probability of receiving a reward. Of course, a variable-ratio schedule is difficult (if not impossible) to use for formal rewards such as pay because it would be too complicated to keep track of who was rewarded when.

Managers wanting to explicitly use reinforcement theory to motivate their employees generally do so with a technique called *behavior modification*, or *OB Mod*.[28] An OB Mod program starts by specifying behaviors that are to be increased (such as producing more units) or decreased (such as coming to work late). These target behaviors are then tied to specific forms or kinds of reinforcement. Although many organizations (such as Procter & Gamble and Ford) have used OB Mod, the best-known application was at Emery Air Freight. Management felt that the containers used to consolidate small shipments into fewer, larger shipments were not being packed efficiently. Through a system of self-monitored feedback and rewards, Emery increased container usage from 45 percent to 95 percent and saved over $3 million during the first three years of the program.[29]

behavior modification (OB Mod)
Method for applying the basic elements of reinforcement theory in an organizational setting

Implications of the Reinforcement Perspectives

Reinforcement in organizations can be a powerful force for maintaining employee motivation. Of course, for reinforcement to be truly effective, managers need to use it in a manner consistent with the various types and schedules of reinforcement discussed above. In addition, managers must understand that they may be inadvertently motivating undesired or dysfunctional behaviors. For instance, if an employee routinely comes to work late but experiences no consequences, both that worker and others will see that it is all right to be late for work.

concept
CHECK

What are the basic kinds and schedules of reinforcement available to managers in organizations?

Describe a time when each of the different kinds of reinforcement affected your behavior.

Popular Motivational Strategies

Although the various theories discussed thus far provide a solid explanation for motivation, managers must use various techniques and strategies to actually apply them. Among the most popular motivational strategies today are empowerment and participation and alternative forms of work arrangements. Various forms of performance-based reward systems, discussed in the next section, also reflect efforts to boost motivation and performance.

Empowerment and Participation

Empowerment and participation represent important methods that managers can use to enhance employee motivation. *Empowerment* is the process of enabling workers to set their own work goals, make decisions, and solve problems within their sphere of responsibility and authority. *Participation* is the process of giving employees a voice in making decisions about their own work. Thus empowerment is a

empowerment
The process of enabling workers to set their own work goals, make decisions, and solve problems within their sphere of responsibility and authority

participation
The process of giving employees a voice in making decisions about their own work

somewhat broader concept that promotes participation in a wide variety of areas, including but not limited to work itself, work context, and work environment.[30]

The role of participation and empowerment in motivation can be expressed in terms of both content perspectives and expectancy theory. Employees who participate in decision making may be more committed to executing decisions properly. Furthermore, the successful process of making a decision, executing it, and then seeing the positive consequences can help satisfy one's need for achievement, provide recognition and responsibility, and enhance self-esteem. Simply being asked to participate in organizational decision making also may enhance an employee's self-esteem. In addition, participation should help clarify expectancies; that is, by participating in decision making, employees may better understand the linkage between their performance and the rewards they want most.

Areas of Participation   At one level, employees can participate in addressing questions and making decisions about their own job. Instead of just telling them how to do their job, for example, managers can ask employees to make their own decisions about how to do it. Based on their own expertise and experience with their tasks, workers might be able to improve their own productivity. In many situations, they might also be well qualified to make decisions about what materials to use, what tools to use, and so forth.

It might also be helpful to let workers make decisions about administrative matters, such as work schedules. If jobs are relatively independent of one another, employees might decide when to change shifts, take breaks, go to lunch, and so forth. A work group or team might also be able to schedule vacations and days off for all of its members. Furthermore, employees are getting increasing opportunities to participate in broader issues of product quality. Such participation has become a hallmark of successful Japanese and other international firms, and many U.S. companies have followed suit.

Techniques and Issues in Empowerment   In recent years, many organizations have actively sought ways to extend participation beyond the traditional areas. Simple techniques, such as suggestion boxes and question-and-answer meetings, allow a certain degree of participation, for example. The basic motive has been to better capitalize on the assets and capabilities inherent in all employees. Thus many managers today prefer the term *empowerment* to *participation* because of its more comprehensive character.

One method used to empower workers is the use of work teams. Such teams are collections of employees empowered to plan, organize, direct, and control their own work. Their supervisor, rather than being a traditional "boss," plays more the role of a coach. The other method for empowerment is to change the team's overall method of organizing. The basic pattern is for an organization to eliminate layers from its hierarchy, thereby become much more decentralized. Power, responsibility, and authority are delegated as far down the organization as possible, placing the control over work squarely in the hands of those who actually do it.[31]

Regardless of the specific technique or method used, however, empowerment will enhance organizational effectiveness only if certain conditions exist. First of all, the organization must be sincere in its efforts to spread power and autonomy to lower levels of the organization. Token efforts to promote participation in only a few areas are not likely to succeed. Second, the organization must be committed to maintaining participation and empowerment. Workers will be resentful if they are given more control, only to later have it reduced or taken away altogether. Third, workers must truly believe that they and their managers are working together in their joint best interests. In some factory settings, for instance, high-performing workers routinely conceal the secrets of their high output. They fear that if management learns those secrets, it will use them to ratchet up performance expectations.[32]

In addition, the organization must be systematic and patient in its efforts to empower workers. Turning over too much control too quickly can spell disaster. And finally, the organization must be prepared to increase its commitment to training. Employees given more freedom in how they work will quite likely need additional training to help them exercise that freedom most effectively.[33]

Alternative Forms of Work Arrangements

Many organizations today are also experimenting with a variety of alternative work arrangements. These alternative arrangements are generally intended to enhance employee motivation and performance by providing employees with greater flexibility in how and when they work. Among the more popular alternative work arrangements are variable work schedules, flexible work schedules, job sharing, and telecommuting.[34]

Variable Work Schedules   Although there are many exceptions, of course, the traditional work schedule starts at 8:00 or 9:00 in the morning and ends at 5:00 in the evening, five days a week (and, of course, many managers work additional hours outside of these times). Unfortunately, this schedule makes it difficult to attend to routine personal business—going to the bank, seeing a doctor or dentist for a routine checkup, having a parent-teacher conference, getting an automobile serviced, and so forth. At a surface level, then, employees locked into this sort of arrangement may find it necessary to take a sick day or a vacation day to handle these activities. At a more unconscious level, some people may also feel so powerless and constrained by their job schedule as to feel increased resentment and frustration.

> **compressed work schedule**
> Working a full 40-hour week in fewer than the traditional five days

To help counter these problems, some businesses have adopted a ***compressed work schedule***, working a full 40-hour week in fewer than the traditional five days.[35] One approach involves working 10 hours a day for four days, leaving an extra day off. Another alternative is for employees to work slightly less than 10 hours a day, but to complete the 40 hours by lunchtime on Friday. And a few firms have tried having employees work 12 hours a day for three days, followed by four days off. Organizations that have used these forms of compressed workweeks include John Hancock, BP Amoco, and Philip Morris. One problem with this schedule is that when employees put in too much time in a single day, they tend to get tired and perform at a lower level later in the day.

A schedule that some organizations today are beginning to use is what they call a "nine-eighty" schedule. Under this arrangement, an employee works a traditional schedule one week and a compressed schedule the next, getting every other Friday off. In other words, they work 80 hours (the equivalent of two weeks of full-time work) in nine days. By alternating the regular and compressed schedules across half of its workforce, the organization can be fully staffed at all times, while still giving employees two full days off each month. Shell Oil and BP Amoco Chemicals are two of the firms that currently use this schedule.

Flexible Work Schedules   Another promising alternative work arrangement is *flexible work schedules*, sometimes called *flextime*. Flextime gives employees more personal control over the times they work. The workday is broken down into two categories: flexible time and core time. All employees must be at their workstation during core time, but they can choose their own schedules during flexible time. Thus one employee may choose to start work early in the morning and leave in midafternoon, another to start in the late morning and work until late afternoon, and still another to start early in the morning, take a long lunch break, and work until late afternoon. Organizations that have used the flexible work schedule method for arranging work include Hewlett-Packard, Compaq Computer, Microsoft, and Texas Instruments.

Job Sharing   Yet another potentially useful alternative work arrangement is job sharing. In *job sharing*, two part-time employees share one full-time job. One person may perform the job from 8:00 A.M. to noon and the other from 1:00 P.M. to 5:00 P.M. Job sharing may be desirable for people who want to work only part time or when job markets are tight. For its part, the organization can accommodate the preferences of a broader range of employees and may benefit from the talents of more people.

> *job sharing*
> When two part-time employees share one full-time job

Telecommuting   An increasingly popular approach to alternative work arrangements is *telecommuting*—allowing employees to spend part of their time working offsite, usually at home. By using e-mail, the Internet, and other forms of information technology, many employees can maintain close contact with their organization and still get just as much work done at home as if they were in their office. The increased power and sophistication of modern communication technology is making telecommuting easier and easier. About 15 percent of the U.S. workforce does at least some telecommuting, and in some businesses it's much higher. At IBM, for instance, 40 percent of the workforce has no corporate workstation or office; at AT&T, the figure is 35 percent, and at Sun Microsystems, it's 50 percent.[36]

> *telecommuting*
> Allowing employees to spend part of their time working offsite, usually at home

> " I get to sit here and look out my window while I talk to customers—and watch the leaves changing, squirrels running around, and kids going off to school."
> Walt Swanson, Agilent Technologies customer service representative
> (*BusinessWeek*, December 12, 2005, p. 79)

concept CHECK

Summarize the basic concepts underlying employee empowerment and participation.

What work schedule would be most attractive to you? Least attractive?

Using Reward Systems to Motivate Performance

Aside from these types of motivational strategies, an organization's reward system is its most basic tool for managing employee motivation. An organizational *reward system* is the formal and informal mechanisms by which employee performance is defined, evaluated, and rewarded. Rewards that are tied specifically to performance, of course, have the greatest impact on enhancing both motivation and actual performance.

> *reward system*
> The formal and informal mechanisms by which employee performance is defined, evaluated, and rewarded

Performance-based rewards play a number of roles and address a variety of purposes in organizations. The major purposes involve the relationship of rewards to

Managers sometimes resort to unusual rewards as a way to retain valuable employees. Mercer Management, a consulting firm, was having trouble holding on to its best consultants, who were beginning to feel a bit restless. Mercer found that some of them were leaving to help implement strategies they had developed for Mercer clients. So, the firm now allows its consultants to take a leave of absence of up to one year to work for other companies. Mercer consultant Gregg Dixon, for example, helped Binney & Smith develop a new strategy for its popular Crayola crayons. He then went to work for Binney & Smith to help implement the strategy. After he has finished, he will return to his old job at Mercer Management.

---

merit pay
Pay awarded to employees on the basis of the relative value of their contributions to the organization

---

merit pay plan
Compensation plan that formally bases at least some meaningful portion of compensation on merit

---

motivation and to performance. Specifically, organizations want employees to perform at relatively high levels and need to make it worth their effort to do so. When rewards are associated with higher levels of performance, employees will presumably be motivated to work harder to achieve those awards. At that point, their own self-interests coincide with the organization's interests. Performance-based rewards are also relevant regarding other employee behaviors, such as retention and citizenship.

Merit Reward Systems

Merit reward systems are one of the most fundamental forms of performance-based rewards. **Merit pay** generally refers to pay awarded to employees on the basis of the relative value of their contributions to the organization. Employees who make greater contributions are given higher pay than those who make lesser contributions. **Merit pay plans**, then, are compensation plans that formally base at least some meaningful portion of compensation on merit.

The most general form of merit pay plan is to provide annual salary increases to individuals in the organization based on their relative merit. Merit, in turn, is usually determined or defined based on the individual's performance and overall contributions to the organization. For example, an organization using such a traditional merit pay plan might instruct its supervisors to give all their employees an average pay raise of, say, 4 percent. But the individual supervisor is further instructed to differentiate among high, average, and low performers. Under a simple system, for example, a manager might give the top 25 percent of her employees a 6 percent pay raise, the middle 50 percent a 4 percent or average pay raise, and the bottom 25 percent a 2 percent pay raise.

Incentive Reward Systems

Incentive reward systems are among the oldest forms of performance-based rewards. For example, some companies were using individual piece-rate incentive plans over 100 years ago.[37] Under a **piece-rate incentive plan**, the organization pays an employee a certain amount of money for every unit she or he produces. For example, an employee might be paid $1 for every dozen units of products that are successfully completed. But such simplistic systems fail to account for such facts as minimum wage levels and rely very heavily on the assumptions that performance is totally under an individual's control and that the individual employee does a single task continuously throughout his or her work time. Thus most organizations today that try to use incentive compensation systems use more sophisticated methodologies.

Incentive Pay Plans Generally speaking, *individual incentive plans* reward individual performance on a real-time basis. In other words, rather than increasing a person's base salary at the end of the year, an individual instead receives some level of salary increase or financial reward in conjunction with demonstrated outstanding performance in close proximity to when that performance occurred. Individual incentive systems are most likely to be used in cases in which performance can be objectively assessed in terms of number of units of output or similar measures, rather than on a subjective assessment of performance by a superior.

Some variations on a piece-rate system are still fairly popular. Although many of these still resemble the early plans in most ways, a well-known piece-rate system at Lincoln Electric illustrates how an organization can adapt the traditional model to achieve better results. For years, Lincoln's employees were paid individual incentive payments based on their performance. However, the amount of money shared (or the incentive pool) was based on the company's profitability. There was also a well-organized system whereby employees could make suggestions for increasing productivity. There was motivation to do this because the employees received one-third of the profits (another third went to the stockholders, and the last share was retained for improvements and seed money). Thus the pool for incentive payments was determined by profitability, and an employee's share of this pool was a function of his or her base pay and rated performance based on the piece-rate system. Lincoln Electric was most famous, however, because of the stories (which were apparently typical) of production workers' receiving a year-end bonus payment that equaled their yearly base pay.[38] In recent years, Lincoln has partially abandoned its famous system for business reasons, but it still serves as a benchmark for other companies seeking innovative piece-rate pay systems.

Perhaps the most common form of individual incentive is *sales commissions* that are paid to people engaged in sales work. For example, sales representatives for consumer products firms and retail sales agents may be compensated under this type of commission system. In general, the person might receive a percentage of the total volume of attained sales as her or his commission for a period of time. Some sales jobs are based entirely on commission, whereas others use a combination of base minimum salary with additional commission as an incentive. Notice that these plans put a considerable amount of the salespersons' earnings "at risk." In other words, although organizations often have drawing accounts to allow the salesperson to live during lean periods (the person then "owes" this money back to the organization), if he or she does not perform well, he or she will not be paid much. The portion of salary based on commission is simply not guaranteed and is paid only if sales reach some target level.

Other Forms of Incentive   Occasionally organizations may also use other forms of incentives to motivate people. For example, a nonmonetary incentive, such as additional time off or a special perk, might be a useful incentive. For example, a company might establish a sales contest in which the sales group that attains the highest level of sales increase over a specified period of time will receive an extra week of paid vacation, perhaps even at an arranged place, such as a tropical resort or a ski lodge.[39]

A major advantage of incentives relative to merit systems is that incentives are typically a one-shot reward and do not accumulate by becoming part of the individual's base salary. Stated differently, an individual whose outstanding performance entitles him or her to a financial incentive gets the incentive only one time, based on that level of performance. If the individual's performance begins to erode in the future, then the individual may receive a lesser incentive or perhaps no incentive in the future. As a consequence, his or her base salary remains the same or is perhaps increased at a relatively moderate pace; he or she receives one-time

piece-rate incentive plan
Reward system wherein the organization pays an employee a certain amount of money for every unit she or he produces

incentive rewards as recognition for exemplary performance. Furthermore, because these plans, by their very nature, focus on one-time events, it is much easier for the organization to change the focus of the incentive plan. At a simple level, for example, an organization can set up an incentive plan for selling one product during one quarter, but then shift the incentive to a different product the next quarter, as the situation requires. Automobile companies like Ford and GM routinely do this by reducing sales incentives for models that are selling very well and increasing sales incentives for models that are selling below expectations or are about to be discontinued.

Team and Group Incentive Reward Systems

The merit compensation and incentive compensation systems described in the preceding sections deal primarily with performance-based reward arrangements for individuals. There also exists a different set of performance-based reward programs that are targeted for teams and groups. These programs are particularly important for managers to understand today, given the widespread trends toward team and group-based methods of work and organizations.[40]

Common Team and Group Reward Systems   There are two commonly used types of team and group reward systems. One type used in many organizations is an approach called gainsharing. ***Gainsharing programs*** are designed to share the cost savings from productivity improvements with employees. The underlying assumption of gainsharing is that employees and the employer have the same goals and thus should appropriately share in incremental economic gains.[41]

gainsharing programs
Designed to share the cost savings from productivity improvements with employees

In general, organizations that use gainsharing start by measuring team- or group-level productivity. It is important that this measure be valid and reliable and that it truly reflect current levels of performance by the team or group. The team or work group itself is then given the charge of attempting to lower costs and otherwise improve productivity through any measures that its members develop and its manager approves. Resulting cost savings or productivity gains that the team or group is able to achieve are then quantified and translated into dollar values. A predetermined formula is then used to allocate these dollar savings between the employer and the employees themselves. A typical formula for distributing gainsharing savings is to provide 25 percent to the employees and 75 percent to the company.

One specific type of gainsharing plan is an approach called the Scanlon plan. This approach was developed by Joseph Scanlon in 1927. The ***Scanlon plan*** has the same basic strategy as gainsharing plans, in that teams or groups of employees are encouraged to suggest strategies for reducing costs. However, the distribution of these gains is usually tilted much more heavily toward employees, with employees usually receiving between two-thirds and three-fourths of the total cost savings that the plan achieves. Furthermore, the distribution of cost savings resulting from the plan is given not just to the team or group that suggested and developed the ideas, but across the entire organization.

Scanlon plan
Similar to gainsharing, but the distribution of gains is tilted much more heavily toward employees

Other Types of Team and Group Rewards   Although gainsharing and Scanlon-type plans are among the most popular group incentive reward systems, there are other systems that are also used by some organizations. Some companies, for example, have begun to use true incentives at the team or group level. Just as with individual incentives, team or group incentives tie rewards directly to performance increases. And, like individual incentives, team or group incentives are paid as they are earned rather than being added to employees' base salary. The incentives are distributed at the team or group level, however, rather than at the individual level. In some cases, the distribution may be based on the existing salary of each employee, with incentive bonuses' being given on a proportionate basis. In other settings, each member of the team or group receives the same incentive pay.

Some companies also use nonmonetary rewards at the team or group level—most commonly in the form of prizes and awards. For example, a company might designate the particular team in a plant or subunit of the company that achieves the highest level of productivity increase, the highest level of reported customer satisfaction, or a similar index of performance. The reward itself might take the form of additional time off, as described earlier in this chapter, or a tangible award, such as a trophy or plaque. In any event, the idea is that the reward is at the team level and serves as recognition of exemplary performance by the entire team.

There are also other kinds of team or group level incentives that go beyond the contributions of a specific work group. These are generally organization-wide kinds of incentives. One long-standing method for this approach is *profit sharing*. In a profit-sharing approach, at the end of the year some portion of the company's profits is paid into a profit-sharing pool that is then distributed to all employees. Either this amount is distributed at that time, or it is put into an escrow account and payment is deferred until the employee retires.

The basic rationale behind profit-sharing systems is that everyone in the organization can expect to benefit when the company does well. But, on the other side of the coin, during bad economic times, when the company is perhaps achieving low or perhaps no profits, then no profit sharing is paid out. This sometimes results in negative reactions from employees, who have perhaps come to feel that profit sharing is really a part of their annual compensation.

Employee stock ownership plans (ESOPs) also represent a group-level reward system that some companies use. Under the employee stock ownership plan, employees are gradually given a major stake in ownership of a corporation. The typical form of this plan involves the company's taking out a loan, which is then used to buy a portion of its own stock in the open market. Over time, company profits are then used to pay off this loan. Employees, in turn, receive a claim on ownership of some portion of the stock held by the company, based on their seniority and perhaps on their performance. Eventually, each individual becomes an owner of the company.

Executive Compensation

The top-level executives of most companies have separate compensation programs and plans. These are intended to reward these executives for their performance and for the performance of the organization.

Standard Forms of Executive Compensation   Most senior executives receive their compensation in two forms. One form is a *base salary*. As with the base salary of any staff member or professional member of an organization, the base salary of an executive is a guaranteed amount of money that the individual will be paid. For example, in 2005 Yahoo! paid its CEO, Terry Semel, $600,000 in base salary.

Above and beyond this base salary, however, most executives also receive one or more forms of incentive pay. The traditional method of incentive pay for executives is in the form of bonuses. Bonuses, in turn, are usually determined by the performance of the organization. Thus, at the end of the year, some portion of a corporation's profits may be diverted into a bonus pool. Senior executives then receive a bonus expressed as a percentage of this bonus pool. The chief executive officer and president are obviously likely to get a larger percentage bonus than a vice president. The exact distribution of the bonus pool is usually specified ahead of time in the individual's employment contract. Some organizations intentionally leave the distribution unspecified, so that the board of directors has the flexibility to give larger rewards to those individuals deemed to be most deserving. Yahoo!'s Terry Semel received a cash bonus of about $250,000 in 2005.

Special Forms of Executive Compensation   Beyond base salary and bonuses, many executives receive other kinds of compensation as well. A form of executive compensation that has received a lot of attention in recent years has been various kinds of stock options. A ***stock option plan*** is established to give senior managers the option to buy company stock in the future at a predetermined fixed price. The basic idea underlying stock option plans is that if the executives contribute to higher levels of organizational performance, then the company stock should increase in value. Then the executive will be able to purchase the stock at the predetermined price, which theoretically should be lower than its future market price. The difference then becomes profit for the individual. Yahoo! awarded Terry Semel stock options with a potential value of $230,000,000.

Stock options continue to grow in popularity as a means of compensating top managers. Options are seen as a means of aligning the interests of the manager with those of the stockholders, and given that they do not cost the organization much (other than some possible dilution of stock values), they will probably be even more popular in the future. In fact, a recent study by KPMG Peat Marwick indicates that for senior management whose salary exceeds $250,000, stock options represent the largest share of the salary mix (relative to salary and other incentives). Furthermore, when we consider all of top management (annual salary over $750,000), stock options comprise a full 60 percent of their total compensation. And the Peat Marwick report indicates that even among exempt employees at the $35,000-a-year level, stock options represent 13 percent of total compensation.

But events in recent years have raised serious questions about the use of stock options as incentives for executives. For example, several executives at Enron allegedly withheld critical financial information from the markets, cashed in their stock options (while Enron stock was trading at $80 a share), and then watched as the financial information was made public and the stock fell to less than $1 a share. Of course, these actions (if proven) are illegal, but they raise questions in the public's mind about the role of stock options and about the way organizations treat stock options from an accounting perspective. Most organizations have *not* treated stock options as liabilities, even though, when exercised, they are exactly that. There is concern that by not carrying stock options as liabilities, the managers are overstating the value of the company, which, of course, can help raise the stock price. Finally, when stock markets generally fell during the middle of 2002, many executives found that their options were worthless, as the price of the stock fell below the option price. When stock options go "under water" in this way, they have no value to anyone.

---

stock option plan
Established to give senior managers the option to buy company stock in the future at a predetermined fixed price

Aside from stock option plans, other kinds of executive compensation are also used by some companies. Among the more popular are such perquisites as memberships in private clubs, access to company recreational facilities, and similar considerations. Some organizations also make available to senior executives low- or no-interest loans. These are often given to new executives whom the company is hiring from other companies and serve as an incentive for the individual to leave his or her current job to join a new organization.

Criticisms of Executive Compensation   In recent years, executive compensation has come under fire for a variety of reasons. One major reason is that the levels of executive compensation attained by some managers seem simply too large for the average shareholder to understand. It is not uncommon, for instance, for a senior executive of a major corporation to earn total income from his or her job in a given year of well in excess of $1 million. Sometimes the income of chief executive officers can be substantially more than this. Coca-Cola's Douglas Daft earned a total of $55 million in 2001 from all sources combined. Thus, just as the typical person has difficulty comprehending the astronomical salaries paid to some movie stars and sports stars, so, too, would the average person be aghast at the astronomical salaries paid to some senior executives.

Compounding the problem created by perceptions of executive compensation is the fact that there often seems to be little or no relationship between the performance of the organization and the compensation paid to its senior executives.[42] Certainly, if an organization is performing at an especially high level and its stock price is increasing consistently, then most observers would agree that the senior executives responsible for this growth should be entitled to attractive rewards.[43] However, it is more difficult to understand a case in which executives are paid huge salaries and other forms of rewards when their company is performing at only a marginal level, yet this is fairly common today. For example, in 2002 Oracle's CEO, Lawrence Ellison, pocketed over $700 million from the sale of previously granted stock options, while the value of Oracle stock was dropping by 57 percent.

Finally, we should note that the gap between the earnings of the CEO and the earnings of a typical employee is enormous. First of all, the size of the gap has been increasing in the United States. In 1980 the typical CEO earned 42 times the earnings of an ordinary worker, but by 1990 this ratio had increased to 85 times the earnings of an ordinary worker. In Japan, on the other hand, the relationship in 1990 was that a typical CEO made less than 20 times the earnings of an ordinary worker.[44]

New Approaches to Performance-Based Rewards

Some organizations have started to recognize that they can leverage the value of the incentives that they offer to their employees and to groups in their organization by allowing those individuals and groups to have a say in how rewards are distributed. For example, at the extreme, a company could go so far as to grant salary increase budgets to work groups and then allow the members of those groups themselves to determine how the rewards are going to be allocated among the various members of the group. This strategy would appear to hold considerable promise if everyone understands the performance arrangements that exist in the work group and everyone is committed to being fair and equitable. Unfortunately, it can also create problems if people in a group feel that rewards are not being distributed fairly.[45]

Organizations are also getting increasingly innovative in their incentive programs. For example, some now offer stock options to all their employees, rather than just to top executives. In addition, some firms are looking into ways to purely individualize reward systems. For instance, a firm might offer one employee a paid three-month sabbatical every two years in exchange for a 20 percent reduction in salary. Another employee in the same firm might be offered a 10 percent salary increase in exchange for a 5 percent reduction in company contributions to the person's retirement account. Corning, General Electric, and Microsoft are among the firms closely studying this option.[46]

Regardless of the method used, however, it is also important that managers in an organization effectively communicate what rewards are being distributed and the basis for that distribution. In other words, if incentives are being distributed on the basis of perceived individual contributions to the organization, then members of the organization should be informed of that fact. This will presumably better enable them to understand the basis on which pay increases and other incentives and performance-based rewards have been distributed.

concept
CHECK

Summarize the essential elements of merit and incentive reward systems.

What are your personal opinions regarding executive compensation?

Summary of Learning Objectives and Key Points

1. Characterize the nature of motivation, including its importance and basic historical perspectives.
   - Motivation is the set of forces that cause people to behave in certain ways.
   - Motivation is an important consideration for managers because it, along with ability and environmental factors, determines individual performance.
   - Thinking about motivation has evolved from the traditional view through the human relations approach to the human resource view.

2. Identify and describe the major content perspectives on motivation.
   - Content perspectives on motivation are concerned with what factor or factors cause motivation.
   - Popular content theories include Maslow's needs hierarchy, the ERG theory, and Herzberg's two-factor theory.
   - Other important needs are the needs for achievement, affiliation, and power.

3. Identify and describe the major process perspectives on motivation.
   - Process perspectives on motivation deal with how motivation occurs.
   - Expectancy theory suggests that people are motivated to perform if they believe that their effort will result in high performance, that this performance will lead to rewards, and that the positive aspects of the outcomes outweigh the negative aspects.
   - Equity theory is based on the premise that people are motivated to achieve and maintain social equity.
   - Attribution theory is a new process theory.

4. Describe reinforcement perspectives on motivation.
   - The reinforcement perspective focuses on how motivation is maintained.
   - Its basic assumption is that behavior that results in rewarding consequences is likely to be repeated, whereas behavior resulting in negative consequences is less likely to be repeated.

- Reinforcement contingencies can be arranged in the form of positive reinforcement, avoidance, punishment, and extinction, and they can be provided on fixed-interval, variable-interval, fixed-ratio, or variable-ratio schedules.

5. Identify and describe popular motivational strategies.
   - Managers use a variety of motivational strategies derived from the various theories of motivation.
   - Common strategies include empowerment and participation and alternative forms of work arrangements, such as variable work schedules, flexible work schedules, and telecommuting.

6. Describe the role of organizational reward systems in motivation.
   - Reward systems also play a key role in motivating employee performance.
   - Popular methods include merit reward systems, incentive reward systems, and team and group incentive reward systems.
   - Executive compensation is also intended to serve as motivation for senior managers but has currently come under close scrutiny and criticism.

Discussion Questions

Questions for Review

1. Each historical perspective on motivation built on the earlier perspectives and differed from them in some ways. Describe the similarities and differences between the traditional approach and the human relations approach. Then describe the similarities and differences between the human relations approach and the human resource approach.

2. Compare and contrast content, process, and reinforcement perspectives on motivation.

3. Explain how goal-setting theory works. How is goal setting different from merely asking a worker to "do your best"?

4. Describe some new forms of working arrangements. How do these alternative arrangements increase motivation?

Questions for Analysis

5. Choose one theory from the content perspectives and one from the process perspectives. Describe actions that a manager might take to increase worker motivation under each of the theories. What differences do you see between the theories in terms of their implications for managers?

6. Can factors from both the content and the process perspectives be acting on a worker at the same time?

Explain why or why not. Whether you answered yes or no to the previous question, explain the implications for managers.

7. How do rewards increase motivation? What would happen if an organization gave too few rewards? What would happen if it gave too many?

Questions for Application

8. Think about the worst job you have held. What approach to motivation was used in that organization? Now think about the best job you have held. What approach to motivation was used there? Can you base any conclusions on this limited information? If so, what are they?

9. Interview both a manager and a worker (or administrator and faculty member) from a local organization.

What views of or approaches to motivation seem to be in use in that organization? Do the manager's views differ from the worker's? If so, how do you explain the differing perceptions?

10. Consider a class you have taken. Using just that one class, offer examples of times when the professor used positive reinforcement, avoidance, punishment, and extinction to manage students' behavior.

Building Effective Interpersonal and Communication Skills

Exercise Overview

Interpersonal skills refer to the manager's ability to understand and motivate individuals and groups, and communication skills refer to the ability to effectively send and receive information. This exercise shows in a very explicit way how essential understanding and communicating are for motivating workers.

Exercise Background

One implication of reinforcement theory is that both positive reinforcement (reward) and punishment can be effective in altering employee behavior. However, the use of punishment may also cause resentment on the worker's part, which can reduce the effectiveness of punishment over the long term. Therefore, positive reinforcement is more effective over time.

Exercise Task

Your professor will ask for volunteers to perform a demonstration in front of the class. Consider volunteering or observe the demonstration. Then answer the following questions:

1. Based on what you saw, which is more effective: positive reinforcement or punishment?
2. How did positive reinforcement and punishment affect the "employee" in the demonstration? How did it affect the "boss"?
3. What do you think are the likely long-term consequences of positive reinforcement and punishment?

Building Effective Decision-Making Skills

Exercise Overview

Decision-making skills include the manager's ability to recognize and define situations correctly and to select courses of action. This exercise allows you to build decision-making skills while using goal-setting theory to help you plan your career.

Exercise Background

Lee Iacocca started his career at Ford in 1946 in an entry-level engineering job. By 1960 he was a vice president and in charge of the group that designed the Mustang. By 1970 he was a president of the firm. After being fired from Ford in 1978, he became a president at Chrysler and rose to the CEO spot, retiring in 1992. What is really remarkable in Iacocca's rise to power is that he had it all planned out, even before he completed college.

As legend has it, Iacocca wrote out a list, while he was still an undergraduate, of all the positions he would like to hold throughout his career. The first item on his list was "engineer at an auto maker." He then wrote down all the career steps he planned to make, ending with CEO. He also wrote down a timetable for his promotions. He put the list on a three-by-five-inch card, which he folded and stowed in his wallet. The story tells us that Iacocca took out that card frequently to look at it and that, each time he did so, he gained fresh confidence and drive. Apparently he reached the pinnacle several years earlier than he anticipated, but he followed the career path faithfully. Iacocca used goal-setting theory to motivate himself to reach his ultimate career aspirations, and you can do the same.

Exercise Task

1. Consider what position you would like to hold at the peak of your career. It may be CEO, or it may be owner of a chain of stores, or partner in a law or accounting firm, or president of a university. It may be something less lofty. Whatever it is, write it down.

2. Choose a career path that will lead you toward that goal. It may help to work "backwards," that is, to start with your final positions and work backwards in time, back to an entry-level position. If you do not know the career path that will lead to your ultimate goal, do some research. You can talk to someone in that career field, ask a professor in that subject, or get online. For example, the AICPA has a section titled "Career Resources," which includes information about career paths and position descriptions for accounting.

3. Write down each step in your path on a card or a sheet of paper.

4. If you were to carry this paper with you and refer to it often, do you think it would help you achieve your ultimate goals? Why or why not?

CHAPTER CLOSING CASE

EXTREME MOTIVATION

To thrive, every business needs to keep employees motivated. The most innovative products, the lowest prices, the best customer service—each of these can be achieved only through the hard work and enthusiasm of workers. There are many motivational techniques, covering a wide array of situations and price ranges. Most companies can accomplish their motivation goals with simple, tried-and-true methods.

Jack Welch, former CEO of General Electric and co-author of *Winning*, is a traditionalist. In his opinion, financial rewards are the most important tool in the motivator's toolbox. He writes, "Some people aren't motivated by financial rewards, but they rarely gravitate toward business. That's why, when you think about motivation, you need to think about money first." He goes on to note four other effective means of increasing motivation, including recognition, celebration, a clear mission, and a balance between recognizing past successes and calling for further achievement. Yet he is quick to point out that money is paramount, saying, "[Other rewards] can never be given in lieu of money. They are

an addendum. Plaques gather dust. Checks can be cashed. And employees know the difference in their bones." He adds, "It's not always how much you give people, though. Sometimes it's how much you give them relative to their peers. . . . Money is a way of keeping score."

Pay-for-performance motivation systems are a popular approach to motivation through financial rewards. They work well, perhaps too well. Michael Beer and Mark Cannon, management professors studying pay-for-performance, write, "[These rewards] motivate employees to focus excessively on doing what they need to do to gain rewards, sometimes at the expense of other things that would help the organization." In the 1990s, Hewlett-Packard instituted a teams-based pay-for-performance compensation system intended to increase motivation and productivity. Instead, it backfired. When goals were not reached, jeopardizing pay, teams began to blame their problems on other teams, increasing conflict dramatically. High-performing teams refused to accept new members. Competition among teams led them to guard their work

methods, reducing knowledge transfer. Employees found the new system too unpredictable and could not easily adjust their lifestyles as their pay fluctuated. Hewlett-Packard quickly dropped the entire program.

For some organizations, simpler methods aren't enough. Seagate, a Silicon Valley firm that is the world's largest maker of hard drives, was facing a severe motivation crisis. In 1996, following a merger and subsequent layoffs, employees from both of the merged firms were deeply unhappy. Concerned about their jobs, hostile towards outsiders, the corporate culture was a mess. "We needed to create a different culture—one that was open, honest, and encouraged people to work together," says CEO Bill Watkins. Watkins knew how to teach team building. "Put [employees] in an environment where they have to ask for help." Seagate's top team decided that the drastic circumstances called for drastic measures. They enrolled 200 managers in a week-long adventure race in New Zealand.

Seagate managers compete for a spot at the annual event. Each day, teams of employees spend the morning learning about the key attributes of a strong, vital culture, including trust, accountability, and healthy competition. The afternoons are devoted to mastering one of the four essential skills for adventure racing: orienteering, rappelling, mountain biking, or kayaking. The final day is devoted to the race itself, a demanding course over rugged terrain that takes from six to ten hours to complete. Over the five days, employees test themselves, open up to their colleagues, and learn to trust team members anchoring the rappelling line. By the event's conclusion, everyone loves it. "For me, the race is anticlimactic," says COO David Wickersham. "You learn so much about yourself in the first four days and, personally, I'm surprised by how much people let their guard down."

The retreat is expensive for Seagate, costing $1.8 million annually.

Yet that is just a fraction of the firm's $40 million total budget for training. CFO Charles Pope was initially skeptical, saying, "I don't like to schmooze for the sake of schmoozing." But by the end he's a believer: "I consider this an investment." Pope will be responsible for the post-event follow up, asking participants to translate the lessons they learned in New Zealand into specific plans for their divisions.

Seagate's six-year experiment with extreme offsites has yielded some real benefits. In January 2006, *Forbes* named Seagate as its "Company of the Year," based on innovation, growth, and efficiency. The firm beat out 1,000 publicly traded companies for the honor. The award is great, but hardly a surprise for Seagate's motivated workforce. Seagate's managers have learned the most important lesson—use a motivation approach that fits the situation.

CASE QUESTIONS

1. Use Maslow's hierarchy of needs to classify each of the rewards mentioned in this case. How do each of these rewards increase motivation?
2. Which theories of motivation seem to fit most closely with Jack Welch's ideas about rewards? Explain.
3. Use one or more approaches to motivation to explain why Seagate's retreats are motivating to workers.

CASE REFERENCES

Martha Lagace, "Pay-for-Performance," Harvard Business School Working Knowledge, April 14, 2003, www.hbs.edu on May 1, 2006; Sarah Max, "Seagate's Moraleathon," *BusinessWeek*, April 3, 2006, www.businessweek.com on April 3, 2006; "Seagate Named 2006 Company of the Year by *Forbes* Magazine," Seagate website, www.seagate.com on May 1, 2006; Jack and Suzy Welch, "Keeping Your People Pumped," *BusinessWeek*, March 27, 2006, p. 122.

YOU MAKE THE CALL

Better Work/Life Balance as a Motivator

1. When you graduate and start your professional career, what factors will be your motivators?
2. How do you envision your primary motivators changing later in your life?
3. Some young people today accept high-stress, high-paying jobs for what they anticipate will be only a short period of time. That is, they say they are willing to sacrifice work/life balance now in order to get a head start on their financial base. Does this option appeal to you? Why or why not?
4. Suppose you found yourself in a job that was demanding more and more of your time. What would you do?
5. In Germany, if employees do not take all of their vacation time by the end of each year their employer is fined. Would you favor such a practice? Why or why not?
6. Being as realistic as possible, describe your "ideal" job and then relate it to the concept of work/life balance.

Test Prepper

college.hmco.com/business/students

Choose the correct answer. Answers are found at the back of the book.

1. T F Herzberg argues in his two-factor theory of motivation that satisfaction and dissatisfaction are at opposite ends of a single continuum.

2. T F In expectancy theory, outcomes that are attractive have positive valence.

3. T F Equity theory and its implications have been shown to be obsolete in the modern workplace.

4. T F Managers who want to use reinforcement theory to motivate their employees generally do so with a technique called behavior modification, or OB Mod.

5. T F Gainsharing programs are designed to reward groups or teams, not individual employees.

6. Thomas believes that if he works hard enough, he'll be able to reach the performance goals his manager set for him. He also believes that performing at this level will lead to a variety of outcomes, such as faster promotions, more challenging work, additional responsibility and bigger pay raises. If you wanted to use expectancy theory to predict Thomas's motivation, you would also need to know

   A. how much Thomas desired to be in control of his environment.
   B. how much Thomas had a need for acceptance from his co-workers.
   C. how much equity Thomas has in the company.
   D. how much work Thomas is currently performing.
   E. how much Thomas values the particular outcomes.

7. According to the expanded goal-setting theory of motivation, goal-directed effort depends on each of the following goal attributes EXCEPT

   A. acceptance.
   B. specificity.
   C. commitment.

   D. difficulty.
   E. expectancy.

8. The most powerful reinforcement schedule in terms of maintaining desired behaviors is the

   A. continuous schedule.
   B. variable-ratio schedule.
   C. fixed-ratio schedule.
   D. variable-interval schedule.
   E. fixed-interval schedule.

9. Empowerment will enhance organizational effectiveness only if certain conditions exist. Which of the following is NOT one of these necessary conditions?

   A. The organization must be sincere in its efforts to spread power and autonomy.
   B. The organization must be committed to maintaining empowerment.
   C. Workers must truly believe that they and their managers are working together.
   D. The organization must attempt to turn over as much control as quickly as possible.
   E. The organization must be prepared to increase its commitment to training.

10. Which of the following accurately describes a stock option plan?

   A. A company takes out a loan to purchase a portion of its own stock, which in turn it gives employees as part of their compensation.
   B. Senior managers are allowed to purchase company stock in the future at a predetermined fixed price.
   C. Employees are given the choice of whether to take a fixed proportion of profits or a regular salary as their compensation.
   D. Union employees' compensation is based on the level of current inventory rather than on individual employees' seniority.
   E. None of these.

chapter 17

Managing Leadership and Influence Processes

LEARNING OBJECTIVES

After studying this chapter, you should be able to:

1. Describe the nature of leadership and relate leadership to management.
2. Discuss and evaluate the two generic approaches to leadership.
3. Identify and describe the major situational approaches to leadership.
4. Identify and describe three related approaches to leadership.
5. Describe three emerging approaches to leadership.
6. Discuss political behavior in organizations and how it can be managed.

FIRST THINGS FIRST

A Cycle of Leadership at Intel

"If I had relied on [former CEO Gordon Moore's] leadership style, I would have been in deep trouble. . . . My role was to be exactly the opposite of Moore."

—ANDREW GROVE, FORMER CEO, INTEL

Intel, the largest maker of semiconductor chips in the world, dominates that industry. It produces twice as many chips as its nearest competitor and has revenues of $700 million per month. Clearly, the chipmaker commands many resources. One of its most important resources, though, is leadership. The firm's five leaders have possessed different strengths and used different approaches, yet each has contributed to Intel's remarkable success.

Bob Noyce helped build the first commercially sold integrated circuit and the first microprocessor. He began Intel in 1969 with Gordon Moore, serving as CEO until 1975. As a scientist, Noyce was called a brilliant inventor and a technological genius. As a leader, Noyce was a "nice guy." He was loyal and agonized over

Intel has relied on the leadership talents of several key executives during its 40-year history. Current CEO Paul Otellini seems to be following capably in the successful footsteps of his predecessors.

decisions. His personality was risk-taking and charismatic. Noyce inspired loyalty in his subordinates too, and would often tell them, "Do something great." Under Noyce, Intel developed a culture that emphasized technical proficiency over profits.

Gordon Moore led Intel from 1975 until 1987. Like Noyce, he was a brilliant engineer and the firm's primary technology innovator. In 1965, Moore put forth Moore's Law, the observation that hardware computing power doubled every two years. Intel scientists used Moore's Law as a goal, and it has been consistently achieved. Moore's management style was similar to Noyce's but was even more hands-off and focused on technology. Moore was quiet and often let others make decisions. Moore contributed at Intel by attentive mentoring of subordinates, including future CEO Andy Grove.

Grove was a doctor of physics and Intel's fourth employee. Moore took Grove under his wing and promoted him to president in 1979. Grove now says, "If [Moore] hadn't been there, I would have been a happy, productive engineer . . . but I don't think I would have ended up running the company." The partnership between the two men was long-lasting and effective. Grove became CEO in 1987, and under his leadership, Intel created the "Intel Inside" ads to raise consumer awareness and developed state-of-the-art manufacturing techniques. Grove's leadership style was competitive, blunt, arrogant, and decisive. He translated Moore's ideas into action. "If I had relied on his leadership style, I would have been in deep trouble because Moore is not an activist," says Grove. "My role was to be exactly the opposite of Moore." For his part, Moore says with wry humor, "[Without Grove, Intel] would have been a much more pleasant place, and a whole lot smaller."

Management guru Peter Drucker sees three chief roles for a CEO: a "thought man," a "man of action," and a "front man." According to Grove, Noyce was Intel's public face or "front man," Moore was the "thought man," and Grove was the "man of action."

Craig Barrett, a Ph.D. engineer, was a Stanford professor prior to joining Intel. Barrett took over the president's position in 1977. One year later, he was CEO. During his rise to power, the Grove-Barrett mentorship paralleled the earlier Moore-Grove pairing. Grove became the visionary and Barrett the implementer. His most important contribution was the shift away from technical proficiency toward a greater emphasis on customers. As a leader, Barrett was quieter, more disciplined, and more approachable than Grove, but was still a perfectionist. He brought Intel's various departments together, giving marketing a role in research and development plans, for example.

In 2005, Paul Otellini became Intel's newest CEO. Repeating the earlier pattern, Otellini, as president, was the implementer of Barrett's programs. His background is in finance, and he is the first nonengineer to lead Intel. While assigned to marketing, he developed Intel's strategy of multiple chips with multiple price points, creating the Pentium and Celeron brands. Otellini is even more customer-focused than Barrett. He is less egotistical and more interested in the bottom line than in gee-whiz technology. He's not afraid to challenge Intel's deepest beliefs, but updating Intel's product-driven culture will be tough.

To accomplish his goals, Otellini plans to conduct a massive reorganization, hire more outsiders, and move into new technologies.

Throughout its history, Intel has found the right leader at the right time. Want to know where Intel is headed? You should look at the current crop of executive and senior vice presidents. When you see that one of them is appointed president, you'll be looking at the future of Intel.[1]

The story of Intel provides several vivid examples of the roles and importance of leadership. Different circumstances call for different kinds of leadership. Intel has benefited enormously by always having just the right leader in place at just the right time. If a different leader had been in place during different stages of Intel's history, the firm might look very different (and much worse) than it does today. Likewise, had any of Intel's leaders worked for other companies, they might never have achieved the success they enjoyed at Intel.

This chapter examines people like Paul Otellini and his predecessors more carefully by focusing on leadership and its role in management. We characterize the nature of leadership and trace through the three major approaches to studying leadership—traits, behaviors, and situations. After examining other perspectives on leadership, we conclude by describing another approach to influencing others—political behavior in organizations.

The Nature of Leadership

In Chapter 16, we described various models and perspectives on employee motivation. From the manager's standpoint, trying to motivate people is an attempt to influence their behavior. In many ways, leadership, too, is an attempt to influence the behavior of others. In this section, we first define leadership, then differentiate it from management, and conclude by relating it to power.

Leadership is a vital force in organizations today, and effective leadership can spell the difference between success and failure. Japanese auto maker Nissan, for instance, was struggling along just a few years ago and seemed destined to be taken over by another company. But the company brought in Carlos Ghosn (center) for a final shot at turning things around. Ghosn had already demonstrated strong management and leadership abilities at Renault, an Italian company that had bought 33 percent ownership of Nissan. He has subsequently led the firm back to strong profitability and solidified its position as Japan's number two auto maker (behind Toyota). Ghosn is shown here with two of his Japanese colleagues at a recent press conference.

The Meaning of Leadership

Leadership is both a process and a property.[2] As a process—focusing on what leaders actually do—leadership is the use of noncoercive influence to shape the group or organization's goals, motivate behavior toward the achievement of those goals, and help define group or organizational culture.[3] As a property, leadership is the set of characteristics attributed to individuals who are perceived to be leaders. Thus *leaders* are people who can influence the behaviors of others without having to rely on force or people whom others accept as leaders.

> **leadership**
> As a process, the use of noncoercive influence to shape the group's or organization's goals, motivate behavior toward the achievement of those goals, and help define group or organizational culture; as a property, the set of characteristics attributed to individuals who are perceived to be leaders

Leadership and Management

From these definitions, it should be clear that leadership and management are related, but they are not the same. A person can be a manager, a leader, both, or neither.[4] Some of the basic distinctions between the two are summarized in Table 17.1. At the left side of the table are four elements that differentiate leadership from management. The two columns show how each element differs when considered from a management and from a leadership point of view. For example, when executing plans, managers focus on monitoring results, comparing them with goals, and correcting deviations. In contrast, the leader focuses on energizing people to overcome bureaucratic hurdles to reach goals.

> **leaders**
> People who can influence the behaviors of others without having to rely on force; those accepted by others as leaders

Organizations need both management and leadership if they are to be effective. Leadership is necessary to create change, and management is necessary to achieve

Table 17.1

DISTINCTIONS BETWEEN MANAGEMENT AND LEADERSHIP

Management and leadership are related, but distinct, constructs. Managers and leaders differ in how they create an agenda, develop a rationale for achieving the agenda, and execute plans, and in the types of outcomes they achieve.

Activity	Management	Leadership
Creating an agenda	*Planning and Budgeting.* Establishing detailed steps and timetables for achieving needed results; allocating the resources necessary to make those needed results happen	*Establishing Direction.* Developing a vision of the future, often the distant future, and strategies for producing the changes needed to achieve that vision
Developing a human network for achieving the agenda	*Organizing and Staffing.* Establishing some structure for accomplishing plan requirements, staffing that structure with individuals, delegating responsibility and authority for carrying out the plan, providing policies and procedures to help guide people, and creating methods or systems to monitor implementation	*Aligning People.* Communicating the direction by words and deeds to everyone whose cooperation may be needed to influence the creation of teams and coalitions that understand the visions and strategies and accept their validity
Executing plans	*Controlling and Problem Solving.* Monitoring results versus planning in some detail, identifying deviations, and then planning and organizing to solve these problems	*Motivating and Inspiring.* Energizing people to overcome major political, bureaucratic, and resource barriers by satisfying very basic, but often unfulfilled, human needs
Outcomes	Produces a degree of predictability and order and has the potential to produce consistently major results expected by various stakeholders (for example, for customers, always being on time; for stockholders, being on budget)	Produces change, often to a dramatic degree, and has the potential to produce extremely useful change (for example, new products that customers want, new approaches to labor relations that help make a firm more competitive)

Source: Reprinted with permission of The Free Press, a division of Simon & Schuster Adult Publishing Group, from *A Force for Change: How Leadership Differs from Management* by John P. Kotter. Copyright © 1990 by John P. Kotter, Inc.

Leaders can rely on several kinds of power to influence others. Take this construction supervisor (in the orange vest), for example. She has legitimate power by virtue of her position at the construction company. She also controls rewards for those who work in her crew. In addition, she has expert power because of the construction skills she learned during her own training. Moreover, her personality and charisma provide her with referent power as well.

orderly results. Management in conjunction with leadership can produce orderly change, and leadership in conjunction with management can keep the organization properly aligned with its environment. Indeed, perhaps part of the reason why executive compensation has soared in recent years is the belief that management and leadership skills reflect a critical but rare combination that can lead to organizational success.

Leadership and Power

To fully understand leadership, it is necessary to understand power. *Power* is the ability to affect the behavior of others. One can have power without actually using it. For example, a football coach has the power to bench a player who is not performing up to par. The coach seldom has to use this power because players recognize that the power exists and work hard to keep their starting positions. In organizational settings, there are usually five kinds of power: legitimate, reward, coercive, referent, and expert power.[5]

> **power**
> The ability to affect the behavior of others

> **legitimate power**
> Power granted through the organizational hierarchy; the power defined by the organization to be accorded to people occupying particular positions

> **reward power**
> The power to give or withhold rewards, such as salary increases, bonuses, promotions, praise, recognition, and interesting job assignments

> **coercive power**
> The power to force compliance by means of psychological, emotional, or physical threat

Legitimate Power *Legitimate power* is power granted through the organizational hierarchy; it is the power defined by the organization to be accorded to people occupying a particular position. A manager can assign tasks to a subordinate, and a subordinate who refuses to do them can be reprimanded or even fired. Such outcomes stem from the manager's legitimate power as defined and vested in her or him by the organization. Legitimate power, then, is authority. All managers have legitimate power over their subordinates. The mere possession of legitimate power, however, does not by itself make someone a leader. Some subordinates follow only orders that are strictly within the letter of organizational rules and policies. If asked to do something not in their job descriptions, they refuse or do a poor job. The manager of such employees is exercising authority but not leadership.

Reward Power *Reward power* is the power to give or withhold rewards. Rewards that a manager may control include salary increases, bonuses, promotion recommendations, praise, recognition, and interesting job assignments. In general, the greater the number of rewards a manager controls and the more important the rewards are to subordinates, the greater is the manager's reward power. If the subordinate sees as valuable only the formal organizational rewards provided by the manager, then he or she is not a leader. If the subordinate also wants and appreciates the manager's informal rewards, such as praise, gratitude, and recognition, however, then the manager is also exercising leadership.

Coercive Power *Coercive power* is the power to force compliance by means of psychological, emotional, or physical threat. In the past, physical coercion in organizations was relatively common. In most organizations today, however, coercion is limited to verbal reprimands, written reprimands, disciplinary layoffs, fines, demotion, and termination. Some managers occasionally go so far as to use verbal abuse, humiliation, and psychological coercion in an attempt to manipulate subordinates. (Of course, most people would agree that these are not appropriate managerial behaviors.) James Dutt, a legendary former CEO of Beatrice Company, once told a subordinate that if his wife and family got in the way of his working a 24-hour day seven days a week, he should get rid of them.[6] The more punitive the elements under a manager's control and the more important they are to subordinates, the more coercive power the manager possesses. On the other hand, the more a manager uses coercive power, the more likely he is to provoke resentment and hostility and the less likely he is to be seen as a leader.[7]

Referent Power   Compared with legitimate, reward, and coercive power, which are relatively concrete and grounded in objective facets of organizational life, **referent power** is abstract. It is based on identification, imitation, loyalty, or charisma. Followers may react favorably because they identify in some way with a leader, who may be like them in personality, background, or attitudes. In other situations, followers might choose to imitate a leader with referent power by wearing the same kind of clothes, working the same hours, or espousing the same management philosophy. Referent power may also take the form of charisma, an intangible attribute of the leader that inspires loyalty and enthusiasm. Thus a manager might have referent power, but it is more likely to be associated with leadership.

> *referent power*
> The personal power that accrues to someone based on identification, imitation, loyalty, or charisma

Expert Power   *Expert power* is derived from information or expertise. A manager who knows how to interact with an eccentric but important customer, a scientist who is capable of achieving an important technical breakthrough that no other company has dreamed of, and a secretary who knows how to unravel bureaucratic red tape all have expert power over anyone who needs that information. The more important the information and the fewer the people who have access to it, the greater is the degree of expert power possessed by any one individual. In general, people who are both leaders and managers tend to have a lot of expert power.

> *expert power*
> The personal power that accrues to someone based on the information or expertise that they possess

Using Power   How does a manager or leader use power? Several methods have been identified.[8] One method is the *legitimate request,* which is based on legitimate power. The manager requests that the subordinate comply because the subordinate recognizes that the organization has given the manager the right to make the request. Most day-to-day interactions between manager and subordinate are of this type. Another use of power is *instrumental compliance,* which is based on the reinforcement theory of motivation. In this form of exchange, a subordinate complies to get the reward the manager controls. Suppose that a manager asks a subordinate to do something outside the range of the subordinate's normal duties, such as working extra hours on the weekend, terminating a relationship with a long-standing buyer, or delivering bad news. The subordinate complies and, as a direct result, reaps praise and a bonus from the manager. The next time the subordinate is asked to perform a similar activity, that subordinate will recognize that compliance will be instrumental in her getting more rewards. Hence the basis of instrumental compliance is clarifying important performance-reward contingencies.

A manager is using *coercion* when she suggests or implies that the subordinate will be punished, fired, or reprimanded if he does not do something. *Rational persuasion* occurs when the manager can convince the subordinate that compliance is in the subordinate's best interests. For example, a manager might argue that the subordinate should accept a transfer because it would be good for the subordinate's career. In some ways, rational persuasion is like reward power, except that the manager does not really control the reward.

Still another way a manager can use power is through *personal identification.* A manager who recognizes that she has referent power over a subordinate can shape the behavior of that subordinate by engaging in desired behaviors: The manager consciously becomes a model for the subordinate and exploits personal identification. Sometimes a manager can induce a subordinate to do something consistent with a set of higher ideals or values through *inspirational appeal.* For example, a plea for loyalty represents an inspirational appeal. Referent power plays a role in determining the extent to which an inspirational appeal is successful because its effectiveness depends at least in part on the persuasive abilities of the leader.

A dubious method of using power is through *information distortion.* The manager withholds or distorts information to influence subordinates' behavior. For example,

> " I had to make sure that we got rid of the saboteurs, built a strong cadre of disciples, and moved all of the fence sitters to the positive side. "
>
> A. G. Lafley, CEO of Procter & Gamble
> (*Fortune*, December 12, 2005, special insert)

The Business of Ethics

Political Behaviors of Enron's Leaders

Following the Enron scandal and bankruptcy in 2001, Kenneth Lay and Jeffrey Skilling, former CEOs, received criminal indictments for fraud and conspiracy. Lay and Skilling were both responsible for the corruption that riddled Enron's top echelon. As their trials unfolded in early 2006, the misuse of power by both Lay and Skilling, and the terrible consequences, became apparent.

Lay was intelligent, with a Ph.D. in economics. He founded Enron in 1985 and headed it for the next 16 years. His defense, therefore, was difficult to believe. Lay and his lawyers used what is commonly referred to as the "idiot" or the "ostrich" defense. Lay claimed, repeatedly and under oath, that he was unaware of any problems at Enron.

As CEO of Enron, Lay had legitimate power but exercised little restraint over subordinates. Jeffrey Sonnenfeld, management professor at Yale, says, "When [Lay] sensed dangerous truths, he saw his job as one of containment, rather than showing courage or character." Lay's testimony in court made it hard to tell whether he was a skillful liar, self-deluded, or horribly incompetent. It's not hard to see, however, that Lay made $300 million on the sale of Enron stock from 1998 to 2001.

Jeffrey Skilling was CEO for six months in 2001. Skilling, intelligent and highly educated, was hired by Lay in 1990. Like Lay, Skilling sold Enron stock—$60 million worth. His "idiot" defense seemed as implausible as Lay's. Many believe that Skilling designed and carried out the fraudulent schemes, with Lay's support.

Fortune reporters Bethany McLean and Peter Elkind, in their exposé novel *The Smartest Guys in the Room*, note that Lay did not exercise his leadership power appropriately. "[Lay] avoided the sort of tough decisions that were certain to make others mad," they say. "He would let someone else take the heat or would throw money at the problem." According to McLean and Elkind, the CEO's shortcomings convinced Skilling and other executives that "they could do whatever they wanted and Lay would never say no."

Lay was found guilty on all six charges of conspiracy and fraud; he died of a heart attack shortly thereafter. Skilling was convicted of 19 counts of conspiracy, fraud, false statements, and insider trading; he faces prison time and may pay fines totaling millions. Yet these punishments are insignificant compared to the $35 billion in lost shareholder value and the 31,000 workers who lost their jobs and retirement funds.

References: Alexei Barrionuevo and Kurt Eichenwald, "For Ken Lay, Enron's Riches Turning to Ruin," *New York Times*, February 26, 2006, pp. N1, 23; Anthony Bianco, "Ken Lay's Audacious Ignorance," *BusinessWeek*, February 6, 2006, pp. 58–59; "Enron: The Trial," *Fortune*, February 6, 2006, p. 14; Bethany McLean and Peter Elkind, "The Smartest Guys in the Room: The Amazing Rise and Scandalous Fall of Enron," *Portfolio Publishing*, 2004; Michael Orey, "Something a Jury Can See," *BusinessWeek*, March 20, 2006, p. 38.

if a manager has agreed to allow everyone to participate in choosing a new group member but subsequently finds one individual whom she really prefers, she might withhold some of the credentials of other qualified applicants so that the desired member is selected. This use of power is dangerous. It may be unethical, and if subordinates find out that the manager has deliberately misled them, they will lose their confidence and trust in that manager's leadership.[9] *The Business of Ethics* underscores some of the problems that can result from misdirected or excessive power.

concept
CHECK

Summarize the key differences between leadership and management.

Identify an example you have experienced or observed to illustrate each of the five types of power discussed in this section.

Generic Approaches to Leadership

Early approaches to the study of leadership adopted what might be called a "universal" or "generic" perspective. Specifically, they assumed that there was one set of answers to the leadership puzzle. One generic approach focused on leadership traits, and the other looked at leadership behavior.

Leadership Traits

The first organized approach to studying leadership analyzed the personal, psychological, and physical traits of strong leaders. The trait approach assumed that some basic trait or set of traits existed that differentiated leaders from nonleaders. If those traits could be defined, potential leaders could be identified. Researchers thought that leadership traits might include intelligence, assertiveness, above-average height, good vocabulary, attractiveness, self-confidence, and similar attributes.[10]

During the first half of the twentieth century, hundreds of studies were conducted in an attempt to identify important leadership traits. For the most part, the results of the studies were disappointing. For every set of leaders who possessed a common trait, a long list of exceptions was also found, and the list of suggested traits soon grew so long that it had little practical value. Alternative explanations usually existed even for relationships between traits and leadership that initially appeared valid. For example, it was observed that many leaders have good communication skills and are assertive. Rather than those traits being the cause of leadership, however, successful leaders may begin to display those traits after they have achieved a leadership position.

Although most researchers gave up trying to identify traits as predictors of leadership ability, many people still explicitly or implicitly adopt a trait orientation.[11] For example, politicians are all too often elected on the basis of personal appearance, speaking ability, or an aura of self-confidence. In addition, traits like honesty and integrity may very well be fundamental leadership traits that do serve an important purpose. Intelligence also seems to play a meaningful role in leadership.[12]

Leadership Behaviors

Spurred on by their lack of success in identifying useful leadership traits, researchers soon began to investigate other variables, especially the behaviors or actions of leaders.

The new hypothesis was that effective leaders somehow behaved differently than less-effective leaders. Thus the goal was to develop a fuller understanding of leadership behaviors.

Michigan Studies   Researchers at the University of Michigan, led by Rensis Likert, began studying leadership in the late 1940s.[13] Based on extensive interviews with both leaders (managers) and followers (subordinates), this research identified two basic forms of leader behavior: job centered and employee centered. Managers using ***job-centered leader behavior*** pay close attention to subordinates' work, explain work procedures, and are keenly interested in performance. Managers using ***employee-centered leader behavior*** are interested in developing a cohesive work group and ensuring that employees are satisfied with their jobs. Their primary concern is the welfare of subordinates.

> *job-centered leader behavior*
> The behavior of leaders who pay close attention to the job and work procedures involved with that job

The two styles of leader behavior were presumed to be at the ends of a single continuum. Although this suggests that leaders may be extremely job centered, extremely employee centered, or somewhere in between, Likert studied only the two end styles for contrast. He argued that employee-centered leader behavior generally tends to be more effective. We should also note the similarities between Likert's leadership research and his Systems 1 through 4 organization designs (discussed in Chapter 12). Job-centered leader behavior is consistent with the System 1 design (rigid and bureaucratic), whereas employee-centered leader behavior is consistent with the System 4 design (organic and flexible). When Likert advocates moving organizations from System 1 to System 4, he is also advocating a transition from job-centered to employee-centered leader behavior.

> *employee-centered leader behavior*
> The behavior of leaders who develop cohesive work groups and ensure employee satisfaction

Ohio State Studies   At about the same time that Likert was beginning his leadership studies at the University of Michigan, a group of researchers at Ohio State University also began studying leadership.[14] The extensive questionnaire surveys conducted during the Ohio State studies also suggested that there are two basic leader behaviors or styles: initiating-structure behavior and consideration behavior. When using ***initiating-structure behavior***, the leader clearly defines the leader-subordinate role so that everyone knows what is expected, establishes formal lines of communication, and determines how tasks will be performed. Leaders using ***consideration behavior*** show concern for subordinates and attempt to establish a warm, friendly, and supportive climate. The behaviors identified at Ohio State are similar to those described at Michigan, but there are important differences. One major difference is that the Ohio State researchers did not interpret leader behavior as being one-dimensional; each behavior was assumed to be independent of the other. Presumably, then, a leader could exhibit varying levels of initiating structure and at the same time varying levels of consideration.

> *initiating-structure behavior*
> The behavior of leaders who define the leader-subordinate role so that everyone knows what is expected, establish formal lines of communication, and determine how tasks will be performed

> *consideration behavior*
> The behavior of leaders who show concern for subordinates and attempt to establish a warm, friendly, and supportive climate

At first, the Ohio State researchers thought that leaders who exhibit high levels of both behaviors would tend to be more effective than other leaders. A study at International Harvester (now Navistar International), however, suggested a more complicated pattern.[15] The researchers found that employees of supervisors who ranked high on initiating structure were high performers but expressed low levels of satisfaction and had a higher absence rate. Conversely, employees of supervisors who ranked high on consideration had low performance ratings but high levels of satisfaction and few absences from work. Later research isolated other variables that make consistent prediction difficult and determined that situational influences also occurred. (This body of research is discussed in the section on situational approaches to leadership.[16])

Managerial Grid   Yet another behavioral approach to leadership is the Managerial Grid.[17] The Managerial Grid provides a means for evaluating leadership styles and then training managers to move toward an ideal style of behavior. The Managerial Grid is shown in Figure 17.1. The horizontal axis represents ***concern for production*** (similar to job-centered and initiating-structure behaviors), and the vertical axis represents ***concern for people*** (similar to employee-centered and consideration behaviors). Note the five extremes of managerial behavior: the 1,1 manager (impoverished management), who exhibits minimal concern for both production and people; the 9,1 manager (authority-compliance), who is highly concerned about production but exhibits little concern for people; the 1,9 manager (country club management), who has exactly opposite concerns from the 9,1 manager; the 5,5 manager (middle-of-the-road management), who maintains adequate concern for both people and production; and the 9,9 manager (team management), who exhibits maximum concern for both people and production.

According to this approach, the ideal style of managerial behavior is 9,9. There is a six-phase program to assist managers in achieving this style of behavior. A. G. Edwards, Westinghouse, the FAA, Equicor, and other companies have used the Managerial Grid with reasonable success. However, there is little published scientific evidence regarding its true effectiveness.

concern for production
The part of the Managerial Grid that deals with the job and task aspects of leader behavior

concern for people
The part of the Managerial Grid that deals with the human aspects of leader behavior

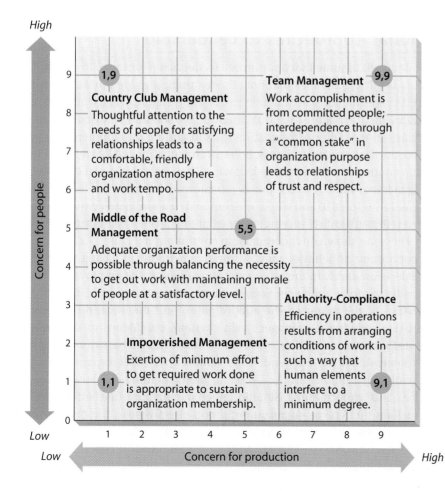

Figure 17.1
THE LEADERSHIP GRID

The Leadership Grid® is a method of evaluating leadership styles. The overall objective of an organization using the Grid® is to train its managers using organization development techniques so that they are simultaneously more concerned for both people and production (9,9 style on the Grid®).

Source: The Leadership Grid Figure for *Leadership Dilemmas—Grid Solutions* by Robert R. Blake and Anne Adams McCanse. (Formerly *The Managerial Grid* by Robert R. Blake and Jane S. Mouton.) Houston: Gulf Publishing Company, p. 29. Copyright © 1997 by Grid International, Inc. Reproduced by permission of the owners.

The leader-behavior theories have played an important role in the development of contemporary thinking about leadership. In particular, they urge us not to be preoccupied with what leaders are (the trait approach) but to concentrate on what leaders do (their behaviors). Unfortunately, these theories also make universal generic prescriptions about what constitutes effective leadership. When we are dealing with complex social systems composed of complex individuals, however, few, if any, relationships are consistently predictable, and certainly no formulas for success are infallible. Yet the behavior theorists tried to identify consistent relationships between leader behaviors and employee responses in the hope of finding a dependable prescription for effective leadership. As we might expect, they often failed. Other approaches to understanding leadership were therefore needed. The catalyst for these new approaches was the realization that although interpersonal and task-oriented dimensions might be useful for describing the behavior of leaders, they were not useful for predicting or prescribing it. The next step in the evolution of leadership theory was the creation of situational models.

concept
CHECK

Describe the basic types of leader behavior identified in the generic approaches to leadership.

Setting aside the validity of the concept, what traits would you see as being most important for effective leadership?

Situational Approaches to Leadership

Situational models assume that appropriate leader behavior varies from one situation to another. The goal of a situational theory, then, is to identify key situational factors and to specify how they interact to determine appropriate leader behavior. Before discussing the major situational theories, we should first discuss an important early model that laid the foundation for subsequent developments. In a 1958 study of the decision-making process, Robert Tannenbaum and Warren H. Schmidt proposed a continuum of leadership behavior. Their model is much like the original Michigan framework.[18] Besides purely job-centered behavior (or "boss-centered" behavior, as they termed it) and employee-centered ("subordinate-centered") behavior, however, they identified several intermediate behaviors that a manager might consider. These are shown on the leadership continuum in Figure 17.2.

This continuum of behavior moves from one extreme, of having the manager make the decision alone, to the other extreme, of having the employees make the decision with minimal guidance. Each point on the continuum is influenced by characteristics of the manager, the subordinates, and the situation. Managerial characteristics include the manager's value system, confidence in subordinates, personal inclinations, and feelings of security. Subordinate characteristics include the subordinates' need for independence, readiness to assume responsibility, tolerance for ambiguity, interest in the problem, understanding of goals, knowledge, experience, and expectations. Situational characteristics that affect decision making include the type of organization, group effectiveness, the problem itself, and time pressures. Although this framework pointed out the importance of situational factors, it was only speculative. It remained for others to develop more comprehensive and integrated theories. In the following sections, we describe four of

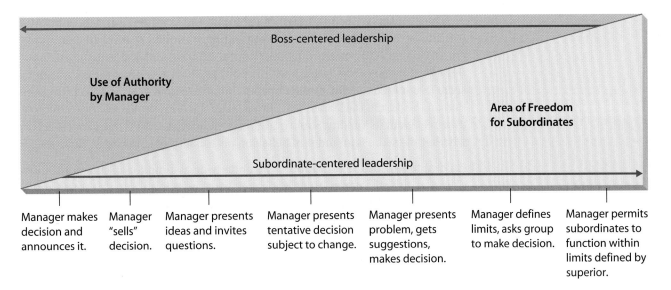

Figure 17.2

TANNENBAUM AND SCHMIDT'S LEADERSHIP CONTINUUM

The Tannenbaum and Schmidt leadership continuum was an important precursor to modern situational approaches to leadership. The continuum identifies seven levels of leadership, which range between the extremes of boss-centered and subordinate-centered leadership.

Source: Reprinted by permission of the *Harvard Business Review*. An exhibit from "How to Choose a Leadership Pattern" by Robert Tannenbaum and Warren Schmidt (May–June 1973). Copyright © 1973 by the President and Fellows of Harvard College; all rights reserved.

the most important and widely accepted situational theories of leadership: the LPC theory, the path-goal theory, Vroom's decision tree approach, and the leader-member exchange approach.

LPC Theory

The **LPC theory**, developed by Fred Fiedler, was the first truly situational theory of leadership.[19] As we will discuss later, LPC stands for least-preferred coworker. Beginning with a combined trait and behavioral approach, Fiedler identified two styles of leadership: task oriented (analogous to job-centered and initiating-structure behavior) and relationship oriented (similar to employee-centered and consideration behavior). He went beyond the earlier behavioral approaches by arguing that the style of behavior is a reflection of the leader's personality and that most personalities fall into one of his two categories—task oriented or relationship oriented by nature. Fiedler measures leadership style by means of a controversial questionnaire called the **least-preferred coworker (LPC) measure**. To use the measure, a manager or leader is asked to describe the specific person with whom he or she is able to work least well—the LPC—by filling in a set of 16 scales anchored at each end by a positive or negative adjective. For example, 3 of the 16 scales are:

> **LPC theory**
> A theory of leadership that suggests that the appropriate style of leadership varies with situational favorableness

> *least-preferred coworker (LPC) measure*
> The measuring scale that asks leaders to describe the person with whom he or she is able to work least well

Helpful									Frustrating
	8	7	6	5	4	3	2	1	

Tense									Relaxed
	1	2	3	4	5	6	7	8	

Boring									Interesting
	1	2	3	4	5	6	7	8	

The leader's LPC score is then calculated by adding up the numbers below the line checked on each scale. Note in these three examples that the higher numbers are associated with positive qualities (helpful, relaxed, and interesting), whereas the negative qualities (frustrating, tense, and boring) have low point values. A high total score is assumed to reflect a relationship orientation and a low score a task orientation on the part of the leader. The LPC measure is controversial because researchers disagree about its validity. Some question exactly what an LPC measure reflects and whether the score is an index of behavior, personality, or some other factor.[20]

Favorableness of the Situation   The underlying assumption of situational models of leadership is that appropriate leader behavior varies from one situation to another. According to Fiedler, the key situational factor is the favorableness of the situation from the leader's point of view. This factor is determined by leader-member relations, task structure, and position power. *Leader-member relations* refer to the nature of the relationship between the leader and the work group. If the leader and the group have a high degree of mutual trust, respect, and confidence, and if they like one another, relations are assumed to be good. If there is little trust, respect, or confidence, and if they do not like one another, relations are poor. Naturally, good relations are more favorable.

Task structure is the degree to which the group's task is well defined. The task is structured when it is routine, easily understood, and unambiguous, and when the group has standard procedures and precedents to rely on. An unstructured task is nonroutine, ambiguous, and complex, with no standard procedures or precedents. You can see that high structure is more favorable for the leader, whereas low structure is less favorable. For example, if the task is unstructured, the group will not know what to do, and the leader will have to play a major role in guiding and directing its activities. If the task is structured, the leader will not have to get so involved and can devote time to nonsupervisory activities.

Position power is the power vested in the leader's position. If the leader has the power to assign work and to reward and punish employees, position power is assumed to be strong. But, if the leader must get job assignments approved by someone else and does not administer rewards and punishment, position power is weak, and it is more difficult to accomplish goals. From the leader's point of view, strong position power is clearly preferable to weak position power. However, position power is not as important as task structure and leader-member relations.

Favorableness and Leader Style   Fiedler and his associates conducted numerous studies linking the favorableness of various situations to leader style and the effectiveness of the group.[21] The results of these studies—and the overall framework of the theory—are shown in Figure 17.3. To interpret the model, look first at the situational factors at the top of the figure. Good or bad leader-member relations, high or low task structure, and strong or weak leader position power can be combined to yield six unique situations. For example, good leader-member relations, high task structure, and strong leader position power (at the far left) are presumed to define the most favorable situation; bad leader-member relations, low task structure, and weak leader power (at the far right) are the least favorable. The other combinations reflect intermediate levels of favorableness.

Below each set of situations are shown the degree of favorableness and the form of leader behavior found to be most strongly associated with effective group performance for those situations. When the situation is most and least favorable, Fiedler found

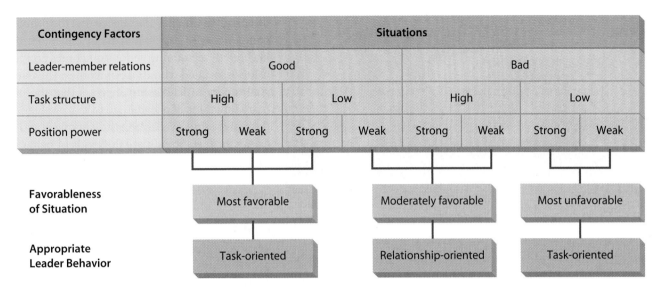

Contingency Factors	Situations							
Leader-member relations	Good				Bad			
Task structure	High		Low		High		Low	
Position power	Strong	Weak	Strong	Weak	Strong	Weak	Strong	Weak

Figure 17.3

THE LEAST-PREFERRED COWORKER THEORY OF LEADERSHIP

Fiedler's LPC theory of leadership suggests that appropriate leader behavior varies as a function of the favorableness of the situation. Favorableness, in turn, is defined by task structure, leader-member relations, and the leader's position power. According to the LPC theory, the most and least favorable situations call for task-oriented leadership, whereas moderately favorable situations suggest the need for relationship-oriented leadership.

that a task-oriented leader is most effective. When the situation is only moderately favorable, however, a relationship-oriented leader is predicted to be most effective.

Flexibility of Leader Style   Fiedler argued that, for any given individual, leader style is essentially fixed and cannot be changed; leaders cannot change their behavior to fit a particular situation because it is linked to their particular personality traits. Thus, when a leader's style and the situation do not match, Fiedler argued that the situation should be changed to fit the leader's style. When leader-member relations are good, task structure low, and position power weak, the leader style that is most likely to be effective is relationship oriented. If the leader is task oriented, a mismatch exists. According to Fiedler, the leader can make the elements of the situation more congruent by structuring the task (by developing guidelines and procedures, for instance) and increasing power (by requesting additional authority or by other means).

Fiedler's contingency theory has been attacked on the grounds that it is not always supported by research, that his findings are subject to other interpretations, that the LPC measure lacks validity, and that his assumptions about the inflexibility of leader behavior are unrealistic.[22] However, Fiedler's theory was one of the first to adopt a situational perspective on leadership. It has helped many managers recognize the important situational factors they must contend with, and it has fostered additional thinking about the situational nature of leadership. Moreover, in recent years Fiedler has attempted to address some of the concerns about his theory by revising it and adding such additional elements as cognitive resources.

Path-Goal Theory

The ***path-goal theory*** of leadership—associated most closely with Martin Evans and Robert House—is a direct extension of the expectancy theory of motivation

---

path-goal theory
A theory of leadership suggesting that the primary functions of a leader are to make valued or desired rewards available in the workplace and to clarify for the subordinate the kinds of behavior that will lead to those rewards

The path-goal theory of leadership suggests that leaders must clarify the paths to goal attainment for their followers. United Airlines ticketing agent Ludy Gerardi, left, gives Pete McDonald, right, United Airlines' chief operating officer, the thumbs-up sign as he visits and thanks employees in the United terminal at Chicago's O'Hare International Airport. United, the No. 2 airline in the United States, recently emerged from bankruptcy. McDonald played a key role in getting United back on solid ground. Among other things, he helped convince United employees that they shared a common goal (restoring the firm's financial strength) and that if they all worked together to achieve that goal, they would save jobs and eliminate the pay cuts that had been necessary to keep the airline flying.

discussed in Chapter 16.[23] Recall that the primary components of expectancy theory included the likelihood of attaining various outcomes and the value associated with those outcomes. The path-goal theory of leadership suggests that the primary functions of a leader are to make valued or desired rewards available in the workplace and to clarify for the subordinate the kinds of behavior that will lead to goal accomplishment and valued rewards—that is, the leader should clarify the paths to goal attainment.

Leader Behavior The most fully developed version of path-goal theory identifies four kinds of leader behavior. *Directive leader behavior* lets subordinates know what is expected of them, gives guidance and direction, and schedules work. *Supportive leader behavior* is being friendly and approachable, showing concern for subordinate welfare, and treating members as equals. *Participative leader behavior* includes consulting with subordinates, soliciting suggestions, and allowing participation in decision making. *Achievement-oriented leader* behavior means setting challenging goals, expecting subordinates to perform at high levels, encouraging subordinates, and showing confidence in subordinates' abilities.

In contrast to Fiedler's theory, path-goal theory assumes that leaders can change their style or behavior to meet the demands of a particular situation. For example, when encountering a new group of subordinates and a new project, the leader may be directive in establishing work procedures and in outlining what needs to be done. Next, the leader may adopt supportive behavior to foster group cohesiveness and a positive climate. As the group becomes familiar with the task and as new problems are encountered, the leader may exhibit participative behavior to enhance group members' motivation. Finally, achievement-oriented behavior may be used to encourage continued high performance.

Situational Factors Like other situational theories of leadership, path-goal theory suggests that appropriate leader style depends on situational factors. Path-goal theory focuses on the situational factors of the personal characteristics of subordinates and environmental characteristics of the workplace.

Important personal characteristics include the subordinates' perception of their own abilities and their locus of control. If people perceive that they are lacking in abilities, they may prefer directive leadership to help them understand path-goal relationships better. If they perceive themselves to have a lot of abilities, however, employees may resent directive leadership. Locus of control is a personality trait. People who have an internal locus of control believe that what happens to them is a function of their own efforts and behavior. Those who have an external locus of control assume that fate, luck, or "the system" determines what happens to them. A person with an internal locus of control may prefer participative leadership, whereas a person with an external locus of control may prefer directive leadership. Managers can do little or nothing to influence the personal characteristics of subordinates, but they can shape the environment to take advantage of these personal characteristics by, for example, providing rewards and structuring tasks.

Environmental characteristics include factors outside the subordinates' control. Task structure is one such factor. When structure is high, directive leadership is less effective than when structure is low. Subordinates do not usually need their boss to continually tell them how to do an extremely routine job. The formal authority system is another important environmental characteristic. Again, the higher the degree of formality, the less directive is the leader behavior that will be accepted by subordinates. The nature of the work group also affects appropriate leader behavior. When the work group provides the employee with social support and satisfaction, supportive leader behavior is less critical. When social support and satisfaction cannot be derived from the group, the worker may look to the leader for this support.

The basic path-goal framework as illustrated in Figure 17.4 shows that different leader behaviors affect subordinates' motivation to perform. Personal and environmental characteristics are seen as defining which behaviors lead to which outcomes. The path-goal theory of leadership is a dynamic and incomplete model. The original intent was to state the theory in general terms so that future research could explore a variety of interrelationships and modify the theory. Research that has been done suggests that the path-goal theory is a reasonably good description of the leadership process and that future investigations along these lines should enable us to discover more about the link between leadership and motivation.[24]

Vroom's Decision Tree Approach

The third major contemporary approach to leadership is ***Vroom's decision tree approach***. The earliest version of this model was proposed by Victor Vroom and Philip Yetton and later revised and expanded by Vroom and Arthur Jago.[25] Most recently, Vroom has developed yet another refinement of the original model.[26] Like the path-goal theory, this approach attempts to prescribe a leadership style appropriate to a given situation. It also assumes that the same leader may display different leadership styles. But Vroom's approach concerns itself with only a single aspect of leader behavior: subordinate participation in decision making.

Basic Premises Vroom's decision tree approach assumes that the degree to which subordinates should be encouraged to participate in decision making depends on

Vroom's decision tree approach
Predicts what kinds of situations call for different degrees of group participation

Figure 17.4
THE PATH-GOAL FRAMEWORK

The path-goal theory of leadership suggests that managers can use four types of leader behavior to clarify subordinates' paths to goal attainment. Personal characteristics of the subordinate and environmental characteristics within the organization both must be taken into account when determining which style of leadership will work best for a particular situation.

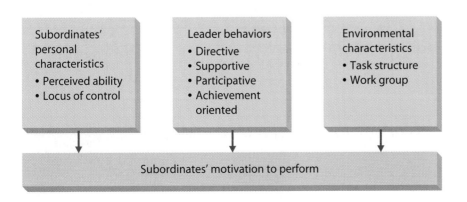

the characteristics of the situation. In other words, no one decision-making process is best for all situations. After evaluating a variety of problem attributes (characteristics of the problem or decision), the leader determines an appropriate decision style that specifies the amount of subordinate participation.

Vroom's current formulation suggests that managers use one of two different decision trees.[27] To do so, the manager first assesses the situation in terms of several factors. This assessment involves determining whether the given factor is high or low for the decision that is to be made. For instance, the first factor is decision significance. If the decision is extremely important and may have a major impact on the organization (such as choosing a location for a new plant), its significance is high. But, if the decision is routine and its consequences are not terribly important (selecting a color for the firm's softball team uniforms), its significance is low. This assessment guides the manager through the paths of the decision tree to a recommended course of action. One decision tree is to be used when the manager is interested primarily in making the decision as quickly as possible; the other is to be used when time is less critical and the manager is interested in helping subordinates to improve and develop their own decision-making skills.

The two decision trees are shown in Figures 17.5 and 17.6. The problem attributes (situational factors) are arranged along the top of the decision tree. To use the model, the decision maker starts at the left side of the diagram and assesses the first

Figure 17.5

VROOM'S TIME-DRIVEN DECISION TREE

This matrix is recommended for situations where time is of the highest importance in making a decision. The matrix operates like a funnel. You start at the left with a specific decision problem in mind. The column headings denote situational factors that may or may not be present in that problem. You progress by selecting high or low (H or L) for each relevant situational factor. Proceed down the funnel, judging only those situational factors for which a judgment is called, until you reach the recommended process.

Source: Adapted and reprinted from *Organizational Dynamics,* Vol. 28, no. 4, Victor H. Vroom, "Leadership and the Decision-Making Process," pp. 82–94, Copyright 2000, with permission from Elsevier.

Decision Significance	Importance of Commitment	Leader Expertise	Likelihood of Commitment	Group Support	Group Expertise	Team Competence	
H	H	H	H	—	—	—	Decide
H	H	H	L	H	H	H	Delegate
H	H	H	L	H	H	L	Consult (group)
H	H	H	L	H	L	—	Consult (group)
H	H	H	L	L	—	—	Consult (group)
H	H	L	H	H	H	H	Facilitate
H	H	L	H	H	H	L	Consult (individually)
H	H	L	H	H	L	—	Consult (individually)
H	H	L	H	L	—	—	Consult (individually)
H	H	L	L	H	H	H	Facilitate
H	H	L	L	H	H	L	Consult (group)
H	H	L	L	H	L	—	Consult (group)
H	H	L	L	L	—	—	Consult (group)
H	L	H	—	—	—	—	Decide
H	L	L	—	H	H	H	Facilitate
H	L	L	—	H	H	L	Consult (individually)
H	L	L	—	H	L	—	Consult (individually)
H	L	L	—	L	—	—	Consult (individually)
L	H	—	H	—	—	—	Decide
L	H	—	L	—	—	H	Delegate
L	H	—	L	—	—	L	Facilitate
L	L	—	—	—	—	—	Decide

PROBLEM STATEMENT

Problem Statement	Decision Significance	Importance of Commitment	Leader Expertise	Likelihood of Commitment	Group Support	Group Expertise	Team Competence	
PROBLEM STATEMENT	H	H	H	H	H	H	H	Decide
							L	Facilitate
						L	—	Consult (group)
					L	—	—	Consult (group)
			—	L	H	H	H	Delegate
							L	Facilitate
						L	—	Facilitate
					L	—	—	Consult (group)
		L	—	—	H	H	H	Delegate
							L	Facilitate
						L	—	Consult (group)
					L	—	—	Consult (group)
	L	H	—	H	—	—	—	Decide
				L	—	—	—	Delegate
		L	—	—	—	—	—	Decide

Figure 17.6
VROOM'S DEVELOPMENT-DRIVEN DECISION TREE

This matrix is to be used when the leader is more interested in developing employees than in making the decision as quickly as possible. Just as with the time-driven tree shown in Figure 17.5, the leader assesses up to seven situational factors. These factors, in turn, funnel the leader to a recommended process for making the decision.

Source: Adapted and reprinted from *Organizational Dynamics,* Vol. 28, no. 4, Victor H. Vroom, "Leadership and the Decision-Making Process," pp. 82–94, Copyright 2000, with permission from Elsevier.

problem attribute (decision significance). The answer determines the path to the second node on the decision tree, where the next attribute (importance of commitment) is assessed. This process continues until a terminal node is reached. In this way, the manager identifies an effective decision-making style for the situation.

Decision-Making Styles   The various decision styles reflected at the ends of the tree branches represent different levels of subordinate participation that the manager should attempt to adopt in a given situation. The five styles are defined as follows:

- *Decide.* The manager makes the decision alone and then announces or "sells" it to the group.
- *Consult (individually).* The manager presents the program to group members individually, obtains their suggestions, and then makes the decision.
- *Consult (group).* The manager presents the problem to group members at a meeting, gets their suggestions, and then makes the decision.
- *Facilitate.* The manager presents the problem to the group at a meeting, defines the problem and its boundaries, and then facilitates group member discussion as they make the decision.
- *Delegate.* The manager allows the group to define for itself the exact nature and parameters of the problem and then to develop a solution.

Vroom's decision tree approach represents a very focused but quite complex perspective on leadership. To compensate for this difficulty, Vroom has developed elaborate expert system software to help managers assess a situation accurately and quickly and then to make an appropriate decision regarding employee participation.[28] Many firms, including Halliburton Company, Litton Industries, and Borland International, have provided their managers with training in how to use the various versions of this model.

Evaluation and Implications   Because Vroom's current approach is relatively new, it has not been fully scientifically tested. The original model and its subsequent refinement, however, attracted a great deal of attention and generally was supported by research.[29] For example, there is some support for the idea that individuals who make decisions consistent with the predictions of the model are more effective than those who make decisions inconsistent with it. The model therefore appears to be a tool that managers can apply with some confidence in deciding how much subordinates should participate in the decision-making process.

The Leader-Member Exchange Approach

Because leadership is such an important area, managers and researchers continue to study it. As a result, new ideas, theories, and perspectives are continuously being developed. The ***leader-member exchange (LMX) model*** of leadership, conceived by George Graen and Fred Dansereau, stresses the importance of variable relationships between supervisors and each of their subordinates.[30] Each superior-subordinate pair is referred to as a "vertical dyad." The model differs from earlier approaches in that it focuses on the differential relationship leaders often establish with different subordinates. Figure 17.7 shows the basic concepts of the leader-member exchange theory.

The model suggests that supervisors establish a special relationship with a small number of trusted subordinates, referred to as "the in-group." The in-group usually receives special duties requiring responsibility and autonomy; they may also receive special privileges. Subordinates who are not a part of this group are called "the out-group," and they receive less of the supervisor's time and attention. Note in the figure that the leader has a dyadic, or one-to-one, relationship with each of the five subordinates.

Early in his or her interaction with a given subordinate, the supervisor initiates either an in-group or an out-group relationship. It is not clear how a leader selects members of the in-group, but the decision may be based on personal compatibility and subordinates' competence. Research has confirmed the existence of in-groups and out-groups. In addition, studies generally have found that in-group members have a higher level of performance and satisfaction than do out-group members.[31]

> **leader-member exchange (LMX) model**
> Stresses that leaders have different kinds of relationships with different subordinates

concept CHECK

Summarize the essential elements of each of the situational approaches to leadership.

Which situational approach do you think is most useful and which the least useful for managers in organizations?

Figure 17.7
THE LEADER-MEMBER EXCHANGE (LMX) MODEL

The LMX model suggests that leaders form unique independent relationships with each of their subordinates. As illustrated here, a key factor in the nature of this relationship is whether the individual subordinate is in the leader's out-group or in-group.

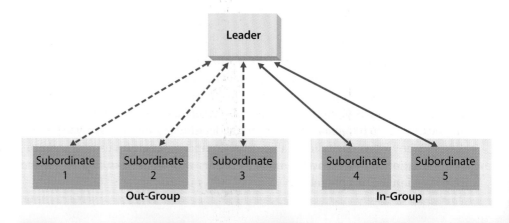

Related Approaches to Leadership

Because of its importance to organizational effectiveness, leadership continues to be the focus of a great deal of research and theory building. New approaches that have attracted much attention are the concepts of substitutes for leadership and transformational leadership.

Substitutes for Leadership

The concept of **substitutes for leadership** was developed because existing leadership models and theories do not account for situations in which leadership is not needed.[32] They simply try to specify what kind of leader behavior is appropriate. The substitutes concept, however, identifies situations in which leader behaviors are neutralized or replaced by characteristics of the subordinate, the task, and the organization. For example, when a patient is delivered to a hospital emergency room, the professionals on duty do not wait to be told what to do by a leader. Nurses, doctors, and attendants all go into action without waiting for directive or supportive leader behavior from the emergency room supervisor.

> **substitutes for leadership**
> A concept that identifies situations in which leader behaviors are neutralized or replaced by characteristics of subordinates, the task, and the organization

Characteristics of the subordinate that may serve to neutralize leader behavior include ability, experience, need for independence, professional orientation, and indifference toward organizational rewards. For example, employees with a high level of ability and experience may not need to be told what to do. Similarly, a subordinate's strong need for independence may render leader behavior ineffective. Task characteristics that may substitute for leadership include routineness, the availability of feedback, and intrinsic satisfaction. When the job is routine and simple, the subordinate may not need direction. When the task is challenging and intrinsically satisfying, the subordinate may not need or want social support from a leader.

Organizational characteristics that may substitute for leadership include formalization, group cohesion, inflexibility, and a rigid reward structure. Leadership may not be necessary when policies and practices are formal and inflexible, for example. Similarly, a rigid reward system may rob the leader of reward power and thereby decrease the importance of the role. Preliminary research has provided support for the concept of substitutes for leadership.[33]

Charismatic Leadership

The concept of **charismatic leadership**, like trait theories, assumes that charisma is an individual characteristic of the leader. **Charisma** is a form of interpersonal attraction that inspires support and acceptance. All else being equal, then, someone with charisma is more likely to be able to influence others than is someone without charisma. For example, a highly charismatic supervisor will be more successful in influencing subordinate behavior than a supervisor who lacks charisma. Thus influence is again a fundamental element of this perspective.

> **charismatic leadership**
> Assumes that charisma is an individual characteristic of the leader

> **charisma**
> A form of interpersonal attraction that inspires support and acceptance

Robert House first proposed a theory of charismatic leadership, based on research findings from a variety of social science disciplines.[34] His theory suggests that charismatic leaders are likely to have a lot of self-confidence, a firm conviction in their beliefs and ideals, and a strong need to influence people. They also tend to communicate high expectations about follower performance and express confidence in followers. Donald Trump is an excellent example of a charismatic leader. Even though he has made his share of mistakes and generally is perceived as only an "average" manager, many people view him as larger than life.[35]

There are three elements of charismatic leadership in organizations that most experts acknowledge today.[36] First, the leader needs to be able to envision the future, set high expectations, and model behaviors consistent with meeting those expectations. Next, the charismatic leader must be able to energize others through a demonstration of personal excitement, personal confidence, and patterns of success. And, finally, the charismatic leader enables others by supporting them, empathizing with them, and expressing confidence in them.[37]

Charismatic leadership ideas are quite popular among managers today and are the subject of numerous books and articles. Unfortunately, few studies have attempted to specifically test the meaning and impact of charismatic leadership. There are also lingering ethical issues about charismatic leadership, however, that trouble some people. For instance, President Bill Clinton was a charismatic leader. But some of his critics argued that this very charisma caused his supporters to overlook his flaws and to minimize some of his indiscretions.

Transformational Leadership

transformational leadership
Leadership that goes beyond ordinary expectations by transmitting a sense of mission, stimulating learning experiences, and inspiring new ways of thinking

Another new perspective on leadership has been called by a number of labels: charismatic leadership, inspirational leadership, symbolic leadership, and transformational leadership. We use the term ***transformational leadership*** and define it as leadership that goes beyond ordinary expectations by transmitting a sense of mission, stimulating learning experiences, and inspiring new ways of thinking.[38] Because of rapid change and turbulent environments, transformational leaders are increasingly being seen as vital to the success of business.[39]

A recent article in the popular press identified seven keys to successful leadership: trusting one's subordinates, developing a vision, keeping cool, encouraging risk, being an expert, inviting dissent, and simplifying things.[40] Although this list was the result of a simplistic survey of the leadership literature, it is nevertheless consistent with the premises underlying transformational leadership. So, too, are recent examples cited as effective leadership. Take the case of 3M. The firm's new CEO is working to make the firm more efficient and profitable while simultaneously keeping its leadership role in new product innovation. He has also changed the reward system, overhauled procedures, and restructured the entire firm. And so far, at least, analysts have applauded these changes.[41]

"Turnaround or growth, it's getting your people focused on the goal that is still the job of leadership."
Anne Mulcahy, CEO of Xerox
(*BusinessWeek*, January 10, 2005, p. 62)

concept
CHECK

What are leadership substitutes? What specific substitutes might work in a classroom setting?

Identify a person you would consider to be a charismatic leader and describe why the person fits the definition.

Emerging Approaches to Leadership

Recently, three potentially very important new approaches to leadership have emerged. One is called "strategic leadership"; the others deal with cross-cultural leadership and ethical leadership.

Strategic Leadership

Strategic leadership is a new concept that explicitly relates leadership to the role of top management. We define ***strategic leadership*** as the capability to understand the complexities of both the organization and its environment and to lead change in the organization in order to achieve and maintain a superior alignment between the organization and its environment. This definition reflects an integration of the leadership concepts covered in this chapter with our discussion of strategic management in Chapter 8. One key element of effective strategic leadership, the board of directors, is the subject of this chapter's *Diversity in Action* feature.

To be effective in this role, a manager needs to have a thorough and complete understanding of the organization—its history, its culture, its strengths, and its weaknesses. In addition, the leader needs a firm grasp of the organization's environment. This understanding must encompass current conditions and circum-

TSX Welcomes Tim Hortons

Tim Hortons is a fast-growing Canadian restaurant chain. The company specializes in fresh coffee, top-quality baked goods, and home-style lunches. Tim Hortons opened its first store in 1964 and has grown steadily ever since. With annual revenues topping $1 billion, the company expanded into the United States a few years ago; its stock is now listed on both the Toronto and the New York Stock Exchanges. Strong and consistent strategic leadership by top managers has played a major role in the firm's long-run success.

stances as well as significant trends and issues on the horizon. The strategic leader also needs to recognize how the firm is currently aligned with its environment—where it relates effectively and where it relates less effectively with that environment. Finally, looking at environmental trends and issues, the strategic leader works to improve both the current alignment and the future alignment.[42]

Jeffrey Immelt (CEO of General Electric), Hector Ruiz (CEO of Advanced Micro Devices), Michael Dell (founder and CEO of Dell Computer), Anne Mulcahy (CEO of Xerox) and A. G. Lafley (CEO of Procter & Gamble) have all been recognized as strong strategic leaders. Reflecting on his dramatic turnaround at Procter & Gamble, for instance, Lafley commented, "I have made a lot of symbolic, very physical changes so people understand we are in the business of leading change." On the other hand, Raymond Gilmartin (CEO of Merck), Scott Livengood (CEO of Krispy Kreme), and Howard Pien (CEO of Chiron) have been cited as less effective strategic leaders. Under Livengood's leadership, for instance, Krispy Kreme's stock has plummeted by 80 percent, and the firm is under investigation by the SEC; moreover, most critics believe that the chain has expanded far too rapidly.[43]

> **strategic leadership**
> The capability to understand the complexities of both the organization and its environment and to lead change in the organization in order to achieve and maintain a superior alignment between the organization and its environment

Cross-Cultural Leadership

Another new approach to leadership is based on cross-cultural issues. In this context, culture is used as a broad concept to encompass both international differences and diversity-based differences within one culture. For instance, when a Japanese firm sends an executive to head the firm's operations in the United States, that person will need to become acclimated to the cultural differences that exist between the two countries and to change his or her leadership style accordingly. As noted in Chapter 5, Japan is generally characterized by collectivism, whereas the United States is based more on individualism. The Japanese executive, then, will

Working with Diversity

The Next Step for Diverse Corporate Boards

"A diverse board [of directors] translates into a more profitable business," claims Pat Ryan, board chairman of Aon. Philip Guarascio, Arbitron's chairman agrees, adding that minorities "add to the richness of the discussion." American corporations must concur because the makeup of boards is becoming more diverse. Now, advocates of diverse boards are shifting attention from mere quantities to issues regarding quality and methodology.

Minorities on corporate boards have increased dramatically. In 1987, just 80 African American directors sat on the boards of the largest 200 corporations. Today, that number has doubled, with 84 percent of these companies including at least one African American. In fact, African Americans make up 10 percent of the directors of *Fortune* 100 firms. That is close to the proportion of blacks in the United States—13 percent in 2004.

The next initiative for diversity supporters is to encourage firms to look beyond the short list of the top minority CEOs. More companies should find board members from the growing ranks of diverse middle managers and academics. Boards want to recruit well-known minority CEOs, such as Richard Parsons, who heads Time Warner. Yet prominent African American men hold more than their share of board positions. The Executive Leadership Council, a nonprofit organization to support blacks in business, helps boards identify and recruit less-famous candidates from the 250,000 African American executives working today.

More public disclosure of corporation's diversity efforts is another goal. While board members are public and visible, the company's overall ethnic composition is often semi-secret. Of the 100 largest firms, only Citigroup, HP, IBM, Coca-Cola, and Merck disclose workforce diversity information. Those calling for full disclosure maintain that investors and job seekers need diversity information to make more informed decisions. Requiring full disclosure would promote greater diversity too.

Finally, diversity champions are calling for companies to expand diversity to other minorities, including other racial minority groups and women. Females, for example, hold just 17 percent of *Fortune* 100 board seats. Hispanics make up 13 percent of the population but hold 4 percent of positions, while the Asian American proportion is 3 percent but a mere 1 percent of seats.

Clearly, U.S. businesses can do more to promote diversity. Feedback to corporate America: "Keep up the good work!"

References: Roger O. Crockett, "The Rising Stock of Black Directors," *BusinessWeek*, February 27, 2006, p. 34; "EEO-1 Reporting," Social Investment Research Analyst Network website, www.siran.org on May 1, 2006; "Women and Minorities on Fortune 100 Boards," The Executive Leadership Council website, www.elcinfo.com on May 1, 2006.

find it necessary to recognize the importance of individual contributions and rewards, as well as the differences in individual and group roles, that exist in Japanese and U.S. businesses.

Similarly, cross-cultural factors play a growing role in organizations as their workforces become more and more diverse. Most leadership research, for instance, has been conducted on samples or case studies involving white male leaders (until several years ago, most business leaders were white males). But, as more females, African Americans, and Latinos achieve leadership positions, it may be necessary to reassess how applicable current theories and models of leadership are when applied to an increasingly diverse pool of leaders.

Ethical Leadership

Most people have long assumed that top managers are ethical people. But in the wake of recent corporate scandals, faith in top managers has been shaken. Perhaps now more than ever, high standards of ethical conduct are being held up as a prerequisite for effective leadership. More specifically, top managers are being called on to maintain high ethical standards for their own conduct, to exhibit ethical behavior unfailingly, and to hold others in their organization to the same standards.

The behaviors of top leaders are being scrutinized more than ever, and those responsible for hiring new leaders for a business are looking more and more closely at the background of those being considered. And the emerging pressures for stronger corporate governance models are likely to further increase commitment to selecting only those individuals with high ethical standards and to hold them more accountable than in the past for both their actions and the consequences of those actions.[44]

> **"Reputation is everything."**
> Ken Chenault, CEO of American Express
> (*USA Today*, April 25, 2005, p. 1B)

concept CHECK

What are the three emerging approaches to leadership, and why are they important?

Can you identify any other emerging leadership issues that are likely to become important in the future?

Political Behavior in Organizations

Another common influence on behavior is politics and political behavior. ***Political behavior*** describes activities carried out for the specific purpose of acquiring, developing, and using power and other resources to obtain one's preferred outcomes.[45] Political behavior may be undertaken by managers dealing with their subordinates, subordinates dealing with their managers, and managers and subordinates dealing with others at the same level. In other words, it may be directed upward, downward, or laterally. Decisions ranging from where to locate a manufacturing plant to where to put the company coffee maker are subject to political action. In any situation, individuals may engage in political behavior to further their own ends, to protect themselves from others, to further goals they sincerely believe to be in the organization's best interests, or simply to acquire and exercise power. And power may be sought by individuals, by groups of individuals, or by groups of groups.[46]

Although political behavior is difficult to study because of its sensitive nature, one early survey found that many managers believed that politics influenced salary and hiring decisions in their firm. Many also believed that the incidence of political behavior was greater at the upper levels of their organization and lesser at the lower levels. More than half of the respondents felt that organizational politics was bad, unfair, unhealthy, and irrational, but most suggested that successful executives have to be good politicians and be political to get ahead.[47]

> **political behavior**
> The activities carried out for the specific purpose of acquiring, developing, and using power and other resources to obtain one's preferred outcomes

Common Political Behaviors

Research has identified four basic forms of political behavior widely practiced in organizations.[48] One form is *inducement*, which occurs when a manager offers to give something to someone else in return for that individual's support. For example, a product manager might suggest to another product manager that she will put in a good word with his boss if he supports a new marketing plan that she has developed. By most accounts, former WorldCom CEO Bernard Ebbers made frequent use of this tactic to retain his leadership position in the company. For example, he allowed board members to use the corporate jet whenever they wanted and invested heavily in their pet projects.

A second tactic is *persuasion,* which relies on both emotion and logic. An operations manager wanting to construct a new plant on a certain site might persuade others to support his goal on grounds that are objective and logical (is less expensive; taxes are lower) as well as subjective and personal. Ebbers also used this approach. For instance, when one board member attempted to remove him from his position, he worked behind the scenes to persuade the majority of board members to allow him to stay on.

A third political behavior involves the *creation of an obligation.* For example, one manager might support a recommendation made by another manager for a new advertising campaign. Although he might really have no opinion on the new campaign, he might think that by going along, he is incurring a debt from the other manager and will be able to "call in" that debt when he wants to get something done and needs additional support. Ebbers loaned WorldCom board members money, for example, but then forgave the loans in exchange for their continued support.

Coercion is the use of force to get one's way. For example, a manager may threaten to withhold support, rewards, or other resources as a way to influence someone else. This, too, was a common tactic used by Ebbers. He reportedly belittled any board member who dared question him, for example. In the words of one former director, "Ebbers treated you like a prince—as long as you never forgot who was king."[49]

Impression Management

Impression management is a subtle form of political behavior that deserves special mention. **Impression management** is a direct and intentional effort by someone to enhance his or her image in the eyes of others. People engage in impression management for a variety of reasons. For one thing, they may do so to further their own careers. By making themselves look good, they think they are more likely to receive rewards, to be given attractive job assignments, and to receive promotions. They may also engage in impression management to boost their self-esteem. When people have a solid image in an organization, others make them aware of it through compliments, respect, and so forth. Still another reason people use impression management is in an effort to acquire more power and hence more control.

People attempt to manage how others perceive them through a variety of mechanisms. Appearance is one of the first things people think of. Hence, a person motivated by impression management will pay close attention to choice of attire, selection of language, and use of manners and body posture. People interested in impression management are also likely to jockey for association only with successful projects. By being assigned to high-profile projects led by highly successful managers, a person can begin to link his or her own name with such projects in the minds of others.

Sometimes people too strongly motivated by impression management become obsessed with it and may resort to dishonest or unethical means. For example, some people have been known to take credit for others' work in an effort to make themselves look better. People have also been known to exaggerate or even falsify their personal accomplishments in an effort to build an enhanced image.[50]

Managing Political Behavior

By its very nature, political behavior is tricky to approach in a rational and systematic way. But managers can handle political behavior so that it does not do excessive damage.[51] First, managers should be aware that, even if their actions are not

impression management
A direct and intentional effort by someone to enhance his or her image in the eyes of others

politically motivated, others may assume that they are. Second, by providing subordinates with autonomy, responsibility, challenge, and feedback, managers reduce the likelihood of political behavior by subordinates. Third, managers should avoid using power if they want to avoid charges of political motivation. Fourth, managers should get disagreements out in the open so that subordinates will have less opportunity for political behavior through using conflict for their own purposes. Finally, managers should avoid covert activities. Behind-the-scenes activities give the impression of political intent, even if none really exists.[52] Other guidelines include clearly communicating the bases and processes for performance evaluation, tying rewards directly to performance, and minimizing competition among managers for resources.[53]

Of course, these guidelines are much easier to list than they are to implement. The well-informed manager should not assume that political behavior does not exist or, worse yet, attempt to eliminate it by issuing orders or commands. Instead, the manager must recognize that political behavior exists in virtually all organizations and that it cannot be ignored or stamped out. It can, however, be managed in such a way that it will seldom inflict serious damage on the organization. It may even play a useful role in some situations.[54] For example, a manager may be able to use his or her political influence to stimulate a greater sense of social responsibility or to heighten awareness of the ethical implications of a decision.

concept CHECK

What are the most common forms of political behavior in organizations?

Have you ever intentionally used impression management? When might impression management be an acceptable behavior, and when might it be an unacceptable behavior?

Summary of Learning Objectives and Key Points

1. Describe the nature of leadership and relate leadership to management.
   - As a process, leadership is the use of noncoercive influence to shape the group's or organization's goals, motivate behavior toward the achievement of those goals, and help define group or organization culture.
   - As a property, leadership is the set of characteristics attributed to those who are perceived to be leaders.
   - Leadership and management are often related but are also different.
   - Managers and leaders use legitimate, reward, coercive, referent, and expert power.

2. Discuss and evaluate the two generic approaches to leadership.
   - The trait approach to leadership assumed that some basic trait or set of traits differentiated leaders from nonleaders.

   - The leadership behavior approach to leadership assumed that the behavior of effective leaders was somehow different from the behavior of nonleaders.
   - Research at the University of Michigan and Ohio State University identified two basic forms of leadership behavior—one concentrating on work and performance and the other concentrating on employee welfare and support.
   - The Managerial Grid attempts to train managers to exhibit high levels of both forms of behavior.

3. Identify and describe the major situational approaches to leadership.
   - Situational approaches to leadership recognize that appropriate forms of leadership behavior are not universally applicable and attempt to specify situations in which various behaviors are appropriate.
   - The LPC theory suggests that a leader's behaviors should be either task oriented or relationship

oriented, depending on the favorableness of the situation.

- The path-goal theory suggests that directive, supportive, participative, or achievement-oriented leader behaviors may be appropriate, depending on the personal characteristics of subordinates and the environment.
- Vroom's decision tree approach maintains that leaders should vary the extent to which they allow subordinates to participate in making decisions as a function of problem attributes.
- The leader-member exchange model focuses on individual relationships between leaders and followers and on in-group versus out-group considerations.

4. Identify and describe three related approaches to leadership.
   - Related leadership perspectives are
     - the concept of substitutes for leadership

- charismatic leadership
- the role of transformational leadership in organizations

5. Describe three emerging approaches to leadership.
   - Emerging approaches include
     - strategic leadership
     - cross-cultural leadership
     - ethical leadership

6. Discuss political behavior in organizations and how it can be managed.
   - Political behavior is another influence process frequently used in organizations.
   - Impression management, one especially important form of political behavior, is a direct and intentional effort by someone to enhance his or her image in the eyes of others.
   - Managers can take steps to limit the effects of political behavior.

Discussion Questions

Questions for Review

1. What activities do managers perform? What activities do leaders perform? Do organizations need both managers and leaders? Why or why not?
2. What are the situational approaches to leadership? Briefly describe each and compare and contrast their findings.

3. Describe the subordinate's characteristics, leader behaviors, and environmental characteristics used in path-goal theory. How do these factors combine to influence motivation?
4. In your own words, define political behavior. Describe four political tactics and give an example of each.

Questions for Analysis

5. Even though the trait approach to leadership has no empirical support, it is still widely used. In your opinion, why is this so? In what ways is the use of the trait approach helpful to those who use it? In what ways is it harmful to those who use it?
6. The behavioral theories of leadership claim that an individual's leadership style is fixed. Do you agree or disagree? Give examples to support your position. The behavioral theories also claim that the ideal style is the same in every situation. Do you agree or disagree? Again, give examples.

7. A few universities are experimenting with alternative approaches, such as allowing students to design their own majors, develop a curriculum for that major, choose professors and design courses, or self-direct and self-evaluate their studies. These are examples of substitutes for leadership. Do you think this will lead to better outcomes for students than a traditional approach? Would you personally like to have that type of alternative approach at your school? Explain your answers.

Questions for Application

8. Consider the following list of leadership situations. For each situation, describe in detail the kinds of power the leader has. If the leader were the same but the situation changed—for example, if you thought of

the president as the head of his family rather than of the military—would your answers change? Why?
   - The president of the United States is commander-in-chief of the U.S. military.

- An airline pilot is in charge of a particular flight.
- Fans look up to a movie star.
- Your teacher is the head of your class.

9. Think about a decision that would affect you as a student. Use Vroom's decision tree approach to decide whether the administrator making that decision should involve students in the decision. Which parts of the model seem most important in making that decision? Why?

10. Describe a time when you or someone you know was part of an in-group or an out-group. What was the relationship between each of the groups and the leader? What was the relationship between the members of the two different groups? What was the outcome of the situation for the leader? For the members of the two groups? For the organization?

Building Effective Diagnostic Skills

Exercise Overview

Diagnostic skills help a manager visualize appropriate responses to a situation. One situation managers often face is how to use different types of power to most effectively respond to different situations.

Exercise Background

In 1599 Shakespeare's *Henry V* was performed for the first time. The play's themes of war, leadership, brotherhood, and treachery are just as relevant today. *Henry V* also contains a speech, the "St. Crispin's Day speech," that is widely considered to be the most inspiring speech ever written.

To set the scene: In 1415, England, under Henry's leadership, has attacked France to regain control of some disputed lands, which are currently held by France. (England's claim is legitimate, in Shakespeare's play, and the war is therefore "just.") England's 6,000 soldiers won several key battles, moving from the coast into the interior of France. The English are sick, cold, hungry, and dispirited. They arrive at the French town of Agincourt and face an army of 25,000 soldiers who are well rested and much better equipped, with horses and armor. Through a mixture of courage, strategy, and plain luck, the English are victorious, losing only 200 men, as they inflict over 5,000 casualties on the French. The French crown prince is injured, their commanding general is killed, and they surrender to the English.

This short scene occurs just before the start of the battle of Agincourt. Henry's officers are worried about their chances of victory, and Henry motivates them to plunge into battle and do their best. If you find it hard to understand Shakespeare's English, your professor has a transcript of the scene.

Exercise Task

View the short excerpt from *Henry V* that your professor will show in class. (The film was made in 1989 and was directed by and stars Kenneth Branagh.) In addition, read the transcript of Henry's monologue. Then answer the following questions:

1. What types of power is Henry using in this speech? Give specific examples of each type.

2. Henry had a rebellious and wayward youth before becoming king. Does his past tend to increase or decrease his referent power, in your opinion? Why?

3. In Shakespeare's play, Henry's speech inspired his soldiers to an almost impossible victory. Is this speech inspiring to you? Why or why not?

Building Effective Conceptual Skills

Exercise Overview

Conceptual skills refer to the manager's ability to think in the abstract. This exercise allows you to analyze one practical approach to assessing leadership skills and to relate practice to theory.

Exercise Background

Current publications contain an abundance of practical advice on leadership. (On the top ten business best-sellers' list in early 2003 were *Good to Great*, by Jim Collins; *First, Break All the Rules*, by Marcus Buckingham; and *Execution: The Discipline of Getting Things Done*, by Larry Bossidy.) Some of these books, such as *Jack: Straight from the Gut*, by former General Electric CEO Jack Welch, are written by managers with years of experience. Others are written by consultants, professors, or reporters. But many—in fact, most—of these books do not have a strong theoretical foundation, nor are their suggestions supported by scientific evidence.

Many of these books contain ideas that may nevertheless be of use to managers. However, learning how to analyze publications in the popular press and to investigate them carefully is an important skill for today's managers. This exercise gives you practice in doing just that.

Exercise Task

1. Visit *Fortune* magazine's website at **www.fortune.com/ fortune/quizzes/careers/boss_quiz.html**. Complete the leadership assessment quiz that was written by management guru Stephen Covey. Then look at Covey's scoring and comments.

2. Look carefully at each of the questions and the suggested answers. Do you see any correlation between the questions and the theoretical models presented to you in this chapter? Which model or models do you think Covey is using? What led you to that conclusion?

3. Use the Internet to discover something about Stephen Covey's background, training, and experiences. Does the information you found give you any clues about Covey's attitudes and beliefs about leadership? Do you see any connection between Covey's attitudes and the items on the quiz? Explain.

4. Based on what you found, how confident are you that the quiz is an accurate measure of leadership ability? Explain.

CHAPTER CLOSING CASE

LEADERSHIP SECRETS OF SUCCESSFUL CEOs

Now, more than ever, leading U.S. businesses is tough. The current passion for "lean and mean" leads to fewer and fewer workers doing more and more work. Globalization requires leaders to understand cross-cultural differences. Knowledge industries present unique leadership challenges, requiring communication skills and flexibility. Technology advances create a flood of communications that overwhelms efforts to respond effectively. What suggestions do top U.S. business leaders have for those who want to follow in their footsteps?

In many industries, workers suffer from overwork—a demanding schedule, stress, and long working hours. For example, U.S. airlines today service 100 million more passengers annually than they did just four years ago, but with 70,000 fewer workers. One leader says, "I used to manage my time; now I manage my energy." Personal energy enables managers to complete their tasks; lack of energy is disabling. Most top corporate leaders work 80 to 100 hours weekly, but they need a way to rebuild and refresh.

Carlos Ghosn, CEO of Nissan, believes in regular breaks. "I do not bring my work home. I play with my four children and spend time with my family on weekends," Ghosn says. "I come up with good ideas as a result of becoming stronger after being recharged." Marissa Mayer, a vice president for Google, says, "I can get by on four to six hours of sleep," but also takes a weeklong vacation three times per year. Many leaders report playing competitive racquetball, running marathons, or just regular exercise and yoga as a way to recover from overwork.

Effective leaders control information flows. Mayer uses many sources of information, saying, "I always have my laptop with me" and "I adore my cellphone." Howard Schultz, Starbucks CEO, receives a morning voice-mail summarizing the previous day's sales results. News is important too: Schultz reads three newspapers daily; Mayer watches news all day; Bill Gross, a securities portfolio manager, examines six monitors displaying real-time investments data.

Gross needs time to concentrate. He says, "Eliminating the noise is critical. . . . I only pick up the phone three or four times a day. . . . I don't want to be connected—I want to be disconnected." To handle a schedule that requires weekly travel to another continent, Ghosn uses bilingual assistants to translate and screen information—one for Europe, one for Japan, and one for the United States. Clothing designer and CEO Vera Wang uses an assistant to filter information. "The barrage of calls is so enormous that if I just answered calls I would do nothing else. . . . If I were to go near email, there would be even more obligations, and I would be in Bellevue with a white jacket on."

Leaders of knowledge workers must motivate and retain talented individuals who have many other options for employment. Bill Gates, founder of Microsoft, states that if the 20 smartest people left, Microsoft would be an insignificant company. This puts enormous pressure on leaders to keep these workers satisfied and productive. Mayer holds office hours, a regularly scheduled time every day when she listens to any and all employee concerns. Schultz visits at least 25

stores each week. Jane Friedman, CEO of publisher HarperCollins, parties. "Authors, who are the most important people in our company, really appreciate it when the CEO turns up at their event."

Hank Paulson, CEO of Goldman Sachs, concentrates on recruiting, visiting business schools personally. He called the company's top 60 CEO customers to wish them a happy new year, resulting in new information and closer relationships. Paul says, "I taught more than 25 sessions to all 1,200 of our managing directors in Asia, Europe and the U.S. That's culture-building." Wang is also interested in strengthening relationships with customers and states, "All businesses are personal businesses."

Leaders must be able to do it all. "[Leadership is] a game of pinball, and you're the ball," says U.S. Senator John McCain. So here's recommendations from effective leaders. Develop a routine that keeps personal energy levels high to help cope with very long hours. Low need for sleep and dedication to regular exercise are plusses. Be a

sponge for information, using many sources and technologies for communications, but don't neglect face-to-face conversations. Carve out time for quiet reflection and concentration. And focus on inspiring and satisfying your organization's most important stakeholders.

CASE QUESTIONS

1. Which bases of power are used by the leaders cited in this article?

2. Which examples of leader behavior described in this article seem to fit best with job-centered leader behavior? Which are most like employee-centered leader behavior?

3. Do the leaders cited in this article exhibit the elements of charismatic leadership? Explain.

CASE REFERENCES

Geoffrey Colvin, "Catch a Rising Star," *Fortune*, February 6, 2006, pp. 46–50; "How I Work," *Fortune*, March 20, 2006, pp. 66–85; "Star Power," *Fortune*, February 6, 2006, pp. 55–66; Jerry Useem, "Making Your Work Work for You," *Fortune*, March 20, 2006, pp. 60–62.

YOU MAKE THE CALL

A Cycle of Leadership at Intel

1. Which Intel CEO's style of leadership most closely resembles your own?

2. Which of the five CEOs profiled would you most like to work for?

3. Intel appears to rely heavily on mentoring and long-term leadership development. What are the pros and cons of such an approach?

4. Suppose you were responsible for a work unit that is in need of a strong-handed, task-oriented leader. You have two options: one is the better manager but isn't particularly task-oriented; the other is task-oriented but not as effective as a manager. Which would you select?

5. Would you want to work for Intel? Why or why not?

Test Prepper

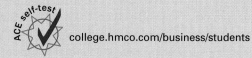

college.hmco.com/business/students

Choose the correct answer. Answers are found at the back of the book.

1. T   F   By definition, leaders are employee oriented, not job oriented.

2. T   F   Situational models assume that appropriate leader behavior varies from one situation to another.

3. T   F   According to LPC theory, the most favorable situation is one in which tasks are highly structured.

4. T   F   According to path-goal theory, people with an internal locus of control will likely prefer directive leadership.

5. T   F   Vroom's decision tree approach helps managers know how much to involve subordinates in decision making.

6. Caroline follows the leader of her company because she identifies with the leader and has attitudes about the company that are similar to the leader's attitudes. What kind of power does this illustrate?

   A. Referent
   B. Reward
   C. Expert
   D. Coercive
   E. Legitimate

7. The studies at the University of Michigan and Ohio State University each identified two similar categories of leadership behaviors: employee-oriented behaviors and job-oriented behaviors. The difference was the Ohio State researchers concluded that

   A. most leaders were employee oriented.
   B. most leaders were job oriented.
   C. employee-oriented leaders demanded higher salaries than did job-oriented leaders.

   D. a person could exhibit high levels of both types of behaviors.
   E. a person was either employee oriented or job oriented, but not both.

8. All of the following describe members of the "in-group," as explained in the leader-member exchange model, EXCEPT

   A. they receive special duties.
   B. they receive special privileges.
   C. they have higher levels of performance.
   D. they are more satisfied.
   E. they have reached minimum levels of seniority in the "out-group."

9. For someone to truly be a strategic leader, he or she must

   A. raise barriers to entry and increase the supply of the organization's product.
   B. achieve a superior alignment between the organization and the environment.
   C. improve the level of human and financial capital in the organization.
   D. limit the power of suppliers in the environment.
   E. limit the power of buyers in the environment.

10. Samuel wears dress slacks and a tie to work each day even though the other employees dress down in jeans and T-shirts. Samuel dresses the way he does because he thinks it will give him a better chance at getting a promotion, and he simply feels better about himself when he dresses more professionally. Samuel has engaged in which form of political behavior?

   A. Inducement
   B. Coercion
   C. Creation of an obligation
   D. Impression management
   E. Unsolicited

Managing Interpersonal Relations and Communication

LEARNING OBJECTIVES

After studying this chapter, you should be able to:

1. Describe the interpersonal nature of organizations.
2. Describe the role and importance of communication in the manager's job.
3. Identify the basic forms of communication in organizations.
4. Discuss informal communication, including its various forms and types.
5. Describe how the communication process can be managed to recognize and overcome barriers.

FIRST THINGS FIRST

Communicating in Phone Interviews

"[On phone interviews,] you cannot be seen. Use this to your advantage."

—COLLEGEGRAD.COM, A JOB-SEARCH WEBSITE

Interviews are stressful. The unfamiliar dress clothes, the need to make an instant good impression, the unexpected questions that leave the job-seeker grasping about for any answer. Surely phone interviews are easier, right? Wrong? Job interviews conducted on the phone have all of the challenges of a face-to-face interview, and then some.

Every interview, whether in person or over the phone, requires the same level and type of preparation. Candidates should sell themselves, tell interesting stories, remain poised, anticipate questions and have answers ready, and ask relevant questions. Many job-seekers, however, feel that phone interviews are

Telephone interviews are becoming an increasingly common way for employers to communicate with prospective employees. This young woman is shown talking to a prospective employer on her cell phone.

somehow less formal, less thorough, or require less preparation. They couldn't be more wrong. Many corporations today conduct phone interviews to pre-screen applicants and many rely on phone interviews exclusively, especially for candidates located far away. Phone interviews save time and money for both the candidate and the employer. However, applicants should be aware of the communication challenges and have solutions ready.

Problem: Scheduling. The interviewer may call at a mutually-agreed-upon time. Or he or she may deliberately make an unscheduled call or call at an odd time. Some want to assess a candidate's ability to think quickly and are looking for unscripted responses. Yet a call is inconvenient when the kids are screaming for dinner or a roommate is hosting an unruly party.

Solution. If the interviewer calls at a time when conversation is truly impossi-ble, you will have to call back. Be aware, however, that some interviewers are put off by the request. If the call will be difficult but not impossible, it's best to carry on with the interview. Ask for a moment to "close the door," then do just that. Ask for quiet, get to a clear space, and take some deep breaths before pick-ing up the phone again.

Problem: Preparation. Phone interviews require the same preparation, but have an added benefit. "You cannot be seen. Use this to your advantage," says CollegeGrad.com, a leading website for entry-level job-seekers. While phone interviews can help alleviate nervousness for some candidates, candidates should not relax entirely.

Solution. Prepare notes about the points you want to cover and arrange them near the phone so you can look at them during the conversation. Include paper and a pen to take notes. Have a copy of your résumé too, so you can answer questions. Dress professionally. While the interviewer cannot see you, studies show that job candidates sound more articulate and more intelligent when they are appropriately dressed for work.

Problem: Noise. Phone conversations are subject to many different types of noise, including a noisy environment, a poor phone connection, and sudden loss of cell phone batteries. Gum chewing, eating, and drinking are also noisy and distracting.

Solution: Shut the door and maintain quiet. Ask the interviewer to speak up if the connection is poor. Recharge those batteries! Never eat, drink, or chew gum during an interview.

Problem: Lack of context cues. An in-person conversation contains many nonverbal context cues. Only a small portion of the conversation's meaning is carried by the words themselves. A phone interview allows for just one nonver-bal element—tone of voice. Every other nonverbal element is eliminated, includ-ing gesture, body language, facial expression, and dress. Applicants must find a way to get their message across with a limited set of tools.

Solution: Even though the interviewer cannot see you, smile. Your speech will change as you do, conveying richer information and making you sound friendlier. In fact, many experts recommend that you use gestures, expression, body language, and so on, just as you would during a face-to-face interview. Many phone sales professionals stand or even walk around the room, to sound more energetic and focused. Finally, if the interviewer seems hesitant, ask if he or she has any questions or concerns. This allows you to explicitly address any weak areas and will compensate to some extent for the lack of context cues.

Job-seekers list "difficulty in making phone calls" as their second-most important problem. But as *Fortune* writer Anne Fisher says, "Making these calls gets easier the more often you do it." So brush up on those communications skills, and then hit the phones![1]

Businesses continue to look for effective ways to communicate with their employees, as well as job seekers, customers, and investors. The idea of telephone interviews for job seekers may seem odd to some people, but many firms are finding this method of screening prospective employees to be both efficient and effective. Of course, as noted, there are both advantages and disadvantages to telephone interviews. Communication has always been a vital part of managerial work. Indeed, managers around the world agree that communication is one of their most important tasks. It is important for them to communicate with others in order to convey their vision and goals for the organization. And it is important for others to communicate with them so that they will better understand what is going on in their environment and how they and their organization can become more effective.

This chapter is the first of two that focuses on interpersonal processes in organizations. We first establish the interpersonal nature of organizations and then discuss communication, one of the most basic forms of interaction among people. We begin by examining communication in the context of the manager's job. We then identify and discuss forms of interpersonal, group, and organizational communication. After discussing informal means of communication, we describe how organizational communication can be effectively managed. In our next chapter, we discuss other elements of interpersonal relations: group and team processes and conflict.

The Interpersonal Nature of Organizations

In Chapter 1, we noted how much of a manager's job involves scheduled and unscheduled meetings, telephone calls, e-mail, and related activities. Indeed, a great deal of what all managers do involves interacting with other people, both directly and indirectly and both inside and outside of the organization. The schedule that follows is a typical day for the president of a Houston-based company, part of a larger firm headquartered in California. He kept a log of his activities for several different days so that you could better appreciate the nature of managerial work.

7:45–8:15 A.M.   Arrive at work; review hardcopy mail sorted by assistant.

8:15–8:30 A.M.   Scan the *Wall Street Journal*; read and respond to e-mail.

8:30–9:00 A.M.   Meet with labor officials and plant manager to resolve minor labor disputes.

9:00–9:30 A.M.   Review internal report; read and respond to new e-mail.

9:30–10:00 A.M.   Meet with two marketing executives to review advertising campaign; instruct them to fax approvals to advertising agency.

By their very nature, organizations are built on interpersonal relations. From the shop floor to the executive suite, much of the work that takes place in an organization involves people interacting and communicating with one another. Take this Home Depot loading dock, for example. These three employees are reviewing various shipping documents to make sure that the right mix of products and building materials is coming into and leaving the store. Without interacting with each other, this group of employees would find their jobs much harder to perform.

10:00–11:30 A.M.   Meet with company executive committee to discuss strategy, budgetary issues, and competition (this committee meets weekly).

11:30–12:00 noon.   Send several e-mails; read and respond to new e-mail.

12:00–1:15 P.M.   Lunch with the financial vice president and two executives from another subsidiary of the parent corporation. Primary topic of discussion is the Houston Rockets basketball team. Place three calls from cell phone en route to lunch and receive one call en route back to office.

1:15–1:45 P.M.   Meet with human resource director and assistant about a recent OSHA inspection; establish a task force to investigate the problems identified and to suggest solutions.

1:45–2:00 P.M.   Read and respond to new e-mail.

2:00–2:30 P.M.   Conference call with four other company presidents.

2:30–3:00 P.M.   Meet with financial vice president about a confidential issue that came up at lunch (unscheduled).

3:00–3:30 P.M.   Work alone in office; read and respond to new e-mail; send several e-mails.

3:30–4:15 P.M.   Meet with a group of sales representatives and the company purchasing agent.

4:15–5:30 P.M.   Work alone in office.

5:30–7:00 P.M.   Play racquetball at nearby athletic club with marketing vice president.

9:00–9:30 P.M.   Read and respond to e-mail from home; send e-mail to assistant about an emergency meeting to be scheduled for the next day.

How did this manager spend his time? He spent most of it working, communicating, and interacting with other people. And this compressed daily schedule does not include several other brief telephone calls, brief conversations with his assistant, and brief conversations with other managers. Clearly, interpersonal relations, communication, and group processes are a pervasive part of all organizations and a vital part of all managerial activities.[2]

Interpersonal Dynamics

The nature of interpersonal relations in an organization is as varied as the individual members themselves. At one extreme, interpersonal relations can be personal and positive. This occurs when the two parties know each other, have mutual respect and affection, and enjoy interacting. Two managers who have known each other for years, play golf together on weekends, and are close personal friends will likely interact at work in a positive fashion. At the other extreme, interpersonal dynamics can be personal but negative. This is most likely when the parties dislike each other, do not have mutual respect, and do not enjoy interacting. Suppose a manager has fought openly for years to block the promotion of another manager within the organization. Over the objections of the first manager, however, the other manager eventually gets promoted to the same rank. When the two of them must interact, it will most likely be in a negative manner.

Most interactions fall between these extremes, as members of the organization interact in a professional way focused primarily on goal accomplishment. The interaction deals with the job at hand, is relatively formal and structured, and is task directed. Two managers may respect each other's work and recognize the professional competence that each brings to the job. However, they may also have few common interests and little to talk about besides the job they are doing. These different types of interactions may occur between individuals, between groups, or between individuals and groups, and they can change over time. The two managers in the second scenario, for example, might decide to bury the hatchet and adopt a detached, professional manner. The two managers in the third example could find more common ground than they anticipated and evolve to a personal and positive interaction.

Outcomes of Interpersonal Behaviors

A variety of things can happen as a result of interpersonal behaviors. Recall from Chapter 16, for example, that numerous perspectives on motivation suggest that people have social needs. Interpersonal relations in organizations can be a primary source of need satisfaction for many people. For a person with a strong need for affiliation, high-quality interpersonal relations can be an important positive element in the workplace. However, when this same person is confronted with poor-quality working relationships, the effect can be just as great in the other direction.

Interpersonal relations also serve as a solid basis for social support. Suppose that an employee receives a poor performance evaluation or is denied a promotion. Others in the organization can lend support because they share a common frame of reference—an understanding of the causes and consequences of what happened. Good interpersonal relations throughout an organization can also be a source of synergy. People who support one another and who work well together can accomplish much more than people who do not support one another and who do not work well together. Another outcome, implied earlier, is conflict—people may leave an interpersonal exchange feeling angry or hostile. But a common thread is woven through all of these outcomes—communication between people in the organization.[3]

concept
CHECK

What kinds of interpersonal interactions can be identified in organizational settings?

How much of your daily life involves interacting with other people?

Communication and the Manager's Job

As evidenced by the daily log presented earlier, a typical day for a manager includes doing desk work, attending scheduled meetings, placing and receiving telephone calls, reading and answering correspondence (both print and electronic), attending unscheduled meetings, and making tours.[4] Most of these activities involve communication. In fact, managers usually spend over half their time on some form of communication. Communication always involves two or more people, so other behavioral processes, such as motivation, leadership, and group and team interactions, all come into play. Top executives must handle communication effectively if they are to be true leaders.

A Definition of Communication

Imagine three managers working in an office building. The first is all alone but is nevertheless yelling for a subordinate to come help. No one appears, but he continues to yell. The second is talking on the telephone to a subordinate, but static on the line causes the subordinate to misunderstand some important numbers being provided by the manager. As a result, the subordinate sends 1,500 crates of eggs to 150 Fifth Street, when he should have sent 150 crates of eggs to 1500 Fifteenth Street. The third manager is talking in her office with a subordinate who clearly hears and understands what is being said. Each of these managers is attempting to communicate, but with different results.

communication
The process of transmitting information from one person to another

Communication is the process of transmitting information from one person to another. Did any of our three managers communicate? The last did, and the first did not. How about the second? In fact, she did communicate. She transmitted information, and information was received. The problem was that the message transmitted and the message received were not the same. The words spoken by the manager were distorted by static and noise. *Effective communication*, then, is the process of sending a message in such a way that the message received is as close in meaning as possible to the message intended. Although the second manager engaged in communication, it was not effective.

effective communication
The process of sending a message in such a way that the message received is as close in meaning as possible to the message intended

Our definition of effective communication is based on the ideas of meaning and consistency of meaning. Meaning is the idea that the individual who initiates the communication exchange wishes to convey. In effective communication, the meaning is transmitted in such a way that the receiving person understands it. For example, consider these messages:

1. The high today will be only 40 degrees.
2. It will be cold today.
3. Ceteris paribus.
4. Xn1gp bo5cz4ik ab19.

You probably understand the meaning of the first statement. The second statement may seem clear at first, but it is somewhat less clear than the first statement because cold is a relative condition and the word can mean different things to different people. Fewer still understand the third statement, because it is written in Latin. None of you understands the last statement because it is written in a secret code that your author developed as a child.

The Role of Communication in Management

We noted earlier the variety of activities that fill a manager's day. Meetings, telephone calls, and correspondence are all a necessary part of every manager's job—and all clearly involve communication. On a typical Monday, Aylwin Lewis, CEO of Sears Holding Corporation, attended 5 scheduled meetings and 2 unscheduled meetings; had 15 telephone conversations; received and/or sent over 100 e-mails and 29 letters, memos, and reports; and dictated 10 letters.[5]

To better understand the linkages between communication and management, recall the variety of roles that managers must fill. Each of the ten basic managerial roles discussed in Chapter 1 (see Table 1.2) would be impossible to fill without communication.[6] Interpersonal roles involve interacting with supervisors, subordinates, peers, and others outside the organization. Decisional roles require managers to seek out information to use in making decisions and then communicate those decisions to others. Informational roles focus specifically on acquiring and disseminating information.

Communication also relates directly to the basic management functions of planning, organizing, leading, and controlling. Environmental scanning, integrating planning-time horizons, and decision making, for example, all necessitate communication. Delegation, coordination, and organization change and development also entail communication. Developing reward systems and interacting with subordinates as a part of the leading function would be impossible without some form of communication. And communication is essential to establishing standards, monitoring performance, and taking corrective actions as a part of control. Clearly, then, communication is a pervasive part of virtually all managerial activities.[7]

The Communication Process

Figure 18.1 illustrates how communication generally takes place between people. The process of communication begins when one person (the sender) wants to transmit a fact, idea, opinion, or other information to someone else (the receiver). This fact, idea, or opinion has meaning to the sender, whether it be simple and concrete or complex and abstract. For example, Linda Porter, a marketing representative at Canon, recently landed a new account and wanted to tell her boss about it. This fact and her motivation to tell her boss represented meaning.

The next step is to encode the meaning into a form appropriate to the situation. The encoding might take the form of words, facial expressions, gestures, or even artistic expressions and physical actions. For example, the Canon representative

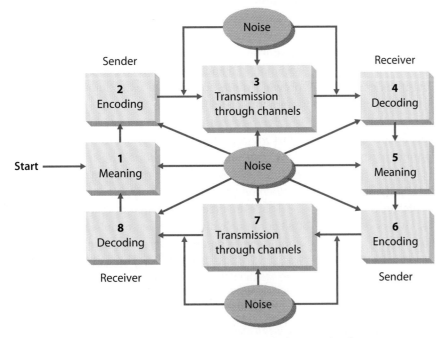

The numbers indicate the sequence in which steps take place.

Figure 18.1

THE COMMUNICATION PROCESS

As the figure shows, noise can disrupt the communication process at any step. Managers must therefore understand that a conversation in the next office, a fax machine out of paper, and the receiver's worries may all thwart the manager's best attempts to communicate.

might have said, "I just landed the Acme account," "We just got some good news from Acme," "I just spoiled Xerox's day," "Acme just made the right decision," or any number of other things. She actually chose the second message. Clearly, the encoding process is influenced by the content of the message, the familiarity of sender and receiver, and other situational factors.

After the message has been encoded, it is transmitted through the appropriate channel or medium. The channel by which this encoded message is being transmitted to you is the printed page. Common channels in organizations include meetings, e-mail, memos, letters, reports, and telephone calls. Linda Porter might have written her boss a note, sent him an e-mail, called him on the telephone, or dropped by his office to convey the news. Because both she and her boss were out of the office when she got the news, she called and left a message for him on his voicemail.

After the message is received, it is decoded back into a form that has meaning for the receiver. As noted earlier, the consistency of this meaning can vary dramatically. Upon hearing about the Acme deal, the sales manager at Canon might have thought, "This'll mean a big promotion for both of us," "This is great news for the company," or "She's blowing her own horn too much again." His actual feelings were closest to

Working with Diversity

The New Mainstream

A television ad: A father explains Toyota's hybrid engine. "[The car] runs on gas and electricity. Mira. Mira aquí. (Look. Look here.) It uses both," the father says. The son replies, "Like you, with English and Spanish." The father answers, "Sí."

As U.S. society changes, organizations need to communicate with diverse customers. Toyota's television spot reflects revolutionary changes in the way companies address buyers from different cultures. Firms once assumed that Hispanics living in the United States were immigrants, spoke no English, and held Old-World values. Yet the truth is, over 22 million of the country's 40 million Hispanics were born in the States. Most Spanish speakers know English and mix elements of U.S. and Latino culture. "This group is not about nostalgia for the home country," says Jaime Fortuno, partner in a U.S. ad agency that is Latin-owned.

The Milk Board's old, targeted ad: A grandmother prepares tres leches cake in a crowded kitchen, under the slogan "Familia, amor, y leche (Family, love, and milk.)" The new ad: Commuters hold on to train steps with their teeth. The slogan says, "Toma leche (Drink milk.)"

Formerly, advertisers relied on mainstream ads. As the purchasing power of minorities became evident, companies developed targeted ads, often delivered through language-targeted media. Corporations pay $4 billion each year for Hispanic-themed ads, for example. Today, companies are beginning to realize that there is a tremendous variety of Hispanic customers, just as there are many segments in a mainstream market. In 2004, about one-third of ads targeted to Hispanics were presented in English, and that proportion is growing.

Latino-targeted ads are catching up to mainstream ads, with wacky, irreverent humor. White marketers, unfamiliar with Hispanics, turn to positive stereotyping, resulting in bland ads. However, Latinos and whites are growing more comfortable with humor that explicitly refers to racial differences.

Energizer battery ad: In Spanish, a man says, "When I lost my arm, I got a new one. From a Japanese guy. Now I can't stop taking pictures." He compulsively takes pictures everywhere—of himself in the shower, in bed, in the men's room, until a fight ensues.

That's an effective and memorable ad. And it shows that communications between people of different races, about race, is getting easier—and funnier.

References: David Kiley, "Laughing Out Loud in Spanish," *Business-Week*, March 13, 2006, www.businessweek.com on May 2, 2006; Stephanie Mehta, "Speaking the Wrong Language," *Fortune*, April 27, 2006, www.fortune.com on May 2, 2006; Laurel Wentz, "Full-Service Hispanic Ad Agencies Dominate Media Buying," *Advertising Age*, February 6, 2006, www.adage.com on May 2, 2006.

the second statement. In many cases, the meaning prompts a response, and the cycle is continued when a new message is sent by the same steps back to the original sender. The manager might have called the sales representative to offer congratulations, written her a personal note of praise, offered praise in an e-mail, or sent a formal letter of acknowledgment. Linda's boss wrote her a personal note.

"Noise" may disrupt communication anywhere along the way. Noise can be the sound of someone coughing, a truck driving by, or two people talking close at hand. It can also include disruptions such as a letter lost in the mail, a dead telephone line, an interrupted cell phone call, an e-mail misrouted or infected with a virus, or one of the participants in a conversation being called away before the communication process is completed. If the note written by Linda's boss had gotten lost, she might have felt unappreciated. As it was, his actions positively reinforced not only her efforts at Acme but also her effort to keep him informed. Another form of noise might be difficulties in understanding messages due to language barriers. *Diversity in Action* discusses how some companies are attempting to address such problems in communicating with Latino consumers by airing commercials using the Spanish language.

concept
CHECK

Distinguish between communication and effective communication.

Recall a recent communication exchange in which you participated and analyze it in terms of the model in Figure 18.1.

Forms of Communication in Organizations

Managers need to understand several kinds of communication that are common in organizations today.[8] These include interpersonal communication, communication in networks and teams, organizational communication, and electronic communication.

Interpersonal Communication

Interpersonal communication generally takes one of two forms: oral and written. As we will see, each has clear strengths and weaknesses.

Oral Communication *Oral communication* takes place in conversations, group discussions, telephone calls, and other situations in which the spoken word is used to express meaning. One study (conducted before the advent of e-mail) demonstrated the importance of oral communication by finding that most managers spent between 50 and 90 percent of their time talking to people.[9] Oral communication is so prevalent for several reasons. The primary advantage of oral communication is that it promotes prompt feedback and interchange in the form of verbal questions or agreement, facial expressions, and gestures. Oral communication is also easy (all the sender needs to do is talk), and it can be done with little preparation (though careful preparation is advisable in certain situations). The sender does not need pencil and paper, typewriter, or other equipment. In another survey, 55 percent of the executives sampled felt that their own written communication skills were fair or poor, so they chose oral communication to avoid embarrassment![10]

oral communication
Face-to-face conversation, group discussions, telephone calls, and other circumstances in which the spoken word is used to transmit meaning

People in organizations use many different forms of communication. For years Toyota used a process it called "tacit understanding" to pass job knowledge from one worker to another. Under this model, little was written down; the information was shared verbally from senior workers to more junior workers. But as Toyota has grown and moved its manufacturing operations into other countries, this system has proved to be less effective. So, for the first time, the company is creating how-to manuals and developing practice drills to transfer knowledge to overseas workers. Kazuo Hyodo, a 30-year veteran on Toyota assembly lines, is shown here teaching Ray Hawley, right, of South Africa, the proper method for tightening bolts.

---

written communication
Memos, letters, reports, notes, and other circumstances in which the written word is used to transmit meaning

---

However, oral communication also has drawbacks. It may suffer from problems of inaccuracy if the speaker chooses the wrong words to convey meaning or leaves out pertinent details, if noise disrupts the process, or if the receiver forgets part of the message.[11] In a two-way discussion, there is seldom time for a thoughtful, considered response or for introducing many new facts, and there is no permanent record of what has been said. In addition, although most managers are comfortable talking to people individually or in small groups, fewer enjoy speaking to larger audiences.[12]

Written Communication   "Putting it in writing" in a letter, report, memorandum, handwritten note, or e-mail can solve many of the problems inherent in oral communication. Nevertheless, and perhaps surprisingly, ***written communication*** is not as common as one might imagine, nor is it a mode of communication much respected by managers. One sample of managers indicated that only 13 percent of the printed mail they received was of immediate use to them.[13] Over 80 percent of the managers who responded to another survey indicated that the written communication they received was of fair or poor quality.[14]

The biggest single drawback of traditional forms of written communication is that they inhibit feedback and interchange. When one manager sends another manager a letter, it must be written or dictated, typed, mailed, received, routed, opened, and read. If there is a misunderstanding, it may take several days for it to be recognized, let alone rectified. Although the use of e-mail is, of course, much faster, both sender and receiver must still have access to a computer, and the receiver must open and read the message for it to actually be received. A phone call could settle the whole matter in just a few minutes. Thus written communication often inhibits feedback and interchange and is usually more difficult and time consuming than oral communication.

Of course, written communication offers some advantages. It is often quite accurate and provides a permanent record of the exchange. The sender can take the time to collect and assimilate the information and can draft and revise it before it is transmitted. The receiver can take the time to read it carefully and can refer to it repeatedly, as needed. For these reasons, written communication is generally preferable when important details are involved. At times it is important to one or both parties to have a written record available as evidence of exactly what took place. Julie Regan, founder of Toucan-Do, an importing company based in Honolulu, relies heavily on formal business letters in establishing contacts and buying merchandise from vendors in Southeast Asia. She believes that such letters give her an opportunity to carefully think through what she wants to say, tailor her message to each individual, and avoid later misunderstandings.

Choosing the Right Form   Which form of interpersonal communication should the manager use? The best medium will be determined by the situation. Oral communication or e-mail is often preferred when the message is personal, nonroutine, and brief. More formal written communication is usually best when the message is more impersonal, routine, and longer. And, given the prominent role that e-mails have played in several recent court cases, managers should always use discretion when sending messages electronically.[15] For example, private e-mails made public during legal proceedings have played major roles in litigation involving Enron, Tyco, WorldCom, and Morgan Stanley.[16]

> "I'm not a big e-mailer. I prefer face-to-face whenever possible."
>
> A. G. Lafley, Procter & Gamble CEO
> (*Fortune,* December 12, 2005, leadership insert)

The manager can also combine media to capitalize on the advantages of each. For example, a quick telephone call to set up a meeting is easy and gets an immediate response. Following up the call with a reminder e-mail or handwritten note helps ensure that the recipient will remember the meeting, and it provides a record of the meeting's having been called. Electronic communication, discussed more fully later, blurs the differences between oral and written communication and can help each be more effective.

Communication in Networks and Work Teams

Although communication among team members in an organization is clearly interpersonal in nature, substantial research also focuses specifically on how people in networks and work teams communicate with one another. A **communication network** is the pattern through which the members of a group or team communicate. Researchers studying group dynamics have discovered several typical networks in groups and teams consisting of three, four, and five members. Representative networks among members of five-member teams are shown in Figure 18.2.[17]

> *communication network*
> The pattern through which the members of a group communicate

In the wheel pattern, all communication flows through one central person, who is probably the group's leader. In a sense, the wheel is the most centralized network because one person receives and disseminates all information. The Y pattern is slightly less centralized—two people are close to the center. The chain offers a more even flow of information among members, although two people (the ones at each end) interact with only one other person. This path is closed in the circle pattern.

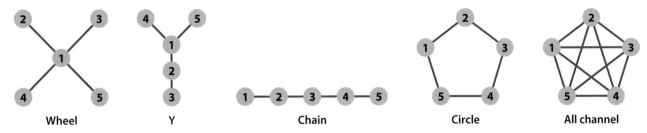

| Wheel | Y | Chain | Circle | All channel |

Figure 18.2

TYPES OF COMMUNICATION NETWORKS

Research on communication networks has identified five basic networks for five-person groups. These networks vary in terms of information flow, position of the leader, and effectiveness for different types of tasks. Managers might strive to create centralized networks when group tasks are simple and routine. Alternatively, managers can foster decentralized groups when group tasks are complex and nonroutine.

Finally, the all-channel network, the most decentralized, allows a free flow of information among all group members. Everyone participates equally, and the group's leader, if there is one, is not likely to have excessive power.

Research conducted on networks suggests some interesting connections between the type of network and group performance. For example, when the group's task is relatively simple and routine, centralized networks tend to perform with greatest efficiency and accuracy. The dominant leader facilitates performance by coordinating the flow of information. When a group of accounting clerks is logging incoming invoices and distributing them for payment, for example, one centralized leader can coordinate things efficiently. When the task is complex and nonroutine, such as making a major decision about organizational strategy, decentralized networks tend to be most effective because open channels of communication permit more interaction and a more efficient sharing of relevant information. Managers should recognize the effects of communication networks on group and organizational performance and should try to structure networks appropriately.

Organizational Communication

Still other forms of communication in organizations are those that flow among and between organizational units or groups. Each of these involves oral or written communication, but each also extends to broad patterns of communication across the organization.[18] As shown in Figure 18.3, two of these forms of communication follow vertical and horizontal linkages in the organization.

---

vertical communication
Communication that flows up and down the organization, usually along formal reporting lines; takes place between managers and their superiors and subordinates and may involve several different levels of the organization

---

Vertical Communication *Vertical communication* is communication that flows up and down the organization, usually along formal reporting lines—that is, it is the communication that takes place between managers and their superiors and subordinates. Vertical communication may involve only two people, or it may flow through several different organizational levels. A common perspective on vertical communication that exists in some organizations is illustrated in the cartoon.

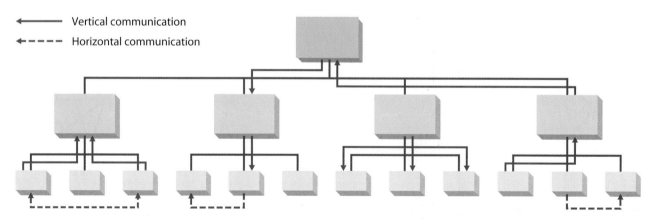

Figure 18.3
FORMAL COMMUNICATION IN ORGANIZATIONS

Formal communication in organizations follows official reporting relationships or prescribed channels. For example, vertical communication, shown here with the solid lines, flows between levels in the organization and involves subordinates and their managers. Horizontal communication, shown with dashed lines, flows between people at the same level and is usually used to facilitate coordination.

Upward communication consists of messages from subordinates to superiors. This flow is usually from subordinates to their direct superior, then to that person's direct superior, and so on up the hierarchy. Occasionally, a message might bypass a particular superior. The typical content of upward communication is requests, information that the lower-level manager thinks is of importance to the higher-level manager, responses to requests from the higher-level manager, suggestions, complaints, and financial information. Research has shown that upward communication is more subject to distortion than is downward communication. Subordinates are likely to withhold or distort information that makes them look bad. The greater the degree of difference in status between superior and subordinate and the greater the degree of distrust, the more likely the subordinate is to suppress or distort information.[19] For example, subordinates might choose to withhold information about problems from their boss if they think the news will make him angry and if they think they can solve the problem themselves without his ever knowing about it.

Downward communication occurs when information flows down the hierarchy from superiors to subordinates. The typical content of these messages is directives on how something is to be done, the assignment of new responsibilities, performance feedback, and general information that the higher-level manager thinks will be of value to the lower-level manager. Vertical communication can and usually should be two-way in nature. In other words, give-and-take communication with active feedback is generally likely to be more effective than one-way communication.[20]

Horizontal Communication   Whereas vertical communication involves a superior and a subordinate, ***horizontal communication*** involves colleagues and peers at the same level of the organization. For example, an operations manager might communicate to a marketing manager that inventory levels are running low and that projected delivery dates should be extended by two weeks. Horizontal communication probably occurs more among managers than among nonmanagers.

This type of communication serves a number of purposes.[21] It facilitates coordination among interdependent units. For example, a manager at Motorola was once researching the strategies of Japanese semiconductor firms in Europe. He found a great deal of information that was relevant to his assignment. He also uncovered some additional information that was potentially important to another department, so he passed it along to a colleague in that department, who used it to improve his own operations. Horizontal communication can also be used for joint problem solving, as when two plant managers at Northrop Grumman got together to work out a new method to improve productivity. Finally, horizontal communication plays a major role in work teams with members drawn from several departments.

> *horizontal communication*
> Communication that flows laterally within the organization; involves colleagues and peers at the same level of the organization and may involve individuals from several different organizational units

Electronic Communication

Finally, as already noted, electronic communication has taken on much greater importance for managers in recent times. Both formal information systems and personal information technology have reshaped how managers communicate with one another. *Technology Toolkit* profiles an emerging form of electronic communication, the blog.

Formal Information Systems   Most larger businesses manage at least a portion of their organizational communication through information systems. Some firms go so far as to create a position for a chief information officer, or CIO. General Mills,

Technology Toolkit

Blog the Corporation!

Cell phones and fax machines? Grandparents use them. Video conferencing? Been there, done that. The Internet? Old news. E-mail? Of course. PDA or Blackberry? Standard equipment for managers.

The explosion of digital communication technologies over the last 20 years has created many new media. Many corporations rely extensively on these new technologies, which have changed the way we work. Virtual teams, global workforces, outsourcing, just-in-time inventory—there are so many widely accepted business tools and methods that could never have existed without these new developments. Today, another new technology is at the cutting-edge: web logs, also called blogs.

According to Wikipedia, the online encyclopedia, "A blog is a web-based publication consisting primarily of periodic articles, most often in reverse chronological order." Blogs are similar to a journal, where a blogger expresses his or her thoughts over a period of time. Most blogs allow readers to post their own comments in response to the original posts.

Blogs allow groups to share thoughts, and for some readers, they supplement or replace traditional news media. Blogs are a form of grapevine network. Like a face-to-face grapevine, blogs can contain information that is suppressed elsewhere, as well as information that is inaccurate or even malicious.

Organizations as disparate as General Motors, the Dallas Cowboys, Microsoft, and organic dairy Stonyfield Farm maintain popular corporate blogs. They provide a way for companies to communicate frankly with customers and employees. Blogs have other uses too. Umbria, a customer research firm, extracts information from blogs and sells it to corporate marketing departments. Umbria's data is valuable because bloggers are often early product adopters and their blog opinions show up quickly. Blog scanning routinely surveys 20 million blogs and costs just $60,000 per year.

Blogging makes corporate communications more egalitarian, as anyone can "talk" with top managers. In addition, "the blogsphere is overflowing with brutally honest opinion," says Howard Kaushansky, Umbria CEO. It can be scary because it's controlled by readers, not corporations.

So far, only about 5 percent of *Fortune* 500 companies blog. But more will. With 20 million blogs worldwide, 350,000 daily posts, and 70,000 new blogs appearing daily, this technology is set to change corporate communications.

References: Matthew Boyle, "Do's and Don'ts of Corporate Blogging," *Fortune*, February 28, 2006, www.fortune.com on May 3, 2006; Heather Green, "Roger Staubach CEO Blogger?" *BusinessWeek*, September 13, 2005, www.businessweek.com on May 3, 2006; Justin Martin, "What Bloggers Think of Your Business," *Fortune*, December 7, 2005, www.fortune.com on May 3, 2006.

Xerox, and Burlington Industries all have such a position. The CIO is responsible for determining the information-processing needs and requirements of the organization and then putting in place systems that facilitate smooth and efficient organizational communication.

Part of the CIO's efforts also involves the creation of one or more formal information systems linking all relevant managers, departments, and facilities in the organization. Most enterprise resource-planning systems play this role very effectively. In the absence of such a system, a marketing manager, for example, may need to call a warehouse manager to find out how much of a particular product is in stock before promising shipping dates to a customer. An effective formal information system allows the marketing manager to get the information more quickly, and probably more accurately, by plugging directly into a computerized information system. Because of the increased emphasis on and importance of these kinds of information systems, we cover them in detail in Chapter 22.

Personal Electronic Technology   In recent years, the nature of organizational communication has changed dramatically, mainly because of breakthroughs in personal electronic communication technology, and the future promises even more change. Electronic typewriters and photocopying machines were early breakthroughs. The photocopier, for example, makes it possible for a manager to have a typed report distributed to large numbers of other people in an extremely short time. Personal computers have accelerated the process even more. E-mail networks, the Internet, and corporate intranets are carrying communication technology even further.

It is also becoming common to have teleconferences in which managers stay at their own location (such as offices in different cities) but are seen on television or computer monitors as they "meet." A manager in New York can keyboard a letter or memorandum at her personal computer, point and click with a mouse, and have it delivered to hundreds or even thousands of colleagues around the world in a matter of seconds. Highly detailed information can be retrieved with ease from large electronic databanks. This has given rise to a new version of an old work arrangement—cottage industry. In cottage industry, people work at home (in their "cottage") and periodically bring the products of their labors in to the company. "Telecommuting" is the label given to a new electronic cottage industry. In telecommuting, people work at home on their computers and transmit their work to their companies via telephone line or cable modem.

Cellular telephones and facsimile machines have made it even easier for managers to communicate with one another. Many now use cell phones to make calls while commuting to and from work, and carry them in their briefcases so that they can receive calls while at lunch. Facsimile machines make it easy for people to use written communication media and get rapid feedback. And newer personal computing devices, such as Palm Pilots and Blackberrys, are further revolutionizing how people communicate with one another.

Psychologists, however, are beginning to associate some problems with these communication advances. For one thing, managers who are seldom in their "real" offices are likely to fall behind in their fields and to be victimized by organizational politics because they are not present to keep in touch with what is going on and to protect themselves. They drop out of the organizational grapevine and miss out on much of the informal communication that takes place. Moreover, the use of electronic communication at the expense of face-to-face meetings and conversations makes it hard to build a strong culture, develop solid working relationships, and create a mutually supportive atmosphere of trust and cooperativeness.[22] Finally, electronic communication is also opening up new avenues for dysfunctional employee behavior, such as the passing of lewd or offensive materials to others. For example, the *New York Times* once fired almost 10 percent of its workers at one of its branch offices for sending inappropriate e-mails at work.[23]

concept
CHECK

What are the primary forms of communication that are used by managers in organizations today?

What kinds of electronic communication have you used in the last 24 hours?

Informal Communication in Organizations

The forms of organizational communication discussed in the previous section all represent planned and relatively formal communication mechanisms. However, in many cases some of the communication that takes place in an organization

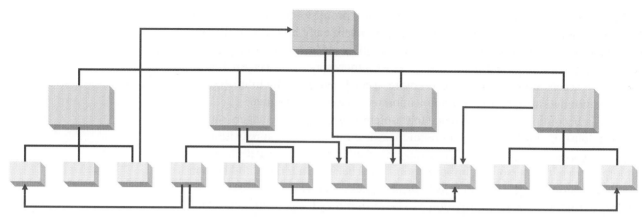

Figure 18.4
INFORMAL COMMUNICATION IN ORGANIZATIONS

Informal communication in organizations may or may not follow official reporting relationships or prescribed channels. It may cross different levels and different departments or work units, and may or may not have anything to do with official organizational business.

transcends these formal channels and instead follows any of several informal methods. Figure 18.4 illustrates numerous examples of informal communication. Common forms of informal communication in organizations include the grapevine, management by wandering around, and nonverbal communication.

The Grapevine

> **grapevine**
> An informal communication network among people in an organization

The **grapevine** is an informal communication network that can permeate an entire organization. Grapevines are found in all organizations except the very smallest, but they do not always follow the same patterns as, nor do they necessarily coincide with, formal channels of authority and communication. Research has identified several kinds of grapevines.[24] The two most common are illustrated in Figure 18.5. The gossip chain occurs when one person spreads the message to many other people. Each one, in turn, may either keep the information confidential or pass it on to others. The gossip chain is likely to carry personal information. The other common grapevine is the cluster chain, in which one person passes the information to a selected few individuals. Some of the receivers pass the information to a few other individuals; the rest keep it to themselves.

Figure 18.5
COMMON GRAPEVINE CHAINS FOUND IN ORGANIZATIONS

The two most common grapevine chains in organizations are the gossip chain (in which one person communicates messages to many others) and the cluster chain (in which many people pass messages to a few others).

Gossip Chain
One person tells many

Cluster Chain
Many people tell a few

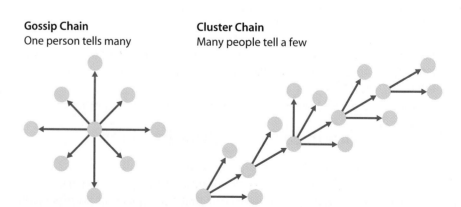

There is some disagreement about how accurate the information carried by the grapevine is, but research is increasingly finding it to be fairly accurate, especially when the information is based on fact rather than speculation. One study found that the grapevine may be between 75 percent and 95 percent accurate.[25] That same study also found that informal communication is increasing in many organizations for two basic reasons. One contributing factor is the recent increase in merger, acquisition, and takeover activity. Because such activity can greatly affect the people within an organization, it follows that they may spend more time talking about it.[26] The second contributing factor is that as more and more corporations move facilities from inner cities to suburbs, employees tend to talk less and less to others outside the organization and more and more to one another.

Attempts to eliminate the grapevine are fruitless, but fortunately the manager does have some control over it. By maintaining open channels of communication and responding vigorously to inaccurate information, the manager can minimize the damage the grapevine can do. The grapevine can actually be an asset. By learning who the key people in the grapevine are, for example, the manager can partially control the information they receive and use the grapevine to sound out employee reactions to new ideas, such as a change in human resource policies or benefit packages. The manager can also get valuable information from the grapevine and use it to improve decision making.[27]

Management by Wandering Around

Another increasingly popular form of informal communication is called, interestingly enough, **management by wandering around**.[28] The basic idea is that some managers keep in touch with what is going on by wandering around and talking with people—immediate subordinates, subordinates far down the organizational hierarchy, delivery people, customers, or anyone else who is involved with the company in some way. Bill Marriott, for example, frequently visits the kitchens, loading docks, and custodial work areas whenever he tours a Marriott hotel. He claims that, by talking with employees throughout the hotel, he gets new ideas and has a better feel for the entire company. And, when Continental Airlines CEO Larry Kellner travels, he makes a point of talking to flight attendants and other passengers to gain continuous insights into how the business can be run more effectively.

A related form of organizational communication that really has no specific term is the informal interchange that takes place outside the normal work setting. Employees attending the company picnic, playing on the company softball team, or taking fishing trips together will almost always spend part of their time talking about work. For example, Texas Instruments engineers at TI's Lewisville, Texas, facility often frequent a local bar in town after work. On any given evening, they talk about the Dallas Cowboys, the newest government contract received by the company, the weather, their boss, the company's stock price, local politics, and problems at work. There is no set agenda, and the key topics of discussion vary from group to group and from day to day. Still, the social gatherings serve an important role. They promote a strong culture and enhance understanding of how the organization works.

> *management by wandering around*
> An approach to communication that involves the manager's literally wandering around and having spontaneous conversations with others

Nonverbal Communication

Nonverbal communication is a communication exchange that does not use words or uses words to carry more meaning than the strict definition of the words themselves.

> *nonverbal communication*
> Any communication exchange that does not use words or uses words to carry more meaning than the strict definition of the words themselves

Nonverbal communication is a powerful but little-understood form of communication in organizations. It often relies on facial expressions, body movements, physical contact, and gestures. One study found that as much as 55 percent of the content of a message is transmitted by facial expressions and body posture and that another 38 percent derives from inflection and tone. Words themselves account for only 7 percent of the content of the message.[29]

Research has identified three kinds of nonverbal communication practiced by managers—images, settings, and body language.[30] In this context, images are the kinds of words people elect to use. "Damn the torpedoes, full speed ahead" and "Even though there are some potential hazards, we should proceed with this course of action" may convey the same meaning. Yet the person who uses the first expression may be perceived as a maverick, a courageous hero, an individualist, or a reckless and foolhardy adventurer. The person who uses the second might be described as aggressive, forceful, diligent, or narrow minded and resistant to change. In short, our choice of words conveys much more than just the strict meaning of the words themselves.

The setting for communication also plays a major role in nonverbal communication. Boundaries, familiarity, the home turf, and other elements of the setting are all important. Much has been written about the symbols of power in organizations. The size and location of an office, the kinds of furniture in the office, and the accessibility of the person in the office all communicate useful information. For example, H. Ross Perot positions his desk so that it is always between him and a visitor. This keeps him in charge. When he wants a less formal dialogue, he moves around to the front of the desk and sits beside his visitor. Michael Dell of Dell Computer has his desk facing a side window so that, when he turns around to greet a visitor, there is never anything between them.

A third form of nonverbal communication is body language.[31] The distance we stand from someone as we speak has meaning. In the United States, standing very close to someone you are talking to generally signals either familiarity or aggression. The English and Germans stand farther apart than Americans when talking, whereas the Arabs, Japanese, and Mexicans stand closer together.[32] Eye contact is another effective means of nonverbal communication. For example, prolonged eye contact might suggest either hostility or romantic interest. Other kinds of body language include body and hand movement, pauses in speech, and mode of dress.

The manager should be aware of the importance of nonverbal communication and recognize its potential impact. Giving an employee good news about a reward with the wrong nonverbal cues can destroy the reinforcement value of the reward. Likewise, reprimanding an employee but providing inconsistent nonverbal cues can limit the effectiveness of the sanctions. The tone of the message, where and how the message is delivered, facial expressions, and gestures can all amplify or weaken the message or change the message altogether.

concept
CHECK

What are the three fundamental kinds of informal communication that occur in an organization?	*Spend 30 minutes observing other people and note the various kinds of nonverbal communication they exhibit.*

Many managers would like to improve communication effectiveness in their organizations. While there are several basic things that can be done, they sometimes seek out unusual and creative methods as well. Ellen Moore (left), for instance, is a professional ethnographer—someone who studies cultures and societies through first-hand observation. Moore works as a communications consultant to several businesses. She spends time watching how people interact and communicate with each other and then offers suggestions for making those processes more effective.

Managing Organizational Communication

In view of the importance and pervasiveness of communication in organizations, it is vital for managers to understand how to manage the communication process.[33] Managers should understand how to maximize the potential benefits of communication and minimize the potential problems. We begin our discussion of communication management by considering the factors that might disrupt effective communication and how to deal with them.

Barriers to Communication

Several factors may disrupt the communication process or serve as barriers to effective communication.[34] As shown in Table 18.1, these may be divided into two classes: individual barriers and organizational barriers.

Individual Barriers	Organizational Barriers
Conflicting or inconsistent signals	Semantics
Credibility about the subject	Status or power differences
Reluctance to communicate	Different perceptions
Poor listening skills	Noise
Predispositions about the subject	Overload
	Language differences

Table 18.1
BARRIERS TO EFFECTIVE COMMUNICATION

Numerous barriers can disrupt effective communication. Some of these barriers involve individual characteristics and processes. Others are functions of the organizational context in which communication is taking place.

Individual Barriers   Several individual barriers may disrupt effective communication. One common problem is conflicting or inconsistent signals. A manager is sending conflicting signals when she says on Monday that things should be done one way, but then prescribes an entirely different procedure on Wednesday. Inconsistent signals are being sent by a manager who says that he has an "open door" policy and wants his subordinates to drop by, but keeps his door closed and becomes irritated whenever someone stops in.

Another barrier is lack of credibility. Credibility problems arise when the sender is not considered a reliable source of information. He may not be trusted or may not be perceived as knowledgeable about the subject at hand. When a politician is caught withholding information or when a manager makes a series of bad decisions, the extent to which he or she will be listened to and believed thereafter diminishes. In extreme cases, people may talk about something they obviously know little or nothing about.

Some people are simply reluctant to initiate a communication exchange. This reluctance may occur for a variety of reasons. A manager may be reluctant to tell subordinates about an impending budget cut because he knows they will be unhappy about it. Likewise, a subordinate may be reluctant to transmit information upward for fear of reprisal or because it is felt that such an effort would be futile.

Poor listening habits can be a major barrier to effective communication. Some people are simply poor listeners. When someone is talking to them, they may be daydreaming, looking around, reading, or listening to another conversation. Because they are not concentrating on what is being said, they may not comprehend part or all of the message. They may even think that they really are paying attention, only to realize later that they cannot remember parts of the conversation.

Receivers may also bring certain predispositions to the communication process. They may already have their minds made up, firmly set in a certain way. For example, a manager may have heard that his new boss is unpleasant and hard to work with. When she calls him in for an introductory meeting, he may go into that meeting predisposed to dislike her and discount what she has to say.

Organizational Barriers   Other barriers to effective communication involve the organizational context in which the communication occurs. Semantics problems arise when words have different meanings for different people. Words and phrases such as *profit, increased output,* and *return on investment* may have positive meanings for managers but less positive meanings for labor.

Communication problems may also arise when people of different power or status try to communicate with each other. The company president may discount a suggestion from an operating employee, thinking, "How can someone at that level help me run my business?" Or, when the president goes out to inspect a new plant, workers may be reluctant to offer suggestions because of their lower status. The marketing vice president may have more power than the human resource vice president and consequently may not pay much attention to a staffing report submitted by the human resource department.

If people perceive a situation differently, they may have difficulty communicating with one another. When two managers observe that a third manager has not spent much time in her office lately, one may believe that she has been to several important meetings, and the other may think she is "hiding out." If they need to talk about her in some official capacity, problems may arise because one has a positive impression and the other a negative impression.

VIP

Comm

Organizational Skills
Follow up
Regulate information flows
Understand the richness of media

Table 18.2
OVERCOMING BARRIERS TO COMMUNICATION

Because communication is so important, managers have developed several methods of overcoming barriers to effective communication. Some of these methods involve individual skills, whereas others are based on organizational skills.

pt effective communication. As mentioned earlier, noise may affect communication in many ways. Similarly, overload may be a problem when the receiver is being sent more information than he or she can effectively handle. As e-mail becomes increasingly common, many managers report getting so many messages each day as to sometimes feel overwhelmed.[35] And, when the manager gives a subordinate many jobs on which to work and at the same time the subordinate is being told by family and friends to do other things, overload may result and communication effectiveness diminishes.

Finally, as businesses become more and more global, different languages can create problems. To counter this problem, some firms are adopting an "official language." For example, when the German chemical firm Hoechst merged with the French firm Rhone-Poulenc, the new company adopted English as its official language. Indeed, English is increasingly becoming the standard business language around the world.[36]

Improving Communication Effectiveness

Considering how many factors can disrupt communication, it is fortunate that managers can resort to several techniques for improving communication effectiveness.[37] As shown in Table 18.2, these techniques include both individual and organizational skills.

Individual Skills   The single most important individual skill for improving communication effectiveness is being a good listener.[38] Being a good listener requires that the individual be prepared to listen, not interrupt the speaker, concentrate on both the words and the meaning being conveyed, be patient, and ask questions as appropriate.[39] So important are good listening skills that companies like Delta, IBM, and Boeing conduct programs to train their managers to be better listeners. Figure 18.6 illustrates the characteristics of poor listeners versus good listeners.

> " . . . being a good listener for as long as you can stand it is the most important thing [for a new leader] to do. "
>
> Henry Schacht, former CEO of Lucent Technologies
> (*Fortune*, January 24, 2005, p. 112)

In addition to being a good listener, several other individual skills can promote effective communication. Feedback, one of the most important, is facilitated by two-way communication. Two-way communication allows the receiver to ask questions, request clarification, and express opinions that let the sender know whether he or she has been understood. In general, the more complicated the message, the more useful two-way communication is. In addition, the sender should be aware of the meanings that different receivers might attach to various words. For example, when addressing stockholders, a manager might use the word *profits* often. When addressing labor leaders, however, she may choose to use *profits* less often.

Figure 18.6
MORE AND LESS EFFECTIVE
LISTENING SKILLS

Effective listening skills are a vital part of communication in organizations. There are several barriers that can contribute to poor listening skills by individuals in organizations. Fortunately, there are also several practices for improving listening skills.

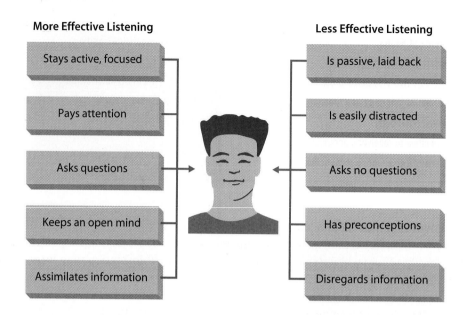

More Effective Listening	Less Effective Listening
Stays active, focused	Is passive, laid back
Pays attention	Is easily distracted
Asks questions	Asks no questions
Keeps an open mind	Has preconceptions
Assimilates information	Disregards information

Furthermore, the sender should try to maintain credibility. This can be accomplished by not pretending to be an expert when one is not, by "doing one's homework" and checking facts, and by otherwise being as accurate and honest as possible. The sender should also try to be sensitive to the receiver's perspective. A manager who must tell a subordinate that she has not been recommended for a promotion should recognize that the subordinate will be frustrated and unhappy. The content of the message and its method of delivery should be chosen accordingly. The manager should be primed to accept a reasonable degree of hostility and bitterness without getting angry in return.[40]

Finally, the receiver should also try to be sensitive to the sender's point of view. Suppose that a manager has just received some bad news—for example, that his position is being eliminated next year. Others should understand that he may be disappointed, angry, or even depressed for a while. Thus they might make a special effort not to take too much offense if he snaps at them, and they might look for signals that he needs someone to talk to.[41]

Organizational Skills   Three useful organizational skills can also enhance communication effectiveness for both the sender and the receiver—following up, regulating information flow, and understanding the richness of different media. Following up simply involves checking at a later time to be sure that a message has been received and understood. After a manager mails a report to a colleague, she might call a few days later to make sure the report has arrived. If it has, the manager might ask whether the colleague has any questions about it.

Regulating information flow means that the sender or receiver takes steps to ensure that overload does not occur. For the sender, this could mean not passing too much information through the system at one time. For the receiver, it might mean calling attention to the fact that he is being asked to do too many things at once. Many managers limit the influx of information by periodically weeding out the list of journals and routine reports they receive, or they train their assistant to screen phone calls and visitors. Indeed, some executives now get so much e-mail that they have it routed to an assistant. That person reviews the e-mail, discards those that are not useful (such as "spam"), responds to those that are routine, and passes on to the executive only those that require her or his personal attention.

Both parties should also understand the richness associated with different media. When a manager is going to lay off a subordinate temporarily, the message should be delivered in person. A face-to-face channel of communication gives the manager an opportunity to explain the situation and answer questions. When the purpose of the message is to grant a pay increase, written communication may be appropriate because it can be more objective and precise. The manager could then follow up the written notice with personal congratulations.

---

concept
CHECK

What are the primary barriers to communication in organizations, and how can they most effectively be overcome?

Think of two recent situations in which you encountered a barrier to communication. How was it—or how might it have been—overcome?

Summary of Learning Objectives and Key Points

1. Describe the interpersonal nature of organizations.
   - Communication is the process of transmitting information from one person to another.
   - Effective communication is the process of sending a message in such a way that the message received is as close in meaning as possible to the message intended.

2. Describe the role and importance of communication in the manager's job.
   - Communication is a pervasive and important part of the manager's world.
   - The communication process consists of a sender's encoding meaning and transmitting it to one or more receivers, who receive the message and decode it into meaning.
   - In two-way communication, the process continues with the roles reversed.
   - Noise can disrupt any part of the overall process.

3. Identify the basic forms of communication in organizations.
   - Several forms of organizational communication exist. Interpersonal communication focuses on communication among a small number of people.
   - Two important forms of interpersonal communication, oral and written, both offer unique advantages and disadvantages.
   - The manager should weigh the pros and cons of each when choosing a medium for communication.

   - Communication networks are recurring patterns of communication among members of a group or work team.
   - Vertical communication between superiors and subordinates may flow upward or downward.
   - Horizontal communication involves peers and colleagues at the same level in the organization.
   - Organizations also use information systems to manage communication.
   - Electronic communication is having a profound effect on managerial and organizational communication.

4. Discuss informal communication, including its various forms and types.
   - There is also a great deal of informal communication in organizations.
   - The grapevine is the informal communication network among people in an organization.
   - Management by wandering around is also a popular informal method of communication.
   - Nonverbal communication includes facial expressions, body movement, physical contact, gestures, and inflection and tone.

5. Describe how the communication process can be managed to recognize and overcome barriers.
   - Managing the communication process necessitates recognizing the barriers to effective

- communication and understanding how to overcome them.
- Barriers can be identified at both the individual and the organizational levels.

- Both individual and organizational skills can be used to overcome these barriers.

Discussion Questions

Questions for Review

1. Describe the difference between communication and effective communication. How can a sender verify that a communication was effective? How can a receiver verify that a communication was effective?
2. Which form of interpersonal communication is best for long-term retention? Why? Which form is best for getting across subtle nuances of meaning? Why?
3. What are the similarities and differences of oral and written communication? What kinds of situations call for the use of oral methods? What situations call for written communication?
4. Describe the individual and organizational barriers to effective communication. For each barrier, describe one action that a manager could take to reduce the problems caused by that barrier.

Questions for Analysis

5. "Personal friendships have no place at work." Do you agree or disagree with this statement, and why?
6. At what points in the communication process can problems occur? Give examples of how noise can interfere with the communication process. What can managers do to reduce problems and noise?
7. How are electronic communication devices (cell phones, e-mail, and websites) likely to affect the communication process in the future? Describe both the advantages and the disadvantages of these three devices over traditional communication methods, such as face-to-face conversations, written notes, and phone calls.

Questions for Application

8. What forms of communication have you experienced today? What form of communication is involved in a face-to-face conversation with a friend? A telephone call from a customer? A traffic light or crossing signal? A picture of a cigarette in a circle with a slash across it? An area around machinery defined by a yellow line painted on the floor?
9. Keep track of your own activities over the course of a few hours of leisure time to determine what forms of communication you encounter. Which forms were most common? If you had been tracking your communications while at work, how would the list be different? Explain why the differences occur.
10. For each of the following situations, tell which form of communication you would use. Then ask the same question of someone who has been in the workforce for at least ten years. For any differences that occur, ask the worker to explain why his or her choice is better than yours. Do you agree with his or her assessment? Why or why not?

- Describing complex changes in how health-care benefits are calculated and administered to every employee of a large firm
- Asking your boss a quick question about how she wants something done
- Telling customers that a new two-for-one promotion is available at your store
- Reprimanding an employee for excessive absences on the job
- Reminding workers that no smoking is allowed in your facility

Building Effective Technical Skills

Exercise Overview

Technical skills are the skills necessary to perform the work of the organization. This exercise will help you develop and apply technical skills involving the Internet and its potential for gathering information relevant to making important decisions.

Exercise Background

Assume that you are a manager for a large national retailer. You have been assigned the responsibility for identifying potential locations for the construction of a warehouse and distribution center. The idea behind such a center is that the firm can use its enormous purchasing power to buy many products in bulk quantities at relatively low prices. Individual stores can then order the specific quantities they need from the warehouse.

The location will need an abundance of land. The warehouse itself, for example, will occupy more than four square acres of land. In addition, it must be close to railroads and major highways because shipments will be arriving by both rail and truck, although outbound shipments will be exclusively by truck. Other important variables are that land prices and the cost of living should be relatively low and weather conditions should be mild (to minimize disruptions to shipments).

The firm's general experience is that small to midsize communities work best. Moreover, warehouses are already in place in the western and eastern parts of the United States, so this new one will most likely be in the central or south-central area. Your boss has asked you to identify three or four possible sites.

Exercise Task

With the information above as a framework, do the following:

1. Use the Internet to identify as many as ten possible locations.

2. Using additional information from the Internet, narrow the set of possible locations to three or four.

3. Again using the Internet, find out as much as possible about the potential locations.

Building Effective Interpersonal Skills

Exercise Overview

A manager's interpersonal skills include his or her abilities to understand and to motivate individuals and groups. This in-class demonstration gives you practice in understanding the nonverbal and verbal behavior of a pair of individuals.

Exercise Background

Nonverbal communication conveys more than half of the information in any face-to-face exchange, and body language is a significant part of our nonverbal behavior. Consider, for example, the impact of a yawn or a frown or a shaking fist. At the same time, however, nonverbal communication is often neglected by managers. The result can be confusing and misleading signals.

In this exercise, you will examine interactions between two people without sound, with only visual clues to meaning. Then you will examine those same interactions with both visual and verbal clues.

Exercise Task

1. Observe the silent video segments that your professor shows to the class. For each segment, describe the nature of the relationship and interaction between the two individuals. What nonverbal clues did you use in reaching your conclusions?

2. Next, observe the same video segments, but this time with audio included. Describe the interaction again, along with any verbal clues you used.

3. How accurate were your assessments when you had only visual information? Explain why you were or were not accurate.

4. What does this exercise show you about the nature of nonverbal communication? What advice would you now give managers about their nonverbal communication?

CHAPTER CLOSING CASE

COMMUNICATING GREATNESS

What do legendary leaders Herb Kelleher, Donald Trump, Rudy Giuliani, and Steve Jobs have in common? One hint: They share this trait with CEOs John Chambers (Cisco), Larry Ellison (Oracle), John Chen (Sybase), Jeff Taylor (Monster.com), Norman Mayne (Dorothy Lane Markets), and other effective managers. Still stumped? It's communication skill. Each of these managers, along with many others, have mastered the art of communicating to convey information, inspire workers, establish personal rapport, and persuade customers.

One of the most important techniques that successful leaders use is personalizing communication. An easy way to do this is to look into the audience's eyes, whether that audience is one person or a thousand. "In my role as communications coach, I've found that failing to maintain eye contact ranks as the No. 1 problem—but also the easiest to fix," says Carmine Gallo, author and communications consultant. Gallo goes on to add, "We like people who look us in the eye. . . . People associate eye contact with honesty, trustworthiness, sincerity, confidence—all the traits you strive toward to make yourself a great business communicator."

Speakers should maintain eye contact for 70 to 80 percent of a face-to-face conversation, but should keep their eyes on the audience 90 to 95 percent of the time when addressing a group. One trick with large groups is to shift focus from one section of the room to another. Within a section, choose one or a few individuals and look at them directly. By doing this, "I make everyone feel as though I'm talking to them, not at them. I'm not lecturing, but conversing," says Fox News journalist Stuart Varney.

To help in making eye contact, great communicators do not use notes. Rudy Giuliani, mayor of New York, was known for making lengthy, detailed speeches completely without notes. So are Jobs, Ellison, and Chambers. Each of these leaders knows his material so well that he has the confidence to rely on memory instead of written notes. Listeners are distracted and energy is lost when a speaker has to glance at or, even worse, read from his or her notes. Donald Trump dislikes watching people read from notes so much that he fired an apprentice who used a notepad. Interviewers tell about the negative impression made when a job candidate relies on notes. When listeners ask for a copy of the speech follow-

ing a presentation delivered by Kelleher, his staff says, "[Sorry,] even Herb doesn't have a copy."

For effective communications, practice makes perfect. To deliver a complex presentation without notes, Giuliani practices for up to four months. CEO Chambers is another example. He spends hours rehearsing every component of a speech, including the slide show, where he will stand and walk, how the lights work, and so on. Barbara Corcoran, CEO of a real estate firm, worked up her confidence through practice. "Years ago I'd speak to groups of 30, 50, or 100," she says. "Now it's 500 or more and I'm much more comfortable with 1,000." Of course, not every communication calls for such elaborate preparation. Yet even a simple conversation or a phone call can be mentally "scripted and rehearsed" ahead of time.

Another important skill is making the message short. When addressing a crowd, studies have shown that an audience's attention will wander after about 18 minutes. Lincoln's Gettysburg Address lasted just 3 minutes and followed a two-hour speech by a famous orator. Lincoln's speech, which contained a mere 272 words arranged in 10 sentences, was shockingly brief, yet it remains one of the most-loved and often-quoted presentations. Corcoran says, "Give them just enough, and then stop." Veteran communicators whet the appetite for more information and then give additional facts when questioned.

Finally, leaders communicate best when they speak with passion. When speaking one to one, relevant and memorable facts have maximum impact. For example, Mayne, CEO of a chain of supermarkets, meets with newly hired employees to emphasize the need to keep expenses low. "On a $25 grocery order, how much profit do you think we make?" he asks. Recruits are usually astonished to learn that profits are only 75 cents, and the example vividly demonstrates the importance of cost control. Chambers is compared to "an evangelist

or a television talk-show host" because he talks passionately, getting close to ask questions or touch someone's shoulder. He has been referred to as "the most electrifying speaker in corporate America today." Not everyone will reach his level, but everyone can learn to become a more effective communicator, with a few simple techniques and practice, practice, practice.

CASE QUESTIONS

1. How do the communication techniques mentioned in this article increase communication effectiveness? That is, how do they help to ensure that the received message is close in meaning to the intended message?
2. This article focuses on oral communication. Is oral communication likely to be more frequent for top managers than written communication? Explain why or why not.
3. When delivering a speech, what are the potential advantages and disadvantages of speaking without notes? Remember to consider both verbal and nonverbal modes in your answer.

CASE REFERENCES

Carmine Gallo, "When Speaking in Public, It's All in the Eyes," MSNBC website, October 21, 2005, www.msnbc.msn.com on May 3, 2006; Sharon McDonnell, "Grading the CEO Speech," *New York Times,* September 27, 2005, www.nytimes.com on May 3, 2006; Kenneth McFarland, "Getting Personal with Your Staff," *BusinessWeek,* April 19, 2006, www.businessweek.com on May 3, 2006; "Presentation Tips," *BusinessWeek,* www.businessweek.com on May 3, 2006.

YOU MAKE THE CALL

Communicating in Phone Interviews

1. As a job seeker, would you prefer a telephone interview or a face-to-face interview? Why?
2. Experts suggest that you should dress professionally for a telephone interview even though the interviewer cannot see you. Do you agree that this is important? Why or why not?
3. In preparing for a telephone interview for a new job, what would be the three or four things you would be most prepared for?

4. If you were interviewing someone else for a job, what would be the three or four major things you would expect to learn?
5. Video cameras linked with computers are becoming increasingly popular. How might this technology be used in conjunction with telephone interviews?
6. Could the concept of telephone interviews be effectively extended to other forms of communication such as text messaging? Why or why not?

Test Prepper

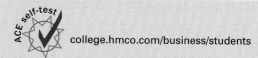

college.hmco.com/business/students

Choose the correct answer. Answers are found at the back of the book.

1. T F Effective communication has taken place when a group of workers has little or no conflict.

2. T F In the encoding step of the communication process, meaning may take the form of words, facial expressions, or gestures.

3. T F Managers who use electronic communication technology extensively and who are seldom in their "real" offices are likely to be victimized by organizational politics.

4. T F Nearly all the content of a message is transmitted by verbal rather than nonverbal communication.

5. T F Conflicting or inconsistent signals will act as barriers to communication between two individuals.

6. Which of the following is the most common form of communication in organizations?

   A. Oral
   B. Written
   C. Nonverbal
   D. Electronic
   E. Memorandum

7. The typical content of upward communication in organizations includes all of the following EXCEPT

   A. requests.
   B. information.
   C. assignments.
   D. suggestions.
   E. complaints.

8. What position is sometimes created in large organizations that rely on formal information systems?

   A. Technological systems specialist
   B. Executive empowerment officer
   C. Director of public relations
   D. Vice president of communications
   E. Chief information officer

9. What should a manager do to eliminate the grapevine, the informal communication network that can permeate an entire organization?

   A. Reorganize teams frequently.
   B. Suppress horizontal communication.
   C. Keep vertical lines of communication open.
   D. Create a culture that supports formal communication.
   E. Nothing; attempts to eliminate the grapevine are fruitless.

10. Mark recently met one of the nation's leading experts in interpersonal communication. The expert told Mark the single most important individual skill for improving communication effectiveness is

   A. documenting all communication.
   B. being a good listener.
   C. allowing subordinates to participate in decision making.
   D. following up on sent messages.
   E. keeping meetings brief.

Managing Work Groups and Teams

chapter 19

FIRST THINGS FIRST

Teamwork for the Tampa Bay Devil Rays

"'What do these kids know? . . . How much baseball will they grasp?' I say, give them a chance."
—DON ZIMMER, SENIOR ADVISOR AND COACH,
TAMPA BAY DEVIL RAYS

In 2004, Andrew Friedman spent his days sitting behind a desk at a private equity firm in New Jersey and his nights online, playing fantasy baseball. Today, he is living his fantasy as executive vice president with the Tampa Bay Devil Rays. Friedman is part of an innovative leadership team at the struggling Devil Rays. The new management team, headed by a former Goldman Sachs executive, recruited its members from the rising-star personnel of investments firms. Team members have a thorough grasp of financial markets and decades of collective experience applying that knowledge in a practical way. But can Wall-Street-style teamwork fix a troubled sports team?

It began with Stuart Sternberg, a partner who managed options trading for a New York firm. Sternberg, who loved baseball as a child, learned that the Rays were up for sale. At first glance the Rays, who are ranked last in Major League Baseball with a value of $176 million, seemed hopeless. Fans didn't turn out for games, the stadium was unattractive, and management was weak.

LEARNING OBJECTIVES

After studying this chapter, you should be able to:

1. Define and identify types of groups and teams in organizations, discuss reasons why people join groups and teams, and list the stages of group and team development.

2. Identify and discuss four essential characteristics of groups and teams.

3. Discuss interpersonal and intergroup conflict in organizations.

4. Describe how organizations manage conflict.

A new management team is attempting to improve the Tampa Bay Devil Rays' performance both on and off the field.

Yet Sternberg was intrigued. "I'm a buy-low guy, and if you pay the right price for something, I don't care what it is, you can't go very wrong," he says. Sternberg and five former colleagues paid $48 million for 48 percent of the Devil Rays in 2004. General partner Vince Naimoli, who obtained the MLB franchise in 1995, owns an additional 15 percent. Limited partners, who have no management role, own the rest. In 2006, Naimoli stepped aside, giving management control to Sternberg and his team.

Sternberg's vision is a complete transformation of every aspect of team management. He wants to upgrade Tropicana Park, more tightly control costs, cultivate a deep roster of young talent, and perhaps even change the team's nickname and colors. To do that, he enlisted the help of a protégé, Matthew Silverman. Silverman, also a childhood baseball geek, worked with Sternberg at Goldman Sachs. The 29-year-old was named president of the Tampa Bay team, with responsibility for managing team finances and operations. Rounding out the team is Friedman, also 29, in charge of managing players.

The team is young and inexperienced in baseball management, although clearly intelligent and knowledgeable about finance. Yet Sternberg does not think this poses a problem. He says, "On Wall Street, you want younger, hungry people." The Rays are ready to take risks and everything is under review. "We love where we are right now," says Sternberg, "[but] we'll look at anything that might be more appealing. . . . If somebody knocks our socks off, . . . we're going there."

In Sternberg's view, other teams' managers might be more willing to negotiate with Friedman over player trades, for example, because they are less intimidated by him than by older, more famous team managers. Tampa players, including catcher Toby Hall, like what the new team has done so far. "Obviously I liked what Sternberg said: They don't fail," says Hall.

The trio are very close, joking around more like fraternity brothers than professional colleagues. A *New York Times* journalist writes, "There is a distinct boys-club feel to the slap-happy camaraderie that binds Mr. Sternberg to his two young executives. It mixes the testosterone of the Wall Street trading floor with the geekiness of those who spend an inordinate amount of time breaking down earned-run averages."

Sternberg, Silverman, and Friedman plan to manage the team like an investments portfolio. Friedman says, "I am purely market driven. I love players I think I can get for less than they are worth. It's positive arbitrage, the valuation asymmetry in the game." Friedman is a believer in "mark-to-market" accounting, in which an asset is valued at its current market price, not the price originally or currently paid for it. For example, Friedman thinks that pitcher Scott Kazmir, who earns just $370,000, is worth $7 million annually to the team. Using mark-to-market, Friedman values the Devil Rays' payroll at $50 million, about 50 percent more than its actual value of $35 million.

Clearly, Friedman talks and thinks like the Harvard-trained economist that he is. At times, he and the other New Yorkers conflict with the rest of the team's staff, who take a more traditional approach. Don Zimmer, a senior coach with 57 years' experience in baseball, doesn't use economic models when evaluating players. He often disagrees with Friedman, but is taking a wait-and-see approach. "People say to me, 'What do these kids know? They look like they are 20 years old. How much baseball will they grasp?'" Zimmer says. "I say, give them a chance."[1]

Andrew Friedman, Stuart Sternberg, and Matthew Silverman are working together as a team. And their goal is to enhance the performance of another team, the Tampa Bay Devil Rays professional baseball franchise. Each member of the management team clearly recognizes the importance of teamwork in organizations. They know, for instance, that if the team is poorly managed it will not succeed. They also recognize that if they do their jobs effectively, then the team will become increasingly competitive.

This chapter is about processes that lead to and follow from activities like those at the Tampa Bay Devil Rays. In our last chapter we established the interpersonal nature of organizations. We extend that discussion here by first introducing basic concepts of group and team dynamics. Subsequent sections explain the characteristics of groups and teams in organizations. We then describe interpersonal and intergroup conflict. Finally, we conclude with a discussion of how conflict can be managed.

Groups and Teams in Organizations

Groups are a ubiquitous part of organizational life. They are the basis for much of the work that gets done, and they evolve both inside and outside the normal structural boundaries of the organization. We will define a ***group*** as two or more people who interact regularly to accomplish a common purpose or goal.[2] The purpose of a group or team may range from preparing a new advertising campaign, to informally sharing information, to making important decisions, to fulfilling social needs.

group
Consists of two or more people who interact regularly to accomplish a common purpose or goal

Types of Groups and Teams

In general, three basic kinds of groups are found in organizations—functional groups, informal or interest groups, and task groups and teams.[3] These are illustrated in Figure 19.1.

A task group is one that is created by the organization to accomplish a relatively narrow range of purposes within a stated or implied time horizon. In the aftermath of the crash of the space shuttle Columbia, numerous task groups were assembled to collect debris, analyze information, and attempt to determine what went wrong. This team, for instance, is working on debris from the wreckage in a hangar at Cape Canaveral. By attempting to reconstruct sections of the shuttle, the team hopes to develop new methods for avoiding future disasters.

Figure 19.1
TYPES OF GROUPS IN ORGANIZATIONS

Every organization has many different types of groups. In this hypothetical organization, a functional group is shown within the purple area, a cross-functional team within the yellow area, and an informal group within the green area.

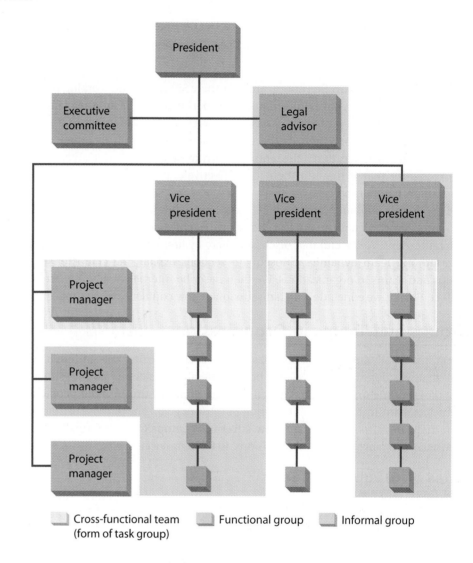

Cross-functional team (form of task group)   Functional group   Informal group

---

functional group
A permanent group created by the organization to accomplish a number of organizational purposes with an unspecified time horizon

Functional Groups A ***functional group*** is a permanent group created by the organization to accomplish a number of organizational purposes with an unspecified time horizon. The advertising department at Target, the management department at the University of North Texas, and the nursing staff at the Mayo Clinic are functional groups. The advertising department at Target, for example, seeks to plan effective advertising campaigns, increase sales, run in-store promotions, and develop a unique identity for the company. It is assumed that the functional group will remain in existence after it attains its current objectives—those objectives will be replaced by new ones.

informal or interest group
Created by its members for purposes that may or may not be relevant to those of the organization

Informal or Interest Groups An ***informal or interest group*** is created by its own members for purposes that may or may not be relevant to organizational goals. It also has an unspecified time horizon. A group of employees who lunch together every day may be discussing productivity, money embezzling, or local politics and sports. As long as the group members enjoy eating together, they will probably continue to do so. When lunches cease to be pleasant, they will seek other company or a different activity.

Informal groups can be a powerful force that managers cannot ignore.[4] One writer described how a group of employees at a furniture factory subverted their boss's efforts to increase production. They tacitly agreed to produce a reasonable amount of work but not to work too hard. One man kept a stockpile of completed work hidden as a backup in case he got too far behind. In another example, auto workers described how they left out gaskets and seals and put soft-drink bottles inside doors.[5] Of course, informal groups can also be a positive force, as demonstrated recently when Continental Airlines employees worked together to buy a new motorcycle for Gordon Bethune, the company's CEO, to show their support and gratitude for his excellent leadership.

In recent years the Internet has served as a platform for the emergence of more and different kinds of informal or interest groups. Just as one example, Yahoo! includes a wide array of interest groups that bring together people with common interests. And increasingly workers who lose their jobs as a result of layoffs are banding together electronically to offer moral support to one another and to facilitate networking as they all look for new jobs.[6]

Task Groups A ***task group*** is a group created by the organization to accomplish a relatively narrow range of purposes within a stated or implied time horizon. Most committees and task forces are task groups. The organization specifies group membership and assigns a relatively narrow set of goals, such as developing a new product or evaluating a proposed grievance procedure. The time horizon for accomplishing these purposes is either specified (a committee may be asked to make a recommendation within 60 days) or implied (the project team will disband when the new product is developed).

> **task group**
> A group created by the organization to accomplish a relatively narrow range of purposes within a stated or implied time horizon

Teams are a special form of task group that have become increasingly popular.[7] In the sense used here, a ***team*** is a group of workers that functions as a unit, often with little or no supervision, to carry out work-related tasks, functions, and activities. Table 19.1 lists and defines some of the various types of teams that are being used today. Earlier forms of teams included autonomous work groups and quality circles. Today, teams are also sometimes called "self-managed teams," "cross-functional teams," or "high-performance teams." Many firms today are routinely using teams to carry out most of their daily operations.[8]

> **team**
> A group of workers that functions as a unit, often with little or no supervision, to carry out work-related tasks, functions, and activities

Organizations create teams for a variety of reasons. For one thing, they give more responsibility for task performance to the workers who are actually performing the tasks. They also empower workers by giving them greater authority and

Problem-Solving Team Most popular type of team; comprises knowledge workers who gather to solve a specific problem and then disband

Management Team Consists mainly of managers from various functions like sales and production; coordinates work among other teams

Work Team An increasingly popular type of team; work teams are responsible for the daily work of the organization; when empowered, they are self-managed teams

Virtual Team A new type of work team that interacts by computer; members enter and leave the network as needed and may take turns serving as leader

Quality Circle Declining in popularity, quality circles, comprising workers and supervisors, meet intermittently to discuss workplace problems

Source: From *Fortune*, September 5, 2004. Copyright © 2004 Time Inc. All rights reserved.

Table 19.1
TYPES OF TEAMS

decision-making freedom. In addition, they allow the organization to capitalize on the knowledge and motivation of their workers. Finally, they enable the organization to shed its bureaucracy and to promote flexibility and responsiveness. Ford used teams to design its new Thunderbird and Focus models. Similarly, General Motors used a team to develop its new model of the Chevrolet Blazer.

When an organization decides to use teams, it is essentially implementing a major form of organization change, as discussed in Chapter 13. Thus it is important to follow a logical and systematic approach to planning and implementing teams in an existing organization design. It is also important to recognize that resistance may be encountered. This resistance is most likely from first-line managers who will be giving up much of their authority to the team. Many organizations find that they must change the whole management philosophy of such managers away from being a supervisor to being a coach or facilitator.[9]

After teams are in place, managers should continue to monitor their contributions and how effectively they are functioning. In the best circumstances, teams will become very cohesive groups with high performance norms. To achieve this state, the manager can use any or all of the techniques described later in this chapter for enhancing cohesiveness. If implemented properly, and with the support of the workers themselves, performance norms will likely be relatively high. In other words, if the change is properly implemented, the team participants will understand the value and potential of teams and the rewards they may expect to get as a result of their contributions. On the other hand, poorly designed and implemented teams will do a less effective job and may detract from organizational effectiveness.[10]

> **"**If a team can't be fed by two pizzas, it's too large.**"**
>
> Jeff Bezos, founder and CEO of Amazon.com
> (*Fortune,* June 12, 2006, p. 122)

People join groups for a variety of reasons. Members of a classic boat club are decked out in pink-flamingo hats as they participate in the opening day boat parade held in conjunction with the annual Windermere Cup race in Seattle, WA. They joined the club because they enjoy boating and love classic boats. They also use things like the flamingo hats to promote group identity and to build camaraderie.

Why People Join Groups and Teams

People join groups and teams for a variety of reasons. They join functional groups simply by virtue of joining organizations. People accept employment to earn money or to practice their chosen professions. Once inside the organization, they are assigned to jobs and roles and thus become members of functional groups. People in existing functional groups are told, are asked, or volunteer to serve on committees, task forces, and teams. People join informal or interest groups for a variety of reasons, most of them quite complex.[11] Indeed, the need to be a team player has grown so strong today that many organizations will actively resist hiring someone who does not want to work with others.[12]

Interpersonal Attraction One reason why people choose to form informal or interest groups is that they are attracted to one another. Many different factors contribute to interpersonal attraction. When people see a lot of each other, pure proximity increases the likelihood that interpersonal attraction will develop. Attraction is increased when people have similar attitudes, personalities, or economic standings.

Group Activities   Individuals may also be motivated to join a group because the activities of the group appeal to them. Jogging, playing bridge, bowling, discussing poetry, playing war games, and flying model airplanes are all activities that some people enjoy. Many of them are more enjoyable to participate in as a member of a group, and most require more than one person. Many large firms like Shell Oil and Apple Computer have a football, softball, or bowling league. A person may join a bowling team, not because of any noticeable attraction to other group members, but simply because being a member of the group allows that person to participate in a pleasant activity. Of course, if the group's level of interpersonal attraction is very low, a person may choose to forgo the activity rather than join the group.

Group Goals   The goals of a group may also motivate people to join. The Sierra Club, which is dedicated to environmental conservation, is a good example of this kind of interest group. Various fund-raising groups are another illustration. Members may or may not be personally attracted to the other fundraisers, and they probably do not enjoy the activity of knocking on doors asking for money, but they join the group because they subscribe to its goal. Workers join unions like the United Auto Workers because they support its goals.

> "Give us people who are dedicated to making the team work, as opposed to a bunch of talented people with big egos, and we'll win every time."
>
> John McConnell, CEO of Worthington Industries
> (*Fortune*, June 12, 2006, p. 88)

Need Satisfaction   Still another reason for joining a group is to satisfy the need for affiliation. New residents in a community may join the Newcomers Club partially as a way to meet new people and partially just to be around other people. Likewise, newly divorced people often join support groups as a way to have companionship.

Instrumental Benefits   A final reason why people join groups is that membership is sometimes seen as instrumental in providing other benefits to the individual. For example, it is fairly common for college students entering their senior year to join several professional clubs or associations because listing such memberships on a résumé is thought to enhance the chances of getting a good job. Similarly, a manager might join a certain racquet club not because she is attracted to its members (although she might be) and not because of the opportunity to play tennis (although she may enjoy it). The club's goals are not relevant, and her affiliation needs may be satisfied in other ways. However, she may feel that being a member of this club will lead to important and useful business contacts. The racquet club membership is instrumental in establishing those contacts. Membership in civic groups such as the Junior League and Rotary may be solicited for similar reasons.

Stages of Group and Team Development

Imagine the differences between a collection of five people who have just been brought together to form a group or team and a group or team that has functioned like a well-oiled machine for years. Members of a new group or team are unfamiliar with how they will function together and are tentative in their interactions. In a group or team with considerable experience, members are familiar with one another's strengths and weaknesses and are more secure in their roles in the group. The former

Figure 19.2
STAGES OF GROUP DEVELOPMENT

As groups mature, they tend to evolve through four distinct stages of development. Managers must understand that group members need time to become acquainted, accept one another, develop a group structure, and become comfortable with their roles in the group before they can begin to work directly to accomplish goals.

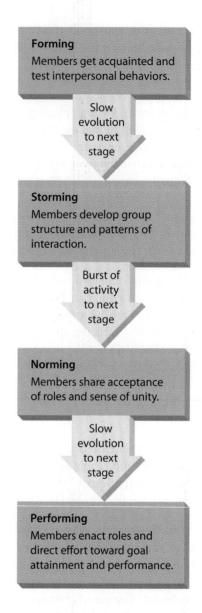

group or team is generally considered to be immature; the latter, mature. To progress from the immature phase to the mature phase, a group or team must go through certain stages of development, as shown in Figure 19.2.[13]

The first stage of development is called *forming*. The members of the group or team get acquainted and begin to test which interpersonal behaviors are acceptable and which are unacceptable to the other members. The members are very dependent on others at this point to provide cues about what is acceptable. The basic ground rules for the group or team are established, and a tentative group structure may emerge.[14] At Reebok, for example, a merchandising team was created to handle its sportswear business. The team leader and his members were barely acquainted and had to spend a few weeks getting to know one another.

The second stage of development, often slow to emerge, is *storming*. During this stage, there may be a general lack of unity and uneven interaction patterns. At the same time, some members of the group or team may begin to exert themselves to become recognized as the group leader or at least to play a major role in shaping the group's agenda. In Reebok's team, some members advocated a rapid expansion into the marketplace; others argued for a slower entry. The first faction won, with disastrous results. Because of the rush, product quality was poor and deliveries were late. As a result, the team leader was fired and a new manager placed in charge.

The third stage of development, called *norming*, usually begins with a burst of activity. During this stage, each person begins to recognize and accept her or his role and to understand the roles of others. Members also begin to accept one another and to develop a sense of unity. There may also be temporary regressions to the previous stage. For example, the group or team might begin to accept one particular member as the leader. If this person later violates important norms or otherwise jeopardizes his or her claim to leadership, conflict might reemerge as the group rejects this leader and searches for another. Reebok's new leader transferred several people away from the team and set up a new system and structure for managing things. The remaining employees accepted his new approach and settled into doing their jobs.

Performing, the final stage of group or team development, is also slow to develop. The team really begins to focus on the problem at hand. The members enact the roles they have accepted, interaction occurs, and the efforts of the group are directed toward goal attainment. The basic structure of the group or team is no longer an issue but has become a mechanism for accomplishing the purpose of the group. Reebok's sportswear business is now growing consistently and has successfully avoided the problems that plagued it at first.

---

concept
CHECK

What are the basic types of groups and teams in organizations?

Identify four groups that you belong to and describe why you joined each one.

Characteristics of Groups and Teams

As groups and teams mature and pass through the four basic stages of development, they begin to take on four important characteristics—a role structure, norms, cohesiveness, and informal leadership.[15]

Role Structures

Each individual in a team has a part, or **role**, to play in helping the group reach its goals. Some people are leaders, some do the work, some interface with other teams, and so on. Indeed, a person may take on a *task specialist role* (concentrating on getting the group's task accomplished) or a *socioemotional role* (providing social and emotional support to others on the team). A few people, usually the leaders, perform both roles; a few others may do neither. The group's **role structure** is the set of defined roles and interrelationships among those roles that the group or team members define and accept. Each of us belongs to many groups and therefore plays multiple roles—in work groups, classes, families, and social organizations.[16]

Role structures emerge as a result of role episodes, as shown in Figure 19.3. The process begins with the expected role—what other members of the team expect the individual to do. The expected role gets translated into the sent role—the messages and cues that team members use to communicate the expected role to the individual.

roles
The parts individuals play in groups in helping the group reach its goals

role structure
The set of defined roles and interrelationships among those roles that the group members define and accept

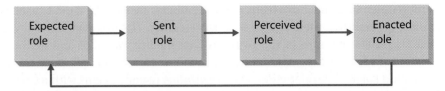

Figure 19.3
THE DEVELOPMENT OF A ROLE

Roles and role structures within a group generally evolve through a series of role episodes. The first two stages of role development are group processes, as the group members let individuals know what is expected of them. The other two parts are individual processes, as the new group members perceive and enact their roles.

The perceived role is what the individual perceives the sent role to mean. Finally, the enacted role is what the individual actually does in the role. The enacted role, in turn, influences future expectations of the team. Of course, role episodes seldom unfold this easily. When major disruptions occur, individuals may experience role ambiguity, conflict, or overload.[17]

> **role ambiguity**
> Arises when the sent role is unclear and the individual does not know what is expected of him or her

Role Ambiguity *Role ambiguity* arises when the sent role is unclear. If your instructor tells you to write a term paper but refuses to provide more information, you will probably experience role ambiguity. You do not know what the topic is, how long the paper should be, what format to use, or when the paper is due. In work settings, role ambiguity can stem from poor job descriptions, vague instructions from a supervisor, or unclear cues from coworkers. The result is likely to be a subordinate who does not know what to do. Role ambiguity can be a significant problem for both the individual who must contend with it and the organization that expects the employee to perform.

> **role conflict**
> Occurs when the messages and cues composing the sent role are clear but contradictory or mutually exclusive

Role Conflict *Role conflict* occurs when the messages and cues composing the sent role are clear but contradictory or mutually exclusive.[18] One common form is *interrole conflict*—conflict between roles. For example, if a person's boss says that one must work overtime and on weekends to get ahead, and the same person's spouse says that more time is needed at home with the family, conflict may result. In a matrix organization, interrole conflict often arises between the roles one plays in different teams as well as between team roles and one's permanent role in a functional group.

Intrarole conflict may occur when the person gets conflicting demands from different sources within the context of the same role. A manager's boss may tell her that she needs to put more pressure on subordinates to follow new work rules. At the same time, her subordinates may indicate that they expect her to get the rules changed. Thus the cues are in conflict, and the manager may be unsure about which course to follow. *Intrasender conflict* occurs when a single source sends clear but contradictory messages. This might arise if the boss says one morning that there can be no more overtime for the next month but after lunch tells someone to work late that same evening. *Person-role conflict* results from a discrepancy between the role requirements and the individual's personal values, attitudes, and needs. If a person is told to do something unethical or illegal, or if the work is distasteful (for example, firing a close friend), person-role conflict is likely. Role conflict of all varieties is of particular concern to managers. Research has shown that conflict may occur in a variety of situations and lead to a variety of adverse consequences, including stress, poor performance, and rapid turnover.

Role Overload   A final consequence of a weak role structure is ***role overload***, which occurs when expectations for the role exceed the individual's capabilities. When a manager gives an employee several major assignments at once, while increasing the person's regular workload, the employee will probably experience role overload. Role overload may also result when an individual takes on too many roles at one time. For example, a person trying to work extra hard at work, run for election to the school board, serve on a committee in church, coach Little League baseball, maintain an active exercise program, and be a contributing member to her or his family will probably encounter role overload.

> *role overload*
> Occurs when expectations for the role exceed the individual's capabilities to perform

In a functional group or team, the manager can take steps to avoid role ambiguity, conflict, and overload. Having clear and reasonable expectations and sending clear and straightforward cues go a long way toward eliminating role ambiguity. Consistent expectations that take into account the employee's other roles and personal value system may minimize role conflict. Role overload can be avoided simply by recognizing the individual's capabilities and limits. In friendship and interest groups, role structures are likely to be less formal; hence, the possibility of role ambiguity, conflict, or overload may not be so great. However, if one or more of these problems does occur, they may be difficult to handle. Because roles in friendship and interest groups are less likely to be partially defined by a formal authority structure or written job descriptions, the individual cannot turn to those sources to clarify a role.

> "Some of the worst teams I've ever seen have been those where everybody was a potential CEO."
>
> David Nadler, consultant
> (*Fortune*, June 12, 2006, p. 88)

Behavioral Norms

Norms are standards of behavior that the group or team accepts for and expects of its members. Most committees, for example, develop norms governing their discussions. A person who talks too much is perceived as doing so to make a good impression or to get his or her own way. Other members may not talk much to this person, may not sit nearby, may glare at the person, and may otherwise "punish" the individual for violating the norm. Norms, then, define the boundaries between acceptable and unacceptable behavior.[19] Some groups develop norms that limit the upper bounds of behavior to "make life easier" for the group—for example, do not make more than two comments in a committee discussion or do not produce any more than you have to. In general, these norms are counterproductive. Other groups may develop norms that limit the lower bounds of behavior—for example, do not come to meetings unless you have read the reports to be discussed or produce as much as you can. These norms tend to reflect motivation, commitment, and high performance. Managers can sometimes use norms for the betterment of the organization. For example, Kodak has successfully used group norms to reduce injuries in some of its plants.[20] *The Business of Ethics* discusses another instance where norms can affect unethical behavior in team settings.

> *norms*
> Standards of behavior that the group accepts for and expects of its members

Norm Generalization   The norms of one group cannot always be generalized to another group. Some academic departments, for example, have a norm that suggests that faculty members dress up on teaching days. People who fail to observe

The Business of Ethics

MBAs: Team Players or Ambitious Rivals?

About 300 universities in the United States offer a Master of Business Administration (MBA) degree. MBA-granting institutions, or B-schools, emphasize three sets of skills: business skills; quantitative or "hard" skills; and people or "soft" skills, which can include leadership, ethics, and teamwork. Businesses increasingly rely on groups and teams, so it seems obvious that business leaders need to be team players. However, graduate schools of business are competitive places. Many MBA seekers see, and demonstrate, plenty of self-serving and unethical actions.

Among the problematic behaviors are refusing to share notes with classmates, removing required readings from the library, and spreading false rumors. One MBA admits, "Before an exam, I would ask students a nonsense question like, 'What's the Dr. Seuss Method of stock valuation?' They spent their last minutes in a panic, leafing frantically through notes, while I remained confident." This MBA, like many others, put her own interests ahead of the team's.

Kerry Patterson, an MBA professor, blames the organizational culture. "Teams of students are brutal to each other. Calling a group of students a team doesn't make them one," Patterson explains. He believes the typical university environment discourages team activities. "Professors work in a system that discourages collaboration and teamwork. . . . University faculties are just a little more cohesive than six people who just met in an elevator."

To reduce the temptation to act unethically, some B-schools do not disclose grades. Professors at these schools hope reducing grade pressure will improve collaboration. Harvard, a top MBA program, only discloses categories of achievement: the top 20 percent, the middle 70 percent, and the bottom 10 percent. Teamwork proponents believe the system decreases competition, but there is no factual evidence. Moreover, some educators feel the nongraded courses encourage laziness and diminish academic rigor.

A small but growing group of experts believes that an overemphasis on teamwork may teach students to seek social acceptance and popularity over honesty and effectiveness. Steve Spurrier, a successful football coach, claims, "If people like you too much, it's probably because they're beating you."

On the other hand, unethical tactics should not be tolerated. MBAs must find a way to balance ambition and acceptance in a competitive environment, without resorting to unethical measures.

References: Grant Allen, "Learning to Juggle," *BusinessWeek*, February 24, 2006, www.businessweek.com on May 20, 2006; Jeffrey Gangemi, "Harvard: No More Grade Secrets," *BusinessWeek*, December 16, 2005, www.businessweek.com on May 20, 2006; Jeffrey Gangemi, "Taking on the 'Cutthroat Culture' of B-School," *BusinessWeek*, May 17, 2006, www.businessweek.com on May 20, 2006; Jeffrey Pfeffer, "You Don't Have to Be Well Liked to Succeed," *Business 2.0*, May 16, 2006, www.cnnmoney.com on May 20, 2006.

this norm are "punished" by sarcastic remarks or even formal reprimands. In other departments, the norm may be casual clothes, and the person unfortunate enough to wear dress clothes may be punished just as vehemently. Even within the same work area, similar groups or teams can develop different norms. One team may strive always to produce above its assigned quota; another may maintain productivity just below its quota. The norm of one team may be to be friendly and cordial to its supervisor; that of another team may be to remain aloof and distant. Some differences are due primarily to the composition of the teams.

Norm Variation   In some cases, there can also be norm variation within a group or team. A common norm is that the least senior member of a group is expected to perform unpleasant or trivial tasks for the rest of the group. These tasks might be to wait on customers who are known to be small tippers (in a restaurant), to deal with complaining customers (in a department store), or to handle the low-commission line of merchandise (in a sales department). Another example is when certain individuals, especially informal leaders, may violate some norms. If the team is going to meet at 8:00 A.M., anyone arriving late will be chastised for holding things up. Occasionally, however, the informal leader may arrive a few minutes late. As long as this does not happen too often, the group probably will not do anything about it.

Norm Conformity   Four sets of factors contribute to norm conformity. First, factors associated with the group are important. For example, some groups or teams may exert more pressure for conformity than others. Second, the initial stimulus that prompts behavior can affect conformity. The more ambiguous the stimulus (for example, news that the team is going to be transferred to a new unit), the more pressure there is to conform. Third, individual traits determine the individual's propensity to conform (for example, more intelligent people are often less susceptible to pressure to conform). Finally, situational factors, such as team size and unanimity, influence conformity. As an individual learns the group's norms, he can do several different things. The most obvious is to adopt the norms. For example, the new male professor who notices that all the other men in the department dress up to teach can also start wearing a suit. A variation is to try to obey the "spirit" of the norm while retaining individuality. The professor may recognize that the norm is actually to wear a tie; thus he might succeed by wearing a tie with his sport shirt, jeans, and sneakers.

The individual may also ignore the norm. When a person does not conform, several things can happen. At first the group may increase its communication with the deviant individual to try to bring her back in line. If this does not work, communication may decline. Over time, the group may begin to exclude the individual from its activities and, in effect, ostracize the person. Finally, we need to briefly consider another aspect of norm conformity—socialization. **Socialization** is generalized norm conformity that occurs as a person makes the transition from being an outsider to being an insider. A newcomer to an organization, for example, gradually begins to learn about such norms as dress, working hours, and interpersonal relations. As the newcomer adopts these norms, she is being socialized into the organizational culture. Some organizations, like Texas Instruments, work to actively manage the socialization process; others leave it to happenstance.

Cohesiveness

A third important team characteristic is cohesiveness. **Cohesiveness** is the extent to which members are loyal and committed to the group. In a highly cohesive team, the members work well together, support and trust one another, and are generally effective at achieving their chosen goals.[21] In contrast, a team that lacks cohesiveness is not very coordinated, its members do not necessarily support one another fully, and it may have a difficult time reaching

socialization
Generalized norm conformity that occurs as a person makes the transition from being an outsider to being an insider in the organization

cohesiveness
The extent to which members are loyal and committed to the group; the degree of mutual attractiveness within the group

Group cohesiveness can play an important role in organizational performance. As part of the infrastructure needed to host the 2012 Olympics, London is building several new rail links and train stations. A team of workers at the newly completed Stratford international station is shown here saluting fellow colleagues as they ride down a new section of track. The management team developed a strong bond as they worked long hours to get this part of the project completed ahead of schedule.

Table 19.2

FACTORS THAT INFLUENCE GROUP COHESIVENESS

Several different factors can influence the cohesiveness of a group. For example, a manager can establish intergroup competition, assign compatible members to the group, create opportunities for success, establish acceptable goals, and foster interaction to increase cohesiveness. Other factors can be used to decrease cohesiveness.

Factors That Increase Cohesiveness	Factors That Reduce Cohesiveness
Intergroup competition	Group size
Personal attraction	Disagreement on goals
Favorable evaluation	Intragroup competition
Agreement on goals	Domination
Interaction	Unpleasant experiences

goals. Of particular interest are the factors that increase and reduce cohesiveness and the consequences of team cohesiveness. These are listed in Table 19.2.

Factors That Increase Cohesiveness   Five factors can increase the level of cohesiveness in a group or team. One of the strongest is intergroup competition. When two or more groups are in direct competition (for example, three sales groups competing for top sales honors or two football teams competing for a conference championship), each group is likely to become more cohesive. Second, just as personal attraction plays a role in causing a group to form, so, too, does attraction seem to enhance cohesiveness. Third, favorable evaluation of the entire group by outsiders can increase cohesiveness. Thus a group's winning a sales contest or a conference title or receiving recognition and praise from a superior tends to increase cohesiveness.

Similarly, if all the members of the group or team agree on their goals, cohesiveness is likely to increase.[22] And the more frequently members of the group interact with one another, the more likely the group is to become cohesive. A manager who wants to foster a high level of cohesiveness in a team might do well to establish some form of intergroup competition, assign members to the group who are likely to be attracted to one another, provide opportunities for success, establish goals that all members are likely to accept, and allow ample opportunities for interaction.

Factors That Reduce Cohesiveness   There are also five factors that are known to reduce team cohesiveness. First of all, cohesiveness tends to decline as a group increases in size. Second, when members of a team disagree on what the goals of the group should be, cohesiveness may decrease. For example, when some members believe the group should maximize output and others think output should be restricted, cohesiveness declines. Third, intragroup competition reduces cohesiveness. When members are competing among themselves, they focus more on their own actions and behaviors than on those of the group.

Fourth, domination by one or more persons in the group or team may cause overall cohesiveness to decline. Other members may feel that they are not being given an opportunity to interact and contribute, and they may become less attracted to the group as a consequence. Finally, unpleasant experiences that result from group membership may reduce cohesiveness. A sales group that comes in last in a sales contest, an athletic team that sustains a long losing streak, and a work group reprimanded for poor-quality work may all become less cohesive as a result of their unpleasant experiences.

Consequences of Cohesiveness   In general, as teams become more cohesive, their members tend to interact more frequently, conform more to norms, and become more satisfied with the team. Cohesiveness may also influence team

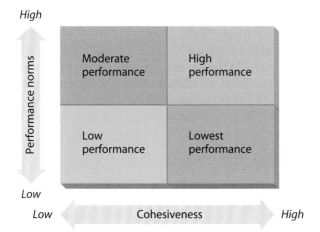

Figure 19.4

THE INTERACTION BETWEEN COHESIVENESS AND PERFORMANCE NORMS

Group cohesiveness and performance norms interact to determine group performance. From the manager's perspective, high cohesiveness combined with high performance norms is the best situation, and high cohesiveness with low performance norms is the worst situation. Managers who can influence the level of cohesiveness and performance norms can greatly improve the effectiveness of a work group.

performance. However, performance is also influenced by the team's performance norms. Figure 19.4 shows how cohesiveness and performance norms interact to help shape team performance.

When both cohesiveness and performance norms are high, high performance should result because the team wants to perform at a high level (norms) and its members are working together toward that end (cohesiveness). When norms are high and cohesiveness is low, performance will be moderate. Although the team wants to perform at a high level, its members are not necessarily working well together. When norms are low, performance will be low, regardless of whether group cohesiveness is high or low. The least desirable situation occurs when low performance norms are combined with high cohesiveness. In this case, all team members embrace the standard of restricting performance (owing to the low performance norm), and the group is united in its efforts to maintain that standard (owing to the high cohesiveness). If cohesiveness were low, the manager might be able to raise performance norms by establishing high goals and rewarding goal attainment or by bringing in new group members who are high performers. But a highly cohesive group is likely to resist these interventions.[23]

Formal and Informal Leadership

Most functional groups and teams have a formal leader—that is, one appointed by the organization or chosen or elected by the members of the group. Because friendship and interest groups are formed by the members themselves, however, any formal leader must be elected or designated by the members. Although some groups do designate such a leader (a softball team may elect a captain, for example), many do not. Moreover, even when a formal leader is designated, the group or team may also look to others for leadership. An ***informal leader*** is a person who engages in leadership activities but whose right to do so has not been formally recognized. The formal and the informal leader in any group or team may be the same person, or they may be different people. We noted earlier the distinction between the task specialist and socioemotional roles within groups. An informal leader is likely to be a person capable of carrying out both roles effectively. If the formal leader can fulfill one role but not the other, an informal leader often emerges to supplement the formal leader's functions. If the formal leader can fill neither role, one or more informal leaders may emerge to carry out both sets of functions.

informal leader
A person who engages in leadership activities but whose right to do so has not been formally recognized by the organization or group

Is informal leadership desirable? In many cases informal leaders are quite powerful because they draw from referent or expert power. When they are working in the best interests of the organization, they can be a tremendous asset. Notable athletes like Brett Favre and Mia Hamm are classic examples of informal leaders. However, when informal leaders work counter to the goals of the organization, they can cause significant difficulties. Such leaders may lower performance norms, instigate walkouts or wildcat strikes, or otherwise disrupt the organization.

concept
CHECK

| Identify and describe the fundamental characteristics of groups and teams. | Assume you were assigned to manage a highly cohesive group with low performance norms. What would you do to try to change things? |

Interpersonal and Intergroup Conflict

Of course, when people work together in an organization, things do not always go smoothly. Indeed, conflict is an inevitable element of interpersonal relationships in organizations. In this section, we look at how conflict affects overall performance. We also explore the causes of conflict between individuals, between groups, and between an organization and its environment.

The Nature of Conflict

> **conflict**
> A disagreement among two or more individuals or groups

Conflict is a disagreement among two or more individuals, groups, or organizations. This disagreement may be relatively superficial or very strong. It may be short-lived or exist for months or even years, and it may be work related or personal. Conflict may manifest itself in a variety of ways. People may compete with one another, glare at one another, shout, or withdraw. Groups may band together to protect popular members or oust unpopular members. Organizations may seek legal remedies.

Most people assume that conflict is something to be avoided because it connotes antagonism, hostility, unpleasantness, and dissension. Indeed, managers and management theorists have traditionally viewed conflict as a problem to be avoided.[24] In recent years, however, we have come to recognize that, although conflict can be a major problem, certain kinds of conflict may also be beneficial.[25] For example, when two members of a site selection committee disagree over the best location for a new plant, each may be forced to more thoroughly study and defend his or her preferred alternative. As a result of more systematic analysis and discussion, the committee may make a better

Conflict can be very disruptive in an organization. These striking service workers and supporters march at the University of Miami in Coral Gables, Florida. About a quarter of the 425 janitors and other contract workers employed at the university went on strike over alleged unfair labor practices. They want to form a union, but their employer has fought their organizing tactics. Such strong conflict may affect relations between the organization and its workers for years.

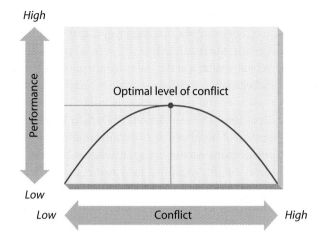

Figure 19.5

THE NATURE OF ORGANIZATIONAL CONFLICT

Either too much or too little conflict can be dysfunctional for an organization. In either case, performance may be low. However, an optimal level of conflict that sparks motivation, creativity, innovation, and initiative can result in higher levels of performance.

decision and be better prepared to justify it to others than if everyone had agreed from the outset and accepted an alternative that was perhaps less well analyzed.

As long as conflict is being handled in a cordial and constructive manner, it is probably serving a useful purpose in the organization. On the other hand, when working relationships are being disrupted and the conflict has reached destructive levels, it has likely become dysfunctional and needs to be addressed.[26] We discuss ways of dealing with such conflict later in this chapter.

Figure 19.5 depicts the general relationship between conflict and performance for a group or organization. If there is absolutely no conflict in the group or organization, its members may become complacent and apathetic. As a result, group or organizational performance and innovation may begin to suffer. A moderate level of conflict among group or organizational members, on the other hand, can spark motivation, creativity, innovation, and initiative, and raise performance. Too much conflict, though, can produce such undesirable results as hostility and lack of cooperation, which lower performance. The key for managers is to find and maintain the optimal amount of conflict that fosters performance. Of course, what constitutes optimal conflict varies with both the situation and the people involved.[27]

Causes of Conflict

Conflict may arise in both interpersonal and intergroup relationships. Occasionally conflict between individuals and groups may be caused by particular organizational strategies and practices. A third arena for conflict is between an organization and its environment.

Interpersonal Conflict   Conflict between two or more individuals is almost certain to occur in any organization, given the great variety in perceptions, goals, attitudes, and so forth among its members. William Gates, founder and CEO of Microsoft, and Kazuhiko Nishi, a former business associate from Japan, ended a long-term business relationship because of interpersonal conflict. Nishi accused Gates of becoming too political, while Gates charged that Nishi became too unpredictable and erratic in his behavior.[28]

A frequent source of interpersonal conflict in organizations is what many people call a "personality clash"—when two people distrust each other's motives, dislike each other, or for some other reason simply cannot get along.[29] Conflict may also arise between people who have different beliefs or perceptions about some aspect of their work or their organization. For example, one manager might want the organization to require that all employees use Microsoft Office software, to promote standardization. Another manager might believe that a variety of software packages should be allowed, in order to recognize individuality. Similarly, a male manager may disagree with his female colleague over whether the organization is guilty of discriminating against women in promotion decisions. Defense Secretary Donald Rumsfeld frequently has conflicts with others because of his abrasive and confrontational style.[30]

Conflict can also result from excess competitiveness among individuals. Two people vying for the same job, for example, may resort to political behavior in an effort to gain an advantage. If either competitor sees the other's behavior as inappropriate, accusations are likely to result. Even after the "winner" of the job is determined, such conflict may continue to undermine interpersonal relationships, especially if the reasons given in selecting one candidate are ambiguous or open to alternative explanations. Robert Allen resigned as CEO of Delta Air Lines a few years ago because he disagreed with other key executives over how best to reduce the carrier's costs. After he began looking for a replacement for one of his rivals without the approval of the firm's board of directors, the resultant conflict and controversy left him no choice but to leave.[31] More recently, similar problems have plagued Boeing as its top executives have publicly disagreed over routine matters and sometimes gone to great lengths to make each other look bad.[32]

Intergroup Conflict   Conflict between two or more organizational groups is also quite common. For example, the members of a firm's marketing group may disagree with the production group over product quality and delivery schedules. Two sales groups may disagree over how to meet sales goals, and two groups of managers may have different ideas about how best to allocate organizational resources.

Many intergroup conflicts arise more from organizational causes than from interpersonal causes. In Chapter 11, we described three forms of group interdependence—pooled, sequential, and reciprocal. Just as increased interdependence makes coordination more difficult, it also increases the potential for conflict. For example, recall that in sequential interdependence, work is passed from one unit to another. Intergroup conflict may arise if the first group turns out too much work (the second group will fall behind), too little work (the second group will not meet its own goals), or poor-quality work.

At one J. C. Penney department store, conflict arose between stockroom employees and sales associates. The sales associates claimed that the stockroom employees were slow in delivering merchandise to the sales floor so that it could be priced and shelved. The stockroom employees, in turn, claimed that the sales associates were not giving them enough lead time to get the merchandise delivered and failed to understand that they had additional duties besides carrying merchandise to the sales floor.

Just like people, different departments often have different goals. Further, these goals may often be incompatible. A marketing goal of maximizing sales, achieved partially by offering many products in a wide variety of sizes, shapes, colors, and models, probably conflicts with a production goal of minimizing costs, achieved partially by long production runs of a few items. Reebok recently confronted this very situation. One group of managers wanted to introduce a new sportswear line as quickly as possible, but other managers wanted to expand more deliberately and cautiously. Because the two groups were not able to reconcile their differences effectively, conflict between the two factions led to quality problems and delivery delays that plagued the firm for months.

Competition for scarce resources can also lead to intergroup conflict. Most organizations—especially universities, hospitals, government agencies, and businesses in depressed industries—have limited resources. In one New England town, for example, the public works department and the library battled over funds from a federal construction grant. The Buick, Pontiac, and Chevrolet divisions of General Motors have frequently fought over the right to manufacture various new products developed by the company.

Conflict Between Organization and Environment   Conflict that arises between one organization and another is called *interorganizational conflict. Technology Toolkit* discusses a very timely example of such conflict. A moderate amount of interorganizational conflict resulting from business competition is expected, of course, but sometimes conflict becomes more extreme. For example, the owners of Jordache Enterprises, Inc., and Guess?, Inc., battled in court for years over ownership

Technology Toolkit
Blackberry's Battle

Unlike healthy competition, extreme interorganizational conflicts waste resources, constrict consumer choice, and obstruct free markets. Long-running conflict between two organizations is creating problems for the personal digital assistant (PDA) market.

PDAs, or "handheld computers," are a significant and growing industry in the United States, where 15 million were sold in 2005. Research in Motion (RIM), maker of the Blackberry brand, sold more than 800,000. In 2002, RIM was sued by NTP, a company that administers patents developed by engineer Thomas Campana over a decade earlier.

Campana's patents described delivery of electronic mail to portable devices, a primary function of PDAs. RIM argued that the concept was too obvious to be patentable. A judge found in NTP's favor, ordering RIM to pay damages and stop production. As RIM appealed all the way to the Supreme Court and lost, it seemed that Blackberries were finished. A last-minute agreement was reached, although the $450 million fee was never paid. Whatever the suit's outcome, a lawsuit does not resolve the larger issue.

Consider the music recording industry. Faced with threats from illegal downloads and pirated copies, recording companies responded in several ways. The first line of attack was directed against file-sharing software programs such as Kazaa and Napster. These services have

been shut down or drastically reduced, for the most part. Some companies tried to copy-protect CDs, making it impossible to use the CDs with a PC. This tactic was so unpopular with consumers that some brought a lawsuit against music companies for failing to disclose their copy protection schemes.

A selling strategy emerged that proved more palatable to consumers and more profitable for the record companies. Apple's iTunes online music store was the first to offer a wide range of songs for legal download at an affordable price. iTunes' success has led to a host of imitators and alternatives, including MusicMatch, PassAlong, and eMusic. Thus, a new industry was born, with profits and products for all.

Courts are not the only or even the best places to solve interorganizational conflicts. Free market competition can function better, especially when innovative technology is at stake.

References: Charles Jade, "Gartner Says PDA Market Is Expanding, But Not What a PDA Is," Ars Technica website, August 3, 2005, arttechnica .com on May 20, 2006; George H. Pike, "Blackberry: Lawsuit and Patent Reform," *Information Today,* May 2006, www.infotoday.com on May 20, 2006; Tom Spring, "Face the Music: Suits Pending over Copy Controls," *PC World,* April 11, 2002, www.pcworld.com on May 20, 2006; Lamont Wood, "Blackberry Lawsuit FAQ: What You Need to Know," *Computerworld,* February 7, 2006, www.computerworld.com on May 20, 2006.

of the Guess? label, allegations of design theft, and several other issues.[33] Similarly, General Motors and Volkswagen went to court to resolve a bitter conflict that spanned more than four years. It all started when a key GM executive, Jose Ignacio Lopez de Arriortua, left for a position at Volkswagen. GM claimed that he took with him key secrets that could benefit its German competitor. After the messy departure, dozens of charges and countercharges were made by the two firms, and only a court settlement was able to put the conflict to an end.[34]

Conflict can also arise between an organization and other elements of its environment. For example, an organization may conflict with a consumer group over claims it makes about its products. McDonald's faced this problem a few years ago when it published nutritional information about its products that omitted details about fat content. A manufacturer might conflict with a governmental agency such as the federal Occupational Safety and Health Administration (OSHA). For example, the firm's management may believe it is in compliance with OSHA regulations, whereas officials from the agency itself believe that the firm is not in compliance. Or a firm might conflict with a supplier over the quality of raw materials. The firm may think the supplier is providing inferior materials, while the supplier thinks the materials are adequate. Finally, individual managers obviously may have disagreements with groups of workers. For example, a manager may think her workers are doing poor-quality work and that they are unmotivated. The workers, on the other hand, may believe they are doing good jobs and that the manager is doing a poor job of leading them.

<u>concept</u>
CHECK

Define conflict and identify its primary causes.

Try to think of a time when you were involved in conflict that had a positive outcome.

Managing Conflict in Organizations

How do managers cope with all this potential conflict? Fortunately, as Table 19.3 shows, there are ways to stimulate conflict for constructive ends, to control conflict before it gets out of hand, and to resolve it if it does. Below we look at ways of managing conflict.[35]

Stimulating Conflict

In some situations, an organization may stimulate conflict by placing individual employees or groups in competitive situations. Managers can establish sales contests, incentive plans, bonuses, or other competitive stimuli to spark competition. As long as the ground rules are equitable and all participants perceive the contest as fair, the conflict created by the competition is likely to be constructive because each participant will work hard to win (thereby enhancing some aspect of organizational performance).

Another useful method for stimulating conflict is to bring in one or more outsiders who will shake things up and present a new perspective on organizational practices. Outsiders may be new employees, current employees assigned to an existing work group, or consultants or advisors hired on a temporary basis. Of course, this action can also provoke resentment from insiders who feel they were qualified for the

Table 19.3

METHODS FOR MANAGING CONFLICT

Conflict is a powerful force in organizations and has both negative and positive consequences. Thus managers can draw on several different techniques to stimulate, control, or resolve and eliminate conflict, depending on their unique circumstances.

Stimulating Conflict
Increase competition among individuals and teams.
Hire outsiders to shake things up.
Change established procedures.

Controlling Conflict
Expand resource base.
Enhance coordination of interdependence.
Set superordinate goals.
Match personalities and work habits of employees.

Resolving and Eliminating Conflict
Avoid conflict.
Convince conflicting parties to compromise.
Bring conflicting parties together to confront and negotiate conflict.

position. The Beecham Group, a British company, once hired an executive from the United States for its CEO position, expressly to change how the company did business. His arrival brought with it new ways of doing things and a new enthusiasm for competitiveness. Unfortunately, some valued employees also chose to leave Beecham because they resented some of the changes that were made.

Changing established procedures, especially procedures that have outlived their usefulness, can also stimulate conflict. Such actions cause people to reassess how they perform their job and whether they perform it correctly. For example, one university president announced that all vacant staff positions could be filled only after written justification had received his approval. Conflict arose between the president and the department heads, who felt they were having to do more paperwork than was necessary. Most requests were approved, but because department heads now had to think through their staffing needs, a few unnecessary positions were appropriately eliminated.

Controlling Conflict

One method of controlling conflict is to expand the resource base. Suppose a top manager receives two budget requests for $100,000 each. If she has only $180,000 to distribute, the stage is set for conflict because each group will believe its proposal is worth funding and will be unhappy if it is not fully funded. If both proposals are indeed worthwhile, it may be possible for the manager to come up with the extra $20,000 from some other source and thereby avoid difficulty.

As noted earlier, pooled, sequential, and reciprocal interdependence can all result in conflict. If managers use an appropriate technique for enhancing coordination, they can reduce the probability that conflict will arise. Techniques for coordination (described in Chapter 11) include making use of the managerial hierarchy, relying on rules and procedures, enlisting liaison people, forming task forces, and integrating departments. At the J. C. Penney store mentioned earlier, the conflict was addressed by providing salespeople with clearer forms on which to specify the merchandise they needed and in what sequence. If one coordination technique does not have the desired effect, a manager might shift to another one.

Competing goals can also be a source of conflict among individuals and groups. Managers can sometimes focus employee attention on higher-level, or superordinate, goals as a way of eliminating lower-level conflict. When labor unions like the

United Auto Workers make wage concessions to ensure survival of the automobile industry, they are responding to a superordinate goal. Their immediate goal may be higher wages for members, but they realize that, without the automobile industry, their members would not even have jobs.

Finally, managers should try to match the personalities and work habits of employees so as to avoid conflict between individuals. For instance, two valuable subordinates, one a chain smoker and the other a vehement antismoker, probably should not be required to work together in an enclosed space. If conflict does arise between incompatible individuals, a manager might seek an equitable transfer for one or both of them to other units.

Resolving and Eliminating Conflict

Despite everyone's best intentions, conflict sometimes flares up. If it is disrupting the workplace, creating too much hostility and tension, or otherwise harming the organization, attempts must be made to resolve it. Some managers who are uncomfortable dealing with conflict choose to avoid the conflict and hope it will go away. Avoidance may sometimes be effective in the short run for some kinds of interpersonal disagreements, but it does little to resolve long-run or chronic conflicts. Even more unadvisable, though, is "smoothing"—minimizing the conflict and telling everyone that things will "get better." Often the conflict only worsens as people continue to brood over it.

Compromise is striking a middle-range position between two extremes. This approach can work if it is used with care, but in most compromise situations, someone wins and someone loses. Budget problems are one of the few areas amenable to compromise because of their objective nature. Assume, for example, that additional resources are not available to the manager mentioned earlier. She has $180,000 to divide, and each of two groups claims to need $100,000. If the manager believes that both projects warrant funding, she can allocate $90,000 to each. The fact that the two groups have at least been treated equally may minimize the potential conflict.

The confrontational approach to conflict resolution—also called *interpersonal problem solving*—consists of bringing the parties together to confront the conflict. The parties discuss the nature of their conflict and attempt to reach an agreement or a solution. Confrontation requires a reasonable degree of maturity on the part of the participants, and the manager must structure the situation carefully. If handled well, this approach can be an effective means of resolving conflict. In recent years, many organizations have experimented with a technique called *alternative dispute resolution*, using a team of employees to arbitrate conflict in this way.[36]

Regardless of the approach, organizations and their managers should realize that conflict must be addressed if it is to serve constructive purposes and be prevented from bringing about destructive consequences. Conflict is inevitable in organizations, but its effects can be constrained with proper attention. For example, Union Carbide sent 200 of its managers to a three-day workshop on conflict management. The managers engaged in a variety of exercises and discussions to learn with whom they were most likely to come in conflict and how they should try to resolve it. As a result, managers at the firm later reported that hostility and resentment in the organization had been greatly diminished and that people in the firm reported more pleasant working relationships.[37]

What techniques are available to managers to stimulate, control, and resolve conflict?

What are the primary risks involved if a manager decides to stimulate conflict?

Summary of Learning Objectives and Key Points

1. Define and identify types of groups and teams in organizations, discuss reasons why people join groups and teams, and list the stages of group and team development.
   - A group is two or more people who interact regularly to accomplish a common purpose or goal.
   - General kinds of groups in organizations are
     - functional groups
     - task groups and teams
     - informal or interest groups
   - A team is a group of workers that functions as a unit, often with little or no supervision, to carry out organizational functions.

2. Identify and discuss four essential characteristics of groups and teams.
   - People join functional groups and teams to pursue a career.
   - Their reasons for joining informal or interest groups include interpersonal attraction, group activities, group goals, need satisfaction, and potential instrumental benefits.
   - The stages of team development include testing and dependence, intragroup conflict and hostility, development of group cohesion, and focusing on the problem at hand.
   - Four important characteristics of teams are role structures, behavioral norms, cohesiveness, and informal leadership.

- Role structures define task and socioemotional specialists and may be disrupted by role ambiguity, role conflict, or role overload.
- Norms are standards of behavior for group members.
- Cohesiveness is the extent to which members are loyal and committed to the team and to one another.
- Informal leaders are those leaders whom the group members themselves choose to follow.

3. Discuss interpersonal and intergroup conflict in organizations.
   - Conflict is a disagreement between two or more people, groups, or organizations.
   - Too little or too much conflict may hurt performance, but an optimal level of conflict may improve performance.
   - Interpersonal and intergroup conflict in organizations may be caused by personality differences or by particular organizational strategies and practices.

4. Describe how organizations manage conflict.
   - Organizations may encounter conflict with one another and with various elements of the environment.
   - Three methods of managing conflict are
     - to stimulate it
     - to control it
     - to resolve and eliminate it

Discussion Questions

Questions for Review

1. What is a group? Describe the several different types of groups and indicate the similarities and differences between them. What is the difference between a group and a team?

2. What are the stages of group development? Do all teams develop through all the stages discussed in this chapter? Why or why not? How might the management of a mature team differ from the management of teams that are not yet mature?

3. Describe the development of a role within a group. Tell how each role leads to the next.

4. Describe the causes of conflict in organizations. What can a manager do to control conflict? To resolve and eliminate conflict?

Questions for Analysis

5. Individuals join groups for a variety of reasons. Most groups contain members who joined for different reasons. What is likely to be the result when members join a group for different reasons? What can a group leader do to reduce the negative impact of a conflict in reasons for joining the group?

6. Consider the case of a developed group, where all members have been socialized. What are the benefits to the individuals of norm conformity? What are the benefits of not conforming to the group's norms? What are the benefits to an organization of conformity? What are the benefits to an organization of non-conformity?

7. Do you think teams are a valuable new management technique that will endure, or are they just a fad that will be replaced with something else in the near future?

Questions for Application

8. Think of several groups of which you have been a member. Why did you join each? Did each group progress through the stages of development discussed in this chapter? If not, why do you think it did not?

9. Describe the behavioral norms that are in effect in your management class. To what extent are the norms generalized; in other words, how severely are students "punished" for not observing norms? To what extent is there norm variation; that is, are some students able to "get away" with violating norms to which others must conform?

10. Describe a case of interpersonal conflict that you have observed in an organization. Describe a case of inter-group conflict that you have observed. (If you have not observed any, interview a worker or manager to obtain examples.) In each case, was the conflict beneficial or harmful to the organization, and why?

Building Effective Conceptual Skills

Exercise Overview

Groups and teams are becoming ever more important in organizations. This exercise will allow you to practice your conceptual skills as they apply to work teams in organizations.

Exercise Background

Several highly effective groups exist outside the boundaries of typical business organizations. For example, a basketball team, a military squadron, a government policy group such as the president's cabinet, a student committee, and the leadership of a church or religious organization are all teams.

Exercise Task

1. Use the Internet to identify an example of a real team. Choose one that (a) is not part of a normal for-profit business and (b) you can argue is highly effective.

2. Determine the reasons for the team's effectiveness. (*Hint:* You might look for websites sponsored by that group, look at online news sources for current articles, or enter the group's name as a search term in a search engine.) Consider team characteristics and activities, such as role structures, norms, cohesiveness, and conflict management.

3. What can a manager learn from this particular team? How can this team's success factors be used in a business setting?

Building Effective Communication Skills

Exercise Overview

Communication skills are essential to effective teamwork because teams depend on members' ability to accurately send and receive information. This game demonstrates how good communication skills can lead to improved teamwork and team performance.

Exercise Background

This game is played three times. The first time, you act alone. The second time, you work in a small group, sharing information. The third time, you again work in a small group, but you also have the benefit of some suggestions for performance improvement. Typically, students find that performance improves over the three turns. Creativity is enhanced when information is shared.

Exercise Task

1. Play the "Name Game" that your professor will describe to you. The first time, work out your answers individually. Report your individual score to the class.
2. The second time you play, join a small group of three to five students. Work out your answers together, writing them on a single answer sheet. Allow each group member to look at the sheet. If you can do so without being overheard by other groups, whisper your answers to your group members. Report your group score to the class.
3. Then ask the highest-performing individuals and groups to share their methods with everyone. Your professor may also have some suggestions. Make sure that you understand at least two strategies for improving your score.
4. Play the game for a third time, working together in the same small group in which you participated before. Report your group scores to the class.
5. Did the average group scores improve on the average individual scores? Why or why not?
6. Did the average group scores rise after discussing methods for improvement? Why or why not?
7. What does this game teach you about teamwork and effectiveness? Share your thoughts with the class.

CHAPTER CLOSING CASE

WHO CAN HEAD TEAM NIKE?

Successful entrepreneurs become so attached to their organizations, so identified with organizational people and products, that it can be almost impossible for them to let others take over. One journalist refers to this pattern as "The Return of the Founder." Jeffrey Sonnenfeld, Yale professor, says "It's just such a predictable script." The latest star of such a drama is Nike, where founder Phil Knight forced out CEO William Perez just 13 months after picking him. Perez had valuable experience, yet according to Knight, he failed to understand and effectively deploy Nike's management teams.

From the company's founding in 1971, Nike's organization culture has been legendary. Athlete culture reigns, and top managers are all competitive athletes. "Nike's early management meetings were rowdy, drunken affairs," writes journalist Daniel Roth. "When fights broke out . . . Knight would rarely interrupt. He liked to see the passion." The culture today remains intense and competitive. Knight is emotional too and has cried "countless times" at athletic events.

A few superstars are brought in from outside, yet Nike's managerial talent is mostly homegrown. Executives rotate through various departments to broaden their experience. Thus, for any job, several people in the company can help the current jobholder. A matrix organization means everyone answers to multiple bosses, increasing information sharing. The promote-from-within mentality, strong cross-training, and horizontal communications create a management team that is highly cohesive.

Knight hires bright, ambitious managers who love sports and then gives them a tremendous amount of freedom. He does and says very little, allowing executives to interpret his silences. For example, when a top manager started a new division, Knight's only instructions were to "sell shoes." "He is less likely to sit down and break it down for you. He believes you can figure it out," says former Nike manager Liz Dolan. "He focuses more on talking to you one-on-one to get the best out of you."

Managers look to him as an inspiration, visionary, and father figure, but in fact, he meets rarely and cares little for details. Knight does not take a stand on most issues and often says, "I reserve the right to change my mind tomorrow." Executives make their own decisions. "It's been 40 years that the company has grown around my idiosyncrasies," says Knight. "They don't even know that they're idiosyncrasies anymore, and of course neither do I."

Perez is shy and introspective, as is Knight, but was a novice in the industry. Perez's knowledge of a consumer products company with diverse product lines was desirable at Nike, which was expanding its offerings in athletic wear and equipment. Perez also oversaw many acquisitions at S. C. Johnson and seemed well equipped to help Nike grow.

Perez ruffled feathers immediately. "Perez started asking questions of 20-to-30 year veterans that have never been asked before," says one manager. Perez claims that Knight interfered with his decisions. "From virtually the day I arrived, Phil was as engaged in the company as he ever was. He was talking to my direct reports. It was confusing for the people and frustrating for me," Perez relates.

Perez questioned Nike's award-winning ads, irking many marketing executives. "He relied more on the spreadsheet, analytical approach as opposed to having a good creative marketing sense," says a marketing manager. In fact, Perez battled with numerous executives, including Mark Parker and Charlie Denson, two Nike lifers who competed for the CEO position.

Knight blames Perez, saying, "I think the failure to really kind of get his arms around this company and this industry led to confusion on behalf of the management team." Perez blames Nike insiders, who he claims are resistant to change. Knight, for example, is making his third leadership flip-flop. "It's almost like a death wish, coming into that company from outside," says Stephanie Joseph, a corporate board expert. Observers blame the board of directors for not being able to envision the company without its founder. "The core challenge of corporate governance is getting past the concept of the imperial CEO," says governance expert Ric Marshall.

After Perez's departure, long-time Nike managers Parker and Denson became president and CEO, respectively. However, the 67-year-old Knight continues to age, and

Nike needs succession planning. The company could benefit from new ideas too. Yet Knight may not be able to let go. The board can ease the transition by making lines of responsibility clear and finding something interesting for Knight to do. Managers, even those passed over for the job, must support the new leader or step aside. Stephen Mader, an executive headhunter, sums up the dilemma. "The message about filling shoes is that you can't. You've got to design new shoes."

CASE QUESTIONS

1. List some of the norms held by work teams at Nike. How much norm conformity seems to exist at the firm?

2. What are some of the likely positive consequences of the highly cohesive Nike teams? What are some of the likely negative consequences?

3. Outsider William Perez experienced interpersonal and intergroup conflict while CEO of Nike. In your opinion, was there too much conflict, the appropriate amount of conflict, or too little conflict? Was the conflict handled correctly? Explain your answers.

CASE REFERENCES

Stanley Holmes, "Nike: Can Perez Fill Knight's Shoes?" *BusinessWeek*, November 19, 2004, www.businessweek.com on May 20, 2006; Stanley Holmes, "Inside the Coup at Nike," *BusinessWeek*, February 6, 2006, www.businessweek.com on May 20, 2006; Stanley Holmes, "Nike's CEO Gets the Boot," *BusinessWeek*, January 24, 2006, www.businessweek.com on May 20, 2006; Daniel Roth, "Can Nike Still Do It Without Phil Knight?" *Fortune*, April 4, 2005, www.fortune.com on May 20, 2006.

Managing Work Groups and Teams

YOU MAKE THE CALL

Teamwork for the Tampa Bay Devil Rays

1. How would working for a sports team be similar to and different from working in a more traditional business setting?

2. Would you have an interest in working in sports management? Why or why not?

3. How might someone interested in sports management best prepare themselves for such a career?

4. In what ways might managing in one type of sports league (e.g., baseball) be similar to and different from another league (e.g., basketball)?

5. If you were going to work in sports management, what would be the relative advantages and disadvan-

tages of working for a strong and established franchise (such as the New York Yankees or the Dallas Cowboys) versus working for a relatively new and emerging franchise (such as the Tamp Bay Devil Rays or the Houston Texans)?

6. If you owned a professional sports franchise and needed a new executive team, what would be the relative advantages and disadvantages of bringing in managers from outside the sports industry versus bringing in managers already working in the industry?

Test Prepper

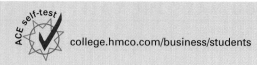

Choose the correct answer. Answers are found at the back of the book.

1. T   F   When an organization decides to use teams, it is essentially implementing a major form of organizational change.

2. T   F   Person-role conflict results from contradictory messages that come from a single source.

3. T   F   Individuals who ignore group norms may initially receive more communication from other group members.

4. T   F   Intragroup competition reduces cohesiveness.

5. T   F   One method of controlling conflict is to expand the resource base.

6. Organizations create teams for all of the following reasons EXCEPT

   A. they give more responsibility for task performance to those performing the tasks.
   B. they give workers more authority and decision-making freedom.
   C. they increase the number of supervisors in the organization.
   D. they allow the organization to promote flexibility and responsiveness.
   E. they allow the organization to capitalize on the knowledge of workers.

7. Groups and teams follow which sequence of stages as they develop?

   A. Storming, forming, norming, performing
   B. Norming, performing, forming, storming
   C. Performing, storming, norming, forming
   D. Forming, storming, norming, performing
   E. Forming, norming, storming, performing

8. When major disruptions in a role episode occur, all of the following may result EXCEPT

   A. role ambiguity.
   B. interrole conflict.
   C. intrasender conflict.
   D. person-role conflict.
   E. role generalization.

9. Which of the following does NOT influence the level of norm conformity?

   A. The level of pressure from the team to conform
   B. Whether the team is a cross-functional team or a high-performance team
   C. Individual traits, such as intelligence
   D. Situational factors, such as team size
   E. The degree of ambiguity in the initial stimulus that prompts behavior

10. Two managers working on separate projects for the same client both want to use company's limited printing resources at the same time. Once the managers realize that unless they both succeed, they both will lose the client, the level of conflict decreases. Which of the following has helped control the conflict?

   A. Expanded resource base
   B. Enhanced coordination
   C. Superordinate goal
   D. Interpersonal problem solving
   E. Alternative dispute resolution

Basic Elements of Control

chapter 20

FIRST THINGS FIRST

Chasing Dimon's Dream for J. P. Morgan Chase

"Waste will hurt our customers. Cars, phones, clubs, perks—what's that got to do with customers?"

—JAMIE DIMON, CEO, J. P. MORGAN CHASE

Jamie Dimon, a new MBA, and industry veteran Sandy Weill spent 12 years transforming Citigroup, through acquisitions, into the largest financial corporation in the United States. The relationship eventually soured, though, and Dimon was fired. He then revitalized Bank One before selling it to J. P. Morgan Chase in 2004. One year later, he was CEO of J. P. Morgan Chase, now the third-largest U.S. bank. Dimon's dream is to surpass his former employer, which has revenues 50 percent greater than Chase's.

LEARNING OBJECTIVES

After studying this chapter, you should be able to:

1. Explain the purpose of control, identify different types of control, and describe the steps in the control process.

2. Identify and explain the three forms of operations control.

3. Describe budgets and other tools for financial control.

4. Identify and distinguish between two opposing forms of structural control.

5. Discuss the relationship between strategy and control, including international strategic control.

6. Identify characteristics of effective control, why people resist control, and how managers can overcome this resistance.

Jamie Dimon, CEO of J. P. Morgan Chase, is using a variety of control measures to reduce costs and boost profits at the company.

Yet Dimon isn't just a dreamer, he's a doer. First, he will increase oversight and control of Bank One's operations and expenses. He expects cost saving measures to free up $3 billion annually by 2007. The cash will then finance new ventures ranging from more ATM machines to the creation of new products. With additional revenues and improved fundamentals, stock price should rise, freeing further funds for new growth. Finally, Dimon wants to build a Citi-like financial empire, merging with firms to jumpstart growth in underserved regional and international markets. Once the basics are right, says Dimon, "you earn the right to do a deal."

A large organization "can get arrogant and full of hubris and lose focus, like the Roman Empire," according to Dimon. J. P. Morgan Chase had high sales, but was spending much more than frugal Bank One, leading to ho-hum profits. Also, the company Dimon inherited underwent multiple mergers with little attempt at integration, resulting in a collection of incompatible systems. Results from different divisions were combined, so "strong businesses were subsidizing weak ones, but the numbers didn't jump out at you," says CFO Michael Cavanagh. "With the results mashed together, it was easy for managers to hide."

Dimon's operational oversight covers virtually every aspect of J. P. Morgan Chase. Here's a sample:

- Dimon reviews each operating unit monthly. Managers must first submit a 50-page report showing financial ratios and results, sales of every product, and even the detailed expenses of every worker. Then Dimon and the leaders spend hours combing through the data, with the CEO asking tough questions and demanding frank answers.
- Dimon prepares a detailed "to do" list every week. "I make my list by business, by person, and try to think about what I might be avoiding, what I have to do," he relates. "It's hard to see the truth—it's even harder to do something about it."
- Dimon slashes bloated budgets. "Waste will hurt our customers," says Dimon. "Cars, phones, clubs, perks—what's that got to do with customers?" He has eliminated fresh flowers, lavish expense accounts, oversized offices, and the in-house gym. Dimon once asked a line of limousine drivers to give the names of the managers they were waiting for. He then called each executive, yelling into the phone, "Too good for the subway?" and "Why don't you try walking?" Dimon denies the story, yet limo use is way down.
- Dimon looks at compensation too. Regional bank managers at J. P. Morgan Chase once earned $2 million annually, compared to Bank One's modest $400,000. "I'd tell people they were way overpaid," the blunt Dimon says. "And guess what? They already knew it." Pay was cut 20 to 50 percent for most staff, yet almost all stayed on. Now a strict pay-for-performance formula keeps compensation in line.
- Dimon gathers outcome data from each manager. "In a big company, it's easy for people to b.s. you. A lot of them have been practicing for decades," Dimon claims. He asks low-level staffers for information and calls suppliers for a

candid performance critique. Steve Black, co-head of investment banking, says, "If you just want to run your business on your own and report results, you won't like working for Jamie."

- Dimon believes that IT is central to the firm's long-term strategy and once cancelled a long-running contract with IBM for information services. "When you're outsourcing . . . people don't care. We want patriots, not mercenaries," Dimon adds. He will pay $2 billion for technology developed in-house over the next year, but considers it money well spent.

   Dimon's long-run goal isn't merely control; it's growth. "It's offensive . . . to be called a cost cutter," he notes. A company analyst describes the changes, saying, "It's the thousand-mile march, and not everyone will survive." Dimon keeps the company focused on the ultimate goal, a firm that can rival Citigroup and dominate U.S. banking.[1]

Jamie Dimon is almost single-handedly remaking J. P. Morgan Chase. Among other things, he is bringing compensation in line with industry standards, cutting costs, streamlining operations, and slashing budgets. He is also setting clear targets for profitability and growth, and managers throughout the company are then being held accountable for meeting these targets. At the heart of all these efforts is a comprehensive control system that helps him monitor all aspects of performance. In a nutshell, effective control helps managers like Jamie Dimon decide where they want their business to go, point it in that direction, and monitor results to keep it on track. Ineffective control, on the other hand, can result in a lack of focus, weak direction, and poor overall performance.

As we discuss in Chapter 1, control is one of the four basic managerial functions that provide the organizing framework for this book. This is the first of three chapters devoted to this important area. In the first section of the chapter we explain the purpose of control. We then look at types of control and the steps in the control process. The rest of the chapter examines the four levels of control that most organizations must employ to remain effective: operations, financial, structural, and strategic control. We conclude by discussing the characteristics of effective control, noting why some people resist control and describing what organizations can do to overcome this resistance. The remaining two chapters in this part focus on managing operations and managing information.

The Nature of Control

Control is the regulation of organizational activities so that some targeted element of performance remains within acceptable limits. Without this regulation, organizations have no indication of how well they are performing in relation to their goals. Control, like a ship's rudder, keeps the organization moving in the proper direction. At any point in time, it compares where the organization is in terms of performance (financial, productive, or otherwise) to where it is supposed to be. Like a rudder, control provides an organization with a mechanism for adjusting its course if performance falls outside of acceptable boundaries. For example, FedEx has a performance goal of delivering 99.8 percent of its packages on time. If on-time

> **control**
> The regulation of organizational activities in such a way as to facilitate goal attainment

Figure 20.1
THE PURPOSE OF CONTROL

Control is one of the four basic management functions in organizations. The control function, in turn, has four basic purposes. Properly designed control systems can fulfill each of these purposes.

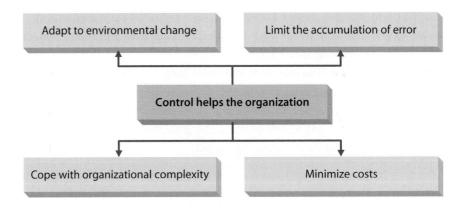

deliveries fall to 99.5 percent, control systems will signal the problem to managers, so that they can make necessary adjustments in operations to regain the target level of performance.[2] An organization without effective control procedures is not likely to reach its goals—or, if it does reach them, to know that it has!

The Purpose of Control

As Figure 20.1 illustrates, control provides an organization with ways to adapt to environmental change, to limit the accumulation of error, to cope with organizational complexity, and to minimize costs. These four functions of control are worth a closer look.

Adapting to Environmental Change   In today's complex and turbulent business environment, all organizations must contend with change.[3] If managers could establish goals and achieve them instantaneously, control would not be needed. But between the time a goal is established and the time it is reached, many things can happen in the organization and its environment to disrupt movement toward the goal—or even to change the goal itself. A properly designed control system can help managers anticipate, monitor, and respond to changing circumstances.[4] In contrast, an improperly designed system can result in organizational performance that falls far below acceptable levels.

For example, Michigan-based Metalloy, a 46-year-old, family-run metal-casting company, signed a contract to make engine-seal castings for NOK, a big Japanese auto parts maker. Metalloy was satisfied when its first 5,000-unit production run yielded 4,985 acceptable castings and only 15 defective ones. NOK, however, was quite unhappy with this performance and insisted that Metalloy raise its standards. In short, global quality standards in most industries are such that customers demand near-perfection from their suppliers. A properly designed control system can help managers like those at Metalloy stay better attuned to rising standards.

Limiting the Accumulation of Error   Small mistakes and errors do not often seriously damage the financial health of an organization. Over time, however, small errors may accumulate and become very serious. For example, Whistler Corporation, a large radar detector manufacturer, was once faced with such rapidly escalating demand that quality essentially became irrelevant. The defect rate rose from 4 percent to 9 percent to 15 percent and eventually reached 25 percent. One day, a manager realized that 100 of the firm's 250 employees were spending all their time fixing defective units and that $2 million worth of inventory was awaiting repair.

Had the company adequately controlled quality as it responded to increased demand, the problem would never have reached such proportions. Similarly, Fleetwood Enterprises, a large manufacturer of recreational vehicles, suffered because its managers did not adequately address several small accounting and production problems years ago. As these small problems grew into large ones, the firm struggled with how to correct them.[5]

Coping with Organizational Complexity When a firm purchases only one raw material, produces one product, has a simple organization design, and enjoys constant demand for its product, its managers can maintain control with a very basic and simple system. But a business that produces many products from myriad raw materials and has a large market area, a complicated organization design, and many competitors needs a sophisticated system to maintain adequate control. When large firms merge, the short-term results are often disappointing. The typical reason for this is that the new enterprise is so large and complex that the existing control systems are simply inadequate. Hewlett-Packard and Compaq Computer faced just this problem when HP acquired Compaq and had to address myriad issues to transform the two firms into one.

Minimizing Costs When it is practiced effectively, control can also help reduce costs and boost output. For example, Georgia-Pacific Corporation, a large wood products company, learned of a new technology that could be used to make thinner blades for its saws. The firm's control system was used to calculate the amount of wood that could be saved from each cut made by the thinner blades relative to the costs used to replace the existing blades. The results have been impressive—the wood that is saved by the new blades each year fills 800 rail cars. As Georgia-Pacific discovered, effective control systems can eliminate waste, lower labor costs, and improve output per unit of input. In their bids to further reduce costs, businesses are cutting back on everything from health insurance coverage to overnight shipping to business lunches for clients.[6]

> "Right now, everything looks O.K. in terms of meeting our entry-into-service dates for the [Boeing] 787. But as you know, new airplanes are really hard to do."
>
> Michael Bair, Boeing Vice President
> (*BusinessWeek,* June 19, 2006, p. 40)

Types of Control

The examples of control given thus far have illustrated the regulation of several organizational activities, from producing quality products to coordinating complex organizations. Organizations practice control in a number of different areas and at different levels, and the responsibility for managing control is widespread.

Areas of Control Control can focus on any area of an organization. Most organizations define areas of control in terms of the four basic types of resources they use: physical, human, information, and financial.[7] Control of physical resources includes inventory management (stocking neither too few nor too many units in inventory), quality control (maintaining appropriate levels of output quality), and equipment control (supplying the necessary facilities and machinery). Control of human resources includes selection and placement, training and development, performance appraisal, and compensation. Control of information resources includes sales and marketing forecasting, environmental analysis, public relations, production scheduling, and economic forecasting.[8] Financial control involves managing the organization's debt so that it does not become excessive, ensuring that the firm always has enough cash on hand to meet its obligations but does not have excess cash in a checking account, and ensuring that receivables are collected and bills are paid on a timely basis.

In many ways, the control of financial resources is the most important area, because financial resources are related to the control of all the other resources in an organization. Too much inventory leads to storage costs; poor selection of personnel leads to termination and rehiring expenses; inaccurate sales forecasts lead to disruptions in cash flows and other financial effects. Financial issues tend to pervade most control-related activities.

The crisis in the U.S. airline industry precipitated by the terrorist attacks on September 11, an economic downturn that reduced business travel, and rising fuel costs can be fundamentally traced back to financial issues. Essentially, airline revenues dropped while their costs increased. Because of high labor costs and other expenses, the airlines have faced major problems in making appropriate adjustments.[9] United Airlines, for instance, spends over half of its revenues on labor; in contrast, JetBlue spends only 25 percent of its revenues on labor.[10]

Levels of Control   Just as control can be broken down by area, Figure 20.2 shows that it can also be broken down by level within the organizational system. ***Operations control*** focuses on the processes the organization uses to transform resources into products or services.[11] Quality control is one type of operations control. ***Financial control*** is concerned with the organization's financial resources. Monitoring receivables to make sure customers are paying their bills on time is an example of financial control. ***Structural control*** is concerned with how the elements of the organization's structure are serving their intended purpose. Monitoring the administrative ratio to make sure staff expenses do not become excessive is an example of structural control. Finally, ***strategic control*** focuses on how effectively the organization's corporate, business, and functional strategies are succeeding in helping the organization meet its goals. For example, if a corporation has been unsuccessful in implementing its strategy of related diversification, its managers need to identify the reasons and either change the strategy or renew their efforts to implement it. We discuss these four levels of control more fully later in this chapter.

Responsibilities for Control   Traditionally, managers have been responsible for overseeing the wide array of control systems and concerns in organizations. They

---

operations control
Focuses on the processes the organization uses to transform resources into products or services

financial control
Concerned with the organization's financial resources

structural control
Concerned with how the elements of the organization's structure are serving their intended purpose

strategic control
Focuses on how effectively the organization's strategies are succeeding in helping the organization meet its goals

Figure 20.2
LEVELS OF CONTROL

Managers use control at several different levels. The most basic levels of control in organizations are strategic, structural, operations, and financial control. Each level must be managed properly if control is to be most effective.

decide which types of control the organization will use, and they implement control systems and take actions based on the information provided by control systems. Thus ultimate responsibility for control rests with all managers throughout an organization.

Most larger organizations also have one or more specialized managerial positions called *controller*. A **controller** is responsible for helping line managers with their control activities, for coordinating the organization's overall control system, and for gathering and assimilating relevant information. Many businesses that use an H-form or M-form organization design have several controllers: one for the corporation and one for each division. The job of controller is especially important in organizations where control systems are complex.[12]

> *controller*
> A position in organizations that helps line managers with their control activities

In addition, many organizations are also beginning to use operating employees to help maintain effective control. Indeed, employee participation is often used as a vehicle for allowing operating employees an opportunity to help facilitate organizational effectiveness. For example, Whistler Corporation increased employee participation in an effort to turn its quality problems around. As a starting point, the quality control unit, formerly responsible for checking product quality at the end of the assembly process, was eliminated. Next, all operating employees were encouraged to check their own work and told that they would be responsible for correcting their own errors. As a result, Whistler has eliminated its quality problems and is now highly profitable once again.

Steps in the Control Process

Regardless of the type or levels of control systems an organization needs, there are four fundamental steps in any control process.[13] These are illustrated in Figure 20.3.

Establishing Standards   The first step in the control process is establishing standards. A **control standard** is a target against which subsequent performance will be compared.[14] Employees at a Taco Bell fast-food restaurant, for example, work toward the following service standards:

> *control standard*
> A target against which subsequent performance will be compared

1. A minimum of 95 percent of all customers will be greeted within 3 minutes of their arrival.

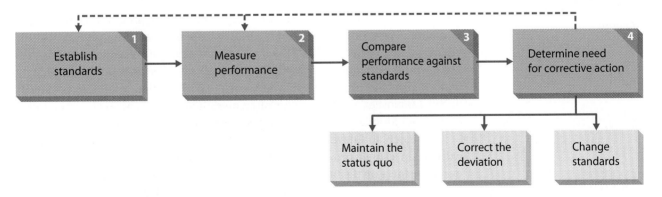

Figure 20.3
STEPS IN THE CONTROL PROCESS

Having an effective control system can help ensure that an organization achieves its goals. Implementing a control system, however, is a systematic process that generally proceeds through four interrelated steps.

Establishing standards, measuring performance, comparing performance against standards, and correcting deviations are parts of the control process. In the European Union, all eggs must now be electronically marked for identification. This marking system provides information about the environment in which the chicken was raised, the country where the eggs were produced, and the specific producer who brought the eggs to market. This information, in turn, is useful in monitoring quality and eliminating any public health hazards that might arise.

2. Preheated tortilla chips will not sit in the warmer more than 30 minutes before they are served to customers or discarded.

3. Empty tables will be cleaned within 5 minutes after being vacated.

Standards established for control purposes should be expressed in measurable terms. Note that standard 1 above has a time limit of 3 minutes and an objective target of 95 percent of all customers. In standard 3, the objective target of "all" empty tables is implied.

Control standards should also be consistent with the organization's goals. Taco Bell has organizational goals involving customer service, food quality, and restaurant cleanliness. A control standard for a retailer like Home Depot should be consistent with its goal of increasing its annual sales volume by 25 percent within five years. A hospital trying to shorten the average hospital stay for a patient will have control standards that reflect current averages. A university reaffirming its commitment to academics might adopt a standard of graduating 80 percent of its student athletes within five years of their enrollment. Control standards can be as narrow or as broad as the level of activity to which they apply and must follow logically from organizational goals and objectives.

A final aspect of establishing standards is to identify performance indicators. Performance indicators are measures of performance that provide information that is directly relevant to what is being controlled. For example, suppose an organization is following a tight schedule in building a new plant. Relevant performance indicators could be buying a site, selecting a building contractor, and ordering equipment. Monthly sales increases are not, however, directly relevant. On the other hand, if control is being focused on revenue, monthly sales increases are relevant, whereas buying land for a new plant is less relevant.

Measuring Performance The second step in the control process is measuring performance. Performance measurement is a constant, ongoing activity for most organizations. For control to be effective, performance measures must be valid. Daily, weekly, and monthly sales figures measure sales performance, and production performance may be expressed in terms of unit cost, product quality, or volume produced. Employees' performance is often measured in terms of quality or quantity of output, but for many jobs measuring performance is not so straightforward.

A research and development scientist at Merck, for example, may spend years working on a single project before achieving a breakthrough. A manager who takes over a business on the brink of failure may need months or even years to turn things around. Valid performance measurement, however difficult to obtain, is nevertheless vital in maintaining effective control, and performance indicators usually can be developed. The scientist's progress, for example, may be partially assessed by peer review,

"We know what measures we need to take to improve the company."
Osamu Masuko, President of Mitsubishi
(*BusinessWeek,* October 24, 2005, p. 56)

and the manager's success may be evaluated by her ability to convince creditors that she will eventually be able to restore profitability.

Comparing Performance Against Standards   The third step in the control process is comparing measured performance against established standards. Performance may be higher than, lower than, or identical to the standard. In some cases comparison is easy. The goal of each product manager at General Electric is to make the product either number one or number two (on the basis of total sales) in its market. Because this standard is clear and total sales are easy to calculate, it is relatively simple to determine whether this standard has been met. Sometimes, however, comparisons are less clear-cut. If performance is lower than expected, the question is how much deviation from standards to allow before taking remedial action. For example, is increasing sales by 7.9 percent when the standard was 8 percent close enough?

The timetable for comparing performance to standards depends on a variety of factors, including the importance and complexity of what is being controlled. For longer-run and higher-level standards, annual comparisons may be appropriate. In other circumstances, more frequent comparisons are necessary. For example, a business with a severe cash shortage may need to monitor its on-hand cash reserves daily.

Considering Corrective Action   The final step in the control process is determining the need for corrective action. Decisions regarding corrective action draw heavily on a manager's analytic and diagnostic skills. For example, as healthcare costs have risen, many firms have sought ways to keep their own expenses in check. Some have reduced benefits; others have opted to pass on higher costs to their employees.[15]

After comparing performance against control standards, one of three actions is appropriate: maintain the status quo (do nothing), correct the deviation, or change the standards. Maintaining the status quo is preferable when performance essentially matches the standards, but it is more likely that some action will be needed to correct a deviation from the standards.

Sometimes, performance that is higher than expected may also cause problems for organizations. For example, when DaimlerChrysler first introduced its PT Cruiser, demand was so strong that customers were placed on waiting lists, and many customers were willing to pay more than the suggested retail price to obtain a car. The company was reluctant to increase production, primarily because it knew demand would eventually drop. At the same time, however, it did not want to alienate potential customers. Consequently, the firm decided to simply reduce its advertising. This curtailed demand a bit and limited customer frustration.

Changing an established standard usually is necessary if it was set too high or too low at the outset. This is apparent if large numbers of employees routinely beat the standard by a wide margin or if no employees ever meet the standard. Also, standards that seemed perfectly appropriate when they were established may need to be adjusted because circumstances have since changed.

concept
CHECK

What are the basic purposes and types of control used in organizations?

Identify a goal you have set for yourself (such as raising your grade point average or buying a car) and then outline a control framework patterned after Figure 20.3 for achieving that goal.

Final inspections are a common part of postaction control systems. Maria Martinez, for example, is shown here inspecting batches of Chiquita brand bananas that have been grown on a plantation in Panama and are being prepared for export. She carefully assesses their weight, size, and appearance to ensure that they meet the company's standards.

---

operations control
Focuses on the processes the organization uses to transform resources into products or services

---

preliminary control
Attempts to monitor the quality or quantity of financial, physical, human, and information resources before they actually become part of the system

---

Operations Control

One of the four levels of control practiced by most organizations, **operations control**, is concerned with the processes the organization uses to transform resources into products or services. As Figure 20.4 shows, the three forms of operations control—preliminary, screening, and postaction—occur at different points in relation to the transformation processes used by the organization.

Preliminary Control

Preliminary control concentrates on the resources—financial, material, human, and information—the organization brings in from the environment. Preliminary control attempts to monitor the quality or quantity of these resources before they enter the organization. Firms like PepsiCo and General Mills hire only college graduates for their management training programs, and even then only after applicants satisfy several interviewers and selection criteria. In this way, they control the quality of the human resources entering the organization. When Sears orders merchandise to be manufactured under its own brand name, it specifies rigid standards of quality, thereby controlling physical inputs. Organizations also control financial and information resources. For example, privately held companies like UPS and Mars limit the extent to which outsiders can buy their stock, and television networks verify the accuracy of news stories before they are broadcast.

Screening Control

Screening control focuses on meeting standards for product or service quality or quantity during the actual transformation process itself. Screening control relies heavily on feedback processes. For example, in a Dell Computer assembly factory, computer system components are checked periodically as each unit is being assembled. This is done to ensure that all the components that have been assembled up to that point are working properly. The periodic quality checks provide feedback to workers so that they know what, if any, corrective actions to take. Because they are useful in identifying the cause of problems, screening controls tend to be used more often than other forms of control.

More and more companies are adopting screening controls because they are an effective way to promote employee participation and catch problems early in the overall transformation process. For example, Corning adopted screening controls for use in manufacturing television glass. In the past, finished television screens were inspected only after they were finished. Unfortunately, over 4 percent of them were later returned by customers because of defects. Now the glass screens are inspected at each step in the production process, rather than at the end, and the return rate from customers has dropped to .03 percent.

Postaction Control

Postaction control focuses on the outputs of the organization after the transformation process is complete. Corning's old system was postaction control—final inspection after the product was completed. Although Corning abandoned its postaction control

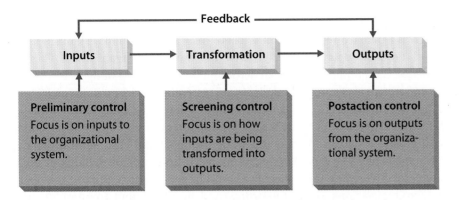

Figure 20.4
FORMS OF OPERATIONS CONTROL

Most organizations develop multiple control systems that incorporate all three basic forms of control. For example, the publishing company that produced this book screens inputs by hiring only qualified employees, typesetters, and printers (preliminary control). In addition, quality is checked during the transformation process, such as after the manuscript is typeset (screening control), and the outputs—printed and bound books—are checked before they are shipped from the bindery (postaction control).

system, this still may be an effective method of control, primarily if a product can be manufactured in only one or two steps or if the service is fairly simple and routine. Although postaction control alone may not be as effective as preliminary or screening control, it can provide management with information for future planning. For example, if a quality check of finished goods indicates an unacceptably high defect rate, the production manager knows that he or she must identify the causes and take steps to eliminate them. Postaction control also provides a basis for rewarding employees. Recognizing that an employee has exceeded personal sales goals by a wide margin, for example, may alert the manager that a bonus or promotion is in order.

Most organizations use more than one form of operations control. For example, Honda's preliminary control includes hiring only qualified employees and specifying strict quality standards when ordering parts from other manufacturers. Honda uses numerous screening controls in checking the quality of components during assembly of cars. A final inspection and test drive as each car rolls off the assembly line is part of the company's postaction control.[16] Indeed, most successful organizations employ a wide variety of techniques to facilitate operations control.

> *screening control*
> Relies heavily on feedback processes during the transformation process

> *postaction control*
> Monitors the outputs or results of the organization after the transformation process is complete

concept
CHECK

Distinguish between preliminary, screening, and postaction control.

Describe how a college or university is likely to use each type of operations control to monitor student progress.

Financial Control

Financial control is the control of financial resources as they flow into the organization (revenues, shareholder investments), are held by the organization (working capital, retained earnings), and flow out of the organization (pay, expenses). Businesses must manage their finances so that revenues are sufficient to cover costs and still return a profit to the firm's owners. Not-for-profit organizations such as universities have the same concerns: Their revenues (from tax dollars or tuition) must cover operating expenses and overhead. U.S. auto makers Ford and General Motors have come to realize that they have to reduce the costs of paying employees they do not need but whom they are obligated to keep due to longstanding labor agreements. Ford has offered to cover the full costs of a college education for certain of its employees if they will resign; GM, for its part, has offered lump-sum payments of varying amounts to some of its workers in return for their resignations.[17] A complete discussion of financial management is beyond the scope of this book, but we will examine the control provided by budgets and other financial control tools.

> *financial control*
> Concerned with the organization's financial resources

Budgetary Control

A ***budget*** is a plan expressed in numerical terms.[18] Organizations establish budgets for work groups, departments, divisions, and the whole organization. The usual time period for a budget is one year, although breakdowns of budgets by the quarter or month are also common. Budgets are generally expressed in financial terms, but they may occasionally be expressed in units of output, time, or other quantifiable factors. When Disney launches the production of a new animated cartoon feature, it creates a budget for how much the movie should cost. Several years ago, when movies like *The Lion King* were raking in hundreds of millions of dollars, Disney executives were fairly flexible about budget overruns. But, on the heels of several animated flops, such as *Atlantis: The Lost Empire* and *Treasure Planet*, the company had to take a much harder line on budget overruns.[19]

Because of their quantitative nature, budgets provide yardsticks for measuring performance and facilitate comparisons across departments, between levels in the organization, and from one time period to another. Budgets serve four primary purposes. They help managers coordinate resources and projects (because they use a common denominator, usually dollars). They help define the established standards for control. They provide guidelines about the organization's resources and expectations. Finally, budgets enable the organization to evaluate the performance of managers and organizational units.

Types of Budgets   Most organizations develop and make use of three different kinds of budgets—financial, operating, and nonmonetary. Table 20.1 summarizes the characteristics of each of these.

A *financial budget* indicates where the organization expects to get its cash for the coming time period and how it plans to use it. Because financial resources are critically important, the organization needs to know where those resources will be coming from and how they are to be used. The financial budget provides answers to both these questions. Usual sources of cash include sales revenue, short- and long-term loans, the sale of assets, and the issuance of new stock.

Table 20.1
DEVELOPING BUDGETS IN ORGANIZATIONS

Organizations use various types of budgets to help manage their control functions. The three major categories of budgets are financial, operating, and nonmonetary. There are several different types of budgets in each category. To be most effective, each budget must be carefully matched with the specific function being controlled.

Types of Budget	What Budget Shows
Financial Budget	*Sources and Uses of Cash*
Cash-flow or cash budget	All sources of cash income and cash expenditures in monthly, weekly, or daily periods
Capital expenditures budget	Costs of major assets such as a new plant, machinery, or land
Balance sheet budget	Forecast of the organization's assets and liabilities in the event all other budgets are met
Operating Budget	*Planned Operations in Financial Terms*
Sales or revenue budget	Income the organization expects to receive from normal operations
Expense budget	Anticipated expenses for the organization during the coming time period
Profit budget	Anticipated differences between sales or revenues and expenses
Nonmonetary Budget	*Planned Operations in Nonfinancial Terms*
Labor budget	Hours of direct labor available for use
Space budget	Square feet or meters of space available for various functions
Production budget	Number of units to be produced during the coming time period

For years Exxon was very conservative in its capital budgeting. As a result, the firm amassed a huge financial reserve but was being overtaken in sales by Royal Dutch/Shell. But executives at Exxon were then able to use their reserves to help finance the firm's merger with Mobil, creating ExxonMobil, and to regain the number-one sales position. Since that time, the firm has become more aggressive in capital budgeting to stay ahead of its European rival.

An *operating budget* is concerned with planned operations within the organization. It outlines what quantities of products or services the organization intends to create and what resources will be used to create them. IBM creates an operating budget that specifies how many of each model of its personal computer will be produced each quarter.

A *nonmonetary budget* is simply a budget expressed in nonfinancial terms, such as units of output, hours of direct labor, machine hours, or square-foot allocations. Nonmonetary budgets are most commonly used by managers at the lower levels of an organization. For example, a plant manager can schedule work more effectively knowing that he or she has 8,000 labor hours to allocate in a week, rather than trying to determine how to best spend $86,451 in wages in a week.

Developing Budgets   Traditionally, budgets were developed by top management and the controller and then imposed on lower-level managers. Although some organizations still follow this pattern, many contemporary organizations now allow all managers to participate in the budget process. As a starting point, top management generally issues a call for budget requests, accompanied by an indication of overall patterns the budgets may take. For example, if sales are expected to drop in the next year, managers may be told up front to prepare for cuts in operating budgets.

As Figure 20.5 shows, the heads of each operating unit typically submit budget requests to the head of their division. An operating unit head might be a department manager in a manufacturing or wholesaling firm or a program director in a

Figure 20.5
DEVELOPING BUDGETS IN
ORGANIZATIONS

Most organizations use the same basic process to develop budgets. Operating units are requested to submit their budget requests to divisions. These divisions, in turn, compile unit budgets and submit their own budgets to the organization. An organizational budget is then compiled for approval by the budget committee, controller, and CEO.

Operating unit
budget requests

Division budget
requests

Organizational budget
• Prepared by budget
  committee
• Approved by budget
  committee, controller,
  and CEO

social service agency. The division heads might include plant managers, regional sales managers, or college deans. The division head integrates and consolidates the budget requests from operating unit heads into one overall division budget request. A great deal of interaction among managers usually takes place at this stage, as the division head coordinates the budgetary needs of the various departments.

Division budget requests are then forwarded to a budget committee. The budget committee is usually composed of top managers. The committee reviews budget requests from several divisions, and once again, duplications and inconsistencies are corrected. Finally, the budget committee, the controller, and the CEO review and agree on the overall budget for the organization, as well as specific budgets for each operating unit. These decisions are then communicated back to each manager.

Strengths and Weaknesses of Budgeting   Budgets offer a number of advantages, but they also have weaknesses. On the plus side, budgets facilitate effective control. Placing dollar values on operations enables managers to monitor operations better and pinpoint problem areas. Budgets also facilitate coordination and communication between departments because they express diverse activities in a common denominator (dollars). Budgets help maintain records of organizational performance and are a logical complement to planning. In other words, as managers develop plans, they should simultaneously consider control measures to accompany them. Organizations can use budgets to link plans and control by first developing budgets as part of the plan and then using those budgets as part of control.

On the other hand, some managers apply budgets too rigidly. Budgets are intended to serve as frameworks, but managers sometimes fail to recognize that changing circumstances may warrant budget adjustments. The process of developing budgets can also be very time consuming. Finally, budgets may limit innovation and change. When all available funds are allocated to specific operating budgets, it may be impossible to procure additional funds to take advantage of an unexpected opportunity. Indeed, for these very reasons, some organizations are working to scale back their budgeting systems. Although most organizations are likely to continue to use budgets, the goal is to make them less confining and rigid.

Other Tools for Financial Control

Although budgets are the most common means of financial control, other useful tools are financial statements, ratio analysis, and financial audits.

financial statement
A profile of some aspect of an organization's financial circumstances

Financial Statements   A *financial statement* is a profile of some aspect of an organization's financial circumstances. There are commonly accepted and required ways that financial statements must be prepared and presented.[20] The two most basic financial statements prepared and used by virtually all organizations are a balance sheet and an income statement.

balance sheet
List of assets and liabilities of an organization at a specific point in time

The *balance sheet* lists the assets and liabilities of the organization at a specific point in time, usually the last day of an organization's fiscal year. For example, the balance sheet may summarize the financial condition of an organization on December 31, 2007. Most balance sheets are divided into current assets (assets that are relatively liquid, or easily convertible into cash), fixed assets (assets that are longer term in nature and less liquid), current liabilities (debts and other obligations that must be paid in the near future), long-term liabilities (payable over an extended period of time), and stockholders' equity (the owners' claim against the assets).

Whereas the balance sheet reflects a snapshot profile of an organization's financial position at a single point in time, the ***income statement*** summarizes financial performance over a period of time, usually one year. For example, the income statement might be for the period January 1, 2007, through December 31, 2007. The income statement summarizes the firm's revenues less its expenses to report net income (profit or loss) for the period. Information from the balance sheet and income statement is used in computing important financial ratios.

> *income statement*
> A summary of financial performance over a period of time

Ratio Analysis Financial ratios compare different elements of a balance sheet or income statement to one another. ***Ratio analysis*** is the calculation of one or more financial ratios to assess some aspect of the financial health of an organization. Organizations use a variety of different financial ratios as part of financial control. For example, *liquidity ratios* indicate how liquid (easily converted into cash) an organization's assets are. *Debt ratios* reflect ability to meet long-term financial obligations. *Return ratios* show managers and investors how much return the organization is generating relative to its assets. *Coverage ratios* help estimate the organization's ability to cover interest expenses on borrowed capital. *Operating ratios* indicate the effectiveness of specific functional areas rather than of the total organization. Walt Disney is an example of a company that relies heavily on financial ratios to keep its financial operations on track.[21]

> *ratio analysis*
> The calculation of one or more financial ratios to assess some aspect of the organization's financial health

Financial Audits ***Audits*** are independent appraisals of an organization's accounting, financial, and operational systems. The two major types of financial audits are the external audit and the internal audit.

> *audit*
> An independent appraisal of an organization's accounting, financial, and operational systems

External audits are financial appraisals conducted by experts who are not employees of the organization.[22] External audits are typically concerned with determining that the organization's accounting procedures and financial statements are compiled in an objective and verifiable fashion. The organization contracts with a certified public accountant (CPA) for this service. The CPA's main objective is to verify for stockholders, the IRS, and other interested parties that the methods by which the organization's financial managers and accountants prepare documents and reports are legal and proper. External audits are so important that publicly held corporations are required by law to have external audits regularly, as assurance to investors that the financial reports are reliable.

Unfortunately, flaws in the auditing process played a major role in the downfall of Enron and several other major firms. The problem can be traced back partially to the auditing groups' problems with conflicts of interest and eventual loss of objectivity. For instance, Enron was such an important client for its auditing firm, Arthur Andersen, that the auditors started letting the firm take liberties with its accounting systems for fear that if they were too strict, Enron might take its business to another auditing firm. In the aftermath of the resulting scandal, Arthur Andersen was forced to close its doors, Enron is a shell of its former self, indictments continue to be handed down, and the entire future of the accounting profession has been called into question.[23]

Some organizations are also starting to employ external auditors to review other aspects of their financial operations. For example, some auditing firms now specialize in checking corporate legal bills. An auditor for the Fireman's Fund Insurance Company uncovered several thousands of dollars in legal fee errors. Other auditors are beginning to specialize in real estate, employee benefits, and pension plan investments.

Whereas external audits are conducted by external accountants, an *internal audit* is handled by employees of the organization. Its objective is the same as that of an external audit—to verify the accuracy of financial and accounting procedures used by the organization. Internal audits also examine the efficiency and appropriateness of financial and accounting procedures. Because the staff members who conduct them are a permanent part of the organization, internal audits tend to be more expensive than external audits. But employees, who are more familiar with the organization's practices, may also point out significant aspects of the accounting system besides its technical correctness. Large organizations like Halliburton and Ford have an internal auditing staff that spends all its time conducting audits of different divisions and functional areas of the organization. Smaller organizations may assign accountants to an internal audit group on a temporary or rotating basis.

The findings of an internal auditor led to the recent financial scandal at World-Com. The firm's new CEO asked an internal auditor to spot-check various records related to capital expenditures. She subsequently discovered that the firm's chief financial officer was misapplying major expenses: Instead of treating them as current expenses, he was treating them as capital expenditures. This treatment, in turn, made the firm look much more profitable than it really was. The CFO was fired, but it will take WorldCom a long time to sort out the $3.8 billion it has so far found to have been handled improperly.[24]

concept
CHECK

| *What are the basic kinds of budgets used in most organizations?* | *Given that financial control relies so heavily on numbers, how can problems like those at Enron occur?* |

Structural Control

Organizations can create designs for themselves that result in very different approaches to control. Two major forms of structural control, bureaucratic control and decentralized control, represent opposite ends of a continuum, as shown in Figure 20.6.[25] The six dimensions shown in the figure represent perspectives adopted by the two extreme types of structural control. In other words, they have different goals, degrees of formality, performance expectations, organization designs, reward systems, and levels of participation. Although a few organizations fall precisely at one extreme or the other, most tend toward one end but may have specific characteristics of either.

Bureaucratic Control

bureaucratic control
A form of organizational control characterized by formal and mechanistic structural arrangements

Bureaucratic control is an approach to organization design characterized by formal and mechanistic structural arrangements. As the term suggests, it follows the bureaucratic model. The goal of bureaucratic control is employee compliance. Organizations that use it rely on strict rules and a rigid hierarchy, insist that employees meet minimally acceptable levels of performance, and often have a tall structure. They focus their rewards on individual performance and allow only limited and formal employee participation.

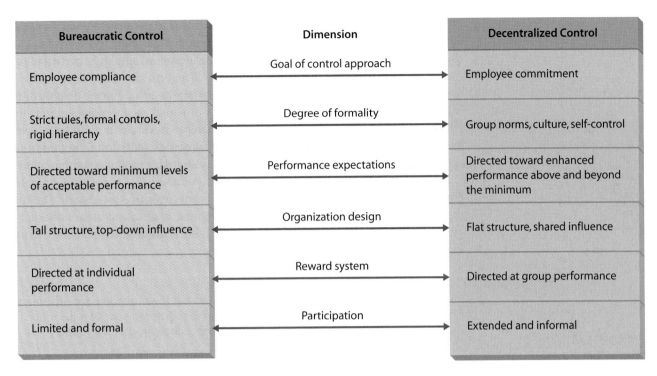

Figure 20.6
ORGANIZATIONAL CONTROL

Organizational control generally falls somewhere between the two extremes of bureaucratic and decentralized control. NBC television uses bureaucratic control, whereas Levi Strauss uses decentralized control.

NBC television applies structural controls that reflect many elements of bureaucracy. The organization relies on numerous rules to regulate employee travel, expense accounts, and other expenses. A new performance appraisal system precisely specifies minimally acceptable levels of performance for everyone. The organization's structure is considerably taller than those of the other major networks, and rewards are based on individual contributions. Perhaps most significantly, many NBC employees have argued that they have too small a voice in how the organization is managed.

In another example, a large oil company recently made the decision to allow employees to wear casual attire to work. But a committee then spent weeks developing a 20-page set of guidelines on what was and was not acceptable. For example, denim pants are not allowed. Similarly, athletic shoes may be worn as long as they are not white. And all shirts must have a collar. Nordstrom, the department store chain, is also moving toward bureaucratic control as it works to centralize all of its purchasing in an effort to lower costs.[26] Similarly, Home Depot is moving more toward bureaucratic control to cut its costs and more effectively compete with its hard-charging rival, Lowe's.[27]

Decentralized Control

Decentralized control, in contrast, is an approach to organizational control characterized by informal and organic structural arrangements. As Figure 20.6 shows, its goal is employee commitment to the organization. Accordingly, it relies heavily on group norms and a strong corporate culture, and gives employees the responsibility

decentralized control
An approach to organizational control based on informal and organic structural arrangements

for controlling themselves. Employees are encouraged to perform beyond minimally acceptable levels. Organizations using this approach are usually relatively flat. They direct rewards at group performance and favor widespread employee participation.

Levi Strauss practices decentralized control. The firm's managers use groups as the basis for work and have created a culture wherein group norms help facilitate high performance. Rewards are subsequently provided to the higher-performing groups and teams. The company's culture also reinforces contributions to the over-all team effort, and employees have a strong sense of loyalty to the organization. Levi's has a flat structure, and power is widely shared. Employee participation is encouraged in all areas of operation.[28] Another company that uses this approach is Southwest Airlines. When Southwest made the decision to "go casual," the firm resisted the temptation to develop dress guidelines. Instead, managers decided to allow employees to exercise discretion over their attire and to deal with clearly inappropriate situations on a case-by-case basis.

concept
CHECK

| Identify the fundamental differences between bureaucratic and decentralized control. | What are the most obvious advantages and disadvantages of bureaucratic versus decentralized control? |

---

strategic control
Control aimed at ensuring that the organization is maintaining an effective alignment with its environment and moving toward achieving its strategic goals

Strategic Control

Given the obvious importance of an organization's strategy, it is also important that the organization assess how effective that strategy is in helping the organization meet its goals.[29] To do this requires that the organization integrate its strategy and control systems. This is especially true for the global organization.

Intel has remained at the forefront of its industry for many years. One key ingredient to Intel's long-term success has been its focus on strategic control. As part of its current strategic initiatives, Intel has opened a new fabrication plan in Chandler, Arizona. These workers are constructing a "clean room" at the new facility. (A clean room is a sterile climate-controlled room used to develop and manufacture delicate electronic components.)

Integrating Strategy and Control

Strategic control generally focuses on five aspects of organizations—structure, leadership, technology, human resources, and information and operational control systems. For example, an organization should periodically examine its structure to determine whether it is facilitating the attainment of the strategic goals being sought. Suppose a firm using a functional (U-form) design has an established goal of achieving a 20 percent sales growth rate per year. However, performance indicators show that it is currently growing at a rate of only 10 percent per year. Detailed analysis might reveal that the current structure is inhibiting growth in some way (for example, by slowing decision making and inhibiting innovation) and that a divisional (M-form) design is more likely to bring about the desired growth (by speeding decision making and promoting innovation).

In this way, strategic control focuses on the extent to which implemented strategy achieves the organization's strategic goals. If, as outlined above, one or more avenues of implementation are inhibiting the attainment of goals, that avenue should be changed. Consequently, the firm might find it necessary to alter its structure, replace key leaders, adopt new technology, modify its human resources, or change its information and operational control systems.

Kohl's department stores essentially redefined how to compete effectively in the midtier retailing market and was on trajectory to leave competitors like Sears and Dillards in its dust. But then the firm inexplicably stopped doing many of the very things that had led to its success—such as keeping abreast of current styles, maintaining low inventories, and keeping its stores neat and clean—and began to stumble. Now, managers are struggling to rejuvenate Kohl's strategic focus and get it back on track.[30] *Technology Toolkit* provides another interesting example of strategic control, one with a more positive spin to it.

> "Kohl's single-handedly turned the department store industry on its ear, a condition that lasted until rivals woke up and said, 'Hey, I can do that, too'."
>
> Kurt Barnard, president, Retail Forecasting
> (*USA Today*, April 8, 2005, p. B1)

Technology Toolkit

Strategic Control Through IT at FedEx

FedEx is committed to accurate and speedy delivery, along with excellent customer service. Information systems are vital to support the firm's complex operations and enable the delivery of 6 million packages daily. IT coordinates 90,000 vehicles, 677 airplanes, and 200,000 employees in 220 countries, while also ensuring that the firm meets it goals of accuracy, speed, and service.

Rob Carter, chief information officer of FedEx, defines the company's business by saying, "We engineer time. We . . . allow you to engineer time to make things happen along time schedules that weren't possible [before]." For example, Texas-based Motion Computing passes customer orders to a Chinese factory. The finished PC is transported by FedEx directly to the consumer in about five days. Scott Eckert, Motion's CEO, says, "We have no inventory tied up in the process anywhere. Frankly, our business is enabled by FedEx."

FedEx CEO Fred Smith famously said that information about a package is as important as the package itself. So FedEx developed an extensive online tracking system. Recently, according to Carter, FedEx "took the whole tracking mechanism and turned it around so that as opposed to having to track a package, you say, 'I want to know what's coming to me today.' You can go out there now and see every inbound package, regardless of whether you knew someone was sending it."

FedEx was the first to recognize the strategic value of information systems, while rival UPS lagged. Carter claims, "I think it's easier to copy than it is to innovate." While acknowledging that both FedEx and UPS offer some of the same information features, he differentiates the two firms. "We've been in a battle on customer-based technology," Carter says. "[FedEx] tends to focus slightly less on operational technology. We focus a little more on revenue-generating, customer-satisfaction-generating, strategic-advantage technology."

Carter adds, "The key focus of my job is driving technology that increases the top line." He puts the emphasis on effectiveness, quality, and satisfaction rather than on "bottom-line" efficiency and cost control. With a successful innovation team and a budget of $1 billion per year, FedEx's IT will be a source of strategic advantage and control for some time to come.

References: Geoffrey Colvin, "The FedEx Edge," *Fortune*, April 3, 2006, pp. 77–84; Dean Foust, "Taking Off Like 'A Rocket Ship,'" *BusinessWeek*, April 3, 2006, p. 76; "For 9th Consecutive Year, FedEx Recognized as One of *Fortune's* '100 Best Companies to Work For,'" *Business Wire*, January 10, 2006, home.businesswire.com on May 23, 2006.

International Strategic Control

Because of both their relatively large size and the increased complexity associated with international business, global organizations must take an especially pronounced strategic view of their control systems. One very basic question that has to be addressed is whether to manage control from a centralized or a decentralized perspective.[31] Under a centralized system, each organizational unit around the world is responsible for frequently reporting the results of its performance to headquarters. Managers from the home office often visit foreign branches to observe firsthand how the units are functioning.

BP, Unilever, Procter & Gamble, and Sony all use this approach. They believe centralized control is effective because it allows the home office to keep better informed of the performance of foreign units and to maintain more control over how decisions are made. For example, BP discovered that its Australian subsidiary was not billing its customers for charges as quickly as were its competitors. By shortening the billing cycle, BP now receives customer payments five days faster than before. Managers believe that they discovered this oversight only because of a centralized financial control system.

Organizations that use a decentralized control system require foreign branches to report less frequently and in less detail. For example, each unit may submit summary performance statements on a quarterly basis and provide full statements only once a year. Similarly, visits from the home office are less frequent and less concerned with monitoring and assessing performance. IBM, Ford, and Shell all use this approach. Because Ford practices decentralized control of its design function, European designers have developed several innovative automobile design features. Managers believe that if they had been more centralized, designers would not have had the freedom to develop their new ideas.

concept
CHECK

How are strategy and control most commonly integrated?

In what ways are domestic and international control issues similar, and in what ways do they differ?

Managing Control in Organizations

Effective control, whether at the operations, financial, structural, or strategic level, successfully regulates and monitors organizational activities. To use the control process, managers must recognize the characteristics of effective control and understand how to identify and overcome occasional resistance to control.[32]

Characteristics of Effective Control

Control systems tend to be most effective when they are integrated with planning and when they are flexible, accurate, timely, and objective.

Integration with Planning   Control should be linked with planning. The more explicit and precise this linkage, the more effective the control system is. The best way to integrate planning and control is to account for control as plans develop. In other words, as goals are set during the planning process, attention should be paid to developing standards that will reflect how well the plan is realized. Managers at

Champion Spark Plug Company decided to broaden their product line to include a full range of automotive accessories—a total of 21 new products. As part of this plan, managers decided in advance what level of sales they wanted to realize from each product for each of the next five years. They established these sales goals as standards against which actual sales would be compared. Thus, by accounting for their control system as they developed their plan, managers at Champion did an excellent job of integrating planning and control.

Flexibility   The control system itself must be flexible enough to accommodate change. Consider, for example, an organization whose diverse product line requires 75 different raw materials. The company's inventory control system must be able to manage and monitor current levels of inventory for all 75 materials. When a change in product line changes the number of raw materials needed, or when the required quantities of the existing materials change, the control system should be flexible enough to handle the revised requirements. The alternative—designing and implementing a new control system—is an avoidable expense. Champion's control system included a mechanism that automatically shipped products to major customers to keep their inventories at predetermined levels. The firm had to adjust this system when one of its biggest customers decided not to stock the full line of Champion products. Because its control system was flexible, though, modifying it for the customer was relatively simple.

Accuracy   Managers make a surprisingly large number of decisions based on inaccurate information. Field representatives may hedge their sales estimates to make themselves look better. Production managers may hide costs to meet their targets. Human resource managers may overestimate their minority recruiting prospects to meet affirmative action goals. In each case, the information that other managers receive is inaccurate, and the results of inaccurate information may be quite dramatic. If sales projections are inflated, a manager might cut advertising (thinking it is no longer needed) or increase advertising (to further build momentum). Similarly, a production manager unaware of hidden costs may quote a sales price much lower than desirable. Or a human resources manager may speak out publicly on the effectiveness of the company's minority recruiting, only to find out later that these prospects have been overestimated. In each case, the result of inaccurate information is inappropriate managerial action.

Timeliness   Timeliness does not necessarily mean quickness. Rather, it describes a control system that provides information as often as is necessary. Because Champion has a wealth of historical data on its sparkplug sales, it does not need information on sparkplugs as frequently as it needs sales feedback for its newer products. Retail organizations usually need sales results daily so that they can manage cash flow and adjust advertising and promotion. In contrast, they may require information about physical inventory only quarterly or annually. In general, the more uncertain and unstable the circumstances, the more frequently measurement is needed.

Objectivity   The control system should provide information that is as objective as possible. To appreciate this, imagine the task of a manager responsible for control of his organization's human resources. He asks two plant managers to submit reports. One manager notes that morale at his plant is "okay," that grievances are "about where they should be," and that turnover is "under control." The other reports that absenteeism at her plant is running at 4 percent, that 16 grievances have been filed this year (compared with 24 last year), and that turnover is 12 percent. The second report will almost always be more useful than the first. Of course, managers also need to look beyond the numbers when assessing performance. For example, a plant manager may be boosting productivity and profit margins by putting too much pressure on workers and using poor-quality materials. As a result, impressive short-run gains may be overshadowed by longer-run increases in employee turnover and customer complaints.

Resistance to Control

Managers sometimes make the mistake of assuming that the value of an effective control system is self-evident to employees. This is not always so, however. Many employees resist control, especially if they feel overcontrolled, if they think control is inappropriately focused or rewards inefficiency, or if they are uncomfortable with accountability.

Overcontrol Occasionally, organizations try to control too many things. This becomes especially problematic when the control directly affects employee behavior. An organization that instructs its employees when to come to work, where to park, when to have morning coffee, and when to leave for the day exerts considerable control over people's daily activities. Yet many organizations attempt to control not only these but other aspects of work behavior as well. Of particular relevance in recent years is some companies' efforts to control their employees' access to private e-mail and the Internet during work hours. Some companies have no policies governing these activities, some attempt to limit it, and some attempt to forbid it altogether.[33]

Troubles arise when employees perceive these attempts to limit their behavior as being unreasonable. A company that tells its employees how to dress, how to arrange their desks, and how to wear their hair may meet with more resistance. Employees at Chrysler who drove non-Chrysler vehicles used to complain because they were forced to park in a distant parking lot. People felt that these efforts to control their personal behavior (what kind of car to drive) were excessive. Managers eventually removed these controls and now allow open parking. Some employees at Abercrombie & Fitch argue that the firm is guilty of overcontrol because of its strict dress and grooming requirements—for example, no necklaces or facial hair for men and only natural nail polish and earrings no larger than a dime for women. Likewise, Enterprise Rent-A-Car has a set of 30 dress-code rules for women and 26 rules for men. The firm was recently sued by one former employee who was fired because of the color of her hair.[34]

Inappropriate Focus The control system may be too narrow, or it may focus too much on quantifiable variables and leave no room for analysis or interpretation. A sales standard that encourages high-pressure tactics to maximize short-run sales may do so at the expense of goodwill from long-term customers. Such a standard is too narrow. A university reward system that encourages faculty members to publish large numbers of articles but fails to consider the quality of the work is also inappropriately focused. Employees resist the intent of the control system by focusing their efforts only at the performance indicators being used.

Rewards for Inefficiency Imagine two operating departments that are approaching the end of their fiscal years. Department 1 expects to have $25,000 of its budget left over; department 2 is already $10,000 in the red. As a result, department 1 is likely to have its budget cut for the next year ("They had money left, so they obviously got too much to begin with"), and department 2 is likely to get a budget increase ("They obviously haven't been getting enough money"). Thus department 1 is punished for being efficient, and department 2 is rewarded for being inefficient. (No wonder departments commonly hasten to deplete their budgets as the end of the year approaches!) As with inappropriate focus, people resist the intent of this control and behave in ways that run counter to the organization's intent.

Too Much Accountability Effective controls allow managers to determine whether employees successfully discharge their responsibilities. If standards are properly set and performance accurately measured, managers know when problems arise and which departments and individuals are responsible. People who do not want to be answerable for their mistakes or who do not want to work as hard as their boss might like therefore resist control. For example, American Express has a system that provides daily information on how many calls each of its customer service representatives handles. If one representative has typically worked at a slower pace and handled fewer calls than other representatives, that individual's deficient performance can now more easily be pinpointed.

Overcoming Resistance to Control

Perhaps the best way to overcome resistance to control is to create effective control to begin with. If control systems are properly integrated with organizational planning and if the controls are flexible, accurate, timely, and objective, the organization will be less likely to overcontrol, to focus on inappropriate standards, or to reward inefficiency. Two other ways to overcome resistance are encouraging employee participation and developing verification procedures.

Encourage Employee Participation Chapter 13 notes that participation can help overcome resistance to change. By the same token, when employees are involved with planning and implementing the control system, they are less likely to resist it. For instance, employee participation in planning, decision making, and quality control at the Chevrolet Gear and Axle plant in Detroit has resulted in increased employee concern for quality and a greater commitment to meeting standards.

Develop Verification Procedures Multiple standards and information systems provide checks and balances in control and allow the organization to verify the accuracy of performance indicators. Suppose a production manager argues that she failed to meet a certain cost standard because of increased prices of raw materials. A properly designed inventory control system will either support or contradict her explanation. Suppose that an employee who was fired for excessive absences argues that he was not absent "for a long time." An effective human resource control system should have records that support the termination. Resistance to control declines because these verification procedures protect both employees and management. If the production manager's claim about the rising cost of raw materials is supported by the inventory control records, she will not be held solely accountable for failing to meet the cost standard, and some action probably will be taken to lower the cost of raw materials.

concept
CHECK

What are the essential characteristics of effective control?

Recall an incident in which you resisted control. What was done, or what might have been done better, to help overcome your resistance?

Summary of Learning Objectives and Key Points

1. Explain the purpose of control, identify different types of control, and describe the steps in the control process.
   - Control is the regulation of organizational activities so that some targeted element of performance remains within acceptable limits.
   - Control provides ways to adapt to environmental change, to limit the accumulation of errors, to cope with organizational complexity, and to minimize costs.
   - Control can focus on financial, physical, information, and human resources and includes operations, financial, structural, and strategic levels.
   - Control is the function of managers, the controller, and, increasingly, of operating employees.
   - Steps in the control process are
     - to establish standards of expected performance
     - to measure actual performance
     - to compare performance to the standards
     - to evaluate the comparison and take appropriate action

2. Identify and explain the three forms of operations control.
   - Operations control focuses on the processes the organization uses to transform resources into products or services.
   - Preliminary control is concerned with the resources that serve as inputs to the system.
   - Screening control is concerned with the transformation processes used by the organization.
   - Postaction control is concerned with the outputs of the organization.
   - Most organizations need multiple control systems because no one system can provide adequate control.

3. Describe budgets and other tools for financial control.
   - Financial control focuses on controlling the organization's financial resources.

   - The foundation of financial control is budgets, which are plans expressed in numerical terms.
   - Most organizations rely on financial, operating, and nonmonetary budgets.
   - Financial statements, various kinds of ratios, and external and internal audits are also important tools organizations use as part of financial control.

4. Identify and distinguish between two opposing forms of structural control.
   - Structural control addresses how well an organization's structural elements serve their intended purpose.
   - Two basic forms of structural control are bureaucratic and decentralized control.
     - Bureaucratic control is relatively formal and mechanistic.
     - Decentralized control is informal and organic.
   - Most organizations use a form of organizational control somewhere between total bureaucratic and total decentralized control.

5. Discuss the relationship between strategy and control, including international strategic control.
   - Strategic control focuses on how effectively the organization's strategies are succeeding in helping the organization meet its goals.
   - The integration of strategy and control is generally achieved through organization structure, leadership, technology, human resources, and information and operational control systems.
   - International strategic control is also important for multinational organizations.
   - The foundation of international strategic control is whether to practice centralized or decentralized control.

6. Identify characteristics of effective control, why people resist control, and how managers can overcome this resistance.
   - One way to increase the effectiveness of control is to fully integrate planning and control.
   - The control system should also be as flexible, accurate, timely, and objective as possible.
   - Employees may resist organizational controls because of overcontrol, inappropriate focus, rewards for inefficiency, and a desire to avoid accountability.
   - Managers can overcome this resistance by improving the effectiveness of controls and by allowing employee participation and developing verification procedures.

Discussion Questions

Questions for Review

1. What is the purpose of organizational control? Why is it important?
2. What are the different levels of control? What are the relationships between the different levels?
3. Describe how a budget is created in most organizations. How does a budget help a manager with financial control?
4. Describe the differences between bureaucratic and decentralized control. What are the advantages and disadvantages of each?

Questions for Analysis

5. How can a manager determine whether his or her firm needs improvement in control? If improvement is needed, how can the manager tell what type of control needs improvement (operations, financial, structural, or strategic)? Describe some steps a manager can take to improve each of these types of control.
6. One company uses strict performance standards. Another has standards that are more flexible. What are the advantages and disadvantages of each system?
7. Are the differences in bureaucratic control and decentralized control related to differences in organization structure? If so, how? If not, why not? (The terms do sound similar to those used to discuss the organizing process.)

Questions for Application

8. Many organizations today are involving lower-level employees in control. Give at least two examples of specific actions that a lower-level worker could do to help his or her organization better adapt to environmental change. Then do the same for limiting the accumulation of error, coping with organizational complexity, and minimizing costs.
9. Describe ways that the top management team, midlevel managers, and operating employees can participate in each step of the control process. Do all participate equally in each step, or are some steps better suited for personnel at one level? Explain your answer.
10. Interview a worker to determine which areas and levels of control exist for him or her on the job. Does the worker resist efforts at control? Why or why not?

Building Effective Time-Management Skills

Exercise Overview

Time-management skills—a manager's ability to prioritize work, to work efficiently, and to delegate appropriately—play a major role in the control function; that is, a manager can use time-management skills to control his or her own work more effectively. This exercise will help demonstrate the relationship between time-management skills and control.

Exercise Background

You are a middle manager in a small manufacturing plant. Today is Monday, and you have just returned from a week of vacation. The first thing you discover is that your assistant will not be in today. His aunt died, and he is out of town at the funeral. He did, however, leave you the following note:

Dear Boss:

Sorry about not being here today. I will be back tomorrow. In the meantime, here are some things you need to know:
Ms. Glinski [your boss] wants to see you today at 4:00.
The shop steward wants to see you as soon as possible about a labor problem.

Mr. Bateman [one of your big customers] has a complaint about a recent shipment.

Ms. Ferris [one of your major suppliers] wants to discuss a change in delivery schedules.

Mr. Prescott from the Chamber of Commerce wants you to attend a breakfast meeting on Wednesday to discuss our expansion plans.

The legal office wants to discuss our upcoming OSHA inspection.

Human resources wants to know when you can interview someone for the new supervisor's position.

Jack Williams, the machinist you fired last month, has been hanging around the parking lot, and his presence is making some employees uncomfortable.

Exercise Task

With the information above as context, do the following:
1. Prioritize the work that needs to be done by sorting the information above into three categories: very timely, moderately timely, and less timely.
2. Are importance and timeliness the same thing?
3. What additional information must you acquire before you can begin to prioritize this work?
4. How would your approach differ if your assistant were in today?

Building Effective Technical Skills

Exercise Overview

Technical skills are the skills necessary to accomplish or understand the specific kind of work being done in an organization. This exercise gives you practice in technical skills related to building a budget and evaluating the effectiveness of a budget.

Exercise Background

Although corporate budgets are much more complicated, the steps in creating a personal budget and creating a corporate budget are much the same. Both begin with estimations of inflow and outflow. They both compare actual results with estimated results. And both end with the development of a plan for corrective action.

Exercise Task

1. Prepare your estimated expenditures and income for one month. This is a budgeted amount, not the amount you actually spend. Instead, it should represent a typical month or a reasonable minimum. For example, is $200 a reasonable amount to spend on groceries? Estimate your necessary monthly expenses for tuition, rent, car payments, childcare, food, utilities, and so on. Then estimate your income from all sources, such as wages, allowance, loans, and funds borrowed on credit cards. Calculate the totals.
2. Write down all of your actual expenses over the last month. Then write down all your actual income. If you do not have exact figures, estimate as closely as you can. Calculate the totals.
3. Compare your estimates to your actual expenses and actual income. Are there any discrepancies? If so, what caused these discrepancies?
4. Did you expect to have a surplus or a deficit for the month? Did you actually have a deficit or a surplus? What are your plans for making up any deficit or managing any surplus?
5. Do you regularly use a personal budget? Is a personal budget likely to be helpful? Why or why not?

CHAPTER CLOSING CASE

IS TOO MUCH CONTROL HURTING DELL?

Michael Dell "broke the paradigm about how to run a computer business," says professor David Yoffie. Among Dell's innovations: direct selling to customers to avoid payments to retailers, flexible manufacturing for customization at a low cost, and just-in-time inventory to keep expenses low. It's clear that Dell's phenomenal success over the last two decades was due to its tightly disciplined operations and relentless controls.

However, the future looks less promising. Customers are flocking to retail stores for the latest electronic gear, which Dell does not carry. The PC maker's customer satisfaction ratings have fallen and complaints are up. Cutthroat competition in desktop PCs, which account for over half of Dell's sales, has squeezed profit margins to a thin 3.8 percent. In February 2006, Dell announced that expected sales growth for the upcoming quarter would be around 7 percent, a drastic drop from last year's 16 percent. Is too much control hurting Dell?

On the positive side, Dell's "value-priced" business model means the firm has done a good job of controlling costs. Dell's new North Carolina plant, opened in October 2005, can produce PCs 40 percent faster with 30 percent less downtime. Unlike older factories, where equipment must be retooled for different types of computers, the new plant can build any of Dell's 40 computer models at any time. Factory designer Richard Komm says, "Other factories have a process-driven flow. [This plant] is focused on one thing: How do we get

[a computer] to the customer in the shortest amount of time?"

Automated robots are not as efficient as humans in certain tasks, such as packing small, delicate items. Instead, robots perform the heavy lifting, such as placing finished machines in shipping boxes. Automating the heavier tasks lowers the injury rate, reducing claims for workers' compensation.

Excellent quality control also reduces costs. Teams of three workers help to build a PC. Each individual has a specialized set of tasks, which eases training, speeds assembly, and reduces errors by 30 percent. Each team includes a tester who performs a quick check when every machine is finished to see that it's wired correctly and will boot. Machines that pass inspection will undergo more extensive testing, but the quick test allows rapid spotting of gross defects. Most defects are now caught in 4 minutes rather than 60, and the overall defect rate is lower. "The faster you get feedback to the operator, the fewer defects," says Komm.

On the negative side, some believe that Dell has gone too far in its quest for control. Some home users, who make up the majority of Dell customers but are half as profitable as business users, are dissatisfied. They complain that much of Dell's customer support staff is located in India, making communications difficult at times. Very long wait times are another concern. "Consumers want to have their cake and eat it too," says Stephen Dukker, CEO of PC maker emachines, Inc. "They want that $300 PC but

expect the same support that came with a machine that 10 years ago cost $2,500." Given today's industry environment, that desire is unrealistic. Dell's least expensive desktop model retails for $299, which would yield a mere $12 in profits, not enough to support much customer service.

To control costs, Dell introduced different levels of customer service to those who pay for pricier models. A buyer of the top-of-the-line XPS model typically waits less than five minutes for phone service, while buyers of $299 models may be put on hold for one to two hours. Dell also plans to sell varying levels of service contracts at various prices. Some standard features will disappear. Sometime in 2006, "free shipping" on low-end models will include delivery only to a local post office. Home delivery will cost extra.

An even bigger concern is Dell's lack of innovation. The company has always assumed that price is paramount, leading to an emphasis on inexpensive, commodity-like products. However, buyers today want tablet PCs, portable music and video players, digital photography, and more. Dell spends less on research and development than rival Apple Computers, despite being four times larger.

Professor Yoffie says, "Michael broke the paradigm," but adds, "They haven't been so great at finding the next paradigm." With competitors imitating Dell's best tactics and gaining on Dell in price and productivity, industry expert Mark Stahlman says, "Dell is singing the same old song. It's time for them to change." Perhaps Dell could afford to give up a little control in exchange for a little more creativity, flexibility, and customer service. Perhaps they can't afford not to.

CASE QUESTIONS

1. What advantages does Dell gain from its tight control system?

What disadvantages does the company experience?

2. Which types of operations controls are mentioned in this case? Give examples of each type.

3. Are Dell's control systems effective? In your opinion, what could Dell do to make its control systems more effective? Explain your responses.

CASE REFERENCES

Amanda Cantrell, "Dell to Get Served by AMD," *Money*, May 18, 2006, www.cnnmoney.com on May 23, 2006; Louise Lee, "Hanging Up on Dell?" *BusinessWeek*, October 10, 2005, www.businessweek.com on May 7, 2006; Louise Lee, "It's Dell vs. The Dell Way," *BusinessWeek*, March 6, 2006, pp. 61–62; Christopher Null, "Dude, You're Getting a Dell—Every Five Seconds," *Business 2.0*, December 1, 2005, www.money.cnn.com on May 15, 2006.

YOU MAKE THE CALL

Chasing Dimon's Dream for J. P. Morgan Chase

1. Would you want to work for Jamie Dimon? Why or why not?
2. How similar or dissimilar is Dimon's management style to the style you might expect to have as a manager?
3. Assume that you are a consultant hired by Dimon. He has asked you to candidly critique his management of J. P. Morgan Chase. What would you have to say?
4. Can you foresee a time when Dimon might need to change his approach to organizational control? What are the factors that might dictate such a change?
5. Would Dimon's approach to control work in other industries? Why or why not?

Test Prepper

college.hmco.com/business/students

Choose the correct answer. Answers are found at the back of the book.

1. T   F   The first step in the control process is measuring performance.

2. T   F   Managers use nonmonetary budgets to quantify resources, such as hours of labor and units of output, into financial terms.

3. T   F   The goal of bureaucratic control is compliance.

4. T   F   A timely control system is not necessarily a quick control system.

5. T   F   Verification procedures lower resistance to control.

6. Which of the following levels of control focuses on the processes organizations use to transform resources into products or services?

    A. Financial
    B. Structural
    C. Operations
    D. Strategic
    E. Managerial

7. When performance matches the standards, a manager should

    A. correct the deviation.
    B. change the standards.
    C. lower employee resistance.
    D. reduce overperformance.
    E. maintain the status quo.

8. Bruce works in a company that produces sensitive electronic equipment. He is confident the components he buys to make this equipment is of high quality, but he knows he must keep a close eye on the production process itself to avoid damaging these components as the equipment is assembled. Bruce needs to emphasize which form of control?

    A. Postaction
    B. Screening
    C. Preliminary
    D. Managerial
    E. Technical

9. Of what benefit to a manager is ratio analysis?

    A. It helps the manager know whether the organization is nondiscriminatory.
    B. It gives the manager a picture of some aspect of the financial health of the firm.
    C. It allows for an independent appraisal of the organization's control system.
    D. It summarizes the financial performance of the organization over the past year.
    E. It avoids the common trap of overcontrol.

10. Bernadette wants to build an effective control system. She should try to include all of the following characteristics EXCEPT

    A. integrated with planning.
    B. timely.
    C. accurate.
    D. rigid.
    E. objective.

chapter 21

Managing Operations, Quality, and Productivity

FIRST THINGS FIRST

Improving the Quality of Hotels

"Our clientele is willing to pay for that quality of service."

—SIMON COOPER, PRESIDENT, MARRIOTT

The luxury traveler can easily find an elegant hotel in New York City. The art deco landmark Waldorf-Astoria and the Plaza, site of the Eloise children's books, for example, are available for nightly rates of $500 and up. "Our clientele is willing to pay for that quality of service," says Simon Cooper of Marriott's Ritz-Carlton. In the 1990s, boutique hotels became popular in New York City. These properties are hip, featuring playful, modern designs, but they also charge

Many hotels today are going to great lengths to improve the level of service they provide for their guests. Indeed, this is becoming a major point of competition.

premium prices. New York offers few options for travelers not willing or able to pay that price.

New York real estate is expensive, so naturally hotel rates are high and rooms are tiny. Hotel restaurants and bars may be fabulous, but amenities such as refrigerators, gyms, and even bathtubs are often scarce. In addition, limited construction of new hotels increases occupancy rates and regularly drives room prices up. A *Frommer's New York City* travel guide says, "There just isn't the range of properties you'd find even in other expensive markets like London and Paris. You've got fleabags, you've got palaces—and not a whole lot in between." Many family and business travelers define a quality hotel as one that offers safety, cleanliness, and comfort. Hotels are starting to recognize the needs of this customer segment.

One obvious solution that has been slow to catch on is the expansion of moderate-priced chain hotels, such as Courtyard by Marriott and Holiday Inn Express. Midlevel brands are just beginning entry into this market. Prices are under $200, a steal for pricey New York.

Another relatively easy fix is an overhaul of existing hotels. For example, Westin hotels found that only 6 percent of guests requested a smoking room. Of those, 90 percent wanted to quit. So it converted all of its rooms to nonsmoking, accomplished by a thorough cleaning and replacement of linens. Other changes include a healthier menu and relaxing fragrances and music. "We view our hotels as a retreat from the rigor of travel," says vice president Sue Brush. "At Westin, we strive to offer a spectrum of products, services, and personal touches that will help our guests walk out of our hotels feeling better than when they arrived."

IDEO is going further, revamping room design in conjunction with Marriott's TownePlace Suites. IDEO designers and anthropologists shadow consumers for days, observing how they use the space, how they spend their time, what they eat, and so on. This deep study can yield surprising insights. IDEO discovered that New York tourists do not need food service because they want to eat in local restaurants. Guests don't appreciate a traditional, overdecorated hotel lobby. They will use their hotel bed as an impromptu desk if none is available.

Hotels can improve the quality of guests' experiences by providing more information about nearby attractions. Lobbies can be simpler, with a few chairs and small tables. A flexible wall unit that can serve as a dining table, TV stand, or desk is desirable and less costly than separate pieces of furniture. Cut back on luxurious frills. Offer more nonsmoking rooms and other inexpensive, health-conscious options. Hotels are learning—when it comes to quality, it can pay to let the guest define it for you.[1]

Managers in the hotel industry are beginning to appreciate the importance of meeting customer needs—most often an optimal blend of price, location, and amenities. Indeed, as is the case in most industries, hotel managers are rethinking all aspects of their operations as they strive to improve quality and boost productivity.

In this chapter we explore operations management, quality, and productivity. We first introduce operations management and discuss its role in general management and organizational strategy. The next three sections discuss the design of operations systems, organizational technologies, and implementing operations systems. We then introduce and discuss various issues in managing for quality and total quality. Finally, we discuss productivity, which is closely related to quality.

The Nature of Operations Management

operations management
The total set of managerial activities used by an organization to transform resource inputs into products, services, or both

Operations management is at the core of what organizations do as they add value and create products and services. But what exactly are operations? And how are they managed? ***Operations management*** is the set of managerial activities used by an organization to transform resource inputs into products and services. When Dell Computer buys electronic components, assembles them into PCs, and then ships them to customers, it is engaging in operations management. When a Pizza Hut employee orders food and paper products and then combines dough, cheese, and tomato paste to create a pizza, he or she is engaging in operations management.

The Importance of Operations

Operations is an important functional concern for organizations because efficient and effective management of operations goes a long way toward ensuring competitiveness and overall organizational performance, as well as quality and productivity. Inefficient or ineffective operations management, on the other hand, will almost inevitably lead to poorer performance and lower levels of both quality and productivity.

In an economic sense, operations management creates value and utility of one type or another, depending on the nature of the firm's products or services. If the product is a physical good, such as a Harley-Davidson motorcycle, operations creates value and provides form utility by combining many dissimilar inputs (sheet metal, rubber, paint, combustion engines, and human skills) to make something

Manufacturing and production are frequently key components of a company's quality management efforts. IGT Corporation makes electronic slot machines that are sold to casinos and other gambling operations around the world. Because of the stringent government regulations that affect this industry, and the potential costs that errors might create, it is extremely important that all machines be of the highest quality. Thus this inspector is closely examining a transparent cover sheet that will announce whether the player has struck it rich!

(a motorcycle) that is more valuable than the actual cost of the inputs used to create it. The inputs are converted from their incoming form into a new physical form. This conversion is typical of manufacturing operations and essentially reflects the organization's technology.

In contrast, the operations activities of American Airlines create value and provide time and place utility through its services. The airline transports passengers and freight according to agreed-upon departure and arrival places and times. Other service operations, such as a Coors beer distributorship or a Gap retail store, create value and provide place and possession utility by bringing together the customer and products made by others. Although the organizations in these examples produce different kinds of products or services, their operations processes share many important features.[2]

Manufacturing and Production Operations

Because manufacturing once dominated U.S. industry, the entire area of operations management used to be called "production management." **Manufacturing** is a form of business that combines and transforms resources into tangible outcomes that are then sold to others. The Goodyear Tire & Rubber Company is a manufacturer because it combines rubber and chemical compounds and uses blending equipment and molding machines to create tires. Broyhill is a manufacturer because it buys wood and metal components, pads, and fabric and then combines them into furniture.

manufacturing
A form of business that combines and transforms resource inputs into tangible outcomes

During the 1970s, manufacturing entered a long period of decline in the United States, primarily because of foreign competition. U.S. firms had grown lax and sluggish, and new foreign competitors came onto the scene with better equipment and much higher levels of efficiency. For example, steel companies in the Far East were able to produce high-quality steel for much lower prices than were U.S. companies like Bethlehem Steel and U.S. Steel (now USX Corporation). Faced with a battle for survival, many companies underwent a long and difficult period of change by eliminating waste and transforming themselves into leaner and more efficient and responsive entities. They reduced their workforces dramatically, closed antiquated or unnecessary plants, and modernized their remaining plants. In the last decade, their efforts have started to pay dividends, as U.S. businesses have regained their competitive positions in many different industries. Although manufacturers from other parts of the world are still formidable competitors, and U.S. firms may never again be competitive in some markets, the overall picture is much better than it was just a few years ago. And prospects continue to look bright.[3]

Service Operations

During the decline of the manufacturing sector, a tremendous growth in the service sector kept the U.S. economy from declining at the same rate. A **service organization** is one that transforms resources into an intangible output and creates time or place utility for its customers. For example, Merrill Lynch makes stock transactions for its customers, Avis leases cars to its customers, and local hairdressers cut clients' hair. In 1947 the service sector was responsible for less than half of the U.S. gross national product (GNP). By 1975, however, this figure reached 65 percent, and by 2006 it was over 80 percent.[4] The service sector has been responsible for almost 90 percent of all new jobs created in the United States during the 1990s. Managers

service organization
An organization that transforms resources into an intangible output and creates time or place utility for its customers

have come to see that many of the tools, techniques, and methods that are used in a factory are also useful to a service firm. For example, managers of automobile plants and hair salons both have to decide how to design their facilities, identify the best locations for them, determine optimal capacities, make decisions about inventory storage, set procedures for purchasing raw materials, and set standards for productivity and quality.

The Role of Operations in Organizational Strategy

It should be clear by this point that operations management is very important to organizations. Beyond its direct impact on such factors as competitiveness, quality, and productivity, it also directly influences the organization's overall level of effectiveness. For example, the deceptively simple strategic decision of whether to stress high quality regardless of cost, lowest possible cost regardless of quality, or some combination of the two has numerous important implications. A highest-possible-quality strategy will dictate state-of-the-art technology and rigorous control of product design and materials specifications. A combination strategy might call for lower-grade technology and less concern about product design and materials specifications. Just as strategy affects operations management, so, too, does operations management affect strategy. Suppose that a firm decides to upgrade the quality of its products or services. The organization's ability to implement the decision is dependent in part on current production capabilities and other resources. If existing technology will not permit higher-quality work, and if the organization lacks the resources to replace its technology, increasing quality to the desired new standards will be difficult.

concept
CHECK

| Distinguish between manufacturing and production operations and service operations. | Why do you think the manufacturing sector of the U.S. economy has declined while the service sector has grown? |

Designing Operations Systems

The problems, challenges, and opportunities faced by operations managers revolve around the acquisition and utilization of resources for conversion. Their goals include both efficiency and effectiveness. A number of issues and decisions must be addressed as operations systems are designed. The most basic ones are product-service mix, capacity, and facilities.

Determining Product-Service Mix

product-service mix
How many and what kinds of products or services (or both) to offer

A natural starting point in designing operations systems is determining the ***product-service mix***. This decision flows from corporate, business, and marketing strategies. Managers have to make a number of decisions about their products and services, starting with how many and what kinds to offer.[5] Procter & Gamble, for example, makes regular, tartar-control, gel, and various other formulas of Crest toothpaste and packages them in several different sizes of tubes, pumps, and other dispensers. Similarly, workers at Subway sandwich shops can combine different breads, vegetables, meats, and condiments to create hundreds of different kinds of sandwiches. Decisions also have to be made regarding the level of quality desired, the optimal cost of each product or service, and exactly how each is to be designed. GE recently reduced the number of parts in its industrial circuit breakers from 28,000 to 1,275. This whole process was achieved by carefully analyzing product design and production methods.

Capacity Decisions

The **capacity** decision involves choosing the amount of products, services, or both that can be produced by the organization. Determining whether to build a factory capable of making 5,000 or 8,000 units per day is a capacity decision. So, too, is deciding whether to build a restaurant with 100 or 150 seats, or a bank with 5 or 10 teller stations. The capacity decision is truly a high-risk one because of the uncertainties of future product demand and the large monetary stakes involved. An organization that builds capacity exceeding its needs may commit resources (capital investment) that will never be recovered. Alternatively, an organization can build a facility with a smaller capacity than expected demand. Doing so may result in lost market opportunities, but it may also free capital resources for use elsewhere in the organization.

A major consideration in determining capacity is demand. A company operating with fairly constant monthly demand might build a plant capable of producing an amount each month roughly equivalent to its demand. But if its market is characterized by seasonal fluctuations, building a smaller plant to meet normal demand and then adding extra shifts staffed with temporary workers or paying permanent workers extra to work more hours during peak periods might be the most effective choice. Likewise, a restaurant that needs 150 seats for Saturday night but never needs more than 100 at any other time during the week would probably be foolish to expand to 150 seats. During the rest of the week, it must still pay to light, heat, cool, and clean the excess capacity. Many customer service departments have tried to improve their capacity to deal with customers while also lowering costs by using automated voice prompts to direct callers to the right representative. However, as discussed in *The Business of Ethics,* this approach is fraught with challenges.

> *capacity*
> The amount of products, services, or both that can be produced by an organization

Facilities Decisions

Facilities are the physical locations where products or services are created, stored, and distributed. Major decisions pertain to facilities location and facilities layout.

Location *Location* is the physical positioning or geographic site of facilities and must be determined by the needs and requirements of the organization. A company that relies heavily on railroads for transportation needs to be located close to rail facilities. GE decided that it did not need six plants to make circuit breakers, so it invested heavily in automating one plant and closed the other five. Different organizations in the same industry may have different facilities requirements. Benetton uses only one distribution center for the entire world, whereas Wal-Mart has several distribution centers in the United States alone. A retail business must choose its location very carefully to be convenient for consumers.

Layout The choice of physical configuration, or the **layout**, of facilities is closely related to other operations decisions. The three entirely different layout alternatives

> *facilities*
> The physical locations where products or services are created, stored, and distributed

> *location*
> The physical positioning or geographic site of facilities

> *layout*
> The physical configuration of facilities, the arrangement of equipment within facilities, or both

The Business of Ethics

Talking to a Human

Consider the frustration associated with customer service call centers and automated phone menus: long waits, hang-ups, numerous transfers. Two contradictory facts emerge: (1) Marketing departments will spend time or even pay money to get a new customer to talk to them. (2) Customer service departments do everything they can to not talk with customers.

This paradox appears on the website **www.gethuman .com**, founded by technology entrepreneur Paul English. On his website, English asks, "Which do you think will result in companies learning how to improve their products and services, and getting more customer revenue? Spending a hundred million dollars on market research and advertising, or loving your existing customers?"

English adds, "I'm not anti-computer. I've been a programmer for 20 years. I'm not anti-capitalist. I'm on my fifth start-up. But I am anti-arrogance. Why do the executives who run these call centers think they can decide when I deserve to speak to a human being and when I don't?"

Lots of folks complain about corporate call centers, but they don't have English's tech skills and industry credibility. First, he wrote about customer service in his blog and created the Get Human site. Then English

decided to get revenge. Based on his own investigations, friends working in corporate IT departments, and strangers who sent suggestions, English posted a "cheat sheet" for popular call centers, from Anheuser Busch to Xbox. The list tells how, by pressing phone buttons, consumers can bypass an automated phone system and talk to a live service representative. Calling CompuServe? Press 1211 without waiting for the prompts. NetZero? Try # # #, then 32.

Companies could respond by making their phone systems even more complex and difficult to use. Or they could take the advice of Jim Kelly, head of customer service at ING Direct. At Kelly's bank, customers call an average of only 1.6 times annually because their online system is so easy to understand. Even so, ING answers every call with a human. "Eliminate most of the problems and complaints," Kelly advises. "The only reason for people to call is to do business. And those are calls you're eager to take."

References: "Blog," "Home," "Tips," Get Human website, www.gethuman .com on May 24, 2006; Burt Helm, "Building Good Web Buzz," *BusinessWeek*, April 17, 2006, www.businessweek.com on May 24, 2006; William C. Taylor, "Your Call Should Be Important to Us, but It's Not," *New York Times*, February 26, 2006, p. BU 3.

---

product layout
A physical configuration of facilities arranged around the product; used when large quantities of a single product are needed

process layout
A physical configuration of facilities arranged around the process; used in facilities that create or process a variety of products

fixed-position layout
A physical configuration of facilities arranged around a single work area; used for the manufacture of large and complex products such as airplanes

shown in Figure 21.1 help demonstrate the importance of the layout decision. A ***product layout*** is appropriate when large quantities of a single product are needed. It makes sense to custom-design a straight-line flow of work for a product when a specific task is performed at each workstation as each unit flows past. Most assembly lines use this format. For example, Dell's personal computer factories use a product layout.

Process layouts are used in operations settings that create or process a variety of products. Auto repair shops and healthcare clinics are good examples. Each car and each person is a separate "product." The needs of each incoming job are diagnosed as it enters the operations system, and the job is routed through the unique sequence of workstations needed to create the desired finished product. In a process layout, each type of conversion task is centralized in a single workstation or department. All welding is done in one designated shop location, and any car that requires welding is moved to that area. This setup is in contrast to the product layout, in which several different workstations may perform welding operations if the conversion task sequence so dictates. Similarly, in a hospital, all X-rays are done in one location, all surgeries in another, and all physical therapy in yet another. Patients are moved from location to location to get the services they need.

The ***fixed-position layout*** is used when the organization is creating a few very large and complex products. Aircraft manufacturers like Boeing and shipbuilders like

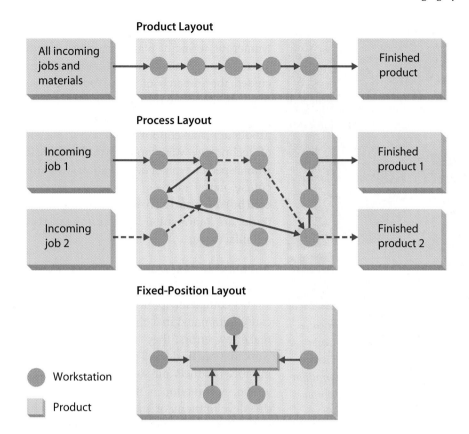

Figure 21.1

APPROACHES TO FACILITIES LAYOUT

When a manufacturer produces large quantities of a product (such as cars or computers), it may arrange its facilities in an assembly line (product layout). In a process layout, the work (such as patients in a hospital or custom pieces of furniture) moves through various workstations. Locomotives and bridges are both manufactured in a fixed-position layout.

Newport News use this method. An assembly line capable of moving one of Boeing's new 787 aircraft would require an enormous plant, so instead the airplane itself remains stationary, and people and machines move around it as it is assembled.

The cellular layout is a relatively new approach to facilities design. **Cellular layouts** are used when families of products can follow similar flow paths. A clothing manufacturer, for example, might create a cell, or designated area, dedicated to making a family of pockets, such as pockets for shirts, coats, blouses, and slacks. Although each kind of pocket is unique, the same basic equipment and methods are used to make all of them. Hence, all pockets might be made in the same area and then delivered directly to different product layout assembly areas where the shirts, coats, blouses, and slacks are actually being assembled.

cellular layout
A physical configuration of facilities used when families of products can follow similar flow paths

concept CHECK

What are the three basic components in designing operations systems? Identify the basic decisions that relate to each.

Think of three local restaurants or other establishments that you have visited recently. Characterize the three components of the operations systems used by each.

Organizational Technologies

One central element of effective operations management is technology. In Chapter 3 we defined **technology** as the set of processes and systems used by organizations to convert resources into products or services.

technology
The set of processes and systems used by organizations to convert resources into products or services

Manufacturing technology continues to become increasingly sophisticated. Ford Motor auto assembly workers Steve Lindgar (left) and Shirley Cosby use a programmable lift to install the engine in a Ford Mustang at Ford's new production plant in Flat Rock, Michigan. Ford invested nearly $700 million in this plant's flexible manufacturing system, which includes programmable platforms that hold the car body on a scissors lift and adjust to the operator's height for improved ergonomics.

automation

The process of designing work so that it can be completely or almost completely performed by machines

Manufacturing Technology

Numerous forms of manufacturing technology are used in organizations. In Chapter 12 we discussed the research of Joan Woodward. Recall that Woodward identified three forms of technology—unit or small batch, large batch or mass production, and continuous process.[6] Each form of technology was thought to be associated with a specific type of organization structure. Of course, newer forms of technology not considered by Woodward also warrant attention. Two of these are automation and computer-assisted manufacturing.

Automation *Automation* is the process of designing work so that it can be completely or almost completely performed by machines. Because automated machines operate quickly and make few errors, they increase the amount of work that can be done. Thus automation helps to improve products and services, and fosters innovation. Automation is the most recent step in the development of machines and machine-controlling devices. Machine-controlling devices have been around since the 1700s. James Watt, a Scottish engineer, invented a mechanical speed control to regulate the speed of steam engines in 1787. The Jacquard loom, developed by a French inventor, was controlled by paper cards with holes punched in them. Early accounting and computing equipment was controlled by similar punched cards.

Automation relies on feedback, information, sensors, and a control mechanism. Feedback is the flow of information from the machine back to the sensor. Sensors are the parts of the system that gather information and compare it to preset standards. The control mechanism is the device that sends instructions to the automatic machine. Early automatic machines were primitive, and the use of automation was relatively slow to develop. These elements are illustrated by the example in Figure 21.2. A thermostat has sensors that monitor air temperature and compare it to a preset low value. If the air temperature falls below the preset value, the thermostat sends an electrical signal to the furnace, turning it on. The furnace heats the air. When the sensors detect that the air temperature has reached a value higher than the low preset value, the thermostat stops the furnace. The last step (shutting off the furnace) is known as *feedback*, a critical component of any automated operation.

The big move to automate factories began during World War II. The shortage of skilled workers and the development of high-speed computers combined to bring about a tremendous interest in automation. Programmable automation (the use of computers to control machines) was introduced during this era, far outstripping conventional automation (the use of mechanical or electromechanical devices to control machines). The automobile industry began to use automatic machines for a variety of jobs. In fact, the term *automation* came into use in the 1950s in the

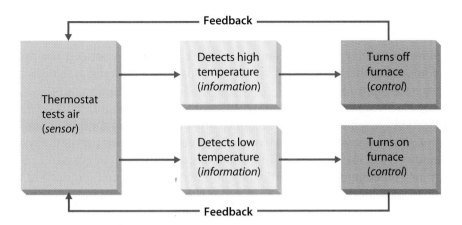

Figure 21.2

A SIMPLE AUTOMATIC CONTROL MECHANISM

All automation includes feedback, information, sensors, and a control mechanism. A simple thermostat is an example of automation. Another example is Benetton's distribution center in Italy. Orders are received, items pulled from stock and packaged for shipment, and invoices prepared and transmitted, with no human intervention.

automobile industry. The chemical and oil-refining industries also began to use computers to regulate production. During the 1990s, automation became a major element in the manufacture of computers and computer components, such as electronic chips and circuits. It is this computerized, or programmable, automation that presents the greatest opportunities and challenges for management today.

The impact of automation on people in the workplace is complex. In the short term, people whose jobs are automated may find themselves without a job. In the long term, however, more jobs are created than are lost. Nevertheless, not all companies are able to help displaced workers find new jobs, so the human costs are sometimes high. In the coal industry, for instance, automation has been used primarily in mining. The output per miner has risen dramatically from the 1950s on. The demand for coal, however, has decreased, and productivity gains resulting from automation have lessened the need for miners. Consequently, many workers have lost their jobs, and the industry has not been able to absorb them. In contrast, in the electronics industry, the rising demand for products has led to increasing employment opportunities despite the use of automation.[7]

Computer-Assisted Manufacturing   Current extensions of automation generally revolve around computer-assisted manufacturing. ***Computer-assisted manufacturing*** is technology that relies on computers to design or manufacture products. One type of computer-assisted manufacturing is *computer-aided design (CAD)*—the use of computers to design parts and complete products and to simulate performance so that prototypes need not be constructed. Boeing uses CAD technology to study hydraulic tubing in its commercial aircraft. Japan's automotive industry uses it to speed up car design. GE used CAD to change the design of circuit breakers, and Benetton uses CAD to design new styles and products. Oneida, the table flatware firm, used CAD to design a new spoon in only two days.[8] CAD is usually combined with *computer-aided manufacturing (CAM)* to ensure that the design moves smoothly to production. The production computer shares the design computer's information and is able to have machines with the proper settings ready when production is needed. A CAM system is especially useful when reorders come in because the computer can quickly produce the desired product, prepare labels and copies of orders, and send the product out to where it is wanted.

Closely aligned with this approach is *computer-integrated manufacturing (CIM)*. In CIM, CAD and CAM are linked together, and computer networks automatically

> **computer-assisted manufacturing**
> A technology that relies on computers to design or manufacture products

adjust machine placements and settings to enhance both the complexity and the flexibility of scheduling. In settings that use these technologies, all manufacturing activities are controlled by the computer network. Because the network can access the company's other information systems, CIM is both a powerful and a complex management control tool.

Flexible manufacturing systems (FMS) usually have robotic work units or workstations, assembly lines, and robotic carts or some other form of computer-controlled transport system to move material as needed from one part of the system to another. FMS like the one at IBM's manufacturing facility in Lexington, Kentucky, rely on computers to coordinate and integrate automated production and materials-handling facilities. And Ford Motor Company used FMS to transform an English factory producing low-cost Ford Escorts into a Jaguar plant making Jaguar luxury cars. Using traditional methods, the plant would have been closed, its workers laid off, and the facility virtually rebuilt from the ground up. But by using FMS, Ford was able to keep the plant open and running continuously while new equipment was being installed and its workers were being retrained in small groups.[9]

These systems are not without disadvantages, however. For example, because they represent fundamental change, they also generate resistance. Additionally, because of their tremendous complexity, CAD systems are not always reliable. CIM systems are so expensive that they raise the break-even point for firms using them. This means that the firm must operate at high levels of production and sales to be able to afford the systems.

Robotics   Another trend in manufacturing technology is computerized robotics. A **robot** is any artificial device that is able to perform functions ordinarily thought to be appropriate for human beings. Robotics refers to the science and technology of the construction, maintenance, and use of robots. The use of industrial robots has steadily increased since 1980 and is expected to continue to increase slowly as more companies recognize the benefits that accrue to users of industrial robots.[10]

Welding was one of the first applications for robots, and it continues to be the area for most applications. A close second is materials handling. Other applications include machine loading and unloading, painting and finishing, assembly, casting, and such machining applications as cutting, grinding, polishing, drilling, sanding, buffing, and deburring. DaimlerChrysler, for instance, replaced about 200 welders with 50 robots on an assembly line and increased productivity about 20 percent. The use of robots in inspection work is increasing. They can check for cracks and holes, and they can be equipped with vision systems to perform visual inspections.

Robots are also beginning to move from the factory floor to all manner of other applications. The Dallas police used a robot to apprehend a suspect who had barricaded himself in an apartment building. The robot smashed a window and reached with its mechanical arm into the building. The suspect panicked and ran outside. At the Long Beach Memorial Hospital in California, brain surgeons are assisted by a robot arm that drills into the patient's skull with excellent precision. Some newer applications involve remote work. For example, the use of robot submersibles controlled from the surface can help divers in remote locations. Surveillance robots fitted with microwave sensors can do things that a human guard cannot do, such as "seeing" through nonmetallic walls and in the dark. In other applications, automated farming (called "agrimation") uses robot harvesters to pick fruit from a variety of trees.

robot
Any artificial device that is able to perform functions ordinarily thought to be appropriate for human beings

Robots are also used by small manufacturers. One robot slices carpeting to fit the inside of custom vans in an upholstery shop. Another stretches balloons flat so that they can be spray-painted with slogans at a novelties company. At a jewelry company, a robot holds class rings while they are engraved by a laser. These robots are lighter, faster, stronger, and more intelligent than those used in heavy manufacturing and are the types that more and more organizations will be using in the future.

> "We can't [reverse outsourcing] unless we use technology—robotics in particular—to increase our factory workers' productivity."
>
> Rodney Brooks, Director, MIT Artificial Intelligence Laboratory
> (*Newsweek*, June 12, 2006, p. 56)

Service Technology

Service technology is also changing rapidly. And it, too, is moving more and more toward automated systems and procedures. In banking, for example, new technological breakthroughs led to automated teller machines and made it much easier to move funds between accounts or between different banks. Many people now have their paycheck deposited directly into a checking account from which many of their bills are then automatically paid. And credit card transactions by Visa customers are recorded and billed electronically.

Hotels use increasingly sophisticated technology to accept and record room reservations (other aspects of their technology are discussed in "First Things First" at the beginning of this chapter). Universities use new technologies to electronically store and provide access to books, scientific journals, government reports, and articles. Hospitals and other healthcare organizations use new forms of service technology to manage patient records, dispatch ambulances and EMTs, and monitor patient vital signs. Restaurants use technology to record and fill customer orders, order food and supplies, and prepare food. Given the increased role that service organizations are playing in today's economy, even more technological innovations are certain to be developed in the years to come.[11]

concept
CHECK

Identify and describe three relatively new manufacturing technologies.

Identify as many examples as you can of how service technology at your college or university has changed in recent times.

Implementing Operations Systems Through Supply Chain Management

After operations systems have been properly designed and technologies developed, they must then be put into use by the organization. Their basic functional purpose is to control transformation processes to ensure that relevant goals are achieved in such areas as quality and costs. Operations management has a number of special purposes within this control framework, including purchasing and inventory management. Indeed, this area of management has become so important in recent years that a new term—*supply chain management*—has been coined. Specifically, **supply chain management** can be defined as the process of managing operations control, resource acquisition and purchasing, and inventory so as to improve overall efficiency and effectiveness.[12]

supply chain management
The process of managing operations control, resource acquisition, and inventory so as to improve overall efficiency and effectiveness

Operations Management as Control

One way of using operations management as control is to coordinate it with other functions. Monsanto Company, for example, established a consumer products division that produces and distributes fertilizers and lawn chemicals. To facilitate control, the operations function was organized as an autonomous profit center. Monsanto finds this effective because its manufacturing division is given the authority to determine not only the costs of creating the product but also the product price and the marketing program.

In terms of overall organizational control, a division like the one used by Monsanto should be held accountable only for the activities over which it has decision-making authority. It would be inappropriate, of course, to make operations accountable for profitability in an organization that stresses sales and market share over quality and productivity. Misplaced accountability results in ineffective organizational control, to say nothing of hostility and conflict. Depending on the strategic role of operations, then, operations managers are accountable for different kinds of results. For example, in an organization using bureaucratic control, accountability will be spelled out in rules and regulations. In a decentralized system, it is likely to be understood and accepted by everyone.

Within operations, managerial control ensures that resources and activities achieve primary goals such as a high percentage of on-time deliveries, low unit-production cost, or high product reliability. Any control system should focus on the elements that are most crucial to goal attainment. For example, firms in which product quality is a major concern (as it is at Rolex) might adopt a screening control system to monitor the product as it is being created. If quantity is a higher priority (as it is at Timex), a postaction system might be used to identify defects at the end of the system without disrupting the manufacturing process itself.

Purchasing Management

| **purchasing management** |
| Buying materials and resources needed to produce products and services |

Purchasing management, also called *procurement,* is concerned with buying the materials and resources needed to create products and services. In many ways, purchasing is at the very heart of effective supply chain management. The purchasing manager for a retailer like Sears, Roebuck is responsible for buying the merchandise the store will sell. The purchasing manager for a manufacturer buys raw materials, parts, and machines needed by the organization. Large companies like GE, IBM, and Siemens have large purchasing departments.[13] The manager responsible for purchasing must balance a number of constraints. Buying too much ties up capital and increases storage costs. Buying too little might lead to shortages and high reordering costs. The manager must also make sure that the quality of what is purchased meets the organization's needs, that the supplier is reliable, and that the best financial terms are negotiated.

Many firms have recently changed their approaches to purchasing as a means to lower costs and improve quality and productivity. In particular, rather than relying on hundreds or even thousands of suppliers, many companies are reducing their number of suppliers and negotiating special production-delivery arrangements.[14] For example, the Honda plant in Marysville, Ohio, found a local business owner looking for a new opportunity. They negotiated an agreement whereby he would start a new company to mount car stereo speakers into plastic moldings. He delivers finished goods to the plant three times a day, and Honda buys all he can manufacture. Thus he has a stable sales base, Honda has a local and reliable supplier, and both companies benefit.

Type	Purpose	Source of Control
Raw materials	Provide the materials needed to make the product	Purchasing models and systems
Work in process	Enable overall production to be divided into stages of manageable size	Shop-floor control systems
Finished goods	Provide ready supply of products on customer demand and enable long, efficient production runs	High-level production scheduling systems in conjunction with marketing
In transit (pipeline)	Distribute products to customers	Transportation and distribution control systems

Table 21.1

INVENTORY TYPES, PURPOSES, AND SOURCES OF CONTROL

JIT is a recent breakthrough in inventory management. With JIT inventory systems, materials arrive just as they are needed. JIT therefore helps an organization control its raw materials inventory by reducing the amount of space it must devote to storage.

Inventory Management

Inventory control, also called *materials control*, is essential for effective operations management. The four basic kinds of inventories are *raw materials, work-in-process, finished-goods,* and *in-transit* inventories. As shown in Table 21.1, the sources of control over these inventories are as different as their purposes. Work-in-process inventories, for example, are made up of partially completed products that need further processing; they are controlled by the shop-floor system. In contrast, the quantities and costs of finished-goods inventories are under the control of the overall production scheduling system, which is determined by high-level planning decisions. In-transit inventories are controlled by the transportation and distribution systems.

Like most other areas of operations management, inventory management changed notably in recent years. One particularly important breakthrough is the *just-in-time (JIT) method*. First popularized by the Japanese, the JIT system reduces the organization's investment in storage space for raw materials and in the materials themselves. Historically, manufacturers built large storage areas and filled them with materials, parts, and supplies that would be needed days, weeks, and even months in the future. A manager using the JIT approach orders materials and parts more often and in smaller quantities, thereby reducing investment in both storage space and actual inventory. The ideal arrangement is for materials to arrive just as they are needed—or just in time.[15]

Recall our example about the small firm that assembles stereo speakers for Honda and delivers them three times a day, making it unnecessary for Honda to carry large quantities of the speakers in inventory. In an even more striking example, Johnson Controls makes automobile seats for DaimlerChrysler and ships them by small truckloads to a DaimlerChrysler plant 75 miles away. Each shipment is scheduled to arrive two hours before it is needed. Clearly, the JIT approach requires high levels of coordination and cooperation between the company and its suppliers. If shipments arrive too early, DaimlerChrysler has no place to store them. If they arrive too late, the entire assembly line may have to be shut down, resulting in enormous expense. When properly designed and used, the JIT method controls inventory very effectively.

inventory control
Managing the organization's raw materials, work in process, finished goods, and products in transit

just-in-time (JIT) method
An inventory system that has necessary materials arriving as soon as they are needed (just in time) so that the production process is not interrupted

concept
CHECK

What is supply chain management? What are its basic components?

Think of four situations in which the just-in-time method might be applicable. Under what circumstances would JIT not be as useful?

Total quality management can sometimes take on unusual dimensions! For instance, researchers in California are developing new standards for air quality that will be imposed on various agricultural facilities. Frank Mitloehner is seen here with some Holstein dairy cows inside a "bio-bubble." Cows are placed inside the "bio-bubbles," which are covered corrals where monitors can measure the gases that the cows emit. Mitloehner's research will be used to help write the state's first air-quality regulations for dairies and could affect regulations nationwide.

Managing Total Quality

Quality and productivity have become major determinants of business success or failure today and are central issues in managing organizations.[16] But, as we will see, achieving higher levels of quality is not an easy accomplishment. Simply ordering that quality be improved is about as effective as waving a magic wand.[17] The catalyst for its emergence as a mainstream management concern was foreign business, especially Japanese. And nowhere was it more visible than in the auto industry. During the energy crisis in the late 1970s, many people bought Toyotas, Hondas, and Nissans because they were more fuel-efficient than U.S. cars. Consumers soon found, however, that not only were the Japanese cars more fuel-efficient, they were also of higher quality than U.S. cars. Parts fit together better, the trim work was neater, and the cars were more reliable. Thus, after the energy crisis subsided, Japanese cars remained formidable competitors because of their reputation for quality.

The Meaning of Quality

The American Society for Quality Control defines ***quality*** as the totality of features and characteristics of a product or service that bear on its ability to satisfy stated or implied needs.[18] Quality has several different attributes. Table 21.2 lists eight basic dimensions that determine the quality of a particular product or service. For example, a product that has durability and is reliable is of higher quality than a product with less durability and reliability.

Quality is also relative. For example, a Lincoln is a higher-grade car than a Mercury Marquis, which, in turn, is a higher-grade car than a Ford Focus. The difference in quality stems from differences in design and other features. The Focus, however,

quality
The totality of features and characteristics of a product or service that bear on its ability to satisfy stated or implied needs

Table 21.2
EIGHT DIMENSIONS OF QUALITY

These eight dimensions generally capture the meaning of quality, which is a critically important ingredient to organizational success today. Understanding the basic meaning of quality is a good first step to managing it more effectively.

1. *Performance*. A product's primary operating characteristic; examples are automobile acceleration and a television's picture clarity
2. *Features*. Supplements to a product's basic functioning characteristics, such as power windows on a car
3. *Reliability*. A probability of not malfunctioning during a specified period
4. *Conformance*. The degree to which a product's design and operating characteristics meet established standards
5. *Durability*. A measure of product life
6. *Serviceability*. The speed and ease of repair
7. *Aesthetics*. How a product looks, feels, tastes, and smells
8. *Perceived quality*. As seen by a customer

Source: Reprinted by permission of *Harvard Business Review*. Exhibit from "Competing on the Eight Dimensions of Quality," by David A. Garvin, November/December 1987. Copyright © 1987 by the Harvard Business School Publishing Corporation; all rights reserved.

is considered a high-quality car relative to its engineering specifications and price. Likewise, the Marquis and Lincoln may also be high-quality cars, given their standards and prices. Thus quality is both an absolute and a relative concept.

Quality is relevant for both products and services. Although its importance for products like cars and computers was perhaps recognized first, service firms ranging from airlines to restaurants have also come to see that quality is a vitally important determinant of their success or failure. Service quality, as we will discuss later in this chapter, has thus also become a major competitive issue in U.S. industry today.[19]

> " [Porsches] . . . cost a lot of money. When you spend that kind of money, you expect things to be right. "
>
> Lynn Kinzig, general manager of Brumos Porsche in Jacksonville, Florida
> (*USA Today*, June 28, 2006, p. 4B)

The Importance of Quality

To help underscore the importance of quality, the U.S. government created the ***Malcolm Baldrige Award***, named after the former secretary of commerce who championed quality in U.S. industry. The award, administered by an agency of the Commerce Department, is given annually to firms that achieve major improvements in the quality of their products or services. In other words, the award is based on changes in quality, as opposed to absolute quality. In addition, numerous other quality awards have been created. For example, the Rochester Institute of Technology and *USA Today* award their Quality Cup award not to entire organizations but to individual teams of workers within organizations. Quality is also an important concern for individual managers and organizations for three very specific reasons: competition, productivity, and costs.[20]

> *Malcolm Baldrige Award*
> Named after a former secretary of commerce, this prestigious award is given to firms that achieve major quality improvements

Competition   Quality has become one of the most competitive points in business today. Ford, DaimlerChrysler, General Motors, and Toyota, for example, each implies that its cars and trucks are higher in quality than the cars and trucks of the others. And American, United, and Continental Airlines each claims that it provides the best and most reliable service. Indeed, it seems that virtually every U.S. business has adopted quality as a major point of competition. Thus a business that fails to keep pace may find itself falling behind not only foreign competition but also other U.S. firms.[21]

Productivity   Managers have also come to recognize that quality and productivity are related. In the past, many managers thought that they could increase output (productivity) only by decreasing quality. Managers today have learned the hard way that such an assumption is almost always wrong. If a firm installs a meaningful quality enhancement program, three things are likely to result. First, the number of defects is likely to decrease, causing fewer returns from customers. Second, because the number of defects goes down, resources (materials and people) dedicated to reworking flawed output will be decreased. Third, because making employees responsible for quality reduces the need for quality inspectors, the organization is able to produce more units with fewer resources.

Costs   Improved quality also lowers costs. Poor quality results in higher returns from customers, high warranty costs, and lawsuits from customers injured by faulty products. Future sales are lost because of disgruntled customers. An organization with quality problems often has to increase inspection expenses just to catch defective products. We noted in Chapter 20, for example, how at one point Whistler Corporation was using 40 percent of its workforce just to fix poorly assembled radar detectors made by the other 60 percent.[22]

Figure 21.3
TOTAL QUALITY MANAGEMENT

Quality is one of the most important issues facing organizations today. Total quality management, or TQM, is a comprehensive effort to enhance an organization's product or service quality. TQM involves the five basic dimensions shown here. Each is important and must be addressed effectively if the organization expects to truly increase quality.

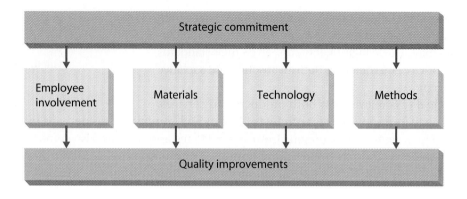

---

total quality management (TQM) (quality assurance)
A strategic commitment by top management to change its whole approach to business in order to make quality a guiding factor in everything it does

Total Quality Management

Once an organization makes a decision to enhance the quality of its products and services, it must then decide how to implement this decision. The most pervasive approach to managing quality has been called *total quality management*, or *TQM* (sometimes called *quality assurance*)—a real and meaningful effort by an organization to change its whole approach to business in order to make quality a guiding factor in everything the organization does.[23] Figure 21.3 highlights the major ingredients in TQM.

Strategic Commitment   The starting point for TQM is a strategic commitment by top management. Such commitment is important for several reasons. First, the organizational culture must change to recognize that quality is not just an ideal but an objective goal that must be pursued.[24] Second, a decision to pursue the goal of quality carries with it some real costs—for expenditures such as new equipment and facilities. Thus, without a commitment from top management, quality improvement will prove to be just a slogan or gimmick, with little or no real change. Just a few years ago Porsche had the lowest reliability of any automobile maker in the world. But a major commitment from top management helped turn the company around. By paying more attention to consumer preferences and using the other methods described below, Porsche shot to the top of global automobile reliability.[25]

Employee Involvement   Employee involvement is another critical ingredient in TQM. Virtually all successful quality enhancement programs involve making the person responsible for doing the job responsible for making sure it is done right.[26] By definition, then, employee involvement is a critical component in improving quality. Work teams, discussed in Chapter 19, are common vehicles for increasing employee involvement.

Technology   New forms of technology are also useful in TQM programs. Automation and robots, for example, can often make products with higher precision and better consistency than can people. Investing in higher-grade machines capable of doing jobs more precisely and reliably often improves quality. For example, Nokia has achieved notable improvements in product quality by replacing many of its machines with new equipment. Similarly, most U.S. auto and electronics firms make regular investments in new technology to help boost quality.

Materials   Another important part of TQM is improving the quality of the materials that organizations use. Suppose that a company that assembles stereos buys chips and circuits from another company. If the chips have a high failure rate, consumers will return defective stereos to the company whose nameplate appears on them, not to the company that made the chips. The stereo firm then loses in two ways: refunds back to customers and a damaged reputation. As a result, many firms have increased the quality requirements they impose on their suppliers as a way of improving the quality of their own products.

Methods   Improved methods can improve product and service quality. Methods are operating systems used by the organization during the actual transformation process. American Express Company, for example, has found ways to cut its approval time for new credit cards from 22 to only 5 days. This results in improved service quality.

TQM Tools and Techniques

Beyond the strategic context of quality, managers can rely also on several specific tools and techniques for improving quality. Among the most popular today are value-added analysis, benchmarking, outsourcing, reducing cycle times, ISO 9000:2000 and ISO 14000, statistical quality control, and Six Sigma.

Value-Added Analysis   *Value-added analysis* is the comprehensive evaluation of all work activities, materials flows, and paperwork to determine the value that they add for customers. Such an analysis often reveals wasteful or unnecessary activities that can be eliminated without jeopardizing customer service. For example, during a value-added analysis, Hewlett-Packard determined that its contracts were unnecessarily long, confusing, and hard to understand. The firm subsequently cut its standard contract form down from 20 to 2 pages and experienced an 18 percent increase in its computer sales.

> *value-added analysis*
> The comprehensive evaluation of all work activities, materials flows, and paperwork to determine the value that they add for customers

Benchmarking   *Benchmarking* is the process of learning how other firms do things in an exceptionally high-quality manner. Some approaches to benchmarking are simple and straightforward. For example, Xerox routinely buys copiers made by other firms and takes them apart to see how they work. This enables the firm to stay abreast of improvements and changes its competitors are using. When Ford was planning the newest version of the Taurus, it identified the 400 features customers identified as being most important to them. It then found the competing cars that did the best job on each feature. Ford's goal was to equal or surpass each of its competitors on those 400 features. Other benchmarking strategies are more indirect. For example, many firms study how L.L. Bean manages its mail-order business, how Disney recruits and trains employees, and how FedEx tracks packages for applications they can employ in their own businesses.[27]

> *benchmarking*
> The process of learning how other firms do things in an exceptionally high quality manner

Outsourcing   Another innovation for improving quality is outsourcing. *Outsourcing* is the process of subcontracting services and operations to other firms that can perform them more cheaply or better. If a business performs each and every one of its own administrative and business services and operations, it is almost certain to be doing at least some of them in an inefficient or low-quality manner. If those areas can be identified and outsourced, the firm will save money and realize a higher-quality service or operation.[28] For example, until recently Eastman Kodak handled all of its own computing operations. Now, however, those operations are subcontracted to IBM, which handles all of Kodak's computing. The result is higher-quality computing systems and operations at Kodak for less money than it was spending before. Firms must be careful in their outsourcing decisions, though, because service or delivery problems can lead to major complications. Boeing's

> *outsourcing*
> Subcontracting services and operations to other firms that can perform them more cheaply or better

"Boeing has never outsourced to this kind of level. They have big technical challenges."

Richard Aboulafia, aviation industry consultant
(*Forbes*, April 17, 2006, p. 82)

new 787 aircraft, for example, has been running several months behind schedule because the firms to which Boeing has outsourced some of its production have been running late.[29] *Technology Toolkit* discusses some of IBM's most recent forays into outsourcing.

Reducing Cycle Time Another popular TQM technique is reducing cycle time. *Cycle time* is the time needed by the organization to develop, make, and distribute products or services.[30] If a business can reduce its cycle time, quality will often improve. A good illustration of the power of cycle time reduction comes from General Electric. At one point the firm needed six plants and three weeks to produce and deliver custom-made industrial circuit breaker boxes. By analyzing and reducing cycle time, the same product can now be delivered in three days, and only a single plant is involved. Table 21.3 identifies a number of basic suggestions that have helped companies reduce the cycle time of their operations. For example, GE found it better to start from scratch with a remodeled plant. GE also wiped out the need for approvals by eliminating most managerial positions and set up teams as a basis for organizing work. Stressing the importance of the schedule helped Motorola build a new plant and start production of a new product in only 18

cycle time
The time needed by the organization to accomplish activities such as developing, making, and distributing products or services

Technology Toolkit

IBM, Meet India. India, IBM.

International Business Machines Corporation (IBM) is the whitest of the white-collar businesses, one of the brands most closely associated with the United States. Yet today the company is under pressure, as are virtually all U.S. firms, to realize cost savings from outsourcing. Over the last ten years, IBM shifted away from hardware manufacturing. Its areas of expertise are now in software and, increasingly, computer services such as integrating diverse information systems. To some extent, the shift to software and services allowed IBM to delay global workforce optimization. Yet the pressure to reduce costs is great in this highly competitive industry that pits IBM against powerful rivals such as Microsoft, Intel, and Dell. "Our customers need us to put the right skills in the right place at the right time," says senior vice president Robert W. Moffat, Jr.

So IBM is increasing its overseas workforce in India and other regions. "Beat 'em at their own game" is IBM's motto in its drive to compete with lower-cost technical staff abroad. The company is replacing expensive U.S. engineers with foreign ones. In India alone, IBM's staff increased from 9,000 in 2004 to 43,000 in 2006. IBM is now the second-largest technical employer in India, after local outsourcing giant Wipro. To manage the complex transition, project Professional Marketplace contains the résumés of thousands of IBMers. The system uses mathematical formulas to automatically choose from any worldwide location the most efficient mix of staff for any project.

Professional Marketplace really pays off. For example, IBM used to manually load software onto clients' PCs. The process required thousands of workers in many locations and cost about $70 per machine. Today, a single facility in Toronto employs 200 workers who send packets of software over the Internet to far-flung clients. The cost is just 20 cents.

IBM "still has a huge way to go to be cost- and price-competitive," says analyst Paul Roehrig. Michael Dell, for one, is skeptical. "It's hard to say you're going to help your customers reduce their own costs when you're the high-cost provider yourself," he says. However, in Moffat's previous position, he managed to shrink manufacturing expenses by $20 billion over four years. Now he seems well positioned to do the same for services.

References: Steve Hamm, "Big Blue Shift," *BusinessWeek*, June 5, 2006, www.busienssweek.com on June 1, 2006; Steve Hamm, "IBM Wakes Up to India's Skills," *BusinessWeek*, June 5, 2006, www.businessweek.com on June 1, 2006; David Kirkpatrick, "IBM Shares Its Secrets," *Fortune*, September 5, 2006, www.fortune.com on June 1, 2006.

1. *Start from scratch*. It is usually easier than trying to do what the organization does now faster.

2. *Minimize the number of approvals needed to do something*. The fewer people who have to approve something, the faster approval will get done.

3. *Use work teams as a basis for organization*. Teamwork and cooperation work better than individual effort and conflict.

4. *Develop and adhere to a schedule*. A properly designed schedule can greatly increase speed.

5. *Do not ignore distribution*. Making something faster is only part of the battle.

6. *Integrate speed into the organization's culture*. If everyone understands the importance of speed, things will naturally get done more quickly.

Source: From *Fortune*, February 13, 1989. Copyright © 1989 Time, Inc. All rights reserved.

Table 21.3

GUIDELINES FOR INCREASING THE SPEED OF OPERATIONS

Many organizations today are using speed for competitive advantage. Listed in the table are six common guidelines that organizations follow when they want to shorten the time they need to get things accomplished. Although not every manager can do each of these things, most managers can do at least some of them.

months. Nokia used to need 12 to 18 months to design new cell phone models, but can do it now in six months.[31]

ISO 9000:2000 and ISO 14000   Still another useful technique for improving quality is ISO 9000. ***ISO 9000:2000*** refers to a set of quality standards created by the International Organization for Standardization; the standards were revised and updated in 2000. These standards cover such areas as product testing, employee training, record keeping, supplier relations, and repair polices and procedures. Firms that want to meet these standards apply for certification and are audited by a firm chosen by the organization's domestic affiliate (in the United States, this is the American National Standards Institute). These auditors review every aspect of the firm's business operations in relation to the standards. Many firms report that merely preparing for an ISO 9000 audit has been helpful. Many firms today, including General Electric, DuPont, Eastman Kodak, British Telecom, and Philips Electronics are urging—or in some cases requiring—that their suppliers achieve ISO 9000 certification.[32] All told, more than 140 countries have adopted ISO 9000 as a national standard, and more than 400,000 certificates of compliance have been issued. ***ISO 14000*** is an extension of the same concept to environmental performance. Specifically, ISO 14000 requires that firms document how they are using raw materials more efficiently, managing pollution, and reducing their impact on the environment.

ISO 9000:2000
A set of quality standards created by the International Organization for Standardization and revised in 2000

ISO 14000
A set of standards for environmental performance

Statistical Quality Control   Another quality control technique is ***statistical quality control (SQC)***. As the term suggests, SQC is concerned primarily with managing quality.[33] Moreover, it is a set of specific statistical techniques that can be used to monitor quality. *Acceptance sampling* involves sampling finished goods to ensure that quality standards have been met. Acceptance sampling is effective only when the correct percentage of products that should be tested (for example, 2, 5, or 25 percent) is determined. This decision is especially important when the test renders the product useless. Batteries, wine, and collapsible steering wheels, for example, are consumed or destroyed during testing. Another SQC method is *in-process sampling*. In-process sampling involves evaluating products during production so that needed changes can be made. The painting department of a furniture company might periodically check the tint of the paint it is using. The company can then adjust the color as necessary to conform to customer standards. The advantage of in-process sampling is that it allows problems to be detected before they accumulate.

statistical quality control (SQC)
A set of specific statistical techniques that can be used to monitor quality; includes acceptance sampling and in-process sampling

Six Sigma Six Sigma was developed in the 1980s for Motorola. The tool can be used by manufacturing or service organizations. The Six Sigma method tries to eliminate mistakes. Although firms rarely obtain Six Sigma quality, it does provide a challenging target. *Sigma* refers to a standard deviation, so a Six Sigma defect rate is 6 standard deviations above the mean rate; 1 sigma quality would produce 690,000 errors per million items. Three sigmas is challenging—66,000 errors per million. Six Sigma is obtained when a firm produces a mere 3.4 mistakes per million. Implementing Six Sigma requires making corrections until errors virtually disappear. At GE, the technique has saved the firm $8 billion in three years. GE is now teaching its customers, including Wal-Mart and Dell, about the approach.

concept
CHECK

What are the basic components of total quality management, and what are the common tools used to manage quality?

Identify and describe three product families that illustrate the concept of absolute versus relative quality.

> **productivity**
> An economic measure of efficiency that summarizes what is produced relative to resources used to produce it

Managing Productivity

Although the current focus on quality by U.S. companies is a relatively recent phenomenon, managers have been aware of the importance of productivity for several years. The stimulus for this attention was a recognition that the gap between productivity in the United States and productivity in other industrialized countries was narrowing. This section describes the meaning of productivity and underscores its importance. After summarizing recent productivity trends, we suggest ways that organizations can increase their productivity.

The Meaning of Productivity

In a general sense, **productivity** is an economic measure of efficiency that summarizes the value of outputs relative to the value of the inputs used to create them.[34] Productivity can be and often is assessed at different levels of analysis and in different forms.

Levels of Productivity By level of productivity we mean the units of analysis used to calculate or define productivity. For example, *aggregate productivity* is the total level of productivity achieved by a country. *Industry productivity* is the total productivity achieved by all the firms in a particular industry. *Company productivity*, just as the term suggests, is the level of productivity achieved by an individual company. *Unit and individual productivity* refer to the productivity achieved by a unit or department within an organization and the level of productivity attained by a single person.

Businesses in highly competitive markets must pay special attention to productivity. Richard Wasilewski, a milk deliverer, surveys his orders for the day's delivery. Wasilewski works for the A. B. Munroe Dairy in East Providence, Rhode Island, and has been delivering milk for them since 1998. He delivers to nearly 400 customers a week in both suburban and rural areas. To maintain profitability, it is important that he make all deliveries on schedule each week. At a time of mega stores and Internet shopping, Munroe Dairy is expanding its home delivery service, in part because of the high productivity of employees like Wasilewski.

Forms of Productivity   There are many different forms of productivity. *Total factor productivity* is defined by the following formula:

$$\text{Productivity} = \frac{\text{Outputs}}{\text{Inputs}}$$

Total factor productivity is an overall indicator of how well an organization uses all of its resources, such as labor, capital, materials, and energy, to create all of its products and services. The biggest problem with total factor productivity is that all the ingredients must be expressed in the same terms—dollars (it is difficult to add hours of labor to number of units of a raw material in a meaningful way). Total factor productivity also gives little insight into how things can be changed to improve productivity. Consequently, most organizations find it more useful to calculate a partial productivity ratio. Such a ratio uses only one category of resource. For example, labor productivity could be calculated by this simple formula:

$$\text{Labor Productivity} = \frac{\text{Outputs}}{\text{Direct Labor}}$$

This method has two advantages. First, it is not necessary to transform the units of input into some other unit. Second, this method provides managers with specific insights into how changing different resource inputs affects productivity. Suppose that an organization can manufacture 100 units of a particular product with 20 hours of direct labor. The organization's labor productivity index is 100/20, or 5 (5 units per labor hour). Now suppose that worker efficiency is increased (through one of the ways to be discussed later in this chapter) so that the same 20 hours of labor result in the manufacture of 120 units of the product. The labor productivity index increases to 120/20, or 6 (6 units per labor hour), and the firm can see the direct results of a specific managerial action.

The Importance of Productivity

Managers consider it important that their firm maintains high levels of productivity for a variety of reasons. Firm productivity is a primary determinant of an organization's level of profitability and, ultimately, of its ability to survive. If one organization is more productive than another, it will have more products to sell at lower prices and have more profits to reinvest in other areas. Productivity also partially determines people's standard of living within a particular country. At an economic level, businesses consume resources and produce goods and services. The goods and services created within a country can be used by that country's own citizens or exported for sale in other countries. The more goods and services the businesses within a country can produce, the more goods and services the country's citizens will have. Even goods that are exported result in financial resources' flowing back into the home country. Thus the citizens of a highly productive country are likely to have a notably higher standard of living than are the citizens of a country with low productivity.

Productivity Trends

The United States has one of the highest levels of productivity in the world. Sparked by gains made in other countries, however, U.S. business has begun to focus more attention on productivity.[35] Indeed, this was a primary factor in the decisions made by U.S. businesses to retrench, retool, and become more competitive in the world marketplace. For example, General Electric's dishwasher plant in Louisville cut its inventory requirements by 50 percent, reduced labor costs from 15 percent to only 10 percent of total manufacturing costs, and cut product development time in half. As a result of these kinds of efforts, productivity trends have now leveled out, and U.S. workers are generally maintaining their lead in most industries.[36]

One important factor that has hurt U.S. productivity indices has been the tremendous growth of the service sector in the United States. Although this sector grew, its productivity levels did not. One part of this problem relates to measurement. For example, it is fairly easy to calculate the number of tons of steel produced at a steel mill and divide it by the number of labor hours used; it is more difficult to determine the output of an attorney or a certified public accountant. Still, virtually everyone agrees that improving service sector productivity is the next major hurdle facing U.S. business.[37]

Figure 21.4 illustrates manufacturing productivity growth since 1970 in terms of annual average percentage of increase. As you can see, that growth slowed during the 1970s but began to rise again in the late 1980s. Some experts believe that productivity in both the United States and abroad will continue to improve at even more impressive rates. Their confidence rests on technology's potential ability to improve operations.

Improving Productivity

How does a business or industry improve its productivity? Numerous specific suggestions made by experts generally fall into two broad categories: improving operations and increasing employee involvement.

Improving Operations   One way that firms can improve operations is by spending more on research and development. Research and development (R&D) spending

Figure 21.4

MANUFACTURING AND SERVICE PRODUCTIVITY GROWTH TRENDS

Both manufacturing productivity and service productivity in the United States continue to grow, although manufacturing productivity is growing at a faster pace. Total productivity, therefore, also continues to grow.

Source: U.S. Bureau of Labor Statistics.

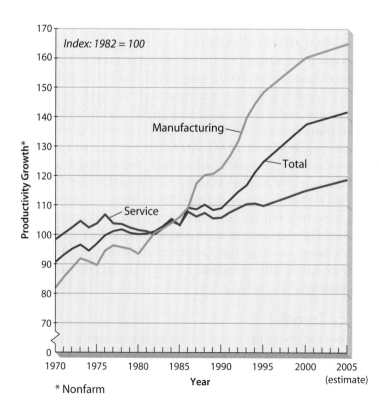

* Nonfarm

helps identify new products, new uses for existing ⌐
making products. Each of these contributes to prod⌐
Lomb almost missed the boat on extended-wear con⌐
pany had neglected R&D. When it became apparent tha⌐
almost a year ahead of Bausch & Lomb in developing th⌐
made R&D a top-priority concern. As a result, the compa⌐
breakthroughs, shortened the time needed to introduce n⌐
enhanced both total sales and profits—and all with a sma⌐
company used to employ. Even though other countries are g⌐
R&D spending, the United States continues to be the world le⌐

Another way firms can boost productivity through operatic⌐
and revamping their transformation facilities. We noted earlie⌐
modernized plants does a better job than six antiquated ones. Ju⌐
factory is no guarantee of success, but IBM, Ford, Caterpillar, and n⌐
nesses have achieved dramatic productivity gains by revamping th⌐
facilities. Facilities refinements are not limited to manufacturers. Mo⌐
restaurants now have drive-through windows, and many have move⌐
dispensers out to the restaurant floor so that customers can get their ⌐
Each of these moves is an attempt to increase the speed with which cust⌐
be served, and thus to increase productivity.

606 PART SIX · The Controlling Process

Summary of Learning Objecti⌐

1. Describe and explain the nature of o⌐
   agement. Operations management i⌐
   • Operations that organiz⌐
     activities and ser⌐
     products ⌐
   • Operations ⌐
     manufa⌐
   • It p⌐

Increasing Employee Involvement The other major thrust in produ⌐tivity enhancement has been toward employee involvement. We noted earlier that participation can enhance quality. So, too, can it boost productivity. Examples of this involvement are an individual worker's being given a bigger voice in how she does her job, a formal agreement of cooperation between management and labor, and total involvement throughout the organization. GE eliminated most of the supervisors at its one new circuit breaker plant and put control in the hands of workers.

Another method popular in the United States is increasing the flexibility of an organization's workforce by training employees to perform a number of different jobs. Such cross-training allows the firm to function with fewer workers because workers can be transferred easily to areas where they are most needed. For example, at one Motorola plant, 397 of 400 employees have learned at least two skills under a similar program.

Rewards are essential to making employee involvement work. Firms must reward people for learning new skills and using them proficiently. At Motorola, for example, workers who master a new skill are assigned for five days to a job requiring them to use that skill. If they perform with no defects, they are moved to a higher pay grade, and then they move back and forth between jobs as they are needed. If there is a performance problem, they receive more training and practice. This approach is fairly new, but preliminary indicators suggest that it can increase productivity significantly. Many unions resist such programs because they threaten job security and reduce a person's identification with one skill or craft.

concept
CHECK

Define productivity and identify the different levels at which it can be assessed.

Will improving productivity always be worth the time and money that might be required? Why or why not?

erations man-

s the set of managerial
ations use in creating their
ices.

anagement is important to both
turing and service organizations.

ays an important role in an organization's
strategy.

2. Identify and discuss the components involved in designing effective operations systems.
   - The starting point in using operations management is designing appropriate operations systems.
   - Key decisions that must be made as part of operations systems design relate to product and service mix, capacity, and facilities.

3. Discuss organizational technologies and their role in operations management.
   - Technology also plays an important role in quality.
   - Automation is especially important today.
   - Numerous computer-aided manufacturing techniques are widely practiced.
   - Robotics is also a growing area.
   - Technology is as relevant to service organizations as to manufacturing organizations.

4. Identify and discuss the components involved in implementing operations systems through supply chain management.

- After an operations system has been designed and put in place, it must then be implemented.
- Major areas of interest during the use of operations systems are purchasing and inventory management.
- Supply chain management is a comprehensive view of managing all of these activities in a more efficient manner.

5. Explain the meaning and importance of managing quality and total quality management.
   - Quality is a major consideration for all managers today.
   - Quality is important because it affects competition, productivity, and costs.
   - Total quality management is a comprehensive, organization-wide effort to enhance quality through a variety of avenues.

6. Explain the meaning and importance of managing productivity, productivity trends, and ways to improve productivity.
   - Productivity is also a major concern to managers.
   - Productivity is a measure of how efficiently an organization is using its resources to create products or services.
   - The United States is a world leader in individual productivity, but firms still work to achieve productivity gains.

Discussion Questions

Questions for Review

1. What is the relationship of operations management to overall organizational strategy? Where do productivity and quality fit into that relationship?
2. Describe three basic decisions that must be addressed in the design of operations systems. For each decision, what information do managers need to make that decision?

3. What are some approaches to facilities layout? How do they differ from one another? How are they similar?
4. What is total quality management? What are the major characteristics of TQM?

Questions for Analysis

5. Is operations management linked most closely to corporate-level, business-level, or functional strategies? Why or in what way?

6. "Automation is bad for the economy because machines will eventually replace almost all human workers, creating high unemployment and

poverty." Do you agree or disagree? Explain your answer.

7. Some quality gurus claim that high-quality products or services are those that are error free. Others claim that high quality exists when customers' needs are satisfied. Still others claim that high-quality products or services must be innovative. Do you subscribe to one of these views? If not, how would you define quality? Explain how the choice of a quality definition affects managers' behavior.

Questions for Application

8. How can a service organization use techniques from operations management? Give specific examples from your college or university (a provider of educational services).

9. Think of a firm that, in your opinion, provides a high-quality service or product. What attributes of the product or service give you the perception of high quality? Do you think that everyone would agree with your judgment? Why or why not?

10. What advice would you give to the manager of a small local service business, such as a pizza parlor or dry cleaner, about improvements in quality and productivity? Would your advice differ if the small business were a manufacturing company—for example, a T-shirt printing firm? Describe any differences you would expect to see.

Building Effective Communication Skills

Exercise Overview

Communication skills refer to a manager's ability to convey ideas and information to others and to receive ideas and information from others. This exercise develops your communication skills in addressing issues of quality.

Exercise Background

Assume that you are a customer service manager of a large auto parts distributor. The general manager of a large auto dealer, one of your best customers, wrote the following letter. It will be your task to write a letter in response.

> Dear Customer Service Manager:
>
> On the first of last month, ABC Autos submitted a purchase order to your firm. Attached to this letter is a copy of the order. Unfortunately, the parts shipment that we received from you did not contain every item on the order. Further, that fact was not noted on the packing slip that accompanied your shipment, and ABC was charged for the full amount of the order. To resolve the problem, please send the missing items immediately. If you are unable to do so by the end of the week, please cancel the remaining items and refund the overpayment. In the future, if you ship a partial order, please notify us at that time and do not bill for items not shipped.
>
> I look forward to your reply and a resolution to my problem.
>
> Sincerely,
> A. N. Owner, ABC Autos
> Attachment: Purchase Order 00001

Exercise Task

1. Write an answer to the above letter, assuming that you now have the parts available.
2. How would your answer differ if ABC Autos were not a valued customer?
3. How would your answer differ if you found out that the parts were in the original shipment but had been stolen by one of your delivery personnel?
4. How would your answer differ if you found out that the owner of ABC Autos made a mistake and the order was filled correctly by your workers?

5. Based on your answers to the questions above, what are the important components of responding effectively to a customer's quality complaint—the tone of the letter, expressing an apology, suggesting a solution, and so on? Explain how you used these components in your response.

Building Effective Diagnostic Skills

Exercise Overview

As noted in the chapter, the quality of a product or service is relative to price and expectations. A manager's diagnostic skills—the ability to visualize responses to a situation—can be useful in helping to position quality relative to price and expectations.

Exercise Background

Think of a recent occasion when you purchased a tangible product—for example, clothing, electronic equipment, luggage, or professional supplies—which you subsequently came to feel was of especially high quality. Now recall another product that you evaluated as having appropriate or adequate quality, and a third that you felt had low or poor quality (three examples total). Next, recall parallel experiences involving purchases of services. Examples might include an airline, a train, or a bus trip; a meal in a restaurant; a haircut; or an oil change for your car (again, three examples total).

Finally, recall three experiences in which both products and services were involved. Examples might include having questions answered by someone about a product you were buying or returning a defective or broken product for a refund or warranty repair. Try to recall instances in which there was an apparent disparity between product and service quality (for instance, a poor-quality product accompanied by outstanding service or a high-quality product accompanied by mediocre service).

Exercise Task

Using the nine examples identified above, do the following:

1. Assess the extent to which the quality you associated with each was a function of price and your expectations.

2. Could the quality of each be improved without greatly affecting price? If so, how?

3. Can high-quality service offset only adequate or even poor product quality? Can outstanding product quality offset only adequate or even poor-quality service?

CHAPTER CLOSING CASE

E-TAILING AT AMAZON.COM

Online retailing, or e-tailing, is Amazon.com's entire business. The firm, unlike online rivals such as Barnes&Noble.com or Walmart.com, has no bricks-and-mortar presence. Customers interact by website, e-mail, or phone. Yet behind the website is one of the world's largest direct-to-consumer distribution operations.

Amazon, founded in 1995 as a bookseller, has gone through many ups and downs. Early investors believed that the promise of online business outweighed the risks associated with a new type of venture, the e-tailer. Giddy expectation soon turned to disappointment because spending soared as rapidly as sales, causing profits to be nonexistent. Amazon diversified into a wide range of products, including toys, music, electronics and software, and household goods. Expansion ate into profits, and huge investments in infrastructure and IT were required before the company went into the black in 2002.

Amazon's business model, although fairly commonplace for online companies today, was revolutionary for its time. Without the need to build numerous stores in high-rent shopping areas, the company chose locations based on cost, as well as convenience to cities and airports. The company's seven distribution centers stock thousands of popular items, but many of the goods are in fact "drop-shipped" directly from the manufacturer. This allows Amazon to carry a multitude of products without high inventory expense. It also can speed delivery times, eliminating one step in the distribution process.

Within Amazon's warehouses, much of the work is automated. Workers use simple, menu-driven computer programs to access and monitor customer orders. Goods are picked from the shelves and placed in a vast system of automated chutes and bins that bundles items appropriately. In the past, Amazon tried to minimize shipping expense by bundling all items for one address into one package. Now, however, they use a more effective sorting algorithm that calculates optimal package size, both to protect items and reduce costs. Automated scanners track the progress of every order. Automated boxers and labelers prepare the goods for shipping.

Software is an increasingly important part of Amazon's operations because better systems enable labor cost reductions, increase accuracy and speed, enhance the customer experience, and support effective planning. Supply chain software uses a complex formula to choose which books should be carried in the warehouse and which should be drop-shipped. Another algorithm constantly recalculates item popularity ratings to choose which books to place in the most-frequented sections of the warehouse.

In addition, Amazon was a pioneer in the development of each of the following operations technologies.

- "One-click" purchasing allows customers to buy products with a single mouse click. Amazon patented this process and licenses it to other companies, for a fee.
- Amazon was one of the first companies to allow customers to post online product reviews. These boost sales and create a sense of community for users.
- Amazon's customers can see a customer order history, create wish lists and favorites lists, share information with friends, get personalized recommendations, receive gift-giving reminders, and tag items with customized category data.

Amazon's software is so popular with other firms that the company has launched a feature called "Amazon Web Services." Through the Internet, independent programmers and merchants gain access to Amazon's library of software, adapting it for their own use. Amazon receives no payment unless the company wants to sell through Amazon.com, in which case Amazon collects a 15 percent commission on each sale. This service has proven so popular that 22 percent of Amazon's sales are made by other merchants.

Some companies rely on Amazon's expertise for management of their websites. Target and Office Depot contract out their online presence to Amazon. Amazon's zshops, which link business websites to Amazon's, are popular. Another initiative is "Amazon Marketplace," an online auction space for used items. The Marketplace is Amazon's attempt to catch up to online auction house eBay.

Sales grew by 26 percent from 2004 to 2005, and R&D spending grew 57 percent. Upcoming enhancements include digital data storage and an online video service to store and share consumers' digital recordings. But wait, there's more. Founder and CEO Jeff Bezos refuses to comment, but rumors are flying that Amazon's next new-technology offering will be a digital music service to rival iTunes. Another rumored improvement is a digital book-selling service that will combat Google's stated intentions to offer downloadable e-books.

Amazon's new technologies are young and not yet profitable, and the company may be spreading itself too thin with too many projects. But watch out! At this rate, Amazon will become the company to beat in many online industries.

CASE QUESTIONS

1. What types of decisions common to manufacturing firms are made at Amazon? What types of decisions common to service firms are made there?

2. Describe Amazon's entire supply chain. Where in the supply chain does Amazon make money? Where in the supply chain do they outsource or contract to outsiders?

3. Give examples of ways in which Amazon's operations allow it to offer a high-quality shopping experience to customers. Give examples of ways in which operations contribute to high productivity.

CASE REFERENCES

"Amazon.com," Amazon website, www.amazon.com on May 24, 2006; Robert Hof, "Amazon's Brighter Horizon?" *Business-Week*, April 26, 2006, www.businessweek.com on May 24, 2006; Robert Hof, "Amazon's Costly Bells and Whistles," *BusinessWeek*, February 3, 2006, www.businessweek.com on May 24, 2006; Paul R. La Monica, "Consumers Keep on Clicking," *Money*, July 26, 2005, www.cnnmoney.com on May 24, 2006.

YOU MAKE THE CALL

Improving the Quality of Hotels

1. What differences might you expect to find in quality dimensions between more and less expensive hotels?

2. As a customer, what are the three biggest quality dimensions on which you would judge a hotel room?

3. Peruse the websites of four hotel chains. Identify the specific quality dimensions promoted by each.

4. Can a hotel focus too much attention on quality? Why or why not?

5. If you were the manager of an upscale hotel, what quality dimensions not currently available in a hotel might you consider adding?

6. If you were the manager of an economy hotel, what quality dimensions not currently available in a hotel might you consider adding?

Test Prepper

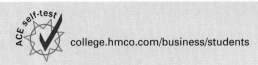

college.hmco.com/business/students

Choose the correct answer. Answers are found at the back of the book.

1. T F The product-service mix is how many and what kinds of employees to hire to manufacture and maintain the organization's goods.

2. T F When an organization is creating a few very large and complex products, such as commercial airplanes, they use a fixed-position layout.

3. T F In-transit inventories are controlled by the transportation and distribution systems.

4. T F A company that has outsourced has acquired more of a critical resource than its competitors.

5. T F Implementing Six Sigma requires making corrections until errors virtually disappear.

6. The main difference between a service organization and a manufacturing organization is that
   A. strategy is more important in manufacturing firms.
   B. service organizations create intangible outputs.
   C. service organizations are more efficient.
   D. manufacturing organizations are more effective.
   E. control is less important in service organizations.

7. Jill is a manager in a company that makes large quantities of a single product. The most appropriate layout for Jill's company is a
   A. process layout.
   B. cellular layout.
   C. product layout.

D. fixed-position layout.
   E. automated layout.

8. A powerful and complex management control tool that combines computer-aided design (CAD), computer-aided manufacturing (CAM) and access to the company's other information systems is called
   A. robotics.
   B. flexible manufacturing systems (FMS).
   C. service technology.
   D. automatic control mechanism (ACM).
   E. computer-integrated manufacturing (CIM).

9. What is the relationship between quality and costs?
   A. Improved quality lowers costs.
   B. Lowered costs improve quality.
   C. Moderate levels of quality are the least expensive; low and high quality are the most expensive.
   D. Moderate levels of quality are the most expensive; low and high quality are the least expensive.
   E. Higher quality requires higher productivity, which in turn increases costs.

10. Why do many unions resist programs in which employees are cross-trained and then rewarded for using their new skills effectively?
    A. Programs like these threaten job security.
    B. Programs like these lower overall productivity.
    C. Programs like these reduce quality.
    D. Programs like these decrease flexibility.
    E. Programs like these increase defects.

chapter 22

Managing Information and Information Technology

FIRST THINGS FIRST

Wikipedia and Other Wikis

"It's important to have efficient, open disclosure . . . [but] we didn't have the tools to practice these amazing concepts until now."

—DARREN LENNARD, MANAGING DIRECTOR,
DRESDNER KLEINWORT WASSERSTEIN BANK

Does information quality depend on the person conveying it? Do experts really know the answers? James Surowiecki claims, "Groups are remarkably intelligent, and are often smarter than the smartest people in them." In his best-seller, *The Wisdom of Crowds*, Surowiecki claims that the masses know more, think more clearly, and make better choices than individuals. Some of the most

Wikipedia has quickly become a standard information source on the Internet. Jimmy Wales, shown here, is the founder of Wikipedia.

interesting developments in today's society spring from the same idea. One is open-source computer software, where many individuals create and improve software code. Nonprofit Wikipedia, an online encyclopedia written entirely by volunteers, is another example.

According to Wikipedia, *wiki* derives from the Hawaiian phrase *wiki wiki*, meaning "quick." A wiki is "a type of website that allows users to add, remove, or otherwise edit all content very quickly and easily, sometimes without the need for registration. This ease of interaction and operation makes a wiki an effective tool for collaborative writing." Wikipedia, whose name combines *wiki* with *encyclopedia*, is an enormous undertaking. By early 2006, the website existed in over 200 languages and encompassed more than 1 million articles in English. Almost all of the technical staff and the 3,000-plus writers are unpaid volunteers and agree to give up all copyrights to their contributions.

The philosophy behind Wikipedia is radical, but simple. The Wikipedia Foundation describes the organization's mission by saying, "Imagine a world in which every single person is given free access to the sum of all human knowledge. That's what we're doing." Founder Jimmy Wales and other early fans, called Wikipedians, gave every user the ability to edit Wikipedia's content. Articles grow and change over time, receiving input from many individuals. Articles are never "finished" but are updated as needed.

Malicious users can disrupt the system by posting false information or removing accurate information, but their changes are quickly found and corrected by Wikipedians. Malicious users are barred from further participation, and the website does not allow illegal or libelous material, but otherwise, the site is uncensored. Instead, the community upholds standards of truth, civility, and neutrality.

Wales believes that Wikipedia reflects an underlying change in society, away from authoritarian experts and toward more democracy and collaboration. He predicts that in the future, traditional encyclopedias will become distrusted and, eventually, obsolete. According to Wales, "People will say, 'This was written by one person? Then looked at by only two or three other people? How can I trust that process?'" Others, especially academics and librarians, disagree. Critics claim that Wikipedia's information is not authoritative because it not attributed to an author, and so reliability cannot be checked. Others worry that Wikipedia is too easily corrupted by a few users with biased points of view. An additional fear is that the site merely reflects popular opinion and that unique or divergent points of view may be excluded.

The technology of Wikipedia is, like its philosophy, radical in its effects but relatively simple to create. The site is hosted on clusters of servers located around the world. The software is built as an extension of an open-source database. Many volunteer programmers collaborate on the creation of the Wikipedia-specific software, which is open-source to comply with the organization's philosophy. The software code has two primary functions: to enable fast, efficient user searches and to provide user-friendly editing capability. The code also generates a "recent changes" list showing the newest edits. This list is a helpful tool to users who want to suppress malicious use.

Wikis are becoming increasingly common in business. Collaboration can be enhanced without the need for an extensive IT staff or a cumbersome process. The Gartner Group, a technology research firm, predicts that at least 50 percent of corporations will adopt wikis by 2009. Whole Foods, for example, uses a corporate wiki to increase collaboration throughout its distribution chain, linking purchasing, stores, and billing staff. Other businesses, including Symantec, Nokia, and Kodak, turn to wikis for bringing together virtual teams, increasing access to company databases, and enabling multiple users to easily work together. Bank manager Darren Lennard shares documents through a corporate wiki instead of e-mail. "It's important to have efficient, open disclosure," Lennard says. "It's just that, as a team, we didn't have the tools to practice these amazing concepts until now."[1]

As the opening vignette clearly demonstrates, information and communications technology continues to evolve at an almost breathtaking pace. Indeed, the very idea of everyone having free and convenient access to all the information they might need, which Wikipedia is trying to provide, would have been viewed as science fiction just a few years ago. Moreover, just as new advances continue to unfold in information technology, those advances are usually integrated into the daily operations of organizations. Managers now routinely turn to digital technology as an integral part of organizational resources and as a means of conducting everyday business. Every major firm's business activities—such as designing services, ensuring product delivery and cash flow, evaluating employees, and creating advertising—are linked to information systems. Effective information management requires a commitment of resources to establish, maintain, and upgrade as new technologies emerge.

This chapter is about advances made by organizations doing this. We describe the role and importance of information to managers, the characteristics of useful information, and information management as control, and we identify the basic building blocks of information systems. We discuss the general and specific determinants of information technology needs. We then discuss the primary types of information technology used in organizations and describe how this technology is managed.

Information and the Manager

Information has always been an integral part of every manager's job. Its importance, however, and therefore the need to manage it, continue to grow at a rapid clip. To appreciate this trend, we need to understand the role of information in the manager's job, characteristics of useful information, and the nature of information management as control.[2]

The Role of Information in the Manager's Job

In Chapters 1 and 18 we highlighted the role of communication in the manager's job. Given that information is a vital part of communication, it follows that management and information are closely related. Indeed, it is possible to conceptualize manage-

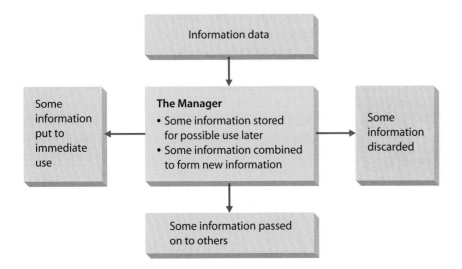

Information data

The Manager
- Some information stored for possible use later
- Some information combined to form new information

Some information put to immediate use

Some information discarded

Some information passed on to others

Figure 22.1

MANAGERS AS INFORMATION PROCESSORS

Managers who receive information and data must decide what to do with it. Some is stored for possible later use, and other information is combined to form new information. Subsequently, some is used immediately, some is passed on to others, and some is discarded.

ment itself as a series of steps involving the reception, processing, and dissemination of information. As illustrated in Figure 22.1, the manager is constantly bombarded with data and information (the difference between the two is noted later).

Suppose that Bob Henderson is an operations manager for a large manufacturing firm. During the course of a normal day, Bob receives many different pieces of information from formal and informal conversations and meetings, telephone calls, personal observation, e-mails, letters, reports, memos, the Internet, and trade publications. He gets a report from a subordinate that explains exactly how to solve a pressing problem, so he calls the subordinate and tells him to put the solution into effect immediately. He scans a copy of a report prepared for another manager, sees that it has no relevance to him, and discards it. He sees a *Wall Street Journal* article that he knows Sara Ferris in marketing should see, so he passes it on to her. He gets an electronic summary of yesterday's production report, but because he knows he will not need to analyze it for another week, he stores it. He observes a worker doing a job incorrectly and realizes that the incorrect method is associated with a mysterious quality problem that someone told him about last week.

A key part of information-processing activity is differentiating between data and information. **Data** are raw figures and facts reflecting a single aspect of reality. The facts that a plant has 35 machines, that each machine is capable of producing 1,000 units of output per day, that current and projected future demand for the units is 30,000 per day, and that workers sufficiently skilled to run the machines make $20 an hour are data.

Information is data presented in a way or form that has meaning.[3] Thus combining and summarizing the four pieces of data given above provides information: The plant has excess capacity and is therefore incurring unnecessary costs. Information has meaning to a manager and provides a basis for action. The plant manager might use the information and decide to sell four machines (perhaps keeping one as a backup) and transfer five operators to other jobs.

A related term is **information technology**, or **IT**. Information technology refers to the resources used by an organization to manage information that it needs to carry out its mission. IT may consist of computers, computer networks, telephones, fax machines, and other pieces of hardware. In addition, IT involves software that

data
Raw figures and facts reflecting a single aspect of reality

information
Data presented in a way or form that has meaning

information technology (IT)
Refers to the resources used by an organization to manage information that it needs in order to carry out its mission

Managers at Ben & Jerry's rely heavily on information to make sure that they have the right flavors of ice cream in the right locations at the right time. But to be of value, of course, the information has to be accurate, timely, complete, and relevant. After all, if a customer wants to buy a carton of Cherry Garcia at the local market today, it's in Ben & Jerry's best interests that the store has an ample supply!

---

accurate information
Provides a valid and reliable reflection of reality

---

complete information
Provides the manager with all the information he or she needs

---

facilitates the system's ability to manage information in a way that is useful for managers.[4]

The grocery industry uses data, information, and information technology to automate inventory and checkout facilities. The average Kroger store, for example, carries over 21,000 items. Computerized scanning machines at the checkout counters can provide daily sales figures for any product. These numbers alone are data and have little meaning in their pure form. But information is created from these data by another computerized system. Using this IT system, managers can identify how any given product or product line is selling in any number of stores over any meaningful period of time.

Characteristics of Useful Information

What factors differentiate between information that is useful and information that is not? In general, information is useful if it is accurate, timely, complete, and relevant. Indeed, part of the reason for the current lack of confidence in business is that stakeholders have long assumed that the accounting information that businesses provided was "true." But myriad scandals and controversies have shown that accounting procedures and reporting formats can vary to make things look much better than they actually are.[5]

Accurate   For information to be of real value to a manager, it must be ***accurate information***. Accuracy means that the information must provide a valid and reliable reflection of reality. A Japanese construction company bought information from a consulting firm about a possible building site in London. The Japanese were told that the land, which would be sold in a sealed-bid auction, would attract bids of close to $250 million. They were also told that the land currently held an old building that could easily be demolished. Thus the Japanese bid $255 million—which ended up being $90 million more than the next-highest bid. And, to make matters worse, a few days later the British government declared the building historic, preempting any thought of demolition. Clearly, the Japanese acted on information that was less than accurate.

Timely   Information also needs to be timely. Timeliness does not necessarily mean speediness; it means only that information needs to be available in time for appropriate managerial action. What constitutes timeliness is a function of the situation facing the manager. When Marriott was gathering information for a new hotel project, managers allowed themselves a six-month period for data collection. They felt this would give them an opportunity to do a good job of getting the information they needed while not delaying things too much. In contrast, Marriott's computerized reservation and accounting systems can provide a manager today with last night's occupancy level at any Marriott facility.

Complete   Information must tell a complete story for it to be useful to a manager. If it is less than ***complete information***, the manager is likely to get an inaccurate or distorted picture of reality. For example, managers at Kroger used to think that house-brand products were more profitable than national brands because they yielded higher unit profits. On the basis of this information, they gave house brands a great deal of shelf space and centered promotional activities around them. As Kroger's managers became more sophisticated in understanding their information, however, they realized that national brands were actually more profitable over time because they sold many more units than house brands during any given period of time. Hence, although a store might sell 10 cans of Kroger coffee in a day, with a profit of 50 cents per can (total profit of $5), it would also sell 15 cans of Maxwell House with a profit of 40 cents per can (total profit of $6) and 10 vacuum bags of Starbucks coffee with a profit of $1 per bag (total profit of $10). With this more complete picture, managers could do a better job of selecting the right mix of Kroger, Maxwell House, and Starbucks coffee to display and promote.

Relevant   Finally, information must be relevant if it is to be useful to managers. *Relevant information*, like *timely information*, is defined according to the needs and circumstances of a particular manager. Operations managers need information on costs and productivity; human resource managers need information on hiring needs and turnover rates; and marketing managers need information on sales projections and advertising rates. As Wal-Mart contemplates countries as possible expansion opportunities, it gathers information about local regulations, customs, and so forth. But the information about any given country is not really relevant until the decision is made to enter that market.

> **relevant information**
> Information that is useful to managers in their particular circumstances for their particular needs

> **timely information**
> Available in time for appropriate managerial action

Information Management as Control

The manager also needs to appreciate the role of information in control—indeed, to see information management as a vital part of the control process in the organization.[6] As already noted, managers receive much more data and information than they need or can use. Accordingly, deciding how to handle each piece of data and information involves a form of control.[7]

The control perspective on information management is illustrated in Figure 22.2. Information enters, is used by, and leaves the organization. For example, Marriott took great pains to make sure it got all the information it needed to plan

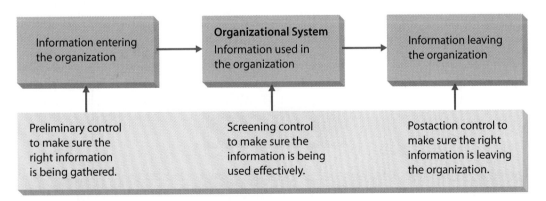

Figure 22.2

INFORMATION MANAGEMENT AS CONTROL

Information management can be part of the control system via preliminary, screening, and postaction control mechanisms. Because information from the environment is just as much a resource as raw materials or finances, it must be monitored and managed to promote its efficient and effective utilization.

for and enter the economy lodging business. Once this preliminary information was gathered, it was necessary to make sure that the information was made available in the proper form to everyone who needed it. In general, the effort to ensure that information is accurate, timely, complete, and relevant is a form of screening control. Finally, Marriott wanted to make sure that its competitors did not learn about its plans until the last possible minute. It also wanted to time and orchestrate news releases, public announcements, and advertising for maximum benefit. These efforts thus served a postaction control function.

> **"**Employees should go to work assuming that Big Brother is going to read over their electronic shoulder when they're sitting at the computer.**"**
>
> Nancy Flynn, executive director of ePolicy Institute
> (*Houston Chronicle*, January 30, 2006, p. D1)

Building Blocks of Information Technology

Information technology is generally of two types—manual or electronic. All information technology, and the systems that it defines, has five basic parts. Figure 22.3 diagrams these parts for a computer-based (electronic) information technology system. The *input medium* is the device that is used to add data and information into the system. For example, the optical scanner at Kroger enters point-of-sale information. Likewise, someone can enter data through a keyboard, with a mouse, using a barcode reader, or from other computers or the Internet.

The data that are entered into the system typically flow first to a processor. The *processor* is the part of the system that is capable of organizing, manipulating, sorting, or performing calculations or other transformations with the data. Most systems also have one or more *storage devices*—places where data can be stored for later use. Floppy disks, hard drives, thumb drives, CD-ROMs, and optical disks are common forms of storage devices. As data are transformed into usable information, the resultant information must be communicated to the appropriate person by means of an *output medium*. Common ways to display output are through video displays, printers, and fax machines, as well as through transmission to other computers or webpages.

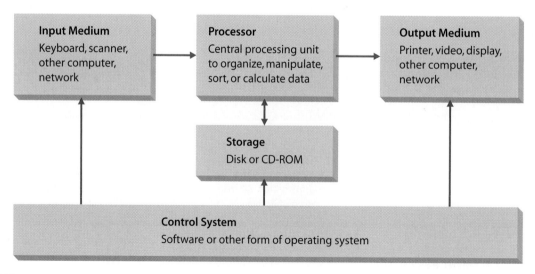

Figure 22.3

BUILDING BLOCKS OF A COMPUTER-BASED INFORMATION SYSTEM

Computer-based information systems generally have five basic components—an input medium, a processor, an output medium, a storage device, and a control system. Noncomputer-based systems use parallel components for the same basic purposes.

Finally, the entire information technology system is operated by a *control system*—most often software of one form or another. Simple systems in smaller organizations can use off-the-shelf software. Microsoft Windows and Linux are general operating systems that control more specialized types of software. Microsoft Word and Word-Perfect are popular systems for word processing. Lotus 123 and Excel are popular spreadsheet programs, and dBase and Access are frequently used for database management. Of course, elaborate systems of the type used by large businesses require a special, customized operating system. When organizations start to link computers together in a network, the operating system must be even more complex. Enterprise resource planning networks are also increasingly being used for this purpose.

As we note earlier, information technology systems need not be computerized. Many small organizations still function quite well with a manual system using paper documents, routing slips, paper clips, file folders, file cabinets, and a single personal computer. Increasingly, however, even small businesses are abandoning their manual systems for computerized ones. As hardware prices continue to drop and software becomes more and more powerful, computerized information systems will likely be within the reach of all businesses that want to have them.

concept
CHECK

What are the characteristics of useful information?

Identify examples of both data and information that you have seen or heard in the last 24 hours.

Types of Information Systems

In a sense, the phrase *information system* may be a misnomer. It suggests that there is one system, but in fact a firm's employees will have different interests, job responsibilities, and decision-making requirements. One information system cannot accommodate such a variety of information requirements. Instead, "the information system" is a complex of several information systems that share information while serving different levels of the organization, different departments, or different operations.

Information systems are required in all kinds of organizational settings. A staff member of the German Aerospace Centre is shown here receiving traffic data from a helicopter at the Stuttgart airport. Local police used a new helicopter-based camera surveillance system to monitor traffic patterns in the Stuttgart region during the FIFA World Cup soccer tournament in 2006. An elaborate information system analyzed the data transmitted from the helicopters to predict emerging traffic patterns. Motorists could then tap into the system and get up-to-the-minute traffic information. The system was credited with helping reduce traffic jams throughout the region.

User Groups and System Requirements

To understand the different kinds of information systems that organizations use, it is instructive to first consider user groups and system requirements. This perspective is illustrated in Figure 22.4. In general, there are four user groups, each with different system requirements: first-line, middle, and top managers, and knowledge workers. Knowledge workers

Figure 22.4

DETERMINANTS OF AN
ORGANIZATION'S INFORMATION-
PROCESSING NEEDS

*Information-processing needs are
determined by user groups and
system requirements, as well as by
such specific managerial factors as
area and level in the organization.*

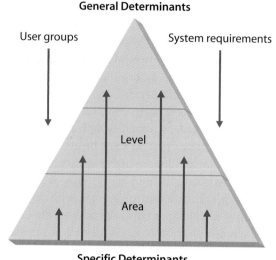

---

knowledge workers
Specialists, usually professionally
trained and certified—engineers, scientists, information technology specialists, psychologists—who rely on
information technology to design new
products or create new business
processes

---

represent a special user category. ***Knowledge workers*** are specialists, usually professionally trained and certified—engineers, scientists, information technology
specialists, psychologists—who rely on information technology to design new
products or create new business processes.

Managers at Different Levels   Because they work on different kinds of problems,
first-line, middle, and top managers, as well as knowledge workers, have different
information needs. First-line (or operational) managers, for example, need information to oversee the day-to-day details of their department or projects. Middle managers need summaries and analyses for setting intermediate and long-range goals
for the department or projects under their supervision. Top management analyzes
broader trends in the economy, the business environment, and overall company
performance to conduct long-range planning for the entire organization. Finally,
knowledge workers need special information for conducting technical projects.

Consider the various information needs for a flooring manufacturer. Sales managers (first-line managers) supervise salespeople, assign territories to the sales force,
and handle customer service and delivery problems. They need current information
on the sales and delivery of products: lists of incoming customer orders and daily
delivery schedules to customers in their territory. Regional managers (middle managers) set sales quotas for each sales manager, prepare budgets, and plan staffing
needs for the upcoming year. They need information on monthly sales by product and
region. Top managers need both external and internal information. Internally, they
use sales data summarized by product, customer type, and geographic region, along
with comparisons to previous years. Equally important is external information on
consumer behavior patterns, the competition's performance, and economic forecasts.
Finally, knowledge workers developing new flooring materials need information on
the chemical properties of adhesives and compression strengths for floor structures.

Functional Areas and Business Processes   Each business function—marketing,
human resources, accounting, operations, finance—has its own information
requirements. In addition, many businesses are organized according to various
business processes, and these process groups also need special information. Each

of these user groups and departments, then, is represented by an information system. When organizations add to these systems the types of systems needed by the four levels of users discussed above, the total number of information systems and applications increases significantly. Top-level finance managers, for example, are concerned with long-range planning for capital expenditures for future facilities and equipment, as well as with determining sources of capital funds.

In contrast, a business process group will include users—both managers and employees—drawn from all organizational levels. The supply chain management group, for instance, may be in the process of trimming down the number of suppliers. The information system supporting this project would contain information ranging across different organizational functions and management levels. The group will need information and expert knowledge on marketing, warehousing and distribution, production, communications technology, purchasing, suppliers, and finance. It will also need different perspectives on operational, technical, and managerial issues: determining technical requirements for new suppliers, specifying task responsibilities for participating firms, and determining future financial requirements.

Major Systems by Level

In this section, we discuss different kinds of systems that provide applications at some organizational levels but not at others. For any routine, repetitive, highly structured decision, a specialized application will suffice. System requirements for knowledge workers, however, will probably vary because knowledge workers often face a variety of specialized problems. Applications of information systems for middle or top-level management decisions must also be flexible, though for different reasons. In particular, they will use a broader range of information collected from a variety of sources, both external and internal.

Transaction-Processing Systems   ***Transaction-processing systems (TPS)*** are applications of information processing for basic day-to-day business transactions. Customer order-taking by online retailers, approval of claims at insurance companies, receipt and confirmation of reservations by airlines, payroll processing and bill payment at almost every company—all are routine business processes. Typically, the TPS for first-level (operational) activities is well defined, with predetermined data requirements, and follows the same steps to complete all transactions in the system.

> *transaction-processing system (TPS)*
> Application of information processing for basic day-to-day business transactions

Systems for Knowledge Workers and Office Applications   Systems for knowledge workers and office applications support the activities of both knowledge workers and employees in clerical positions. They provide assistance for data processing and other office activities, including the creation of communications documents. Like other departments, the IS department includes both knowledge workers and data workers.

Systems for Operations and Data Workers   People who run the company's computer equipment are usually called *system operations workers*. They make sure that the right programs are run in the correct sequence and monitor equipment to ensure that it is operating properly. Many organizations also have employees who enter data into the system for processing.

Figure 22.5

A BASIC MANAGEMENT INFORMATION SYSTEM

A basic management information system relies on an integrated database. Managers in various functional areas can access the database and get the information they need to make decisions. For example, operations managers can access the system to determine sales forecasts by marketing managers, and financial managers can check human resource files to identify possible candidates for promotion into the finance department.

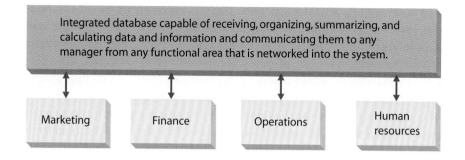

management information system (MIS)
Supports an organization's managers by providing daily reports, schedules, plans, and budgets

Knowledge-Level and Office Systems Needless to say, the explosion of new support systems—word processing, document imaging, desktop publishing, computer-aided design, simulation modeling—has increased the productivity of both knowledge and office workers. Desktop publishing combines graphics and word-processing text to publish professional-quality print and web documents. Document-imaging systems can scan paper documents and images, convert them into digital form for storage on disks, retrieve them, and transmit them electronically to workstations throughout the network.

Management Information Systems *Management information systems (MIS)* support an organization's managers by providing daily reports, schedules, plans, and budgets. A simple MIS is shown in Figure 22.5. Each manager's information activities vary according to his or her functional area (say, accounting or marketing) and management level. Whereas midlevel managers focus mostly on internal activities and information, higher-level managers are also engaged in external activities. Middle managers, the largest MIS user group, need networked information to plan such upcoming activities as personnel training, materials movements, and cash flows. They also need to know the current status of the jobs and projects being carried out in their department: What stage is it at now? When will it be finished? Is there an opening so we can start the next job? Many of a firm's management information systems—cash flow, sales, production scheduling, shipping—are indispensable in helping managers find answers to such questions.

decision support system (DSS)
An interactive system that locates and presents information needed to support the decision-making process

Decision Support Systems Middle and top-level managers receive decision-making assistance from a *decision support system (DSS)*: an interactive system that locates and presents information needed to support the decision-making process. Whereas some DSSs are devoted to specific problems, others serve more general purposes, allowing managers to analyze different types of problems. Thus a firm that often faces decisions on plant capacity, for example, may have a capacity DSS: The manager inputs data on anticipated levels of sales, working capital, and customer delivery requirements. Then the DSS's built-in transaction processors manipulate the data and make recommendations on the best levels of plant capacity for each future time period. In contrast, a general-purpose system, such as a marketing DSS, might respond to a variety of marketing-related problems. It may be programmed to handle "what if" questions, such as "When is the best time to introduce a new product if my main competitor introduces one in three months, our new product has an eighteen-month expected life, demand is seasonal with a peak in autumn, and my goal is to gain the largest possible market share?" The DSS can assist in decisions for which predetermined solutions are unknown by using sophisticated modeling tools and data analysis.

Executive Support Systems An *executive support system (ESS)* is a quick-reference, easy-access application of information systems specially designed for instant access by upper-level managers. ESSs are designed to assist with executive-level decisions and problems, ranging from "What lines of business should we be in five years from now?" to "Based on forecasted developments in electronic technologies, to what extent should our firm be globalized in five years? In ten years?" The ESS also uses a wide range of both internal information and external sources, such as industry reports, global economic forecasts, and reports on competitors' capabilities. Because senior-level managers do not usually possess advanced computer skills, they prefer systems that are easily accessible and adaptable. Accordingly, ESSs are not designed to address only specific, predetermined problems. Instead, they allow the user some flexibility in attacking a variety of problem situations. They are easily accessible by means of simple keyboard strokes or even voice commands.

> **executive support system (ESS)**
> A quick-reference, easy-access application of information systems specially designed for instant access by upper-level managers

Artificial Intelligence and Expert Systems *Artificial intelligence (AI)* can be defined as the construction of computer systems, both hardware and software, to imitate human behavior—in other words, systems that perform physical tasks, use thought processes, and learn. In developing AI systems, knowledge workers—business specialists, modelers, information technology experts—try to design computer-based systems capable of reasoning, so that computers, instead of people, can perform certain business activities.

> **artificial intelligence (AI)**
> The construction of computer systems, both hardware and software, to imitate human behavior, that is, to perform physical tasks, use thought processes, and learn

One example is a credit evaluation system that decides which loan applicants are creditworthy and which ones risky and then composes acceptance and rejection letters accordingly. Another example is an applicant selection system that receives interviewees' job applications, screens them, and then decides which applicants are best matched with each of several job openings. There are also AI systems that possess sensory capabilities, such as lasers that "see," "hear," and "feel." In addition, as machines become more sophisticated in processing natural language, humans can give instructions and ask questions merely by speaking to a computer.

A special form of AI program, the *expert system*, is designed to imitate the thought processes of human experts in a particular field. Expert systems incorporate the rules that an expert applies to specific types of problems, such as the judgments a physician makes in diagnosing illnesses. In effect, expert systems supply everyday users with "instant expertise." General Electric's Socrates Quick Quote, for example, imitates the decisions of a real estate expert and then places a package of recommendations about real estate transactions at the fingertips of real estate dealers on GE's private computer network. A system called MOCA (for Maintenance Operations Center Advisor), by imitating the thought processes of a maintenance manager, schedules routine maintenance for American Airlines' entire fleet.

The Internet

Although not everyone would automatically think of it this way, the Internet is also an information system, one that is becoming more and more important to business every day. The *Internet*—the largest public data communications network—is a gigantic network of networks serving millions of computers; offering information on business, science, and government; and providing communications flows among more than 170,000 separate networks around the world. Originally commissioned

> **Internet (the Net)**
> A gigantic network of networks serving millions of computers; offering information on business, science, and government; and providing communications flows among more than 170,000 separate networks around the world

by the Pentagon as a communications tool for use during wartime, the Internet allows personal computers in virtually any location to be linked together. The Net has gained in popularity because it is an efficient tool for information retrieval that makes available an immense wealth of academic, technical, and business information.

Because it can transmit information quickly and at low cost—lower than long distance phone service, postal delivery, and overnight delivery—the Net has also become the most important e-mail system in the world. For thousands of businesses, therefore, the Net has joined—and is even replacing—the telephone, fax machine, and express mail as a standard means of communication. Although individuals cannot connect directly to the Internet, for a small monthly usage fee they can subscribe to the Net via an ***Internet service provider (ISP)***, such as America Online or Earthlink. An ISP is a commercial firm that maintains a permanent connection to the Net and sells temporary connections to subscribers.[8]

The Internet's popularity continues to grow for both business and personal applications. In 2005 more than 1 billion Net users were active on links connecting every country in the world. Between 2000 and 2005 the number of users increased by 184%. In the United States alone, more than 150 million users are on the Net every day. Its power to change the way business is conducted has been amply demonstrated in both large and small firms as their members use the Net to communicate both within and across organizational boundaries, to buy and sell products and services, and to glean information from myriad sources around the world.

The Net has also benefited small companies, especially as a means of expanding market research and improving customer service, as well as serving as a source of information. In San Leandro, California, for example, TriNet Employer Group subscribes to Ernst & Young's online consulting program, Ernie. For $3,500 a year, TriNet controller Lyle DeWitt sends questions from his computer and gets an answer from an Ernst & Young expert within 48 hours. Aiming for small clients who cannot afford big-name consulting advice, Ernie answers questions on health insurance, benefit plans, immigration issues, and payroll taxes. Of course, as noted in *The Business of Ethics*, the constant expansion of Internet applications is not without risk.

Internet service provider (ISP)
A commercial firm that maintains a permanent connection to the Net and sells temporary connections to subscribers

---

World Wide Web (WWW)
A system with universally accepted standards for storing, retrieving, formatting, and displaying information

---

> "It may sound geeky, but we need a national data-management plan."
>
> Francine Berman, Director, San Diego Supercomputer Center
> (*Newsweek*, June 12, 2006, p. 57)

The World Wide Web Thanks to the ***World Wide Web*** (***WWW***, or simply "the Web"), the Internet is easy to use and allows users around the world to communicate electronically with little effort. The World Wide Web is a system with universally accepted standards for storing, retrieving, formatting, and displaying information.[9] It provides the common language that enables us to "surf" the Net and makes the Internet available to a general audience, rather than only to technical users like computer programmers. To access a website, for example, the user must specify the *Uniform Resource Locator (URL)* that points to the resource's unique address on the Web.

Servers and Browsers Each website opens with a *home page*—a screen display that welcomes the visitor with a greeting that may include graphics, sound, and visual enhancements introducing the user to the site. Additional pages give details on the sponsor's products and explain how to contact help in using the site. Often, they furnish URLs for related websites, to which the user can link by simply pointing

The Business of Ethics

The Digital You

The marriage of information technology and mathematics has revolutionized business before—think about business process modeling, quantitative financial analysis, and data mining. Now, it's about to do so again. Advances in computing capability and mathematical modeling, combined with increasing amounts of personal data stored and accessible online, mean that industry's next modeling subject will be—you. "We turn the world of content into math, and we turn you into math," says Howard Kaushansky, CEO of Umbria, a market analysis firm.

Your buying patterns will likely be analyzed first. Google already sells advertising based on an analysis of customers' online browsing and buying patterns. E-loan, an online lender, uses a complicated algorithm to purchase key-word advertising. The company adjusts the amount it is willing to pay for 250,000 loan-related search terms on a continual basis, changing thousands of bids in an hour. Umbria, hired by PepsiCo, peeked into millions of blogs and found that young men use Gatorade as a cocktail mixer in the hope of reducing hangovers, a use that marketers did not predict.

As the models become more sophisticated, they will begin to analyze smaller and smaller groups, and finally, individuals. IBM, a long-time leader in process modeling, is working to model 50,000 of its IT consul-

tants. Their education, skills, and experiences become quantitative inputs to the system. Their free time can be seen by looking at calendar software, and their global location is revealed by mobile communication devices. Even social savvy is measured, by investigating the traffic patterns and language of e-mails.

Other modeling techniques that can get personal include genetic analysis performed by physicians or insurance companies, demographic and phone pattern data that can unmask terrorists, and virtual libraries that provide customized information based on user reading patterns.

Personal modeling raises ethical issues of privacy. In addition, the techniques may give too much power to the analysts and the companies who hire them. One IBM manager, Samer Takriri, believes that human ingenuity will prevent most abuses. "People are complicated," Takriti says. "If you have a system, they figure out how to game it." To which experts reply that they will simply build models that expect and adjust for human behavior.

References: Stephen Baker, "Math Will Rock Your World," *Business-Week*, January 23, 2006, pp. 54–62; Damien Cave, "16 to 25? Pentagon Has Your Number, and More," *New York Times*, June 24, 2005, www.nytimes.com on June 26, 2005; William Holstein, "An Algorithm as a Pickax," *New York Times*, October 9, 2005; Erik Schonfeld, "The Great Giveaway," *Business 2.0*, April 1, 2005, www.money.cnn.com on May 30, 2006.

and clicking. The person who is responsible for maintaining an organization's website is usually called the *webmaster*. Large websites use dedicated workstations—large computers—known as *web servers*, which are customized for managing, maintaining, and supporting websites.

With hundreds of thousands of new webpages appearing each day, cyberspace is now serving up billions of pages of publicly accessible information. Sorting through this maze would be frustrating and inefficient without access to a **web browser**—the software that enables the user to access information on the Web. A browser runs on the user's PC and supports the graphics and linking capabilities needed to navigate the Web. Microsoft's Internet Explorer is the world's dominant web browser today.

> **web browser**
> The software that enables the user to access information on the Web

Directories and Search Engines The web browser offers additional tools—website directories and search engines—for navigating on the Web. Among the most successful cyberspace enterprises are companies like Yahoo! that maintain free directories of web content. When Yahoo! is notified about new websites, it classifies them in its directory. The user enters one or two key words (say, "compact disk"), and the directory responds by retrieving from the directory a list of websites with titles containing those words.

In contrast to a directory, a search engine will search cyberspace's millions of webpages without preclassifying them into a directory. It searches for webpages that contain the same words as the user's search terms. Then it displays addresses for those that come closest to matching, then the next closest, and so on. A search engine such as Google or Ask.com may respond to more than 10 million inquiries per day. It is thus no surprise that both directories and search engines are packed with paid ads.[10] Yahoo! and Google are the current leaders in *portal sites*—sites used by Net surfers as primary home pages.

Intranets   The success of the Internet has led some companies to extend the Net's technology internally, using it for internal websites containing information about the firm. These private networks, or **intranets**, are accessible only to employees via entry through electronic firewalls. Firewalls, discussed later, are used to limit access to an intranet. At Compaq Computer, the intranet allows employees to shuffle their retirement savings among various investment funds. Ford's intranet connects 120,000 workstations in Asia, Europe, and the United States to thousands of Ford websites containing private information on Ford activities in production, engineering, distribution, and marketing. Sharing such information has helped reduce the lead time for getting models into production from 36 to 24 months. Ford's latest project in improving customer service through internal information sharing is called *manufacturing on demand*. Now, for example, the Mustang that required 50 days' delivery time in 1996 is available in less than two weeks. The savings to Ford, of course, will be billions of dollars in inventory and fixed costs.[11]

> *intranet*
> A communications network similar to the Internet but operating within the boundaries of a single organization

Extranets   Sometimes firms allow outsiders access to their intranets. These so-called **extranets** allow outsiders limited access to a firm's intranet. The most common application allows buyers to enter the seller's system to see which products are available for sale and delivery, thus providing product availability information quickly to outside buyers. Industrial suppliers, too, are often linked into their customers' intranets so that they can see planned production schedules and make supplies ready as needed for customers' upcoming operations.

> *extranet*
> A communications network that allows selected outsiders limited access to an organization's internal information system, or intranet

concept
CHECK

Identify the various different levels of information systems that exist today.	*Identify examples of how you use the Internet for informational purposes.*

Managing Information Systems

At this point, the value and importance of information systems should be apparent. There are still important questions to be answered, however. How are such systems developed, and how are they used on a day-to-day basis? This section provides insights into these issues and related areas.

Creating Information Systems

The basic steps involved in creating an information system are outlined in Figure 22.6. The first step is to determine the information needs of the organization and to

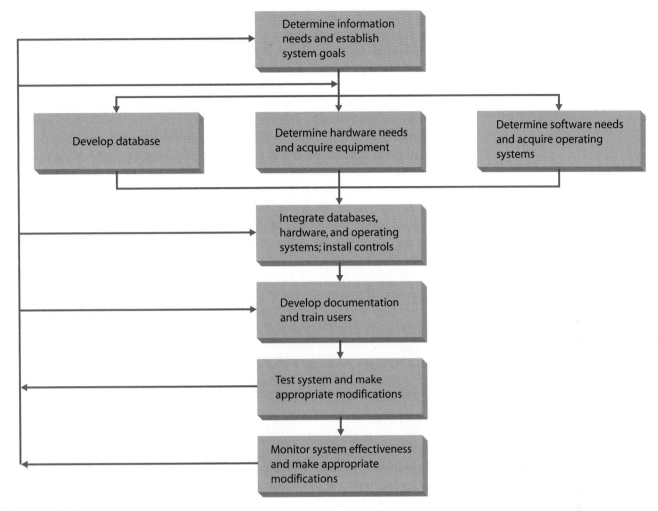

Figure 22.6

ESTABLISHING AN INFORMATION SYSTEM

Establishing an information system is a complex procedure. Managers must realize, however, that the organization's information management needs will change over time, and some steps of the process may have to be repeated in the future.

establish goals for what is to be achieved with the proposed system. It is absolutely imperative that the project have full support and an appropriate financial commitment from top management if it is to be successful. Once the decision has been made to develop and install an information system, a task force is usually constituted to oversee everything. Target users, as discussed earlier, must be well represented on such a task force.

Next, three tasks can be done simultaneously. One task is to develop a database. Most organizations already possess the information they need for an information system, but it is often not in the correct form. The Pentagon has spent large sums of money to transform all of its paper records into computer records. Many other branches of the government are also working hard to computerize their data.[12]

While the database is being assembled, the organization also needs to determine its hardware needs and acquire the appropriate equipment. Some systems rely solely on one large mainframe computer; others are increasingly using personal computers.

Equipment is usually obtained from large manufacturers like IBM, Compaq, Sun, and Dell. Finally, software needs must also be determined and an appropriate operating system obtained. Again, off-the-shelf packages will sometimes work, although most companies find it necessary to do some customization to suit their needs.[13]

The actual information system is created by integrating the databases, hardware, software, and operating system. Obviously, the mechanics of doing this are beyond the scope of this discussion. However, the company usually has to rely on the expertise of outside consulting firms, along with the vendors who provided the other parts of the system, to get it all put together. During this phase, the equipment is installed, cables are strung between units, the data are entered into the system, the operating system is installed and tested, and so forth. During this phase, system controls are also installed. A control is simply a characteristic of the system that limits certain forms of access or limits what a person can do with the system. For example, top managers may want to limit access to certain sensitive data to a few key people. These people may be given private codes that must be entered before the data are made available. It is important to make sure that data cannot be accidentally erased by someone who just happens to press the wrong key.

The next step is to develop documentation of how the system works and to train people in how to use it. *Documentation* refers to manuals, computerized help programs, diagrams, and instruction sheets. Essentially, it tells people how to use the system for different purposes. Beyond pure documentation, however, training sessions are also common. Such sessions allow people to practice using the system under the watchful eyes of experts.

The system must then be tested and appropriate modifications made. Regardless of how well planned an information system is, there will almost certainly be glitches. For example, the system may be unable to generate a report that needs to be made available to certain managers. Or the report may not be in the appropriate format. Or certain people may be unable to access data that they need to get other information from the system. In most cases, the consultants or the internal group that installed the system will be able to make such modifications as the need arises.

The organization must recognize that information management needs will change over time. Hence, even though the glitches get straightened out and the information system is put into normal operation, modifications may still be needed in the future. For example, after Black & Decker acquired General Electric's small-appliance business, it had to overhaul its own information system to accommodate all the new information associated with its new business. Information management is a continuous process. Even if an effective information system can be created and put into use, there is still a good chance that it will occasionally need to be modified to fit changing circumstances.

Integrating Information Systems

In very large and complex organizations, information systems must also be integrated. This integration may involve linkages between different information systems within the same organization or between different organizations altogether. Within an organization, for example, it is probably necessary for the marketing system and the operations system to be able to communicate with each other.

Linking systems together is not as easy. Consider, for example, the complexities involved when Hewlett-Packard acquired Compaq Computer. Each firm had its own complex and integrated information network. But because each firm's network relied on different technologies, hardware, and operating systems, integrating the two firms has been a costly and complex undertaking. Similarly, suppose a firm installs one system in one of its divisions, using Dell equipment and Microsoft software, and then installs a different system in another division, using Hewlett-Packard equipment and Lotus software. Just as with Hewlett-Packard and Compaq, if and when the firm decides to tie its two distinct systems together, it may face considerable difficulties.

There are two ways to overcome this problem. One is to develop everything at once. Unfortunately, doing so is expensive, and sometimes managers simply cannot anticipate today exactly what their needs will be tomorrow. The other method is to adopt a standard type of system at the beginning, so that subsequent additions fit properly.[14] Even then, however, breakthroughs in information system technology may still make it necessary to change approaches in midstream.

Using Information Systems

The real test of the value of an information system is how it can be used. Ideally, an information system should be simple to use and nontechnical—that is, one should not have to be a computer expert to use the system. In theory, a manager should be able to access a modern information system by turning on a computer and clicking an icon with a mouse. The manager should also be able to enter appropriate new data or request that certain kinds of information be provided. The requested information might first be displayed on a computer screen or monitor. After the manager is satisfied, the information can then be printed out in paper form on a standard printer, or the manager can store the information back in the system for possible future use or for use by others.

One implication relates to the span of management and the number of levels of an organization. Innovations in information technology enable a manager to stay in touch with an increasingly large number of managers and subordinates. T. J. Rodgers, CEO of Cypress Semiconductor, uses the firm's information system to check on the progress of each of his employees every week. Using this and related approaches, spans of management are likely to widen and organizational levels to decrease. And some organizations are using their information-processing capabilities to network with other companies. Pacific Intermountain Express, a large western trucking company, gives customers access to its own computer network so they can check on the status of their shipments.

Travelers Insurance has made effective use of its information system by hiring a team of trained nurses to review health insurance claims. The nurses tap into the company's regular information system and analyze the medical diagnoses provided with each claim. They can use this information to determine whether a second opinion is warranted before a particular surgical procedure is approved. They enter their decision directly into the system. When the claim form is printed out, it contains a provision that spells out whether the claimant must seek a second opinion before proceeding with a particular treatment.

Managing Information Security

An increasingly common concern for businesses today is security. Security measures for protection against intrusion are a constant challenge. To gain entry into most systems, users have protected passwords that guard against unauthorized access, but many firms rely on additional protective software as a safeguard. To protect against intrusions by unauthorized outsiders, companies use security devices, called *electronic firewalls,* in their systems. **Firewalls** are software and hardware

> **firewall**
> Software and hardware system that allows employees access to both the Internet and the company's internal computer network while barring access by outsiders

systems that allow employees access to both the Internet and the company's internal computer network while barring entry by outsiders.

Security for electronic communications is an additional concern. Electronic transmissions can be intercepted, altered, and read by intruders. To prevent unauthorized access, many firms rely on *encryption:* use of a secret numeric code to scramble the characters in the message, so that the message is not understandable during transmission. Only personnel with the deciphering codes can read them. Protection for preserving data files and databases is not foolproof and typically involves making backup copies to be stored outside the computer system, usually in a safe. Damaged system files can thus be replaced by backups.

Finally, the most important security factor is the people in the system. At most firms, personnel are trained in the responsibilities of computer use and warned of the penalties for violating system security. For example, each time the computer boots up, a notice displays the warning that software and data are protected and spells out penalties for unauthorized use.[15]

> "Morgan Stanley is in serious trouble because of the way it mishandled an increasingly critical matter for corporations: handing over e-mail and other documents in legal battles."
>
> Susanne Craig, business writer
> (*Wall Street Journal*, May 16, 2005, p. A1)

Understanding Information System Limitations

It is also necessary to recognize the limits of information systems. Several of these are listed in Table 22.1. First of all, as already noted, information systems are expensive and difficult to develop and implement. Thus organizations may try to cut corners too much or install a system in such a piecemeal fashion that its effectiveness suffers.

Information systems simply are not suitable for some tasks or problems. Complex problems requiring human judgment must still be addressed by humans. Information systems are often a useful tool for managers, but they can seldom actually replace managers. Managers also may come to rely too much on information systems. As a consequence, the manager may lose touch with the real-world problems he or she needs to be concerned about. Similarly, access to unlimited information can result in overload, rendering managers less effective than they would be with reduced access to information.[16]

Information may not be as accurate, timely, complete, or relevant as it appears. There is a strong tendency for people to think that because a computer performed the calculations, the answer must be correct—especially if the answer is calculated to several decimal places. But the fact of the matter is that if the initial information was flawed, all resultant computations using it are likely to be flawed as well.

Managers sometimes have unrealistic expectations about what information systems can accomplish. They may believe that the first stage of implementation will

Table 22.1

LIMITATIONS OF INFORMATION SYSTEMS

Although information systems play a vital role in modern organizations, they are not without their limitations. In particular, information systems have six basic limitations. For example, one major limitation of installing an information system is cost. For a large company, an information system might cost several million dollars.

1. Information systems are expensive and difficult to develop and implement.
2. Information systems are not suitable for all tasks or problems.
3. Managers sometimes rely too much on information systems.
4. Information provided to managers may not be as accurate, timely, complete, or relevant as it first appears to be.
5. Managers may have unrealistic expectations of what information systems can do.
6. The information system may be subject to sabotage, computer viruses, or downtime.

result in a full-blown Orwellian communications network that a child could use. When the manager comes to see the flaws and limitations of the system, she or he may become disappointed and as a result not use the system effectively. Finally, the information system may be subject to sabotage, computer viruses, or downtime. Disgruntled employees have been known to enter false data deliberately. And a company that relies too much on a computerized information system may find itself totally paralyzed in the event of a simple power outage or a crippling computer virus.

concept
CHECK

Describe how information systems are created.

Identify personal examples of information system limitations that you have encountered or experienced.

The Impact of Information Systems on Organizations

Information systems are clearly an important part of most modern organizations. Their effects are felt in a variety of ways. Indeed, the rapid growth of information technologies has changed the very structure of business organizations.

Leaner Organizations

Information networks are leading to leaner companies with fewer employees and simpler structures. Because today's networked firm can maintain information linkages among both employees and customers, more work can be accomplished with fewer people. Bank customers, for example, can dial into a twenty-four-hour information system and find out their current balances from a digital voice. In the industrial sector, assembly workers at an IBM plant used to receive instructions from supervisors or special staff. Now instructions are delivered electronically to their workstations.

Widespread reductions in middle-management positions and the shrinkage of layers in organizational structure are possible because information networks now provide direct communications between top managers and workers at lower levels. The operating managers who formerly communicated company policies, procedures, or work instructions to lower-level employees are being replaced by electronic information networks.

More Flexible Operations

Electronic networks allow businesses to offer customers greater variety and faster delivery cycles. Recovery after heart surgery, for example, is expedited by custom-tailored

Breakthroughs in information technology will continue to impact organizations in myriad ways. This Siemens engineer demonstrates one of the newest breakthroughs on the horizon—a virtual keyboard. A mini projector is used to create keys and a mousepad—all the user has to do is touch the worksurface and the keystroke is entered into a computer or other device. Such breakthroughs may be especially significant for use in so-called clean work environments such as medical labs and high-tech research facilities.

rehabilitation programs designed with integrated information systems. Each personalized program integrates the patient's history with information from physicians and rehabilitation specialists and then matches the patient with an electronically monitored exercise regimen. Products such as cellular phones, PCs, and audio systems can be custom-ordered, too, with your choice of features and options and next-day delivery. The underlying principle is called *mass customization*. Although companies produce in large volumes, each unit features the unique variations and options that the customer prefers.

Flexible production and fast delivery depend on an integrated network to coordinate all of the transactions, activities, and process flows necessary to make quick adjustments in the production process. The ability to organize and store massive volumes of information is crucial, as are the electronic linkages between customers, manufacturer, materials suppliers, and shippers.

Increased Collaboration

Collaboration, not only among internal units but with outside firms as well, is on the rise because networked systems make it cheaper and easier to contact everyone, whether other employees or outside organizations.[17] Aided by intranets, more companies are learning that complex problems can be solved better by means of collaboration, either in formal teams or through spontaneous interaction. In the new, networked organization, decisions that were once the domain of individuals are now shared, as both people and departments have become more interdependent. The design of new products, for example, was once an engineering responsibility. Now, in contrast, it can be a shared responsibility because so much information is accessible for evaluation from various perspectives. Marketing, finance, production, engineering, and purchasing can now share their different stores of information and determine a best overall design.

Naturally, networked systems are also helpful in business-to-business (often referred to as "B2B") relationships. Increasingly, organizational buyers and suppliers are becoming so closely networked that they sometimes seem to be working for one organization. In the financial services industry, for example, institutional investors are networked with investment bankers, thus allowing efficient buying and selling of initial stock offerings. In manufacturing, Ford's parts suppliers are linked to Ford's extranet. Because they know Ford's current production schedules and upcoming requirements, they can move materials into Ford plants more quickly and more accurately.

A step toward even greater collaboration between companies—the so-called virtual company—has become possible through networking. As we saw in Chapter 12, a virtual company can be a temporary team assembled by a single organization. But a virtual company can also be created when several firms join forces. Each contributes different skills and resources that collectively result in a competitive business that would not be feasible for any of the collaborators acting alone. A company with marketing and promotional skills, for example, may team up with firms that are experts in warehousing and distribution, engineering, and production. Networking allows collaborators to exchange ideas, plan daily activities, share customer information, and otherwise coordinate their efforts, even if their respective facilities are far apart.

More Flexible Work Sites

Geographic separation of the workplace from the company headquarters is more common than ever because of networked organizations. Employees no longer work only at the office or the factory, nor are all of a company's operations performed at one location. The sales manager for an advertising agency may visit the company office in New York once every two weeks, preferring instead to work over the firm's electronic network from her home office in Florida. A medical researcher for the Cleveland Clinic may work at a home office networked into the clinic's system.[18]

A company's activities may also be geographically scattered but highly coordinated thanks to a networked system. Many e-businesses, for example, conduct no activities at one centralized location. When you order products from an Internet storefront—say, a chair, a sofa, a table, and two lamps—the chair may come from a cooperating warehouse in Philadelphia and the lamps from a manufacturer in California, while the sofa and table may be shipped directly from two manufacturers in North Carolina. All these activities are launched instantaneously by the customer's order and coordinated through the network, just as if all of them were being processed at one location.[19]

Improved Management Processes

Networked systems have changed the very nature of the management process. The activities, methods, and procedures of today's manager differ significantly from those that were common just a few years ago. Once, for example, upper-level managers did not concern themselves with all the detailed information that filtered upward in the workplace. Why? Because it was expensive to gather, slow in coming, and quickly out of date. Workplace management was delegated to middle and first-line managers.

With networked systems, however, instantaneous information is accessible in a convenient, usable format. Consequently, more and more upper managers use it routinely for planning, leading, directing, and controlling operations. Today, a top manager can find out the current status of any customer order, inspect productivity statistics for each workstation, and analyze the delivery performance of any driver and vehicle. More importantly, managers can better coordinate company-wide performance. They can identify departments that are working well together and those that are creating bottlenecks. Hershey's networked system, for example, includes SAP, an enterprise resource-planning model that identifies the current status of any order and traces its progress from order entry through customer delivery and receipt of payment. Progress and delays at intermediate stages—materials ordering, inventory availability, production scheduling, packaging, warehousing, distribution—can be checked continuously to determine which operations should be more closely coordinated with others to improve overall performance.

Changed Employee Behaviors

Information systems also directly affect the behaviors of people in organizations. Some of these effects are positive; others can be negative. On the plus side, information systems usually improve individual efficiency. Some people also enjoy their work more because they have fun using the new technology. Through computerized bulletin boards and e-mail, groups can form across organizational boundaries.

On the negative side, information systems can lead to isolation, as people have everything they need to do their job without interacting with others. Managers can work at home easily, with the possible side effects of being unavailable to others who need them or being removed from key parts of the social system. Computerized working arrangements also tend to be much less personal than other methods. For example, a computer-transmitted "pat on the back" will likely mean less than a real one. Researchers are just beginning to determine how individual behaviors and attitudes are affected by information systems.[20]

concept
CHECK

What are the primary impacts of information systems on organizations?

What are the primary ways in which information systems affect you personally?

Summary of Learning Objectives and Key Points

1. Describe the role and importance of information in the manager's job and identify the basic building blocks of information technology.
   - Information is a vital part of every manager's job.
   - For information to be useful, it must be accurate, timely, complete, and accurate.
   - Information technology is best conceived of as part of the control process.
   - Information technology systems contain five basic components:
     - an input medium
     - a processor
     - an output medium
     - a storage device
     - a control system

2. Discuss the basic factors that determine an organization's information technology needs and describe the basic types of information systems used by organizations.
   - An organization's information technology needs are determined by several factors—most notably, user groups and systems requirements.
   - There are several basic levels of information systems:
     - transaction-processing systems
     - systems for various types of workers
     - basic management information systems

   - decision support systems
   - executive support systems
   - artificial intelligence systems
   - expert systems
   - Each provides certain types of information and is most valuable for specific types of managers.
   - Each should also be matched to the needs of user groups.

3. Discuss how information systems can be managed.
   - Managing information systems involves five basic elements:
     - They must be designed and created information systems.
     - They must be integrated.
     - They must be useable.
     - They must be secure.
     - There limitations must be recognized.

4. Describe how information systems affect organizations.
   - Information systems have an impact on organizations in a variety of ways. Major influences include:
     - leaner organizations
     - more flexible operations
     - increased collaboration
     - more flexible work sites
     - improved management processes
     - changed employee behaviors

Discussion Questions

Questions for Review

1. What are the differences between data and information? Give three examples of data and then show how those data can be turned into information.
2. Who uses information systems in organizations? What types of functions do the systems perform for each type of user?
3. Describe each of the levels of major information technology systems. Give an example of each, other than the examples in the text.
4. What are some of the positive impacts that information technology can have on organizations? What are some of the negative impacts?

Questions for Analysis

5. Very often, managers making decisions in real organizations have to work with information that does not perfectly meet all four criteria for useful information. In that case, should the manager use the imperfect information? What can the manager do to increase the usefulness of imperfect information?
6. At higher organizational levels, the information technology tools used become more sophisticated. Yet, in many organizations, higher-level managers are the least sophisticated and experienced with hands-on use of information technology. How can unsophisticated users effectively employ a sophisticated IT tool? What are some of the potential problems they should be aware of?
7. It has been said that the information revolution is like the Industrial Revolution in terms of the magnitude of its impact on organizations and society. What leads to such a view? Why might that view be an overstatement?

Questions for Application

8. Interview a business manager about the use of information in his or her organization. How is the information managed? Is a computer system used? How well is the information system integrated with other aspects of organizational control?
9. Visit a local organization, such as a university administration office, a restaurant, or a supermarket. Stand in its facility and look around you. How many different information systems can you spot? Do not look just for "computers"; also look for less-obvious examples, such as the digital thermostat on the wall or the electronic cash register. What type of information system is each?
10. A knowledge worker can be defined as "someone who creates, transforms, or repackages information." Choose a knowledge worker occupation that interests you. Use the Internet to investigate the job qualifications for that occupation. What skills, knowledge, and experience are needed? How do the qualifications for knowledge workers differ from the qualifications of white-collar workers?

Building Effective Technical Skills

Exercise Overview

Technical skills are the skills necessary to accomplish or understand the specific kind of work being done in an organization. This exercise asks you to consider the potential benefits and costs of automating a manual process.

Exercise Background

So many innovative information technology products, both hardware and software, are available to businesses today. Yet many firms continue to use manual processes for much of the work they do. Are these businesses unaware of or indifferent to the benefits that technology could bring them? Is the technology just too expensive? Or might there be sound reasons, other than budgetary ones, to limit the use of information technology?

Exercise Task

1. Observe a business that is using a manual process—for example, a hospital that maintains patient records on paper, a receptionist who answers calls and routes them to the appropriate person, or a library that loans books.
2. Use the Internet to find an example of a company that is using information technology to perform that process. (*Hint:* Look for organizations of the same type, such as another hospital. Or look at the websites of companies that provide software or hardware. Many of them will have a section about their clients, called "Case Studies" or "Success Stories.")
3. Investigate and then describe how the business you observed could use information technology.
4. Describe the benefits that you would expect the business to obtain if it automated that process. Then describe the costs, limitations, or potential problems you would expect.
5. Should the business automate? Why or why not?

Building Effective Time-Management Skills

Exercise Overview

Time-management skills refer to the manager's ability to prioritize work, to work efficiently, and to delegate appropriately. This exercise analyzes the ways in which your use of information technology influences your time management.

Exercise Background

One of the biggest implied advantages of modern information technology is time management. Modern technology is supposed to make us more productive and more efficient and to make it easier to communicate with one another. At the same time, most people acknowledge that information technology can also get out of hand.

Think back to your use of information technology over the last week. Consider cell phones, e-mail, the Internet, instant messaging, handheld devices such as Palm Pilots, and so on. Think about ways that each of these forms can both save and waste time.

Exercise Task

With the background information above as context, do the following:

1. List every form of technology that you used. Note how frequently you used it and for how long. (Alternatively, keep track of your use over the upcoming week. Then continue with the exercise.)
2. Which did you use most often? Least often? Which did you use for the longest total time? For the shortest total time? Which performed critically important functions for you? Less important functions? Explain your answers.
3. For each device, list alternative, less technologically sophisticated ways of achieving that same function—for example, use of a pay phone instead of a cell phone.
4. For each type of technology, decide whether that device was a time saver, performing functions more efficiently than the alternatives. Which were time wasters?
5. What ideas does a review of your answers give you about more time-efficient use of technology?

CHAPTER CLOSING CASE

AN MTV MAKEOVER

"Never trust anyone over 30" was a popular saying during the youthful 1960s, but it could just as easily apply to MTV. In 2006, the youth-oriented station, where the primary audience is 12 to 34 years old, turns 25. Few MTV viewers can remember a time before the channel existed. It is now a mature brand and must adapt to avoid decline and obsolescence. Judy McGrath, CEO of MTV, says, "Nobody wants to be who they used to be, including us. Media identities, like market share, are up for grabs." MTV is overdue for an extreme makeover.

The aging of U.S. society is one of the most significant and potentially threatening trends facing the company today. As viewers age, they move out of MTV's youthful target market range, shifting their loyalty to other channels and even other media. MTV grew just 5 percent last year, while VH1, whose viewers are older, grew 17 percent. "More than half the American public is 35 and older, and they dominate the wealth in this country," says John Sykes, MTV's president of network development. "We want to be able to reach that audience instead of watching them fall off a cliff after they leave some of our existing channels."

Another concern for MTV is the proliferation of entertainment media. Traditional cable television dominated entertainment for decades, but today's viewers have options that range from cell phones to online streaming video to DVRs for time-delay viewing. Each of the new technologies presents unique challenges. Video delivered to a cell phone must be short, visually simple, and compelling enough to convince viewers to pay for the broadcast. MTV wants to increase its Internet presence, but it's not yet clear how to make money with an online business model. Advertisers insist on paying less when a significant number of viewers use DVR technology to "skip over" the ads.

MTV is just one of the many brands at Viacom, which also includes BET, Comedy Central, CMT, Logo, Nickelodeon, Noggin, The N, Spike TV, TV Land, VH1, Paramount, and DreamWorks. In addition, Viacom has already made some ventures into online media, through its ifilm, Neopets, Xfire, and GameTrailers.com businesses. Viacom's scope and size provide plenty of resources to support MTV through a transition, and its online experience is also a plus.

To update its customer targeting and support alternative media, MTV has developed a number of solutions. Creating unique products for older viewers, ages 35 to 50 years, is the first phase of MTV's makeover. Viacom's market research showed that these "late baby boomers" were spending more time at home and more time watching television than younger viewers. So MTV is developing several new channels that center around lifestyle, money, and health. "We need to fish where the fish are," Sykes comments.

The second push is into new media. Viacom CEO Tom Freston, who ran MTV for 17 years, says, "I look at the Internet and whole digital interactive world as an amazing opportunity for us. We're the kings of the short attention span." MTV Overdrive is increasing the number of music videos and is developing an online music subscription service called Urge, in conjunction with Microsoft. "We live or die in this next phase," Freston claims. "We go from being TV-centric to brand-centric." MTV plans major forays into online broadband, cell phones, and video games. MTV President Michael J. Wolf believes online revenues can grow from today's $150 million to $500 million in just three years. "The world has come to us. The Internet is no longer about text. It's about video. We produce and own more video than anybody."

MTV has more new plans, among them geographic expansion. From 15 international channels in 1996, MTV today offers 124 channels and still has room to grow. Market penetration of cable and satellite television in much of Europe and Asia is between 35 and 40 percent, where the U.S. market was in the 1980s.

Freston comments on his own career, saying, "One can, if one is so inclined, senselessly prolong one's youth." He could just as well be talking about MTV. Can MTV grow up? Or more accurately, can MTV grow up but stay cool? Stay tuned to find out.

CASE QUESTIONS

1. What information is conveyed by the television technology used by a channel such as MTV?
2. How has the introduction of new technologies such as the Internet, DVRs, and cell phones changed the way that information is communicated in the entertainment industry?
3. How well do you expect MTV to cope with the changes that are taking place in technology? Are there new technologies that MTV should consider as possible new businesses? Explain.

CASE REFERENCES

Jack Ewing, "MTV Networks' Mobile Move," *BusinessWeek*, January 31, 2006, www .businessweek.com on May 30, 2006; Marc Gunther, "Mr. MTV Grows Up," *Fortune*, April 10, 2006, www.cnnmoney.com on May 30, 2006; Tom Lowry, "Can MTV Stay Cool?" *BusinessWeek*, February 20, 2006, www.businessweek.com on May 30, 2006; Tom Lowry, "MTV for Life," *BusinessWeek*, February 20, 2006, www.businessweek.com on May 30, 2006.

YOU MAKE THE CALL

Wikipedia and Other Wikis

1. Do you use Wikipedia? Why or why not?
2. Do you think Wikipedia will eliminate the need for traditional reference sources? Why or why not?
3. Identify three topics that interest you. Locate the discussion of these topics on Wikipedia and comment on their usefulness and accuracy.
4. Identify and describe two potential applications of wiki sites to a business that interests you.
5. How might wiki sites be of value to you as a student?

Test Prepper

college.hmco.com/business/students

Choose the correct answer. Answers are found at the back of the book.

1. T F Relevant information is defined according to the needs and circumstances of a particular manager.

2. T F The information system in an organization is often a complex of several information systems that work together to serve different areas of the organization.

3. T F The Internet frequently benefits large companies, but is rarely of use to small companies.

4. T F The operating managers who formerly communicated company policies and procedures to lower-level employees are being replaced by electronic information networks.

5. T F The use of information systems can lead to isolation of employees who now can perform their jobs without interacting with others.

6. Rachel is a professionally trained engineer who relies on information technology to design new products. Rachel, and others like her, are referred to as

   A. information system analysts.
   B. data contractors.
   C. information technicians.
   D. knowledge workers.
   E. operations managers.

7. Francisco works at a call center for a major airline making flight reservations for passengers. Francisco likely uses a(n) _____ to complete his basic day-to-day work.

   A. transaction-processing system
   B. expert system

   C. management information system
   D. executive support system
   E. decision support system

8. Shawn's firm has extended the Net's technology internally to build a communications network that operates within the boundaries of his company. Shawn's firm has created a(n)

   A. portal site.
   B. firm wide web.
   C. intranet.
   D. extranet.
   E. company service provider.

9. The purpose of an electronic firewall is to

   A. encrypt information so unauthorized others cannot decipher it.
   B. bar access by outsiders to a company's internal computer network.
   C. prevent information from leaking out of an expert system.
   D. simplify the human resource function of terminating employees.
   E. build morale in online team-building exercises.

10. Information systems lead to all the following benefits EXCEPT

   A. leaner organizations.
   B. more flexible operations.
   C. increased collaboration.
   D. reduced prevalence of telecommuting.
   E. improved management processes.

Tools for Planning and Decision Making

This appendix discusses a number of the basic tools and techniques that managers can use to enhance the efficiency and effectiveness of planning and decision making. We first describe forecasting, an extremely important tool, and then discuss several other planning techniques. Next we discuss several tools that relate more to decision making. We conclude by assessing the strengths and weaknesses of the various tools and techniques.

Forecasting

To plan, managers must make assumptions about future events. But unlike Harry Potter and his friends, planners cannot simply look into a crystal ball or wave a wand. Instead, they must develop forecasts of probable future circumstances. **Forecasting** is the process of developing assumptions or premises about the future that managers can use in planning or decision making.

Sales and Revenue Forecasting

As the term implies, **sales forecasting** is concerned with predicting future sales. Because monetary resources (derived mainly from sales) are necessary to finance both current and future operations, knowledge of future sales is of vital importance. Sales forecasting is something that every business, from Exxon Mobil to a neighborhood pizza parlor, must do. Consider, for example, the following questions that a manager might need to answer:

1. How much of each of our products should we produce next week? Next month? Next year?
2. How much money will we have available to spend on research and development and on new-product test marketing?
3. When and to what degree will we need to expand our existing production facilities?
4. How should we respond to union demands for a 5 percent pay increase?
5. If we borrow money for expansion, when can we pay it back?

None of these questions can be answered adequately without some notion of what future revenues are likely to be. Thus, sales forecasting is generally one of the first steps in planning.

Unfortunately, the term *sales forecasting* suggests that this form of forecasting is appropriate only for organizations that have something to sell. But other kinds of organizations also depend on financial resources, and so they also must forecast. The University of South Carolina, for example, must forecast future state aid before planning course offerings, staff size, and so on. Hospitals must forecast their future income from patient fees, insurance payments, and other sources to assess their

---

forecasting
The process of developing assumptions or premises about the future that managers can use in planning or decision making

sales forecasting
The prediction of future sales

ability to expand. Although we will continue to use the conventional term, keep in mind that what is really at issue is ***revenue forecasting***.

Several sources of information are used to develop a sales forecast. Previous sales figures and any obvious trends, such as the company's growth or stability, usually serve as the base. General economic indicators, technological improvements, new marketing strategies, and the competition's behavior all may be added together to ensure an accurate forecast. Once projected, the sales (or revenues) forecast becomes a guiding framework for various other activities. Raw-material expenditures, advertising budgets, sales-commission structures, and similar operating costs are all based on projected sales figures.

Organizations often forecast sales across several time horizons. The longer-run forecasts may then be updated and refined as various shorter-run cycles are completed. For obvious reasons, a forecast should be as accurate as possible, and the accuracy of sales forecasting tends to increase as organizations learn from their previous forecasting experience. But the more uncertain and complex future conditions are likely to be, the more difficult it is to develop accurate forecasts. To offset these problems partially, forecasts are more useful to managers if they are expressed as a range rather than as an absolute index or number. If projected sales increases are expected to be in the range of 10 to 12 percent, a manager can consider all the implications for the entire range. A 10 percent increase could dictate one set of activities; a 12 percent increase could call for a different set of activities.

Technological Forecasting

Technological forecasting is another type of forecasting used by many organizations. It focuses on predicting what future technologies are likely to emerge and when they are likely to be economically feasible. In an era when technological breakthrough and innovation have become the rule rather than the exception, it is important that managers be able to anticipate new developments. If a manager invests heavily in existing technology (such as production processes, equipment, and computer systems) and the technology becomes obsolete in the near future, the company has wasted its resources.

The most striking technological innovations in recent years have been in electronics, especially semiconductors. Personal computers, electronic games, and sophisticated communications equipment such as cell phones with wireless Internet capabilities are all evidence of the electronics explosion. Given the increasing importance of technology and the rapid pace of technological innovation, it follows that managers will grow increasingly concerned with technological forecasting in the years to come.

Other Types of Forecasting

Other types of forecasting are also important to many organizations. Resource forecasting projects the organization's future needs for and the availability of human resources, raw materials, and other resources. General economic conditions are the subject of economic forecasts. For example, some organizations undertake population or market-size forecasting. Some organizations also attempt to forecast future government fiscal policy and various government regulations that might be put into practice. Indeed, almost any component in an organization's environment may be an appropriate area for forecasting.

Forecasting Techniques

To carry out the various kinds of forecasting we have identified, managers use several different techniques.[1] Time-series analysis and causal modeling are two common quantitative techniques.

Time-Series Analysis The underlying assumption of ***time-series analysis*** is that the past is a good predictor of the future. This technique is most useful when the manager has a lot of historical data available and when stable trends and patterns are apparent. In a time-series analysis, the variable under consideration (such as sales or enrollment) is plotted across time, and a "best-fit" line is identified.[2] Figure A.1 shows how a time-series analysis might look. The dots represent the number of units sold for each year from 1997 through 2005. The best-fit line has also been drawn in. It is the line around which the dots cluster with the least variability. A manager who wants to know what sales to expect in 2006 simply extends the line. In this case the projection would be around eighty-two hundred units.

Real time-series analysis involves much more than simply plotting sales data and then using a ruler and a pencil to draw and extend the line. Sophisticated mathematical procedures, among other things, are necessary to account for seasonal and cyclical fluctuations and to identify the true best-fit line. In real situations, data seldom follow the neat pattern found in Figure A.1. Indeed, the data points may be so widely dispersed that they mask meaningful trends from all but painstaking, computer-assisted inspection.

Causal Modeling Another useful forecasting technique is ***causal modeling***. Actually, the term *causal modeling* represents a group of several techniques. Table A.1 summarizes three of the most useful approaches. ***Regression models*** are

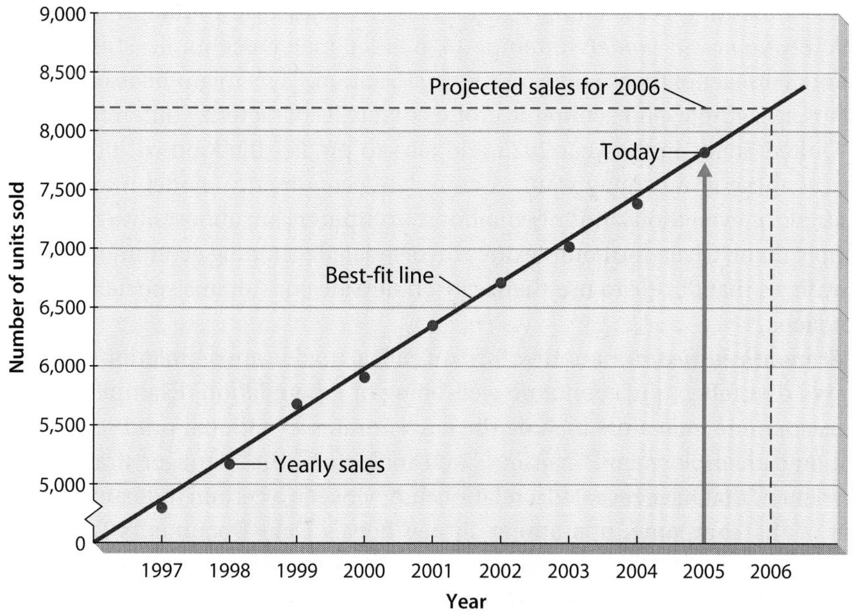

> **time-series analysis**
> A forecasting technique that extends past information into the future through the calculation of a best-fit line

Figure A.1
AN EXAMPLE OF TIME-SERIES ANALYSIS

Because time-series analysis assumes that the past is a good predictor of the future, it is most useful when historical data are available, trends are stable, and patterns are apparent. For example, it can be used for projecting estimated sales for products like shampoo, pens, and automobile tires. (Of course, few time-series analyses yield such clear results because there is almost always considerably more fluctuation in data from year to year.)

Table A.1

SUMMARY OF CAUSAL MODELING
FORECASTING TECHNIQUES

*Managers use several different types
of causal models in planning and
decision making. Three popular
models are regression models,
econometric models, and
economic indicators.*

Regression models	Used to predict one variable (called the dependent variable) on the basis of known or assumed other variables (called independent variables). For example, we might predict future sales based on the values of price, advertising, and economic levels.
Econometric models	Make use of several multiple-regression equations to consider the impact of major economic shifts. For example, we might want to predict what impact the migration toward the Sun Belt might have on our organization.
Economic indicators	Various population statistics, indexes, or parameters that predict organizationally relevant variables such as discretionary income. Examples include cost-of-living index, inflation rate, and level of unemployment.

equations created to predict a variable (such as sales volume) that depends on several other variables (such as price and advertising). The variable being predicted is called the *dependent variable*; the variables used to make the prediction are called *independent variables*. A typical regression equation used by a small business might take this form:

$$y = ax_1 + bx_2 + cx_3 + d$$

where

y = the dependent variable (sales in this case)

$x_1, x_2,$ and x_3 = independent variables (advertising budget, price, and commissions)

$a, b,$ and c = weights for the independent variables calculated during development of the regression model

d = a constant

To use the model, a manager can insert various alternatives for advertising budget, price, and commissions into the equation and then compute y. The calculated value of y represents the forecasted level of sales, given various levels of advertising, price, and commissions.[3]

Econometric models employ regression techniques at a much more complex level. **Econometric models** attempt to predict major economic shifts and the potential impact of those shifts on the organization. They might be used to predict various age, ethnic, and economic groups that will characterize different regions of the United States in the year 2025 and also to predict the kinds of products and services these groups may want. A complete econometric model may consist of hundreds or even thousands of equations. Computers are almost always necessary to apply them. Given the complexities involved in developing econometric models, many firms that decide to use them rely on outside consultants specializing in this approach.

Economic indicators, another form of causal model, are population statistics or indexes that reflect the economic well-being of a population. Examples of widely used economic indicators include the current rates of national productivity, inflation, and unemployment. In using such indicators, the manager draws on past experiences that have revealed a relationship between a certain indicator and some facet of the company's operations. Pitney Bowes Data Documents Division, for example, can predict future sales of its business forms largely on the basis of current GNP estimates and other economic growth indexes.

econometric model
A causal model that predicts major economic shifts and the potential impact of those shifts on the organization

Economic indicators
A key population statistic or index that reflects the economic well-being of a population

Qualitative Forecasting Techniques Organizations also use several qualitative techniques to develop their forecasts. A **qualitative forecasting technique** relies more on individual or group judgment or opinion rather than on sophisticated mathematical analyses. The Delphi procedure, described in Chapter 9 as a mechanism for managing group decision-making activities, can also be used to develop forecasts. A variation of it—the *jury-of-expert-opinion* approach—involves using the basic Delphi process with members of top management. In this instance, top management serves as a collection of experts asked to make a prediction about something—competitive behavior, trends in product demand, and so forth. Either a pure Delphi or a jury-of-expert-opinion approach might be useful in technological forecasting.

The *sales-force-composition* method of sales forecasting is a pooling of the predictions and opinions of experienced salespeople. Because of their experience, these individuals are often able to forecast quite accurately what various customers will do. Management combines these forecasts and interprets the data to create plans. Textbook publishers use this procedure to project how many copies of a new title they might sell.

The *customer evaluation* technique goes beyond an organization's sales force and collects data from customers of the organization. The customers provide estimates of their own future needs for the goods and services that the organization supplies. Managers must combine, interpret, and act on this information. This approach, however, has two major limitations. Customers may be less interested in taking time to develop accurate predictions than members of the organization itself, and the method makes no provision for including any new customers that the organization may acquire. Wal-Mart helps its suppliers use this approach by providing them with detailed projections regarding what it intends to buy several months in advance.

Selecting an appropriate forecasting technique can be as important as applying it correctly. Some techniques are appropriate only for specific circumstances. For example, the sales-force-composition technique is good only for sales forecasting. Other techniques, like the Delphi method, are useful in a variety of situations. Some techniques, such as the econometric models, require extensive use of computers, whereas others, such as customer evaluation models, can be used with little mathematical expertise. For the most part, selection of a particular technique depends on the nature of the problem, the experience and preferences of the manager, and available resources.[4]

> *qualitative forecasting technique*
> One of several techniques that rely on individual or group judgment rather than on mathematical analyses

Other Planning Techniques

Of course, planning involves more than just forecasting. Other tools and techniques that are useful for planning purposes include linear programming, breakeven analysis, and simulations.

Linear Programming

Linear programming is one of the most widely used quantitative tools for planning. **Linear programming** is a procedure for calculating the optimal combination of resources and activities. It is appropriate when there is some objective to be met (such as a sales quota or a certain production level) within a set of constraints (such as a limited advertising budget or limited production capabilities).

To illustrate how linear programming can be used, assume that a small electronics company produces two basic products—a high-quality cable television tuner and a

> *linear programming*
> A planning technique that determines the optimal combination of resources and activities

Table A.2

PRODUCTION DATA FOR TUNERS AND RECEIVERS

Linear programming can be used to determine the optimal number of tuners and receivers an organization might make. Essential information needed to perform this analysis includes the number of hours each product spends in each department, the production capacity for each department, and the profit margin for each product.

Department	Number of Hours Required per Unit		Production Capacity for Day (in Hours)
	Tuners (T)	Receivers (R)	
Production (PR)	10	6	150
Inspection and testing (IT)	4	4	80
Profit margin	$30	$20	

high-quality receiver for picking up television audio and playing it through a stereo amplifier. Both products go through the same two departments, first production and then inspection and testing. Each product has a known profit margin and a high level of demand. The production manager's job is to produce the optimal combination of tuners (T) and receivers (R) that maximizes profits and uses the time in production (PR) and in inspection and testing (IT) most efficiently. Table A.2 gives the information needed for the use of linear programming to solve this problem.

The *objective function* is an equation that represents what we want to achieve. In technical terms, it is a mathematical representation of the desirability of the consequences of a particular decision. In our example, the objective function can be represented as follows:

Maximize profit = $\$30X_T + \$20X_R$

where

R = the number of receivers to be produced

T = the number of tuners to be produced

The $30 and $20 figures are the respective profit margins of the tuner and receiver, as noted in Table A.2. The objective, then, is to maximize profits.

However, this objective must be accomplished within a specific set of constraints. In our example, the constraints are the time required to produce each product in each department and the total amount of time available. These data are also found in Table A.2 and can be used to construct the relevant constraint equations:

$10T + 6R \leq 150$

$4T + 4R \leq 80$

(that is, we cannot use more capacity than is available), and of course,

$T \geq 0$

$R \geq 0$

The set of equations consisting of the objective function and constraints can be solved graphically. To start, we assume that production of each product is maximized when production of the other is at zero. The resultant solutions are then plotted on a coordinate axis. In the PR department, if $T = 0$ then:

$10T + 6R \leq 150$

$10(0) + 6R \leq 150$

$R \leq 25$

In the same department, if $R = 0$ then:

$10T + 6R \leq 150$

$10T + 6(0) \leq 150$

$T \leq 15$

Similarly, in the IT department, if no tuners are produced,

$4T + 4R \leq 80$

$4(0) + 4R \leq 80$

$R \leq 20$

and, if no receivers are produced,

$4T + 4R \leq 80$

$4T + 4(0) \leq 80$

$T \leq 20$

The four resulting inequalities are graphed in Figure A.2. The shaded region represents the feasibility space, or production combinations that do not exceed the capacity of either department. The optimal number of products will be defined at one of the four corners of the shaded area—that is, the firm should produce twenty receivers only (point C), fifteen tuners only (point B), thirteen receivers and seven tuners (point E), or no products at all. With the constraint that production of both tuners and receivers must be greater than zero, it follows that point E is the optimal solution. That combination requires 148 hours in PR and 80 hours in IT and yields $470 in profit. (Note that if only receivers were produced, the profit would be $400; producing only tuners would mean $450 in profit.)

Unfortunately, only two alternatives can be handled by the graphical method, and our example was extremely simple. When there are other alternatives, a complex algebraic method must be employed. Real-world problems may require several

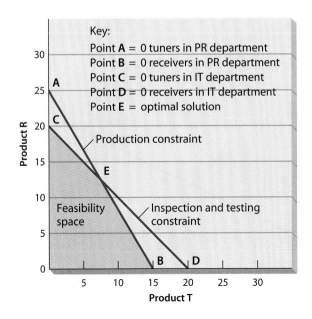

Figure A.2

THE GRAPHICAL SOLUTION OF A LINEAR PROGRAMMING PROBLEM

Finding the graphical solution to a linear programming problem is useful when only two alternatives are being considered. When problems are more complex, computers that can execute hundreds of equations and variables are necessary. Virtually all large firms, such as General Motors, Chevron Texaco, and Sears, use linear programming.

hundred equations and variables. Clearly, computers are necessary to execute such sophisticated analyses. Linear programming is a powerful technique, playing a key role in both planning and decision making. It can be used to schedule production, select an optimal portfolio of investments, allocate sales representatives to territories, or produce an item at some minimum cost.

Breakeven Analysis

Linear programming is called a *normative procedure* because it prescribes the optimal solution to a prolem. Breakeven analysis is a *descriptive procedure* because it simply describes relationships among varables; then it is up to the manager to make decisions. We can defin **breakeven analysis** as a procedure for identifying the point at which revenues start covering their associated costs. It might be used to analyze the effects on profits of different price and output combinations or various levels of output.

Figure A.3 represents the key cost variables in breakeven analysis. Creating most products or services includes three types of costs: fixed costs, variable costs, and total costs. *Fixed costs* are costs that are incurred regardless of what volume of output is being generated. They include rent or mortgage payments on the building, managerial salaries, and depreciation of plant and equipment. *Variable costs* vary with the number of units produced, such as the cost of raw materials and direct labor used to make each unit. *Total costs* are fixed costs plus variable costs. Note that because of fixed costs, the line for total costs never begins at zero.

Other important factors in breakeven analysis are revenue and profit. Revenue, the total dollar amount of sales, is computed by multiplying the number of units sold by the sales price of each unit. *Profit* is then determined by subtracting total costs from total revenues. When revenues and total costs are plotted on the same axes, the breakeven graph shown in Figure A.4 emerges. The point at which the lines representing total costs and total revenues cross is the breakeven point. If the company represented in Figure A.4 sells more units than are represented by point A, it will realize a profit; selling below that level will result in a loss.

Mathematically, the breakeven point (expressed as units of production or volume) is shown by the formula

$$BP = \frac{TFC}{P - VC}$$

where

BP = breakeven point

breakeven analysis
A procedure for identifying the point at which revenues start covering their associated costs

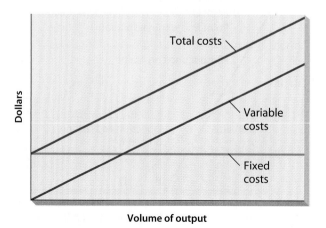

Figure A.3
AN EXAMPLE OF COST FACTORS FOR BREAKEVEN ANALYSIS

To determine the breakeven point for profit on sales for a product or service, the manager must first determine both fixed and variable costs. These costs are then combined to show total costs.

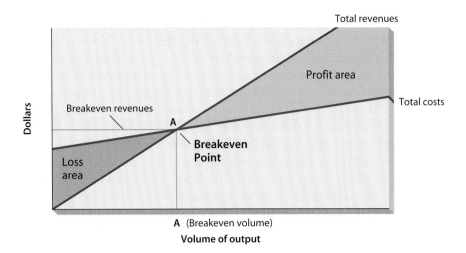

Total revenues

Profit area

Total costs

Breakeven revenues

A

Breakeven Point

Loss area

Dollars

A (Breakeven volume)

Volume of output

Figure A.4
BREAKEVEN ANALYSIS

After total costs are determined and graphed, the manager then graphs the total revenues that will be earned on different levels of sales. The regions defined by the intersection of the two graphs show loss and profit areas. The intersection itself shows the breakeven point—the level of sales at which all costs are covered but no profits are earned.

TFC = total fixed costs

P = price per unit

VC = variable cost per units

Assume that you are considering the production of a new garden hoe with an ergonomically curved handle. You have determined that an acceptable selling price will be $20. You have also determined that the variable costs per hoe will be $15, and you have total fixed costs of $400,000 per year. The question is, How many hoes must you sell each year to break even? Using the breakeven model, you find that

$$BP = \frac{TFC}{P - VC}$$

$$BP = \frac{400,000}{20 - 15}$$

BP = 80,000 units

Thus, you must sell eighty thousand hoes to break even. Further analysis would also show that if you could raise your price to $25 per hoe, you would need to sell only forty thousand to break even, and so on.

The state of New York used a breakeven analysis to evaluate seven variations of prior approvals for its Medicaid service. Comparisons were conducted of the costs involved in each variation against savings gained from efficiency and improved quality of service. The state found that only three of the variations were cost effective.[5]

Breakeven analysis is a popular and important planning technique, but it also has noteworthy weaknesses. It considers revenues only up to the breakeven point, and it makes no allowance for the time value of money. For example, because the funds used to cover fixed and variable costs could be used for other purposes (such as investment), the organization is losing interest income by tying up its money prior to reaching the breakeven point. Thus, managers often use break-even analysis as only the first step in planning. After the preliminary analysis has been completed, more sophisticated techniques (such as rate-of-return analysis or discounted-present-value analysis) are used. Those techniques can help the manager decide whether to proceed or to divert resources into other areas.

Simulations

Another useful planning device is simulation. The word *simulate* means to copy or to represent. An **organizational simulation** is a model of a real-world situation that can be manipulated to discover how it functions. Simulation is a descriptive, rather than a prescriptive, technique. Northern Research & Engineering Corporation is an engineering consulting firm that helps clients plan new factories. By using a sophisticated factory simulation model, the firm recently helped a client cut several machines and operations from a new plant and save over $750,000.

To consider another example, suppose the city of Houston was going to build a new airport. Issues to be addressed might include the number of runways, the direction of those runways, the number of terminals and gates, the allocation of various carriers among the terminals and gates, and the technology and human resources needed to achieve a target frequency of takeoffs and landings. (Of course, actually planning such an airport would involve many more variables than these.) A model could be constructed to simulate these factors, as well as their interrelationships. The planner could then insert several different values for each factor and observe the probable results.

Simulation problems are in some ways similar to those addressed by linear programming, but simulation is more useful in very complex situations characterized by diverse constraints and opportunities. The development of sophisticated simulation models may require the expertise of outside specialists or consultants, and the complexity of simulation almost always necessitates the use of a computer. For these reasons, simulation is most likely to be used as a technique for planning in large organizations that have the required resources.

PERT

A final planning tool that we will discuss is PERT. **PERT**, an acronym for Program Evaluation and Review Technique, was developed by the U.S. Navy to help coordinate the activities of three thousand contractors during the development of the Polaris nuclear submarine, and it was credited with saving two years of work on the project. It has subsequently been used by most large companies in different ways. The purpose of PERT is to develop a network of activities and their interrelationships and thus highlight critical time intervals that affect the overall project. PERT follows six basic steps:

1. Identify the activities to be performed and the events that will mark their completion.
2. Develop a network showing the relationships among the activities and events.
3. Calculate the time needed for each event and the time necessary to get from each event to the next.
4. Identify within the network the longest path that leads to completion of the project. This path is called the critical path.
5. Refine the network.
6. Use the network to control the project.

Suppose that a marketing manager wants to use PERT to plan the test marketing and nationwide introduction of a new product. Table A.3 identifies the basic steps involved in carrying out this project. The activities are then arranged in a network like the one shown in Figure A.5. In the figure, each completed event is rep-

Table A.3

ACTIVITIES AND EVENTS FOR INTRODUCING A NEW PRODUCT

PERT is used to plan schedules for projects, and it is particularly useful when many activities with critical time intervals must be coordinated. Besides launching a new product, PERT is useful for projects like constructing a new factory or building, remodeling an office, or opening a new store.

Activities	Events
a Produce limited quantity for test marketing.	1 Origin of project.
b Design preliminary package.	2 Completion of production for test marketing.
c Locate test market.	3 Completion of design for preliminary package.
d Obtain local merchant cooperation.	4 Test market located.
e Ship product to selected retail outlets.	5 Local merchant cooperation obtained.
f Monitor sales and customer reactions.	6 Product for test marketing shipped to retail outlets.
g Survey customers in test-market area.	7 Sales and customer reactions monitored.
h Make needed product changes.	8 Customers in test-market area surveyed.
i Make needed package changes.	9 Product changes made.
j Mass-produce the product.	10 Package changes made.
k Begin national advertising.	11 Product mass-produced.
l Begin national distribution.	12 National advertising carried out.
	13 National distribution completed.

resented by a number in a circle. The activities are indicated by letters on the lines connecting the events. Notice that some activities are performed independently of one another and that others must be performed in sequence. For example, test production (activity a) and test site location (activity c) can be done at the same time, but test site location has to be done before actual testing (activities f and g) can be done.

The time needed to get from one activity to another is then determined. The normal way to calculate the time between each activity is to average the most optimistic, most pessimistic, and most likely times, with the most likely time weighted by 4. Time is usually calculated with the following formula:

$$\text{Expected time} = \frac{a + 4b + c}{6}$$

Where

a = optimistic time

b = most likely time

c = pessimistic time

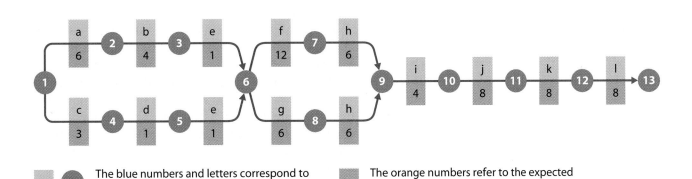

The blue numbers and letters correspond to the numbers and letters used in Table A.3.

The orange numbers refer to the expected number of weeks for each activity.

Figure A.5

A PERT NETWORK FOR INTRODUCING A NEW PRODUCT

critical path
The longest path through a PERT network

The expected number of weeks for each activity in our example is shown in parentheses along each path in Figure A.5. The ***critical path***—or the longest path through the PERT network—is then identified. This path is considered critical because it shows the shortest time in which the project can be completed. In our example, the critical path is 1-2-3-6-7-9-10-11-12-13, totaling fifty-seven weeks. PERT thus tells the manager that the project will take fifty-seven weeks to complete.

The first network may be refined. If fifty-seven weeks to completion is too long a time, the manager might decide to begin preliminary package design before the test products are finished. Or the manager might decide that ten weeks rather than twelve is a sufficient time period to monitor sales. The idea is that if the critical path can be shortened, so too can the overall duration of the project. The PERT network serves as an ongoing framework for both planning and control throughout the project. For example, the manager can use it to monitor where the project is relative to where it needs to be. Thus, if an activity on the critical path takes longer than planned, the manager needs to make up the time elsewhere or live with the fact that the entire project will be late.

Decision-Making Tools

Managers can also use a number of tools that relate more specifically to decision making than to planning. Two commonly used decision-making tools are payoff matrices and decision trees.

Payoff Matrices

payoff matrix
A decision-making tool that specifies the probable value of different alternatives, depending on different possible outcomes associated with each

probability
The likelihood, expressed as a percentage, that a particular event will or will not occur

expected value
When applied to alternative courses of action, the sum of all possible values of outcomes from that action multiplied by their respective probabilities

A ***payoff matrix*** specifies the probable value of different alternatives, depending on different possible outcomes associated with each. The use of a payoff matrix requires that several alternatives be available, that several different events could occur, and that the consequences depend on which alternative is selected and on which event or set of events occurs. An important concept in understanding the payoff matrix, then, is probability. A ***probability*** is the likelihood, expressed as a percentage, that a particular event will or will not occur. If we believe that a particular event will occur seventy-five times out of one hundred, we can say that the probability of its occurring is 75 percent, or .75. Probabilities range in value from 0 (no chance of occurrence) to 1.00 (certain occurrence—also referred to as 100 percent). In the business world, there are few probabilities of either 0 or 1.00. Most probabilities that managers use are based on subjective judgment, intuition, and historical data.

The ***expected value*** of an alternative course of action is the sum of all possible values of outcomes from that action multiplied by their respective probabilities. Suppose, for example, that a venture capitalist is considering investing in a new company. If he believes there is a .40 probability of making $100,000, a .30 probability of making $30,000, and a .30 probability of losing $20,000, the expected value *(EV)* of this alternative is

$$EV = .40(100,000) + .30(30,000) + .30(-20,000)$$

$$EV = 40,000 + 9,000 - 6,000$$

$$EV = \$43,000$$

		High inflation (*probability of .30*)	Low inflation (*probability of .70*)
Investment alternative **1**	Leisure products company	–$10,000	+$50,000
Investment alternative **2**	Energy enhancement company	+$90,000	–$15,000
Investment alternative **3**	Food-processing company	+$30,000	+$25,000

Figure A.6

AN EXAMPLE OF A PAYOFF MATRIX

A payoff matrix helps the manager determine the expected value of different alternatives. A payoff matrix is effective only if the manager ensures that probability estimates are as accurate as possible.

The investor can then weigh the expected value of this investment against the expected values of other available alternatives. The highest *EV* signals the investment that should most likely be selected.

For example, suppose another venture capitalist wants to invest $20,000 in a new business. She has identified three possible alternatives: a leisure products company, an energy enhancement company, and a food-producing company. Because the expected value of each alternative depends on short-run changes in the economy, especially inflation, she decides to develop a payoff matrix. She estimates that the probability of high inflation is .30 and the probability of low inflation is .70. She then estimates the probable returns for each investment in the event of both high and low inflation. Figure A.6 shows what the payoff matrix might look like (a minus sign indicates a loss). The expected value of investing in the leisure products company is

$$EV = .30(-10,000) + .70(50,000)$$

$$EV = -3,000 + 35,000$$

$$EV = \$32,000$$

Similarly, the expected value of investing in the energy enhancement company is

$$EV = .30(90,000) + .70(-15,000)$$

$$EV = 27,000 + (-10,500)$$

$$EV = \$16,500$$

And, finally, the expected value of investing in the food-processing company is

$$EV = .30(30,000) + .70(25,000)$$

$$EV = 9,000 + 17,500$$

$$EV = \$26,500$$

Investing in the leisure products company, then, has the highest expected value.

Other potential uses for payoff matrices include determining optimal order quantities, deciding whether to repair or replace broken machinery, and deciding which of several new products to introduce. Of course, the real key to using payoff matrices effectively is making accurate estimates of the relevant probabilities.

Decision Trees

Decision trees are like payoff matrices because they enhance a manager's ability to evaluate alternatives by making use of expected values. However, they are most appropriate when there are several decisions to be made in sequence.

Figure A.7 illustrates a hypothetical decision tree. The small firm represented wants to begin exporting its products to a foreign market, but limited capacity restricts it to only one market at first. Managers feel that either France or China would be the best place to start. Whichever alternative is selected, sales for the product in that country may turn out to be high or low. In France, there is a .80 chance of high sales and a .20 chance of low sales. The anticipated payoffs in these situations are predicted to be $20 million and $3 million, respectively. In China, the probabilities of high versus low sales are .60 and .40, respectively, and the associated payoffs are presumed to be $25 million and $6 million. As shown in Figure A.7, the expected value of shipping to France is $16,600,000, whereas the expected value of shipping to China is $17,400,000.

The astute reader will note that this part of the decision could have been set up as a payoff matrix. However, the value of decision trees is that we can extend the

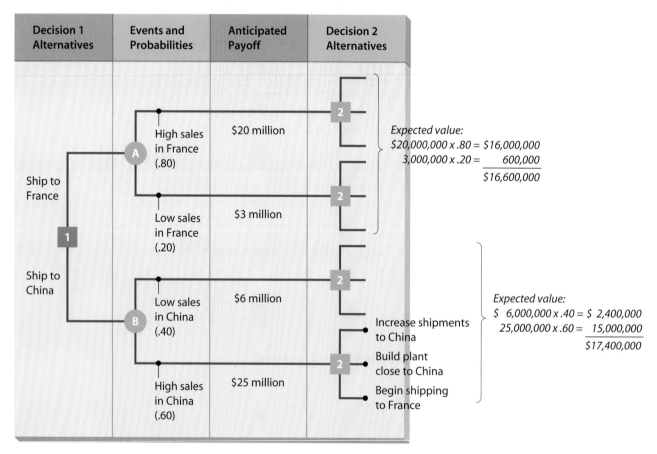

Figure A.7

AN EXAMPLE OF A DECISION TREE

A decision tree extends the basic concepts of a payoff matrix through multiple decisions. This tree shows the possible outcomes of two levels of decisions. The first decision is whether to expand to China or to France. The second decision, assuming that the company expands to China, is whether to increase shipments to China, build a plant close to China, or initiate shipping to France.

model to include subsequent decisions. Assume, for example, that the company begins shipping to China. If high sales do in fact materialize, the company will soon reach another decision situation. It might use the extra revenues to (1) increase shipments to China, (2) build a plant close to China and thus cut shipping costs, or (3) begin shipping to France. Various outcomes are possible for each decision, and each outcome will also have both a probability and an anticipated payoff. It is therefore possible to compute expected values back through several tiers of decisions all the way to the initial one. As it is with payoff matrices, determining probabilities accurately is the crucial element in the process. Properly used, however, decision trees can provide managers with a useful road map through complex decision situations.

Other Techniques

In addition to payoff matrices and decision trees, several other quantitative methods are also available to facilitate decision making.

Inventory Models   *Inventory models* are techniques that help the manager decide how much inventory to maintain. Target Stores uses inventory models to help determine how much merchandise to order, when to order it, and so forth. Inventory consists of both raw materials (inputs) and finished goods (outputs). Polaroid, for example, maintains a supply of the chemicals that it uses to make film, the cartons it packs film in, and packaged film ready to be shipped. For finished goods, both extremes are bad: excess inventory ties up capital, whereas a small inventory may result in shortages and customer dissatisfaction. The same holds for raw materials: too much inventory ties up capital, but if a company runs out of resources, work stoppages may occur. Finally, because the process of placing an order for raw materials and supplies has associated costs (such as clerical time, shipping expenses, and higher unit costs for small quantities), it is important to minimize the frequency of ordering. Inventory models help the manager make decisions that optimize the size of inventory. New innovations in inventory management such as *just-in-time, or JIT*, rely heavily on decision-making models. A JIT system involves scheduling materials to arrive in small batches as they are needed, thereby eliminating the need for a big reserve inventory, warehouse space, and so forth.[6]

> **inventory model**
> A technique that helps managers decide how much inventory to maintain

> **just-in-time (JIT)**
> An inventory management technique in which materials are scheduled to arrive in small batches as they are needed, eliminating the need for resources such as big reserves and warehouse space

Queuing Models   *Queuing models* are intended to help organizations manage waiting lines. We are all familiar with such situations: shoppers waiting to pay for groceries at Kroger, drivers waiting to buy gas at an Exxon station, travelers calling American Airlines for reservations, and customers waiting for a teller at Citibank. Take the Kroger example. If a store manager has only one check-out stand in operation, the store's cost for check-out personnel is very low; however, many customers are upset by the long line that frequently develops. To solve the problem, the store manager could decide to keep twenty check-out stands open at all times. Customers would like the short waiting period, but personnel costs would be very high. A queuing model would be appropriate in this case to help the manager determine the optimal number of check-out stands: the number that would balance personnel costs and customer waiting time. Target Stores uses queuing models to determine how many check-out lanes to put in its retail stores.

> **queuing model**
> A model used to optimize waiting lines in organizations

Distribution Models   A decision facing many marketing managers relates to the distribution of the organization's products. Specifically, the manager must decide where the products should go and how to transport them. Railroads, trucking, and

distribution model
A model used to determine the optimal pattern of distribution across different carriers and routes

game theory
A planning tool used to predict how competitors will react to various activities that an organization might undertake

artificial intelligence (AI)
A computer program that attempts to duplicate the thought processes of experienced decision makers

air freight have associated shipping costs, and each mode of transportation follows different schedules and routes. The problem is to identify the combination of routes that optimize distribution effectiveness and distribution costs. **Distribution models** help managers determine this optimal pattern of distribution.

Game Theory   **Game theory** was originally developed to predict the effect of one company's decisions on competitors. Models developed from game theory are intended to predict how a competitor will react to various activities that an organization might undertake, such as price changes, promotional changes, and the introduction of new products. If Wells Fargo Bank were considering raising its prime lending rate by 1 percent, it might use a game theory model to predict whether Citicorp would follow suit. If the model revealed that Citicorp would do so, Wells Fargo would probably proceed; otherwise, it would probably maintain the current interest rates. Unfortunately, game theory is not yet as useful as it was originally expected to be. The complexities of the real world combined with the limitation of the technique itself restrict its applicability. Game theory, however, does provide a useful conceptual framework for analyzing competitive behavior, and its usefulness may be improved in the future.

Artificial Intelligence   A fairly new addition to the manager's quantitative tool kit is **artificial intelligence (AI)**. The most useful form of AI is the expert system.[7] An expert system is essentially a computer program that attempts to duplicate the thought processes of experienced decision makers. For example, Hewlett-Packard has developed an expert system that checks sales orders for new computer systems and then designs preliminary layouts for those new systems. HP can now ship the computer to a customer in components for final assembly on site. This approach has enabled the company to cut back on its own final-assembly facilities.

Strengths and Weaknesses of Planning Tools

Like all issues confronting management, planning tools of the type described here have several strengths and weaknesses.

Weaknesses and Problems

One weakness of the planning and decision-making tools discussed in this appendix is that they may not always adequately reflect reality. Even with the most sophisticated and powerful computer-assisted technique, reality must often be simplified. Many problems are also not amenable to quantitative analysis because important elements of them are intangible or nonquantifiable. Employee morale or satisfaction, for example, is often a major factor in managerial decisions.

The use of these tools and techniques may also be quite costly. For example, only larger companies can afford to develop their own econometric models. Even though the computer explosion has increased the availability of quantitative aids, some expense is still involved and it will take time for many of these techniques to become widely used. Resistance to change also limits the use of planning tools in some settings. If a manager for a retail chain has always based decisions for new locations on personal visits, observations, and intuition, she or he may be less than eager to begin using a computer-based model for evaluating and selecting sites. Finally, problems may arise when managers have to rely on technical specialists to use sophisticated models. Experts trained in the use of complex mathematical procedures may not understand or appreciate other aspects of management.

Strengths and Advantages

On the plus side, planning and decision-making tools offer many advantages. For situations that are amenable to quantification, they can bring sophisticated mathematical processes to bear on planning and decision making. Properly designed models and formulas also help decision makers "see reason." For example, a manager might not be inclined to introduce a new product line simply because she or he doesn't think it will be profitable. After seeing a forecast predicting first-year sales of one hundred thousand units coupled with a breakeven analysis showing profitability after only twenty thousand, however, the manager will probably change her or his mind. Thus, rational planning tools and techniques force the manager to look beyond personal prejudices and predispositions. Finally, the computer explosion is rapidly making sophisticated planning techniques available in a wider range of settings than ever before.

The crucial point to remember is that planning tools and techniques are a means to an end, not an end in themselves. Just as a carpenter uses a hand saw in some situations and an electric saw in others, a manager must recognize that a particular model may be useful in some situations but not in others that may call for a different approach. Knowing the difference is one mark of a good manager.

Summary of Key Points

Managers often use various tools and techniques as they develop plans and make decisions. Forecasting is one widely used method. Forecasting is the process of developing assumptions or premises about the future. Sales or revenue forecasting is especially important. Many organizations also rely heavily on technological forecasting. Time-series analysis and causal modeling are important forecasting techniques. Qualitative techniques are also widely used.

Managers also use other planning tools and techniques in different circumstances. Linear programming helps optimize resources and activities. Breakeven analysis helps identify how many products or services must be sold to cover costs. Simulations model reality. PERT helps plan how much time a project will require.

Other tools and techniques are useful for decision making. Constructing a payoff matrix, for example, helps a manager assess the expected value of different alternatives. Decision trees are used to extend expected values across multiple decisions. Other popular decision-making tools and techniques include inventory models, queuing models, distribution models, game theory, and artificial intelligence.

Various strengths and weaknesses are associated with each of these tools and techniques, as well as with their use by a manager. The key to success is knowing when each should and should not be used and knowing how to use and interpret the results that each provides.

Notes

CHAPTER 1

1. "Corporate Information," Google website, www.google.com on March 1, 2006; Peter Coy, "The Secret to Google's Success," *BusinessWeek*, March 6, 2006, p. 42; Mara Der Hovanesian and Sarah Lacy, "Reality Check for the Google Boys," *BusinessWeek*, March 13, 2006, p. 43; Alan Deutschman, "Can Google Stay Google?" *Fast Company*, August 2005, www.fastcompany.com on March 1, 2006; Alan Deutschman, "Googling for Courage," *Fast Company*, September 2004, www.fastcompany.com on March 1, 2006; Burt Helm, "Google Shows Surfers the Money," *BusinessWeek*, March 1, 2006, www.businessweek.com on March 1, 2006; Adi Ignatius, "In Search of the Real Google," *Time*, February 20, 2006, pp. 36–49 (quote p. 41).

2. Fred Luthans, "Successful vs. Effective Real Managers," *Academy of Management Executive*, May 1988, pp. 127–132. See also "The Best Performers," *BusinessWeek*, Spring 2006 Special Issue, pp. 61–140.

3. See "The Best (& Worst) Managers of the Year," *BusinessWeek*, January 10, 2005, pp. 55–86.

4. Sumantsa Ghospal and Christopher A. Bartlett, "Changing the Role of Top Management: Beyond Structure to Process," *Harvard Business Review*, January–February 1995, pp. 86–96.

5. Renovating Home Deport," *BusinessWeek*, March 6, 2006, pp. 50–58; see also Ram Charan, "Home Depot's Blueprint for Culture Change," *Harvard Business Review*, April 2006, pp. 60–71.

6. See "Executive Pay," *BusinessWeek*, April 15, 2002, pp. 80–100. See also Jim Collins, "The Ten Greatest CEO's of All Times," *Fortune*, July 21, 2003, pp. 54–68.

7. Rosemary Stewart, "Middle Managers: Their Jobs and Behaviors," in Jay W. Lorsch (ed.), *Handbook of Organizational Behavior* (Englewood Cliffs, N.J.: Prentice-Hall, 1987), pp. 385–391. See also Rosabeth Moss Kanter, "The Middle Manager as Innovator," *Harvard Business Review*, July–August 2004, pp. 150–161.

8. John P. Kotter, "What Effective General Managers Really Do," *Harvard Business Review*, March–April 1999, pp. 145–155. See also Peter Drucker, "What Makes an Effective Executive," *Harvard Business Review*, June 2004, pp. 58–68.

9. Henry Mintzberg, *The Nature of Managerial Work* (New York: Harper & Row, 1973).

10. See Robert L. Katz, "The Skills of an Effective Administrator," *Harvard Business Review*, September–October 1974, pp. 90–102, for a classic discussion of several of these skills.

11. "Ritz-Carlton Opens with Training Tradition," *USA Today*, June 29, 2000, p. 3B.

12. The Best Managers . . . And the Worst," *BusinessWeek*, January 10, 2005, pp. 55–86; "New P&G Chief Is Tough, Praised for People Skills," *Wall Street Journal*, June 6, 2000, pp. B1, B4.

13. See "The Real Reasons You're Working so Hard . . . And What You Can Do About It," *BusinessWeek*, October 3, 2005, pp. 60–68; "I'm Late, I'm Late, I'm Late," *USA Today*, November 26, 2002, pp. 1B, 2B.

14. For a thorough discussion of the importance of time-management skills, see David Barry, Catherine Durnell Cramton, and Stephen J. Carroll, "Navigating the Garbage Can: How Agendas Help Managers Cope with Job Realities," *Academy of Management Executive*, May 1997, pp. 26–42.

15. "Taming the Out-of-Control In-Box," *Wall Street Journal*, February 4, 2000, pp. B1, B4.

16. See Michael A. Hitt, "Transformation of Management for the New Millennium," *Organizational Dynamics*, Winter 2000, pp. 7–17.

17. James H. Davis, F. David Schoorman, and Lex Donaldson, "Toward a Stewardship Theory of Management," *Academy of Management Review*, January 1997, pp. 20–47.

18. Gary Hamel and C. K. Prahalad, "Competing for the Future," *Harvard Business Review*, July–August 1994, pp. 122–128.

19. James Waldroop and Timothy Butler, "The Executive as Coach," *Harvard Business Review*, November–December 1996, pp. 111–117.

20. Walter Kiechel, III, "A Manager's Career in the New Economy," *Fortune*, April 4, 1994, pp. 68–72.

21. "The Executive MBA Your Way," *BusinessWeek*, October 18, 1999, pp. 88–92.

22. Turning B-School into E-School," *BusinessWeek*, October 18, 1999, p. 94.

23. See "Reunion at P&G University," *Wall Street Journal*, June 7, 2000, pp. B1, B4, for a discussion of Procter & Gamble's training programs.

24. For an interesting discussion of these issues, see Rakesh Khurana, "The Curse of the Superstar CEO," *Harvard Business Review*, September 2002, pp. 60–70.

25. James L. Perry and Hal G. Rainey, "The Public-Private Distinction in Organization Theory: A Critique and Research Strategy," *Academy of Management Review*, April 1988, pp. 182–201. See also Ran Lachman, "Public and Private Sector Differences: CEOs' Perceptions of Their Role Environments," *Academy of Management Journal*, September 1985, pp. 671–680.

26. Patricia L. Nemetz and Sandra L. Christensen, "The Challenge of Cultural Diversity: Harnessing a Diversity of Views to Understand Multiculturalism," *Academy of Management Review*, 1996, vol. 21, no. 2, pp. 434–462; Frances J. Milliken and Luis L. Martins, "Searching for Common Threads: Understanding the Multiple Effects of Diversity in Organizational Groups," *Academy of Management Review*, 1996, vol. 21, no. 2, pp. 402–433.

27. Geoffrey Colvin, "The 50 Best Companies for Asians, Blacks, and Hispanics," *Fortune*, July 19, 1999, pp. 52–57; see also Cora Daniels, "Pioneers," *Fortune*, August 22, 2005, pp. 72–88.

28. Craig L. Pearce and Charles P. Osmond, "Metaphors for Change: The ALPS Model of Change Management," *Organizational Dynamics*, Winter 1996, pp. 23–35.

CHAPTER 2

1. Katrina Brooker, "The Pepsi Machine," *Fortune*, January 30, 2006, www.fortune.com on March 2, 2006; Dean Foust, "Neville Isdell: Shaking Up Coke Abroad," *BusinessWeek*, April 4, 2005, www.businessweek.com on March 2, 2006; Devon Jarvis, "Coke Is What?" *Fast Company*, September

2005, www.fastcompany.com on March 2, 2006; Betsy Morris, "The Real Story," *Fortune,* May 31, 2004, www.fortune.com on March 2, 2006; Geri Smith, "Inside Coke's Labor Struggles," *BusinessWeek,* January 23, 2006, www.businessweek.com on March 2, 2006.

2. Terence Mitchell and Lawrence James, "Building Better Theory: Time and the Specification of When Things Happen," *Academy of Management Review,* 2001, vol. 26, no. 4, pp. 530–547.

3. Peter F. Drucker, "The Theory of the Business," *Harvard Business Review,* September–October 1994, pp. 95–104.

4. "Why Business History?" *Audacity,* Fall 1992, pp. 7–15. See also Alan L. Wilkins and Nigel J. Bristow, "For Successful Organization Culture, Honor Your Past," *Academy of Management Executive,* August 1987, pp. 221–227.

5. Daniel Wren, *The Evolution of Management Thought,* 5th ed. (New York: Wiley, 2005); Page Smith, *The Rise of Industrial America* (New York: McGraw-Hill, 1984).

6. Martha I. Finney, "Books That Changed Careers," *HRMagazine,* June 1997, pp. 141–145. See also "Leadership in Literature," *Harvard Business Review,* March 2006, pp. 47–55.

7. See Harriet Rubin, *The Princessa: Machiavelli for Women* (New York: Doubleday/Currency, 1997). See also Nanette Fondas, "Feminization Unveiled: Management Qualities in Contemporary Writings," *Academy of Management Review,* January 1997, pp. 257–282.

8. Alan M. Kantrow (ed.), "Why History Matters to Managers," *Harvard Business Review,* January–February 1986, pp. 81–88.

9. Wren, *The Evolution of Management Theory.*

10. Charles Babbage, *On the Economy of Machinery and Manufactures* (London: Charles Knight, 1832).

11. Wren, *The Evolution of Management Theory.*

12. Frederick W. Taylor, *Principles of Scientific Management* (New York: Harper and Brothers, 1911).

13. Charles D. Wrege and Amedeo G. Perroni, "Taylor's Pig-Tale: A Historical Analysis of Frederick W. Taylor's Pig-Iron Experiment," *Academy of Management Journal,* March 1974, pp. 6–27; Charles D. Wrege and Ann Marie Stoka, "Cooke Creates a Classic: The Story Behind Taylor's Principles of Scientific Management," *Academy of Management Review,* October 1978, pp. 736–749.

14. Robert Kanigel, *The One Best Way* (New York: Viking, 1997); Oliver E. Allen, "'This Great Mental Revolution,'" *Audacity,* Summer 1996, pp. 52–61; Jill Hough and Margaret White, "Using Stories to Create Change: The Object Lesson of Frederick Taylor's 'Pig-Tale,'" *Journal of Management,* 2001, vol. 27, pp. 585–601.

15. Henri Fayol, *General and Industrial Management,* trans. J. A. Coubrough (Geneva: International Management Institute, 1930).

16. Max Weber, *Theory of Social and Economic Organizations,* trans. T. Parsons (New York: Free Press, 1947); Richard M. Weis, "Weber on Bureaucracy: Management Consultant or Political Theorist?" *Academy of Management Review,* April 1983, pp. 242–248.

17. Chester Barnard, *The Functions of the Executive* (Cambridge, Mass.: Harvard University Press, 1938).

18. "The Line Starts Here," *Wall Street Journal,* January 11, 1999, pp. R1, R25.

19. Hugo Munsterberg, *Psychology and Industrial Efficiency* (Boston: Houghton Mifflin, 1913).

20. Wren, *The Evolution of Management Theory,* pp. 255–264.

21. Elton Mayo, *The Human Problems of an Industrial Civilization* (New York: Macmillan, 1933); Fritz J. Roethlisberger and William J. Dickson, *Management and the Worker* (Cambridge, Mass.: Harvard University Press, 1939).

22. Abraham Maslow, "A Theory of Human Motivation," *Psychological Review,* July 1943, pp. 370–396.

23. Douglas McGregor, *The Human Side of Enterprise* (New York: McGraw-Hill, 1960).

24. Sara L. Rynes and Christine Quinn Trank, "Behavioral Science in the Business School Curriculum: Teaching in a Changing Institutional Environment," *Academy of Management Review,* 1999, vol. 24, no. 4, pp. 808–824.

25. See Ricky W. Griffin and Gregory Moorhead, *Organizational Behavior,* 8th ed. (Boston: Houghton Mifflin, 2007), for a recent review of current developments in the field of organizational behavior.

26. Wren, *The Evolution of Management Thought,* Chapter 21.

27. "Math Will Rock Your World," *BusinessWeek,* January 23, 2006, pp. 54–61.

28. "Quantitative Analysis Offers Tools to Predict Likely Terrorist Moves," *Wall Street Journal,* February 17, 2006, p. B1.

29. For more information on systems theory in general, see Ludwig von Bertalanffy, C. G. Hempel, R. E. Bass, and H. Jonas, "General Systems Theory: A New Approach to Unity of Science," I–VI *Human Biology,* vol. 23, 1951, pp. 302–361. For systems theory as applied to organizations, see Fremont E. Kast and James E. Rosenzweig, "General Systems Theory: Applications for Organizations and Management," *Academy of Management Journal,* December 1972, pp. 447–465. For a recent update, see Donde P. Ashmos and George P. Huber, "The Systems Paradigm in Organization Theory: Correcting the Record and Suggesting the Future," *Academy of Management Review,* October 1987, pp. 607–621.

30. "Gillette's New Edge," *BusinessWeek,* February 6, 2006, p. 44.

31. Kathleen M. Eisenhardt and D. Charles Galunic, "Coevolving—At Last, a Way to Make Synergies Work," *Harvard Business Review,* January–February 2000, pp. 91–103.

32. Fremont E. Kast and James E. Rosenzweig, *Contingency Views of Organization and Management* (Chicago: Science Research Associates, 1973).

33. "Welch Memoirs Fetch $7.1M," *USA Today,* July 14, 2000, p. 1B.

34. "The BusinessWeek Best-Seller List," *BusinessWeek,* November 4, 2002, p. 26.

CHAPTER 3

1. "Gold Design Award: MINI_motion Strategy," *BusinessWeek,* July 4, 2005, www.businessweek.com on February 8, 2006; David Kiley, "Suddenly Revved about Small Cars," *BusinessWeek,* January 10, 2006, www.businessweek.com on February 8, 2006 (quote); John Maltras, "2005 Mini Cooper S Convertible," *BusinessWeek,* December 28, 2005, www.businessweek.com on February 8, 2006; "Manufacturing Facility," Mini website, www.miniusa.com on February 8, 2006; Jena McGregor, "High-Tech Achiever: Mini USA," *Fast Company,* October 2004, www.fastcompany

.com on February 8, 2006; Dave Vanderwerp, "MINI Cooper S Convertible," *Car and Driver*, February 8, 2006, www.caranddriver.com on March 3, 2006.

2. Arie de Geus, *The Living Company—Habits for Surviving in a Turbulent Business Environment* (Boston: Harvard Business School Press, 1997). See also John G. Sifonis and Beverly Goldberg, *Corporation on a Tightrope* (New York: Oxford University Press, 1996), for an interesting discussion of how organizations must navigate through the environment.

3. Eric D. Beinhocker, "Robust Adaptive Strategies," *Sloan Management Review*, Spring 1999, pp. 95–105; see also John Crotts, Duncan Dickson, and Robert Ford, "Aligning Organizational Processes with Mission: The Case of Service Excellence," *Academy of Management Executive*, Vol. 19, No. 3, 2005, pp. 54–63.

4. See Jay B. Barney and William G. Ouchi (eds.), *Organizational Economics* (San Francisco: Jossey-Bass, 1986), for a detailed analysis of linkages between economics and organizations.

5. "How Prosperity Is Reshaping the American Economy," *BusinessWeek*, February 14, 2000, pp. 100–110.

6. See "Firms Brace for a Worker Shortage," *Time*, May 6, 2002, p. 44.

7. See Ricky Griffin and Michael Pustay, *International Business: A Managerial Perspective*, 5th ed. (Upper Saddle River, N.J.: Prentice Hall, 2008), for an overview.

8. For example, see Susanne G. Scott and Vicki R. Lane, "A Stakeholder Approach to Organizational Identity," *Academy of Management Review*, 2000, vol. 25, no. 1, pp. 43–62.

9. Richard N. Osborn and John Hagedoorn, "The Institutionalization and Evolutionary Dynamics of Interorganizational Alliances and Networks," *Academy of Management Journal*, April 1997, pp. 261–278. See also "More Companies Cut Risk by Collaborating with Their 'Enemies,'" *Wall Street Journal*, January 31, 2000, pp. A1, A10.

10. "Behind Sony-Samsung Rivalry, An Unlikely Alliance Develops," *Wall Street Journal*, January 13, 2006, p. A1.

11. "The Best & Worst Boards," *BusinessWeek*, October 7, 2002, pp. 104–114. See also Amy Hillman and Thomas Dalziel, "Boards of Directors and Firm Performance: Integrating Agency and Resource Dependence Perspectives," *Academy of Management Review*, 2003, vol. 23, no. 3, pp. 383–396.

12. "The Wild New Workforce," *BusinessWeek*, December 6, 1999, pp. 38–44.

13. "Temporary Workers Getting Short Shrift," *USA Today*, April 11, 1997, pp. 1B, 2B.

14. "Curves Ahead," *Wall Street Journal*, March 10, 1999, pp. B1, B10.

15. Terrence E. Deal and Allan A. Kennedy, *Corporate Cultures: The Rights and Rituals of Corporate Life* (Reading, Mass.: Addison-Wesley, 1982).

16. Sue Zesinger, "Ford's Hip Transplant," *Fortune*, May 10, 1999, pp. 82–92.

17. Jay B. Barney, "Organizational Culture: Can It Be a Source of Sustained Competitive Advantage?" *Academy of Management Review*, July 1986, pp. 656–665.

18. For example, see Carol J. Loomis, "Sam Would Be Proud," *Fortune*, April 17, 2000, pp. 131–144.

19. "Why Wells Fargo Is Circling the Wagons," *Wall Street Journal*, June 9, 1997, pp. 92–93.

20. See Tomothy Galpin, "Connecting Culture to Organizational Change," *HRMagazine*, March 1996, pp. 84–94.

21. For a recent review, see Allen C. Bluedorn, "Pilgrim's Progress: Trends and Convergence in Research on Organizational Size and Environments," *Journal of Management*, 1993, vol. 19, no. 2, pp. 163–191.

22. James D. Thompson, *Organizations in Action* (New York: McGraw-Hill, 1967).

23. Michael E. Porter, *Competitive Strategy: Techniques for Analyzing Industries and Competitors* (New York: Free Press, 1980). See also Joel A. C. Baum and Helaine J. Korn, "Competitive Dynamics of Interfirm Rivalry," *Academy of Management Journal*, April 1996, pp. 255–291.

24. See "Xerox Faces Mounting Challenge to Copier Business," *Wall Street Journal*, December 17, 1999, p. B4.

25. "Plane Maker May Not Seek More 'Sole Supplier' Deals," *USA Today*, June 26, 1997, p. 3B.

26. "Starting Over," *Fortune*, January 21, 2002, pp. 50–68.

27. Bala Chakravarthy, "A New Strategy Framework for Coping with Turbulence," *Sloan Management Review*, Winter 1997, pp. 69–82.

28. "In Wooing AT&T, SBC Has Eye on Business Customers," *Wall Street Journal*, January 28, 2005, pp. A1, A2.

29. Gareth Jones, *Organizational Theory, Design, and Change*, 5th ed. (Upper Saddle River, N.J.: Prentice Hall, 2007).

30. E. Yuchtman and S. Seashore, "A Systems Resource Approach to Organizational Effectiveness," *American Sociological Review*, 1967, vol. 32, pp. 891–903.

31. B. S. Georgopoules and A. S. Tannenbaum, "The Study of Organizational Effectiveness," *American Sociological Review*, 1957, vol. 22, pp. 534–540.

32. Jones, *Organizational Theory, Design, and Change*.

33. Anthony A. Atkinson, John H. Waterhouse, and Robert B. Wells, "A Stakeholder Approach to Strategic Performance Measurement," *Sloan Management Review*, Spring 1997, pp. 25–37.

CHAPTER 4

1. Jennifer Alsever, "Fair Prices for Farmers: Simple Idea, Complex Reality," *New York Times*, March 19, 2006, p. BU5; Leslie Land, "The Straight Stuff," *Money*, February 1, 2004, www.money.com on March 4, 2006; "The Chocolate Industry: Abusive Child Labor and Poverty Behind the Sweetness," Global Exchange website, www.globalexchange.org on March 4, 2006; "Slave Chocolate?" *Forbes*, April 24, 2006, pp. 96–101.

2. See Norman Barry, *Business Ethics* (West Lafayette, Ind.: Purdue University Press, 1999).

3. Thomas Donaldson and Thomas W. Dunfee, "Toward a Unified Conception of Business Ethics: An Integrative Social Contracts Theory," *Academy of Management Review*, 1994, vol. 19, no. 2, pp. 252–284.

4. "Faced with Less Time off, Workers Take More," *USA Today*, October 29, 2002, p. 1A.

5. "Drug Companies Face Assault on Prices," *Wall Street Journal,* May 11, 2000, pp. B1, B4.

6. Jeremy Kahn, "Presto Chango! Sales Are Huge," *Fortune,* March 20, 2000, pp. 90–96; "More Firms Falsify Revenue to Boost Stocks," *USA Today,* March 29, 2000, p. 1B.

7. "How U.S. Concerns Compete in Countries Where Bribes Flourish," *Wall Street Journal,* September 29, 1995, pp. A1, A14; Patricia Digh, "Shades of Gray in the Global Marketplace," *HRMagazine,* April 1997, pp. 90–98.

8. Patricia H. Werhane, *Moral Imagination and Management Decision Making* (New York: Oxford University Press, 1999).

9. "Bad Boys," *Forbes,* July 22, 2002, pp. 99–104.

10. William Dill, "Beyond Codes and Courses," *Selections,* Fall 2002, pp. 21–23.

11. Gerald F. Cavanagh, *American Business Values,* 2nd ed. (Upper Saddle River, N.J.: Prentice-Hall, 1998).

12. See "Restoring Trust in Corporate America," *BusinessWeek,* June 24, 2002, pp. 30–35.

13. "How to Fix Corporate Governance," *BusinessWeek,* May 6, 2002, pp. 68–78. See also Catherine Daily, Dan Dalton, and Albert Cannella, "Corporate Governance: Decades of Dialogue and Data," *Academy of Management Review,* 2003, vol. 28, no. 3, pp. 371–382 and "CEOs Report Stricter Rules," *USA Today,* March 20, 2006, p. 1B.

14. Thomas Donaldson and Lee E. Preston, "The Stakeholder Theory of the Corporation: Concepts, Evidence, and Implications," *Academy of Management Review,* 1995, vol. 20, no. 1, pp. 65–91. See also Jeffrey S. Harrison and R. Edward Freeman, "Stakeholders, Social Responsibility, and Performance: Empirical Evidence and Theoretical Perspectives," *Academy of Management Journal,* 1999, vol. 42, no. 5, pp. 479–495.

15. Aseem Prakash, *Greening the Firm* (Cambridge, U.K.: Cambridge University Press, 2000); Forest L. Reinhardt, *Down to Earth* (Cambridge, Mass.: Harvard Business School Press, 2000).

16. "Oil Companies Strive to Turn a New Leaf to Save Rain Forest," *Wall Street Journal,* July 17, 1997, pp. A1, A8.

17. See J. Alberto Aragon-Correa and Sanjay Sharma, "A Contingent Resource-Based View of Proactive Corporate Environmental Strategy," *Academy of Management Review,* 2003, vol. 28, no. 1, pp. 71–88.

18. Linda Grant, "There's Gold in Going Green," *Fortune,* April 14, 1997, pp. 116–118.

19. "Ford to Reveal Plans for Think Brand," *USA Today,* January 10, 2000, p. 1B. See also "Lean Green Machine," *Forbes,* February 3, 2003, p. 44.

20. Christine Y. Chen and Greg Lindsay, "Will Amazon(.com) Save the Amazon?" *Fortune,* March 20, 2000, pp. 224–226.

21. "Ashland Just Can't Seem to Leave Its Checkered Past Behind," *BusinessWeek,* October 31, 1988, pp. 122–126.

22. For discussions of this debate, see Jean B. McGuire, Alison Sundgren, and Thomas Schneeweis, "Corporate Social Responsibility and Firm Financial Performance," *Academy of Management Journal,* December 1988, pp. 854–872, and Margaret A. Stroup, Ralph L. Neubert, and Jerry W. Anderson, Jr., "Doing Good, Doing Better: Two Views of Social Responsibility," *Business Horizons,* March–April 1987, pp. 22–25.

23. "Is It Rainforest Crunch Time?" *BusinessWeek,* July 15, 1996, pp. 70–71; "Yo, Ben! Yo, Jerry! It's Just Ice Cream," *Fortune,* April 28, 1997, p. 374.

24. Andrew Singer, "Can a Company Be Too Ethical?" *Across the Board,* April 1993, pp. 17–22.

25. "Help or Hype from Exxon?" *BusinessWeek,* August 28, 1995, p. 36.

26. "Inside America's Most Reviled Company," *BusinessWeek,* November 29, 1999, pp. 176–192.

27. "How Barbie is Making Business a Little Better," *USA Today,* March 27, 2006, pp. 1B, 2B.

28. "Legal—But Lousy," *Fortune,* September 2, 2002, p. 192.

29. Lynn Sharp Paine, "Managing for Organizational Integrity," *Harvard Business Review,* March–April 1994, pp. 106–115.

30. "Battling 'Donor Dropsy,'" *Wall Street Journal,* July 19, 2002, pp. B1, B4.

31. "A New Way of Giving," *Time,* July 24, 2000, pp. 48–51. See also Michael Porter and Mark Kramwe, "The Competitive Advantage of Corporate Philanthropy," *Harvard Business Review,* December 2002, pp. 57–66.

32. David M. Messick and Max H. Bazerman, "Ethical Leadership and the Psychology of Decision Making," *Sloan Management Review,* Winter 1996, pp. 9–22.

33. "Ethics in Action: Getting It Right," *Selections,* Fall 2002, pp. 24–27.

34. For a thorough review of the literature on whistle-blowing, see Janet P. Near and Marcia P. Miceli, "Whistle-Blowing: Myth and Reality," *Journal of Management,* 1996, vol. 22, no. 3, pp. 507–526. See also Michael Gundlach, Scott Douglas, and Mark Martinko, "The Decision to Blow the Whistle: A Social Information Processing Framework," *Academy of Management Review,* 2003, vol. 28, no.1, pp. 107–123.

35. For instance, see "The Complex Goals and Unseen Costs of Whistle-Blowing," *Wall Street Journal,* November 25, 2002, pp. A1, A10.

36. "A Whistle-Blower Rocks an Industry," *BusinessWeek,* June 24, 2002, pp. 126–130.

37. "How Green Was My Report Card?" *BusinessWeek,* September 2, 2002, p. 12.

CHAPTER 5

1. "2005 Annual Report," Company Fact Sheet, "Company Timeline," Starbucks Coffee International (quote), Starbucks website, www.starbucks.com on March 5, 2006; Randall Frost, "Global Packaging: The Reality," *BusinessWeek,* January 23, 2006, www.businessweek.com on March 5, 2006; John Pastier, "Starbucks: Selling the American Bean," *BusinessWeek,* December 1, 2005, www.businessweek.com on March 5, 2006; Gianfranco Zaccai, "Global or Local? Make It Both," *BusinessWeek,* August 22, 2005, www.businessweek.com on March 5, 2006.

2. See Ricky W. Griffin and Michael Pustay, *International Business,* 5th ed. (Upper Saddle River, N.J.: Prentice-Hall, 2008), for an overview of international business.

3. See Thomas Begley and David Boyd, "The Need for a Global Mind-Set," *Sloan Management Review,* Winter 2003, pp. 25–36.

4. For a more complete discussion of forms of international business, see Griffin and Pustay, *International Business.*

5. *Hoover's Handbook of American Business 2006* (Austin, Texas: Hoover's Business Press, 2006), pp. 1280–1281.

6. John H. Dunning, *Multinational Enterprises and the Global Economy* (Wokingham, U.K.: Addison-Wesley, 1993); Christopher Bartlett and Sumantra Ghoshal, *Transnational Management* (Homewood, Ill.: Irwin, 1992).

7. "A Company Without a Country?" *BusinessWeek*, May 5, 1997, p. 40.

8. "The Fortune Global 500—World's Largest Corporations," *Fortune*, July 25, 2005, pp. 97–140.

9. "The Fortune Global 500 Ranked Within Industries," *Fortune*, July 25, 2005, pp. 97–140.

10. *Hoover's Handbook of American Business 2006*, pp. 197–198, 570–571.

11. "Going Global—Lessons from Late Movers," *Harvard Business Review*, March–April 2000, pp. 132–142.

12. See "Spanning the Globe," *USA Today*, April 30, 2002, pp. 1C, 2C.

13. "Creating a Worldwide Yen for Japanese Beer," *Financial Times*, October 7, 1994, p. 20.

14. Kenichi Ohmae, "The Global Logic of Strategic Alliances," *Harvard Business Review*, March–April 1989, pp. 143–154.

15. Jeremy Main, "Making Global Alliances Work," *Fortune*, December 17, 1990, pp. 121–126.

16. Hans Mjoen and Stephen Tallman, "Control and Performance in International Joint Ventures," *Organization Science*, May–June 1997, pp. 257–274.

17. "Finally, Coke Gets It Right," *BusinessWeek*, February 10, 2003, p. 47.

18. "The Border," *BusinessWeek*, May 12, 1997, pp. 64–74.

19. Griffin and Pustay, *International Business*.

20. For an excellent discussion of the effects of NAFTA, see "In the Wake of Nafta, a Family Firm Sees Business Go South," *Wall Street Journal*, February 23, 1999, pp. A1, A10.

21. Griffin and Pustay, *International Business*. See also "Overseas Economies Rally, Giving the U.S. a Very Mixed Blessing," *Wall Street Journal*, August 19, 1999, pp. A1, A8.

22. Eileen P. Gunn, "Emerging Markets," *Fortune*, August 18, 1997, pp. 168–173.

23. "In Many Ways, Return of Hong Kong to China Has Already Happened," *Wall Street Journal*, June 9, 1997, pp. A1, A2; "How You Can Win in China," *BusinessWeek*, May 26, 1997, pp. 66–68.

24. "Argentina Cries Foul as Choice Employers Beat a Path Next Door," *Wall Street Journal*, May 2, 2000, pp. A1, A8.

25. "GM Is Building Plants in Developing Nations to Woo New Markets," *Wall Street Journal*, August 4, 1997, pp. A1, A4.

26. For example, see "China Weighs Lifting Curbs on Foreign Firms," *Wall Street Journal*, January 1, 2000, p. A17.

27. Griffin and Pustay, *International Business*.

28. "Oil Companies Strive to Turn a New Leaf to Save Rain Forest," *Wall Street Journal*, July 17, 1997, pp. A1, A8.

29. "Host of Companies Pocket Windfalls from Tariff Law," *Wall Street Journal*, December 5, 2002, pp. A1, A14.

30. "What if There Weren't Any Clocks to Watch?" *Newsweek*, June 30, 1997, p. 14.

31. Geert Hofstede, *Culture's Consequences: International Differences in Work Related Values* (Beverly Hills, Calif.: Sage, 1980).

32. I have taken the liberty of changing the actual labels applied to each dimension for several reasons. The terms I have chosen are more descriptive, simpler, and more self-evident in their meanings.

33. Geert Hofstede, "The Business of International Business Is Culture," *International Business Review*, 1994, vol. 3, no. 1, pp. 1–14.

34. "Crazy for Crunchies," *Newsweek*, April 28, 1997, p. 49.

35. Stratford Sherman, "Are You as Good as the Best in the World?" *Fortune*, December 13, 1993, pp. 95–96.

CHAPTER 6

1. "Black Enterprise Announces List of 50 Most Powerful Women in Business," *Black Enterprise*, January 17, 2006, www.blackenterprise.com on March 6, 2006; Lynette Clemetson, "Chief of BET Plans to Broaden Programming Appeal," *New York Times*, January 10, 2006, www.nytimes.com on March 6, 2006 (quote); "Debra Lee," "Debra Lee Succeeds BET's Bob Johnson," BET website, www.bet.com on March 6, 2006; David Liss, "New Network for African Americans," *BusinessWeek*, September 16, 2003, www.businessweek.com on March 6, 2006.

2. "Then & Now," *HR Magazine*, 50th Anniversary Issue, 2005, p. 80.

3. Gail Robinson and Kathleen Dechant, "Building a Business Case for Diversity," *Academy of Management Executive*, August 1997, pp. 21–31. See also Orlando C. Richard, "Racial Diversity, Business Strategy, and Firm Performance: A Resource-Based View," *Academy of Management Journal*, 2000, vol. 43, no. 2, pp. 164–177.

4. "The Coming Job Bottleneck," *BusinessWeek*, March 24, 1997, pp. 184–185; Linda Thornburg, "The Age Wave Hits," *HR Magazine*, February 1995, pp. 40–46; "How to Manage an Aging Workforce," *The Economist*, February 18, 2006, p. 11.

5. Gary Powell and D. Anthony Butterfield, "Investigating the 'Glass Ceiling' Phenomenon: An Empirical Study of Actual Promotions to Top Management," *Academy of Management Journal*, 1994, vol. 37, no. 1, pp. 68–86.

6. Karen S. Lyness and Donna E. Thompson, "Above the Glass Ceiling? A Comparison of Matched Samples of Female and Male Executives," *Journal of Applied Psychology*, 1997, vol. 82, no. 3, pp. 359–375.

7. "What Glass Ceiling?" *USA Today*, July 20, 1999, pp. 1B, 2B; see also Patricia Sellers, "The 50 Most Powerful Women in Business," *Fortune*, November 14, 2005, pp. 125–170.

8. *Occupational Outlook Handbook* (Washington, D.C.: U.S. Bureau of Labor Statistics, 1990–1991).

9. "Hispanic Nation," *BusinessWeek*, March 15, 2004, pp. 58–70.

10. "The Power of Diversity: Who's Got the Clout?" *Fortune*, August 22, 2005, special issue.

11. "In a Factory Schedule, Where Does Religion Fit In?" *Wall Street Journal*, March 4, 1999, pp. B1, B12.

12. Jane Easter Bahls, "Make Room for Diverse Beliefs," *HR Magazine*, August 1997, pp. 89–95; see also Cliff Edwards, "Coming Out in Corporate America," *BusinessWeek*, December 15, 2003, pp. 64–72.

13. "Immigration Is on the Rise, Again," *USA Today,* February 28, 1997, p. 7A.

14. Based on Taylor H. Cox and Stacy Blake, "Managing Cultural Diversity: Implications for Organizational Competitiveness," *Academy of Management Executive,* August 1991, pp. 45–56. See also Jacqueline A. Gilbert and John M. Ivancevich, "Valuing Diversity: A Tale of Two Organizations," *Academy of Management Executive,* 2000, vol. 14, no. 1, pp. 93–103.

15. Michelle Neely Martinez, "Work-Life Programs Reap Business Benefits," *HR Magazine,* June 1997, pp. 110–119. See also Cox and Blake, "Managing Cultural Diversity: Implications for Organizational Competitiveness."

16. Jonathan Hickman, "America's 50 Best Companies for Minorities," *Fortune,* July 8, 2002, pp. 110–120.

17. For an example, see "A Female Executive Tells Furniture Maker What Women Want," *Wall Street Journal,* June 25, 1999, pp. A1, A11.

18. "Target Makes a Play for Minority Group Sears Has Cultivated," *Wall Street Journal,* April 12, 1999, pp. A1, A8.

19. For example, see Tony Simons, Lisa Hope Pelled, and Ken A. Smith, "Making Use of Difference: Diversity, Debate, and Decision Comprehensiveness in Top Management Teams," *Academy of Management Journal,* 2000, vol. 42, no. 6, pp. 662–673.

20. C. Marlene Fiol, "Consensus, Diversity, and Learning in Organizations," *Organization Science,* August 1994, pp. 403–415.

21. Patrick Reinmoeller and Nicole van Baardwijk, "The Link Between Diversity and Resilience," *MIT Sloan Management Review,* Summer 2005, pp. 61–70.

22. Patricia L. Nemetz and Sandra L. Christensen, "The Challenge of Cultural Diversity: Harnessing a Diversity of Views to Understand Multiculturalism," *Academy of Management Review,* 1996, vol. 21, no. 2, pp. 434–462. See also "Generational Warfare," *Forbes,* March 22, 1999, pp. 62–66; "Do Women Compete in Unhealthy Ways at Work?" *USA Today,* December 30, 2005, p. 1B.

23. Christine M. Riordan and Lynn McFarlane Shores, "Demographic Diversity and Employee Attitudes: An Empirical Examination of Relational Demography Within Work Units," *Journal of Applied Psychology,* 1997, vol. 82, no. 3, pp. 342–358.

24. "Computer Chip Project Brings Rivals Together, But the Cultures Clash," *Wall Street Journal,* May 3, 1994, pp. A1, A8.

25. Cora Daniels, "Women vs. Wal-Mart," *Fortune,* July 21, 2003, pp. 78–82; "How Shoney's, Belted by a Lawsuit, Found the Path to Diversity," *Wall Street Journal,* April 16, 1996, pp. A1, A6; Fay Rice, "Denny's Changes Its Spots," *Fortune,* May 13, 1996, pp. 133–142; "The Ugly Talk on the Texaco Tape," *BusinessWeek,* November 18, 1996, p. 58; "Smith Barney's Woman Problem," *BusinessWeek,* June 3, 1996, pp. 102–106.

26. Jonathan Hickman, "America's 50 Best Companies for Minorities," *Fortune,* July 7, 2003, pp. 103–120.

27. "Firms Address Workers' Cultural Variety," *Wall Street Journal,* February 10, 1989, p. B1.

28. Sara Rynes and Benson Rosen, "What Makes Diversity Programs Work?" *HR Magazine,* October 1994, pp. 67–75.

29. Karen Hildebrand, "Use Leadership Training to Increase Diversity," *HR Magazine,* August 1996, pp. 53–59.

30. "Learning to Accept Cultural Diversity," *Wall Street Journal,* September 12, 1990, pp. B1, B9.

31. "Firms Address Workers' Cultural Variety."

32. Anthony Carneville and Susan Stone, "Diversity—Beyond the Golden Rule," *Training and Development,* October 1994, pp. 22–27.

33. Janice R. W. Joplin and Catherine S. Daus, "Challenges of Leading a Diverse Workforce," *Academy of Management Executive,* August 1997, pp. 32–47.

34. This discussion derives heavily from Taylor H. Cox, "The Multicultural Organization," *Academy of Management Executive,* May 1991, pp. 34–47.

CHAPTER 7

1. "2005 Annual Report," Citigroup website, www.citigroup.com on March 7, 2006; Mara Der Hovanesian, "Rewiring Chuck Prince," *BusinessWeek,* February 20, 2006, pp. 75–78; Marcia Vickers, "The Unlikely Revolutionary," *Fortune,* March 6, 2006, pp. 132–144 (quote).

2. Patrick R. Rogers, Alex Miller, and William Q. Judge, "Using Information-Processing Theory to Understand Planning/Performance Relationships in the Context of Strategy," *Strategic Management Journal,* 1999, vol. 20, pp. 567–577.

3. See Peter J. Brews and Michelle R. Hunt, "Learning to Plan and Planning to Learn: Resolving the Planning School/Learning School Debate," *Strategic Management Journal,* 1999, vol. 20, pp. 889–913.

4. Max D. Richards, *Setting Strategic Goals and Objectives,* 2nd ed. (St. Paul: West, 1986).

5. Jim Collins, "Turning Goals into Results: The Power of Catalytic Mechanisms," *Harvard Business Review,* July–August 1999, pp. 71–81.

6. "GE, No. 2 in Appliances, Is Agitating to Grab Share from Whirlpool," *Wall Street Journal,* July 2, 1997, pp. A1, A6. See also "A Talk with Jeff Immelt," *BusinessWeek,* January 28, 2002, pp. 102–104.

7. Kenneth R. Thompson, Wayne A. Hochwarter, and Nicholas J. Mathys, "Stretch Targets: What Makes Them Effective?" *Academy of Management Executive,* August 1997, pp. 48–58.

8. "A Methodical Man," *Forbes,* August 11, 1997, pp. 70–72.

9. See Thomas Bateman, Hugh O'Neill, and Amy Kenworthy-U'Ren, "A Hierarchical Taxonomy of Top Managers' Goals," *Journal of Applied Psychology,* 2002, vol. 87, no. 6, pp. 1134–1148.

10. John A. Pearce II and Fred David, "Corporate Mission Statements: The Bottom Line," *Academy of Management Executive,* May 1987, p. 109.

11. "Starbucks Mission Statement," Starbucks website, www.starbucks.com/aboutus/environment.asp on May 10, 2006.

12. "Bean Counter," *Forbes,* February 28, 2005, pp. 79–80.

13. "Renovating Home Depot," *BusinessWeek,* March 6, 2006, pp. 50–58; see also Ram Charan, "Home Depot's Blueprint for Culture Change," *Harvard Business Review,* April 2006, pp. 60–71.

14. "Lowe's Is Sprucing Up Its House," *BusinessWeek,* June 3, 2002, pp. 56–58.

15. "Airlines Try Cutting Business Fares, Find They Don't Lose Revenue," *Wall Street Journal,* November 22, 2002, pp. A1, A6.

16. See Charles Hill and Gareth Jones, *Strategic Management,* 6th ed. (Boston: Houghton Mifflin, 2004).

17. *Hoover's Handbook of World Business 2006* (Austin, Tex.: Hoover's Business Press, 2006), pp. 334–335.

18. See "Disney Cuts Strategic-Planning Unit," *Wall Street Journal,* March 28, 2005, pp. A1, A12.

19. K. A. Froot, D. S. Scharfstein, and J. C. Stein, "A Framework for Risk Management," *Harvard Business Review,* November–December 1994, pp. 91–102.

20. "How the Fixers Fended off Big Disasters," *Wall Street Journal,* December 23, 1999, pp. B1, B4.

21. "At Wal-Mart, Emergency Plan Has Big Payoff," *Wall Street Journal,* September 12, 2005, pp. B1, B3.

22. "Next Time," *USA Today,* October 4, 2005, pp. 1B, 2B.

23. Michael Watkins and Max Bazerman, "Predictable Surprises: The Disasters You Should Have Seen Coming," *Harvard Business Review,* March 2003, pp. 72–81.

24. James Brian Quinn, Henry Mintzberg, and Robert M. James, *The Strategy Process* (Englewood Cliffs, N.J.: Prentice-Hall, 1988).

25. Vasudevan Ramanujam and N. Venkatraman, "Planning System Characteristics and Planning Effectiveness," *Strategic Management Journal,* 1987, vol. 8, no. 2, pp. 453–468.

26. "Coca-Cola May Need to Slash Its Growth Targets," *Wall Street Journal,* January 28, 2000, p. B2. See also "Pepsi and Coke Roll Out Flavors to Boost Sales," *Wall Street Journal,* May 7, 2002, pp. B1, B4.

27. "Finally, Coke Gets It Right," *BusinessWeek,* February 10, 2003, p. 47.

28. "Disney, Revisited," *USA Today,* December 14, 1999, pp. 1B, 2B.

29. Andrew Campbell, "Tailored, Not Benchmarked," *Harvard Business Review,* March–April 1999, pp. 41–48.

30. For a review of the strengths and weaknesses of MBO, see Jack N. Kondrasuk, "Studies in MBO Effectiveness," *Academy of Management Review,* July 1981, pp. 419–430 .

CHAPTER 8

1. Ken Belson, "In Sony's Stumble, The Ghost of Betamax," *New York Times,* February 26, 2006, pp. BU 1, 4; James Brightman, "Gamemaker Acclaim Betting on its Brand," *BusinessWeek,* April 7, 2006, www.businessweek.com on April 8, 2006 (quote); Burt Helm, "A Radical New Game Plan," *Business-Week,* March 20, 2006, pp. 54–56; David Kiley, "Rated M for Mad Ave," *BusinessWeek,* February 27, 2006, pp. 76–77.

2. For early discussions of strategic management, see Kenneth Andrews, *The Concept of Corporate Strategy,* rev. ed. (Homewood, Ill.: Dow Jones–Irwin, 1980); and Igor Ansoff, *Corporate Strategy* (New York: McGraw-Hill, 1965). For more recent perspectives, see Michael E. Porter, "What Is Strategy?" *Harvard Business Review,* November–December 1996, pp. 61–78; Kathleen M. Eisenhardt, "Strategy as Strategic Decision Making," *Sloan Management Review,* Spring 1999, pp. 65–74; Sarah Kaplan and Eric Beinhocker, "The Real Value of Strategic Planning," *Sloan Management Review,* Winter 2003, pp. 71–80.

3. *Hoover's Handbook of American Business 2006* (Austin, Tex.: Hoover's Business Press, 2006), pp. 879–881.

4. For a discussion of the distinction between business- and corporate-level strategies, see Charles Hill and Gareth Jones, *Strategic Management: An Integrated Approach,* 6th ed. (Boston: Houghton Mifflin, 2003).

5. See Gary Hamel, "Strategy as Revolution," *Harvard Business Review,* July–August 1996, pp. 69–82.

6. See Henry Mintzberg, "Patterns in Strategy Formulation," *Management Science,* October 1978, pp. 934–948; Henry Mintzberg, "Strategy Making in Three Modes," *California Management Review,* 1973, pp. 44–53.

7. "If It's on the Fritz, Take It to Jane," *BusinessWeek,* January 27, 1997, pp. 74–75.

8. Jay Barney, "Firm Resources and Sustained Competitive Advantage," *Journal of Management,* June 1991, pp. 99–120.

9. Jay Barney, "Strategic Factor Markets," *Management Science,* December 1986, pp. 1231–1241. See also Constantinos C. Markides, "A Dynamic View of Strategy," *Sloan Management Review,* Spring 1999, pp. 55–64.

10. See Michael Porter, *Competitive Strategy* (New York: Free Press, 1980).

11. Porter, *Competitive Strategy.* See also Colin Campbell-Hunt, "What Have We Learned About Generic Competitive Strategy? A Meta-Analysis," *Strategic Management Journal,* 2000, vol. 21, pp. 127–154.

12. Ian C. MacMillan and Rita Gunther McGrath, "Discovering New Points of Differentiation," *Harvard Business Review,* July–August 1997, pp. 133–136.

13. "In a Water Fight, Coke and Pepsi Try Opposite Tacks," *Wall Street Journal,* April 18, 2002, pp. A1, A8.

14. "General Mills Intends to Reshape Doughboy in Its Own Image," *Wall Street Journal,* July 18, 2000, pp. A1, A8.

15. Raymond E. Miles and Charles C. Snow, *Organizational Strategy, Structure, and Process* (New York: McGraw-Hill, 1978); See also Wayne DeSarbo, C. Anthony Benedetto, Michael Song, and Indrajit Sinha, "Revisiting the Miles and Snow Strategic Framework: Uncovering the Interrelationships Between Strategic Types, Capabilities, Environmental Uncertainty, and Firm Performance," *Strategic Management Journal,* 2005, vol. 26, pp. 47–74.

16. See Donald L. Laurie, Yves L. Doz, and Claude P. Sheer, "Creating New Growth Platforms, *Harvard Business Review,* May 2006, pp. 80–91.

17. "Rough Crossing for eBay," *BusinessWeek,* February 7, 2000, p. EB 48.

18. See Eric D. Beinhocker, "Robust Adaptive Strategies," *Sloan Management Review,* Spring 1999, pp. 95–105.

19. See Lawrence G. Hrebiniak, "Obstacles to Effective Strategy Implementation," *Organizational Dynamics,* February 2006, pp. 12–21.

20. Robert Kaplan and David Norton, "How to Implement a New Strategy Without Disrupting Your Organization," *Harvard Business Review,* March 2006, pp. 100–109.

21. See Scott D. Anthony, Matt Eyring, and Lib Gibson, "Mapping Your Innovation Strategy," *Harvard Business Review,* May 2006, pp. 104–113.

22. "At Starbucks, a Blend of Coffee and Music Creates a Potent Mix," *Wall Street Journal,* July 19, 2005, pp. A1, A11.

23. Larry Huston and Nabil Sakkab, "Connect and Develop: Inside Procter & Gamble's New Model for Innovation," *Harvard Business Review,* March 2006, pp. 58–67.

24. Alfred Chandler, *Strategy and Structure: Chapters in the History of the American Industrial Enterprise* (Cambridge, Mass.: MIT Press, 1962); Richard Rumelt, *Strategy, Structure, and Economic Performance* (Cambridge, Mass.: Division of Research, Graduate School of Business Administration, Harvard University, 1974); Oliver Williamson, *Markets and Hierarchies* (New York: Free Press, 1975).

25. "Not the Flavor of the Month," *BusinessWeek,* March 20, 2000, p. 128.

26. K. L. Stimpert and Irene M. Duhaime, "Seeing the Big Picture: The Influence of Industry, Diversification, and Business Strategy on Performance," *Academy of Management Journal,* 1997, vol. 40, no. 3, pp. 560–583.

27. See Chandler, *Strategy and Structure;* Yakov Amihud and Baruch Lev, "Risk Reduction as a Managerial Motive for Conglomerate Mergers," *Bell Journal of Economics,* 1981, pp. 605–617.

28. Chandler, *Strategy and Structure;* Williamson, *Markets and Hierarchies.*

29. "Did Somebody Say McBurrito?" *BusinessWeek,* April 10, 2000, pp. 166–170.

30. For a discussion of the limitations of unrelated diversification, see Jay Barney and William G. Ouchi, *Organizational Economics* (San Francisco: Jossey-Bass, 1986).

31. See Belen Villalonga and Anita McGahan, "The Choice Among Acquisitions, Alliances, and Divestitures," *Strategic Management Journal,* 2005, vol. 26, pp. 1183–1208.

32. "Latest Merger Boom Is Happening in China, and Bears Watching," *Wall Street Journal,* July 30, 1997, pp. A1, A9; "A Breakthrough in Bavaria," *BusinessWeek,* August 4, 1997, p. 54.

33. Kathleen M. Eisenhardt and D. Charles Galunic, "Coevolving—At Last. A Way to Make Synergies Work," *Harvard Business Review,* January–February 2000, pp. 91–100.

34. "MGM Grand Pays $4.4 Billion for Mirage," *USA Today,* March 7, 2000, p. 1B.

35. See Constantinos C. Markides and Peter J. Williamson, "Corporate Diversification and Organizational Structure: A Resource-Based View," *Academy of Management Journal,* April 1996, pp. 340–367; See also Harry Bowen and Margarethe Wiersema, "Foreign-Based Competition and Corporate Diversification Strategy," *Strategic Management Journal,* 2005, vol. 26, pp. 1153–1171.

36. See Barry Hedley, "A Fundamental Approach to Strategy Development," *Long Range Planning,* December 1976, pp. 2–11; Bruce Henderson, "The Experience Curve-Reviewed. IV: The Growth Share Matrix of the Product Portfolio," *Perspectives,* no. 135 (Boston: Boston Consulting Group, 1973).

37. "BMW: Unloading Rover May Not Win the Race," *BusinessWeek,* April 3, 2000, p. 59.

38. Michael G. Allen, "Diagramming G.E.'s Planning for What's WATT," in Robert J. Allio and Malcolm W. Pennington (eds.), *Corporate Planning: Techniques and Applications* (New York: AMACOM, 1979). Limits of this approach are discussed in R. A. Bettis and W. K. Hall, "The Business Portfolio Approach: Where It Falls Down in Practice," *Long Range Planning,* March 1983, pp. 95–105.

39. "Unilever to Sell Specialty-Chemical Unit to ICI of the U.K. for About $8 Billion," *Wall Street Journal,* May 7, 1997, pp. A3, A12; "For Unilever, It's Sweetness and Light," *Wall Street Journal,* April 13, 2000, pp. B1, B4.

40. Howard Thomas, Timothy Pollock, and Philip Gorman, "Global Strategic Analyses: Frameworks and Approaches," *Academy of Management Executive,* 1999, vol. 13, no. 1, pp. 70–80.

41. Kasra Ferdows, "Making the Most of Foreign Factories," *Harvard Business Review,* March–April 1997, pp. 73–88.

42. "Russia Bans U.S. Chicken Shipments, Inspiring Fears of Tough Trade Battle," *Wall Street Journal,* February 23, 1996, p. A2.

43. Anil K. Gupta and Vijay Govindarajan, "Knowledge Flows Within Multinational Corporations," *Strategic Management Journal,* 2000, vol. 21, no. 4, pp. 473–496; See also Jane Lu and Paul Beamish, "International Diversification and Firm Performance: The S-Curve Hypothesis," *Academy of Management Journal,* 2004, vol. 47, pp. 598–609.

44. Christopher A. Bartlett and Sumantra Ghoshal, *Transnational Management,* 2nd ed. (Chicago: Irwin, 1995), pp. 237–242. See also Tatiana Kostova, "Transnational Transfer of Strategic Organizational Practices: A Contextual Perspective," *Academy of Management Review,* 1999, vol. 24, no. 2, pp. 308–324.

45. "At Nokia, a Comeback—And Then Some," *BusinessWeek,* December 2, 1996, p. 106.

CHAPTER 9

1. "About Us," "At a Glance," Barclays Capital website, www.barclayscapital.com on April 8, 2006; Ed Blount, "Breaking Away," *ABA Banking Journal,* October 2005, vol. 97, www.abaj.com on April 10, 2006; Stanley Reed, "Making Barclays Sparkle," *BusinessWeek,* April 10, 2006, www.businessweek.com on April 8, 2006; Stanley Reed, "Barclays: Anything But Stodgy," *BusinessWeek,* April 10, 2006, www.businessweek.com on April 8, 2006.

2. Richard Priem, "Executive Judgment, Organizational Congruence, and Firm Performance," *Organization Science,* August 1994, pp. 421–432. See also R. Duane Ireland and C. Chet Miller, "Decision-Making and Firm Success," *Academy of Management Executive,* 2004, vol. 18, no. 4, pp. 8–12.

3. "Disney-Pixar: It's a Wrap," *BusinessWeek,* January 24, 2006, pp. 56–59.

4. Paul Nutt, "The Formulation Processes and Tactics Used in Organizational Decision Making," *Organization Science,* May 1993, pp. 226–240.

5. For a review of decision making, see E. Frank Harrison, *The Managerial Decision Making Process,* 5th ed. (Boston: Houghton Mifflin, 1999).

6. "Kodak Moment Came Early for CEO Fisher, Who Takes a Stumble," *Wall Street Journal,* July 25, 1997, pp. A1, A6.

7. George P. Huber, *Managerial Decision Making* (Glenview, Ill.: Scott, Foresman, 1980).

8. For an example, see Paul D. Collins, Lori V. Ryan, and Sharon F. Matusik, "Programmable Automation and the Locus of Decision-Making Power," *Journal of Management,* 1999, vol. 25, pp. 29–53.

9. Huber, *Managerial Decision Making*. See also David W. Miller and Martin K. Starr, *The Structure of Human Decisions* (Englewood Cliffs, N.J.: Prentice-Hall, 1976); Alvar Elbing, *Behavioral Decisions in Organizations*, 2nd ed. (Glenview, Ill: Scott, Foresman, 1978).

10. See Alex Taylor III, "Porsche's Risky Recipe," *Fortune*, February 17, 2003, pp. 90–94; "This SUV Can Tow an Entire Carmaker," *BusinessWeek*, January 19, 2004, pp. 40–41. See also "Porsche's Road to Growth Has Real Hazards," *Wall Street Journal*, December 8, 2005, pp. B1, B2.

11. Gerard P. Hodgkinson, Nicola J. Bown, A. John Maule, Keith W. Glaister, and Alan D. Pearman, "Breaking the Frame: An Analysis of Strategic Cognition and Decision Making Under Uncertainty," *Strategic Management Journal*, 1999, vol. 20, pp. 977–985.

12. "Andersen's Fall from Grace Is a Tale of Greed and Miscues," *Wall Street Journal*, June 7, 2002, pp. A1, A6.

13. Glen Whyte, "Decision Failures: Why They Occur and How to Prevent Them," *Academy of Management Executive*, August 1991, pp. 23–31. See also Jerry Useem, "Decisions, Decisions," *Fortune*, June 27, 2005, pp. 55–154.

14. Jerry Useem, "Boeing vs. Boeing," *Fortune*, October 2, 2000, pp. 148–160; "Airbus Prepares to 'Bet the Company' as It Builds a Huge New Jet," *Wall Street Journal*, November 3, 1999, pp. A1, A10.

15. Paul Nutt, "Expanding the Search for Alternatives During Strategic Decision-Making," *Academy of Management Executive*, 2004, vol. 18, no. 4, pp. 13–22.

16. See Paul J. H. Schoemaker and Robert E. Gunther, "The Wisdom of Deliberate Mistakes," *Harvard Business Review*, June 2006, pp. 108–115.

17. "Accommodating the A380," *Wall Street Journal*, November 29, 2005, p. B1; "Boeing Roars Ahead," *BusinessWeek*, November 7, 2005, pp. 44–45; "Boeing's New Tailwind," *Newsweek*, December 5, 2005, p. 45.

18. "The Wisdom of Solomon," *Newsweek*, August 17, 1987, pp. 62–63.

19. "Making Decisions in Real Time," *Fortune*, June 26, 2000, pp. 332–334. See also Eugene Sadler-Smith and Erella Shefy, "The Intuitive Executive: Understanding and Applying 'Gut Feel' in Decision-Making," *Academy of Management Executive*, 2004, vol. 18, no. 4, pp. 76–91.

20. Herbert A. Simon, *Administrative Behavior* (New York: Free Press, 1945). Simon's ideas have been refined and updated in Herbert A. Simon, *Administrative Behavior*, 3rd ed. (New York: Free Press, 1976), and Herbert A. Simon, "Making Management Decisions: The Role of Intuition and Emotion," *Academy of Management Executive*, February 1987, pp. 57–63.

21. Patricia Corner, Angelo Kinicki, and Barbara Keats, "Integrating Organizational and Individual Information Processing Perspectives on Choice," *Organization Science*, August 1994, pp. 294–302.

22. Kimberly D. Elsbach and Greg Elofson, "How the Packaging of Decision Explanations Affects Perceptions of Trustworthiness," *Academy of Management Journal*, 2000, vol. 43, pp. 80–89.

23. Kenneth Brousseau, Michael Driver, Gary Hourihan, and Rikard Larsson, "The Seasoned Executive's Decision-Making Style," *Harvard Business Review*, February 2006, pp. 111–112.

24. Charles P. Wallace, "Adidas—Back in the Game," *Fortune*, August 18, 1997, pp. 176–182.

25. Barry M. Staw and Jerry Ross, "Good Money After Bad," *Psychology Today*, February 1988, pp. 30–33; D. Ramona Bobocel and John Meyer, "Escalating Commitment to a Failing Course of Action: Separating the Roles of Choice and Justification," *Journal of Applied Psychology*, 1994, vol. 79, pp. 360–363.

26. Mark Keil and Ramiro Montealegre, "Cutting Your Losses: Extricating Your Organization When a Big Project Goes Awry," *Sloan Management Review*, Spring 2000, pp. 55–64.

27. Gerry McNamara and Philip Bromiley, "Risk and Return in Organizational Decision Making," *Academy of Management Journal*, 1999, vol. 42, pp. 330–339.

28. For an example, see Brian O'Reilly, "What It Takes to Start a Startup," *Fortune*, June 7, 1999, pp. 135–140.

29. Martha I. Finney, "The Catbert Dilemma—The Human Side of Tough Decisions," *HRMagazine*, February 1997, pp. 70–78.

30. Edwin A. Locke, David M. Schweiger, and Gary P. Latham, "Participation in Decision Making: When Should It Be Used?" *Organizational Dynamics*, Winter 1986, pp. 65–79; Nicholas Baloff and Elizabeth M. Doherty, "Potential Pitfalls in Employee Participation," *Organizational Dynamics*, Winter 1989, pp. 51–62.

31. "The Art of Brainstorming," *BusinessWeek*, August 26, 2002, pp. 168–169.

32. Andre L. Delbecq, Andrew H. Van de Ven, and David H. Gustafson, *Group Techniques for Program Planning* (Glenview, Ill.: Scott, Foresman, 1975); Michael J. Prietula and Herbert A. Simon, "The Experts in Your Midst," *Harvard Business Review*, January–February 1989, pp. 120–124.

33. Norman P. R. Maier, "Assets and Liabilities in Group Problem Solving: The Need for an Integrative Function," in J. Richard Hackman, Edward E. Lawler III, and Lyman W. Porter (eds.), *Perspectives on Business in Organizations*, 2nd ed. (New York: McGraw-Hill, 1983), pp. 385–392.

34. Anthony L. Iaquinto and James W. Fredrickson, "Top Management Team Agreement About the Strategic Decision Process: A Test of Some of Its Determinants and Consequences," *Strategic Management Journal*, 1997, vol. 18, pp. 63–75.

35. Tony Simons, Lisa Hope Pelled, and Ken A. Smith, "Making Use of Difference: Diversity, Debate, and Decision Comprehensiveness in Top Management Teams," *Academy of Management Journal*, 1999, vol. 42, pp. 662–673.

36. Richard A. Cosier and Charles R. Schwenk, "Agreement and Thinking Alike: Ingredients for Poor Decisions," *Academy of Management Executive*, February 1990, pp. 69–78.

37. Irving L. Janis, *Groupthink*, 2nd ed. (Boston: Houghton Mifflin, 1982).

38. Ibid.

CHAPTER 10

1. Michelle Conlin, "You Are What You Post," *BusinessWeek*, March 27, 2006, pp. 52–53; David Kushner, "The Web's Hottest Site: Facebook.com," *Rolling Stone*, April 7, 2006, www.rollingstone.com on April 15, 2006 (quote); Sarah

Michalos, "Facebook Aids in Arrest After Incident," *The [Purdue, Indiana]Exponent* , www.purdueexponent.com; Matt Nagowski, "The Face Behind thefacebook.com," *Current Magazine*, November 30, 2004, www.msnbc.msn.com on February 3, 2006; Steve Rosenbush, "Facebook's on the Block," *BusinessWeek*, March 28, 2006, www.businessweek.com on March 28, 2006.

2. Bro Uttal, "Inside the Deal That Made Bill Gates $350,000,000," *Fortune*, July 21, 1986, pp. 23–33.

3. "The 400 Richest People in America," *Forbes*, October 15, 2005, p. 104.

4. Murray B. Low and Ian MacMillan, "Entrepreneurship: Past Research and Future Challenges," *Journal of Management*, June 1988, pp. 139–159.

5. U.S. Bureau of the Census, *Statistical Abstract of the United States*, 2005 (Washington, D.C.: Government Printing Office, 2005).

6. "Small Business 'Vital Statistics,'" www.sba.gov/aboutsba on May 24, 2000.

7. "Small Business 'Vital Statistics.'"

8. "Workforce Shifts to Big Companies," *USA Today*, March 19, 2002, p. 1B.

9. "Small Business 'Vital Statistics.'"

10. "A Five-Year Journey to a Better Mousetrap," *New York Times*, May 24, 1998, p. 8.

11. "The Top Entrepreneurs," *BusinessWeek*, January 10, 2000, pp. 80–82.

12. "New Entrepreneur, Old Economy," *Wall Street Journal*, May 22, 2000, p. R10.

13. Amar Bhide, "How Entrepreneurs Craft Strategies That Work," *Harvard Business Review*, March–April 1994, pp. 150–163.

14. "Three Men and a Baby Bell," *Forbes*, March 6, 2000, pp. 134–135.

15. *Hoover's Handbook of American Business 2006* (Austin, Tex.: Hoover's Business Press, 2006), pp. 918–919; Wendy Zellner, "Peace, Love, and the Bottom Line," *BusinessWeek*, December 7, 1998, pp. 79–82.

16. "Giving Birth to a Web Business," *New York Times*, October 15, 1998, p. G5.

17. Nancy J. Lyons, "Moonlight over Indiana," *Inc.*, January 2000, pp. 71–74.

18. F. M. Scherer, *Industrial Market Structure and Economic Performance*, 2nd ed. (Boston: Houghton Mifflin, 1980).

19. "Three Biker-Entrepreneurs Take on Mighty Harley," *New York Times*, August 20, 1999, p. F1.

20. The importance of discovering niches is emphasized in Charles Hill and Gareth Jones, *Strategic Management: An Integrative Approach*, 7th ed. (Boston: Houghton Mifflin, 2007).

21. Gregory Patterson, "An American in . . . Siberia?" *Fortune*, August 4, 1997, p. 63; "Crazy for Crunchies," *Newsweek*, April 28, 1997, p. 49.

22. "'Ship Those Boxes; Check the Euro!'" *Wall Street Journal*, February 7, 2003, pp. C1, C7.

23. Thea Singer, "Brandapalooza," *Inc. 500*, 1999, pp. 69–72.

24. "Cheap Tricks," *Forbes*, February 21, 2000, p. 116.

25. U.S. Bureau of the Census, *Statistical Abstract of the United States*, 2005 (Washington, D.C.: Government Printing Office, 2005). See also "Too Much Ventured, Nothing Gained," *Fortune*, November 25, 2002, pp. 135–144.

26. Susan Greco, "get$$$now.com," *Inc.*, September 1999, pp. 35–38.

27. "Internet Industry Surges 'Startling' 62%," *USA Today*, June 6, 2000, p. 1B.

28. "Up-and-Comers," *BusinessWeek*, May 15, 2000, pp. EB70–EB72.

29. Andy Serwer, "There's Something About Cisco," *Fortune*, May 15, 2000, pp. 114–138.

30. "High-Tech Advances Push C.I.A. into New Company," *New York Times*, September 29, 1999, p. A14.

31. "The Courtship of Black Consumers," *New York Times*, August 16, 1998, pp. D1, D5.

32. See *The Wall Street Journal Almanac 1999*, pp. 179, 182.

33. "Women Entrepreneurs Attract New Financing," *New York Times*, July 26, 1998, p. 10.

34. "Women Increase Standing as Business Owners," *USA Today*, June 29, 1999, p. 1B.

35. Norman M. Scarborough and Thomas W. Zimmerer, *Effective Small Business Management: An Entrepreneurial Approach*, 6th ed. (Upper Saddle River, N.J.: Prentice Hall, 2000), pp. 412–413.

36. "Expert Entrepreneur Got Her Show on the Road at an Early Age," *USA Today*, May 24, 2000, p. 5B.

CHAPTER 11

1. Taffy Akner, "How to Be a Late-Night TV Joke Writer," Avant Guild website, www.mediabistro.com on April 12, 2006; "David Letterman, Host," CBS website, www.cbs.com on April 12, 2006; Brian Doben, "Who Ever Said Comedy Had to Be Fun?" *Fast Company,* May 2003, www.fastcompany.com on April 12, 2006 (quote).

2. See David Lei and John Slocum, "Organization Designs to Renew Competitive Advantage," *Organizational Dynamics*, 2002, vol. 31, no. 1, pp. 1–18.

3. For a related discussion, see Kathleen M. Eisenhardt and Shona L. Brown, "Patching—Restitching Business Portfolios in Dynamic Markets," *Harvard Business Review*, May–June 1999, pp. 106–115.

4. Gareth Jones, *Organization Theory, Design, and Change*, 5th ed. (Upper Saddle River, N.J.: Prentice-Hall, 2007). See also "The Office Chart That Really Counts," *BusinessWeek*, February 27, 2006, pp. 48–49.

5. David A. Nadler and Michael L. Tushman, *Competing by Design: The Power of Organizational Architecture* (New York: Oxford University Press, 1997).

6. Ricky W. Griffin and Gary McMahan, "Motivation Through Job Design," in Jerald Greenberg (ed.), *Organizational Behavior: The State of the Science* (Hillsdale, N.J.: Lawrence Erlbaum Associates, 1994), pp. 23–44.

7. Adam Smith, *Wealth of Nations* (New York: Modern Library, 1937; originally published in 1776).

8. Andrea Gabor, *The Capitalist Philosophers* (New York: Times Business, 2000).

9. Ricky W. Griffin, *Task Design* (Glenview, Ill.: Scott Foresman, 1982).

10. Anne S. Miner, "Idiosyncratic Jobs in Formal Organizations," *Administrative Science Quarterly*, September 1987, pp. 327–351.

11. M. D. Kilbridge, "Reduced Costs Through Job Enlargement: A Case," *Journal of Business*, vol. 33, 1960, pp. 357–362.

12. Griffin and McMahan, "Motivation Through Job Enrichment."

13. Kilbridge, "Reduced Costs Through Job Enlargement: A Case."

14. Frederick Herzberg, *Work and the Nature of Man* (Cleveland: World Press, 1966).

15. Robert Ford, "Job Enrichment Lessons from AT&T," *Harvard Business Review*, January–February 1973, pp. 96–106.

16. J. Richard Hackman and Greg R. Oldham, *Work Redesign* (Reading, Mass.: Addison-Wesley, 1980).

17. Jerry Useem, "What's That Spell? Teamwork!" *Fortune*, June 12, 2006, pp. 64–66.

18. For a related discussion, see Etienne C. Wenger and William M. Snyder, "Communities of Practice: The Organizational Frontier," *Harvard Business Review*, January–February 2000, pp. 139–148.

19. Richard L. Daft, *Organization Theory and Design*, 9th ed. (Cincinnati: South-Western, 2007).

20. A. V. Graicunas, "Relationships in Organizations," *Bulletin of the International Management Institute*, March 7, 1933, pp. 39–42.

21. Ralph C. Davis, *Fundamentals of Top Management* (New York: Harper & Row, 1951); Lyndall F. Urwick, *Scientific Principles and Organization* (New York: American Management Association, 1938), p. 8; Ian Hamilton, *The Soul and Body of an Army* (London: Edward Arnold, 1921), pp. 229–230.

22. David D. Van Fleet and Arthur G. Bedeian, "A History of the Span of Management," *Academy of Management Review*, 1977, pp. 356–372.

23. James C. Worthy, "Factors Influencing Employee Morale," *Harvard Business Review*, January 1950, pp. 61–73.

24. Dan R. Dalton, William D. Todor, Michael J. Spendolini, Gordon J. Fielding, and Lyman W. Porter, "Organization Structure and Performance: A Critical Review," *Academy of Management Review*, January 1980, pp. 49–64.

25. See Jerry Useem, "Welcome to the New Company Town," *Fortune*, January 10, 2000, pp. 62–70, for a related discussion. See also "Wherever You Go, You're On the Job," *BusinessWeek*, June 20, 2005, pp. 87–90.

26. David Van Fleet, "Span of Management Research and Issues," *Academy of Management Journal*, September 1983, pp. 546–552.

27. Philip Siekman, "Where 'Build to Order' Works Best," *Fortune*, April 26, 1999, pp. 160C–160V.

28. See Daft, *Organization Theory and Design*.

29. William Kahn and Kathy Kram, "Authority at Work: Internal Models and Their Organizational Consequences," *Academy of Management Review*, 1994, vol. 19, no. 1, pp. 17–50.

30. Carrie R. Leana, "Predictors and Consequences of Delegation," *Academy of Management Journal*, December 1986, pp. 754–774.

31. Jerry Useem, "In Corporate America It's Cleanup Time," *Fortune*, September 16, 2002, pp. 62–70.

32. Norm Brodsky, "Necessary Losses," *Inc.*, December 1997, p. 116–119.

33. "Remote Control," *HRMagazine*, August 1997, pp. 82–90.

34. "Toppling the Pyramids," *Canadian Business*, May 1993, pp. 61–65.

35. Kevin Crowston, "A Coordination Theory Approach to Organizational Process Design," *Organization Science*, March–April 1997, pp. 157–166.

36. James Thompson, *Organizations in Action* (New York: McGraw-Hill, 1967). For a recent discussion, see Bart Victor and Richard S. Blackburn, "Interdependence: An Alternative Conceptualization," *Academy of Management Review*, July 1987, pp. 486–498.

37. Jay R. Galbraith, *Designing Complex Organizations* (Reading, Mass.: Addison-Wesley, 1973) and *Organizational Design* (Reading, Mass.: Addison-Wesley, 1977).

38. Paul R. Lawrence and Jay W. Lorsch, "Differentiation and Integration in Complex Organizations," *Administrative Science Quarterly*, March 1967, pp. 1–47.

CHAPTER 12

1. "2004 Annual Report," "The A&F Brands," Abercrombie & Fitch website, www.abercrombie.com on April 16, 2006; Robert Berner, "Flip-Flops, Torn Jeans—and Control," *BusinessWeek*, May 30, 2005, www.businessweek.com on April 15, 2006 (quote); Parija Bhatnagar, "Abercrombie Looking to 'Ruehl,'" *Money*, August 27, 2004, www.cnnmoney.com on April 16, 2006; Emily Scardino, "Ruehl: A&F's Hip New Retail Concept," *DSN Retailing Today*, September 20, 2004, www.dsnretailingtoday.com on April 16, 2006.

2. See Gareth Jones, *Organization Theory*, 5th ed. (Upper Saddle River, N.J.: Prentice-Hall, 2007).

3. David Lei and John Slocum, "Organization Designs to Renew Competitive Advantage," *Organizational Dynamics*, 2002, vol. 31, no. 1, pp. 1–18.

4. Max Weber, *Theory of Social and Economic Organizations*, trans. T. Parsons (New York: Free Press, 1947).

5. Paul Jarley, Jack Fiorito, and John Thomas Delany, "A Structural Contingency Approach to Bureaucracy and Democracy in U.S. National Unions," *Academy of Management Journal*, 1997, vol. 40, no. 4, pp. 831–861.

6. Rensis Likert, *New Patterns in Management* (New York: McGraw-Hill, 1961), and *The Human Organization* (New York: McGraw-Hill, 1967).

7. William F. Dowling, "At General Motors: System 4 Builds Performance and Profits," *Organizational Dynamics*, Winter 1975, pp. 23–28.

8. Jones, *Organization Theory*. See also "The Great Transformation," *BusinessWeek*, August 28, 2000, pp. 84–99.

9. Joan Woodward, *Industrial Organization: Theory and Practice* (London: Oxford University Press, 1965).

10. Joan Woodward, *Management and Technology, Problems of Progress Industry*, no. 3 (London: Her Majesty's Stationery Office, 1958).

11. William Bridges, "The End of the Job," *Fortune*, September 19, 1994, pp. 62–74.

12. For example, see Michael Russo and Niran Harrison, "Organizational Design and Environmental Performance: Clues from the Electronics Industry," *Academy of Management Journal*, 2005, vol. 48, no. 4, pp. 582–593.

13. Tom Burns and G. M. Stalker, *The Management of Innovation* (London: Tavistock, 1961).

14. Paul R. Lawrence and Jay W. Lorsch, *Organization and Environment* (Homewood, Ill.: Irwin, 1967).

15. Edward E. Lawler III, "Rethinking Organization Size," *Organizational Dynamics*, Autumn 1997, pp. 24–33. See also Tom Brown, "How Big Is Too Big?" *Across the Board*, July–August 1999, pp. 14–20.

16. Derek S. Pugh and David J. Hickson, *Organization Structure in Its Context: The Aston Program I* (Lexington, Mass.: D. C. Heath, 1976).

17. "Can Wal-Mart Get Any Bigger?" *Time*, January 13, 2003, pp. 38–43.

18. Robert H. Miles and Associates, *The Organizational Life Cycle* (San Francisco: Jossey-Bass, 1980). See also "Is Your Company Too Big?" *BusinessWeek*, March 27, 1989, pp. 84–94.

19. Douglas Baker and John Cullen, "Administrative Reorganization and Configurational Context: The Contingent Effects of Age, Size, and Change in Size," *Academy of Management Journal*, 1993, vol. 36, no. 6, pp. 1251–1277. See also Kevin Crowston, "A Coordination Theory Approach to Organizational Process Design," *Organization Science*, March–April 1997, pp. 157–168.

20. See Charles W. L. Hill and Gareth Jones, *Strategic Management: An Integrated Approach*, 7th ed. (Boston: Houghton Mifflin, 2007).

21. See "The Corporate Ecosystem," *BusinessWeek*, August 28, 2000, pp. 166–197.

22. Richard D'Aveni and David Ravenscraft, "Economies of Integration Versus Bureaucratic Costs: Does Vertical Integration Improve Performance?" *Academy of Management Journal*, 1994, vol. 37, no. 5, pp. 1167–1206.

23. Gerardine DeSanctis, Jeffrey Glass, and Ingrid Morris Ensing, "Organizational Designs for R&D," *Academy of Management Executive*, 2002, vol. 16, no. 2, pp. 55–64.

24. Oliver E. Williamson, *Markets and Hierarchies* (New York: Free Press, 1975).

25. Ibid.

26. Michael E. Porter, "From Competitive Advantage to Corporate Strategy," *Harvard Business Review*, May–June 1987, pp. 43–59.

27. Williamson, *Markets and Hierarchies*.

28. Jay B. Barney and William G. Ouchi (eds.), *Organizational Economics* (San Francisco: Jossey-Bass, 1986); Robert E. Hoskisson, "Multidivisional Structure and Performance: The Contingency of Diversification Strategy," *Academy of Management Journal*, December 1987, pp. 625–644. See also Bruce Lamont, Robert Williams, and James Hoffman, "Performance During 'M-Form' Reorganization and Recovery Time: The Effects of Prior Strategy and Implementation Speed," *Academy of Management Journal*, 1994, vol. 37, no. 1, pp. 153–166.

29. Stanley M. Davis and Paul R. Lawrence, *Matrix* (Reading, Mass.: Addison-Wesley, 1977).

30. "Martha, Inc.," *BusinessWeek*, January 17, 2000, pp. 63–72.

31. Davis and Lawrence, *Matrix*.

32. See Lawton Burns and Douglas Wholey, "Adoption and Abandonment of Matrix Management Programs: Effects of Organizational Characteristics and Interorganizational Networks," *Academy of Management Journal*, 1993, vol. 36, no. 1, pp. 106–138.

33. See Michael Hammer and Steven Stanton, "How Process Enterprises Really Work," *Harvard Business Review*, November–December 1999, pp. 108–118.

34. Raymond E. Miles, Charles C. Snow, John A. Mathews, Grant Miles, and Henry J. Coleman, Jr., "Organizing in the Knowledge Age: Anticipating the Cellular Form," *Academy of Management Executive*, November 1997, pp. 7–24.

35. "The Horizontal Corporation," *BusinessWeek*, December 20, 1993, pp. 76–81; Shawn Tully, "The Modular Corporation," *Fortune*, February 8, 1993, pp. 106–114.

36. "Management by Web," *BusinessWeek*, August 28, 2000, pp. 84–96.

37. Peter Senge, *The Fifth Discipline* (New York: Free Press, 1993). See also David Lei, John W. Slocum, and Robert A. Pitts, "Designing Organizations for Competitive Advantage: The Power of Unlearning and Learning," *Organizational Dynamics*, Winter 1999, pp. 24–35.

38. See William G. Egelhoff, "Strategy and Structure in Multinational Corporations: A Revision of the Stopford and Wells Model," *Strategic Management Journal*, 1988, vol. 9, pp. 1–14, for a recent discussion of these issues. See also Ricky W. Griffin and Michael Pustay, *International Business: A Managerial Perspective*, 5th ed. (Upper Saddle River, N.J.: Prentice-Hall, 2007).

CHAPTER 13

1. Kerry Capell, "Ikea," *BusinessWeek*, November 14, 2005, www.businessweek.com on February 2, 2006 (quote); Cora Daniels, "Create Ikea, Make Billions, Take Bus," *Fortune*, May 3, 2004, www.cnnmoney.com on April 15, 2006; "Facts & Figures," Ikea website, www.ikea.com on April 15, 2006; John Leland, "How the Disposable Sofa Conquered America," *New York Times*, December 1, 2002, www.nytimes.com on April 15, 2006; Gianfranco Zaccai, "What Ikea Could Teach Alitalia," *BusinessWeek*, January 19, 2006, www.businessweek.com on February 2, 2006.

2. For an excellent review of this area, see Achilles A. Armenakis and Arthur G. Bedeian, "Organizational Change: A Review of Theory and Research in the 1990s," *Journal of Management*, 1999, vol. 25, no. 3, pp. 293–315.

3. For additional insights into how technological change affects other parts of the organization, see P. Robert Duimering, Frank Safayeni, and Lyn Purdy, "Integrated Manufacturing: Redesign the Organization Before Implementing Flexible Technology," *Sloan Management Review*, Summer 1993, pp. 47–56.

4. Joel Cutcher-Gershenfeld, Ellen Ernst Kossek, and Heidi Sandling, "Managing Concurrent Change Initiatives," *Organizational Dynamics*, Winter 1997, pp. 21–38.

5. Michael A. Hitt, "The New Frontier: Transformation of Management for the New Millennium," *Organizational Dynamics*, Winter 2000, pp. 7–15. See also Michael Beer and Nitin Nohria, "Cracking the Code of Change," *Harvard Business Review*, May–June 2000, pp. 133–144; and Clark Gilbert, "The Disruption Opportunity," *MIT Sloan Management Review*, Summer 2003, pp. 27–32.

6. See Warren Boeker, "Strategic Change: The Influence of Managerial Characteristics and Organizational Growth," *Academy of Management Journal*, 1997, vol. 40, no. 1, pp. 152–170.

7. Alan L. Frohman, "Igniting Organizational Change from Below: The Power of Personal Initiative," *Organizational Dynamics*, Winter 1997, pp. 39–53.

8. Nandini Rajagopalan and Gretchen M. Spreitzer, "Toward a Theory of Strategic Change: A Multi-Lens Perspective

and Integrative Framework," *Academy of Management Review*, 1997, vol. 22, no. 1, pp. 48–79.

9. Anne Fisher, "Danger Zone," *Fortune*, September 8, 1997, pp. 165–167.

10. "Kodak to Cut Staff up to 21% Amid Digital Push," *Wall Street Journal*, January 22, 2005, pp. A1, A7.

11. John P. Kotter and Leonard A. Schlesinger, "Choosing Strategies for Change," *Harvard Business Review*, March–April 1979, p. 106.

12. Clayton M. Christensen and Michael Overdorf, "Meeting the Challenge of Disruptive Change," *Harvard Business Review*, March–April 2000, pp. 67–77.

13. "To Maintain Success, Managers Must Learn How to Direct Change," *Wall Street Journal*, August 13, 2002, p. B1.

14. See Eric Abrahamson, "Change Without Pain," *Harvard Business Review*, July–August 2000, pp. 75–85. See also Gib Akin and Ian Palmer, "Putting Metaphors to Work for Change in Organizations," *Organizational Dynamics*, Winter 2000, pp. 67–76.

15. Erik Brynjolfsson, Amy Austin Renshaw, and Marshall Van Alstyne, "The Matrix of Change," *Sloan Management Review*, Winter 1997, pp. 37–54.

16. Kurt Lewin, "Frontiers in Group Dynamics: Concept, Method, and Reality in Social Science," *Human Relations*, June 1947, pp. 5–41.

17. Michael Roberto and Lynne Levesque, "The Art of Making Change Initiatives Stick," *MIT Sloan Management Review*, Summer 2005, pp. 53–62.

18. "Time for a Turnaround," *Fast Company*, January 2003, pp. 55–61.

19. See Connie J. G. Gersick, "Revolutionary Change Theories: A Multilevel Exploration of the Punctuated Equilibrium Paradigm," *Academy of Management Review*, January 1991, pp. 10–36.

20. For a good illustration of how resistance emerges, see Gerald Andrews, "Mistrust, the Hidden Obstacle to Empowerment, *HRMagazine*, November 1994, pp. 66–74.

21. See Clark Gilbert and Joseph Bower, "Disruptive Change," *Harvard Business Review*, May 2002, pp. 95–104.

22. "RJR Employees Fight Distraction amid Buy-out Talks," *Wall Street Journal*, November 1, 1988, p. A8.

23. Arnon E. Reichers, John P. Wanous, and James T. Austin, "Understanding and Managing Cynicism About Organizational Change," *Academy of Management Executive*, February 1997, pp. 48–59.

24. For a classic discussion, see Paul R. Lawrence, "How to Deal with Resistance to Change," *Harvard Business Review*, January–February 1969, pp. 4–12, 166–176.

25. Lester Coch and John R. P. French, Jr., "Overcoming Resistance to Change," *Human Relations*, August 1948, pp. 512–532.

26. Eric von Hippel, Stefan Thomke, and Mary Sonnack, "Creating Breakthroughs at 3M," *Harvard Business Review*, September–October 1999, pp. 47–54. See also Jerry Useem, "Tape + Light Bulbs = ?" *Fortune*, August 12, 2002, pp. 127–132.

27. Benjamin Schneider, Arthur P. Brief, and Richard A. Guzzo, "Creating a Climate and Culture for Sustainable Organizational Change," *Organizational Dynamics*, Spring 1996, pp. 7–19.

28. "Troubled GM Plans Major Tuneup," *USA Today*, June 6, 2005, pp. 1B, 2B.

29. Paul Bate, Raza Khan, and Annie Pye, "Towards a Culturally Sensitive Approach to Organization Structuring: Where Organization Design Meets Organization Development," *Organization Science*, March–April 2000, pp. 197–211.

30. David Kirkpatrick, "The New Player," *Fortune*, April 17, 2000, pp. 162–168.

31. Jeffrey A. Alexander, "Adaptive Change in Corporate Control Practices," *Academy of Management Journal*, March 1991, pp. 162–193.

32. "Mr. Ryder Rewrites the Musty Old Book at Reader's Digest," *Wall Street Journal*, April 18, 2000, pp. A1, A10.

33. "Struggling Saks Tries Alterations in Management," *Wall Street Journal*, January 10, 2006, pp. B1, B2.

34. Thomas A. Stewart, "Reengineering—The Hot New Managing Tool," *Fortune*, August 23, 1993, pp. 41–48.

35. "Old Company Learns New Tricks," *USA Today*, April 10, 2000, pp. 1B, 2B.

36. Richard Beckhard, *Organization Development: Strategies and Models* (Reading, Mass.: Addison-Wesley, 1969), p. 9.

37. W. Warner Burke, "The New Agenda for Organization Development," *Organizational Dynamics*, Summer 1997, pp. 7–20.

38. Wendell L. French and Cecil H. Bell, Jr., *Organization Development: Behavioral Science Interventions for Organization Improvement*, 2nd ed. (Englewood Cliffs, N.J.: Prentice-Hall, 1978).

39. "Memo to the Team: This Needs Salt!" *Wall Street Journal*, April 4, 2000, pp. B1, B14.

40. Roger J. Hower, Mark G. Mindell, and Donna L. Simmons, "Introducing Innovation Through OD," *Management Review*, February 1978, pp. 52–56.

41. "Is Organization Development Catching On? A Personnel Symposium," *Personnel*, November–December 1977, pp. 10–22.

42. For a recent discussion on the effectiveness of various OD techniques in different organizations, see John M. Nicholas, "The Comparative Impact of Organization Development Interventions on Hard Criteria Measures," *Academy of Management Review*, October 1982, pp. 531–542.

43. Constantinos Markides, "Strategic Innovation," *Sloan Management Review*, Spring 1997, pp. 9–24. See also James Brian Quinn, "Outsourcing Innovation: The New Engine of Growth," *Sloan Management Review*, Summer 2000, pp. 13–21.

44. L. B. Mohr, "Determinants of Innovation in Organizations," *American Political Science Review*, 1969, pp. 111–126; G. A. Steiner, *The Creative Organization* (Chicago: University of Chicago Press, 1965); R. Duncan and A. Weiss, "Organizational Learning: Implications for Organizational Design," in B. M. Staw (ed.), *Research in Organizational Behavior*, vol. 1 (Greenwich, Conn.: JAI Press, 1979), pp. 75–123; J. E. Ettlie, "Adequacy of Stage Models for Decisions on Adoption of Innovation," *Psychological Reports*, 1980, pp. 991–995.

45. See Alan Patz, "Managing Innovation in High Technology Industries," *New Management*, September 1986, pp. 54–59.

46. "Flops," *BusinessWeek*, August 16, 1993, pp. 76–82.

47. "Apple Can't Keep up with Demand for Newest iMac," *USA Today*, August 26, 2002, p. 3B.

48. See Willow A. Sheremata, "Centrifugal and Centripetal Forces in Radical New Product Development Under Time Pressure," *Academy of Management Review*, 2000, vol. 25, no. 2, pp. 389–408. See also Richard Leifer, Gina Colarelli O'Connor, and Mark Rice, "Implementing Radical Innovation in Mature Firms: The Role of Hobs," *Academy of Management Executive*, 2001, vol. 15, no. 3, pp. 102–113.

49. See "Amid Japan's Gloom, Corporate Overhauls Offer Hints of Revival," *Wall Street Journal*, February 21, 2002, pp. A1, A11.

50. Dorothy Leonard and Jeffrey F. Rayport, "Spark Innovation Through Empathic Design," *Harvard Business Review*, November–December 1997, pp. 102–115.

51. See Steven P. Feldman, "How Organizational Culture Can Affect Innovation," *Organizational Dynamics*, Summer 1988, pp. 57–68.

52. Geoffrey Moore, "Innovating Within Established Enterprises," *Harvard Business Review*, July–August 2004, pp. 87–96.

53. See Gifford Pinchot III, *Intrapreneuring* (New York: Harper & Row, 1985).

CHAPTER 14

1. Anne Fisher, "Want a 'Real Job'? Temp While You're Looking," *Fortune*, April 26, 2005, www.fortune.com on April 20, 2006; Anni Layne, "Silicon Valley's Worst-Kept Secret," *Fast Company*, May 2001, www.fastcompany.com on April 20, 2006 (quote); Michael Mandel, "Temporary Jobs: Bah, Humbug?" *BusinessWeek*, December 23, 2005, www.businessweek.com on April 20, 2006; Michael Mandel, "Where's the Wage Growth?" *BusinessWeek*, January 17, 2006, www.businessweek.com on April 20, 2006; Tanya Mohn, "A Way to Try a Job on for Size Before Making a Commitment," *New York Times*, March 12, 2006, p. NJW 1, 3.

2. For a complete review of human resource management, see Angelo S. DeNisi and Ricky W. Griffin, *Human Resource Management*, 3rd ed. (Boston: Houghton Mifflin, 2008).

3. Patrick Wright and Gary McMahan, "Strategic Human Resources Management: A Review of the Literature," *Journal of Management*, June 1992, pp. 280–319.

4. Augustine Lado and Mary Wilson, "Human Resource Systems and Sustained Competitive Advantage: A Competency-Based Perspective," *Academy of Management Review*, 1994, vol. 19, no. 4, pp. 699–727.

5. David Lepak and Scott Snell, "Examining the Human Resource Architecture: The Relationships Among Human Capital, Employment, and Human Resource Configurations," *Journal of Management*, 2002, vol. 28, no. 4, pp. 517–543.

6. "Maryland First to OK 'Wal-Mart Bill,'" *USA Today*, January 13, 2006, p. 1B.

7. "Is Butter Flavoring Ruining Popcorn Workers' Lungs?" *USA Today*, June 20, 2002, pp. 1A, 8A.

8. "While Hiring at Most Firms Chills, Wal-Mart's Heats Up," *USA Today*, August 26, 2002, p. 1B.

9. "The New Workforce," *BusinessWeek*, March 20, 2000, pp. 64–70.

10. John Beeson, "Succession Planning," *Across the Board*, February 2000, pp. 38–41.

11. "Star Search," *BusinessWeek*, October 10, 2005, pp. 66–78.

12. Robert Gatewood, Mary Gowan, and Gary Lautenschlager, "Corporate Image, Recruitment Image, and Initial Job Choice Decisions," *Academy of Management Journal*, 1993, vol. 36, no. 2, pp. 414–427; see also Karen Holcombe Ehrhart and Jonathan Ziegert, "Why Are Individuals Attracted to Organizations?" *Journal of Management*, 2005, vol. 31, no. 6, pp. 901–919.

13. "Firms Cook up New Ways to Keep Workers," *USA Today*, January 18, 2000, p. 1B.

14. Claudio Fernandez-Araoz, "Hiring Without Firing," *Harvard Business Review*, July–August 1999, pp. 109–118.

15. James A. Breaugh and Mary Starke, "Research on Employee Recruiting: So Many Studies, So Many Remaining Questions," *Journal of Management*, 2000, vol. 26, no. 3, pp. 405–434.

16. "Pumping up Your Past," *Time*, June 10, 2002, p. 96.

17. Frank L. Schmidt and John E. Hunter, "Employment Testing: Old Theories and New Research Findings," *American Psychologist*, October 1981, pp. 1128–1137.

18. Robert Liden, Christopher Martin, and Charles Parsons, "Interviewer and Applicant Behaviors in Employment Interviews," *Academy of Management Journal*, 1993, vol. 36, no. 2, pp. 372–386.

19. Paul R. Sackett, "Assessment Centers and Content Validity: Some Neglected Issues," *Personnel Psychology*, 1987, vol. 40, pp. 13–25.

20. Renee DeRouin, Barbara Fritzsche, and Eduardo Salas, "E-Learning in Organizations," *Journal of Management*, 2005, vol. 31, no. 6, pp. 920–940.

21. "'Boeing U': Flying by the Book," *USA Today*, October 6, 1997, pp. 1B, 2B. See also "Is Your Airline Pilot Ready for Surprises?" *Time*, October 14, 2002, p. 72.

22. See Paul Levy and Jane Williams, "The Social Context of Performance Appraisal: A Review and Framework for the Future," *Journal of Management*, 2004, vol. 30, no. 6, pp. 881–905.

23. See Angelo S. DeNisi and Avraham N. Kluger, "Feedback Effectiveness: Can 360-Degree Appraisals Be Improved?" *Academy of Management Executive*, 2000, vol. 14, no. 1, pp. 129–139.

24. Barry R. Nathan, Allan Mohrman, and John Milliman, "Interpersonal Relations as a Context for the Effects of Appraisal Interviews on Performance and Satisfaction: A Longitudinal Study," *Academy of Management Journal*, June 1991, pp. 352–369.

25. "Goodyear to Stop Labeling 10% of Its Workers as Worst," *USA Today*, September 12, 2002, p. 1B.

26. Jaclyn Fierman, "The Perilous New World of Fair Pay," *Fortune*, June 13, 1994, pp. 57–64. See also "The Best vs. the Rest," *Wall Street Journal*, January 30, 2006, pp. B1, B3.

27. Stephanie Armour, "Show Me the Money, More Workers Say," *USA Today*, June 6, 2000, p. 1B.

28. "To Each According to His Needs: Flexible Benefits Plans Gain Favor," *Wall Street Journal*, September 16, 1986, p. 29.

29. "The Future Look of Employee Benefits," *Wall Street Journal*, September 7, 1988, p. 21.

30. See "Companies Chisel Away at Workers' Benefits," *USA Today*, November 18, 2002, pp. 1B, 2B. See also "The Benefits Trap," *BusinessWeek*, July 19, 2004, pp. 64–72.

31. See Sherry E. Sullivan, "The Changing Nature of Careers: A Review and Research Agenda," *Journal of Management*, 1999, vol. 25, no. 3, pp. 457–484.

32. Barbara Presley Nobel, "Reinventing Labor," *Harvard Business Review*, July–August 1993, pp. 115–125.

33. John A. Fossum, "Labor Relations: Research and Practice in Transition," *Journal of Management*, Summer 1987, pp. 281–300.

34. "How Wal-Mart Keeps Unions at Bay," *BusinessWeek*, October 28, 2002, pp. 94–96.

35. Max Boisot, *Knowledge Assets* (Oxford, U.K.: Oxford University Press, 1998).

36. Thomas Stewart, "In Search of Elusive Tech Workers," *Fortune*, February 16, 1998, pp. 171–172.

37. "Need for Computer Experts Is Making Recruiters Frantic," *New York Times*, December 18, 1999, p. C1.

38. "FBI Taps Retiree Experience for Temporary Jobs," *USA Today*, October 3, 2002, p. 1A.

39. "When Is a Temp Not a Temp?" *BusinessWeek*, December 7, 1998, pp. 90–92.

40. "Drivers Deliver Trouble to FedEx by Seeking Employee Benefits," *Wall Street Journal*, January 7, 2005, pp. A1, A8.

CHAPTER 15

1. Paul Babiak and Robert D. Hare, *Snakes in Suits: When Psychopaths Go to Work* (New York: Regan, 2006); Alan Deutschman, "Is Your Boss a Psychopath?" *Fast Company*, July 2005, www.fastcompany.com on April 22, 2006 (quote); Paul Kaihla, "Getting Inside the Boss's Head," *Business 2.0*, November 1, 2003, www.cnnmoney.com on April 22, 2006; "Welcome," The Without Conscience website, www.hare.org on April 22, 2006.

2. Lynn McGarlane Shore and Lois Tetrick, "The Psychological Contract as an Explanatory Framework in the Employment Relationship," in C. L. Cooper and D. M. Rousseau (eds.), *Trends in Organizational Behavior* (London: Wiley, 1994). See also Jacqueline Coyle-Shapiro and Neil Conway, "Exchange Relationships: Examining Psychological Contracts and Perceived Organizational Support," *Journal of Applied Psychology*, 2005, vol. 90, no. 4, pp. 774–781.

3. Elizabeth Wolfe Morrison and Sandra L. Robinson, "When Employees Feel Betrayed: A Model of How Psychological Contract Violation Develops," *Academy of Management Review*, January 1997, pp. 226–256.

4. Lawrence Pervin, "Personality" in Mark Rosenzweig and Lyman Porter (eds.), *Annual Review of Psychology*, vol. 36 (Palo Alto, Calif.: Annual Reviews, 1985), pp. 83–114; S. R. Maddi, *Personality Theories: A Comparative Analysis*, 4th ed. (Homewood, Ill.: Dorsey, 1980).

5. L. R. Goldberg, "An Alternative 'Description of Personality': The Big Five Factor Structure," *Journal of Personality and Social Psychology*, 1990, vol. 59, pp. 1216–1229.

6. Michael K. Mount, Murray R. Barrick, and J. Perkins Strauss, "Validity of Observer Ratings of the Big Five Personality Factors," *Journal of Applied Psychology*, 1994, vol. 79, no. 2, pp. 272–280; Timothy A. Judge, Joseph J. Martocchio, and Carl J. Thoreson, "Five-Factor Model of Personality and Employee Absence," *Journal of Applied Psychology*, 1997, vol. 82, no. 5, pp. 745–755.

7. J. B. Rotter, "Generalized Expectancies for Internal vs. External Control of Reinforcement," *Psychological Monographs*, 1966, vol. 80, pp. 1–28. See also Simon S. K. Lam and John Schaubroeck, "The Role of Locus of Control in Reactions to Being Promoted and to Being Passed Over: A Quasi Experiment," *Academy of Management Journal*, 2000, vol. 43, no. 1, pp. 66–78.

8. Marilyn E. Gist and Terence R. Mitchell, "Self-Efficacy: A Theoretical Analysis of Its Determinants and Malleability," *Academy of Management Review*, April 1992, pp. 183–211.

9. T. W. Adorno, E. Frenkel-Brunswick, D. J. Levinson, and R. N. Sanford, *The Authoritarian Personality* (New York: Harper & Row, 1950).

10. "The Rise and Fall of Dennis Kozlowski," *BusinessWeek*, December 23, 2002, pp. 64–77.

11. Jon L. Pierce, Donald G. Gardner, and Larry L. Cummings, "Organization-Based Self-Esteem: Construct Definition, Measurement, and Validation," *Academy of Management Journal*, 1989, vol. 32, pp. 622–648.

12. Michael Harris Bond and Peter B. Smith, "Cross-Cultural Social and Organizational Psychology," in Janet Spence (ed.), *Annual Review of Psychology*, vol. 47 (Palo Alto, Calif.: Annual Reviews, 1996), pp. 205–235.

13. See Daniel Goleman, *Emotional Intelligence: Why It Can Matter More Than IQ* (New York: Bantam, 1995).

14. Daniel Goleman, "Leadership That Gets Results," *Harvard Business Review*, March–April 2000, pp. 78–90. See also Kenneth Law, Chi-Sum Wong, and Lynda Song, "The Construct and Criterion Validity of Emotional Intelligence and Its Potential Utility for Management Studies," *Journal of Applied Psychology*, 2004, vol. 87, no. 3, pp. 483–496.

15. Leon Festinger, *A Theory of Cognitive Dissonance* (Palo Alto, Calif.: Stanford University Press, 1957).

16. See John J. Clancy, "Is Loyalty Really Dead?" *Across the Board*, June 1999, pp. 15–19.

17. Patricia C. Smith, L. M. Kendall, and Charles Hulin, *The Measurement of Satisfaction in Work and Behavior* (Chicago: Rand-McNally, 1969). See also Steven Currall, Annette Towler, Tomothy Judge, and Laura Kohn, "Pay Satisfaction and Organizational Outcomes," *Personnel Psychology*, 2005, vol. 58, pp. 613–640.

18. "Companies Are Finding Real Payoffs in Aiding Employee Satisfaction," *Wall Street Journal*, October 11, 2000, p. B1.

19. James R. Lincoln, "Employee Work Attitudes and Management Practice in the U.S. and Japan: Evidence from a Large Comparative Study," *California Management Review*, Fall 1989, pp. 89–106.

20. Ibid.

21. Richard M. Steers, "Antecedents and Outcomes of Organizational Commitment," *Administrative Science Quarterly*, 1977, vol. 22, pp. 46–56.

22. For research work in this area, see Jennifer M. George and Gareth R. Jones, "The Experience of Mood and Turnover

Intentions: Interactive Effects of Value Attainment, Job Satisfaction, and Positive Mood," *Journal of Applied Psychology*, 1996, vol. 81, no. 3, pp. 318–325; Larry J. Williams, Mark B. Gavin, and Margaret Williams, "Measurement and Non-measurement Processes with Negative Affectivity and Employee Attitudes," *Journal of Applied Psychology*, 1996, vol. 81, no. 1, pp. 88–101.

23. Kathleen Sutcliffe, "What Executives Notice: Accurate Perceptions in Top Management Teams," *Academy of Management Journal*, 1994, vol. 37, no. 5, pp. 1360–1378.

24. For a classic treatment of attribution, see H. H. Kelley, *Attribution in Social Interaction* (Morristown, N.J.: General Learning Press, 1971).

25. For a recent overview of the stress literature, see Frank Landy, James Campbell Quick, and Stanislav Kasl, "Work, Stress, and Well-Being," *International Journal of Stress Management*, 1994, vol. 1, no. 1, pp. 33–73.

26. Hans Selye, *The Stress of Life* (New York: McGraw-Hill, 1976).

27. M. Friedman and R. H. Rosenman, *Type A Behavior and Your Heart* (New York: Knopf, 1974).

28. "Work & Family," *BusinessWeek*, June 28, 1993, pp. 80–88.

29. Richard S. DeFrank, Robert Konopaske, and John M. Ivancevich, "Executive Travel Stress: Perils of the Road Warrior," *Academy of Management Executive*, 2000, vol. 14, no. 2, pp. 58–67.

30. Steven Rogelberg, Desmond Leach, Peter Warr, and Jennifer Burnfield, "'Not Another Meeting!' Are Meeting Time Demands Related to Employee Well Being?" *Journal of Applied Psychology*, 2006, vol. 91, no. 1, pp. 86–96.

31. "Breaking Point," *Newsweek*, March 6, 1995, pp. 56–62. See also "Rising Job Stress Could Affect Bottom Line," *USA Today*, July 28, 2003, p. 18.

32. John M. Kelly, "Get a Grip on Stress," *HRMagazine*, February 1997, pp. 51–58.

33. "Nice Work if You Can Get It," *BusinessWeek*, January 9, 2006, pp. 56–57.

34. See Richard W. Woodman, John E. Sawyer, and Ricky W. Griffin, "Toward a Theory of Organizational Creativity," *Academy of Management Review*, April 1993, pp. 293–321.

35. Emily Thornton, "Japan's Struggle to be Creative," *Fortune*, April 19, 1993, pp. 129–134.

36. "In Secret Hideaway, Bill Gates Ponders Microsoft's Future," *Wall Street Journal*, March 28, 2005, pp. A1, A13.

37. John Simons, "The $10 Billion Pill," *Fortune*, January 20, 2003, pp. 58–68.

38. Christina E. Shalley, Lucy L. Gilson, and Terry C. Blum, "Matching Creativity Requirements and the Work Environment: Effects on Satisfaction and Intentions to Leave," *Academy of Management Journal*, 2000, vol. 43, no. 2, pp. 215–223. See also Filiz Tabak, "Employee Creative Performance: What Makes It Happen?" *Academy of Management Executive*, 1997, vol. 11, no. 1, pp. 119–122.

39. "That's It, I'm Outa Here," *BusinessWeek*, October 3, 2000, pp. 96–98.

40. For recent findings regarding this behavior, see Philip M. Podsakoff, Scott B. MacKenzie, Julie Beth Paine, and Daniel G. G. Bacharah, "Organizational Citizenship Behaviors: A Critical Review of the Theoretical and Empirical Literature and Suggestions for Future Research," *Journal of Management*, 2000, vol. 26, no. 3, pp. 513–563.

41. Dennis W. Organ "Personality and Organizational Citizenship Behavior," *Journal of Management*, 1994, vol. 20, no. 2, pp. 465–478; Mary Konovsky and S. Douglas Pugh, "Citizenship Behavior and Social Exchange," *Academy of Management Journal*, 1994, vol. 37, no. 3, pp. 656–669; and Jacqueline A-M. Coyle-Shapiro, "A Psychological Contract Perspective on Organizational Citizenship," *Journal of Organizational Behavior*, 2002, vol. 23, pp. 927–946.

42. See Anne O'Leary-Kelly, Ricky W. Griffin, and David J. Glew, "Organization-Motivated Aggression: A Research Framework," *Academy of Management Review*, January 1996, pp. 225–253. See also Ricky Griffin and Yvette Lopez, "'Bad Behavior' in Organization: A Review and Typology for Future Research," *Journal of Management*, 2005, vol. 31, no. 6, pp. 988–1005.

CHAPTER 16

1. Michael Arendt, "Nice Work If You Can Get It," *Business-Week*, January 9, 2006, pp. 56–57; Jody Miller and Matt Miller, "Get a Life!" *Fortune*, November 28, 2005, pp. 109–124 (quote); Danielle Sacks, "Scenes from the Culture Clash," *Fast Company*, January 2006, www.fastcompany.com on May 1, 2006.

2. Richard M. Steers, Gregory A. Bigley, and Lyman W. Porter, *Motivation and Leadership at Work*, 6th ed. (New York: McGraw-Hill, 1996). See also Maureen L. Ambrose and Carol T. Kulik, "Old Friends, New Faces: Motivation Research in the 1990s," *Journal of Management*, 1999, vol. 25, no. 3, pp. 231–292; and Edwin Locke and Gary Lartham, "What Should We Do About Motivation Theory? Six Recommendations for the Twenty-First Century," *Academy of Management Review*, 2004, vol. 29, no. 3, pp. 388–403.

3. See Nigel Nicholson, "How to Motivate Your Problem People," *Harvard Business Review*, January 2003, pp. 57–67. See also Hugo Kehr, "Integrating Implicit Motives, Explicit Motives, and Perceived Abilities: The Compensatory Model of Work Motivation and Volition," *Academy of Management Review*, 2004, vol. 29, no. 3, pp. 479–499.

4. See Jeffrey Pfeffer, *The Human Equation* (Cambridge, Mass.: Harvard Business School Press, 1998).

5. See Craig Pinder, *Work Motivation in Organizational Behavior* (Upper Saddle River, N.J.: Prentice-Hall, 1998).

6. Frederick W. Taylor, *Principles of Scientific Management* (New York: Harper & Brothers, 1911).

7. Elton Mayo, *The Social Problems of an Industrial Civilization* (Cambridge, Mass.: Harvard University Press, 1945); Fritz J. Rothlisberger and W. J. Dickson, *Management and the Worker* (Cambridge, Mass.: Harvard University Press, 1939).

8. For a recent discussion of these questions, see Eryn Brown, "So Rich So Young—But Are They Really Happy?" *Fortune*, September 18, 2000, pp. 99–110.

9. Abraham H. Maslow, "A Theory of Human Motivation," *Psychological Review*, 1943, vol. 50, pp. 370–396; Abraham H. Maslow, *Motivation and Personality* (New York: Harper

& Row, 1954). Maslow's most recent work is Abraham H. Maslow and Richard Lowry, *Toward a Psychology of Being* (New York: Wiley, 1999).

10. For a review, see Pinder, *Work Motivation in Organizational Behavior.*

11. Clayton P. Alderfer, *Existence, Relatedness, and Growth* (New York: Free Press, 1972).

12. Frederick Herzberg, Bernard Mausner, and Barbara Snyderman, *The Motivation to Work* (New York: Wiley, 1959); Frederick Herzberg, "One More Time: How Do You Motivate Employees?" *Harvard Business Review*, January–February 1987, pp. 109–120 (reprinted in *Harvard Business Review*, January 2003, pp. 87–98).

13. Robert J. House and Lawrence A. Wigdor, "Herzberg's Dual-Factor Theory of Job Satisfaction and Motivation: A Review of the Evidence and a Criticism," *Personnel Psychology*, Winter 1967, pp. 369–389; Victor H. Vroom, *Work and Motivation* (New York: Wiley, 1964). See also Pinder, *Work Motivation in Organizational Behavior.*

14. David C. McClelland, *The Achieving Society* (Princeton, N.J.: Van Nostrand, 1961); David C. McClelland, *Power: The Inner Experience* (New York: Irvington, 1975).

15. "Best Friends Good for Business," *USA Today*, December 1, 2004, pp. 1B, 2B.

16. David McClelland and David H. Burnham, "Power Is the Great Motivator," *Harvard Business Review*, March–April 1976, pp. 100–110 (reprinted in *Harvard Business Review*, January 2003, pp. 117–127).

17. See "The Rise and Fall of Dennis Kozlowski," *BusinessWeek*, December 23, 2002, pp. 64–77.

18. Victor H. Vroom, *Work and Motivation* (New York: Wiley, 1964).

19. "Starbucks' Secret Weapon," *Fortune*, September 29, 1997, p. 268.

20. Lyman W. Porter and Edward E. Lawler III, *Managerial Attitudes and Performance* (Homewood, Ill.: Dorsey, 1968).

21. J. Stacy Adams, "Towards an Understanding of Inequity," *Journal of Abnormal and Social Psychology*, November 1963, pp. 422–436.

22. "The Best vs. the Rest," *Wall Street Journal*, January 30, 2006, pp. B1, B3.

23. See Edwin A. Locke, "Toward a Theory of Task Performance and Incentives," *Organizational Behavior and Human Performance*, 1968, vol. 3, pp. 157–189.

24. Gary P. Latham and J. J. Baldes, "The Practical Significance of Locke's Theory of Goal Setting," *Journal of Applied Psychology*, 1975, vol. 60, pp. 187–191.

25. For a recent extension of goal-setting theory, see Yitzhak Fried and Linda Haynes Slowik, "Enriching Goal-Setting Theory with Time: An Integrated Approach," *Academy of Management Review*, 2004, vol. 29, no. 3, pp. 404–422.

26. B. F. Skinner, *Beyond Freedom and Dignity* (New York: Knopf, 1971).

27. Fred Luthans and Robert Kreitner, *Organizational Behavior Modification and Beyond: An Operant and Social Learning Approach* (Glenview, Ill.: Scott, Foresman, 1985).

28. Ibid.; W. Clay Hamner and Ellen P. Hamner, "Behavior Modification on the Bottom Line," *Organizational Dynamics*, Spring 1976, pp. 2–21.

29. "At Emery Air Freight: Positive Reinforcement Boosts Performance," *Organizational Dynamics*, Winter 1973, pp. 41–50; for a recent update, see Alexander D. Stajkovic and Fred Luthans, "A Meta-Analysis of the Effects of Organizational Behavior Modification on Task Performance, 1975–95," *Academy of Management Journal*, 1997, vol. 40, no. 5, pp. 1122–1149.

30. David J. Glew, Anne M. O'Leary-Kelly, Ricky W. Griffin, and David D. Van Fleet, "Participation in Organizations: A Preview of the Issues and Proposed Framework for Future Analysis," *Journal of Management*, 1995, vol. 21, no. 3, pp. 395–421.

31. Robert E. Quinn and Gretchen M. Spreitzer, "The Road to Empowerment: Seven Questions Every Leader Should Consider," *Organizational Dynamics*, Autumn 1997, pp. 37–47.

32. "On Factory Floors, Top Workers Hide Secrets to Success," *Wall Street Journal*, July 1, 2002, pp. A1, A10.

33. Russ Forrester, "Empowerment: Rejuvenating a Potent Idea," *Academy of Management Executive*, 2000, vol. 14, no. 3, pp. 67–77.

34. Baxter W. Graham, "The Business Argument for Flexibility," *HRMagazine*, May 1996, pp. 104–110.

35. A. R. Cohen and H. Gadon, *Alternative Work Schedules: Integrating Individual and Organizational Needs* (Reading, Mass.: Addison-Wesley, 1978).

36. "The Easiest Commute of All," *BusinessWeek*, December 12, 2005, pp. 78–80.

37. Daniel Wren, *The Evolution of Management Theory*, 4th ed. (New York: Wiley, 1994).

38. C. Wiley, "Incentive Plan Pushes Production," *Personnel Journal*, August 1993, p. 91.

39. "When Money Isn't Enough," *Forbes*, November 18, 1996, pp. 164–169.

40. Jacquelyn DeMatteo, Lillian Eby, and Eric Sundstrom, "Team-Based Rewards: Current Empirical Evidence and Directions for Future Research," in L. L. Cummings and Barry Staw (eds.), *Research in Organizational Behavior*, vol. 20 (Greenwich, Conn.: JAI, 1998), pp. 141–183.

41. Theresa M. Welbourne and Luis R. Gomez-Mejia, "Gainsharing: A Critical Review and a Future Research Agenda," *Journal of Management*, 1995, vol. 21, no. 3, pp. 559–609.

42. Harry Barkema and Luis Gomez-Mejia, "Managerial Compensation and Firm Performance: A General Research Framework," *Academy of Management Journal*, 1998, vol. 41, no. 2, pp. 135–145.

43. Rajiv D. Banker, Seok-Young Lee, Gordon Potter, and Dhinu Srinivasan, "Contextual Analysis of Performance Impacts of Outcome-Based Incentive Compensation," *Academy of Management Journal*, 1996, vol. 39, no. 4, pp. 920–948.

44. M. Blair, "CEO Pay: Why Such a Contentious Issue?" *The Brookings Review*, Winter 1994, pp. 23–27.

45. Steve Kerr, "The Best-Laid Incentive Plans," *Harvard Business Review*, January 2003, pp. 27–40.

46. "Now It's Getting Personal," *BusinessWeek*, December 16, 2002, pp. 90–92.

CHAPTER **17**

1. Leslie Berlin, *The Man Behind the Microchip: Robert Noyce and the Invention of Silicon Valley* (New York: Oxford University Press, 2005); Cliff Edwards, "Inside Intel," *BusinessWeek*, January 9, 2006, pp. 47–54; Arik Hesseldahl, "Intel on the Offensive," *BusinessWeek*, April 28, 2006, www.businessweek.com on April 28, 2006; David Kirkpatrick, "Intel Finally Fights Back," *Fortune*, April 27, 2006, www.fortune.com on May 1, 2006; Adam Lashinsky, "Is This the Right Man for Intel?" *Fortune*, April 18, 2005, www.fortune.com on May 1, 2006; Mukul Pandya, et al., *Lasting Leadership: What You Can Learn from the Top 25 Business People of Our Times* (Upper Saddle River, N.J.: Wharton School Publishing, 2004) (quote).

2. See Ronald A. Heifetz and Donald L. Laurie, "The Work of Leadership," *Harvard Business Review*, January–February 1997, pp. 124–134. See also Arthur G. Jago, "Leadership: Perspectives in Theory and Research," *Management Science*, March 1982, pp. 315–336, and "The New Leadership," *BusinessWeek*, August 28, 2000, pp. 100–187.

3. Gary A. Yukl, *Leadership in Organizations*, 3rd ed. (Englewood Cliffs, N.J.: Prentice-Hall, 1994), p. 5. See also Gregory G. Dess and Joseph C. Pickens, "Changing Roles: Leadership in the 21st Century," *Organizational Dynamics*, Winter 2000, pp. 18–28.

4. John P. Kotter, "What Leaders Really Do," *Harvard Business Review*, May–June 1990, pp. 103–111 (reprinted in *Harvard Business Review*, December 2001, pp. 85–93). See also Daniel Goleman, "Leadership That Gets Results," *Harvard Business Review*, March–April 2000, pp. 78–88; and Keith Grints, *The Arts of Leadership* (Oxford, U.K.: Oxford University Press, 2000).

5. John R. P. French and Bertram Raven, "The Bases of Social Power," in Dorwin Cartwright (ed.), *Studies in Social Power* (Ann Arbor, Mich.: University of Michigan Press, 1959), pp. 150–167.

6. Hugh D. Menzies, "The Ten Toughest Bosses," *Fortune*, April 21, 1980, pp. 62–73.

7. Bennett J. Tepper, "Consequences of Abusive Supervision," *Academy of Management Journal*, 2000, vol. 43, no. 2, pp. 178–190.

8. Thomas A. Stewart, "Get with the New Power Game," *Fortune*, January 13, 1997, pp. 58–62.

9. For more information on the bases and uses of power, see Philip M. Podsakoff and Chester A. Schriesheim, "Field Studies of French and Raven's Bases of Power: Critique, Reanalysis, and Suggestions for Future Research," *Psychological Bulletin*, 1985, vol. 97, pp. 387–411; Robert C. Benfari, Harry E. Wilkinson, and Charles D. Orth, "The Effective Use of Power," *Business Horizons*, May–June 1986, pp. 12–16; and Yukl, *Leadership in Organizations*.

10. Bernard M. Bass, *Bass & Stogdill's Handbook of Leadership*, 3rd ed. (Riverside, N.J.: Free Press, 1990).

11. Shelley A. Kirkpatrick and Edwin A. Locke, "Leadership: Do Traits Matter?" *Academy of Management Executive*, May 1991, pp. 48–60. See also Robert J. Sternberg, "Managerial Intelligence: Why IQ Isn't Enough," *Journal of Management*, 1997, vol. 23, no. 3, pp. 475–493.

12. Timothy Judge, Amy Colbert, and Remus Ilies, "Intelligence and Leadership: A Quantitative Review and Test of Theoretical Propositions," *Journal of Applied Psychology*, 2004, vol. 89, no. 3, pp. 542–552.

13. Rensis Likert, *New Patterns of Management* (New York: McGraw-Hill, 1961); Rensis Likert, *The Human Organization* (New York: McGraw-Hill, 1967).

14. The Ohio State studies stimulated many articles, monographs, and books. A good overall reference is Ralph M. Stogdill and A. E. Coons, eds., *Leader Behavior: Its Description and Measurement* (Columbus, Ohio: Bureau of Business Research, Ohio State University, 1957).

15. Edwin A. Fleishman, E. F. Harris, and H. E. Burt, *Leadership and Supervision in Industry* (Columbus, Ohio: Bureau of Business Research, Ohio State University, 1955).

16. See Timothy Judge, Ronald Piccolo, and Remus Ilies, "The Forgotten One? The Validity of Consideration and Initiating Structure in Leadership Research," *Journal of Applied Psychology*, 2004, vol. 89, no. 1, pp. 36–51.

17. Robert R. Blake and Jane S. Mouton, *The Managerial Grid* (Houston: Gulf Publishing, 1964); Robert R. Blake and Jane S. Mouton, *The Versatile Manager: A Grid Profile* (Homewood, Ill.: Dow Jones-Irwin, 1981).

18. Robert Tannenbaum and Warren H. Schmidt, "How to Choose a Leadership Pattern," *Harvard Business Review*, March–April 1958, pp. 95–101.

19. Fred E. Fiedler, *A Theory of Leadership Effectiveness* (New York: McGraw-Hill, 1967).

20. Chester A. Schriesheim, Bennett J. Tepper, and Linda A. Tetrault, "Least Preferred Co-Worker Score, Situational Control, and Leadership Effectiveness: A Meta-Analysis of Contingency Model Performance Predictions," *Journal of Applied Psychology*, 1994, vol. 79, no. 4, pp. 561–573.

21. Fiedler, *A Theory of Leadership Effectiveness*; Fred E. Fiedler and M. M. Chemers, *Leadership and Effective Management* (Glenview, Ill.: Scott, Foresman, 1974).

22. For recent reviews and updates, see Lawrence H. Peters, Darrell D. Hartke, and John T. Pohlmann, "Fiedler's Contingency Theory of Leadership: An Application of the Meta-Analysis Procedures of Schmidt and Hunter," *Psychological Bulletin*, vol. 97, pp. 274–285; and Fred E. Fiedler, "When to Lead, When to Stand Back," *Psychology Today*, September 1987, pp. 26–27.

23. Martin G. Evans, "The Effects of Supervisory Behavior on the Path-Goal Relationship," *Organizational Behavior and Human Performance*, May 1970, pp. 277–298; Robert J. House and Terence R. Mitchell, "Path-Goal Theory of Leadership," *Journal of Contemporary Business*, Autumn 1974, pp. 81–98. See also Yukl, *Leadership in Organizations*.

24. For a recent review, see J. C. Wofford and Laurie Z. Liska, "Path-Goal Theories of Leadership: A Meta-Analysis," *Journal of Management*, 1993, vol. 19, no. 4, pp. 857–876.

25. See Victor H. Vroom and Philip H. Yetton, *Leadership and Decision Making* (Pittsburgh: University of Pittsburgh Press, 1973); and Victor H. Vroom and Arthur G. Jago, *The New Leadership* (Englewood Cliffs, N.J.: Prentice-Hall, 1988).

26. Victor Vroom, "Leadership and the Decision-Making Process," *Organizational Dynamics*, 2000, vol. 28, no. 4, pp. 82–94.

27. Vroom and Jago, *The New Leadership*.

28. Ibid.

29. See Madeline E. Heilman, Harvey A. Hornstein, Jack H. Cage, and Judith K. Herschlag, "Reaction to Prescribed Leader Behavior as a Function of Role Perspective: The Case of the Vroom-Yetton Model," *Journal of Applied Psychology*, February 1984, pp. 50–60; R. H. George Field, "A Test of the Vroom-Yetton Normative Model of Leadership," *Journal of Applied Psychology*, February 1982, pp. 523–532.

30. George Graen and J. F. Cashman, "A Role-Making Model of Leadership in Formal Organizations: A Developmental Approach," in J. G. Hunt and L. L. Larson (eds.), *Leadership Frontiers* (Kent, Ohio: Kent State University Press, 1975), pp. 143–165; Fred Dansereau, George Graen, and W. J. Haga, "A Vertical Dyad Linkage Approach to Leadership Within Formal Organizations: A Longitudinal Investigation of the Role-Making Process," *Organizational Behavior and Human Performance*, 1975, vol. 15, pp. 46–78.

31. See Kathryn Sherony and Stephen Green, "Coworker Exchange: Relationships Between Coworkers, Leader-Member Exchange, and Work Attitudes," *Journal of Applied Psychology*, 2002, vol. 87, no. 3, pp. 542–548.

32. Steven Kerr and John M. Jermier, "Substitutes for Leadership: Their Meaning and Measurement," *Organizational Behavior and Human Performance*, December 1978, pp. 375–403.

33. See Charles C. Manz and Henry P. Sims, Jr., "Leading Workers to Lead Themselves: The External Leadership of Self-Managing Work Teams," *Administrative Science Quarterly*, March 1987, pp. 106–129. See also "Living Without a Leader," *Fortune*, March 20, 2000, pp. 218–219.

34. See Robert J. House, "A 1976 Theory of Charismatic Leadership," in J. G. Hunt and L. L. Larson (eds.), *Leadership: The Cutting Edge* (Carbondale, Ill.: Southern Illinois University Press, 1977), pp. 189–207. See also Jay A. Conger and Rabindra N. Kanungo, "Toward a Behavioral Theory of Charismatic Leadership in Organizational Settings," *Academy of Management Review*, October 1987, pp. 637–647.

35. Stratford P. Sherman, "Donald Trump Just Won't Die," *Fortune*, August 13, 1990, pp. 75–79.

36. David A. Nadler and Michael L. Tushman, "Beyond the Charismatic Leader: Leadership and Organizational Change," *California Management Review*, Winter 1990, pp. 77–97.

37. Jane Howell and Boas Shamir, "The Role of Followers in the Charismatic Leadership Process: Relationships and Their Consequences," *Academy of Management Review*, 2005, vol. 30, no. 1, pp. 96–112.

38. James MacGregor Burns, *Leadership* (New York: Harper & Row, 1978). See also Rajnandini Pillai, Chester A. Schriesheim, and Eric J. Williams, "Fairness Perceptions and Trust as Mediators for Transformational and Transactional Leadership: A Two-Sample Study," *Journal of Management*, 1999, vol. 25, no. 6, pp. 897–933.

39. Robert Rubin, David Munz, and William Bommer, "Leading from Within: The Effects of Emotion Recognition and Personality on Transformational Leadership Behaviors," *Academy of Management Journal*, 2005, vol. 48, no. 5, pp. 845–858.

40. Labich, "The Seven Keys to Business Leadership."

41. Jerry Useem, "Tape + Light Bulbs = ?" *Fortune*, August 12, 2002, pp. 127–132.

42. Dusya Vera and Mary Crossan, "Strategic Leadership and Organizational Learning," *Academy of Management Review*, 2004, vol. 29, no. 2, pp. 222–240.

43. The Best & Worst Managers of the Year," *BusinessWeek*, January 19, 2005, pp. 55–84.

44. See Kurt Dirks and Donald Ferrin, "Trust in Leadership," *Journal of Applied Psychology*, 2002, vol. 87, no. 4, pp. 611–628.

45. Jeffrey Pfeffer, *Power in Organizations* (Marshfield, Mass.: Pitman, 1981), p. 7.

46. Timothy Judge and Robert Bretz, "Political Influence Behavior and Career Success," *Journal of Management*, 1994, vol. 20, no. 1, pp. 43–65.

47. Victor Murray and Jeffrey Gandz, "Games Executives Play: Politics at Work," *Business Horizons*, December 1980, pp. 11–23; Jeffrey Gandz and Victor Murray, "The Experience of Workplace Politics," *Academy of Management Journal*, June 1980, pp. 237–251.

48. Don R. Beeman and Thomas W. Sharkey, "The Use and Abuse of Corporate Power," *Business Horizons*, March–April 1987, pp. 26–30.

49. How Ebbers Kept the Board in His Pocket," *BusinessWeek*, October 14, 2002, pp. 138–139.

50. See William L. Gardner, "Lessons in Organizational Dramaturgy: The Art of Impression Management," *Organizational Dynamics*, Summer 1992, pp. 51–63; Elizabeth Wolf Morrison and Robert J. Bies, "Impression Management in the Feedback-Seeking Process: A Literature Review and Research Agenda," *Academy of Management Review*, July 1991, pp. 522–541.

51. See Chad Higgins, Timothy Judge, and Gerald Ferris, "Influence Tactics and Work Outcomes: A Meta-Analysis," *Journal of Organizational Behavior*, 2003, vol. 24, pp. 89–106.

52. Murray and Gandz, "Games Executives Play."

53. Beeman and Sharkey, "The Use and Abuse of Corporate Power."

54. Stefanie Ann Lenway and Kathleen Rehbein, "Leaders, Followers, and Free Riders: An Empirical Test of Variation in Corporate Political Involvement," *Academy of Management Journal*, December 1991, pp. 893–905.

CHAPTER 18

1. Hugh Anderson, "Phone-Interview Tips for Savvy Candidates," *Wall Street Journal* executive career website, www.careerjournal.com on May 2, 2006; Anne Fisher, "Fear of Phoning," *Fortune*, September 6, 2005, www.fortune.com on May 2, 2006; Anne Fisher, "How Can I Survive a Phone Interview?" *Fortune*, April 19, 2004, www.fortune.com on May 2, 2006; "Phone Interview Success," CollegeGrad.com website, May 2, 2006.

2. See John J. Gabarro, "The Development of Working Relationships," in Jay W. Lorsch (ed.), *Handbook of Organizational Behavior* (Englewood Cliffs, N.J.: Prentice-Hall, 1987), pp. 172–189. See also "Team Efforts, Technology, Add New Reasons to Meet," *USA Today*, December 8, 1997, pp. 1A, 2A.

3. See C. Gopinath and Thomas E. Becker, "Communication, Procedural Justice, and Employee Attitudes: Relationships Under Conditions of Divestiture," *Journal of Management*, 2000, vol. 26, no. 1, pp. 63–83.

4. Henry Mintzberg, *The Nature of Managerial Work* (New York: Harper & Row, 1973).

5. "At Sears, a Great Communicator," *BusinessWeek*, October 31, 2005, pp. 50–52.

6. Ibid.

7. See Batia M. Wiesenfeld, Sumita Charan, and Raghu Garud, "Communication Patterns as Determinants of Organizational Identification in a Virtual Organization," *Organization Science*, 1999, vol. 10, no. 6, pp. 777–790.

8. Bruce Barry and Ingrid Fulmer, "The Medium and the Message: The Adaptive Use of Communication Media in Dyadic Influence," *Academy of Management Review*, 2004, vol. 29, no. 2, pp. 272–292.

9. Mintzberg, *The Nature of Managerial Work*.

10. Reid Buckley, "When You Have to Put It to Them," *Across the Board*, October 1999, pp. 44–48.

11. "'Did I Just Say That?!' How to Recover from Foot-in-Mouth," *Wall Street Journal*, June 19, 2002, p. B1.

12. "Executives Who Dread Public Speaking Learn to Keep Their Cool in the Spotlight," *Wall Street Journal*, May 4, 1990, pp. B1, B6.

13. Mintzberg, *The Nature of Managerial Work*.

14. Buckley, "When You Have to Put It to Them."

15. See "Watch What You Put in That Office Email," *BusinessWeek*, September 30, 2002, pp. 114–115.

16. Nicholas Varchaver, "The Perils of E-mail," *Fortune*, February 17, 2003, pp. 96–102; "How a String of E-Mail Came to Haunt CSFB and Star Banker," *Wall Street Journal*, February 28, 2003, pp. A1, A6; "How Morgan Stanley Botched a Big Case by Fumbling Emails," *Wall Street Journal*, May 16, 2005, pp. A1, A10.

17. A. Vavelas, "Communication Patterns in Task-Oriented Groups," *Journal of the Accoustical Society of America*, 1950, vol. 22, pp. 725–730; Jerry Wofford, Edwin Gerloff, and Robert Cummins, *Organizational Communication* (New York: McGraw-Hill, 1977).

18. Nelson Phillips and John Brown, "Analyzing Communications in and Around Organizations: A Critical Hermeneutic Approach," *Academy of Management Journal*, 1993, vol. 36, no. 6, pp. 1547–1576.

19. Walter Kiechel III, "Breaking Bad News to the Boss," *Fortune*, April 9, 1990, pp. 111–112.

20. Mary Young and James Post, "How Leading Companies Communicate with Employees," *Organizational Dynamics*, Summer 1993, pp. 31–43.

21. For one example, see Kimberly D. Elsbach and Greg Elofson, "How the Packaging of Decision Explanations Affects Perceptions of Trustworthiness," *Academy of Management Journal*, 2000, vol. 43, no. 1, pp. 80–89.

22. Walter Kiechel III, "Hold for the Communicaholic Manager," *Fortune*, January 2, 1989, pp. 107–108.

23. "Those Bawdy E-Mails Were Good for a Laugh—Until the Ax Fell," *Wall Street Journal*, February 4, 2000, pp. A1, A8.

24. Keith Davis, "Management Communication and the Grapevine," *Harvard Business Review*, September–October 1953, pp. 43–49.

25. "Spread the Word: Gossip Is Good," *Wall Street Journal*, October 4, 1988, p. B1.

26. See David M. Schweiger and Angelo S. DeNisi, "Communication with Employees Following a Merger: A Longitudinal Field Experiment," *Academy of Management Journal*, March 1991, pp. 110–135.

27. Nancy B. Kurland and Lisa Hope Pelled, "Passing the Word: Toward a Model of Gossip and Power in the Workplace," *Academy of Management Review*, 2000, vol. 25, no. 2, pp. 428–438.

28. See Tom Peters and Nancy Austin, *A Passion for Excellence* (New York: Random House, 1985).

29. Albert Mehrabian, *Non-verbal Communication* (Chicago: Aldine, 1972).

30. Michael B. McCaskey, "The Hidden Messages Managers Send," *Harvard Business Review*, November–December 1979, pp. 135–148.

31. David Givens, "What Body Language Can Tell You That Words Cannot," *U.S. News & World Report*, November 19, 1984, p. 100.

32. Edward J. Hall, *The Hidden Dimension* (New York: Doubleday, 1966).

33. For a detailed discussion of improving communication effectiveness, see Courtland L. Bovee, John V. Thill, and Barbara E. Schatzman, *Business Communication Today*, 7th ed. (Upper Saddle River, N.J.: Prentice-Hall, 2003).

34. See Otis W. Baskin and Craig E. Aronoff, *Interpersonal Communication in Organizations* (Glenview, Ill.: Scott, Foresman, 1980).

35. See "You Have (Too Much) E-Mail," *USA Today*, March 12, 1999, p. 3B.

36. Justin Fox, "The Triumph of English," *Fortune*, September 18, 2000, pp. 209–212.

37. Joseph Allen and Bennett P. Lientz, *Effective Business Communication* (Santa Monica, Calif.: Goodyear, 1979).

38. See "Making Silence Your Ally," *Across the Board*, October 1999, p. 11.

39. Boyd A. Vander Houwen, "Less Talking, More Listening," *HRMagazine*, April 1997, pp. 53–58.

40. For a discussion of these and related issues, see Eric M. Eisenberg and Marsha G. Witten, "Reconsidering Openness in Organizational Communication," *Academy of Management Review*, July 1987, pp. 418–426.

41. For a recent illustration, see Barbara Kellerman, "When Should a Leader Apologize—and When Not?" *Harvard Business Review*, April 2006, pp. 72–81.

CHAPTER 19

1. Bill Chastain, "Q&A with Stuart Sternberg," Devil Rays website, October 6, 2005, tampabay.devilrays.mlb.com on May 4, 2006; Mark Hyman, "Baseball: Money Can't Buy Me Wins," *BusinessWeek*, October 4, 2005, www.businessweek.com on May 4, 2006; Chris Isidore, "Baseball Spending Spree Ahead," *Money*, October 7, 2005, www.cnnmoney.com on May 4, 2006; Landon Thomas Jr., "Case Study: Fix a Baseball Team," *New York Times*, April 2, 2006, pp. BU 1, 9 (quote).

2. For a review of definitions of groups, see Gregory Moorhead and Ricky W. Griffin, *Organizational Behavior*, 8th ed. (Boston: Houghton Mifflin, 2007).

3. Dorwin Cartwright and Alvin Zander, eds., *Group Dynamics: Research and Theory*, 3rd ed. (New York: Harper & Row, 1968).

4. Rob Cross, Nitin Nohria, and Andrew Parker, "Six Myths About Informal Networks—and How to Overcome Them," *Sloan Management Review*, Spring 2002, pp. 67–77.

5. Robert Schrank, *Ten Thousand Working Days* (Cambridge, Mass.: MIT Press, 1978); Bill Watson, "Counter Planning on the Shop Floor," in Peter Frost, Vance Mitchell, and Walter Nord (eds.), *Organizational Reality*, 2nd ed. (Glenview, Ill.: Scott, Foresman, 1982), pp. 286–294.

6. "After Layoffs, More Workers Band Together," *Wall Street Journal*, February 26, 2002, p. B1.

7. Bradley L. Kirkman and Benson Rosen, "Powering Up Teams," *Organizational Dynamics*, Winter 2000, pp. 48–58.

8. Brian Dumaine, "Payoff from the New Management," *Fortune*, December 13, 1993, pp. 103–110.

9. "Why Teams Fail," *USA Today*, February 25, 1997, pp. 1B, 2B.

10. Brian Dumaine, "The Trouble with Teams," *Fortune*, September 5, 1994, pp. 86–92. See also Susan G. Cohen and Diane E. Bailey, "What Makes Teams Work: Group Effectiveness Research from the Shop Floor to the Executive Suite," *Journal of Management*, 1997, vol. 23, no. 3, pp. 239–290; and John Mathieu, Lucy Gilson, and Thomas Ruddy, "Empowerment and Team Effectiveness: An Empirical Test of an Integrated Model," *Journal of Applied Psychology*, 2006, vol. 91, no. 1, pp. 97–108.

11. Marvin E. Shaw, *Group Dynamics: The Psychology of Small Group Behavior*, 4th ed. (New York: McGraw-Hill, 1985).

12. "How to Avoid Hiring the Prima Donnas Who Hate Teamwork," *Wall Street Journal*, February 15, 2000, p. B1.

13. See Connie Gersick, "Marking Time: Predictable Transitions in Task Groups," *Academy of Management Journal*, June 1989, pp. 274–309. See also Avan R. Jassawalla and Hemant C. Sashittal, "Building Collaborative Cross-Functional New Product Teams," *Academy of Management Review*, 1999, vol. 13, no. 3, pp. 50–60.

14. See Gilad Chen, "Newcomer Adaptation in Teams: Multilevel Antecedents and Outcomes," *Academy of Management Journal*, 2005, vol. 48, no. 1, pp. 101–116.

15. For a review of other team characteristics, see Michael Campion, Gina Medsker, and A. Catherine Higgs, "Relations Between Work Group Characteristics and Effectiveness: Implications for Designing Effective Work Groups," *Personnel Psychology*, Winter 1993, pp. 823–850.

16. David Katz and Robert L. Kahn, *The Social Psychology of Organizations*, 2nd ed. (New York: Wiley, 1978), pp. 187–221. See also Greg L. Stewart and Murray R. Barrick, "Team Structure and Performance: Assessing the Mediating Role of Intrateam Process and the Moderating Role of Task Type," *Academy of Management Journal*, 2000, vol. 43, no. 2, pp. 135–148; and Michael G. Pratt and Peter O. Foreman, "Classifying Managerial Responses to Multiple Organizational Identities," *Academy of Management Review*, 2000, vol. 25, no. 1, pp. 18–42.

17. See Travis C. Tubre and Judith M. Collins, "Jackson and Schuler (1985) Revisited: A Meta-Analysis of the Relationships Between Role Ambiguity, Role Conflict, and Job Performance," *Journal of Management*, 2000, vol. 26, no. 1, pp. 155–169.

18. Robert L. Kahn, D. M. Wolfe, R. P. Quinn, J. D. Snoek, and R. A. Rosenthal, *Organizational Stress: Studies in Role Conflict and Role Ambiguity* (New York: Wiley, 1964).

19. Daniel C. Feldman, "The Development and Enforcement of Group Norms," *Academy of Management Review*, January 1984, pp. 47–53.

20. "Companies Turn to Peer Pressure to Cut Injuries as Psychologists Join the Battle," *Wall Street Journal*, March 29, 1991, pp. B1, B3.

21. James Wallace Bishop and K. Dow Scott, "How Commitment Affects Team Performance," *HRMagazine*, February 1997, pp. 107–115.

22. Anne O'Leary-Kelly, Joseph Martocchio, and Dwight Frink, "A Review of the Influence of Group Goals on Group Performance," *Academy of Management Journal*, 1994, vol. 37, no. 5, pp. 1285–1301.

23. Philip M. Podsakoff, Michael Ahearne, and Scott B. MacKenzie, "Organizational Citizenship Behavior and the Quantity and Quality of Work Group Performance, *Journal of Applied Psychology*, 1997, vol. 82, no. 2, pp. 262–270.

24. Suzy Wetlaufer, "Common Sense and Conflict," *Harvard Business Review*, January–February 2000, pp. 115–125.

25. Kathleen M. Eisenhardt, Jean L. Kahwajy, and L. J. Bourgeois III, "How Management Teams Can Have a Good Fight," *Harvard Business Review*, July–August 1997, pp. 77–89.

26. Thomas Bergmann and Roger Volkema, "Issues, Behavioral Responses and Consequences in Interpersonal Conflicts," *Journal of Organizational Behavior*, 1994, vol. 15, pp. 467–471.

27. Robin Pinkley and Gregory Northcraft, "Conflict Frames of Reference: Implications for Dispute Processes and Outcomes," *Academy of Management Journal*, 1994, vol. 37, no. 1, pp. 193–205.

28. "How 2 Computer Nuts Transformed Industry Before Messy Breakup," *Wall Street Journal*, August 27, 1996, pp. A1, A10.

29. Bruce Barry and Greg L. Stewart, "Composition, Process, and Performance in Self-Managed Groups: The Role of Personality," *Journal of Applied Psychology*, 1997, vol. 82, no. 1, pp. 62–78.

30. "Rumsfeld's Abrasive Style Sparks Conflict with Military Command," *USA Today*, December 10, 2002, pp. 1A, 2A.

31. "Delta CEO Resigns After Clashes with Board," *USA Today*, May 13, 1997, p. B1.

32. "Why Boeing's Culture Breeds Turmoil," *BusinessWeek*, March 21, 2005, pp. 34–36.

33. "A 'Blood War' in the Jeans Trade," *BusinessWeek*, November 13, 1999, pp. 74–81.

34. Peter Elkind, "Blood Feud," *Fortune*, April 14, 1997, pp. 90–102.

35. See Patrick Nugent, "Managing Conflict: Third-Party Interventions for Managers," *Academy of Management Executive*, 2002, vol. 16, no. 1, pp. 139–148.

36. "Solving Conflicts in the Workplace Without Making Losers," *Wall Street Journal*, May 27, 1997, p. B1.

37. "Teaching Business How to Cope with Workplace Conflicts," *BusinessWeek*, February 18, 1990, pp. 136, 139.

CHAPTER 20

1. Mara Der Hovanesian, "Dimon in the Rough," *Business-Week*, March 28, 2005, www.businessweek.com on May 22, 2006; "Dimon's Grand Design," *BusinessWeek*, March 28, 2005, www.businessweek.com on May 22, 2006; "Jamie Dimon, In His Own Words," *BusinessWeek*, March 28, 2005, www.businessweek.com on May 22, 2006 (quote); Shawn Tully, "The Contender: Jamie Dimon, The New CEO of J. P. Morgan Chase," *Fortune*, April 3, 2006, pp. 54–66.

2. For a complete discussion of how FedEx uses control in its operations, see "The FedEx Edge," *Fortune*, April 3, 2006, pp. 77–84. Note also the "Technology Toolkit" elsewhere in this chapter.

3. Thomas A. Stewart, "Welcome to the Revolution," *Fortune*, December 13, 1993, pp. 66–77.

4. William Taylor, "Control in an Age of Chaos," *Harvard Business Review*, November–December 1994, pp. 64–70.

5. "Fleetwood: Not a Happy Camper Company," *Business-Week*, October 9, 2000, pp. 88–90.

6. "An Apple a Day," *BusinessWeek*, October 14, 2002, pp. 122–125; "More Business People Say: Let's Not Do Lunch," *USA Today*, December 24, 2002, p. 1B; David Stires, "The Breaking Point," *Fortune*, March 3, 2003, pp. 107–114.

7. Mark Kroll, Peter Wright, Leslie Toombs, and Hadley Leavell, "Form of Control: A Critical Determinant of Acquisition Performance and CEO Rewards," *Strategic Management Journal*, 1997, vol. 18, no. 2, pp. 85–96.

8. See Karynne Turner and Mona Makhija, "The Role of Organizational Controls in Managing Knowledge," *Academy of Management Review*, 2006, vol. 31, no. 1, pp. 197–217.

9. "It's Showtime for the Airlines," *BusinessWeek*, September 2, 2002, pp. 36–37.

10. "United's Bid to Cut Labor Costs Could Force Rivals to Follow," *Wall Street Journal*, February 25, 2003, pp. A1, A6.

11. Sim Sitkin, Kathleen Sutcliffe, and Roger Schroeder, "Distinguishing Control from Learning in Total Quality Management: A Contingency Perspective," *Academy of Management Review*, 1994, vol. 19, no. 3, pp. 537–564.

12. Robert Lusch and Michael Harvey, "The Case for an Off-Balance-Sheet Controller," *Sloan Management Review*, Winter 1994, pp. 101–110.

13. Edward E. Lawler III and John G. Rhode, *Information and Control in Organizations* (Pacific Palisades, Calif.: Goodyear, 1976).

14. Charles W. L. Hill, "Establishing a Standard: Competitive Strategy and Technological Standards in Winner-Take-All Industries," *Academy of Management Executive*, 1997, vol. 11, no. 2, pp. 7–16.

15. "Shifting Burden Helps Employers Cut Health Costs," *Wall Street Journal*, December 8, 2005, pp. B1, B2.

16. "An Efficiency Guru Refits Honda to Fight Auto Giants," *Wall Street Journal*, September 15, 1999, p. B1.

17. See "To Shed Idled Workers, Ford Offers to Foot Bill for College," *Wall Street Journal*, January 18, 2006, pp. B1, B3; "GM's Employees Buyout Offer," *Fast Company*, May 2006, p. 58.

18. See Belverd E. Needles, Jr., Henry R. Anderson, and James C. Caldwell, *Principles of Accounting*, 2002 ed. (Boston: Houghton Mifflin, 2002).

19. "At Disney, String of Weak Cartoons Leads to Cost Cuts," *Wall Street Journal*, June 18, 2002, pp. A1, A6.

20. Needles, Anderson, and Caldwell, *Principles of Accounting*.

21. "Mickey Mouse, CPA," *Forbes*, March 10, 1997, pp. 42–43.

22. Needles, Anderson, and Caldwell, *Principles of Accounting*.

23. Jeremy Kahn, "Do Accountants Have a Future?" *Fortune*, March 3, 2003, pp. 115–117.

24. "Inside WorldCom's Unearthing of a Vast Accounting Scandal," *Wall Street Journal*, June 27, 2002, pp. A1, A12.

25. William G. Ouchi, "The Transmission of Control Through Organizational Hierarchy," *Academy of Management Journal*, June 1978, pp. 173–192; Richard E. Walton, "From Control to Commitment in the Workplace," *Harvard Business Review*, March–April 1985, pp. 76–84.

26. "Nordstrom Cleans Out Its Closets," *BusinessWeek*, May 22, 2000, pp. 105–108.

27. "Best Managed Companies in America," *Forbes*, January 9, 2006, p. 118.

28. See "In Bow to Retailers New Clout, Levi Strauss Makes Alterations," *Wall Street Journal*, June 17, 2005, pp. A1, A15.

29. Peter Lorange, Michael F. Scott Morton, and Sumantra Ghoshal, *Strategic Control* (St. Paul, Minn.: West, 1986). See also Joseph C. Picken and Gregory G. Dess, "Out of (Strategic) Control," *Organizational Dynamics*, Summer 1997, pp. 35–45.

30. "Kohl's Works to Refill Consumers' Bags," *USA Today*, April 8, 2005, pp. B1, B1.

31. See Hans Mjoen and Stephen Tallman, "Control and Performance in International Joint Ventures," *Organization Science*, May–June 1997, pp. 257–265.

32. For a recent study of effective control, see Diana Robertson and Erin Anderson, "Control System and Task Environment Effects on Ethical Judgment: An Exploratory Study of Industrial Salespeople," *Organization Science*, November 1993, pp. 617–629.

33. "Workers, Surf at Your Own Risk," *BusinessWeek*, June 12, 2000, pp. 105–106.

34. "Enterprise Takes Idea of Dressed for Success to a New Extreme," *Wall Street Journal*, November 20, 2002, p. B1.

CHAPTER 21

1. Lisa Chamberlain, "Going Off the Beaten Path for New Design Ideas," *New York Times*, March 12, 2006, p. BU 28; Roger O. Crockett, "Keeping Ritz Carlton at the Top of Its Game," *BusinessWeek*, May 29, 2006, www.businessweek

.com on May 30, 2006; Holly Hughes, *Frommer's New York City with Kids,* 9th edition (New York: Wiley, 2005); Alison Gregor, "Finding the Middle Ground," *New York Times,* April 16, 2006, p. BU 22; John Holusha, "Where All the Rooms are Nonsmoking," *New York Times,* February 19, 2006, p. BU 22.

2. Paul M. Swamidass, "Empirical Science: New Frontier in Operations Management Research," *Academy of Management Review,* October 1991, pp. 793–814.

3. See Anil Khurana, "Managing Complex Production Processes," *Sloan Management Review,* Winter 1999, pp. 85–98.

4. "Service Sector Grows," *USA Today,* March 3, 2006, p. 1B.

5. For an example, see Robin Cooper and Regine Slagmulder, "Develop Profitable New Products with Target Costing," *Sloan Management Review,* Summer 1999, pp. 23–34.

6. Joan Woodward, *Industrial Organization: Theory and Practice* (London: Oxford University Press, 1965).

7. See "Tight Labor? Tech to the Rescue," *BusinessWeek,* March 20, 2000, pp. 36–37.

8. "Computers Speed the Design of More Workaday Products," *Wall Street Journal,* January 18, 1985, p. 25.

9. "New Plant Gets Jaguar in Gear," *USA Today,* November 27, 2000, p. 4B.

10. "Thinking Machines," *BusinessWeek,* August 7, 2000, pp. 78–86.

11. James Brian Quinn and Martin Neil Baily, "Information Technology: Increasing Productivity in Services," *Academy of Management Executive,* 1994, vol. 8, no. 3, pp. 28–37.

12. See Charles J. Corbett, Joseph D. Blackburn, and Luk N. Van Wassenhove, "Partnerships to Improve Supply Chains," *Sloan Management Review,* Summer 1999, pp. 71–82; and Jeffrey K. Liker and Yen-Chun Wu, "Japanese Automakers, U.S. Suppliers, and Supply-Chain Superiority," *Sloan Management Review,* Fall 2000, pp. 81–93.

13. See "Siemens Climbs Back," *BusinessWeek,* June 5, 2000, pp. 79–82.

14. See M. Bensaou, "Portfolios of Buyer-Supplier Relationships," *Sloan Management Review,* Summer 1999, pp. 35–44.

15. "Just-in-Time Manufacturing Is Working Overtime," *BusinessWeek,* November 8, 1999, pp. 36–37.

16. "Quality—How to Make It Pay," *BusinessWeek,* August 8, 1994, pp. 54–59.

17. Rhonda Reger, Loren Gustafson, Samuel DeMarie, and John Mullane, "Reframing the Organization: Why Implementing Total Quality Is Easier Said Than Done," *Academy of Management Review,* 1994, vol. 19, no. 3, pp. 565–584.

18. Ross Johnson and William O. Winchell, *Management and Quality* (Milwaukee: American Society for Quality Control, 1989). See also Carol Reeves and David Bednar, "Defining Quality: Alternatives and Implications," *Academy of Management Review,* 1994, vol. 19, no. 3, pp. 419–445; and C. K. Prahalad and M. S. Krishnan, "The New Meaning of Quality in the Information Age," *Harvard Business Review,* September–October 1999, pp. 109–120.

19. "Quality Isn't Just for Widgets," *BusinessWeek,* July 22, 2002, pp. 72–73.

20. W. Edwards Deming, *Out of the Crisis* (Cambridge, Mass.: MIT Press, 1986).

21. David Waldman, "The Contributions of Total Quality Management to a Theory of Work Performance," *Academy of Management Review,* 1994, vol. 19, no. 3, pp. 510–536.

22. Joel Dreyfuss, "Victories in the Quality Crusade," *Fortune,* October 10, 1988, pp. 80–88.

23. Thomas Y. Choi and Orlando C. Behling, "Top Managers and TQM Success: One More Look After All These Years," *Academy of Management Executive,* 1997, vol. 11, no. 1, pp. 37–48.

24. James Dean and David Bowen, "Management Theory and Total Quality: Improving Research and Practice Through Theory Development," *Academy of Management Review,* 1994, vol. 19, no. 3, pp. 392–418.

25. See "Porsche Figures Out What Americans Want," *USA Today,* June 28, 2006, p. 4B.

26. Edward E. Lawler, "Total Quality Management and Employee Involvement: Are They Compatible?" *Academy of Management Executive,* 1994, vol. 8, no. 1, pp. 68–79.

27. Jeremy Main, "How to Steal the Best Ideas Around," *Fortune,* October 19, 1992, pp. 102–106.

28. See James Brian Quinn, "Strategic Outsourcing: Leveraging Knowledge Capabilities," *Sloan Management Review,* Summer 1999, pp. 8–22.

29. "Global Gamble," *Forbes,* April 17, 2006, pp. 78–82.

30. Thomas Robertson, "How to Reduce Market Penetration Cycle Times," *Sloan Management Review,* Fall 1993, pp. 87–96.

31. "Speed Demons," *BusinessWeek,* March 27, 2006, pp. 68–76.

32. Ronald Henkoff, "The Hot New Seal of Quality," *Fortune,* June 28, 1993, pp. 116–120. See also Mustafa V. Uzumeri, "ISO 9000 and Other Metastandards: Principles for Management Practice?" *Academy of Management Executive,* 1997, vol. 11, no. 1, pp. 21–28.

33. Paula C. Morrow, "The Measurement of TQM Principles and Work-Related Outcomes," *Journal of Organizational Behavior,* July 1997, pp. 363–376.

34. John W. Kendrick, *Understanding Productivity: An Introduction to the Dynamics of Productivity Change* (Baltimore: Johns Hopkins University Press, 1977).

35. "Study: USA Losing Competitive Edge," *USA Today,* April 25, 1997, p. 9D.

36. "Why the Productivity Revolution Will Spread," *BusinessWeek,* February 14, 2000, pp. 112–118. See also "Productivity Grows in Spite of Recession," *USA Today,* July 29, 2002, pp. 1B, 2B; and "Productivity's Second Wind," *BusinessWeek,* February 17, 2003, pp. 36–37.

37. Michael van Biema and Bruce Greenwald, "Managing Our Way to Higher Service-Sector Productivity," *Harvard Business Review,* July–August 1997, pp. 87–98.

CHAPTER 22

1. Michelle Conlin, "E-mail Is So Five Minutes Ago," *BusinessWeek,* November 28, 2005, www.businessweek.com on May 30, 2006 (quote); Josh Hyatt, "The Wonder of Wikipedia,"

Fortune, June 12, 2006, p. 140; Nathan C. Kaiser, "Jimmy Wales, CEO of Wikipedia," nPost website, www.npost.com on May 30, 2006; Randall Stross, "Anonymous Source Is Not the Same as Open Source," *New York Times*, March 12, 2006, p. BU 5; James Surowiecki, *The Wisdom of Crowds* (New York: Doubleday, 2004); "Wikipedia," Wikipedia website, www.wikipedia.org on May 30, 2006.

2. See Charlie Feld and Donna Stoddard, "Getting IT Right," *Harvard Business Review*, February 2005, pp. 72–80.

3. See Michael H. Zack, "Managing Codified Knowledge," *Sloan Management Review*, Summer 1999, pp. 45–58.

4. Donald A. Marchand, William J. Kettinger, and John D. Rollins, "Information Orientation: People, Technology, and the Bottom Line," *Sloan Management Review*, Summer 2000, pp. 69–79.

5. Justin Fox, "Inside the New Earnings Game," *Fortune*, March 3, 2003, pp. 97–103.

6. William J. Burns, Jr., and F. Warren McFarlin, "Information Technology Puts Power in Control Systems," *Harvard Business Review*, September–October 1987, pp. 89–94.

7. N. Venkatraman, "IT-Enabled Business Transformation: From Automation to Business Scope Redefinition," *Sloan Management Review*, Winter 1994, pp. 73–84.

8. Kenneth C. Laudon and Jane P. Laudon, *Essentials of Management Information Systems*, 3rd ed. (Upper Saddle River, N.J.: Prentice Hall, 1999), p. 267.

9. Laudon and Laudon, *Essentials of Management Information Systems*, p. 270.

10. See "The Killer Ad Machine," *Forbes*, December 11, 2000, pp. 168–178.

11. Mary Cronin, "Ford's Intranet Success," *Fortune*, March 30, 1998, p. 158.

12. "The Messy Business of Culling Company Files," *Wall Street Journal*, May 22, 1997, pp. B1, B2.

13. "Software That Plows Through Possibilities," *BusinessWeek*, August 7, 2000, p. 84.

14. See "Do One Thing, and Do It Well," *BusinessWeek*, June 19, 2000, pp. 94–100.

15. "On the Job, You're Never Alone," *Houston Chronicle*, January 30, 2006, pp. D1, D4.

16. For example, see "Swamped Workers Switch to 'Unlisted' E-Mails," *USA Today*, September 7, 1999, p. 1A. See also

Nicholas Varchaver, "The Perils of E-Mail," *Fortune*, February 17, 2003, pp. 96–103.

17. Robert Kraut, Charles Steinfield, Alice P. Chan, Brian Butler, and Anne Hoag, "Coordination and Virtualization: The Role of Electronic Networks and Personal Relationships," *Organization Science*, 1999, vol. 10, no. 6, pp. 722–740.

18. See Mahmoud M. Watad and Frank J. DiSanzo, "The Synergism of Telecommuting and Office Automation," *Sloan Management Review*, Winter 2000, pp. 85–96.

19. Manju K. Ahuja and Kathleen M. Carley, "Network Structure in Virtual Organizations," *Organization Science*, 1999, vol. 10, no. 6, pp. 741–757.

20. "Worksite Face-Off: Techie vs. User," *USA Today*, June 17, 1997, pp. B1, B2.

APPENDIX

1. For a classic review, see John C. Chambers, S. K. Mullick, and D. Smith, "How to Choose the Right Forecasting Technique," *Harvard Business Review*, July–August 1971, pp. 45–74.

2. Charles Ostrom, *Time-Series Analysis: Regression Techniques* (Beverly Hills, Calif.: Sage Publications, 1980).

3. Fred Kerlinger and Elazar Pedhazur, *Multiple Regression in Behavioral Research* (New York: Holt, 1973).

4. Chambers, Mullick, and Smith, "How to Choose the Right Forecasting Technique"; see also J. Scott Armstrong, *Long-Range Forecasting: From Crystal Ball to Computers* (New York: Wiley, 1978).

5. Edward Hannan, Linda Ryan, and Richard Van Orden, "A Cost-Benefit Analysis of Prior Approvals for Medicaid Services in New York State," *Socio-Economic Planning Sciences*, 1984, Vol. 18, pp. 1–14.

6. Ramon L. Alonso and Cline W. Fraser, "JIT Hits Home: A Case Study in Reducing Management Delays," *Sloan Management Review*, Summer 1991, pp. 59–68.

7. Beau Sheil, "Thinking about Artificial Intelligence," *Harvard Business Review*, July–August 1987, pp. 91–97; and Dorothy Leonard-Barton and John J. Sviokla, "Putting Expert Systems to Work," *Harvard Business Review*, March–April 1988, pp. 91–98.

Answers to Test Preppers

CHAPTER 1
1. F
2. F
3. T
4. T
5. F
6. b
7. d
8. c
9. d
10. e

CHAPTER 2
1. T
2. F
3. T
4. F
5. T
6. d
7. e
8. b
9. e
10. c

CHAPTER 3
1. T
2. F
3. T
4. T
5. T
6. b
7. c
8. d
9. a
10. c

CHAPTER 4
1. F
2. T
3. T
4. T
5. F
6. a
7. e
8. d
9. c
10. b

CHAPTER 5
1. F
2. F
3. T
4. T
5. F
6. a
7. e
8. b
9. b
10. d

CHAPTER 6
1. T
2. F
3. F
4. F
5. F
6. a
7. b
8. a
9. e
10. b

CHAPTER 7
1. T
2. F
3. T
4. T
5. F
6. e
7. b
8. b
9. c
10. c

CHAPTER 8
1. F
2. F
3. T
4. T
5. F
6. a
7. e
8. b
9. b
10. c

CHAPTER 9

1. F
2. T
3. F
4. T
5. F
6. a
7. d
8. d
9. b
10. a

CHAPTER 10

1. F
2. T
3. T
4. F
5. F
6. e
7. b
8. e
9. b
10. c

CHAPTER 11

1. T
2. F
3. F
4. T
5. F
6. d
7. e
8. a
9. c
10. a

CHAPTER 12

1. F
2. T
3. T
4. F
5. T
6. b
7. c
8. e
9. e
10. e

CHAPTER 13

1. T
2. F
3. F
4. T
5. T
6. b
7. a
8. c
9. a
10. c

CHAPTER 14

1. F
2. T
3. T
4. T
5. F
6. a
7. c
8. b
9. d
10. b

CHAPTER 15

1. F
2. F
3. F
4. T
5. F
6. a
7. d
8. e
9. d
10. c

CHAPTER 16

1. F
2. T
3. F
4. T
5. T
6. e
7. e
8. b
9. d
10. b

CHAPTER 17

1. F
2. T
3. T
4. F
5. T
6. a
7. d
8. e
9. b
10. d

CHAPTER 18

1. F
2. T
3. T
4. F
5. T
6. a
7. c
8. e
9. e
10. b

CHAPTER 19

1. T
2. F
3. T
4. T
5. T
6. c
7. d
8. e
9. b
10. c

CHAPTER 20

1. F
2. F
3. T
4. T
5. T
6. c
7. e
8. b
9. b
10. d

CHAPTER 21

1. F
2. T
3. T
4. F
5. T
6. b
7. c
8. e
9. a
10. a

CHAPTER 22

1. T
2. T
3. F
4. T
5. T
6. d
7. a
8. c
9. b
10. d

Photo Credits

Name Index

Organization and Product Index

Subject Index

For Students

This website offers a plethora of valuable assets including ACE Practice Tests; "Your Guide to an A," content that includes Interactive Skills Self-Assessments, Practice Tests, and Interactive Games.

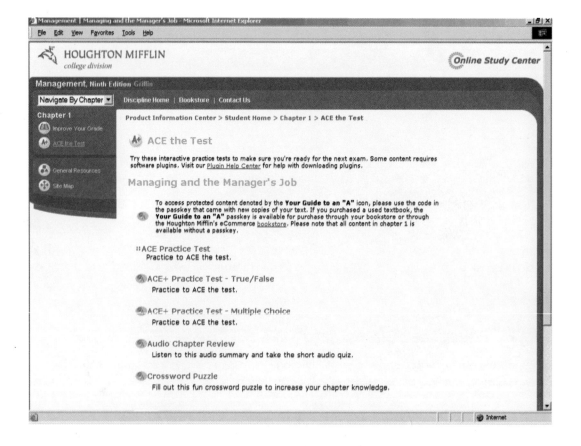